(ex·ploring)
SERIES

1. Investigating in a systematic way: examining. 2. Searching into or ranging over for the purpose of discovery.

Microsoft®

Excel 2016

Comprehensive

Series Editor **Mary Anne Poatsy**

Mulbery | Davidson

Series Created by Dr. Robert T. Grauer

PEARSON

Boston   Columbus   Indianapolis   New York   San Francisco   Hoboken
Amsterdam   Cape Town   Dubai   London   Madrid   Milan   Munich   Paris   Montréal   Toronto
Delhi   Mexico City   São Paulo   Sydney   Hong Kong   Seoul   Singapore   Taipei   Tokyo

Vice President of Career Skills: Andrew Gilfillan
Senior Editor: Samantha Lewis
Team Lead, Project Management: Laura Burgess
Project Manager: Laura Karahalis
Program Manager: Emily Biberger
Development Editor: Barbara Stover
Editorial Assistant: Michael Campbell
Director of Product Marketing: Maggie Waples
Director of Field Marketing: Leigh Ann Sims
Product Marketing Manager: Kaylee Carlson
Field Marketing Managers: Molly Schmidt & Joanna Sabella
Marketing Coordinator: Susan Osterlitz
Senior Operations Specialist: Diane Peirano
Senior Art Director: Diane Ernsberger
Interior and Cover Design: Diane Ernsberger
Cover Photo: Courtesy of Shutterstock® Images
Associate Director of Design: Blair Brown
Senior Product Strategy Manager: Eric Hakanson
Product Manager, MyITLab: Zachary Alexander
Media Producer, MyITLab: Jaimie Noy
Digital Project Manager, MyITLab: Becca Lowe
Media Project Manager, Production: John Cassar
Full-Service Project Management: Jenna Vittorioso, Lumina Datamatics, Inc.
Composition: Lumina Datamatics, Inc.
Efficacy Curriculum Manager: Jessica Sieminski

Credits and acknowledgments borrowed from other sources and reproduced, with permission, in this textbook appear on the appropriate page within text.

Library of Congress Control Number: 2015956945

ISBN 10:   0-13-447944-0
ISBN 13: 978-0-13-447944-6

Dedications

For my husband, Ted, who unselfishly continues to take on more than his share to support me throughout the process; and for my children, Laura, Carolyn, and Teddy, whose encouragement and love have been inspiring.

Mary Anne Poatsy

I dedicate this book to three people who had a significant impact on my career. Penny Sumpter, my high school business teacher, taught me about professionalism and paying attention to details; she inspired me to become a business educator. Dr. Amanda Copeland, the department chair while I completed my bachelor's degree, was an excellent mentor and visionary. Barbra Hoge, my first department chair at Utah Valley State College, was a strong leader and advocate for her faculty; her leadership serves as a role model for me in my capacity as department chair today.

Keith Mulbery

I dedicate this book in loving memory of my grandfather Laurence L. Leggett. A passionate lifelong educator, gifted musician, and incredible role model. I will never forget our time together. I strive every day to make you proud.

Jason Davidson

To my husband Dan, whose encouragement, patience, and love helped make this endeavor possible. Thank you for taking on the many additional tasks at home so that I could focus on writing.

Amy Rutledge

About the Authors

Mary Anne Poatsy, Series Editor, Windows 10 Author

Mary Anne is a senior faculty member at Montgomery County Community College, teaching various computer application and concepts courses in face-to-face and online environments. She holds a B.A. in Psychology and Education from Mount Holyoke College and an M.B.A. in Finance from Northwestern University's Kellogg Graduate School of Management.

Mary Anne has more than 12 years of educational experience. She is currently adjunct faculty at Gwynedd-Mercy College and Montgomery County Community College. She has also taught at Bucks County Community College and Muhlenberg College, as well as conducted personal training. Before teaching, she was Vice President at Shearson Lehman in the Municipal Bond Investment Banking Department.

Dr. Keith Mulbery, Excel Author

Dr. Keith Mulbery is the Department Chair and a Professor in the Information Systems and Technology Department at Utah Valley University (UVU), where he currently teaches systems analysis and design, and global and ethical issues in information systems and technology. He has also taught computer applications, C# programming, and management information systems. Keith served as Interim Associate Dean, School of Computing, in the College of Technology and Computing at UVU.

Keith received the Utah Valley State College Board of Trustees Award of Excellence in 2001, School of Technology and Computing Scholar Award in 2007, and School of Technology and Computing Teaching Award in 2008. He has authored more than 17 textbooks, served as Series Editor for the Exploring Office 2007 series, and served as developmental editor on two textbooks for the Essentials Office 2000 series. He is frequently asked to give presentations and workshops on Microsoft Office Excel at various education conferences.

Keith received his B.S. and M.Ed. in Business Education from Southwestern Oklahoma State University and earned his Ph.D. in Education with an emphasis in Business Information Systems at Utah State University. His dissertation topic was computer-assisted instruction using Prentice Hall's Train and Assess IT program (the predecessor to MyITLab) to supplement traditional instruction in basic computer proficiency courses.

Jason Davidson, Excel Author

Jason Davidson is a faculty member in the College of Business at Butler University, where he teaches Advanced Web Design, Data Networks, Data Analysis and Business Modeling, and introductory information systems courses. He is the co-author of Exploring Microsoft Excel 2013 Comprehensive, Exploring Microsoft Office 2013 Volume 2, Exploring Microsoft Office 2013 Plus, and Exploring VBA for Microsoft Office 2013.

With a background in media development, prior to joining the faculty at Butler, he worked in the technical publishing industry. Along with teaching, he currently serves as an IT consultant for regional businesses in the Indianapolis area. He holds a B.A. in Telecommunication Arts from Butler University and an M.B.A. from Morehead State University. He lives in Indianapolis, Indiana, and in his free time enjoys road biking, photography, and spending time with his family.

Amy Rutledge, Common Features Author

Amy Rutledge is a Special Instructor of Management Information Systems at Oakland University in Rochester, Michigan. She coordinates academic programs in Microsoft Office applications and introductory management information systems courses for the School of Business Administration. Before joining Oakland University as an instructor, Amy spent several years working for a music distribution company and automotive manufacturer in various corporate roles including IT project management. She holds a B.S. in Business Administration specializing in Management Information Systems, and a B.A. in French Modern Language and Literature. She holds an M.B.A from Oakland University. She resides in Michigan with her husband Dan and daughters Emma and Jane.

Dr. Robert T. Grauer, Creator of the Exploring Series

Bob Grauer is an Associate Professor in the Department of Computer Information Systems at the University of Miami, where he is a multiple winner of the Outstanding Teaching Award in the School of Business, most recently in 2009. He has written numerous COBOL texts and is the vision behind the Exploring Office series, with more than three million books in print. His work has been translated into three foreign languages and is used in all aspects of higher education at both national and international levels. Bob Grauer has consulted for several major corporations including IBM and American Express. He received his Ph.D. in Operations Research in 1972 from the Polytechnic Institute of Brooklyn.

Brief Contents

Contents

Microsoft Office 2016

CHAPTER ONE Office 2016 Common Features: Taking the First Step 2

Microsoft Office Excel 2016

CHAPTER ONE Introduction to Excel: Creating and Formatting a Worksheet 68

Acknowledgments

The Exploring team would like to acknowledge and thank all the reviewers who helped us throughout the years by providing us with their invaluable comments, suggestions, and constructive criticism.

Adriana Lumpkin
Midland College

Alan S. Abrahams
Virginia Tech

Alexandre C. Probst
Colorado Christian University

Ali Berrached
University of Houston–Downtown

Allen Alexander
Delaware Technical & Community College

Andrea Marchese
Maritime College, State University of New York

Andrew Blitz
Broward College; Edison State College

Angel Norman
University of Tennessee, Knoxville

Angela Clark
University of South Alabama

Ann Rovetto
Horry-Georgetown Technical College

Astrid Todd
Guilford Technical Community College

Audrey Gillant
Maritime College, State University of New York

Barbara Stover
Marion Technical College

Barbara Tollinger
Sinclair Community College

Ben Brahim Taha
Auburn University

Beverly Amer
Northern Arizona University

Beverly Fite
Amarillo College

Biswadip Ghosh
Metropolitan State University of Denver

Bonita Volker
Tidewater Community College

Bonnie Homan
San Francisco State University

Brad West
Sinclair Community College

Brian Powell
West Virginia University

Carol Buser
Owens Community College

Carol Roberts
University of Maine

Carolyn Barren
Macomb Community College

Carolyn Borne
Louisiana State University

Cathy Poyner
Truman State University

Charles Hodgson
Delgado Community College

Chen Zhang
Bryant University

Cheri Higgins
Illinois State University

Cheryl Brown
Delgado Community College

Cheryl Hinds
Norfolk State University

Cheryl Sypniewski
Macomb Community College

Chris Robinson
Northwest State Community College

Cindy Herbert
Metropolitan Community College–Longview

Craig J. Peterson
American InterContinental University

Dana Hooper
University of Alabama

Dana Johnson
North Dakota State University

Daniela Marghitu
Auburn University

David Noel
University of Central Oklahoma

David Pulis
Maritime College, State University of New York

David Thornton
Jacksonville State University

Dawn Medlin
Appalachian State University

Debby Keen
University of Kentucky

Debra Chapman
University of South Alabama

Debra Hoffman
Southeast Missouri State University

Derrick Huang
Florida Atlantic University

Diana Baran
Henry Ford Community College

Diane Cassidy
The University of North Carolina at Charlotte

Diane L. Smith
Henry Ford Community College

Dick Hewer
Ferris State College

Don Danner
San Francisco State University

Don Hoggan
Solano College

Don Riggs
SUNY Schenectady County Community College

Doncho Petkov
Eastern Connecticut State University

Donna Ehrhart
State University of New York at Brockport

Elaine Crable
Xavier University

Elizabeth Duett
Delgado Community College

Erhan Uskup
Houston Community College–Northwest

Eric Martin
University of Tennessee

Erika Nadas
Wilbur Wright College

Floyd Winters
Manatee Community College

Frank Lucente
Westmoreland County Community College

G. Jan Wilms
Union University

Gail Cope
Sinclair Community College

Gary DeLorenzo
California University of Pennsylvania

Gary Garrison
Belmont University

Gary McFall
Purdue University

George Cassidy
Sussex County Community College

Gerald Braun
Xavier University

Gerald Burgess
Western New Mexico University

Gladys Swindler
Fort Hays State University

Hector Frausto
California State University
Los Angeles

Heith Hennel
Valencia Community College

Henry Rudzinski
Central Connecticut State University

Irene Joos
La Roche College

Iwona Rusin
Baker College; Davenport University

J. Roberto Guzman
San Diego Mesa College

Jacqueline D. Lawson
Henry Ford Community College

Jakie Brown Jr.
Stevenson University

James Brown
Central Washington University

James Powers
University of Southern Indiana

Jane Stam
Onondaga Community College

Janet Bringhurst
Utah State University

Jean Welsh
Lansing Community College

Jeanette Dix
Ivy Tech Community College

Jennifer Day
Sinclair Community College

Jill Canine
Ivy Tech Community College

Jill Young
Southeast Missouri State University

Jim Chaffee
The University of Iowa Tippie College of
Business

Joanne Lazirko
University of Wisconsin–Milwaukee

Jodi Milliner
Kansas State University

John Hollenbeck
Blue Ridge Community College

John Seydel
Arkansas State University

Judith A. Scheeren
Westmoreland County Community College

Judith Brown
The University of Memphis

Juliana Cypert
Tarrant County College

Kamaljeet Sanghera
George Mason University

Karen Priestly
Northern Virginia Community College

Karen Ravan
Spartanburg Community College

Karen Tracey
Central Connecticut State University

Kathleen Brenan
Ashland University

Ken Busbee
Houston Community College

Kent Foster
Winthrop University

Kevin Anderson
Solano Community College

Kim Wright
The University of Alabama

Kristen Hockman
University of Missouri–Columbia

Kristi Smith
Allegany College of Maryland

Laura Marcoulides
Fullerton College

Laura McManamon
University of Dayton

Laurence Boxer
Niagara University

Leanne Chun
Leeward Community College

Lee McClain
Western Washington University

Linda D. Collins
Mesa Community College

Linda Johnsonius
Murray State University

Linda Lau
Longwood University

Linda Theus
Jackson State Community College

Linda Williams
Marion Technical College

Lisa Miller
University of Central Oklahoma

Lister Horn
Pensacola Junior College

Lixin Tao
Pace University

Loraine Miller
Cayuga Community College

Lori Kielty
Central Florida Community College

Lorna Wells
Salt Lake Community College

Lorraine Sauchin
Duquesne University

Lucy Parakhovnik
California State University, Northridge

Lynn Keane
University of South Carolina

Lynn Mancini
Delaware Technical Community College

Mackinzee Escamilla
South Plains College

Marcia Welch
Highline Community College

Margaret McManus
Northwest Florida State College

Margaret Warrick
Allan Hancock College

Marilyn Hibbert
Salt Lake Community College

Mark Choman
Luzerne County Community College

Maryann Clark
University of New Hampshire

Mary Beth Tarver
Northwestern State University

Mary Duncan
University of Missouri–St. Louis

Melissa Nemeth
Indiana University-Purdue University
Indianapolis

Melody Alexander
Ball State University

Michael Douglas
University of Arkansas at Little Rock

Michael Dunklebarger
Alamance Community College

Michael G. Skaff
College of the Sequoias

Michele Budnovitch
Pennsylvania College of Technology

Mike Jochen
East Stroudsburg University

Mike Michaelson
Palomar College

Mike Scroggins
Missouri State University

Mimi Spain
Southern Maine Community College

Muhammed Badamas
Morgan State University

NaLisa Brown
University of the Ozarks

Nancy Grant
Community College of Allegheny County–
South Campus

Nanette Lareau
University of Arkansas Community
College–Morrilton

Nikia Robinson
Indian River State University

Pam Brune
Chattanooga State Community College

Pam Uhlenkamp
Iowa Central Community College

Patrick Smith
Marshall Community and Technical College

Paul Addison
Ivy Tech Community College

Paula Ruby
Arkansas State University

Peggy Burrus
Red Rocks Community College

Peter Ross
SUNY Albany

Philip H. Nielson
Salt Lake Community College

Philip Valvalides
Guilford Technical Community College

Ralph Hooper
University of Alabama

Ranette Halverson
Midwestern State University

Richard Blamer
John Carroll University

Richard Cacace
Pensacola Junior College

Richard Hewer
Ferris State University

Richard Sellers
Hill College

Rob Murray
Ivy Tech Community College

Robert Banta
Macomb Community College

Robert Dušek
Northern Virginia Community College

Robert G. Phipps Jr.
West Virginia University

Robert Sindt
Johnson County Community College

Robert Warren
Delgado Community College

Rocky Belcher
Sinclair Community College

Roger Pick
University of Missouri at Kansas City

Ronnie Creel
Troy University

Rosalie Westerberg
Clover Park Technical College

Ruth Neal
Navarro College

Sandra Thomas
Troy University

Sheila Gionfriddo
Luzerne County Community College

Sherrie Geitgey
Northwest State Community College

Sherry Lenhart
Terra Community College

Sophia Wilberscheid
Indian River State College

Sophie Lee
California State University,
Long Beach

Stacy Johnson
Iowa Central Community College

Stephanie Kramer
Northwest State Community College

Stephen Z. Jourdan
Auburn University at Montgomery

Steven Schwarz
Raritan Valley Community College

Sue A. McCrory
Missouri State University

Sumathy Chandrashekar
Salisbury University

Susan Fuschetto
Cerritos College

Susan Medlin
UNC Charlotte

Susan N. Dozier
Tidewater Community College

Suzan Spitzberg
Oakton Community College

Suzanne M. Jeska
County College of Morris

Sven Aelterman
Troy University

Sy Hirsch
Sacred Heart University

Sylvia Brown
Midland College

Tanya Patrick
Clackamas Community College

Terri Holly
Indian River State College

Terry Ray Rigsby
Hill College

Thomas Rienzo
Western Michigan University

Tina Johnson
Midwestern State University

Tommy Lu
Delaware Technical Community College

Troy S. Cash
Northwest Arkansas Community College

Vicki Robertson
Southwest Tennessee Community

Vickie Pickett
Midland College

Weifeng Chen
California University of Pennsylvania

Wes Anthony
Houston Community College

William Ayen
University of Colorado at Colorado Springs

Wilma Andrews
Virginia Commonwealth University

Yvonne Galusha
University of Iowa

Special thanks to our content development and technical team:

Barbara Stover

Janet Pickard

Lori Damanti

Steven Rubin

Elizabeth Lockley

Lhe Smith

Joyce Nielsen

Mara Zebest

Preface

The Exploring Series and You

Exploring is Pearson's Office Application series that requires students like you to think "beyond the point and click." In this edition, we have worked to restructure the Exploring experience around the way you, today's modern student, actually use your resources.

The goal of Exploring is, as it has always been, to go farther than teaching just the steps to accomplish a task—the series provides the theoretical foundation for you to understand when and why to apply a skill. As a result, you achieve a deeper understanding of each application and can apply this critical thinking beyond Office and the classroom.

The How & Why of This Revision

Outcomes matter. Whether it's getting a good grade in this course, learning how to use Excel so students can be successful in other courses, or learning a specific skill that will make learners successful in a future job, everyone has an outcome in mind. And outcomes matter. That is why we revised our chapter opener to focus on the outcomes students will achieve by working through each Exploring chapter. These are coupled with objectives and skills, providing a map students can follow to get everything they need from each chapter.

Critical Thinking and Collaboration are essential 21st century skills. Students want and need to be successful in their future careers—so we used motivating case studies to show relevance of these skills to future careers and incorporated Soft Skills, Collaboration, and Analysis Cases with Critical Thinking steps in this edition to set students up for success in the future.

Students today read, prepare, and study differently than students used to. Students use textbooks like a tool—they want to easily identify what they need to know and learn it efficiently. We have added key features such as Tasks Lists (in purple), Step Icons, Hands-On Exercise Videos, and tracked everything via page numbers that allow efficient navigation, creating a map students can easily follow.

Students are exposed to technology. The new edition of Exploring moves beyond the basics of the software at a faster pace, without sacrificing coverage of the fundamental skills that students need to know.

Students are diverse. Students can be any age, any gender, any race, with any level of ability or learning style. With this in mind, we broadened our definition of "student resources" to include physical Student Reference cards, Hands-On Exercise videos to provide a secondary lecture-like option of review; and MyITLab, the most powerful and most ADA-compliant online homework and assessment tool around with a direct 1:1 content match with the Exploring Series. Exploring will be accessible to all students, regardless of learning style.

Providing You with a Map to Success to Move Beyond the Point and Click

All of these changes and additions will provide students an easy and efficient path to follow to be successful in this course, regardless of where they start at the beginning of this course. Our goal is to keep students engaged in both the hands-on and conceptual sides, helping achieve a higher level of understanding that will guarantee success in this course and in a future career.

In addition to the vision and experience of the series creator, Robert T. Grauer, we have assembled a tremendously talented team of Office Applications authors who have devoted themselves to teaching the ins and outs of Microsoft Word, Excel, Access, and PowerPoint. Led in this edition by series editor Mary Anne Poatsy, the whole team is dedicated to the Exploring mission of moving students **beyond the point and click**.

Key Features

The **How/Why Approach** helps students move beyond the point and click to a true understanding of how to apply Microsoft Office skills.

- **White Pages/Yellow Pages** clearly distinguish the theory (white pages) from the skills covered in the Hands-On Exercises (yellow pages) so students always know what they are supposed to be doing and why.

- **Case Study** presents a scenario for the chapter, creating a story that ties the Hands-On Exercises together.

- **Hands-On Exercise Videos** are tied to each Hands-On Exercise and walk students through the steps of the exercise while weaving in conceptual information related to the Case Study and the objectives as a whole.

The **Outcomes focus** allows students and instructors to know the higher-level learning goals and how those are achieved through discreet objectives and skills.

- **Outcomes** presented at the beginning of each chapter identify the learning goals for students and instructors.

- **Enhanced Objective Mapping** enables students to follow a directed path through each chapter, from the objectives list at the chapter opener through the exercises at the end of the chapter.
  - **Objectives List:** This provides a simple list of key objectives covered in the chapter. This includes page numbers so students can skip between objectives where they feel they need the most help.
  - **Step Icons:** These icons appear in the white pages and reference the step numbers in the Hands-On Exercises, providing a correlation between the two so students can easily find conceptual help when they are working hands-on and need a refresher.
  - **Quick Concepts Check:** A series of questions that appear briefly at the end of each white page section. These questions cover the most essential concepts in the white pages required for students to be successful in working the Hands-On Exercises. Page numbers are included for easy reference to help students locate the answers.
  - **Chapter Objectives Review:** Appears toward the end of the chapter and reviews all important concepts throughout the chapter. Newly designed in an easy-to-read bulleted format.

- **MOS Certification Guide** for instructors and students to direct anyone interested in prepping for the MOS exam to the specific locations to find all content required for the test.

End-of-Chapter Exercises offer instructors several options for assessment. Each chapter has approximately 11–12 exercises ranging from multiple choice questions to open-ended projects.

- **Multiple Choice, Key Terms Matching, Practice Exercises, Mid-Level Exercises, Beyond the Classroom Exercises, and Capstone Exercises** appear at the end of all chapters.
  - **Enhanced Mid-Level Exercises** include a **Creative Case** (for PowerPoint and Word), which allows students some flexibility and creativity, not being bound by a definitive solution, and an **Analysis Case** (for Excel and Access), which requires students to interpret the data they are using to answer an analytic question, as well as **Discover Steps**, which encourage students to use Help or to problem-solve to accomplish a task.

- **Application Capstone** exercises are included in the book to allow instructors to test students on the entire contents of a single application.

Resources

Instructor Resources

The Instructor's Resource Center, available at **www.pearsonhighered.com**, includes the following:

- **Instructor Manual** provides one-stop-shop for instructors, including an overview of all available resources, teaching tips, as well as student data and solution files for every exercise.

- **Solution Files with Scorecards** assist with grading the Hands-On Exercises and end-of-chapter exercises.

- **Prepared Exams** allow instructors to assess all skills covered in a chapter with a single project.

- **Rubrics** for Mid-Level Creative Cases and Beyond the Classroom Cases in Microsoft Word format enable instructors to customize the assignments for their classes.

- **PowerPoint Presentations** with notes for each chapter are included for out-of-class study or review.

- **Multiple Choice, Key Term Matching, and Quick Concepts Check Answer Keys**

- **Test Bank** provides objective-based questions for every chapter.

- **Scripted Lectures** offer an in-class lecture guide for instructors to mirror the Hands-On Exercises.

- **Syllabus Templates**
  - Outcomes, Objectives, and Skills List
  - Assignment Sheet
  - File Guide

Student Resources

Student Data Files

Access your student data files needed to complete the exercises in this textbook at **www.pearsonhighered.com/exploring**.

Available in MyITLab

- **Hands-On Exercise Videos** allow students to review and study the concepts taught in the Hands-On Exercises.
- **Audio PowerPoints** provide a lecture review of the chapter content, and include narration.
- **Multiple Choice quizzes** enable you to test concepts you have learned by answering auto-graded questions.
- **Book-specific 1:1 Simulations** allow students to practice in the simulated Microsoft Office 2016 environment using hi-fidelity, HTML5 simulations that directly match the content in the Hands-On Exercises.
- **eText** available in some MyITLab courses and includes links to videos, student data files, and other learning aids.
- **Book-specific 1:1 Grader Projects** allow students to complete end-of-chapter Capstone Exercises live in Microsoft Office 2016 and receive immediate feedback on their performance through various reports.

(ex·ploring)

SERIES

1. Investigating in a systematic way: examining. 2. Searching into or ranging over for the purpose of discovery.

Microsoft®

Excel 2016

COMPREHENSIVE

Office 2016 Common Features

LEARNING OUTCOME

You will apply skills common across the Microsoft Office suite to create and format documents and edit content in Office 2016 applications.

OBJECTIVES & SKILLS: After you read this chapter, you will be able to:

CASE STUDY | Spotted Begonia Art Gallery

You are an administrative assistant for Spotted Begonia, a local art gallery. The gallery does a lot of community outreach and tries to help local artists develop a network of clients and supporters. Local schools are invited to bring students to the gallery for enrichment programs.

As the administrative assistant for Spotted Begonia, you are responsible for overseeing the production of documents, spreadsheets, newspaper articles, and presentations that will be used to increase public awareness of the gallery. Other clerical assistants who are familiar with Microsoft Office will prepare the promotional materials, and you will proofread, make necessary corrections, adjust page layouts, save and print documents, and identify appropriate templates to simplify tasks. Your experience with Microsoft Office 2016 is limited, but you know that certain fundamental tasks that are common to Word, Excel, and PowerPoint will help you accomplish your oversight task. You are excited to get started with your work!

Taking the First Step

CHAPTER 1

Konstantin Chagin/Shutterstock

Word 2016, Windows 10, Microsoft Corporation

FIGURE 1.1 Spotted Begonia Art Gallery Memo and Flyer

CASE STUDY | Spotted Begonia Art Gallery

Starting Files	Files to be Submitted
f01h1Letter	f01h2Flyer_LastFirst
f01h2Flyer	f01h3Letter_LastFirst
Blank document	

Office 2016 Common Features • Common Features 2016   3

Getting Started with Office Applications

Organizations around the world rely heavily on Microsoft Office software to produce documents, spreadsheets, presentations, and databases. *Microsoft Office* is a productivity software suite including a set of software applications, each one specializing in a particular type of output. You can use *Word* to produce all sorts of documents, including memos, newsletters, forms, tables, and brochures. *Excel* makes it easy to organize records, financial transactions, and business information in the form of worksheets. With *PowerPoint*, you can create dynamic presentations to inform and persuade audiences. *Access* is a relational database software application that enables you to record and link data, query databases, and create forms and reports.

You will sometimes find that you need to use two or more Office applications to produce your intended output. You might, for example, find that an annual report document you are preparing in Word for an art gallery should also include a chart of recent sales stored in Excel. You can use Excel to prepare the summary and then incorporate the worksheet in the Word document. Similarly, you can integrate Word tables and Excel charts into a PowerPoint presentation. The choice of which software applications to use really depends on what type of output you are producing. Table 1.1 describes the major tasks of the four primary applications in Microsoft Office.

TABLE 1.1 Microsoft Office Software	
Office 2016 Product	**Application Characteristics**
Word	Word processing software used with text to create, edit, and format documents such as letters, memos, reports, brochures, resumes, and flyers.
Excel	Spreadsheet software used to store quantitative data and to perform accurate and rapid calculations with results ranging from simple budgets to financial and statistical analyses.
PowerPoint	Presentation graphics software used to create slide shows for presentation by a speaker, to be published as part of a website, or to run as a stand-alone application on a computer kiosk.
Access	Relational database software used to store data and convert it into information. Database software is used primarily for decision making by businesses that compile data from multiple records stored in tables to produce informative reports.

Pearson Education, Inc.

As you become familiar with Microsoft Office, you will find that although each software application produces a specific type of output, all applications share common features. Such commonality gives a similar feel to each software application so that learning and working with Office software products is easy.

In this section, you will learn how to open an application, log in with your Microsoft account, and open and save a file. You will also learn to identify features common to Office software applications, including interface components such as the Ribbon, Backstage view, and the Quick Access Toolbar. You will experience Live Preview. You will learn how to get help with an application. You will also learn how to search for and install Office add-ins.

Starting an Office Application

STEP 1 ›› Microsoft Office applications are launched from the Start menu. Click the Start button, and then click the app tile for the application in which you want to work. If the application tile is not on the Start menu, you can open the program from All apps, or alternatively, you can click in the search box on the task bar, type the name of the program, and press Enter. The program will open automatically.

Change Your Microsoft Account

Although you can log in to Windows as a local network user, you can also log in using a Microsoft account. When you have a Microsoft account, you can sign in to any Windows computer and you will be able to access the saved settings associated with your Microsoft account. That means the computer will have the same familiar look that you are used to seeing on other computers and devices. Your Microsoft account will automatically sign in to all of the apps and services that use a Microsoft account as the authentication. You can also save your sign-in credentials for other websites that you frequently visit. If you share your computer with another user, each user can have access to his own Microsoft account; you can easily switch between accounts so you can access your own files.

To switch between accounts in an application such as Word, complete the following steps:

1. Click the profile name at the top-right of the application.
2. Select Switch account. Select an account from the list, if the account has already been added to the computer, or add a new account.

Logging in with your Microsoft account also provides additional benefits such as being connected to all of Microsoft's resources on the Internet. These resources include a free Outlook email account and access to OneDrive cloud storage. **Cloud storage** is a technology used to store files and to work with programs that are stored in a central location on the Internet. **OneDrive** is an app used to store, access, and share files and folders. It is accessible using an installed desktop app or as cloud storage using a Web address. For Office applications, OneDrive is the default location for saving files. Documents saved in OneDrive are accessible from any computer that has an Internet connection. As long as the document has been saved in OneDrive, the most recent version of the document will be accessible when you log in from any computer connected to the Internet. Moreover, files and folders stored on the computer's hard drive or saved on a portable storage device can be synced with those on the OneDrive account.

OneDrive enables you to collaborate with others. You can easily share your documents with others or edit a document on which you are collaborating. You can even work with others simultaneously on the same document.

Working with Files

When working with an Office application, you can begin by opening an existing file that has already been saved to a storage medium, or you can begin work on a new file. When you open an application within Office, you can select a template to use as you begin working on a new file.

Create a New File

After opening an Office application, such as Word, Excel, or PowerPoint, you will be presented with template choices. Click Blank document (workbook, presentation, etc.) to start a new blank file. Perhaps you are already working with a document in an Office application but want to create a new file.

To create a new Office file, complete the following steps:

1. Click the File tab and click New.
2. Click Blank.

Open a File

STEP 2 You will often work with a file, save it, and then continue the project at a later time. To open an existing file, you can click a location such as This PC or OneDrive and navigate to the folder or drive where your document is stored. Once you make your way to the file to be opened, double-click the file name to open the file (see Figure 1.2).

To open a file, complete the following steps:

1. Open the application.
2. Click Open Other Documents (Workbooks, etc.).
3. Click the location for your file (such as This PC or OneDrive).
4. Navigate to the folder or drive and double-click the file to open it.

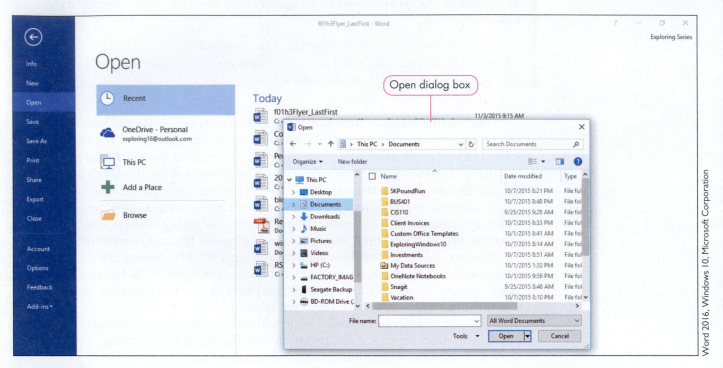

FIGURE 1.2 The Open Dialog Box

Office simplifies the task of reopening the file by providing a Recent documents list with links to your most recently opened files. Previously saved files, such as the data files for this book, are available in the Recent documents list, shown in Figure 1.3. If you just opened the application, the recent list displays at the left. If you do not see your file listed, you can click the link to Open Other Documents (or Workbooks, Presentations, etc.)

To access the Recent documents list, complete the following steps:

1. Open the application.
2. Click any file listed in the Recent documents list to open that document.

The list constantly changes to reflect only the most recently opened files, so if it has been quite some time since you worked with a particular file, you might have to browse for your file instead of using the Recent documents list to open the file.

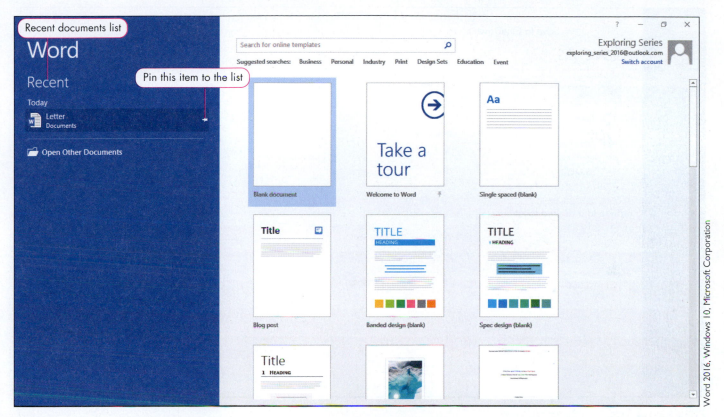

FIGURE 1.3 Recent Documents List

Save a File

STEP 3 ❱❱ Saving a file enables you to later open it for additional updates or reference. Files are saved to a storage medium such as a hard drive, CD, flash drive, or to the cloud on OneDrive.

The first time that you save a file, you should indicate where the file will be saved and assign a file name. Of course, you will want to save the file in an appropriately named folder so that you can find it easily later. Thereafter, you can quickly save the file with the same settings, or you can change one or more of those settings, perhaps saving the file to a different storage device as a backup copy. Figure 1.4 shows a typical Save As pane for Office that enables you to select a location before saving the file.

It is easy to save a previously saved file with its current name and file location; click the Save icon on Quick Access Toolbar. There are instances where you may want to rename the file or save it to a different location. For example, you might reuse an event flyer for another event and simply update some of the details for the new event.

To save a file with a different name and/or file location, complete the following steps:

1. Click the File tab.
2. Click Save As.
3. Select a location or click Browse to navigate to the desired file storage location.
4. Type the file name.
5. Click Save.

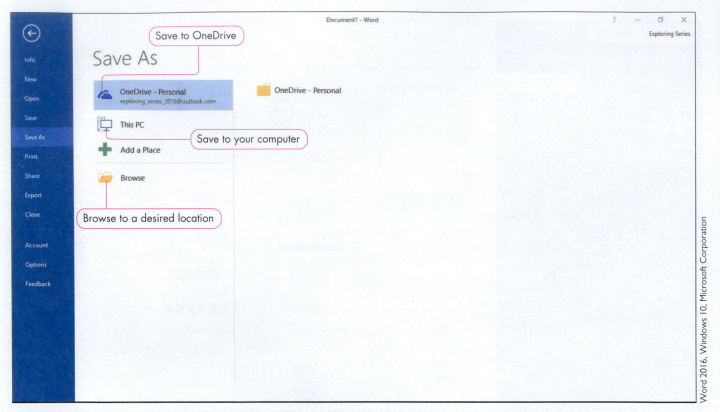

FIGURE 1.4 Save As in Backstage View

As previously mentioned, signing in to your Microsoft account enables you to save files to OneDrive and access them from virtually anywhere. To save a file to your OneDrive account follow the same steps as saving a file to your hard drive but select OneDrive and then the desired storage location on your OneDrive. You must be connected to the Internet in order to complete this action.

Using Common Interface Components

When you open any Office application you will first notice the title bar and Ribbon. The *title bar* identifies the current file name and the application in which you are working. It also includes Ribbon display options and control buttons that enable you to minimize, restore down, or close the application window (see Figure 1.5). The Quick Access Toolbar, on the left side of the title bar, enables you to save the file, and undo or redo editing. Located just below the title bar is the Ribbon. The *Ribbon* is the command center of Office applications. It is the long bar located just beneath the title bar, containing tabs, groups, and commands.

FIGURE 1.5 The Title Bar and Quick Access Toolbar

Use the Ribbon

The Ribbon is composed of tabs. Each **tab** is designed to appear much like a tab on a file folder, with the active tab highlighted. The File tab is located at the far left of the Ribbon. The File tab provides access to Backstage view which contains Save and Print, as well as additional functions. Other tabs on the Ribbon enable you to modify a file. The active tab in Figure 1.6 is the Home tab.

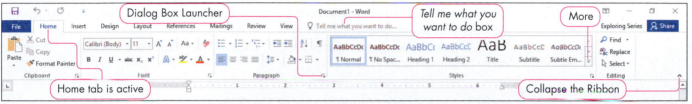

FIGURE 1.6 The Ribbon

Office applications enable you to work with objects such as images, shapes, charts, and tables. When you include such objects in a project, they are considered separate components that you can manage independently. To work with an object, you must select it. When you select an object, the Ribbon is modified to include one or more **contextual tabs** that contain groups of commands related to the selected object. Figure 1.7 shows a contextual tab related to a selected picture in a Word document. When you click away from the selected object, the contextual tab disappears.

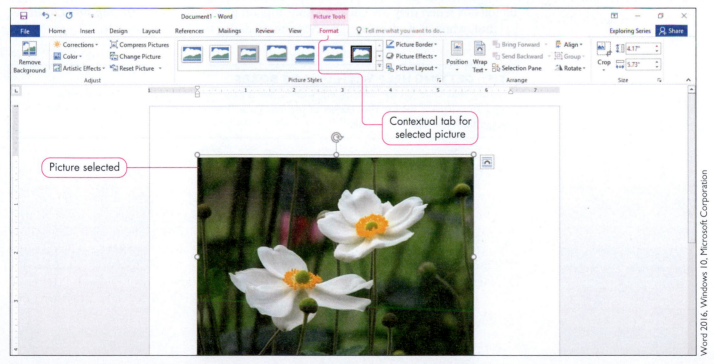

FIGURE 1.7 A Contextual Tab

On each tab, the Ribbon displays several task-oriented groups, with each group containing related commands. A *group* is a subset of a tab that organizes similar tasks together. A *command* is a button or area within a group that you click to perform tasks. Office is designed to provide the most functionality possible with the fewest clicks. For that reason, the Home tab, displayed when you first open a document in an Office software application, contains groups and commands that are most commonly used. For example, because you often want to change the way text is displayed, the Home tab in each Office application includes a Font group with commands related to modifying text. Similarly, other tabs contain groups of related actions, or commands, many of which are unique to the particular Office application.

Word, PowerPoint, Excel, and Access all share a similar Ribbon structure. Although the specific tabs, groups, and commands vary among the Office programs, the way in which you use the Ribbon and the descriptive nature of tab titles is the same regardless of which program you are using. For example, if you want to insert a chart in Excel, a header in Word, or a shape in PowerPoint, you will click the Insert tab in any of those programs. The first thing that you should do as you begin to work with an Office application is to study the Ribbon. Take a look at all tabs and their contents. That way, you will have a good idea of where to find specific commands and how the Ribbon with which you are currently working differs from one that you might have used in another application.

If you are working with a large project, you can maximize your workspace by temporarily hiding the Ribbon.

To hide the Ribbon, complete one of the following steps:

- Double-click the active tab to hide the Ribbon.
- Click Collapse the Ribbon (refer to Figure 1.6), located at the right side of the Ribbon.

To unhide the Ribbon, double-click any tab to redisplay the Ribbon.

Some actions do not display on the Ribbon because they are not as commonly used, but are related to commands displayed on the Ribbon. For example, you might want to change the background of a PowerPoint slide to include a picture. In that case, you will work with a *dialog box* that provides access to more precise, but less frequently used, commands. Figure 1.8 shows the Font dialog box in Word. Some commands display a dialog box when they are clicked. Other Ribbon groups include a *Dialog Box Launcher* ⬚ that, when clicked, opens a corresponding dialog box (see Figure 1.8).

> **TIP: GETTING HELP WITH DIALOG BOXES**
> Getting help while you are working with a dialog box is easy. Click the Help button that displays as a question mark in the top-right corner of the dialog box. The subsequent Help window will offer suggestions relevant to your task.

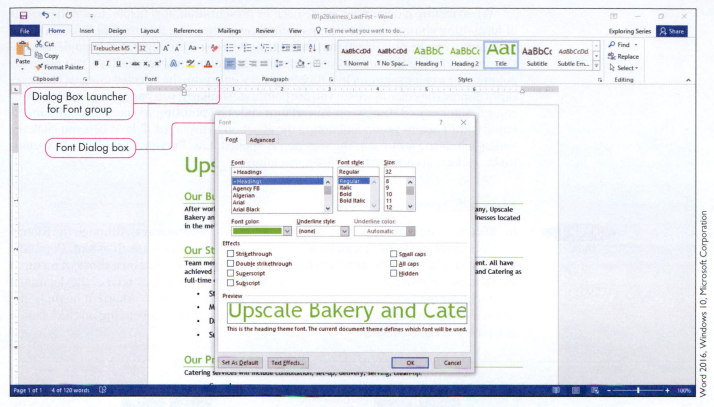

FIGURE 1.8 The Font Dialog Box

The Ribbon contains many selections and commands, but some selections are too numerous to include in the Ribbon's limited space. For example, Word provides far more text styles than it can easily display at once, so additional styles are available in a ***gallery***. A gallery also provides a choice of Excel chart styles and PowerPoint transitions. Figure 1.9 shows an example of a PowerPoint Themes gallery. Most often, you can display a gallery of additional choices by clicking the More button ▼ (refer to Figure 1.6) that is found in some Ribbon selections.

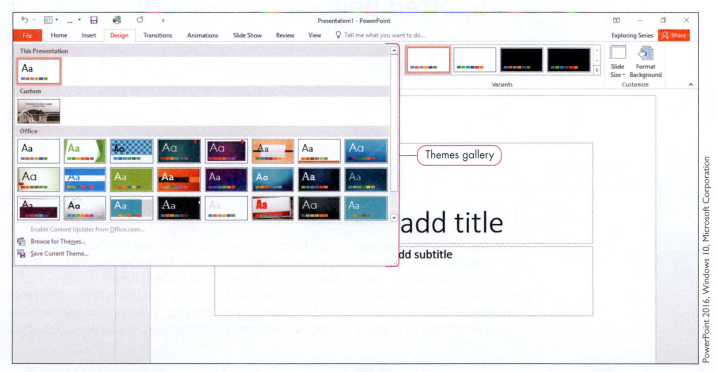

FIGURE 1.9 The Themes Gallery in PowerPoint

When editing a document, worksheet, or presentation, it is helpful to see the results of formatting changes before you make final selections. The feature that displays a preview of the results of a selection is called **Live Preview**. You might, for example, be considering modifying the color of an image in a document or worksheet. As you place the pointer over a color selection in a Ribbon gallery or group, the selected image will temporarily display the color to which you are pointing. Similarly, you can get a preview of how color designs would display on PowerPoint slides by pointing to specific themes in the PowerPoint Themes group and noting the effect on a displayed slide. When you click the item, such as the font color, the selection is applied. Live Preview is available in various Ribbon selections among the Office applications.

Use a Shortcut Menu

STEP 4 ❱❱ In Office, you can usually accomplish the same task in several ways. Although the Ribbon provides ample access to formatting and Clipboard commands (such as Cut, Copy, and Paste), you might find it convenient to access the same commands on a shortcut menu. A **shortcut menu** provides choices related to the object, selection, or area of the document at which you right-click, such as the one shown in Figure 1.10. A shortcut menu is also called a *context menu* because the contents of the menu vary depending on the location at which you right-clicked.

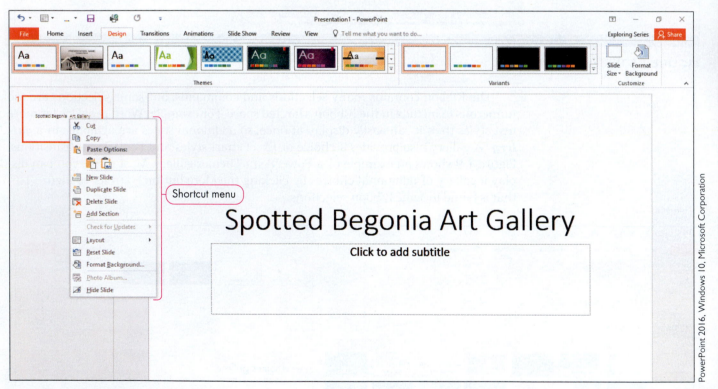

FIGURE 1.10 A Shortcut Menu in PowerPoint

Use Keyboard Shortcuts

You might find that you prefer to use keyboard shortcuts, which are keyboard equivalents for software commands, when they are available. Universal keyboard shortcuts in Office include Ctrl+C (Copy), Ctrl+X (Cut), Ctrl+V (Paste), and Ctrl+Z (Undo). To move to the beginning of a Word document, to cell A1 in Excel, or to the first PowerPoint slide, press Ctrl+Home. To move to the end of those items, press Ctrl+End. There are many other keyboard shortcuts. To discover a keyboard shortcut for a commonly used command, press

Alt to display Key Tips for commands available on the Ribbon and Quick Access Toolbar. You can press the letter or number corresponding to Ribbon commands to invoke the action from the keyboard. Press Alt again to remove the Key Tips.

> **TIP: USING RIBBON COMMANDS WITH ARROWS**
> Some commands, such as Paste in the Clipboard group, contain two parts: the main command and an arrow. The arrow may be below or to the right of the command, depending on the command, window size, or screen resolution. Instructions in the *Exploring* series use the command name to instruct you to click the main command to perform the default action (e.g., Click Paste). Instructions include the word *arrow* when you need to select the arrow to access an additional option (e.g., Click the Paste arrow).

Customize the Ribbon

The Ribbon provides access to commands to develop, edit, save, share, and print documents. Office applications enable users to personalize the Ribbon, giving them easier access to a frequently used set of commands that are unique to them or their business. You can create and name custom tabs on the Ribbon, add groups of commands to custom or existing tabs, and alter the positioning of tabs on the Ribbon (see Figure 1.11). By default, the command list displays popular commands associated with other tabs (e.g. Paste, Delete, Save As), but all available commands can be displayed in the list's respective menu. The custom tabs are unique to the Office program in which they are created. You can add and remove Ribbon tabs, as well as rename them.

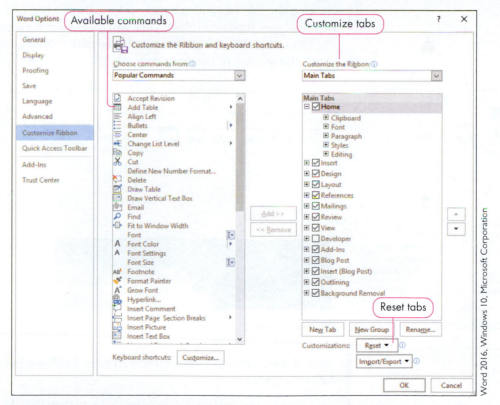

FIGURE 1.11 Customize the Ribbon in Word

To customize the Ribbon, complete the following steps:

1. Click the File tab and click Options.
2. Click Customize Ribbon. By deselecting a tab name, you can remove it from the Ribbon. Later, you can select it again to redisplay it.
3. Click a tab name and click Rename to change the name of the tab.
4. Type a new name and press Enter.

To return to showing all of the original tabs, click Reset and click Reset all customizations (refer to Figure 1.11).

Use the Quick Access Toolbar

The *Quick Access Toolbar*, located at the top-left corner of any Office application window (refer to Figure 1.5), provides one-click access to commonly executed tasks such as saving a file or undoing recent actions. By default, the Quick Access Toolbar includes buttons for saving a file and for undoing or redoing recent actions. You can recover from a mistake by clicking Undo on the Quick Access Toolbar. If you click the arrow beside Undo—known as the Undo arrow—you can select from a list of previous actions in order of occurrence. The Undo list is not maintained when you close a file or exit the application, so you can only erase an action that took place during the current Office session. Similar to Undo, you can also Redo (or Replace) an action that you have just undone. You can also customize the Quick Access Toolbar to include buttons you frequently use for commands such as printing or opening files. Because the Quick Access Toolbar is onscreen at all times, the most commonly accessed tasks are just a click away.

Customize the Quick Access Toolbar

There are certain actions in an Office application that you use often, and for more convenient access, you can add a button for each action to the Quick Access Toolbar (see Figure 1.12). One such action you may want to add is a Quick Print button. Rather than clicking the File tab and selecting print options, you can add a Quick Print icon to the Quick Access Toolbar, and one click will print your document with the default settings of the Print area. Other buttons can also be added such as Spelling & Grammar to quickly check the spelling of the document.

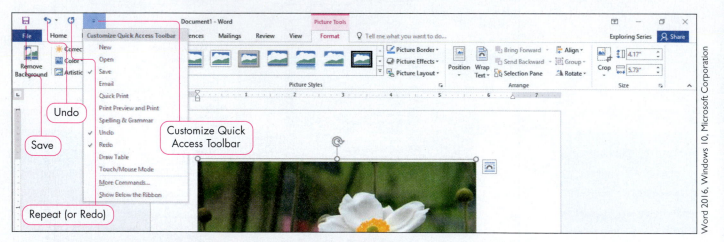

FIGURE 1.12 Customize the Quick Access Toolbar

> **To add a command to the Quick Access Toolbar, complete one of the following steps:**
>
> - Click Customize Quick Access Toolbar and then click More Commands near the bottom of the menu options. Then, select commands from a list and click Add.
> - Right-click the command on the Ribbon and click Add to Quick Access Toolbar.

Similarly, remove a command from the Quick Access Toolbar by right-clicking the icon on the Quick Access Toolbar and clicking *Remove from Quick Access Toolbar*. If you want to display the Quick Access Toolbar beneath the Ribbon, click *Customize Quick Access Toolbar* and click *Show Below the Ribbon*.

Getting Help

One of the most frustrating things about learning new software is determining how to complete a task. Microsoft includes comprehensive help with Office so that you are less likely to feel such frustration. As you work with any Office application, you can access help online as well as within the current software installation.

Use the *Tell me what you want to do Box*

STEP 5 New to Office 2016 is the *Tell me what you want to do* box. The ***Tell me what you want to do box***, located to the right of the last tab (see Figure 1.13), not only enables you to search for help and information about a command or task you want to perform, but it will also present you with a shortcut directly to that command and in some instances (like Bold) it will complete the action for you. Perhaps you want to find an instance of a word in your document and replace it with another word but cannot locate the command on the Ribbon. You can type *find and replace* in the *Tell me what you want to do* box and a list of commands related to the skill will display. For example, in Figure 1.13, you see that Replace displays as an option in the list. If you click this option, the Find and Replace dialog box opens without you having to locate the button to do so.

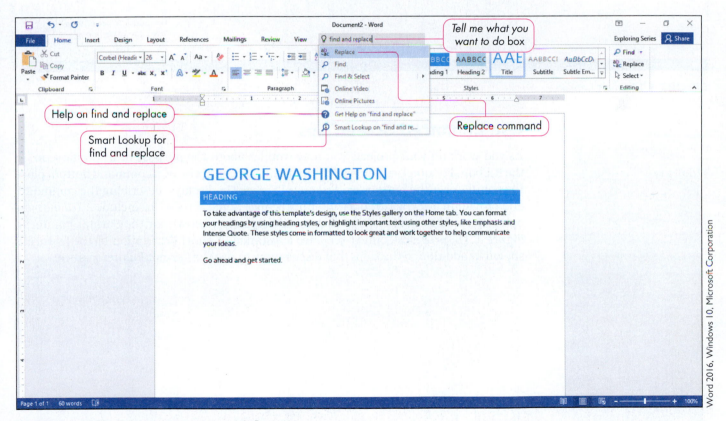

FIGURE 1.13 The *Tell me what you want to do* Box

Should you want to read about the feature instead of apply it, you can click *Get Help on "find and replace"* option, which will open Office Help for the feature. Another new feature is Smart Lookup. This feature opens the Insights pane that shows results from a Bing search on the task description typed in the box (see Figure 1.14). **Smart Lookup** provides information about tasks or commands in Office, and can also be used to search for general information on a topic such as *President George Washington*. Smart Lookup is also available on the shortcut menu when you right-click text.

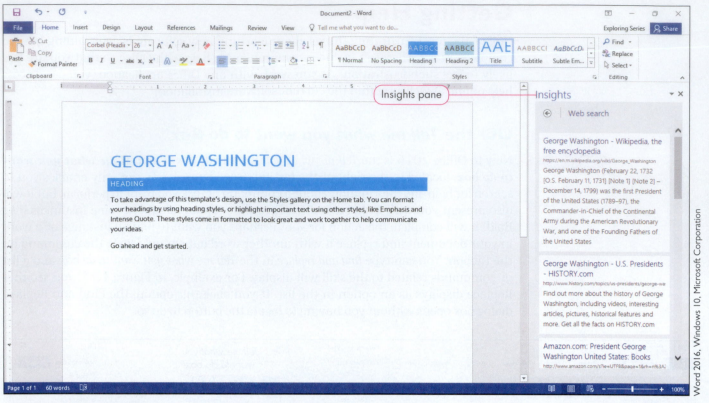

FIGURE 1.14 Smart Lookup

Use Enhanced ScreenTips

As you work on your projects you may wonder about the purpose of a specific icon on the Ribbon. For quick summary information on the purpose of a command button, place the pointer over the button. An **Enhanced ScreenTip** displays, describing the command, and providing a keyboard shortcut, if applicable. Some ScreenTips include a *Tell me more* option for additional help. The Enhanced ScreenTip, shown for the Format Painter in Figure 1.15, provides context-sensitive assistance. A short description of the feature is shown in addition to the steps that discuss how to use the Format Painter feature.

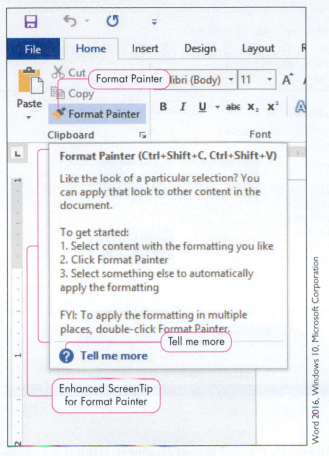

FIGURE 1.15 Enhanced ScreenTip

Installing Add-ins

Sometimes it is helpful to extend the functionality of Office programs by adding a Microsoft or third-party add-in to the program. An ***add-in*** is a custom program or additional command that extends the functionality of a Microsoft Office program (see Figure 1.16). Some add-ins are available for free while others may have a cost associated with them. For example, in PowerPoint you could add a Poll Everywhere poll that enables you to interact with your audience by having them respond to a question you have asked. The audience's electronic responses will appear on a slide as a real-time graph or word cloud. In Excel, add-ins provide additional functionality that can help with statistics and data mining.

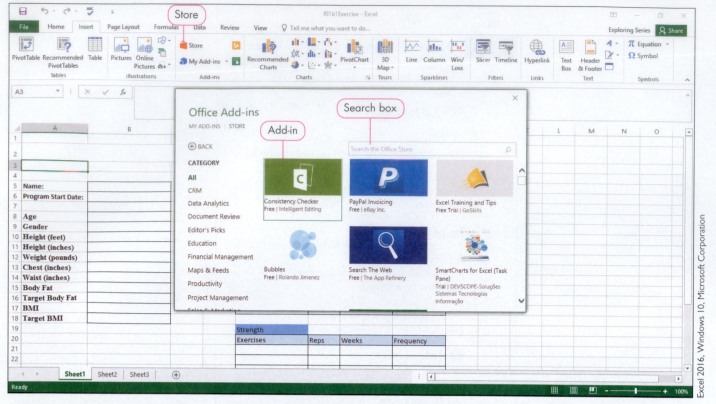

FIGURE 1.16 Add-Ins for Excel

To search for and install an add-in from the Microsoft Store, complete the following steps:

1. Click the Insert tab.
2. Click Store (refer to Figure 1.16). Browse the list of add-ins or use the search box.
3. Click the add-in. A box will display with information about the add-in such as its purpose, the cost (if any), and information it may access.
4. Click Trust It to add the add-in to your application. The newly added add-in will be available for future use in the My Add-ins list located on the Insert tab.

Quick Concepts

1. What are the benefits of logging in with your Microsoft account? *p. 5*
2. What is the purpose of the Quick Access Toolbar? *p. 14*
3. You are having trouble completing a task in Microsoft Word. What are some of the Office application features you could use to assist you in getting help with that task? *pp. 15–17*

1 Getting Started with Office Applications

The Spotted Begonia Art Gallery just hired several new clerical assistants to help you develop materials for the various activities coming up throughout the year. A coworker sent you a letter and asked for your assistance in making a few minor formatting changes. The letter is to thank the ABC Arts Foundation for its generous donation to the *Discover the Artist in You!* program and to invite them to the program's kickoff party. To begin, you will open Word and then open an existing document. You will use the Shortcut menu to make simple changes to the document. Finally, you will use the *Tell me what you want to do* box to apply a style to the first line of text.

STEP 1 ›› OPEN A MICROSOFT OFFICE APPLICATION

You start Microsoft Word from the Windows Start menu. Refer to Figure 1.17 as you complete Step 1.

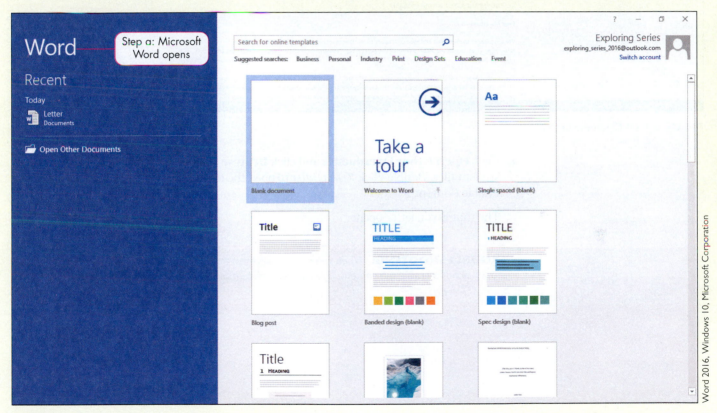

FIGURE 1.17 Open Word

a. Start your computer and log into your Microsoft account. On the Start menu, click **All apps** and click **Word 2016**.

Microsoft Word displays.

You open a thank-you letter that you will later modify. Refer to Figure 1.18 as you complete Step 2.

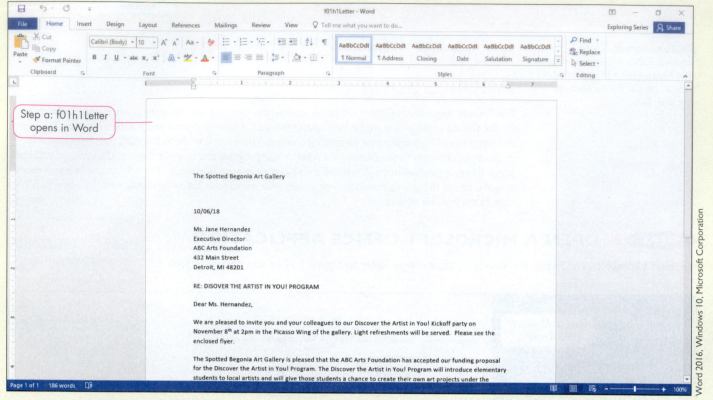

Step a: f01h1Letter
opens in Word

FIGURE 1.18 Open the Letter

a. Click **Open Other Documents** and click **Browse**. Navigate to the location of your student files. Double-click *f01h1Letter* to open the file shown in Figure 1.18. Click Enable Content.

The thank-you letter opens.

TROUBLESHOOTING: When you open an file from the student files associated with this book, you will need to enable the content. You may be confident of the trustworthiness of the files for this book.

You save the document with a different name, to preserve the original file. Refer to Figure 1.19 as you complete Step 3.

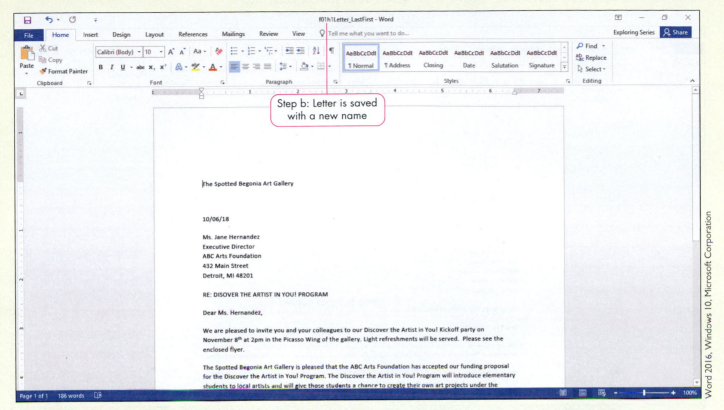

FIGURE 1.19 Save the Letter with a New Name

a. Click the **File tab**, click **Save As**, and then click **Browse** to display the Save As dialog box. Click **This PC** or click the location where you are saving your files.

b. Click in the **File name box** and type **f01h1Letter_LastFirst**.

When you save files, use your last and first names. For example, as the Common Features author, I would name my document "f01h1Letter_RutledgeAmy".

> **TROUBLESHOOTING:** If you make any major mistakes in this exercise, you can close the file, open *f01h1Letter* again, and then start this exercise over.

c. Click **Save**.

The file is now saved as f01h1Letter_LastFirst. You can check the title bar of the workbook to confirm that the file has been saved with the correct name.

You would like to apply italics to the *Discover the Artist in You!* text in the first sentence of the letter. You will select the text and use the shortcut menu to apply italics to the text. Refer to Figure 1.20 as you complete Step 4.

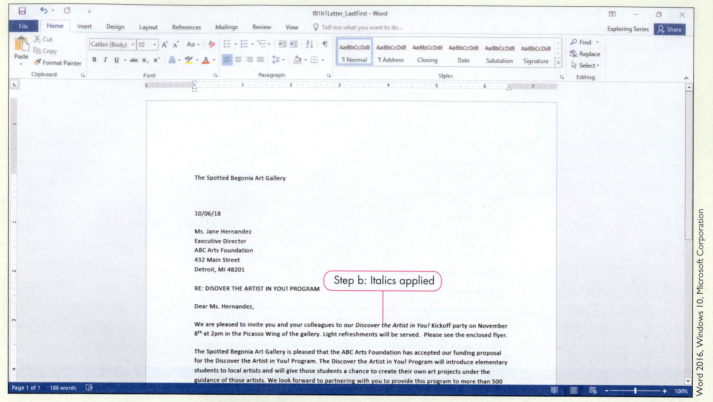

FIGURE 1.20 Apply Italics Using the Shortcut Menu

a. Select the text **Discover the Artist in You!** in the first sentence of the letter that starts with *We are pleased*.

   The text is selected.

b. Right-click the selected text. Click **Font** on the Shortcut menu. Click **Italic** under Font style, and click **OK**.

   Italics is applied to the text.

c. Click **Save** on the Quick Access Toolbar.

You would like to apply a style to the first line in the letter. Since you do not know how to complete the task, you use the *Tell me what you want to do* box to search for and apply the change. Refer to Figure 1.21 as you complete Step 5.

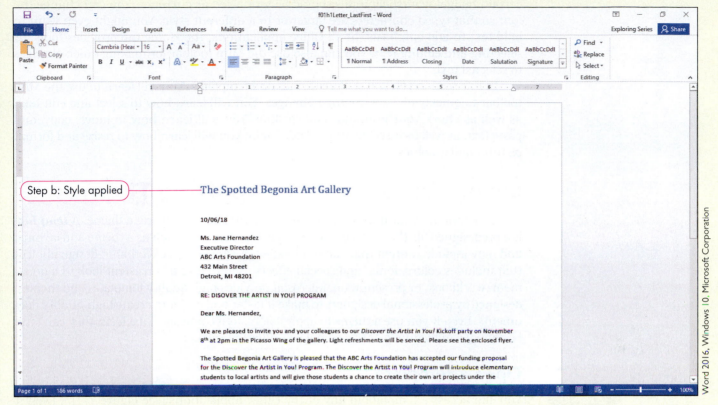

FIGURE 1.21 Change the Text Style Using the *Tell me what you want to do* Box

    a. Triple-click the entire first line of the letter that starts with *The Spotted Begonia Art Gallery* to select it. Click the ***Tell me what you want to do* box**, and type **heading 1**.

       A list of options appears below the box.

    b. Click **Promote to Heading1** to apply the style to the selected text.

       The Heading 1 style is applied to the text.

    c. Save the document. Keep the document open if you plan to continue with the next Hands-On Exercise. If not, save and close the workbook, and exit Word.

Format Document Content

After creating a document, worksheet, or presentation, you will probably want to make some formatting changes. You might prefer to center a title, or maybe you think that certain budget worksheet totals should be formatted as currency. You can change the font so that typed characters are larger or in a different style. You might even want to bold text to add emphasis. In all Office applications, the Home tab provides tools for selecting and editing text. You can also use the Mini toolbar for making quick changes to selected text.

In this section you will explore themes and templates. You will learn to use the Mini toolbar to quickly make formatting changes. You will learn how to select and edit text, as well as check your grammar and spelling. You will learn how to move, copy, and paste text, as well as insert pictures. And, finally, you will learn how to resize and format pictures and graphics.

Using Templates and Applying Themes

You can enhance your documents by using a template or applying a theme. A *template* is a predesigned file that incorporates formatting elements, such as a theme and layouts, and may include content that can be modified. A *theme* is a collection of design choices that includes colors, fonts, and special effects used to give a consistent look to a document, workbook, or presentation. Microsoft provides high quality templates and themes, designed by professional designers to make it faster and easier to create high-quality documents. Even if you use a theme to apply colors, fonts, and special effects, they can later be changed individually or to a completely different theme.

Open a Template

STEP 1 ▶▶ You can access a template in any of the Office applications (see Figure 1.22). Even if you know only a little bit about the software, you could then make a few changes so that the file would accurately represent your specific needs. The document also would be prepared much more quickly than if you designed it yourself from a blank file. For example, you might want to prepare a home budget using an Excel template, such as the Family monthly budget planner template, that is available by typing *Budget* in the *Suggested searches* template list.

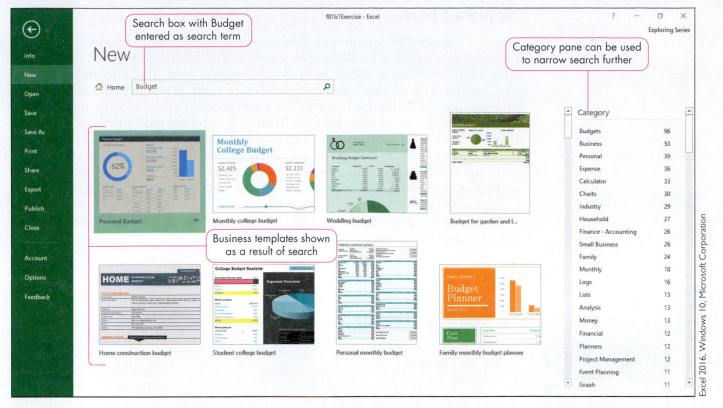

FIGURE 1.22 Templates in Excel

The Templates list is comprised of template groups available within each Office application. The search box enables you to locate other templates that are available online. When you click one of the Suggested searches, additional choices are displayed. Once you select a template, you can view more information about the template including author information, a general overview about the template, and additional views (if applicable).

> **To search for and use a template, complete the following steps:**
>
> 1. Open the Microsoft application with which you will be working.
> 2. Type a search term in the *Search for online templates box*, or click one of the Suggested search terms.
> 3. Scroll through the template options or use the pane at the right to narrow your search further.
> 4. Select a template, and review its information in the window that opens.
> 5. Click Create to open the template in the application.

A Help window may display along with the worksheet template. Read it for more information about the template, or close it to continue working.

Apply a Theme

Applying a theme enables you to visually coordinate various page elements. Themes are a bit different for each of the Office applications. In Word, a theme is a set of coordinating fonts, colors, and special effects, such as shadowing or glows that are combined into a package to provide a stylish appearance (see Figure 1.23). In PowerPoint, a theme is a file that includes the formatting elements like a background, a color scheme, and slide layouts that position content placeholders. Themes in Excel are similar to those in Word in that they are a set of coordinating fonts, colors, and special effects. Themes in Excel will not only change the color of the fill in a cell, but will also affect any SmartArt or charts in the workbook. Access also has a set of themes that coordinate the appearance of fonts and colors for objects such as Forms and Reports. In Word and PowerPoint, themes can be accessed from the Design tab. In Excel they can be accessed from the Page Layout tab. In Access, themes can be applied to forms and reports. To apply a theme, click the Themes arrow, and select a theme from the Themes gallery.

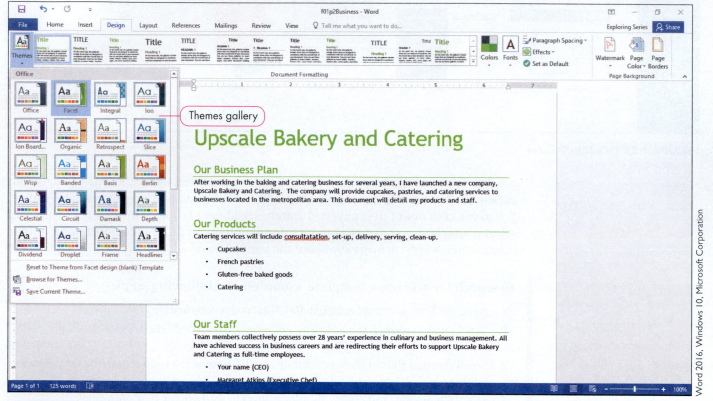

FIGURE 1.23 Themes in Word

Modifying Text

Formatting and modifying text in documents, worksheets, or presentations is an essential function when using Office applications. Centering a title, formatting cells, or changing the font color or size are tasks that occur frequently. In all Office applications, the Home tab provides tools for editing selected text. You can also use the Mini toolbar for making quick changes to selected text.

Select Text

STEP 2 Before making any changes to existing text or numbers, you must first select the characters. A general rule that you should commit to memory is "Select, then do." A foolproof way to select text or numbers is to place the pointer before the first character of the text you want to select, and then drag to highlight the intended selection. Before you drag, be sure that the pointer takes on the shape of the letter *I*, called the *I-beam* $\boxed{\text{I}}$. Although other methods for selecting exist, if you remember only one way, it should be the click-and-drag method. If your attempted selection falls short of highlighting the intended area, or perhaps highlights too much, click outside the selection and try again.

Sometimes it can be difficult to precisely select a small amount of text, such as a single word or sentence. Other times, the task can be overwhelming large, such as when selecting an entire 550-page document. In either case there are shortcuts to selecting text. The shortcuts shown in Table 1.2 are primarily applicable to text in Word and PowerPoint. When working with Excel, you will more often need to select multiple cells. To select multiple cells, drag the intended selection when the pointer displays as a large white plus sign $\boxed{\Leftrightarrow}$.

TABLE 1.2 Shortcut Selection in Word and PowerPoint	
Item Selected	**Action**
One word	Double-click the word.
One line of text	Place the pointer at the left of the line, in the margin area. When the pointer changes to a right-pointing arrow, click to select the line.
One sentence	Press and hold Ctrl, and click in the sentence to select it.
One paragraph	Triple-click in the paragraph.
One character to the left of the insertion point	Press and hold Shift, and press the left arrow on the keyboard.
One character to the right of the insertion point	Press and hold Shift, and press the right arrow on the keyboard.
Entire document	Press and hold Ctrl, and press A on the keyboard.

Once you have selected the desired text, besides applying formatting, you can delete or simply type over to replace the text.

Edit Text

At times, you will want to make the font size larger or smaller, change the font color, or apply other font attributes. For example, if you are creating a handout for a gallery show opening, you may want to apply a different font to emphasize key information such as dates and times. Because such changes are commonplace, Office places those formatting commands in many convenient places within each Office application.

You can find the most common formatting commands in the Font group on the Home tab. As noted earlier, Word, Excel, and PowerPoint all share very similar Font groups that provide access to tasks related to changing the character font. Remember that you can place the pointer over any command icon to view a summary of the icon's purpose, so although the icons might at first appear cryptic, you can use the pointer to quickly determine the purpose and applicability to your desired text change.

The way characters display onscreen or print in documents, including qualities such as size, spacing, and shape, is determined by the font. Office applications have a default font, Calibri, which is the font that will be in effect unless you change it. Other font attributes include bold, italic, and font color, all of which can be applied to selected text. Some formatting commands, such as Bold and Italic, are called ***toggle commands***. They act somewhat like light switches that you can turn on and off. Once you have applied bold formatting to text, the Bold command is highlighted on the Ribbon when that text is selected again. To undo bold formatting, click Bold again.

If you want to apply a different font to a section of your project for added emphasis or interest, you can make the change by selecting a font from within the Font group on the Home tab. You can also change the font by selecting from the Mini toolbar.

If the font change that you plan to make is not included as a choice on either the Home tab or the Mini toolbar, you can find what you are looking for in the Font dialog box. Click the Dialog Box Launcher in the bottom-right corner of the Font group. Figure 1.24 shows a sample Font dialog box. Because the Font dialog box provides many formatting choices in one window, you can make several changes at once. Depending on the application, the contents of the Font dialog box vary slightly, but the purpose is consistent—providing access to choices related to modifying characters.

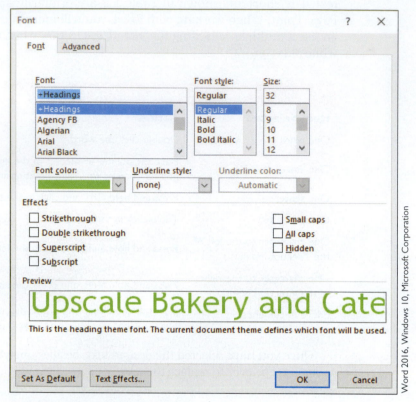

FIGURE 1.24 The Font Dialog Box

Use the Mini Toolbar

You have learned that you can always use commands on the Home tab of the Ribbon to change selected text within a document, worksheet, or presentation. Although using the Ribbon to select commands is simple enough, the *Mini toolbar* provides an even faster way to accomplish some of the same formatting changes. When you select any amount of text within a worksheet, document, or presentation, move the pointer slightly within the selection to display the Mini toolbar (see Figure 1.25). The Mini toolbar provides access to the most common formatting selections, such as bold or italic, or font type or color. Unlike the Quick Access Toolbar, the Mini toolbar is not customizable, which means that you cannot add or remove options from the toolbar.

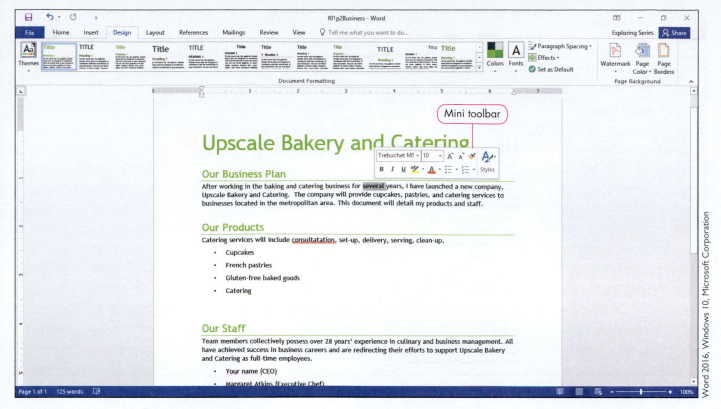

FIGURE 1.25 The Mini Toolbar

The Mini toolbar is displayed only when text is selected. The closer the pointer is to the Mini toolbar, the darker the toolbar becomes. As you move the pointer away from the selected text, the Mini toolbar eventually fades away. If the Mini toolbar is no longer displayed, you can right-click the selection to make the Mini toolbar appear again. To make selections from the Mini toolbar, click a command on the toolbar. To temporarily remove the Mini toolbar from view, press Esc.

To permanently disable the Mini toolbar so that it does not display in any open file when text is selected, complete the following steps:

1. Click the File tab and click Options.
2. Click General.
3. Click the *Show Mini toolbar on selection* check box to deselect it.
4. Click OK.

Copy Formats with Format Painter

 Using *Format Painter*, you can copy all formatting from one area to another in Word, PowerPoint, and Excel (see Figure 1.26). If, for example, a heading in Word includes multiple formatting features, you will save time by copying the entire set of formatting options to the other headings. In so doing, you will ensure the consistency of formatting for all headings because they will appear exactly alike.

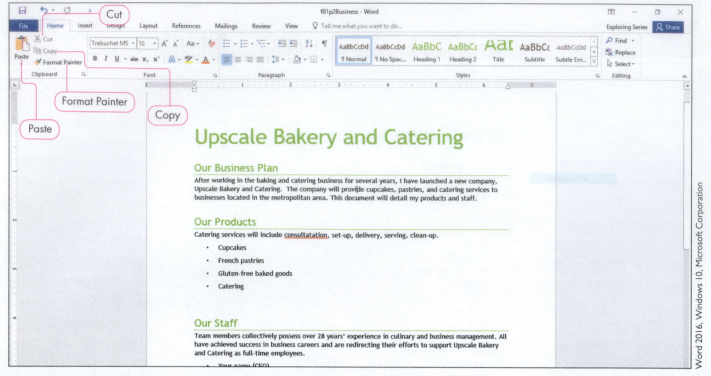

FIGURE 1.26 Format Painter

To copy a format, complete the following steps:

1. Select the text containing the desired format.
2. Single-click Format Painter if you want to copy the format to only one other selection. If, however, you plan to copy the same format to multiple areas, double-click Format Painter.
3. Select the area to which the copied format should be applied.

If you single-clicked Format Painter to copy the format to one other selection, Format Painter turns off once the formatting has been applied. If you double-clicked Format Painter to copy the format to multiple locations, continue selecting text in various locations to apply the format. Then, to turn off Format Painter, click Format Painter again or press Esc.

Relocating Text

On occasion, you will want to relocate a section of text from one area to another. Suppose that you have included text on a PowerPoint slide that you believe would be more appropriate on a different slide. Or perhaps an Excel formula should be copied from one cell to another because both cells should be totaled in the same manner. You can move the slide text or copy the Excel formula by using the cut, copy, and paste features found in the Clipboard group on the Home tab. The Office **Clipboard** is an area of memory reserved to temporarily hold selections that have been cut or copied and allows you to paste the selections. When the computer is shut down or loses power, the contents of the Clipboard are erased, so it is important to finalize the paste procedure during the current session.

Cut, Copy, and Paste Text

STEP 4 ➤➤ To **cut** means to remove a selection from the original location and place it in the Office Clipboard. To **copy** means to duplicate a selection from the original location and place a copy in the Office Clipboard. Although the Clipboard can hold up to 24 items at one time, the usual procedure is to paste the cut or copied selection to its final destination fairly quickly. To **paste** means to place a cut or copied selection into another location. In addition to using the Clipboard group icons, you can also cut, copy, and paste in any of the ways listed in Table 1.3.

TABLE 1.3	Cut, Copy, and Paste Options
Command	**Actions**
Cut	• Click Cut in Clipboard group. • Right-click selection and select Cut. • Press Ctrl+X.
Copy	• Click Copy in Clipboard group. • Right-click selection and select Copy. • Press Ctrl+C.
Paste	• Click in destination location and select Paste in Clipboard group. • Click in destination location and press Ctrl+V. • Click Clipboard Dialog Box Launcher to open Clipboard pane. Click in destination location. With Clipboard pane open, click arrow beside intended selection and select Paste.

Pearson Education, Inc.

To cut or copy text, complete the following steps:

1. Select the text you want to cut or copy.
2. Click the appropriate icon in the Clipboard group either to cut or copy the selection. Remember that cut or copied text is actually placed in the Clipboard, remaining there even after you paste it to another location. It is important to note that you can paste the same item multiple times, because it will remain in the Clipboard until you power down your computer or until the Clipboard exceeds 24 items.
3. Click the location where you want the cut or copied text to be placed. The location can be in the current file or in another open file within any Office application.
4. Click Paste in the Clipboard group on the Home tab.

When you paste text you may not want to paste the text with all of its formatting. In some instances, you may want to paste only the text, unformatted, so that it fits in with the formatting of its new location. When pasting text, there are several options available and those options will depend on the program you are using.

Use the Office Clipboard

When you cut or copy selections, they are placed in the Office Clipboard. Regardless of which Office application you are using, you can view the Clipboard by clicking the Clipboard Dialog Box Launcher, as shown in Figure 1.27.

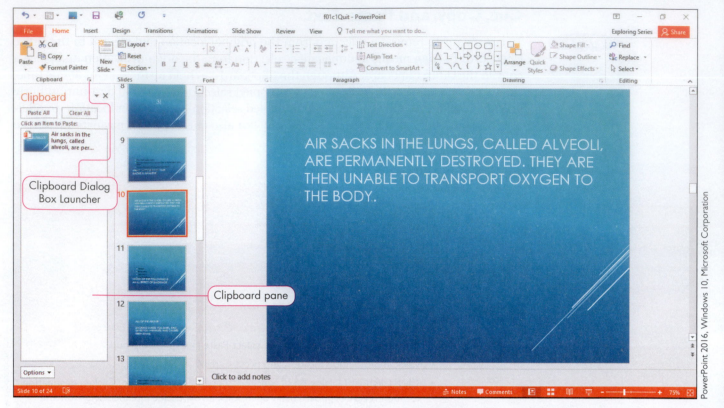

FIGURE 1.27 The Office Clipboard

Unless you specify otherwise when beginning a paste operation, the most recently added Clipboard item is pasted. You can, however, select an item from the Clipboard pane to paste. Click the item in the list to add it to the document. You can also delete items from the Clipboard by clicking the arrow next to the selection in the Clipboard pane and then clicking Delete. You can remove all items from the Clipboard by clicking Clear All. The Options button in the Clipboard pane enables you to control when and where the Clipboard is displayed. Close the Clipboard pane by clicking the Close ☒ button in the top-right corner of the pane or by clicking the arrow in the title bar of the Clipboard pane and selecting Close.

Checking Spelling and Grammar

STEP 5 ▶▶ As you create or edit a file you will want to make sure no spelling or grammatical errors exist. You will also be concerned with wording, being sure to select words or phrases that best represent the purpose of the document, worksheet, or presentation. On occasion, you might even find yourself at a loss for an appropriate word. Word, Excel, and PowerPoint all provide standard tools for proofreading, including a spelling and grammar checker and thesaurus.

Word and PowerPoint check your spelling and grammar as you type. If a word is unrecognized, it is flagged as misspelled or grammatically incorrect. Even though Excel does not check your spelling as you type, it is important to run the spelling checker in Excel. Excel's spelling checker will review charts, pivot tables, and other reports that all need to be spelled correctly. Misspellings are identified with a red wavy underline, grammatical problems are underlined in green, and word usage errors (such as using bear instead of bare) have a blue underline.

To check the spelling for an entire file, complete the following steps:

1. Click the Review tab.
2. Click Spelling and Grammar.

Beginning at the top of the document, each identified error is highlighted in a pane similar to Figure 1.28. You can then choose how to address the problem by making a selection from the options in the pane.

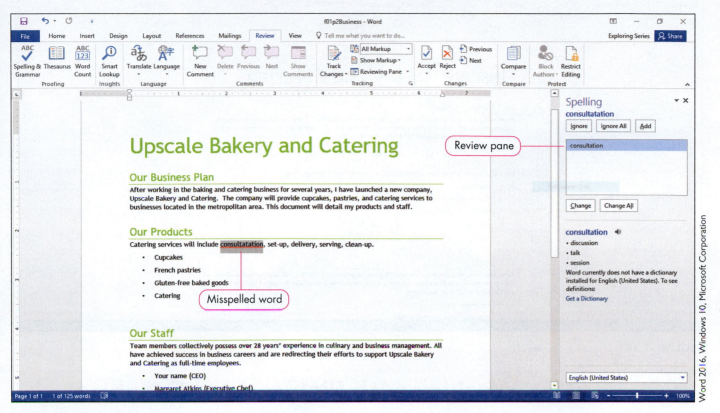

FIGURE 1.28 Checking for Spelling and Grammatical Errors

If the word or phrase is truly in error—that is, it is not a person's name or an unusual term that is not in the application's dictionary—you can correct it manually, or you can let the software correct it for you. If you right-click a word or phrase that is identified as a mistake, you will see a shortcut menu similar to that shown in Figure 1.29. If the Office dictionary makes a suggestion with the correct spelling, you can click to accept the suggestion and make the change. If a grammatical rule is violated, you will have an opportunity to select a correction. However, if the text is actually correct, you can click Ignore or Ignore All (to bypass all occurrences of the flagged error in the current document). Click *Add to Dictionary* if you want the word to be considered correct whenever it appears in any document. Similar selections on a shortcut menu enable you to ignore grammatical mistakes if they are not errors.

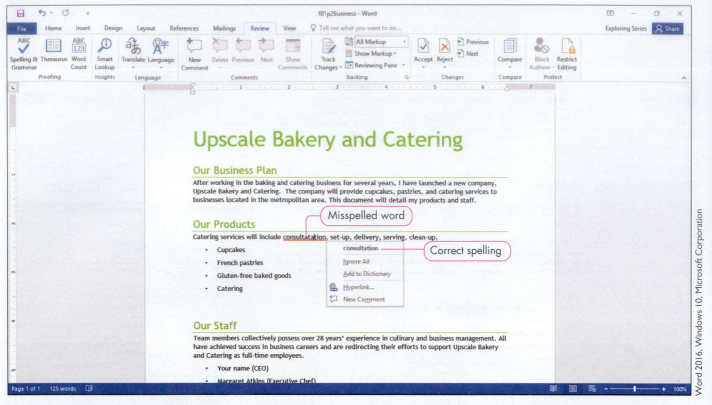

FIGURE 1.29 Correcting Misspelling

Working with Pictures and Graphics

Documents, worksheets, and presentations can include much more than just words and numbers. You can add energy and additional description to a project by including pictures and other graphic elements. Although a *picture* is usually just that—a digital photo—it is actually defined as a graphic element.

Insert Pictures and Graphics

 You can insert pictures from your own library of digital photos you have saved on your hard drive, OneDrive, or another storage medium, or you can initiate a Bing Image Search for online pictures directly inside the Office program you are using. The Bing search filters are set to use the Creative Commons license system. These are images and drawings that can be used more freely than images from websites. You should read the Creative Commons license for each image you use to avoid copyright infringement. You can also insert a picture from social media sites, such as Facebook, by clicking the Facebook icon at the bottom of the Online Pictures dialog box.

To insert an online picture from a Bing Image Search, complete the following steps:

1. Click in the file where you want the picture to be placed.
2. Click the Insert tab.
3. Click Online Pictures in the Illustrations group.
4. Type a search term in the Bing Image Search box and press Enter.
5. Select your desired image and click Insert (see Figure 1.30).

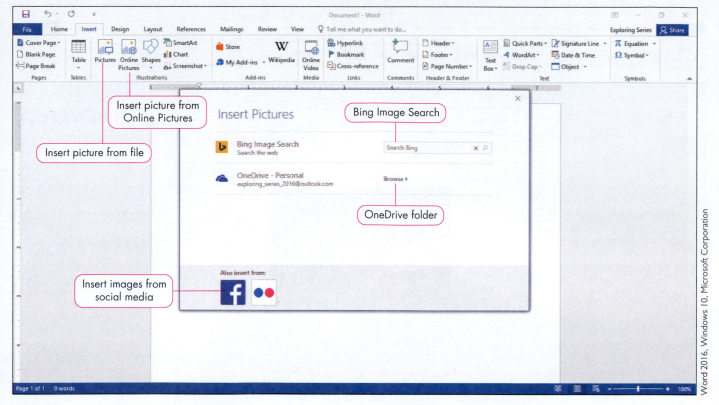

FIGURE 1.30 Inserting Online Pictures

To insert a picture from a file stored on your computer, complete the following steps:

1. Click in the file where you want the picture to be placed.
2. Click the Insert tab.
3. Click Pictures in the Illustrations group to search for a file located on your computer.
4. Locate the file and select it. Click Insert at the bottom of the dialog box to insert the file into your document.

Resize and Format Pictures and Graphics

You have learned how to add a picture to your document, but quite often, a picture is inserted in a size that is too large or too small for your purposes. To resize a picture, you can drag a corner sizing handle. You should never resize a picture by dragging a center sizing handle, as doing so would skew the picture. You can also resize a picture by adjusting settings in the Size group of the Picture Tools Format tab. When a picture is selected, the Picture Tools Format tab includes options for modifying a picture (see Figure 1.31). You can apply a picture style or effect, as well as add a picture border, from selections in the Picture Styles group. Click More (see Figure 1.31) to view a gallery of picture styles. As you point to a style, the style is shown in Live Preview, but the style is not applied until you click it. Options in the Adjust group simplify changing a color scheme, applying creative artistic effects, and even adjusting the brightness, contrast, and sharpness of an image.

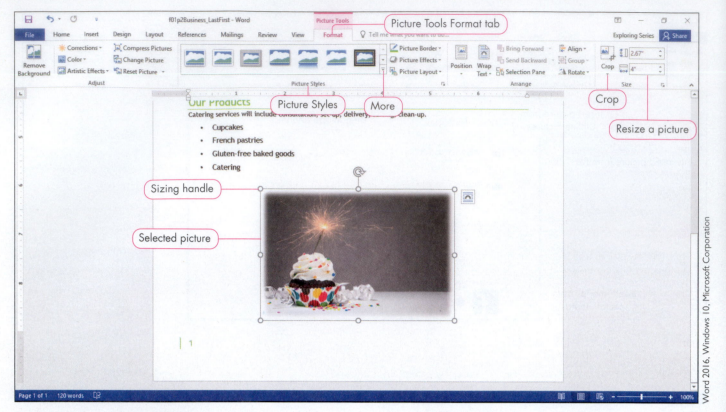

FIGURE 1.31 Formatting a Picture

If a picture contains more detail than is necessary, you can crop it, which is the process of trimming edges that you do not want to display. The Crop tool is located on the Picture Tools Format tab (refer to Figure 1.31). Even though cropping enables you to adjust the amount of a picture that displays, it does not actually delete the portions that are cropped out unless you actually compress the picture. Therefore, you can later recover parts of the picture, if necessary. Cropping a picture does not reduce the file size of the picture or the document in which it displays.

Quick Concepts

4. What is the difference between a theme and a template? *p. 24*

5. Give an example of when Format Painter could be used. *p. 29*

6. When will an Office application identify a word as misspelled that is not actually misspelled? *p. 33*

Hands-On Exercises

Watch the Video for this Hands-On Exercise!

MyITLab®
HOE2 Training

Skills covered: Open a Template • Select Text • Edit Text • Use the Mini Toolbar • Format Painter • Cut, Copy, and Paste Text • Check Spelling and Grammar • Insert a Picture

2 Format Document Content

As the administrative assistant for the Spotted Begonia Art Gallery, you want to create a flyer to announce the *Discover the Artist in You!* kickoff event. You decide to use a template to help you get started more quickly. You will modify the flyer created with the template by adding and editing text and a photo.

STEP 1 ›› OPEN A TEMPLATE

To expedite the process of creating a flyer, you will review the templates that are available in Microsoft Word. You search for flyers and finally choose one that is appropriate for the gallery, knowing that you will be able to replace the photos with your own. Refer to Figure 1.32 as you complete Step 1.

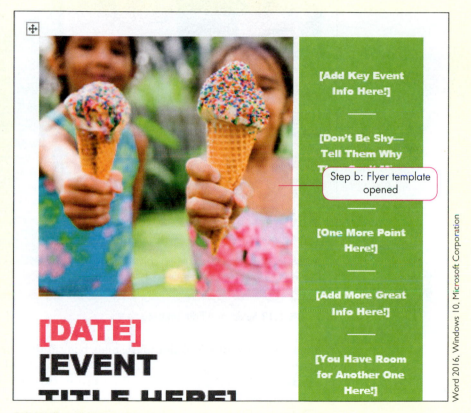

Word 2016, Windows 10, Microsoft Corporation

FIGURE 1.32 Use a Template

a. Start Word. In the *Search for online templates* box type the search term **event flyer** to search for event flyer templates Click **Search**.

Your search results in a selection of event flyer templates.

b. Locate the event flyer template in Figure 1.32 and click to select it. The template appears in a preview. Click **Create** to open the flyer template.

The flyer template that you selected opens in Word.

> **TROUBLESHOOTING:** If you do not find the template in the figure, you may access the template from the student data files – *f01h2Flyer*.

c. Click **Save** on the Quick Access Toolbar. Save the document as **f01h2Flyer_LastFirst**. Because this is the first time to save the flyer file, the Save button on the Quick Access Toolbar opens a dialog box in which you must indicate the location of the file and the file name.

You will replace the template text to create the flyer, adding information such as a title, date, and description. After adding the text to the document, you will modify the organization name in the flyer so it is more like the logo text. Refer to Figure 1.33 as you complete Step 2.

FIGURE 1.33 Select and Edit Text

a. Click the [Date] **placeholder** in the main body of the text and type **May 31, 2018** in the placeholder. Click the [Event Title Here] **placeholder** and type **Discover the Artist in You!** in the placeholder. Press **Enter** and continue typing **Spotted Begonia Art Gallery**. Click the [Event Description Heading] **placeholder** and type **A Special Childrens Event**. (Ignore the misspelling at this time.)

You modify the placeholders to customize the flyer for your purposes.

b. Point to the text **Discover the Artist in You!** until the pointer becomes an I-beam. Click and drag to select the text. Click the **Font arrow** on the Mini toolbar. Select **Eras Bold ITC**.

The font is changed.

c. Select the text, **May 31, 2018**. Click the **Font Size arrow** on the Mini toolbar. Select **26** on the Font Size menu.

The font size is changed to 26 pt.

d. Click Save on the Quick Access Toolbar to save the document.

USE FORMAT PAINTER

You want the gallery name font to match that of the event description heading in the flyer. You recently learned about using the Format Painter tool to quickly apply font attributes to text. Refer to Figure 1.34 as you complete Step 3.

Step a: Text format changed using Format Painter

Word 2016, Windows 10, Microsoft Corporation

FIGURE 1.34 Use Format Painter

a. Click the **Home tab**. Select the text **A Special Childrens Event**, and click **Format Painter** in the Clipboard group. Drag to select the text **Spotted Begonia Art Gallery**.

The text is now modified to match the font and size of the event description heading.

b. Save the document.

STEP 4 **CUT, COPY, AND PASTE TEXT**

You decide that one of the paragraphs in the flyer would be best near the end of the document. You cut the paragraph and paste it in the new location. Refer to Figure 1.35 as you complete Step 4.

Step a: Text moved

Word 2016, Windows 10, Microsoft Corporation

FIGURE 1.35 Move Text

a. Point to the text **Spotted Begonia Art Gallery** until the pointer becomes an I-beam. Click and drag to select the text. Press **Ctrl+X**.

The paragraph text is cut from the document and placed in the Office Clipboard.

b. Click before the word *May*. Press **Ctrl+V** to paste the previously cut text.

The text is now moved above the event date.

c. Save the document.

Because this flyer will be seen by the public, it is important to check the spelling and grammar for your document. Refer to Figure 1.36 as you complete Step 5.

FIGURE 1.36 Check Spelling and Grammar

a. Press **Ctrl+Home**. Click the **Review tab**, and click **Spelling & Grammar**. in the Proofing group Click **Change** to accept the suggested change to *Children's* in the Spelling pane. Click **OK** to close the dialog box.

The spelling and grammar check is complete.

b. Save the document.

You want to add an image saved on your computer that was taken at a previous children's event held at the gallery. Refer to Figure 1.37 as you complete Step 6.

FIGURE 1.37 Insert Picture

a. Click the **image** to select it. Click the **Insert tab** and then click **Pictures**. Browse to your student data files and locate the *f01h2Art* picture file. Click **Insert**.

The child's image is inserted into the flyer and replaces the template image of the children with ice cream.

b. Save and close the document. You will submit this file to your instructor at the end of the last Hands-On Exercise.

Modify Document Layout and Properties

When working with a document, at some point you must get it ready for distribution and/or printing. Before you send a document or print it, you will want to view the final product to make sure that your margins and page layout are as they should be.

In this section you will learn about Backstage view and explore how to view and edit document properties. You will learn about views and how to change a document view to suit your needs. Additionally, you will learn how to modify the page layout including page orientation and margins as well as how to add headers and footers. Finally, you will explore Print Preview and the various printing options available to you.

Using Backstage View

Backstage view is a component of Office that provides a concise collection of commands related to a file. Using Backstage view, you can view or specify settings related to protection, permissions, versions, and properties. A file's properties include the author, file size, permissions, and date modified. Backstage view also includes options for customizing program settings, signing in to your Office account, and exiting the application. You can create a new document, as well as open, save, print, share, export, and close files using Backstage view. Backstage view also enables you to exit the application.

Click the File tab to see Backstage view (see Figure 1.38). Backstage view will occupy the entire application window, hiding the file with which you are working. You can return to the application in a couple of ways. Either click the Back arrow in the top-left corner or press Esc on the keyboard.

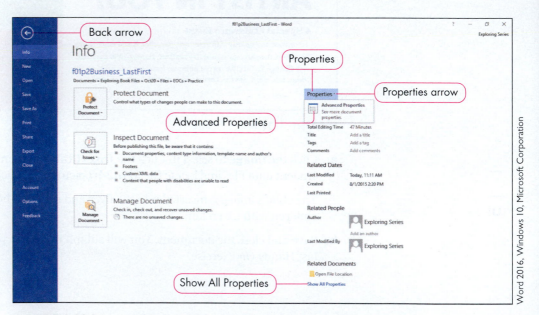

FIGURE 1.38 Backstage View and Document Properties

Customize Application Options

General settings in the Office application in which you are working can also be customized (see Figure 1.39). For example, you can change the AutoRecover settings, a feature that enables Word to recover a previous version of a document, such as the location and save frequency. You can alter how formatting, spelling, and grammar are checked by the application such as ignoring words in all uppercase letters. You can also modify the AutoCorrect feature. Additionally, you can change the language in which the application is displayed or the language for spelling and grammar checking, which may be helpful for a language course.

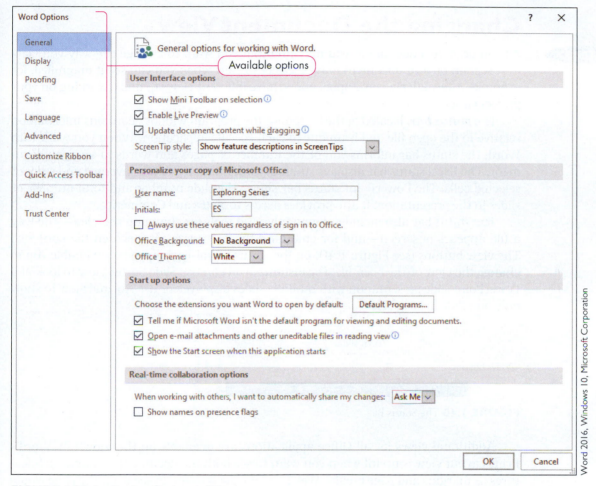

FIGURE 1.39 Application Options in Word

To customize an Office application, complete the following steps:

1. Click the File tab.
2. Click Options and select the option of your choice.
3. Click OK.

View and Edit Document Properties

STEP 1 ▶▶ It is good to include information that identifies a document, such as the author, document purpose, intended audience, or general comments. Those data elements, or metadata, are saved with the document, but do not appear in the document as it displays onscreen or is printed. You can use the Document Properties, located in Backstage view, to display descriptive information. You can even search for a file based on metadata you assign a document. For example, suppose you apply a tag of *Picasso* to all documents you create that are associated with that particular artist. Later, you can use that keyword as a search term, locating all associated documents. Statistical information related to the current document such as file size, number of pages, and total words are located on the Info page of Backstage view. You can modify some document information, such as adding a title or comments, but for more possibilities, display the Advanced Properties (refer to Figure 1.38).

To display the Advanced Properties, complete the following steps:

1. Click the File tab.
2. Click the Properties arrow on the Info page.

Changing the Document View

STEP 2 ›› As you prepare a document, you may find that you want to change the way you view it. A section of your document may be easier to view when you can see it magnified, for example. Alternatively, some applications have different views to make working on your project easier.

The *status bar*, located at the bottom of the program window, contains information relative to the open file and is unique to each specific application. When you work with Word, the status bar informs you of the number of pages and words in an open document. The Excel status bar displays summary information, such as average and sum, of selected cells. The PowerPoint status bar shows the slide number and total number of slides in the presentation. It also provides access to Notes and Comments.

The status bar also includes commonly used tools for changing the *view*—the way a file appears onscreen—and for changing the zoom size of onscreen file contents. The view buttons (see Figure 1.40) on the status bar of each application enable you to change the view of the open file. For instance, you can use Slide Sorter view to look at a PowerPoint slide presentation with multiple slides displayed or use Normal view to show only one slide in large size.

Zoom slider

View buttons

Word 2016,
Windows 10,
Microsoft Corporation

FIGURE 1.40 The Status Bar

Additional views for all Office applications are available on the View tab. Word's Print Layout view is useful when you want to see both the document text and such features as margins and page breaks. Web Layout view is useful to see what the page would look like on the Internet. Read Mode view provides a clean look that displays just the content without the Ribbon or margins. It is ideal for use on a tablet where the screen may be smaller than on a laptop or computer. PowerPoint, Excel, and Access also provide other unique view options. As you learn more about Office applications, you will become aware of the views that are specific to each application.

The *Zoom slider* is a horizontal bar on the bottom-right side of the status bar that enables you to increase or decrease the size of the document onscreen. You can drag the tab along the slider in either direction to increase or decrease the magnification of the file (refer to Figure 1.40). Be aware, however, that changing the size of text onscreen does not change the font size when the file is printed or saved.

Changing the Page Layout

When you prepare a document or worksheet, you are concerned with the way the project appears onscreen and possibly in print. The Layout tab in Word and the Page Layout tab in Excel provide access to a full range of options such as margin settings and page orientation. PowerPoint does not have a Page Layout tab, since its primary purpose is displaying contents onscreen rather than in print.

Because a document or workbook is most often designed to be printed, you may need to adjust margins and change the page orientation for the best display. In addition, perhaps the document or spreadsheet should be centered on the page vertically or the text should be aligned in columns. You will find these and other common page settings in the Page Setup group on the Layout (or Page Layout) tab. For less common settings, such as determining whether headers should print on odd or even pages, you use the Page Setup dialog box.

Change Margins

STEP 3 ⟫ A ***margin*** is the area of blank space that displays to the left, right, top, and bottom of a document or worksheet. Margins display when you are in Print Layout or Page Layout view, or in Backstage view previewing a document to print. As shown in Figure 1.41, you can change the margins by clicking Margins in the Page Setup group. You can also change margins in the Print area on Backstage view.

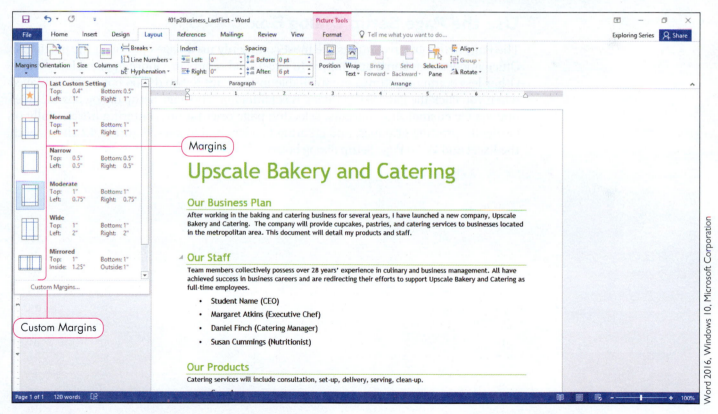

FIGURE 1.41 Page Margins in Word

To change margins in Word and Excel, complete the following steps:

1. Click the Layout (or Page Layout) tab.
2. Click Margins in the Page Setup group.
3. Select a preset margin option or click Custom Margins (refer to Figure 1.41) to display the Page Setup dialog box where you can apply custom margin settings.
4. Click OK to accept the settings and close the dialog box.

Change Page Orientation

Documents and worksheets can be displayed in different page orientations. A page displayed or printed in *portrait orientation* is taller than it is wide. A page in *landscape orientation* is wider than it is tall. Word documents are usually more attractive displayed in portrait orientation, whereas Excel worksheets are often more suited to landscape orientation.

To change the page orientation, complete the following steps:

1. Click the Layout (or Page Layout) tab.
2. Click Orientation in the Page Setup group.
3. Select Portrait or Landscape.

Orientation is also an option in the Print area of Backstage view.

Use the Page Setup Dialog Box

The Page Setup group contains the most commonly used page options in the particular Office application. Some are unique to Excel, and others are more applicable to Word. Other less common settings are available in the Page Setup dialog box only, displayed when you click the Page Setup Dialog Box Launcher. The Page Setup dialog box includes options for customizing margins, selecting page orientation, centering horizontally or vertically, printing gridlines, and creating headers and footers. Figure 1.42 shows both the Excel and Word Page Setup dialog boxes.

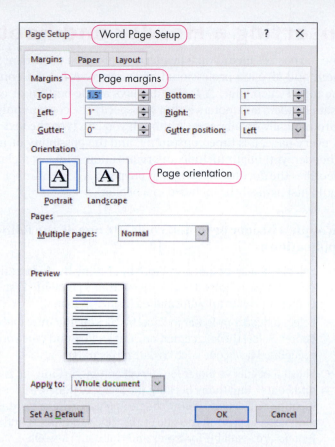

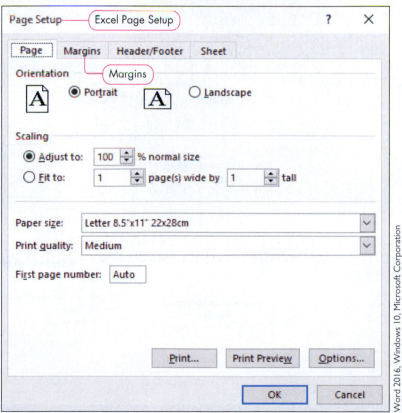

FIGURE 1.42 Page Setup Dialog Boxes in Word and Excel

Word 2016, Windows 10, Microsoft Corporation

Inserting a Header and Footer

STEP 4 » The purpose of including a header or footer in a document is to better identify the document and give it a professional appearance. A *header* consists of one or more lines at the top of each page. A *footer* displays at the bottom of each page. One advantage of using headers and footers is that you specify the content only once, after which it displays automatically on all pages. Although you can type the text yourself at the top or bottom of every page, it is time-consuming, and the possibility of making a mistake is great. As a header, you might include an organization name or a class number so that each page identifies the document's origin or purpose. A page number is a typical footer, although it could just as easily be included in a header.

To apply a header or footer, complete one of the following steps (based on the application):

- Select a header or footer in Word by clicking the Insert tab and then clicking Header or Footer (see Figure 1.43). Choose from a predefined list, or click Edit Header (or Edit Footer) to create an unformatted header or footer.

- Select a header or footer in Excel by clicking the Insert tab and clicking Header and Footer. Select the left, center, or right section and type your own footer or use a predefined field code such as date or file name.

- Select a header or footer for PowerPoint by clicking the Insert tab, clicking Header and Footer, and then checking the footer option for slides. In PowerPoint, a footer's location will depend on the theme applied to the presentation. For some themes, the footer will appear on the side of the slide rather than at the bottom. Headers and footers are available for Notes and Handouts as well.

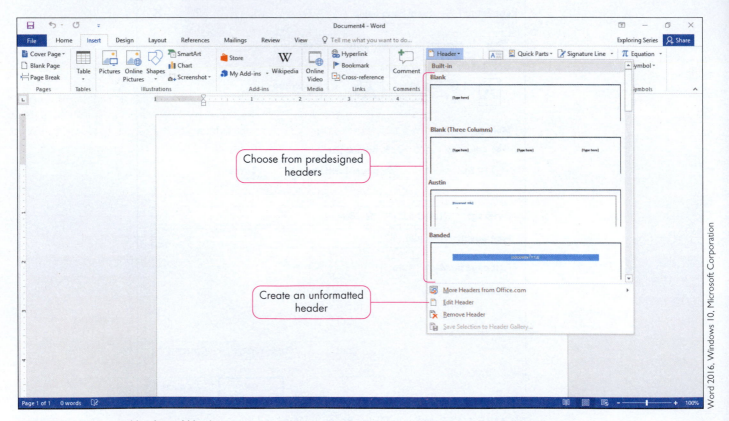

FIGURE 1.43 Insert Header in Word

After typing a header or footer, it can be formatted like any other text. It can be formatted in any font or font size. In Word or Excel, when you want to leave the header and footer area and return to the document, click Close Header and Footer (see Figure 1.44).

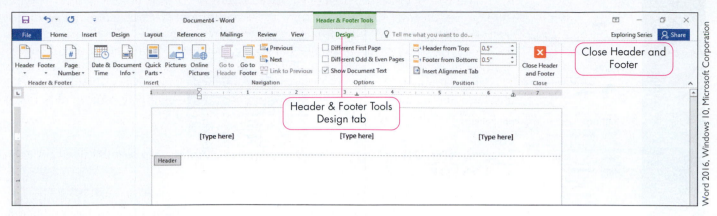

FIGURE 1.44 Close Header and Footer

Previewing and Printing a File

STEP 5 When you want to print an Office file, you can select from various print options, including the number of copies and the specific pages to print. It is a good idea to take a look at how your document or worksheet will appear before you print it. The Print Preview feature of Office enables you to do just that. In the Print Preview pane, you will see all items, including any headers, footers, graphics, and special formatting.

To view a file before printing, complete the following steps:

1. Click the File tab.
2. Click Print.

The subsequent Backstage view shows the file preview on the right, with print settings located in the center of the Backstage screen. Figure 1.45 shows a typical Backstage Print view. If you know that the page setup is correct and that there are no unique print settings to select, you can simply print without adjusting any print settings.

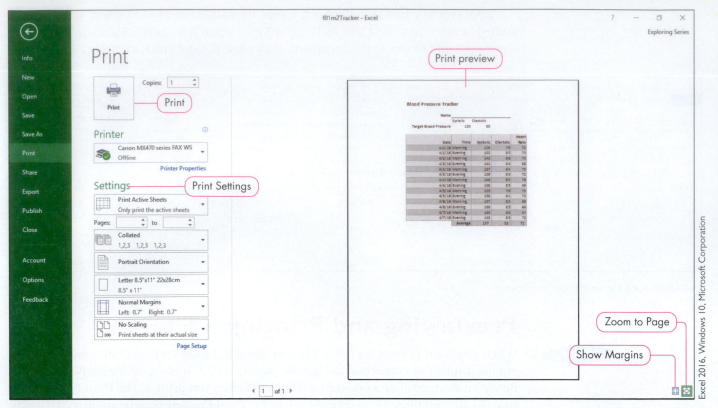

FIGURE 1.45 Backstage Print View in Excel

Excel 2016, Windows 10, Microsoft Corporation

Options to show the margins (*Show Margins*) and to increase the size of the print preview (*Zoom to Page*) are found on the bottom-right corner of the preview (refer to Figure 1.45). Remember that increasing the font size by adjusting the zoom applies to the current display only; it does not actually increase the font size when the file is printed or saved. To return the preview to its original view, click *Zoom to Page* once more.

Other options in the Backstage Print view vary depending on the application in which you are working. For example, PowerPoint's Backstage Print view includes options for printing slides and handouts in various configurations and colors, whereas Excel's focuses on worksheet selections and Word's includes document options. Regardless of the Office application, you will be able to access Settings options from Backstage view, including page orientation (landscape or portrait), margins, and paper size. To print a file, click the Print button (refer to Figure 1.45).

Quick Concepts

7. What functions and features are included in Backstage view? **p. 42**

8. Why would you need to change the view of a document? **p. 44**

9. What is the purpose of a header or footer? **p. 48**

Hands-On Exercises

Skills covered: Enter Document Properties • Change the Document View • Change Margins • Insert a Footer • Preview a File • Change Page Orientation

3 Modify Document Layout and Properties

You continue to work on the thank-you letter you previously started. As the administrative assistant for the Spotted Begonia Art Gallery, you must be able to search for and find documents previously created. You know that by adding tags to your letter you will more easily be able to find it at a later time. You will review and add document properties, and prepare the document to print and distribute by changing the page setup. Additionally, you will add a footer with Spotted Begonia's information. Finally, you will explore printing options, and save the letter.

STEP 1 >> ENTER DOCUMENT PROPERTIES

You will add document properties, which will help you locate the file when performing a search of your hard drive. Refer to Figure 1.46 as you complete Step 1.

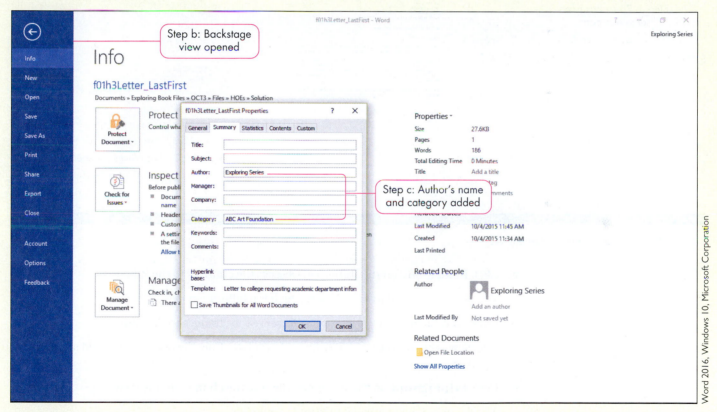

FIGURE 1.46 Backstage View

Word 2016, Windows 10, Microsoft Corporation

a. Open *f01h1Letter_LastFirst* if you closed it at the end of Hands-On Exercise 1, and save it as **f01h3Letter_LastFirst**, changing h1 to h3.

The letter is now open in Word.

b. Click the **File tab** and click **Properties** at the top-right of Backstage view. Click **Advanced Properties**.

The Properties dialog box opens so you can make changes.

c. Select the **Author box** and type your first and last name. Select the **Category box** and type **ABC Art Foundation**. Click **OK**.

You added the Author and Category properties to your document.

d. Save the document.

STEP 2 >> **CHANGE THE DOCUMENT VIEW**

To get a better perspective on your letter, you want to explore the various document views available in Word. Refer to Figure 1.47 as you complete Step 2.

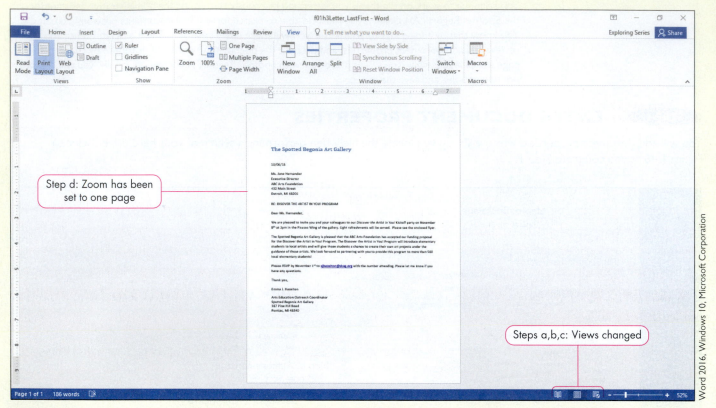

FIGURE 1.47 Change the Document View

a. Click **Read Mode** on the status bar. Observe the changes to the Ribbon.

The view is changed to Read Mode, which is a full-screen view.

b. Click **Web Layout** on the status bar. Observe the changes to the view.

The view is changed to Web Layout and simulates how the document would appear on the Web.

c. Click **Print Layout** on the status bar. Observe the changes to the view.

The document has returned to Print Layout view.

d. Click the **View tab** and click **Zoom** in the Zoom group. Click the **One Page option**. Click **OK**.

The entire letter is displayed.

While the letter was displayed in One Page zoom, you observed that the margins were too large. You will change the margins so they are narrower. Refer to Figure 1.48 as you complete Step 3.

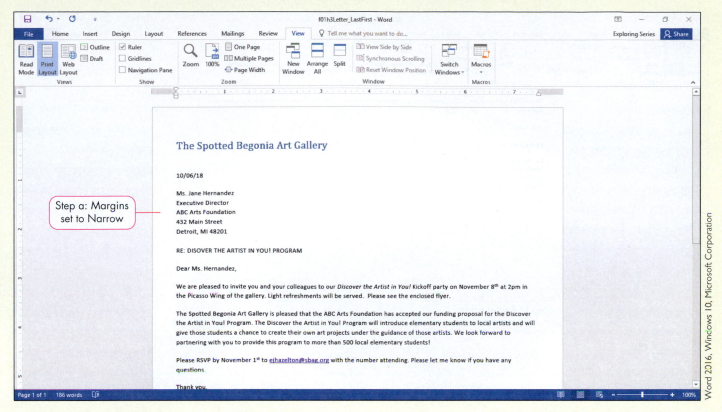

FIGURE 1.48 Change Margins

a. Click the **Layout tab** and click **Margins** in the Page Setup group. Select **Narrow**. Observe the changes.

The document margins were changed to Narrow.

b. Click the **View tab** and click **100%** in the Zoom group.

The document returns to its previous view.

c. Save the document.

Additional information such as a phone number and website need to be added to the letter. You decide to add these to the letter as a footer. Refer to Figure 1.49 as you complete Step 4.

FIGURE 1.49 Footer

a. Click the **Insert tab** and click **Footer** in the Header & Footer group. Click the **Blank (three columns)** footer.

The document opens in Header and Footer view. You select a footer with little formatting.

b. Click **[Type here]** on the far left of the footer. Type **Spotted Begonia Art Gallery** in that placeholder. Click **[Type here]** in the center of the footer. Type **www.sbag.org** in that placeholder. Click **[Type here]** on the far right of the footer. Type **Pontiac, MI** in that placeholder. On the Header & Footer Tools Design tab, click **Close Header and Footer** in the Close group.

The footer information is entered.

c. Save the document.

You have reviewed and finalized the letter, so you will print the document so it can be sent to its recipient. You will first preview the document as it will appear when printed. Refer to Figure 1.50 as you complete Step 5.

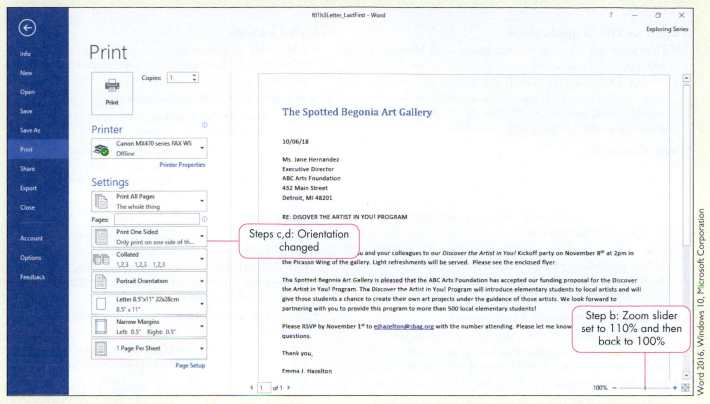

FIGURE 1.50 Backstage Print View

a. Click the **File tab** and click **Print**.

It is always a good idea to check the way a file will look when printed before actually printing it.

b. Drag the **Zoom slider on the status bar** to increase the document view to 110%. Click **Zoom to Page** (located at the far right of the status bar).

Your print preview returns to the original size.

c. Click **Portrait Orientation** in the Settings area. Click **Landscape Orientation**.

The letter appears in a wider and shorter view.

d. Return to Portrait Orientation to see the original view.

You decide that the flyer is more attractive in portrait orientation, so you return to that setting.

e. Save and close the file. Based on your instructor's directions, submit the following:

f01h2Flyer_LastFirst

f01h3Letter_LastFirst

Chapter Objectives Review

After reading this chapter, you have accomplished the following objectives:

1. **Start an Office application.**
   - Your Microsoft account connects you to all of Microsoft's Internet-based resources.
   - Change a Microsoft account: If you share your computer with another user, each user can have access to his own Microsoft account; you can easily switch between accounts so you can access your own files.

2. **Work with files.**
   - Create a new file: You can create a document as a blank document or with a template.
   - Open a file: You can open an existing file using the Open dialog box. Previously saved files can be accessed using the Recent documents list.
   - Save a file: Saving a file enables you to open it later for additional updates or reference. Files are saved to a storage medium such as a hard drive, CD, flash drive, or to the cloud on OneDrive.

3. **Use common interface components.**
   - Use the Ribbon: The Ribbon, the long bar located just beneath the title bar containing tabs, groups, and commands, is the command center of Office applications.
   - Use a shortcut menu: A shortcut menu provides choices related to the object, selection, or area of the document on which you right-click.
   - Use keyboard shortcuts: Keyboard shortcuts are keyboard equivalents for software commands. Universal keyboard shortcuts in Office include Ctrl+C (Copy), Ctrl+X (Cut), Ctrl+V (Paste), and Ctrl+Z (Undo).
   - Customize the Ribbon: You can personalize the Ribbon in your Office applications, giving you easier access to a frequently used set of commands that are unique to you or your business.
   - Use the Quick Access Toolbar: The Quick Access Toolbar, located at the top-left corner of any Office application window, provides one-click access to commonly executed tasks such as saving a file or undoing recent actions.
   - Customize the Quick Access Toolbar: You use certain actions in an Office application often, and for more convenient access, you can add a button for each action to the Quick Access Toolbar.

4. **Get help.**
   - Use the *Tell me what you want to do* box: The *Tell me what you want to do* box not only links to online resources and technical support but also provides quick access to functions.
   - Use Enhanced ScreenTips: An Enhanced ScreenTip describes a command and provides a keyboard shortcut, if applicable.

5. **Install add-ins.**
   - Add-ins are custom programs or additional commands that extend the functionality of a Microsoft Office program.

6. **Use templates and apply themes.**
   - Open a template: Templates are a convenient way to save time when designing a document.
   - Apply a theme: Themes are a collection of design choices that include colors, fonts, and special effects used to give a consistent look to a document, workbook, or presentation.

7. **Modify text.**
   - Select text: To select text or numbers, place the pointer before the first character or digit you want to select, and then drag to highlight the intended selection. Before you drag, be sure that the pointer takes on the shape of the letter *I*, called the I-beam.
   - Edit text: You can edit the font, font color, size, and many other attributes.
   - Use the Mini toolbar: The Mini toolbar provides instant access to common formatting commands after text is selected.
   - Copy formats with the Format Painter: Easily apply formatting from one selection to another by using Format Painter.

8. **Relocate text.**
   - Cut, copy, and paste text: To cut means to remove a selection from the original location and place it in the Office Clipboard. To copy means to duplicate a selection from the original location and place a copy in the Office Clipboard. To paste means to place a cut or copied selection into another location.
   - Use the Office Clipboard: When you cut or copy selections, they are placed in the Office Clipboard. You can paste the same item multiple times; it will remain in the Clipboard until you power down your computer or until the Clipboard exceeds 24 items.

9. **Check spelling and grammar.**
   - Office applications check and mark spelling and grammar errors as you type for later correction. The Thesaurus enables you to search for synonyms.

10. **Work with pictures and Graphics.**
    - Insert pictures and graphics: You can insert pictures from your own library of digital photos you have saved on your hard drive, OneDrive, or another storage medium, or you can initiate a Bing search for online pictures directly inside the Office program you are using.
    - Resize and format pictures and graphics: To resize a picture, drag a corner sizing handle; never resize a picture by dragging a center sizing handle. You can apply

a picture style or effect, as well as add a picture border, from selections in the Picture Styles group.

11. Use Backstage view.

- Customize application options: You can customize general settings in the Office application in which you are working, such as AutoRecover settings and location and save frequency.
- View and edit document properties: Information that identifies a document, such as the author, document purpose, intended audience, or general comments can be added to the document's properties. Those data elements are saved with the document, but do not appear in the document as it displays onscreen or is printed.

12. Change the document view.

- The status bar provides information relative to the open file and quick access to View and Zoom level options. Each application has a set of views specific to the application.

13. Change the page layout.

- Change margins: A margin is the area of blank space that displays to the left, right, top, and bottom of a document or worksheet.

- Change page orientation: Documents and worksheets can be displayed in different page orientations. Portrait orientation is taller than it is wide; landscape orientation is wider than it is tall.
- Use the Page Setup dialog box: The Page Setup dialog box includes options for customizing margins, selecting page orientation, centering horizontally or vertically, printing gridlines, and creating headers and footers.

14. Insert a header and footer.

- A footer displays at the bottom of each page.
- A header consists of one or more lines at the top of each page.

15. Preview and print a file.

- It is important to review your file before printing.
- Print options can be set in Backstage view and include page orientation, the number of copies, and the specific pages to print.

Key Terms Matching

Match the key terms with their definitions. Write the key term letter by the appropriate numbered definition.

a. Access

b. Add-in

c. Clipboard

d. Backstage view

e. Cloud storage

f. Format Painter

g. Footer

h. Group

i. Header

j. Margin

k. Microsoft Office

l. Mini toolbar

m. OneDrive

n. Quick Access Toolbar

o. Ribbon

p. Status bar

q. Tab

r. *Tell me what you want to do* box

s. Template

t. Theme

1. _____ A tool that copies all formatting from one area to another. **p. 29**

2. _____ Stores up to 24 cut or copied selections for use later on in your computing session. **p. 30**

3. _____ A task-oriented section of the Ribbon that contains related commands. **p. 10**

4. _____ An online app used to store, access, and share files and folders. **p. 5**

5. _____ Custom programs or additional commands that extend the functionality of a Microsoft Office program. **p. 17**

6. _____ A component of Office that provides a concise collection of commands related to an open file and includes save and print options. **p. 42**

7. _____ A tool that displays near selected text that contains formatting commands. **p. 28**

8. _____ Relational database software used to store data and convert it into information. **p. 4**

9. _____ Consists of one or more lines at the bottom of each page. **p. 48**

10. _____ A predesigned file that incorporates formatting elements, such as a theme and layouts, and may include content that can be modified. **p. 24**

11. _____ A collection of design choices that includes colors, fonts, and special effects used to give a consistent look to a document, workbook, or presentation. **p. 24**

12. _____ A component of the Ribbon that is designed to appear much like a tab on a file folder. **p. 9**

13. _____ Provides handy access to commonly executed tasks such as saving a file and undoing recent actions. **p. 14**

14. _____ The long bar at the bottom of the screen that houses the Zoom slider and various View buttons. **p. 44**

15. _____ A productivity software suite including a set of software applications, each one specializing in a particular type of output. **p. 4**

16. _____ Allows you to search for help and information about a command or task you want to perform, and will also present you with a shortcut directly to that command. **p. 15**

17. _____ The long bar located just beneath the title bar containing tabs, groups, and commands. **p. 8**

18. _____ The area of blank space that displays to the left, right, top, and bottom of a document or worksheet **p. 45**

19. _____ A technology used to store files and to work with programs that are stored in a central location on the Internet. **p. 5**

20. _____ Consists of one or more lines at the top of each page. **p. 48**

Multiple Choice

1. The Recent documents list shows documents that have been previously:
   - (a) Printed.
   - (b) Opened.
   - (c) Saved in an earlier software version.
   - (d) Deleted.

2. In Word or PowerPoint a quick way to select an entire paragraph is to:
   - (a) Place the pointer at the left of the line, in the margin area, and click.
   - (b) Triple-click inside the paragraph.
   - (c) Double-click at the beginning of the paragraph.
   - (d) Press Ctrl+C inside the paragraph.

3. When you want to copy the format of a selection but not the content, you should:
   - (a) Double-click Copy in the Clipboard group.
   - (b) Right-click the selection and click Copy.
   - (c) Click Copy Format in the Clipboard group.
   - (d) Click Format Painter in the Clipboard group.

4. Which of the following is *not* a benefit of using OneDrive?
   - (a) Save your folders and files to the cloud.
   - (b) Share your files and folders with others.
   - (c) Hold video conferences with others.
   - (d) Simultaneously work on the same document with others.

5. What does a red wavy underline in a document, spreadsheet, or presentation mean?
   - (a) A word is misspelled or not recognized by the Office dictionary.
   - (b) A grammatical mistake exists.
   - (c) An apparent word usage mistake exists.
   - (d) A word has been replaced with a synonym.

6. Which of the following is *true* about headers and footers?
   - (a) They can be inserted from the Layout tab.
   - (b) Headers and footers only appear on the last page of a document.
   - (c) Headers appear at the top of every page in a document.
   - (d) Only page numbers can be included in a header or footer.

7. Live Preview:
   - (a) Opens a predesigned document or spreadsheet that is relevant to your task.
   - (b) Provides a preview of the results of a choice you are considering before you make a final selection.
   - (c) Provides a preview of an upcoming Office version.
   - (d) Enlarges the font onscreen.

8. You can get help when working with an Office application in which one of the following areas?
   - (a) The *Tell me what you want to do* box
   - (b) Status bar
   - (c) Backstage view
   - (d) Quick Access Toolbar

9. In PowerPoint, a file that includes formatting elements such as a background, a color scheme, and slide layout is a:
   - (a) Theme.
   - (b) Template.
   - (c) Scheme.
   - (d) Variant.

10. A document or worksheet printed in landscape orientation is:
    - (a) Taller than it is wide.
    - (b) Wider than it is tall.
    - (c) A document with 2" left and right margins.
    - (d) A document with 2" top and bottom margins.

Practice Exercises

1 Designing Webpages

You have been asked to make a presentation to the local business association. With the mayor's renewed emphasis on growing the local economy, many businesses are interested in establishing a Web presence. The business owners would like to know a little bit more about how webpages are designed. In preparation for the presentation, you will proofread and edit your PowerPoint file. You decide to insert an image to enhance your presentation. Refer to Figure 1.51 as you complete this exercise.

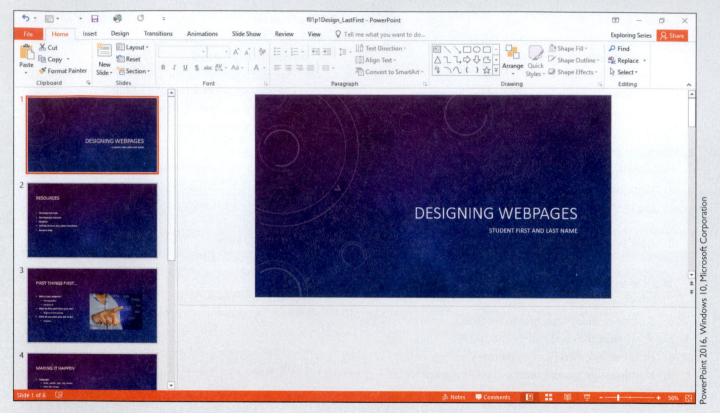

FIGURE 1.51 Designing Webpages Presentation

a. Open *f01p1Design*. Click the **File tab**, click **Save As**, and save the file as **f01p1Design_LastFirst**.

b. Ensure that Slide 1 is visible, select the text *Firstname Lastname*, and type your own first and last names. Click an empty area of the slide to cancel the selection.

c. Click the **Design tab**, then click the **Celestial theme** in the Themes group to apply it to all slides.

d. Click the **Review tab** and click **Spelling** in the Proofing group. In the Spelling pane, click **Change** or **Ignore** to make changes as needed. Most identified misspellings should be changed. The words *KompoZer* and *Nvu* are not misspelled, so you should ignore them when they are flagged. Click **OK** when you have finished checking spelling.

e. Click the **Slide Show tab**. Click **From Beginning** in the Start Slide Show group. Click each slide to view the show and press **Esc** when you reach the last slide, slide 6.

f. Click **Slide 2** in the Slides pane on the left. Triple-click to select the **Other tools** text on the slide and press **Backspace** on the keyboard to delete the text.

g. Click **Slide 4** in the Slides pane. Triple-click to select the **FrontPage,Nvu** text and press **Backspace** to delete the text.

h. Click the **Insert tab**. Click **Header & Footer** in the Text group. Click the **Slide number check box** to select it and click **Apply to All**.

i. Press **Ctrl+End** to place the insertion point at the end of *Templates* on Slide 4 and press **Enter**. Type **Database Connectivity** to create a new bulleted item.

j. Click **Slide 3** in the Slides pane. Click the **Insert tab** and click **Pictures** in the Images group. Browse to the student data files, locate and select *f01p1website*, and then click **Insert**.

k. Click the **Shape height box** in the Size group on the Picture Tools Format tab. Type **4** and then press Enter.

l. Click **Slide 6** in the Slides pane. Click the **Insert tab**, and then click **Store** in the Add-ins group. In the search box, type **multiple response poll**. Press **Enter**. The add-in will resize if the window or resolution is small.

m. Click the **Multiple Response Poll** and then click **Trust It** to insert it into the slide.

n. Click the **Insert question here text box** in the poll window, and type **Do you have a website?**

o. Click the first **Insert option here text box** and type **Yes**. Click the second **Insert option here text box** and type **No**. Click **Preview** in the poll window.

p. Click the **File tab** and click **Print**. Click the **Full Page Slides arrow** and click **6 Slides Horizontal** to see a preview of all of the slides as a handout. Click the **Back arrow**.

q. Click **Slide 1** in the Slides pane to move to the beginning of the presentation.

r. Drag the **Zoom slider** on the status bar to the right to **130%** to magnify the text. Use the **Zoom slider** to move to **60%**.

s. Save and close the file. Based on your instructor's directions, submit f01p1Design_LastFirst.

You have always been interested in baking and have worked in the field for several years. You now have an opportunity to devote yourself full time to your career as the CEO of a company dedicated to baking cupcakes and pastries, and to catering. One of the first steps in getting the business off the ground is developing a business plan so that you can request financial support. You will use Word to develop your business plan. Refer to Figure 1.52 as you complete this exercise.

a. Open *f01p2Business*. Click the **File tab**, click **Save As**, and save the file as **f01p2Business_LastFirst**.

b. Click the **Review tab** and click **Spelling & Grammar** in the Proofing group. Click **Change** for all suggestions and then click OK.

c. Select the paragraphs beginning with *Our Staff* and ending with *(Nutritionist)*. Click the **Home tab** and click **Cut** in the Clipboard group. Click to the left of *Our Products* and click **Paste**.

Upscale Bakery and Catering

Our Business Plan

After working in the baking and catering business for several years, I have launched a new company, Upscale Bakery and Catering. The company will provide cupcakes, pastries, and catering services to businesses located in the metropolitan area. This document will detail my products and staff.

Our Staff

Team members collectively possess over 28 years' experience in culinary and business management. All have achieved success in business careers and are redirecting their efforts to support Upscale Bakery and Catering as full-time employees.

- Student Name (CEO)
- Margaret Atkins (Executive Chef)
- Daniel Finch (Catering Manager)
- Susan Cummings (Nutritionist)

Our Products

Catering services will include consultation, set-up, delivery, serving, clean-up.

- Cupcakes
- French pastries
- Gluten-free baked goods
- Catering

1

Word 2016, Windows 10, Microsoft Corporation

FIGURE 1.52 Upscale Bakery Business Plan

d. Select the text **Your name** in the first bullet in the *Our Staff* section and replace it with your first and last names. Select the entire bullet list, click the **Font Size arrow** and then click **11**.

e. Double-click **Format Painter** in the Clipboard group on the Home tab. Drag the Format Painter pointer to change the other *Our Staff* bullets' font size to **11 pt**. Drag across all four *Our Products* bullets. Click Format Painter to deselect it.

f. Click the *Tell me what you want to do* box, and type **Footer**. Click **Add a Footer** scroll to locate the **Sideline footer**, click to add it to the page. Click **Close Header and Footer** on the Header & Footer Tools Design tab.

g. Select the last line in the document, which says *Insert and position picture here*, and press **Delete**. Click the **Insert tab** and click **Online Pictures** in the Illustrations group.

- Click in the **Bing Image Search box**, type **Cupcakes**, and then press **Enter**.
- Select any cupcake image and click **Insert**. Do not deselect the image.

> **TROUBLESHOOTING:** If you are unable to find a cupcake image in the Bing Image Search then you can use f01p2Cupcake from the student data files.

- Ensure the **Picture Tools Format tab** is active, and in the Picture Styles group, click the **Soft Edge Rectangle**.
- Click the **Shape width box** in the Size group and change the width to **4**.
- Click outside the picture.

h. Click the **File tab**. In the Properties section, add the tag **Business Plan**. Add your first and last name to the Author property.

i. Click **Print** in Backstage view. Change Normal Margins to **Moderate Margins**. Click the **Back arrow**.

j. Click the **picture** and click **Center** in the Paragraph group on the Home tab.

k. Save and close the file. Based on your instructor's directions, submit f01p2Business_LastFirst.

Mid-Level Exercises

1 Reference Letter

You are an instructor at a local community college. A student asked you to provide her with a letter of reference for a job application. You have used Word to prepare the letter, but now you want to make a few changes before it is finalized.

a. Open *f01m1RefLetter* and save it as **f01m1RefLetter_LastFirst**.

b. Select the date and point to several font sizes on the Mini toolbar. Use Live Preview to compare them. Click **11**.

c. Change the rest of the letter (below the date) to font size 11.

d. Apply bold to the student's name, *Stacy VanPatten*, in the first sentence.

e. Customize the Quick Access Toolbar so that a Spelling and Grammar button is added.

f. Use the button you just added to correct all errors using Spelling & Grammar. Stacy's last name is spelled correctly.

g. Select the word *intelligent* in the second paragraph, and use the Thesaurus to find a synonym. Replace *intelligent* with **gifted**. Change the word *an* to **a** just before the new word. Close the Thesaurus.

h. Add the tag **reference letter** to the Properties for the file in Backstage view.

i. Move the last paragraph—beginning with *In my opinion*—to position it before the second paragraph—beginning with *Stacy is a gifted*.

j. Move the insertion point to the beginning of the document.

k. Change the margins to **Narrow**.

l. Preview the document as it will appear when printed.

m. Save and close the file. Based on your instructor's directions, submit f01m1RefLetter_LastFirst.

2 Medical Monitoring

You are enrolled in a Health Informatics program of study in which you learn to manage databases related to health fields. For a class project, your instructor requires that you monitor your blood pressure, recording your findings in an Excel worksheet. You have recorded the week's data and will now make a few changes before printing the worksheet for submission.

a. Open *f01m2Tracker* and save it as **f01m2Tracker_LastFirst**.

b. Preview the worksheet as it will appear when printed. Change the orientation of the worksheet to **Landscape**. Close the Preview.

c. Click in the cell to the right of *Name* and type your first and last names. Press **Enter**.

d. Change the font of the text in **cell C1** to **Verdana**. Use Live Preview to try some font sizes. Change the font size to **20**.

e. Add the Spelling and Grammar feature to the Quick Access Toolbar, and then check the spelling for the worksheet to ensure that there are no errors.

 f. Get help on showing decimal places. You want to increase the decimal places for the values in **cells E22**, **F22**, and **G22** so that each value shows one place to the right of the decimal. Select the cells and then use the *Tell me what you want to do* box to immediately apply the changes. You might use **Increase Decimals** as a search term. When you find the answer, increase the decimal places to **1**.

 g. Click **cell A1** and insert an Online Picture of your choice related to blood pressure. Resize and position the picture so that it displays in an attractive manner. Apply the **Soft Edges** picture effect to the image and set to **5 pt**.

h. Change the page margins to **Wide**.

i. Insert a footer with the page number in the center of the spreadsheet footer area. Click on any cell in the worksheet.

j. Change the View to **Normal**.

k. Open Backstage view and adjust print settings to print two copies. You will not actually print two copies unless directed by your instructor.

l. Save and close the file. Based on your instructor's directions, submit f01m2Tracker_LastFirst.

3 Today's Musical Artists

With a few of your classmates, you will use PowerPoint to create a single presentation on your favorite musical artists. Each student must create at least one slide and then all of the slides will be added to the presentation. Because everyone's schedule is varied, you will use your OneDrive to pass the presentation file among the group.

a. Designate one student to create a new presentation and save it as **f01m3Music_GroupName**.

b. Add your group member names to the Author Properties in Backstage view.

c. Add a theme to the presentation.

d. Add one slide that contains the name of an artist, the genre, and two or three interesting facts about the artist.

e. Insert a picture of the artist or clip art that represents the artist.

f. Put your name on the slide that you created. Save the presentation.

g. Pass the presentation to the next student so that he or she can perform the same tasks in Steps d–f and save the presentation before passing it on to the next student. Continue until all group members have created a slide in the presentation.

h. Save and close the file. Based on your instructor's directions, submit f01m3Music_GroupName.

Beyond the Classroom

Fitness Planner
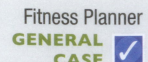
GENERAL CASE

You will use Microsoft Excel to develop a fitness planner. Open *f01b1Exercise* and save it as **f01b1Exercise_LastFirst**. Because the fitness planner is a template, the exercise categories are listed, but without actual data. You will personalize the planner. Change the orientation to **Landscape**. Move the contents of **cell A2** (*Exercise Planner*) to **cell A1**. Click **cell A8** and use Format Painter to copy the format of that selection to **cells A5** and **A6**. Increase the font size of **cell A1** to **18**. Use the *Tell me what you want to do* box to learn how to insert a header and put your name in the header. Begin the fitness planner, entering at least one activity in each category (warm-up, aerobics, strength, and cool-down). Insert a picture from a Bing Image Search that is appropriate for the planner. You may want to use **exercise** as your search term. Check the spelling in the workbook. Add the tag **Exercise Planner** to the Properties in Backstage view. Review the document in Print Preview. Ensure that the tracker fits on a single sheet of paper when printed. Resize the image if necessary to fit on the page. Save and close the file. Based on your instructor's directions, submit f01b1Exercise_LastFirst.

Household Records
DISASTER RECOVERY

FROM SCRATCH

Use Microsoft Excel to create a detailed (fictional) record of valuables in your household. In case of burglary or disaster, an insurance claim is expedited if you are able to itemize what was lost along with identifying information such as serial numbers. You will then make a copy of the record on another storage device for safekeeping outside your home (in case your home is destroyed by a fire or weather-related catastrophe). Design a worksheet listing at least five fictional appliances and pieces of electronic equipment along with the serial number of each. Change the orientation to **Landscape**. Use the *Tell me what you want to do* box to learn how to insert a header and put your name in the header. Return to Normal view. Insert a picture from a Bing Image Search that is appropriate for the record. You may want to use **appliances** as your search term. Review the document in Print Preview. Ensure that the records fit on a single sheet of paper when printed. Move and resize the image as necessary so that it fits on the page when printed. Check the spelling in the workbook. Add the tag **Disaster Recovery** to the Properties in Backstage view. Save the workbook as **f01b2Household_LastFirst**. Save and close the file. Based on your instructor's directions, submit f01b2Household_LastFirst.

Capstone Exercise

You are a member of the Student Government Association (SGA) at your college. As a community project, the SGA is sponsoring a Stop Smoking drive designed to provide information on the health risks posed by smoking cigarettes and to offer solutions to those who want to quit. The SGA has partnered with the local branch of the American Cancer Society as well as the outreach program of the local hospital to sponsor free educational awareness seminars. As the secretary for the SGA, you will help prepare a PowerPoint presentation that will be displayed on screens around campus and used in student seminars. The PowerPoint presentation has come back from the reviewers with only one comment: A reviewer suggested that you spell out Centers for Disease Control and Prevention, instead of abbreviating it. You will use Microsoft Office to help with those tasks.

Open and Save Files

You will open, review, and save a PowerPoint presentation.

a. Open *f01c1Quit* and save it as **f01c1Quit_LastFirst**.

Select Text, Move Text, and Format Text

A reviewer commented that you should modify the text on slide 12. The last sentence in the paragraph should be first since it is the answer to the question on the previous slide. You also add emphasis to the sentence.

a. Click **Slide 12**, and select the text **Just one cigarette – for some people**.

b. Cut the selected text and then paste it at the beginning of the paragraph.

c. Use the Mini toolbar to apply **Italics** to the text *Just one cigarette – for some people*.

Apply a Theme and Change the View

There is a blank theme for the slides, so you apply a different theme to the presentation.

a. Apply the **Metropolitan** theme to the presentation.

b. Change the View to Slide Sorter. Click **Slide 2** and drag to move Slide 2 to the end of the presentation. It will become the last slide (Slide 22).

c. Return to Normal view.

Insert and Modify a Picture

You will add a picture to the first slide and then resize it and position it.

a. Click **Slide 1**, and insert an online picture appropriate for the topic of **smoking**.

b. Resize the picture and reposition it.

c. Click outside the picture to deselect it.

Use the *Tell me what you want to do* Box

A reviewer suggested that you spell out Centers for Disease Control and Prevention, instead of abbreviating it. You know that there is a find and replace option to do this but you cannot remember where it is. You use the *Tell me what you want to do* box to help you with this function. You then replace the text.

a. Use the *Tell me what you want to do* box to search **replace**.

b. Use the results from your search to find a function that will find and then replace the single occurrence of *CDC* with **Centers for Disease Control and Prevention**.

Customize the Quick Access Toolbar

You often preview and print your presentations and find it would be easier to have a button on the Quick Access Toolbar to do so. You customize the toolbar by adding this shortcut.

a. Add the Print Preview button to the Quick Access Toolbar.

b. Add the Print button to the Quick Access Toolbar.

Use Print Preview, Change Print Layout, and Print

To get an idea of how the presentation will look when printed, you will preview the presentation. You decide to print the slides so that two slides will appear on one page.

a. Preview the document as it will appear when printed.

b. Change the Print Layout to **2 Slides** (under the Handouts section).

c. Preview the document as it will appear when printed.

d. Adjust the print settings to print two copies. You will not actually print two copies unless directed by your instructor.

Check Spelling and Change View

Before you call the presentation complete, you will correct any spelling errors and view the presentation as a slide show.

a. Check the spelling. The word *hairlike* is not misspelled, so it should not be corrected.

b. View the slide show. Click after reviewing the last slide to return to the presentation.

c. Save and close the file. Based on your instructor's directions, submit f01c1Quit_LastFirst.

Introduction to Excel

LEARNING OUTCOME You will create and format a basic Excel worksheet.

OBJECTIVES & SKILLS: After you read this chapter, you will be able to:

CASE STUDY | OK Office Systems

Alesha Bennett, the general manager at OK Office Systems (OKOS), asked you to calculate the retail price, sale price, and profit analysis for selected items on sale this month. Using markup rates provided by Alesha, you will calculate the retail price, the amount OKOS charges its customers for the products. You will calculate sale prices based on discount rates between 10% and 30%. Finally, you will calculate the profit margin to determine the percentage of the final sale price over the cost.

After you create the initial pricing spreadsheet, you will be able to change values and see that the formulas update the results automatically. In addition, you will insert data for additional sale items or delete an item based on the manager's decision. After inserting formulas, you will format the data in the worksheet to have a professional appearance.

Creating and Formatting a Worksheet

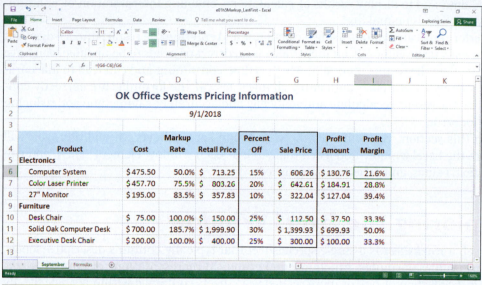

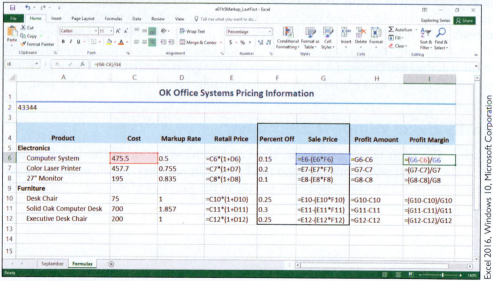

FIGURE 1.1 Completed OKOS Worksheet

CASE STUDY | OK Office Systems

Starting File	File to be Submitted
e01h1Markup	**e01h5Markup_LastFirst**

Introduction to Spreadsheets

Organizing, calculating, and evaluating quantitative data are important skills needed today for personal and managerial decision making. You track expenses for your household budget, maintain a savings plan, and determine what amount you can afford for a house or car payment. Retail managers create and analyze their organizations' annual budgets, sales projections, and inventory records. Charitable organizations track the donations they receive, the distribution of those donations, and overhead expenditures.

You should use a spreadsheet to maintain data and perform calculations. A *spreadsheet* is an electronic file that contains a grid of columns and rows used to organize related data and to display results of calculations, enabling interpretation of quantitative data for decision making.

Performing calculations using a calculator and entering the results into a ledger can lead to inaccurate values. If an input value is incorrect or needs to be updated, you have to recalculate the results manually, which is time-consuming and can lead to inaccuracies. A spreadsheet makes data entry changes easy. If the formulas are correctly constructed, the results recalculate automatically and accurately, saving time and reducing room for error.

In this section, you will learn how to design spreadsheets. In addition, you will explore the Excel window and learn the name of each window element. Then, you will enter text, values, and dates in a spreadsheet.

Exploring the Excel Window

In Excel, a *worksheet* is a single spreadsheet that typically contains descriptive labels, numeric values, formulas, functions, and graphical representations of data. A *workbook* is a collection of one or more related worksheets contained within a single file. By default, new workbooks contain one worksheet. Storing multiple worksheets within one workbook helps organize related data together in one file and enables you to perform calculations among the worksheets within the workbook. For example, you might want to create a budget workbook of 13 worksheets, one for each month to store your personal income and expenses and a final worksheet to calculate totals across the entire year.

Identify Excel Window Elements

Like other Microsoft Office programs, the Excel window contains the Quick Access Toolbar, the title bar, sizing buttons, and the Ribbon. In addition, Excel contains unique elements. Figure 1.2 identifies elements specific to the Excel window, and Table 1.1 lists and describes the Excel window elements.

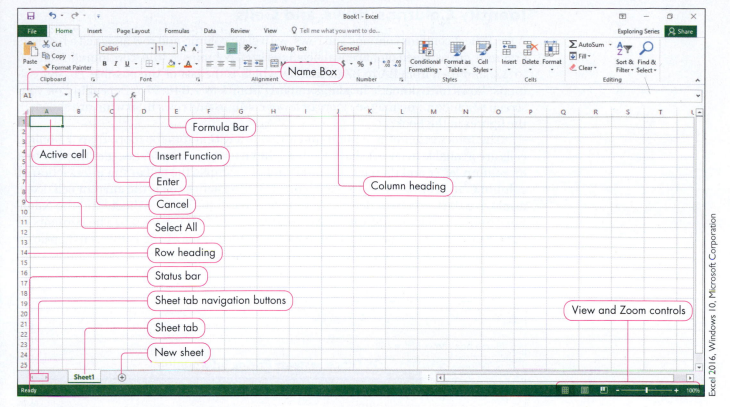

FIGURE 1.2 Excel Window

TABLE 1.1	Excel Elements
Element	**Description**
Name Box	An element located below the Ribbon and displays the address of the active cell. Use the Name Box to go to a cell, assign a name to one or more cells, or select a function.
Cancel ☒	When you enter or edit data, click Cancel to cancel the data entry or edit, and revert back to the previous data in the cell, if any. Cancel changes from gray to red when you position the pointer over it.
Enter ☑	When you enter or edit data, click Enter to accept data typed in the active cell and keep the current cell active. Enter changes from gray to blue when you position the pointer over it.
Insert Function f_x	Click to display the Insert Function dialog box to search for and select a function to insert into the active cell. The Insert Function icon changes from gray to green when you position the pointer over it.
Formula Bar	An element located below the Ribbon and to the right of the Insert Function command. Shows the contents of the active cell. You enter or edit cell contents here or directly in the active cell. Drag the bottom border of the Formula Bar down to increase the height of the Formula Bar to display large amounts of data or a long formula contained in the active cell.
Select All ◲	The triangle at the intersection of the row and column headings in the top-left corner of the worksheet. Click it to select everything contained in the active worksheet.
Column headings	The letters above the columns. For example, B is the letter above the second column.
Row headings	The numbers to the left of the rows, such as 1, 2, 3, and so on. For example, 3 is the row heading for the third row.
Active cell	The current cell, which is indicated by a dark green border.
Sheet tab	A visual label that looks like a file folder tab. A sheet tab shows the name of a worksheet contained in the workbook. When you create a new Excel workbook, the default worksheet is named Sheet1.
New sheet ⊕	Click to insert a new worksheet to the right of the current worksheet.
Sheet tab navigation	If your workbook contains several worksheets, Excel may not show all the sheet tabs at the same time. Use the buttons to display the first, previous, next, or last worksheet.
Status bar	The row at the bottom of the Excel window. It displays information about a selected command or operation in progress. For example, it displays *Select destination and press ENTER or choose Paste* after you use the Copy command.
View controls	Icons on the right side of the status bar that control how the worksheet is displayed. Click a view control to display the worksheet in Normal, Page Layout, or Page Break Preview. **Normal view** displays the worksheet without showing margins, headers, footers, and page breaks. **Page Layout view** shows the margins, header and footer area, and a ruler. **Page Break Preview** indicates where the worksheet will be divided into pages.
Zoom control	Drag the zoom control to increase the size of the worksheet onscreen to see more or less of the worksheet data.

Identify Columns, Rows, and Cells

A worksheet contains columns and rows, with each column and row assigned a heading. Columns are assigned alphabetical headings from columns A to Z, continuing from AA to AZ, and then from BA to BZ until XFD, which is the last of the possible 16,384 columns. Rows have numeric headings ranging from 1 to 1,048,576. Depending on your screen resolution, you may see more or fewer columns and rows than what are shown in the figures in this book.

The intersection of a column and a row is a *cell*; a total of more than 17 billion cells are available in a worksheet. Each cell has a unique *cell address*, identified by first its column letter and then its row number. For example, the cell at the intersection of column C and row 6 is cell C6 (see Figure 1.3). The active cell is the current cell. Excel displays a dark green border around the active cell in the worksheet, and the Name Box shows the location of the active cell, which is C6 in Figure 1.3. The contents of the active cell, or the formula used to calculate the results of the active cell, appear in the Formula Bar. Cell references are useful when referencing data in formulas, or in navigation.

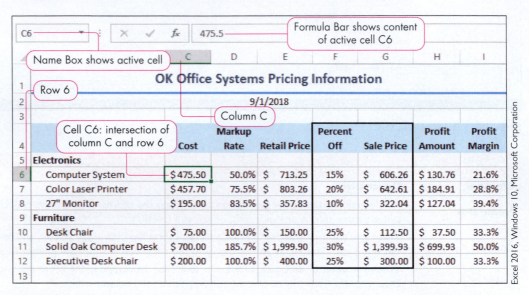

FIGURE 1.3 Columns, Rows, and Cells

Navigate in and Among Worksheets

To navigate to a new cell, click it or use the arrow keys on the keyboard. When you press Enter, the next cell down in the same column becomes the active cell. If you work in a large worksheet, use the vertical and horizontal scroll bars to display another area of the worksheet and click in the desired cell to make it the active cell. The keyboard contains several keys that can be used in isolation or in combination with other keys to navigate in a worksheet. Table 1.2 lists the keyboard navigation methods. The Go To command is helpful for navigating to a cell that is not visible onscreen.

TABLE 1.2 Keystrokes and Actions

Keystroke	Used to
↑	Move up one cell in the same column.
↓	Move down one cell in the same column.
←	Move left one cell in the same row.
→	Move right one cell in the same row.
Tab	Move right one cell in the same row.
Page Up	Move the active cell up one screen.
Page Down	Move the active cell down one screen.
Home	Move the active cell to column A of the current row.
Ctrl+Home	Make cell A1 the active cell.
Ctrl+End	Make the rightmost, lowermost active corner of the worksheet—the intersection of the last column and row that contains data—the active cell. Does not move to cell XFD1048576 unless that cell contains data.
F5 or Ctrl+G	Display the Go To dialog box to enter any cell address.

Pearson Education, Inc.

To display the contents of another worksheet within the workbook, click the sheet tab at the bottom of the workbook window, above the status bar. After you click a sheet tab, you can then navigate within that worksheet.

Entering and Editing Cell Data

You should plan the structure of a worksheet before you start entering data. Using the OKOS case presented at the beginning of the chapter as an example, use the following steps to plan the worksheet design, enter and format data, and complete the workbook. Refer to Figure 1.1 for the completed workbook.

Plan the Worksheet Design

1. **State the purpose of the worksheet.** The purpose of the OKOS worksheet is to store data about products on sale and to calculate important details, such as the retail price based on markup, the sales price based on a discount rate, and the profit margin.

2. **Decide what outputs are needed to achieve the purpose of the worksheet.** Outputs are the results you need to calculate. For the OKOS worksheet, the outputs include columns to calculate the retail price (i.e., the selling price to your customers), the sale price, and the profit margin. In some worksheets, you might want to create an *output area*, the region in the worksheet to contain formulas dependent on the values in the input area.

3. **Decide what input values are needed to achieve the desired output.** Input values are the initial values, such as variables and assumptions. You may change these values to see what type of effects different values have on the end results. For the OKOS worksheet, the input values include the costs OKOS pays the manufacturers, the markup rates, and the proposed discount rates for the sale. In some worksheets, you should create an *input area*, a specific region in the worksheet to store and change the variables used in calculations. For example, if you applied the same Markup Rate and same Percent Off for all products, it would be easier to create an input area at the top of the worksheet to change the values in one location rather than in several locations.

Enter and Format the Data

4. **Enter the labels, values, and formulas in Excel.** Use the design plan (steps 2–3) as you enter labels, input values, and formulas to calculate the output. In the OKOS worksheet, descriptive labels (the product names) appear in the first column to indicate that the values on a specific row pertain to a specific product. Descriptive labels appear at the top of each column, such as Cost and Retail Price, to describe the values in the respective column. Change the input values to test that your formulas produce correct results. If necessary, correct any errors in the formulas to produce correct results. For the OKOS worksheet, change some of the original costs and markup rates to ensure the calculated retail price, selling price, and profit margin percentage results update correctly.

5. **Format the numerical values in the worksheet.** Align decimal points in columns of numbers and add number formats and styles. In the OKOS worksheet, you will use Accounting Number Format and the Percent Style to format the numerical data. Adjust the number of decimal places as needed.

6. **Format the descriptive titles and labels.** Add bold and color to headings so that they stand out and are attractive. Apply other formatting to headings and descriptive labels. In the OKOS worksheet, you will center the main title over all the columns, bold and center column labels over the columns, and apply other formatting to the headings.

Complete the Workbook

7. **Document the workbook as thoroughly as possible.** Include the current date, your name as the workbook author, assumptions, and purpose of the workbook. Some people provide this documentation in a separate worksheet within the workbook. You can also add some documentation in the Properties section when you click the File tab.

8. **Save and share the completed workbook.** Preview and prepare printouts for distribution in meetings, send an electronic copy of the workbook to those who need it, or upload the workbook on a shared network drive or in the cloud.

Enter Text

STEP 1 ⟩⟩ *Text* is any combination of letters, numbers, symbols, and spaces not used in calculations. Excel treats phone numbers, such as 555-1234, and Social Security numbers, such as 123-45-6789, as text entries. You enter text for a worksheet title to describe the contents of the worksheet, as row and column labels to describe data, and as cell data. In Figure 1.4, the cells in column A contain text, such as Class. Text aligns at the left cell margin by default.

To enter text in a cell, complete the following steps:

1. Make sure the cell is active where you want to enter text.
2. Type the text. If you want to enter a numeric value as text, such as a class section number, type an apostrophe and the number, such as '002.
3. Make another cell the active cell after entering data by completing one of the following steps:
   - Press Enter on the keyboard.
   - Press an arrow key on the keyboard.
   - Press Tab on the keyboard.

   Keep the current cell active after entering data by completing one of the following steps:
   - Press Ctrl+Enter on the keyboard.
   - Click Enter (the check mark between the Name Box and the Formula Bar).

As soon as you begin typing a label into a cell, the **AutoComplete** feature searches for and automatically displays any other label in the same column that matches the letters you type. The top half of Figure 1.4 shows Spreadsheet Apps is typed in cell A3. When you start to type *Sp* in cell A4, AutoComplete displays Spreadsheet Apps because a text entry in the same column already starts with *Sp*. Press Enter to accept the repeated label, or continue typing to enter a different label, such as Spanish II. The bottom half of Figure 1.4 shows that '002 was entered in cell B4 to start the text with a 0. Otherwise, Excel would have eliminated the zeros in the class section number. Ignore the error message that displays when you intentionally use an apostrophe to enter a number which is not actually a value.

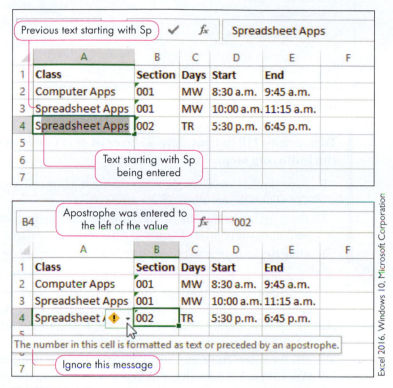

FIGURE 1.4 Entering Text

Use Auto Fill to Complete a Sequence

STEP 2 ›› While AutoComplete helps to complete a label that is identical to another label in the same column, **Auto Fill** is a feature that helps you complete a sequence of words or values. For example, if you enter January in a cell, use Auto Fill to fill in the rest of the months in adjacent cells so that you do not have to type the rest of the month names. Auto Fill can help you complete other sequences, such as quarters (Qtr 1, etc.), weekdays, and weekday abbreviations after you type the first item in the sequence. Figure 1.5 shows the results of filling in months, abbreviated months, quarters, weekdays, abbreviated weekdays, and increments of 5.

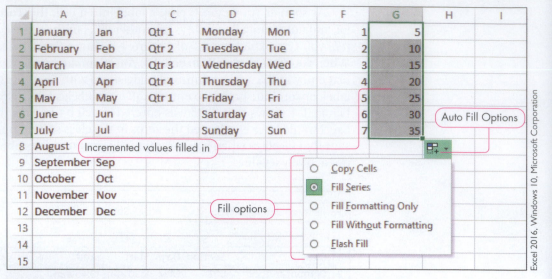

FIGURE 1.5 Auto Fill Examples

To use Auto Fill to complete a series of text (such as month names), complete the following steps:

1. Type the first label (e.g., January) in the starting cell (e.g., cell A1) and press Ctrl+Enter to keep that cell the active cell.

2. Point to the *fill handle* (a small green square in the bottom-right corner of the active cell) until the pointer changes to a thin black plus sign.

3. Drag the fill handle to repeat the content in other cells (e.g., through cell A12).

Immediately after you use Auto Fill, Excel displays Auto Fill Options in the bottom-right corner of the filled data (refer to Figure 1.5). Click Auto Fill Options to display several fill options: Copy Cells, Fill Series, Fill Formatting Only, Fill Without Formatting, or Flash Fill. The menu will also include other options, depending on the cell content: Fill Months for completing months; Fill Weekdays for completing weekdays; and Fill Days, Fill Weekdays, Fill Months, Fill Years to complete dates. Select Fill Formatting Only when you want to copy the formats but not complete a sequence. Select Fill Without Formatting when you want to complete the sequence but do not want to format the rest of the sequence.

To use Auto Fill to fill a sequence of consecutive numbers (such as 1, 2, 3, etc.), complete the following steps:

1. Type the first number in the starting cell (e.g., cell F1) and press Ctrl+Enter to keep that cell the active cell.

2. Drag the fill handle to fill the content in other cells. Excel will copy the same number for the rest of the cells.

3. Click Auto Fill Options and select Fill Series. Excel will change the numbers to be in sequential order, starting with the original value you typed.

For non-consecutive numeric sequences, you must specify the first two values in sequence. For example, if you want to fill in 5, 10, 15, and so on, you must enter 5 and 10 in two adjacent cells before using Auto Fill so that Excel knows to increment by 5.

> **To use Auto Fill to fill a sequence of number patterns (such as 5, 10, 15, 20 shown in the range G1:G7 in Figure 1.5), complete the following steps:**
>
> 1. Type the first two numbers of the sequence in adjoining cells.
> 2. Select those two cells containing the starting two values.
> 3. Drag the fill handle to fill in the rest of the sequence.

> **TIP: FLASH FILL**
> Flash Fill is a similar feature to Auto Fill in that it can quickly fill in data for you; however, *Flash Fill* uses data in previous columns as you type in a new label in an adjoining column to determine what to fill in. For example, assume that column A contains a list of first and last names (such as Penny Sumpter in cell A5), but you want to have a column of just first names. To do this, type Penny's name in cell B5, click Fill in the Editing group on the Home tab and select Flash Fill to fill in the rest of column B with people's first names based on the data entered in column A.

Enter Values

STEP 3 ⟫ *Values* are numbers that represent a quantity or a measurable amount. Excel usually distinguishes between text and value data based on what you enter. The primary difference between text and value entries is that value entries can be the basis of calculations, whereas text cannot. In Figure 1.3, the data below the Cost, Markup Rates, and Percent Off labels are values. Values align at the right cell margin by default. After entering values, align decimal places and apply formatting by adding characters, such as $ or %. Entering values is the same process as entering text: Type the value in a cell and click Enter or press Enter.

> **TIP: ENTERING VALUES WITH TRAILING ZEROS OR PERCENTAGES**
> You do not need to type the last 0 in 475.50 shown in cell C6 in Figure 1.3. Excel will remove or add the trailing 0 depending on the decimal place formatting. Similarly, you do not have to type the leading 0 in a percentage before the decimal point. Type a percent in the decimal format, such as .5 for 50%. You will later format the value.

Enter Dates and Times

STEP 4 ⟫ You can enter dates and times in a variety of formats. You should enter a static date to document when you create or modify a workbook or to document the specific point in time when the data were accurate, such as on a balance sheet or income statement. Later, you will learn how to use formulas to enter dates that update to the current date. In Figure 1.6, the data in column A contains the date 9/1/2018 but in different formats. Dates are values, so they align at the right side of a cell. The data in column C contains the time 2:30 PM but in different formats.

◢	A	B	C	D
1	9/1/2018		2:30:00 PM	
2	Saturday, September 1, 2018		14:30	
3	9/1		2:30 PM	
4	9/1/18		14:30:00	
5	09/01/18		2:30:00 PM	
6	1-Sep			
7	1-Sep-18			
8	September 1, 2018			
9				

Excel 2016, Windows 10, Microsoft Corporation

FIGURE 1.6 Date and Time Examples

Excel displays dates differently from the way it stores dates. For example, the displayed date 9/1/2018 represents the first day in September in the year 2018. Excel stores dates as serial numbers starting at 1 with January 1, 1900, so that you can create formulas, such as to calculate how many days exist between two dates. For example, 9/1/2018 is stored as 43344.

Edit and Clear Cell Contents

After entering data in a cell, you may need to change it. For example, you may want to edit a label to make it more descriptive, such as changing a label from OKC Office Systems Information to OKC Office Systems Pricing Information. Furthermore, you might realize a digit is missing from a value and need to change 500 to 5000.

To edit the contents of a cell, compete the following steps:

1. Click the cell.
2. Click in the Formula Bar or press F2 to put the cell in edit mode. The insertion point displays on the right side of the data in the cell when you press F2.
3. Make the changes to the content in the cell.
4. Click or press Enter.

You may want to clear or delete the contents in a cell if you no longer need data in a cell.

To clear the contents of a cell, complete the following steps:

1. Click the cell.
2. Press Delete or click the cell, click Clear in the Editing group on the Home tab, and select the desired option (see Figure 1.7).

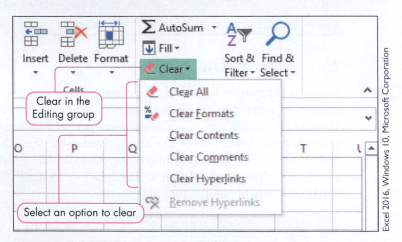

FIGURE 1.7 Clear Options

Quick Concepts

1. What are two major advantages of using an electronic spreadsheet instead of a paper-based ledger? *p. 70*

2. What are the visual indicators that a cell is the active cell? *p. 72*

3. What steps should you perform before entering data into a worksheet? *pp. 73-74*

4. What three types of content can you can enter into a cell? Give an example (different from those in the book) for each type. *pp. 74-77*

Hands-On Exercises

Skills covered: Enter Text
• Use Auto Fill to Complete a Sequence • Enter Values • Enter a Date • Clear Cell Contents

1 Introduction to Spreadsheets

As the assistant manager of OKOS, you will create a worksheet that shows the cost (the amount OKOS pays its suppliers), the markup percentage (the amount by which the cost is increased), and the retail selling price. You also will list the discount percentage (such as 25% off) for each product, the sale price, and the profit margin percentage.

STEP 1 ›› ENTER TEXT

Now that you have planned the OKOS worksheet, you are ready to enter labels for the product names in the first column. Refer to Figure 1.8 as you complete Step 1.

	A	B	C	D	E	F	G	H	I
1	OK Office Sys...	mation							
2									
3									
4	Product	Code	Cost	Markup R...	Retail Pric	Percent O	Sale Price	Profit Margin	
5	Computer System					0.15			
6	Color Laser Printer					0.2			
7	Filing Cabinet					0.1			
8	Desk Chair					0.25			
9	Solid Oak Computer Desk					0.3			
10	27" Monitor					0.1			
11									
12									

Step b: Enter text for first product

Steps b and c: Labels extend into empty column B

Step c: Name of products

Excel 2016, Windows 10, Microsoft Corporation

FIGURE 1.8 Text Entered in Cells

a. Open *e01h1Markup* and save it as **e01h1Markup_LastFirst**.

When you save files, use your last and first names. For example, as the Excel author, I would save my workbook as *e01h1Markup_MulberyKeith*.

> **TROUBLESHOOTING:** If you make any major mistakes in this exercise, you can close the file, open *e01h1Markup* again, and then start this exercise over.

b. Click **cell A5**, type **Computer System**, and then press **Enter**.

When you press Enter, the next cell down—cell A6 in this case—becomes the active cell. The text does not completely fit in cell A5, and some of the text appears in cell B5. If you make cell B5 the active cell, the Formula Bar is empty, indicating that nothing is stored in that cell.

c. Type **Color Laser Printer** in **cell A6** and press **Enter**.

When you start typing C in cell A6, AutoComplete displays a ScreenTip suggesting a previous text entry starting with C—Computer System—but keep typing to enter Color Laser Printer instead.

d. Continue typing the rest of the text in **cells A7** through **A10** as shown in Figure 1.8. Text in column A appears to flow into column B.

You just entered the product labels to describe the data in each row.

e. Click **Save** on the Quick Access Toolbar to save the changes you made to the workbook.

You should develop a habit of saving periodically. That way if your system unexpectedly shuts down, you will not lose everything you worked on.

STEP 2 >> USE AUTO FILL TO COMPLETE A SEQUENCE

You want to assign a product code for each product on sale. You will assign consecutive numbers 101 to 106. After typing the first code number, you will use Auto Fill to complete the rest of the series. Refer to Figures 1.9 and 1.10 as you complete Step 2.

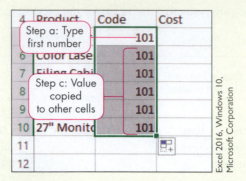

FIGURE 1.9 Auto Fill Copied Original Value

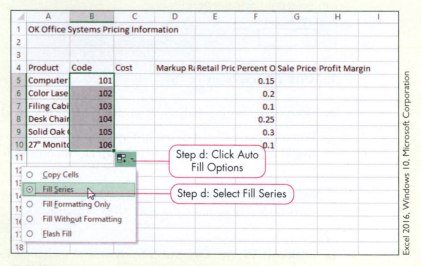

FIGURE 1.10 Auto Fill Sequence

a. Click **cell B5**, type **101**, and then press **Ctrl+Enter**.

The product name Computer System no longer overlaps into column B after you enter data into cell B5. The data in cell A5 is not deleted; the rest of the label is hidden until you increase the column width later.

b. Position the pointer on the fill handle in the bottom-right corner of **cell B5**.

The pointer looks like a black plus sign when you point to a fill handle.

c. Double-click the **cell B6 fill handle**.

Excel copies 101 as the item number for the rest of the products. Excel stops inserting item numbers in column B when it detects the last label in cell A10 (refer to Figure 1.9).

d. Click **Auto Fill Options** and select **Fill Series**. Save the workbook.

Excel changes the duplicate values to continue sequentially in a series of numbers.

STEP 3 ›› **ENTER VALUES**

Now that you have entered the descriptive labels and item numbers, you will enter the cost and markup rate for each product. Refer to Figure 1.11 as you complete Step 3.

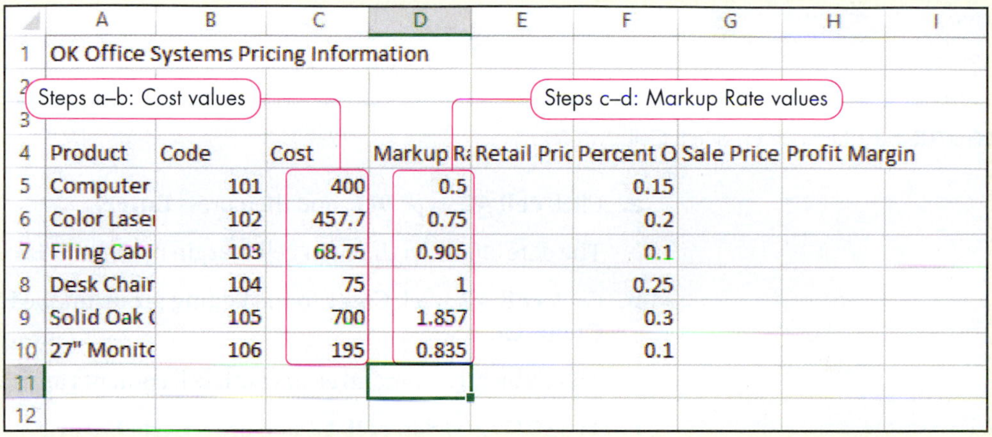

	A	B	C	D	E	F	G	H	I
1	OK Office Systems Pricing Information								
2	Steps a–b: Cost values				Steps c–d: Markup Rate values				
3									
4	Product	Code	Cost	Markup Ra	Retail Pric	Percent O	Sale Price	Profit Margin	
5	Computer	101	400	0.5		0.15			
6	Color Lase	102	457.7	0.75		0.2			
7	Filing Cabi	103	68.75	0.905		0.1			
8	Desk Chair	104	75	1		0.25			
9	Solid Oak (	105	700	1.857		0.3			
10	27" Monitc	106	195	0.835		0.1			
11									
12									

Excel 2016, Windows 10, Microsoft Corporation

FIGURE 1.11 Values Entered in Cells

a. Click **cell C5**, type **400**, and then press **Enter**.

b. Type the remaining costs in **cells C6** through **C10** shown in Figure 1.11.

To improve your productivity, use the number keypad (if available) on the right side of your keyboard. It is much faster to type values and press Enter on the number keypad rather than to use the numbers on the keyboard. Make sure Num Lock is active before using the number keypad to enter values.

c. Click **cell D5**, type **0.5**, and then press **Enter**.

You entered the markup rate as a decimal instead of a percentage. You will apply Percent Style later, but now you will concentrate on data entry.

d. Type the remaining values in **cells D6** through **D10** as shown in Figure 1.11. Save the workbook.

As you review the worksheet, you realize you need to provide a date to indicate when the sale starts. Refer to Figure 1.12 as you complete Step 4.

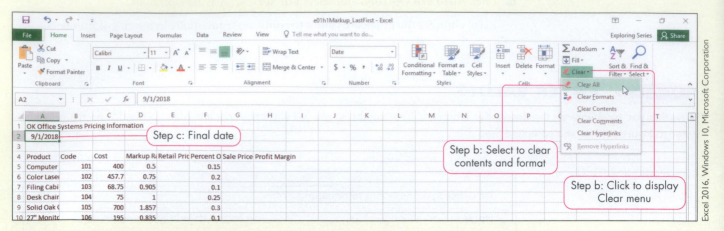

FIGURE 1.12 Date Entered in a Cell

a. Click **cell A2**, type **9/1**, and then press **Enter**.

The date aligns on the right cell margin by default. Excel displays 1-Sep instead of 9/1.

b. Click **cell A2**, click **Clear** in the Editing group on the Home tab, and then select **Clear All**.

The Clear All command clears both cell contents and formatting in the selected cell(s).

c. Type **9/1/2018** in **cell A2** and press **Ctrl+Enter**.

> **TROUBLESHOOTING:** If you did not use Clear All and typed 9/1/2018 in cell A2, Excel would have retained the previous date format and displayed 1-Sep again.

When you type the month, day, and year such as 9/1/2018, Excel enters the date in that format (unless it has a different date format applied).

d. Save the workbook. Keep the workbook open if you plan to continue with the next Hands-On Exercise. If not, close the workbook, and exit Excel.

Mathematical Operations and Formulas

A **formula** combines cell references, arithmetic operations, values, and/or functions used in a calculation. Formulas transform static numbers into meaningful results that update as values change. For example, a payroll manager can build formulas to calculate the gross pay, deductions, and net pay for an organization's employees, or a doctoral student can create formulas to perform various statistical calculations to interpret his or her research data.

In this section, you will learn how to use mathematical operations in Excel formulas. You will refresh your memory of the mathematical order of operations and learn how to construct formulas using cell addresses so that when the value of an input cell changes, the result of the formula changes without you having to modify the formula.

Creating Formulas

Use formulas to help you analyze how results will change as the input data changes. You can change the value of your assumptions or inputs and explore the results quickly and accurately. For example, if your rent increases, how does that affect your personal budget? Analyzing different input values in Excel is easy after you build formulas. Simply change an input value and observe the change in the formula results. In the OKOS product sales worksheet, the results for the Retail Price, Sale Price, and Profit Margin labels were calculated by using formulas (refer to Figure 1.1).

Use Cell References in Formulas

STEP 1 ▶▶ You should use cell references instead of values in formulas where possible. You may include values in an input area—such as dates, salary, or costs—that you will need to reference in formulas. Referencing these cells in your formulas, instead of typing the value of the cell to which you are referring, keeps your formulas accurate if you change values to perform a what-if analysis.

Figure 1.13 shows a worksheet containing input values and results of formulas. The figure also displays the actual formulas used to generate the calculated results. For example, cell E2 contains the formula =B2+B3. Excel uses the value stored in cell B2 (10) and adds it to the value stored in cell B3 (2). The result (12) appears in cell E2 instead of the actual formula. The Formula Bar displays the formula entered into the active cell.

| E2 | ▾ | ⋮ | ✕ | ✓ | f_x | =B2+B3 | |

◢	A	B	C	D	E	F
						Formulas in
1	**Description**	**Values**		**Description**	**Results**	**Column E**
2	First input value	10		Sum of 10 and 2	12	=B2+B3
3	Second input value	2		Difference between 10 and 2	8	=B2-B3
4				Product of 10 and 2	20	=B2*B3
5				Results of dividing 10 by 2	5	=B2/B3
6				Results of 10 to the 2nd power	100	=B2^B3

FIGURE 1.13 Formula Results

Excel 2016, Windows 10, Microsoft Corporation

To enter a formula, complete the following steps:

1. Click the cell.
2. Type an equal sign (=), followed by the arithmetic expression, using cell references instead of values. Do not include any spaces in the formula.
3. Click Enter or press Enter.

> **TIP: EQUAL SIGN NEEDED**
> If you type B2+B3 without the equal sign, Excel does not recognize that you entered a formula and stores the "formula" as text.

> **TIP: UPPER OR LOWERCASE**
> When you create a formula, type the cell references in uppercase, such as =B2+B3, or lowercase, such as =b2+b3. Excel changes cell references to uppercase automatically.

In Figure 1.13, cell B2 contains 10, and cell B3 contains 2. Cell E2 contains =B2+B3 but shows the result 12. If you change the value of cell B3 to 5, cell E2 displays the new result, which is 15. However, if you had typed actual values in the formula, =10+2, you would have to edit the formula to =10+5, even though the value in cell B3 was changed to 5. Using values in formulas can cause problems as you might forget to edit the formula or you might have a typographical error if you edit the formula. Always design worksheets in such a way as to be able to place those values that might need to change as input values. Referencing cells with input values in formulas instead of using the values themselves will avoid having to modify your formulas if an input value changes later.

> **TIP: WHEN TO USE A VALUE IN A FORMULA**
> Use cell references instead of actual values in formulas, unless the value will never change. For example, if you want to calculate how many total months are in a specified number of years, enter a formula such as =B5*12, where B5 contains the number of years. You might want to change the number of years, so you type that value in cell B5. However, every year always has 12 months, so you can use the value 12 in the formula.

Apply the Order of Operations

The *order of operations* (also called order of precedence) are rules that controls the sequence in which arithmetic operations are performed, which affects the result of the calculation. Excel performs mathematical calculations left to right in this order: **P**arentheses, **E**xponentiation, **M**ultiplication or **D**ivision, and finally **A**ddition or **S**ubtraction. Some people remember the order of operations with the phrase *Please Excuse My Dear Aunt Sally*.

Table 1.3 lists the primary order of operations. Use Help to learn about the complete order of precedence.

TABLE 1.3	Order of Operations	
Order	**Description**	**Symbols**
1	Parentheses	( )
2	Exponentiation	^
3	Multiplication and Division	* and / (respectively)
4	Addition and Subtraction	+ and − (respectively)

Pearson Education, Inc.

Figure 1.14 shows formulas, the sequence in which calculations occur, calculations, the description, and the results of each order of operations. The highlighted results are the final formula results. This figure illustrates the importance of symbols and use of parentheses.

	A	B	C	D	E	F
1	**Input**		**Formula**	**Sequence**	**Description**	**Result**
2	2		=A2+A3*A4+A5	1	3 (cell A3) * 4 (cell A4)	12
3	3			2	2 (cell A2) + 12 (order 1)	14
4	4			3	14 (order 2) + 5 (cell A5)	19
5	5					
6			=(A2+A3)*(A4+A5)	1	2 (cell A2) + 3 (cell A3)	5
7				2	4 (cell A4) + 5 (cell A5)	9
8				3	5 (order 1) * 9 (order 2)	45
9						
10			=A2/A3+A4*A5	1	2 (cell A2) / 3 (cell A3)	0.666667
11				2	4 (cell A4) * 5 (cell A5)	20
12				3	0.666667 (order 1) + 20 (order 2)	20.66667
13						
14			=A2/(A3+A4)*A5	1	3 (cell A3) + 4 (cell A4)	7
15				2	2 (cell A2) / 7 (order 1)	0.285714
16				3	0.285714 (order 2) * 5 (cell A5)	1.428571
17						
18			=A2^2+A3*A4%	1	4 (cell A4) is converted to percentage	0.04
19				2	2 (cell A2) to the power of 2	4
20				3	3 (cell A3) * 0.04 (order 1)	0.12
21				4	4 (order 2) + 0.12 (order 3)	4.12

Excel 2016, Windows 10, Microsoft Corporation

FIGURE 1.14 Formula Results Based on Order of Operations

Use Semi-Selection to Create a Formula

STEP 2 ▶▶ To decrease typing time and ensure accuracy, use **semi-selection**, a process of selecting a cell or range of cells for entering cell references as you create formulas. Semi-selection is often called **pointing** because you use the pointer to select cells as you build the formula. Some people prefer using the semi-selection method instead of typing a formula so that they can make sure they use the correct cell references as they build the formula.

To use the semi-selection technique to create a formula, complete the following steps:

1. Click the cell where you want to create the formula.
2. Type an equal sign (=) to start a formula.
3. Click the cell that contains the value to use in the formula. A moving marquee appears around the cell or range you select, and Excel displays the cell or range reference in the formula.
4. Type a mathematical operator.
5. Continue clicking cells, selecting ranges, and typing operators to finish the formula. Use the scroll bars if the cell is in a remote location in the worksheet, or click a worksheet tab to see a cell in another worksheet.
6. Press Enter to complete the formula.

Copy Formulas

STEP 3 After you enter a formula in a cell, you duplicate the formula without retyping the formula for other cells that need a similar formula. Previously, you learned about the Auto Fill feature that enables you to use the fill handle to fill in a series of values, months, quarters, and weekdays. You can also use the fill handle to copy the formula in the active cell to adjacent cells down a column or across a row, depending on how the data are organized. Cell references in copied formulas adjust based on their relative locations to the original formula.

> **To copy a formula to other cells using the fill handle, complete the following steps:**
>
> 1. Click the cell with the content you want to copy to make it the active cell.
> 2. Point to the fill handle in the bottom-right corner of the cell until the pointer changes to the fill pointer (a thin black plus sign).
> 3. Drag the fill handle to copy the formula.

Displaying Cell Formulas

STEP 4 Excel shows the result of the formula in the cell (see the top half of Figure 1.15); however, you might want to display the formulas instead of the calculated results in the cells (see the bottom half of Figure 1.15). Displaying the cell formulas may help you double-check all your formulas at one time or troubleshoot a problem with a formula instead of clicking in each cell containing a formula and looking at just the Formula Bar.

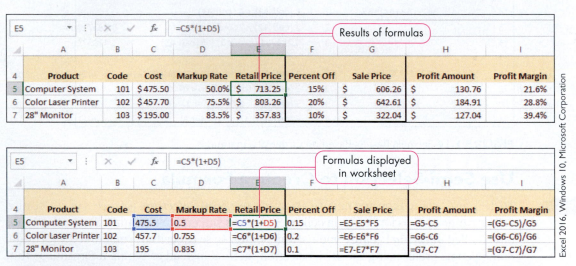

FIGURE 1.15 Formulas and Formula Results

> **To display cell formulas in the worksheet, complete one of the following steps:**
>
> • Press Ctrl and the grave accent (`) key, sometimes referred to as the tilde key, in the top-left corner of the keyboard, below the Esc key.
> • Click Show Formulas in the Formula Auditing group on the Formulas tab.

To hide the formulas and display the formula results again, repeat the preceding process.

Quick Concepts

5. What is the order of operations? Provide and explain two examples that use four different operators: one with parentheses and one without. *p. 84*

6. Why should you use cell references instead of typing values in formulas? *p. 84*

7. When would it be useful to display formulas instead of formula results in a worksheet? *p. 86*

Hands-On Exercises

 Watch the Video for this Hands-On Exercise!

 MyITLab® HOE2 Training

Skills covered: Use Cell References in Formulas • Apply the Order of Operations • Use Semi-Selection to Create a Formula • Copy Formulas • Display Cell Formulas

2 Mathematical Operations and Formulas

In Hands-On Exercise 1, you created the basic worksheet for OKOS by entering text, values, and a date for items on sale. Now you will insert formulas to calculate the missing results—specifically, the retail (before sale) price, sale price, and profit margin. You will use cell addresses in your formulas, so when you change a referenced value, the formula results will update automatically.

STEP 1 ›› USE CELL REFERENCES IN A FORMULA AND APPLY THE ORDER OF OPERATIONS

The first formula you create will calculate the retail price. The retail price is the price you originally charge. It is based on a percentage of the original cost so that you earn a profit. Refer to Figure 1.16 as you complete Step 1.

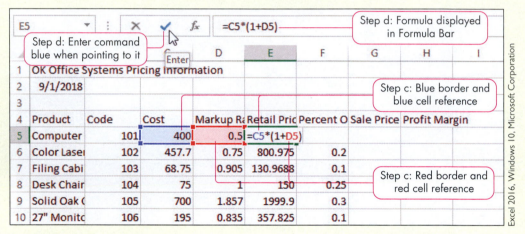

FIGURE 1.16 Retail Price Formula

a. Open *e01h1Markup_LastFirst* if you closed it at the end of Hands-On Exercise 1 and save it as **e01h2Markup_LastFirst**, changing h1 to h2.

b. Click **cell E5**.

Cell E5 is the cell where you will enter the formula to calculate the retail selling price of the first item.

c. Type **=C5*(1+D5)** and view the formula and the colored cells and borders on the screen.

As you build or edit a formula, each cell address in the formula displays in a specific color, and while you type or edit the formula, the cells referenced in the formula have a temporary colored border. For example, in the formula =C5*(1+D5), C5 appears in blue, and D5 appears in red. Cell C5 has a temporarily blue border and light blue shading, and cell D5 has a temporarily red border with light red shading to help you identify cells as you construct your formulas (refer to Figure 1.16).

You enclosed 1+D5 in parentheses to control the order of operations so that 1 is added to the value in cell D5 (0.5). The result is 1.5, which represents 150% of the cost. That result is then multiplied by the value in C5 (400). If you did not use the parentheses, Excel would multiply the value in C5 by 1 (which would be 400) and add that result to the value in D5 (0.5) for a final result of 400.5, which would have given you incorrect results.

An alternative formula also calculates the correct retail price: =C5*D5+C5 or =C5+C5*D5. In this formula, 400 (cell C5) is multiplied by 0.5 (cell D5); that result (200) represents the dollar value of the markup. Excel adds the value 200 to the original cost of 400 to obtain 600, the retail price. You were instructed to enter =C5*(1+D5) to demonstrate the order of operations.

d. Click **Enter** ✓ (between the Name Box and the Formula Bar) and view the formula in the Formula Bar to check it for accuracy.

The result of the formula, 600, appears in cell E5, and the formula displays in the Formula Bar. This formula first adds 1 (the decimal equivalent of 100%) to 0.5 (the value stored in cell D5). Excel multiplies that sum of 1.5 by 400 (the value stored in cell C5). This calculation reflects a retail price is 150% of the original cost.

> **TROUBLESHOOTING:** If the result is not correct, click the cell and look at the formula in the Formula Bar. Click in the Formula Bar, edit the formula to match the formula shown in Step c, and click Enter (the check mark between the Name Box and the Formula Bar). Make sure you start the formula with an equal sign.

e. Position the pointer on the **cell E5 fill handle**. When the pointer changes from a white plus sign to a thin black plus sign, double-click the **fill handle**.

Excel copies the retail price formula for the remaining products in your worksheet. Excel detects when to stop copying the formula when it detects the last label in the dataset.

f. Click **cell E6**, the cell containing the first copied retail price formula, look at the Formula Bar, and then save the workbook.

The formula in cell E6 is =C6*(1+D6). It was copied from the formula in cell E5, which is =C5*(1+D5). Excel adjusts the row references in this formula as you copied the formula down a column so that the results are based on each row's data.

> **TROUBLESHOOTING:** The result in cell E7 may show more decimal places than shown in Figure 1.16. Do not worry about this slight difference.

STEP 2 ›› **USE SEMI-SELECTION AND APPLY THE ORDER OF OPERATIONS TO CREATE A FORMULA**

Now that you have calculated the retail price, you will calculate a sale price. This week, the computer is on sale for 15% off the retail price. Refer to Figure 1.17 as you complete Step 2.

G6		✕ ✓ *fx*	=E6-(E6*F6)					
	A	B	C	D	E	F	G	H	I
1	OK Office Systems Pricing Information								
2	9/1/2018								
3									
4	Product	Code	Cost	Markup Ra	Retail Pric	Percent O	Sale Price	Profit Margin	
5	Computer	101	400	0.5	600	0.15	510		
6	Color Lase	102	457.7	0.75	800.975	0.2	640.78		
7	Filing Cabi	103	68.75	0.905	130.9688	0.1	117.8719		
8	Desk Chair	104	75	1	150	0.25	112.5		
9	Solid Oak (	105	700	1.857	1999.9	0.3	1399.93		
10	27" Monitc	106	195	0.835	357.825	0.1	322.0425		

Step e: Formula for second product

Steps b–c: Type original formula in cell G5

Step d: Results of copied formula

Excel 2016, Windows 10, Microsoft Corporation

FIGURE 1.17 Sale Price Formula

a. Click **cell G5**, the cell where you will enter the formula to calculate the sale price.

b. Type =, click **cell E5**, type -, click **cell E5**, type *, and then click **cell F5**. Notice the color-coding in the cell addresses. Press **Ctrl+Enter** to keep the current cell the active cell.

You used the semi-selection method to enter a formula. The result is 510. Looking at the formula, you might think E5–E5 equals zero; remember that because of the order of operations, multiplication is calculated before subtraction. The product of 600 (cell E5) and 0.15 (cell F5) equals 90, which is then subtracted from 600 (cell E5), so the sale price is 510.

> **TROUBLESHOOTING:** You should check the result for logic. Use a calculator to spot-check the accuracy of formulas. If you mark down merchandise by 15% of its regular price, you are charging 85% of the regular price. You should spot-check your formula to ensure that 85% of 600 is 510 by multiplying 600 by 0.85.

c. Click **cell G5**, type **=E5-(E5*F5)**, and then click **Enter**.

Although the parentheses are not needed because the multiplication occurs before the subtraction, it may be helpful to add parentheses to make the formula easier to interpret.

d. Double-click the **cell G5 fill handle** to copy the formula down column G.

e. Click **cell G6**, the cell containing the first copied sale price formula, view the Formula Bar, and save the workbook.

The original formula was =E5-(E5*F5). The copied formula in cell G6 is adjusted to =E6-(E6*F6) so that it calculates the sales price based on the data in row 6.

STEP 3 ›› **USE CELL REFERENCES IN A FORMULA AND APPLY THE ORDER OF OPERATIONS**

After calculating the sale price, you want to know the profit margin OKOS will earn. OKOS paid $400 for the computer and will sell it for $510. The profit of $110 is then divided by the $400 cost, which gives OKOS a profit margin of 0.215686, which will be formatted later as a percent 21.6%. Refer to Figure 1.18 as you complete Step 3.

	A	B	C	D	E	F	G	H
	H5				fx	=(G5-C5)/G5		
1	OK Office Systems Pricing Information							
2	9/1/2018							
3								
4	Product	Code	Cost	Markup Ra	Retail Pric	Percent O	Sale Price	Profit Margin
5	Computer	101	400	0.5	600	0.15	510	0.215686
6	Color Lase	102	457.7	0.75	800.975	0.2	640.78	0.285714
7	Filing Cabi	103	68.75	0.905	130.9688	0.1	117.8719	0.41674
8	Desk Chair	104	75	1	150	0.25	112.5	0.333333
9	Solid Oak (	105	700	1.857	1999.9	0.3	1399.93	0.499975
10	27" Monitc	106	195	0.835	357.825	0.1	322.0425	0.39449
11								
12								

Step b: Formula in Formula Bar

Step c: Results after copying the formula

Excel 2016, Windows 10, Microsoft Corporation

FIGURE 1.18 Profit Margin Formula

a. Click **cell H5**, the cell where you will enter the formula to calculate the profit margin.

The profit margin is the profit (difference in sales price and cost) percentage of the sale price.

b. Type **=(G5-C5)/G5** and notice the color-coding in the cell addresses. Press **Ctrl+Enter**.

The formula must first calculate the profit, which is the difference between the sale price (510) and the original cost (400). The difference (110) is then divided by the sale price (510) to determine the profit margin of 0.215686, or 21.6%.

c. Double-click the **cell H5 fill handle** to copy the formula down the column.

d. Click **cell H6**, the cell containing the first copied profit margin formula, look at the Formula Bar, and then save the workbook.

The original formula was =(G5-C5)/G5, and the copied formula in cell H6 is =(G6-C6)/G6.

STEP 4 ›› DISPLAY CELL FORMULAS

You want to see how the prices and profit margins are affected when you change some of the original cost values. For example, the supplier might notify you that the cost to you will increase. In addition, you want to see the formulas displayed in the cells temporarily. Refer to Figures 1.19 and 1.20 as you complete Step 4.

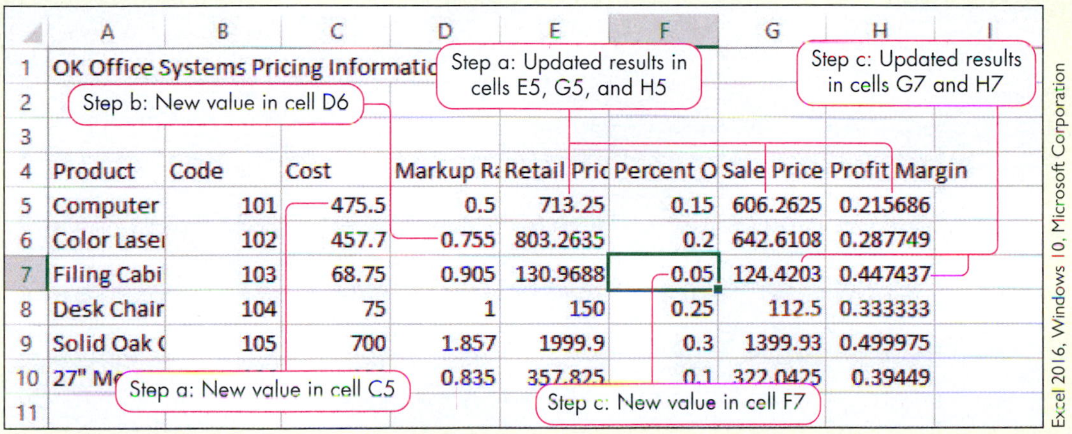

FIGURE 1.19 Results of Changed Values

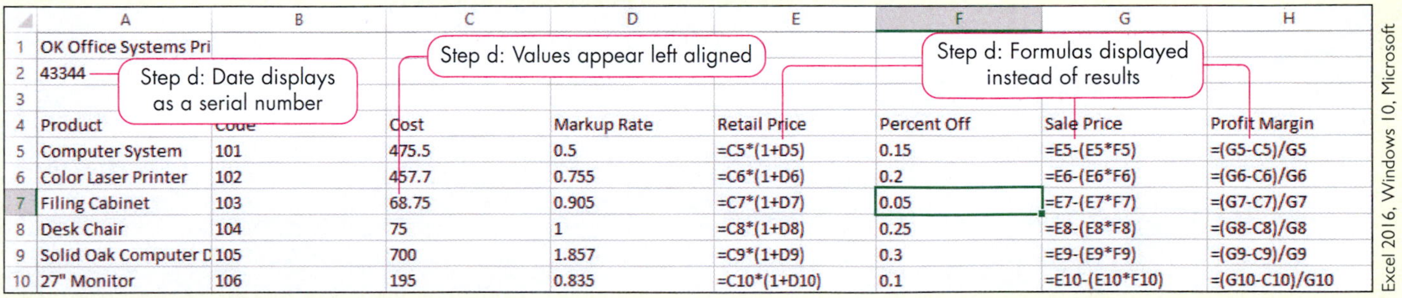

FIGURE 1.20 Formulas Displayed in the Worksheet

a. Click **cell C5**, type **475.5**, and then press **Enter**.

The results of the retail price, sale price, and profit margin formulas change based on the new cost.

b. Click **cell D6**, type **0.755**, and then press **Enter**.

The results of the retail price, sale price, and profit margin formulas change based on the new markup rate.

c. Click **cell F7**, type **0.05**, and then press **Ctrl+Enter**.

The results of the sale price and profit margin formulas change based on the new markdown rate. Note that the retail price did not change because that formula is not based on the markup rate.

d. Press **Ctrl+`** (the grave accent mark).

The workbook now displays the formulas rather than the formula results (refer to Figure 1.20). This is helpful when you want to review several formulas at one time. Numbers are left-aligned, and the date displays as a serial number when you display formulas.

e. Press **Ctrl+`** (the grave accent mark).

The workbook now displays the formula results in the cells again.

f. Save the workbook. Keep the workbook open if you plan to continue with the next Hands-On Exercise. If not, close the workbook, and exit Excel.

Worksheet Structure and Clipboard Tasks

Although you plan worksheets before entering data, you might need to insert a new row to accommodate new data, delete a column that you no longer need, hide a column of confidential data before printing worksheets for distribution, or adjust the size of columns and rows so that the data fit better. Furthermore, you may decide to move data to a different location in the same worksheet or even to a different worksheet. Instead of deleting the original data and typing it in the new location, select and move data from one cell to another. In some instances, you might want to create a copy of data entered so that you can explore different values and compare the results of the original data set and the copied and edited data set.

In this section, you will learn how to make changes to columns and rows. Furthermore, you will also learn how to select ranges, move data to another location, copy data to another range, and use the Paste Special feature.

Managing Columns and Rows

As you enter and edit worksheet data, you might need to adjust the row and column structure to accommodate new data or remove unnecessary data. You can add rows and columns to add new data and delete data, columns, and rows that you no longer need. Adjusting the height and width of rows and columns, respectively, can often present the data better.

Insert Cells, Columns, and Rows

STEP 1 ▶▶ After you construct a worksheet, you might need to insert cells, columns, or rows to accommodate new data. For example, you might want to insert a new column to perform calculations or insert a new row to list a new product.

> **To insert a new column or row, complete the following steps:**
>
> 1. Click in the column or row.
> 2. Click the Insert arrow in the Cells group on the Home tab (see Figure 1.21).
> 3. Select Insert Sheet Columns or Insert Sheet Rows.

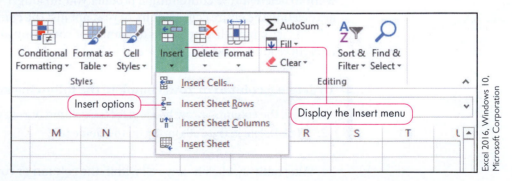

FIGURE 1.21 Insert Menu

Alternatively, you can use a shortcut menu. Right-click the column (letter) or row (number) heading. Then select Insert from the shortcut menu.

Excel inserts new columns to the left of the current column and new rows above the active row. If the current column is column C and you insert a new column, the new column becomes column C, and the original column C data are now in column D. Likewise, if the current row is 5 and you insert a new row, the new row is row 5, and the original row 5 data are now in row 6. When you insert cells, rows, and columns, cell addresses in formulas adjust automatically.

Inserting a cell is helpful when you realize that you left out an entry after you have entered all of the data. Instead of inserting a new row or column, you just want to move the existing content down or over to enter the missing value. You can insert a single cell in a particular row or column.

To insert one or more cells, complete the following steps:

1. Click in the cell where you want the new cell.
2. Click the Insert arrow in the Cells group on the Home tab.
3. Select Insert Cells.
4. Select an option from the Insert dialog box (see Figure 1.22) to position the new cell and click OK.

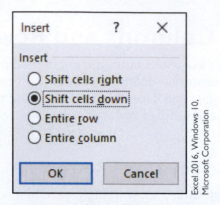

FIGURE 1.22 Insert Dialog Box

Alternatively, click Insert in the Cells group. The default action of clicking Insert is to insert a cell at the current location, which moves existing data down in that column only.

Delete Cells, Columns, and Rows

STEP 2 ▶▶ If you no longer need a cell, column, or row, you should delete it. For example, you might want to delete a row containing a product you no longer carry. In these situations, you are deleting the entire cell, column, or row, not just the contents of the cell to leave empty cells. As with inserting new cells, columns, or rows, any affected formulas adjust the cell references automatically.

To delete a column or row, complete the following steps:

1. Click the column or row heading for the column or row you want to delete.
2. Click Delete in the Cells group on the Home tab.

Alternatively, click in any cell within the column or row you want to delete, click the Delete arrow in the Cells group on the Home tab (see Figure 1.23), and then select Delete Sheet Columns or Delete Sheet Rows. Another alternative is to right-click the column letter or row number for the column or row you want to delete and then select Delete from the shortcut menu.

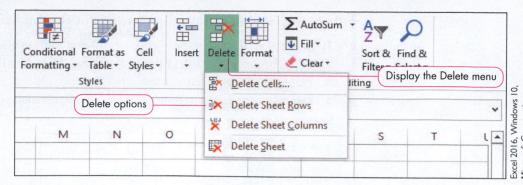

FIGURE 1.23 Delete Menu

To delete a cell or cells, complete the following steps:

1. Select the cell(s).
2. Click the Delete arrow in the Cells group.
3. Select Delete Cells to display the Delete dialog box (see Figure 1.24).
4. Click the appropriate option to shift cells left or up and click OK.

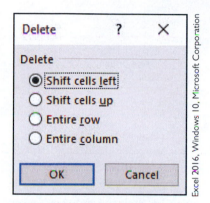

FIGURE 1.24 Delete Dialog Box

Alternatively, click Delete in the Cells group. The default action of clicking Delete is to delete the active cell, which moves existing data up in that column only.

Hide and Unhide Columns and Rows

If your worksheet contains information you do not want to display, hide some columns and/or rows before you print a copy for public distribution. However, the column or row is not deleted. If you hide column B, you will see columns A and C side by side. If you hide row 3, you will see rows 2 and 4 together. Figure 1.25 shows that column B and row 3 are hidden. Excel displays a double line between column headings (such as between A and C), indicating one or more columns are hidden, and a double line between row headings (such as between 2 and 4), indicating one or more rows are hidden.

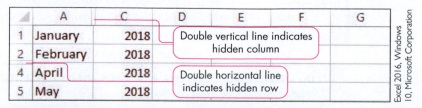

FIGURE 1.25 Hidden Columns and Rows

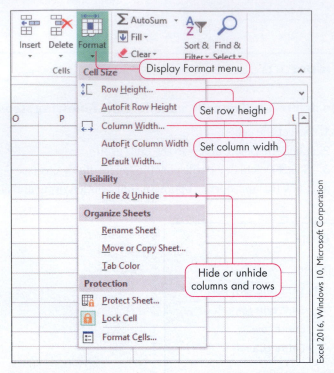

FIGURE 1.26 Format Menu

Alternatively, you can right-click the column or row heading(s) you want to hide. Then select Hide.

You can hide multiple columns and rows at the same time. To select adjacent columns (such as columns B through E) or adjacent rows (such as rows 2 through 4), drag across the adjacent column or row headings and use the Hide command.

> **TIP: UNHIDING COLUMN A, ROW 1, AND ALL HIDDEN ROWS/COLUMNS**
> Unhiding column A or row 1 is different because you cannot select the row or column on either side. To unhide column A or row 1, type A1 in the Name Box and press Enter. Click Format in the Cells group on the Home tab, point to Hide & Unhide, and select Unhide Columns or Unhide Rows to display column A or row 1, respectively. If you want to unhide all columns and rows, click Select All (the triangle above the row 1 heading and to the left of the column A heading) and use the Hide & Unhide submenu.

Adjust Column Width

STEP 3 ▶▶ After you enter data in a column, you often need to adjust the *column width*—the horizontal measurement of a column in a table or a worksheet. In Excel, column width is measured by the number of characters or pixels. For example, in the worksheet you created in Hands-On Exercises 1 and 2, the labels in column A displayed into column B when those adjacent cells were empty. However, after you typed values in column B, the labels in column A appeared cut off. You will need to widen column A to show the full name of all of your products.

> **TIP: POUND SIGNS DISPLAYED**
> Numbers and dates appear as a series of pound signs (######) when the cell is too narrow to display the complete value, and text appears to be truncated.

To widen a column to accommodate the longest label or value in a column, complete one of the following sets of steps:

- Point to the right vertical border of the column heading. When the pointer displays as a two-headed arrow, double-click the border. For example, if column B is too narrow to display the content in that column, double-click the right vertical border of the column B heading.
- Click Format in the Cells group on the Home tab (refer to Figure 1.26) and select AutoFit Column Width.

To adjust the width of a column to an exact width, complete the following sets of steps:

- Drag the vertical border to the left to decrease the column width or to the right to increase the column width. As you drag the vertical border, Excel displays a ScreenTip specifying the width (see Figure 1.27) from 0 to 255 characters and in pixels.
- Click Format in the Cells group on the Home tab (refer to Figure 1.26), select Column Width, type a value that represents the maximum number of characters to display in the Column width box in the Column Width dialog box, and then click OK.

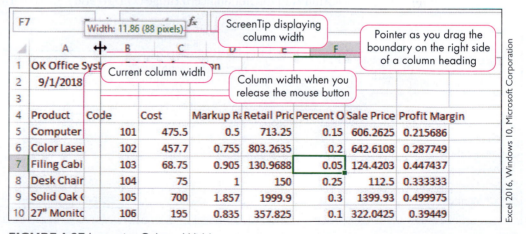

FIGURE 1.27 Increasing Column Width

Adjust Row Height

You can adjust the *row height*—the vertical measurement of the row—in a way similar to how you change column width by double-clicking the border between row numbers or by selecting Row Height or AutoFit Row Height from the Format menu (refer to Figure 1.26). In Excel, row height is a value between 0 and 409 based on point size (abbreviated as pt) and pixels. Whether you are measuring font sizes or row heights, one point size is equal to 1/72 of an inch. Your row height should be taller than your font size. For example, with an 11-pt font size, the default row height is 15.

> **TIP: MULTIPLE COLUMN WIDTHS AND ROW HEIGHTS**
> You can set the size for more than one column or row at a time to make the selected columns or rows the same size. Drag across the column or row headings for the area you want to format, and set the size using any method.

Selecting, Moving, Copying, and Pasting Data

You may already know the basics of selecting, cutting, copying, and pasting data in other programs, such as Microsoft Word. These tasks are somewhat different when working in Excel.

Select a Range

STEP 4 ➤➤ A *range* refers to a group of adjacent or contiguous cells in a worksheet. A range may be as small as a single cell or as large as the entire worksheet. It may consist of a row or part of a row, a column or part of a column, or multiple rows or columns, but will always be a rectangular shape, as you must select the same number of cells in each row or column for the entire range. A range is specified by indicating the top-left and bottom-right cells in the selection. For example, in Figure 1.28, the date is a single-cell range in cell A2, the Color Laser Printer data are stored in the range A6:H6, the cost values are stored in the range C5:C10, and the sales prices and profit margins are stored in range G5:H10. A *nonadjacent range* contains multiple ranges, such as D5:D10 and F5:F10. At times, you will select nonadjacent ranges so that you can apply the same formatting at the same time, such as formatting the nonadjacent range D5:D10 and F5:F10 with Percent Style.

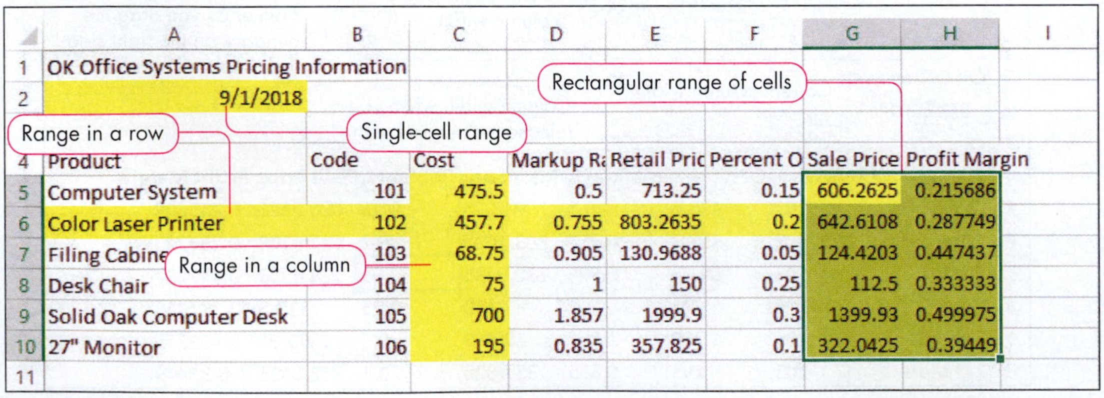

FIGURE 1.28 Sample Ranges

Table 1.4 lists methods to select ranges, including nonadjacent ranges.

TABLE 1.4	Selecting Ranges
To Select:	**Do This:**
A range	Drag until you select the entire range. Alternatively, click the first cell in the range, press and hold Shift, and click the last cell in the range.
An entire column	Click the column heading.
An entire row	Click the row heading.
Current range containing data, including headings	Click in the range of data and press Ctrl+A.
All cells in a worksheet	Click Select All or press Ctrl+A twice.
Nonadjacent range	Select the first range, press and hold Ctrl, and select additional range(s).

Pearson Education, Inc.

A green border appears around a selected range. Any command you execute will affect the entire range. The range remains selected until you select another range or click in any cell in the worksheet.

> **TIP: NAME BOX**
> Use the Name Box to select a range by clicking in the Name Box, typing a range address such as B15:D25, and pressing Enter.

Move a Range

You can move cell contents from one range to another. For example, you might want to move an input area from the right side of the worksheet to above the output range. When you move a range containing text and values, the text and values do not change. However, any formulas that refer to cells in that range will update to reflect the new cell addresses.

To move a range, complete the following steps:

1. Select the range.
2. Click Cut in the Clipboard group to copy the range to the Clipboard (see Figure 1.29). Unlike cutting data in other Microsoft Office applications, the data you cut in Excel remain in their locations until you paste them elsewhere. A moving dashed green border surrounds the selected range and the status bar displays *Select destination and press ENTER or choose Paste.*
3. Ensure the destination range—the range where you want to move the data—is the same size or greater than the size of the cut range.
4. Click in the top-left corner of the destination range, and use the Paste command (see Figure 1.29). If any cells within the destination range contain data, Excel overwrites that data when you use the Paste command.

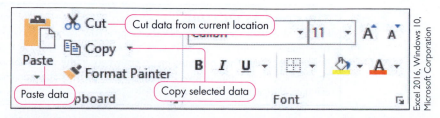

FIGURE 1.29 Cut, Copy, Paste

Copy and Paste a Range

STEP 5 You may want to copy cell contents from one range to another. When you copy a range, the original data remain in their original locations. For example, you might copy your January budget to another worksheet to use as a model for creating your February budget. Cell references in copied formulas adjust based on their relative locations to the original data. Furthermore, you want to copy formulas from one range to another range. In this situation where you cannot use the fill handle, you will use the Copy and Paste functions to copy the formula.

> **To copy a range, complete the following steps:**
>
> 1. Select the range.
> 2. Click Copy in the Clipboard group (refer to Figure 1.29) to copy the contents of the selected range to the Clipboard. A moving dashed green border surrounds the selected range and the status bar displays *Select destination and press ENTER or choose Paste*.
> 3. Ensure the destination range—the range where you want to copy the data—is the same size or greater than the size of the copied range.
> 4. Click in the top-left corner of the destination range where you want the duplicate data, and click Paste (refer to Figure 1.29). If any cells within the destination range contain data, Excel overwrites that data when you use the Paste command. The original range still has the moving dashed green border, and the pasted copied range is selected with a solid green border. Figure 1.30 shows a selected range (A4:H10) and a copy of the range (J4:Q10). Immediately after you click Paste, the **Paste Options button** displays in the bottom-right corner of the pasted data. Click the arrow to select a different result for the pasted data.
> 5. Press Esc to turn off the moving dashed border around the originally selected range.

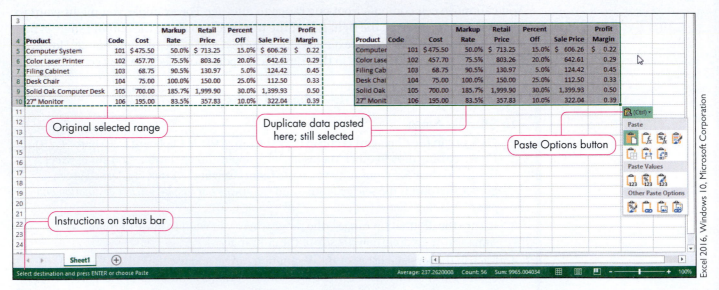

FIGURE 1.30 Copied and Pasted Range

> **TIP: COPY AS PICTURE**
>
> Instead of clicking Copy, if you click the Copy arrow in the Clipboard group, you can select Copy (the default option) or Copy as Picture. When you select Copy as Picture, you copy an image of the selected data. Then paste the image elsewhere in the workbook or in a Word document or PowerPoint presentation. However, when you copy the data as an image, you cannot edit individual cell data after you paste the image.

Use Paste Options and Paste Special

STEP 6 »» Sometimes you might want to paste data in a different format than they are in the Clipboard. For example, you might want to preserve the results of calculations before changing the original data. To do this, you can paste the data as values. If you want to copy data from Excel and paste them into a Word document, you can paste the Excel data as a worksheet object, as unformatted text, or in another format.

To paste data from the Clipboard into a different format, complete the following steps:

1. Click the Paste arrow in the Clipboard group (see Figure 1.31).
2. Point to command to see a ScreenTip and a preview of how the pasted data will look.
3. Click the option you want to apply.

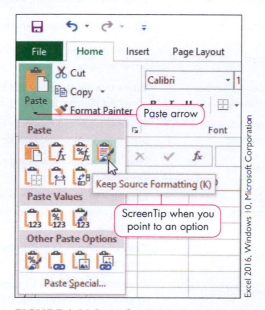

FIGURE 1.31 Paste Options

Table 1.5 lists and describes some of the options in the Paste gallery that opens when you click the Paste arrow in the Clipboard or the Paste Options button that displays immediately after you use Paste. Paste options enable you to paste content or attributes, such as a formula or format.

TABLE 1.5 Paste Options

Icon	Option Name	Paste Description
	Paste	Cell contents and all formatting from copied cells
	Formulas	Formulas, but no formatting, from copied cells
	Formulas & Number Formatting	Formulas and number formatting, such as Currency, but no font formatting, such as font color, fill color, or borders
	Keep Source Formatting	Cell contents and formatting from copied cells
	No Borders	Cell contents, number formatting, and text formatting except borders
	Keep Source Column Widths	Cell contents, number and text formatting, and the column width of the source data when pasting in another column
	Transpose	Transposes data from rows to columns and columns to rows
	Values	Unformatted values that are the results of formulas, not the actual formulas
	Values & Number Formatting	Values that are the results of formulas, not the actual formulas; preserves number formatting but not text formatting
	Values & Source Formatting	Values that are the results of formulas, not the actual formulas; preserves number and text formatting
	Formatting	Number and text formatting only from the copied cells; no cell contents
	Paste Link	Creates a reference to the source cells (such as =$G$15), not the cell contents; preserves number formatting but not text formatting
	Picture	Creates a picture image of the copied data; pasted data is not editable
	Linked Picture	Creates a picture with a reference to the copied cells; if the original cell content changes, so does the picture
	Paste Special	Opens the Paste Special dialog box (see Figure 1.32)

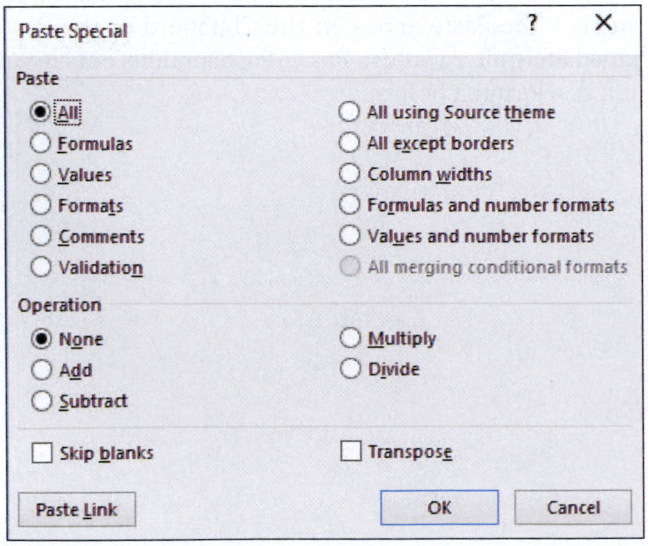

FIGURE 1.32 Paste Special Dialog Box

TIP: TRANSPOSING COLUMNS AND ROWS

After entering data into a worksheet, you might want to transpose the columns and rows so that the data in the first column appear as column labels across the first row, or the column labels in the first row appear in the first column. Figure 1.33 shows the original data with the months in column A and the utility costs in columns B, C, and D. In the transposed data, the months are shown in the first row, and each row contains utility information. The original formats (bold and right-aligned) are copied in the transposed data.

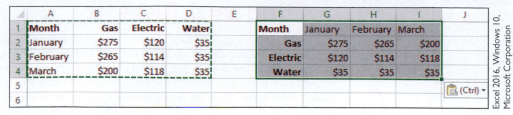

FIGURE 1.33 Transposed Data

Copy Excel Data to Other Programs

You can copy Excel data and use it in other applications, such as in a Word document or in a PowerPoint slide show. For example, you might perform statistical analyses in Excel and copy the data into a research paper in Word. Or, you might want to create a budget in Excel and copy the data into a PowerPoint slide show for a meeting.

After selecting and copying a range in Excel, you must decide how you want the data to appear in the destination application. Click the Paste arrow in the destination application to see a gallery of options or to select the Paste Special option.

Quick Concepts

8. Give an example of when you would delete a column versus when you would hide a column. **pp. 94-95**

9. When should you adjust column widths instead of using the default width? **p. 97**

10. Why would you use the Paste Special options in Excel? **p. 101**

Skills covered: Insert Columns and Rows • Delete a Row • Hide a Column • Adjust Column Width • Adjust Row Height • Select a Range • Move a Range • Copy and Paste a Range • Use Paste Special

3 Worksheet Structure and Clipboard Tasks

You want to insert a column to calculate the amount of markup and delete a row containing data you no longer need. You also want to adjust column widths to display the labels in the columns. In addition, your supervisor asked you to enter data for a new product. Because it is almost identical to an existing product, you will copy the original data and edit the copied data to save time. You also want to experiment with the Paste Special option to see the results of using it in the OKOS workbook.

STEP 1 ›› INSERT A COLUMN AND ROWS

You decide to add a column to display the amount of profit. Because profit is a dollar amount, you want to keep the profit column close to another column of dollar amounts. Therefore, you will insert the profit column before the profit margin (percentage) column. You will insert new rows for product information and category names. Refer to Figure 1.34 as you complete Step 1.

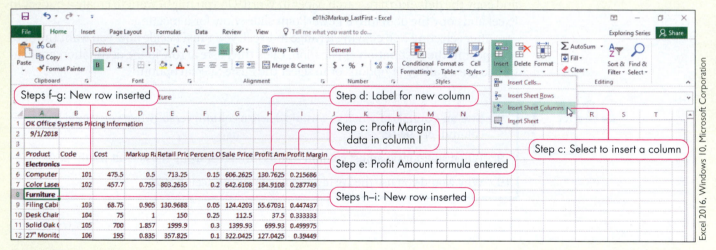

FIGURE 1.34 Column and Rows Inserted

a. Open *e01h2Markup_LastFirst* if you closed it at the end of Hands-On Exercise 2 and save it as **e01h3Markup_LastFirst**, changing h2 to h3.

b. Click **cell H5** (or any cell in column H).

You want to insert a column between the Sale Price and Profit Margin columns so that you can calculate the profit amount in dollars.

c. Click the **Insert arrow** in the Cells group and select **Insert Sheet Columns**.

You inserted a new blank column H. The data in the original column H are now in column I.

d. Click **cell H4**, type **Profit Amount**, and then press **Enter**.

e. Ensure the active cell is **cell H5**. Type **=G5-C5** and click **Enter**. Double-click the **cell H5 fill handle**.

You calculated the profit amount by subtracting the original cost from the sale price and then copied the formula down the column.

f. Right-click the **row 5 heading** and select **Insert** from the shortcut menu.

You inserted a new blank row 5, which is selected. The original rows of data move down a row each.

g. Click **cell A5**. Type **Electronics** and press **Ctrl+Enter**. Click **Bold** in the Font group on the Home tab.

You typed and applied bold formatting to the category name Electronics above the list of electronic products.

h. Right-click the **row 8 heading** and select **Insert** from the shortcut menu.

You inserted a new blank row 8. The data that was originally on row 8 is now on row 9.

i. Click **cell A8**. Type **Furniture** and press **Ctrl+Enter**. Click **Bold** in the Font group on the Home tab and save the workbook.

You typed and applied bold formatting to the category name Furniture above the list of furniture products.

STEP 2 ▶▶ DELETE A ROW AND HIDE A COLUMN

You just realized that you do not have enough filing cabinets in stock to offer on sale, so you need to delete the Filing Cabinet row. The item numbers are meaningful to you, but the numbers are not necessary for the other employees. Before distributing the worksheet to the employees, you want to hide column B. Because you might need to see that data later, you will hide it rather than delete it. Refer to Figure 1.35 as you complete Step 2.

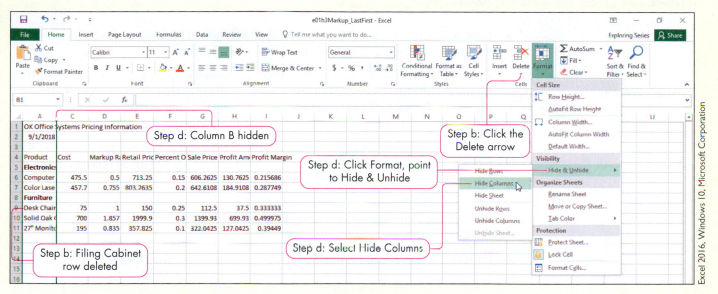

FIGURE 1.35 Row Deleted and Column Hidden

a. Click **cell A9** (or any cell on row 9), the row that contains the Filing Cabinet data.

b. Click the **Delete arrow** in the Cells group and select **Delete Sheet Rows**.

The Filing Cabinet row is deleted, and the remaining rows move up one row.

> **TROUBLESHOOTING:** If you accidentally delete the wrong row or accidentally selected Delete Sheet Columns instead of Delete Sheet Rows, click Undo on the Quick Access Toolbar to restore the deleted row or column.

c. Click the **column B heading**.

d. Click **Format** in the Cells group, point to **Hide & Unhide**, and then select **Hide Columns**.

Excel hides column B. You see a gap in column heading letters A and C, indicating column B is hidden instead of deleted.

e. Save the workbook.

As you review your worksheet, you notice that the labels in column A appear cut off. You will increase the width of that column to display the entire product names. In addition, you want to make row 1 taller. Refer to Figure 1.36 as you complete Step 3.

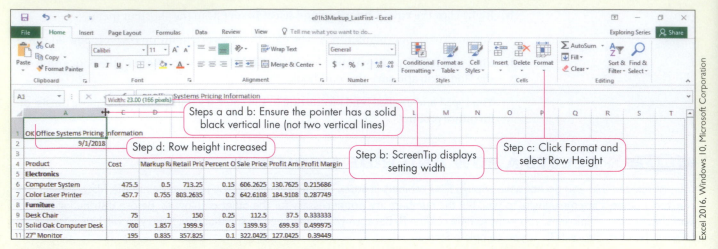

FIGURE 1.36 Column Width and Row Height Changed

a. Point to the right border of column A. When the pointer looks like a double-headed arrow with a solid black vertical line, double-click the border.

When you double-click the border between two columns, Excel adjusts the width of the column on the left side of the border to fit the contents of that column. Excel increased the width of column A based on the cell containing the longest content (the title in cell A1). You decide to adjust the column width to the longest product name instead.

b. Point to the right border of column A until the double-headed arrow appears. Drag the border to the left until the ScreenTip displays **Width: 23.00 (166 pixels)**. Release the mouse button.

You decreased the column width to 23 for column A. The longest product name is visible. You will not adjust the other column widths until after you apply formats to the column headings in Hands-On Exercise 4.

c. Click **cell A1**. Click **Format** in the Cells group and select **Row Height**.

The Row Height dialog box opens so that you can adjust the height of the current row.

d. Type **30** in the **Row height box** and click **OK**. Save the workbook.

You increased the height of the row that contains the worksheet title so that it is more prominent.

You want to move the 27" Monitor product to be immediately after the Color Laser Printer product. Before moving the 27" Monitor row, you will insert a blank row between the Color Laser Printer and Furniture rows. Refer to Figure 1.37 as you complete Step 4.

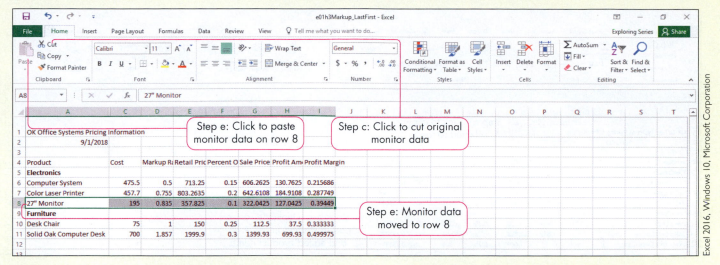

FIGURE 1.37 Row Moved to New Location

a. Right-click the **row 8 heading** and select **Insert** from the menu.

You will insert a blank row so that you can move the 27" Computer Monitor data to be between the Color Laser Printer and Furniture rows.

b. Select the **range A12:I12**.

You selected the range of cells containing the 27" Monitor data.

c. Click **Cut** in the Clipboard group.

A moving dashed green border outlines the selected range. The status bar displays the message *Select destination and press ENTER or choose Paste.*

d. Click **cell A8**.

This is the first cell in the destination range. If you cut and paste a row without inserting a new row first, Excel will overwrite the original row of data, which is why you inserted a new row in step a.

e. Click **Paste** in the Clipboard group and save the workbook.

The 27" Monitor product data is now located on row 8.

Alesha told you that a new chair is on its way. She asked you to enter the data for the Executive Desk Chair. Because most of the data is the same as the Desk Chair data, you will copy the original Desk Chair data, edit the product name, and change the cost to reflect the cost of the second chair. Refer to Figure 1.38 as you complete Step 5.

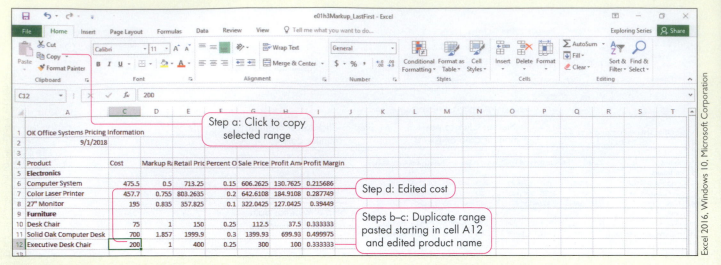

FIGURE 1.38 Data Copied and Edited

a. Select the **range A10:I10** and click **Copy** in the Clipboard group.

You copied the row containing the Desk Chair product data to the Clipboard.

b. Click **cell A12**, click **Paste** in the Clipboard group, and then press **Esc**.

The pasted range is selected in row 12.

c. Click **cell A12**, press **F2** to activate Edit Mode, press **Home**, type **Executive**, press **Spacebar**, and then press **Enter**.

You edited the product name to display Executive Desk Chair.

d. Change the value in **cell C12** to **200**. Save the workbook.

The formulas calculate the results based on the new cost of 200 for the Executive Desk Chair.

STEP 6 ❱❱ **USE PASTE SPECIAL**

During your lunch break, you want to experiment with some of the Paste Special options. Particularly, you are interested in pasting Formulas and Value & Source Formatting. First, you will apply bold and a font color to the title to help you test these Paste Special options. Refer to Figure 1.39 as you complete Step 6.

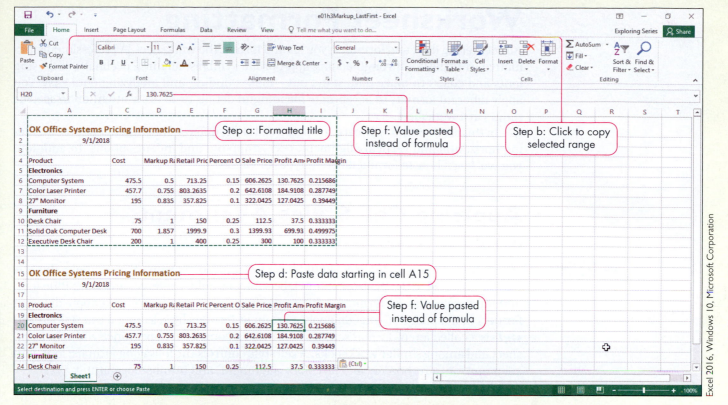

FIGURE 1.39 Paste Special Results

a. Click **cell A1**. Change the font size to **14**, click **Bold**, click the **Font Color arrow** in the Font group and then select **Gold, Accent 4, Darker 50%**.

You will format text to see the effects of using different Paste Special options.

b. Select the **range A1:I12** and click **Copy** in the Clipboard group.

c. Click **cell A15**, the top-left corner of the destination range.

d. Click the **Paste arrow** in the Clipboard group and point to **Formulas**, the second icon from the left in the Paste group.

Without clicking the command, Excel shows you a preview of what that option would do. The pasted copy would not contain the font formatting you applied to the title or the bold on the two category names. In addition, the pasted date would appear as a serial number. The formulas would be maintained.

e. Position the pointer over **Values & Source Formatting**, the first icon from the right in the Paste Values group.

This option would preserve the formatting, but it would convert the formulas into the current value results.

f. Click **Values & Source Formatting**, click **cell H6** to see a formula, and then click **cell H20**. Press **Esc** to turn off the border.

Cell H6 contains a formula, but in the pasted version, the equivalent cell H20 has converted the formula result into an actual value. If you were to change the original cost on row 20, the contents of cell H20 would not change. In a working environment, this is useful only if you want to capture the exact value in a point in time before making changes to the original data.

g. Save the workbook. Keep the workbook open if you plan to continue with the next Hands-On Exercise. If not, close the workbook and exit Excel.

Worksheet Formatting

After entering data and formulas, you should format the worksheet. A professionally formatted worksheet—through adding appropriate symbols, aligning decimals, and using fonts and colors to make data stand out—makes finding and analyzing data easy. You apply different formats to accentuate meaningful details or to draw attention to specific ranges in a worksheet.

In this section, you will learn to apply a cell style, different alignment options, including horizontal and vertical alignment, text wrapping, and indent options. In addition, you will learn how to format different types of values.

Applying Cell Styles, Alignment, and Font Options

STEP 1 ›› Different areas of a worksheet should have different formatting. For example, the title may be centered in 16-pt size; column labels may be bold, centered, and Dark Blue font; and input cells may be formatted differently from output cells. You can apply different formats individually, or you can apply a group of formats by selecting a cell style. A *cell style* is a collection of format settings to provide a consistent appearance within a worksheet and among similar workbooks. A cell style controls the following formats: font, font color and font size, borders and fill colors, alignment, and number formatting.

> **To apply a cell style to a cell or a range of cells, complete the following steps:**
>
> 1. Click Cell Styles in the Styles group on the Home tab to display the Cell Styles gallery (see Figure 1.40).
> 2. Position the pointer over a style name to see a Live Preview of how the style will affect the selected cell or range. The gallery provides a variety of built-in styles to apply to your worksheet data.
> 3. Click a style to apply it to the selected cell or range.

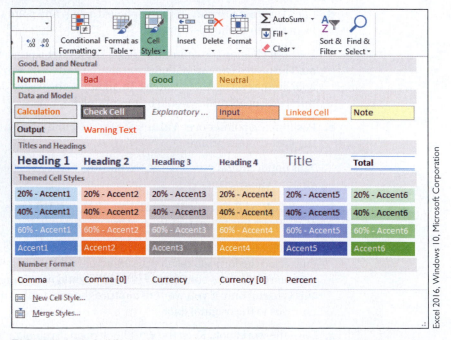

FIGURE 1.40 Cell Styles

Alignment refers to how data are positioned in the boundaries of a cell. Each type of data has a default alignment. Text aligns at the left cell margin, and dates and values align at the right cell margin. You should change the alignment of cell contents to improve the appearance of data within the cells. The Alignment group (see Figure 1.41) on the Home tab contains several commands to help you align and format data.

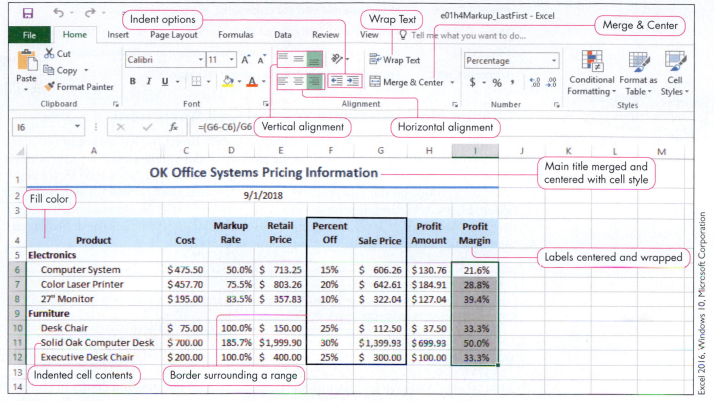

FIGURE 1.41 Alignment and Font Settings Applied

> **TIP: ALIGNMENT OPTIONS**
> The Format Cells dialog box contains additional alignment options. To open the Format Cells dialog box, click the Dialog Box Launcher in the Alignment group on the Home tab. The Alignment tab in the dialog box contains the options for aligning data.

Merge and Center Labels

You may want to place a title at the top of a worksheet and center it over the columns of data in the worksheet. You can center main titles over all columns in the worksheet, and you can center category titles over groups of related columns. You can also merge cells on adjacent rows.

To merge and center cells, complete the following steps:

1. Enter the text in the top left cell of the range.
2. Select the range of cells across which you want to center the label.
3. Click Merge & Center in the Alignment group on the Home tab.

Only data in the far left cell (or top-right cell) are merged. Any other data in the merged cells are deleted. Excel merges the selected cells together into one cell, and the merged cell address is that of the original cell on the left. The data are centered within the merged cell.

If you want to split a merged cell into multiple cells, click the merged cell and click Merge & Center. Unmerging places the data in the top-left cell.

For additional options, click the Merge & Center arrow. Table 1.6 lists the four merge options.

TABLE 1.6	Merge Options
Option	**Results**
Merge & Center	Merges selected cells and centers data into one cell.
Merge Across	Merges the selected cells but keeps text left aligned or values right aligned.
Merge Cells	Merges a range of cells on multiple rows as well as in multiple columns.
Unmerge Cells	Separates a merged cell into multiple cells again.

Pearson Education, Inc.

Change Horizontal and Vertical Cell Alignment

STEP 2 ❱❱ *Horizontal alignment* specifies the position of data between the left and right cell margins, and *vertical alignment* specifies the position of data between the top and bottom cell margins. Bottom Align is the default vertical alignment (as indicated by the light green background on the Ribbon), and Align Left is the default horizontal alignment for text. In Figure 1.41, the labels on row 4 have Center horizontal alignment and the title in row 1 has Middle Align vertical alignment. To change alignments, click the desired alignment setting(s) in the Alignment group on the Home tab.

> **TIP: ROTATE CELL DATA**
> People sometimes rotate headings in cells. To rotate data in a cell, click Orientation in the Alignment group and select an option, such as Angle Clockwise.

Wrap Text

Sometimes you have to maintain specific column widths, but the data do not fit entirely. Use *wrap text* to make data appear on multiple lines by adjusting the row height to fit the cell contents within the column width. Excel wraps the text on two or more lines within the cell. In Figure 1.41, the Markup Rate and Percent Off labels on row 4 are examples of wrapped text.

To wrap text within a cell, complete the following steps:

1. Click the cells or select the range of cells that contain labels that need to be wrapped.
2. Click Wrap Text in the Alignment group.

> **TIP: LINE BREAK IN A CELL**
> If a long text label does not fit well in a cell even after you have applied wrap text, you might want to insert a line break to display the text label on multiple lines within the cell. To insert a line break while you are typing a label, press Alt+Enter where you want to start the next line of text within the cell.

Increase and Decrease Indent

STEP 3 ❱❱ Cell content is left-aligned or right-aligned based on the default data type. However, you can *indent* the cell contents to offset the data from its current alignment. For example, text is left-aligned, but you can indent it to offset it from the left side. Indenting helps others see the hierarchical structure of data. Accountants often indent the word Totals in financial statements so that it stands out from a list of items above the total row. Values are right-aligned by default, but you can indent a value to offset it from the right side of the cell. In Figure 1.41, Computer System and Desk Chair are indented.

To increase or decrease the indent of data in a cell, complete the following steps:

1. Click the cell that contains data.
2. Click Increase Indent or Decrease Indent in the Alignment group.

TIP: INDENTING VALUES

Values are right aligned by default. You should align the decimal places in a column of values. If the column label is wide, the values below it appear too far on the right. To preserve the values aligning at the decimal places, use the Align Right horizontal alignment and click Increase Indent to shift the values over to the left a little for better placement.

Apply Borders and Fill Color

STEP 4 ❯❯ You can apply a border or fill color to accentuate data in a worksheet. A **border** is a line that surrounds a cell or a range of cells. Use borders to offset some data from the rest of the worksheet data. To apply a border, select the cell or range that you want to have a border, click the Borders arrow in the Font group, and select the desired border type. In Figure 1.41, a border surrounds the range F4:G12. To remove a border, select No Border from the Borders menu.

Add some color to your worksheets to emphasize data or headers by applying a fill color. **Fill color** is a background color that displays behind the data in a cell so that the data stand out. You should choose a fill color that contrasts with the font color. For example, if the font color is Black, Text 1, you might choose Yellow fill color. If the font color is White, Background 1, you might apply Blue or Dark Blue fill color. The color palette contains two sections: Theme Colors and Standard Colors. The Theme Colors section displays variations of colors that match the current theme applied in the worksheet. For example, it contains shades of blue, such as Blue, Accent 5, Lighter 80%. The Standard Colors section contains basic colors, such as Dark Red and Red.

To apply a fill color, complete the following steps:

1. Select the cell or range that you want to have a fill color.
2. Click the Fill Color arrow on the Home tab to display the color palette.
3. Select the color choice from the Fill Color palette. In Figure 1.41, the column labels in row 4 contain the Blue, Accent 1, Lighter 80% fill color. If you want to remove a fill color, select No Fill from the bottom of the palette. Select More Colors to open the Colors dialog box, click the Standard tab or Custom tab, and then click a color.

For additional border and fill color options, complete the following steps:

1. Click the Dialog Box Launcher in the Font group to display the Format Cells dialog box.
2. Click the Border tab to select border options, including the border line style and color.
3. Click the Fill tab to set the background color, fill effects, and patterns.

Applying Number Formats

Values have no special formatting when you enter data. However, you should apply **number formats**, settings that control how a value is displayed in a cell. For example, you might want to apply either the Accounting or Currency number format to monetary values. Changing the number format changes the way the number displays in a cell, but the format does not change the stored value. If, for example, you enter 123.456 into a cell and format the cell with the Currency number type, the value shows as $123.46 onscreen, but the actual value 123.456 is used for calculations. When you apply a number format, specify the number of decimal places to display onscreen.

Apply a Number Format

STEP 5 ›› The default number format is General, which displays values as you originally enter them. General number format does not align decimal points in a column or include symbols, such as dollar signs, percent signs, or commas. Table 1.7 lists and describes the primary number formats in Excel.

TABLE 1.7 Number Formats	
Format Style	**Display**
General	A number as it was originally entered. Numbers are shown as integers (e.g., 12345), decimal fractions (e.g., 1234.5), or in scientific notation (e.g., 1.23E+10) if the number exceeds 11 digits.
Number	A number with or without the 1,000 separator (e.g., a comma) and with any number of decimal places. Negative numbers can be displayed with parentheses and/or red.
Currency	A number with the 1,000 separator and an optional dollar sign (which is placed immediately to the left of the number). Negative values are preceded by a minus sign or are displayed with parentheses or in red. Two decimal places display by default.
Accounting Number Format	A number that contains the $ on the left side of the cell and formats the value with a comma for every three digits on the left side of the decimal point and displays two digits to the right of the decimal point. Negative values display in parentheses, and zero values display as hyphens.
Comma Style	A number is formatted with a comma for every three digits on the left side of the decimal point and displays two digits to the right of the decimal point. Used in conjunction with Accounting Number Format to align commas and decimal places.
Date	The date in different ways, such as Long Date (March 14, 2016) or Short Date (3/14/16 or 14-Mar-16).
Time	The time in different formats, such as 10:50 PM or 22:50 (military time).
Percent Style	The value as it would be multiplied by 100 (for display purpose), with the percent symbol. The default number of decimal places is zero if you click Percent Style in the Number group or two decimal places if you use the Format Cells dialog box. However, you should typically increase the number of decimal points to show greater accuracy.
Fraction	A number as a fraction; use when no exact decimal equivalent exists. A fraction is entered into a cell as a formula such as =1/3. If the cell is not formatted as a fraction, the formula results display.
Scientific	A number as a decimal fraction followed by a whole number exponent of 10; for example, the number 12345 would appear as 1.23E+04. The exponent, +04 in the example, is the number of places the decimal point is moved to the left (or right if the exponent is negative). Very small numbers have negative exponents.
Text	The data left aligned; is useful for numerical values that have leading zeros and should be treated as text, such as postal codes or phone numbers. Apply Text format before typing a leading zero so that the zero displays in the cell.
Special	A number with editing characters, such as hyphens in a Social Security number.
Custom	Predefined customized number formats or special symbols to create your own customized number format.

The Number group on the Home tab contains commands for applying **Accounting Number Format**, **Percent Style**, and **Comma Style** numbering formats. You can click the Accounting Number Format arrow and select other denominations, such as English pounds or euros. For other number formats, click the Number Format arrow and select the numbering format you want to use. For more specific numbering formats than those provided, select More Number Formats from the Number Format menu or click the Number Dialog Box Launcher to open the Format Cells dialog box with the Number tab options readily available. Figure 1.42 shows different number formats applied to values.

	A	B
1	General	1234.567
2	Number	1234.57
3	Currency	$1,234.57
4	Accounting	$ 1,234.57
5	Comma	1,234.57
6	Percent	12%
7	Short Date	3/1/2018
8	Long Date	Thursday, March 1, 2018

Excel 2016, Windows 10, Microsoft Corporation

FIGURE 1.42 Number Formats

Increase and Decrease Decimal Places

After applying a number format, you may need to adjust the number of decimal places that display. For example, if you have an entire column of monetary values formatted in Accounting Number Format, Excel displays two decimal places by default. If the entire column of values contains whole dollar values and no cents, displaying *.00* down the column looks cluttered. Decrease the number of decimal places to show whole numbers only.

To change the number of decimal places displayed, complete the following steps:

1. Click the cell or select a range of cells containing values that need to have fewer or more decimal places.
2. Click Increase Decimal in the Number group on the Home tab to display more decimal places for greater precision or Decrease Decimal to display fewer or no decimal places.

Quick Concepts

11. What is the importance of formatting a worksheet? *p. 110*

12. Describe five alignment and font formatting techniques used to format labels that are discussed in this section. *p. 110*

13. What are the main differences between Accounting Number Format and Currency format? Which format has its own command on the Ribbon? *p. 114*

Hands-On Exercises

Skills covered: Apply a Cell Style • Merge and Center Data • Change Cell Alignment • Wrap Text • Increase Indent • Apply a Border • Apply Fill Color • Apply Number Formats • Increase and Decrease Decimal Places

4 Worksheet Formatting

In the first three Hands-On Exercises, you entered data about products on sale, created formulas to calculate markup and profit, and inserted new rows and columns to accommodate the labels Electronics and Furniture to identify the specific products. You are ready to format the worksheet. Specifically, you will center the title, align text, format values, and apply other formatting to enhance the readability of the worksheet.

STEP 1 ›› APPLY A CELL STYLE AND MERGE AND CENTER THE TITLE

To make the title stand out, you want to apply a cell style and center it over all the data columns. You will use the Merge & Center command to merge cells and center the title at the same time. Refer to Figure 1.43 as you complete Step 1.

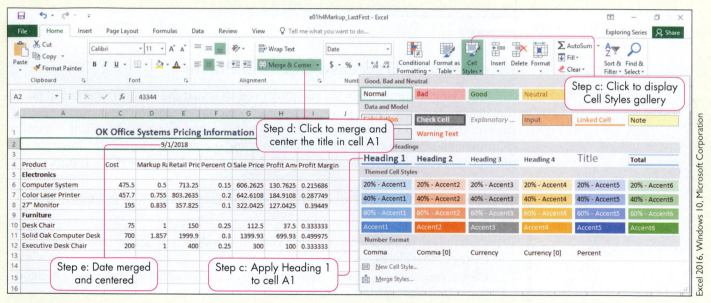

FIGURE 1.43 Cell Style Applied; Data Merged and Centered

a. Open *e01h3Markup_LastFirst* if you closed it at the end of Hands-On Exercise 3 and save it as **e01h4Markup_LastFirst**, changing h3 to h4.

b. Select the **range A15:I26** and press **Delete**.

You maintained a copy of your Paste Special results in the *e01h3Markup_LastFirst* workbook, but you do not need it to continue.

c. Select the **range A1:I1**, click **Cell Styles** in the Styles group on the Home tab, and then click **Heading 1**.

You applied the Heading 1 style to the range A1:I1. This style formats the contents with 15-pt font size, Blue-Gray, Text 2 font color, and a thick blue bottom border.

d. Click **Merge & Center** in the Alignment group.

Excel merges cells in the range A1:I1 into one cell and centers the title horizontally within the merged cell, which is cell A1.

> **TROUBLESHOOTING:** If you merge too many or not enough cells, unmerge the cells and start again. To unmerge cells, click in the merged cell. The Merge & Center command is shaded in green when the active cell is merged. Click Merge & Center to unmerge the cell. Then select the correct range to merge and use Merge & Center again.

e. Select the **range A2:I2**. Click **Merge & Center** in the Alignment group. Save the workbook.

> **TROUBLESHOOTING:** If you try to merge and center data in the range A1:I2, Excel will keep the top-left data only and delete the date. To merge separate data on separate rows, you must merge and center data separately.

STEP 2 ›› **CHANGE CELL ALIGNMENT**

You will wrap the text in the column headings to avoid columns that are too wide for the data, but which will display the entire text of the column labels. In addition, you will horizontally center column labels between the left and right cell margins. Refer to Figure 1.44 as you complete Step 2.

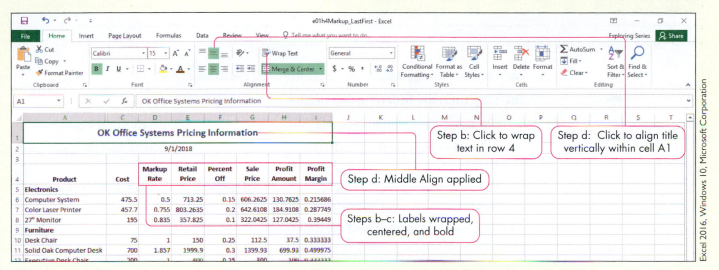

FIGURE 1.44 Formatted Column Labels

a. Select the **range A4:I4** to select the column labels.

b. Click **Wrap Text** in the Alignment group.

The multiple-word column headings are now visible on two lines within each cell.

c. Click **Center** in the Alignment group and click **Bold** in the Font group to format the selected column headings.

The column headings are centered horizontally between the left and right edges of each cell.

d. Click **cell A1**, which contains the title, click **Middle Align** in the Alignment group, and then save the workbook.

Middle Align vertically centers data between the top and bottom edges of the cell.

As you review the first column, you notice that the category names, Electronics and Furniture, do not stand out. You decide to indent the labels within each category to better display which products are in each category. Refer to Figure 1.45 as you complete Step 3.

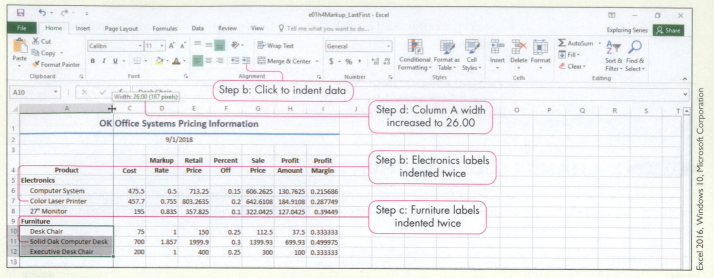

FIGURE 1.45 Indented Cell Contents

a. Select the **range A6:A8**, the cells containing Electronic products labels.

b. Click **Increase Indent** in the Alignment group twice.

The three selected product names are indented below the Electronics heading.

c. Select the **range A10:A12**, the cells containing furniture products, and click **Increase Indent** twice.

The three selected product names are indented below the Furniture heading. Notice that the one product name appears cut off.

d. Increase the column A width to **26.00**. Save the workbook.

You want to apply a light blue fill color to highlight the column headings. In addition, you want to emphasize the percent off and sale prices. You will do this by applying a border around that range. Refer to Figure 1.46 as you complete Step 4.

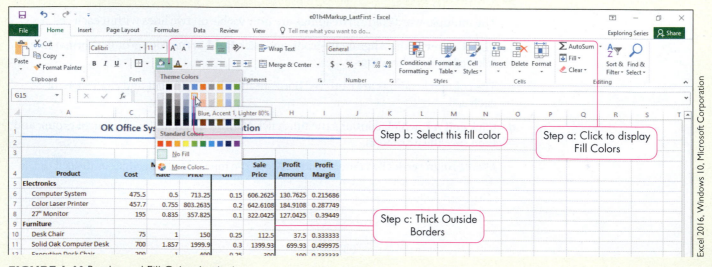

FIGURE 1.46 Border and Fill Color Applied

a. Select the **range A4:I4** and click the **Fill Color arrow** in the Font group.

b. Click **Blue, Accent 1, Lighter 80%** in the Theme Colors section (second row, fifth column).

You applied a fill color to the selected cells to draw attention to these cells.

c. Select the **range F4:G12**, click the **Border arrow** in the Font group, and then select **Thick Outside Borders**.

You applied a border around the selected cells.

d. Click in an empty cell below the columns of data to deselect the cells. Save the workbook.

STEP 5 » APPLY NUMBER FORMATS AND INCREASE AND DECREASE DECIMAL PLACES

You need to format the values to increase readability and look more professional. You will apply number formats and adjust the number of decimal points displayed. Refer to Figure 1.47 as you complete Step 5.

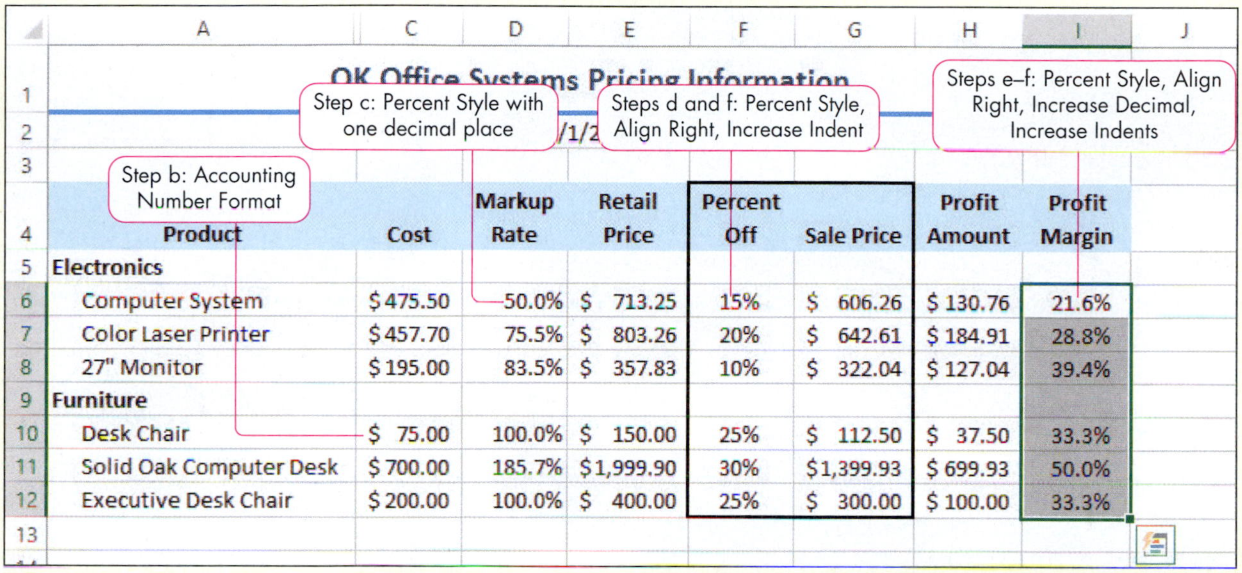

	A	C	D	E	F	G	H	I	J
1	OK Office Systems Pricing Information								
2			/1/2						
3									
4	Product	Cost	Markup Rate	Retail Price	Percent Off	Sale Price	Profit Amount	Profit Margin	
5	Electronics								
6	Computer System	$ 475.50	50.0%	$ 713.25	15%	$ 606.26	$ 130.76	21.6%	
7	Color Laser Printer	$ 457.70	75.5%	$ 803.26	20%	$ 642.61	$ 184.91	28.8%	
8	27" Monitor	$ 195.00	83.5%	$ 357.83	10%	$ 322.04	$ 127.04	39.4%	
9	Furniture								
10	Desk Chair	$ 75.00	100.0%	$ 150.00	25%	$ 112.50	$ 37.50	33.3%	
11	Solid Oak Computer Desk	$ 700.00	185.7%	$1,999.90	30%	$1,399.93	$ 699.93	50.0%	
12	Executive Desk Chair	$ 200.00	100.0%	$ 400.00	25%	$ 300.00	$ 100.00	33.3%	
13									

Excel 2016, Windows 10, Microsoft Corporation

FIGURE 1.47 Number Formats and Decimal Places

a. Select the **range C6:C12.** Press and hold **Ctrl** as you select the **ranges E6:E12** and **G6:H12**.

Because you want to apply the same format to nonadjacent ranges, you hold down Ctrl while selecting each range.

b. Click **Accounting Number Format** in the Number group. If some cells display pound signs, increase the column widths as needed.

You formatted the selected nonadjacent ranges with the Accounting Number Format. The dollar signs align on the left cell margins and the decimals align.

c. Select the **range D6:D12,** click **Percent Style** in the Number group, and then click **Increase Decimal** in the Number group.

You formatted the values in the selected range with Percent Style and increased the decimal to show one decimal place to avoid misleading your readers by displaying the values as whole percentages.

d. Apply **Percent Style** to the **range F6:F12**.

e. Select the **range I6:I12**, apply **Percent Style**, and then click **Increase Decimal**.

f. Select the **range F6:F12**, click **Align Right**, and then click **Increase Indent** twice. Select the **range I6:I12**, click **Align Right**, and then click **Increase Indent**.

With values, you want to keep the decimal points aligned, but you can then use Increase Indent to adjust the indent so that the values appear more centered below the column labels.

g. Save the workbook. Keep the workbook open if you plan to continue with the next Hands-On Exercise. If not, close the workbook and exit Excel.

Worksheets, Page Setup, and Printing

When you start a new blank workbook in Excel, the workbook contains one worksheet named Sheet1. However, you can add additional worksheets. The text, values, dates, and formulas you enter into the individual worksheets are saved under one workbook file name. Having multiple worksheets in one workbook is helpful to keep related items together.

Although you might distribute workbooks electronically as email attachments or you might upload workbooks to a corporate server, you should prepare the worksheets in case you need to print them or in case others who receive an electronic copy of your workbook want to print the worksheets.

In this section, you will copy, move, and rename worksheets. You will also select options on the Page Layout tab. Specifically, you will use the Page Setup, Scale to Fit, and Sheet Options groups. After selecting page setup options, you will learn how to print your worksheet.

Managing Worksheets

Creating a multiple-worksheet workbook takes some planning and maintenance. Worksheet tab names should reflect the contents of the respective worksheets. In addition, you can insert, copy, move, and delete worksheets within the workbook. You can even apply background color to the worksheet tabs so that they stand out onscreen. Figure 1.48 shows a workbook in which the sheet tabs have been renamed, colors have been applied to worksheet tabs, and a worksheet tab has been right-clicked so that the shortcut menu appears.

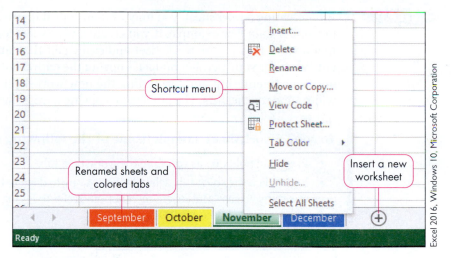

FIGURE 1.48 Worksheet Tabs

The active sheet tab has a green horizontal bar below the sheet name, and the sheet name is bold and green. If a color (such as Red) has been applied to the sheet tab, the tab shows in the full color when it is not active. When that sheet is active, the sheet tab color is a gradient of the selected color.

Insert and Delete a Worksheet

Sometimes you need more than one worksheet in the workbook. For example, you might want one worksheet for each month to track your monthly income and expenses for one year. When tax time comes around, you have all your data stored in one workbook file. You can insert additional, rename, copy, and move worksheets. Adding worksheets within one workbook enables to you save related sheets of data together.

To insert a new worksheet, complete one of the following sets of steps:

- Click New sheet to the right of the last worksheet tab.
- Click the Insert arrow (either to the right or below Insert) in the Cells group on the Home tab and select Insert Sheet.
- Right-click any sheet tab, select Insert from the shortcut menu (refer to Figure 1.48), click Worksheet in the Insert dialog box, and click OK.
- Press Shift+F11.

If you no longer need the data in a worksheet, delete the worksheet. Doing so will eliminate extra data in a file and reduce file size.

To delete a worksheet in a workbook, complete one of the following sets of steps:

- Click the Delete arrow (either to the right or below Delete) in the Cells group on the Home tab and select Delete Sheet.
- Right-click any sheet tab and select Delete from the shortcut menu (refer to Figure 1.48).

If the sheet you are trying to delete contains data, Excel will display a warning: *Microsoft Excel will permanently delete this sheet. Do you want to continue?* Click Delete to delete the worksheet, or click Cancel to keep the worksheet. If you try to delete a blank worksheet, Excel will not display a warning; it will immediately delete the sheet.

Copy or Move a Worksheet

STEP 1 ❯❯ After creating a worksheet, you may want to copy it to use as a template or starting point for similar data. For example, if you create a worksheet for your September budget, you might want to copy the worksheet and easily edit the data on the copied worksheet to enter data for your October budget. Copying the entire worksheet saves you a lot of valuable time in entering and formatting the new worksheet, and it preserves the column widths and row heights. The process for copying a worksheet is similar to moving a sheet.

To copy a worksheet, complete one of the following sets of steps:

- Press and hold Ctrl as you drag the worksheet tab.
- Right-click the sheet tab, select Move or Copy to display the Move or Copy dialog box, select the *To book* and *Before sheet* options (refer to Figure 1.49), click the *Create a copy* check box, and then click OK.

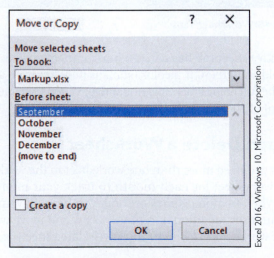

FIGURE 1.49 Move or Copy Dialog Box

You can arrange the worksheet tabs in a different sequence. For example, if the December worksheet is to the left of the October and November worksheets, move the December worksheet to be in chronological order.

To move a worksheet, complete one of the following sets of steps:

- Drag a worksheet tab to the desired location. As you drag a sheet tab, the pointer resembles a piece of paper. A down-pointing triangle appears between sheet tabs to indicate where the sheet will be placed when you release the mouse button.
- Click Format in the Cells group on the Home tab (refer to Figure 1.35) and select Move or Copy Sheet.
- Right-click the sheet tab you want to move and select Move or Copy to display the Move or Copy dialog box. You can move the worksheet within the current workbook or to a different workbook. In the *Before sheet* list, select the worksheet you want to come after the moved worksheet and click OK.

Rename a Worksheet

The default worksheet name Sheet1 does not describe the contents of the worksheet. You should rename worksheet tabs to reflect the sheet contents. For example, if your budget workbook contains monthly worksheets, name the worksheets September, October, etc. Although you can have spaces in worksheet names, keep worksheet names relatively short. The longer the worksheet names, the fewer sheet tabs you will see at the bottom of the workbook window without scrolling.

To rename a worksheet, complete one of the following sets of steps:

- Double-click a sheet tab, type the new name, and then press Enter.
- Click the sheet tab for the sheet you want to rename, click Format in the Cells group on the Home tab (refer to Figure 1.35), select Rename Sheet, type the new sheet name, and then press Enter.
- Right-click the sheet tab, select Rename from the shortcut menu (refer to Figure 1.48), type the new sheet name, and then press Enter.

> **TIP: CHANGE TAB COLOR**
> You can change the color of each worksheet tab to emphasize the difference among the sheets. For example, you might apply red to the September tab and yellow to the October tab. Right-click a sheet tab, select Tab Color, and select a color from the color palette.

Selecting Page Setup Options

The Page Setup group on the Page Layout tab contains options to set the margins, select orientation, specify page size, select the print area, and apply other options (see Figure 1.50). The Scale to Fit group contains options for adjusting the scaling of the spreadsheet on the printed page. When possible, use the commands in these groups to apply page settings. Table 1.8 lists and describes the commands in the Page Setup group.

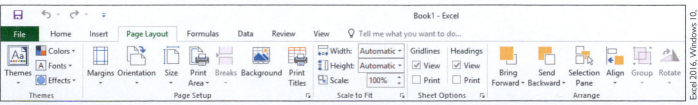

FIGURE 1.50 Page Layout Tab

TABLE 1.8   Page Setup Commands

Command	Description
Margins	Displays a menu to select predefined margin settings. The default margins are 0.75" top and bottom and 0.7" left and right. You will often change these margin settings to balance the worksheet data better on the printed page. If you need different margins, select Custom Margins.
Orientation	Displays orientation options. The default page orientation is portrait, which is appropriate for worksheets that contain more rows than columns. Select landscape orientation when worksheets contain more columns than can fit in portrait orientation. For example, the OKOS worksheet might appear better balanced in landscape orientation because it has eight columns.
Size	Displays a list of standard paper sizes. The default size is 8 ½" by 11". If you have a different paper size, such as legal paper, select it from the list.
Print Area	Displays a list to set or clear the print area. When you have very large worksheets, you might want to print only a portion of that worksheet. To do so, select the range you want to print, click Print Area in the Page Setup group, and select Set Print Area. When you use the Print commands, only the range you specified will be printed. To clear the print area, click Print Area and select Clear Print Area.
Breaks	Displays a menu to insert or remove page breaks.
Background	Enables you to select an image to appear as the background behind the worksheet data when viewed onscreen (backgrounds do not appear when the worksheet is printed).
Print Titles	Enables you to select column headings and row labels to repeat on multiple-page printouts.

Pearson Education, Inc.

TIP: APPLYING PAGE SETUP OPTIONS TO MULTIPLE WORKSHEETS
When you apply Page Setup options, those settings apply to the current worksheet only. However, you can apply page setup options, such as margins or a header, to multiple worksheets at the same time. To select adjacent sheets, click the first sheet tab, press and hold Shift, and click the last sheet tab. To select nonadjacent sheets, press and hold Ctrl as you click each sheet tab. Then choose the Page Setup options to apply to the selected sheets. When you are done, right-click a sheet tab and select Ungroup Sheets.

Specify Page Options

STEP 2 ❯❯ To apply several page setup options at once or to access options not found on the Ribbon, click the Page Setup Dialog Box Launcher. The Page Setup dialog box organizes options into four tabs: Page, Margins, Header/Footer, and Sheet. All tabs contain Print and Print Preview buttons. Figure 1.51 shows the Page tab.

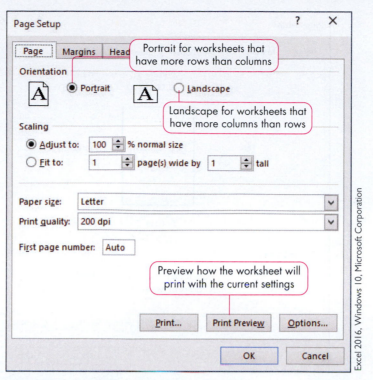

FIGURE 1.51 Page Setup Dialog Box: Page Tab

The Page tab contains options to select the orientation and paper size. In addition, it contains scaling options that are similar to the options in the Scale to Fit group on the Page Layout tab. You use scaling options to increase or decrease the size of characters on a printed page, similar to using a zoom setting on a photocopy machine. You might want to use the *Fit to* option to force the data to print on a specified number of pages.

Set Margin Options

The Margins tab (see Figure 1.52) contains options for setting the specific margins. In addition, it contains options to center the worksheet data horizontally or vertically on the page, which are used to balance worksheet data equally between the left and right margins or top and bottom margins, respectively.

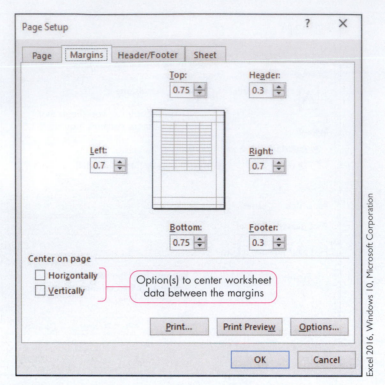

FIGURE 1.52 Page Setup Dialog Box: Margins Tab

Create Headers and Footers

STEP 3 ⟫ The Header/Footer tab (see Figure 1.53) lets you create a header and/or footer that appears at the top and/or bottom of every printed page. Click the arrows to choose from several preformatted entries, or alternatively, click Custom Header or Custom Footer, insert text and other objects, and click the appropriate formatting button to customize the headers and footers. Use headers and footers to provide additional information about the worksheet. You can include your name, the date the worksheet was prepared, and page numbers, for example.

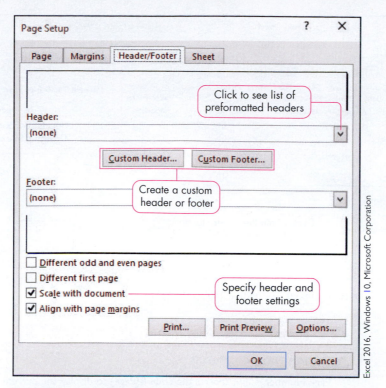

FIGURE 1.53 Page Setup Dialog Box: Header/Footer Tab

You can create different headers or footers on different pages, such as one header with the file name on odd-numbered pages and a header containing the date on even-numbered pages. Click the *Different odd and even pages* check box to select it in the Page Setup dialog box (see Figure 1.53).

You might want the first page to have a different header or footer from the rest of the printed pages, or you might not want a header or footer to show up on the first page but want the header or footer to display on the remaining pages. Click the *Different first page* check box to select it in the Page Setup dialog box to specify a different first page header or footer.

Instead of creating headers and footers using the Page Setup dialog box, you can click the Insert tab and click Header & Footer in the Text group. Excel displays the worksheet in Page Layout view with the insertion point in the center area of the header. Click inside the left, center, or right section of a header or footer. When you click inside a section within the header or footer, Excel displays the Header & Footer Tools Design contextual tab (see Figure 1.54). Enter text or insert data from the Header & Footer Elements group on the tab. Table 1.9 lists and describes the options in the Header & Footer Elements group. To get back to Normal view, click any cell in the worksheet and click Normal in the Workbook Views group on the View tab.

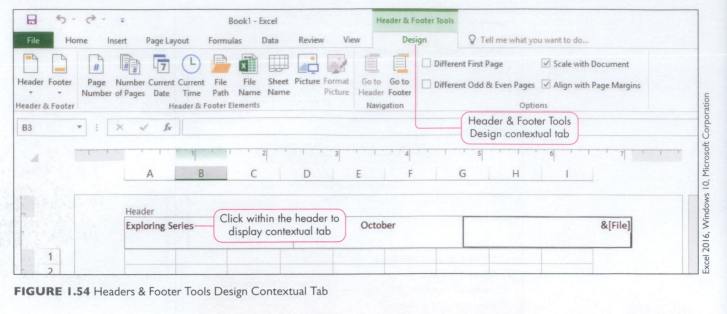

FIGURE 1.54 Headers & Footer Tools Design Contextual Tab

TABLE 1.9	Header & Footer Elements Options
Option Name	**Result**
Page Number	Inserts the code &[Page] to display the current page number.
Number of Pages	Inserts the code &[Pages] to display the total number of pages that will print.
Current Date	Inserts the code &[Date] to display the current date, such as 5/19/2018. The date is updated to the current date when you open or print the worksheet.
Current Time	Inserts the code &[Time] to display the current time, such as 5:15 PM. The time is updated to the current time when you open or print the worksheet.
File Path	Inserts the code &[Path]&[File] to display the path and file name, such as C:\Users\Keith\Documents\e01h4Markup. This information changes if you save the workbook with a different name or in a different location.
File Name	Inserts the code &[File] to display the file name, such as e01h4Markup. This information changes if you save the workbook with a different name.
Sheet Name	Inserts the code &[Tab] to display the worksheet name, such as September. This information changes if you rename the worksheet.
Picture	Inserts the code &[Picture] to display and print an image as a background behind the data, not just the worksheet.
Format Picture	Enables you to adjust the brightness, contrast, and size of an image after you use the Picture option.

> **TIP: VIEW TAB**
> If you click the View tab and click Page Layout, Excel displays an area *Click to add header* at the top of the worksheet.

Select Sheet Options

The Sheet tab (see Figure 1.55) contains options for setting the print area, print titles, print options, and page order. Some of these options are also located in the Sheet Options group on the Page Layout tab.

By default, Excel displays gridlines onscreen to show you each cell's margins, but the gridlines do not print unless you specifically select the Gridlines check box in the Page Setup dialog box or the Print Gridlines check box in the Sheet Options group on the Page Layout tab. In addition, Excel displays row (1, 2, 3, etc.) and column (A, B, C, etc.) headings onscreen. However, these headings do not print unless you click the *Row and column headings* check box in the Page Setup dialog box or click the Print Headings check box in the Sheet Options group on the Page Layout tab. For most worksheets, you do not need to print gridlines and row/column headings. However, when you want to display and print cell formulas instead of formula results, you might want to print the gridlines and row/column headings. Doing so will help you analyze your formulas. The gridlines help you see the cell boundaries, and the headings help you identify what data are in each cell. At times, you might want to display gridlines to separate data on a regular printout to increase readability.

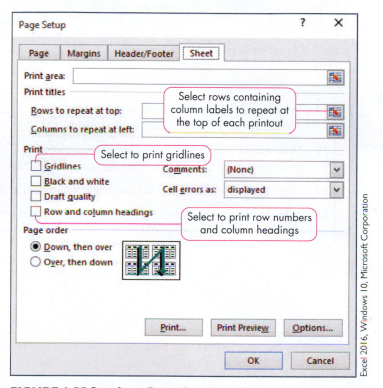

FIGURE 1.55 Page Setup Dialog Box: Sheet Tab

> **TIP: REPEATING ROWS AND COLUMNS**
> If you have spreadsheet data that would take more than one printed page, open the Page Setup dialog box, click the Sheet tab, click in the *Rows to repeat at top* box, and then select the row(s) containing column labels. That way, when the pages print, the rows containing the descriptive column labels will repeat at the top of each printed page so that you can easily know what data is in each column. Likewise, if the spreadsheet has too many columns to print on one page, you can click in the *Columns to repeat at left* box on the Sheet tab within the Page Setup dialog box and select the column(s) so that the row labels will display on the left side of each printed page.

Previewing and Printing a Worksheet

STEP 4 ›› Microsoft Office Backstage view displays print options and displays the worksheet in print preview mode. Print preview helps you see before printing if the data are balanced on the page or if data will print on multiple pages.

You can specify the number of copies to print and which printer to use to print the worksheet. The first option in the Settings area specifies what to print. The default option is Print Active Sheets. You might want to choose other options, such as Print Entire Workbook or Print Selection, or specify which pages to print. If you are connected to a printer capable of duplex printing, you can print on only one side or print on both sides. You can also collate, change the orientation, specify the paper size, adjust the margins, and adjust the scaling.

The bottom of the Print window indicates how many pages will print. If you do not like how the worksheet will print, click Page Setup at the bottom of the print settings to open the Page Setup dialog box so that you can adjust margins, scaling, column widths, and so on until the worksheet data appear the way you want them to print.

> **TIP: PRINTING MULTIPLE WORKSHEETS**
> To print more than one worksheet at a time, select the sheets you want to print. To select adjacent sheets, click the first sheet tab, press and hold Shift, and click the last sheet tab. To select nonadjacent sheets, press and hold Ctrl as you click each sheet tab. When you display the Print options in Microsoft Office Backstage view, Print Active Sheets is one of the default settings. If you want to print all of the worksheets within the workbook, change the setting to Print Entire Workbook.

Quick Concepts

14. Why would you insert several worksheets of data in one workbook instead of creating a separate workbook for each worksheet? *p. 121*

15. Why would you select a *Center on page* option in the Margins tab within the Page Setup dialog box if you have already set the margins? *p. 125*

16. List at least five elements you can insert in a header or footer. *p. 128*

17. Why would you want to print gridlines and row and column headings? *p. 129*

Hands-On Exercises

Watch the Video for this Hands-On Exercise!

MyITLab®
HOE5 Training

Skills covered: Copy or Move a Worksheet • Rename a Worksheet • Group Worksheets • Set Page Orientation • Select Scaling Options • Set Margin Options • Create a Header or Footer • View in Print Preview • Print a Worksheet

5 Worksheets, Page Setup, and Printing

You are ready to complete the OKOS worksheet. You want to copy the existing worksheet so that you display the results on the original sheet and display formulas on the duplicate sheet. Before printing the worksheet for your supervisor, you want to make sure the data will appear professional when printed. You will adjust some page setup options to put the finishing touches on the worksheet.

STEP 1 ›› COPY, MOVE, AND RENAME A WORKSHEET

You want to copy the worksheet, move it to the right side of the original worksheet, and rename the duplicate worksheet so that you can show formulas on the duplicate sheet. Refer to Figure 1.56 as you complete Step 1.

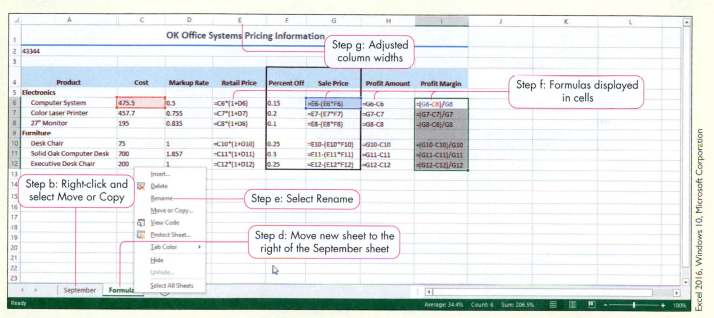

FIGURE 1.56 Worksheets

a. Open *e01h4Markup_LastFirst* if you closed it at the end of Hands-On Exercise 4 and save it as **e01h5Markup_LastFirst**, changing h4 to h5.

b. Right-click the **Sheet1 tab** at the bottom of the worksheet and select **Move or Copy**.

The Move or Copy dialog box opens so that you can move the existing worksheet or make a copy of it.

c. Click the **Create a copy check box** to select it and click **OK**.

The duplicate worksheet is named Sheet1 (2) and is placed to the left of the original worksheet.

d. Drag the **Sheet1 (2) worksheet tab** to the right of the Sheet1 worksheet tab.

The duplicate worksheet is now on the right side of the original worksheet.

e. Right-click the **Sheet1 sheet tab**, select **Rename**, type **September**, and then press **Enter**. Rename Sheet1 (2) as **Formulas**.

You renamed the original worksheet as September to reflect the September sales data, and you renamed the duplicate worksheet as Formulas to indicate that you will keep the formulas displayed on that sheet.

f. Press **Ctrl+`** to display the formulas in the Formulas worksheet.

g. Change these column widths in the Formulas sheet:

- Column A **(13.00)**
- Columns C and D **(6.00)**
- Columns E, G, H, and I **(7.00)**
- Column F **(5.00)**

You reduced the column widths so that the data will fit on a printout better.

h. Save the workbook.

STEP 2 ›› **SET PAGE ORIENTATION, SCALING, AND MARGIN OPTIONS**

Because the worksheet has several columns, you decide to print it in landscape orientation. You want to set a 1" top margin and center the data between the left and right margins. Furthermore, you want to make sure the data fits on one page on each sheet. Currently, if you were to print the Formulas worksheet, the data would print on two pages. Refer to Figure 1.57 as you complete Step 2.

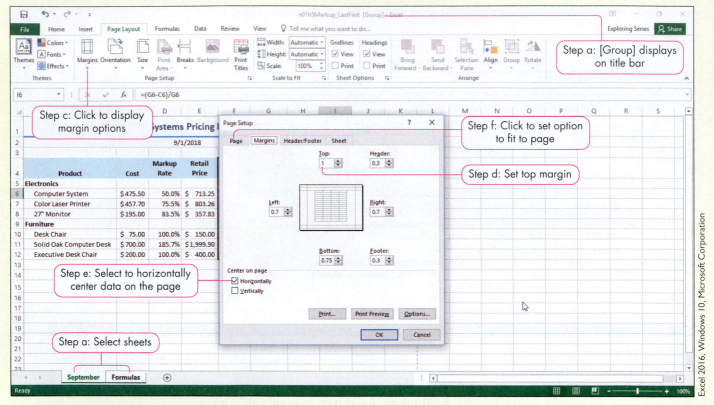

FIGURE 1.57 Page Setup Options Applied

a. Click the **September sheet tab**, press and hold down **Ctrl**, and then click the **Formulas sheet tab**.

Both worksheets are grouped together as indicated by [Group] after the file name on the title bar. Anything you do on one sheet affects both sheets.

b. Click the **Page Layout tab**, click **Orientation** in the Page Setup group, and then select **Landscape** from the list.

Because both worksheets are grouped, both worksheets are formatted in landscape orientation.

c. Click **Margins** in the Page Setup group on the Page Layout tab and select **Custom Margins**.

The Page Setup dialog box opens with the Margins tab options displayed.

d. Click the **Top spin arrow** to display **1**.

Because both worksheets are grouped, the 1" top margin is set for both worksheets.

e. Click the **Horizontally check box** to select it in the Center on page section.

Because both worksheets are grouped, the data on each worksheet are centered between the left and right margins.

f. Click the **Page tab** within the Page Setup dialog box, click **Fit to** in the Scaling section, and then click **OK**. Save the workbook.

The Fit to option ensures that each sheet fits on one page.

STEP 3 ▸▸ CREATE A HEADER

To document the grouped worksheets, you want to include your name, the sheet name, and the file name in a header. Refer to Figure 1.58 as you complete Step 3.

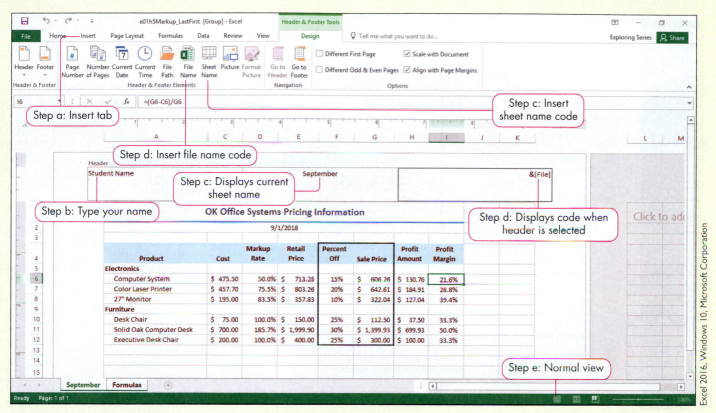

FIGURE 1.58 Header

a. Ensure the worksheets are still grouped, click the **Insert tab**, and then click **Header & Footer** in the Text group.

Excel displays the Header & Footer Tools Design contextual tab and the worksheet displays in Page Layout view, which displays the header area, margin space, and ruler. The insertion point blinks inside the center section of the header.

b. Click in the left section of the header and type your name.

c. Click in the center section of the header and click **Sheet Name** in the Header & Footer Elements group on the Design tab.

Excel inserts the code &[Tab]. This code displays the name of the worksheet. If you change the worksheet tab name, the header will reflect the new sheet name.

d. Click in the right section of the header and click **File Name** in the Header & Footer Elements group on the Design tab.

Excel inserts the code &[File]. This code displays the name of the file. Because the worksheets were grouped when you created the header, a header will appear on both worksheets. The file name will be the same; however, the sheet names will be different.

e. Click in any cell in the worksheet, click **Normal** on the status bar, and then save the workbook.

   Normal view displays the worksheet, but does not display the header or margins.

f. Click the **Review tab** and click **Spelling** in the Proofing group. Correct all errors, if any, and click **OK** when prompted with the message, *Spell check complete. You're good to go!* Save the workbook.

   You should always spell-check a workbook before publishing it.

STEP 4 ▶▶ VIEW IN PRINT PREVIEW AND PRINT

Before printing the worksheets, you should preview it. Doing so helps you detect margin problems and other issues, such as a single row or column of data flowing onto a new page. Refer to Figure 1.59 as you complete Step 4.

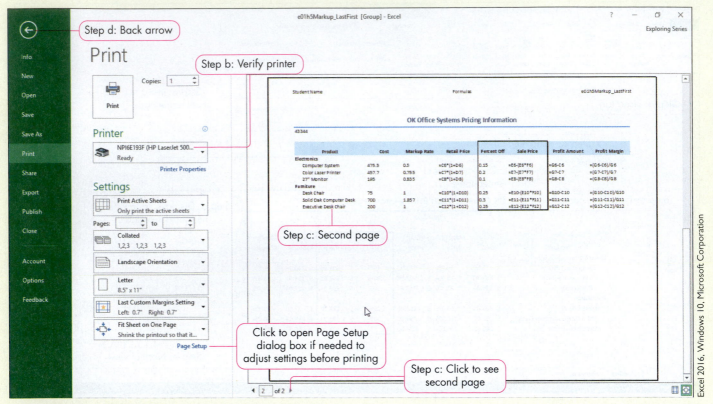

FIGURE 1.59 Worksheet in Print Preview

a. Click the **File tab** and click **Print**.

   The Microsoft Office Backstage view displays print options and a preview of the worksheet.

b. Verify the Printer box displays the printer that you want to use to print your worksheet, and verify the last Settings option displays Fit Sheet on One Page.

   The bottom of Backstage shows 1 of 2, indicating two pages will print.

c. Click **Next Page** to see the second page, which is the data on the Formulas worksheet, and verify the last Settings option displays Fit Sheet on One Page.

   Check the Print Preview window to make sure the data are formatted correctly and would print correctly.

d. Click the **Back arrow** and save the workbook.

   Although you did not print the worksheets, all the print options are saved.

e. Save and close the file. Based on your instructor's directions, submit e01h5Markup_LastFirst. Once the file is closed, the Formulas sheet may not display the formulas when you open the workbook again. If that happens, press **Ctrl+`** again.

Chapter Objectives Review

After reading this chapter, you have accomplished the following objectives:

1. Explore the Excel window.

- A worksheet is a single spreadsheet containing data. A workbook is a collection of one or more related worksheets contained in a single file.
- Identify Excel window elements: The Name Box displays the name of the current cell. The Formula Bar displays the contents of the current cell. The active cell is the current cell. A sheet tab shows the name of the worksheet.
- Identify columns, rows, and cells: Columns have alphabetical headings, such as A, B, C. Rows have numbers, such as 1, 2, 3. A cell is the intersection of a column and row and is indicated with a column letter and a row number.
- Navigate in and among worksheets: Use the arrow keys to navigate within a sheet, or use the Go To command to go to a specific cell. Click a sheet tab to display the contents on another worksheet.

2. Enter and edit cell data.

- You should plan the worksheet design by stating the purpose, deciding what output you need, and then identifying what input values are needed. Next, you enter and format data in a worksheet. Finally, you document, save, and then share a workbook.
- Enter text: Text may contain letters, numbers, symbols, and spaces. Text aligns at the left side of a cell.
- Use Auto Fill to complete a sequence. Auto Fill can automatically fill in sequences, such as month names or values, after you enter the first label or value. Double-click the fill handle to fill in the sequence.
- Enter values: Values are numbers that represent a quantity. Values align at the right side of a cell by default.
- Enter dates and times: Excel stores dates and times as serial numbers so that you can calculate the number of days between dates or times.
- Edit and clear contents: You might want to edit the contents of a cell to correct errors or to make labels more descriptive. Use the Clear option to clear the cell contents and/or formats.

3. Create formulas.

- A formula is used to perform a calculation. The formula results display in the cell.
- Use cell references in formulas: Use references, such as =B5+B6, instead of values within formulas.
- Apply the order of operations: The most commonly used operators are performed in this sequence: Parentheses, exponentiation, multiplication, division, addition, and subtraction.

- Use semi-selection to create a formula: When building a formula, click a cell containing a value to enter that cell reference in the formula.
- Copy formulas with the fill handle: Double-click the fill handle to copy a formula down a column.

4. Display cell formulas.

- By default, the results of formulas appear in cells.
- Display formulas by pressing Ctrl+`.

5. Manage columns and rows.

- Insert cells, columns, and rows: Insert a cell to move the remaining cells down or to the right. Insert a new column or row for data.
- Delete cells, columns, and rows: You should delete cells, columns, and rows you no longer need.
- Hide and unhide columns and rows: Hiding rows and columns protects confidential data from being displayed.
- Adjust column width: Double-click between the column headings to widen a column based on the longest item in that column, or drag the border between column headings to increase or decrease a column width.
- Adjust row height: Drag the border between row headings to increase or decrease the height of a row.

6. Select, move, copy, and paste data.

- Select a range: A range may be a single cell or a rectangular block of cells.
- Move a range to another location: After selecting a range, cut it from its location. Then select the top-left corner of the destination range to make it the active cell and paste the range there.
- Copy and paste a range: After selecting a range, click Copy, click the top-left corner of the destination range, and then click Paste to make a copy of the original range.
- Use Paste Options and Paste Special: The Paste Special option enables you to specify how the data are pasted into the worksheet.
- Copy Excel data to other programs: You can copy Excel data and paste it in other programs, such as in Word or PowerPoint.

7. Apply cell styles, alignment, and font options.

- Cell styles contain a collection of formatting, such as font, font color, font size, fill, and borders. You can apply an Excel cell style to save formatting time.
- Merge and center labels: Type a label in the left cell, select a range including the data you typed, and then click Merge & Center to merge cells and center the label within the newly merged cell.

- Change horizontal and vertical cell alignment: The default horizontal alignment depends on the data entered, and the default vertical alignment is Bottom Align.
- Wrap text: Use the Wrap Text option to present text on multiple lines in order to avoid having extra-wide columns.
- Increase and decrease indent: To indicate hierarchy of data or to offset a label, increase or decrease how much the data are indented in a cell.
- Apply borders and fill colors: Borders and fill colors help improve readability of worksheets.

8. Apply number formats.

- Apply a number format: The default number format is General, which does not apply any particular format to values. Apply appropriate formats to values to present the data with the correct symbols and decimal alignment. For example, Accounting Number Format is a common number format for monetary values.
- Increase and decrease decimal places: After applying a number format, you might want to increase or decrease the number of decimal places displayed.

9. Manage worksheets.

- Insert and delete a worksheet: You can insert new worksheets to include related data within one workbook, or you can delete extra worksheets you do not need.

- Copy or move a worksheet: Drag a sheet tab to rearrange the worksheets. You can copy a worksheet within a workbook or to another workbook.
- Rename a worksheet: The default worksheet tab name is Sheet1, but you should change the name to describe the contents of the worksheet.

10. Select page setup options.

- The Page Layout tab on the Ribbon contains options for setting margins, selecting orientation, specifying page size, selecting the print area, and applying other settings.
- Specify page options: Page options include orientation, paper size, and scaling.
- Set margin options: You can set the left, right, top, and bottom margins. In addition, you can center worksheet data horizontally and vertically on a page.
- Create headers and footers: Insert a header or footer to display documentation, such as your name, date, time, and worksheet tab name.
- Select sheet options: Sheet options control the print area, print titles, print options, and page order.

11. Preview and print a worksheet.

- Before printing a worksheet, you should display a preview to ensure the data will print correctly. The Print Preview helps you see if margins are correct or if isolated rows or columns will print on separate pages.
- After making appropriate adjustments, you can print the worksheet.

Key Terms Matching

Match the key terms with their definitions. Write the key term letter by the appropriate numbered definition.

a. Alignment
b. Auto Fill
c. Cell
d. Column width
e. Fill color
f. Fill handle
g. Formula
h. Formula Bar
i. Input area
j. Name Box

k. Order of operations
l. Output area
m. Range
n. Row height
o. Sheet tab
p. Text
q. Value
r. Workbook
s. Worksheet
t. Wrap text

1. _____ A spreadsheet that contains formulas, functions, values, text, and visual aids. **p. 70**

2. _____ A file containing related worksheets. **p. 70**

3. _____ A range of cells containing values for variables used in formulas. **p. 73**

4. _____ A range of cells containing results based on manipulating the variables. **p. 73**

5. _____ Identifies the address of the current cell. **p. 71**

6. _____ Displays the content (text, value, date, or formula) in the active cell. **p. 71**

7. _____ Displays the name of a worksheet within a workbook. **p. 71**

8. _____ The intersection of a column and row. **p. 72**

9. _____ Includes letters, numbers, symbols, and spaces. **p. 74**

10. _____ A number that represents a quantity or an amount. **p. 77**

11. _____ Rules that control the sequence in which Excel performs arithmetic operations. **p. 84**

12. _____ Enables you to copy the contents of a cell or cell range or to continue a sequence by dragging the fill handle over an adjacent cell or range of cells. **p. 75**

13. _____ A small green square at the bottom-right corner of a cell. **p. 76**

14. _____ The horizontal measurement of a column. **p. 97**

15. _____ The vertical measurement of a row. **p. 98**

16. _____ A rectangular group of cells. **p. 98**

17. _____ The position of data between the cell margins. **p. 111**

18. _____ Formatting that enables a label to appear on multiple lines within the current cell. **p. 112**

19. _____ The background color appearing behind data in a cell. **p. 113**

20. _____ A combination of cell references, operators, values, and/or functions used to perform a calculation. **p. 83**

Multiple Choice

1. Which step is *not* part of planning a worksheet design?

   (a) Decide what input values are needed.

   (b) State the purpose of the worksheet.

   (c) Decide what outputs are needed to achieve the purpose.

   (d) Enter labels, values, and formulas.

2. You just copied a range of data containing formulas. However, you want to preserve the formula results and the original number and text formatting in the pasted range. Which paste option would you select?

   (a) Formulas

   (b) Keep Source Formatting

   (c) Values & Source Formatting

   (d) Values & Number Formatting

3. Given the formula =B1*B2+B3/B4^2, what operation is calculated first?

   (a) B1*B2

   (b) B2+B3

   (c) B3/B4

   (d) B4^2

4. How can you display formulas within the cells instead of the cell results?

   (a) Press Ctrl+G.

   (b) Press Ctrl+`.

   (c) Click Cell References on the Home tab.

   (d) Press Ctrl+C.

5. What is a fast way to apply several formats at one time?

   (a) Click each one individually.

   (b) Apply a cell style.

   (c) Use Auto Fill.

   (d) Use Copy and Paste options.

6. Which of the following is *not* an alignment option?

   (a) Increase Indent

   (b) Merge & Center

   (c) Fill Color

   (d) Wrap Text

7. Which of the following characteristics is *not* applicable to the Accounting Number Format?

   (a) Dollar sign immediately on the left side of the value

   (b) Commas to separate thousands

   (c) Two decimal places

   (d) Zero values displayed as hyphens

8. You selected and copied worksheet data containing formulas. However, you want the pasted copy to contain the current formula results rather than formulas. What do you do?

   (a) Click Paste in the Clipboard group on the Home tab.

   (b) Click the Paste arrow in the Clipboard group and select Formulas.

   (c) Click the Paste arrow in the Clipboard group and select Values & Source Formatting.

   (d) Display the Paste Special dialog box and select Formulas & Number Formatting.

9. Assume that the data on a worksheet consume a whole printed page and a couple of columns on a second page. You can do all of the following *except* what to force the data to print all on one page?

   (a) Decrease the Scale value.

   (b) Increase the left and right margins.

   (c) Decrease column widths if possible.

   (d) Select a smaller range as the print area.

10. What should you do if you see pound signs (###) instead of values or results of formulas?

    (a) Increase the zoom percentage.

    (b) Delete the column.

    (c) Adjust the row height.

    (d) Increase the column width.

Practice Exercises

1 Mathematics Review

You want to brush up on your math skills to test your logic by creating formulas in Excel. You realize that you should avoid values in formulas most of the time. Therefore, you created an input area that contains values you will use in your formulas. To test your knowledge of formulas, you will create an output area that will contain a variety of formulas using cell references from the input area. You will include a formatted title, the date prepared, and your name. After creating and verifying formula results, you will change input values and observe changes in the formula results. You want to display cell formulas, so you will create a picture copy of the formulas view. Refer to Figure 1.60 as you complete this exercise.

▲	A	B	C	D	E
1				**Excel Formulas and Order of Precedence**	
2	Date Created:	42614		Student Name	
3					
4	**Input Area:**			**Output Area:**	
5	First Value	2		Sum of 1st and 2nd values	=B5+B6
6	Second Value	4		Difference between 4th and 1st values	=B8-B5
7	Third Value	6		Product of 2nd and 3rd values	=B6*B7
8	Fourth Value	8		Quotient of 3rd and 1st values	=B7/B5
9				2nd value to the power of 3rd value	=B6^B7
10				1st value added to product of 2nd and 4th values and difference between sum and 3rd value	=B5+B6*B8-B7
11				Product of sum of 1st and 2nd and difference between 4th and 3rd values	=(B5+B6)*(B8-B7)
12				Product of 1st and 2nd added to product of 3rd and 4th values	=(B5*B6)+(B7*B8)

FIGURE 1.60 Formula Practice

a. Open *e01p1Math* and save it as **e01p1Math_LastFirst**.

b. Type the current date in **cell B2** in this format: 9/1/2018. Type your first and last names in **cell D2**.

c. Adjust the column widths by doing the following:
   - Click in any cell in column A and click **Format** in the Cells group.
   - Select **Column Width**, type **12.57** in the Column width box, and then click **OK**.
   - Click in any cell in column B and set the width to **11**.
   - Click in any cell in column D and set the width to **35.57**.

d. Select the **range A1:E1**, click **Merge & Center** in the Alignment group, click **Bold** in the Font group, and then change the font size to **14**.

e. Select the **range B5:B8** and click **Center** in the Alignment group.

f. Select the **range D10:D12** and click **Wrap Text** in the Alignment group.

g. Enter the following formulas in column E:
   - Click **cell E5**. Type **=B5+B6** and press **Enter**. Excel adds the value stored in cell B5 (1) to the value stored in cell B6 (2). The result (3) appears in cell E5, as described in cell D5.
   - Enter appropriate formulas in **cells E6:E8**, pressing **Enter** after entering each formula. Subtract to calculate a difference, multiply to calculate a product, and divide to calculate a quotient.
   - Type **=B6^B7** in **cell E9** and press **Enter**. Calculate the answer: 2*2*2 = 8.
   - Enter **=B5+B6*B8-B7** in **cell E10** and press **Enter**. Calculate the answer: 2*4 = 8; 1+8 = 9; 9-3 = 6. Multiplication occurs first, followed by addition, and finally subtraction.
   - Enter **=(B5+B6)*(B8-B7)** in **cell E11** and press **Enter**. Calculate the answer: 1+2 = 3; 4-3 = 1; 3*1 = 3. This formula is almost identical to the previous formula; however, calculations in parentheses occur before the multiplication.
   - Enter **=B5*B6+B7*B8** in **cell E12** and press **Enter**. Calculate the answer: 1*2 = 2; 3*4 = 12; 2+12 = 14.

h. Edit a formula and the input values:

- Click **cell E12** and click in the Formula Bar to edit the formula. Add parentheses as shown: **=(B5*B6)+(B7*B8)** and click **Enter** to the left side of the Formula Bar. The answer is still 14. The parentheses do not affect order of operations because multiplication occurred before the addition. The parentheses help improve the readability of the formula.
- Type **2** in **cell B5**, **4** in **cell B6**, **6** in **cell B7**, and **8** in **cell B8**.
- Double-check the results of the formulas using a calculator or your head. The new results in cells E5:E12 should be 6, 6, 24, 3, 4096, 28, 12, and 56, respectively.

i. Double-click the **Sheet1 tab**, type **Results**, and then press **Enter**. Right-click the **Results sheet tab**, select **Move or Copy**, click **(move to end)** in the *Before sheet* section, click the **Create a copy check box** to select it, and click **OK**. Double-click the **Results (2) sheet tab**, type **Formulas**, and then press **Enter**.

j. Ensure that the Formulas sheet tab is active, click the **Formulas sheet tab** and click **Show Formulas** in the Formula Auditing group. Double-click between the column A and column B headings to adjust the column A width. Double-click between the column B and column C headings to adjust the column B width. Set **24.00 width** for column D.

k. Ensure that the Formulas worksheet is active, click the **Page Layout tab**, and do the following:

- Click the **Gridlines Print check box** to select it in the Sheet Options group.
- Click the **Headings Print check box** to select it in the Sheet Options group.

l. Click the **Results sheet tab**, press and hold **Ctrl**, and click the **Formulas sheet tab** to select both worksheets. Do the following:

- Click **Orientation** in the Page Setup group and select **Landscape**.
- Click the **Insert tab**, click **Header & Footer** in the Text group. Click **Go to Footer** in the Navigation group.
- Type your name on the left side of the footer.
- Click in the center section of the footer and click **Sheet Name** in the Header & Footer Elements group.
- Click in the right section of the footer and click **File Name** in the Header & Footer elements group.

m. Click in the worksheet, press **Ctrl+Home**, and click **Normal View** on the status bar.

n. Click the **File tab** and click **Print**. Verify that each worksheet will print on one page. Press **Esc** to close the Print Preview, and right-click the worksheet tab and click **Ungroup Sheets**.

o. Save and close the file. Based on your instructor's directions, submit e01p1Math_LastFirst.

2 Calendar Formatting

You want to create a calendar for July 2018. The calendar will enable you to practice alignment settings, including center, merge and center, and indents. In addition, you will need to adjust column widths and increase row height to create cells large enough to enter important information, such as birthdays, in your calendar. You will create a formula and use Auto Fill to complete the days of the week and the days within each week. To improve the appearance of the calendar, you will add fill colors, font colors, and borders to create a red, white, and blue effect to celebrate Independence Day. Refer to Figure 1.61 as you complete this exercise.

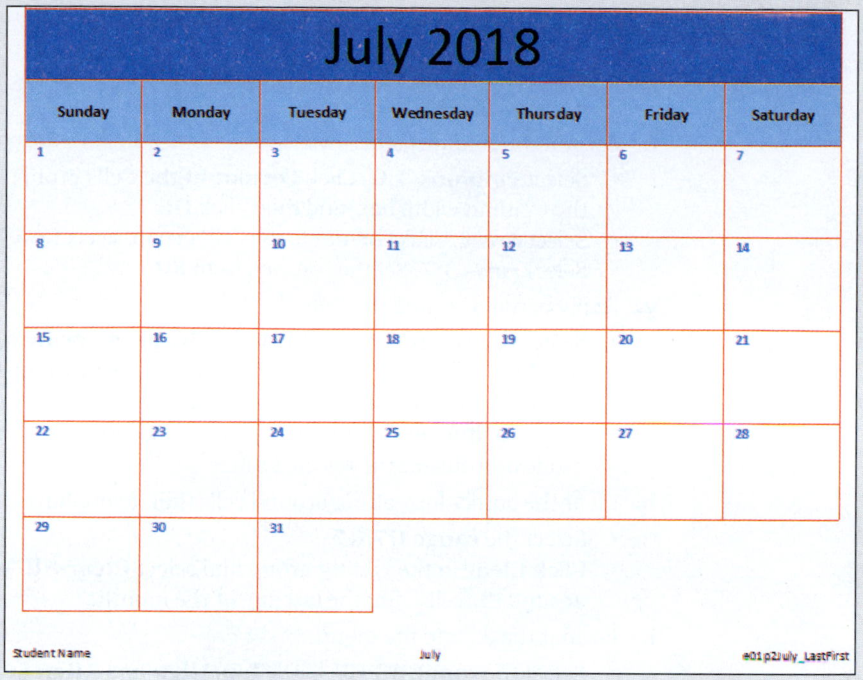
July 2018
Sunday
Monday
Tuesday
Wednesday
Thursday
Friday
Saturday
1 2 3 4 5 6 7
8 9 10 11 12 13 14
15 16 17 18 19 20 21
22 23 24 25 26 27 28
29 30 31
Student Name
July
e01p2July_LastFirst

Excel 2016, Windows 10, Microsoft Corporation

FIGURE 1.61 Calendar

a. Click the **File tab**, select **New**, and click **Blank workbook**. Save the workbook as **e01p2July_LastFirst**.

b. Type **'July 2018** in **cell A1** and click **Enter** on the left side of the Formula Bar.

> **TROUBLESHOOTING:** If you do not type the apostrophe before July 2018, the cell will display July-18 instead of July 2018.

c. Format the title:
- Select the **range A1:G1** and click **Merge & Center** in the Alignment group.
- Change the font size to **48**.
- Click the **Fill Color arrow** and click **Blue** in the Standard Colors section of the color palette.
- Click **Middle Align** in the Alignment group.

d. Complete the days of the week:
- Type **Sunday** in **cell A2** and click **Enter** to the left side of the Formula Bar.
- Drag the **cell A2 fill handle** across the row through **cell G2** to use Auto Fill to complete the rest of the weekdays.
- Ensure that the **range A2:G2** is selected. Click the **Fill Color arrow** and select **Blue, Accent 1, Lighter 40%** in the Theme Colors section of the color palette.
- Apply bold and change the font size to **14 size** to the selected range.
- Click **Middle Align** and click **Center** in the Alignment group to format the selected range.

e. Complete the days of the month:
- Type **1** in **cell A3** and press **Ctrl+Enter**. Drag the **cell A3 fill handle** across the row through **cell G3**.
- Click **Auto Fill Options** in the bottom-right corner of the copied data and select **Fill Series** to change the numbers to 1 through 7.
- Type **=A3+7** in **cell A4** and press **Ctrl+Enter**. Usually you avoid numbers in formulas, but the number of days in a week is always 7. Drag the **cell A4 fill handle** down through **cell A7** to get the date for each Sunday in July.

- Keep the **range A4:A7** selected and drag the fill handle across through **cell G7**. This action copies the formulas to fill in the days in the month.
- Select the **range D7:G7** and press **Delete** to delete the extra days 32 through 35 because July has only 31 days.

f. Format the columns and rows:

- Select **columns A:G**. Click **Format** in the Cells group, select **Column Width**, type **16** in the Column width box, and then click **OK**.
- Select **row 2**. Click **Format** in the Cells group, select **Row Height**, type **54**, and then click **OK**.
- Select **rows 3:7**. Set the row height to **80**.

g. Apply borders around the cells:

- Select the **range A1:G7**. Click the **Borders arrow** in the Font group and select **More Borders** to display the Format Cells dialog box with the Border tab selected.
- Click the **Color arrow** and select **Red**.
- Click **Outline** and **Inside** in the Presets section. Click **OK**. This action applies a red border inside and outside the selected range.

h. Clear the border formatting around cells that do not have days:

- Select the **range D7:G7**.
- Click **Clear** in the Editing group and select **Clear All**. This action removes the red borders around the cells after the last day of the month.

i. Format the days in the month:

- Select the **range A3:G7**. Click **Top Align** and **Align Left** in the Alignment group.
- Click **Increase Indent** in the Alignment group to offset the days from the border.
- Click **Bold** in the Font group, click the **Font Color arrow** and select **Blue**, and click the **Font Size arrow**, and then select **12**.

j. Double-click the **Sheet1 tab**, type **July**, and then press **Enter**.

k. Deselect the range and click the **Page Layout tab** and do the following:

- Click **Orientation** in the Page Setup group and select **Landscape**.
- Click **Margins** in the Page Setup group and select **Custom Margins**. Click the **Horizontally check box** to select it in the *Center on page* section and click **OK**.

l. Click the **Insert tab** and click **Header & Footer** in the Text group and do the following:

- Click **Go to Footer** in the Navigation group.
- Click in the left side of the footer and type your name.
- Click in the center of the footer and click **Sheet Name** in the Header & Footer Elements group on the Design tab.
- Click in the right side of the footer and click **File Name** in the Header & Footer Elements group on the Design tab.
- Click in any cell in the workbook, press **Ctrl+Home**, and then click **Normal** on the status bar.

m. Save and close the file. Based on your instructor's directions, submit e01p2July_LastFirst.

You are the assistant manager at Downtown Theatre, where touring Broadway plays and musicals are performed. You will analyze ticket sales by completing a worksheet that focuses on seating charts for each performance. The spreadsheet will identify the seating sections, total seats in each section, and the number of seats sold for a performance. You will then calculate the percentage of seats sold and unsold. Refer to Figure 1.62 as you complete this exercise.

	A	B	C	D	E	F
1	**Downtown Theatre**					
2	Ticket Sales by Seating Section					
3	3/31/2018					
4						
5	**Section**	**Available Seats**	**Seats Sold**	**Percentage Sold**	**Percentage Unsold**	
6	Box Seats	25	12	48.0%	52.0%	
7	Front Floor	120	114	95.0%	5.0%	
8	Back Floor	132	108	81.8%	18.2%	
9	Tier 1	40	40	100.0%	0.0%	
10	Mezzanine	144	138	95.8%	4.2%	
11	Balcony	106	84	79.2%	20.8%	

FIGURE 1.62 Theatre Seating Data

Excel 2016, Windows 10, Microsoft Corporation

a. Open *e01p3TicketSales* and save it as **e01p3TicketSales_LastFirst**.

b. Double-click the **Sheet1 sheet tab**, type **Seating**, and press **Enter**.

c. Type **3/31/2018** in **cell A3** and press **Enter**.

d. Format the title:
   - Select the **range A1:E1** and click **Merge & Center** in the Alignment group.
   - Click **Cell Styles** in the Styles group and select **Title** in the Titles and Headings section.
   - Click **Bold** in the Font group.

e. Format the subtitle and date:
   - Use the Merge & Center command to merge the **range A2:E2** and center the subtitle.
   - Use the Merge & Center command to merge the **range A3:E3** and center the date.

f. Select the **range A5:E5**, click **Wrap Text**, click **Center**, and click **Bold** to format the column labels.

g. Right-click the **row 9 heading** and select **Insert** from the shortcut menu to insert a new row. Type the following data in the new row: **Back Floor**, **132**, **108**.

h. Move the Balcony row to be the last row by doing the following:
   - Click the **row 6 heading** and click **Cut** in the Clipboard group on the Home tab.
   - Right-click the **row 12 heading** and select **Insert Cut Cells** from the menu.

i. Adjust column widths by doing the following:
   - Double-click between the column A and column B headings.
   - Select **columns B** and **C headings** to select the columns, click **Format** in the Cells group, select **Column Width**, type **9** in the **Column width box**, and then click **OK**. Because columns B and C contain similar data, you set the same width for these columns.
   - Set the width of columns D and E to **12**.

j. Select the **range B6:C11**, click **Align Right** in the Alignment group, and then click **Increase Indent** twice in the Alignment group.

k. Click **cell D6** and use semi-selection to calculate and format the percentage of sold and unsold seats by doing the following:

- Type **=**, click **cell C6**, type **/**, and then click **cell B6** to enter =C6/B6.
- Press **Tab** to enter the formula and make cell E6 the active cell. This formula divides the number of seats sold by the total number of Box Seats.
- Type **=(B6-C6)/B6** and click **Enter** on the left side of the Formula Bar to enter the formula and keep cell E6 the active cell. This formula must first subtract the number of sold seats from the available seats to calculate the number of unsold seats. The difference is divided by the total number of available seats to determine the percentage of unsold seats.
- Select the **range D6:E6**, click **Percent Style** in the Number group, and then click **Increase Decimal** in the Number group. Keep the range selected.
- Double-click the **cell E6 fill handle** to copy the selected formulas down their respective columns. Keep the range selected.
- Click **Align Right** in the Alignment group and click **Increase Indent** twice in the Alignment group. These actions will help center the data below the column labels. Do not click Center; doing so will center each value and cause the decimal points not to align. Deselect the range.

l. Display and preserve a screenshot of the formulas by doing the following:

- Click **New sheet**, double-click the **Sheet1 sheet tab**, type **Formulas**, and then press **Enter**.
- Click the **View tab** and click **Gridlines** in the Show group to hide the gridlines on the Formulas worksheet. This action will prevent the cell gridlines from bleeding through the screenshot you are about to embed.
- Click the **Seating sheet tab**, click the **Formulas tab** on the Ribbon, and then click **Show Formulas** in the Formula Auditing group to display cell formulas.
- Click **cell A1** and drag down to **cell E11** to select the range of data.
- Click the **Home tab**, click **Copy arrow** in the Clipboard group, select **Copy as Picture**, and then click **OK** in the Copy Picture dialog box.
- Click the **Formulas sheet tab**, click **cell A1**, and then click **Paste**.
- Click the **Page Layout tab**, click **Orientation** in the Page Setup group, and then select **Landscape** to change the orientation for the Formulas sheet.
- Click the **Seating sheet tab**, click the **Formulas tab**, and then click **Show Formulas** in the Formula Auditing group to hide the cell formulas.

m. Click the **Seating sheet tab**, press **Ctrl** and click the **Formulas sheet tab** to group the two sheets. Click the **Page Layout tab**, click **Margins** in the Page Setup group, and then select **Custom Margins**. Click the **Horizontally check box** to select it and click **Print Preview**. Excel centers the data horizontally based on the widest item in each worksheet. Verify that the worksheets each print on one page. If not, go back into the Page Setup dialog box for each worksheet and reapply settings if needed. Press **Esc** to leave the Print Preview mode.

n. Click the **Page Setup Dialog Box Launcher**, click the **Header/Footer tab** in the Page Setup dialog box, click **Custom Footer**. Click in the left section of the footer and type your name. Click in the center section of the footer and, click **Insert Sheet Name**. Click in the right section of the footer, click **Insert File Name**, and then click **OK** to close the Footer dialog box. Click **OK** to close the Page Setup dialog box.

o. Right-click the **Seating sheet tab** and select **Ungroup Sheets**.

p. Save and close the file. Based on your instructor's directions, submit e01p3TicketSales_LastFirst.

Mid-Level Exercises

1 Guest House Rental Rates

ANALYSIS CASE

You manage a beach guest house in Ft. Lauderdale containing three types of rental units. Prices are based on peak and off-peak times of the year. You want to calculate the maximum daily revenue for each rental type, assuming all units are rented. In addition, you will calculate the discount rate for off-peak rental times. Finally, you will improve the appearance of the worksheet by applying font, alignment, and number formats.

a. Open *e01m1Rentals* and save it as **e01m1Rentals_LastFirst**.

b. Apply the **Heading 1** cell style to the **range A1:G1** and the **20% - Accent1** cell style to the **range A2:G2**.

c. Merge and center Peak Rentals in the **range C4:D4**, over the two columns of peak rental data. Apply **Dark Red fill color** and **White, Background 1 font color**.

d. Merge and center Off-Peak Rentals in the **range E4:G4** over the three columns of off-peak rental data. Apply **Blue fill color** and **White, Background 1 font color**.

e. Center and wrap the headings on row 5. Adjust the width of columns D and F, if needed. Center the data in the **range B6:B8**.

f. Create and copy the following formulas:
- Calculate the Peak Rentals Maximum Revenue by multiplying the number of units by the peak rental price per day.
- Calculate the Off-Peak Rentals Maximum Revenue by multiplying the number of units by the off-peak rental price per day.
- Calculate the Discount rate for the Off-Peak rental price per day. For example, using the peak and off-peak per day values, the studio apartment rents for 75% of its peak rental rate. However, you need to calculate and display the off-peak discount rate, which is .20 for the Studio Apartment. To calculate the discount rate, divide the off-peak per day rate by the peak per day rate. Subtract that result from 1, which represents 100%.

g. Format the monetary values with **Accounting Number Format**. Format the Discount Rate formula results in **Percent Style** with one decimal place. Adjust column widths if necessary to display the data.

DISCOVER

h. Apply **Blue, Accent 1, Lighter 80% fill color** to the **range E5:G8**.

i. Select the **range C5:D8** and apply a custom color with **Red 242**, **Green 220**, and **Blue 219**.

j. Answer the four questions below the worksheet data. If you change any values to answer the questions, change the values back to the original values.

k. Create a copy of the Rental Rates worksheet, place the new sheet to the right side of the original worksheet, and rename the new sheet **Formulas**. Display cell formulas on the Formulas sheet.

l. Group the worksheets and do the following:
- Select landscape orientation.
- Set **1"** top, bottom, left, and right margins. Center the data horizontally on the page.
- Insert a footer with your name on the left side, the sheet name code in the center, and the file name code on the right side.
- Apply the setting to fit to one page.

m. Click the **Formulas sheet tab** and set options to print gridlines and headings. Adjust column widths.

n. Save and close the file. Based on your instructor's directions, submit e01m1Rentals_LastFirst.

You are a small real estate agent in Indianapolis. You track the real estate properties you list for clients. You want to analyze sales for selected properties. Yesterday, you prepared a workbook with a worksheet for recent sales data and another worksheet listing several properties you listed. You want to calculate the number of days that the houses were on the market and their sales percentage of the list price. In one situation, the house was involved in a bidding war between two families that really wanted the house. Therefore, the sale price exceeded the list price.

a. Open *e01m2Sales* and save it as **e01m2Sales_LastFirst**.

b. Delete the row that has incomplete sales data. The owners took their house off the market.

c. Type **2018-001** in **cell A5** and use Auto Fill to complete the series to assign a property ID to each property.

d. Calculate the number of days each house was on the market in column C. Copy the formula down that column.

e. Format list prices and sold prices with **Accounting Number Format** with zero decimal places.

f. Calculate the sales price percentage of the list price in cell H5. The second house was listed for $500,250, but it sold for only $400,125. Therefore, the sale percentage of the list price is 79.99%. Format the percentages with two decimal places.

g. Wrap the headings on row 4.

h. Insert a new column between the Date Sold and List Price columns. Do the following:
- Move the Days on Market range C4:C13 to the new column.
- Delete the empty column C.

i. Edit the list date of the 41 Chestnut Circle house to be **4/22/2018**. Edit the list price of the house on Amsterdam Drive to be **$355,000**.

j. Select the property rows and set a **25 row height** and apply **Middle Align**.

k. Apply the **All Borders** border style to the **range A4:H12**. Adjust column widths as necessary.

l. Apply **Align Right** and indent twice the values in the **range E5:E12**.

m. Apply **120% scaling**.

n. Delete the Properties worksheet.

o. Insert a new worksheet and name it **Formulas**.

p. Use the Select All feature to select all data on the Houses Sold worksheet and copy it to the Formulas worksheet.

q. Complete the following steps on the Formulas worksheet:
- Hide the Date Listed and Date Sold columns.
- Display cell formulas.
- Set options to print gridlines and row and column headings.
- Adjust column widths.

r. Group the worksheets and do the following:
- Set landscape orientation.
- Center the page horizontally and vertically between the margins.
- Insert a footer with your name on the left side, the sheet tab code in the center, and the file name code on the right side.

s. Save and close the file. Based on your instructor's directions, submit e01m2Sales_LastFirst.

3 Problem Solving with Classmates

COLLABORATION CASE

Your instructor wants all students in the class to practice their problem-solving skills. Pair up with a classmate so that you can create errors in a workbook and then see how many errors your classmate can find in your worksheet and how many errors you can find in your classmate's worksheet.

a. Create a folder named **Exploring** on your OneDrive and give access to that drive to a classmate and your instructor.

b. Open *e01h5Markup_LastFirst*, which you created in the Hands-On Exercises, and save it as **e01m3Markup_LastFirst**, changing h5 to m3.

c. Edit each main formula to have a deliberate error (such as a value or incorrect cell reference) in it and then copy the formulas down the columns.

d. Save the workbook to your shared folder on your OneDrive.

e. Open the workbook your classmate saved on his or her OneDrive and save the workbook with your name after theirs, such as *e01m3Markup_MulberyKeith_KrebsCynthia*.

f. Find the errors in your classmate's workbook, insert comments to describe the errors, and then correct the errors.

g. Save the workbook back to your classmate's OneDrive and close the file. Based on your instructor's directions, submit e01m3Markup_LastFirst_LastFirst.

Beyond the Classroom

Tip Distribution

GENERAL CASE

You are a server at a restaurant in Portland. You must tip the bartender 13% of each customer's drink sales and the server assistant 1.75% of the food sales plus 2% of the drink sales. You want to complete a worksheet that shows the sales, tips, and your net tip. Open *e01b1Server* and save it as **e01b1Server_LastFirst**.

Insert a column between the Drinks and Tip Left columns. Type the label **Subtotal** in cell D6. Calculate the food and drinks subtotal for the first customer and copy the formula down the column. In column F, enter a formula to calculate the amount of the tip as a percentage of the subtotal for the first customer's sales. Format the results with Percent Style with one decimal place. Type **13%** in cell G7, type **1.75%** in cell H7, and type **2%** in cell I7. Copy these percentage values down these three columns. Horizontally center the data in the three percentage columns.

In cell J7, calculate the bartender's tip for the first customer, using the rule specified in the first paragraph. In cell K7, calculate the assistant's tip for the first customer, using the rule specified in the first paragraph. In cell L7, calculate your net tip after giving the bartender and server their share of the tips. Copy the formulas from the range J7:L7 down their respective columns. Merge and center **Customer Subtotal and Tip** in the range B5:E5, **Tip Rates** in the range F5:I5, and **Tip Amounts** in the range J5:L5. Apply Currency format to the monetary values. Apply borders around the Tip Rates and Tip Amounts sections similar to the existing border around the Customer Subtotal and Tip section. For the range A6:L6, apply **Orange, Accent 2, Lighter 40%** fill color, center horizontal alignment, and wrap text. Apply **Orange, Accent 2, Lighter 80%** fill color to the values in the Tip Left column and the My Net Tip column.

Set 0.2" left and right margins, select Landscape orientation, and set the scaling to fit to one page. Include a footer with your name on the left footer, the sheet name code in the center, and file name code on the right side. Copy the worksheet and place the copied worksheet on the right side of the original worksheet. Rename the copied worksheet as **Tip Formulas**. On the Tip Formulas worksheet, display cell formulas, print gridlines, print headings, and adjust the column widths. Change the Tips sheet tab color to **Orange, Accent 2**, and change the Tip Formulas sheet tab color to **Orange, Accent 2, Darker 25%**. Save and close the file. Based on your instructor's directions, submit e01b1Server_LastFirst.

Net Proceeds from House Sale

DISASTER RECOVERY

Daryl Patterson is a real estate agent. He wants his clients to have a realistic expectation of how much money they will receive when they sell their houses. Sellers know they have to pay a commission to the agent and pay off their existing mortgages; however, many sellers forget to consider they might have to pay some of the buyer's closing costs, title insurance, and prorated property taxes. The realtor commission and estimated closing costs are based on the selling price and the respective rates. The estimated property taxes are prorated based on the annual property taxes and percentage of the year. For example, if a house sells three months into the year, the seller pays 25% of the property taxes. Daryl created a worksheet to enter values in an input area to calculate the estimated deductions at closing and calculate the estimated net proceeds the seller will receive. However, the worksheet contains errors. Open *e01b2Proceeds* and save it as **e01b2Proceeds_LastFirst**. Review the font formatting and alignment for consistency.

Use Help to learn how to insert comments into cells. As you identify the errors, insert comments in the respective cells to explain the errors. Correct the errors, including formatting errors. Apply Landscape orientation, 115% scaling, 1.5" top margin, and center horizontally. Insert your name on the left side of the header, the sheet name code in the center, and the file name code on the right side. Save and close the file. Based on your instructor's directions, submit e01b2Proceeds_LastFirst.

Capstone Exercise

You are a division manager for a regional hearing-aid company in Cheyenne, Wyoming. Your sales managers travel frequently to some of the offices in the western region. You need to create a travel expense report for your managers to use to record their budgeted and actual expenses for their travel reports. The draft report contains a title, input areas, and a detailed expense area.

Format the Title and Complete the Input Areas

Your first tasks are to format the title and complete the input area. The input area contains two sections: Standard Inputs that are identical for all travelers and Traveler Inputs that the traveler enters based on his or her trip.

a. Open *e01c1Travel* and save it as **e01c1Travel_LastFirst**.

b. Merge and center the title over the **range A1:E1** and set the row height for the first row to **40**.

c. Apply the **Input cell style** to the **ranges B3:B6, E3:E4**, and **E6:E7**, and then apply the **Calculation cell style** to **cell E5**. Part of the borders are removed when you apply these styles.

d. Select the **ranges A3:B6** and **D3:E7**. Apply **Thick Outside Borders**.

e. Enter **6/1/2018** in **cell E3** for the departure date, **6/5/2018** in **cell E4** for the return date, **149** in **cell E6** for the hotel rate per night, and **18%** in **cell E7** for the hotel tax rate.

f. Enter a formula in **cell E5** to calculate the number of days between the return date and the departure date.

Insert Formulas

The Detailed Expenses section contains the amount budgeted for the trip, the actual expenses reported by the traveler, percentage of the budget spent on each item, and the amount the actual expense went over or under budget. You will insert formulas for this section. Some budgeted amounts are calculated based on the inputs. Other budgeted amounts, such as airfare, are estimates.

a. Enter the amount budgeted for Mileage to/from Airport in **cell B12**. The amount is based on the mileage rate and roundtrip to the airport from the Standard Inputs section.

b. Enter the amount budgeted for Airport Parking in **cell B13**. This amount is based on the airport parking daily rate and the number of total days traveling (the number of nights + 1) to include both the departure and return dates. For example, if a person departs on June 1 and returns on June 5, the total number of nights at a hotel is 4, but the total number of days the vehicle is parked at the airport is 5.

c. Enter the amount budgeted for Hotel Accommodations in **cell B16**. This amount is based on the number of nights, the hotel rate, and the hotel tax rate.

d. Enter the amount budgeted for Meals in **cell B17**. This amount is based on the daily meal allowance and the total travel days (# of hotel nights + 1).

e. Enter the % of Budget in **cell D12**. This percentage indicates the percentage of actual expenses to budgeted expenses. Copy the formula to the **range D13:D18**.

f. Enter the difference between the actual and budgeted expenses in **cell E12**. Copy the formula to the **range E13:E18**. If the actual expenses exceeded the budgeted expenses, the result should be positive. If the actual expenses were less than the budgeted expense, the result should be negative, indicating under budget.

Add Rows, Indent Labels, and Move Data

The Detailed Expenses section includes a heading Travel to/from Destination. You want to include two more headings to organize the expenses. Then you will indent the items within each category. Furthermore, you want the monetary columns together, so you will insert cells and move the Over or Under column to the right of the Actual column.

a. Insert a new row 15. Type **Destination Expenses** in **cell A15**. Bold the label.

b. Insert a new row 19. Type **Other** in **cell A19**. Bold the label.

c. Indent twice the labels in the **ranges A12:A14, A16:A18**, and **A20**.

d. Select the **range D10:D21** and insert cells to shift the selected cells to the right.

e. Cut the **range F10:F21** and paste it in the **range D10:D21** to move the Over or Under data in the new cells you inserted.

Format the Detailed Expenses Section

You are ready to format the values to improve readability. You will apply Accounting Number Format to the monetary values on the first and total rows, Comma Style to the monetary values in the middle rows, and Percent Style for the percentages.

a. Apply **Accounting Number Format** to the **ranges B12:D12** and **B21:D21**.

b. Apply **Comma Style** to the **range B13:D20**.

c. Apply **Percent Style** with one decimal place to the **range E12:E20**.

d. Underline the **range: B20:D20**. Do not use the border feature.

e. Apply the cell style **Bad** to **cell D21** because the traveler went over budget.

f. Select the **range A10:E21** and apply **Thick Outside Borders**.

g. Select the **range A10:E10**, apply **Blue-Gray, Text 2, Lighter 80% fill color**, apply **Center** alignment, and apply **Wrap Text**.

Manage the Workbook

You will apply page setup options, insert a footer, and, then duplicate the Expenses statement worksheet.

a. Spell-check the workbook and make appropriate corrections.

b. Set a **1.5"** top margin and select the margin setting to center the data horizontally on the page.

c. Insert a footer with your name on the left side, the sheet name code in the center, and the file name code on the right side.

d. Copy the Expenses worksheet, move the new worksheet to the end, and rename it **Formulas**.

e. Display the cell formulas on the Formulas worksheet, change to landscape orientation, and adjust column widths. Use the Page Setup dialog box or the Page Layout tab to print gridlines and row and column headings.

f. Save and close the file. Based on your instructor's directions, submit e01c1Travel_LastFirst.

Formulas and Functions

LEARNING OUTCOME

You will apply formulas and functions to calculate and analyze data.

OBJECTIVES & SKILLS: After you read this chapter, you will be able to:

CASE STUDY | Townsend Mortgage Company

You are an assistant to Erica Matheson, a mortgage broker at the Townsend Mortgage Company. Erica spends her days reviewing mortgage rates and trends, meeting with clients, and preparing paperwork. She relies on your expertise in using Excel to help analyze mortgage data.

Today, Erica provided you with sample mortgage data: loan number, house cost, down payment, mortgage rate, and the length of the loan in years. She asked you to perform some basic calculations so that she can check the output provided by her system to verify if it is calculating results correctly. She wants you to calculate the amount financed, the periodic interest rate, the total number of payment periods, the percent of the house cost that is financed, and the payoff year for each loan. In addition, you will calculate totals, averages, and other basic statistics.

Furthermore, she has asked you to complete another worksheet that uses functions to look up interest rates from a separate table, calculate the monthly payments, and determine how much (if any) the borrower will have to pay for private mortgage insurance (PMI).

Performing Quantitative Analysis

CHAPTER 2

	A	B	C	D	E	F	G	H	I	J	K
1	**Townsend Mortgage Company**										
2											
3	**Input Area**										
4	Today's Date:	10/2/2018									
5	Pmts Per Year:	12									
6											
7	Loan #	House Cost	Down Payment	Amount Financed	Mortgage Rate	Rate Per Period	Years	# of Pmt Periods	% Financed	Date Financed	Payoff Year
8	452786	$ 400,000	$ 80,000	$ 320,000	3.625%	0.302%	25	300	80.0%	5/1/2016	2041
9	453000	$ 425,000	$ 60,000	$ 365,000	3.940%	0.328%	30	360	85.9%	11/3/2016	2046
10	453025	$ 175,500	$ 30,000	$ 145,500	3.550%	0.296%	25	300	82.9%	4/10/2017	2042
11	452600	$ 265,950	$ 58,000	$ 207,950	2.500%	0.208%	15	180	78.2%	10/14/2017	2032
12	452638	$ 329,750	$ 65,000	$ 264,750	3.250%	0.271%	30	360	80.3%	2/4/2018	2048
13											
14	**Summary Statistics**										
15	Statistics	House Cost	Down Payment	Amount Financed							
16	Total	$ 1,596,200	$ 293,000	$ 1,303,200							
17	Average	$ 319,240	$ 58,600	$ 260,640							
18	Median	$ 329,750	$ 60,000	$ 264,750							
19	Lowest	$ 175,500	$ 30,000	$ 145,500							
20	Highest	$ 425,000	$ 80,000	$ 365,000							
21	# of Mortgages	5	5	5							

Details | Payment Info | (+)

Ready

Excel 2016, Windows 10, Microsoft Corporation

FIGURE 2.1 Townsend Mortgage Company Worksheet

CASE STUDY | Townsend Mortgage Company

Starting File	File to be Submitted
e02h1Loans	**e02h3Loans_LastFirst**

Formula Basics

When you increase your understanding of formulas, you can build robust workbooks that perform a variety of calculations for quantitative analysis. Your ability to build sophisticated workbooks and to interpret the results increases your value to any organization. By now, you should be able to build simple formulas using cell references and mathematical operators and use the order of operations to control the sequence of calculations in formulas.

In this section, you will create formulas in which cell addresses change or remain fixed when you copy them.

Using Relative, Absolute, and Mixed Cell References in Formulas

When you copy a formula, Excel either adjusts or preserves the cell references in the copied formula based on how the cell references appear in the original formula. Excel uses three different ways to reference a cell in a formula: relative, absolute, and mixed. Relative references change when a formula is copied. For example, if a formula containing the cell A1 is copied down one row in the column, the reference would become A2. In contrast, absolute references remain constant, no matter where they are copied. Mixed references are a combination of both absolute and relative, where part will change and part will remain constant.

When you create a formula that you will copy to other cells, ask yourself the following question: Do the cell references contain constant or variable values? In other words, should the cell references be adjusted or always refer to the same cell location, regardless of where the copied formula is located?

Use a Relative Cell Reference

STEP 1 ❯❯ A *relative cell reference* is the default method of referencing in Excel. It indicates a cell's relative location, such as five rows up and one column to the left, from the original cell containing the formula. When you copy a formula containing a relative cell reference, the cells referenced in the copied formula change relative to the position of the copied formula. Regardless of where you paste the formula, the cell references in the copied formula maintain the same relative distance from the cell containing the copied formula, as the cell references the relative location to the original formula cell.

In Figure 2.2, the formulas in column F contain relative cell references. When you copy the original formula =D2-E2 from cell F2 down one row to cell F3, the copied formula changes to =D3-E3. Because you copy the formula *down* the column to cell F3, the column letters in the formula stay the same, but the row numbers change to reflect the row to which you copied the formula. Using relative referencing is an effective time saving tool. For example, using relative cell addresses to calculate the amount financed ensures that each borrower's down payment is subtracted from his or her respective house cost.

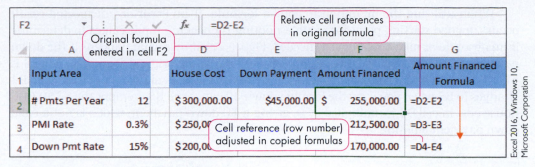

FIGURE 2.2 Relative Cell References

Use an Absolute Cell Reference

STEP 2 ▶▶ In many calculations there are times in which a value should remain constant, such as an interest rate or payoff date. In these situations absolute cell references are utilized. An **absolute cell reference** provides a constant reference to a specific cell. When you copy a formula containing an absolute cell reference, the cell reference in the copied formula does not change, regardless of where you copy the formula. An absolute cell reference appears with a dollar sign before both the column letter and row number, such as $B$4.

In Figure 2.3, the down payment is calculated by multiplying the house cost by the down payment rate (15%). Each down payment calculation uses a different purchase price and constant down payment rate, therefore an absolute reference is required. Cell E2 contains =D2*$B$4 ($300,000*15.0%) to calculate the first borrower's down payment ($45,000). When you copy the formula down to the next row, the copied formula in cell E3 is =D3*$B$4. The relative cell reference D2 changes to D3 (for the next house cost) and the absolute cell reference $B$4 remains the same to refer to the constant 15.0% down payment rate. This formula ensures that the cell reference to the house cost changes for each row but that the house cost is always multiplied by the rate in cell B4.

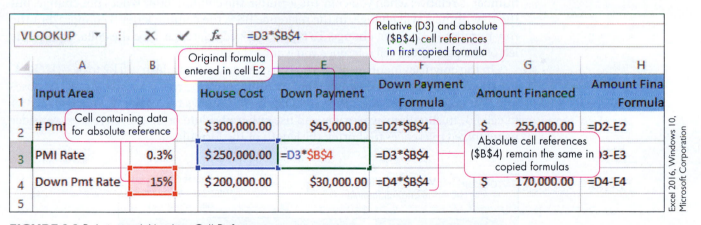

FIGURE 2.3 Relative and Absolute Cell References

TIP: INPUT AREA AND ABSOLUTE CELL REFERENCES

To illustrate the effect of modifying an assumption (e.g., the down payment rate changes from 15% to 20%), it is efficient to enter the new input value in only one cell (e.g., B4) rather than including the same value in a string of formulas. In Figure 2.3, values that can be modified, such as the down payment rate, are put in an input area. Generally, formulas use absolute references to the cells in the input area. For example, B4 is an absolute cell reference in all the down payment calculations. If the value in B4 is modified, Excel recalculates the amount of down payment for all the down payment formulas. By using cell references from an input area, you can perform what-if analyses very easily.

When utilizing the fill option to copy a formula, if an error or unexpected result occurs, a good starting point for troubleshooting is checking input values to determine if an absolute or mixed reference is needed. Figure 2.4 shows what happens if the down payment formula used a relative reference to cell B4. If the original formula in cell E2 is =D2*B4, the copied formula becomes =D3*B5 in cell E3. The relative cell reference to B4 changes to B5 when you copy the formula down. Because cell B5 is empty, the $350,000 house cost in cell D3 is multiplied by 0, giving a $0 down payment, which is not a valid down payment amount.

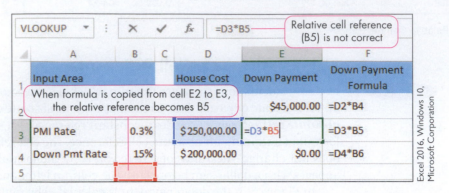

FIGURE 2.4 Error in Formula

Use a Mixed Cell Reference

STEP 3 ›› A *mixed cell reference* combines an absolute cell reference with a relative cell reference. When you copy a formula containing a mixed cell reference, either the column letter or the row number that has the absolute reference remains fixed while the other part of the cell reference that is relative changes in the copied formula. $B4 and B$4 are examples of mixed cell references. In the reference $B4, the column B is absolute, and the row number is relative; when you copy the formula, the column letter B does not change, but the row number will change. In the reference B$4, the column letter B changes, but the row number, 4, does not change. To create a mixed reference, type the dollar sign to the left of the part of the cell reference you want to be absolute.

In the down payment formula, you can change the formula in cell E2 to be =D2*B$4. Because you are copying down the same column, only the row reference 4 must be absolute; the column letter stays the same. Figure 2.5 shows the copied formula =D3*B$4 in cell E3. In situations where you can use either absolute or mixed references, consider using mixed references to shorten the length of the formula.

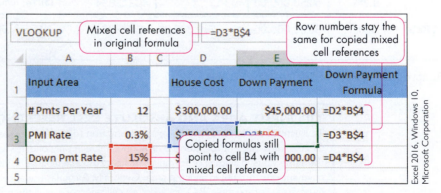

FIGURE 2.5 Relative and Mixed Cell References

TIP: THE F4 KEY
The F4 key toggles through relative, absolute, and mixed references. Click a cell reference within a formula on the Formula Bar and press F4 to change it. For example, click in B4 in the formula =D2*B4. Press F4 and the relative cell reference (B4) changes to an absolute cell reference ($B$4). Press F4 again and $B$4 becomes a mixed reference (B$4); press F4 again and it becomes another mixed reference ($B4). Press F4 a fourth time and the cell reference returns to the original relative reference (B4).

Quick
Concepts

1. What happens when you copy a formula containing a relative cell reference one column to the right? *p. 154*

2. Why would you use an absolute reference in a formula? *p. 155*

3. What is the benefit of using a mixed reference? *p. 156*

Hands-On Exercises

Watch the Video
for this Hands-On
Exercise!

MyITLab®
HOE1 Training

Skills covered: Use a Relative
Cell Reference • Use an Absolute
Cell Reference • Use a Mixed Cell
Reference

1 Formula Basics

Erica prepared a workbook containing data for five mortgages financed with the Townsend Mortgage
Company. The data include house cost, down payment, mortgage rate, number of years to pay off the
mortgage, and the financing date for each mortgage.

STEP 1 ›› USE A RELATIVE CELL REFERENCE

You will calculate the amount financed by each borrower by creating a formula with relative cell references that calculates the
difference between the house cost and the down payment. After verifying the results of the amount financed by the first borrower,
you will copy the formula down the Amount Financed column to calculate the other borrowers' amounts financed. Refer to
Figure 2.6 as you complete Step 1.

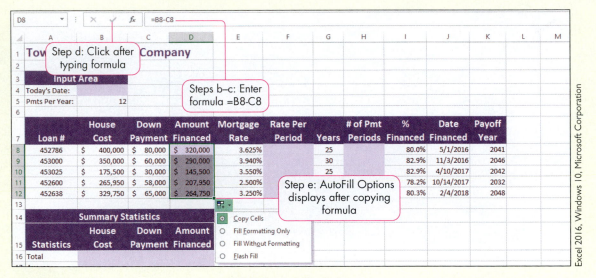

FIGURE 2.6 Formula Containing Relative Cell Reference Copied

a. Open *e02h1Loans* and save it as **e02h1Loans_LastFirst**.

> **TROUBLESHOOTING:** If you make any major mistakes in this exercise, you can close the file,
> open *e02h1Loans* again, and then start this exercise over.

The workbook contains two worksheets: Details (for Hands-On Exercises 1 and 2) and
Payment Info (for Hands-On Exercise 3). You will enter formulas in the shaded cells.

b. Click **cell D8** in the Details sheet. Type = and click **cell B8**, the cell containing the first
borrower's house cost.

c. Type **-** and click **cell C8**, the cell containing the down payment by the first borrower.

d. Click **Enter** ☑ (the check mark between the Name Box and Formula Bar) to complete the
formula.

The first borrower financed (i.e., borrowed) $320,000, the difference between the cost
($400,000) and the down payment ($80,000).

e. Double-click the **cell D8 fill handle**.

You copied the formula down the Amount Financed column for each mortgage row.

f. Click **cell D9** and view the formula in the Formula Bar.

The formula in cell D8 is =B8-C8. The formula copied to cell D9 is =B9-C9. Because the original formula contained relative cell references, when you copy the formula down to the next row, the row numbers for the cell references change. Each result represents the amount financed for that particular borrower.

g. Press ⬇ and look at the cell references in the Formula Bar to see how the references change for each formula you copied. Save the workbook with the new formula you created.

STEP 2 ›› USE AN ABSOLUTE CELL REFERENCE

Column E contains the mortgage rate for each loan. Because the borrowers will make monthly payments, you will modify the given annual interest rate (APR) to a monthly rate by dividing it by 12 (the number of payments in one year) for each borrower. Refer to Figure 2.7 as you complete Step 2.

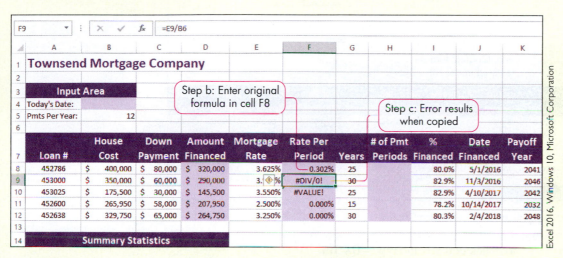

FIGURE 2.7 Formula Containing Incorrect Relative Cell Reference Copied

a. Click **cell F8**.

You will create a formula to calculate the monthly interest rate for the first borrower.

b. Type **=E8/B5** and click **Enter** (the check mark between the Name Box and the Formula Bar).

Typically, you should avoid typing values directly in formulas. Therefore, you use a reference to cell B5, where the number of payments per year is placed in the input area, so that the company can change the payment period to bimonthly (24 payments per year) or quarterly (four payments per year) without adjusting the formula.

c. Double-click the **cell F8 fill handle**, click **cell F9**, and then view the results (see Figure 2.7).

An error icon displays to the left of cell F9, which displays #DIV/0!, and cell F10 displays #VALUE!. The original formula was =E8/B5. Because you copied the formula =E8/B5 down the column, the first copied formula is =E9/B6, and the second copied formula is =E10/B7. Although you want the mortgage rate cell reference (E8) to change (E9, E10, etc.) from row to row, you do not want the divisor (cell B5) to change. You need all formulas to divide by the value stored in cell B5, so you will edit the formula to make B5 an absolute reference.

d. Click **Undo** in the Quick Access Toolbar to undo the AutoFill process. With F8 as the active cell, click to the right of **B5** in the Formula Bar.

e. Press **F4** and click **Enter** (the check mark between the Name Box and the Formula Bar).

Excel changes the cell reference from B5 to $B$5, making it an absolute cell reference.

f. Double-click the fill handle to copy the formula down the Rate Per Period column. Click **cell F9** and view the formula in the Formula Bar.

The formula in cell F9 is =E9/$B$5. The reference to E9 is relative and the reference to B5 is absolute. The results of all the calculations in the Rate Per Period column are now correct.

g. Save the workbook.

The next formula you create will calculate the total number of payment periods for each loan. Refer to Figure 2.8 as you complete Step 3.

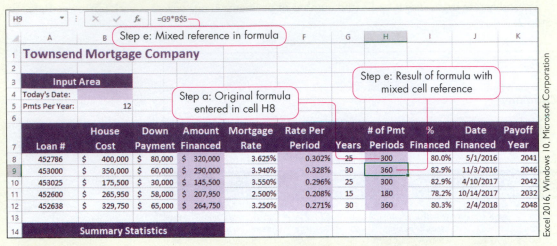

FIGURE 2.8 Formula Containing Mixed Cell Reference Copied

a. Click **cell H8** and type **=G8*B5**.

You will multiply the number of years (25) by the number of payment periods in one year (12) using cell references.

b. Press **F4** to make the B5 cell reference absolute and click **Enter**.

You want B5 to be absolute so that the cell reference remains B5 when you copy the formula. The product of 25 years and 12 months is 300 months or payment periods.

c. Copy the formula down the # of Pmt Periods column.

The first copied formula is =G9*$B$5, and the result is 360. You want to see what happens if you change the absolute reference to a mixed reference and copy the formula again. Because you are copying down a column, the column letter B can be relative because it will not change either way, but the row number 5 must be absolute.

d. Ensure that cell H8 is the active cell and click **Undo** on the Quick Access Toolbar to undo the copied formulas.

e. Click within the **$B$5 cell reference** in the Formula Bar. Press **F4** to change the cell reference to a mixed cell reference: B$5. Press **Ctrl+Enter** and copy the formula down the # of Pmt Periods column. Click **cell H9**.

The first copied formula is =G9*B$5 and the result is still 360. In this situation, using either an absolute reference or a mixed reference provides the same results.

f. Save the workbook. Keep the workbook open if you plan to continue with the next Hands-On Exercise. If not, close the workbook and exit Excel.

Function Basics

An Excel *function* is a predefined computation that simplifies creating a formula that performs a complex calculation. Excel contains more than 400 functions, which are organized into 14 categories. Table 2.1 lists and describes the primary function categories used in this chapter.

TABLE 2.1 Function Categories and Descriptions

Category	Description
Date & Time	Provides methods for manipulating date and time values.
Financial	Performs financial calculations, such as payments, rates, present value, and future value.
Logical	Performs logical tests and returns the value of the tests. Includes logical operators for combined tests, such as AND, OR, and NOT.
Lookup & Reference	Looks up values, creates links to cells, or provides references to cells in a worksheet.
Math & Trig	Performs standard math and trigonometry calculations.
Statistical	Performs common statistical calculations, such as averages and standard deviations.

Pearson Education, Inc.

When using functions, you must adhere to correct *syntax*, the rules that dictate the structure and components required to perform the necessary calculations. Start a function with an equal sign, followed by the function name, and then its arguments enclosed in parentheses.

- The function name describes the purpose of the function. For example, the function name SUM indicates that the function sums, or adds, values.

- A function's *arguments* specify the inputs—such as cells, values, or arithmetic expressions—that are required to complete the operation. In some cases, a function requires multiple arguments separated by commas.

In this section, you will learn how to insert common functions using the keyboard and the Insert Function and Function Arguments dialog boxes.

Inserting a Function

To insert a function by typing, first type an equal sign, and then begin typing the function name. *Formula AutoComplete* displays a list of functions and defined names that match letters as you type a formula. For example, if you type =SU, Formula AutoComplete displays a list of functions and names that start with *SU* (see Figure 2.9). You can double-click the function name from the list or continue typing the function name. You can even point to a list item and see the ScreenTip describing the function.

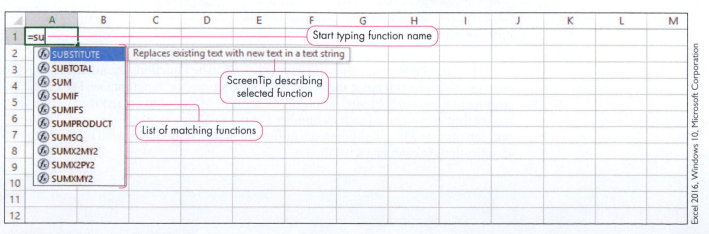

FIGURE 2.9 Formula AutoComplete

After you type the function name and opening parenthesis, Excel displays the *function ScreenTip*, a small pop-up description that displays the function's arguments. The argument you are currently entering is bold in the function ScreenTip (see Figure 2.10). Square brackets indicate optional arguments. For example, the SUM function requires the number1 argument, but the number2 argument is optional. Click the argument name in the function ScreenTip to select the actual argument in the formula you are creating if you want to make changes to the argument.

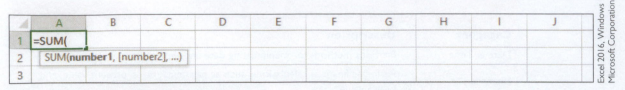

FIGURE 2.10 Function ScreenTip

You can also use the Insert Function dialog box to search for a function, select a function category, and select a function from the list (see Figure 2.11). The dialog box is helpful if you want to browse a list of functions, especially if you are not sure of the function you need and want to see descriptions.

To display the Insert Function dialog box, click Insert Function f_x (located between the Name Box and the Formula Bar) or click Insert Function in the Function Library group on the Formulas tab. From within the dialog box, select a function category, such as Most Recently Used, and select a function to display the syntax and a brief description of that function. Click *Help on this function* to display details about the selected function.

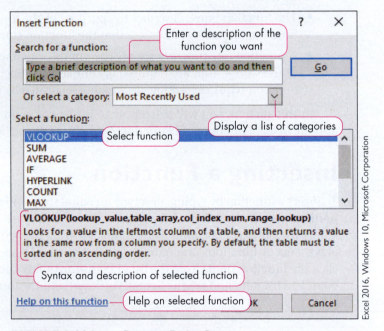

FIGURE 2.11 Insert Function Dialog Box

When you find the function you want, click OK. The Function Arguments dialog box opens so that you can enter the arguments for that specific function (see Figure 2.12). Argument names in bold (such as number1 in the SUM function) are required. Argument names that are not bold (such as number2 in the SUM function) are optional. The function can operate without the optional argument, which is used when you need additional specifications to calculate a result.

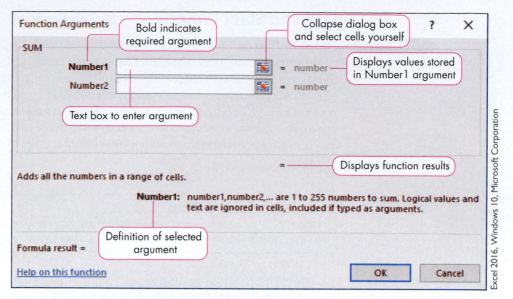

FIGURE 2.12 Function Arguments Dialog Box

Type the cell references in the argument boxes, or click a collapse button to the right side of an argument box to collapse the dialog box and select the cell or range of cells in the worksheet to designate as that argument. If you click the collapse button to select a range, you need to click the expand button to expand the dialog box again. You also have the ability to manually select the cells for the argument without clicking the collapse button. The collapse button is best used if the desired cells for the arguments view is obstructed. The value, or results, of a formula contained in the argument cell displays on the right side of the argument box (such as 5; 10; 15; 20; 25—the values stored in the range A1:A5 used for the number1 argument). If the argument is not valid, Excel displays an error description on the right side of the argument box.

The bottom of the Function Arguments dialog box displays a description of the function and a description of the argument containing the insertion point. As you enter arguments, the bottom of the dialog box also displays the results of the function, such as 75.

> **TIP: #NAME?**
>
> If you enter a function and #NAME? displays in the cell, you might have mistyped the function name. To avoid this problem, select the function name from the Formula AutoComplete list as you type the function name, or use the Insert Function dialog box. You can type a function name in lowercase letters. If you type the name correctly, Excel converts the name to all capital letters when you press Enter, indicating that you spelled the function name correctly.

Inserting Basic Math and Statistics Functions

Excel includes commonly used math and statistical functions that you can use for a variety of calculations. For example, you can insert functions to calculate the total amount you spend on dining out in a month, the average amount you spend per month purchasing music online, your highest electric bill, and your lowest time to run a mile this week. When using these functions, a change in the values within the ranges referenced will change the results of the function.

Use the SUM Function

STEP I)) The **SUM function** totals values in one or more cells and displays the result in the cell containing the function. This function is more efficient to create when you need to add the values contained in three or more contiguous cells. For example, to add the contents of cells A2 through A14, you could enter =A2+A3+A4+A5+A6+A7+A8+A9+A10+ A11+A12+A13+A14, which is time-consuming and increases the probability of entering an inaccurate cell reference, such as entering a cell reference twice or accidentally leaving out a cell reference. Instead, you should use the SUM function, =SUM(A2:A14).

=SUM(number1, [number2],…)

> **TIP: FUNCTION SYNTAX**
> In this book, the function syntax lines are highlighted. Brackets [ ] indicate optional arguments; however, do not actually type the brackets when you enter the argument.

The SUM function contains one required argument (number1) that represents a range of cells to add. The range, such as A2:A14, specifies the first and last of an adjacent group of cells containing values to SUM. Excel will sum all cells within that range. The number2 optional argument is used when you want to sum values stored in nonadjacent cells or ranges, such as =SUM(A2:A14,F2:F14). The ellipsis in the function syntax indicates that you can add as many additional ranges as desired, separated by commas.

> **TIP: AVOIDING FUNCTIONS FOR BASIC FORMULAS**
> Do not use a function for a basic mathematical expression. For example, although =SUM(B4/C4) produces the same result as =B4/C4, the SUM function is not needed to perform the basic arithmetic division. Furthermore, someone taking a quick look at that formula might assume it performs addition instead of division. Use the most appropriate, clear-cut formula, =B4/C4.

To insert the SUM function (for example, to sum the values of a range), complete one of the following steps:

- Type =SUM(type the range), and press Enter.
- Type =SUM(drag to select the range, then type the closing) and press Enter.
- Click a cell, click Sum in the Editing group on the Home tab, press Enter to select the suggested range (or drag to select a range), and then press Enter.
- Click in a cell, click AutoSum in the Function Library group on the Formulas tab, either press Enter to select the suggested range or type the range, and then press Enter.
- Click the cell directly underneath the range you would like to SUM and press Alt=.

Figure 2.13 shows the result of using the SUM function in cell D2 to total scores (898).

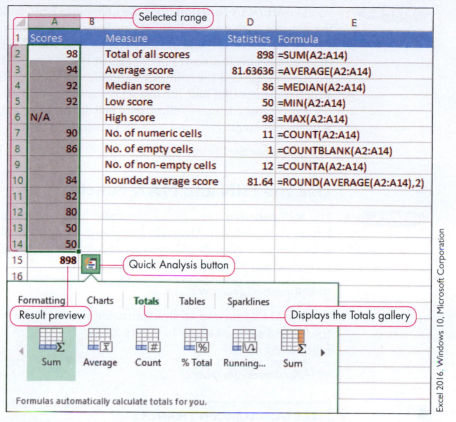

FIGURE 2.13 Function Results

TIP: SUM ARROW

If you click Sum in the Editing group on the Home tab or in the Function Library group on the Formulas tab, Excel inserts the SUM function. However, if you click the Sum arrow, Excel displays a list of basic functions to select: Sum, Average, Count Numbers, Max, and Min. If you want to insert another function, select More Functions from the list.

TIP: NEST FUNCTIONS AS ARGUMENTS

A *nested function* occurs when one function is embedded as an argument within another function. Each function has its own set of arguments that must be included. For example, cell D10 in Figure 2.13 contains =ROUND(AVERAGE(A2:A14),2). The ROUND function requires two arguments: number (the number to be rounded) and num_digits (the number of decimals to which the number is to be rounded).

The AVERAGE function is used to create the number to be rounded, and is nested in the number argument of the ROUND function. AVERAGE(A2:A14) returns 81.63636. That value is then rounded to two decimal places, indicated by 2 in the num_digits argument. The result is 81.64. If you change the second argument from 2 to 0, such as =ROUND(AVERAGE (A2:A14),0), the result would be 82.

Use the AVERAGE and MEDIAN Functions

STEP 2 ▶▶ People often describe data based on central tendency, which means that values tend to cluster around a central value. Excel provides two functions to calculate central tendency: AVERAGE and MEDIAN. The ***AVERAGE function*** calculates the arithmetic mean, or average, for the values in a range of cells. You can use this function to calculate the class average on a biology test or the average number of points scored per game by a basketball player. In Figure 2.13, =AVERAGE(A2:A14) in cell D3 returns 81.63636 as the average test score. The AVERAGE function ignores empty cells and cells containing N/A or text.

=AVERAGE (number1,[number2],…)

STEP 3 ❯❯ The ***MEDIAN function*** finds the midpoint value, which is the value that one half of the data set is above or below. The median is particularly useful because extreme values often influence arithmetic mean calculated by the AVERAGE function. In Figure 2.13, the two extreme test scores of 50 distort the average. The rest of the test scores range from 80 to 98. Cell D4 contains =MEDIAN(A2:A14). The median for test scores is 86, which indicates that half the test scores are above 86 and half the test scores are below 86. This statistic is more reflective of the data set than the average. The MEDIAN function ignores empty cells and cells containing N/A or text.

=MEDIAN(number1,[number2],…)

Use the MIN and MAX Functions

STEP 4 ❯❯ The ***MIN function*** analyzes an argument list to determine the lowest value, such as the lowest score on a test. Manually inspecting a range of values to identify the lowest value is inefficient, especially in large spreadsheets. In Figure 2.13, =MIN(A2:A14) in cell D5 identifies that 50 is the lowest test score.

=MIN(number1,[number2],…)

The ***MAX function*** analyzes an argument list to determine the highest value, such as the highest score on a test. In Figure 2.13, =MAX(A2:A14) in cell D6 identifies 98 as the highest test score.

=MAX(number1,[number2],…)

> **TIP: NONADJACENT RANGES**
> In most basic aggregate functions such as SUM, MIN, MAX, and AVERAGE, you can use multiple ranges as arguments, such as finding the largest number within two nonadjacent (nonconsecutive) ranges. For example, you can find the highest test score where some scores are stored in cells A2:A14 and others are stored in cells K2:K14. Separate each range with a comma in the argument list, so that the formula is =MAX(A2:A14,K2:K14).

Use the COUNT Functions

Excel provides three basic count functions—COUNT, COUNTBLANK, and COUNTA—to count the cells in a range that meet a particular criterion. The ***COUNT function*** tallies the number of cells in a range that contain values you can use in calculations, such as numerical and date data, but excludes blank cells or text entries from the tally. In Figure 2.13, the selected range spans 13 cells; however, =COUNT(A2:A14) in cell D7 returns 11, the number of cells that contain numerical data. It does not count the cell containing the text *N/A* or the blank cell.

The ***COUNTBLANK function*** tallies the number of cells in a range that are blank. In Figure 2.13, =COUNTBLANK(A2:A14) in cell D8 identifies that one cell in the range A2:A14 is blank. The ***COUNTA function*** tallies the number of cells in a range that are not blank, that is, cells that contain data, whether a value, text, or a formula. In Figure 2.13, =COUNTA(A2:A14) in cell D9 returns 12, indicating that the range A2:A14 contains 12 cells that contain some form of data. It does not count the blank cell; however, it will count cells that contain text such as cell A6.

=COUNT(value1,[value2],…)

=COUNTBLANK(range)

=COUNTA(value1,[value2],…)

Perform Calculations with Quick Analysis Tools

Quick Analysis is a set of analytical tools you can use to apply formatting, create charts or tables, and insert basic functions. When you select a range of data, the Quick Analysis button displays adjacent to the bottom-right corner of the selected range. Click the Quick Analysis button to display the Quick Analysis gallery and select the analytical tool to meet your needs.

Figure 2.13 shows the Totals gallery options so that you can sum, average, or count the values in the selected range. Select % Total to display the percentage of the grand total of two or more columns. Select Running Total to provide a cumulative total at the bottom of multiple columns. Additional options can be seen by clicking the right expansion arrow.

Using Date Functions

In order to maximize the use of dates and date functions in Excel, it is important to understand how they are handled in the program. Excel assigns serial numbers to dates. The date January 1, 1900 is the equivalent to the number 1. The number 2 is the equivalent of January 2, 1900 and so on. Basically, Excel adds 1 to every serial number as each day passes. Therefore the newer the date, the bigger the equivalent serial number. For example, assume today is January 1, 2018, and you graduate on May 6, 2018. To determine how many days until graduation, subtract today's date from the graduation date. Excel uses the serial numbers for these dates (43101 and 43226) to calculate the difference of 125 days.

Insert the TODAY Function

STEP 5 ❯❯ The **TODAY function** displays the current date in a cell. Excel updates the TODAY function results when you open or print the workbook. The TODAY() function does not require arguments, but you must include the parentheses. If you omit the parentheses, Excel displays #NAME? in the cell with a green triangle in the top-left corner of the cell. When you click the cell, an error icon appears that you can click for more information.

`=TODAY()`

Insert the NOW Function

The **NOW function** uses the computer's clock to display the current date and military time that you last opened the workbook. (Military time expresses time on a 24-hour period where 1:00 is 1 a.m. and 13:00 is 1 p.m.) The date and time will change every time the workbook is opened. Like the TODAY function, the NOW function does not require arguments, but you must include the parentheses. Omitting the parentheses creates a #NAME? error.

`=NOW()`

Quick Concepts

4. What visual features help guide you through typing a function directly in a cell? *p. 162*

5. What type of data do you enter in a Function Arguments dialog box, and what are four things the dialog box tells you? *p. 163*

6. What is the difference between the AVERAGE and MEDIAN functions? *pp. 165–166*

7. What is a nested function, and why would you create one? *p. 165*

Skills covered: Insert a Function • Insert a Function Using Formula AutoComplete • Use the Insert Function Dialog Box • Use the SUM Function • Use the AVERAGE and MEDIAN Functions • Use the MIN and MAX Functions • Use the COUNT Functions • Use the TODAY Function

2 Function Basics

The Townsend Mortgage Company worksheet contains an area in which you will enter summary statistics. In addition, you will include the current date.

STEP 1 ›› USE THE SUM FUNCTION

The first summary statistic you calculate is the total value of the houses bought by the borrowers. You will use the SUM function. Refer to Figure 2.14 as you complete Step 1.

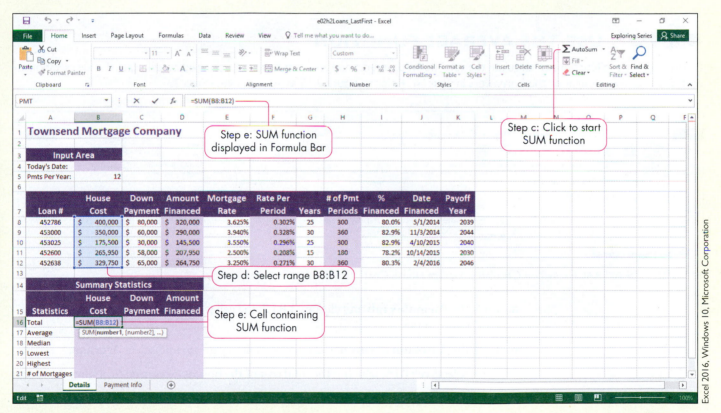

FIGURE 2.14 SUM Function Calculates Total House Cost

a. Open *e02h1Loans_LastFirst* if you closed it at the end of Hands-On Exercise 1 and save it as **e02h2Loans_LastFirst**, changing h1 to h2.

b. Ensure that the Details worksheet is active and click **cell B16**, the cell where you will enter a formula for the total house cost.

c. Click **AutoSum** ∑ AutoSum ▾ in the Editing group on the Home tab.

Excel anticipates the range of cells containing values you want to sum based on where you enter the formula—in this case, A8:D15. This is not the correct range, so you must enter the correct range.

> **TROUBLESHOOTING:** AutoSum, like some other commands in Excel, contains two parts: the main command button and an arrow. Click the main command button when instructed to click Sum to perform the default action. Click the arrow when instructed to click the Sum arrow for additional options. If you accidentally clicked the arrow instead of Sum, press Esc to cancel the SUM function from being completed and try Step c again.

d. Select the **range B8:B12**, the cells containing house costs.

As you use the semi-selection process, Excel enters the range in the SUM function.

> **TROUBLESHOOTING:** If you entered the function without changing the arguments, repeat Steps b–d or edit the arguments in the Formula Bar by deleting the default range, typing B8:B12 between the parentheses and pressing Enter.

e. Click **Enter**.

Cell B16 contains the function = SUM(B8:B12), and the result is $1,521,200.

f. Save the workbook.

STEP 2 ›› USE THE AVERAGE FUNCTION

Before copying the functions to calculate the total down payments and amounts financed, you want to calculate the average house cost of the houses bought by the borrowers in your list. Refer to Figure 2.15 as you complete Step 2.

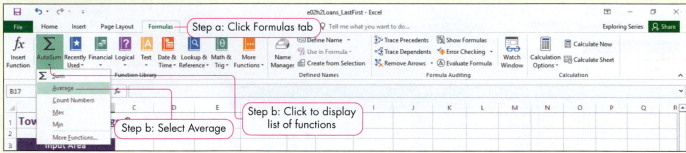

FIGURE 2.15 AVERAGE Function Calculates Average House Cost

Excel 2016, Windows 10, Microsoft Corporation

a. Click the **Formulas tab** and click **cell B17**, the cell where you will display the average cost of the houses.

b. Click the **AutoSum arrow** in the Function Library group and select **Average**.

Excel selects cell B16, which is the total cost of the houses. You need to change the range.

c. Select the **range B8:B12**, the cells containing the house costs.

The function is =AVERAGE(B8:B12).

d. Press **Enter**, making cell B18 the active cell.

The average house cost is $304,240.

e. Save the workbook.

You realize that extreme house costs may distort the average. Therefore, you decide to identify the median house cost to compare it to the average house cost. Refer to Figure 2.16 as you complete Step 3.

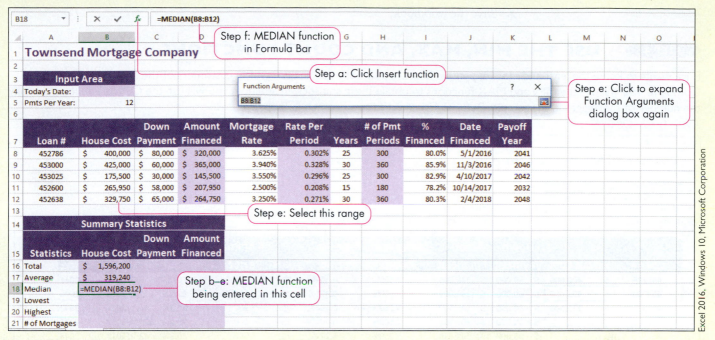

FIGURE 2.16 MEDIAN Function Calculates the Median House Cost

a. Ensure that cell B18 is the active cell. Click **Insert Function** f_x between the Name Box and the Formula Bar, or in the Function Library group on the Formulas tab.

The Insert Function dialog box opens. Use this dialog box to select the MEDIAN function because it is not available on the Ribbon.

b. Type **median** in the *Search for a function box* and click **Go**.

Excel displays a list of functions in the *Select a function* list. The MEDIAN function is selected at the top of the list; the bottom of the dialog box displays the syntax and the description.

c. Read the MEDIAN function description and click **OK**.

The Function Arguments dialog box opens. It contains one required argument, Number1, representing a range of cells containing values. It has an optional argument, Number2, which you can use if you have nonadjacent ranges that contain values.

d. Click **Collapse Dialog Box** to the right of the Number1 box.

You collapsed the Function Arguments dialog box so that you can select the range.

e. Select the **range B8:B12** and click **Expand Dialog Box** in the Function Arguments dialog box.

The Function Arguments dialog box expands, displaying B8:B12 in the Number1 box.

f. Click **OK** to accept the function arguments and close the dialog box.

Half of the houses purchased cost more than the median, $329,750, and half of the houses cost less than this value. Notice the difference between the median and the average: The average is lower because it is affected by the lowest-priced house, $175,500.

g. Save the workbook.

STEP 4 ›› USE THE MIN, MAX, AND COUNT FUNCTIONS

Erica wants to know the least and most expensive houses so that she can analyze typical customers of the Townsend Mortgage Company. You will use the MIN and MAX functions to obtain these statistics. In addition, you will use the COUNT function to tally the number of mortgages in the sample. Refer to Figure 2.17 as you complete Step 4.

	A	B	C	D	E	F	G	H	I	J	K	L
1	**Townsend Mortgage Company**											
2												
3	**Input Area**											
4	Today's Date:											
5	Pmts Per Year:											
6												
7	Loan #	House Cost	Down Payment	Amount Financed	Mortgage Rate	Rate Per Period	Years	# of Pmt Periods	% Financed	Date Financed	Payoff Year	
8	452786	$ 400,000	$ 80,000	$ 320,000	3.625%	0.302%	25	300	80.0%	5/1/2016	2041	
9	453000	$ 425,000	$ 60,000	$ 365,000	3.940%	0.328%	30	360	85.9%	11/3/2016	2046	
10	453025	$ 175,500	$ 30,000	$ 145,500	3.550%	0.296%	25	300	82.9%	4/10/2017	2042	
11	452		$ 58,000	$ 207,950	2.500%	0.208%	15	180	78.2%	10/14/2017	2032	
12	452		$ 65,000	$ 264,750	3.250%	0.271%	30	360	80.3%	2/4/2018	2048	
13												
14	**Summary Statistics**											
15	Statistics	House Cost	Down Payment	Amount Financed								
16	Total	$ 1,596,200	$ 293,000	$ 1,303,200								
17	Average	$ 319,240	$ 58,600	$ 260,640								
18	Median	$ 329,750	$ 60,000	$ 264,750								
19	Lowest	$ 175,500	$ 30,000	$ 145,500								
20	Highest	$ 425,000	$ 80,000	$ 365,000								
21	# of Mortgages	5	5	5								

Callouts in figure:
- Step g: Value changed in cell B9
- Step b: Cell contains MIN function
- Step f: Formulas copied to these columns
- Step c: Cell contains MAX function
- Step d: Cell contains COUNT function

FIGURE 2.17 MIN, MAX, and COUNT Function Results

a. Click **cell B19**, the cell to display the cost of the least expensive house.

b. Click the **AutoSum arrow** in the Function Library group, select **Min**, select the **range B8:B12**, and then press **Enter**.

The MIN function identifies that the least expensive house is $175,500.

c. Click **cell B20**. Click the **AutoSum arrow** in the Function Library group, select **Max**, select the **range B8:B12**, and then press **Enter**.

The MAX function identifies that the highest-costing house is $400,000.

d. Click **cell B21**. Type **=COUNT(B8:B12)** and press **Enter**.

As you type the letter C, Formula AutoComplete suggests functions starting with C. As you continue typing, the list of functions narrows. After you type the beginning parenthesis, Excel displays the function ScreenTip, indicating the arguments for the function. The range B8:B12 contains five cells.

e. Select the **range B16:B21**.

You want to select the range of original statistics to copy the cells all at one time to the next two columns.

f. Drag the fill handle to the right by two columns to copy to the range C16:D21. Click **cell D21**.

Because you used relative cell references in the functions, the range in the function changes from =COUNT(B8:B12) to =COUNT(D8:D12).

g. Click **cell B9**, change the cell value to **425000**, and then click **Enter**.

The results of all formulas and functions change, including the total, average, and max house costs.

h. Save the workbook.

Before finalizing the worksheet you will insert the current date. You will use the TODAY function to display the current date. Refer to Figure 2.18 as you complete Step 5.

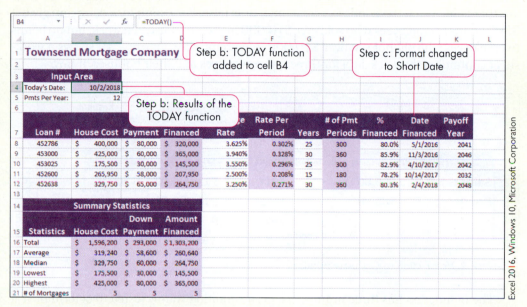

FIGURE 2.18 Insert the Current Date with the TODAY Function

a. Click **cell B4**, the cell to contain the current date.

b. Click **Date & Time** in the Function Library group, select **TODAY** to display the Function Arguments dialog box, and then click **OK** to close the dialog box.

The Function Arguments dialog box opens, although no arguments are necessary for this function. Excel displays TODAY() in the Edit formula bar, and inserts the current date in Short Date format, such as 6/1/2018, based on the computer system's date.

c. Click the **Format arrow** from the Cells group and select **AutoFit Column Width**.

d. Save the workbook. Keep the workbook open if you plan to continue with the next Hands-On Exercise. If not, close the workbook and exit Excel.

Logical, Lookup, and Financial Functions

As you prepare complex spreadsheets using functions, you will frequently use three function categories: logical, lookup and reference, and finance. Logical functions test the logic of a situation and return a particular result. Lookup and reference functions are useful when you need to look up a value in a list to identify the applicable value. Financial functions are useful to anyone who plans to take out a loan or invest money.

In this section, you will learn how to use the logical, lookup, and financial functions.

Determining Results with the IF Function

STEP 3 ▶▶ The most common logical function is the *IF function*, which tests specified criteria to see if it is true or false, then returns one value when a condition is met, or is true, and returns another value when the condition is not met, or is false. For example, a company gives a $500 bonus to employees who sold *over* $10,000 in merchandise in a week, but no bonus to employees who did not sell over $10,000 in merchandise. Figure 2.19 shows a worksheet containing the sales data for three representatives and their bonuses, if any.

F2			:	×	✓	f_x	=IF(E2>B$2,B$3,0)		Result if condition is false

⊿	A	B	C	D	E	F	G
1	Input Are	Condition to be tested		Sales Rep	Sales	Bonus	
2	Sales Goal	$10,000.00		Tiffany	$11,000.00	$500.00	
3	Bonus	$ 500.00		Jose	$10,000.00	$ -	
4				Rex	$ 9,000.00	$ -	
5			Result if condition is true				

FIGURE 2.19 Function to Calculate Bonus

The IF function has three arguments: (1) a condition that is tested to determine if it is either true or false, (2) the resulting value if the condition is true, and (3) the resulting value if the condition is false.

=IF(logical_test,[value_if_true],[value_if_false])

You might find it helpful to create two flowcharts to illustrate an IF function. First, construct a flowchart that uses words and numbers to illustrate the condition and results. For example, the left flowchart in Figure 2.20 illustrates the condition to see if sales are greater than $10,000, and the $500 bonus if the condition is true or $0 if the condition is false. Then, create a second flowchart—similar to the one on the right side of Figure 2.20—that replaces the words and values with actual cell references. Creating these flowcharts can help you construct the IF function that is used in cell F2 in Figure 2.19.

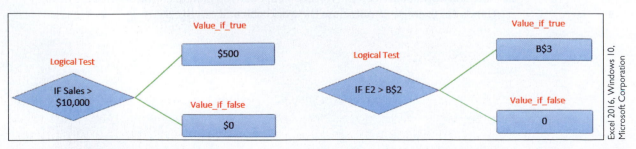

FIGURE 2.20 Flowcharts Illustrating IF Function

Design the Logical Test

The first argument for the IF function is the logical test. The **logical test** contains either a value or an expression that evaluates to true or false. The logical test requires a comparison between at least two variables, such as the values stored in cells E2 and B2. In this example a salesperson receives a bonus IF he or she sells more than the $10,000 quota. The variable of total sales is in cell E2 and the constant of the sales quota is in cell B2. Therefore the logical test IF E2 > B2 translates into the following: if the amount of sales generated is greater than $10,000. Table 2.2 lists and describes in more detail the logical operators to make the comparison in the logical test.

In Figure 2.19, cell F2 contains an IF function where the logical test is E2>$B$2 to determine if Tiffany's sales in cell E2 are greater than the sales goal in cell B2. Copying the function down the column will compare each sales representative's sales with the $10,000 value in cell B2.

TABLE 2.2	Comparison Operators
Operator	**Description**
=	Equal to
<>	Not equal to
<	Less than
>	Greater than
<=	Less than or equal to
>=	Greater than or equal to

Pearson Education, Inc.

Design the Value_If_True and Value_If_False Arguments

The second and third arguments of an IF function are value_if_true and value_if_false. When Excel evaluates the logical test, the result is either true or false. If the logical test is true, the value_if_true argument executes. If the logical test is false, the value_if_false argument executes. Only one of the last two arguments is executed; both arguments cannot be executed, because the logical test is either true or false but not both.

The value_if_true and value_if_false arguments can contain text, cell references, formulas, or constants. In Figure 2.19, cell F2 contains an IF function in which the value_if_true argument is B$3 and the value_if_false argument is 0. Because the logical test (E2>B$2) is true—that is, Tiffany's sales of $11,000 are greater than the $10,000 goal—the value_if_true argument is executed, and the result displays $500, the value that is stored in cell B3.

Jose's sales of $10,000 are *not* greater than $10,000, and Rex's sales of $9,000 are *not* greater than $10,000. Therefore, the value_if_false argument is executed and returns no bonus in cells F3 and F4.

> **TIP: AT LEAST TWO POSSIBLE RIGHT ANSWERS**
> Every IF function can have at least two right solutions to produce the same results. Since the logical test is a comparative expression, it can be written two ways. For example, comparing whether E2 is greater than B2 can be written using greater than (E2>B2) or the reverse can also be compared to see if B2 is less than E2 (B2<E2). Depending on the logical test, the value if true and value if false arguments will switch.

Figure 2.21 illustrates several IF functions, how they are evaluated, and their results. The input area contains values that are used in the logical tests and results. You can create this worksheet with the input area and IF functions to develop your understanding of how IF functions work.

⏴	A	B	C
1	Input Values		
2	$ 1,000.00		
3	$ 2,000.00		
4	10%		
5	5%		
6	$ 250.00		
7			
8	IF Function	Evaluation	Result
9	=IF(A2=A3,A4,A5)	$1,000 is equal to $2,000: FALSE	5%
10	=IF(A2<A3,A4,A5)	$1,000 is less than $2,000: TRUE	10%
11	=IF(A2<>A3,"Not Equal","Equal")	$1,000 and $2,000 are not equal: TRUE	Not Equal
12	=IF(A2>A3,A2*A4,A2*A5)	$1,000 is greater than $2,000: FALSE	$ 50.00
13	=IF(A2>A3,A2*A4,MAX(A2*A5,A6))	$1,000 is greater than $2,000: FALSE	$ 250.00
14	=IF(A2*A4=A3*A5,A6,0)	$100 (A2*A4) is equal to $100 (A3*A5): TRUE	$ 250.00

Excel 2016, Windows 10, Microsoft Corporation

FIGURE 2.21 Sample IF Functions

- **Cell A9.** The logical test A2=A3 compares the values in cells A2 and A3 to see if they are equal. Because $1,000 is not equal to $2,000, the logical test is false. The value_if_false argument is executed, which displays 5%, the value stored in cell A5.

- **Cell A10.** The logical test A2<A3 determines if the value in cell A2 is less than the value in A3. Because $1,000 is less than $2,000, the logical test is true. The value_if_true argument is executed, which displays the value stored in cell A4, which is 10%.

- **Cell A11.** The logical test A2<>A3 determines if the values in cells A2 and A3 are not equal. Because $1,000 and $2,000 are not equal, the logical test is true. The value_if_true argument is executed, which displays the text Not Equal.

- **Cell A12.** The logical test A2>A3 is false. The value_if_false argument is executed, which multiplies the value in cell A2 ($1,000) by the value in cell A5 (5%) and displays $50. The parentheses in the value_if_true (A2*A4) and value_if_false (A2*A5) arguments are optional. They are not required but may help you read the function arguments better.

- **Cell A13.** The logical test A2>A3 is false. The value_if_false argument, which contains a nested MAX function, is executed. The MAX function, MAX(A2*A5,A6), multiplies the values in cells A2 ($1,000) and A5 (5%) and returns the higher of the product ($50) and the value stored in cell A6 ($250).

- **Cell A14.** The logical test A2*A4=A3*A5 is true. The contents of cell A2 ($1,000) are multiplied by the contents of cell A4 (10%) for a result of $100. That result is then compared to the result of A3*A5, which is also $100. Because the logical test is true, the function returns the value of cell A6 ($250).

TIP: TEXT AND NESTED FUNCTIONS IN IF FUNCTIONS

You can use text within a formula. For example, you can build a logical test comparing the contents of cell A1 to specific text, such as A1="Input Values". The IF function in cell A11 in Figure 2.21 uses "Not Equal" and "Equal" in the value_if_true and value_if_false arguments. When you use text in a formula or function, you must enclose the text in quotation marks. However, do not use quotation marks around formulas, cell references, or values. You can also nest functions in the logical test, value_if_true, and value_if_false arguments of the IF function. When you nest functions as arguments, make sure the nested function contains the required arguments for it to work and that you nest the function in the correct argument to calculate accurate results. For example, cell C13 in Figure 2.21 contains a nested MAX function in the value_if_false argument.

Using Lookup Functions

You can use lookup and reference functions to quickly find data associated with a specified value. For example, when you order merchandise on a website, the webserver looks up the shipping costs based on weight and distance; or at the end of a semester, your professor uses your average, such as 88%, to look up the letter grade to assign, such as B+. There are numerous lookup functions in Excel, including HLOOKUP, INDEX, LOOKUP, MATCH, and VLOOKUP. Each lookup function can be used to identify and return information based, in part, on how the data is organized.

Use the VLOOKUP function

STEP 1 ▶▶ The **VLOOKUP function** accepts a value and looks for the value in the left column of a specified table array and returns another value located in the same row from a specified column. Use VLOOKUP to search for exact matches or for the nearest value that is less than or equal to the search value, such as assigning a B grade for a class average between 80% and 89%. The VLOOKUP function has the following three required arguments and one optional argument: (1) lookup_value, (2) table_array, (3) col_index_num, and (4) range_lookup.

=VLOOKUP(lookup_value,table_array,col_index_num,[range_lookup])

Figure 2.22 shows a partial grade book that contains a vertical lookup table, as well as the final scores and letter grades. The function in cell F3 is =VLOOKUP(E3,$A$3:$B$7,2).

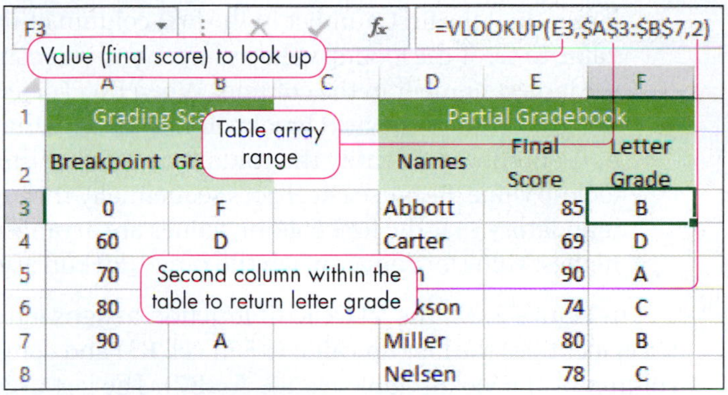

FIGURE 2.22 VLOOKUP Function for Grade Book

The **lookup value** is the cell reference of the cell that contains the value to look up. The lookup value for the first student is cell E3, which contains 85. The **table array** is the range that contains the lookup table: $A$3:$B$7. The table array range must be absolute, the value you want to look up must be located in the first column, and cannot include column labels for the lookup table. The **column index number** is the column number in the lookup table that contains the return values. In this example, the column index number is 2, which corresponds to the letter grades in column B.

> **TIP: USING VALUES IN FORMULAS**
> You know to avoid using values in formulas because the input values in a worksheet cell might change. However, as shown in Figure 2.22, the value 2 is used in the col_index_number argument of the VLOOKUP function. The 2 refers to a particular column within the lookup table and is an acceptable use of a number within a formula.

The last argument in the VLOOKUP function is the optional *range_lookup*. This argument determines how the VLOOKUP function handles lookup values that are not an exact match for the data in the lookup table. By default, the range_lookup is set to TRUE, which is appropriate to look up values in a range. Omitting the optional argument or typing TRUE in it enables the VLOOKUP function to find the nearest value that is less than or equal in the table to the lookup value. For this reason, the first column in a VLOOKUP table array should be sorted from smallest to largest (or A to Z alphabetically) when defaulting to TRUE.

To look up an exact match, enter FALSE in the range_lookup argument. For example, if you are looking up product numbers, you must find an exact match to display the price. The function would look like this: =VLOOKUP(D15,$A$1:$B$50,2,FALSE). The function returns a value for the first lookup value that matches the first column of the lookup table. If no exact match is found, the function returns #N/A.

Here is how the VLOOKUP function works:

1. The first argument of the function evaluates the value to be located in the left column of lookup table.

2. Excel searches the first column of the lookup table until it (a) finds an exact match (if possible) or (b) identifies the correct range if an exact match is not required.

3. If Excel finds an exact match, it moves across the table to the column designated by the column index number on that same row, and returns the value stored in that cell. If the last argument is TRUE or omitted, then Excel is looking for an approximate value (NOT an exact value). In this example, if the lookup value is larger than the first number in the first column of the table, it looks to the next value to see if the lookup value is larger and will continue to do so until reaching the largest number in the column. When Excel detects that the lookup value is not greater than the next breakpoint, it stays on that row. It then uses the column index number to identify the column containing the value to return for the lookup value. Because Excel goes sequentially through the breakpoint values, it is mandatory that the first column values are arranged from the lowest value to the highest value for ranges when the range_lookup argument is TRUE or omitted.

In Figure 2.22, the VLOOKUP function assigns letter grades based on final scores. Excel identifies the lookup value (85 in cell E3) and compares it to the values in the first column of the lookup table (range A3:B7). The last argument is omitted, so Excel tries to find an exact match of 85 or an approximate match; and because the table contains breakpoints rather than every conceivable score and the first column of the lookup table is arranged from the lowest to the highest breakpoints, Excel detects that 85 is greater than 80 but is not greater than 90. Therefore, it stays on the 80 row. Excel looks at the second column (column index number of 2) and returns the letter grade of B. The B grade is then displayed in cell F3.

Create the Lookup Table

A *lookup table* is a range containing a table of values and text from which data can be retrieved. The table should contain at least two rows and two columns, not including headings. Figure 2.23 illustrates a college directory with three columns. The first column contains professors' names. You look up a professor's name in the first column to see his or her office (second column) and phone extension (third column).

Name	Office	Extension
Brazil, Estivan	GT 218b	7243
Fiedler, Zazilia	CS 417	7860
Lam, Kaitlyn	SC 124a	7031
Rodriquez, Lisa	GT 304	7592
Yeung, Braden	CS 414	7314

FIGURE 2.23 College Directory Lookup Table Analogy

It is important to plan the table so that it conforms to the way in which Excel can utilize the data in it. Excel cannot interpret the structure of Table 2.3. If the values you look up are exact values, you can arrange the first column in any logical order. However, to look up an approximate value in a range (such as the range 80–89), you must arrange data from the lowest to the highest value and include only the lowest value in the range (such as 80) instead of the complete range (as demonstrated in Table 2.3). The lowest value for a category or in a series is the ***breakpoint***. Table 2.4 shows how to construct the lookup table in Excel. The first column contains the breakpoints—such as 60, 70, 80, and 90—or the lowest values to achieve a particular grade. The lookup table contains one or more additional columns of related data to retrieve.

TABLE 2.3 Grading Scale

Range	Grade
90–100	A
80–89	B
70–79	C
60–69	D
Below 60	F

TABLE 2.4 Grades Lookup Table

Range	Grade
0	F
60	D
70	C
80	B
90	A

You can nest functions as arguments inside the VLOOKUP function. For example, Figure 2.24 illustrates shipping amounts that are based on weight and location (Boston or Chicago). In the VLOOKUP function in cell C3, the lookup_value argument looks up the weight of a package in cell A3. That weight (14 pounds) is compared to the data in the table array argument, which is $E$3:$G$5. To determine which column of the lookup table to use, an IF function is nested as the column_index_number argument. The nested IF function compares the city stored in cell B3 to the text Boston. If cell B3 contains Boston, it returns 2 to use as the column_index_number to identify the shipping value for a package that is going to Boston. If cell B3 does not contain Boston (i.e., the only other city in this example is Chicago), the column_index_number is 3.

C3 =VLOOKUP(A3,$E$3:$G$5,IF(B3="Boston",2,3))

	A	B	C	D	E	F	G	H
1	Customer Data				Lookup Data			
2	Weight	Location	Shipping		Weight	Boston	Chicago	
3	14	Boston	$ 19.95		0	$ 9.95	$ 12.95	
4	4	Chicago	$ 12.95		5	$ 14.95	$ 16.95	
5	8	Boston	$ 14.95		10	$ 19.95	$ 22.95	

FIGURE 2.24 IF Function Nested in VLOOKUP Function

Use the HLOOKUP Function

Lookup functions are not limited to only vertical tables. In situations in which data is better organized horizontally, you can design a lookup table where the first row contains the values for the basis of the lookup or the breakpoints, and additional rows contain data to be retrieved. With a horizontal lookup table, use the **HLOOKUP function**. Table 2.5 shows how quarterly sales data would look in a horizontal lookup table.

TABLE 2.5	Horizontal Lookup Table			
Region	**Qtr1**	**Qtr2**	**Qtr3**	**Qtr4**
North	3495	4665	4982	5010
South	8044	7692	7812	6252
East	5081	6089	5982	6500
West	4278	4350	4387	7857

Pearson Education, Inc.

The syntax is almost the same as the syntax for the VLOOKUP function, except the third argument is row_index_num instead of col_index_num.

=HLOOKUP(lookup_value,table_array,row_index_num,[range_lookup])

Calculating Payments with the PMT Function

STEP 2 >> Excel contains several financial functions to help you perform calculations with monetary values. If you take out a loan to purchase a car, you need to know the monthly payment, which depends on the price of the car, the down payment, and the terms of the loan, in order to determine if you can afford the car. The decision is made easier by developing the worksheet in Figure 2.25 and by changing the various input values as indicated.

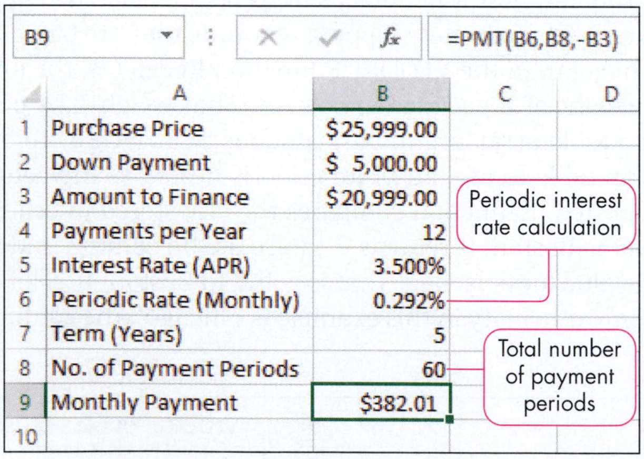

B9		:	× ✓ fx	=PMT(B6,B8,-B3)	
▲	A		B	C	D
1	Purchase Price		$25,999.00		
2	Down Payment		$ 5,000.00		
3	Amount to Finance		$20,999.00	Periodic interest	
4	Payments per Year		12	rate calculation	
5	Interest Rate (APR)		3.500%		
6	Periodic Rate (Monthly)		0.292%		
7	Term (Years)		5	Total number	
8	No. of Payment Periods		60	of payment	
9	Monthly Payment		$382.01	periods	
10					

Excel 2016, Windows 10, Microsoft Corporation

FIGURE 2.25 Car Loan Worksheet

Creating a loan model helps you evaluate options. You realize that the purchase of a $25,999 car is prohibitive because the monthly payment is $382.01. Purchasing a less expensive car, coming up with a substantial down payment, taking out a longer-term loan, or finding a better interest rate can decrease your monthly payments.

The **PMT function** calculates payments for a loan with a fixed amount at a fixed periodic rate for a fixed time period. The PMT function uses three required arguments and up to two optional arguments: (1) rate, (2) nper, (3) pv, (4) fv, and (5) type.

=PMT(rate,nper,pv,[fv],[type])

The **rate** is the interest rate per payment period. If the annual percentage rate (APR) is 12% and you make monthly payments, the periodic rate is 1% (12%/12 months). With the same APR and quarterly payments, the periodic rate is 3% (12%/4 quarters). Divide the APR by the number of payment periods in one year. However, instead of calculating the periodic interest rate within the PMT function, you can calculate it in a separate cell and refer to that cell in the PMT function, as is done in cell B6 of Figure 2.25.

The **nper** is the total number of payment periods. The term of a loan is usually stated in years; however, you make several payments per year. For monthly payments, you make 12 payments per year. To calculate the nper, multiply the number of years by the number of payments in one year. You can either calculate the number of payment periods in the PMT function, or calculate the number of payment periods in cell B8 and use that calculated value in the PMT function.

The **pv** is the present value of the loan. The result of the PMT function is a negative value because it represents your debt. However, you can display the result as a positive value by typing a minus sign in front of the present value cell reference in the PMT function.

> **TIP: FINANCIAL FUNCTIONS AND NEGATIVE VALUES**
>
> When utilizing the PMT and other financial functions in Excel, you will often receive negative numbers. This happens because Excel understands accounting cash flow and the negative value represents a debt or outgoing monetary stream. It is important to understand why this happens and also to understand in some situations this should be a positive number, for example, if you are the company that granted the loan. In this situation you would receive an incoming cash flow, which should be a positive number. In contrast, if you are the requester of a loan, the payment should be negative as you will have a cash outflow each payment period. This can be manipulated by changing the pv argument of the PMT function between positive and negative values or by adding—in front of the PMT function.

Quick Concepts

8. Describe the three arguments for an IF function. **p. 175**

9. How should you structure a vertical lookup table if you need to look up values in a range? **pp. 178–179**

10. What are the first three arguments of a PMT function? Why would you divide by or multiply an argument by 12? **p. 181**

Hands-On Exercises

Skills covered: Use the VLOOKUP Function • Use the PMT Function • Use the IF Function

3 Logical, Lookup, and Financial Functions

Erica wants you to complete another model that she might use for future mortgage data analysis. As you study the model, you realize you need to incorporate logical, lookup, and financial functions.

STEP 1 ►► USE THE VLOOKUP FUNCTION

Rates vary based on the number of years to pay off the loan. Erica created a lookup table for three common mortgage years, and she entered the current APR. The lookup table will provide efficiency later when the rates change. You will use the VLOOKUP function to display the correct rate for each customer based on the number of years of the respective loans. Refer to Figure 2.26 as you complete Step 1.

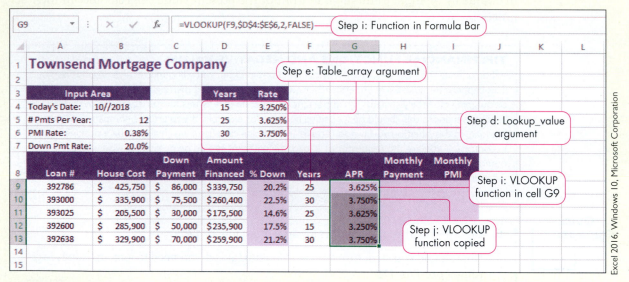

FIGURE 2.26 VLOOKUP Function to Determine APR

a. Open *e02h2Loans_LastFirst* if you closed it at the end of Hands-On Exercise 2 and save it as **e02h3Loans_LastFirst**, changing h2 to h3.

b. Click the **Payment Info worksheet tab** to display the worksheet containing the data to complete. Click **cell G9**, the cell that will store the APR for the first customer.

c. Click the **Formulas tab**, click **Lookup & Reference** in the Function Library group, and then select **VLOOKUP**.

The Function Arguments dialog box opens.

d. Ensure that the insertion point is in the Lookup_value box, click the **Collapse Dialog Box**, click **cell F9** to enter F9 in the Lookup_value box, and then click the **Expand Dialog Box** to return to Function Arguments dialog box.

Cell F9 contains the value you need to look up from the table: 25 years.

e. Press **Tab**, click **Collapse Dialog Box** to the right of the Table_array box, select the **range D4:E6**, and then click **Expand Dialog Box** to return to the Function Arguments dialog box.

This is the range that contains that data for the lookup table. The Years values in the table are arranged from lowest to highest. Do *not* select the column labels for the range.

Anticipate what will happen if you copy the formula down the column. What do you need to do to ensure that the cell references always point to the exact location of the table? If your answer is to make the table array cell references absolute, then you answered correctly.

f. Press **F4** to make the range references absolute.

The Table_array box now contains $D$4:$E$6.

g. Press **Tab** and type **2** in the Col_index_num box.

The second column of the lookup table contains the Rates that you want to return and display in the cells containing the formulas.

h. Press **Tab** and type **False** in the Range_lookup box.

To ensure an exact match to look up in the table, you enter *False* in the optional argument.

i. Click **OK**.

The VLOOKUP function uses the first loan's term in years (25) to find an exact match in the first column of the lookup table, and then returns the corresponding rate from the second column, which is 3.625%.

j. Copy the formula down the column.

Spot-check the results to make sure the function returned the correct APR based on the number of years.

k. Save the workbook.

STEP 2 » USE THE PMT FUNCTION

The worksheet now has all the necessary data for you to calculate the monthly payment for each loan: the APR, the number of years for the loan, the number of payment periods in one year, and the initial loan amount. You will use the PMT function to calculate the monthly payment, which includes paying back the principal amount with interest. This calculation does not include escrow amounts, such as property taxes or insurance. Refer to Figure 2.27 as you complete Step 2.

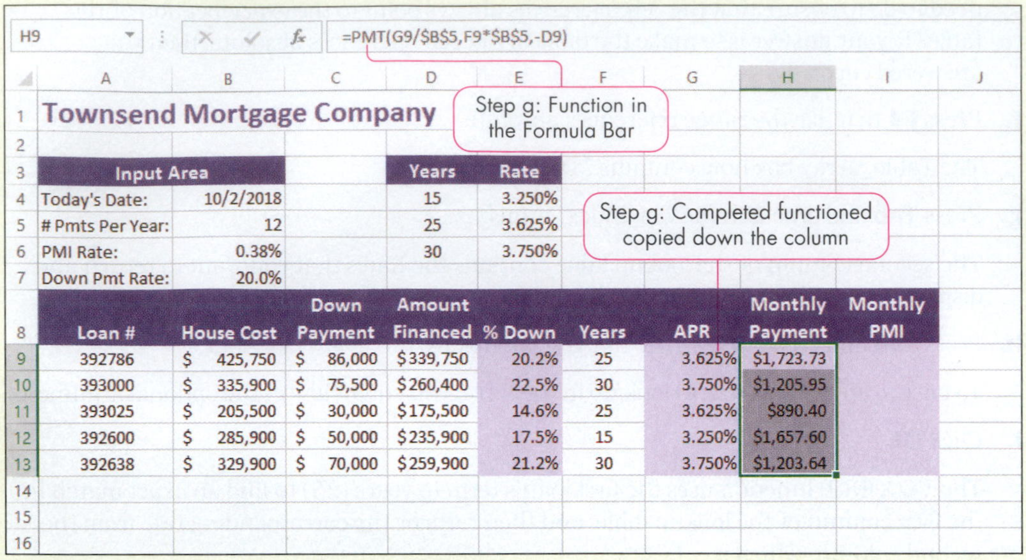

H9 =PMT(G9/$B$5,F9*$B$5,-D9)

	A	B	C	D	E	F	G	H	I
1	Townsend Mortgage Company								
2									
3	Input Area			Years	Rate				
4	Today's Date:	10/2/2018		15	3.250%				
5	# Pmts Per Year:	12		25	3.625%				
6	PMI Rate:	0.38%		30	3.750%				
7	Down Pmt Rate:	20.0%							
8	Loan #	House Cost	Down Payment	Amount Financed	% Down	Years	APR	Monthly Payment	Monthly PMI
9	392786	$ 425,750	$ 86,000	$339,750	20.2%	25	3.625%	$1,723.73	
10	393000	$ 335,900	$ 75,500	$260,400	22.5%	30	3.750%	$1,205.95	
11	393025	$ 205,500	$ 30,000	$175,500	14.6%	25	3.625%	$890.40	
12	392600	$ 285,900	$ 50,000	$235,900	17.5%	15	3.250%	$1,657.60	
13	392638	$ 329,900	$ 70,000	$259,900	21.2%	30	3.750%	$1,203.64	

FIGURE 2.27 PMT Function to Calculate Monthly Payment

a. Click **cell H9**, the cell that will store the payment for the first customer.

b. Click **Financial** in the Function Library group, scroll through the list, and then select **PMT**.

The Function Arguments dialog box opens.

> **TROUBLESHOOTING:** Make sure you select PMT, not PPMT. The PPMT function calculates the principal portion of a particular monthly payment, not the total monthly payment itself.

c. Type **G9/B5** in the Rate box.

Think about what will happen if you copy the formula. The argument will be G10/B6 for the next customer. Are those cell references correct? G10 does contain the APR for the next customer, but B6 does not contain the correct number of payments in one year. Therefore, you need to make B5 an absolute cell reference because the number of payments per year does not vary.

d. Press **F4** to make the reference to cell B5 absolute.

e. Press **Tab** and type **F9*$B$5** in the Nper box.

You calculate the nper by multiplying the number of years by the number of payments in one year. You must make B5 an absolute cell reference so that it does not change when you copy the formula down the column.

f. Press **Tab** and type **-D9** in the Pv box.

The bottom of the dialog box indicates that the monthly payment is 1723.73008 or $1,723.73.

TROUBLESHOOTING: If the payment displays as a negative value, you probably forgot to type the minus sign in front of the D9 reference in the Pv box. Edit the function and type the minus sign in the correct place.

g. Click **OK**. Copy the formula down the column.

h. Save the workbook.

STEP 3 ›› USE THE IF FUNCTION

Lenders often want borrowers to have a 20% down payment. If borrowers do not put in 20% of the cost of the house as a down payment, they pay a private mortgage insurance (PMI) fee. PMI serves to protect lenders from absorbing loss if the borrower defaults on the loan, and it enables borrowers with less cash to secure a loan. The PMI fee is about 0.38% of the amount financed. Some borrowers have to pay PMI for a few months or years until the balance owed is less than 80% of the appraised value. The worksheet contains the necessary values in the input area. You use the IF function to determine which borrowers must pay PMI and how much they will pay. Refer to Figure 2.28 as you complete Step 3.

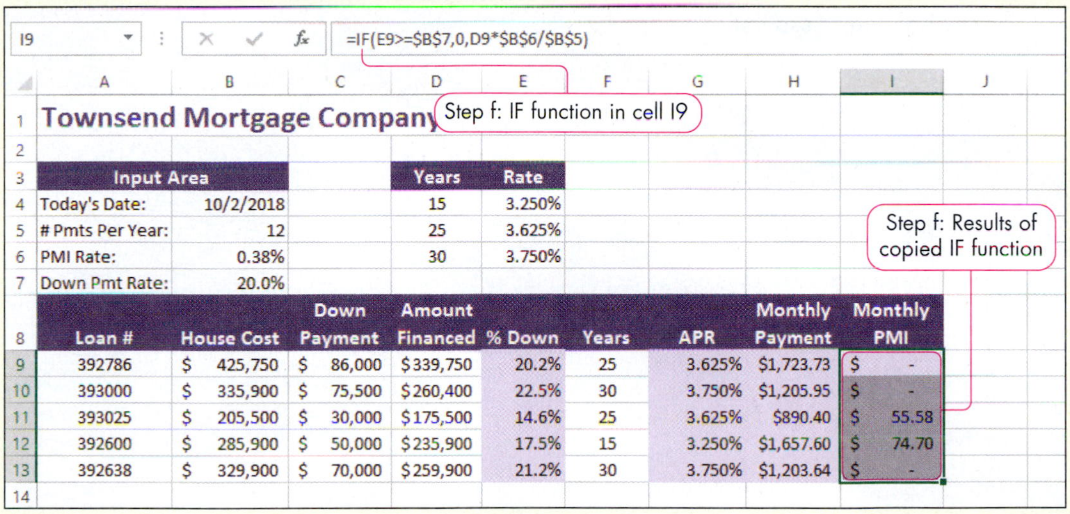

	A	B	C	D	E	F	G	H	I
1	Townsend Mortgage Company								
2									
3	Input Area			Years	Rate				
4	Today's Date:	10/2/2018		15	3.250%				
5	# Pmts Per Year:	12		25	3.625%				
6	PMI Rate:	0.38%		30	3.750%				
7	Down Pmt Rate:	20.0%							
8	Loan #	House Cost	Down Payment	Amount Financed	% Down	Years	APR	Monthly Payment	Monthly PMI
9	392786	$ 425,750	$ 86,000	$339,750	20.2%	25	3.625%	$1,723.73	$ -
10	393000	$ 335,900	$ 75,500	$260,400	22.5%	30	3.750%	$1,205.95	$ -
11	393025	$ 205,500	$ 30,000	$175,500	14.6%	25	3.625%	$890.40	$ 55.58
12	392600	$ 285,900	$ 50,000	$235,900	17.5%	15	3.250%	$1,657.60	$ 74.70
13	392638	$ 329,900	$ 70,000	$259,900	21.2%	30	3.750%	$1,203.64	$ -
14									

Excel 2016, Windows 10, Microsoft Corporation

FIGURE 2.28 IF Function to Calculate Monthly PMI

a. Click **cell I9**, the cell that will store the PMI, if any, for the first customer.

b. Click **Logical** in the Function Library group and select **IF**.

The Function Arguments dialog box opens. You will enter the three arguments.

c. Type **E9>=$B$7** in the Logical_test box.

The logical test compares the down payment percentage to see if the customer's down payment is at least 20%, the threshold stored in B7, of the amount financed. The customer's percentage cell reference is relative so that it will change when you copy it down the column; however, cell B7 must be absolute because it contains a value that should remain constant when the formula is copied to other cells.

d. Press **Tab** and type **0** in the Value_if_true box.

If the customer makes a down payment that is at least 20% of the purchase price, the customer does not pay PMI, so a value of 0 will display whenever the logical test is true. The first customer paid 20% of the purchase price, so he or she does not have to pay PMI.

e. Press **Tab** and type **D9*$B$6/$B$5** in the Value_if_false box.

If the logical test is false, the customer must pay PMI, which is calculated by multiplying the amount financed (D9) by the periodic PMI rate (the result of dividing the yearly PMI (B6) by the number of payments per year (B5)).

f. Click **OK** and copy the formula down the column.

The first, second, and fifth customers paid 20% of the purchase price, so they do not have to pay PMI. The third and fourth customers must pay PMI because their respective down payments were less than 20% of the purchase price.

> **TROUBLESHOOTING:** If the results are not as you expected, check the logical operators. People often mistype < and > or forget to type = for >= situations. Correct any errors in the original formula and copy the formula again.

g. Set the worksheets to print on one page. Add a footer with your name on the left, sheet code in the middle, and the file name code on the right.

h. Save and close the file. Based on your instructor's directions, submit e02h3Loans_LastFirst.

Chapter Objectives Review

After reading this chapter, you have accomplished the following objectives:

1. Use relative, absolute, and mixed cell references in formulas.

- Use a relative cell address: A relative reference indicates a cell's location relative to the formula cell. When you copy the formula, the relative cell reference changes.
- Use an absolute cell reference: An absolute reference is a permanent pointer to a particular cell, indicated with $ before the column letter and the row number, such as $B$5. When you copy the formula, the absolute cell reference does not change.
- Use a mixed cell reference: A mixed reference contains part absolute and part relative reference, such as $B5 or B$5. Either the column or the row reference changes, while the other remains constant when you copy the formula.

2. Insert a function.

- A function is a predefined formula that performs a calculation. It contains the function name and arguments. Formula AutoComplete, function ScreenTips, and the Insert Function dialog box help you select and create functions. The Function Arguments dialog box guides you through the entering requirements for each argument.

3. Insert basic math and statistics functions.

- Use the SUM function: The SUM function calculates the total of a range of values. The syntax is =SUM(number1,[number2],...).
- Use the AVERAGE and MEDIAN functions: The AVERAGE function calculates the arithmetic mean of values in a range. The MEDIAN function identifies the midpoint value in a set of values.
- Use the MIN and MAX functions: The MIN function identifies the lowest value in a range, whereas the MAX function identifies the highest value in a range.
- Use the COUNT functions: The COUNT function tallies the number of cells in a range, that contain values, whereas the COUNTBLANK function tallies the number of blank cells in a range, and COUNTA tallies the number of cells that are not empty.

- Perform calculations with Quick Analysis tools: With the Quick Analysis tools you can apply formatting, create charts or tables, and insert basic functions.

4. Use date functions.

- Insert the TODAY function: The TODAY function displays the current date.
- Insert the NOW function: The NOW function displays the current date and time.

5. Determine results with the IF function.

- Design the logical test: The IF function is a logical function that evaluates a logical test using logical operators, such as <, >, and =, and returns one value if the condition is true and another value if the condition is false.
- Design the value_if_true and value_if_false arguments: The arguments can contain cell references, text, or calculations. If a logical test is true, Excel executes the value_if_true argument. If a logical test is false, Excel executes the value_if_false argument.
- You can nest or embed other functions inside one or more of the arguments of an IF function to create more complex formulas.

6. Use lookup functions.

- Use the VLOOKUP function: The VLOOKUP function contains the required arguments lookup_value, table_array, and col_index_num and one optional argument, range_lookup.
- Create the lookup table: Design the lookup table using exact values or the breakpoints for ranges. If using breakpoints, the breakpoints must be in ascending order.
- Use the HLOOKUP function: The HLOOKUP function looks up values by row (horizontally) rather than by column (vertically).

7. Calculate payments with the PMT function.

- The PMT function calculates periodic payments for a loan with a fixed interest rate and a fixed term. The PMT function requires the periodic interest rate, the total number of payment periods, and the original value of the loan.

Key Terms Matching

Match the key terms with their definitions. Write the key term letter by the appropriate numbered definition.

a. Absolute cell reference

b. Argument

c. AVERAGE function

d. COUNT function

e. IF function

f. Logical test

g. Lookup table

h. MAX function

i. MEDIAN function

j. MIN function

k. Mixed cell reference

l. NOW function

m. PMT function

n. Relative cell reference

o. SUM function

p. Syntax

q. TODAY function

r. VLOOKUP function

1. _____ A set of rules that governs the structure and components for properly entering a function. **p. 161**

2. _____ Displays the current date. **p. 167**

3. _____ Indicates a cell's specific location; the cell reference does not change when you copy the formula. **p. 155**

4. _____ An input, such as a cell reference or value, needed to complete a function. **p. 161**

5. _____ Identifies the highest value in a range. **p. 166**

6. _____ Tallies the number of cells in a range that contain values. **p. 166**

7. _____ Looks up a value in a vertical lookup table and returns a related result from the lookup table. **p. 177**

8. _____ A range that contains data for the basis of the lookup and data to be retrieved. **p. 178**

9. _____ Calculates the arithmetic mean, or average, of values in a range. **p. 165**

10. _____ Identifies the midpoint value in a set of values. **p. 166**

11. _____ Displays the current date and time. **p. 167**

12. _____ Evaluates a condition and returns one value if the condition is true and a different value if the condition is false. **p. 174**

13. _____ Calculates the total of values contained in one or more cells. **p. 164**

14. _____ Calculates the periodic payment for a loan with a fixed interest rate and fixed term. **p. 181**

15. _____ Indicates a cell's location from the cell containing the formula; the cell reference changes when the formula is copied. **p. 154**

16. _____ Contains both an absolute and a relative cell reference in a formula; the absolute part does not change but the relative part does when you copy the formula. **p. 156**

17. _____ An expression that evaluates to true or false. **p. 175**

18. _____ Displays the lowest value in a range. **p. 166**

Multiple Choice

1. If cell E15 contains the formula =$C$5*J$15, what type of cell reference is the J$15 in the formula?

   (a) Relative reference

   (b) Absolute reference

   (c) Mixed reference

   (d) Syntax

2. What function would most efficiently accomplish the same thing as =(B5+C5+D5+E5+F5)/5?

   (a) =SUM(B5:F5)/5

   (b) =AVERAGE(B5:F5)

   (c) =MEDIAN(B5:F5)

   (d) =COUNT(B5:F5)

3. When you start to type =AV, what feature displays a list of functions and defined names?

   (a) Function ScreenTip

   (b) Formula AutoComplete

   (c) Insert Function dialog box

   (d) Function Arguments dialog box

4. A formula containing the entry =$B3 is copied to a cell one column to the right and two rows down. How will the entry appear in its new location?

   (a) =$B3

   (b) =B3

   (c) =$C5

   (d) =$B5

5. Which of the following functions should be used to insert the current date and time in a cell?

   (a) =TODAY()

   (b) =CURRENT()

   (c) =NOW()

   (d) =DATE

6. Which of the following is not an argument of the IF function?

   (a) value_if_true

   (b) value_if_false

   (c) logical_test

   (d) lookup_value

7. Which of the following is *not* true about the VLOOKUP function?

   (a) The lookup table must be in ascending order.

   (b) The lookup table must be in descending order.

   (c) The default match type is approximate.

   (d) The match type must be false when completing an exact match.

8. The function =PMT(C5,C7,-C3) is stored in cell C15. What must be stored in cell C5?

   (a) APR

   (b) Periodic interest rate

   (c) Loan amount

   (d) Number of payment periods

9. Which of the following is *not* an appropriate use of the SUM function?

   (a) =SUM(B3:B45)

   (b) =SUM(F1:G10)

   (c) =SUM(A8:A15,D8:D15)

   (d) =SUM(D15-C15)

10. What is the keyboard shortcut to create an absolute reference?

   (a) F2

   (b) F3

   (c) F4

   (d) Alt

Practice Exercises

1 Hamilton Heights Auto Sales

You are the primary loan manager for Hamilton Heights Auto Sales, an auto sales company located in Missouri. In order to most efficiently manage the auto loans your company finances, you have decided to create a spreadsheet to perform several calculations. You will insert the current date, calculate down payment and interest rates based on credit score, calculate periodic payment amounts, and complete the project with basic summary information. Refer to Figure 2.29 as you complete this exercise.

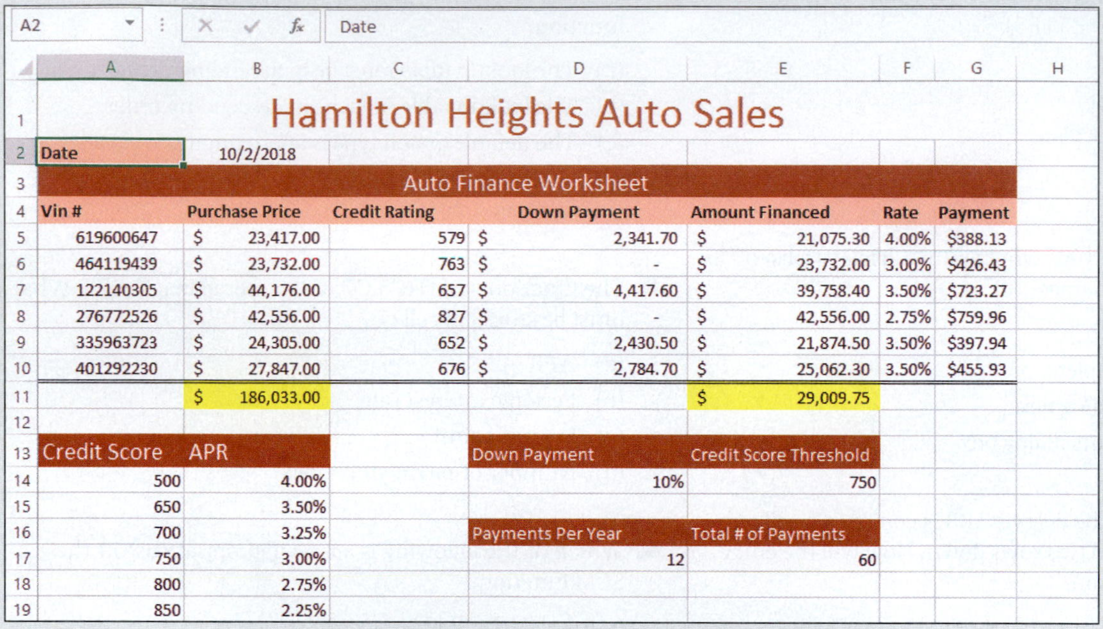

FIGURE 2.29 Hamilton Heights Auto Sales

a. Open *e02p1AutoSales* and save it as **e02p1AutoSales_LastFirst**.

b. Click **cell B2**, click the **Formulas tab**, click **Date & Time** in the Function Library group, select **NOW**, and then click **OK** to enter today's date in the cell.

c. Click **cell D5** on the Formulas tab, click **Logical** in the Function Library group, and select **IF**.

d. Type **C5<=$E$14** in the Logical_test box, type **$D$14*B5** in the Value_if_true box, type **0** in the Value_if_false box, and then click **OK**.

   This uses the IF function to calculate the required down payment based on credit score. If the customer has a credit score higher than 750 a down payment is not required. All clients with credits scores lower than 750 must pay a required 10% down payment in advance.

e. Use the fill handle to copy the contents of **cell D5** down the column, click **Auto Fill Options** to the lower-right of the copied cells, and then click **Fill Without Formatting** to ensure that the **Bottom Double border** remains applied to cell D10.

f. Calculate the Amount Financed by doing the following:
   - Click **cell E5** and type **=B5-D5**.
   - Use **cell E5's fill handle** to copy the function down the column.
   - Apply **Bottom Double border** to cell E10.

g. Calculate the Rate by doing the following:
   - Click **cell F5**. Click **Lookup & Reference** in the Function Library group and select **VLOOKUP**.
   - Type **C5** in the Lookup_value box, type **$A$14:$B$19** in the Table_array box, type **2** in the Col_index_num box, and then click **OK**
   - Double-click **cell F5's fill handle** to copy the function down the column.
   - Click **Auto Fill Options**, and click **Fill Without Formatting**.

h. Calculate the required periodic payment by doing the following:
  - Click **cell G5**, click **Financial** in the Function Library Group, and then click **PMT**.
  - Type **F5/$D$17** in the Rate box, type **$E$17** in the Nper box, type **–E5** in the Pv box, and then click **OK**.
  - Double-click **cell G5's** fill handle to copy the function down the column.
  - Click the **Auto Fill Options** button, and click **Fill Without Formatting**.

i. Select the **range B5:B10**, click the **Quick Analysis button**, click **TOTALS**, and select **Sum** from the Quick Analysis Gallery.

j. Click **cell E11** and type **=AVERAGE(E5:E10)** to calculate the average amount financed.

k. Create a footer with your name on the left side, the sheet name code in the center, and the file name on the right side.

l. Save and close the workbook. Based on your instructor's directions, submit e02p1AutoSales_LastFirst.

2 Lockridge Marketing Analytics

As a business analyst for Lockridge Marketing Analytics, you have been tasked with awarding performance bonuses. You prepare a model to calculate employee bonuses based on average customer satisfaction survey results. The survey is based on a scale of 1 to 5 with 5 being the highest rating. Employees with survey results where ratings are between 1 and 2.9 do not receive bonuses, scores between 3 and 3.9 earn a 2% one-time bonus on their monthly salary, and scores of 4 or higher receive a 5% bonus. In addition, you calculate basic summary data for reporting purposes. Refer to Figure 2.30 as you complete this exercise.

J10		× ✓ fx				
	A	B	C	D	E	F
1	Lockridge Marketing Analytics					
2						
3	**Inputs and Constants**				**Bonus Data**	
4	Today:	10/2/2018		**Rating**	1	3
5	Employees Surveyed	6		**Bonus**	0%	2%
6						
7						
8						
9	**Survey Code**	**Current Salary**	**Monthly Salary**	**Survey Score**	**Rating Bonus**	**Monthly Take Home**
10	38078	$ 50,000	$ 4,166.67	5	$ 208.33	$ 4,375.00
11	41105	$ 75,250	$ 6,270.83	3.5	$ 125.42	$ 6,396.25
12	39752	$ 67,250	$ 5,604.17	4.2	$ 280.21	$ 5,884.38
13	37872	$ 45,980	$ 3,831.67	3	$ 76.63	$ 3,908.30
14	40616	$ 58,750	$ 4,895.83	4.2	$ 244.79	$ 5,140.63
15	40347	$ 61,000	$ 5,083.33	4.5	$ 254.17	$ 5,337.50
16						
17						
18	**Statistics**					
19	Lowest Bonus	$ 76.63				
20	Average Bonus	$ 198.26				
21	Highest Bonus	$ 280.21				

Excel 2016, Windows 10, Microsoft Corporation

FIGURE 2.30 Lockridge Marketing Analytics

a. Open *e02p2Bonus* and save it as **e02p2Bonus_LastFirst**.

b. Click **cell B4**, click the **Formulas tab**, click **Date & Time** in the Function Library group, select **TODAY**, and then click **OK** to enter today's date in the cell.

   c. Click **cell B5**, click the **AutoSum arrow** in the Function Library group, and then select **Count Numbers**. Select the **range A10:A15** and press **Enter**.

   d. Click **cell C10**, type **=B10/12**, press **Ctrl+Enter**, and then double-click the **fill handle**.

   e. Enter the Rating Bonus based on survey average by doing the following:
- Click **cell E10** and type **=C10***.
- Click **Lookup & Reference** in the Function Library group and select **HLOOKUP**.
- Type **D10** in the Lookup_value box, type **E$4:G$5** in the Table_array box, type **2** in the Col_index_num box, and then click **OK**.
- Double-click the **cell E10 fill handle** to copy the formula down the Rating Bonus column.

   f. Calculate each employee's monthly take-home by doing the following:
- Click **cell F10** and type **=C10+E10**.
- Double-click the **cell F10 fill handle**.

   g. Calculate basic summary statistics by doing the following:
- Click **cell B19**, click the **Formulas tab**, click the **AutoSum arrow**, and then select **MIN**.
- Select the **range E10:E15** and then press **Enter**.
- In **cell B20**, click the **AutoSum arrow**, select **AVERAGE**, select the **range E10:E15**, and then press **Enter**.
- In **cell B21**, click the **AutoSum arrow**, select **MAX**, select the **range E10:E15**, and then press **Enter**.

   h. Create a footer with your name on the left side, the sheet name in the center, and the file name code on the right side.

   i. Save and close the workbook. Based on your instructor's directions, submit e02p2Bonus_LastFirst.

Mid-Level Exercises

1 Metropolitan Zoo Gift Shop Weekly Payroll

ANALYSIS CASE

As manager of the gift shop at the Metropolitan Zoo, you are responsible for managing the weekly payroll. Your assistant developed a partial worksheet, but you need to enter the formulas to calculate the regular pay, overtime pay, gross pay, taxable pay, withholding tax, FICA, and net pay. In addition, you want to include total pay columns and calculate some basic statistics. As you construct formulas, make sure you use absolute and relative cell references correctly in formulas.

a. Open the *e02m1Payroll* workbook and save it as **e02m1Payroll_LastFirst**.

b. Study the worksheet structure and read the business rules in the Notes section.

c. Use IF functions to calculate the regular pay and overtime pay based on a regular 40-hour workweek in **cells E5** and **F5**. Pay overtime only for overtime hours. Calculate the gross pay based on the regular and overtime pay. Abram's regular pay is $398. With 8 overtime hours, Abram's overtime pay is $119.40.

d. Create a formula in **cell H5** to calculate the taxable pay. Multiply the number of dependents by the deduction per dependent and subtract that from the gross pay. With two dependents, Abram's taxable pay is $417.40.

e. Use a VLOOKUP function in **cell I5** to identify and calculate the federal withholding tax. With a taxable pay of $417.40, Abram's tax rate is 25% and the withholding tax is $104.35. The VLOOKUP function returns the applicable tax rate, which you must then multiply by the taxable pay.

f. Calculate FICA in **cell J5** based on gross pay and the FICA rate, and calculate the net pay in cell K5.

g. Copy all formulas down their respective columns.

h. Use Quick Analysis tools to calculate the total regular pay, overtime pay, gross pay, taxable pay, withholding tax, FICA, and net pay on **row 17**.

i. Apply **Accounting Number Format** to the **range C5:C16**. Apply **Accounting Number Format** to the first row of monetary data and to the total row. Apply the **Comma style** to the monetary values for the other employees. Underline the last employee's monetary values and use the Format Cells dialog box to apply Top and Double Bottom borders for the totals.

j. Insert appropriate functions to calculate the average, highest, and lowest values in the Summary Statistics area (the **range I21:K23**) of the worksheet. Format the # of hours calculations as **Number format** with one decimal and the remaining calculations with **Accounting Number Format**.

k. Insert a new sheet named **Overtime**. List the number of overtime hours for the week. Calculate the yearly gross amount spent on overtime assuming the same number of overtime hours per week. Add another row with only half the overtime hours (using a formula). What is your conclusion and recommendation on overtime? Format this worksheet.

l. Insert a footer with your name on the left side, the sheet name in the center, and the file name code on the right side of both worksheets.

m. Save and close the workbook. Based on your instructor's directions, submit e02m1Payroll_LastFirst.

FROM SCRATCH

As a financial consultant, you work with a family who plans to purchase a $35,000 car. You want to create a worksheet containing variable data (the price of the car, down payment, date of the first payment, and borrower's credit rating) and constants (sales tax rate, years, and number of payments in one year). Borrowers pay 0.5% sales tax on the purchase price of the vehicle and their credit rating determines the required down payment percentage and APR. Your worksheet needs to perform various calculations.

a. Start a new Excel workbook, save it as **e02m2Loan_LastFirst**, and then rename Sheet1 **Payment**.

b. Type **Auto Loan Calculator** in cell A1, and then merge and center the title on the first row in the **range A1:F1**. Apply **bold, 18 pt** font size, and **Gold, Accent 4, Darker 25%** font color.

c. Type the labels in the **range A3:A12**. For each label, such as *Negotiated Cost of Vehicle*, merge the cells, such as the **range A4:B4**. Use the Format Painter to copy the formatting to the remaining nine labels. Next type and format the Inputs and Constants values in **column C**.

d. Type **Credit**, **Down Payment**, and **APR** in the **range A14:C14**, type the four credit ratings in the first column, the required down payment percentages in the second column, and the respective APRs in the third column. Next format the percentages, and then indent the percentages in the cells as needed.

e. Type labels in the Intermediate Calculations *and* Outputs sections in **column E**.

f. Enter formulas in the Intermediate Calculations and Outputs sections to calculate the following:

- **APR** based on credit rating: Use a Lookup function that references the borrower's credit rating and the table array in range. Include the range_lookup argument to ensure an exact match.

DISCOVER

- **Minimum down payment required**: Use a lookup function and calculation. Use the credit rating as the lookup value, and the **table array A15:C18**. Include the range_lookup argument to ensure an exact match. Multiply the function results by the negotiated cost of the house.
- **Sales tax**: Multiply the negotiated cost of the vehicle by the sales tax rate.
- **Total down payment**: The sum of the minimum down payment required and any additional down payment made.
- **Amount of the loan**: The difference between the negotiated cost of the house and the total down payment.
- **Monthly payment**: Principal and interest using the PMT function.

g. Format each section with fill color, bold, underline, number formats, borders, and column widths as needed.

h. Insert a footer with your name on the left side, the sheet name in the center, and the file name code on the right side of both sheets.

i. Save and close the workbook. Based on your instructor's directions, submit e02m2Loan_LastFirst.

3 Facebook and Blackboard

COLLABORATION CASE

FROM SCRATCH

Social media extends past friendships to organizational and product "fan" pages. Organizations such as Lexus, Pepsi, and universities create pages to provide information about their organizations. Some organizations even provide product details, such as for the Lexus ES350. Facebook includes a wealth of information about Microsoft Office products. People share information, pose questions, and reply with their experiences.

a. Log in to your Facebook account. If you do not have a Facebook account, sign up for one and add at least two classmates as friends. Search for Microsoft Excel 2016 and click **Like**.

b. Review postings on the Microsoft Excel wall. Notice that some people post what they like most about Excel or how much it has improved their productivity. Post a note about one of your favorite features about Excel that you have learned so far or how you have used Excel in other classes or on the job.

c. Click the **Discussions link** on the Microsoft Excel Facebook page and find topics that relate to IF or HLOOKUP functions. Post a response to one of the discussions. Take a screenshot of your posting and insert it into a Word document. Save the Word document **as e02m3_LastFirst**.

d. Create a team of three students. Create one discussion that asks people to describe their favorite use of any of the nested functions used in this chapter. Each team member should respond to the posting. Monitor the discussion and, when you have a few responses, capture a screenshot of the dialogue and insert it into your Word document.

e. Go to www.youtube.com and search for one of these Excel topics: absolute references, mixed references, semi-selection, IF function, VLOOKUP function, or PMT function.

f. Watch several video clips and find one of particular interest to you.

g. Post the URL on your Facebook wall. Specify the topic and describe why you like this particular video.

h. Watch videos from the links posted by other students on their Facebook walls. Comment on at least two submissions. Point out what you like about the video or any suggestions you have for improvement.

i. Insert screenshots of your postings in a Word document, if required by your instructor. Save and close the file. Based on your instructor's directions submit e02m3_LastFirst.

Beyond the Classroom

Auto Finance

After graduating from college and obtaining your first job, you have decided to purchase a new vehicle. Before purchasing the car, you want to create a worksheet to estimate the monthly payment based on the purchase price, APR, down payment, and years. Your monthly budget is $500 and you will use conditional logic to automatically determine if you can afford the cars you are evaluating. Open the workbook *e02b1CarLoan* and save it as **e02b1CarLoan_LastFirst**.

Insert a function to automatically enter the current date in cell A4. Starting in cell B12 enter a formula to calculate the down payment for each vehicle price range based on the down payment percentage listed in cell D4. Be sure to use the appropriate absolute or mixed reference and copy the formula to complete range B13:B16. Before calculating the periodic payment for each vehicle, you will need to research the current vehicle interest rates. Conduct an Internet search to determine the current interest rate for a five-year auto loan and enter the value in cell D5. In cell C12 type a function that calculates the periodic payment for the first vehicle based on the input information in range D4:D7. Be sure to use the appropriate absolute or mixed reference and copy the formula to complete range C12:C16. In column D, use an IF function to determine if the first vehicle is financially viable; display either Test Drive or NA based on the criteria in cell D8. Be sure to use the appropriate absolute or mixed reference and copy the formula to complete range D12:D16.

Include a footer with your name on the left side, the date in the center, and the file name on the right side. Save and close the workbook. Based on your instructor's directions, submit e02b1CarLoan_LastFirst.

Park City Condo Rental

You and some friends are planning a Labor Day vacation to Park City, Utah. You have secured a four-day condominium that costs $1,200. Some people will stay all four days; others will stay part of the weekend. One of your friends constructed a worksheet to help calculate each person's cost of the rental. The people who stay Thursday night will split the nightly cost evenly. To keep the costs down, everyone agreed to pay $30 per night per person for Friday, Saturday, and/or Sunday nights. Depending on the number of people who stay each night, the group may owe more money. Kyle, Ian, Isaac, and Daryl agreed to split the difference in the total rental cost and the amount the group members paid. Open the workbook *e02b2ParkCity*, and save it as **e02b2ParkCity_LastFirst**.

Review the worksheet structure, including the assumptions and calculation notes at the bottom of the worksheet. Check the formulas and functions, making necessary corrections. With the existing data, the number of people staying each night is 5, 8, 10, and 7, respectively. The total paid given the above assumptions is $1,110, giving a difference of $90 to be divided evenly among the first four people. Kyle's share should be $172.50. In the cells containing errors, insert comments to describe the error and fix the formulas. Verify the accuracy of formulas by entering an IF function in cell I1 to ensure that the totals match. Nick, James, and Body inform you they cannot stay Sunday night, and Rob wants to stay Friday night. Change the input accordingly. The updated total paid is now $1,200, and the difference is $150. Include a footer with your name on the left side, the date in the center, and the file name on the right side. Save and close the workbook. Based on your instructor's directions, submit e02b2ParkCity_LastFirst.

Capstone Exercise

You are an account manager for Inland Jewelers, a regional company that makes custom class rings for graduating seniors. Your supervisor requested a workbook to report on new accounts created on payment plans. The report should provide details on total costs to the student as well as payment information. Each ring financed has a base price that can fluctuate based on ring personalization.

Insert Current Date

You open the starting workbook you previously created, and insert the current date and time.

a. Open the *e02c1ClassRing* workbook, and then save it as **e02c1ClassRing_LastFirst**.

b. Insert a function in **cell B2** to display the current date and format as a **Long Date**.

c. Set column B's width to **Autofit**.

Calculate Cost

You are ready to calculate the cost of each class ring ordered. The rings are priced based on their base metal as displayed in the range A15:B19.

a. Insert a lookup function in **cell C5** to display the ring cost for the first student.

b. Copy the function from **cell C5** down through **C11** to complete column C.

c. Apply **Accounting Number Format** to **column C**.

Determine the Total Due

You will calculate the total due for each student's order. The total is the base price of the ring plus an additional charge for personalization if applicable.

a. Insert an IF function in **cell E5** to calculate the total due. If the student has chosen to personalize the ring,

there is an additional charge of 5% located in **cell B21** that must be applied; if not, the student pays only the base price. Use appropriate relative and absolute cell references.

b. Copy the function from **cell E5** down through **E11** to complete column E.

c. Apply **Accounting Number Format** to **column E**.

Calculate the Monthly Payment

Your next step is to calculate the periodic payment for each student's account. The payments are based on the years financed in column F and the annual interest rate in cell B22. All accounts are paid on a monthly basis.

a. Insert the function in **cell G5** to calculate the first student's monthly payment, using appropriate relative and absolute cell references.

b. Copy the formula down the column.

c. Apply **Accounting Number Format** to **column G**.

Finalize the Workbook

You perform some basic statistical calculations and finalize the workbook with formatting and page setup options.

a. Calculate totals in **cells C12**, **E12**, and **G12**.

b. Apply **Accounting Number Format** to the **cells C12, E12**, and **G12**.

c. Set **0.3"** left and right margins and ensure that the page prints on only one page.

d. Insert a footer with your name on the left side, the sheet name in the center, and the file name on the right side.

e. Save and close the workbook. Based on your instructor's directions, submit e02c1ClassRing_LastFirst.

Charts

LEARNING OUTCOME You will create charts and insert sparklines to represent data visually.

OBJECTIVES & SKILLS: After you read this chapter, you will be able to:

CASE STUDY | Computer Job Outlook

You are an academic advisor for the School of Computing at a private university in Seattle, Washington. You will visit high schools over the next few weeks to discuss the computing programs at the university and to inform students about the job outlook in the computing industry. Your assistant, Doug Demers, researched growing computer-related jobs in the *Occupational Outlook Handbook* published by the Bureau of Labor Statistics on the U.S. Department of Labor's website. In particular, Doug listed seven jobs, the number of those jobs in 2010, the projected number of jobs by 2020, the growth in percentage increase and number of jobs, and the 2010 median pay. This dataset shows an 18%–31% increase in computer-related jobs in that 10-year time period.

To prepare for your presentation to encourage students to enroll in your School of Computing, you will create several charts that depict the job growth in the computer industry. You know that different charts provide different perspectives on the data. After you complete the charts, you will be able to use them in a variety of formats, such as presentations, fliers, and brochures.

Depicting Data Visually

Everything possible/
Shutterstock

CHAPTER 3

FIGURE 3.1 Computer Job Outlook Charts

Excel 2016, Windows 10, Microsoft Corporation

CASE STUDY | Computer Job Outlook

Starting File	File to be Submitted
e03h1Jobs	e03h3Jobs_LastFirst

Chart Basics

A **chart** is a visual representation of numerical data that compares data and reveals trends or patterns to help people make informed decisions. An effective chart depicts data in a clear, easy-to-interpret manner and contains enough data to be useful without overwhelming your audience.

In this section, you will select the data source, choose the best chart type to represent numerical data, and designate the chart's location.

Selecting the Data Source

Look at the structure of the worksheet—the column labels, the row labels, the quantitative data, and the calculated values. Before creating a chart, make sure the worksheet data are organized so that the values in columns and rows use the same value system (such as dollars or units), make sure labels are descriptive, and delete any blank rows or columns that exist in the dataset. Decide what you want to convey to your audience by answering these questions:

- Does the worksheet hold a single set of data, such as average snowfall at one ski resort, or multiple sets of data, such as average snowfall at several ski resorts?

- Do you want to depict data for one specific time period or over several time periods, such as several years or decades?

Figure 3.2 shows a worksheet containing computer-related job titles, the number of jobs in 2010, the projected number of jobs by 2020, other details, and a chart. Row 3 contains labels merged and centered over individual column labels in row 5. Row 4 is blank and hidden. It is a good practice to insert a blank row between merged labels and individual column labels to enable you to sort the data correctly.

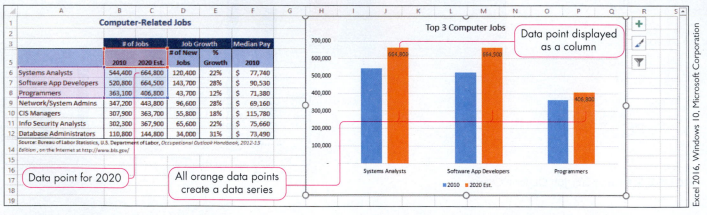

FIGURE 3.2 Dataset and Chart

Each cell containing a value is a **data point**. For example, the value 664,800 in cell C6 is a data point for the estimated number of Systems Analysts in 2020. Each data point in the worksheet creates an individual data point in the chart. A group of related data points that display in row(s) or column(s) in the worksheet create a **data series**. For example, the values 664,800, 664,500, and 406,800 comprise the number of estimated jobs by 2020 data series, which is indicated by the orange columns in the chart.

Identify the data range by selecting values and labels that you want to include in the chart. If the values and labels are not stored in adjacent cells, hold Ctrl while selecting the nonadjacent ranges. Do not select worksheet titles or subtitles; doing so would add unnecessary data to the chart. To create the chart in Figure 3.2, select the range A5:C8. It is important to select parallel ranges. A parallel range is one that consists of the same starting and end point as another similar range. For example, the range C5:C12 is a parallel range to A5:A12. Including the column headings on row 5 (even though cell A5 is blank) is necessary to include the years in the legend at the bottom of the chart area.

Excel transforms the selected data into a chart. A chart may include several chart elements or components. Table 3.1 lists and describes some of these elements. Figure 3.3 shows a chart area that contains these elements.

TABLE 3.1	Chart Elements
Chart Element	**Description**
Chart area	The container for the entire chart and all of its elements.
Plot area	Region containing the graphical representation of the values in the data series. Two axes form a border around the plot area.
X-axis	The horizontal border that provides a frame of reference for measuring data left to right.
Y-axis	The vertical border that provides a frame of reference for measuring data up and down.
Legend	A key that identifies the color, gradient, picture, texture, or pattern assigned to each data series in a chart. For example, blue might represent values for 2010, and orange might represent values for 2020.

Pearson Education, Inc.

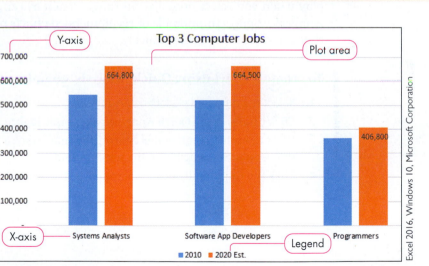

FIGURE 3.3 Chart Elements

Excel refers to the axes as the category axis and value axis. The ***category axis*** is the axis that displays descriptive labels for the data points plotted in a chart. The category axis labels are typically text contained in the first column of worksheet data (such as job titles) used to create the chart. The ***value axis*** is the axis that displays incremental numbers to identify the approximate values (such as number of jobs or revenue) of data points in a chart.

Choosing a Chart Type

You can create different charts from the same dataset; each chart type tells a different story. Select a chart type that appropriately represents the data and tells a story. For example, one chart might compare the number of computer-related jobs between 2010 and 2020, and another chart might indicate the percentage of new jobs by job title. The most commonly used chart types are column, bar, line, pie, and combo (see Table 3.2). Each chart type is designed to provide a unique perspective to the selected data.

TABLE 3.2	Common Chart Types	
Chart	**Chart Type**	**Description**
	Column	Displays values in vertical columns where the height represents the value; the taller the column, the larger the value. Categories display along the horizontal (category) axis.
	Bar	Displays values in horizontal bars where the length represents the value; the longer the bar, the larger the value. Categories display along the vertical (category) axis.
	Line	Displays category data on the horizontal axis and value data on the vertical axis. Appropriate to show continuous data to depict trends over time, such as months, years, or decades.
	Pie	Shows proportion of individual data points to the total or whole of all those data points.
	Combo	Combines two chart types (such as column and line) to plot different data types (such as values and percentages)

Pearson Education, Inc.

Quick Analysis. When you select a range of adjacent cells (such as the range A5:C12) and position the pointer over that selected range, Excel displays Quick Analysis in the bottom-right corner of the selected area. However, Quick Analysis does not display when you select nonadjacent ranges, such as ranges A6:A12 and D6:D12. Quick Analysis displays thumbnails of recommended charts based on the data you selected so that you can create a chart quickly.

To create a chart using Quick Analysis, complete the following steps:

1. Select the data and click Quick Analysis.
2. Click Charts in the Quick Analysis gallery (see Figure 3.4).
3. Point to each recommended chart thumbnail to see a preview of the type of chart that would be created from the selected data.
4. Click the thumbnail of the chart you want to create.

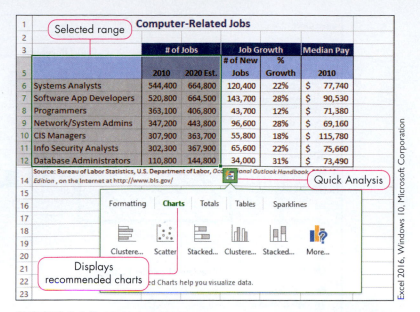

FIGURE 3.4 Quick Analysis Tool

Insert Tab. The Insert tab contains commands for creating a variety of charts. You must use the Insert tab to create a chart when you select nonadjacent ranges, but you can also use the Insert tab to create a chart when you select adjacent ranges. Clicking a particular chart on the Insert tab displays a gallery of icons representing more specific types of charts.

To create a chart using the Insert tab, complete the following steps:

1. Select the data and click the Insert tab.
2. Complete one of the following steps to select the chart type:
   - Click the chart type (such as Column) in the Charts group and click a chart subtype (such as Clustered Column) from the chart gallery (see Figure 3.5).
   - Click Recommended Charts in the Charts group to open the Insert Chart dialog box, click a thumbnail of the chart you want in the Recommended Charts tab or click the All Charts tab (see Figure 3.6) and click a thumbnail, and then click OK.

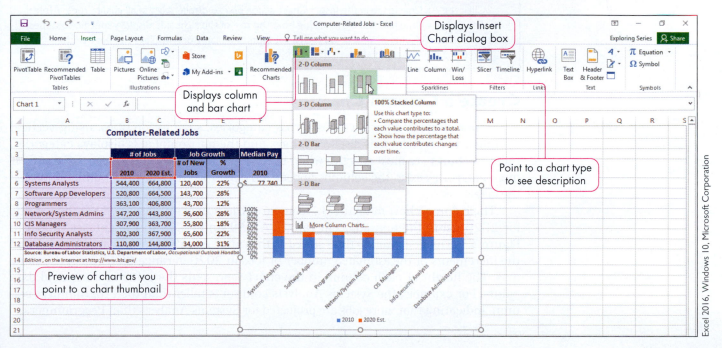

FIGURE 3.5 Chart Gallery

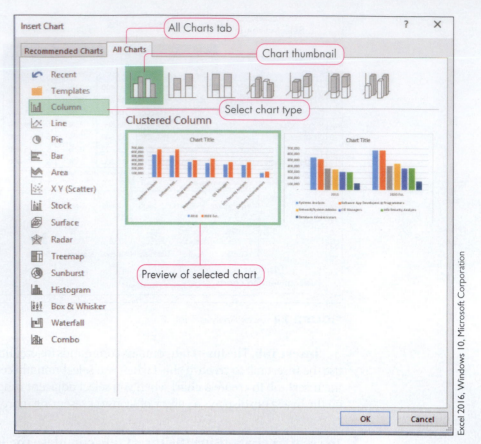

FIGURE 3.6 Insert Chart Dialog Box

TIP: RECOMMENDED VS. LIST OF ALL CHARTS

If you are unsure which type of chart would be a good choice for the selected data, click Recommended Charts in the Chart group. Excel will analyze the selected data and display thumbnails of recommended charts in the Insert Chart dialog box. Click a thumbnail to see a larger visualization of how your selected data would look in that chart type. The dialog box displays a message indicating the purpose of the selected chart, such as *A clustered bar chart is used to compare values across a few categories. Use it when the chart shows duration or when the category text is long.*

Click the All Charts tab in the Insert Chart dialog box to display a list of all chart types. After you click a type on the left side of the dialog box, the top of the right side displays specific subtypes, such as Clustered Column. When you click a subtype, the dialog box displays an image of that subtype using the selected data.

Create a Column Chart

STEP 1 ❯❯ A ***column chart*** compares values across categories, such as job titles, using vertical columns. The vertical axis displays values, and the horizontal axis displays categories. Column charts are most effective when they are limited to seven or fewer categories. If more categories exist, the columns appear too close together, making it difficult to read the labels.

The column chart in Figure 3.7 compares the number of projected jobs by job title for 2020 using the non-adjacent ranges A5:A9 and C5:C9 in the dataset shown in Figure 3.5. The first four job titles stored in the range A6:A9 form the category axis, and the increments of the estimated number of jobs in 2020 in range C6:C9 form the value axis. The height of each column in the chart represents the value of individual data points. For example, the Systems Analysts column is taller than the Programmers column, indicating that more jobs are projected for Systems Analysts than Programmers.

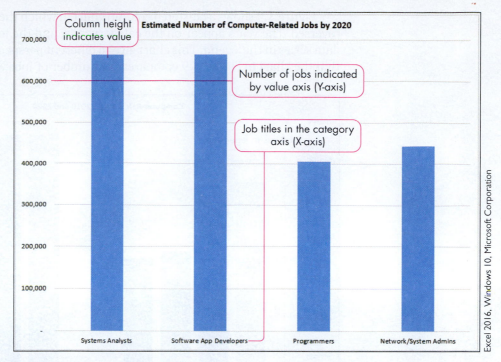

FIGURE 3.7 Column Chart

A ***clustered column chart*** compares groups—or clusters—of columns set side by side. The clustered column chart facilitates quick comparisons across data series, and it is effective for comparing several data points among categories. Figure 3.8 shows a clustered column chart created from the adjacent range A5:C9 in the dataset shown in Figure 3.5. By default, the job titles in the range A6:A9 appear on the category axis, and the yearly data points appear as columns with the value axis showing incremental numbers. Excel assigns a different color to each yearly data series and includes a legend so that you know what color represents which data series. The 2010 data series is light blue, and the 2020 data series is dark blue. This chart makes it easy to compare the predicted job growth from 2010 to 2020 for each job title and then to compare the trends among job titles.

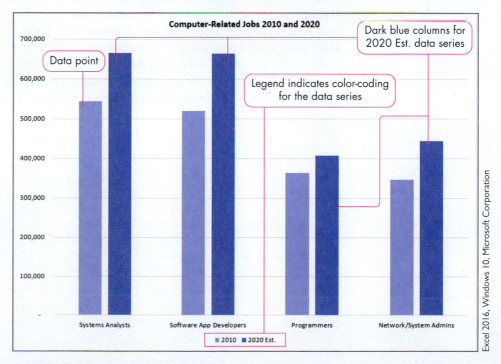

FIGURE 3.8 Clustered Column Chart

Figure 3.9 shows a clustered column chart in which the categories and data series are reversed. The years appear on the category axis, and the job titles appear as color-coded data series in the legend. This chart gives a different perspective from that in Figure 3.8 in that the chart in Figure 3.9 compares the number of jobs within a given year.

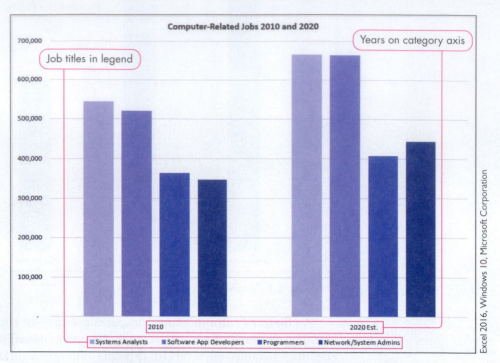

FIGURE 3.9 Clustered Column Chart: Category Axis and Legend Reversed

A **_stacked column chart_** shows the relationship of individual data points to the whole category. A stacked column chart displays only one column for each category. Each category within the stacked column is color-coded for one data series. Use the stacked column chart when you want to compare total values across categories, as well as to display the individual category values. Figure 3.10 shows a stacked column chart in which a single column represents each categorical year, and each column stacks color-coded data-point segments representing the different jobs. The stacked column chart enables you to compare the total number of computer-related jobs for each year. The height of each color-coded data point enables you to identify the relative contribution of each job to the total number of jobs for a particular year. A disadvantage of the stacked column chart is that the segments within each column do not start at the same point, making it more difficult to compare individual segment values across categories.

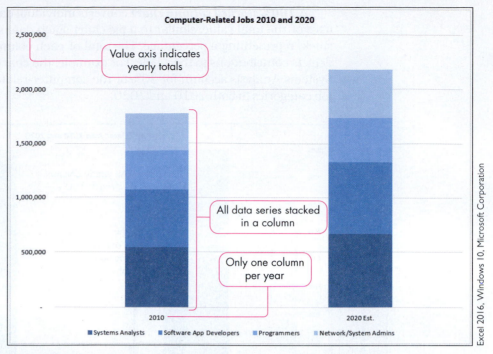

FIGURE 3.10 Stacked Column Chart

When you create a stacked column chart, make sure data are additive: Each column represents a sum of the data for each segment. Figure 3.10 correctly uses years as the category axis and the jobs as data series. For each year, Excel adds the number of jobs, and the columns display the total number of jobs. For example, the estimated total number of the four computer-related jobs in 2020 is about 2,180,000. Figure 3.11 shows a meaningless stacked column chart because the yearly number of jobs by job title is *not* additive. Adding the number of current actual jobs to the number of estimated jobs in the future does not make sense. It is incorrect to state that about 1,200,000 Systems Analysts jobs exist. Be careful when constructing stacked column charts to ensure that they lead to logical interpretation of data.

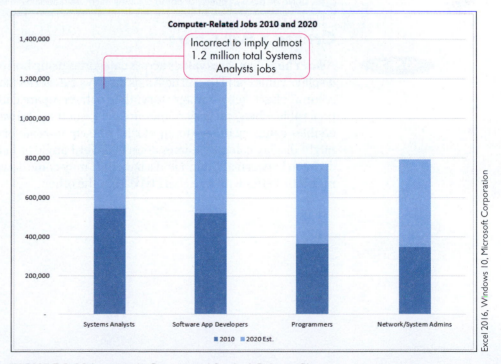

FIGURE 3.11 Incorrectly Constructed Stacked Column Chart

A **100% stacked column chart** converts individual data points (values) into percentages of the total value, similar to a pie chart. Each data series is a different color of the stack, representing a percentage. The total of each column is 100%. This type of chart depicts contributions to the whole. For example, the chart in Figure 3.12 illustrates that Systems Analysts account for 30% of the computer-related jobs represented by the four job categories in both 2010 and 2020.

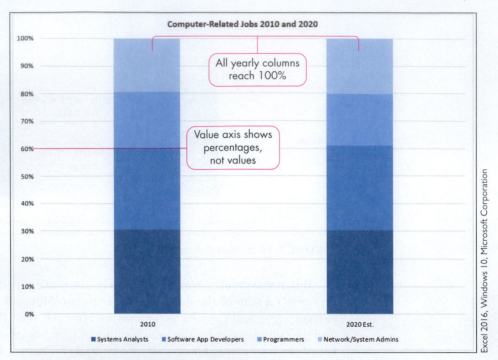

FIGURE 3.12 100% Stacked Column Chart

> **TIP: AVOID 3-D CHARTS**
> Avoid creating 3-D charts, because the third dimension is a superficial enhancement that usually distorts the charted data. For example, some columns appear taller or shorter than they actually are because of the angle of the 3-D effect, or some columns might be hidden by taller columns in front of them.

Create a Bar Chart

STEP 2 ▶▶ A **bar chart** compares values across categories using horizontal bars. The horizontal axis displays values, and the vertical axis displays categories (see Figure 3.13). Bar charts and column charts tell a similar story: they both compare categories of data. A bar chart is preferable when category names are long, such as *Software App Developers*. A bar chart enables category names to appear in an easy-to-read format, whereas a column chart might display category names at an awkward angle or in a smaller font size. The overall decision between a column and a bar chart may come down to the fact that different data may look better with one chart type than the other.

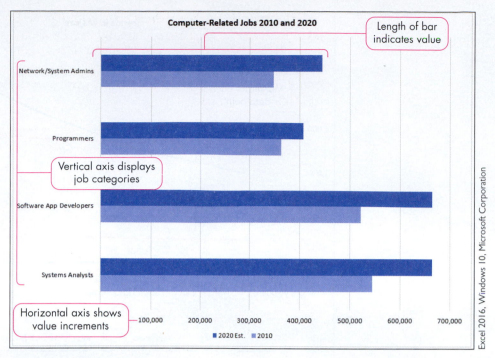

FIGURE 3.13 Clustered Bar Chart

Change the Chart Type

After you create a chart, you may decide that the data would be better represented by a different type of chart. For example, you might decide a bar chart would display the labels better than a column chart, or you might want to change a clustered bar chart to a stacked bar chart to provide a different perspective for the data. Use the Change Chart Type feature to change a chart to a different type of chart.

To change the type of an existing chart, complete the following steps:

1. Select the chart and click the Design tab.
2. Click Change Chart Type in the Type group to open the Change Chart Type dialog box (which is similar to the Insert Chart dialog box).
3. Click the All Charts tab within the dialog box.
4. Click a chart type on the left side of the dialog box.
5. Click a chart subtype on the right side of the dialog box and click OK.

Create a Line Chart

A **line chart** displays lines connecting data points to show trends over equal time periods. Excel displays each data series with a different line color. The category axis (X-axis) represents time, such as 10-year increments, whereas the value axis (Y-axis) represents a value, such as money or quantity. A line chart enables you to detect trends because the line continues to the next data point. To show each data point, choose the Line with Markers chart type. Figure 3.14 shows a line chart indicating the number of majors from 2005 to 2020 (estimated) at five-year increments. The number of Arts majors remains relatively constant, but the number of Tech & Computing majors increases significantly over time, especially between the years 2010 and 2020.

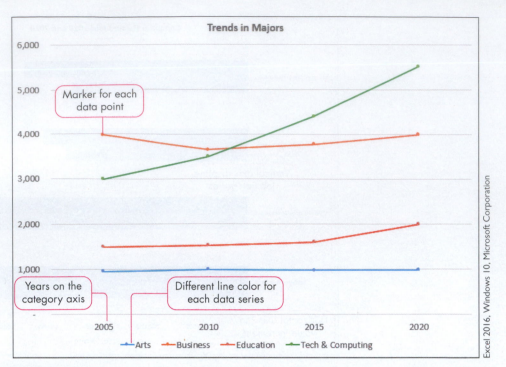

FIGURE 3.14 Line Chart

Excel 2016, Windows 10, Microsoft Corporation

Create a Pie Chart

STEP 4 ⟩⟩ A *pie chart* shows each data point as a proportion to the whole data series. The pie chart displays as a circle, or "pie," where the entire pie represents the total value of the data series. Each slice represents a single data point. The larger the slice, the larger percentage that data point contributes to the whole. Use a pie chart when you want to convey percentage. Unlike column, bar, and line charts that typically chart multiple data series, pie charts represent a single data series only.

The pie chart in Figure 3.15 divides the pie representing the estimated number of new jobs into seven slices, one for each job title. The size of each slice is proportional to the percentage of total computer-related jobs depicted in the worksheet for that year. For example, Systems Analysts account for 21% of the estimated total number of new computer-related jobs in 2020. Excel creates a legend to indicate which color represents which pie slice. When you create a pie chart, limit it to about seven data points. Pie charts with too many slices appear too busy to interpret, or shades of the same color scheme become too difficult to distinguish.

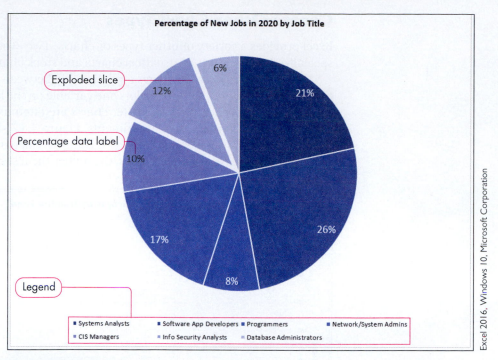

FIGURE 3.15 Pie Chart

Create a Combo Chart

STEP 5 A *combo chart* is a chart that combines two chart types, such as column and line charts. This type of chart is useful to show two different but related data types. For example, you might want to show the number of new jobs in columns and the percentage growth of new jobs in a line within the same chart (see Figure 3.16). A combo chart has a primary and a secondary axis. The primary axis displays on the left side of the chart. In this case, the primary axis indicates the number of jobs represented in the columns. The secondary axis displays on the right side of the chart. In this case, the secondary axis indicates the percentage of new jobs created as represented by the line.

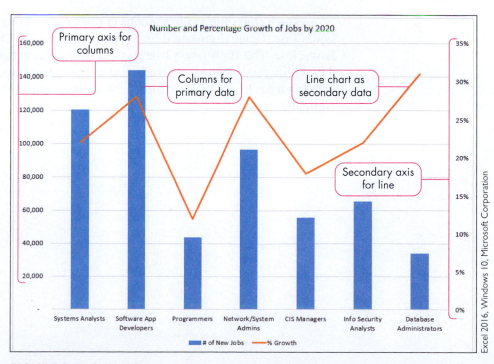

FIGURE 3.16 Combo Chart

Create Other Chart Types

Excel provides a variety of other types of charts. Two other chart types that are used for specialized analysis are X Y (scatter) charts and stock charts.

An **_X Y (scatter) chart_** shows a relationship between two numerical variables using their X and Y coordinates. Excel plots one variable on the horizontal X-axis and the other variable on the vertical Y-axis. Scatter charts are often used to represent data in educational, scientific, and medical experiments. Figure 3.17 shows the relationship between the number of minutes students view a training video and their test scores. The more minutes of a video a student watches, the higher the test score.

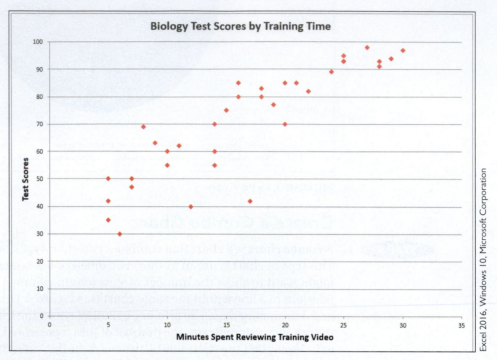

FIGURE 3.17 X Y (Scatter) Chart

A **_stock chart_** shows fluctuations in stock prices. Excel has four stock subtypes: High-Low-Close, Open-High-Low-Close, Volume-High-Low-Close, and Volume-Open-High-Low-Close. The High-Low-Close stock chart marks a stock's trading range on a given day with a vertical line from the lowest to the highest stock prices. Rectangles mark the opening and closing prices. Figure 3.18 shows three days of stock prices for a particular company.

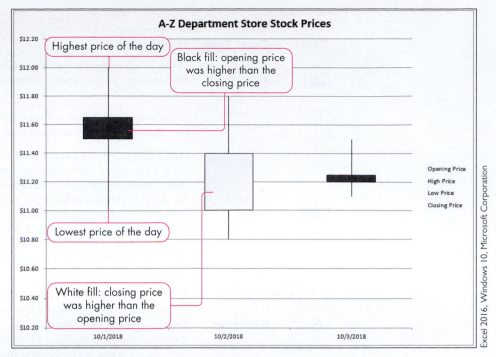

FIGURE 3.18 Stock Chart

The rectangle represents the difference in the opening and closing prices. If the rectangle has a white fill, the closing price is higher than the opening price. If the rectangle has a black fill, the opening price is higher than the closing price. In Figure 3.18, on October 1, the opening price was $11.65, and the closing price was $11.50, indicated by the top and bottom of the black rectangle. A line below the rectangle indicates that the lowest trading price is lower than the opening and closing prices. The lowest price was $11.00 on October 1. A line above the rectangle indicates that the highest trading price is higher than the opening and closing prices. The highest price was $12.00 on October 1. If no line exists below the rectangle, the lowest price equals either the opening or closing price, and if no line exists above the rectangle, the highest price equals either the opening or closing price.

TIP: ARRANGE DATA FOR A STOCK CHART

To create an Open-High-Low-Close stock chart, you must arrange data with Opening Price, High Price, Low Price, and Closing Price as column labels in that sequence. If you want to create other variations of stock charts, you must arrange data in a structured sequence required by Excel.

Table 3.3 lists and describes some of the other types of charts you can create in Excel.

TABLE 3.3	Other Chart Types	
Chart	**Chart Type**	**Description**
	Area	Similar to a line chart in that it shows trends over time; however, the area chart displays colors between the lines to help illustrate the magnitude of changes.
	Surface	Represents numeric data and numeric categories. Displays trends using two dimensions on a continuous curve.
	Radar	Uses each category as a spoke radiating from the center point to the outer edges of the chart. Each spoke represents each data series, and lines connect the data points between spokes, similar to a spider web. A radar chart compares aggregate values for several data series. For example, a worksheet could contain the number of specific jobs for 2015, 2016, 2017, and 2018. Each year would be a data series containing the individual data points (number of specific jobs) for that year. The radar chart would aggregate the total number of jobs per year for all four data series.
	Histogram	A histogram is similar to a column chart. The category axis shows bin ranges (intervals) where data is aggregated into bins, and the vertical axis shows frequencies. For example, your professor might want to show the number (frequency) of students who earned a score within each grade interval, such as 60-69, 70-79, 80-89, and 90-100.

Pearson Education, Inc.

Moving, Sizing, and Printing a Chart

 Excel inserts the chart as an embedded object in the current worksheet, often to the right of, but sometimes on top of and covering up, the data area. After you insert a chart, you usually need to move it to a different location and adjust its size. If you need to print a chart, decide whether to print the chart only or the chart and its data source.

Move a Chart

When you create a chart, Excel displays the chart in the worksheet, often on top of existing worksheet data. Therefore, you should move the chart so that it does not cover up data. If you leave the chart in the same worksheet, you can print the data and chart on the same page.

To move a chart on an active worksheet, complete the following steps:

1. Point to the chart area to display the Chart Area ScreenTip and the pointer includes the white arrowhead and a four-headed arrow.
2. Drag the chart to the desired location.

You might want to place the chart in a separate worksheet, called a ***chart sheet***. A chart sheet contains a single chart only; you cannot enter data and formulas on a chart sheet. If you want to print or view a full-sized chart, move the chart to its own chart sheet.

To move a chart to another sheet or a chart sheet, complete the following steps:

1. Select the chart.
2. Click the Design tab and click Move Chart in the Location group (or right-click the chart and select Move Chart) to open the Move Chart dialog box (see Figure 3.19).
3. Select one of these options to indicate where you want to move the chart:
   - Click *New sheet* to move the chart to its own sheet. The default chart sheet for the first chart is Chart1, but you can rename it in the Move Chart dialog box or similarly to the way you rename other sheet tabs.
   - Click *Object in*, click the *Object in* arrow, and select the worksheet to which you want to move the chart.
4. Click OK.

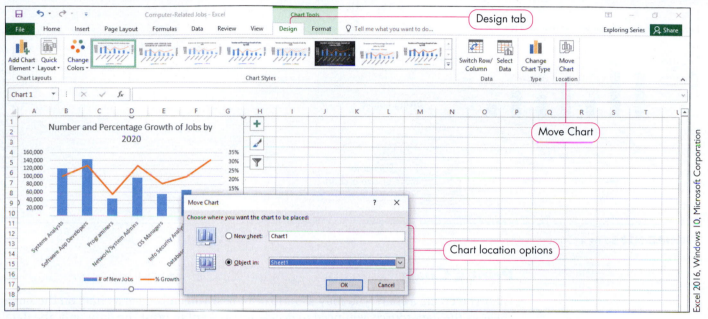

FIGURE 3.19 Design Tab and Move Chart Dialog Box

Size a Chart

If you move a chart to a chart sheet, the chart is enlarged to fill the entire sheet. If you keep a chart embedded within a worksheet, you might want to size the chart to fit in a particular range or to ensure the chart elements are proportional. Use the sizing handles or the Format tab on the Ribbon to change the size of the chart.

To change the chart size with sizing handles, complete the following steps:

1. Select the chart. Excel displays a line border and sizing handles around the chart when you select it. *Sizing handles* are eight circles that display around the four corners and outside middle sections of a chart when you select it.
2. Point to the outer edge of the chart where the sizing handles are located until the pointer changes to a two-headed arrow.
3. Drag the border to adjust the chart's height or width. Drag a corner sizing handle to increase or decrease the height and width of the chart at the same time. Press and hold Shift as you drag a corner sizing handle to change the height and width proportionately.

1. Select the chart.
2. Click the Format tab.
3. Change the value in the Height and Width boxes in the Size group (see Figure 3.20).

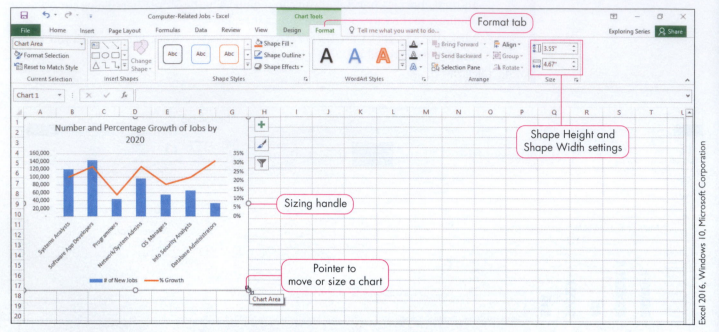

FIGURE 3.20 Sizing a Chart

Print a Chart

After you create a chart, you may want to print it. If you embedded a chart on the same sheet as the data source, you need to decide if you want to print the data only, the data and the chart, or the chart only.

To print the data only, complete the following steps:

1. Select the data.
2. Click the File tab and click Print.
3. Click the first arrow in the Settings section and select Print Selection.
4. Click Print.

To print only the chart as a full page, complete the following steps:

1. Select the chart if it is on a worksheet that also contains data.
2. Click the File tab and click Print.
3. Make sure the default setting is Print Selected Chart.
4. Click Print.

If the data and chart are on the same worksheet, print the worksheet contents to print both, but do not select either the chart or the data before displaying the Print options. The preview shows you what will print. Make sure it displays what you want to print before clicking Print.

If you moved the chart to a chart sheet, the chart is the only item on that worksheet. When you display the print options, the default is Print Active Sheets, and the chart will print as a full-page chart.

Quick Concepts

1. Why should you not include aggregates, such as totals or averages, along with individual data points in a chart? *p. 201*

2. Describe the purpose of each of these chart types: (a) column, (b) bar, (c) line, (d) pie, and (e) combo. *p. 202*

3. How can you use Quick Analysis to create a chart? *p. 202*

4. How do you decide whether to move a chart within the worksheet where you created it or move it to a chart sheet? *p. 214*

Hands-On Exercises

Watch the Video for this Hands-On Exercise!

MyITLab®
HOE1 Training

Skills covered: Select an Adjacent Range • Create a Clustered Column Chart • Move a Chart to a New Chart Sheet • Select a Nonadjacent Range • Create a Bar Chart • Change the Chart Type • Move a Chart Within a Worksheet • Size a Chart • Create a Pie Chart • Create a Combo Chart

1 Chart Basics

Doug Demers, your assistant, gathered data about seven computer-related jobs from the *Occupational Outlook Handbook* online. He organized the data into a structured worksheet that contains the job titles, the number of jobs in 2010, the projected number of jobs by 2020, and other data. Now you are ready to transform the data into visually appealing charts.

STEP 1 ⟫ CREATE A CLUSTERED COLUMN CHART

You want to compare the number of jobs in 2010 to the projected number of jobs in 2020 for all seven computer-related professions that Doug entered into the worksheet. You decide to create a clustered column chart to depict this data. After you create this chart, you will move it to its own chart sheet. You will format the charts in Hands-On Exercise 2. Refer to Figure 3.21 as you complete Step 1.

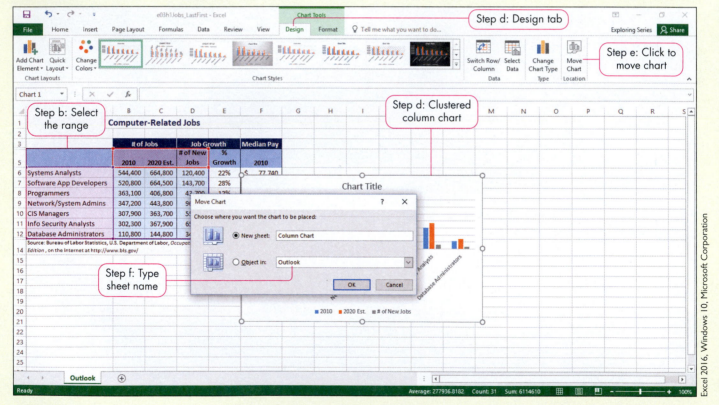

FIGURE 3.21 Clustered Column Chart

a. Open *e03h1Jobs* and save it as **e03h1Jobs_LastFirst**.

> **TROUBLESHOOTING:** If you make any major mistakes in this exercise, you can close the file, open *e03h1Jobs* again, and then start this exercise over.

CHAPTER 3 • Hands-On Exercise 1

b. Select the **range A5:D12**.

You selected the job titles, the number of jobs in 2010, the projected number of jobs in 2020, and the number of new jobs. Because you are selecting three data series (three columns of numerical data), you must also select the column headings on row 5.

c. Click **Quick Analysis** at the bottom-right corner of the selected range and click **Charts**.

The Quick Analysis gallery displays recommended charts based on the selected range.

d. Point to **Clustered Column** (the third thumbnail in the Charts gallery) to see a preview of what the chart would look like and click **Clustered Column**.

Excel inserts a clustered column chart based on the selected data. The Design tab displays on the Ribbon while the chart is selected.

e. Click **Move Chart** in the Location group.

The Move Chart dialog box opens for you to specify where to move the chart.

f. Click **New sheet**, type **Column Chart**, and then click **OK**. Save the workbook.

Excel moves the clustered column chart to a new sheet called Column Chart.

STEP 2 ›› CREATE A BAR CHART

You want to create a bar chart to depict the number of jobs in 2010 and the number of new jobs that will be created by 2020. Finally, you want to change the chart to a stacked bar chart to show the total jobs in 2020 based on the number of jobs in 2010 and the number of new jobs. Refer to Figure 3.22 as you complete Step 2.

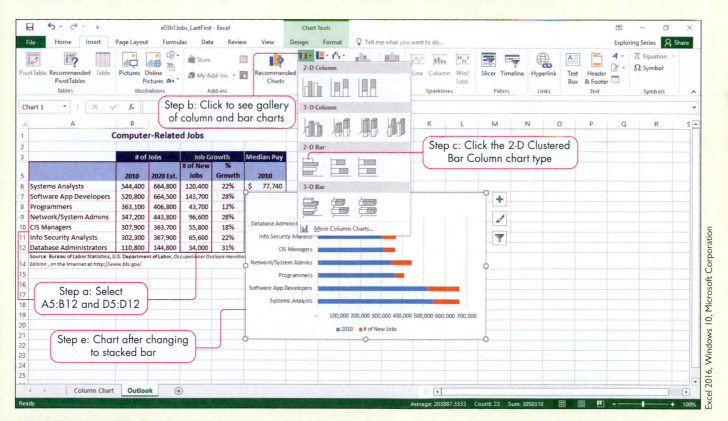

FIGURE 3.22 Bar Chart

a. Click the **Outlook sheet tab**, select the **range A5:B12**, press and hold **Ctrl**, and then select the **range D5:D12**.

You used Ctrl to select nonadjacent ranges: the job title labels, the number of jobs in 2010, and the number of new jobs.

> **TIP: PARALLEL RANGES**
> Nonadjacent ranges should be parallel so that the legend will correctly reflect the data series. This means that each range should contain the same number of related cells. For example, A5:A12, B5:B12, and D5:D12 are parallel ranges. Even though cell A5 is blank, you must select it to have a parallel range with the other two selected ranges that include cells on row 5.

b. Click the **Insert tab** and click **Insert Column or Bar Chart** in the Charts group.

The gallery shows both column and bar chart thumbnails.

c. Click **Clustered Bar** in the 2-D Bar section to create a clustered bar chart.

Excel inserts the clustered bar chart in the worksheet.

d. Click **Change Chart Type** in the Type group on the Design tab.

The Change Chart Type dialog box opens. The left side of the dialog box lists all chart types. The top-right side displays thumbnails of various bar charts, and the lower section displays a sample of the selected chart.

e. Click **Stacked Bar** in the top center of the dialog box and click **OK**. Save the workbook.

Excel displays the number of jobs in 2010 in blue and stacks the number of new jobs in orange into one bar per job title. This chart tells the story of how the total projected number of jobs in 2020 is calculated: the number of existing jobs in 2010 (blue) and the number of new jobs (orange).

STEP 3 ›› MOVE AND SIZE A CHART

The bar chart is displayed in the middle of the worksheet. You decide to position it below the job outlook data and adjust its size to make it larger so that it is as wide as the dataset and a little taller for better proportions. Refer to Figure 3.23 as you complete Step 3.

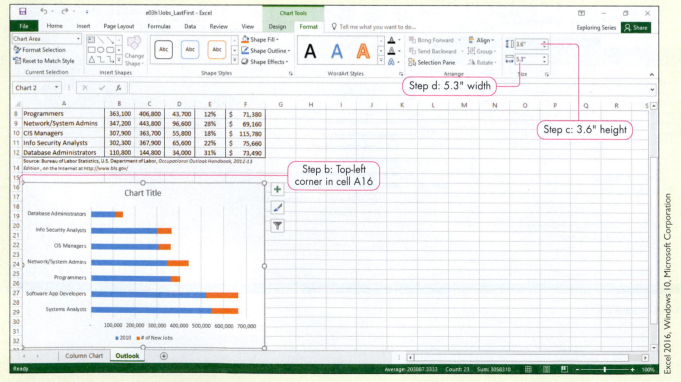

FIGURE 3.23 Stacked Bar Chart Moved and Sized

a. Point to an empty part of the chart area.

The pointer displays a four-headed arrow with the regular white arrowhead, and the Chart Area ScreenTip displays.

> **TROUBLESHOOTING:** Make sure you see the Chart Area ScreenTip as you perform Step b. If you move the pointer to another chart element—such as the legend—you will move or size that element instead of moving the entire chart.

b. Drag the chart so that the top-left corner of the chart appears in **cell A16**.

You positioned the chart below the worksheet data.

c. Click the **Format tab**, select the value in the **Shape Height box**, type **3.6**, and then press **Enter**.

The chart is now 3.6" tall.

d. Select the value in the **Shape Width box**, type **5.3**, and then press **Enter**. Save the workbook.

The chart is now 5.3" wide.

STEP 4 ›› **CREATE A PIE CHART**

You decide to create a pie chart that depicts the percentage of new jobs by job title calculated from the total number of new jobs created for the seven job titles Doug researched. After creating the pie chart, you will move it to its own sheet. Refer to Figure 3.24 as you complete Step 4.

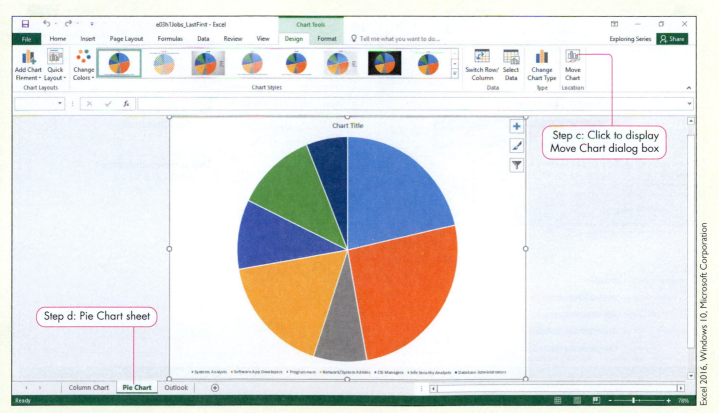

FIGURE 3.24 Pie Chart

a. Select the **range A6:A12**, press and hold **Ctrl**, then select the **range D6:D12**.

> **TROUBLESHOOTING:** Do not select cells A5 and D5 this time because you are creating a pie chart. When creating a chart from a single data series (e.g., # of New Jobs), you do not need to select the column headings.

b. Click the **Insert tab**, click **Insert Pie or Doughnut Chart** in the Charts group, and then select **Pie** in the 2-D Pie group on the gallery.

The pie chart displays in the worksheet.

c. Click **Move Chart** in the Location group on the Design tab.

The Move Chart dialog box opens.

d. Click **New sheet**, type **Pie Chart**, and then click **OK**. Save the workbook.

Excel creates a new sheet called Pie Chart. The pie chart is the only object on that sheet.

STEP 5 ›› **CREATE A COMBO CHART**

You want to create a combo chart that shows the number of new jobs in columns and the percentage of new jobs created in a line on the secondary axis. Although the number of new jobs may appear low as represented by the smallest column (such as 34,000 new database administrators), the actual percentage of new jobs created between 2010 and 2020 may be significant as represented by the steep incline of the orange line (such as 31% growth for database administrators). Refer to Figure 3.25 as you complete Step 5.

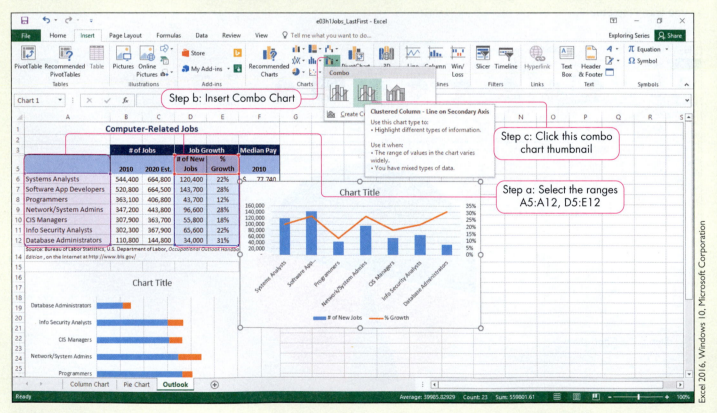

FIGURE 3.25 Combo Chart

Excel 2016, Windows 10, Microsoft Corporation

a. Click the **Outlook sheet tab**, select the **range A5:A12**, press and hold **Ctrl**, then select the **range D5:E12**.

b. Click the **Insert tab** and click **Insert Combo Chart** in the Charts group.

The Combo Chart gallery of thumbnails displays.

c. Click the **Clustered Column – Line on Secondary Axis thumbnail**, which is the middle thumbnail.

Excel creates a combo chart based on the thumbnail you selected. The number of new jobs displays in blue columns, and the percentage growth displays as an orange line.

d. Click **Move Chart** in the Location group on the Design tab, click **New sheet**, type **Combo Chart**, and then click **OK**.

e. Save the workbook. Keep the workbook open if you plan to continue with the next Hands-On Exercise. If not, close the workbook, and exit Excel.

Chart Elements

After creating a chart, you should add appropriate chart elements. A **chart element** is a component that completes or helps clarify the chart. Some chart elements, such as chart titles, should be included in every chart. Other elements are optional. Table 3.4 describes the chart elements, and Figure 3.26 illustrates several chart elements.

TABLE 3.4	Chart Elements
Element	**Description**
Axis title	Label that describes the category or value axes. Display axis titles, such as In Millions of Dollars or Top 7 Computer Job Titles, to clarify the axes. Axis titles are not displayed by default.
Chart title	Label that describes the entire chart. It should reflect the purpose of the chart. For example, Houses Sold is too generic, but Houses Sold in Seattle in 2018 indicates the what (Houses), the where (Seattle), and the when (2018). The default text is Chart Title.
Data label	Descriptive label that shows the exact value or name of a data point. Data labels are not displayed by default.
Data table	A grid that contains the data source values and labels. If you embed a chart on the same worksheet as the data source, you might not need to include a data table. Only add a data table with a chart that is on a chart sheet.
Error bars	Visuals that indicate the standard error amount, a percentage, or a standard deviation for a data point or marker. Error bars are not displayed by default.
Gridlines	Horizontal or vertical lines that display in the plot area, designed to help people identify the values plotted by the visual elements, such as a column.
Legend	A key that identifies the color, gradient, picture, texture, or pattern assigned to each data series. The legend is displayed by default for some chart types.
Trendline	A line that depicts trends or helps forecast future data, such as estimating future sales or number of births in a region. Add a trendline to column, bar, line, stock, scatter, and bubble charts. Excel will analyze the current trends and display a line indicating future values based on those trends.

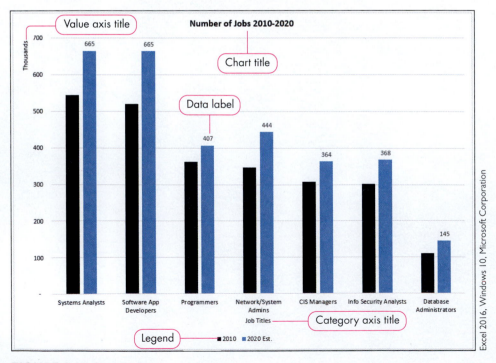

FIGURE 3.26 Chart Elements

In this section, you will learn how to add, edit, and format chart elements. Specifically, you will learn how to type a chart title, add axis titles, add data labels, and position the legend. Furthermore, you will learn how to format these elements as well as format axes, position the legend, and add gridlines. Finally, you will learn how to format the chart area, plot area, data series, and a data point.

Adding, Editing, and Formatting Chart Elements

After you create a chart, you usually need to add elements to provide labels to describe the chart. Adding descriptive text for labels provides information for the reader to comprehend the chart without knowing or seeing the underlying data. When you create a chart, one or more elements may display by default. For example, when you created the charts in Hands-On Exercise 1, Excel displayed a placeholder for the chart title and displayed a legend so that you know which color represents each data series.

When a chart is selected, three icons display to the right of the chart: Chart Elements, Chart Styles, and Chart Filters. In addition, the Design tab contains the Chart Layouts group that allows you to add and customize chart elements and change the layout of the chart.

When you point to a chart element, Excel displays a ScreenTip with the name of that element. To select a chart element, click it when you see the ScreenTip, or click the Format tab, click the Chart Elements arrow in the Current Selection group, and select the element from the list.

Edit, Format, and Position the Chart Title

STEP 1 ›› Excel includes the placeholder text *Chart Title* above the chart. You should replace that text with a descriptive title. In addition, you might want to format the chart title by applying bold and changing the font, font size, font color, and fill color.

> **To edit and format the chart title, complete the following steps:**
>
> 1. Select the chart title.
> 2. Type the text you want to appear in the title and press Enter.
> 3. Click the Home tab.
> 4. Apply the desired font formatting, such as increasing the font size and applying bold.
> 5. Click the chart to deselect the chart title.

> **TIP: FONT COLOR**
> The default font color for the chart title, axes, axes titles, and legend is Black, Text 1, Lighter 35%. If you want these elements to stand out, change the color to Black, Text 1 or another solid color.

By default, the chart title displays centered above the plot area. Although this is a standard location for the chart, you might want to position it elsewhere.

To change the position of the chart title, complete the following steps:

1. Select the chart title and click Chart Elements to the right of the chart.
2. Point to the Chart Title and click the triangle on the right side of the menu option, Chart Title (see Figure 3.27).
3. Select one of the options:
   - Above Chart: Centers the title above the plot area, decreasing the plot area size to make room for the chart title.
   - Centered Overlay: Centers the chart title horizontally without resizing the plot area; the title displays over the top of the plot area.
   - More Options: Opens the Format Chart Title task pane to apply fill, border, and alignment settings. A **task pane** is a window of options to format and customize chart elements. The task pane name and options change based on the selected chart element. For example, when you double-click the chart title, the Format Chart Title task pane displays.
4. Click Chart Elements to close the menu.

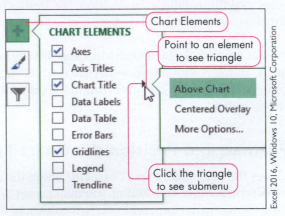

FIGURE 3.27 Chart Elements List

TIP: LINKING A CHART TITLE OR AN AXIS TITLE TO A CELL

Instead of typing text directly in the Chart Title or Axis Title placeholder, you can link the title to a label in a cell. Click the Chart Title or Axis Title placeholder, type = in the Formula Bar, click the cell containing the label you want for the title, and then press Enter. Excel will enter the sheet name and cell reference, such as =Outlook!$A$1, in the Formula Bar. If you change the worksheet label, Excel will also change the title in the chart.

Add, Format, and Position Axis Titles

STEP 2 ⟩⟩ Axis titles are helpful to provide more clarity about the value or category axis. Axis titles also help you conform to ADA compliance requirements. For example, if the values are abbreviated as 7 instead of 7,000,000 you should indicate the unit of measurement on the value axis as In Millions. You might want to further clarify the labels on the category axis by providing a category axis title, such as Job Titles.

To add an axis title, complete the following steps:

1. Select the chart and click Chart Elements to the right of the chart.
2. Point to Axis Titles and click the triangle on the right side.
3. Select one or more of these options:
   - Primary Horizontal: Displays a title for the primary horizontal axis.
   - Primary Vertical: Displays a title for the primary vertical axis.
   - Secondary Horizontal: Displays a title for the secondary horizontal axis in a combo chart.
   - Secondary Vertical: Displays a title for the secondary vertical axis in a combo chart.
   - More Options: Opens the Format Axis Title task pane to apply fill, border, and alignment settings.
4. Click Chart Elements to close the menu.

To use the Design tab to add a chart element, complete the following steps:

1. Click the Design tab.
2. Click Add Chart Element in the Chart Layouts group.
3. Point to an element and select from that element's submenu (see Figure 3.28).

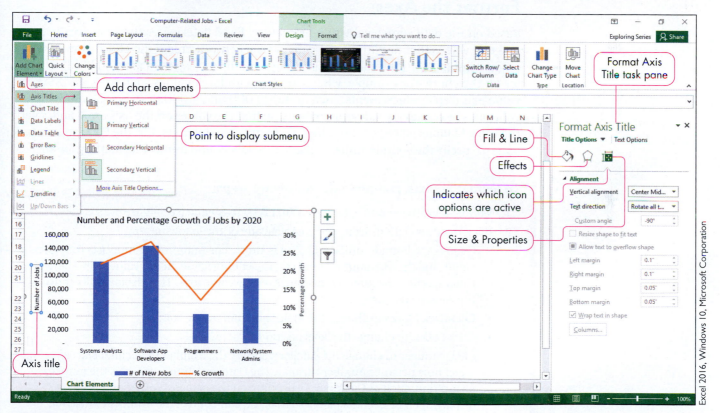

FIGURE 3.28 Chart Elements Menu and Format Axis Title Task Pane

The horizontal axis title displays below the category labels, and the rotated vertical axis title displays on the left side of the value axis. After including an axis title, click the title, type the text for the title, and then press Enter similarly to editing text for a chart title. You might want to apply font formatting (such as font size and color) to the axis titles similarly to formatting a chart title. Use the Format Axis Title task pane to customize and format the axis title.

To position and format the axis title, complete the following:

1. Double-click the axis title to open the Format Axis Title task pane (refer to Figure 3.28). Each task pane has categories, such as Title Options and Text Options. Below these categories are icons, such as Fill & Line, Effects, and Size & Properties.

2. Click Title Options and click the Size & Properties icon. The options in the task pane change to display options related to the icon you click. A thin horizontal gray line separates the icons from the options. The line contains a partial triangle that points to the icon that is active to indicate which options are displayed. Figure 3.28 shows the triangle is pointing to Size & Properties.

3. Change the *Vertical alignment* or *Horizontal alignment* option to the desired position.

4. Click other icons, such as Fill & Line, and select the desired options.

5. Close the Format Axis Title task pane.

6. Click the Home tab and apply font formatting, such as Font Color.

TIP: REMOVE AN ELEMENT

To remove an element, click Chart Elements and click a check box to deselect the check box. Alternatively, click Add Chart Element in the Chart Layouts group on the Chart Tools Design tab, point to the element name, and then select None. You can also select a chart element and press Delete to remove it.

Format the Axes

Based on the data source values and structure, Excel determines the start, incremental, and end values that display on the value axis when you create the chart. However, you might want to adjust the value axis so that the numbers displayed are simplified or fit better on the chart. For example, when working with large values such as 4,567,890, the value axis displays increments, such as 4,000,000 and 5,000,000. You can simplify the value axis by displaying values in millions, so that the values on the axis are 4 and 5 with the word Millions placed by the value axis to indicate the units. Use the Format Axis task pane to specify the bounds, units, display units, labels, and number formatting for an axis.

To format an axis, complete the following steps:

1. Double-click the axis to open the Format Axis task pane (see Figure 3.29).

2. Click the Axis Options icon, and complete any of the following steps:
   - Change the bounds, units, and display units. The Minimum Bound sets the starting value, and the Maximum Bound sets the ending value on the value axis. The Major Units specifies the intervals of values on the value axis. The Display units converts the values, such as to Millions.
   - Click Tick Marks to change the major and minor tick marks.
   - Click Labels to change the label position.
   - Click Number to change the category, specify the number of decimal places, select how negative numbers display. The Category option specifies the number formatting, such as Currency. Depending on the category, other options may display, such as Decimal places so that you can control the number of decimal places on the value axis.

3. Close the Format Axis task pane.

4. Click the Home tab and apply font formatting, such as Font Color.

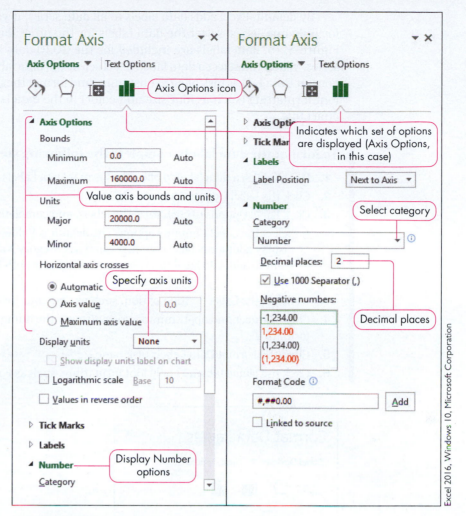

FIGURE 3.29 Format Axis Task Pane

> **TIP: DISPLAYING OPTIONS WITHIN TASK PANES**
> A diagonal black triangle next to a category, such as Axis Options, indicates that all of a category's options are displayed (expanded). A triangle with a white fill, such as the one next to Tick Marks, indicates that the category options are not displayed (collapsed).

Add, Position, and Format Data Labels

STEP 3 ➤➤ A data label is descriptive text that shows the exact value or name of a data point. Data labels are useful to indicate specific values for data points you want to emphasize. Typically, you would add data labels only to specific data points, and not all data points. Use either Chart Elements or the Design tab to display data labels.

To add and position data labels, complete the following steps:

1. Select the chart and click Chart Elements to the right of the chart.
2. Click the Data Labels check box to display data labels.
3. Click the arrow to the right of the Data Labels item to select the position, such as Center or Outside End.
4. Click Chart Elements to close the menu.

By default, Excel adds data labels to all data series. If you want to display data labels for only one series, select the data labels for the other data series and press Delete. In Figure 3.26, data labels are included for the 2020 data series but not the 2010 data series. When you select a data label, Excel selects all data labels in that data series. Use the Format Data Labels task pane to customize and format the data labels. You can also apply font formatting (such as font size and color) to the data labels similarly to formatting a chart title.

To format the data labels, complete the following steps:

1. Double-click a data label to open the Format Data Labels task pane (see Figure 3.30).
2. Click the Label Options icon.
3. Click Label Options to customize the labels, and complete any of the following steps:
   - Select the Label Contains option. The default is Value, but you might want to display additional label contents, such as Category Name. For example, you might want to add data labels to a pie chart to indicate both Percentage and Category Names.
   - Select the Label Position option, such as Center or Inside End.
4. Click Number and apply number formatting if the numeric data labels are not formatted.
5. Close the Format Data Labels task pane.
6. Click the Home tab and apply font formatting, such as Font Color.

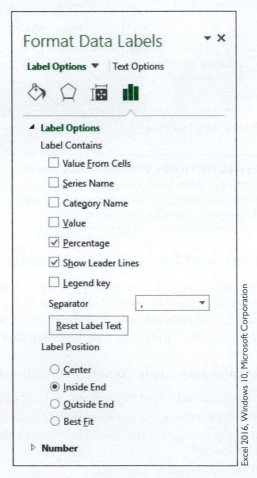

FIGURE 3.30 Format Data Labels Task Pane

Position and Format the Legend

When you create a multiple series chart, the legend displays, providing a key to the color-coded data series. Position the legend to the right, top, bottom, or left of the plot area, similarly to choosing the position for a chart title using Chart Elements. Make sure that the columns, bars, or lines appear proportionate and well balanced after you position the legend. Use the Format Legend task pane to customize and format the legend.

To format the legend, complete the following steps:

1. Double-click the legend to open the Format Legend task pane.
2. Click the Legend Options icon.
3. Select the position of the legend: Top, Bottom, Left, Right, or Top Right.
4. Click the Fill & Line icon, click Border, and set border options if you want to change the border settings for the legend.
5. Close the Format Legend task pane.
6. Click the Home tab and apply font formatting, such as Font Color.

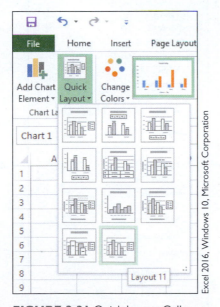

FIGURE 3.31 Quick Layout Gallery

Add and Format Gridlines

Gridlines are horizontal or vertical lines that span across the plot area of the chart to help people identify the values plotted by the visual elements, such as a column. Excel displays horizontal gridlines for column, line, scatter, stock, surface, and bubble charts and vertical gridlines for bar charts. Click either Chart Elements or Add Chart Elements in the Chart Layouts group on the Design tab to add gridlines.

Format gridlines by double-clicking a gridline to open the Format Major Gridlines task pane. You can change the line type, color, and width of the gridlines.

> **TIP: ALTERNATIVE FOR OPENING FORMAT TASK PANES**
> Another way to display a task pane is to right-click the chart element and choose Format <element>, where <element> is the specific chart element. If you do not close a task pane after formatting a particular element, such as gridlines, and then click another chart element, the task pane will change so that you can format that particular chart element.

Format the Chart Area, Plot Area, and Data Series

STEP 4 >> Apply multiple settings, such as fill colors and borders, at once using the Format task pane for an element. To open a chart element's task pane, double-click the chart element. Figure 3.32 displays the Format Chart Area, Format Plot Area, and Format Data Series task panes with different fill options selected to display the different options that result. All three task panes include the same fill and border elements. For example, you might want to change the fill color of a data series from blue to green. After you select a fill option, such as *Gradient fill*, the remaining options change in the task pane.

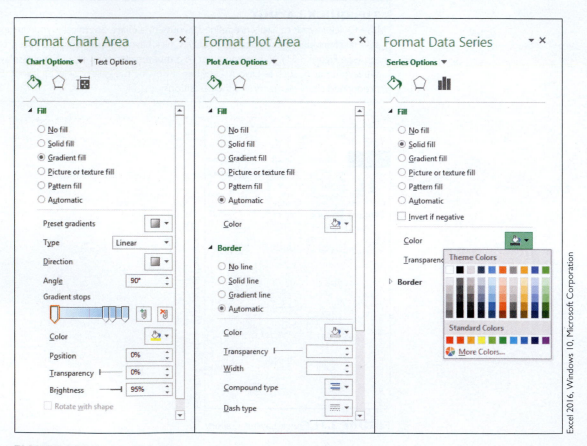

FIGURE 3.32 Format Task Panes

Excel 2016, Windows 10, Microsoft Corporation

Format a Data Point

Earlier in this chapter, you learned that a data point reflects a value in a single cell in a worksheet. You can select that single data point in a chart and format it differently from the rest of the data series. Select the data point you want to format, display the Format Data Point task pane, and make the changes you want. For example, you might want to focus a person's attention on a particular slice by separating one or more slices from the rest of the chart in an ***exploded pie chart*** (refer to Figure 3.15).

To format a pie slice data point, complete the following steps:

1. Click within the pie chart, pause, and then click the particular slice you want to format.
2. Right-click the selected pie slice and select Format Data Point to open the Format Data Point task pane.
3. Click the Fill & Line icon and click the desired option (such as Solid fill) in the Fill category.
4. Click the Color arrow and select a color for a solid fill; select a *Preset gradient*, type, color, and other options for a gradient fill; or insert a picture or select a texture for a picture or texture fill.
5. Click the Series Options icon and drag the Point Explosion to the right to explode the selected pie slice, such as to 12% (see Figure 3.33).
6. Close the Format Data Point task pane.

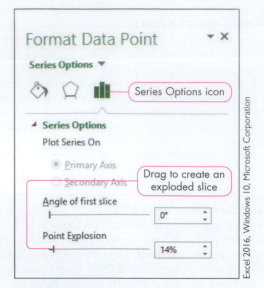

FIGURE 3.33 Format Data Point Task Pane

> **TIP: DRAG TO EXPLODE A PIE SLICE**
> Another way to explode a pie slice is to select the specific slice and then drag it away from the pie.

Use the Chart Tools Format Tab

The Format tab contains options to select a chart element, insert shapes, apply shape styles, apply WordArt styles, arrange objects, and specify the size of an object. Table 3.5 lists and describes the groups on the Format tab.

TABLE 3.5	Chart Tools Format Tab
Group	**Description**
Current Selection	Selects a chart element, displays the task pane to format the selected element, and clears custom formatting of the selected element.
Insert Shapes	Inserts a variety of shapes in a chart.
Shape Styles	Specifies a shape style, fill color, outline color, and shape effect.
WordArt Styles	Adds artistic style, text fill, and text effects to an object.
Arrange	Brings an object forward or backward to layer multiple objects; aligns, groups, and rotates objects.
Size	Adjusts the height and width of the selected object.

Quick Concepts

5. List at least four types of appropriate labels that describe chart elements. What types of things can you do to customize these labels? ***p. 224***

6. What is the purpose of exploding a slice on a pie chart? ***p. 233***

7. What are some of the fill options you can apply to a chart area or a plot area? ***p. 232***

Watch the Video for this Hands-On Exercise!

MyITLab®
HOE2 Training

Skills covered: Edit and Format Chart Titles • Add and Format Axes Titles • Format Axes • Add, Position, and Format Data Labels • Format the Chart Area • Format a Data Point

2 Chart Elements

You want to enhance the computer job column, bar, and pie charts by adding some chart elements. In particular, you will enter a descriptive chart title for each chart, add and format axis titles for the bar chart, add and format data labels for the pie chart, and change fill colors in the pie chart.

STEP 1 ›› EDIT AND FORMAT CHART TITLES

When you created the column, bar, and pie charts in Hands-On Exercise 1, Excel displayed *Chart Title* at the top of each chart. You will add a title that appropriately describes each chart. In addition, you want to format the chart titles by applying bold and enlarging the font sizes. Refer to Figure 3.34 as you complete Step 1.

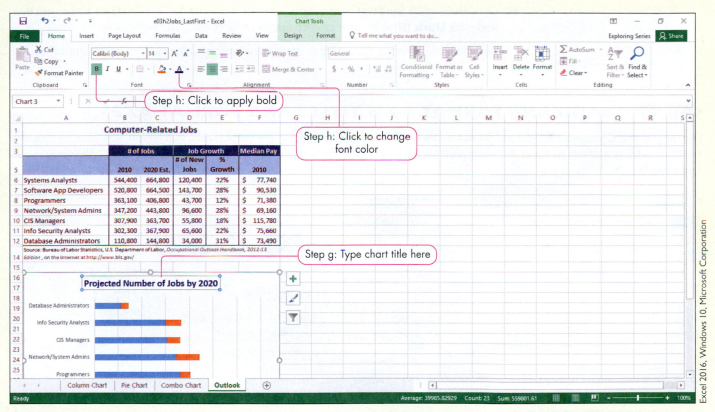

FIGURE 3.34 Formatted Chart Title

a. Open *e03h1Jobs_LastFirst* if you closed it at the end of the Hands-On Exercise 1, and save it as **e03h2Jobs_LastFirst**, changing h1 to h2.

b. Make sure the Combo Chart sheet is the active sheet, select the **Chart Title** placeholder, type **Number of New Computer-Related Jobs by 2020**, and then press **Enter**.

As you type a chart title, Excel displays the text in the Formula Bar. The text does not appear in the chart title until after you press Enter.

> **TROUBLESHOOTING:** If you double-click a title and type directly into the title placeholder, do not press Enter after typing the new title. Doing so will add a blank line.

c. Click the **Home tab**, click **Bold**, click the **Font Color arrow**, and then select **Black, Text 1**.

You applied font formats so that the chart title stands out.

d. Click the **Pie Chart sheet tab**, select the **Chart Title** placeholder, type **New Computer-Related Jobs by 2020**, and then press **Enter**.

Excel displays the text you typed for the chart title.

e. Click the **Home tab**, click **Bold**, click the **Font Size arrow** and select **18**, and then click the **Font Color arrow** and select **Black, Text 1**.

You formatted the pie chart title so that it stands out.

f. Click the **Column Chart sheet tab**, select the **Chart Title** placeholder, type **Number of Computer-Related Jobs 2010 and 2020**, and then press **Enter**. Click **Bold**, click the **Font Size arrow**, and then select **18**. Click the **Font Color arrow** and click **Black, Text 1** font color to the chart title.

g. Click the **Outlook sheet tab**, select the **Chart Title** placeholder, type **Projected Number of Jobs by 2020**, and then press **Enter**.

h. Click **Bold**, click the **Font Size arrow**, and then select **14**. Click the **Font Color arrow** and click **Dark Blue** in the Standard Colors section. Save the workbook.

You formatted the bar chart title to have a similar font color as the worksheet title.

STEP 2 ›› ADD AND FORMAT AXIS TITLES AND FORMAT AXES

For the bar chart, you want to add and format a title to describe the job titles on the vertical axis. In addition, you want to simplify the horizontal axis values to avoid displaying *,000* for each increment and add the title *Thousands*. Refer to Figure 3.35 as you complete Step 2.

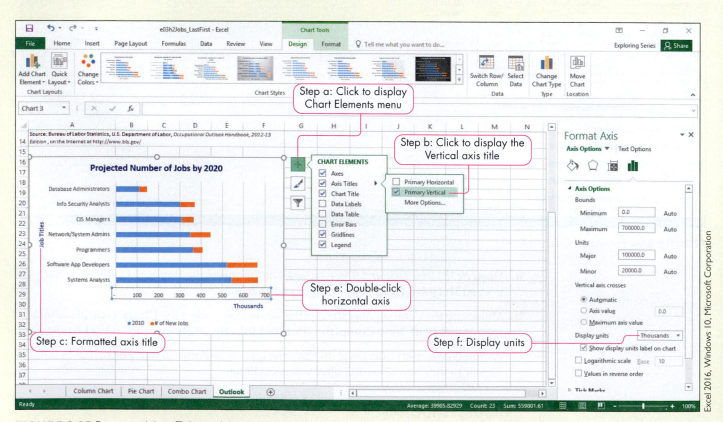

FIGURE 3.35 Formatted Axis Titles and Axes

a. Ensure that the bar chart is selected in the Outlook worksheet and click **Chart Elements** to the right of the chart.

Excel displays the Chart Elements menu.

b. Point to **Axis Titles**, click the **Axis Titles arrow**, and then click the **Primary Vertical check box** to select it. Close the menu.

Excel displays Axis Title on the left side of the vertical axis.

c. Ensure that the Axis Title placeholder is selected, type **Job Titles**, and then press **Enter**.

d. Click **Font Color** to apply the default Dark Blue font color to the selected axis title.

e. Point to the **horizontal axis**. When you see the ScreenTip, Horizontal (Value) Axis, double-click the values on the horizontal axis.

The Format Axis task pane opens for you to format the value axis.

f. Click the **Display units arrow** and select **Thousands**.

> **TROUBLESHOOTING:** If the Display units is not shown, click the Axis Options icon, and click Axis Options to display the options.

The axis now displays values such as 700 instead of 700,000. The title Thousands displays in the bottom-right corner of the horizontal axis.

g. Click the **Home tab**, select the title **Thousands**, and then apply **Dark Blue font color** in the Font group. Close the Format Axis task pane. Save the workbook.

STEP 3 ›› ADD AND FORMAT DATA LABELS

The pie chart includes a legend to identify which color represents each computer-related job; however, it does not include numerical labels to help you interpret what percentage of all computer-related jobs will be hired for each position. You want to insert and format percentage value labels. Refer to Figure 3.36 as you complete Step 3.

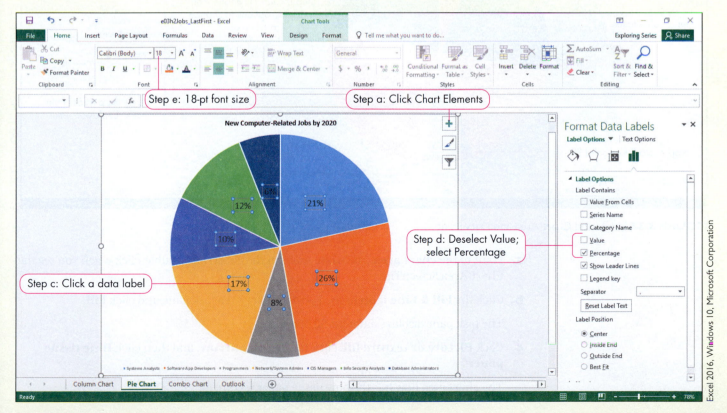

FIGURE 3.36 Formatted Data Labels

a. Click the **Pie Chart sheet tab** and click **Chart Elements**.

b. Click the **Data Labels arrow** and select **Center**. Close the Chart Elements menu.

You added data labels to the pie slices. The default data labels show the number of new jobs in the pie slices.

c. Right-click one of the data labels and select **Format Data Labels** to open the Format Data Label task pane.

d. Click **Label Options**, click the **Percentage check box** to select it, and then click the **Value check box** to deselect it. Close the Format Data Labels task pane.

Typically, pie chart data labels show percentages instead of values.

e. Change the font size to **18** to make the data labels larger. Save the workbook.

STEP 4 ›› **FORMAT THE CHART AREA AND A DATA POINT**

You want to apply a texture fill to the chart area and change the fill colors for the Software Apps Developers and the Database Administrators slices. Refer to Figure 3.37 as you complete Step 4.

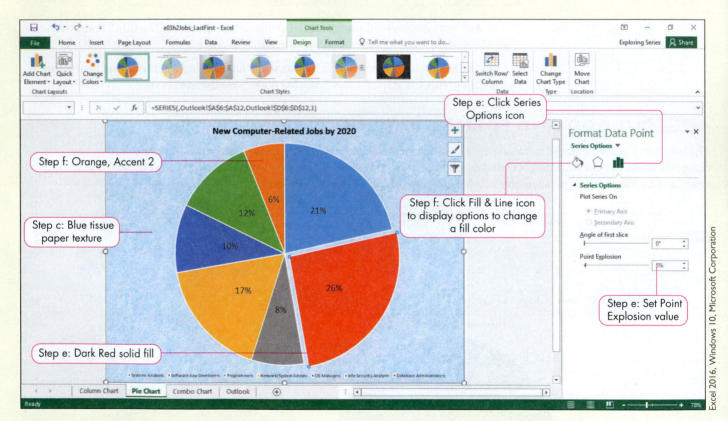

FIGURE 3.37 Formatted Chart Area and Data Point

a. Point to the **chart area** (the white space in the chart) and double-click when you see the Chart Area ScreenTip.

b. Click the **Fill & Line icon** in the Format Chart Area task pane and click **Fill**.

The task pane displays different fill options.

c. Click **Picture or texture fill**, click the **Texture arrow**, and then click **Blue tissue paper**.

The chart area now has the blue tissue paper texture fill.

d. Click the **26% Orange, Accent 2 slice**, pause, and then click the **26% Orange, Accent 2 slice** again to select just that data point (slice).

The first click selects all slices of the pie. The second click selects only the Software App Developers slice so that you can format that data point. Because you did not close the Format Chart Area task pane after Step c, Excel changes to the Format Data Point task pane when you select a data point.

e. Complete the following steps to format the selected data point:

- Click the **Fill & Line icon**, click **Solid fill**, click the **Color arrow**, and then click **Dark Red** in the Standard Colors section.
- Click the **Series Options icon** in the Format Data Point task pane and click the **Point Explosion increment** to **5%**.

You changed the fill color and exploded the slice for the selected data point.

f. Click the **6% Database Administrators slice**, click the **Fill & Line icon** in the Format Data Point task pane, click **Solid fill**, click the **Color arrow**, and then click **Orange, Accent 2**. Close the Format Data Point task pane.

The new color for the Database Administrators slice makes it easier to read the percentage data label.

g. Save the workbook. Keep the workbook open if you plan to continue with the next Hands-On Exercise. If not, close the workbook and exit Excel.

Chart Design and Sparklines

After you add and format chart elements, you might want to experiment with other features to enhance a chart. The Chart Tools Design tab contains two other groups: Chart Styles and Data. These groups enable you to apply a different style or color scheme to a chart or manipulate the data that are used to build a chart. You can also click Chart Styles and Chart Filters to the right of a chart to change the design of a chart.

At times, you might want to insert small visual chart-like images within worksheet cells to illustrate smaller data series rather than a large chart to illustrate several data points. Excel enables you to create small chart-like images in close proximity to individual data points to help you visualize the data.

In this section, you will learn how to apply chart styles and colors, filter chart data, and insert and customize miniature charts (sparklines) within individual cells.

Applying a Chart Style and Colors

STEP 1 ≫ A *chart style* is a collection of formatting that controls the color of the chart area, plot area, and data series. Styles, such as flat, 3-D, or beveled, also affect the look of the data series. Figure 3.38 shows the options when you click Chart Styles to the right of the chart, and Figure 3.39 shows the Chart Styles gallery that displays when you click Chart Styles on the Design tab. The styles in the Chart Styles gallery reflect what is available for the currently selected chart, such as a pie chart. If you select a different type of chart, the gallery will display styles for that particular type of chart.

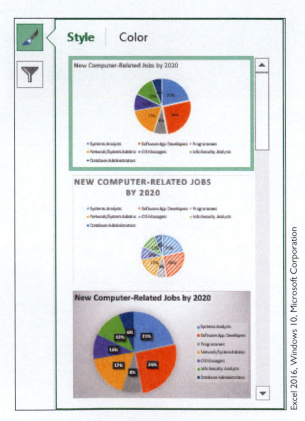

FIGURE 3.38 Chart Styles

Excel 2016, Windows 10, Microsoft Corporation

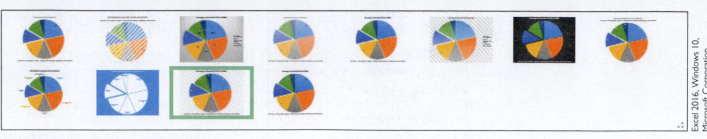

FIGURE 3.39 Chart Styles Gallery

Excel 2016, Windows 10, Microsoft Corporation

> **TIP: CHOOSING APPROPRIATE CHART STYLES**
> When choosing a chart style, make sure the style complements the chart data and is easy to read. Also, consider whether you will display the chart onscreen in a presentation or print the chart. If you will display the chart in a presentation, consider selecting a style with a black background.

To change the color scheme of the chart, complete the following steps:

1. Click Chart Styles to the right of the chart.
2. Click Color or click Change Colors in the Chart Styles group on the Design tab.
3. Select from the Colorful and Monochromatic sections.

Modifying the Data Source

The data source is the range of worksheet cells that are used to construct a chart. Although you should select the data source carefully before creating a chart, you may decide to alter that data source after you create and format the chart. The Data group on the Design tab is useful for adjusting the data source. Furthermore, you can apply filters to display or hide a data series without adjusting the entire data source.

Apply Chart Filters

STEP 2 ❱❱ A *chart filter* controls which data series and categories are visible in a chart. By default, all the data you selected to create the chart are used to construct the data series and categories. However, you can apply a chart filter to focus on particular data. For example, you might want to focus on just one job title at a time. Click Chart Filters to the right of the chart to display the options (see Figure 3.40). A check mark indicates the data series or categories currently displayed in the chart. Click a check box to deselect or hide a data series or a category.

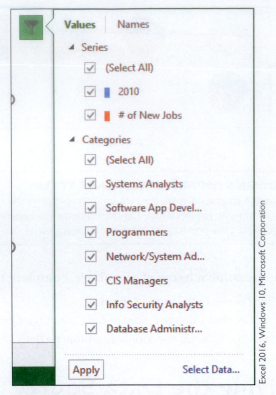

FIGURE 3.40 Chart Filter Options

Click Select Data in the Data group on the Design tab to open the Select Data Source dialog box (see Figure 3.41). This dialog box is another way to filter which categories and data series are visible in your chart. Furthermore, this dialog box enables you to change the chart data range, as well as add, edit, or remove data that is being used to create the chart. For example, you might want to add another data series or remove an existing data series from the chart.

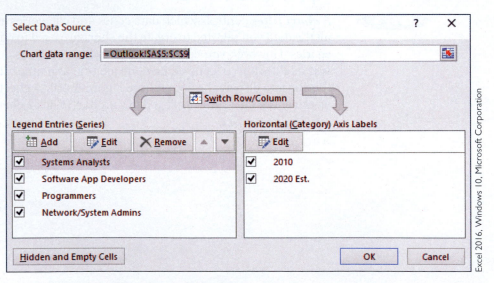

FIGURE 3.41 Select Data Source Dialog Box

Switch Row and Column Data

You might want to switch data used to create the horizontal axis and the legend to give a different perspective and to change the focus on the data. For example, you might want to display years as data series to compare different years for categories, and then you might want to switch the data to show years on the category axis to compare job titles within the same year. In Figure 3.42, the chart on the left uses the job titles to build the data series and legend, and the years display on the horizontal axis. The chart on the right shows the results after switching the data: the job titles build the horizontal axis, and the years build the data series and legend.

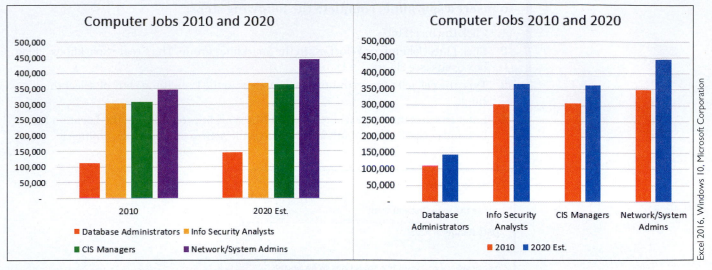

FIGURE 3.42 Original Chart and Chart with Switched Rows/Columns

To switch the row and column data, complete the following steps:

1. Select the chart.
2. Click Switch Row/Column in the Data group on the Design tab.

Creating and Customizing Sparklines

A *sparkline* is a small line, column, or win/loss chart contained in a single cell. The purpose of a sparkline is to present a condensed, simple, succinct visual illustration of data. Unlike a regular chart, a sparkline does not include any of the standard chart labels, such as a chart title, axis label, axis titles, legend, or data labels. Inserting sparklines next to data helps to create a visual "dashboard" to help you understand the data quickly without having to look at a full-scale chart.

Figure 3.43 shows three sample sparklines: line, column, and win/loss. The line sparkline shows trends over time, such as each student's trends in test scores. The column sparkline compares test averages. The win/loss sparkline depicts how many points a team won or lost each game.

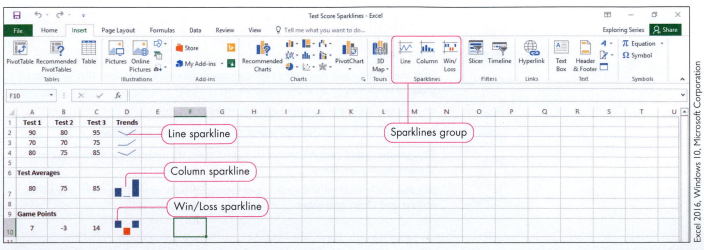

FIGURE 3.43 Sample Sparklines

Insert a Sparkline

STEP 3 ▶▶ Before creating a sparkline, identify the data range you want to depict (such as A2:C2 for the first person's test score) and where you want to place the sparkline (such as cell D2).

> **To insert a sparkline, complete the following steps:**
>
> 1. Click the Insert tab.
> 2. Click Line, Column, or Win/Loss in the Sparklines group. The Create Sparklines dialog box opens (see Figure 3.44).
> 3. Type the cell references containing the values in the Data Range box or select the range.
> 4. Enter or select the range where you want the sparkline to display in the Location Range box and click OK. The default cell location is the active cell unless you change it.

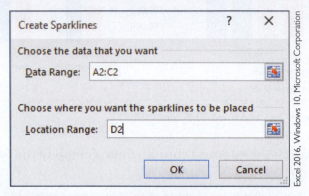

FIGURE 3.44 Create Sparklines Dialog Box

Customize a Sparkline

After you insert a sparkline, the Sparkline Tools Design tab displays (see Figure 3.45), with options to customize the sparkline. Table 3.6 lists and describes the groups on the Sparkline Tools Design tab.

FIGURE 3.45 Sparkline Tools Design Tab

Excel 2016, Windows 10, Microsoft Corporation

TABLE 3.6	Sparkline Tools Design Tab
Group	**Description**
Sparkline	Edits the location and data source for a group or individual data point that generates a group of sparklines or an individual sparkline.
Type	Changes the selected sparkline type (line, column, win/loss).
Show	Displays points, such as the high points, or markers within a sparkline.
Style	Changes the sparkline style, similar to a chart style, changes the sparkline color, or changes the marker color.
Group	Specifies the horizontal and vertical axis settings, groups objects together, ungroups objects, and clears sparklines.

Pearson Education, Inc.

Quick Concepts ✓

8. What are two ways to change the color scheme of a chart? *p. 241*

9. How can you change a chart so that the data in the legend are on the X-axis and the data on the X-axis are in the legend? *pp. 242–243*

10. What is a sparkline, and why would you insert one? *p. 243*

Hands-On Exercises

Skills covered: Apply a Chart Style • Apply Chart Filters • Insert a Sparkline • Customize Sparklines

3 Chart Design and Sparklines

Now that you have completed the pie chart, you want to focus again on the bar chart. You are not satisfied with the overall design and want to try a different chart style. In addition, you would like to include sparklines to show trends for all jobs between 2010 and 2020.

STEP 1 ►► APPLY A CHART STYLE

You want to give more contrast to the bar chart. Therefore, you will apply the Style 2 chart style. That style changes the category axis labels to all capital letters and displays data labels inside each segment of each bar. Refer to Figure 3.46 as you complete Step 1.

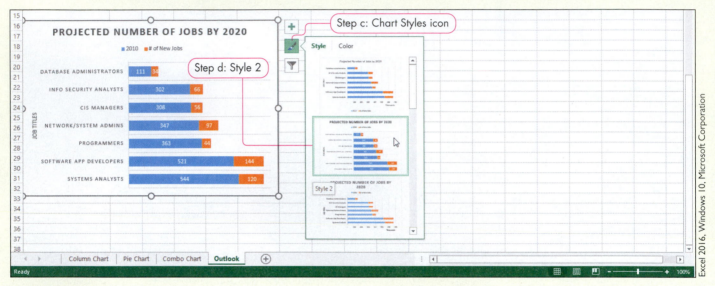

FIGURE 3.46 Chart Style Applied

a. Open *e03h2Jobs_LastFirst* if you closed it at the end of the Hands-On Exercise 2, and save it as **e03h3Jobs_LastFirst**, changing h2 to h3.

b. Click the **Outlook sheet tab** and click the bar chart to select it.

c. Click **Chart Styles** to the right of the chart.

The gallery of chart styles opens.

d. Point to **Style 2**. When you see the ScreenTip that identifies Style 2, click **Style 2**. Click **Chart Styles** to close the gallery. Save the workbook.

Excel applies the Style 2 chart style to the chart, which displays value data labels in white font color within each stack of the bar chart. The chart title and the category labels display in all capital letters. The legend displays above the plot area.

When you first created the clustered column chart, you included the number of new jobs as well as the number of 2010 jobs and the projected number of 2020 jobs. However, you decide that the number of new jobs is implied by comparing the 2010 to the 2020 jobs. Therefore, you want to set a chart filter to exclude the number of new jobs. Refer to Figure 3.47 as you complete Step 2.

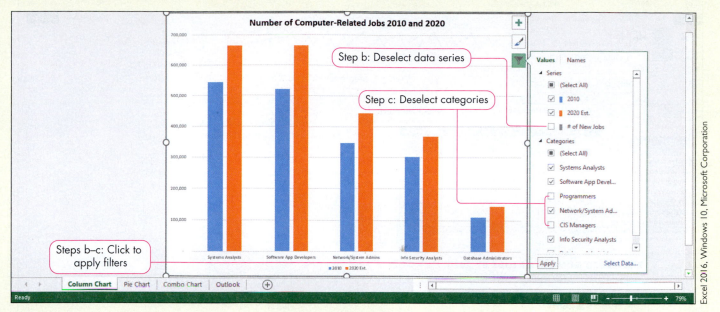

FIGURE 3.47 Chart Filters

a. Click the **Column Chart sheet tab** and click **Chart Filters** on the right of the chart area.

b. Point to the various filter options to see a preview of the filtered data. Click the **# of New Jobs check box** in the Series group to deselect it and click **Apply** at the bottom of the filter window.

The number of new jobs (gray) data series no longer displays in the clustered column chart.

c. Click the **Programmers check box** to deselect the category, click the **CIS Managers check box** to deselect it, and then click **Apply**. Click **Chart Filters** to close the menu. Save the workbook.

The Programmers and CIS Managers categories no longer display in the clustered column chart.

You want to insert sparklines to show the trends between 2010 and 2020. After inserting the sparklines, you want to display the high points to show that all jobs will have major increases by 2020. Refer to Figure 3.48 as you complete Step 3.

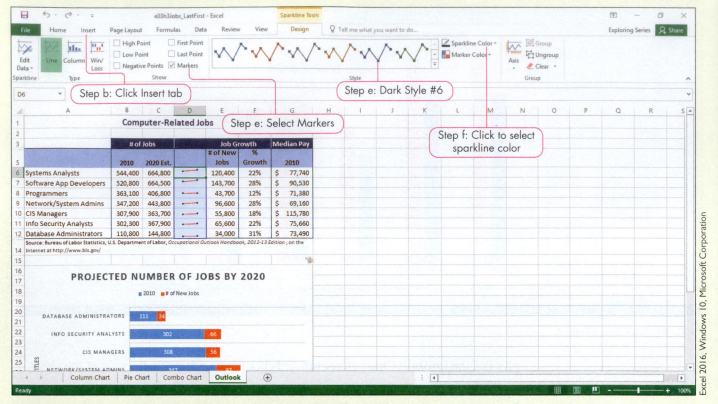

FIGURE 3.48 Sparkline Tools Design Tab

a. Click the **Outlook sheet tab**, select **cell D6**, click the **Insert arrow** in the Cells group, and then select **Insert Sheet Columns**.

   You inserted a new column so that you can place the sparklines close to the data you want to visualize.

b. Click the **Insert tab** and click **Line** in the Sparklines group.

c. Select the **range B6:C12** to enter that range in the Data Range box.

   You selected multiple rows at one time to create a group of sparklines.

d. Press **Tab** and select the **range D6:D12** to enter that range in the Location Range box. Click **OK**.

   Excel inserts sparklines in the range D6:D12 with each sparkline representing data on its respective row. The Sparkline Tools Design tab displays.

e. Click the **Markers check box** in the Show group to select it and click **Sparkline Style Dark #6** in the Style group.

f. Click **Sparkline Color** in the Style group and click **Red** in the Standard Colors section.

g. Click **Axis** in the Group group and click **Same for All Sparklines** in the Vertical Axis Minimum Value Options section. Click **Axis** again and click **Same for All Sparklines** in the Vertical Axis Maximum Value Options section.

   Because the sparklines look identical in trends, you changed the axis settings to set the minimum and maximum values as relative to the sparkline values in the entire selected range of rows rather than the default setting that bases the minimum and maximum for each row.

h. Save and close the file. Based on your instructor's directions, submit e03h3Jobs_LastFirst.

Chapter Objectives Review

After reading this chapter, you have accomplished the following objectives:

1. Select the data source.
- Decide which data you want to include in a chart. Each value is a data point, and several related data points create a data series in a chart.
- Select the range of data, including appropriate labels. The labels become the legend and the category axis.

2. Choose a chart type.
- After selecting a range, click Quick Analysis and click Charts to display a gallery of recommended chart types.
- Create a column chart: A clustered column chart compares groups of side-by-side columns where the height of the column indicates its value. The taller the column, the larger the value. A stacked column chart shows relationships of individual data points to the whole.
- Create a bar chart: A bar chart compares values across categories using horizontal bars where the width of the bar indicates its value. The wider the bar, the larger the value. A stacked bar chart shows relationships of individual data points to the whole.
- Change the chart type: After creating a chart, you might want to change it to a different type by clicking Change Chart Type in the Type group on the Design tab.
- Create a line chart: A line chart compares trends over time. Values are displayed on the value axis, and time periods are displayed on the category axis.
- Create a pie chart: A pie chart indicates the proportion to the whole for one data series. The size of the slice indicates the size of the value. The larger the pie slice, the larger the value.
- Create a combo chart: A combo chart combines elements of two chart types, such as column and line, to depict different data, such as individual data points compared to averages or percentages.
- Create other chart types: An X Y (scatter) chart shows a relationship between two numerical variables. A stock chart shows fluctuations in prices of stock, such as between the opening and closing prices on a particular day.

3. Move, size, and print a chart.
- Move a chart: The Move Chart dialog box enables you to select a new sheet and name the new chart sheet. To move a chart within a worksheet, click and drag the chart to the desired area.
- Size a chart: Adjust the chart size by dragging a sizing handle or specifying exact measurements in the Size group on the Format tab.
- Print a chart: To print a chart with its data series, the chart needs to be on the same worksheet as the data source. To ensure both the data and the chart print, make sure the chart is not selected. If the chart is on its own sheet or if you select the chart on a worksheet containing other data, the chart will print as a full-sized chart.

4. Add, edit, and format chart elements.
- Click Chart Elements to add elements. Chart elements include a chart title, axis titles, data labels, legend, gridlines, chart area, plot area, data series, and data point.
- Edit, format, and position the chart title: The default chart title is Chart Title, but you should edit it to provide a descriptive title for the chart. Apply font formats, such as bold and font size, to the chart title. Position the chart title above the chart, centered and overlaid, or in other locations.
- Add, format, and position axis titles: Display titles for the value and category axes to help describe the axes better. Apply font formats, such as bold and font size, to the axis titles.
- Format the axes: Change the unit of display for the value axis, such as converting values to In Millions.
- Add, position, and format data labels: Data labels provide exact values for a data series. Select the position of the data labels and the content of the data labels. Apply font formats, such as bold and font size, to the data labels.
- Position and format the legend: Position the legend to the right, top, bottom, or left of the plot area. Change the font size to adjust the label sizes within the legend.
- Add and format gridlines: Gridlines help the reader read across a column chart. Adjust the format of the major and minor gridlines.
- Format the chart area, plot area, and data series: The Format task panes enable you to apply fill colors, select border colors, and apply other settings.
- Format a data point: Format a single data point, such as changing the fill color for a single pie slice or specifying the percentage to explode a slice in a pie chart. Apply font formats, such as bold and font size, to the data points.
- Use the Chart Tools Format tab: Use this tab to select a chart element and insert and format shapes.

5. Apply a chart style and colors.
- Apply a chart style: This feature applies predetermined formatting, such as the background color and the data series color.

6. Modify the data source.

- Add or remove data from the data source to change the data in the chart.
- Apply chart filters: The Select Data Source dialog box enables you to modify the ranges used for the data series. When you deselect a series, Excel removes that series from the chart.
- Switch row and column data: You can switch the way data is used to create a chart by switching data series and categories.

7. Create and customize sparklines.

- Create a sparkline: A sparkline is a miniature chart in a cell representing a single data series.
- Customize a sparkline: Change the data source, location, and style. Display markers and change line or marker colors.

Key Terms Matching

Match the key terms with their definitions. Write the key term letter by the appropriate numbered definition.

a. Axis title
b. Bar chart
c. Category axis
d. Chart area
e. Chart title
f. Clustered column chart
g. Combo chart
h. Data label
i. Data point
j. Data series

k. Gridline
l. Legend
m. Line chart
n. Pie chart
o. Plot area
p. Sizing handle
q. Sparkline
r. Task pane
s. Value axis
t. X Y (scatter) chart

1. _____ Chart that groups columns side by side to compare data points among categories. **p. 205**

2. _____ Miniature chart contained in a single cell. **p. 243**

3. _____ Chart type that shows trends over time in which the value axis indicates quantities and the horizontal axis indicates time. **p. 209**

4. _____ Label that describes the entire chart. **p. 224**

5. _____ Label that describes either the category axis or the value axis. **p. 224**

6. _____ Key that identifies the color, gradient, picture, texture, or pattern fill assigned to each data series in a chart. **p. 201**

7. _____ Chart type that compares categories of data horizontally. **p. 208**

8. _____ Chart that shows each data point in proportion to the whole data series. **p. 210**

9. _____ Numeric value that describes a single value on a chart. **p. 200**

10. _____ Chart that contains two chart types, such as column and line, to depict two types of data, such as individual data points and percentages. **p. 211**

11. _____ A circle that enables you to adjust the height or width of a selected chart. **p. 215**

12. _____ Horizontal or vertical line that extends from the horizontal or vertical axis through the plot area. **p. 224**

13. _____ Chart type that shows the relationship between two variables. **p. 212**

14. _____ Group of related data points that display in row(s) or column(s) in a worksheet. **p. 200**

15. _____ Window of options to format and customize chart elements. **p. 226**

16. _____ Provides descriptive labels for the data points plotted in a chart. **p. 201**

17. _____ Section of a chart that contains graphical representation of the values in a data series. **p. 201**

18. _____ A container for the entire chart and all of its elements. **p. 201**

19. _____ An identifier that shows the exact value of a data point in a chart. **p. 224**

20. _____ Displays incremental numbers to identify approximate values, such as dollars or units, of data points in a chart. **p. 201**

Multiple Choice

1. Which type of chart is the *least* appropriate for depicting yearly rainfall totals for five cities for four years?

    (a) Pie chart

    (b) Line chart

    (c) Column chart

    (d) Bar chart

2. Look at the stacked bar chart in Figure 3.35. Which of the following is a category on the category axis?

    (a) Thousands

    (b) Job Titles

    (c) CIS Managers

    (d) 700

3. Which of the following is not a type of sparkline?

    (a) Line

    (b) Bar

    (c) Column

    (d) Win-Loss

4. If you want to show exact values for a data series in a bar chart, which chart element should you display?

    (a) Chart title

    (b) Legend

    (c) Value axis title

    (d) Data labels

5. The value axis currently shows increments such as 50,000 and 100,000. What option would you select to display the values in increments of 50 and 100?

    (a) More Primary Vertical Axis Title Options

    (b) Show Axis in Thousands

    (c) Show Axis in Millions

    (d) Show Right to Left Axis

6. You want to create a single chart that shows the proportion of yearly sales for five divisions for each year for five years. Which type of chart can accommodate your needs?

    (a) Pie chart

    (b) Surface chart

    (c) Clustered bar chart

    (d) 100% stacked column chart

7. Currently, a column chart shows values on the value axis, years on the category axis, and state names in the legend. What should you do if you want to organize data with the states on the category axis and the years shown in the legend?

    (a) Change the chart type to a clustered column chart.

    (b) Click Switch Row/Column in the Data group on the Design tab.

    (c) Click Layout 2 in the Chart Layouts group on the Design tab and apply a different chart style.

    (d) Click Legend in the Labels group on the Layout tab and select Show Legend at Bottom.

8. What do you click to remove a data series from a chart so that you can focus on other data series?

    (a) Chart Elements

    (b) Chart Series

    (c) Chart Filters

    (d) Chart Styles

9. Which of the following does not display automatically when you create a clustered column chart?

    (a) Data labels

    (b) Chart title placeholder

    (c) Gridlines

    (d) Legend

10. After you create a line type sparkline, what option should you select to display dots for each data point?

    (a) High Point

    (b) Negative Point

    (c) Sparkline Color

    (d) Markers

Practice Exercises

1 Hulett Family Utility Expenses

Your cousin, Alex Hulett, wants to analyze his family's utility expenses for 2018. He gave you his files for the electric, gas, and water bills for the year. You created a worksheet that lists the individual expenses per month, along with yearly totals per utility type and monthly totals. You will create some charts to depict the data. Refer to Figure 3.49 as you complete this exercise.

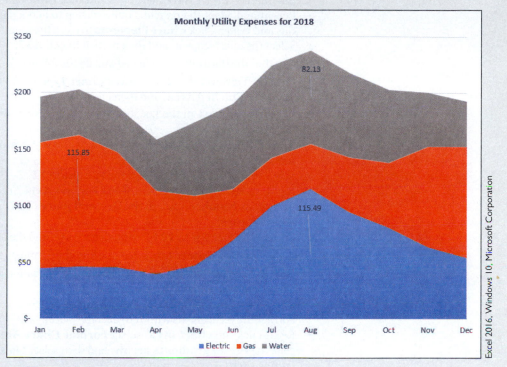

FIGURE 3.49 Hulett Family Utility Expenses

a. Open *e03p1Utilities* and save it as **c03p1Utilities_LastFirst**.

b. Select the **range A4:E17**, click **Quick Analysis**, click **Charts**, and then click **Clustered Column**.

c. Click **Chart Filters** to the right of the chart and do the following:
  - Deselect the **Monthly Totals check box** in the Series group.
  - Scroll through the Categories group and deselect the **Yearly Totals check box**.
  - Click **Apply** to remove totals from the chart. Click **Chart Filters** to close the menu.

d. Point to the **chart area**. When you see the Chart Area ScreenTip, drag the chart so that the top-left corner of the chart is in **cell A21**.

e. Click the **Format tab** and change the size by doing the following:
  - Click in the **Shape Width box** in the Size group, type **6"**, and then press **Enter**.
  - Click in the **Shape Height box** in the Size group, type **3.5"**, and then press **Enter**.

f. Click the **Design tab**, click **Quick Layout** in the Chart Layouts group, and then click **Layout 3**.

g. Select the **Chart Title placeholder**, type **Monthly Utility Expenses for 2018**, and then press **Enter**.

h. Click the chart, click the **More button** in the Chart Styles group, and then click **Style 6**.

i. Click **Copy** on the Home tab, click **cell A39**, and then click **Paste**. With the second chart selected, do the following:

- Click the **Design tab**, click **Change Chart Type** in the Type group, click **Line** on the left side of the dialog box, select **Line with Markers** in the top-center section, and then click **OK**.
- Click the **Electric data series line** to select it and click the highest marker to select only that marker. Click **Chart Elements** and click **Data Labels**.
- Repeat and adapt the previous bulleted step to add a data label to the highest markers for Gas and Water. Click **Chart Elements** to close the menu.
- Select the chart, copy it, and then paste it in **cell A57**.

j. Ensure that the third chart is selected and do the following:

- Click the **Design tab**, click **Change Chart Type** in the Type group, select **Area** on the left side, click **Stacked Area**, and then click **OK**.
- Click **Move Chart** in the Location group, click **New sheet**, type **Area Chart**, and then click **OK**.
- Select each data label and change the font size to **12**. Move each data label up closer to the top of the respective shaded area.
- Select the value axis and change the font size to **12**.
- Right-click the value axis and select **Format Axis**. Scroll down in the Format Axis task pane, click **Number**, click in the **Decimal places box**, and then type **0** . Close the Format Axis task pane.
- Change the font size to **12** for the category axis and the legend.

k. Click the **Expenses sheet tab**, select the line chart, and do the following:

- Click the **Design tab**, click **Move Chart** in the Location group, click **New sheet**, type **Line Chart**, and then click **OK**.
- Change the font size to **12** for the value axis, category axis, data labels, and legend.
- Format the vertical axis with zero decimal places.
- Right-click the **chart area**, select **Format Chart Area**, click **Fill**, click **Gradient fill**, click the **Preset gradients arrow**, and then select **Light Gradient – Accent 1**. Close the Format Chart Area task pane.

l. Click the **Expenses sheet**, select the **range B5:D16** and do the following:

- Click the **Insert tab**, click **Line** in the Sparkline group, click in the **Location Range box**, type **B18:D18**, and then click **OK**.
- Click the **High Point check box** to select it and click the **Low Point check box** to select it in the Show group with all three sparklines selected.

m. Create a footer with your name on the left side, the sheet name code in the center, and the file name code on the right of each sheet.

n. Save and close the file. Based on your instructor's directions, submit e03p1Utilities_LastFirst.

2 Trends in Market Value of Houses on Pine Circle

You live in a house on Pine Circle, a quiet cul-de-sac in a suburban area. Recently, you researched the market value and square footage of the five houses on Pine Circle. Now, you want to create charts to visually depict the data to compare values for the houses in the cul-de-sac. Refer to Figure 3.50 as you complete this exercise.

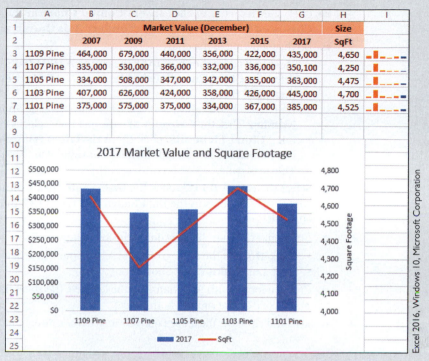

▲	A	B	C	D	E	F	G	H	I
1		Market Value (December)						Size	
2		2007	2009	2011	2013	2015	2017	SqFt	
3	1109 Pine	464,000	679,000	440,000	356,000	422,000	435,000	4,650	
4	1107 Pine	335,000	530,000	366,000	332,000	336,000	350,100	4,250	
5	1105 Pine	334,000	508,000	347,000	342,000	355,000	363,000	4,475	
6	1103 Pine	407,000	626,000	424,000	358,000	426,000	445,000	4,700	
7	1101 Pine	375,000	575,000	375,000	334,000	367,000	385,000	4,525	

Excel 2016, Windows 10, Microsoft Corporation

FIGURE 3.50 Market Values

a. Open *e03p2Pine* and save it as **e03p2Pine_LastFirst**.

b. Select the **range A2:G7**, click **Quick Analysis**, click **Charts**, and then click **Line**.

c. Click **Move Chart** in the Location group, click **New sheet**, type **Line**, and then click **OK**.

d. Select the **Chart Title placeholder** and do the following:
- Type **Market Value of Pine Circle Houses** and press **Enter**.
- Apply bold to the chart title, change the font size to **20**, and then select **Olive Green, Accent 3, Darker 50% font color**.

e. Click the **value axis** on the left side of the chart and do the following:
- Change the font size to 12 and select **Olive Green, Accent 3, Darker 50% font color**.
- Double-click the value axis to open the Format Axis task pane.
- Type **300000** in the Minimum Bounds box and press **Enter**. The Maximum Bounds box should change to 700000 automatically.
- Scroll down in the Format Axis task pane and click **Number** to display those options.
- Click the **Category arrow** and select **Currency**.
- Close the Format Axis task pane.

f. Click **Chart Elements**, click the **Axis Titles triangle**, and then click the **Primary Vertical check box** to select it. Type **December Market Values** in the **Axis Title placeholder** and press **Enter**.

g. Make sure the Chart Elements menu is showing, click the **Gridlines triangle**, and then click the **Primary Minor Horizontal check box** to select it.

h. Click the blue **1109 Pine data series line**, click the **Data Labels check box** to select it, and then click **Chart Elements** to close the menu.

i. Click the data labels you just created, click the **Home tab**, click the **Font Color arrow**, and then select **Blue** in the Standard Colors section.

j. Select the category axis, change the font size to **12**, and select **Olive Green, Accent 3, Darker 50% font color**.

k. Right-click the legend and select **Format Legend**. Click **Top** in the Legend Position section of the Format Legend task pane and close the task pane.

l. Click the **Pine Circle sheet tab** and select the **ranges A2:A7** and **G2:H7**.

m. Click the **Insert tab**, click **Insert Combo Chart** in the Charts group, and then click the **Clustered Column – Line on Secondary Axis thumbnail**.

n. Do the following to the chart:
- Move and resize the chart to fill the **range A10:H25**.
- Select the **Chart Title placeholder**, type **2017 Market Value and Square Footage**, and then press **Enter**.
- Double-click the value axis on the left side, scroll down in the Format Axis task pane, click **Number**, click the **Category arrow**, and then select **Currency**.
- Click **Chart Elements**, click the **Axis Titles triangle**, click the **Secondary Vertical check box** to select it, type **Square Footage**, and then press **Enter**. Close the Format Axis Title task pane.

o. Select the **range B3:G7**, click the **Insert tab**, click **Column** in the Sparklines group, make sure B3:G7 displays in the Data Range box, type **I3:I7** in the Location Range box, and then click **OK**.

p. Customize the sparklines by doing the following:
- Click **More** in the Style group and select **Sparkline Style Accent 6, Darker 25%**.
- Click **Last Point** in the Show group.

q. Create a footer with your name on the left side, the sheet name code in the center, and the file name code on the right of both sheets.

r. Save and close the file. Based on your instructor's directions, submit e03p2Pine_LastFirst.

Mid-Level Exercises

1 Airport Passenger Counts

ANALYSIS CASE

As an analyst for the airline industry, you track the number of passengers at the top five major U.S. airports: Atlanta, Chicago, Los Angeles, Dallas/Fort Worth, and Denver. You researched passenger data at http://www.aci-na.org. One worksheet you created lists the number of total yearly passengers at the top five airports for a six-year period. To prepare for an upcoming meeting, you need to create a clustered column chart to compare the number of passengers at each airport. Next, you will create a bar chart to compare the passenger count for the latest year of data available and then emphasize the airport with the largest number of passenger traffic. Finally, you want to insert sparklines to visually represent trends in passengers at each airport over the six-year period. You can then refer to the sparklines and clustered column chart to write a paragraph analyzing the trends to detect.

a. Open *e03m1Airports* and save it as **e03m1Airports_LastFirst**.

b. Create a clustered column chart for the **range A4:G9**. Position and resize the chart to fit in the **range A15:G34**.

c. Customize the chart by doing the following:
   - Swap the data on the category axis and in the legend.
   - Apply the **Style 6 chart style**.
   - Select **Color 12** in the Monochromatic section of the Change Colors gallery.
   - Apply the **Light Gradient – Accent 1** preset gradient fill to the chart area.

DISCOVER

   - Change the fill color of the 2013 data series to **Dark Blue** and change the fill color of the 2008 data series to **Blue, Accent 5, Lighter 60%**.
   - Use Help and add a solid **Blue border** around the legend.

d. Type **Passengers by Top U.S. Airports** as the chart title. Change the font color to **Blue**.

DISCOVER

e. Adjust the value axis by doing the following:
   - Change the display units to **Millions** for the value axis.
   - Edit the axis title to display **Millions of Passengers**.

f. Display data labels above the columns for the 2013 data series only.

g. Create a clustered bar chart for the **range A5:A9** and **G5:G9** and then do the following:
   - Move the bar chart to a chart sheet named **Bar Chart**.
   - Enter **Passengers at Top 5 U.S. Airports in 2013** as the chart title.
   - Apply the **Style 3 chart style**.
   - Change the font color to **Dark Blue** on the chart title, category axis, and the value axis.
   - Format the Atlanta data point with **Dark Blue fill color**.

h. Display the Passenger worksheet and insert **Line sparklines** in the **range H5:H9** to illustrate the data in the **range B5:G9**. This should insert a sparkline to represent yearly data for each airport.

i. Customize the sparklines by doing the following:
   - Show the high and low points in each sparkline.
   - Apply **Black, Text 1 color** to the high point marker in each sparkline.

DISCOVER

   - Apply **Dark Red color** to the low point marker in each sparkline.

 j. Click **cell A36** and compose a paragraph that analyzes the trends depicted by the airport sparklines. Notice the overall trends in decreased and increased number of passengers and any unusual activity for an airport. Spell-check the worksheet and correct any errors.

k. Set **0.2"** left and right margins and scale to fit to 1 page for the Passenger worksheet.

l. Insert a footer with your name on the left side, the sheet name code in the center, and the file name code on the right on all worksheets.

m. Save and close the file. Based on your instructor's directions, submit e03m1Airports_LastFirst.

You are a teaching assistant for Dr. Monica Unice's introductory psychology class. You have maintained her grade book all semester, entering three test scores for each student and calculating the final average. You created a section called Final Grade Distribution that contains calculations to identify the number of students who earned an A, B, C, D, or F. Dr. Unice wants you to create a chart that shows the percentage of students who earn each letter grade. Therefore, you decide to create and format a pie chart. You will also create a bar chart to show a sample of the students' test scores. Furthermore, Dr. Unice wants to see if a correlation exists between attendance and students' final grades; therefore, you will create a scatter chart depicting each student's percentage of attendance with his or her respective final grade average.

a. Open *e03m2Psych* and save it as **e03m2Psych_LastFirst**.

b. Create a pie chart from the Final Grade Distribution data located below the student data in the **range F38:G42** and move the pie chart to its own sheet named **Grades Pie**.

c. Customize the pie chart with these specifications:
- Apply the **Style 7 chart style.**
- Type **PSY 2030 Final Grade Distribution - Fall 2018** for the chart title.
- Explode the B grade slice by **10%**.
- Remove the legend.

d. Add centered data labels and customize the labels with these specifications:
- Display these data labels: **Percentage** and **Category Name**. Remove other data labels.
- Change the font size to **20** and apply **Black, Text 1** font color.

e. Create a clustered bar chart using the **range A7:D12** and move the bar chart to its own sheet named **Students Bar Chart**.

f. Customize the bar chart with these specifications:
- Apply the **Style 5 chart style**.
- Type **Sample Student Test Scores** for the chart title.
- Position the legend on the right side.
- Add data labels in the Outside End position for the Final Exam data series.
- Arrange the categories in reverse order so that Atkin is listed at the top and Ethington is listed at the bottom of the bar chart.

DISCOVER **g.** Create a scatter chart using the **range E7:F33**, the attendance record and final averages from
DISCOVER the Grades worksheet. Move the scatter chart to its own sheet named **Scatter Chart**.

h. Apply these label settings to the scatter chart:
- Remove the legend.
- Type **Attendance-Final Average Relationship** for the chart title.
- Add the following primary horizontal axis title: **Percentage of Attendance**.
- Add the following primary vertical axis title: **Student Final Averages**.

DISCOVER **i.** Use Help to learn how to apply the following axis settings:
- Vertical axis: 40 minimum bound, 100 maximum bound, 10 major units, and a number format with zero decimal places
- Horizontal axis: 40 minimum bound, 100 maximum bound, automatic units

j. Change the font size to **12** on the vertical axis title, vertical axis, horizontal axis title, and horizontal axis. Bold the chart title and the two axes titles.

k. Add the **Parchment texture fill** to the plot area.

l. Insert a linear trendline.

m. Insert Line sparklines in the **range H8:H33** using the three tests score columns. Change the sparkline color to **Purple** and show the low points.

n. Insert a footer with your name on the left, the sheet name code in the center, and the file name code on the right on all the sheets.

o. Save and close the file. Based on your instructor's directions, submit e03m2Psych_LastFirst.

3 Box Office Movies

You and two of your friends like to follow the popularity of new movies at the theater. You will research current movies that have been showing for four weeks and decide which movies on which to report. Work in teams of three for this activity. After obtaining the data, your team will create applicable charts to illustrate the revenue data. Team members will critique each other's charts.

a. Have all three team members log in to a chat client and engage in a dialogue about which movies are currently playing. Each member should research a different theater to see what is playing at that theater. Decide on six movies that have been in theaters for at least four weeks to research. Save a copy of your instant message dialogue and submit based on your instructor's directions.

b. Divide the six movies among the three team members. Each member should research the revenue reported for two movies for the past four weeks. Make sure your team members use the same source to find the data.

Student 1:

c. Create a new Excel workbook and enter appropriate column labels and the four-week data for all six movies. Name Sheet1 **Data**.

d. Format the data appropriately. Save the workbook as **e03m3Movies_GroupName**. Upload the workbook to a shared location, such as OneDrive, invite the other students to share this location, and send a text message to the next student.

Student 2:

e. Create a line chart to show the trends in revenue for the movies for the four-week period.

f. Add a chart title, format the axes appropriately, select a chart style, and then apply other formatting.

g. Move the chart to its own sheet named **Trends**. Save the workbook, upload it to the shared location, and send a text message to the next student.

Student 3:

h. Add a column to the right of the four-week data and total each movie's four-week revenue.

i. Create a pie chart depicting each movie's percentage of the total revenue for your selected movies.

j. Add a chart title, explode one pie slice, add data labels showing percentages and movie names, and then apply other formatting.

k. Move the chart to its own sheet named **Revenue Chart**. Save the workbook, upload it to the shared location, and send a text message to the next student.

Student 1:

l. Critique the charts. Insert a new worksheet named **Chart Critique** that provides an organized critique of each chart. Type notes that list each team member's name and specify what each student's role was in completing this exercise.

m. Save the workbook, upload it to the shared location, and send a text message to the next student.

Student 2:

n. Read the critique of the line chart and make any appropriate changes for the line chart. On the critique worksheet, provide a response to each critique and why you made or did not make the suggested change.

o. Save the workbook, upload it to the shared location, and send a text message to the next student.

Student 3:

p. Read the critique of the pie chart and make any appropriate changes for the pie chart. On the critique worksheet, provide a response to each critique and why you made or did not make the suggested change.

q. Save and close the file. Based on your instructor's directions, submit e03m3Movies_GroupName.

Beyond the Classroom

Historical Stock Prices

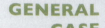

GENERAL CASE

FROM SCRATCH

You are interested in investing in the stock market. First, you need to research the historical prices for a particular stock. Launch a Web browser, go to finance.yahoo.com, type a company name, such as Apple, and then select the company name from a list of suggested companies. Click the Historical Prices link. Copy the stock data (date, high, low, open, close, volume) for a six-month period and paste it in a new workbook, adjusting the column widths to fit the data. Save the workbook as **e03b1StockData_LastFirst**. Rename Sheet1 **Data**. Display data for only the first date listed for each month; delete rows containing data for other dates. Sort the list from the oldest date to the newest date. Use Help if needed to learn how to sort data and how to create a Volume-Open-High-Low-Close chart. Then rearrange the data columns in the correct sequence. Format the data and column labels.

Insert a row to enter the company name and insert another row to list the company's stock symbol, such as AAPL. Copy the URL from the Web browser and paste it as a source below the list of data and the date you obtained the data. Merge the cells containing the company name and stock symbol through the last column of data and word-wrap the URL.

Create a Volume-Open-High-Low-Close chart on a new chart sheet named **Stock Chart**. Type an appropriate chart title. Set the primary vertical axis (left side) unit measurement to millions and include an axis title **Volume in Millions**. Include a secondary vertical axis (right side) title **Stock Prices**. Apply the Currency number style with 0 decimal places for the secondary axis values. Change the font size to 11 and the font color to Black, Text 1 on the vertical axes and category axis. Hide the legend.

Use Help to research how to insert text boxes. Insert a text box that describes the stock chart: white fill rectangles indicate the closing price was higher than the opening price; black fill rectangles indicate the closing price was lower than the opening price; etc. Create a footer with your name, the sheet name code, and the file name code on both worksheets. Save and close the file. Based on your instructor's directions, submit e03b1StockData_LastFirst.

Harper County Houses Sold

DISASTER RECOVERY

You want to analyze the number of houses sold by type (e.g., rambler, two story, etc.) in each quarter in Harper County. You entered quarterly data for 2018, calculated yearly total number of houses sold by each type, and quarterly total number of houses sold. You asked an intern to create a stacked column chart for the data, but the chart contains a lot of errors.

Open *e03b2Houses* and save it as **e03b2Houses_LastFirst**. Identify the errors and poor design for the chart. Below the chart, list the errors and your corrections in a two-column format. Then correct the problems in the chart. Link the chart title to the cell containing the most appropriate label in the worksheet. Create a footer with your name, the sheet name code, and the file name code. Adjust the margins and scaling to print the worksheet data, including the error list, and the chart on one page. Save and close the file. Based on your instructor's directions, submit e03b2Houses_LastFirst.

Capstone Exercise

You are an analyst for the airline industry. You created a workbook that lists overall airline arrival statistics for several years. In particular, you listed the percentage and number of on-time arrivals, late arrivals, canceled flights, and diverted flights based on information provided by the Bureau of Transportation Statistics. You want to create charts and insert sparklines that show the trends to discuss with airline and airport managers.

Insert and Format Sparklines

The first dataset shows the percentages. You want to insert sparklines that show the trends in the five-year data. The sparklines will help show any trends in on-time arrivals compared to late arrivals, canceled flights, and diverted flights.

a. Open the *e03c1Arrivals* workbook and save it as **e03c1Arrivals_LastFirst**.

b. Insert Line sparklines in the **range G4:G7**, using the data for the five years.

c. Display the high and low points for the sparklines.

d. Change the high point marker color to **Green**.

Create a Pie Chart

You want to focus on the arrival percentages for 2014. Creating a pie chart will help people visualize the breakdown of all operations for that year. After you create the chart, you will move it to its own chart sheet and edit the chart title to reflect 2014 flight arrivals.

a. Select the **range A4:A7** and the **range F4:F7**.

b. Create a pie chart and move it to a chart sheet named **Pie Chart**.

c. Change the chart title to **2014 Flight Arrivals**.

Add and Format Chart Elements

You want to format the chart by applying a different chart style and positioning the legend above the plot area. Furthermore, you need to add data labels so that you will know the percentages for the arrival categories. Finally, you want to emphasize the canceled flights in Dark Red and explode the late arrival pie slice.

a. Apply the **Style 12 chart style** to the pie chart.

b. Format the chart title with **Blue font color**.

c. Position the legend between the chart title and the plot area.

d. Add data labels to the Best Fit position and display.

e. Apply bold to the data labels and change the font size to **12**.

f. Format the Canceled data point with **Dark Red fill color** and format the Late Arrival data point in **Green**.

g. Explode the Late Arrival data point by **5%**.

Create and Size a Column Chart

To provide a different perspective, you will create a clustered column chart using the actual number of flights. The Total Operations row indicates the total number of reported (scheduled) flights. After creating the chart, you will position and size the chart below the source rows.

a. Create a clustered column chart using the **range A10:F15** in the Arrivals sheet.

b. Edit the chart title: **On-Time and Late Flight Arrivals**.

c. Position the clustered column chart so that the top-left corner is in **cell A20**.

d. Change the width to **5.75"** and the height to **3.5"**.

Format the Column Chart

Now that you have created the column chart, you realize that some data seems irrelevant. You will filter out the unneeded data, format the value axis to remove digits, insert a vertical axis title, apply a color change, and format the chart area.

a. Apply chart filters to remove the canceled, diverted, and total operations data.

b. Select the value axis, set **500000** for the Major unit, display the axis units **in Millions**, select category **Number** format with **1** decimal place.

c. Add a primary vertical axis title **Number of Flights**.

d. Apply the **Color 2 chart color** to the chart.

e. Apply the **Light Gradient – Accent 3** fill to the chart area.

Finalizing the Workbook

You want to prepare the workbook in case someone wants to print the data and charts. The margins and scaling have already been set. You just need to insert a footer.

a. Create a footer on each worksheet with your name, the sheet name code, and the file name code.

b. Save and close the file. Based on your instructor's direction, submit e03c1Arrivals_LastFirst.

Datasets and Tables

LEARNING OUTCOME

You will demonstrate how to manage and analyze large sets of data.

OBJECTIVES & SKILLS: After you read this chapter, you will be able to:

CASE STUDY | Reid Furniture Store

Vicki Reid owns Reid Furniture Store in Portland, Oregon. She divided her store into four departments: Living Room, Bedroom, Dining Room, and Appliances. All merchandise is categorized into one of these four departments for inventory records and sales. Vicki has four sales representatives: Chantalle Desmarais, Jade Gallagher, Sebastian Gruenewald, and Ambrose Sardelis. The sales system tracks which sales representative processed each transaction.

The business has grown rapidly, and Vicki hired you to analyze the sales data in order to increase future profits. For example, which department generates the most sales? Who is the leading salesperson? Do most customers purchase or finance? Are sales promotions necessary to promote business, or will customers pay the full price?

You downloaded March 2018 data from the sales system into an Excel workbook. To avoid extraneous data that is not needed in the analysis, you did not include customer names, accounts, or specific product numbers. The downloaded file contains transaction numbers, dates, sales representative names, departments, general merchandise descriptions, payment types, transaction types, and the total price.

Managing Large Volumes of Data

CHAPTER 4

Page 1 — March Totals worksheet

Trans_No	Operator	Sales_First	Sales_Last	Date	Department	Furniture	Pay_Type	Trans_Type	Amount
						Reid Furniture Store			
				Monthly Transactions:		March 2018			
				Down Payment Requirement:		25%			
2018-001	KRM	Sebastian	Gruenewald	3/1/2018	Bedroom	Mattress	Finance	Promotion	2,788
2018-002	RKM	Sebastian	Gruenewald	3/1/2018	Bedroom	Mattress	Finance	Promotion	3,245
2018-003	MAP	Jade	Gallagher	3/1/2018	Living Room	Sofa, Loveseat, Chair Package	Finance	Promotion	10,000
2018-004	MAP	Jade	Gallagher	3/1/2018	Living Room	End Tables	Finance	Promotion	1,000
2018-005	MAP	Jade	Gallagher	3/1/2018	Appliances	Washer and Dryer	Finance	Promotion	2,750
2018-006	COK	Ambrose	Sardelis	3/1/2018	Living Room	Sofa, Loveseat, Chair Package	Finance	Promotion	12,000
2018-006	COK	Ambrose	Sardelis	3/1/2018	Living Room	Sofa, Loveseat, Chair Package	Finance	Promotion	12,000
2018-007	MAP	Jade	Gallagher	3/1/2018	Dining Room	Dining Room Table	Finance	Promotion	3,240
2018-008	COK	Chantalle	Desmarais	3/1/2018	Dining Room	Dining Room Table	Finance	Promotion	4,080
2018-009	KRM	Sebastian	Gruenewald	3/1/2018	Appliances	Washer and Dryer	Finance	Promotion	2,750
2018-010	MAP	Jade	Gallagher	3/2/2018	Dining Room	Dining Room Table and Chairs	Finance	Standard	6,780
2018-011	COK	Chantalle	Desmarais	3/2/2018	Dining Room	Dining Room Table and Chairs	Finance	Standard	10,000
2018-012	KRM	Ambrose	Sardelis	3/2/2018	Appliances	Washer	Paid in Full	Promotion	1,100
2018-013	COK	Chantalle	Desmarais	3/3/2018	Living Room	Recliners	Finance	Standard	2,430
2018-014	COK	Jade	Gallagher	3/3/2018	Dining Room	Dining Room Table and Chairs	Paid in Full	Standard	4,550
2018-015	MAP	Chantalle	Desmarais	3/3/2018	Living Room	Sofa, Loveseat, Chair Package	Finance	Standard	6,784
2018-016	MAP	Jade	Gallagher	3/4/2018	Appliances	Dishwasher	Paid in Full	Standard	640
2018-017	MAP	Jade	Gallagher	3/4/2018	Appliances	Refrigerator, Oven, Microwave Combo	Finance	Promotion	8,490
2018-018	KRM	Sebastian	Gruenewald	3/4/2018	Appliances	Refrigerator, Oven, Microwave Combo	Finance	Promotion	6,780

Page 1   Page 2

March Totals | March Individual

Page 2 — March Individual worksheet

Reid Furniture
Monthly Transactions: March 2018
Down Payment Requirement: 25%

Trans_No	Date	Sales_First	Sales_Last	Department	Furniture	Pay_Type	Trans_Type	Amou	Down_Pa	Owe
2018-001	3/1/2018	Sebastian	Gruenewald	Bedroom	Mattress	Finance	Promotion	2,788	697.00	2,091.00
2018-002	3/1/2018	Sebastian	Gruenewald	Bedroom	Mattress	Finance	Promotion	3,245	811.25	2,433.75
2018-003	3/1/2018	Jade	Gallagher	Living Room	Sofa, Loveseat, Chair Package	Finance	Promotion	10,000	2,500.00	7,500.00
2018-004	3/1/2018	Jade	Gallagher	Living Room	End Tables	Finance	Promotion	1,000	250.00	750.00
2018-005	3/1/2018	Jade	Gallagher	Appliances	Washer and Dryer	Finance	Promotion	2,750	687.50	2,062.50
2018-006	3/1/2018	Ambrose	Sardelis	Living Room	Sofa, Loveseat, Chair Package	Finance	Promotion	12,000	3,000.00	9,000.00
2018-007	3/1/2018	Jade	Gallagher	Dining Room	Dining Room Table	Finance	Promotion	3,240	810.00	2,430.00
2018-008	3/1/2018	Chantalle	Desmarais	Dining Room	Dining Room Table	Finance	Promotion	4,080	1,020.00	3,060.00
2018-009	3/1/2018	Sebastian	Gruenewald	Appliances	Washer and Dryer	Finance	Promotion	2,750	687.50	2,062.50
2018-010	3/2/2018	Jade	Gallagher	Dining Room	Dining Room Table and Chairs	Finance	Standard	6,780	1,695.00	5,085.00
2018-011	3/2/2018	Chantalle	Desmarais	Dining Room	Dining Room Table and Chairs	Finance	Standard	10,000	2,500.00	7,500.00
2018-012	3/2/2018	Ambrose	Sardelis	Appliances	Washer	Paid in Full	Promotion	1,100	1,100.00	-
2018-013	3/3/2018	Chantalle	Desmarais	Living Room	Recliners	Finance	Standard	2,430	607.50	1,822.50
2018-014	3/3/2018	Jade	Gallagher	Dining Room	Dining Room Table and Chairs	Paid in Full	Standard	4,550	4,550.00	-
2018-015	3/3/2018	Chantalle	Desmarais	Living Room	Sofa, Loveseat, Chair Package	Finance	Standard	6,784	1,696.00	5,088.00
2018-016	3/4/2018	Jade	Gallagher	Appliances	Dishwasher	Paid in Full	Standard	640	640.00	-
2018-017	3/4/2018	Jade	Gallagher	Appliances	Refrigerator, Oven, Microwave Combo	Finance	Promotion	8,490	2,122.50	6,367.50
2018-018	3/4/2018	Sebastian	Gruenewald	Appliances	Refrigerator, Oven, Microwave Combo	Finance	Promotion	6,780	1,695.00	5,085.00
2018-019	3/5/2018	Jade	Gallagher	Living Room	Sofa	Paid in Full	Standard	2,500	2,500.00	-

March Totals | March Individual

FIGURE 4.1 Reid Furniture Store Datasets

CASE STUDY | Reid Furniture Store

Starting File	File to be Submitted
e04h1Reid	e04h4Reid_LastFirst

Large Datasets

So far you have worked with worksheets that contain small datasets, a collection of structured, related data in a limited number of columns and rows. In reality, you will probably work with large datasets consisting of hundreds or thousands of rows and columns of data. When you work with small datasets, you can usually view most or all of the data without scrolling. When you work with large datasets, you probably will not be able to see the entire dataset onscreen even on a large, widescreen monitor set at high resolution. You might want to keep the column and row labels always in view, even as you scroll throughout the dataset. Figure 4.2 shows Reid Furniture Store's March 2018 sales transactions. Because it contains a lot of transactions, the entire dataset is not visible. You could decrease the zoom level to display more transactions; however, doing so decreases the text size onscreen, making it hard to read the data.

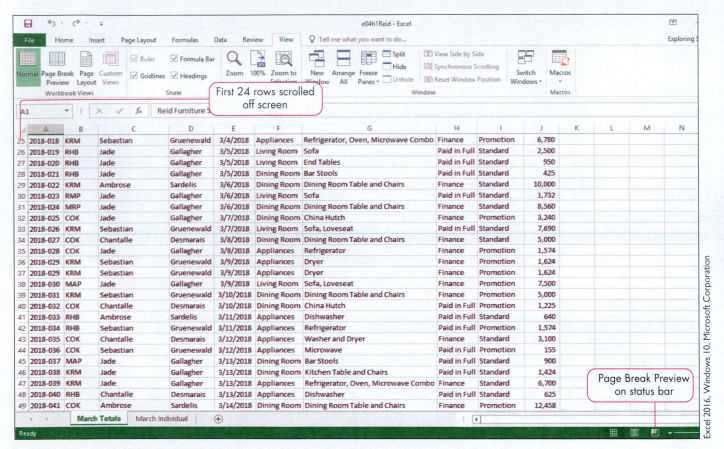

FIGURE 4.2 Large Dataset

As you work with larger datasets, realize that the data will not always fit on one page when it is printed. You will need to preview the automatic page breaks and probably insert some manual page breaks in more desirable locations, or you might want to print only a selected range within the large dataset to distribute to others.

In this section, you will learn how to keep labels onscreen as you scroll through a large dataset. In addition, you will learn how to manage page breaks, print only a range instead of an entire worksheet, and print column labels at the top of each page of a large dataset.

TIP: GO TO A SPECIFIC CELL

You can navigate through a large worksheet by using the Go To command. Click Find & Select in the Editing group on the Home tab and select Go To (or press F5 or Ctrl+G) to display the Go To dialog box, enter the cell address in the Reference box, and then press Enter to go to the cell. You can also click in the Name Box, type the cell reference, and then press Enter to go to a specific cell.

Freezing Rows and Columns

STEP 1 When you scroll to parts of a dataset not initially visible, some rows and columns, such as headings, disappear from view. When the row and column labels scroll off the screen, you may not remember what each column or row represents. You can keep labels onscreen by freezing them. ***Freezing*** is the process of keeping rows and/or columns visible onscreen at all times even when you scroll through a large dataset. Table 4.1 describes the three freeze options.

TABLE 4.1 Freeze Options

Option	Description
Freeze Panes	Keeps both rows and columns above and to the left of the active cell visible as you scroll through a worksheet.
Freeze Top Row	Keeps only the top row visible as you scroll through a worksheet.
Freeze First Column	Keeps only the first column visible as you scroll through a worksheet.

To freeze one or more rows and columns, use the Freeze Panes option. Before selecting this option, make the active cell one row below and one column to the right of the rows and columns you want to freeze. For example, to freeze the first five rows and the first column, make cell B6 the active cell before clicking the Freeze Panes option. As Figure 4.3 shows, Excel displays a horizontal line below the last frozen row (row 5) and a vertical line to the right of the last frozen column (column F). Unfrozen rows (such as rows 6–14) and unfrozen columns (such as columns G and H) are no longer visible as you scroll down and to the right, respectively.

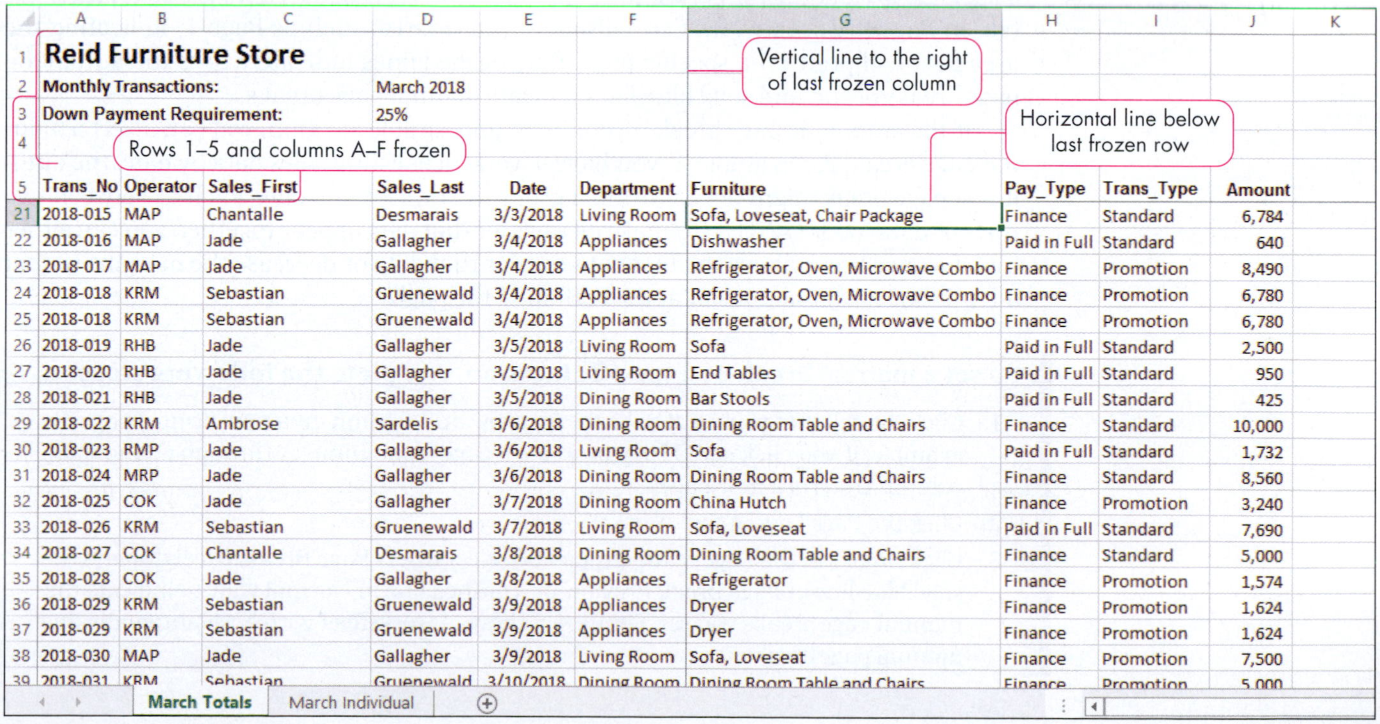

	A	B	C	D	E	F	G	H	I	J
1	Reid Furniture Store									
2	Monthly Transactions:			March 2018						
3	Down Payment Requirement:			25%						
4										
5	Trans_No	Operator	Sales_First	Sales_Last	Date	Department	Furniture	Pay_Type	Trans_Type	Amount
21	2018-015	MAP	Chantalle	Desmarais	3/3/2018	Living Room	Sofa, Loveseat, Chair Package	Finance	Standard	6,784
22	2018-016	MAP	Jade	Gallagher	3/4/2018	Appliances	Dishwasher	Paid in Full	Standard	640
23	2018-017	MAP	Jade	Gallagher	3/4/2018	Appliances	Refrigerator, Oven, Microwave Combo	Finance	Promotion	8,490
24	2018-018	KRM	Sebastian	Gruenewald	3/4/2018	Appliances	Refrigerator, Oven, Microwave Combo	Finance	Promotion	6,780
25	2018-018	KRM	Sebastian	Gruenewald	3/4/2018	Appliances	Refrigerator, Oven, Microwave Combo	Finance	Promotion	6,780
26	2018-019	RHB	Jade	Gallagher	3/5/2018	Living Room	Sofa	Paid in Full	Standard	2,500
27	2018-020	RHB	Jade	Gallagher	3/5/2018	Living Room	End Tables	Paid in Full	Standard	950
28	2018-021	RHB	Jade	Gallagher	3/5/2018	Dining Room	Bar Stools	Paid in Full	Standard	425
29	2018-022	KRM	Ambrose	Sardelis	3/6/2018	Dining Room	Dining Room Table and Chairs	Finance	Standard	10,000
30	2018-023	RMP	Jade	Gallagher	3/6/2018	Living Room	Sofa	Paid in Full	Standard	1,732
31	2018-024	MRP	Jade	Gallagher	3/6/2018	Dining Room	Dining Room Table and Chairs	Finance	Standard	8,560
32	2018-025	COK	Jade	Gallagher	3/7/2018	Dining Room	China Hutch	Finance	Promotion	3,240
33	2018-026	KRM	Sebastian	Gruenewald	3/7/2018	Living Room	Sofa, Loveseat	Paid in Full	Standard	7,690
34	2018-027	COK	Chantalle	Desmarais	3/8/2018	Dining Room	Dining Room Table and Chairs	Finance	Standard	5,000
35	2018-028	COK	Jade	Gallagher	3/8/2018	Appliances	Refrigerator	Finance	Promotion	1,574
36	2018-029	KRM	Sebastian	Gruenewald	3/9/2018	Appliances	Dryer	Finance	Promotion	1,624
37	2018-029	KRM	Sebastian	Gruenewald	3/9/2018	Appliances	Dryer	Finance	Promotion	1,624
38	2018-030	MAP	Jade	Gallagher	3/9/2018	Living Room	Sofa, Loveseat	Finance	Promotion	7,500
39	2018-031	KRM	Sebastian	Gruenewald	3/10/2018	Dining Room	Dining Room Table and Chairs	Finance	Promotion	5,000

FIGURE 4.3 Freeze Panes Set

To unlock the rows and columns from remaining onscreen as you scroll, click Freeze Panes in the Window group and select Unfreeze Panes, which only appears on the menu when you have frozen rows and/or columns. After you unfreeze the panes, the Freeze Panes option appears instead of Unfreeze Panes on the menu again.

When you freeze panes and press Ctrl+Home, the first unfrozen cell is the active cell instead of cell A1. For example, with column F and rows 1 through 5 frozen in Figure 4.3, pressing Ctrl+Home makes cell G6 the active cell. If you want to edit a cell in the frozen area, click the particular cell to make it active and edit the data.

Printing Large Datasets

For a large dataset, some columns and rows may print on several pages. Analyzing the data on individual printed pages is difficult when each page does not contain column and row labels. To prevent wasting paper, always use Print Preview. Doing so enables you to adjust page settings until you are satisfied with how the data will print.

The Page Layout tab (see Figure 4.4) contains options to help you prepare large datasets to print. Previously, you changed the page orientation, set different margins, and adjusted the scaling. In addition, you can manage page breaks, set the print area, and print titles.

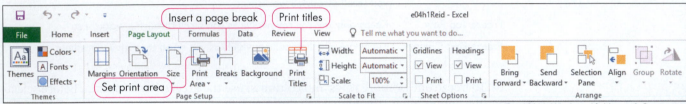

FIGURE 4.4 Page Setup Options

Excel 2016, Windows 10, Microsoft Corporation

Display and Change Page Breaks

STEP 2 ❯❯ Based on the paper size, orientation, margins, and other settings, Excel identifies how much data can print on a page. Then it displays a *page break*, indicating where data will start on another printed page. To identify where these automatic page breaks will occur, click Page Break Preview on the status bar or in the Workbook Views group on the View tab. In Page Break Preview, Excel displays watermarks, such as Page 1, indicating the area that will print on a specific page. Blue dashed lines indicate where the automatic page breaks occur, and solid blue lines indicate manual page breaks.

If the automatic page breaks occur in an undesirable location, you can insert a manual page break. For example, if you have a worksheet listing sales data by date, the automatic page break might occur within a group of rows for one date, such as between two rows of data for 3/1/2018. To make all rows for that date appear together, you can either insert a page break above the first data row for that date or decrease the margins so that all 3/1/2018 transactions fit at the bottom of the page.

To set a manual break at a specific location, complete the following steps:

1. Click the cell that you want to be the first row and column on a new printed page. For example, if you click cell D50, you create a page for columns A through C, and then column D starts a new page.
2. Click the Page Layout tab.
3. Click Breaks in the Page Setup group and select Insert Page Break. Excel displays a solid blue line in Page Break Preview or a dashed line in Normal view to indicate the manual page breaks you set. Figure 4.5 shows a worksheet with both automatic and manual page breaks.

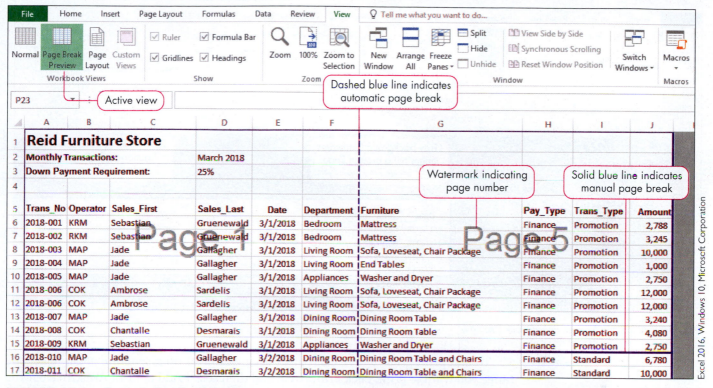

FIGURE 4.5 Page Breaks in Page Break Preview

TIP: USING THE POINTER TO MOVE PAGE BREAKS
To use the pointer to adjust a page break, point to the page break line to see the two-headed arrow and drag the line to the location where you want the page break to occur.

Set and Clear a Print Area

STEP 3 ▶▶ The default Print settings send an entire dataset on the active worksheet to the printer. However, you might want to print only part of the worksheet data. If you display the worksheet in Page Break view, you can identify which page(s) you want to print. Then click the File tab and select Print. Under Settings, type the number(s) of the page(s) you want to print. For example, to print page 2 only, type 2 in the Pages text box and in the *to* text box.

You can further restrict what is printed by setting the ***print area***, which is the range of cells that will print. For example, you might want to print only an input area or just the transactions that occurred on a particular date.

In Page Break Preview, the print area has a white background and solid blue border; the rest of the worksheet has a gray background (see Figure 4.6). In Normal view or Page Layout view, the print area is surrounded by thin gray lines.

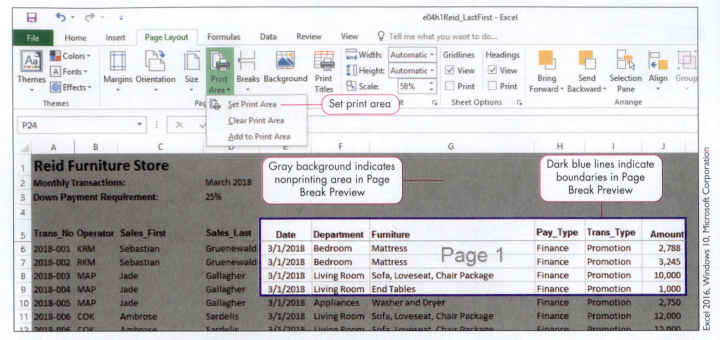

FIGURE 4.6 Print Area in Page Break Preview

To add print areas where each print area will print on a separate page, select the range you want to print, click Print Area, and then select Add to Print Area. To clear the print area, click Print Area in the Page Setup group and select Clear Print Area.

TIP: PRINT A SELECTION

Another way to print part of a worksheet is to select the range you want to print. Click the File tab and click Print. Click the first arrow in the Settings section and select Print Selection. This provides additional flexibility compared to using a defined print area in situations in which you may be required to print materials outside a consistent range of cells.

Print Titles

STEP 4 ❯❯ When you print large datasets, it is helpful if every page contains descriptive column and row labels. When you click Print Titles in the Page Setup group on the Page Layout tab, Excel opens the Page Setup dialog box with the Sheet tab active so that you can select which row(s) and/or column(s) to repeat on each page of a printout (see Figure 4.7).

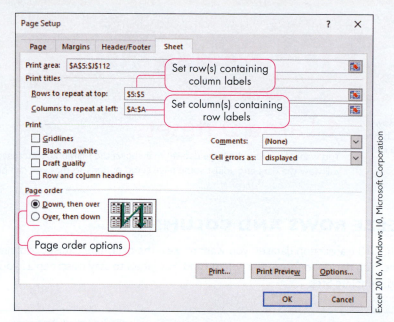

FIGURE 4.7 Sheet Tab Options

To repeat rows or columns at the top or left of each page when printed, select the row(s) that contain the labels or titles (such as row 5) in the *Rows to repeat at top* box to display $5:$5. To print the row labels at the left side of each page, select the column(s) that contain the labels or titles (such as column A) in the *Columns to repeat at left* box to display AA.

Control Print Page Order

Print order is the sequence in which the pages are printed. By default, the pages print in this order: top-left section, bottom-left section, top-right section, and bottom-right section. However, you might want to print the entire top portion of the worksheet before printing the bottom portion. To change the print order, open the Page Setup dialog box, click the Sheet tab, and then select the desired Page order option (refer to Figure 4.7).

Quick Concepts

1. What is the purpose of freezing panes in a worksheet? **p. 265**

2. Why would you want to insert page breaks instead of using the automatic page breaks? **p. 266**

3. What steps should you take to ensure that column labels display on each printed page of a large dataset? **pp. 268–269**

Hands-On Exercises

Watch the Video for this Hands-On Exercise!

MyITLab®
HOE1 Training

Skills covered: Freeze Rows and Columns • Display and Change Page Breaks • Set and Clear a Print Area • Print Titles

1 Large Datasets

You want to review the large dataset that shows the March 2018 transactions for Reid Furniture Store. You will view the data and adjust some page setup options so that you can print necessary labels on each page.

STEP 1 ▶▶ FREEZE ROWS AND COLUMNS

Before printing the March 2018 transaction dataset, you want to view the data. The dataset contains more rows than will display onscreen at the same time. You decide to freeze the column and row labels to stay onscreen as you scroll through the transactions. Refer to Figure 4.8 as you complete Step 1.

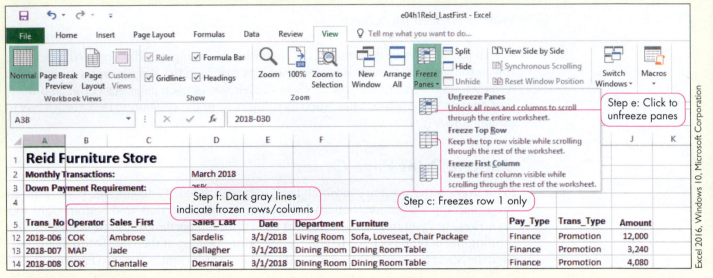

FIGURE 4.8 Freeze Panes Activated

a. Open *e04h1Reid* and save it as **e04h1Reid_LastFirst**.

> **TROUBLESHOOTING:** If you make any major mistakes in this exercise, you can close the file, open *e04h1Reid* again, and then start this exercise over.

The workbook contains two worksheets: March Totals (for Hands-On Exercises 1–3) and March Individual (for Hands-On Exercise 4).

b. Press **Page Down** four times to scroll through the dataset. Then press **Ctrl+Home** to go back to the top of the worksheet.

After you press Page Down, the column labels in row 5 scroll off the screen, making it challenging to remember what type of data are in some columns.

c. Click the **View tab**, click **Freeze Panes** in the Window group, and then select **Freeze Top Row**.

A dark gray horizontal line displays between rows 1 and 2.

d. Press **Page Down** to scroll down through the worksheet.

As rows scroll off the top of the Excel window, the first row remains frozen onscreen. The title by itself is not helpful; you need to freeze the column labels as well.

> **TROUBLESHOOTING:** Your screen may differ from Figure 4.8 due to different Windows resolution settings. If necessary, continue scrolling right and down until you see columns and rows scrolling offscreen.

e. Click **Freeze Panes** in the Window group and select **Unfreeze Panes**.

f. Click **cell B6**, the cell below the row and one column to the right of what you want to freeze. Click **Freeze Panes** in the Window group and select **Freeze Panes**.

Excel displays a vertical line between columns A and B, indicating that column A is frozen, and a horizontal line between rows 5 and 6, indicating the first five rows are frozen.

g. Press **Ctrl+G**, type **Q112** in the Reference box of the Go To dialog box, and then click **OK** to make cell Q112 the active cell.

Rows 6 through 96 and columns B and C are not visible because they scrolled off the screen. Note that the results will vary slightly based on screen resolution.

h. Save the workbook.

You plan to print the dataset so that you and Vicki Reid can discuss the transactions in your weekly meeting. Because the large dataset will not fit on one page, you want to see where the automatic page breaks are and then insert a manual page break. Refer to Figure 4.9 as you complete Step 2.

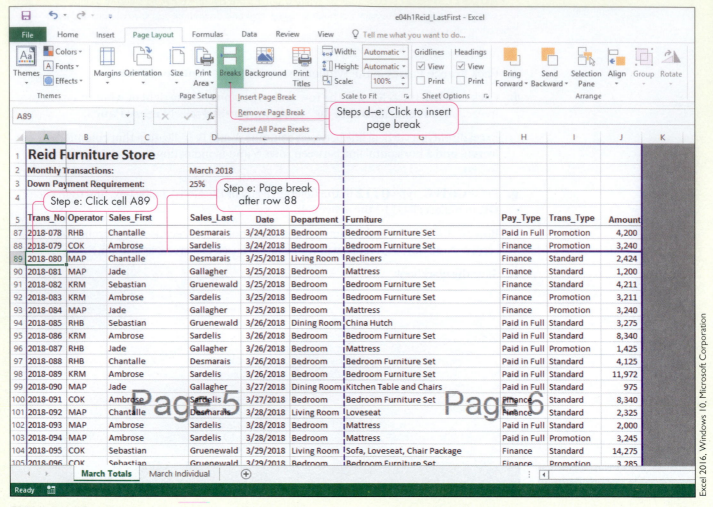

FIGURE 4.9 Page Breaks

a. Press **Ctrl+Home** to move to **cell B6**, the first cell in the unfrozen area. Click the **View tab** and click **Page Break Preview** in the Workbook Views group or on the status bar.

Excel displays blue dashed lines to indicate the automatic page breaks.

b. Scroll down until you see row 44 below the frozen column labels.

The automatic horizontal page break is between rows 46 and 47 (or between rows 45 and 46). You do not want transactions for a particular day to span between printed pages, so you need to move the page break up to keep all 3/13/2018 transactions together.

c. Click **cell A45**, the first cell containing 3/13/2018 data and the cell to start the top of the second page.

d. Click the **Page Layout tab**, click **Breaks** in the Page Setup group, and then select **Insert Page Break**.

You inserted a page break between rows 44 and 45 so that the 3/13/2018 transactions will be on one page.

e. Click **cell A89**, click **Breaks** in the Page Setup group, and then select **Insert Page Break**.

You inserted a page break between rows 88 and 89 to keep the 3/25/2018 transactions on the same page.

f. Save the workbook.

You want to focus on the transactions for only March 1, 2018. To avoid printing more data than you need, you will set the print area to print transactions for only that day. Refer to Figure 4.10 as you complete Step 3.

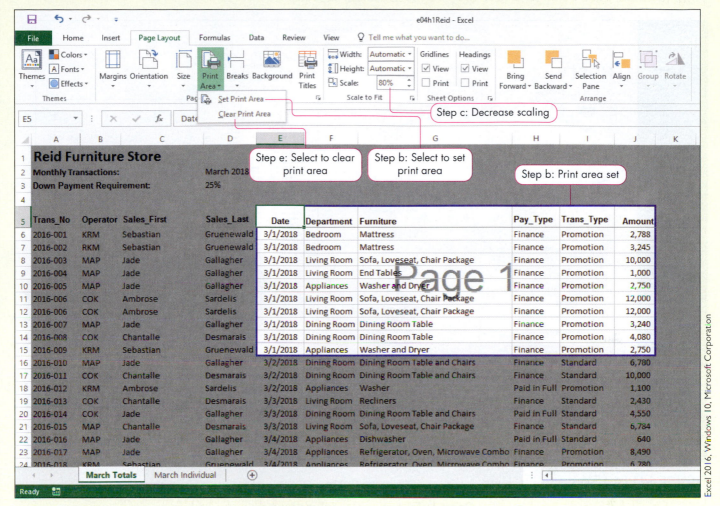

FIGURE 4.10 Print Area Set

a. Select the **range E5:J15**, the range of data for March 1, 2018.

b. Click the **Page Layout tab**, click **Print Area** in the Page Setup group, and then select **Set Print Area**.

   Excel displays the print area with a border. The rest of the worksheet displays with a gray background.

c. Click **cell E5** and click the **Scale arrow** down four times to display 80% in the Scale to Fit group.

   The selected print area will print on one page.

d. Press **Ctrl+P** to see that only the print area will print. Press **Esc**.

e. Click **Print Area** in the Page Setup group and select **Clear Print Area**.

f. Save the workbook.

Only the first page will print both row and column labels. Pages 2 and 3 will print the remaining row labels, page 4 will print the remaining column labels, and pages 5 and 6 will not print either label. You want to make sure the column and row labels print on all pages. To do this, you will print titles. Refer to Figure 4.11 as you complete Step 4.

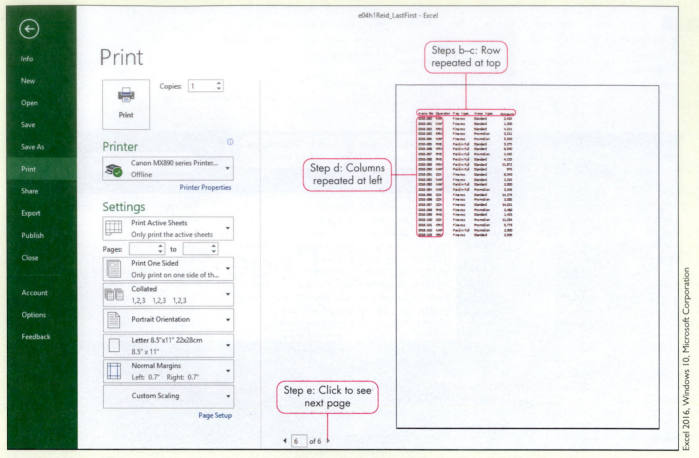

FIGURE 4.11 Print Titles

a. Click **Print Titles** in the Page Setup group.

The Page Setup dialog box opens, displaying the Sheet tab.

b. Click **Collapse Dialog Box** on the right side of the *Rows to repeat at top* box.

Clicking Collapse Dialog Box reduces the dialog box so that you can select a range in the worksheet easily.

c. Click the **row 5 heading** and click **Expand Dialog Box** within the *Page Setup: Rows to repeat at top* dialog box.

You selected the fifth row, which contains the column labels, and expanded the Page Setup dialog box back to its full size.

d. Click in the **Columns to repeat at left box**, type **A:B**, click the **Over, then down** Page order, and then click **Print Preview**.

You have manually entered the columns that contain the heading you want to repeat.

e. Click **Next Page** at the bottom of the Print Preview. Click **Next Page** until the sixth page displays.

Figure 4.11 shows a preview of the sixth page. The column labels and the first two columns appear on all pages.

f. Click the **Back arrow**.

g. Save the workbook. Keep the workbook open if you plan to continue with the next Hands-On Exercise. If not, close the workbook, and exit Excel.

Excel Tables

All organizations maintain lists of data. Businesses maintain inventory lists, educational institutions maintain lists of students and faculty, and governmental entities maintain lists of contracts. Although more complicated related data should be stored in a database management program, such as Access, you can manage basic data structure in Excel tables. A *table* is a structured range that contains related data organized in a method that increases the capability to manage and analyze information.

In this section, you will learn table terminology and rules for structuring data. You will create a table from existing data, manage records and fields, and remove duplicates. You will then apply a table style to format the table.

Understanding the Benefits of Data Tables

When dealing with large datasets it is imperative that documents are strategically organized to maintain data integrity and ease of use. Thus far you have worked with the manipulation of data ranges, and while you can use many tools in Excel to analyze simple data ranges, tables provide many additional analytical and time saving benefits. Using tables in Excel can help create and maintain data structure. *Data structure* is the organization method used to manage multiple data points within a dataset. For example, a dataset of students may include names, grades, contact information, and intended majors of study. The data structure of this dataset would define how the information is stored, organized, and accessed. Although you can manage and analyze data structure as a range in Excel, a table provides many advantages:

- Column headings remain onscreen without having to use Freeze Panes.
- Filter arrows let you sort and filter efficiently.
- Table styles easily format table rows and columns with complementary fill colors.
- Calculated columns let you create and edit formulas that copy down the columns automatically.
- A calculated total row lets you implement a variety of summary functions.
- You can use structured references instead of cell references in formulas.
- You can export table data to a SharePoint list.

Designing and Creating Tables

A table is a group of related data organized in a series of rows and columns that is managed independently from any other data on the worksheet. Once a data range is converted into a table, each column represents a *field*, which is an individual piece of data, such as last names or quantities sold. Each field should represent the smallest possible unit of data. For example, instead of a Name field, separate name data into First Name and Last Name fields. Instead of one large address field, separate address data into Street Address, City, State, and ZIP Code fields. Separating data into the smallest units possible enables you to manipulate the data in a variety of ways for output. Each row in a table represents a *record*, which is a collection of related data about one entity. For example, all data related to one particular transaction form a record in the Reid Furniture Store worksheet.

You should plan the structure before creating a table. The more thoroughly you plan, the fewer changes you will have to make to gain information from the data in the table after you create it. To help plan your table, follow these guidelines:

- Enter field (column) names on the top row of the table.
- Keep field names short, descriptive, and unique. No two field names should be identical.

- Format the field names so that they stand out from the data.
- Enter data for each record on a row below the field names.
- Do not leave blank rows between records or between the field names and the first record.
- Delete any blank columns between fields in the dataset.
- Make sure each record has something unique, such as a transaction number or ID.
- Insert at least one blank row and one blank column between the table and other data, such as the main titles. When you need multiple tables in one workbook, a best practice is to place each table on a separate worksheet.

Create a Table

STEP 1 ❯❯ While it is possible to create a table from random unorganized data, it is a best practice first to plan the data structure. When your worksheet data is structured correctly, you can easily create a table. Furthermore, by taking the time to create an organized data structure you will ensure that the data can be used to identify specific information easily, is easy to manage, and is scalable.

To create a table from existing data, complete the following steps:

1. Click within the existing range of data.
2. Click the Insert tab and click Table in the Tables group. The Create Table dialog box opens (see Figure 4.12), prompting you to enter the range of data.
   - Select the range for the *Where is the data for your table* box if Excel does not correctly predict the range.
   - Select the *My table has headers* check box if the existing range contains column labels.
3. Click OK to create the table.

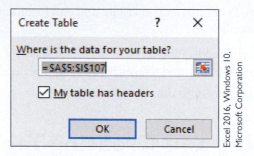

Excel 2016, Windows 10, Microsoft Corporation

FIGURE 4.12 Create Table Dialog Box

TIP: QUICK ANALYSIS TABLE CREATION
You can also create a table by selecting a range, clicking the Quick Analysis button, clicking Tables (see Figure 4.13) in the Quick Analysis gallery, and then clicking Table. While Quick Analysis is efficient for tasks such as creating a chart, it may take more time to create a table because you have to select the entire range first. Some people find that it is faster to create a table on the Insert tab.

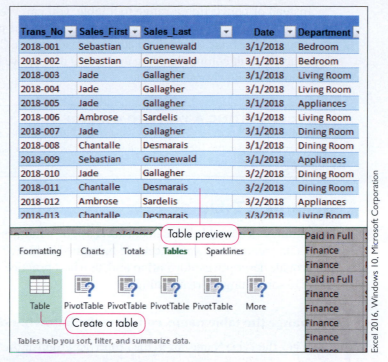

FIGURE 4.13 Quick Analysis Gallery

After you create a table, the Table Tools Design tab displays. Excel applies the default Table Style Medium 2 style to the table, and each cell in the header row has filter arrows (see Figure 4.14). This book uses the term *filter arrows* for consistency.

> **TIP: FILTER ARROWS**
> Click the Filter Button check box in the Table Style Options group on the Design tab to display or hide the filter arrows (see Figure 4.14). For a range of data instead of a table, click Filter in the Sort & Filter group on the Data tab to display or hide the filter arrows.

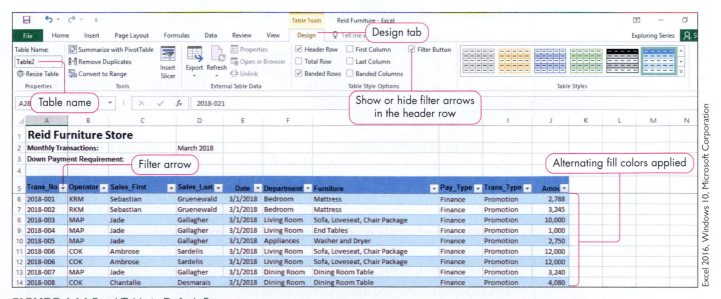

FIGURE 4.14 Excel Table in Default Format

Instead of converting a range to a table, you can create a table structure first and add data to it later. Select an empty range and follow the previously listed steps to create the range for the table. The default column headings are Column1, Column2, and so on. Click each default column heading and type a descriptive label. Then enter the data into each row of the newly created table.

> **TIP: CONVERTING A TABLE TO A RANGE**
> To convert a table back to a range, click within the table range, click the Table Tools Design tab, click Convert to Range in the Tools group, and then click Yes in the message box asking, *Do you want to convert the table to a normal range?*

Rename a Table

STEP 2 ⟫ By default, when a table is created, Excel assigns a name automatically. For example, the first table created in a worksheet will be named Table1. The default nomenclature does not provide descriptive information and, as a best practice, you should change the default name to something more meaningful.

To change the table name, complete the following steps:

1. Click the Table Name box in the Properties group of the Table Tools Design tab.
2. Type a new name using the same rules you applied when assigning range names, and press Enter.

Once a name has been assigned to a table, it can be used when building functions in place of the traditional absolute reference.

Add and Delete Fields

STEP 3 ⟫ After creating a table, you may need to insert a new field. For example, you might want to add a field for product numbers to the Reid Furniture Store transaction table.

To insert a field, complete the following steps:

1. Click in any data cell (other than the cell containing the field name) in a field that will be to the right of the new field. For example, to insert a new field between the fields in columns A and B, click any cell in column B.
2. Click the Home tab and click the Insert arrow in the Cells group.
3. Select Insert Table Columns to the Left.

If you want to add a field at the end of the right side of a table, click in the cell to the right of the last field name and type a label. Excel will extend the table to include that field and will format the cell as a field name.

You can also delete a field if you no longer need any data for that particular field. Although deleting records and fields is easy, you must make sure not to delete data erroneously. If you accidentally delete data, click Undo immediately.

To delete a field, complete the following steps:

1. Click a cell in the field that you want to delete.
2. Click the Delete arrow in the Cells group on the Home tab.
3. Select Delete Table Columns.

Add, Edit, and Delete Records

STEP 4 ▶▶ After you begin storing data in your newly created table, you might want to add new records, such as adding a new client or a new item to an inventory table. One of the advantages to using tables in Excel is the ability to easily add, edit, or delete records within the dataset.

To add a record to a table, complete the following steps:

1. Click a cell in the record below which you want the new record inserted. If you want to add a new record below the last record, click the row containing the last record.
2. Click the Home tab and click the Insert arrow in the Cells group.
3. Select Insert Table Rows Above to insert a row above the current row, or select Insert Table Row Below if the current row is the last one and you want a row below it.

You can also add a record to the end of a table by clicking in the row immediately below the table and typing. Excel will extend the table to include that row as a record in the table and will apply consistent formatting.

You might need to change data for a record. For example, when a client moves, you need to change the client's address. You edit data in a table the same way you edit data in a regular worksheet cell.

Finally, you can delete records. For example, if you maintain an inventory of artwork in your house and sell a piece of art, delete that record from the table.

To delete a record from the table, complete the following steps:

1. Click a cell in the record that you want to delete.
2. Click the Home tab and click the Delete arrow in the Cells group.
3. Select Delete Table Rows.

Remove Duplicate Rows

STEP 5 ▶▶ A table might contain duplicate records, which can give false results when totaling or performing other calculations on the dataset. For a small table, you might be able to detect duplicate records by scanning the data. For large tables, it is more difficult to identify duplicate records by simply scanning the table with the eye.

To remove duplicate records, complete the following steps:

1. Click within the table and click the Design tab.
2. Click Remove Duplicates in the Tools group to display the Remove Duplicates dialog box (see Figure 4.15). As an alternate method, you can also click the Data tab and click Remove Duplicates in the Data Tools group to open the Remove Duplicates dialog box.
3. Click Select All to set the criteria to find a duplicate for every field in the record and click OK. If you select individual column(s), Excel looks for duplicates in the specific column(s) only and deletes all but one record of the duplicated data. Excel will display a message box informing you of how many duplicate rows it removed.

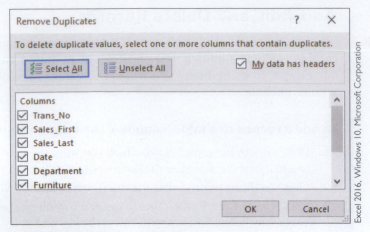

FIGURE 4.15 Remove Duplicates Dialog Box

Applying a Table Style

STEP 6 ›› When you create a table, it is automatically formatted with a table style of alternating colored rows and a bold style for the header row. ***Table styles*** control the fill color of the header row (the row containing field names) and rows of records. In addition, table styles specify bold and border lines. You can change the table style to a color scheme that complements your organization's color scheme or to emphasize data in the header rows or columns. Click the More button in the Table Styles group to display the Table Styles gallery (see Figure 4.16). To see how a table style will format your table using Live Preview, point to a style in the Table Styles gallery. After you identify a style you want, click it to apply it to the table.

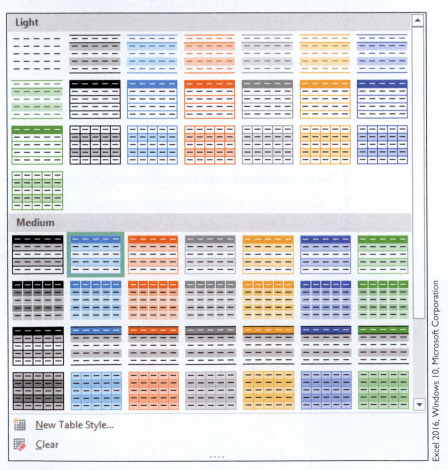

FIGURE 4.16 Table Styles Gallery

After you select a table style, you can control what the style formats. The Table Style Options group contains check boxes to select specific format actions in a table. Table 4.2 lists the options and the effect of each check box. Avoid overformatting the table. Applying too many formatting effects may obscure the message you want to present with the data.

TABLE 4.2 Table Style Options	
Check Box	**Action**
Header Row	Displays the header row (field names) when checked; removes field names when not checked. Header Row formatting takes priority over column formats.
Total Row	Displays a total row when selected. Total Row formatting takes priority over column formats.
First Column	Applies a different format to the first column so that the row headings stand out. First Column formatting takes priority over Banded Rows formatting.
Last Column	Applies a different format to the last column so that the last column of data stands out; effective for aggregated data, such as grand totals per row. Last Column formatting takes priority over Banded Rows formatting.
Banded Rows	Displays alternate fill colors for even and odd rows to help distinguish records.
Banded Columns	Displays alternate fill colors for even and odd columns to help distinguish fields.
Filter Button	Displays a filter button on the right side of each heading in the header row.

Quick Concepts

4. List at least four guidelines for planning a table in Excel. **pp. 275–276**

5. Why would you convert a range of data into an Excel table? **p. 276**

6. What are six options you can control after selecting a table style? **p. 281**

Hands-On Exercises

Skills covered: Create a Table • Rename a Table • Add and Delete Fields • Add, Edit, and Delete Records • Remove Duplicate Rows • Apply a Table Style

2 Excel Tables

You want to convert the March Totals data to a table. As you review the table, you will delete the unnecessary Operator field, add two new fields, insert a missing furniture sale transaction, and remove duplicate transactions. Finally, you will enhance the table appearance by applying a table style.

STEP 1 ❯❯ CREATE A TABLE

Although Reid Furniture Store's March transaction data are organized in an Excel worksheet, you know that you will have additional functionality if you convert the range to a table. Refer to Figure 4.17 as you complete Step 1.

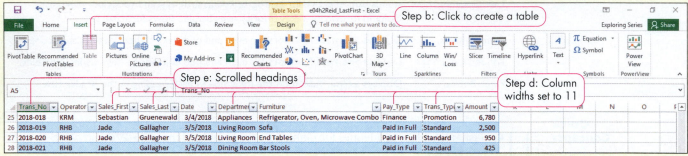

FIGURE 4.17 Range Converted to a Table

Excel 2016, Windows 10, Microsoft Corporation

a. Open *e04h1Reid_LastFirst* if you closed it at the end of Hands-On Exercise 1, and save it as **e04h2Reid_LastFirst**, changing h1 to h2. Click **Normal** on the status bar.

b. Click in any cell within the transactional data, click the **Insert tab**, and then click **Table** in the Tables group.

The Create Table dialog box opens. The *Where is the data for your table?* box displays =$A$5:$J$112. Keep the *My table has headers* check box selected so that the headings on the fifth row become the field names for the table.

c. Click **OK** and click **cell A5**.

Excel creates a table from the data range and displays the Design tab, filter arrows, and alternating fill colors for the records. The columns widen to fit the field names, although the wrap text option is still applied to those cells.

d. Set the column width to **11** for the Sales_First, Sales_Last, Department, Pay_Type, and Trans_Type fields.

e. Unfreeze the panes and scroll through the table.

With a regular range of data, column labels scroll off the top of the screen if you do not freeze panes. When you scroll within a table, the table's header row remains onscreen by moving up to where the Excel column (letter) headings usually display (see Figure 4.17). Note that it will not retain the bold formatting when scrolling.

f. Save the workbook.

After creating the table, you will change the name from the default "Table1" to a more descriptive title that meets your business standards. Refer to Figure 4.18 as you complete Step 2.

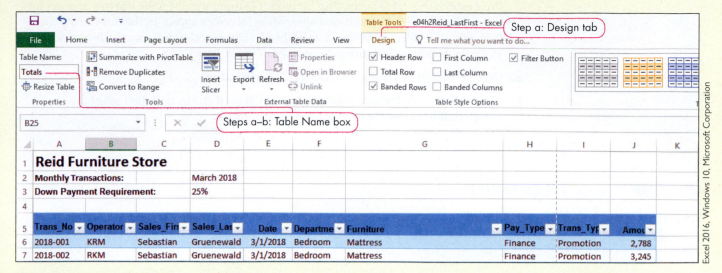

FIGURE 4.18 Rename the Table

a. Click the **Design tab** and click the **Table Name box** in the Properties group.

b. Type **Totals** in the Table Name box and press **Enter**.

> When a table is created, Excel assigns the default name "table" and a sequential number based on the number of tables in the document. For example, if there were two tables in the document the default name for the second table would be "Table2." In this step you have added a custom name that will be used throughout the rest of the project.

STEP 3 ▶▶ ADD AND DELETE FIELDS

The original range included a column for the data entry operators' initials. You will delete this column because you do not need it for your analysis. In addition, you want to add a field to display down payment amounts in the future. Refer to Figure 4.19 as you complete Step 3.

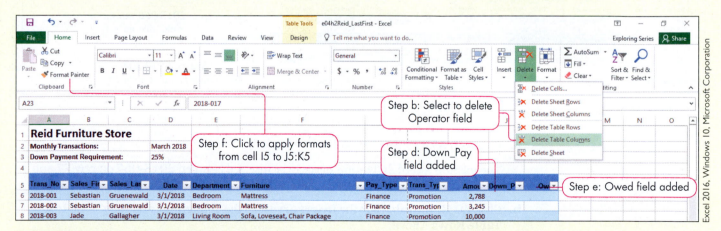

FIGURE 4.19 Newly Created Fields

a. Click any cell containing a value in the Operator column.

> You need to make a cell active in the field you want to remove.

b. Click the **Home tab**, click the **Delete arrow** in the Cells group, and then select **Delete Table Columns**.

> Excel deletes the Operator column and may adjust the width of other columns.

c. Set the widths of columns E, F, and G to AutoFit. Click **cell J5**, the first blank cell on the right side of the field names.

d. Type **Down_Pay** and press **Ctrl+Enter**.

Excel extends the table formatting to column J automatically. A filter arrow appears for the newly created field name, and alternating fill colors appear in the rows below the field name. The fill color is the same as the fill color for other field names; however, the font color is White, Background 1, instead of Black Text 1.

e. Click **cell K5**, type **Owed**, and then press **Ctrl+Enter**.

f. Click **cell I5**, click **Format Painter** in the Clipboard group, and then select the **range J5:K5** to copy the format. Save the workbook.

STEP 4 ›› ADD RECORDS

As you review the March 2018 transaction table, you notice that two transactions are missing: 2018-068 and 2018-104. After finding the paper invoices, you are ready to add records with the missing transaction data. Refer to Figure 4.20 as you complete Step 4.

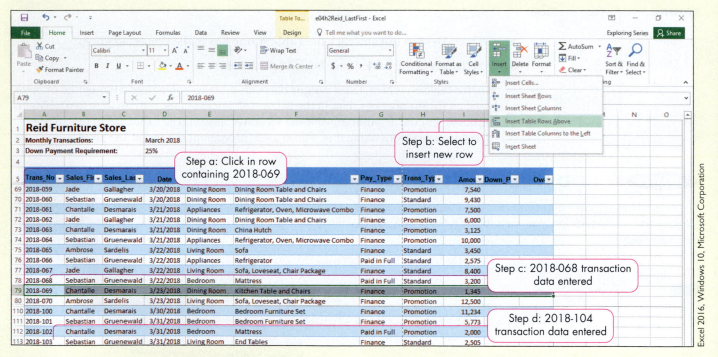

FIGURE 4.20 Missing Records Added

a. Click **cell A78**.

The missing record 2018-068 needs to be inserted between 2018-067 on row 77 and 2018-069 on row 78.

b. Click the **Home tab**, click the **Insert arrow** in the Cells group, and then select **Insert Table Rows Above**.

Excel inserts a new table row on row 78, between the 2018-067 and 2018-069 transactions.

c. Enter the following data in the respective fields on the newly created row:

2018-068, **Sebastian**, **Gruenewald**, **3/22/2018**, **Bedroom**, **Mattress**, **Paid in Full**, **Standard**, **3200**

d. Click **cell A114** and enter the following data in the respective fields:

2018-104, Ambrose, Sardelis, 3/31/2018, Appliances, Refrigerator, Paid in Full, Standard, 1500

When you start typing 2018-104 in the row below the last record, Excel immediately includes and formats row 114 as part of the table. Review Figure 4.20 to ensure that you inserted the records in the correct locations. In the figure, rows 81–109 are hidden to display both new records in one screenshot.

e. Save the workbook.

STEP 5 ›› REMOVE DUPLICATE ROWS

You noticed that the 2018-006 transaction is duplicated on rows 11 and 12 and that the 2018-018 transaction is duplicated on rows 24 and 25. You think the table may contain other duplicate rows. To avoid having to look at the entire table row by row, you will have Excel find and remove the duplicate rows for you. Refer to Figure 4.21 as you complete Step 5.

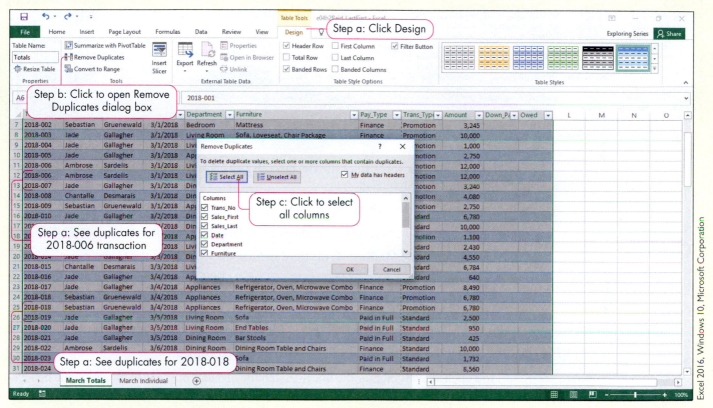

FIGURE 4.21 Remove Duplicate Records

a. Click a cell in the table. Scroll to see rows 11 and 12. Click the **Design tab**.

The records on rows 11 and 12 are identical. Rows 24 and 25 are also duplicates. You need to remove the extra rows.

b. Click **Remove Duplicates** in the Tools group.

The Remove Duplicates dialog box opens.

c. Click **Select All**, make sure the *My data has headers* check box is selected, and then click **OK**.

Excel displays a message box indicating *5 duplicate records found and removed; 104 unique values remain.*

d. Click **OK** in the message box. Click **cell A109** to view the last record in the table. Save the workbook.

Transaction 2018-104 is located on row 109 after the duplicate records are removed.

Now that you have finalized the fields and added missing records to the March 2018 transaction table, you want to apply a table style to format the table. Refer to Figure 4.22 as you complete Step 6.

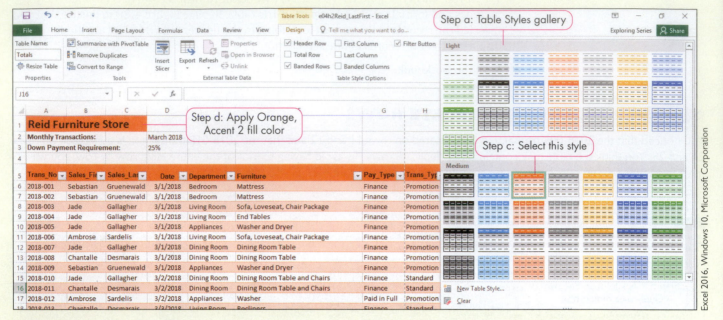

FIGURE 4.22 Table Style Applied

a. Click a cell in the table. Click the **Design tab** and click **More** in the Table Styles group to open the Table Styles gallery.

b. Point to the fourth style on the second row in the Light section.

Live Preview shows the table with the Table Style Light 10 style but does not apply it.

c. Click **Table Style Medium 3**, the third style on the first row in the Medium section.

Excel formats the table with the Medium 3 table style, which applies Orange, Accent 2 fill color to the table header row and Orange, Accent 2, Lighter 80% fill color to every other record.

d. Press **Ctrl+Home**. Select the **range A1:C1**, click the **Fill Color arrow** in the Font group on the Home tab, and then click **Orange, Accent 2**.

You applied a fill color for the title to match the fill color of the field names on the header row in the table.

e. Save the workbook. Keep the workbook open if you plan to continue with the next Hands-On Exercise. If not, close the workbook, and exit Excel.

Table Manipulation

Along with maintaining data structure, tables have a variety of options to enhance and manipulate data, in addition to managing fields, adding records, and applying table styles. You can build formulas and functions, arrange records in different sequences to get different perspectives on the data, and restrict the onscreen appearance of data using filtering. For example, you can arrange the transactions by sales representative. Furthermore, you can display only particular records instead of the entire dataset to focus on a subset of the data. For example, you might want to focus on the financed transactions.

In this section, you will learn how to create structured references, and how to sort records by text, numbers, and dates in a table. In addition, you will learn how to filter data based on conditions you set.

Creating Structured References in Formulas

STEP 1 Your experience in building formulas involves using cell references, such as =SUM(B1:B15) or =H6*$B$3. Cell references in formulas help to identify where the content is on a worksheet, but does not tell the user what the content represents. An advantage to Excel tables is that they use structured references to clearly indicate which type of data is used in the calculations. A *structured reference* is a tag or use of a table element, such as a field heading, as a reference in a formula. As shown in Figure 4.23, structured references in formulas clearly indicate which type of data is used in the calculations.

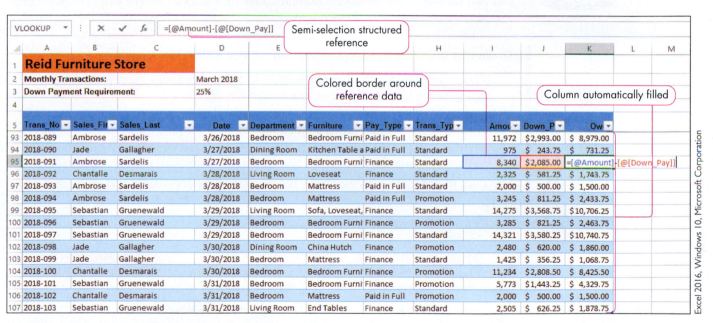

FIGURE 4.23 Structured Reference

When creating a formula in a table using structured references, field headings are set off by brackets around column headings or field names, such as =[Amount]–[Down_Pay]. The use of field headings without row references in a structured formula is called an *unqualified reference*. After you type the equal sign to begin your formula, type an opening bracket, and then Formula AutoComplete displays a list of field headings. Type or double-click the column name from the list and type the closing bracket. Excel displays a colored border around the referenced column that coordinates with the structured reference in the formula, similar to Excel identifying cell references and their worksheet placement. When you enter a formula using structured references, Excel copies the formula down the rest of the table column automatically, compared to typing references in formulas and using the fill handle to copy the formula down a column.

You can also use the semi-selection process to create a formula. As you click cells to enter a formula in a table, Excel builds a formula like this: =[@Amount]–[@Down_Pay], where the @ indicates the current row. If you use the semi-selection process to create a formula outside the table, the formula includes the table and field names, such as =Table1[@Amount]–Table1[@Down_Pay]. Table1 is the name of the table; Amount and Down_Pay are field names. This structured formula that includes references, such as table name, is called a *fully qualified structured reference*. When you build formulas *within* a table, you can use either unqualified or fully qualified structured references. If you need to use table data in a formula *outside* the table boundaries, you must use fully qualified structured references.

Sorting Data

Sometimes if you rearrange the order of records, new perspective is gained making the information easier to understand. In Figure 4.2, the March 2018 data are arranged by transaction number. You might want to arrange the transactions so that all of the transactions for a particular sales representative are together. *Sorting* is the process of arranging records by the value of one or more fields within a table. Sorting is not limited to data within tables; normal data ranges can be sorted as well.

Sort One Field

STEP 2 ›› You can sort data in a table or a regular range in a worksheet. For example, you could sort by transaction date or department.

> **To sort by only one field, complete one of the following steps:**
>
> - Click in a cell within the field you want to sort and click Sort & Filter in the Editing group on the Home tab, and select a desired sort option.
> - Click in a cell within the field you want to sort and click Sort A to Z, Sort Z to A, or Sort in the Sort & Filter group on the Data tab.
> - Right-click the field to sort, point to Sort on the shortcut menu, and then select the type of sort you want.
> - Click the filter arrow in the header row and select the desired sort option.

Table 4.3 lists sort options by data type.

TABLE 4.3	Sort Options	
Data Type	**Options**	**Explanation**
Text	Sort A to Z	Arranges data in alphabetical order.
	Sort Z to A	Arranges data in reverse alphabetical order.
Dates	Sort Oldest to Newest	Displays data in chronological order, from oldest to newest.
	Sort Newest to Oldest	Displays data in reverse chronological order, from newest to oldest.
Values	Sort Smallest to Largest	Arranges values from the smallest value to the largest.
	Sort Largest to Smallest	Arranges values from the largest value to the smallest.
Color	Sort by Cell Color	Arranges data together for cells containing a particular fill color.
	Sort by Font Color	Arranges data together for cells containing a particular font color.

Sort Multiple Fields

STEP 3 After sorting, if a second sort is applied the original sort will be removed. However, at times, sorting by only one field does not yield the desired outcome. Using multiple level sorts enables like records in the primary sort to be further organized by additional sort levels. For example, you could sort by date of transaction and then by last name. Excel enables you to sort data on 64 different levels.

To perform a multiple level sort, complete the following steps:

1. Click in any cell in the table.
2. Click Sort in the Sort & Filter group on the Data tab to display the Sort dialog box.
3. Select the primary sort level by clicking the Sort by arrow, selecting the field to sort by, and then clicking the Order arrow and selecting the sort order from the list.
4. Click Add Level, select the second sort level by clicking the Then by arrow, select the column to sort by, click the Order arrow, and then select the sort order from the list.
5. Continue to click Add Level and add sort levels until you have entered all sort levels (see Figure 4.24). Click OK.

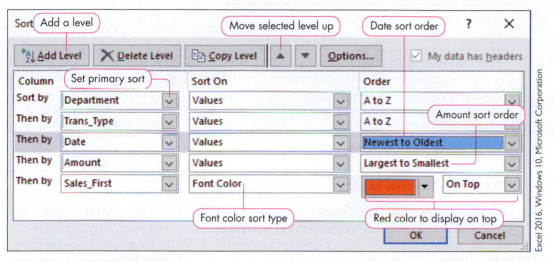

FIGURE 4.24 Sort Dialog Box

Create a Custom Sort

STEP 4 Excel arranges data in alphabetical or numerical order. For example, days of the week are sorted alphabetically: Friday, Monday, Saturday, Sunday, Thursday, Tuesday, and Wednesday. However, you might want to create a custom sort sequence. For example, you can create a custom sort to arrange days of the week in order from Sunday to Saturday.

To create a custom sort sequence, complete the following steps:

1. Click Sort in the Sort & Filter group on the Data tab.
2. Click the Order arrow and select Custom List to display the Custom Lists dialog box (see Figure 4.25).
3. Select an existing sort sequence in the Custom lists box, or select NEW LIST.
4. Type the entries in the desired sort sequence in the List entries box, pressing Enter between entries.
5. Click Add and click OK.

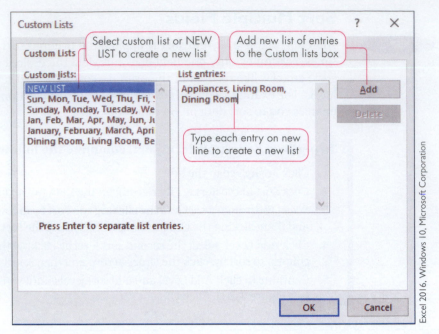

FIGURE 4.25 Custom Lists Dialog Box

> **TIP: NAME SORTS**
> Always check the data to determine how many levels of sorting you need to apply. If your table contains several people with the same last name but different first names, you would first sort by the Last Name field, then sort by First Name field. All the people with the last name Desmarais would be grouped together and further sorted by first name, such as Amanda and then Bradley.

Filtering Data

In some situations you might want to display only a subset of the data available, for example, the data to show transactions for only a particular sales representative. In these situations, you could apply a filter to achieve the desired results. In Excel, you have the ability to filter using various criteria such as date, value, text, and color. ***Filtering*** is the process of specifying conditions to display only those records that meet certain conditions.

> **TIP: COPYING BEFORE FILTERING DATA**
> Often, you need to show different filters applied to the same dataset. You can copy the worksheet and filter the data on the copied worksheet to preserve the original dataset.

Apply Text Filters

 When you apply a filter to a text field, the filter menu displays each unique text item. You can select one or more text items from the list to be filtered. Once completed only the selected text will be displayed.

To apply a text filter, complete the following steps:

1. Click any cell in the range of data to be filtered.
2. Click the Data tab and click Filter in the Sort & Filter group to display the filter arrows.
3. Click the filter arrow for the column you will filter.
4. Deselect the (Select All) check mark and click the check boxes for the text you would like to remain visible in the dataset. Click OK.

You can also select Text Filters to see a submenu of additional options, such as Begins With, to select all records for which the name begins with the letter G, for example.

Figure 4.26 shows the Sales_Last filter menu with two names selected. Excel displays records for these two reps only. The records for the other sales reps are hidden but not deleted. The filter arrow displays a filter icon, indicating which field is filtered. Excel displays the row numbers in blue, indicating that you applied a filter. The missing row numbers indicate hidden rows of data. When you remove the filter, all the records display again.

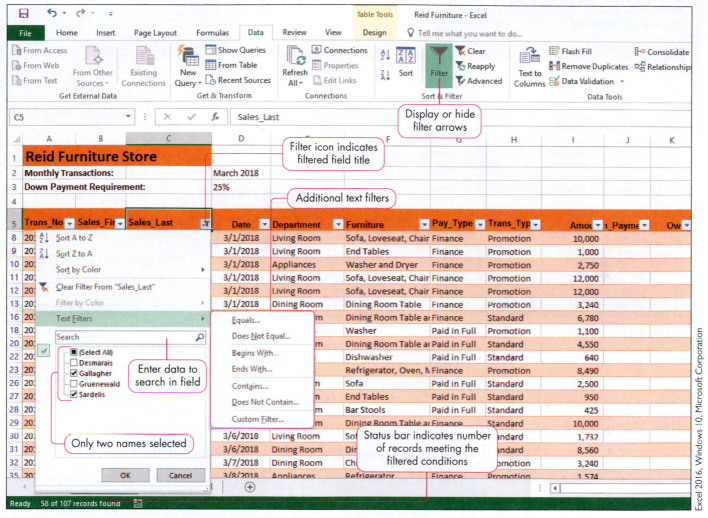

FIGURE 4.26 Filtered Text

Apply Number Filters

STEP 6 ▶▶ Excel contains a variety of number filters that enable you to display specific numbers, or a range of numbers such as above average or top 10 values. When you filter a field of numbers, you can select specific numbers. Or, you might want to filter numbers by a range, such as numbers greater than $5,000 or numbers between $4,000 and $5,000. If the field contains a large number of unique entries, you can click in the Search box and enter a value to display all matching records. For example, if you enter $7, the list will display only values that start with $7. The filter submenu enables you to set a variety of number filters. In Figure 4.27, the amounts are filtered to show only those that are above the average amount. In this situation, Excel calculates the average amount as $4,512. Only records above that amount display.

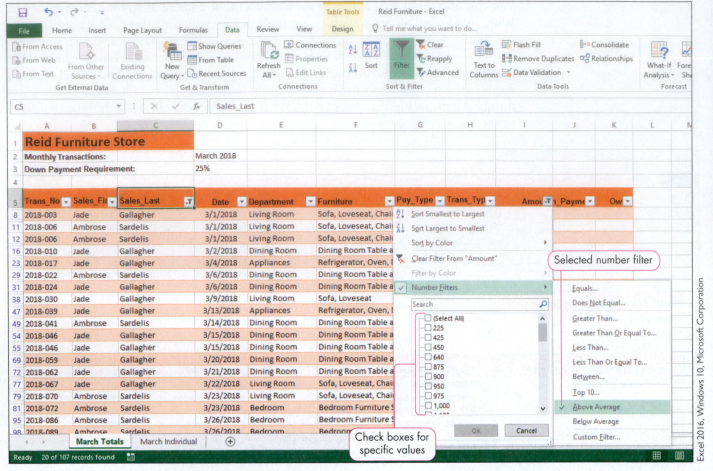

FIGURE 4.27 Filtered Numbers

The Top 10 option enables you to specify the top records. Although the option name is Top 10, you can specify the number or percentage of records to display. For example, you can filter the list to display only the top five or the bottom 7%. Figure 4.28 shows the Top 10 AutoFilter dialog box.

> **To filter using the custom Top 10 AutoFilter, complete the following steps:**
>
> 1. Click anywhere in the range or table, click the Data tab, and click Filter in the Sort & Filter group.
> 2. Click the filter arrow for the column that contains the data you would like to manipulate, point to Number Filters, and select Top 10.
> 3. Choose Top or Bottom value, click the last arrow to select either Items or Percent, and click OK.

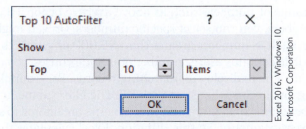

FIGURE 4.28 Top 10 AutoFilter Dialog Box

Apply Date Filters

STEP 7 >> When you filter a field of dates, you can select specific dates or a date range, such as dates after 3/15/2018 or dates between 3/1/2018 and 3/7/2018. The submenu enables you to set a variety of date filters. For more specific date options, point to Date Filters, point to *All Dates in the Period*, and then select a period, such as Quarter 2 or October. Figure 4.29 shows the Date Filters menu.

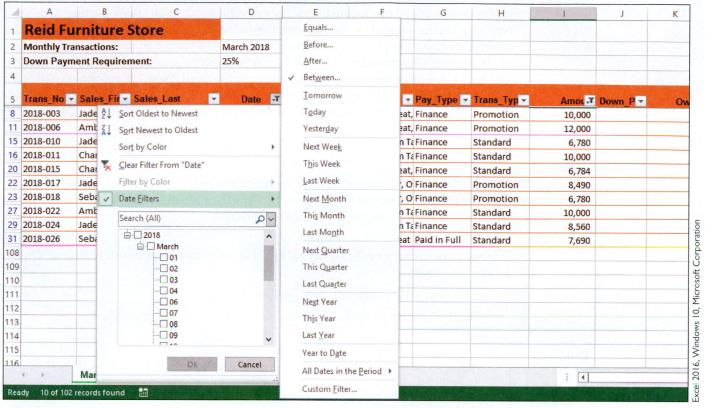

FIGURE 4.29 Filtered Dates

Apply a Custom Filter

Suppose as the manager of a furniture store, you are only interested in marketing directly to people who spent between $500 and $1,000 in the last month. To quickly identify the required data, you could use a custom AutoFilter. If you select options such as Greater Than or Between, Excel displays the Custom AutoFilter dialog box (see Figure 4.30). You can also select Custom Filter from the menu to display this dialog box, which is designed for more complex filtering requirements.

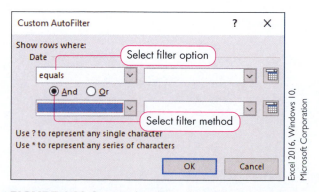

FIGURE 4.30 Custom AutoFilter Dialog Box

The dialog box indicates the column being filtered. To set the filters, click the arrows to select the comparison type, such as equals or contains. Click the arrow on the right to select a specific text, value, or date entry, or type the data yourself. For ranges of dates or values, click And, and then specify the comparison operator and value or date for the next condition row. For text, click Or. For example, if you want both Gallagher and Desmarais, you must select Or because each data entry contains either Gallagher or Desmarais but not both at the same time.

When filtering, you can use wildcards to help locate information in which there are multiple criteria and no custom filters. For example, to select all states starting with New, type *New** in the second box; this will obtain results such as New York or New Mexico. The asterisk (*) is used in exchange for the text after "New" and can represent any number of characters. Therefore this wildcard filter would return states New York, New Mexico, and New Hampshire because they all begin with the word "New." If you want a wildcard for only a single character, type the question mark (?). For example when filtering departments, "R?om" would return any department with room in the name as would "Room*."

Clear Filters

You can remove the filters from one or more fields to expand the dataset again. To remove only one filter and keep the other filters, click the filter arrow for the field from which you wish to clear the filter and select Clear Filter From.

To remove all filters and display all records in a dataset, complete one of the following steps:

- Click Clear in the Sort & Filter group on the Data tab.
- Click Sort & Filter in the Editing group on the Home tab and select Clear.

Quick Concepts

7. What is the purpose of sorting data in a table? ***p. 288***

8. What are two ways to arrange (sort) dates? ***p. 288***

9. List at least five ways you can filter numbers. ***p. 291***

10. Assume you are filtering a list and want to display records for people who live in Boston or New York. What settings do you enter in the Custom AutoFilter dialog box for that field? ***p. 293***

Hands-On Exercises

Watch the Video for this Hands-On Exercise!

MyITLab®
HOE3 Training

Skills covered: Create a Structured Reference in a Formula • Sort One Field • Sort Multiple Fields • Create a Custom Sort • Apply Text Filters • Apply a Number Filter • Apply a Date Filter

3 Table Manipulation

You want to start analyzing the March 2018 transactions for Reid Furniture Store by calculating the totals owed, then sorting and filtering data in a variety of ways to help you understand the transactions better.

STEP 1 ›› CREATE A STRUCTURED REFERENCE IN A FORMULA

First, you want to calculate the down payment owed by each customer. You will then calculate the total amount owed by subtracting the down payment from the total down payment. You will use structured references to complete these tasks. Refer to Figure 4.31 as you complete Step 1.

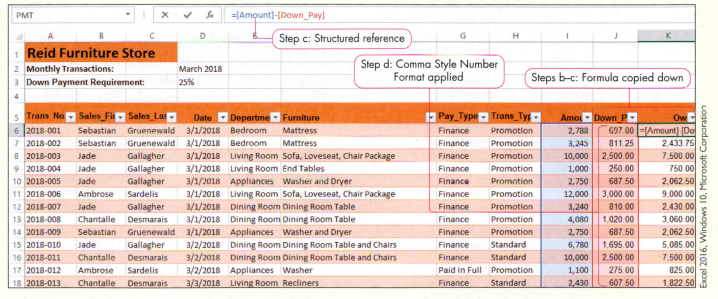

FIGURE 4.31 Create a Structured Reference

a. Open *e04h2Reid_LastFirst* if you closed it at the end of Hands-On Exercise 2. Save it as **e04h3Reid_LastFirst**, changing h2 to h3.

b. Click **cell J6**. Type the formula **=[Amount]*$D$3** and press **Enter**.

The down payment required is 25% of the total purchase price. Structured reference format is used for Amount to create the formula that calculates the customer's down payment. Excel copies the formula down the column.

c. Click **cell K6**. Type the formula **=[Amount]-[Down_Pay]** and press **Enter**.

The formula calculates the total value owed to the sales rep and copies the formula down the column.

d. Select the **range J6:K109** and apply the **Comma Style Number Format**.

e. Save the workbook.

You want to compare the number of transactions by sales rep, so you will sort the data by the Sales_Last field. After reviewing the transactions by sales reps, you then want to arrange the transactions to show the one with the largest purchase first and the smallest purchase last. Refer to Figure 4.32 as you complete Step 2.

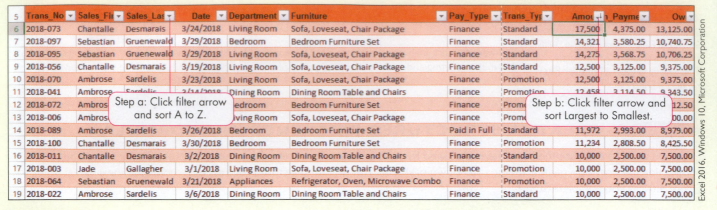

FIGURE 4.32 Sorted Data

a. Click the **Sales_Last filter arrow** and select **Sort A to Z**.

Excel arranges the transactions in alphabetical order by last name, starting with Desmarais. Within each sales rep, records display in their original sequence by transaction number. If you scan the records, you can see that Gallagher completed the most sales transactions in March. The up arrow icon on the Sales_Last filter arrow indicates that records are sorted in alphabetical order by that field.

b. Click the **Amount filter arrow** and select **Sort Largest to Smallest**.

The records are no longer sorted by Sales_Last. When you sort by another field, the previous sort is not saved. In this case, Excel arranges the transactions from the one with the largest amount to the smallest amount, indicated by the down arrow icon in the Amount filter arrow.

c. Save the workbook.

You want to review the transactions by payment type (financed or paid in full). Within each payment type, you further want to compare the transaction type (promotion or standard). Finally, you want to compare costs within the sorted records by displaying the highest costs first. You will use the Sort dialog box to perform a three-level sort. Refer to Figure 4.33 as you complete Step 3.

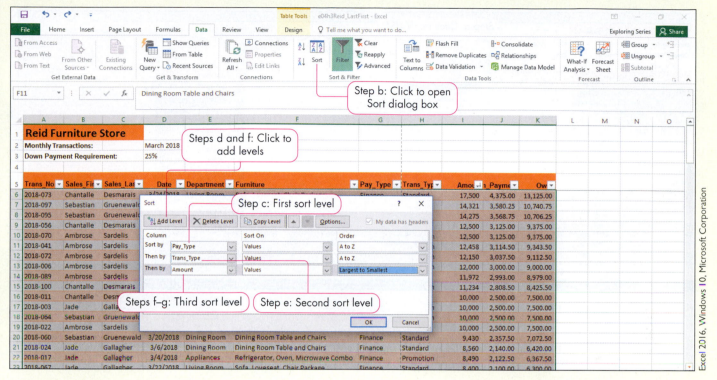

FIGURE 4.33 Three-Level Sort

a. Click inside the table and click the **Data tab**.

   Both the Data and Home tabs contain commands to open the Sort dialog box.

b. Click **Sort** in the Sort & Filter group to open the Sort dialog box.

c. Click the **Sort by arrow** and select **Pay_Type**. Click the **Order arrow** and select **A to Z**.

   You start by specifying the column for the primary sort. In this case, you want to sort the records first by the Payment Type column.

d. Click **Add Level**.

   The Sort dialog box adds the Then by row, which adds a secondary sort.

e. Click the **Then by arrow** and select **Trans_Type**.

   The default order is A to Z, which will sort in alphabetical order by Trans_Type. Excel will first sort the records by the Pay_Type (Finance or Paid in Full). Within each Pay_Type, Excel will further sort records by Trans_Type (Promotion or Standard).

f. Click **Add Level** to add another Then by row. Click the second **Then by arrow** and select **Amount**.

g. Click the **Order arrow** for the Amount sort and select **Largest to Smallest**.

   Within the Pay_Type and Trans_Type sorts, this will arrange the records with the largest amount first in descending order to the smallest amount.

h. Click **OK** and scroll through the records. Save the workbook.

   Most customers finance their purchases instead of paying in full. For the financed transactions, more than half were promotional sales. For merchandise paid in full, a majority of the transactions were standard sales, indicating that people with money do not necessarily wait for a promotional sale to purchase merchandise.

For the month of March you want to closely monitor sales of the Dining Room and Living Room departments. After completing the prior sort, you will add an additional level to create a custom sort of the department's data. Refer to Figure 4.34 as you complete Step 4.

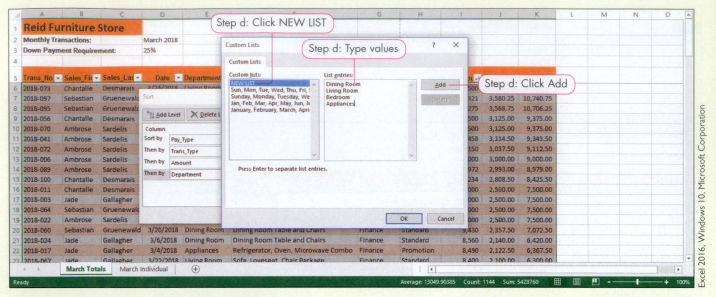

FIGURE 4.34 Custom Sort

a. Click inside the table and click **Sort** in the Sort & Filter group to open the Sort dialog box.

The Sort dialog box will open with the prior sort criteria displayed.

b. Click the **last level added** in the prior step and click **Add Level**.

c. Select **Department**. Click the **Order arrow** and select **Custom List**.

This will open the Custom Lists dialog box, enabling you to manually specify the sort order.

d. Click **NEW LIST** in the Custom lists box, click the **List entries box** and type **Dining Room, Living Room, Bedroom, Appliances**. Click **Add**, click **OK**, and then click **OK** again to complete to return to the worksheet.

After completing the custom list, the data in column E will be sorted by Dining Room, Living Room, Bedroom, and Appliances as the last step within the custom sort.

e. Save the workbook.

Now that you know Jade Gallagher had the most transactions for March, you will filter the table to focus on her sales. You notice that she sells more merchandise from the Dining Room department, so you will filter out the other departments. Refer to Figure 4.35 as you complete Step 5.

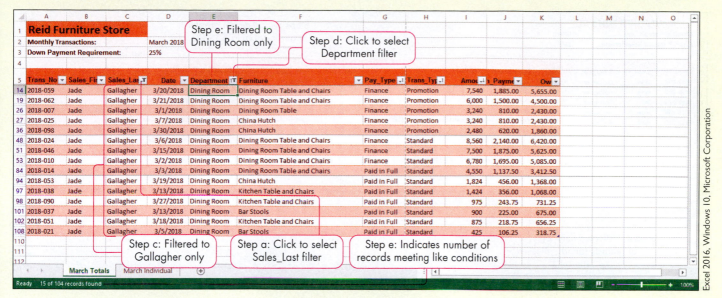

FIGURE 4.35 Apply Text Filters

a. Click the **Sales_Last filter arrow**.

   The (Select All) check box is selected.

b. Click the **(Select All) check box** to deselect all last names.

c. Click the **Gallagher check box** to select it and click **OK**.

   The status bar indicates that 33 out of 104 records meet the filtering condition. The Sales_Last filter arrow includes a funnel icon, indicating that this column is filtered.

d. Click the **Department filter arrow**.

e. Click the **(Select All) check box** to deselect all departments, click the **Dining Room check box** to focus on that department, and then click **OK**. Save the workbook.

   The remaining 15 records show Gallagher's dining room sales for the month. The Department filter arrow includes a funnel icon, indicating that this column is also filtered.

Vicki is considering giving a bonus to employees who sold high-end dining room furniture during a specific time period (3/16/2018 to 3/31/2018). You want to determine if Jade Gallagher qualifies for this bonus. In particular, you are interested in how much gross revenue she generated for dining room furniture that cost at least $5,000 or more. Refer to Figure 4.36 as you complete Step 6.

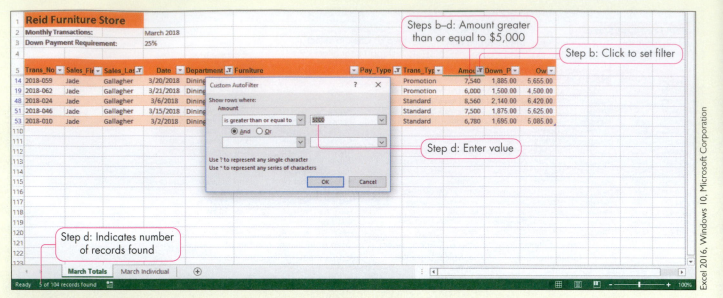

FIGURE 4.36 Filtered to Amounts Greater Than or Equal to $5,000

a. Select the **range I14:I108** of the filtered list and then view the status bar.

The average transaction amount is $3,754 with 15 transactions (i.e., 15 filtered records).

b. Click the **Amount filter arrow**.

c. Point to **Number Filters** and select **Greater Than Or Equal To**.

The Custom AutoFilter dialog box opens.

d. Type **5000** in the box to the right of *is greater than or equal to* and click **OK**. Save the workbook.

When typing numbers, you can type raw numbers such as 5000 or formatted numbers such as $5,000. Out of Gallagher's original 15 dining room transactions, only 5 transactions (one-third of her sales) were valued at $5,000 or more.

STEP 7 ›› APPLY A DATE FILTER

Finally, you want to study Jade Gallagher's sales records for the last half of the month. You will add a date filter to identify those sales records. Refer to Figure 4.37 as you complete Step 7.

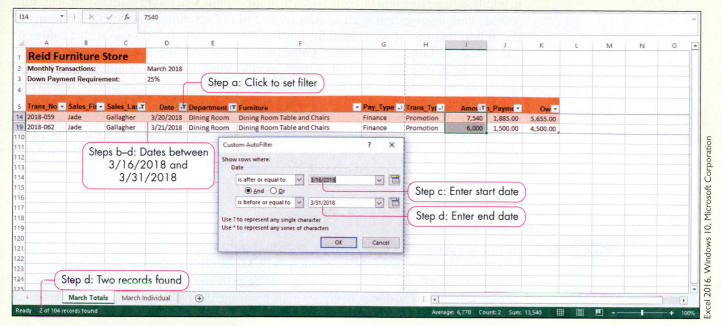

FIGURE 4.37 Filtered by Dates Between 3/16/2018 and 3/31/2018

a. Click the **Date filter arrow**.

b. Point to **Date Filters** and select **Between**.

   The Custom AutoFilter dialog box opens. The default comparisons are *is after or equal to* and *is before or equal to*, ready for you to enter the date specifications.

c. Type **3/16/2018** in the box on the right side of *is after or equal to*.

   You specified the starting date of the range of dates to include. You will keep the *And* option selected.

d. Type **3/31/2018** in the box on the right side of *is before or equal to*. Click **OK**.

   Gallagher had only two dining room sales greater than $5,000 during the last half of March.

e. Save the workbook. Keep the workbook open if you plan to continue with the next Hands-On Exercise. If not, close the workbook, and exit Excel.

Table Aggregation and Conditional Formatting

In addition to sorting and filtering tables to analyze data, you might want to add fields that provide data aggregation such as Average or Sum of amount purchased. Furthermore, you might want to apply special formatting to cells that contain particular values or text using conditional formatting. **Conditional formatting** applies special formatting to highlight or emphasize cells that meet specific conditions. For example, a sales manager might want to highlight employees that have reached their sales goal, or a professor might want to highlight test scores that fall below the average. You can also apply conditional formatting to point out data for a specific date or duplicate values in a range.

In this section, you will learn how to add a total row to a table along with learning about the five conditional formatting categories and how to apply conditional formatting to a range of values based on a condition you set.

Adding a Total Row

STEP 1 ▶▶ At times, aggregating data provides insightful information. For regular ranges of data, you use basic statistical functions, such as SUM, AVERAGE, MIN, and MAX, to provide summary analysis for a dataset. An Excel table provides the advantage of being able to display a total row automatically without creating the aggregate function yourself. A **total row** displays below the last row of records in an Excel table and enables you to display summary statistics, such as a sum of values displayed in a column.

To display and use the total row, complete the following steps:

1. Click any cell in the table.
2. Click the Design tab.
3. Click Total Row in the Table Style Options group. Excel displays the total row below the last record in the table. Excel displays Total in the first column of the total row.
4. Click a cell in the total row, click that cell's total row arrow, and then select the function result that you desire. Excel calculates the summary statistics for values, but if the field is text, the only summary statistic that can be calculated is Count.
5. Add a summary statistic to another column click in the empty cell for that field in the total row and click the arrow to select the desired function. Select None to remove the function.

Figure 4.38 shows the active total row with totals applied to the Amount, Down_Pay, and Owed fields. A list of functions displays to change the function for the last field.

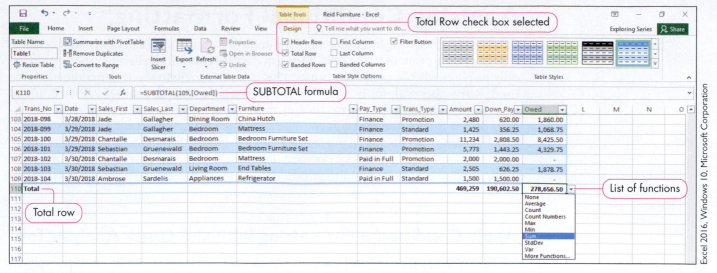

FIGURE 4.38 Total Row

The calculations on the total row use the SUBTOTAL function. The **SUBTOTAL function** calculates an aggregate value, such as totals or averages, for displayed values in a range, table, or database. If you click in a calculated total row cell, the SUBTOTAL function displays in the Formula Bar. The function for the total row looks like this: =SUBTOTAL(function_num,ref1). The function_num argument is a number that represents a function (see Table 4.4). The ref1 argument indicates the range of values to calculate. The SUBTOTAL function used to total the values in the Owed field would be =SUBTOTAL(109,[Owed]), where the number 109 represents the SUM function, and [Owed] represents the Owed field. A benefit of the SUBTOTAL function is that it subtotals data for filtered records, so you have an accurate total for the visible records.

=SUBTOTAL(function_num,ref1,…)

TABLE 4.4	Subtotal Function Numbers	
Function	**Function Number**	**Table Number**
AVERAGE	1	101
COUNT	2	102
COUNTA	3	103
MAX	4	104
MIN	5	105
PRODUCT	6	106
STDEV.S	7	107
STDEV.P	8	108
SUM	9	109
VAR.S	10	110
VAR.P	11	111

Pearson Education, Inc.

TIP: FILTERING DATA AND SUBTOTALS
If you filter the data and display the total row, the SUBTOTAL function's 109 argument ensures that only the displayed data are summed; data for hidden rows are not calculated in the aggregate function.

Applying Conditional Formatting

Conditional formatting helps you and your audience understand a dataset better because it adds a visual element to the cells. The term is called conditional because the formatting only displays when a condition is met. This is similar logic to the IF function you have used. Remember with an IF function, you create a logical test that is evaluated. If the logical or conditional test is true, the function produces one result. If the logical or conditional test is false, the function produces another result. With conditional formatting, if the condition is true, Excel formats the cell automatically based on that condition. If the condition is false, Excel does not format the cell. If you change a value in a conditionally formatted cell, Excel examines the new value to see if it should apply the conditional format.

Apply Conditional Formatting with the Quick Analysis Tool

When you select a range and click the Quick Analysis button, the Formatting options display in the Quick Analysis gallery. Point to a thumbnail to see how it will affect the selected range (see Figure 4.39). You can also apply conditional formatting by clicking Conditional Formatting in the Styles group on the Home tab.

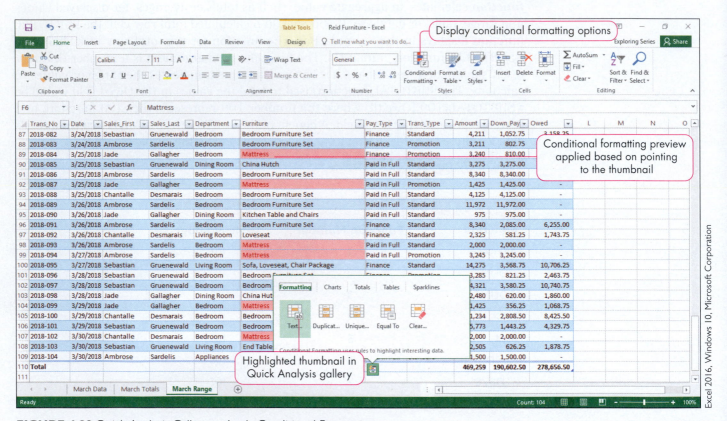

FIGURE 4.39 Quick Analysis Gallery to Apply Conditional Formatting

Table 4.5 describes the conditional formatting options in the Quick Analysis gallery.

TABLE 4.5	Conditional Formatting Options in Quick Analysis Gallery
Options	**Description**
Text Contains	Formats cells that contain the text in the first selected cell. In Figure 4.39, the first selected cell contains Mattress. If a cell contains Mattress and Springs, Excel would format that cell also because it contains Mattress.
Duplicate Values	Formats cells that are duplicated in the selected range.
Unique Values	Formats cells that are unique; that is, no other cell in the selected range contains the same data.
Equal To	Formats cells that are exactly like the data contained in the first selected cell.
Clear Format	Removes the conditional formatting from the selected range.

Pearson Education, Inc.

Table 4.6 lists and describes a number of different conditional formats that you can apply if you want more specific rules.

TABLE 4.6	Conditional Formatting Options
Options	**Description**
Highlight Cells Rules	Highlights cells with a fill color, font color, or border (such as Light Red Fill with Dark Red Text) if values are greater than, less than, between two values, equal to a value, or duplicate values; text that contains particular characters; or dates when a date meets a particular condition, such as *In the last 7 days*.
Top/Bottom Rules	Formats cells with values in the top 10 items, top 10%, bottom 10 items, bottom 10%, above average, or below average. You can change the exact values to format the top or bottom items or percentages, such as top 5 or bottom 15%.
Data Bars	Applies a gradient or solid fill bar in which the width of the bar represents the current cell's value compared relatively to other cells' values.
Color Scales	Formats different cells with different colors, assigning one color to the lowest group of values and another color to the highest group of values, with gradient colors to other values.
Icon Sets	Inserts an icon from an icon palette in each cell to indicate values compared to each other.

Pearson Education, Inc.

To apply a conditional format, complete the following steps:

1. Select the cells for which you want to apply a conditional format, click the Home tab, and click Conditional Formatting in the Styles group.
2. Select the conditional formatting category you want to apply.

Apply Highlight Cells Rules

STEP 2 ▶▶ The Highlight Cells Rules category enables you to apply a highlight to cells that meet a condition, such as cells containing values greater than a particular value. This option contains predefined combinations of fill colors, font colors, and/or borders. For example, suppose you are a sales manager who developed a worksheet containing the sales for each day of a month. You are interested in sales between $5000 and $10,000. You might want to apply a conditional format to cells that contain values within the desired range. To apply this conditional formatting, you would select Highlight Cells Rules and then select Between. In the Between dialog box (see Figure 4.40), type 5000 in the first value box and 10000 in the second value box, select the type of conditional formatting, such as Light Red Fill with Dark Red Text, and then click OK to apply the formats.

FIGURE 4.40 Between Dialog Box

Figure 4.41 shows two columns of data that contain conditional formats. The Department column is conditionally formatted to highlight text with a Light Red Fill with Dark Red Text for cells that contain Living Room, and the Amount column is conditionally formatted to highlight values between $5,000 and $10,000 with a Dark Red Border.

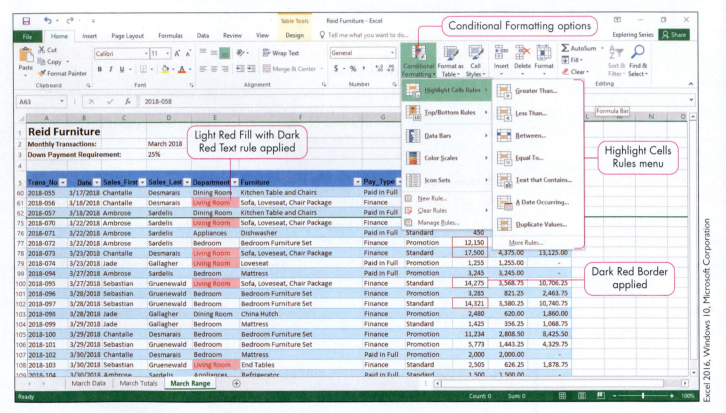

FIGURE 4.41 Highlight Cells Rules Conditional Formatting

Specify Top/Bottom Rules

STEP 3 ❯❯ You might be interested in identifying the top five sales to reward the sales associates, or want to identify the bottom 15% of of sales for more focused marketing. The Top/Bottom Rules category enables you to specify the top or bottom number, top or bottom percentage, or values that are above or below the average value in a specified range. In Figure 4.42, the Amount column is conditionally formatted to highlight the top five amounts. (Some rows are hidden so that all top five values display in the figure.) Although the menu option is Top 10 Items, you can specify the exact number of items to format.

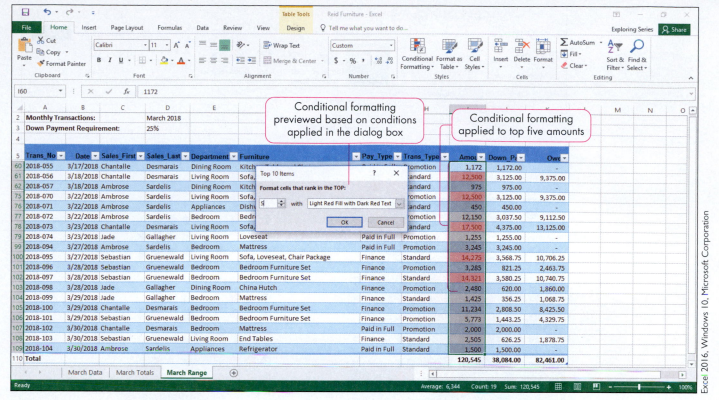

FIGURE 4.42 Top 10 Items Dialog Box

Display Data Bars, Color Scales, and Icon Sets

STEP 4 ➤➤ **Data bars** apply a gradient or solid fill bar in which the width of the bar represents the current cell's value compared relatively to other cells' values (see Figure 4.43). The width of the data bar represents the value in a cell, with a wider bar representing a higher value and a narrower bar a lower value. Excel locates the largest value and displays the widest data bar in that cell. Excel then finds the smallest value and displays the smallest data bar in that cell. Excel sizes the data bars for the remaining cells based on their values relative to the high and low values in the column. If you change the values, Excel updates the data bar widths. Excel uses the same color for each data bar, but each bar differs in size based on the value in the respective cells.

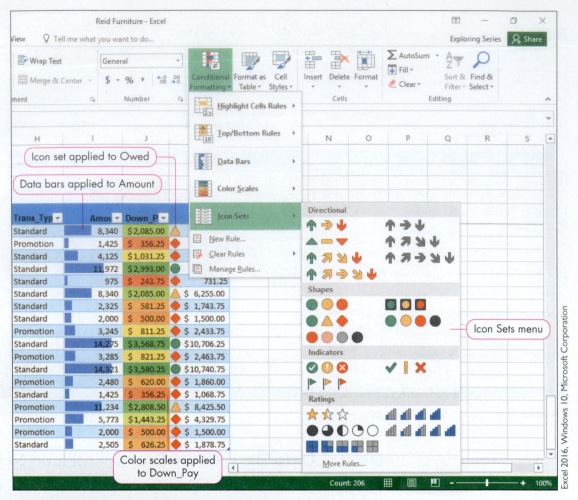

FIGURE 4.43 Data Bars, Color Scales, and Icon Sets

Color scales format cells with different colors based on the relative value of a cell compared to other selected cells. You can apply a two- or three-color scale. This scale assists in comparing a range of cells using gradations of those colors. The shade of the color represents higher or lower values. In Figure 4.43, for example, the red color scales display for the lowest values, the green color displays for the highest values, and gradients of yellow and orange represent the middle range of values in the Down_Pay column. Use color scales to understand variation in the data to identify trends, for example, to view good stock returns and weak stock returns.

Icon sets are symbols or signs that classify data into three, four, or five categories, based on the values in a range. Excel determines categories of value ranges and assigns an icon to each range. In Figure 4.43, a three-icon set was applied to the Owed column. Excel divided the range of values between the lowest value of $0 and the highest value of $13,125 into thirds. The red diamond icon displays for the cells containing values in the lowest third ($0 to $4,375), the yellow triangle icon displays for cells containing the values in the middle third ($4,376 to $8,750), and the green circle icon displays for cells containing values in the top third ($8,751 to $13,125). Most purchases fall into the lowest third.

> **TIP: DON'T OVERDO IT!**
> Although conditional formatting helps identify trends, you should use this feature wisely and sparingly. Apply conditional formatting only when you want to emphasize important data. When you decide to apply conditional formatting, think about which category is best to highlight the data.

Creating a New Rule

The default conditional formatting categories provide a variety of options. Excel also enables you to create your own rules to specify different fill colors, borders, or other formatting if you do not want the default settings. Excel provides three ways to create a new rule.

To create a new Conditional Formatting rule, complete one of the following steps:

- Click Conditional Formatting in the Styles group and select New Rule.
- Click Conditional Formatting in the Styles group, select Manage Rules to open the Conditional Formatting Rules Manager dialog box, and then click New Rule.
- Click Conditional Formatting in the Styles group, select a rule category such as Highlight Cells Rules, and then select More Rules.

When creating a new rule, the New Formatting Rule dialog box opens (see Figure 4.44) so that you can define the conditional formatting rule. First, select a rule type, such as *Format all cells based on their values*. The *Edit the Rule Description* section changes, based on the rule type you select. With the default rule type selected, you can specify the format style (2-Color Scale, 3-Color Scale, Data Bar, or Icon Sets). You can then specify the minimum and maximum values, the fill colors for color sets or data bars, or the icons for icon sets. After you edit the rule description, click OK to save your new conditional format.

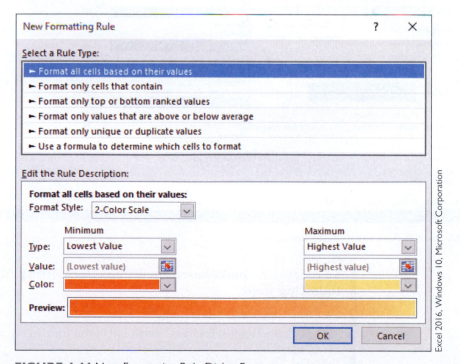

FIGURE 4.44 New Formatting Rule Dialog Box

If you select any rule type except the *Format all cells based on their values* rule, the dialog box contains a Format button. When you click Format, the Format Cells dialog box opens so that you can specify number, font, border, and fill formats to apply to your rule.

> **TIP: FORMAT ONLY CELLS THAT CONTAIN A SPECIFIC VALUE**
> When creating new Conditional Formatting rules, you have the option to format only cells that contain a specific value. This option provides a wide array of things you can format: values, text, dates, blanks, no blanks, errors, or no errors. Formatting blanks is helpful to see where you are missing data, and formatting cells containing errors helps you find those errors quickly. These options can be accessed from the Select a Rule Type box in the New Formatting Rule dialog box when creating a Conditional Formatting rule.

Use Formulas in Conditional Formatting

STEP 5 ❯❯ Suppose you want to format merchandise amounts of financed items *and* amounts that are $10,000 or more. You can use a formula to create a conditional formatting rule to complete the task. Figure 4.45 shows the Edit Formatting Rule dialog box and the corresponding conditional formatting applied to cells.

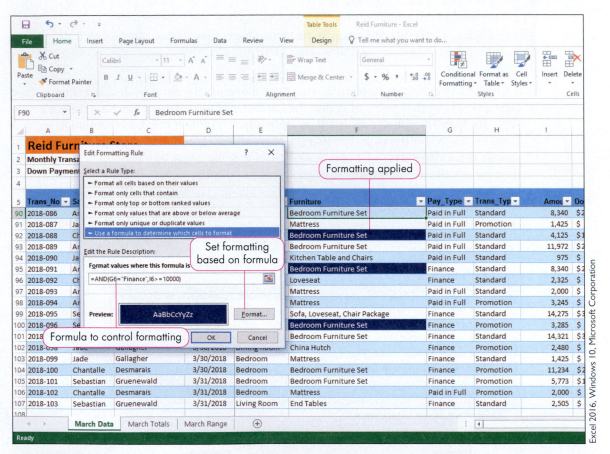

FIGURE 4.45 Formula Rule Created and Applied

> **To create a formula-based conditional formatting rule, complete the following steps:**
>
> 1. Select the desired data range.
> 2. Click the Home tab, click Conditional Formatting in the Styles group, and click New Rule.
> 3. Select *Use a formula to determine which cells to format* and type the formula, using cell references in the first row, in the *Format values where this formula is true* box.

Once complete, Excel applies the general formula to the selected range, substituting the appropriate cell reference as it makes the comparisons. In the Figure 4.45 example, =AND(G6="Finance",I6>=10000) requires that the text in the Pay_Type column (column G) contain Finance and the Amount column (column I) contain a value that is greater than or equal to $10,000. The AND function requires that both logical tests be met to apply the conditional formatting. A minimum of two logical tests are required; however, you can include additional logical tests. Note that *all* logical tests must be true to apply the conditional formatting.

= AND(logical1,logical2,…)

Manage Rules

Periodically conditional formatting rules may need to be updated, moved, or completely deleted.

To edit or delete conditional formatting rules you create, click Conditional Formatting in the Styles group and select Manage Rules. The Conditional Formatting Rules Manager dialog box opens (see Figure 4.46). Click the *Show formatting rules for* arrow and select from *current selection, the entire worksheet,* or *this table.* Select the rule, click Edit Rule or Delete Rule, and click OK after making the desired changes. To remove conditional formatting from a range of cells, select the cells. Then click Conditional Formatting, point to Clear Rules, and select Clear Rules from Selected Cells.

To clear all conditional formatting from the entire worksheet, complete the following steps:

1. Click Conditional Formatting in the Styles group on the Home tab.
2. Point to Clear Rules, and then select Clear Rules from Entire Sheet.

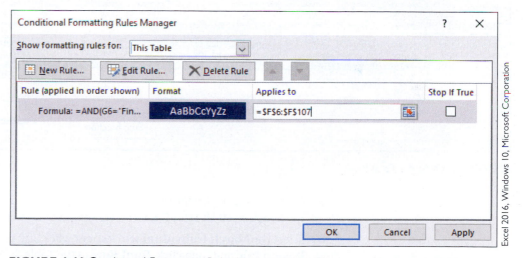

FIGURE 4.46 Conditional Formatting Rules Manager Dialog Box

Quick Concepts

11. How is conditional formatting similar to an IF function? *p. 304*

12. What conditional formatting would be helpful to identify the three movies with the highest revenue playing at theaters? *pp. 306–307*

13. How is data bar conditional formatting helpful when reviewing a column of data? *p. 307*

Hands-On Exercises

Watch the Video for this Hands-On Exercise!

MyITLab® HOE4 Training

4 Table Aggregation and Conditional Formatting

Vicki Reid wants to review the transactions with you. She is interested in Sebastian Gruenewald's sales record and the three highest transaction amounts. In addition, she wants to compare the down payment amounts visually. Finally, she wants you to analyze the amounts owed for sales completed by Sebastian.

STEP 1 » ADD A TOTAL ROW

You want to see the monthly totals for the Amount, Down_Pay, and Owed columns. You will add a total row to calculate the values. Refer to Figure 4.47 as you complete Step 1.

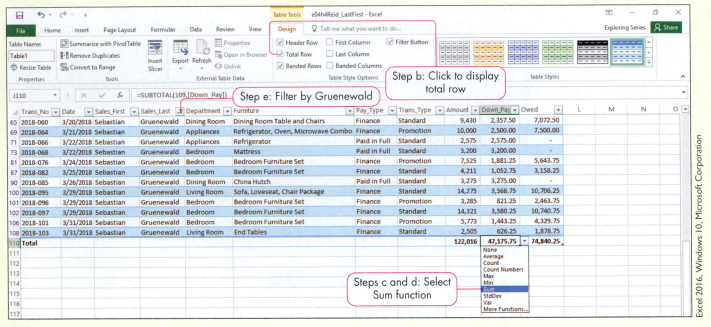

FIGURE 4.47 Add a Total Row

a. Open *e04h3Reid_LastFirst* if you closed it at the end of Hands-On Exercise 3. Save the workbook as **e04h4Reid_LastFirst**, changing h3 to h4.

b. Select the **March Individual worksheet**, click any cell inside the table, click the **Design tab**, and then click **Total Row** in the Table Style Options group.

Excel displays the total row after the last record. It sums the last field of values automatically. The total amount customers owe is $278,656.50.

c. Click the **Down_Pay cell** in row 110, click the **total arrow**, and then select **Sum**.

You added a total to the Down_Pay field. The total amount of down payment collected is $190,602.50. The formula displays as =SUBTOTAL(109,[Down_Pay]) in the Formula Bar.

d. Click the **Amount cell** in row 110, click the **total arrow**, and then select **Sum**.

You added a total to the Amount column. The total amount of merchandise sales is $469,259. The formula displays as =SUBTOTAL(109,[Amount]) in the Formula Bar.

e. Click the **Sales_Last filter arrow**, click the **(Select All) check box**, click the **Gruenewald check box** to select it, and then click **OK**.

The total row values change to display the totals for only Gruenewald: $122,016 (Amount), 47,175.75 (Down_Pay), and 74,840.25 (Owed). This is an advantage of using the total row, which uses the SUBTOTAL function, as opposed to if you had inserted the SUM function manually. The SUM function would provide a total for all data in the column, not just the filtered data.

f. Click the **Data tab** and click **Clear** in the Sort & Filter group to remove all filters.

g. Save the workbook.

STEP 2 ›› APPLY HIGHLIGHT CELLS RULES

You want to identify Sebastian's sales for March 2018 without filtering the data. You will set a conditional format to apply a fill and font color so cells that document appliance sales stand out. Refer to Figure 4.48 as you complete Step 2.

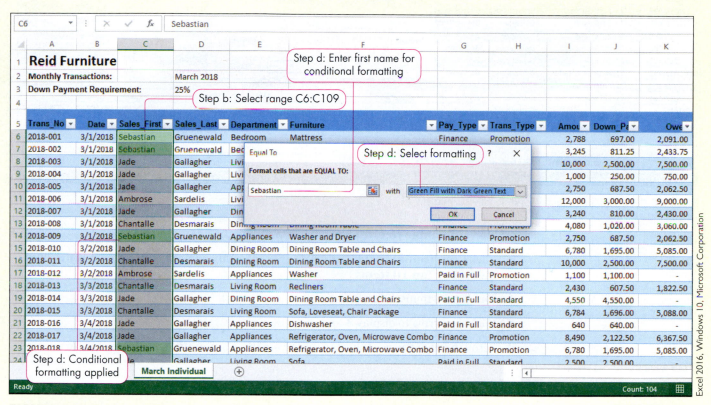

FIGURE 4.48 Conditional Formatting Rules Manager Dialog Box

a. Select **row headings 6 through 109** in the March Individual worksheet. Click the **Home tab**, click the **Fill Color arrow**, and then select **No Fill**.

You removed the previous table style. This will avoid having too many fill colors when you apply conditional formatting rules.

b. Select the **range C6:C109**.

c. Click **Conditional Formatting** in the Styles group, point to **Highlight Cells Rules**, and then select **Text that Contains**.

The Text that Contains dialog box opens.

d. Type **Sebastian** in the box, click the **with arrow**, and then select **Green Fill with Dark Green Text**. Click **OK**. Deselect the range and save the workbook.

Excel formats only cells that contain Sebastian with the fill and font color.

Vicki is now interested in identifying the highest three sales transactions in March. Instead of sorting the records, you will use the Top/Bottom Rules conditional formatting. Refer to Figure 4.49 as you complete Step 3.

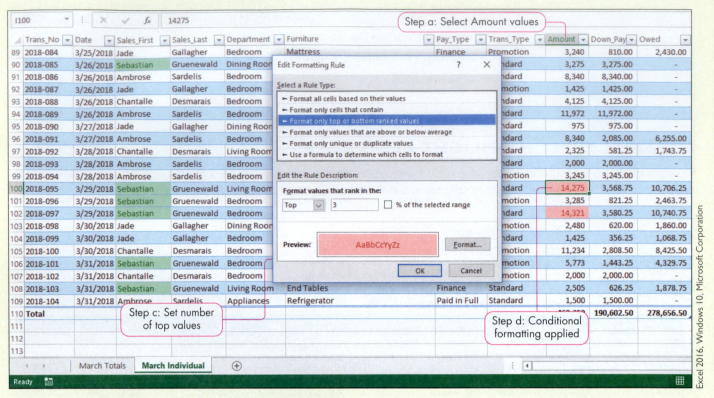

FIGURE 4.49 Top 3 Amounts Conditionally Formatted

a. Select the **range I6:I109**, the range containing the amounts.

b. Click **Conditional Formatting** in the Styles group, point to **Top/Bottom Rules**, and then select **Top 10 Items**.

The Top 10 Items dialog box opens.

c. Click the arrow to display **3** and click **OK**.

d. Scroll through the worksheet to see the top three amounts. Save the workbook.

Vicki wants to compare all of the down payments. Data bars would add a nice visual element as she compares down payment amounts. Refer to Figure 4.50 as you complete Step 4.

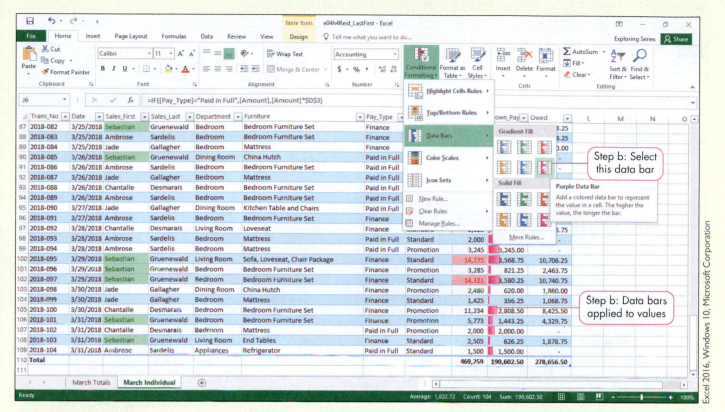

FIGURE 4.50 Data Bars Conditional Formatting

a. Select the **range J6:J109**, which contains the down payment amounts.

b. Click **Conditional Formatting** in the Styles group, point to **Data Bars**, and then select **Purple Data Bar** in the Gradient Fill section. Scroll through the list and save the workbook.

Excel displays data bars in each cell. The larger bar widths help Vicki quickly identify the largest down payments. However, the largest down payments are identical to the original amounts when the customers pay in full. This result illustrates that you should not accept the results at face value. Doing so would provide you with an inaccurate analysis.

Vicki's next request is to analyze the amounts owed by Sebastian's customers. In particular, she wants to highlight the merchandise for which more than $5,000 is owed. To do this, you realize you need to create a custom rule that evaluates both the Sales_First column and the Owed column. Refer to Figure 4.51 as you complete Step 5.

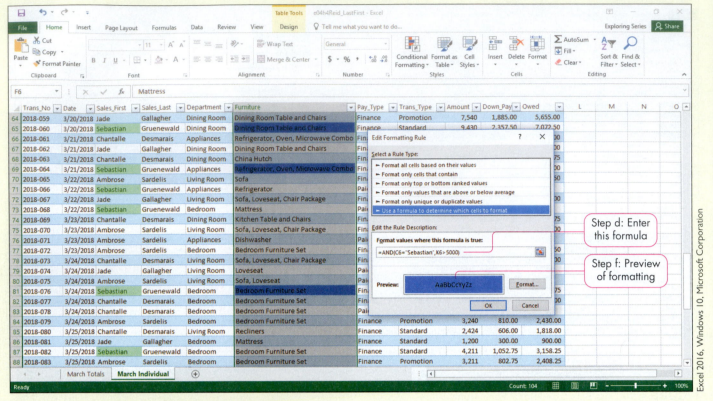

FIGURE 4.51 Custom Rule Created

a. Select the **range F6:F109**, which contains the furniture merchandise.

b. Click **Conditional Formatting** in the Styles group and select **New Rule**.

   The New Formatting Rule dialog box opens.

c. Select **Use a formula to determine which cells to format**.

d. Type **=AND(C6="Sebastian",K6>5000)** in the *Format values where this formula is true* box.

   Because you are comparing the contents of cell C6 to text, you must enclose the text within quotation marks.

e. Click **Format** to open the Format Cells dialog box.

f. Click the **Font tab**, and click **Bold** in the Font style list. Click the **Border tab**, click the **Color arrow**, select **Blue, Accent 5**, and then click **Outline**. Click the **Fill tab**, click **Blue, Accent 5 background color** (the second color from the right on the first row), and then click **OK**.

   Figure 4.51 shows the Edit Formatting Rule dialog box, but the options are similar to the New Formatting Rule dialog box.

g. Click **OK** in the New Formatting Rule dialog box and scroll through the list to see which amounts owed are greater than $5,000 for Sebastian only.

> **TROUBLESHOOTING:** If the results seem incorrect, click Conditional Formatting and select Manage Rules. Edit the rule you just created and make any corrections to the formula.

h. Save and close the file. Based on your instructor's directions, submit the file e04h4Reid_LastFirst.

Chapter Objectives Review

After reading this chapter, you have accomplished the following objectives:

1. Freeze rows and columns.

- The Freeze Panes setting freezes the row(s) above and the column(s) to the left of the active cell. When you scroll, those rows and columns remain onscreen.
- Use Unfreeze Panes to clear the frozen rows and columns.

2. Print large datasets.

- Display and change page breaks: Display the data in Page Break Preview to see the automatic page breaks. Dashed blue lines indicate automatic page breaks. You can insert manual page breaks, indicated by solid blue lines.
- Set and clear a print area: If you do not want to print an entire worksheet, select a range and set a print area.
- Print titles: Select rows to repeat at top and/or columns to repeat at left to print the column and row labels on every page of a printout of a large dataset.
- Control print page order: You can control the sequence in which the pages will print.

3. Understand the benefits of data tables.

- A table is a structured range that contains related data. Tables have several benefits over regular ranges. The column labels, called field names, display on the first row of a table. Each row is a complete set of data for one record.

4. Design and create tables.

- Plan a table before you create it. Create unique field names on the first row of the table and enter data below the field names, avoiding blank rows.
- Create a table: You can create a table from existing data. Excel applies the Table Style Medium 2 format and assigns a name, such as Table1, to the table. When the active cell is within a table, the Table Tools Design tab displays.
- Rename a table: When a table is created, Excel assigns a generic name and enables you to edit the default to a more suitable name.
- Add and delete fields: You can insert and delete table rows and columns to adjust the structure of a table.
- Add, edit, and delete records: You can add table rows, edit records, and delete table rows.
- Remove duplicate rows: Use the Remove Duplicates dialog box to remove duplicate records in a table. Excel will display a dialog box telling you how many records are deleted.

5. Apply a table style.

- Table styles control the fill color of the header row and records within the table.

6. Create structured references in formulas.

- Structured references use tags as field headings that can be used in formulas in place of cell references.

7. Sort data.

- Sort one field: You can sort text in alphabetical or reverse alphabetical order, values from smallest to largest or largest to smallest, and dates from oldest to newest or newest to oldest. Click the filter arrow and select the sort method from the list.
- Sort multiple fields: Open the Sort dialog box and add column levels and sort orders.
- Create a custom sort: You can create a custom sort for unique data, such as ensuring that the months sort in sequential order rather than alphabetical order.

8. Filter data.

- Filtering is the process of specifying conditions for displaying records in a table. Only records that meet those conditions display; the other records are hidden.
- Apply text filters: A text filter can find exact text, text that does not equal a condition, text that begins with a particular letter, and so forth.
- Apply number filters: A number filter can find exact values, values that do not equal a particular value, values greater than or equal to a value, and so on.
- Apply date filters: You can set filters to find dates before or after a certain date, between two dates, yesterday, next month, and so forth.
- Apply a custom filter: You can create a custom AutoFilter to filter values by options such as Greater Than, Less Than, or Before.
- Clear filters: If you do not need filters, you can clear the filters.

9. Add a total row.

- You can display a total row after the last record. You can add totals or select a different function, such as Average.

10. Apply conditional formatting.

- Apply conditional formatting with the Quick Analysis Tool: After selecting text, click Formatting in the Quick Analysis gallery to apply a conditional format.
- Apply a highlight cells rule: This rule highlights cell contents with a fill color, font color, and/or border color where the contents match a particular condition.
- Specify a top/bottom rule: This rule enables you to highlight the top or bottom x number of items or percentage of items.
- Display data bars, color scales, and icon sets: Data bars compare values within the selected range. Color scales indicate values that occur within particular ranges. Icon sets display icons representing a number's relative value compared to other numbers in the range.

11. Create a new rule.

- You can create conditional format rules. The New Formatting Rule dialog box enables you to select a rule type.
- Use formulas in conditional formatting: You can create rules based on content in multiple columns.
- Manage rules: Use the Conditional Formatting Rules Manager dialog box to edit and delete rules.

Key Terms Matching

Match the key terms with their definitions. Write the key term letter by the appropriate numbered definition.

a. Color scale
b. Conditional formatting
c. Data bar
d. Field
e. Filtering
f. Freezing
g. Icon set
h. Page break
i. Print area

j. Print order
k. Record
l. Sorting
m. Structured reference
n. SUBTOTAL function
o. Table
p. Table style
q. Total row

1. _____ A conditional format that displays a horizontal gradient or solid fill indicating the cell's relative value compared to other selected cells. **p. 307**

2. _____ The process of listing records or text in a specific sequence, such as alphabetically by last name. **p. 288**

3. _____ The process of specifying conditions to display only those records that meet those conditions. **p. 290**

4. _____ A set of rules that applies specific formatting to highlight or emphasize cells that meet specifications. **p. 302**

5. _____ A group of related fields representing one entity, such as data for one person, place, event, or concept. **p. 275**

6. _____ The rules that control the fill color of the header row, columns, and records in a table. **p. 280**

7. _____ An indication of where data will start on another printed page. **p. 266**

8. _____ A table row that appears below the last row of records in an Excel table and displays summary or aggregate statistics, such as a sum or an average. **p. 302**

9. _____ A conditional format that displays a particular color based on the relative value of the cell contents to the other selected cells. **p. 308**

10. _____ The sequence in which the pages are printed. **p. 269**

11. _____ A tag or use of a table element, such as a field label, as a reference in a formula. **p. 287**

12. _____ Symbols or signs that classify data into three, four, or five categories, based on the values in a range. **p. 308**

13. _____ The range of cells within a worksheet that will print. **p. 267**

14. _____ A predefined formula that calculates an aggregate value, such as totals, for values in a range, a table, or a database. **p. 303**

15. _____ The smallest data element contained in a table, such as first name, last name, address, and phone number. **p. 275**

16. _____ A structure that organizes data in a series of records (rows), with each record made up of a number of fields (columns). **p. 275**

17. _____ The process of keeping rows and/or columns visible onscreen at all times even when you scroll through a large dataset. **p. 265**

Multiple Choice

1. You have a large dataset that will print on several pages. You want to ensure that related records print on the same page with column and row labels visible and that confidential information is not printed. You should apply all of the following page setup options *except* which one to accomplish this task?
   (a) Set a print area.
   (b) Print titles.
   (c) Adjust page breaks.
   (d) Change the print page order.

2. You are working with a large worksheet. Your row headings are in column A. Which command(s) should be used to see the row headings and the distant information in columns X, Y, and Z?
   (a) Freeze Panes command
   (b) Hide Rows command
   (c) New Window command and cascade the windows
   (d) Split Rows command

3. Which statement is *not* a recommended guideline for designing and creating an Excel table?
   (a) Avoid naming two fields with the same name.
   (b) Ensure that no blank columns separate data columns within the table.
   (c) Leave one blank row between records in the table.
   (d) Include field names on the first row of the table.

4. Which of the following characters are wildcards in Excel? (Check all that apply.)
   (a) *
   (b) #
   (c) ?
   (d) $

5. What should you do to ensure that records in a table are unique?
   (a) Do nothing; a logical reason probably exists to keep identical records.
   (b) Use the Remove Duplicates command.
   (c) Look at each row yourself and manually delete duplicate records.
   (d) Find the duplicate records and change some of the data to be different.

6. Which Conditional Formatting rule is best suited to apply formatting to the top five values in a range of values?
   (a) Above Average
   (b) Greater Than
   (c) Top 10 Items
   (d) Between

7. Which date filter option enables you to restrict the view to only dates that occur in March of 2018?
   (a) Equals
   (b) Before
   (c) After
   (d) Between

8. Which of the following is an unqualified structured reference?
   (a) =[Purchase_Price]-[Down_Payment]
   (b) =Sales[Purchase_Price]-Sales[Down_Payment]
   (c) =Purchase_Price-Down_Payment
   (d) =[Sales]Purchase_Price-[Sales]Down_Payment

9. Which of the following is not an aggregate function that can be applied in a total row?
   (a) MAX
   (b) AVERAGE
   (c) COUNT
   (d) VLOOKUP

10. If you would like to set a conditional formatting rule based on the function =AND(G6="Finance", H7<7000), which formatting rule type is needed?
    (a) Format all cells based on their values
    (b) Format only cells that contain
    (c) Use a formula to determine which cells to format
    (d) Format only values that are above or below average

Practice Exercises

1 Collectables and Replacement Values

Marie Maier has collected dinnerware, from a fine china company, since 1986. Between 1986 and 2012, the company produced 30 colors, each with a unique name. Marie created a table in Word that lists the name, number, year introduced, and year retired (if applicable) for each color. She created another table in Word that lists the item number, item, replacement value, and source of information for each item in her collection. Her main sources for replacement values are Homer Laughlin (www.fiestafactorydirect.com), Replacements, Ltd. (www.replacements.com), eBay (www.ebay.com), and two local antique stores. She needs your help to convert the data to Excel tables, apply table formatting, delete duplicate records, insert functions, and sort and filter the data. Refer to Figure 4.52 as you complete this exercise.

	A	B	C	D	E	F	G	H
1	Color Number	Year Introduced	Year Retired	Status	Color	Item Number	Item	Replacement Value
31	102	2000	2010	Retired	Cinnabar	571	Canister Small	49.99
32	102	2000	2010	Retired	Cinnabar	830	5 Piece Place Setting	35.99
33	102	2000	2010	Retired	Cinnabar	484	Pitcher Large Disc	34.99
34	102	2000	2010	Retired	Cinnabar	467	Chop Plate	25.00
35	102	2000	2010	Retired	Cinnabar	497	Salt and Pepper Set	20.00
36	102	2000	2010	Retired	Cinnabar	465	Luncheon Plate	12.50
37	102	2000	2010	Retired	Cinnabar	439	Spoon Rest	11.99
38	102	2000	2010	Retired	Cinnabar	570	Java Mug	9.99
39	102	2000	2010	Retired	Cinnabar	453	Mug	8.49
40	102	2000	2010	Retired	Cinnabar	446	Tumbler	6.99
41	103	1986	2005	Retired	Rose	494	Covered Coffee Server	75.00
42	103	1986	2005	Retired	Rose	495	Covered Casserole	65.00
43	103	1986	2005	Retired	Rose	489	Pyramid Candleholders	59.99
44	103	1986	2005	Retired	Rose	486	Sauceboat	39.99
45	103	1986	2005	Retired	Rose	830	5 Piece Place Setting	35.00
46	103	1986	2005	Retired	Rose	821	Sugar/Cream Tray Set	29.99
47	103	1986	2005	Retired	Rose	484	Pitcher Large Disc	24.99
48	103	1986	2005	Retired	Rose	478	AD Cup and Saucer	19.99
49	103	1986	2005	Retired	Rose	471	Bowl Large 1 qt	19.99
50	103	1986	2005	Retired	Rose	497	Salt and Pepper Set	18.00
51	103	1986	2005	Retired	Rose	467	Chop Plate	16.95
52	103	1986	2005	Retired	Rose	451	Rim Soup	12.50

FIGURE 4.52 Fiesta® Collection

a. Open *e04p1Collectables* and save it as **e04p1Collectables_LastFirst**.

b. Select the **range A2:D31** on the Colors Data sheet, click in the **Name Box**, type **Colors**, and then press **Enter** to assign the name *Colors* to the selected range.

c. Click **cell A2** on the Items sheet, click the **View tab**, click **Freeze Panes** in the Window group, and then select **Freeze Top Row**.

d. Click the **Insert tab**, click **Table** in the Tables group, and then click **OK** in the Create Table dialog box.

e. Click **More Styles** in the Table Styles group and click **Table Style Medium 5**.

f. Click the **Data tab**, click **Remove Duplicates** in the Data Tools group, and then click **OK** in the Remove Duplicates dialog box. Click **OK** in the message box that informs you that 6 duplicate values were found and removed; 356 unique values remain.

g. Click **cell A2**, click the **Home tab**, click **Sort & Filter** in the Editing group, and then select **Sort Smallest to Largest**.

h. Click **cell B2**, click the **Insert arrow** in the Cells group, and then select **Insert Table Columns to the Left**. Insert two more columns to the left. Do the following to insert functions and customize the results in the three new table columns:

- Type **Year Introduced** in **cell B1**, **Year Retired** in **cell C1**, and **Color** in **cell D1**.
- Click **cell B2**, type **=VLOOKUP([Color Number],colors,3,False)**, and then press **Enter**. Excel copies the function down the Year Introduced column. This function looks up each item's color number using the structured reference *[Color Number]*, looks up that value in the colors table, and then returns the year that color was introduced, which is in the third column of that table.
- Click **cell B2**, click **Copy**, click **cell C2**, and then click **Paste**. Change the *3* to **4** in the col_index_num argument of the pasted function and press **Enter**. Excel copies the function down the Year Retired column. This function looks up each item's color number using the structured reference *[Color Number]*, looks up that value in the colors table, and then returns the year that color was retired, if applicable, which is in the fourth column of that table. The function returns 0 if the retired cell in the lookup table is blank.

- Click the **File tab**, click **Options**, click **Advanced**, scroll down to the Display options for this worksheet section, click the **Show a zero in cells that have zero value check box** to deselect it, and then click **OK**. The zeros disappear. (This option hides zeros in the active worksheet. While this is not desirable if you need to show legitimate zeros, this worksheet is designed to avoid that issue.)
- Click **cell C2**, click **Copy**, click **cell D2**, and then click **Paste**. Change the *4* to **2** in the col_index_num argument of the pasted function and press **Enter**. Excel copies the function down the Color column. This function looks up each item's color number using the structured reference *[Color Number]* to look up that value in the colors table and returns the color name, which is in the second column of that table.

i. Apply wrap text, horizontal centering, and **30.50 row height** to the column labels row. Adjust column widths to AutoFit. Center data horizontally in the Color Number, Year Introduced, Year Retired, and Item Number columns. Apply **Comma Style** to the Replacement Values. Deselect the data.

j. Click **Sort & Filter** in the Editing group and select **Custom Sort** to display the Sort dialog box. Do the following in the Sort dialog box:

- Click the **Sort by arrow** and select **Color**.
- Click **Add Level**, click the **Then by arrow**, and then select **Replacement Value**.
- Click the **Order arrow** and select **Largest to Smallest**.
- Click **Add Level**, click the **Then by arrow**, and select **Source**.
- Click the **Order arrow**, select **Custom List**, and type the following entries: **Ebay Auction, Downtown Antique Store, The Homer Laughlin China Co., Replacements LTD., Keith's Antique Store**. Click **Add** and click **OK**. Click **OK**.

k. Right-click the **Items sheet tab**, select **Move or Copy**, click **(move to end)**, click the **Create a copy check box** to select the option, and then click **OK**. Rename the copied sheet **Retired**.

l. Ensure that Retired is the active sheet. Insert a table column between the Year Retired and Color columns.

- Type **Status** in **cell D1** as the column label.
- Click **cell D2**, type **=IF([Year Retired]=0, "Current","Retired")**, and then press **Enter**. This function determines that if the cell contains a 0 (which is hidden), it will display the word *Current*. Otherwise, it will display *Retired*.

m. Click the **Status filter arrow**, deselect the **Current check box**, and then click **OK** to filter out the current colors and display only retired colors.

n. Click the **Design tab** and click **Total Row** in the Table Style Options group. Click **cell I358**, click the **Source total cell** (which contains a count of visible items), click the **Source total arrow**, and then select **None**. Click **cell H358**, the Replacement Value total cell, click the **Replacement Value total arrow**, and then select **Sum**.

o. Prepare the Retired worksheet for printing by doing the following:

- Set **0.2"** left and right page margins.
- Select the **range E1:I358**, click the **Page Layout tab**, click **Print Area** in the Page Setup group, and then select **Set Print Area**.
- Click **Print Titles** in the Page Setup group, click the **Rows to repeat at top Collapse Dialog Box**, click the **row 1 header**, and then click **Expand Dialog Box**. Click **OK**.
- Click the **View tab** and click **Page Break Preview** in the Workbook Views group. Decrease the top margin to avoid having only one or two records print on the last page.

p. Create a footer with your name on the left side, the sheet name code in the center, and the file name code on the right side of each worksheet.

q. Save and close the file. Based on your instructor's directions, submit e04p1Collectables_LastFirst.

2 Sunny Popcorn, Inc.

You are a financial analyst for Sunny Popcorn, Inc. and have been given the task of compiling a workbook to detail weekly sales information. The current information provided detailed sales rep information, flavors ordered, account type, and volume ordered. The owners are specifically interested in local sales that are generating at least $150.00 a week. To complete the document you will sort, filter, use table tools, and apply conditional formatting. Refer to Figure 4.53 as you complete this exercise.

	First Name	Last Name	Account type	Flavor	Volume in lbs	Price per lb	Deposit	Amount Due
1	Sunny Popcorn Inc							
2	Date	10/6/2018						
3	Deposit	5%						
22	Helen	Sanchez	Local	Regular	58	$2.25	$ 6.53	$ 123.98
23	Yoshio	Guo	Local	Cheese	88	$2.00	$ 8.80	$ 167.20
24	Yong	Lopez	Local	Regular	91	$2.25	$ 10.24	$ 194.51
25	Dalia	Azizi	Local	Regular	33	$2.25	$ 3.71	$ 70.54
26	Kyung	Rodriguez	Local	Carmel	99	$1.50	$ 7.43	$ 141.08
27	Jasmine	Bettar	Local	Cheese	67	$2.00	$ 6.70	$ 127.30
28	Yukio	He	Local	Low Salt	64	$2.25	$ 7.20	$ 136.80
29	Dai	Zhu	Local	Chocolate	62	$2.00	$ 6.20	$ 117.80
30	Nam	Sato	Local	Cheese	66	$2.00	$ 6.60	$ 125.40
31	Ryung	Inoue	Local	Chocolate	17	$2.00	$ 1.70	$ 32.30
32	Raul	Martinez	Local	Crunch	31	$2.25	$ 3.49	$ 66.26
33	Yoshio	Flores	Local	Low Salt	27	$2.25	$ 3.04	$ 57.71
34	Diego	Sun	Local	Low Salt	16	$2.25	$ 1.80	$ 34.20
35	Helen	Cho	Local	Cheese	48	$2.00	$ 4.80	$ 91.20
36	Yoshio	Seo	Local	Chocolate	32	$2.00	$ 3.20	$ 60.80
37	Sang	Allen	Local	Carmel	53	$1.50	$ 3.98	$ 75.53
38	Raj	Hong	Local	Cheese	41	$2.00	$ 4.10	$ 77.90
39	Javier	Hyat	Local	Cheese	100	$2.00	$ 10.00	$ 190.00
40	Brian	Hernandez	Local	Low Salt	16	$2.25	$ 1.80	$ 34.20

Sales

Ready

Excel 2016, Windows 10, Microsoft Corporation

FIGURE 4.53 Sunny Popcorn Inc

a. Open *e04p2Popcorn* and save it as **e04p2Popcorn_LastFirst**.

b. Click **cell C7**, click the **Home tab**, click the **Sort & Filter arrow** in the Editing group, and select **Sort A to Z**. This sorts the data by account type in Column C.

c. Click the **Insert tab**, click **Table** in the Tables group, and click **OK** in the Create Table dialog box.

d. Click **Table Style Medium 3** in the Table Styles group on the Design tab.

e. Click cell **G7** and type **=[Price per lb]*[Volume in lbs]*$B$3** and press **Enter**.

f. Click cell **H7** and type **=[Price per lb]*[Volume in lbs]-[Deposit]** and press **Enter**

g. Select the **range G7:H106**, click the **Home tab**, and click **Accounting Number Format** in the Number group.

h. Click the **Design tab** and click **Total Row** in the Table Style Options group.

i. Click the **Deposit Total Row arrow**, and select **Sum**, click the **Volume in lbs Total Row arrow**, and then select **Average**. Apply **Number Style Format** to the results in **cell E107**.

j. Click the **filter arrow** of the Account type column, click the **Select All check box** to deselect it, click **Local**, and click **OK**.

k. Select the **range H22:H51**, click **Quick Analysis**, and then select **Greater Than**. Type **150.00** in the Format cells that are GREATER THAN box, select **Green Fill with Dark Green Text**, and click **OK**.

l. Select the **range E22:E51**, click **Quick Analysis**, and then select **Data Bars**.

m. Click the **Page Layout tab**, click the **Scale box** in the Scale to Fit group, and then type **85%**.

n. Create a footer with your name on the left side, the sheet name code in the center, and the file name code on the right side of each worksheet.

o. Save and close the file. Based on your instructor's directions, submit e04p2Popcorn_LastFirst.

Mid-Level Exercises

1 Crafton's Pet Supplies

You are the inventory manager for Crafton's Pet Supplies. You are currently preforming analysis to determine inventory levels, as well as the total value of inventory on hand. Your last steps will be to check the report for duplicate entries and format for printing.

a. Open *e04m1Inventory* and save it as **e04m1Inventory_LastFirst**.

b. Freeze the panes so that the column labels do not scroll offscreen.

c. Convert the data to a table and name the table **Inventory2018**.

d. Apply **Table Style Medium 3** to the table.

e. Sort the table by Warehouse (A to Z), then Department, and then by Unit Price (smallest to largest). Create a custom sort order for Department so that it appears in this sequence: Food & Health, Collars & Leashes, Toys, Clothes, Training, and Grooming.

f. Remove duplicate records from the table. Excel should find and remove one duplicate record.

g. Create an unqualified structured reference in column G to determine the value of the inventory on hand and apply **Accounting Number Format**. To calculate the inventory on hand multiply the **Unit Price** and the **Amount on Hand.**

h. Apply a **Total Row** to the Inventory2018 table, set the Inventory Value to Sum, and the Amount on Hand to Average. Format the results to display with two decimal points.

i. Create a new conditional formatting rule that displays any Inventory Value for the **Food & Health** department with a value of $30,000 or more as **Red Accent 2 fill color**. There will be two qualifying entries.

j. Ensure the warehouse information is not broken up between pages when printed. Add a page break to make sure that each warehouse prints on its own consecutive page.

k. Set the worksheet to **Landscape orientation**, and repeat row 1 labels on all pages.

l. Display the Inventory sheet in Page Break Preview.

m. Insert a footer with your name on the left side, the sheet name code in the center, and the file name code on the right side of all four sheets.

n. Save and close the file. Based on your instructor's directions, submit e04m1Inventory_LastFirst.

2 Artwork

You work for a gallery that is an authorized Greenwich Workshop fine art dealer (www.greenwichworkshop.com). Customers in your area are especially fond of James C. Christensen's art. Although customers can visit the website to see images and details about his work, they have requested a list of all his artwork. Your assistant prepared a list of artwork: art, type, edition size, release date, and issue price. In addition, you included a column to identify which pieces are sold out at the publisher, indicating the rare, hard-to-obtain artwork that is available on the secondary market. You now want to convert the data to a table so that you can provide information to your customers.

a. Open *e04m2FineArt* and save it as **e04m2FineArt_LastFirst**.

b. Convert the data to a table and apply **Table Style Medium 5**.

c. Add a row (below the record for *The Yellow Rose*) for this missing piece of art: **The Yellow Rose**, **Masterwork Canvas Edition**, **50** edition size, **May 2009** release date, **$895** issue price. Enter **Yes** to indicate the piece is sold out.

d. Sort the table by Type in alphabetical order and then by Release Date from newest to oldest.

e. Add a total row that shows the largest edition size and the most expensive issue price. Delete the Total label in **cell A205** and **cell H205**. Add a descriptive label in **cell C205** to reflect the content on the total row.

f. Create a custom conditional format for the Issue Price column with these specifications:
- **4 Traffic Lights** icon set (Black, Red, Yellow, Green)
- **Red icon** when the number is greater than 1000
- **Yellow icon** when the number is less than or equal to 1000 and greater than 500
- **Green icon** when the number is less than or equal to 500 and greater than 250
- **Black icon** when the number is less than or equal to 250.

DISCOVER

g. Filter the table by the **Red Traffic Light** conditional formatting icon.

h. Answer the questions in the range D213:D217 based on the filtered data.

i. Set the print area to print the **range C1:H205**, select the **first row to repeat at the top of each printout**, set **1"** top and bottom margins, set **0.3"** left and right margins, and then select **Landscape orientation**. Set the option to fit the data to 1 page.

j. Wrap text, and horizontally center column labels and adjust column widths and row heights as needed.

k. Create a footer with your name on the left side, the sheet name code in the center, and the file name code on the right side.

l. Save and close the file. Based on your instructor's directions, submit e04m2FineArt_LastFirst.

3 Party Music

You are planning a weekend party and want to create a mix of music so that most people will appreciate some of the music you will play at the party. To help you decide what music to play, you have asked five classmates to help you create a song list. The entire class should decide on the general format, capitalization style, and the sequence: Song, Artist, Genre, Released, and approximate song length.

a. Conduct online research to collect data for your favorite 25 songs.

b. Enter the data into a new workbook in the format, capitalization style, and sequence that was decided by the class.

c. Save the workbook as **e04m3PlayList_LastFirst**.

d. Upload the file to a shared folder on OneDrive or Dropbox that everyone in the class can access.

e. Download four workbooks from friends and copy and paste data from their workbooks into yours.

f. Convert the data to a table and apply a table style of your choice.

g. Detect and delete duplicate records. Make a note of the number of duplicate records found and deleted.

h. Sort the data by genre using the custom list: Pop, Rock, R&B, and Jazz, then by artist in alphabetical order, and then by release date with the oldest year first.

i. Set a filter to display songs that were released before 2018.

j. Display the total row and select the function to count the number of songs displayed.

k. Insert comments in the workbook to indicate which student's workbooks you used, the number of duplicate records deleted, and the number of filtered records.

l. Save and close the file. Based on your instructor's directions, submit e04m3PlayList_LastFirst.

Beyond the Classroom

Flight Arrival Status

GENERAL CASE

FROM SCRATCH

As an analyst for an airport, you want to study the flight arrivals for a particular day. Select an airport and find its list of flight arrival data. Some airport websites do not list complete details, so search for an airport that does, such as Will Rogers World Airport or San Diego International Airport. Copy the column labels and arrival data (airline, flight number, city, gate, scheduled time, status, etc.) for one day and paste them in a new workbook. The columns may be in a different sequence from what is listed here. However, you should format the data as needed. Leave two blank rows below the last row of data and enter the URL of the webpage from which you got the data, the date, and the time. Save the workbook as **e04b1Flights_LastFirst**. Convert the list to a table and apply a table style.

Sort the table by scheduled time and then by gate number. Apply conditional formatting to the Status column to highlight cells that contain the text Delayed (or similar text). Add a total row to calculate the MODE for the gate number and arrival time. The MODE is the number that appears the most frequently in the dataset. You must select **More Functions** from the list of functions in the total row and search for and select **MODE**. Change the total row label in the first column from Total to **Most Frequent**. Use Help to refresh your memory on how to nest an IF function inside another IF function. Add a calculated column on the right side of the table using a nested IF function and structured references to display **Late** if the actual time was later than the scheduled time, **On Time or Early** if the actual time was earlier than or equal to the scheduled time, or **Incomplete** if the flight has not landed yet.

Name the worksheet **Arrival Time**. Copy the worksheet and name the copied worksheet **Delayed**. Filter the list by delayed flights. Include a footer with your name on the left side, the sheet name code in the center, and the file name code on the right side of both worksheets. Adjust the margins on both worksheets as necessary. Save and close the file. Based on your instructor's directions, submit e04b1Flights_LastFirst.

Dairy Farm

DISASTER RECOVERY

You are the product manager for Schaefer Dairy farm, a local organic farm that produces dairy products. Each month you must run an inventory report to identify and discard expired products before they are sold. Open *e04b2Dairy* and save it as **e04b2Dairy_LastFirst**. Convert the **range A5:E105** to a table, give the table a name, and apply a table style.

Freeze all data above row 6 and create a conditional formatting rule that highlights any package date that is 30 days or older than the manufacture date in B4. Sort the table first by the newly created highlight color then by department. Next, in column E create an IF function using structured referencing to determine the course of action for expired products. The function should display **discard** if the product is expired and nothing if the product is still sellable. Filter the table to display only items that should be discarded, then add a total row that counts the number of items to discard. Format the table so the column headings print at the top of each page and create a footer with your name, the sheet name code, and the file name code. Save and close the file. Based on your instructor's directions, submit e04b2Dairy_LastFirst.

Capstone Exercise

You work for Rockville Auto Sales and have been asked to aid in the development of a spreadsheet to manage sales and inventory information. You will start the task with a prior worksheet that contains vehicle information and sales data for 2018. You need to convert the data to a table. You will manage the large worksheet, prepare the worksheet for printing, sort and filter the table, include calculations, and then format the table.

Prepare the Large Worksheet as a Table

You will freeze the panes so that labels remain onscreen. You also want to convert the data to a table so that you can apply table options.

a. Open the *e04c1AutoSales* workbook and save it as **e04c1AutoSales_LastFirst**.

b. Freeze the first row on the Fleet Information worksheet.

c. Convert the data to a table, name the table **Inventory**, and apply the **Table Style Medium 19**.

d. Remove duplicate records.

Sort and Print the Table

To help the sales agents manage vehicle inventory, you will sort the data. Then you will prepare the large table to print.

a. Sort the table by Make in alphabetical order, add a second level to sort by Year, and a third level to sort by Sticker Price smallest to largest.

b. Repeat the field names on all pages.

c. Change page breaks so each vehicle make is printed on a separate page.

d. Add a footer with your name on the left side, the sheet name code in the center, and the file name code on the right side.

Add Calculated Fields and a Total Row

For tax purposes, the accounting department needs you to calculate the number of vehicles sold, the total value of sticker prices, and actual sales price for vehicles sold in the first quarter.

a. Click the Sales Information worksheet and convert the data to a table, name the table Sales, and apply the **Table Style Dark 11**.

b. Create a formula with structured references to calculate the percentage of the Sticker Price in column E.

c. Format the **range E2:E30** with **Percentage Style** Number Format.

d. Add a total row to display the Average of % of Sticker Price and Sum of Sticker Price and Sale Price.

e. Adjust the width of **columns B:E** to show the total values.

Apply Conditional Formatting

You want to help the office manager visualize the differences among the sales. To highlight sales trends, you will apply data bar conditional formatting to the % of Value column.

a. Apply **Data Bars conditional formatting** to the % of Sticker Price data.

b. Create a new conditional format that applies yellow fill and bold font to values that sold for less than 60% of the list price.

c. Edit the conditional format you created so that it formats values 70% or less.

Copy and Filter the Data

In order to isolate first quarter sales, you will filter the data. To keep the original data intact for the sales agents, you will copy the table data to a new sheet and use that sheet to display the filtered data.

a. Copy the Sales Information sheet and place the duplicate sheet to the right of the original sheet tab.

b. Rename the duplicate worksheet **First Quarter Sales**.

c. Rename the table **FirstQuarter**.

d. Display the filter arrows for the data.

e. Filter the data to display January, February, and March sales.

Finalize the Workbook

You are ready to finalize the workbook by adding a footer to the new worksheet and saving the final workbook.

a. Add a footer with your name on the left side, the sheet name code in the center, and the file name code on the right side.

b. Select **Landscape orientation** for all sheets and set appropriate margins so that the data will print on one page.

c. Save and close the file. Based on your instructor's directions, submit e04c1AutoSales_LastFirst.

Excel

Subtotals, PivotTables, and PivotCharts

LEARNING OUTCOME

You will manage and analyze data by creating subtotals, PivotTables, and PivotCharts.

OBJECTIVES & SKILLS: After you read this chapter, you will be able to:

CASE STUDY | Ivory Halls Publishing Company

You are the new vice president of the Sociology Division at Ivory Halls Publishing Company. The sociology domain has many disciplines, such as Family, Introductory, and Race/Class/Gender. Ivory Halls publishes several textbooks in each discipline to appeal to a vast array of university professors and students. Your assistant has prepared a worksheet containing these columns of data for the sociology textbooks:

- **Discipline.** Textbooks are classified by the overall discipline, such as Family.
- **Area.** Within each discipline, books are further classified by area. For example, the Family discipline is further classified into two areas: (1) Family Interaction and (2) Marriage and Family.
- **Units Sold Wholesale.** This column lists the number of books sold to wholesale buyers, such as college bookstores.
- **Unit Price Wholesale.** This column lists the price per book for wholesale buyers.
- **Sales: Wholesale.** This is the sales amount resulting by multiplying the Units Sold Wholesale by the Unit Price Wholesale.

Summarizing and Analyzing Data

CHAPTER 5

- **Units Sold Retail.** This column lists the number of books sold to online customers, such as individual students.
- **Unit Price Retail.** This column lists the price per book for an online customer.
- **Sales: Unit Price.** This is the sales amount resulting by multiplying the Units Sold Retail by the Unit Price Retail.
- **Total Book Sales:** This is the total amount of wholesale and retail sales.

You want to analyze sales for all books published in the Sociology Division. To do this, you will organize data so that you can group data by discipline and then insert subtotal rows. You will also create PivotTables to gain a variety of perspectives of aggregated data, including data from multiple tables. Finally, you will create a PivotChart to depict the aggregated data visually.

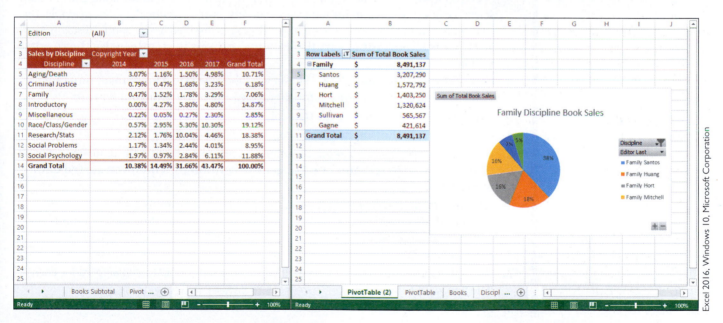

FIGURE 5.1 Ivory Halls Publishing Company PivotTables

CASE STUDY | Ivory Halls Publishing Company

Starting Files	Files to be Submitted
e05h1Sociology e05h4Sociology	e05h3Sociology_LastFirst e05h4Sociology_LastFirst

Subtotals, PivotTables, and PivotCharts • Excel 2016   **329**

Subtotals and Outlines

Data alone are meaningless; data translated into meaningful information increase your knowledge so that you can make well-informed decisions. Previously, you used analytical tools such as sorting, filtering, conditional formatting, tables, and charts. These tools help translate raw data into information so that you can identify trends, patterns, and anomalies in a dataset. Now you are ready to explore other functionalities that help you analyze larger amounts of data.

In this section, you will learn how to insert subtotals within a dataset. Then you will learn how to group data to create an outline, collapse and expand groups within the outline, and ungroup data to return them to their original state.

Subtotaling Data

STEP 1 ❯❯ When a dataset is sorted by categories, you can use the Subtotals command to display a total for columns containing values in each category. The Subtotal command inserts a *subtotal row*, which is a row that includes one or more aggregate functions, such as a sum or average, of values within each category within a dataset. This command saves you time so that you do not have to manually insert a blank row for each category and then insert a function on each subtotal row. After you use the Subtotal command, you can then compare the subtotals among categories to analyze the data. Furthermore, when you use the Subtotals command, you can collapse and expand details without having to manually hide and unhide individual rows.

To add subtotals to a dataset, complete the following steps:

1. Sort the dataset using the column that you want to use to group the data. You should select a column that contains multiple occurrences of the same data. For example, the Discipline column contains several books that are classified in the Family discipline. **NOTE: It is important to sort the data into groups first; otherwise the results will be incorrect.**

2. Convert the table to range (if the dataset is a table). **NOTE: The dataset must be converted to a range, not a table, before you use the Subtotal feature.**

3. Click in the dataset and click the Data tab.

4. Click Subtotal in the Outline group to open the Subtotal dialog box.

5. Click the *At each change in* arrow and select the column by which the data are sorted (see Figure 5.2). **NOTE: You must select the column by which you sorted data in Step 1.**

6. Click the *Use function* arrow and select the function you want to apply. For columns that contain values, select a function such as Sum, Min, Max, or Count. For text columns, use the Count function to count the number of rows within the group.

7. Select the appropriate column heading check boxes in the *Add subtotal to* list for each field you want to subtotal.

8. Select any other check boxes you want to use and click OK.

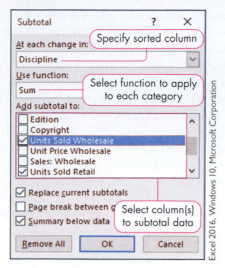

FIGURE 5.2 Subtotal Dialog Box

For the Ivory Halls Publishing Company, the sociology textbook dataset is sorted by discipline. The Subtotal command inserts a subtotal row, a row within the dataset containing at least one aggregated value when the category you specified in the *At a change in* option changes. For example, when Excel detects a change from the Research/Stats discipline to the Social Problems discipline, a subtotal row is inserted on row 70. Figure 5.3 shows the subtotal rows highlighted in yellow; however, the Subtotal feature does not add highlighting.

	Discipline	Area	Book Title	Units Sold Wholesale	Unit Price Wholesale	Sales: Wholesale	Units Sold Retail	Unit Price Retail	Sales: Retail	Total Book Sales
77	Research/Stats	Social Statistics	Statistical Procedures for Sociology	14,875	$ 95	$ 1,413,125	112	$ 124	$ 13,888	$ 1,427,013
78	Research/Stats	Social Statistics	Statistics for Social Sciences	7,550	$ 115	$ 868,250	88	$ 150	$ 13,200	$ 881,450
79	**Research/Stats Total**			203,707			5,452			$ 22,091,701
80	Social Problems	Alcohol/Drugs	Current Trends in Alcohol and Drug Abuse	4,500	$ 90	$ 405,000	312	$ 117	$ 36,504	$ 441,504
81	Social Problems	Alcohol/Drugs	Understanding Alcohol and Human Behavior	3,798	$ 75	$ 284,850	68	$ 98	$ 6,664	$ 291,514
		pproach	A Conflict Approach to Social Problems	3,500	$ 75	$ 262,500	24	$ 98	$ 2,352	$ 264,852
			Addressing Social Problems	11,342	$ 115	$ 1,304,330	87	$ 150	$ 13,050	$ 1,317,380
			Current Social Problems	20,300	$ 115	$ 2,334,500	118	$ 150	$ 17,700	$ 2,352,200
85	Social Problems	General	Social Inequalities Around the Globe	11,329	$ 90	$ 1,019,610	154	$ 117	$ 18,018	$ 1,037,628
			Social Problems	14,333	$ 100	$ 1,433,300	93	$ 130	$ 12,090	$ 1,445,390
		Abuse	Child Abuse in Today's World	3,500	$ 125	$ 437,500	43	$ 163	$ 7,009	$ 444,509
88	Social Problems	Violence/Abuse	Domestic Violence: Trends and Preventions	9,876	$ 115	$ 1,135,740	22	$ 150	$ 3,300	$ 1,139,040
89	Social Problems	Violence/Abuse	Increasing Violence in Our Schools	15,374	$ 130	$ 1,998,620	110	$ 169	$ 18,590	$ 2,017,210
90	**Social Problems Total**			97,852			1,031			$ 10,751,227
91	Social Psychology	General	An Introduction to Symbolic Interactionism	18,750	$ 135	$ 2,531,250	1,023	$ 176	$ 180,048	$ 2,711,298
92	Social Psychology	General	Modern Perspectives on Social Psychology	25,983	$ 115	$ 2,988,045	853	$ 150	$ 127,950	$ 3,115,995
93	Social Psychology	General	Readings in Social Psychology	15,502	$ 75	$ 1,162,650	73	$ 98	$ 7,154	$ 1,169,804
94	Social Psychology	General	Social Psychology	17,353	$ 105	$ 1,822,065	650	$ 137	$ 89,050	$ 1,911,115
	Social Psychology		ology: An interaction Approach	8,034	$ 95	$ 763,230	123	$ 124	$ 15,252	$ 778,482
		action	and Society	5,321	$ 85	$ 452,285	11	$ 111	$ 1,221	$ 453,506
97	Social Psychology	Symbolic Interactionism	Symbolic Interactionism: An Introduction	18,950	$ 125	$ 2,368,750	1,654	$ 163	$ 269,602	$ 2,638,352
98	Social Psychology	Symbolic Interactionism	Symbolic Interactionism: Brief Edition	15,768	$ 95	$ 1,497,960	143	$ 124	$ 17,732	$ 1,515,692
99	**Social Psychology Total**			125,661			4,530			$ 14,294,244
100	**Grand Total**			1,119,529			33,219			$ 120,233,644

Retail Price Rate (Based on Wholesale): 130%
Standard Author Royalty Rate: 10%

F90 =SUBTOTAL(9,F80:F89)

Outline symbols — SUBTOTAL function — Data sorted by discipline

Subtotal row inserted for Research/Stats discipline

Social Problems subtotal

Social Psychology subtotal — Grand total

FIGURE 5.3 Subtotaled Data

In Figure 5.3, the Subtotal command calculates the number of books sold in the Units Sold Wholesale, Units Sold Retail, and the Total Book Sales columns for each discipline. Adding subtotals helps identify which disciplines contribute the highest revenue for the company and which disciplines produce the lowest revenue. You can then analyze the data to determine whether to continue publishing books in high revenue-generating areas or discontinue the publication of books in low-selling areas.

The publisher sold 97,852 wholesale books in the Social Problems discipline compared to 203,707 wholesale books in the Research/Stats discipline, indicating that the number of Research/Stats books sold was more than double the number of Social Problems books sold. A grand total row is inserted at the end of the dataset to indicate that 1,119,529 total wholesale books were sold.

For each subtotal row, Excel inserts a **SUBTOTAL function**, a math & trig function that calculates a subtotal for values contained in a specified range. Cell F90 contains =SUBTOTAL(9,F80:F89) to sum the number of books sold contained in the range F80:F89. The first argument indicates which summary function is used to calculate the subtotal. In this case, the argument 9 sums all values in the range specified in the second argument. Excel inserts the function and its arguments automatically so that you do not have to memorize what the arguments represent. Table 5.1 lists some of the summary functions and their respective argument values.

TABLE 5.1 SUBTOTAL Function_Num Argument	
Summary Function	**Argument**
AVERAGE	1
COUNT	2
COUNTA	3
MAX	4
MIN	5
SUM	9

Add a Second Level of Subtotals

STEP 2 ▶▶ You can add a second level of subtotals to a dataset. Adding a second level preserves the primary subtotals and adds another level of subtotals for subcategories. For example, you might want to display subtotals for each discipline and the areas within each discipline for the sociology books.

To add a second level of subtotals, complete the following steps:

1. Perform a two-level sort based on primary and secondary categorical data.
2. Click the Data tab and click Subtotal in the Outline group.
3. Click the *At a change in* arrow and specify the column that was used for the secondary sort.
4. Select the function and columns to be subtotaled.
5. Click the *Replace current subtotals* check box to deselect it and click OK.

> **TIP: REMOVING SUBTOTALS**
> The subtotal rows are temporary. To remove the rows of subtotals, display the Subtotals dialog box and click Remove All.

Collapse and Expand the Subtotals

STEP 3 ▶▶ The Subtotal command creates an **outline**, a hierarchical structure of data that you can group related data to summarize. When a dataset has been grouped into an outline, you can **collapse** the outlined data to show only main rows, such as subtotals, or expand the outlined data to show all the details. Table 5.2 explains the outline symbols that appear on the left side of the subtotaled data. Figure 5.4 shows a dataset that is collapsed to display the discipline subtotals and the grand total after clicking 2. The number of outline symbols depends on the total number of subtotals created. If two subtotal levels are applied, four outline symbols display. Clicking the last number displays the entire list. You can ***expand*** the dataset to display the detailed rows in the subtotaled or outlined dataset.

TABLE 5.2 Outline Symbols

Symbol	Description
1	Collapses outline to display the grand total only.
2	Displays subtotals by the main subtotal category and the grand total.
3	Displays the entire list.
+	Expands an outline group to see its details.
–	Collapses an outline group to see its category name only.

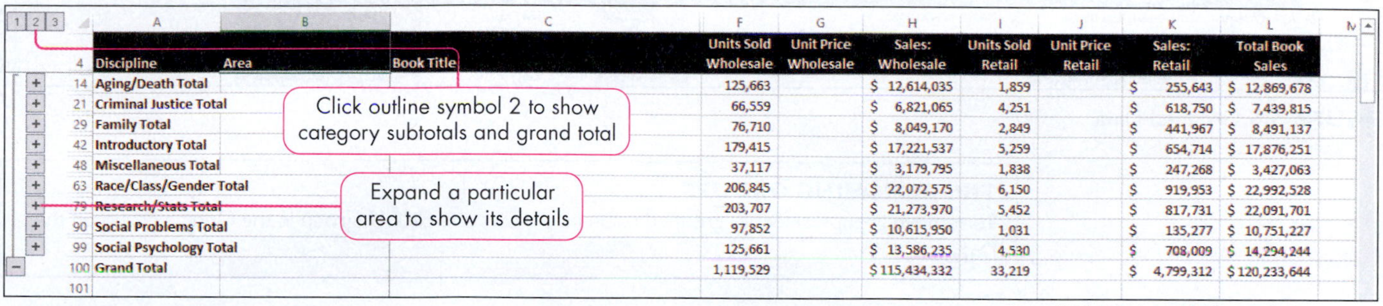

4	Discipline	Area	Book Title	Units Sold Wholesale	Unit Price Wholesale	Sales: Wholesale	Units Sold Retail	Unit Price Retail	Sales: Retail	Total Book Sales
14	Aging/Death Total			125,663		$ 12,614,035	1,859		$ 255,643	$ 12,869,678
21	Criminal Justice Total			66,559		$ 6,821,065	4,251		$ 618,750	$ 7,439,815
29	Family Total			76,710		$ 8,049,170	2,849		$ 441,967	$ 8,491,137
42	Introductory Total			179,415		$ 17,221,537	5,259		$ 654,714	$ 17,876,251
48	Miscellaneous Total			37,117		$ 3,179,795	1,838		$ 247,268	$ 3,427,063
63	Race/Class/Gender Total			206,845		$ 22,072,575	6,150		$ 919,953	$ 22,992,528
79	Research/Stats Total			203,707		$ 21,273,970	5,452		$ 817,731	$ 22,091,701
90	Social Problems Total			97,852		$ 10,615,950	1,031		$ 135,277	$ 10,751,227
99	Social Psychology Total			125,661		$ 13,586,235	4,530		$ 708,009	$ 14,294,244
100	Grand Total			1,119,529		$ 115,434,332	33,219		$ 4,799,312	$ 120,233,644
101										

FIGURE 5.4 Subtotaled Data Collapsed

Excel 2016, Windows 10, Microsoft Corporation

Grouping and Ungrouping Data

STEP 4 The Subtotals command outlines data into categories by rows. You can create outlines by columns of related data as well. For Excel to outline by columns, the dataset must contain columns with formulas or aggregate functions. If Excel cannot create the outline, it displays the message box *Cannot create an outline*.

To create an outline by columns, complete the following steps:

1. Click the Data tab.
2. Click the Group arrow in the Outline group.
3. Select Auto Outline.

For more control in creating an outline, you can create groups. ***Grouping*** is the process of joining rows or columns of related data together into a single entity so that groups can be collapsed or expanded for data analysis. After you create groups in the dataset, you can click a collapse button [–] to collapse a group to show the outside column or click the expand button [+] to expand groups of related columns to view the internal columns of data. Grouping enables you to hide raw data while you focus on key calculated results.

To group subtotaled data, complete the following steps:

1. Select the rows or columns you want to group. For column groups, you often select columns containing details but not aggregate columns, such as totals or averages. (Rows are automatically grouped if you use the Subtotals feature.)
2. Click the Data tab.
3. Click Group in the Outline group. If the Group dialog box opens, click *Rows* to group the data by rows or click *Columns* to group the data by columns. Click OK.

In Figure 5.5, the data is grouped by columns. Because the Units Sold Retail and Unit Price Retail columns are grouped, click – above Sales: Retail to collapse the columns and focus on the Sales: Retail column. Click + above the Sales: Wholesale column to expand (display) the related wholesale columns.

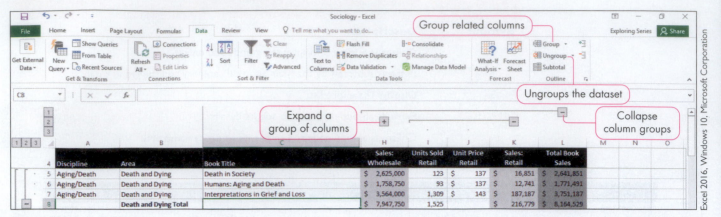

FIGURE 5.5 Grouped Data

TIP: REMOVING GROUPS
To remove groups, select all grouped columns or rows and click Ungroup in the Outline group on the Data tab.

Quick Concepts ✓

1. Discuss why a dataset must be sorted by a category before using the Subtotal feature. *p. 330*

2. Describe the two arguments used in the SUBTOTAL function. *p. 332*

3. What is the purpose of grouping and outlining columns in a worksheet? *p. 333*

Watch the Video for this Hands-On Exercise!

MyITLab®
HOE1 Training

Skills covered: Sort Multiple Fields • Subtotal Data • Add a Second Subtotal • Collapse and Expand the Subtotals • Group Data • Ungroup Data

1 Subtotals and Outlines

As vice president of the Sociology Division, you want to analyze your textbook publications. Each textbook falls within a general discipline, and each discipline is divided into several areas. The company tracks units sold, unit prices, and gross sales by two major types of sales: (1) wholesale sales to bookstores and (2) retail sales to individual customers. Your assistant applied Freeze Panes to keep the column headings in row 4 and the disciplines and areas in columns A and B visible regardless of where you scroll.

STEP 1 ›› SUBTOTAL DATA BASED ON THE PRIMARY SORT

Before you use the Subtotal command, you must sort the data by discipline and then by area. After sorting the data, you will insert subtotals for each discipline. You want to see the totals for the wholesale sales, retail sales, and total book sales. Refer to Figure 5.6 as you complete Step 1.

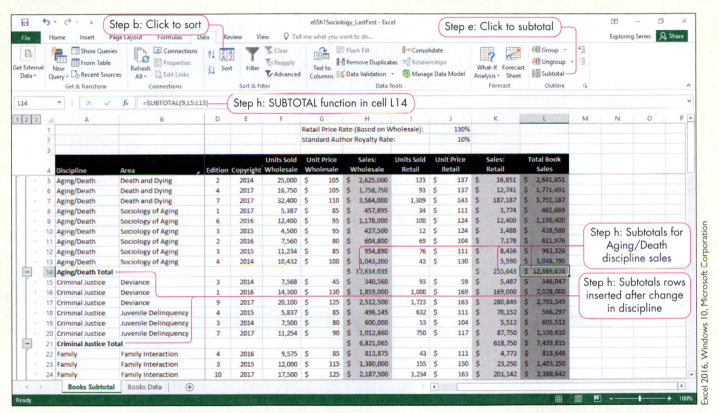

FIGURE 5.6 Discipline Subtotal Rows

a. Open *e05h1Sociology* and save it as **e05h1Sociology_LastFirst**.

> **TROUBLESHOOTING:** If you make any major mistakes in this exercise, you can close the file, open *e05h1Sociology* again, and then start this exercise over.

The workbook contains two worksheets: Books Subtotal for Hands-On Exercise 1 and Books Data for Hands-On Exercises 2–3.

b. Click the **Data tab** and click **Sort** in the Sort & Filter group.

c. Click the **Sort by arrow** and select **Discipline** in the Sort dialog box.

d. Click **Add Level**, click the **Then by arrow**, and then select **Area**. Click **OK**.

Excel sorts the data by discipline in alphabetical order. Within each discipline, Excel sorts the data further by area. The data are sorted first by disciplines so that you can apply subtotals to each discipline.

e. Click **Subtotal** in the Outline group.

The Subtotal dialog box opens. The default *At each change in* is the Discipline column, and the default *Use function* is Sum. These settings are correct.

f. Click the **Sales: Wholesale check box** to select it in the *Add subtotal to* section.

g. Click the **Sales: Retail check box** to select it in the *Add subtotal to* section.

Excel selected the last column—Total Book Sales—automatically. You selected the other two sales columns to total. Leave the *Replace current subtotals* and *Summary below data* check boxes selected.

h. Click **OK**.

Excel inserts subtotal rows after each discipline category. The subtotal rows include discipline labels and subtotals for the Sales: Wholesale, Sales: Retail, and Total Book Sales columns.

i. Scroll to the right to see the subtotals and click **cell L14**. Save the workbook

Cell L14 contains the SUBTOTAL function for the total book sales for the Aging/Death discipline. The first argument, 9, indicates the SUM function, and L5:L13 is the range of data (all books on Aging/Death) being subtotaled.

> **TROUBLESHOOTING:** If your subtotals do not match the totals in Figure 5.6, open the Subtotal dialog box, click Remove All, click OK, and repeat steps b through i again.

STEP 2 ›› ADD A SECOND SUBTOTAL

Now you want to add another level to see subtotals for each area within each discipline. You already added subtotals for the primary category (Discipline). Now you will add a subtotal to the second category (Area). When you use the Subtotal dialog box, you will keep the original subtotals intact. Refer to Figure 5.7 as you complete Step 2.

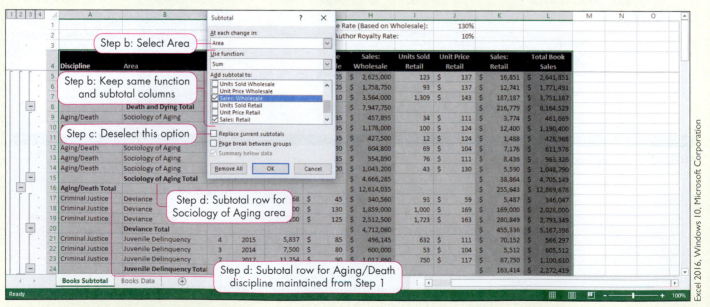

FIGURE 5.7 Discipline and Area Subtotal Rows

a. Click **Subtotal** in the Outline group to open the Subtotal dialog box again.

b. Click the **At each change in arrow** and select **Area**.

Use function is still Sum, and Excel remembers the last columns you selected in the *Add subtotal to* section—Sales: Wholesale, Sales: Retail, and Total Book Sales.

c. Click the **Replace current subtotals check box** to deselect it.

Deselecting this check box will keep the discipline subtotals.

d. Click **OK** and click **cell L15**. Save the workbook.

Excel inserts subtotal rows after each area. The Formula Bar displays =SUBTOTAL(9,L9:L14). Your data have discipline subtotals and area subtotals within each discipline.

> **TROUBLESHOOTING:** If you subtotal the area first and then the disciplines, Excel adds several discipline subtotals, which repeat the area subtotals. That is why you must subtotal by the primary category first and then subtotal by the secondary category.

STEP 3 ›› COLLAPSE AND EXPAND THE SUBTOTALS

You want to compare wholesale, retail, and book sales among the disciplines and then among areas within a discipline. Refer to Figure 5.8 as you complete Step 3.

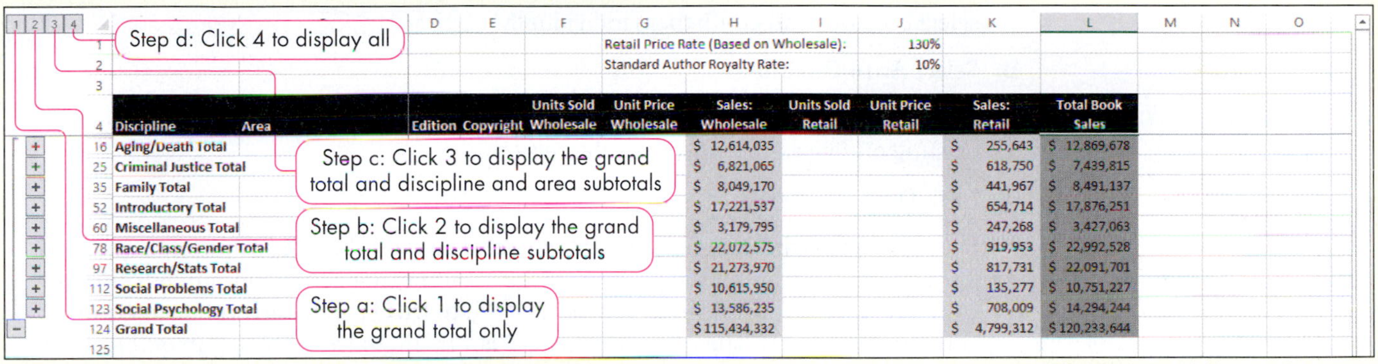

FIGURE 5.8 Collapsed Subtotals at Level 2

Excel 2016, Windows 10, Microsoft Corporation

a. Click the **1 outline symbol** in the top-left outline area (to the left of the column headings).

You collapsed the outline to show the grand totals only for wholesale, retail, and total book sales.

b. Click the **2 outline symbol** in the top-left outline area (see Figure 5.8).

You expanded the outline to show the grand and discipline subtotals. Which two disciplines had the highest wholesale and retail sales? Which discipline had the lowest total sales?

c. Click the **3 outline symbol** in the top-left outline area.

You expanded the outline to show the grand, discipline, and area subtotals. Within the Introductory discipline, which area had the lowest sales? How do wholesale and retail sales compare? Are they proportionally the same within each area?

d. Click the **4 outline symbol** in the top-left outline area. Save the workbook.

You expanded the outline to show all details again. If you had not added the second subtotal, the outline would have had three levels instead of four.

You want to apply an outline to the columns so that you can collapse or expand the Units Sold and Unit Price columns. Refer to Figure 5.9 as you complete Step 4.

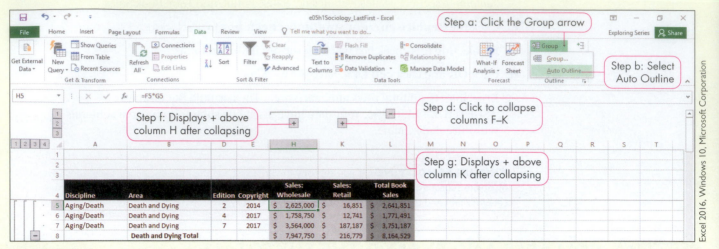

FIGURE 5.9 Groups of Columns Outlined

a. Click the **Group arrow** in the Outline group on the Data tab.

You want to see if Excel can create a column outline for you so that you do not have to select columns and group them individually.

b. Select **Auto Outline**.

Excel displays the message box *Modify existing outline?* because it recognizes that an existing outline exists—the row subtotals outline.

c. Click **OK**.

Excel maintains the outlined subtotal rows and adds outlines the columns. Horizontal lines and collapse buttons appear above the columns that contain formulas (columns H, K, and L). The formula in cell H5 is =F5*G5, so Excel creates an outline to group columns F, G, and H. The formula in cell K5 is =I5*J5, so Excel creates an outline to group columns I, J, and K. It also creates a higher-level outline of columns F through K, because the formula in column L sums the values in columns H and K.

d. Click the **collapse button** - above column L.

You collapsed columns F through K to display disciplines, areas, and total sales by title.

e. Click the **expand button** + above column L.

You expanded the outline to show columns F through K again.

f. Click the **collapse button** - above column H.

You collapsed the outline to hide columns F and G so you can focus on the wholesale sales without the distraction of the Units Sold or Unit Price columns.

g. Click the **collapse button** - above column K.

You collapsed the outline to hide columns I and J so you can focus on the retail sales without the distraction of the Units Sold or Unit Price columns.

h. Save the workbook. Keep the workbook open if you plan to continue with the next Hands-On Exercise. If not, save and close the workbook, and exit Excel.

PivotTable Basics

Analyzing large amounts of data is important for making solid business decisions. Entering data is the easy part; retrieving data in a structured, meaningful way is more challenging. **Data mining** is the process of analyzing large volumes of data, using advanced statistical techniques, and identifying trends and patterns in the data. Managers use data-mining techniques to address a variety of questions, such as the following:

- What snack foods do customers purchase most when purchasing Pepsi® products?

- What age group from what geographic region downloads the most top 10 songs from iTunes?

- What hotel chain and rental car combinations are most popular among Delta Air Lines passengers flying into Salt Lake City?

Questions similar to those above help organizations prepare their marketing plans to capitalize on consumer spending patterns. The more you know about your customer demographics, the better you can focus your strategic plans to increase market share.

A **PivotTable report**, commonly referred to as a *PivotTable*, is an interactive table that uses calculations to consolidate and summarize data from a data source into a separate table. PivotTables enable you to analyze data in a dataset without altering the dataset itself. PivotTables are dynamic: You can easily and quickly pivot, or rearrange, data to analyze data from different viewpoints. Looking at data from different perspectives helps identify trends and patterns among the variables that might not be obvious from looking at hundreds or thousands of rows of data yourself.

In this section, you will create a PivotTable. You will learn how to organize and group data into rows and columns, remove and rearrange fields, and change the settings for value fields.

Creating a PivotTable

Before you create a PivotTable, ensure that the data source is well structured by applying the rules for good table design. Use meaningful column labels, ensure data accuracy, and avoid blank rows and columns in the dataset. At least one column must have duplicate values, such as the same discipline or area name for several records, to create categories for organizing and summarizing data. Another column must have numeric values that can be aggregated to produce quantitative summaries, such as averages or sums.

> **TIP: PIVOTTABLE OR SUBTOTALS?**
> PivotTables are similar to subtotals because they both produce subtotals, but PivotTables provide more flexibility than subtotals. If you need complex subtotals cross-referenced by two or more categories with filtering and other specifications, create a PivotTable. Furthermore, using the Subtotals command inserts subtotals rows within the dataset, whereas creating a PivotTable does not change the dataset.

Create a Recommended PivotTable

STEP 1 ›› You can create a PivotTable from the Quick Analysis gallery or from the Recommended PivotTables command in the Tables group on the Insert tab. One benefit of these methods is that Excel displays previews of recommended PivotTables based on the data in the dataset. Creating a recommended PivotTable is beneficial when you first start using PivotTables so that you can see potential ways to depict the dataset before starting to create PivotTables from scratch.

To create a PivotTable using Quick Analysis, complete the following steps:

1. Right-click within a dataset and select Quick Analysis on the shortcut menu.
2. Click Tables in the Quick Analysis gallery.
3. Point to a PivotTable thumbnail to see a preview of the different recommended PivotTables (see Figure 5.10).
4. Click a PivotTable thumbnail to create the desired PivotTable.

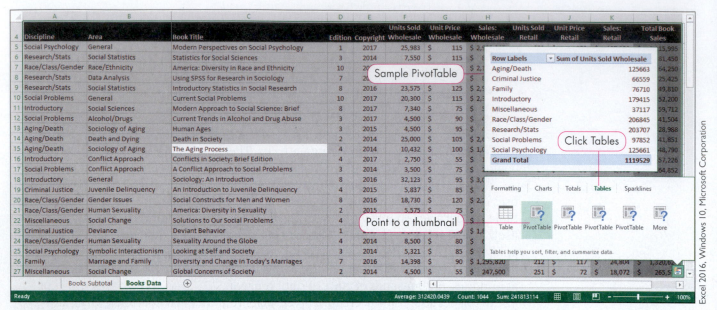

FIGURE 5.10 Quick Analysis Gallery to Create a Recommended PivotTable

To create a PivotTable from the Recommended PivotTables dialog box, complete the following steps:

1. Click inside the dataset (the range of cells or table).
2. Click the Insert tab and click Recommended PivotTables in the Tables group to open the Recommended PivotTables dialog box (see Figure 5.11).
3. Point to a thumbnail in the gallery on the left side of the dialog box to display a preview of the PivotTable on the right side.
4. Click a thumbnail to select it and click OK to create the desired PivotTable.

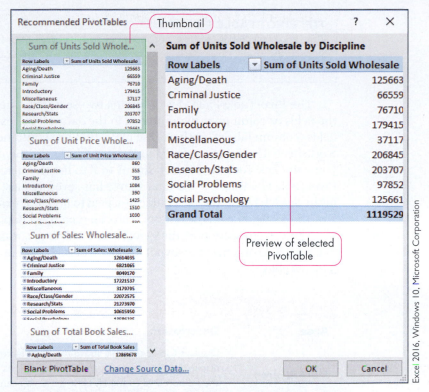

FIGURE 5.11 Recommended PivotTable Dialog Box

When you select a PivotTable, Excel creates a PivotTable on a new worksheet (see Figure 5.12) to the left of the worksheet containing the dataset. The ***PivotTable Fields List***, a task pane that displays the list of fields in a dataset and areas to place the fields to create the layout to organize data in columns, rows, values, and filters in a PivotTable, displays on the right side of the worksheet. In addition, the Ribbon displays the PivotTable Tools Analyze and Design tabs. If you click outside the PivotTable, the contextual tabs and PivotTable Fields List are no longer displayed. Click within the PivotTable to display these elements again.

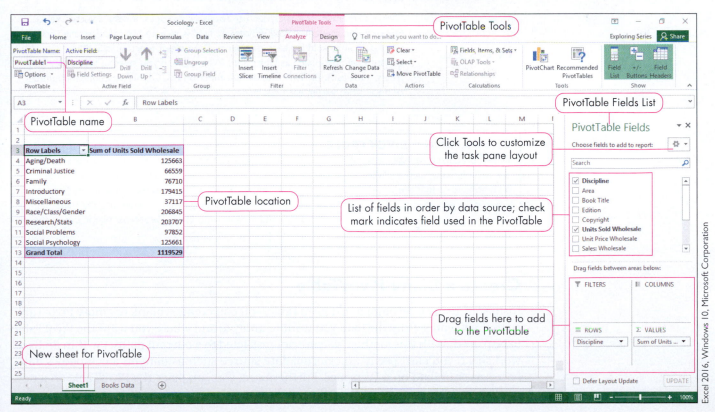

FIGURE 5.12 Recommended PivotTable

The PivotTable Fields List contains two sections. The top section contains a list of the fields or column labels contained in the dataset. For example, Figure 5.12 shows the fields (column labels), such as Discipline, that are contained on row 4 in the Books Data worksheet. The fields are listed in the same order as the original data source; however, you can click Tools and select Sort A to Z to list the fields in alphabetical order in the PivotTable Fields List. If the data source has several fields, scroll through the list or click in the Search box and type a name of a field to find. For example, Figure 5.12 shows only 7 of the 12 fields from the dataset. You can type Total Book Sales to search for that field.

The bottom section of the PivotTable Fields List contains four areas where you can place fields to organize the layout of the PivotTable. Table 5.3 describes the four areas of a PivotTable.

TABLE 5.3	Areas of a PivotTable
Area	**Description**
FILTERS Area	Displays top-level filters above the PivotTable so that you can set filters to display results based on particular conditions you set. For example, if you drag the Edition field to the FILTERS area, you can then set a filter to display sales for a particular edition, such as for first editions.
COLUMNS Area	Displays columns of summarized data for the selected field(s). For example, if you drag Copyright to the COLUMNS area, the PivotTable displays one column of data for each unique copyright year contained in the dataset.
ROWS Area	Groups the data into categories in the first column based on the selected field(s). For example, the Discipline field is placed in the ROWS area. Each unique discipline label (such as Family) is listed only one time in alphabetical order in the first column regardless how many times the label is present in the original dataset. These labels identify the content on each row.
VALUES Area	Displays summary statistics, such as totals or averages, for the selected field. For example, the Units Sold Wholesale field is selected to calculate the total wholesale units sold for each discipline. The default function is SUM for quantitative fields, such as Units Sold Wholesale. If you select a field containing labels, such as Book Title, the default function is COUNT to count the number of book titles within each discipline.

Pearson Education, Inc.

Create a Blank PivotTable

Instead of using a recommended PivotTable, you can create a blank or empty PivotTable so that you can specify the data you want to analyze and where you want the PivotTable to be placed. With this method, you are not restricted to a current dataset within an Excel worksheet; you can specify an external data source such as data on a company's database server or data on a Web page. Furthermore, you can place the PivotTable on a new worksheet or on an existing worksheet.

To create a blank PivotTable, complete the following steps:

1. Click the Insert tab and click PivotTable in the Tables group to open the Create PivotTable dialog box.
2. Select the data that you want to analyze (table or range within the open workbook or a connection to an external dataset).
3. Select where you want to place the PivotTable: New Worksheet or Existing Worksheet. If you click Existing Worksheet, then specify the sheet tab name in the Location box.
4. Click OK to create the PivotTable.

The PivotTable Tools Analyze and Design tabs display, the PivotTable Fields List displays on the right side, and a blank PivotTable is located on the left side (see Figure 5.13). The PivotTable layout is developed when you drag fields to the areas in the PivotTable Fields List.

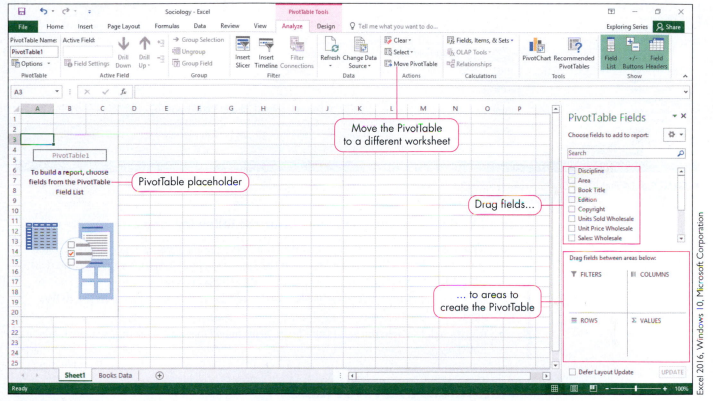

FIGURE 5.13 Blank PivotTable

TIP: MOVE A PIVOTTABLE

After creating a PivotTable, you might want to move it to another worksheet. To move a PivotTable, click within the PivotTable, click Move PivotTable in the Actions group on the Analyze tab to open the Move PivotTable dialog box. Click New Worksheet or click Existing Worksheet and specify the existing sheet name and the cell in the top-left corner to locate the PivotTable, and then click OK.

Modifying a PivotTable

After you create a PivotTable, you might want to modify it to see the data from a different perspective. For example, you might want to add fields to the ROWS, COLUMNS, and VALUES areas in a PivotTable. In addition, you might want to collapse the PivotTable to show fewer details or expand it to show more details.

Add Rows to a PivotTable

STEP 2 ▶▶ You can add one or more fields to the PivotTable to provide a more detailed analysis. The sequence of the fields within the ROWS area dictates the hierarchy. For example, you might want to show the Areas within each Discipline for the Ivory Halls textbook list. To show this hierarchy, list the Discipline field first and Area field second in the ROWS area (see Figure 5.14).

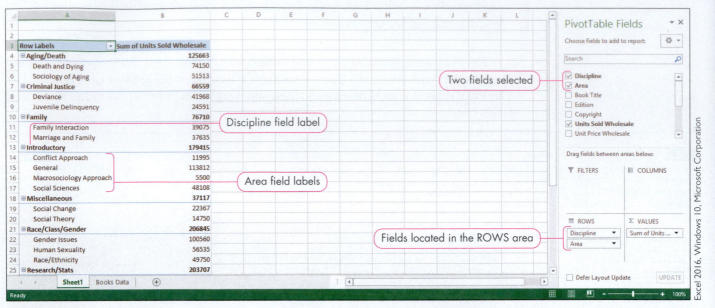

FIGURE 5.14 Fields in ROWS Area

To add a field as a row, complete one of the following steps:

- Click the field's check box to select it in the *Choose fields to add to report* section. Excel adds the field to a PivotTable based on the type of data stored in the field. If the field contains text, Excel usually places that field in the ROWS area.
- Drag the field from the *Choose fields to add to report* section and drop it in the ROWS area.
- Right-click the field name in the *Choose fields to add to report* section and select *Add to Row Labels*.

Add Values in a PivotTable

A PivotTable has meaning when you include quantitative fields, such as quantities and monetary values, to aggregate the data. You can add other quantitative fields. For example, you might want to add the Book Titles and Sales: Wholesale fields (see Figure 5.15). Excel sums the values for each field listed in the ROWS area. For example, the total number of units sold wholesale for the Family discipline is 76,710, and the total wholesale sales revenue is $8,049,170. If you place a text field, such as Book Title, in the VALUES area, Excel counts the number of records for each group listed in the ROWS area. In this case, Excel counts seven books in the Family discipline.

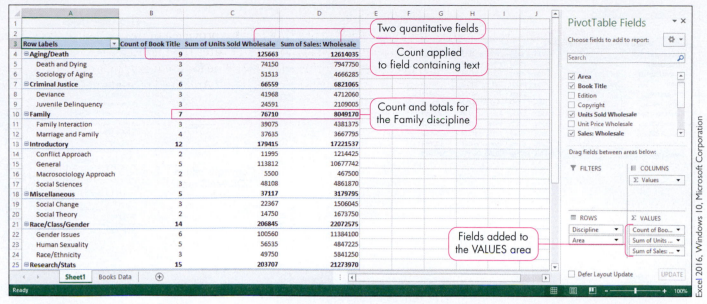

FIGURE 5.15 Fields in VALUES Area

To add values to the PivotTable, complete one of the following steps:

- Click the field's check box to select it in the *Choose fields to add to report* section. Excel makes the value an aggregate, such as *Sum of Sales*.
- Drag the field from the *Choose fields to add to report* section and drop it in the VALUES area.
- Right-click the field name in the *Choose fields to add to report* section and select *Add to Values*.

Add Columns to a PivotTable

Although you can create subdivisions of data by adding more fields to the ROWS area, you might want to arrange the subdivision categories in columns. Doing so minimizes the redundancy of duplicating subdivision row labels and helps consolidate data. To subdivide data into columns, drag a field from the *Choose fields to add to report* section and drop it in the COLUMNS area. Excel updates the aggregated values by the combination of row and column categories.

Figure 5.16 shows a PivotTable that uses the Discipline field as rows, the *Sum of Units Sold Wholesale* field as values, and Copyright field as columns. Each discipline label and each copyright year label appears only once in the PivotTable. This added level of detail enables you to see the total sales for each discipline based on its copyright year. The PivotTable includes grand totals for each discipline and grand totals for each year.

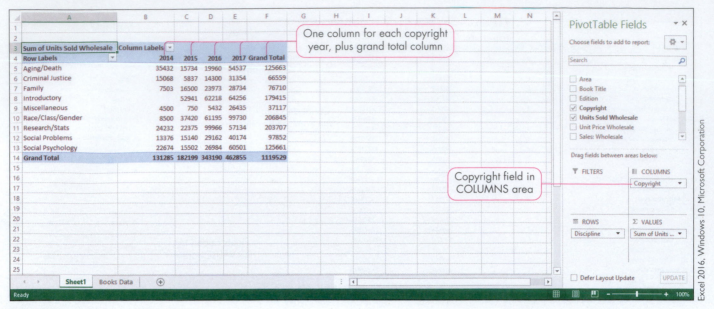

FIGURE 5.16 Fields in COLUMNS Area

Collapse and Expand Items in a PivotTable

If you include two or more fields as ROWS, the PivotTable displays more depth but may be overwhelming. You can hide or collapse the secondary field rows, as needed. For example, if the PivotTable contains both Discipline and Area row labels, you might want to collapse areas for some disciplines. The collapse and expand buttons display to the left of the row labels (see Figure 5.17). If the buttons do not display, click +/− Buttons in the Show group on the Analyze tab.

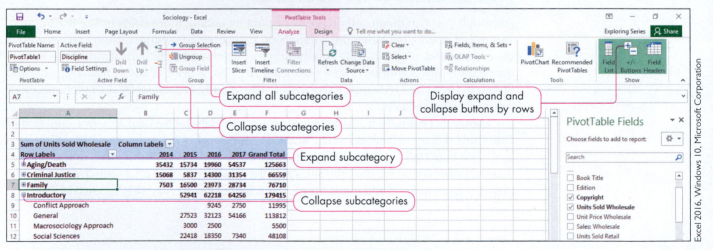

FIGURE 5.17 Collapse and Expand PivotTable

To collapse or expand a category, complete one of the following steps:

- Click the collapse button $-$ on the left side of the specific category you want to collapse. Excel hides the subcategories for that particular category and shows only the aggregated totals for the category. Continue collapsing other categories as needed to focus on a particular category's details.
- Click the expand button $+$ on the left side of the category labels to expand the subcategories again.

Remove Fields from a PivotTable

STEP 3 ›› As you continue adding and arranging fields, the PivotTable may contain too much data to be useful or the needs have changed, making it necessary to remove fields. You can remove fields to reduce the amount of data to analyze.

To remove a field from the PivotTable, complete one of the following steps:

- Click the field name in the *Drag fields between areas below* section and select Remove Field.
- Click the check box next to the field name to deselect it in the *Choose fields to add to report* section.
- Drag a field name in the *Drag fields between areas below* section outside the PivotTable Fields List.

Rearrange Fields in a PivotTable

A primary benefit of creating a PivotTable is that you can rearrange (or pivot) fields to view and summarize data from different perspectives. PivotTables provide ease and flexibility in changing the layout and level of depth depicted. As you rearrange the fields within the four areas, you gain a different perspective on the data and provide an easier layout to interpret the data. You might want to pivot the data by moving a field from the COLUMNS area to the ROWS area. As you move fields from one area to another in the PivotTable Fields List, the PivotTable immediately reflects the new layout. For example, your PivotTable might include the Discipline and Copyright fields in the ROWS so that you can view details for each discipline by copyright year. You might want to move the Copyright field to the COLUMNS area to provide a more distinct analysis of revenue for each discipline by copyright year.

To move a field from one PivotTable area to another, complete one of the following steps:

- Drag the field in the *Drag fields between areas below* section.
- Click the field arrow within the area and select Move to Report Filter, Move to Row Labels, Move to Column Labels, or Move to Values.

You can also move a field within its area. Table 5.4 explains the Move options.

TABLE 5.4 Move Options

Option	Moves the Field . . .
Move Up	Up one position in the hierarchy within the same area
Move Down	Down one position in the hierarchy within the same area
Move to Beginning	To the beginning of all fields in the same area
Move to End	To the end of all fields in the same area
Move to Report Filter	To the end of the FILTERS area of the PivotTable
Move to Row Labels	To the end of the ROWS area of the PivotTable
Move to Column Labels	To the end of the COLUMNS area of the PivotTable
Move to Values	To the end of the VALUES area of the PivotTable

Change the Values Field Settings

STEP 4 ›› Excel uses the SUM function as the default summary statistic for numerical fields and COUNT as the default statistic for text field. However, you can select a different function for numerical fields. For example, you might want to calculate the average, lowest, or highest value within each group, or identify the lowest sales for each discipline/copyright year combination to see if the older books have decreased sales.

In addition to changing the summary statistic, you might want to change the column label that appears above the summary statistic. By default, words indicate the summary statistic function applied, such as *Sum of Total Sales by Book* or *Average of Total Sales by Book*, depending on the summary statistic applied to the values. Finally, you might need to format the aggregated values.

To modify any of these value settings, complete the following steps:

1. Click a value in the appropriate field in the PivotTable and click Field Settings in the Active Field group on the Analyze tab. Alternatively, click the field's arrow in the VALUES area of the PivotTable Fields List and select Value Field Settings. The Value Field Settings dialog box opens (see Figure 5.18).

2. Type the name you want to appear as the column label in the Custom Name box. For example, you might want the heading to appear as *Total Sales* instead of *Sum of Total Book Sales*.

3. Select the summary statistical function you want to use to summarize the values in the *Summarize value field by* list.

4. Click Number Format to open an abbreviated version of the Format Cells dialog box. Select a number type, such as Accounting, in the Category list; select other settings, such as number of decimal places in the *Decimal places* box; and then click OK.

5. Click OK in the Value Field Settings dialog box.

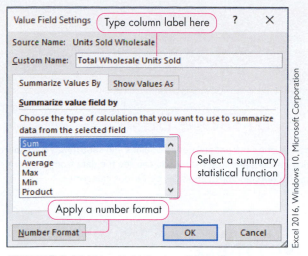

FIGURE 5.18 Value Field Settings Dialog Box

> **TIP: MULTIPLE SUMMARY STATISTICS**
> You can display more than one function for a field. For example, you might want to show both the total book sales and the average book sales. To display multiple summary statistics, drag another copy of the same field to the VALUES area and set each value setting separately.

Refresh a PivotTable

STEP 5 ▶▶ Although PivotTables are powerful, they are not automatically updated if you make any changes to the underlying data in the data source. For example, if you change a sales value or delete a row in the data source, the PivotTable does not reflect the changed data. Unfortunately, this causes PivotTable summary statistics to become outdated with inaccurate results.

To update the PivotTable, complete the following steps:

1. Click in the PivotTable.
2. Click the Analyze tab.
3. Click Refresh in the Data group to refresh the current PivotTable only, or click the Refresh arrow and select Refresh All to refresh all PivotTables in the workbook.

PivotTables should be current when you open a workbook. However, you can specify a setting to ensure that the PivotTables are updated when you open a workbook containing PivotTables.

To ensure PivotTables are up to date when you open a workbook, complete the following steps:

1. Click the Analyze tab.
2. Click the Options in the PivotTable group to open the PivotTable Options dialog box.
3. Click the Data tab, select the *Refresh data when opening the file* check box, and then click OK.

> **TIP: CHANGE THE DATA SOURCE**
> To change the data source used to create the PivotTable, click Change Data Source in the Data group on the Analyze tab, select the new range containing the data to pivot, and click OK in the Change Data Source dialog box.

Quick Concepts

4. What are the advantages of using a PivotTable instead of a subtotal? *p. 339*

5. What is the main benefit of creating a PivotTable using Quick Analysis or from the Recommended PivotTables dialog box over creating a blank PivotTable? *p. 339*

6. Describe the four areas of a PivotTable. *p. 342*

Hands-On Exercises

 Watch the Video for this Hands-On Exercise!

 MyITLab® HOE2 Training

Skills covered: Create a Recommended PivotTable • Rename a PivotTable • Add Rows to a PivotTable • Add Columns to a PivotTable • Remove Fields from a PivotTable • Rearrange Fields in a PivotTable • Change Value Field Settings • Refresh a PivotTable

2 PivotTable Basics

After exhausting the possibilities of outlines and subtotals, you want to create a PivotTable to analyze the sociology book sales. You realize you can see the data from different perspectives, enabling you to have a stronger understanding of the sales by various categories.

STEP 1 ›› CREATE A PIVOTTABLE

Because you want to keep the subtotals you created in the Books Subtotal worksheet, you will create a PivotTable from the Books Data worksheet. Refer to Figures 5.11 and 5.19 as you complete Step 1.

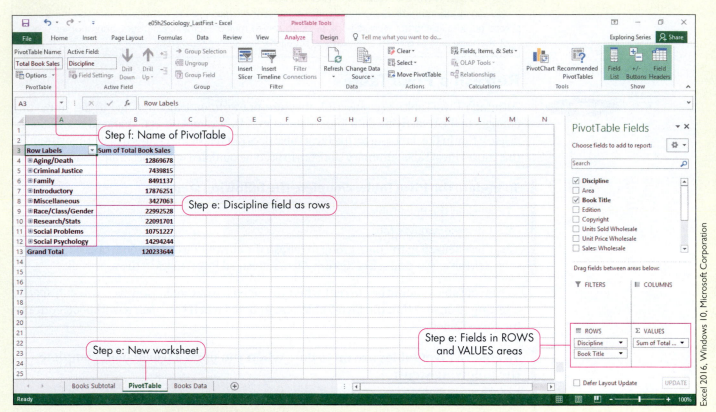

FIGURE 5.19 PivotTable for Total Book Sales

a. Open *e05h1Sociology_LastFirst* if you closed it at the end of Hands-On Exercise 1 and save it as **e05h2Sociology_LastFirst**, changing h1 to h2.

b. Click the **Books Data sheet tab**.

Excel does not let you create a PivotTable using subtotaled data. To preserve the subtotals you created in Hands-On Exercise 1, you will use the dataset in the Books Data worksheet.

c. Click **cell A5**, click the **Insert tab**, and then click **Recommended PivotTables** in the Tables group.

The Recommended PivotTables dialog box opens (refer to Figure 5.11).

d. Scroll the thumbnails of recommended PivotTables and click the **Sum of Total Book Sales by Discipline thumbnail**. (NOTE: Point to each thumbnail to see the full name.)

You selected this PivotTable to show the overall total book sales for each discipline. The dialog box shows a preview of the selected PivotTable.

e. Click **OK**. Rename Sheet1 as **PivotTable**.

Excel inserts a new Sheet1 worksheet, which you renamed as PivotTable, with the PivotTable on the left side and the PivotTable Fields List on the right side (see Figure 5.19).

f. Click the **PivotTable Name box** in the PivotTable group on the Analyze tab, type **Total Book Sales**, and then press **Enter**. Save the workbook.

You changed the name of the PivotTable from PivotTable1 to Total Book Sales to comply with accessibility standards and to give meaningful names to the PivotTables within your workbook.

STEP 2 ›› ADD FIELDS TO ROWS AND COLUMNS

You want to compare sales combinations by discipline, copyright year, and edition. The Discipline field is already in the PivotTable, so you will add the copyright year and edition fields. Refer to Figure 5.20 as you complete Step 2.

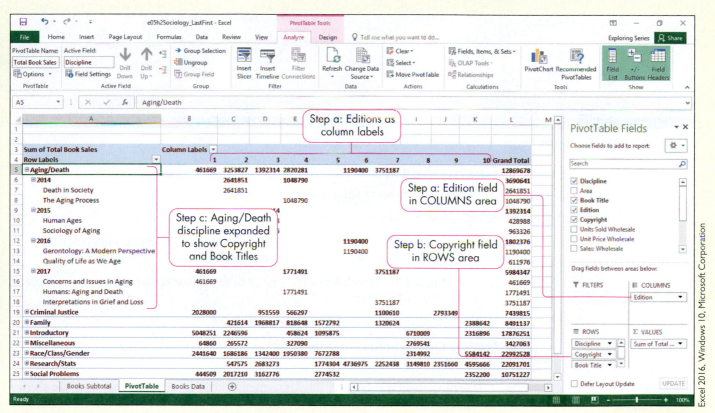

FIGURE 5.20 Fields Added to Rows and Columns Sales

a. Drag the **Edition field** to the COLUMNS area in the PivotTable Fields List.

Excel displays the total book sales by a combination of discipline and edition. This enables you to compare sales of current editions within each discipline. Blanks appear in the PivotTable when a discipline does not have a specific edition. For example, the Family discipline does not have any first-edition books currently being published.

b. Drag the **Copyright field** between the Discipline and Book Title fields in the ROWS area of the PivotTable Fields List.

The Copyright and Book Titles are not showing in the PivotTable because they are collapsed within the Discipline rows.

c. Click the **Aging/Death expand button** +. Save the workbook.

You expanded the Aging/Death discipline to show the copyright years and titles.

Although it is informative to compare sales by edition, you think that the PivotTable contains too much detail, so you will remove the Edition field. In addition, the ROWS area contains the Book Titles field, but those data are collapsed; therefore, you will remove it as well. After you remove the fields, you will rearrange other fields to simplify the PivotTable. Refer to Figure 5.21 as you complete Step 3.

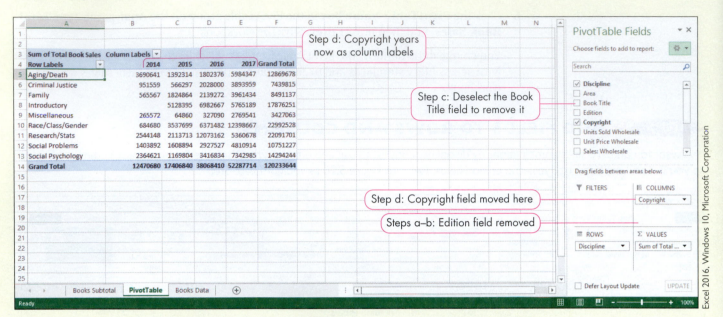

FIGURE 5.21 PivotTable After Removing and Rearranging Fields

a. Click the **Edition arrow** in the COLUMNS area.

Excel displays a menu of options to apply to this field.

b. Select **Remove Field** on the menu.

You removed the Edition field from the PivotTable. Instead of several sales columns, Excel consolidates the sales into one sales column.

c. Click the **Book Title check box** to deselect it in the *Choose fields to add to report* section of the PivotTable Fields List.

You removed the Book Title field from the PivotTable.

d. Drag the **Copyright field** from the ROWS area to the COLUMNS area. Save the workbook.

This arrangement consolidates the data better. Instead of repeating the copyright years for each discipline, the copyright years are listed only once each at the top of the sales columns.

After selecting the PivotTable fields, you want to improve the appearance of the sociology textbook PivotTable. You will format the values with the Accounting Number Format and replace the generic Row Labels description with a label that indicates the sociology disciplines. Refer to Figure 5.22 as you complete Step 4.

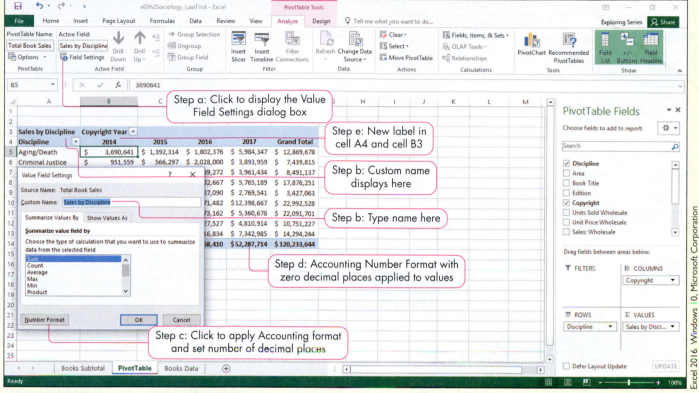

FIGURE 5.22 Formatted Values and Labels

a. Click **cell B5** and click **Field Settings** in the Active Field group on the Analyze tab.

The Value Field Settings dialog box opens so that you can format the field.

b. Type **Sales by Discipline** in the Custom Name box. Leave Sum as the selected calculation type in the *Summarize value field by* section.

You created a customized name for the calculated field and retained the calculation to sum the values. The Value Field Settings dialog box is still open so that you can format the field.

c. Click **Number Format**.

Excel opens a Format Cells dialog box with only the Number tab.

d. Click **Accounting** in the Category list, change the **Decimal places value** to **0**, click **OK** in the Format Cells dialog box, and then click **OK** in the Value Field Settings dialog box.

You formatted the values with Accounting Number Format with no decimal places, and the heading *Sales by Discipline* displays in cell A3.

e. Type **Discipline** in **cell A4** and type **Copyright Year** in **cell B3**.

You replaced the generic *Row Labels* heading with *Discipline* to describe the contents of the first column, and you replaced the *Column Labels* heading with *Copyright Year*. Although you can create custom names for values, you cannot create custom names for row and column labels. However, you can edit the labels directly in the cells.

f. Select the **range B4:F4** and center the labels horizontally. Save the workbook.

After consulting with the Accounting Department, you realize that the retail prices are incorrect. The unit retail prices are based on a percentage of the wholesale price. The retail unit price is 30% more than the wholesale unit price, but it should be 25%. You will edit the input cell in the original worksheet and refresh the PivotTable to see the corrected results. Refer to Figure 5.23 as you complete Step 5.

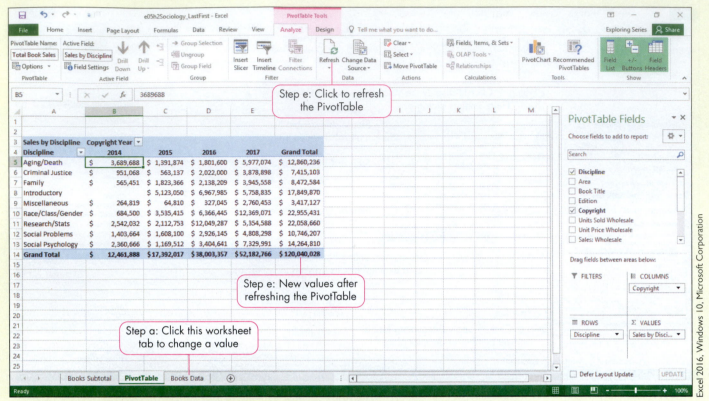

FIGURE 5.23 Refreshed PivotTable

a. Look at **cell F14**.

The current grand total is $120,233.644.

b. Click the **Books Data sheet tab**.

You need to locate and change the retail price percentage.

c. Click **cell J1**, the cell that contains the current retail price percentage.

d. Type **125** and press **Enter**. Save the workbook.

You changed the retail price rate, which changes the results shown in columns J, K, and L in the Books Data worksheet. However, the PivotTable values are not updated yet.

e. Click the **PivotTable sheet tab**.

Notice that the PivotTable aggregate values did not change. The grand total is still $120,233,644. You must refresh the PivotTable.

f. Click the **Analyze tab** and click **Refresh** in the Data group.

Excel updates the PivotTable values based on the change you made in the Books Data worksheet. The grand total is now $120,040,028.

g. Save the workbook. Keep the workbook open if you plan to continue with the next Hands-On Exercise. If not, close the workbook and exit Excel.

PivotTable Options

As you have experienced, PivotTables consolidate and aggregate large amounts of data to facilitate data analysis. You can use the Analyze tab to customize the PivotTable for more in-depth analysis. You can add filters, insert slicers, and insert a timeline to include or exclude data from being represented in a PivotTable. In addition, you can perform a variety of calculations and show specific calculation results. Furthermore, you can change the design to control the overall appearance of the PivotTable.

In this section, you will learn how to filter data in a PivotTable. In addition, you will create a calculated field and display subtotals. Finally, you will change the style of the PivotTable.

Filtering and Slicing a PivotTable

PivotTables display aggregated data for each category. However, you may want to set a filter to exclude particular categories or values. You can specify a particular field to filter the PivotTable. In addition, you can include slicers to easily set filters to designate which specific data to include in the PivotTable.

Add Filters

STEP 1 ❯❯ You can apply filters to show only a subset of the PivotTable. Similar to applying filters to an Excel table, when you add filters in a PivotTable, the filters only temporarily remove some data from view. The PivotTable displays only data that reflects the filters you enabled. Drag a field to the FILTERS area in the PivotTable Fields List when you want to engage a filter based on a particular field. For example, you might want to filter the PivotTable to show only aggregates for first- and second-edition books. When you drag a field to the FILTERS area, Excel displays the filters above the PivotTable. The first field in the FILTERS area displays in cell A1 with a filter arrow in cell B1. Additional fields added to the FILTERS area display in the subsequent rows.

> **To set a PivotTable filter, complete the following steps:**
>
> 1. Drag a field to the FILTERS area in the PivotTable Fields List.
> 2. Click the filter arrow in cell B1 to open the Filter menu and complete one of the following steps:
>   - Select the value in the list to filter the data by that value only.
>   - Click the Select Multiple Items check box if you want to select more than one value to filter the PivotTable. Click the check boxes by each value you want to set (see Figure 5.24).
>   - Type a value in the Search box if the list is long and you want to find a value quickly.
> 3. Click OK.

The PivotTable displays only a subset of the data that meet those conditions and calculates the summary statistics based on the filtered data rather than the complete dataset. The filter arrow displays an icon of a funnel when the PivotTable is being filtered.

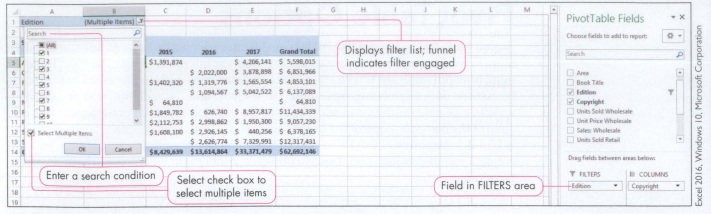

FIGURE 5.24 Filter Menu

Cell B1 displays (All) when no filter is enabled, the value if one filter is enabled, or (Multiple Items) if more than one item is selected. If you no longer need a filter, you can remove it.

> **To remove a filter from a PivotTable, complete one of the following steps:**
>
> - Drag the field from the FILTER area in the PivotTable Fields List to remove the entire filter.
> - Click the Filter arrow in cell B1, select (All), and then click OK to remove the filter settings but keep the field in the FILTERS area on the PivotTable Fields List.

You can apply additional filters for rows and columns. For example, you can apply date filters to display summary statistics for data occurring within a particular time frame or apply filters for values within a designated range.

> **To apply row or column filters in a PivotTable, complete the following steps:**
>
> 1. Click the Row Labels or Column Labels arrow in the PivotTable (see Figure 5.25) to open a filter menu.
> 2. Click the (Select All) check box on the menu to deselect all items.
> 3. Click the check boxes by the item(s) you want to display and click OK.

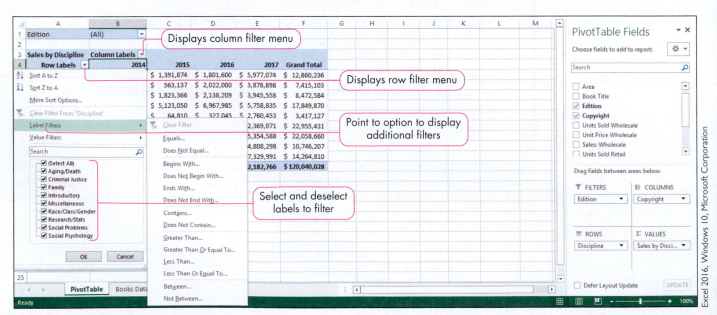

FIGURE 5.25 Row and Column Filtering

Insert a Slicer to Filter a PivotTable

STEP 2 ⟩⟩ You can insert a *slicer*, a small window containing one button for each unique item in a field so that you can filter the PivotTable quickly. The visual representation is easier to manipulate than adding more fields to the FILTERS area and then setting each field's filter.

To insert a slicer, complete the following steps:

1. Click the Analyze tab.
2. Click Insert Slicer in the Filter group to open the Insert Slicers dialog box (see Figure 5.26).
3. Click one or more field check boxes to display one or more slicers and click OK.

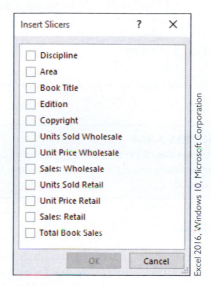

FIGURE 5.26 Insert Slicers Dialog Box

For each field check box you select, Excel inserts a slicer into the worksheet. You can manipulate a slicer by doing one of the following:

- **Move the Slicer.** Drag a slicer to move it in the Excel window to avoid overlapping the slicer and PivotTable.

- **Filter Data by One Value.** Click the slicer button to filter by the value represented by the button. For example, to set a filter to display only 1st editions, click 1 on the Edition filter. Excel displays the slicer buttons in three different colors to indicate selected items, items filtered out, and items that are not applicable due to other filters set. This color coding makes it clear how you filtered the PivotTable.

- **Filter Data by Multiple Values.** Click Multi-Select to be able to click more than one button to filter data for multiple values. For example, to set a filter to display first and second editions, click Multi-Select and click 1 and 2. In Figure 5.27, the Discipline field is filtered by Family, Introductory, and Social Problems. Although no filter has been enabled for the Edition field, the 6th and 9th edition buttons are unavailable because the three disciplines selected do not have books that are in their sixth or ninth editions.

- **Clear a Filter.** Click Clear Filter in the top-right corner of the slicer to clear the filters for that field.

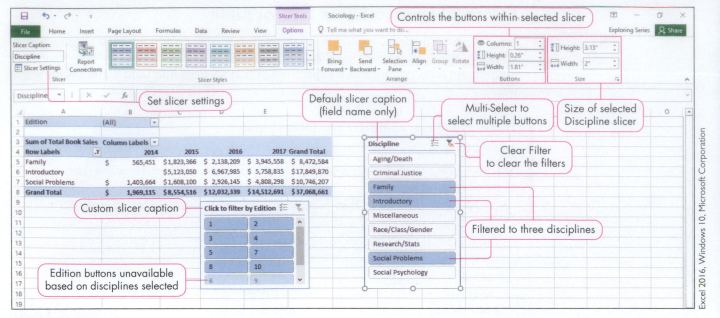

FIGURE 5.27 Slicers

TIP: SLICERS VS. FILTERS AREA

The benefit of using slicers over the FILTERS area is that slicers display color-coded buttons to show which fields are being filtered, whereas using the filter arrows within the PivotTable do not show what fields are currently being filtered.

Customize a Slicer

When you select a slicer, the Slicer Tools Options tab displays so that you can customize a slicer. The default slicer caption displays the field name only. The **slicer caption** is text that displays in the header at the top of the slicer window, similar to a title bar, to identify the data in the field. However, you can customize the slicer by changing its caption. In Figure 5.27, the caption for the Edition slicer displays an instruction to the user, whereas the caption for the Discipline slicer displays the default field name. Table 5.5 lists and describes the commands on the Slicer Tools Options tab.

TABLE 5.5 Slicer Tools Commands

Group	Commands
Slicer	Enables you to change the slicer caption, display the Slicer Settings dialog box for further customization, and manage the PivotTable connected to the slicer. The Edition slicer has been sorted in ascending order. The light blue items 6 and 9 do not apply to the selected disciplines.
Slicer Styles	Applies a style to the slicer by specifying the color of the filtered item in the slicer. For example, given the workbook theme, the default active filters appear in blue and unavailable items appear in light blue.
Arrange	Specifies the slicer's placement in relation to other groups, such as placing a slicer on top of other slicers.
Buttons	Defines how many columns are displayed in the selected slicer and the height and width of each button inside the slicer. For example, the Edition slicer contains two columns, and the Discipline slicer contains one column.
Size	Sets the height and width of the slicer window. For example, the Discipline slicer's height is 3.13".

Insert a Timeline to Filter a PivotTable

When a PivotTable is based on a dataset that contains dates, you might want to filter data to a particular date or range of dates to analyze the data. Insert a *PivotTable timeline* to filter the data based on the date range you want. A PivotTable timeline is a small window that starts with the first date and ends with the last date in the data source. It contains horizontal tiles that you can click to filter data by day, month, quarter, or year.

To insert a timeline and filter data on a timeline in a PivotTable, complete the following steps:

1. Click the Analyze tab.
2. Click Insert Timeline in the Filter group to open the Insert Timelines dialog box, which displays field names of fields that contain date-formatted data.
3. Click a field check box and click OK. Excel displays a timeline in the worksheet, and the Timeline Tools Options tab displays (see Figure 5.28) so that you can change the timeline caption, apply a style, adjust the size, and show items on the timeline.
4. Click the arrow by the current time level and select a time period: YEARS, QUARTERS, MONTHS, or DAYS. The timeline displays that time period.
5. Click a tile on the timeline to filter data. For example, click March 2018 to filter data in the PivotTable for that particular month. To select multiple time periods, click the tile representing the first time period and drag across the tiles to select consecutive time periods. For non-consecutive time periods (such as the 1st quarter of each year), press and hold Ctrl while you click various time periods on the timeline. To clear the timeline filter, click Clear Filter in the top-right corner of the timeline.

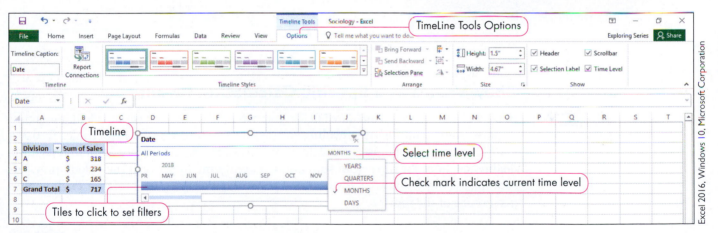

FIGURE 5.28 Timeline

Creating a Calculated Field

STEP 3 ⟫ You can create a *calculated field*, which is a user-defined field that derives its value based on performing calculations in other fields in a PivotTable. The calculated field does not exist in the original dataset. For example, you can create a calculated field that converts totals to percentages for easier relative comparison among categories, or you might want to create a calculated field that determines the number of units sold generated by a 10% increase for the upcoming year.

To create a calculated field, complete the following steps:

1. Select a cell within the PivotTable.
2. Click the Analyze tab.
3. Click Fields, Items, & Sets in the Calculations group and select Calculated Field to display the Insert Calculated Field dialog box (see Figure 5.29).
4. Type a descriptive label for the calculated field in the Name box.
5. Build a formula starting with the equal sign (=). Instead of using cell references, insert the field names and other operands. For example, = 'Total Book Sales'*.1 calculates a 10% royalty amount on the total book sales.
6. Click OK to insert the calculated field in the PivotTable. Format the numerical values in the calculated field column as needed.

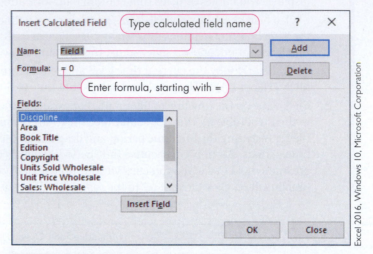

FIGURE 5.29 Insert Calculated Field Dialog Box

Show Values as a Specific Calculation Result

STEP 4 ▶▶ In addition to creating calculated fields, you can apply built-in custom calculations that display relationships between values in rows and columns in the PivotTable. To use a value as a calculation, insert the field in the VALUES area. You might want to repeat the field twice: once for the actual sum and a second time to perform the calculation. For example, you can show each value as a percentage of the grand total or each value's percentage of the row total.

To display values in relation to others, complete the following steps:

1. Click the field in the VALUES area of the PivotTable Fields List and select Value Field Settings (or click within the field in the PivotTable and click Field Settings in the Active Field group on the Analyze tab).
2. Click the Show Values As tab within the Value Field Settings dialog box.
3. Click the *Show values as* arrow and select the desired calculation type. Table 5.6 lists and describes some of the calculation options.
4. Click Number Format to set number formats, click OK to close the Format Cells dialog box, and then click OK to close the Value Field Settings dialog box.

TABLE 5.6 Calculation Options

Option	Description
% of Grand Total	Displays each value as a percentage of the grand total.
% of Column Total	Displays each value as a percentage of the respective column total. The values in each column total 100%.
% of Row Total	Displays each value as a percentage of the respective row total. The values in each row total 100%.
% of Parent Row Total	Displays values as: (value for the item) / (value for the parent item on rows). Two fields should be contained in the ROWS area where the first field is a parent of the second field. For example, if Discipline is the first field and Area is the second field, Family would be the parent for the Family Interaction and Marriage and Family areas. The calculation would divide the Family Interaction value by the total value in the Family parent row.
Running Total	Displays values as running totals.
Rank Smallest to Largest	Displays the rank of values in a specific field where 1 represents the smallest value.
Rank Largest to Smallest	Displays the rank of values in a specific field where 1 represents the largest value.

Pearson Education, Inc.

Figure 5.30 illustrates the use of the Total Sales field inserted three times in the VALUES area: (1) sum of the totals for each discipline and area, (2) % of Parent Row Total, and (3) % of Grand Total. The Discipline and Area fields are contained in the ROWS area. The Disciplines are the parents to the respective Areas. In the % of Parent Row column, the Death and Dying sales ($3,751,187) are 66.92% of its Aging/Death parent sales of $5,606,170. The Sociology of Aging sales ($1,853,983) are 33.08% of the Aging/Death parent sales. The percentages for the areas within the Aging/Death discipline must add up to 100%. The Aging/Death discipline sales of $5,605,170 is 8.93% of its parent sales, the grand total of $62,796,185.

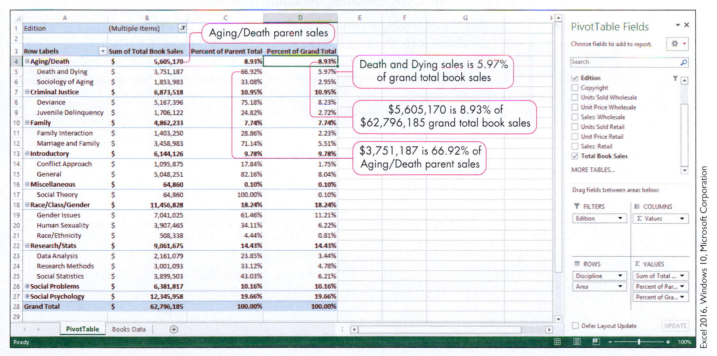

FIGURE 5.30 PivotTable Tools Design Tab

In the Percent of Grand Total column, each parent's sale is the percentage of the grand total, and each area's sales is a percentage of the grand total. The bold discipline (parent) percentages equal 100%, and the area percentages also equal 100% of the total sales.

> **TIP: SHOW CALCULATIONS AS HELP**
> Use Help within the Value Field Settings dialog box for more information and examples about these calculations.

Changing the PivotTable Design

Excel applies basic formatting to PivotTables. For example, it formats primary row labels in bold to distinguish those categories from the subcategories. In addition, the subtotals are bold to offset these values from the subcategory values. The PivotTable Tools Design tab contains commands for enhancing the format of a PivotTable (see Figure 5.31).

FIGURE 5.31 PivotTable Tools Design Tab

Excel 2016, Windows 10, Microsoft Corporation

Change the PivotTable Style

 A *PivotTable style* controls bold formatting, font colors, shading colors, and border lines. For example, the default Pivot Style Light 16 displays a light blue fill color for the field filters in cells A1 and B1, the column and row labels, and the grand total row.

> **To change the style, complete the following steps:**
>
> 1. Click the PivotTable Tools Design tab.
> 2. Click More in the PivotTable Styles group to display the PivotTable Styles gallery (see Figure 5.32).
> 3. Point to a thumbnail on the gallery. Excel shows a preview of how that style will affect the PivotTable.
> 4. Click a style to apply it to the PivotTable.

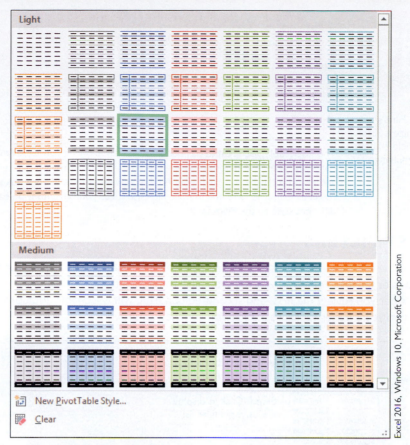

FIGURE 5.32 PivotTable Styles

The PivotTable Style Options group on the Design tab controls which areas of the PivotTable are affected by the style. Click Row Headers to apply special formatting for the first row, Column Headers to apply special formatting to the first column, Banded Rows to format odd and even rows differently, and Banded Columns to format odd and even columns differently.

Change the PivotTable Layout

The Layout group on the Design tab controls the layout of the PivotTable elements. These commands control whether subtotals and grand totals are displayed or hidden. You can customize the location of subtotals by clicking Subtotals in the Layout group on the Design tab. For example, displaying the subtotals at the top of the group draws attention to the totals and enables you to scroll to view all of the supporting data if necessary.

The Report Layout controls the overall format. You can select a compact, outline, or tabular layout. The Report Layout also controls whether item labels are repeated when multiple fields are located in the ROWS area of the PivotTable Fields List. The Blank Rows command enables you to insert blank rows between items or remove blank rows.

Quick Concepts

7. What is the purpose of applying a filter to a PivotTable? What types of filters can you apply? **p. 355**

8. What is a slicer? What is the purpose of a slicer? **p. 357**

9. When would you create a calculated field in a PivotTable? **p. 359**

Hands-On Exercises

Skills covered: Set Filters • Insert a Slicer • Customize a Slicer • Create a Calculated Field • Show Values as Calculations • Change the PivotTable Style

3 PivotTable Options

The PivotTable you created has benefited you by allowing you to review sales data by discipline for each copyright year. In addition, you have used the PivotTable to compare grand total sales among disciplines and grand totals by copyright year. Now you want to extend your analysis. You will calculate author royalties from the sales and impose filters to focus your attention on each analysis. Finally, you will apply a different style to the PivotTable.

STEP 1 ▶▶ SET FILTERS

The level of success of the first two editions especially determines the likelihood of approving subsequent revisions and editions. To display aggregated sales for these editions, you will set a filter to remove the other editions so they are not included in the calculated sales data. After you review the first- and second-edition data, you will enable additional filters to review books published in the past two years. Refer to Figure 5.33 as you complete Step 1.

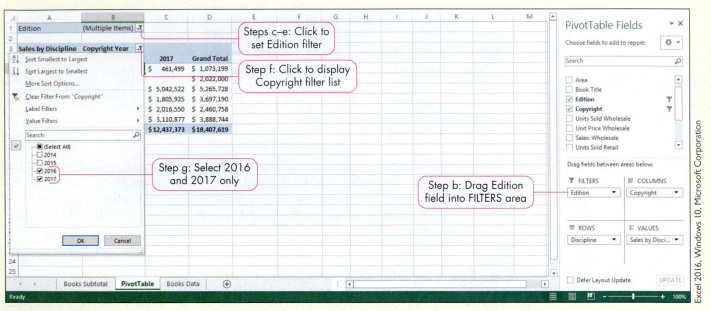

FIGURE 5.33 Filters Enabled

a. Open *e05h2Sociology_LastFirst* if you closed it at the end of Hands-On Exercise 2 and save it as **e05h3Sociology_LastFirst**, changing h2 to h3.

> **TROUBLESHOOTING:** Click in the PivotTable to display the PivotTable Fields List if necessary.

b. Make sure the PivotTable worksheet tab is active and drag the **Edition field** from the *Choose fields to add to report* section to the FILTERS area.

   You can now filter the PivotTable based on the Edition field. Cell A1 displays the field name, and cell B1 displays (All) and the filter arrow.

c. Click the **Edition filter arrow** in **cell B1** and click the **Select Multiple Items check box** to select it.

   The list displays a check box for each item.

d. Click the **(All) check box** to deselect it.

e. Click the **1** and **2 check boxes** and click **OK**.

The summary statistics reflect sales data for only first- and second-edition publications. The filter arrow changes to a funnel icon in cell B1. Cell B1 also changes from (All) to (Multiple Items), indicating that multiple items are included in the filter.

f. Click the **Copyright Year filter arrow** in **cell B3** and click the **(Select All) check box** to deselect it.

g. Click the **2016** and **2017 check boxes**, click **OK**, and save the workbook.

Excel filters out data for years that do not meet the condition you set. The filter arrow changes to a funnel icon in cell B3.

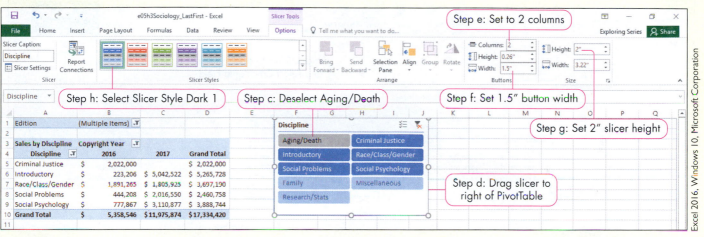

STEP 2 ›› INSERT AND CUSTOMIZE A SLICER

You might distribute the workbook to colleagues who are not as skilled in Excel as you are. To help them set their own filters, you want to insert slicers. Refer to Figure 5.34 as you complete Step 2.

FIGURE 5.34 Slicer

a. Click **Insert Slicer** in the Filter group on the Analyze tab.

The Insert Slicers dialog box opens, listing each field name.

b. Click **Discipline** and click **OK**.

Excel inserts the Discipline slicer in the worksheet. Six slicer buttons are blue, indicating that those disciplines are selected. The grayed-out buttons at the bottom of the slicer indicate those disciplines are not applicable based on other engaged filters you set (first and second editions and 2016 and 2017 copyright years).

c. Press and hold **Ctrl** as you click **Aging/Death** in the Discipline slicer.

This deselects the Aging/Death discipline.

> **TROUBLESHOOTING:** Because several disciplines are selected, if you click Aging/Death instead of pressing Ctrl as you click it, you set Aging/Death as the only discipline. The others are filtered out. If this happens, immediately click Undo and repeat step c.

d. Drag the slicer to the right of the PivotTable.

You moved the slicer so that it does not cover up data in the PivotTable.

e. Change the **Columns value** to **2** in the Buttons group on the Options tab. Change the button **Width** to **1.5"** in the Buttons group.

The slicer now displays buttons in two columns. You changed the width of the buttons to 1.5" to display the full discipline names within the buttons.

f. Change the slicer **Height** to **2** in the Size group.

The slicer window is now only 2" tall.

g. Click **More** in the Slicer Styles group and click **Slicer Style Dark 1**. Save the workbook.

Based on the selected workbook theme, Slicer Style Dark 1 applies a dark blue fill color for selected disciplines, dark gray and black font for available but not currently selected disciplines, and light blue fill with medium blue font color for non-applicable disciplines.

STEP 3 ›› CREATE A CALCULATED FIELD

You want to calculate the amount of the sales returned to the authors as royalties. Although the 10% royalty rate is stored in cell J2 in the Books Data worksheet, the value must be used in the calculated field because range names and cell references outside the PivotTable cannot be used. Refer to Figure 5.35 as you complete Step 3.

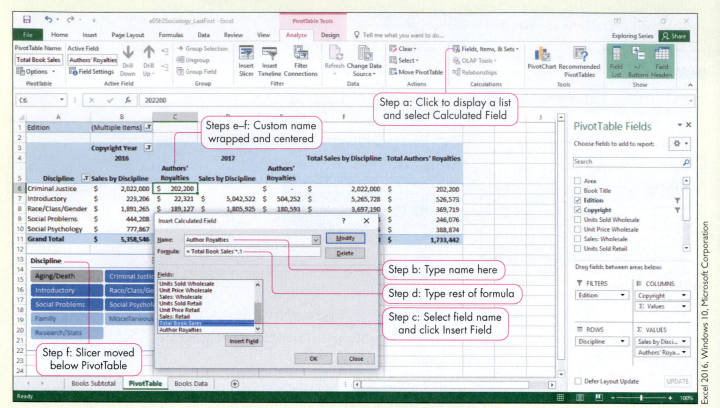

FIGURE 5.35 Calculated Field

a. Click within the PivotTable, click the **Analyze tab**, click **Fields, Items, & Sets** in the Calculations group, and then select **Calculated Field**.

The Insert Calculated Field dialog box opens.

b. Type **Author Royalties** in the Name box.

c. Scroll down the Fields list, click **Total Book Sales**, and then click **Insert Field**.

Excel starts to build the formula, which is currently = 'Total Book Sales'.

d. Type ***.1** at the end of the Formula box and click **OK**.

Excel adds Sum of Author Royalties calculated field columns, one for each copyright year category. It calculates the authors' royalties as 10% of the total sales for each copyright year.

e. Click **cell C5**, click **Field Settings** in the Active Field group on the Analyze tab, type **Authors' Royalties** in the Custom Name box in the Value Field Settings dialog box, and then click **OK**.

f. Move the slicer below the PivotTable so that the top-left corner is in **cell A13**.

g. Select **cells C5** and **E5**, click the **Home tab**, and then click **Center** and **Wrap Text** in the Alignment group. Click **Format** in the Cells group and select **Row Height**, type **30**, and click **OK**. Click **Format**, select **Column Width**, type **12**, and click **OK**.

h. Save the workbook.

You want to see which copyright year generated the largest sales for each discipline, which discipline contributes the largest percentage of the total sociology sales, and which introductory book has the largest sales contribution within that discipline. Refer to Figure 5.36 as you complete Step 4.

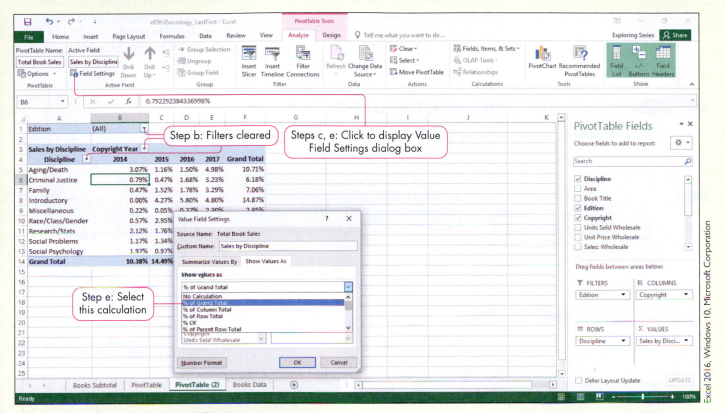

FIGURE 5.36 Percentage of Grand Total

a. Right-click the **PivotTable sheet tab**, select **Move or Copy**, click **Books Data** in the *Before sheet* list, click the **Create a copy check box** to select it, and then click **OK**.

You copied the PivotTable worksheet to maintain the previous tasks you completed as evidence. You will work with the PivotTable (2) worksheet, which is the active worksheet.

b. Do the following to remove filters, slicer, and Authors' Royalties field:

- Click the **Edition filter** in **cell B1**, click the **(All) check box** to select it, and then click **OK** to clear the Edition filter.
  When you click (All), all edition numbers are selected again, as indicated by the check marks.
- Click the **Discipline filter** in **cell A5** and select **Clear Filter From "Discipline"**.
- Click the **Copyright Year filter** in **cell B3** and select **Clear Filter From "Copyright"**.
- Select the slicer and press **Delete**.
- Click **Authors' Royalties** in the VALUES area of the PivotTable Fields List and select **Remove Field**.

c. Click within any value in the PivotTable, click the **Analyze tab**, and then click **Field Settings** in the Active Field group.

The Value Field Settings dialog box opens.

d. Click the **Show Values As tab**, click the **Show values as arrow**, select **% of Row Total**, and then click **OK**.

Excel displays each copyright year's values as percentages for that discipline. All disciplines except Introductory and Research/Stats had the highest percentage of sales for the books with a 2017 copyright. These two disciplines had their highest percentage of sales for books with a 2016 copyright.

e. Click the **Field Settings** in the Active Field group, click the **Show Values As tab** within the dialog box, click the **Show values as arrow**, select **% of Grand Total**, and then click **OK**. Save the workbook.

Refer to Figure 5.36. Each discipline's yearly value displays as a percentage of the total sales. Which discipline and for what copyright year produces the highest percentage of total sales? Answer: 2017 Race/Class/Gender with 10.30%, followed closely by the 2016 Research/Stats with 10.04%. In general, the Race/Class/Gender discipline contributed the highest percentage of the total sales with 19.12%.

STEP 5 ›› CHANGE THE PIVOTTABLE STYLE

To enhance the readability of the sociology textbook PivotTable, you will change the PivotTable style. Refer to Figure 5.37 as you complete Step 5.

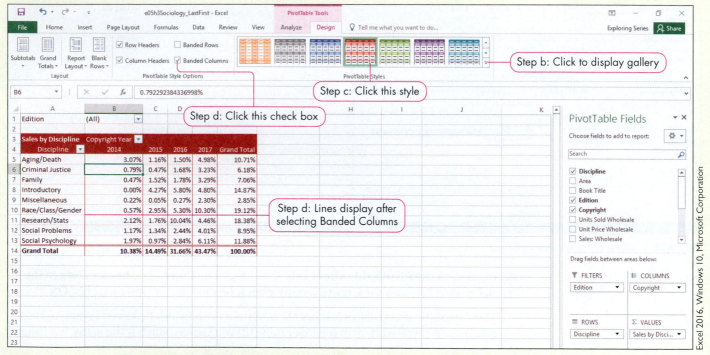

FIGURE 5.37 PivotTable Style

a. Make sure the PivotTable (2) sheet tab is active. Click a cell within the PivotTable, click the **Design tab**, and then click **More** in the PivotTable Styles group.

The PivotTable Style gallery displays styles that you can apply.

b. Click **Pivot Style Medium 3** to apply a dark red style to the PivotTable.

c. Click the **Banded Columns check box** to select it in the PivotTable Style Options group to add dark red vertical lines between the columns.

d. Save and close the workbook. You will submit this file to your instructor at the end of the last Hands-On Exercise.

Data Modeling and PivotCharts

When you created a PivotTable earlier in this chapter, you created it from a dataset in a single worksheet. However, the data is often contained in multiple sources, such as multiple worksheets or databases. Excel enables you to use related data to create a PivotTable.

You can create PivotCharts, which like other charts you have created in Excel, provide visual representations of numerical data. Charts help reveal trends or patterns in the data because people can often interpret visual aids easier than reviewing an entire dataset.

In this section, you will select multiple datasets, create a relationship between the datasets, and then create a PivotTable. Finally, you will create and format a PivotChart.

Creating a Data Model

So far, you have been working with data from one table. Often, however, you will want to analyze data contained in multiple tables. A **data model** is a collection of related tables that contain structured data used to create a database. You can create a relationship between two or more Excel tables that have some commonality and relationship, similar to how you can create relationships among common tables in an Access database. You can then perform complex data analysis to make insightful decisions.

Create a Relationship Between Tables

STEP 1 ❱❱ A **relationship** is an association or connection between two tables where both tables contain a common field of data. Similar to how a VLOOKUP function looks up data from a range to find matching data in another range, you can create relationships between tables. For example, you want to generate a report that contains sales representatives' names and their respective data, but the data is stored in one table, and the representatives' names are stored in another table. To combine the names and data into one report, you must establish a link (or relationship) between the two tables using the sales representatives' IDs, which is contained in both tables.

> **To create a relationship between two tables in Excel, complete the following steps:**
>
> 1. Click the Data tab and click Relationships in the Data Tools group to open the Manage Relationships dialog box.
> 2. Click New in the dialog box to open the Create Relationship dialog box (see Figure 5.38).
> 3. Click the Table arrow and select the name of the primary table. The primary table in this example is SALES.
> 4. Click the Column (Foreign) arrow and select the name of the column that contains a relationship to the related or lookup table. For example, Rep ID is the column that relates to a column in the other table.
> 5. Click the Related Table arrow and select the name of the related or lookup table. For example, the related table is REPS.
> 6. Click the Related Column (Primary) arrow and select the name of the column that is related to the primary table. For example, the ID column in the REPS table relates to the Rep ID column in the SALES table.
> 7. Click OK in the Create Relationships dialog box and click Close in the Manage Relationships dialog box.

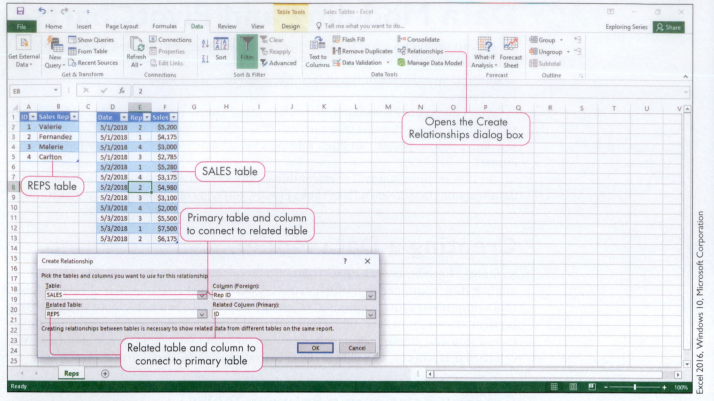

FIGURE 5.38 Relating Tables

TIP: CREATING MULTIPLE RELATIONSHIPS

You can create multiple relationships with one table similar to creating relationships among several tables in an Access database. To create multiple relationships, you must create a relationship between two tables at a time. Each combination of tables must have a common field. After creating the first relationship, repeat the process to create a relationship between two other tables.

TIP: EDITING A RELATIONSHIP

If you want to edit the relationship, click Relationships in the Data Tools group to open the Manage Relationships dialog box. Select the relationship you want to edit, click Edit to open the Edit Relationships dialog box (which looks like the Create Relationships dialog box), make the changes, click OK, and then click Close.

Create a PivotTable from Related Tables

STEP 2 ▶▶ After you create a relationship between tables, you can create a PivotTable from both tables. The fields from both tables are available from which to choose, giving you more detailed analysis of the data. When selecting fields, use the common field. For example, if both tables contain sales representatives' IDs, you can use the actual names instead of their IDs for better descriptions in the PivotTable.

To create a PivotTable from the data model, complete the following steps:

1. Click within the primary table.
2. Click the Insert tab and click PivotTable in the Tables group to open the Create PivotTable dialog box (see Figure 5.39).
3. Make sure the primary table name is displayed in the Table/Range box.
4. Click the *Add this data to the Data Model* check box to select it and click OK.

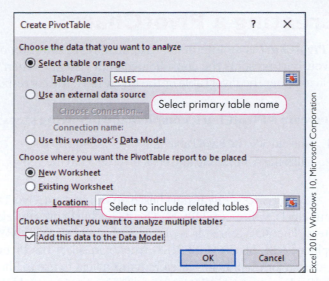

FIGURE 5.39 Create PivotTable Dialog Box

In the PivotTable Fields List, click ALL to display the names of all related tables. Click the table names to display the field names. You then can arrange the fields in the different area boxes at the bottom of the PivotTable Fields List (see Figure 5.40).

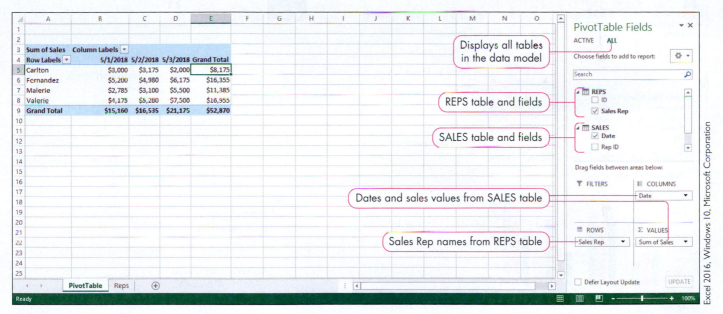

FIGURE 5.40 PivotTable Created from Related Tables

> **TIP: POWER PIVOT TABLES**
> Power Pivot is an add-in that enables you to relate tables and external data from multiple data sources. You can use this add-in to create PivotTables as well as perform other sophisticated analyses. Use the Excel Help feature to look up the topic Power Pivot to learn more about the Power Pivot functionality.

Creating a PivotChart

STEP 3 ▶▶ A *PivotChart* is an interactive graphical representation of the data in a PivotTable. A PivotChart presents the consolidated data visually. When you change the position of a field in either the PivotTable or the PivotChart, the corresponding object changes as well.

> **To create a PivotChart, complete the following steps:**
>
> 1. Click inside the PivotTable.
> 2. Click the Analyze tab and click PivotChart in the Tools group.

Excel creates a PivotChart based on the current PivotTable settings—row labels, column labels, values, and filters. The PivotChart contains elements that enable you to set filters. The ROWS area is replaced with AXIS (CATEGORY), and the COLUMNS area is replaced with LEGEND (SERIES) when you select the PivotChart (see Figure 5.41). The field used for the FILTERS area remains a field to use to filter data within the PivotChart. The field used for VALUES in a PivotTable remains a field that builds the plot area within the PivotChart.

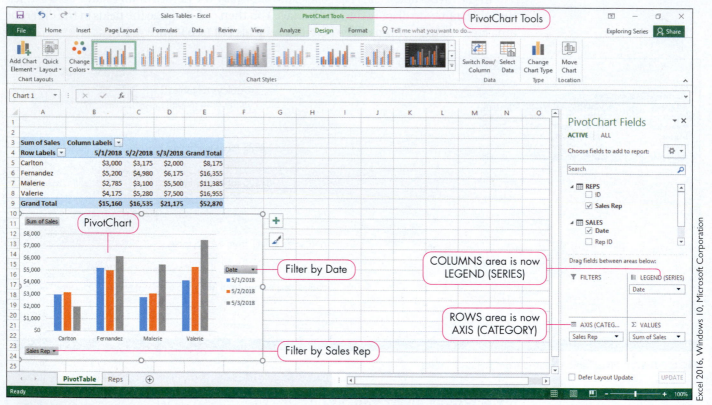

FIGURE 5.41 PivotTable and PivotChart

Modify the PivotChart

STEP 4 ▶▶ Although Excel creates the PivotChart based on the current PivotTable settings, you can change the settings using the PivotChart Fields List. Click the FILTERS arrow and select values to filter the chart. Click the AXIS (CATEGORY) arrows to sort or filter the categories and subcategories in rows. Click the LEGEND (SERIES) to filter the chart based on the values. Changes you make to the PivotChart also affect the corresponding PivotTable. For example, if you apply a filter to the PivotChart, Excel also filters the PivotTable. If you click Switch Rows/Column to change how the data is plotted in the PivotChart, Excel changes the rows and columns in the PivotTable.

The PivotChart Tools Analyze tab contains the same options that you used to customize a PivotTable. You can enter a name in the Chart Name box in the PivotChart group, insert slicers and timelines to filter the data depicted in the chart, and refresh the chart after changing the data source. In addition, the Actions group contains the Move Chart option so that you can move a PivotChart to a different worksheet.

The PivotChart Tools Design tab contains the Chart Layouts, Chart Styles, Data, Type, and Location groups, similar to the groups on the Chart Tools Design tab. Table 5.7 describes the commands in these groups.

TABLE 5.7	PivotChart Tools Design Tab
Group	**Commands**
Chart Layouts	Add chart elements (such as a chart title and data labels) and apply a layout to the PivotChart.
Chart Styles	Apply a different chart style to the PivotChart and then customize the chart by changing the color scheme.
Data	Switch how rows and columns of data are represented in the PivotChart and change the data source used to create the chart.
Type	Change the chart type, such as changing a column chart to a bar chart.
Location	Move the chart to a different sheet in the workbook.

Pearson Education, Inc.

The Chart Elements and Chart Styles buttons display to the right of a PivotChart when it is selected, similar to these buttons that display when a regular chart is selected. When you click the Chart Elements button, a menu displays to add or remove chart elements, such as the chart title, data labels, and legend. When you click the Chart Styles button, a gallery of chart styles displays so that you can apply a different style to the chart.

When you double-click a chart element, the applicable task pane displays on the right side of the screen so that you can customize that element. For example, if you double-click the chart title, the Format Chart Title task pane displays. If you double-click a slice of a pie in a pie chart, the Format Data Point task pane displays so that you can change the fill color for that slice. Use Excel Help to learn more about customizing PivotCharts.

Quick Concepts

10. When is it beneficial to create a relationship between two tables? *p. 369*

11. What PivotTable areas are used to create the elements in a PivotChart? *p. 372*

12. What happens when you set filters and change fields used in a PivotChart? *p. 372*

Skills covered: Create Relationships • Create a PivotTable from Related Tables • Create a PivotChart • Modify the PivotChart

4 Data Modeling and PivotCharts

You are converting the data into separate tables to improve the database design of the books data. Your new workbook contains a Books table, an Editor table, and a Discipline table. The Books table uses numbers to code the editor assigned to each book and the discipline for each book. You will build relationships among these tables, create a PivotTable to analyze data by discipline and editor, and then create a PivotChart for the Family discipline.

STEP 1 ›› CREATE RELATIONSHIPS

The BOOKS table contains codes instead of discipline categories, and a new column contains editor IDs. You will create relationships between the BOOKS table and the DISCIPLINE and EDITOR tables to build a data model. Refer to Figure 5.42 as you complete Step 1.

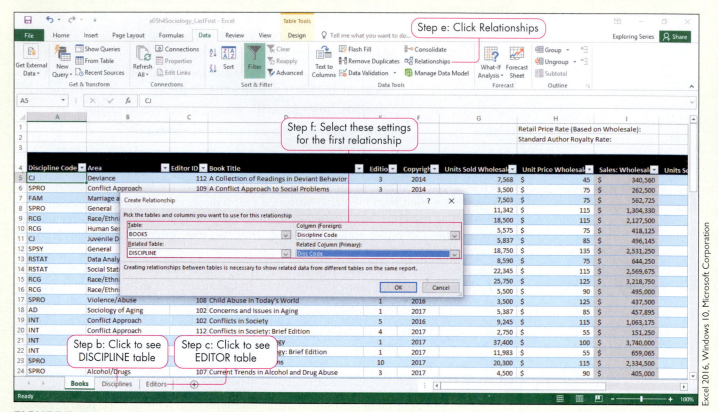

FIGURE 5.42 Relating Tables

a. Open *e05h4Sociology* and save it as **e05h4Sociology_LastFirst**.

The Books sheet tab contains the BOOKS table. Notice that the discipline category names have been replaced with discipline codes in the first column. The third column contains codes that represent editor names.

b. Click the **Disciplines sheet tab**.

The Disciplines sheet contains the DISCIPLINE table. Each discipline code and category name is listed only once. For example, FAM is the code for the Family discipline.

c. Click the **Editors sheet tab**.

The Editors sheet contains the EDITOR table. Each editor is listed only once. For example, 101 is Melissa Hort.

d. Click the **Books sheet tab** and click **cell A5**.

e. Click the **Data tab** and click **Relationships** in the Data Tools group.

The Manage Relationships dialog box opens.

f. Click **New** to open the Create Relationship dialog box and do the following:

- Click the **Table arrow** and select **BOOKS**.
- Click the **Column (Foreign) arrow** and select **Discipline Code**.
- Click the **Related Table arrow** and select **DISCIPLINE**.
- Click the **Related Column (Primary) arrow** and select **Disc Code**.
- Click **OK**.

You created a relationship between the BOOKS and DISCIPLINE tables based on the common data, the discipline codes. The Manage Relationships dialog box now displays the relationship you created. You will now add a second relationship before closing the dialog box.

g. Click **New** to open the Create Relationship dialog box and do the following:

- Click the **Table arrow** and select **BOOKS**.
- Click the **Column (Foreign)** and select **Editor ID**.
- Click the **Related Table arrow** and select **EDITOR**.
- Click the **Related Column (Primary)** and select **Editor ID**.
- Click **OK**.

You created a relationship between the BOOKS and EDITOR tables based on the common data, the Editor IDs. The Manage Relationships dialog box now displays the relationship you created.

h. Click **Close** and then save the workbook.

STEP 2 ›› CREATE A PIVOTTABLE FROM RELATED TABLES

Now that the BOOKS table is related to both the DISCIPLINE and EDITOR tables, you are ready to create a PivotTable using the three tables. Refer to Figure 5.43 as you complete Step 2.

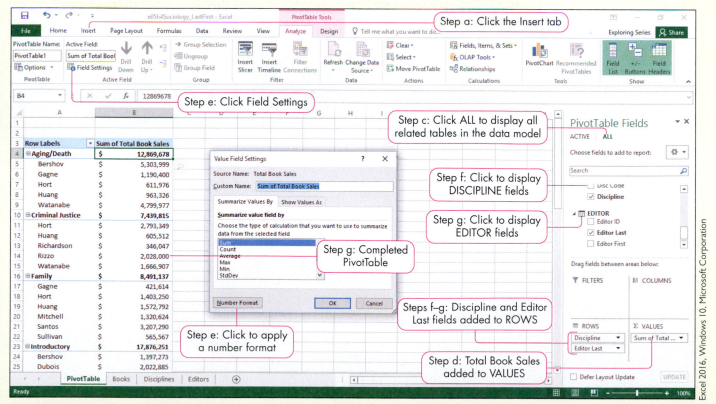

FIGURE 5.43 PivotTable for Related Tables

a. Click within the dataset on the Books sheet, click the **Insert tab** and click **PivotTable** in the Tables group.

The Create PivotTable dialog box opens with BOOKS as the selected Table/Range.

b. Click the **Add this data to the Data Model check box** to select it and click **OK**.

Excel inserts Sheet1 with a blank PivotTable on the left side.

c. Click **ALL** at the top of the PivotTable Fields List.

The PivotTable Fields List shows BOOKS, DISCIPLINE, and EDITOR table names.

d. Click **BOOKS** to display the fields in the BOOKS table, scroll through the fields, and then click the **Total Book Sales check box** to select it.

The Total Book Sales field is added to the VALUES area.

e. Click **Field Settings** in the Active Field group on the Analyze tab to open the Value Field Settings dialog box and complete the following steps:

- Click **Number Format** to open the Number Format dialog box.
- Click **Accounting** in the Category list.
- Change the **Decimal places** to **0**.
- Click **OK** in the Format Cells dialog box.
- Click **OK** in the Value Field Settings dialog box.

The value is formatting with Accounting Number Format with zero decimal places.

f. Click **DISCIPLINE** in the PivotTable Fields List to display the fields in the DISCIPLINE table and click the **Discipline check box** to select it.

The Discipline field is added to the ROWS area.

g. Scroll down and click **EDITOR** to display the fields in the EDITOR table, and then click the **Editor Last check box** to select it.

The Editor Last field is added below the Discipline field in the ROWS area.

h. Double-click the **Sheet1 sheet tab**, type **PivotTable**, and press **Enter**. Save the workbook.

You want to create a PivotChart to depict the sales data by editor for the Family discipline. Refer to Figure 5.44 as you complete Step 3.

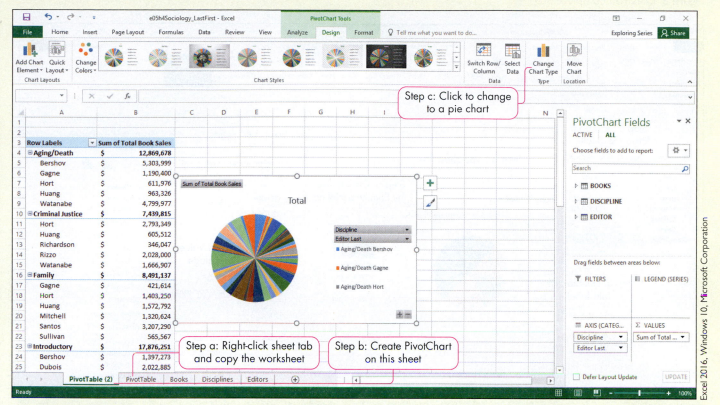

FIGURE 5.44 PivotChart

a. Right-click the **PivotTable sheet tab**, select **Move or Copy**, click the **Create a copy check box** to select it, and click **OK**.

You created a copy of the PivotTable so that you can preserve that PivotTable settings, modify the duplicate PivotTable, and then create a PivotChart based on the modified PivotTable.

b. Ensure the PivotTable (2) sheet tab is active, click **PivotChart** in the Tools group to open the Insert Chart dialog box, and then click **OK**.

Excel creates a clustered column chart from the PivotTable.

c. Click the **Design tab**.

d. Click **Change Chart Type** in the Type group, click **Pie**, and click **OK**. Save the workbook.

You changed the chart type from a clustered column chart to a pie chart.

The PivotChart depicts too many data points. You will set a filter to display data for the Family discipline only. You will add a descriptive chart title and then display slices from largest to smallest. Finally, you will display percentage data labels. Refer to Figure 5.45 as you complete Step 4.

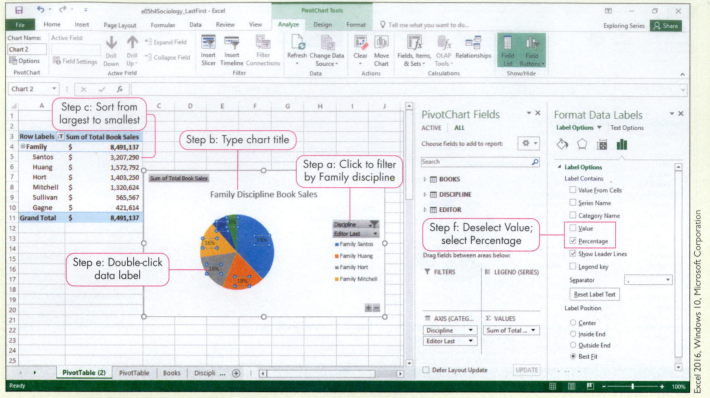

FIGURE 5.45 Modified PivotChart

a. Click the **Discipline arrow** within the PivotChart, click the **(Select All) check box** to deselect all disciplines, click the **Family check box**, and click **OK**.

This action filtered both the PivotChart and the PivotTable to display only Family discipline data.

b. Click **Total** in the chart title, type **Family Discipline Book Sales**, and then press **Enter**.

You changed the chart title to be more descriptive.

c. Click **cell B5** in the PivotTable, click the **Data tab**, and then click **Sort Largest to Smallest** in the Sort & Filter group.

This action sorts the values from largest to smallest in both the PivotTable and in the PivotChart.

d. Click the PivotChart, click **Chart Elements** on the right of the PivotChart and then click the **Data Labels check box** to select it.

You added data labels to the PivotChart.

e. Double-click a data label to display the Format Data Labels task pane.

f. Click the **Value check box** to deselect the values and click the **Percentage check box** to display percentage data labels. Close the Format Data Labels task pane.

g. Save and close the file. Based on your instructor's directions, submit the following:

e05h3Sociology_LastFirst

e05h4Sociology_LastFirst

Chapter Objectives Review

After reading this chapter, you have accomplished the following objectives:

1. Subtotal data.

- The Subtotal dialog box enables you to insert subtotals, such as sums or averages, based on sorted data. This feature detects changes between categories arranged in rows to insert the subtotal rows.
- Add a second level of subtotals: To keep the first level and add a second level, deselect the *Replace current subtotals* check box in the Subtotals dialog box.
- Collapse and expand the subtotals: Click the outline level buttons to collapse the subtotals to the grand total, grand total and subtotals, or entire dataset. Click a particular collapse button to collapse a category, or click an expand button to expand a particular category.

2. Group and ungroup data.

- If the data contain columns of formulas based on other columns and/or row subtotals, use Auto Outline to create an outline based on the data structure. You can then collapse and expand the outline as you review the data. If you no longer need grouped data, select and ungroup the data again.

3. Create a PivotTable.

- Create a Recommended PivotTable: When you use Quick Analysis or Recommended PivotTable, Excel analyzes the dataset to provide recommended PivotTables. The PivotTable displays on a new worksheet, and the PivotTable Fields List displays on the right side of that worksheet. The PivotTable Fields List contains a list of fields in the dataset and areas to control the layout of the PivotTable.
- Create a Blank PivotTable: Use the Ribbon to create a blank PivotTable layout. You can then add fields to design the PivotTable.

4. Modify a PivotTable.

- Add rows to a PivotTable: Add fields to the ROWS area of the PivotTable Fields List to add row categories. The order of the fields within the ROWS area dictates the hierarchy.
- Add values in a PivotTable: Add numerical fields to the VALUES area to display aggregated totals for that field. You can add a field multiple times with a different aggregate for each instance. If you add a field containing text, the default calculation is to provide a count of data.
- Add columns to a PivotTable: Drag fields to the COLUMNS area to add additional columns of details.
- Collapse and expand items in a PivotTable: Click the collapse button to collapse subcategory rows and click the expand button to expand a subcategory of details.
- Remove fields from a PivotTable: Click a field name in the respective area of the PivotTable Fields List and select Remove Field.
- Rearrange fields in a PivotTable: Drag fields from one area to another in the PivotTable Fields List to rearrange fields in the PivotTable.

- Change the value field settings: You can select a different function to calculate the statistics in the PivotTable. You can also apply number formatting, such as Currency, and specify a custom column heading for value columns.
- Refresh a PivotTable: PivotTables do not update automatically if you change the original dataset. You must click Refresh to update the PivotTable.

5. Filter and slice a PivotTable.

- Add filters: Drag a field to the FILTERS area of the PivotTable Fields List and click the Filter arrow above the PivotTable to set the filter conditions. You can also click the row labels arrow in cell A4 to set row filters and click the column arrow in cell B3 to set column filters.
- Insert a slicer to filter a PivotTable: A slicer is a small window containing the values for a particular field. You click buttons in the slicer to set filters for that particular field.
- Customize a slicer: You can specify the slicer's style and size. You can specify how many columns of buttons appear in the slicer and the size of those buttons.
- Insert a timeline to filter a PivotTable: A timeline is a small window that enables you to filter a PivotTable to a particular time period, such as years, quarters, months, or dates.

6. Create a calculated field.

- A calculated field is a user-defined field based on other fields. This field does not exist in the original dataset. You can use basic arithmetic operations, but you cannot use cell references or range names in the calculated field syntax.
- Show values as a specific calculation result: You can apply predefined calculations, such as *% of Grand Total*, for displaying the values in the PivotTable.

7. Change the PivotTable design.

- Change the PivotTable style: A PivotTable style controls bold formatting, font colors, shading colors, and border lines. The PivotTable Styles gallery displays thumbnails of styles from which to choose. When you point to a thumbnail, Excel shows a preview of that style in the PivotTable. Click a style to actually apply it to the PivotTable.
- Change the PivotTable layout: The layout commands control whether subtotals and grand totals are displayed, specifies the location of subtotals, and controls the overall layout.

8. Create a data model.

- Create a relationship between tables: You can create relationships between two or more related tables within one workbook. The relationship is based on a common field, such as IDs, in the tables.

- Create a PivotTable from related tables: After creating the relationships, you can create a PivotTable that uses fields from the related tables. The PivotTable Fields List displays the names of the related tables in the data model.

9. Create a PivotChart.
- A PivotChart is similar to a regular chart, except it is based on the categories and structure of the PivotTable, not the original dataset. You can customize a PivotChart with the same methods you use to customize a regular chart. If you change fields or sort in either the PivotTable or the PivotChart, Excel automatically adjusts the corresponding pivot object.
- Modify the PivotChart: You can modify the PivotChart like a regular chart. You can add a chart title, change the chart type, and add chart elements such as data labels. If you change the fields or set filters for the PivotChart, Excel applies those same changes to the related PivotTable.

Key Terms Matching

Match the key terms with their definitions. Write the key term letter by the appropriate numbered definition.

a. Calculated field

b. COLUMNS area

c. Data mining

d. Data model

e. FILTERS area

f. Grouping

g. Outline

h. PivotChart

i. PivotTable Fields List

j. PivotTable report

k. PivotTable style

l. PivotTable timeline

m. Relationship

n. ROWS area

o. Slicer

p. Slicer caption

q. Subtotal

r. VALUES area

1. _____ An association created between two tables where both tables contain a common field of data. **p. 369**

2. _____ A hierarchical structure of data that you can group related data to summarize. **p. 332**

3. _____ A row that contains at least one aggregate calculation, such as SUM or AVERAGE, that applies for a group of sorted data within a dataset. **p. 330**

4. _____ A process of joining related rows or columns of related data into a single entity so that groups can be collapsed or expanded. **p. 333**

5. _____ The process of analyzing large volumes of data to identify trends and patterns in the data. **p. 339**

6. _____ An interactive table that uses calculations to consolidate and summarize data from a data source into a separate table to enable a person to analyze the data in a dataset without altering the actual data. **p. 339**

7. _____ A user-defined field that performs a calculation based on other fields in a PivotTable. **p. 359**

8. _____ A window listing all unique items in a field so that the user can click button to filter data by that particular item or value. **p. 357**

9. _____ A section within the PivotTable Fields List used to place a field that will display labels to organize data horizontally in a PivotTable. **p. 342**

10. _____ A section within the PivotTable Fields List used to place a field to display summary statistics, such as totals or averages in a PivotTable. **p. 342**

11. _____ A section within the PivotTable Fields List used to place a field so that the user can then filter the data by that field. **p. 342**

12. _____ A section within the PivotTable Fields List used to place a field that will display labels to organize summarized data vertically in a PivotTable. **p. 342**

13. _____ A graphical representation of aggregated data derived from a PivotTable. **p. 372**

14. _____ A task pane that displays the fields in a dataset and enables a user to specify what fields are used to create a layout to organize the data in columns, rows, values, and filters in a PivotTable. **p. 341**

15. _____ The text or field name that appears as a header or title at the top of a slicer to identify the data in that field. **p. 358**

16. _____ A small window that starts with the first date and ends with the last date in the data source. It contains horizontal tiles that you can click to filter data by day, month, quarter, or year. **p. 359**

17. _____ A collection of related tables that contain structured data used to create a database. **p. 369**

18. _____ A set of formatting that controls bold, font colors, shading colors, and border lines. **p. 362**

Multiple Choice

1. A worksheet contains a list of graduates at your university. The worksheet contains these columns in this sequence: Student Last Name, Student First Name, College, Major, and GPA. Data are sorted by College, then by Major, and then by Student Last Name. What is the default *At a change in* setting within the Subtotal dialog box, and what would be a more appropriate setting?

    (a) Student Last Name (default field), GPA (correct field)

    (b) Student First Name (default field), Student Last Name (correct field)

    (c) College (default field), Student Last Name (correct field)

    (d) Student Last Name (default field), College (correct field)

2. You created an outline within a worksheet. What does the ⏤ button indicate to the left of a row heading?

    (a) You can click it to collapse the details of that category.

    (b) You can click it to expand the details of that category.

    (c) You can add a new row at that location only.

    (d) One or more columns are hidden.

3. A worksheet contains a PivotTable placeholder and the PivotTable Fields List. No fields have been added to the PivotTable yet. If you click the College Major field check box in the PivotTable Fields List, where does Excel place this field?

    (a) FILTERS area

    (b) COLUMNS area

    (c) ROWS area

    (d) VALUES area

4. You created a PivotTable to summarize commissions earned by employees in each department. What is the default summary statistic for the commissions field when you add it to the PivotTable?

    (a) Average

    (b) Count

    (c) Min

    (d) Sum

5. You have created a PivotTable and made some changes to values in the original dataset from which the PivotTable was created. How does this affect the PivotTable?

    (a) The PivotTable is updated automatically when you make changes to the dataset.

    (b) Changes in the dataset do not affect the PivotTable until you refresh the PivotTable.

    (c) You must create a new PivotTable if you want updated results in a PivotTable.

    (d) The PivotTable is deleted from the workbook because it is not up to date.

6. What settings should you select for a PivotTable if you want to apply a different color scheme and display different fill colors for main category rows and horizontal lines within the PivotTable?

    (a) Banded Rows and Banded Columns check boxes

    (b) Banded Columns check box and a different PivotTable style

    (c) Banded Rows check box and a different PivotTable style

    (d) A different PivotTable style only

7. You have just created a slicer for the State field in a PivotTable. Which of the following does *not* characterize the initial slicer?

    (a) The slicer buttons are set to filter out all records.

    (b) The slicer caption is State.

    (c) The slicer contains one column of state names or abbreviations.

    (d) The slicer may display on top of the PivotTable data.

8. Which PivotTable calculated field is correctly constructed to calculate a 20% tip on a meal at a restaurant?

    (a) =Meal Cost * 20%

    (b) ='Meal Cost'*.2

    (c) ="Meal Cost"*.2

    (d) =B5*1.2

9. You have created a PivotChart showing sales by quarter by sales rep. Before presenting it to management, you notice the name of a rep who has since been fired. How do you remove this rep from the chart without deleting the data?

    (a) Make the employee's data points and axis titles invisible.

    (b) You cannot delete the rep from the chart without first deleting the data.

    (c) Filter the Sales Rep field in the PivotChart and deselect the employee's check box.

    (d) Hide that rep's row(s) in the underlying list, which automatically removes that rep from the chart.

10. Currently, the House Types field is in the ROWS area, the Real Estate Agent field is in the COLUMNS area, and Sum of List Prices is in the VALUES area. How can you modify the PivotTable to display the agent names as subcategories within the house types in the first column?

(a) Drag the Real Estate Agent field from the COLUMNS area and drop it above the House Types field in the ROWS area.

(b) Drag the House Types field from the ROWS area and drop it below the Real Estate Agent field in the COLUMNS area.

(c) Drag the House Types field from the ROWS area to the FILTERS area and drag the Real Estate Agent field from the COLUMNS area to the ROWS area.

(d) Drag the Real Estate Agent field from the COLUMNS area and drop it below the House Types field in the ROWS area.

Practice Exercises

1 January Restaurant Revenue

Your cousin Anthony owns a restaurant in Columbus, Ohio. The restaurant manager tracks daily revenue for the lunch and dinner hours. Anthony wants to analyze revenue by weekday for both the lunch and dinner hours for January. You will add subtotals of revenue by days of the week and by meal time for Anthony. At the end of the year, he wants to analyze data by days of the week and quarters for the whole year. You will create a PivotTable and a PivotChart to organize the data. Refer to Figure 5.46 as you complete this exercise.

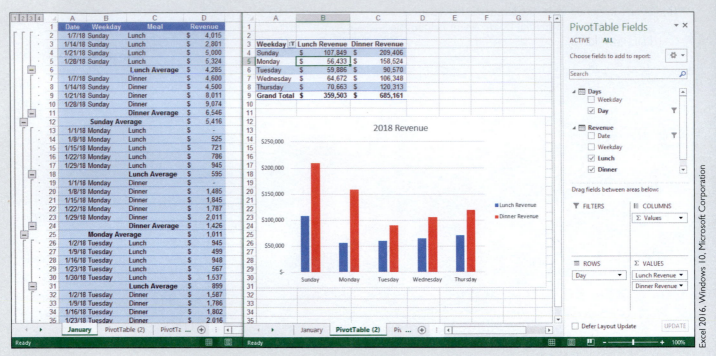

FIGURE 5.46 Revenue Subtotals, PivotTable, and PivotChart

a. Open *e05p1Revenue* and save it as **e05p1Revenue_LastFirst**.

b. Ensure that the January worksheet is active. Complete the following steps to sort the data:
   - Click the **Data tab** and click **Sort** in the Sort & Filter group to open the Sort dialog box.
   - Click the **Sort by arrow** and select **Weekday**.
   - Click the **Order arrow** and select **Custom List** to open the Custom Lists dialog box. Select **Sunday, Monday, Tuesday** in the *Custom lists* section and click **OK**.
   - Click **Add Level** in the Sort dialog box, click the **Then by arrow**, and then select **Meal**.
   - Click the **Order arrow** for Meal, select **Z to A** to list Lunch before Dinner, and click **OK**.

c. Click **Subtotal** in the Outline group. Complete the following steps in the Subtotal dialog box:
   - Click the **At each change in arrow** and select **Weekday**.
   - Click the **Use function arrow** and select **Average**.
   - Keep the Revenue check box selected and click **OK**.

d. Add a second-level subtotal by meal by completing the following steps:
   - Click **Subtotal** in the Outline group.
   - Click the **At each change in arrow** and select **Meal**.
   - Keep the Average function selected and keep the Revenue check box selected.
   - Click the **Replace current subtotals check box** to deselect it. Click **OK**.

e. Click the **2 outline symbol** to collapse the list to see the weekday and grand averages. Which weekday produced the highest revenue? (Saturday) Which weekday produced the lowest revenue? (Monday) Click the **3 outline symbol** to expand the list to see weekday subtotals for lunch and dinner. Increase the width of column C so that the labels fully display.

f. Click the **Yearly Data sheet tab**. The Revenue table lists lunch and dinner revenue for every day in 2018. The Weekday column is coded where 1 = Sunday and 7 = Saturday. Click the **Weekdays sheet tab**. The Days table contains two columns: the Weekday codes with their respective weekday in the Day column. Click the **Yearly Data sheet tab**.

g. Click the **Data tab**, click **Relationships** in the Data Tools group to open the Manage Relationships dialog box, and then and complete the following steps:
- Click **New** to open the Create Relationship dialog box.
- Click the **Table arrow** and select **Revenue** (the main table). Click the **Column (Foreign) arrow** and select **Weekday**.
- Click the **Related Table arrow** and select **Days**. Click the **Related Column (Primary) arrow** and select **Weekday**.
- Click **OK** to close the Create Relationship dialog box. Click **Close** to close the Manage Relationships dialog box.

h. Complete the following steps to create a PivotTable using the related tables:
- Click the **Insert tab** and click **PivotTable** in the Tables group to open the Create PivotTable dialog box.
- Click the **Add this data to the Data Model check box** in the *Choose whether you want to analyze multiple tables* section. Click **OK**. Double-click the **Sheet1 tab**, type **PivotTable**, and then press **Enter**.
- Click **ALL** at the top of the PivotTable Fields List to display all table names.
- Click **Revenue** at the top of the PivotTable Fields List to display the fields for the Revenue table.
- Click the **Lunch** and **Dinner check boxes** in the PivotTable Fields List to display these fields in the VALUES area.
- Click **Days** in the PivotTable Fields List to display the fields for the Days table.
- Click the **Day check box** in the PivotTable Fields List to add this field to the ROWS area.

i. Modify the PivotTable by doing the following:
- Click the **Row Labels arrow** in **cell A3** and select **Sort A to Z**. (Note that this action sorts in sequential order by weekday, not alphabetical order by weekday name.)
- Type **Weekday** in **cell A3** and press **Enter**.
- Click the **Design tab**, click the **More button** in the PivotTable Styles group, and then click **Pivot Style Light 17**.
- Click the **Banded Rows check box** in the PivotTable Style Options group.

j. Format the values by doing the following:
- Click **cell B4**, click the **Analyze tab**, and then click **Field Settings** in the Active Field group.
- Type **Lunch Revenue** in the Custom Name box.
- Click **Number Format**, click **Accounting**, click the **Decimal places arrow** to display **0**, click **OK** in the Format Cells dialog box, and then click **OK** in the Value Field Settings dialog box.
- Click **cell C4** and click **Field Settings** in the Active Field group.
- Type **Dinner Revenue** in the Custom Name box.
- Click **Number Format**, click **Accounting**, click the **Decimal places arrow** to display **0**, click **OK** in the Format Cells dialog box, and then click **OK** in the Value Field Settings dialog box.
- Click the **PivotTable Name box** in the PivotTable group on the Analyze tab, type **Weekday Revenue**, and then press **Enter**.

k. Insert a timeline by completing the following steps:
- Click **Insert Timeline** in the Filter group to open the Insert Timelines dialog box.
- Click the **Date check box** and click **OK** to display the Date timeline. Move the Date timeline so that the top-left corner starts in **cell A13**.
- Click the **MONTHS arrow** in the Date timeline and select **QUARTERS**.
- Click the tile below **Q4** in the timeline to filter the data to reflect weekday totals for the fourth quarter only (October through December).

l. Create a PivotChart from the PivotTable by doing the following.
- Right-click the **PivotTable sheet tab**, select **Move or Copy**, click **PivotTable** in the *Before sheet* list, click the **Create a copy check box** to select it, and then click **OK**.

- Ensure that the PivotTable (2) sheet tab is active. Click the **Date timeline window** and press **Delete**.
- Click the **Analyze tab**, click **PivotChart** in the Tools group, and then click **OK** in the Insert Chart dialog box to create a default clustered column chart.
- Click the **Day arrow** in the bottom-left corner of the PivotChart, click the **Friday** and **Saturday check boxes** to deselect these weekdays so that you can focus on the other days of the week where sales are lower. Click **OK**.
- Click the **Shape Height box** in the Size group on the Format tab, type **3.5**, and then press **Enter**. Click in the **Shape Width box**, type **6**, and then press **Enter**.
- Click **CHART ELEMENTS** on the right of the chart, click the **Chart Title check box**, and click **CHART ELEMENTS** to close the menu.
- Click the **Chart Title placeholder**, type **2018 Revenue**, and then press **Enter**.
- Move the chart so that the top-left corner starts in **cell A12**.
- Click the **Analyze tab**, click the **Field Buttons arrow** in the Show/Hide group, and then select **Hide All** to hide the buttons within the chart area.

   m. Create a footer with your name on the left side, the sheet name code in the center, and the file name code on the right side on each worksheet.

   n. Save and close the file. Based on your instructor's directions, submit e05p1Revenue_LastFirst.

2 Suburbia Regional Hospital

Alesha Rogers is the Nurse Manager for the Neuro Acute Care Division at Suburbia Regional Hospital. The 12-hour nursing shifts are divided into day and graveyard. Alesha collects data on the number of patients that start each shift, the number of patients admitted, the number of patients discharged, and the number of patients at the end of each shift. She also notes how many nurses worked each shift. Because of your expertise in using Excel to analyze data, she has provided you a basic spreadsheet and asked you to help consolidate the data for her to analyze. She is interested in the number of nurses per daily shift (such as all Sunday graveyard shifts) for the month of April. Refer to Figure 5.47 as you complete this exercise.

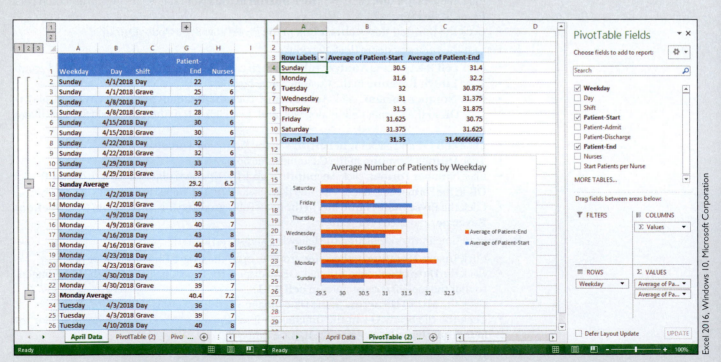

FIGURE 5.47 Suburbia Regional Hospital

a. Open *e05p2Patients* and save it as **e05p2Patients_LastFirst**.

b. Ensure that the **April Data worksheet** is active. Complete the following steps to sort the data:
   - Click the **Data tab** and click **Sort** in the Sort & Filter group.
   - Click the **Sort by arrow** and select **Weekday**.
   - Click the **Order arrow** and select **Custom List** to open the Custom Lists dialog box. Select **Sunday, Monday, Tuesday** in the *Custom lists* section and click **OK**. Click **OK** in the Sort dialog box.

c. Click **Subtotal** in the Outline group. Complete the following steps in the Subtotal dialog box:
   - Click the **At each change in arrow** and select **Weekday**.
   - Click the **Use function arrow** and select **Average**.
   - Click the **Patient-End check box** to select it, keep the Nurses check box selected, and then click **OK**.

d. Click the **Group arrow** in the Outline group on the Data tab, select **Auto Outline**, and then click **OK**. Click the **collapse button** above column G to collapse the outline.

e. Click the **April Table sheet tab**, click the **Insert tab**, click **Recommended PivotTables** in the Tables group, click the **Sum of Patient-Start by Weekday and Shift thumbnail**, and then click **OK**.

f. Complete the following steps to modify the PivotTable:
   - Click the **Day check box** in the PivotTable Fields List to add that field to the ROWS area.
   - Move the **Shift field** from the COLUMNS area to the FILTERS area in the PivotTable Fields List.
   - Click the **Shift arrow** in **cell B1**, select **Day**, and click **OK** to filter the records to show totals for only the day shifts.
   - Click the **PivotTable Name box** in the PivotTable group on the Analyze tab, type **Patients-Nurses**, and then press **Enter**.
   - Rename Sheet1 as **PivotTable**.

g. Complete the following steps to create a calculated field:
   - Click the **Analyze tab**, click **Fields, Items, & Sets** in the Calculations group, and then select **Calculated Field**.
   - Type **Start Patients per Nurse** in the Name box in the Insert Calculated Field dialog box.
   - Double-click **Patient-Start** in the Fields list, type **/**, and double-click **Nurses** in the Fields list. Click **OK**.
   - Click **cell C3**, click **Field Settings** in the Active Field group, click **Number Format**, click **Number** in the Category list, click the **Decimal places** setting to **0**, click **OK** in the Format Cells dialog box, and then click **OK** in the Value Field Settings dialog box.

h. Click **Insert Slicer** in the Filter group, click the **Weekday check box** in the Insert Slicers dialog box, and then click **OK**.

i. Complete the following steps to customize the filter:
   - Move the filter to start in **cell F3**.
   - Click **More** in the Slicer Styles group on the Options tab and click **Slicer Style Dark 5**.
   - Change the **Width** to **1.5** in the Buttons group on the Options tab.
   - Press **Ctrl** and click **Sunday** and **Saturday** in the Weekday slicer to filter out these two days.

j. Copy the PivotTable sheet tab and place the PivotTable (2) sheet tab between the April Data and PivotTable sheet tabs. Ensure that the PivotTable (2) sheet is active and complete the following steps:
   - Click the **Shift check box** in the PivotTable Fields List to remove it from the FILTERS area.
   - Click the **Day check box** in the PivotTable Fields List to remove it from the ROWS area.
   - Click **Multi-Select** in the Weekday slicer window, click **Sunday**, and then click **Saturday** so that all seven days will display.

k. Click in the PivotTable, click the **Analyze tab**, click **PivotChart** in the Tools group, and then complete the following steps:

- Click **Bar** in the Insert Chart dialog box and click **OK**.
- Click the **Sum of Start Patients per Nurse arrow** in the VALUES area of the PivotTable Fields List and select **Remove Field**.
- Click the **Sum of Patients Start arrow** in the VALUES area of the PivotTable Fields List, click **Value Field Settings**, select **Average**, click **Number Format**, select **Number** in the Category list, click **OK** in the Format Cells dialog box, and then click **OK** in the Value Field Settings dialog box.
- Click the **Sum of Patients End arrow** in the VALUES area of the PivotTable Fields List, click **Value Field Settings**, select **Average**, click **Number Format**, select **Number** in the Category list, click **OK** in the Format Cells dialog box, and then click **OK** in the Value Field Settings dialog box.
- Click the **Analyze tab**, click the **Field Buttons arrow** in the Show/Hide group, and then select **Hide All**.
- Click the **Chart Title placeholder**, type **Average Number of Patients by Weekday**, and then press **Enter**.
- Move the chart so that the top-left corner starts in **cell A13**.

l. Create a footer with your name on the left side, the sheet name code in the center, and the file name code on the right side on each worksheet.

m. Save and close the file. Based on your instructor's directions, submit e05p2Patients_LastFirst.

Mid-Level Exercises

1 Mountain View Realty

ANALYSIS CASE

You are a real estate analyst who works for Mountain View Realty in the North Utah County area. You have consolidated a list of houses sold during the past few months and want to analyze the data. For a simple analysis, you will outline the data and use the Subtotal feature. You will then create two PivotTables and a PivotChart to give you a way to perform more in-depth analysis.

a. Open *e05m1RealEstate* and save it as **e05m1RealEstate_LastFirst**.

b. Make sure the Sales Subtotals worksheet is the active sheet and insert the following formulas:

- Insert a formula in **cell G2** to calculate the selling price percentage of the asking price, format it with **Percent Style** with **1** decimal place, and then copy the formula down the column.
- Insert a formula in **cell J2** to calculate the number of days between the listing date and sale date. Copy the formula down the column.

c. Sort the list by city in alphabetical order, then by selling agent in alphabetical order, and finally by listing date in chronological order.

d. Use the Subtotal feature to calculate the average selling price, percentage of asking price, and days on market by city.

e. Apply an automatic outline to the columns and complete the following steps:

- Collapse the outline to hide the listing and sale dates.
- Click the outline symbol to display the grand average and city average rows only. Format the average days on market to zero decimal places.
- Apply wrap text for **cells G1** and **J1**.
- Select individually columns G and J and change the column width to **10.00**.
- Change the row height to **24** for the first row.
- Set a print area for the **range C1:J88**.

f. Go to **cell C101** in the Sales Subtotals worksheet. Read the questions and provide the appropriate answers in the respective highlighted cells in the **range G102:G106**. Apply **Accounting Number Format** with **0** decimal places to **cell G102**.

g. Click the **Sales Data sheet tab** and create a blank PivotTable on a new worksheet. Name the new worksheet **PivotTable**. Name the PivotTable **Average City Prices**.

h. Place the **City field** in rows, the **Selling Agent field** in columns, and the **Asking Price** and **Selling Price fields** as values.

i. Modify the PivotTable by completing the following steps:

- Display averages rather than sums with **Accounting Number Format** with **0** decimal places for the two value fields.
- Pivot the data by moving the **City field** below the Values field in the COLUMNS area and moving the **Selling Agents field** to ROWS area.
- Add a filter in **cell B3** to display only Alpine and Cedar Hills.

j. Complete the following steps to change the format of the PivotTable:

- Change the widths of columns A, B, C, D, and E to **11**.
- Change the widths of columns F and G to **14**.
- Wrap text and center horizontally data in **cells B4**, **D4**, **F4**, and **G4**.
- Apply the **Bottom Border** to the **range B4:E4**.
- Change the label in **cell A5** to **Agent**. Change the height of row 4 to **40**.

k. Display the contents on the Sales Data worksheet. You realize that a selling price is incorrect. Change the selling price for Number 40 from *$140,000* to **$1,400,000**. Refresh the PivotTable. Adjust the column widths to match the instructions in step j.

l. Display the contents on the Sales Data worksheet. Create a recommended PivotTable using the **Sum of Selling Price by City** thumbnail. Change the name of the new PivotTable worksheet to **Selling Price**. Make these changes to the new PivotTable:

- Change the value to display averages not sums.
- Apply the **Accounting Number Format** with **0** decimal places to the values.
- Apply **Pivot Style Medium 2** to the PivotTable.

m. Create a column PivotChart from the PivotTable on the Selling Price worksheet. Move the chart to a chart sheet named **Sales Chart**. Complete the following steps for the chart:

- Change the chart title to **Average Selling Price by City** and apply **Dark Blue font color**.
- Remove the legend.
- Apply **Dark Blue fill color** to the data series.

n. Create a footer with your name on the left side, the sheet name code in the center, and the file name code on the right side all worksheets. Adjust page scaling if needed.

o. Save and close the file. Based on your instructor's directions, submit e05m1RealEstate_LastFirst.

2 Fiesta® Collection

Your Aunt Laura has been collecting Fiesta dinnerware, a popular brand from the Homer Laughlin China Company, since 1986. You help her maintain an inventory. So far, you and Aunt Laura have created a table of color numbers, color names, year introduced, and year retired, if applicable. In a second table, you entered color numbers, item numbers, items, current value, and source. Previously, you helped her research current replacement costs from Homer Laughlin's website (www.hlchina.com), Replacements, Ltd. (www.replacements.com), and eBay (www.ebay.com); however, you believe the retired colors may be worth more now. Laura is especially interested in the values of retired colors so that she can provide this information for her insurance agent. You will build a PivotTable and add slicers to help her with the analysis.

a. Open *e05m2Fiesta* and save it as **e05m2Fiesta_LastFirst**.

b. Create a relationship between the Items table using the Color Number field and the Colors table using the Color Number field.

c. Create a blank PivotTable from within the Items table on the Collection worksheet to analyze multiple tables. Add the data to the data model. Place the PivotTable on a new worksheet and name the worksheet **Retired Colors**. Name the PivotTable **Retired**.

d. Display the names of both tables in the PivotTable Fields List.

e. Display the **Color field** as rows and the sum of the Replacement Value field as values.

f. Add a filter to display aggregates for retired colors only using the **Retired field**. Note that current colors do not have a retirement date, so you must filter out the blanks.

g. Apply the **Pivot Style Medium 7**.

h. Format the values with **Accounting Number Format** with **2** decimal places. Create a custom name **Replacement Value**. Change *Row Labels* in **cell A3** to **Retired Colors**.

DISCOVER

i. Add a column to show calculations by completing the following steps:

- Add a second Replacement Value field below the current field in the VALUES area.
- Select the option to display the values as percentages of the grand total.
- Type the custom name **Percent of Total**.

j. Add a slicer for the **Color field**. Select these colors to display: **Apricot**, **Chartreuse**, **Lilac**, **Marigold**, **Pearl Gray**, and **Sapphire**.

k. Customize the slicer by completing the following steps:

- Apply the **Slicer Style Light 6 style**.
- Display 3 columns within the slicer window.
- Change the button width to **1.5"**. Move the slicer so that the top-left corner starts in **cell E2**.

l. Create a clustered column PivotChart and place it on a new chart sheet named **Retired PivotChart**.

m. Modify the chart by completing these steps:

- Change the chart title to **Replacement Value of Retired Items**.
- Change the Lilac data point fill color to **Purple**.
- Change the value axis font size to **11** and apply **Black, Text 1** font color.

- Change the category axis font size to **11** and apply **Black, Text 1** font color.
- Hide the field buttons on the PivotChart.

n. Create a footer with your name on the left side, the sheet name code in the center, and the file name code on the right side of all worksheets.

o. Save and close the file. Based on your instructor's directions, submit e05m2Fiesta_LastFirst.

3 Facebook® Social Phenomenon

COLLABORATION CASE

FROM SCRATCH

Facebook has experienced phenomenal growth since its creation in 2004. What is it that has made Facebook a huge success story, starting a decade after many of the other Web company startups? To understand how people use Facebook, look at its applications. Work with another student to conduct this research, obtain data, and create PivotTables.

a. Open a Web browser and conduct a search to learn about Facebook's history.

b. Start a new Excel workbook and save it as **e05m3Facebook_LastFirst**.

c. Build a worksheet that lists at least 200 application leaders for 10 categories, two of which must be Business and Just For Fun. Each student should find 100 different application leaders. Use collaboration tools to make sure you and your team member use the same format and do not duplicate data.

d. Include data for these columns: Category, Name, Daily Average Use (DAU), Monthly Average Use (MAU), and Daily Growth.

e. Copy your team member's worksheet as a new worksheet in your workbook. Then create a third worksheet to combine the data. Name the sheets appropriately.

f. Format the data and headings appropriately in the combined worksheet.

g. Create a PivotTable based on the data to reflect one perspective of analysis. Format the values and apply desired filters.

h. Have your teammate copy the combined sheet and create his or her own PivotTable with a different perspective, formatting, and desired filters.

i. Discuss your analysis with your team member.

j. Create a footer with your name and your team member's name on the left side, sheet name code in the center, and the file name code on the right side of each worksheet.

k. Save and close the file. Based on your instructor's directions, submit e05m3FaceBook_LastFirst.

Beyond the Classroom

Departing Flights

GENERAL CASE

FROM SCRATCH

You want to research morning flight departures from Tulsa International Airport (TUL) using data obtained from flightstats.com website. Find the airport's departing flight schedule for yesterday morning and copy the flight information on a worksheet in a new workbook. Name the workbook **e05b1Tulsa_LastFirst**. Clean up the data after copying it. Name the worksheet **Departures**. Copy the worksheet and name the duplicate sheet **Morning Departures**. Sort the data on the Departures sheet by destination and then by airline. Insert subtotals at a change in destination, counting the number of flights. Collapse the subtotals to display the subtotals and grand totals.

Create a blank PivotTable from the Morning Departures sheet. Display the Destination and Airline fields in rows. Display the Status field in columns to display canceled, on-time, and delayed flights. Display the Flight field in the values area and change the field settings to the Count function. Display the Departure Time as a filter and set a filter to include only departure times from 6 to 9 a.m. Name the PivotTable **Morning Departure Status**. Apply **PivotStyle Medium 13 style**. Adjust column widths as needed. Name the worksheet **PivotTable**.

Create a PivotChart from the original dataset. Name the sheet **PivotChart**. Use the Destination field as the axis and the Flight # as the value. Change the value to the Count function. Change the chart type to a bar chart. Set 3.75" chart height and 5.75" chart width. Insert a slicer for the Status field and click the slicer button to display only on-time departures. Add a chart title **On-Time Departures**. Create a footer with your name, the sheet name code, and the file name code on each worksheet. Save and close the file. Based on your instructor's directions, submit e05b1Tulsa_LastFirst.

Innovative Game Studio

DISASTER RECOVERY

You work as an assistant to Terry Park, the producer for a video game studio in Phoenix, Arizona. The company produces games for the PlayStation®, Xbox®, and Wii™ consoles. The producer tracks salaries and performance for everyone on a particular team, which consists of artists, animators, programmers, and so forth. Terry tried to create a PivotTable to organize the data by department and then by title within department. He also wants to display total salaries by these categories and filter the data to show aggregates for team members who earned only Excellent and Good performance ratings. In addition, he wants to see what the percentages of total salaries for each job title are of each department's budget. For example, the total salary for Senior Artists is $263,300. That represents 50.27% of the Art Department's salary budget ($523,800) for Excellent- and Good-rated employees. However, the percentages are not displayed correctly. Terry called you in to correct his PivotTable.

Open *e05b2Games* and save it as **e05b2Games_LastFirst**. Identify the errors and make a list of these errors starting on row 41 in the PivotTable worksheet. Correct the errors and improve the format, including a medium Pivot Style, throughout the PivotTable. Create a footer with your name, the sheet name code, and the file name code. Save and close the file. Based on your instructor's directions, submit e05b2Games_LastFirst.

Capstone Exercise

You are an analyst for an authorized Greenwich Workshop® fine art dealer (www.greenwichworkshop.com). Customers are especially fond of James C. Christensen's art. You prepared a list of his artwork: Title (title of each piece of art), Type (the medium, such as Limited Edition Print or Anniversary Edition Canvas), Edition Size (how many copies were produced for purchase), Release Date (the month and year the art was released), Issue Price (the original retail price when the art was released), and Est. Value (the estimated current market value). Studying the data will help you discuss value trends with art collectors.

Sort, Subtotal, and Outline Data

You want to organize data to facilitate using the Subtotal feature to display the average issue price and estimated value by Type.

a. Open *e05c1FineArt* and save it as **e05c1FineArt_LastFirst**.

b. Click the **Subtotals sheet tab**. Sort the data by Type and further sort it by the Title, both in alphabetical order.

c. Use the Subtotal feature to insert subtotal rows by Type to identify the highest Issue Price and Est. Value.

d. Collapse the data by displaying only the subtotals and grand total rows.

e. Set a print area for the **range D1:I247**. Set the scaling to fit to one page.

Create a PivotTable

You want to create a PivotTable to analyze the art by Type, Issue Price, and Est. Value. In addition, you will rename the worksheet and the PivotTable.

a. Click the **Christensen sheet tab** and create a blank PivotTable on a new worksheet.

b. Name the worksheet **Sold Out**.

c. Use the **Type** and **Issue Price fields**, enabling Excel to determine where the fields go.

d. Add the **Est. Value field** to the VALUES area.

e. Name the PivotTable **Average Price by Type**.

Change Value Field Settings and Create a Calculated Field

Excel displays the sum of the values by Type. However, you want to calculate the average values for each art type. In addition, you will calculate the percentage change from the Issue Price to the Est. Value. Finally, you will format the values and enter clear headings in the PivotTable.

a. Modify the value fields to determine the average Issue Price and average Est. Value by type.

b. Customize the value fields by completing the following steps:
- Change the custom names to **Average Issue Price** and **Average Est. Value**, respectively for the two value fields.
- Apply **Currency** number format with **0** decimal places to the two value fields.

c. Insert a calculated field to determine percent change in values between the Est. Value and Issue Price.

d. Customize the calculated field by completing the following steps:
- Change the custom name to **Percent Change in Value**.
- Apply **Percentage** number format with **2** decimal places.

e. Select the **range B3:D3** and apply these formats: wrap text, **Align Right** horizontal alignment, **30** row height, and **10** column widths.

f. Type **Type of Art** in **cell A3** and type **Average of All Art** in **cell A18**.

Filter the PivotTable and Apply a Style

You want to focus on average values for sold-out art because these pieces typically increase in value on the secondary market. The Sold Out column indicates Yes if the art is sold out, blank if the art is still available, or Limited Availability if the art is still available but in limited supply. In addition, you want to narrow the list to particular types. After filtering the data, you will apply a different style to the PivotTable.

a. Set a filter to display only sold-out art (indicated by **Yes**).

b. Set a Type filter to filter out these types Hand Colored Print, Limited Edition Hand Colored Print, Open Edition Canvas, Open Edition Print, and Poster.

c. Apply **Pivot Style Light 23**.

d. Display banded columns.

Insert a Slicer and Timeline

You want to preserve the original PivotTable but create a duplicate so that you can filter data by a timeline and slicer. You will insert a slicer for the Sold Out field and a timeline for the Release Date field. You will then use these elements to filter the data to show only sold-out art for the years 2000 to 2005.

a. Copy the Sold Out worksheet, move the duplicate sheet tab to the left of the Sold Out sheet tab, and rename the new sheet **Types**.

b. Reset the Sold Out filter and then remove the Sold Out field from the FILTERS area.

c. Insert a slicer for the Sold Out field and complete the following steps to customize the slicer:

- Change the slicer height to **1.5"**.
- Apply **Slicer Style Dark 1**.
- Click the **Yes slicer button** to filter the PivotTable to list averages for only sold-out art.

d. Insert a timeline for the Release Date field and complete the following steps:

- Change the time period to **YEARS**.
- Set the timeline to filter to display **2000** to **2005**.
- Change the timeline width to **4"**.

Create a PivotChart

To help interpret the consolidated values of the art, you want to create a PivotChart. You realize that displaying both monetary values and percentages on the same chart is like mixing apples and oranges. If you modify the PivotChart, you will change the PivotTable; therefore, you will copy the Sold Out worksheet and then create a PivotChart from the duplicate worksheet.

a. Copy the Sold Out worksheet, move the duplicate sheet tab to the left of the Types sheet tab, and rename the new sheet **PivotChart**.

b. Create a PivotChart selecting the **Clustered Bar** type.

c. Modify the PivotChart by completing the following steps:

- Move the PivotChart so that the top-left corner starts in **cell A14**.
- Change the chart height to **3.5"** and the width to **6.5"**.
- Hide the field buttons in the PivotChart.
- Remove the Percentage Change field.

d. Add a chart title and type **Values for Sold-Out Christensen Art**.

e. Set the upper limit of the value axis to **3000**.

f. Change the chart style to **Style 12**.

g. Select the category labels in the PivotChart and sort the labels from Z to A.

Finalizing Your Workbook

You will finalize your workbook by adding a footer to the worksheets you changed and created.

a. Create a footer on all worksheets (except Christensen) with your name, the sheet name code, and the file name code.

b. Save and close the file. Based on your instructor's directions, submit e05c1FineArt_LastFirst.

What-If Analysis

LEARNING OUTCOME — You will demonstrate how to use decision-making tools.

OBJECTIVES & SKILLS: After you read this chapter, you will be able to:

CASE STUDY | Personal Finance: Buying Your First Home

After several years of living with friends after college, you have decided to purchase your first home. After doing some preliminary research on prices, you developed a spreadsheet to help you calculate your monthly mortgage payment, total amount to repay the loan, and the total amount of interest you will pay. Your total budget for the home is $150,000 including taxes, closing costs, and other miscellaneous fees. You plan to take $10,000 out of your savings account for a down payment. You are currently investigating loan interest rates at various banks and credit unions. You realize that you may need to find a less expensive home or increase your down payment to reach a monthly payment you can afford. Although you can change input values to see how different values affect the monthly payment, you want to be able to see the comparisons at the same time. In addition, you want to look at your budget to review the impact of purchasing a new home on your income and expenses.

Using Decision-Making Tools

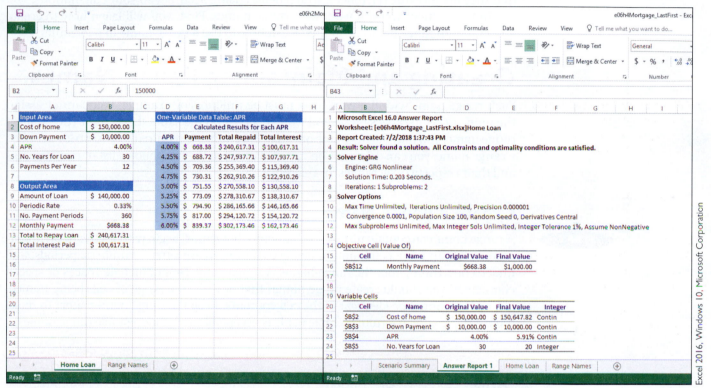

FIGURE 6.1 Home Loan Worksheet

You will use Excel to help you create a worksheet that analyzes the variables that affect the mortgage payment, total amount to repay the loan, and the total interest paid. To help you make a decision, you will use several what-if analysis tools, each with specific purposes, benefits, and restrictions. With these tools, you will have a better understanding of how a mortgage payment will affect your overall budget.

CASE STUDY | Personal Finance: Buying Your First Home

Starting File	File to be submitted
e06h1Mortgage	e06h4Mortgage_LastFirst

Range Names

In order to complete the required mortgage analysis, you will use several financial functions in conjunction with analysis tools within Excel. To simplify entering ranges into these functions, you can use range names. A ***range name*** is a word or string of characters assigned to one or more cells. Think of range names in this way: Your college identifies you by your student ID; however, your professors call you by an easy-to-remember name, such as Terrance or Valerie. Similarly, instead of using cell addresses, you can use descriptive range names in formulas. For example, when calculating a periodic mortgage payment using the PMT function, instead of using the function =PMT(B3,C3,-D3), you could assign easy to understand range names to the cell references modifying the function to =PMT(Periodic_Rate,Payments,-Cost). Another benefit of using range names is that they are absolute references, which helps ensure accuracy in your calculations.

In this section, you will work with range names. First, you will learn how to create and maintain range names. You then learn how to use a range name in a formula.

Creating and Maintaining Range Names

Each range name within a workbook must be unique. For example, you cannot assign the name *COST* to ranges on several worksheets or on the same sheet. After you create a range name, you may edit its name or range if a change is required. If you no longer need a range name, you can delete it. You can also insert in the workbook a list of range names and their respective cell ranges for reference.

Create a Range Name

STEP 1 ❯❯ A range name can contain up to 255 characters, but it must begin with a letter or an underscore. You can use a combination of upper- or lowercase letters, numbers, periods, and underscores throughout the range name. A range name cannot include spaces or special characters. You should create range names that describe the range of cells being named, but names cannot be identical to the cell contents. Keep the range names short to make them easier to use in formulas. Table 6.1 lists acceptable and unacceptable range names.

TABLE 6.1 Range Names	
Name	**Description**
Grades	Acceptable range name
COL	Acceptable abbreviation for *cost of living*
Tax_Rate	Acceptable name with underscore
Commission Rate	Unacceptable name; cannot use spaces in names
Discount Rate %	Unacceptable name; cannot use special symbols and spaces
2018_Rate	Unacceptable name; cannot start with a number
Rate_2018	Acceptable name with underscore and numbers

Pearson Education, Inc.

To create a range name, select the range you want to name, and complete one of the following steps:

- Click in the Name Box, type the range name, and then press Enter.
- Click the Formulas tab, click Define Name in the Defined Names group to open the New Name dialog box (see Figure 6.2), type the range name in the Name Box, and then click OK.
- Click the Formulas tab, click Name Manager in the Defined Names group to open the Name Manager dialog box, click New, type the range name in the Name Box, click OK, and then click Close.

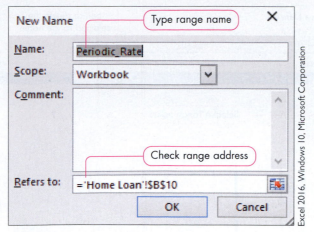

FIGURE 6.2 New Name Dialog Box

You can create several range names at the same time if your worksheet includes ranges with values and descriptive labels. To do this, select the range of cells containing the labels that you want to become names and the cells that contain the values to name, click Create from Selection in the Defined Names group on the Formulas tab, and then select an option in the Create Names from Selection dialog box (see Figure 6.3).

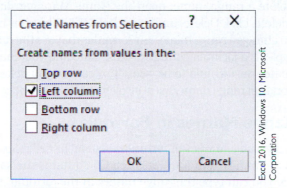

FIGURE 6.3 Create Names from Selection Dialog Box

> **TIP: GO TO A RANGE NAME**
> Use the Go To dialog box to go to the top-left cell in a range specified by a range name.

Edit or Delete a Range Name

STEP 2 ›› Use the Name Manager dialog box to edit, delete, and create range names. To open the Name Manager dialog box shown in Figure 6.4, click Name Manager in the Defined Names group on the Formulas tab. To edit a range or range name, click the range name in the list and click Edit. In the Edit Name dialog box, make your edits and click OK.

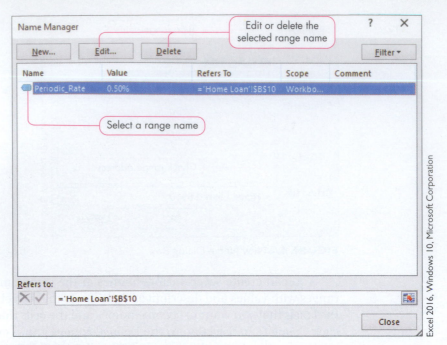

FIGURE 6.4 Name Manager Dialog Box

To delete a range name, open the Name Manager dialog box, select the name you want to delete, click Delete, and then click OK in the confirmation message box.

If you change a range name, any formulas that use the range name reflect the new name. For example, if a formula contains =Cost*Rate and you change the name rate to tax_rate, Excel updates the formula to be =cost*tax_rate. If you delete a range name and a formula depends on that range name, Excel displays #NAME?—indicating an Invalid Name error.

Use Range Names in Formulas

STEP 3 You can use range names in formulas instead of cell references. For example, if cell C15 contains a purchase amount, and cell C5 contains the sales tax rate, instead of typing =C15*C5, you can type the range names in the formula, such as =Purchase*Tax_Rate. When you type a formula, Formula AutoComplete displays a list of range names, as well as functions, that start with the letters you use as you type (see Figure 6.5). Double-click the range name to insert it in the formula.

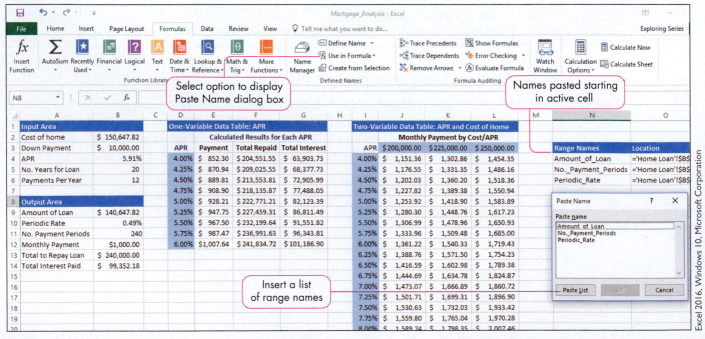

FIGURE 6.5 Paste Name Dialog Box and List of Range Names

Another benefit of using range names is that if you have to copy the formula, you do not have to make the cell reference absolute in the formula. Furthermore, if you share your workbook with others, range names in formulas help others understand what values are used in the calculations.

> **TIP: PASTE NAME**
> The Paste Name dialog box can be used as an alternate method of inserting range names into a function or formula. To access the Paste Name dialog box press F3 on your keyboard.

Insert a List of Range Names

 STEP 4 You can document a workbook by inserting a list of range names in a worksheet. To insert a list of range names, click Use in Formula in the Defined Names group on the Formulas tab and select Paste Names. The Paste Name dialog box opens (see Figure 6.6), listing all range names in the current workbook. Click Paste List to insert a list of range names in alphabetical order. The first column contains a list of range names, and the second column contains the worksheet names and range locations.

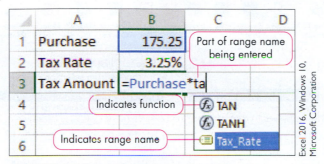

FIGURE 6.6 Range Names Inserted in a Formula

> **TIP: LIST OF RANGE NAMES**
> When you paste range names, the list will overwrite any existing data in a worksheet, so consider pasting the list in a separate worksheet. If you add, edit, or delete range names, the list does not update automatically. To keep the list current, you need to paste the list again.

Quick Concepts ✔

1. What is a range name? **p. 398**

2. List at least five guidelines and rules for naming a range. **p. 398**

3. What is the purpose of inserting a list of range names in a worksheet? What is contained in the list, and how is it arranged? **p. 401**

Hands-On Exercises

Skills covered: Create a Range Name • Edit or Delete a Range Name • Use Range Names in Formulas • Insert a List of Range Names

1 Range Names

You decide to simplify the PMT function you are using to calculate your mortgage by adding range names for the Amount of Loan, Periodic Rate, and No. of Payments instead of the actual cell references. After creating the range names, you will modify the names and create a list of range names.

STEP 1 ›› CREATE A RANGE NAME

You want to assign a range name to the Amount of Loan, Periodic Rate, and No. of Payments. Refer to Figure 6.7 as you complete Step 1.

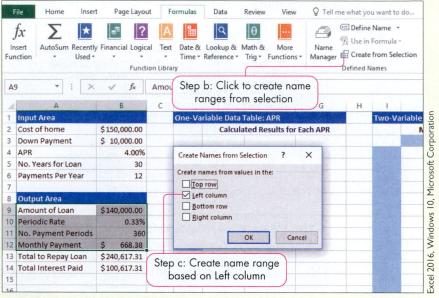

FIGURE 6.7 Range Name

a. Open *e06h1Mortgage* and save it as **e06h1Mortgage_LastFirst**.

> **TROUBLESHOOTING:** If you make any major mistakes in this exercise, you can close the file, open *e06h1Mortgage* again, and then start this exercise over.

b. Select the **range A9:B12**, click the **Formulas tab**, select **Create from Selection** in the Defined Names group, and then ensure **Left column** is checked.

This automatically assigns range names to values based on the row labels in Column A.

c. Click **OK** in the Create Names from Selection dialog box.

Range names are created for cells B9:B12 and when any cell in that range is selected, the name will appear in Name Box.

d. Save the workbook.

You noticed that an extra row was selected when the name ranges were created. You will use the Name Manager dialog box to view and delete the unneeded name range. Refer to Figure 6.8 as you complete Step 2.

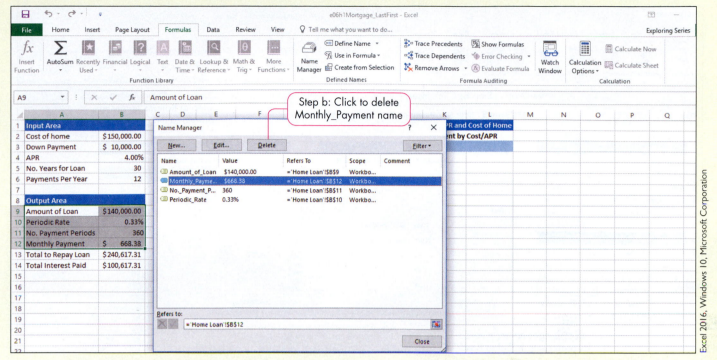

FIGURE 6.8 Editing Range Names

a. Click **Name Manager** in the Defined Names group on the Formulas tab.

The Name Manager dialog box opens.

b. Select **Monthly_Payment** in the list of named ranges and click **Delete**, read the warning message box, and then click **OK** to confirm the deletion of the Monthly_Payment range name.

This range name applies to the cell that will contain the monthly payment function which does not required a named range.

c. Click **Close**.

d. Save the workbook.

You will modify the PMT function by replacing the existing references with the corresponding range names. This will help interpret the PMT function. Refer to Figure 6.9 as you complete Step 3.

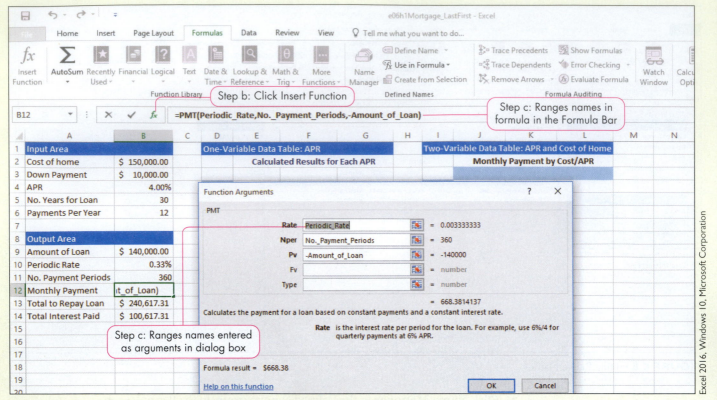

FIGURE 6.9 Range Names in a Formula

a. Click **cell B12**, the cell containing the PMT function.

b. Click **Insert Function** (between the Name Box and the Formula Bar) to open the Function Arguments dialog box.

c. Click in the **Rate box**, click **cell B10**, and then press **Tab**. Click **cell B11**, press **Tab**, and type **-**, and then click **B9**.

The new function is =PMT(Periodic_Rate,No._Payment_Periods,-Amount_of_Loan).

d. Click **OK**.

e. Save the workbook.

To ensure continuity moving forward, you want to create a documentation worksheet that lists all of the range names in the workbook. Refer to Figure 6.10 as you complete Step 4.

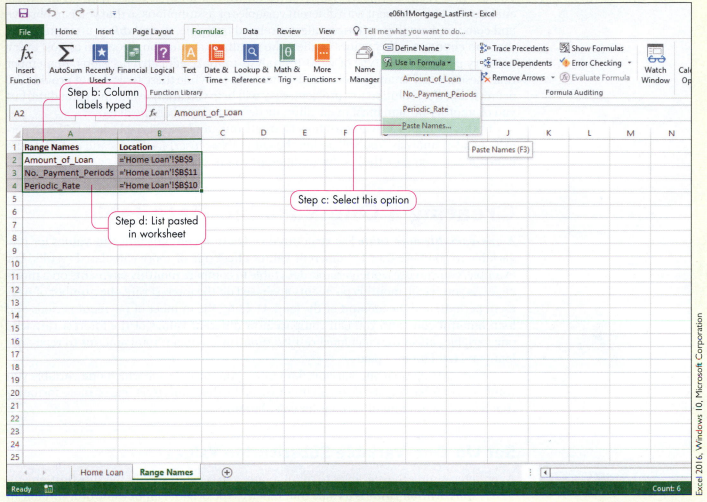

FIGURE 6.10 Range Names Inserted in a Formula

a. Click **New sheet** to the right of the Home Loan tab, and double-click the default sheet name **Sheet1**. Type **Range Names** and press **Enter**.

You inserted and renamed the new worksheet to reflect the data you will add to it.

b. Type **Range Names** in **cell A1** and type **Location** in **cell B1**. Bold these headings.

These column headings will display above the list of range names.

c. Click **cell A2**, click **Use in Formula** in the Defined Names group on the Formulas tab, and then select **Paste Names**.

The Paste Name dialog box opens, displaying all of the range names in the workbook.

d. Click **Paste List**.

Excel pastes an alphabetical list of range names starting in cell A2. The second column displays the locations of the range names.

e. Increase the widths of columns A and B to fit the data.

f. Save the workbook. Keep the workbook open if you plan to continue with the next Hands-On Exercise. If not, close the workbook and exit Excel.

One- and Two-Variable Data Tables

You are now ready to explore Excel's powerful what-if analysis tools. *What-if analysis* enables you to experiment with different variables or assumptions so that you can observe and compare how these changes affect a related outcome. A *variable* is an input value that can change to other values to affect the results of a situation. People in almost every industry perform some type of what-if analysis to make educated decisions. Remember that these what-if analysis tools are just that—tools. While these tools do not provide the definitive, perfect solution to a problem, they will help you analyze and interpret data, but you or another human must make ultimate decisions based on the data.

In this section, you will learn how to create one- and two-variable data tables to perform what-if analysis. You will design the data tables, insert formulas, and complete the data tables to compare the results for different values of the variables.

Creating a One-Variable Data Table

A *one-variable data table* is a structured range that contains different values for one variable to compare how the different values affect one or more calculated results. For example, you can use a one-variable data table to compare monthly payments on a mortgage. As you recall, monthly payments are based on the interest rate, the number of payment periods, and the amount of the loan. Holding the number of payment periods and loan amount constant, you can compare how different values of the interest rate (the one variable) affect the calculated results: monthly payment, total amount to repay the loan, and total interest paid.

When setting up a one-variable data table, you must decide which one variable you want to use. After you decide on an input variable, then you select one or more formulas that depend on that input variable for calculations.

Set Up One-Variable Substitution Values

STEP 1 ❯❯ After determining the variables to manipulate, you need to specify the substitution values. A *substitution value* is a value that replaces the original input value of a variable in a data table. For example, the original interest rate is 4.5%, but you might want to substitute 5%, 5.5%, 6%, 6.5%, and 7% in place of the 4.5% to see how these different interest rates affect the results.

To set up the one-variable data table, locate a range to the right of, or below, the regular worksheet data to create the one-variable data table. Leave at least one blank row and one blank column between the dataset and the data table. Enter the substitution values down one column or across one row. With one variable and several results, a vertical orientation for the substitution values is recommended because people often look for a value in the first column of a table and then read across to see corresponding values.

You can enter the substitution values yourself or use the Series dialog box to help complete a series of values. See Figure 6.11.

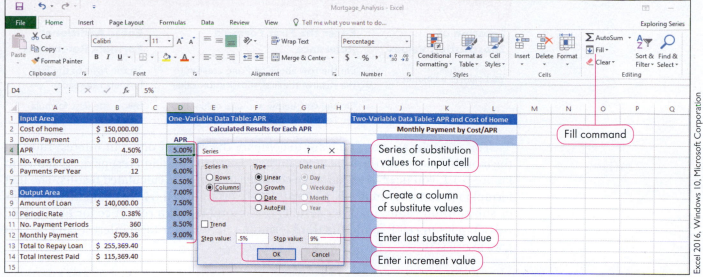

FIGURE 6.11 Series Dialog Box

To use the Series dialog box, complete the following steps:

1. Type the first substitution value (such as 5%) in cell D4 and keep that cell as the active cell.

2. Click the Home tab, click Fill in the Editing group, and then select Series to open the Series dialog box.

3. Click Rows to place the series of substitution values across a row or click Columns to place the series of substitution values down a column.

4. Enter the value increment in the *Step value* box and enter the ending value for the series in the *Stop value* box.

5. Click OK. Excel fills in a series of values.

TIP: AUTOFILL A SERIES OF SUBSTITUTION VALUES

Instead of using the Series dialog box, you can use AutoFill to complete a series of substitution values. To do this, enter the first two substitution values (such as 5% and 5.5%). Select the cells containing these two values and drag the fill handle down until the ScreenTip displays the last substitution value you want. Excel sets the increment pattern based on the difference between the first two values.

Add Formulas to a One-Variable Data Table

STEP 2 ▶▶ After you enter the substitution values in either a column or row, you must add one or more formulas that relate mathematically to the variable for which you are using substitution values. Although you can create formulas directly in the data table, referencing cells containing existing formulas outside the data table is preferable because the formulas are often already created. You can save time and reduce errors by referencing the original formula. Within the data table range, the formula references must be entered in a specific location based on the location of the substitution values (see Table 6.2).

TABLE 6.2 Locations for Formula References

Location of Substitution Values	Enter the First Formula Reference	Enter Additional Formula References
Vertically in a column	On the row above and one column to the right of the first substitution value	To the right of the first formula reference
Horizontally in a row	On the row below and one column to the left of the first substitution value	Below the first formula reference

For example, assume you want to compare the effect of different interest rates on the monthly payment, the total amount repaid, and the total interest paid. As shown in Figure 6.12, you need to set up three columns to show the calculated results. The first formula reference for monthly payment (=B12) goes in cell E3. To compare the effects of substitution values on other results, the second formula reference for total repaid (=B13) goes in cell F3, and the third formula reference for total interest paid (=B14) goes in cell G3.

Calculate Results

STEP 3 ❱❱ It is important that you enter the substitution values and formula references in the correct locations. This sets the left and top boundaries of the soon-to-be-completed data table.

To complete the one-variable data table, complete the following steps:

1. Select the data table boundaries, starting in the blank cell in the top-left corner of the data table. Drag down and to the right, if there is more than one column, to select the last blank cell at the intersection of the last substitution value and the last formula reference.

2. Click the Data tab, click What-If Analysis in the Forecast group, and then select Data Table to open the Data Table dialog box (see Figure 6.12).

3. Enter the cell reference of the cell containing the original variable for which you are substituting values. If you listed the substitution values in a row, enter the original variable cell reference in the *Row input cell* box. If you listed the substitution values in a column, enter the original variable cell reference in the *Column input cell* box. In Figure 6.12, for example, click cell B4—the original interest rate variable—in the *Column input cell* box because the substitution interest rates are in a column. Note that the cell reference is automatically made absolute so that Excel always refers to the original input cell as it performs calculations in the data table.

4. Click OK.

Pearson Education, Inc.

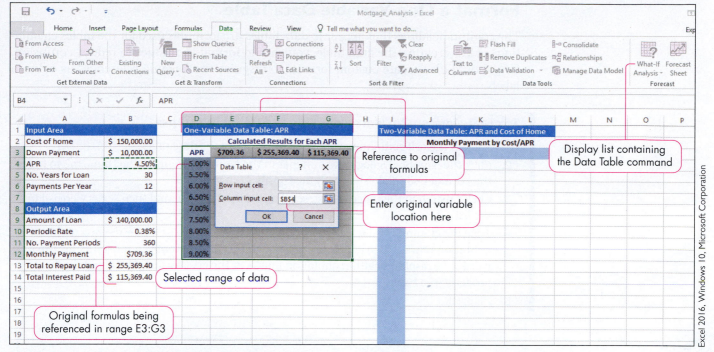

FIGURE 6.12 Data Table Dialog Box

When you create the one-variable data table, Excel uses the substitution values individually to replace the original variable's value, which is then used in the formulas to produce the results in the body of the data table. In Figure 6.13, the data table shows the substitution values of different interest rates, the calculated monthly payments (column E), total payments (column F), and total interest paid (column G) for the respective interest rates.

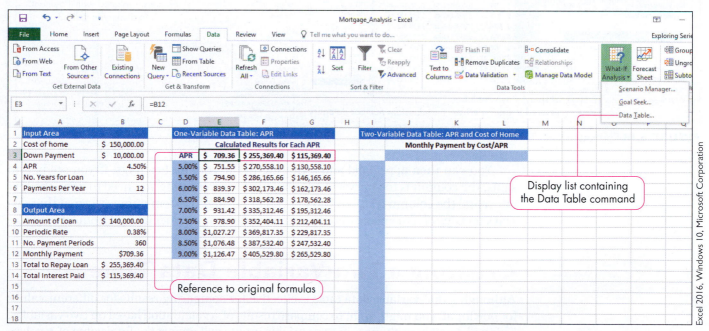

FIGURE 6.13 Completed Data Table

Format a One-Variable Data Table

The column headings that appear in data tables are formulas used for the tables calculations. After creating the data table, you should format the values to reduce confusion. You should also create custom formats to disguise the formula references as column labels.

To create custom formats, complete the following steps:

1. Click in the cell containing a formula reference in the data table.
2. Click the Number Dialog Box Launcher in the Number group on the Home tab to open the Format Cells dialog box with the Number tab active.
3. Click Custom in the Category list, scroll up in the Type list, and then select General in the list.
4. Type the column heading in the Type box above the Type list. Enter the text within quotation marks, such as "Payment" and click OK. Note that you must include the word to be displayed within quotation marks or the custom format will not display properly (see Figure 6.14).
5. Click OK.

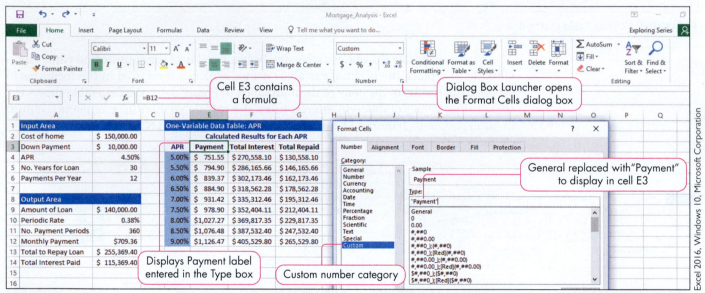

FIGURE 6.14 Formatted Data Table

You can then apply bold and centering to the column headings. If you see pound signs, the column is too narrow to display the text, indicating you need to wrap the text or expand the column width. Although you are using a custom number format that displays text, Excel remembers that the actual contents are values derived from formulas.

Creating a Two-Variable Data Table

Although a one-variable data table is effective for comparing results for different values for one input, you might want to compare results of a calculation based on two variables. This will detail how changes in two variable inputs will impact the final value of a calculation. For example, you might want to compare the combined effects of various interest rates (such as 5%, 5.5%, and 6%) and different down payments (such as $10,000, $15,000, and $20,000) on the monthly payment. A ***two-variable data table*** is a structured range that contains different values for two variables to compare how these differing values affect the results for one calculated value.

Set Up the Substitution Values for Two Variables

STEP 4 ❯❯ Create the two-variable data table separate from regular worksheet data, similar to the method used for a one-variable data table. For a two-variable data table, you use the top row for one variable's substitution values and the first column for the other variable's substitution values. Figure 6.15 shows substitution interest rates in the first column (range D4:D12) and substitution down payments in the first row (range E3:G3).

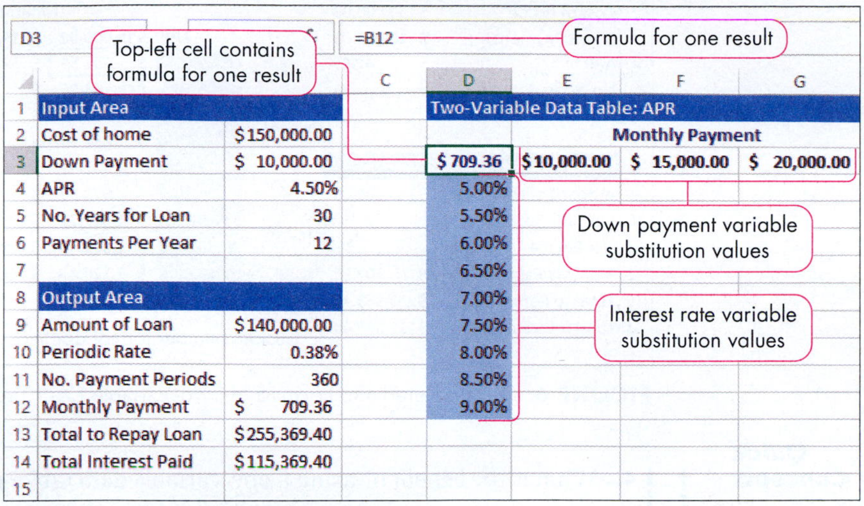

FIGURE 6.15 Substitution Values and Formula for a Two-Variable Data Table

Add a Formula to the Data Table

The two-variable data table enables you to use two variables, but you are restricted to only one result instead of multiple results. With the one-variable data table, you use the interest rate variable to compare multiple results: monthly payment, total to repay the loan, and total interest paid. However, for the two-variable data table, decide which result you want to focus on based on the two variables. In the case of a home loan, you might want to focus on the effects that changes in interest rates and down payments (the two variables) have on different monthly payments (the result). Enter the formula or reference to the original formula in the blank cell in the top-left corner. For example, enter the cell reference for the monthly payment (=B12) in cell D3 as shown in Figure 6.15.

Calculate Results for a Two-Variable Data Table

STEP 5 ❯❯ After entering the substitution values and the reference to one formula result, you are ready to complete the table to see the results.

To finish the two-variable data table, complete the following steps:

1. Select the data table boundaries, starting in the top-left corner of the data table. Drag down and to the right to select the last blank cell at the intersection of the last substitution value for both the column and the row.
2. Click the Data tab, click What-If Analysis in the Forecast group, and then select Data Table. The Data Table dialog box opens.
3. Enter the cell that contains the original value for the substitution values in the first row in the *Row input cell* box. Enter the cell that contains the original value for the substitution values in the first column in the *Column input cell* box. For example, the original row (down payment) variable value is stored in cell B3, and the original column (APR) variable value is stored in cell B4.
4. Click OK.

After you complete the data table, to reduce confusion, you should format the results by applying a custom number format to the formula cell to appear as a heading and add a merged heading above the row substitution values (see Figure 6.16).

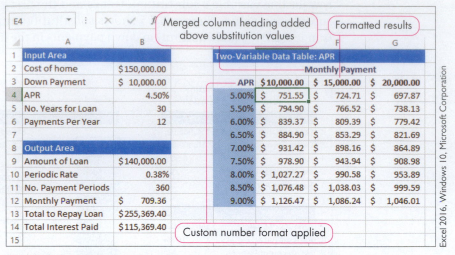

FIGURE 6.16 Completed and Formatted Two-Variable Data Table

Quick Concepts ✓

4. What is the benefit of using a one-variable data table? *p. 406*

5. Why is it preferable to reference formula cells outside of a one-variable data table versus entering the formula manually? *p. 407*

6. What is the difference between a one- and two-variable data table? *p. 410*

Hands-On Exercises

Skills covered: Set Up One-Variable Substitution Values • Add Formulas to a One-Variable Data Table • Calculate Results • Format a One-Variable Data Table • Set Up Two-Variable Substitution Values • Add a Formula to the Data Table • Calculate Results for a Two-Variable Data Table

2 One- and Two-Variable Data Tables

As you consider different options for a home purchase, you want to use data tables to compare how different interest rates and prices will affect your monthly payment. You decide to create both one- and two-variable data tables to analyze the results.

STEP 1 ►► SET UP ONE-VARIABLE SUBSTITUTION VALUES

You want to compare monthly mortgage payments, total amounts to repay a loan, and total interest you will pay based on several interest rates—the variable. The interest rates range from 4% to 6% in 0.25% increments. Your first step is to enter a series of substitution values for the interest rate. Refer to Figure 6.17 as you complete Step 1.

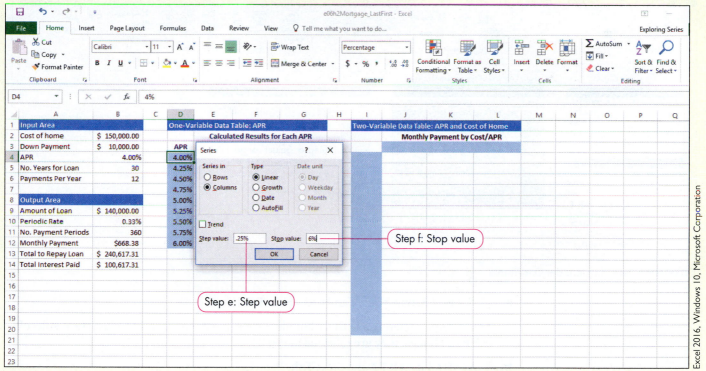

FIGURE 6.17 Substitution Values

a. Open *e06h1Mortgage_LastFirst* if you closed it at the end of Hands-On Exercise 1, and save it as **e06h2Mortgage_LastFirst**, changing h1 to h2.

b. Make the **Home Loan** worksheet active, click **cell D4**, type **4** and then press **Ctrl+Enter**.

Cell D4 is the first cell containing a substitution value. Make sure cell D4 is still the active cell.

c. Click **Fill** in the Editing group on the Home tab and select **Series**.

The Series dialog box opens.

d. Click **Columns**.

You changed the *Series in* option to Columns because you want the series of substitution values listed vertically in column D.

e. Delete the existing value in the Step value box and type **0.25%**.

f. Type **6%** in the Stop value box and click **OK**.

Excel fills in the series of values.

> **TROUBLESHOOTING:** If you forget to type the decimal point in Step e and/or the percent sign in Steps e or f, the series will be incorrect. If this happens, click Undo and repeat Steps c through f.

STEP 2 ›› **ADD FORMULAS TO A ONE-VARIABLE DATA TABLE AND CALCULATE RESULTS**

In the next steps, you will enter references to the monthly payment, total amount to repay the loan, and total interest formulas. Then, you will complete the table to compare the results for different interest rates ranging from 4% to 6%. Refer to Figure 6.18 as you complete Step 2.

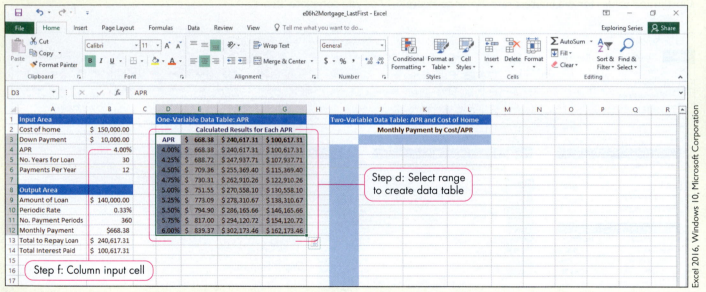

FIGURE 6.18 Complete the Data Table

a. Click **cell E3**, type **=B12**, and then press **Tab**.

You entered a reference to the original monthly payment formula. When the results of cell B12 change, they are reflected in cell E3.

b. Type **=B13** in **cell F3** and press **Tab**.

You entered a reference to the original total amount to repay the loan.

c. Type **=B14** in **cell G3** and press **Enter**.

You entered a reference to the original total interest paid.

d. Select the **range D3:G12**.

You select the entire range of the data table, starting in the blank cell in the top-left corner. Note that you did not select the titles or headings in cells D1:G2.

e. Click the **Data tab**, click **What-If Analysis** in the Forecast group, and then select **Data Table**.

f. Click in the **Column input cell box**, click **cell B4**, and then click **OK**. Save the workbook.

Because the substitution values are in a column, you reference cell B4 in the Column input box. Excel inserts the TABLE array function in the empty result cells and substitutes the values in range D4:D12 individually for the original APR to calculate the respective monthly payments, total amounts, and total interest payments. The higher the APR, the higher the monthly payment, total amount to repay the loan, and total interest.

STEP 3 ›› **FORMAT A ONE-VARIABLE DATA TABLE**

You want to format the results to show dollar signs and to display rounded values to the nearest penny. In addition, you want to add column headings to provide more detail to the data table and add custom formats to the cells to appear as column headings. Refer to Figure 6.19 as you complete Step 3.

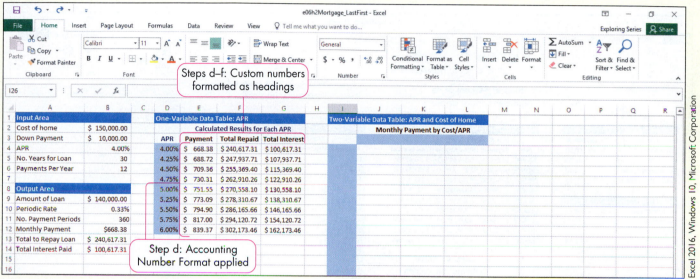

FIGURE 6.19 Formatted Data Table

a. Select the **range E4:G12**, click the **Home tab**, and then click **Accounting Number Format** in the Number group.

The values look more professional now that you have formatted them.

b. Click **cell D3**, type **APR**, and then press **Tab**.

Because cell D3 was empty, you can type the label directly in the cell without adding a custom format. Cell E3 should now be the active cell.

c. Click **Number Format** in the Number group on the Home tab.

d. Select **Custom** in the Category list, scroll up through the Type list, and select **General** in the list.

e. Select the existing text in the **Type box**, type **"Payment"** (make sure you include the quotation marks), and Click **OK**.

The custom format is applied and Payment displays instead of =B12.

f. Repeat and adapt steps c through e to enter the following custom number formats: **"Total Repaid"** for **cell F3** and **"Total Interest"** for **cell G3**.

g. Center and bold the **range E3:G3**.

h. Save the workbook.

STEP 4 ▶▶ SET UP TWO-VARIABLE SUBSTITUTION VALUES AND ADD A FORMULA TO THE DATA TABLE

Now you want to focus on how a combination of interest rates and different costs will affect just the monthly payment. The interest rates range from 4% to 8% at .25% increments with costs of $150,000, $175,000, $200,000. Refer to Figure 6.20 as you complete Step 4.

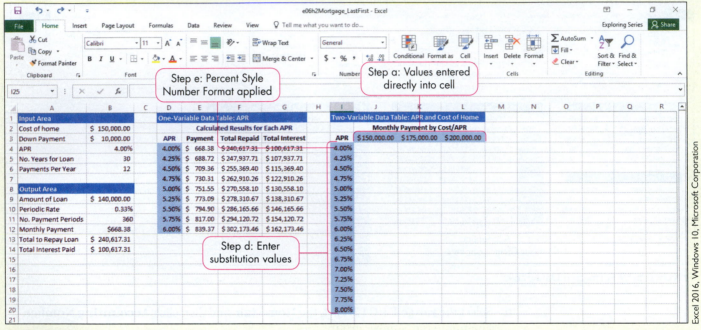

FIGURE 6.20 Substitution Values

a. Enter **150000**, **175000**, and **200000** in the **range J3:L3**. Format these values with **Accounting Number Format**. Expand the column width if pound signs (#) appear.

b. Click **cell I4**, type **4%**, and then press **Ctrl+Enter**.

c. Click **Fill** in the Editing group on the Home tab, select **Series**, and then click **Columns**.

d. Replace the existing value in the Step value box with **0.25%**, type **8%** in the Stop value box, and then click **OK**.

e. Format the **range I4:I20** with two decimal places.

f. Click **cell I3**, type **=B12**, and then press **Ctrl+Enter**. Expand the column width if pound signs (#) appear. Save the workbook.

You inserted the reference to the formula in the top-left cell of the two-variable data table. The cell displays pound signs, indicating the column is too narrow to display the value; you will apply a custom number format in Step 5.

STEP 5 ›› CALCULATE RESULTS FOR A TWO-VARIABLE DATA TABLE

You complete the data table, format the monthly payment results, and apply a custom number format to the cell containing the formula reference so that it displays the text APR. Refer to Figure 6.21 as you complete Step 5.

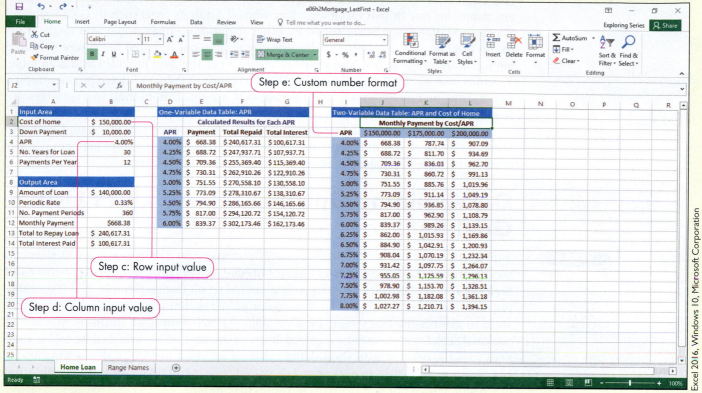

FIGURE 6.21 Completed Two-Variable Data Table

a. Select the **range I3:L20**.

b. Click the **Data tab**, click **What-If Analysis** in the Forecast group, and then select **Data Table**.

c. Click **cell B2** to enter that cell reference in the Row input cell box.

Because you entered the purchase price substitution values in the top row of the data table, you entered the reference to the cell containing the original cost in the Row input cell box.

d. Click in the **Column input cell box**, click **cell B4**, and then click **OK**.

Because you entered the interest rate substitution values in the left column of the data table, you entered the reference to the cell containing the original APR variable in the Column input cell box.

e. Click **cell I3** and apply a custom number format to display **APR**. Center and bold the contents in **cell I3**.

f. Save the workbook. Keep the workbook open if you plan to continue with Hands-On Exercise 3. If not, close the workbook and exit Excel.

Goal Seek and Scenario Manager

Although data tables are useful for particular situations to compare effects of different values for one or two variables, other what-if analysis tools such as Goal Seek and Scenario Manager are better suited for other situations. For example, you might want to use Goal Seek to determine exactly the down payment required to acquire a desired payment. In this situation, you would not need all of the data provided by a data table. You may also want to weigh the options between various values of down payments, purchase costs, and interest rates using Scenario Manager. If more than two variables are required, data tables would not be a viable option.

In this section, you will learn when and how to use both Goal Seek and Scenario Manager to assist you in making decisions. These tools enable you to perform what-if analysis to make forecasts or predictions involving quantifiable data.

Determining Optimal Input Values Using Goal Seek

STEP 1 ❱❱ Suppose the most you can afford for a monthly payment on a mortgage is $800. How can you determine the down payment amount needed to meet that monthly payment? *Goal Seek* is a tool that enables you to specify a desired result from a formula ($800 monthly payment) without knowing what input value achieves that goal. Goal Seek works backward to identify the exact value for a variable to reach your goal. In this case, you can use Goal Seek to determine the required down payment. Unlike variable data tables, Goal Seek uses the original worksheet data to change an input instead of displaying various combinations of results in a separate table. Goal Seek manipulates only one variable and one result; it does not produce a list of values to compare.

> **To use Goal Seek, complete the following steps:**
>
> 1. Click What-If Analysis in the Forecast group on the Data tab.
> 2. Select Goal Seek to open the Goal Seek dialog box.
> 3. Enter the cell reference for the cell to be optimized in the *Set cell* box. This cell must contain a formula, such as the monthly payment.
> 4. Enter the result you want to achieve (such as the $800 goal) in the *To value* box.
> 5. Enter the cell reference that contains the variable to adjust (such as the down payment) in the *By changing cell* box as shown in Figure 6.22. This cell must be a value, not a formula, which has a mathematical relationship with the cell containing the formula or goal.
> 6. Click OK.

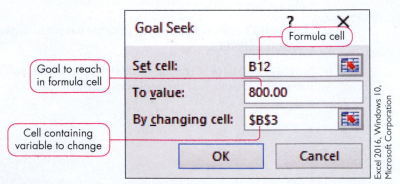

FIGURE 6.22 Goal Seek Dialog Box

Excel varies the input value until the desired result is achieved, if possible, and displays the Goal Seek Status dialog box. Click OK to accept the target value and change the value of the input cell you entered in Step 5 to achieve the goal you specified in Steps 3 and 4. Click Cancel to keep the original input cell value instead of changing it. If Excel cannot determine a solution given the input cell and the desired results, it displays a message box.

Using Scenario Manager

You may want to compare several variables and their combined effects on multiple calculated results. This type of analysis involves identifying and setting up *scenarios*, which are detailed sets of values that represent different possible situations. Business managers often create a best-case scenario, worst-case scenario, and most likely scenario to compare outcomes. For example, a best-case scenario could reflect an increase in units sold and lower production costs. A worst-case scenario could reflect fewer units sold and higher production costs.

Scenario Manager is a what-if analysis tool that enables you to define and manage up to 32 scenarios to compare their effects on calculated results. You can perform more sophisticated what-if analyses with Scenario Manager with the increased number of variables and results than with data tables. The Scenario Manager dialog box (see Figure 6.23) enables you to create, edit, and delete scenario names. Each scenario represents different sets of what-if conditions to assess the outcome of spreadsheet models. Each scenario is stored under its own name and defines cells whose values change from scenario to scenario.

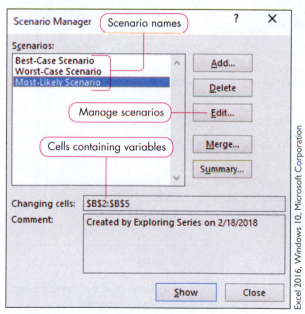

FIGURE 6.23 Scenario Manager Dialog Box

> **TIP: SCENARIOS ON DIFFERENT WORKSHEETS**
> When you create scenarios, Excel maintains those scenarios on the worksheet that was active when you created them. You can create scenarios for each worksheet in a workbook. The Scenario Manager dialog box displays only those scenarios you have created on the active worksheet.

Create Scenarios

STEP 2 ›› Before you start the Scenario Manager, identify cells that contain the variables you want to change or manipulate. For example, in evaluating home loans, you might want to manipulate the values for these variables: cost, down payment, interest rate, and the duration of the loan. You enter the cell references for these variables as the changing cells because you change the values to compare the results. After identifying the variables you want to change, identify one or more cells containing formulas that generate results you want to compare. Note these formulas must be directly impacted by the changing cell.

To create a scenario, complete the following steps:

1. Click What-If Analysis in the Forecast group on the Data tab.
2. Select Scenario Manager to open the Scenario Manager dialog box.
3. Click Add to open the Add Scenario dialog box (see Figure 6.24).
4. Enter a meaningful name in the *Scenario name* box.
5. Enter the input cells for the scenario in the *Changing cells* box. These are the cells containing variable values that Scenario Manager will adjust or change. Ranges can be used and commas are required between nonadjacent cells. The changing cells must be identical cell references across all scenarios.
6. Click in the Comment box. Excel enters the name of the person who created the scenarios in the Comment box; however, you can change the name and enter additional descriptions and rationales for the scenarios.
7. Click OK to open the Scenario Values dialog box (see Figure 6.25), which lists the changing cell references that you specified in the previous dialog box. In each respective box, type the value you want to use for that particular scenario.

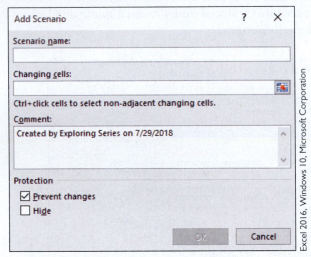

FIGURE 6.24 Add Scenario Dialog Box

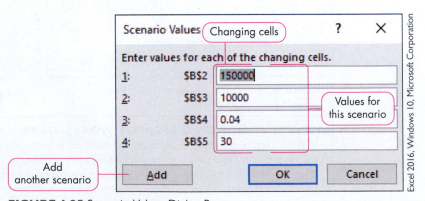

FIGURE 6.25 Scenario Values Dialog Box

Add and Edit Scenarios

STEP 3 ▶▶ After creating a scenario, you may want to edit the original values or add more scenarios for additional review.

> **TIP: RANGE NAMES**
>
> To help you know what data to enter for the changing cells, you might want to assign a range name to the variable cells before using Scenario Manager. If you do this, the range names, rather than the cell references, appear in the Scenario Values dialog box.

If you need to modify the parameters of a scenario, such as the name or input values, open the Scenario Manager dialog box, select the scenario you want to modify in the Scenarios list, and then click Edit. The Edit Scenario dialog box opens so that you can change the values. Click OK after making the necessary changes.

If you have scenarios in several worksheets or workbooks, you can combine them. Click Merge in the Scenario Manager dialog box to open the Merge Scenarios dialog box. Select the workbook and worksheet and click OK. Use Help to learn more about merging scenarios.

View Scenarios

After you create the scenarios, you can view each of them. To view the scenarios, click What-If Analysis in the Forecast group on the Data tab, select Scenario Manager, select the name of the scenario you want to view in the Scenarios list, and then click Show. Excel places the defined values in the respective changing cells and displays the results.

Generate a Scenario Summary Report

STEP 4 ▶▶ Although you can view the defined values and their results individually, you will probably want to compare all scenarios in a table. A ***scenario summary report*** is an organized structured table of the scenarios, their input values, and their respective results. The summary report displays in the form of a worksheet outline and enables you to compare the results based on different values specified by the respective scenarios. Excel can produce two types of reports: Scenario Summary and Scenario PivotTable report. PivotTable reports summarize the data in a pivot table. This provides the same functionality as any other pivot table. Scenario summary reports display the results of each scenario in a new worksheet. The data reported in the summary are formatted without gridlines, and the report is easily printable.

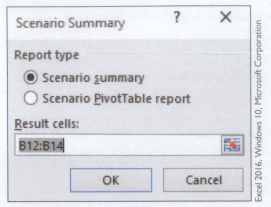

FIGURE 6.26 Scenario Summary Dialog Box

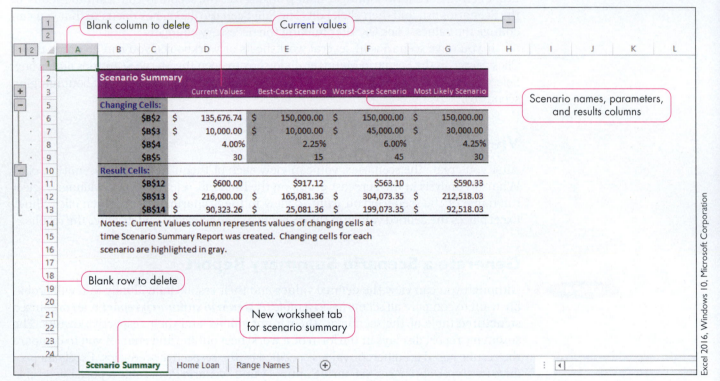

FIGURE 6.27 Scenario Summary

The scenario summary contains a column listing the changing and resulting cell references, current values and result values, and a column of values and results for each defined scenario. This organized structure helps you compare the results as you analyze the scenarios. You should modify the structure and format the data for a more professional look. Typically, you should do the following:

- Delete the blank row 1 and the blank column A.

- Delete the Current Values column if it duplicates a defined scenario or if you do not want that data.

- Replace cell reference labels with descriptive labels in the first column.

- Delete the explanatory paragraph below the table and replace it with a narrative analysis relevant to the data.

Quick Concepts

7. What are the limitations of Goal Seek? *p. 418*

8. What is the difference between a scenario summary report and a PivotTable report? *p. 421*

9. What are the benefits of using Scenario Manager? *p. 419*

Watch the Video for this Hands-On Exercise!

MyITLab®
HOE3 Training

Skills covered: Determine Optimal Input Values Using Goal Seek • Create Scenarios • Add and Edit Scenarios • Generate a Scenario Summary Report

3 Goal Seek and Scenario Manager

You want to use Goal Seek and Scenario Manager to perform additional what-if analyses with your mortgage data.

STEP 1 ›› DETERMINE OPTIMAL INPUT VALUES USING GOAL SEEK

Given the current interest rate with a 30-year mortgage and your planned down payment, you want to identify the most that you can afford and maintain a $600.00 monthly payment. You will use Goal Seek to work backward from your goal to identify the ideal home purchase price. Refer to Figure 6.28 as you complete Step 1.

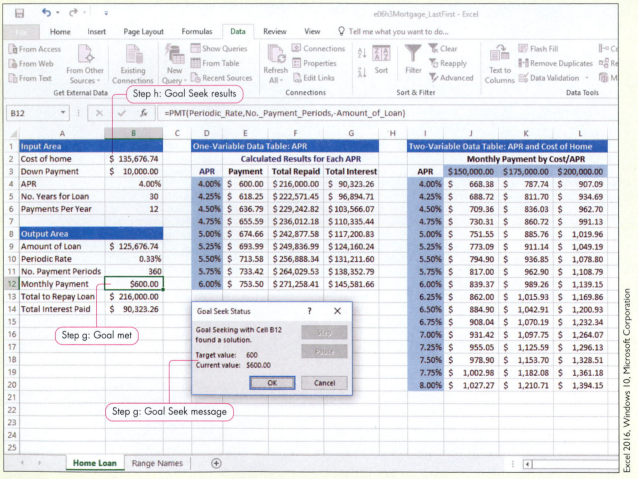

FIGURE 6.28 Goal Seek

a. Open the *e06h2Mortgage_LastFirst* workbook if you closed it at the end of Hands-On Exercise 2, and save it as **e06h3Mortgage_LastFirst**, changing h2 to h3.

b. Click the **Data tab**.

c. Click **What-If Analysis** in the Forecast group and select **Goal Seek**.

   The Goal Seek dialog box opens.

d. Click **cell B12** to enter the cell reference for the monthly payment in the *Set cell box*.

   You indicated which cell contains the formula that produces the goal.

e. Click in the **To value box** and type **600**.

   You want the monthly payment to be $600.

f. Click in the **By changing cell box** and click **cell B2**, the cell containing the cost of the home.

Cell B2 is the cell whose value will be determined using the Goal Seek analysis tool.

g. Click **OK**.

The Goal Seek Status dialog box opens, indicating that it reached the target monthly payment goal of $600.

h. Click **OK** to accept the solution and to close the Goal Seek Status dialog box. Save the workbook.

To achieve a $600 monthly mortgage payment, you need to purchase a home that costs up to $135,676.74, instead of the original $150,000, assuming the other variables (down payment, interest rate, and term of loan) stay the same.

STEP 2 ›› CREATE A SCENARIO

You want to use Scenario Manager to explore different scenarios. Your first scenario is a best-case scenario with these parameters: $150,000 home, $10,000 down payment, special reduced interest financing for 15 years. Refer to Figure 6.29 as you complete Step 2.

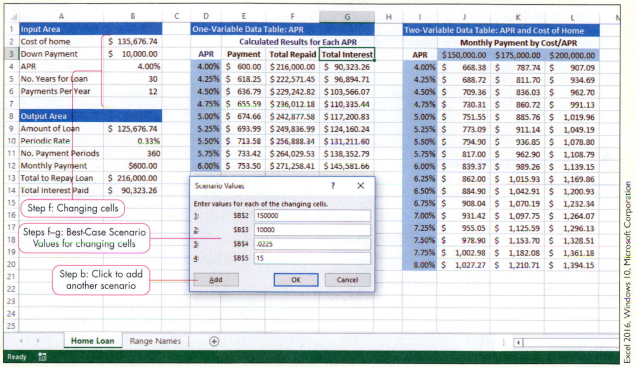

FIGURE 6.29 First Scenario's Values

a. Click **What-If Analysis** in the Forecast group on the Data tab, and then select **Scenario Manager**.

The Scenario Manager dialog box opens.

b. Click **Add**.

The Add Scenario dialog box opens so that you can assign a scenario name and select the changing cells.

c. Click in the **Scenario name box** and type **Best-Case Scenario**.

d. Delete existing contents in the *Changing cells* box and select the **range B2:B5**.

Excel enters this range in the Changing cells box. These are the variable cells cost of the home, down payment, and interest rate that will be changed in the various scenarios.

e. Ensure the Comment box displays your name and the date the scenario is created, such as "Created by Jason Davidson on 8/01/2018," and click **OK**.

The Scenario Values dialog box opens so that you can enter the parameters for the scenario.

f. Type **150000** in the $B$2 box and press **Tab** twice to accept the current $10,000 down payment.

You entered 150000 as the cost of the home.

g. Type **.0225** in the $B$4 box, press **Tab**, and then type **15** in the $B$5 box.

h. Click **OK** and click **Close**. Save the workbook.

While you could have kept the Scenario Values dialog box open to continue to the next step, you closed it so that you could save the workbook.

STEP 3 ›› **ADD SCENARIOS**

You will add two more scenarios: a worst-case scenario and a most likely scenario. In the worst-case scenario, you assume you will have to settle for a higher down payment, higher interest rate, and a longer loan period. In the most likely scenario, you will enter values that are between those in the other two scenarios. Refer to Figure 6.30 as you complete Step 3.

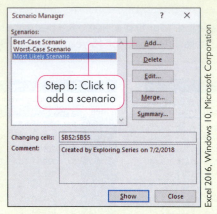

FIGURE 6.30 Add Scenarios

a. Click **What-If Analysis** in the Forecast group and select **Scenario Manager**.

b. Click **Add**, type **Worst-Case Scenario**, and then click **OK**.

The *Changing cells* box displays B2:B5, the range you selected for the first scenario.

c. Type the following values in the respective changing cells boxes:

Changing Cell Box	Value
$B$2	150000
$B$3	45000
$B$4	6%
$B$5	45

For the cell $B$4 box, you can enter the value as a percentage (6%) or as a decimal equivalent (0.06).

d. Click **Add**.

e. Type **Most Likely Scenario** and click **OK** in the Add Scenario dialog box.

f. Type the following values in the respective changing cells boxes:

Changing Cell Box	Value
$B$2	150000
$B$3	30000
$B$4	4.25%
$B$5	30

g. Click **OK**.

The Scenario Manager dialog box lists the three scenarios you created.

TROUBLESHOOTING: If you believe you made any data entry errors, or if you want to double-check your values, select a scenario and click Edit. You can then change values in the Edit Scenario dialog box and click OK.

h. Click **Close** to close the Scenario Manager dialog box. Save the workbook.

You want to generate a scenario summary report to compare the three home loan scenarios you created. Refer to Figures 6.27 and 6.31 as you complete Step 4.

Step e: Descriptive labels

Step c: Scenario results

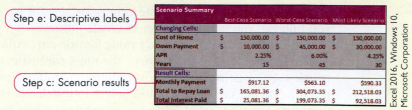

Scenario Summary		Best-Case Scenario	Worst-Case Scenario	Most Likely Scenario
Changing Cells:				
Cost of Home	$ 150,000.00	$ 150,000.00	$ 150,000.00	
Down Payment	$ 10,000.00	$ 45,000.00	$ 30,000.00	
APR	2.25%	6.00%	4.25%	
Years	15	45	30	
Result Cells:				
Monthly Payment	$917.12	$563.10	$590.33	
Total to Repay Loan	$ 165,081.36	$ 304,073.35	$ 212,518.03	
Total Interest Paid	$ 25,081.36	$ 199,073.35	$ 92,518.03	

Excel 2016, Windows 10, Microsoft Corporation

FIGURE 6.31 Scenario Summary

a. Click **What-If Analysis** in the Forecast group and select **Scenario Manager**.

b. Click **Summary**.

Excel may select a range within a data table.

c. Select the **range B12:B14** to enter it in the Result cells box and click **OK**.

Excel generates the summary on a new worksheet named Scenario Summary. The report details the changes in payment amounts based on the variable inputs. The results are similar to Figure 6.27. You need to make a few deletions and add descriptive labels.

d. Delete the following:

- Column A
- Row 1
- Current Values column
- Notes in the **range A13:A15**

e. Enter descriptive labels in the following cells:

- **Cost of Home** in cell A5
- **Down Payment** in cell A6
- **APR** in cell A7
- **Years** in cell A8
- **Monthly Payment** in cell A10
- **Total to Repay Loan** in cell A11
- **Total Interest Paid** in cell A12

The labels describe data contained in each row. Now you can delete column B, which displays the cell references. Note, if range names are used with Scenario Manager, they will appear in the scenario summary report.

f. Delete column B and increase the width of column A.

The Best-Case Scenario provides the lowest monthly payment. Based on the scenario summary report we learn that the Worst-Case scenario provides the lowest payment but has the highest interest charges and longest repayment duration. We also learned the Best-Case scenario has the highest payment but the shortest repayment duration and lowest interest charges. This leaves the Most-Likely scenario which offers a monthly payment in-between Best and Worst-Case options while offering lower interest charges and a reduced repayment duration compared to the Worst-Case scenario.

g. Save the workbook. Keep the workbook open if you plan to continue with Hands-On Exercise 4. If not, close the workbook and exit Excel.

TIP: SCENARIO WORKSHEETS

Each time you generate a summary, Excel inserts another Scenario Summary worksheet. You can delete a summary worksheet if you no longer need the data.

Solver

Add-ins are programs that can be added to Excel to provide enhanced functionality. **Solver** is an add-in application that searches for the best or optimum solution to a problem by manipulating the values for several variables within restrictions that you impose. You can use Solver to create optimization models. **Optimization models** find the highest, lowest, or exact value for one particular result by adjusting values for selected variables. Solver is one of the most sophisticated what-if analysis tools, and people use Solver in a variety of situations and industries. For example, a cellular phone manufacturing facility could use Solver to maximize the number of phones made or minimize the number of labor hours required while conforming to other production specifications. A financial planner might use Solver to help a family adjust its expenses to stay within its monthly income.

In this section, you will learn how to load the Solver add-in. Then, you will use Solver to set a target, select changing cells, and create constraints.

Loading the Solver Add-In

STEP 1 ❯❯ Because other companies create the add-ins, they are not active by default. You must load the Solver add-in before you can use it.

> **To load Solver, complete the following steps:**
>
> 1. Click the File tab and select Options.
> 2. Click Add-ins to see a list of active and inactive add-in applications. The Active Application Add-ins list displays currently enabled add-ins, and the Inactive Application Add-ins list displays add-ins that are not currently enabled.
> 3. Click the Manage arrow at the bottom of the dialog box, select Excel Add-ins, and then click Go to open the Add-ins dialog box (see Figure 6.32).
> 4. Click the Solver Add-in check box in the Add-ins available list and click OK.

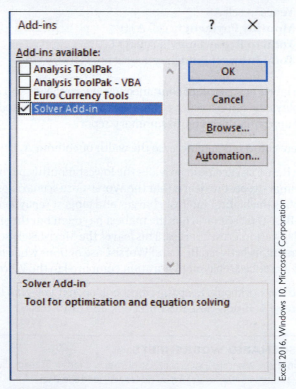

Excel 2016, Windows 10, Microsoft Corporation

FIGURE 6.32 Add-Ins Dialog Box

When you load Solver, Excel displays Solver in the Analyze group on the Data tab (see Figure 6.33), where it remains until you remove the Solver add-in. However, if you are in a campus computer lab that resets software settings when you log off, you will have to load Solver again each time you log into the lab's network.

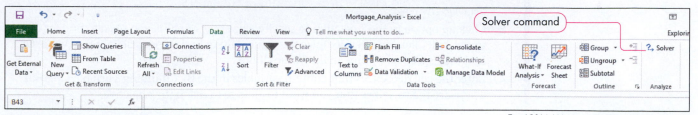

FIGURE 6.33 Solver on Data Tab

Excel 2016, Windows 10, Microsoft Corporation

> **TIP: SOLVER**
>
> If you are working in a campus computer lab, your institution may prevent you from loading applications, such as Solver. Check with your instructor if your system in the lab prevents you from loading Solver.

Optimizing Results with Solver

Solver may be the best what-if analysis tool to solve complex linear and nonlinear problems. You can use it for complex equation solving and for constrained optimization, where a set of constraints is specified and you want the outcome to be minimized or maximized. With Solver, you are able to change the values of several variables at once to achieve the desired result. For example, a business analyst might want to use Solver to maximize profits by changing selected variables while adhering to required limitations. Or a fulfillment company might want to determine the lowest shipping costs to transfer merchandise from a distribution center to retail stores.

Identify the Objective Cell and Changing Cells

STEP 2 ❯❯ Before using Solver, review your spreadsheet as you specify the goal, identify one or more variables that can change to reach the desired goal, and determine the limitations of the model. You will use these data to specify three parameters in Solver: objective cell, changing cells, and constraints.

The ***objective cell*** specifies the cell that contains a formula that produces a value that you want to optimize (that is, maximize, minimize, or set to a value) by manipulating values of one or more variables. The formula in the objective cell relates directly or indirectly to the changing cells and constraints. Using the mortgage case study as an example, the objective cell is B14 (the cell containing the total interest paid formula), and your goal is to minimize the total interest.

The ***changing variable cells*** are the cells containing variables whose values change within the constraints until the objective cell reaches its optimum value. The changing variable cells typically contain values, not formulas, but these cells have a mathematical relationship to the formula in the objective. In the home loan example, the changing variable cells are B3 (down payment) and B5 (number of years). You can select up to 200 changing variable cells.

To specify the objective and changing cells, complete the following steps:

1. Click Solver in the Analyze group on the Data tab to open the Solver Parameters dialog box (see Figure 6.34).

2. Enter the cell containing the formula for which you want to optimize its value in the *Set Objective* box.

3. Click an option in the *To* section to specify what type of value you need to find for the target cell. Click Max to maximize the value, Min to find the lowest value, or Value Of, and then specify the value in the Value Of box.

4. Enter the cell references that contain variables in the By Changing Variable Cells box. These are the variables that you want to change to reach the objective.

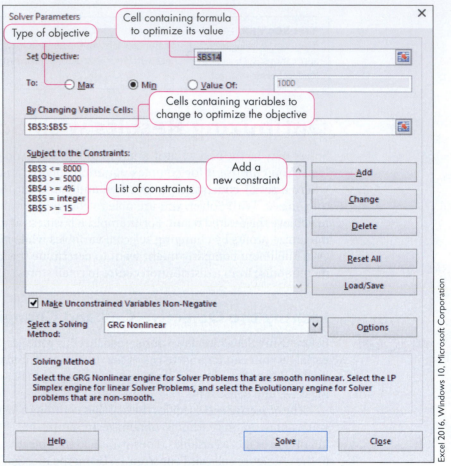

FIGURE 6.34 Solver Parameters Dialog Box

Define Constraints

STEP 3 ▶▶ The **constraints** specify the restrictions or limitations imposed on a spreadsheet model as Solver determines the optimum value for the objective cell. Rules govern every business model, based on historical requirements, physical limitations, and other decisions. Probably the most challenging process in using Solver is identifying all legitimate limitations. You may identify limitations through conversations with your supervisor, by reading policy statements, gathering information in meetings, and so on. Even after you enter data into Solver and run a report, you may gain knowledge of other limitations that you must build into the model. Using the home loan example, a constraint might be that the down payment must be between $5,000 and $8,000.

To add constraints to the Solver, complete the following steps:

1. Click Add to the right of the *Subject to the Constraints* list in Solver Parameters to open the Add Constraint dialog box.

2. Enter the cell reference, the operator to test the cell reference, and the constraint the cell needs to match (see Figure 6.35). The cell reference contains a variable whose value you want to constrain or restrict to a particular value or range. The operator defines the relationship between the variable and the constraint. For example, cell B3 (the down payment) is restricted to being less than or equal to $8,000. Solver will not allow the down payment to be higher than this value.

3. Click OK to add the constraint and return to the Solver Parameters dialog box, or click Add to add the constraint and create another constraint.

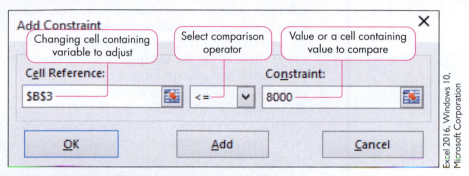

FIGURE 6.35 Add Constraint Dialog Box

> **TIP: INTEGER CONSTRAINT**
> One of the constraint operators is *integer*. This constraint requires the changing variable cell to be an integer, or whole number. For example, a manufacturing plant does not produce partial units such as 135.62 units, and a department store does not sell 18.32 shirts. To ensure that Solver produces realistic results, you should create integer constraints for these types of quantities. In Figure 6.34, the constraint $B$5 = integer limits the number of years for the loan to be a whole number.

To modify a constraint's definition, select the constraint in the *Subject to the Constraints* list and click Change. Make changes in the Change Constraint dialog box and click OK to update the definition. If you no longer need a constraint, select it in the *Subject to the Constraints* list and click Delete. Be careful when using Delete; Solver does not prompt you to confirm the deletion. Solver deletes the selected constraint immediately, and you cannot restore the deleted constraint.

> **TIP: GREATER-THAN-ZERO CONSTRAINT**
> Another often overlooked constraint is the requirement that the value of a variable cell be greater than or equal to zero. Physically, it makes no sense to produce a negative number of products in any category. Mathematically, however, a negative value in a changing variable cell may produce a higher value for the objective cell. By default, the Make Unconstrained Variables Non-Negative check box is selected to ensure variable values are greater than or equal to zero. If you want to allow the lower end of a variable's value to be a negative value, you can create a constraint such as B2>=-100. That constraint takes priority over the Make Unconstrained Variables Non-Negative check box.

Create a Solver Report

STEP 4 ›› After defining the objective, changing variable cells, and constraints, select a solving method. Solver uses the selected solving method to determine which type of algorithms it executes to reach the objective. The Solver add-in for Excel contains these solving methods: GRG Nonlinear, Simplex LP, and Evolutionary. Look up *Solver* in Help to link to a specific set of descriptions of these methods. You can also review additional information and download additional add-ins on www.solver.com. For the purposes of this chapter, accept the default option, GRG Nonlinear.

You are now ready to use Solver to find a solution to the problem. Solver uses an iterative process of using different combinations of values in the changing variable cells to identify the optimum value for the objective cell. It starts with the current values and adjusts those values in accordance with the constraints. Once it finds the best solution, given the parameters you set, it identifies the values for the changing variable cells and shows you the optimum value in the objective value. If Solver cannot determine an optimum value, it does not enable you to generate summary reports.

To create a Solver report, complete the following steps:

1. Click Solve in the Solver Parameters dialog box. When Solver completes the iterative process, the Solver Results dialog box appears (see Figure 6.36). If it finds a solution, the Reports list displays available report types. If Solver cannot reach an optimal solution, no reports are available. Solutions are unattainable if a logic error exists or if the constraints do not allow sufficient elasticity to achieve a result. For example, a constraint between 10 and 11 may not allow sufficient flexibility, or a constraint greater than 20 but also less than 10 is illogical. If this happens, check each constraint for range constraints or errors in logic.

2. Click Keep Solver Solution to keep the changed objective and variable values, or click Restore Original Values to return to the original values in the worksheet. If you keep the changed values, Excel makes those changes to the actual worksheet. Do this if you are comfortable with those changes. If you want to maintain the original values, you should restore the original values.

3. Select a report from the Reports list. Generating a report is appropriate to see what changes Solver made while preserving the original values in the worksheet from Step 2.

4. Click OK to generate the summary on a separate worksheet.

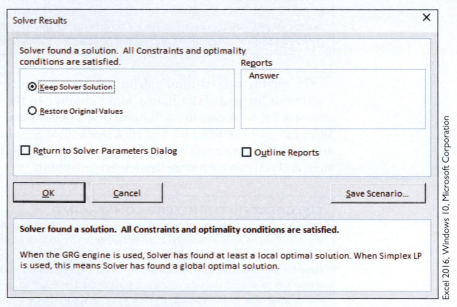

FIGURE 6.36 Solver Results Dialog Box

Solver creates a new worksheet for the Solver summary report containing four major sections (see Figure 6.37). The first section displays information about the Solver report. Specifically, it displays the report type, file name and worksheet containing the dataset, date and time the report was generated, Solver Engine details, and Solver Options that were set at the time the report was generated.

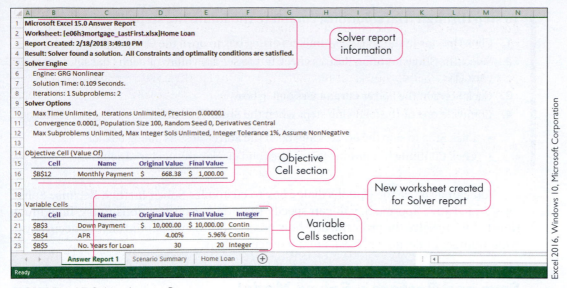

FIGURE 6.37 Solver Answer Report

The remaining sections of the report help you analyze the results. The section displays the objective cell information. Specifically, this section shows the original and final objective cell values. For example, using the original worksheet values, the original total interest paid in cell B14 was $100,617.31. The final minimized total interest paid is $47,064.23.

The third section displays the variable cells. Specifically, it displays the cell references, the variable cell names, original values, and final values. For example, the original down payment was $10,000, and the final value is $8,000.

The final section lists the constraints. It displays the cell reference, description, new cell value, formula, status, and slack for each defined constraint. In this case, the down payment slack ($3,000) is the difference between the lower constraint ($5,000) and the final value ($8,000). The Status column indicates Binding or Not Binding. A **binding constraint** is a rule that Solver has to enforce to reach the objective value. That is, the value hits the maximum allowable value for a less-than-or-equal-to, minimum allowable value for a greater-than-or-equal-to, equal to, or integer constraint. For example, $B$3<=8000 is a binding constraint. That is, the down payment was raised to its maximum limit of $8,000 to identify the optimal least amount of total interest paid. If this constraint had not been set, Solver could have identified a higher down payment to obtain a lower value for the objective cell. A **nonbinding constraint** is one that does not restrict the target value that Solver finds. For example, $B$3>=5000 is nonbinding. Solver did not have to stop at a lowest down payment of $5,000 to reach the optimal total interest paid value.

If you change any of the Solver parameters—objective cell, changing variable cells, or constraints—you need to generate another report. Solver does not update the report automatically. Each time you generate a report, Solver creates another new worksheet with names like Answer Report 1, Answer Report 2, and so on. Delete any reports you no longer need to minimize the file size of your workbook.

> **TIP: SAVE SCENARIO**
> If you want to save the solution parameters to use in Scenario Manager, click Save Scenario in the Solver Results dialog box and type a name for the scenario in the *Scenario name* box.

Configure Solver

You can closely monitor the trial solutions prior to reaching the final solution. Solver is a mathematical modeling operation, and you can determine solutions using the associated mathematics. However, stepping through Solver enables you to view the steps Solver performs.

You can also use the Options dialog box to customize Solver further. Because Solver uses an iterative approach, you can specify the number of iterations to try, how much time to take to solve the problem, and how precise the answer should be (i.e., accuracy to what number of decimal places), among other settings.

Save and Restore a Solver Model

When you use Solver, Excel keeps track of your settings and saves only the most recent Solver settings. In some cases, you may want to save the parameters of a model so that you can apply them again in the future. Saving a Solver model is helpful if the original data source might change and you want to compare results by generating multiple Solver answer reports. When you save a Solver model, you save the objective value, the changing variable cells, and the constraints.

When you save a Solver model, Excel places the information in a small block of cells on a worksheet. The number of cells required to save the Solver model is dependent on the number of constraints in the model.

If you want to use an existing Solver model with new or updated data, you must return to a previous Solver model.

Quick Concepts

10. What is the advantage of using Solver over Goal Seek? *p. 428*

11. What three optimization goals can Solver calculate? *p. 429*

12. When using Solver why would you define a constraint as an integer? *p. 431*

Watch the Video for this Hands-On Exercise!

MyITLab®
HOE4 Training

Skills covered: Load the Solver Add-In • Identify the Objective Cell and Changing Cells • Define Constraints • Create a Solver Report

4 Solver

Although Goal Seek and Scenario Manager were helpful in further analyzing your home purchase, you want to ensure the spreadsheet model imposes constraints on the situation. Therefore, you will continue your analysis by using Solver.

STEP 1 ›› LOAD THE SOLVER ADD-IN

Before you can use Solver to analyze your home loan model, you need to load Solver. If Solver is already loaded, skip Step 1 and start with Step 2. Refer to Figure 6.38 as you complete Step 1.

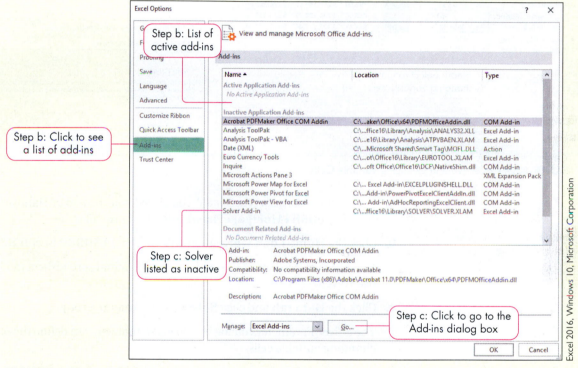

FIGURE 6.38 Excel Options Dialog Box

a. Click the **File tab** and click **Options**.

The Excel Options dialog box opens so that you can customize Excel settings.

b. Click **Add-ins** on the left side of the Excel Options dialog box.

The Excel Options dialog box displays a list of active and inactive application add-ins.

c. Check to see where Solver is listed. If Solver is listed in the Active Application Add-ins list, click **Cancel**, and then skip Step d. If Solver is listed in the Inactive Application Add-ins list, click the **Manage arrow**, select **Excel Add-ins,** and then click **Go**.

The Add-Ins dialog box opens, containing a list of available add-in applications.

d. Click the **Solver Add-in check box** in the Add-ins available list and click **OK**.

Before using Solver, you want to reset the variables to their original values. After entering the original variable values again, you will specify the monthly payment cell as the objective cell and the home cost, down payment, APR, and number of years for the loan as the changing variable cells. Refer to Figure 6.39 as you complete Step 2.

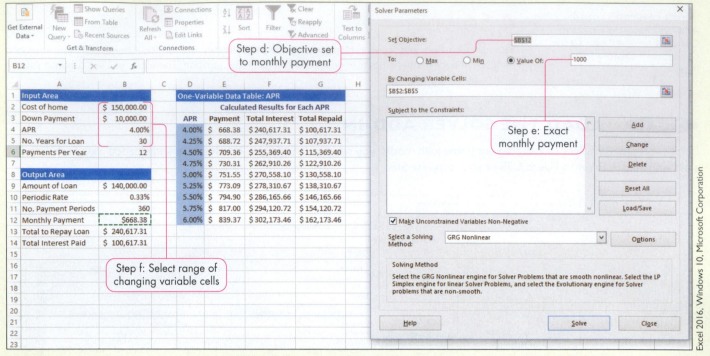

FIGURE 6.39 Objective and Changing Variable Cells

a. Open *e06h3Mortgage_LastFirst* if you closed it at the end of Hands-On Exercise 3, and save it as **e06h4Mortgage_LastFirst**, changing h3 to h4.

b. Click the **Home Loan worksheet tab** and type **150000** in **cell B2**. Press **Ctrl+Enter**.

Now that you have reset the values to your original spreadsheet model, you are ready to use Solver.

c. Click the **Data tab** and click **Solver** in the Analyze group.

The Solver Parameters dialog box opens so that you can define the objective and changing variable cells.

d. Click **cell B12** to enter it in the Set Objective box.

You set the objective cell as the monthly payment.

e. Click **Value Of** and type **1000** in the Value Of box.

You specified that you want an exact $1,000 monthly home payment.

f. Click in the **By Changing Variable Cells box** and select the **range B2:B5**. Click **Close**.

> **TROUBLESHOOTING:** Be careful to select the correct range. If you accidentally select cell B6, Solver might produce inaccurate results.

g. Save the workbook.

You define the constraints: $100,000 to $300,000 cost, $5,000 to $10,000 down payment, 4% to 6% APR, and 15- to 30-year loan. In addition, you set an integer constraint for the years so that Solver does not produce a fractional year, such as 5.71. Refer to Figure 6.40 as you complete Step 3.

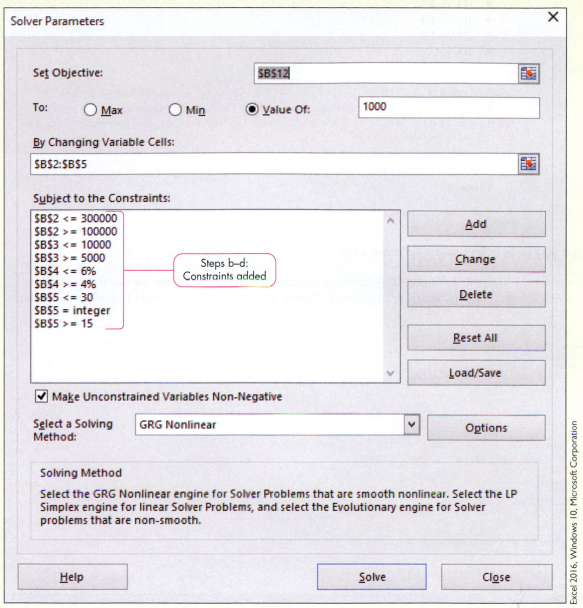

FIGURE 6.40 Constraints

a. Click **Solver** in the Analyze group and click **Add**.

The Add Constraint dialog box opens so that you can define the first constraint.

b. Click **cell B2**, make sure **<=** is selected, click in the **Constraint box**, and then type **300000**.

You defined a constraint that the total home cost cannot exceed $300,000.

c. Click **Add** to define another constraint. Click **cell B2**, click the **operator arrow**, select **>=**, click in the **Constraint box**, and then type **100000**.

The second constraint specifies that the cost of the home must be at least $100,000.

d. Add the following constraints in a similar manner. After you enter the last constraint, click **OK** in the *Add Constraint* dialog box.

- **B3<=10000**
- **B3>=5000**
- **B4<=6%**
- **B4>=4%**
- **B5<=30**
- **B5>=15**
- **B5 int**

> **TROUBLESHOOTING:** Click Add to complete the current constraint and open an Add Constraint dialog box to enter another constraint. Click OK in the Add Constraint dialog box only when you have completed the last constraint and want to return to the Solver Parameters dialog box to solve the problem.

e. Check the constraints carefully against those shown in Figure 6.39 and Step d. Click **Close**.

f. Save the workbook.

STEP 4 ▶▶ **CREATE A SOLVER REPORT**

Now that you have completed the parameters for restricting the result based on the cost of the home, the down payment, the APR, and the number of years for the loan, you are ready to generate a Solver report. Refer to Figure 6.41 as you complete Step 4.

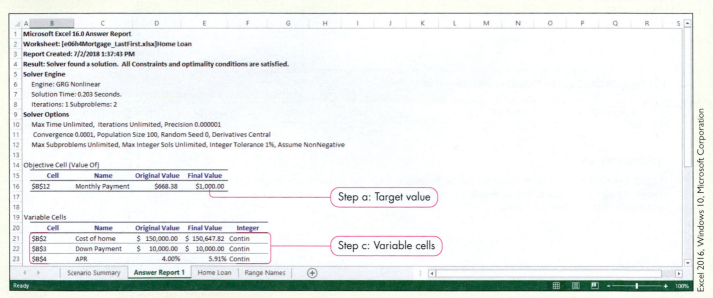

FIGURE 6.41 Solver Answer Report

a. Click **Solver** in the Analyze group and click **Solve**.

The Solver Results dialog box opens. Look at the worksheet data, the new values appear in the changing cells, and the $1000 target monthly payment appears in cell B12.

b. Select **Answer** in the Reports list and click **OK**.

Solver generates a report and displays it in a new worksheet named Answer Report 1.

> **TROUBLESHOOTING:** If you see the error message, *Solver: An unexpected internal error occurred, or available memory was exhausted*, close Solver, click Undo, remove Solver as an add-in, save and close the workbook, open the workbook again, and then enable the Solver add-in again. Then click Solver in the Analyze group, click Solve, select Answer Report, and then click OK.

c. Click the **Answer Report 1 worksheet tab**.

Solver adjusts the values in the changing cells B2:B5 to obtain the exact value of $1000 for the objective cell B12. The report shows the previous and final values of the objective and variable cells. Your final values may vary slightly from those shown in the figure.

d. Scroll down through the worksheet to see the constraints.

In addition, the report displays the constraints—cell references, descriptive labels, current cell values, formulas, status (binding/not binding), and slack. Although not specified, integer constraints are always binding. Had you not constrained the years to a whole number, Solver might have found different values for the variable cells. However, you need to enforce that constraint because the term of the mortgage is a whole year. The 4% APR constraint is binding, meaning that Solver found the lowest possible APR to produce its answer. Finally, the 30-year limit is binding, meaning that Solver could not use a larger number of years for the loan to derive its answer.

e. Save and close the file. Based on your instructor's directions, submit e06h4Mortgage_LastFirst.

Chapter Objectives Review

After reading this chapter, you have accomplished the following objectives:

1. Create and maintain range names.

- Create a range name: You can use range names in formulas to make the formulas easier to interpret by using a descriptive name for the value(s) contained in a cell or range.
- Edit or delete a range name: Once created, ranges names can be added, edited, or deleted.
- Use range names in formulas: Range names can be used in formulas and will replace the traditional cell reference when using autocomplete.
- Insert a list of range names: A list of range names can automatically be inserted into a workbook for documentation purposes.

2. Create a one-variable data table.

- A one-variable data table enables you to compare different values for one variable to compare the effects on one or more results.
- Set up one-variable substitution values: Substitution values replace the original value of a variable in a data table.
- Add formulas to the one-variable data table: After entering a substitution value, a formula must be added to relate mathematically to the substitution values.
- Calculate results: Excel uses the substitution values individually to replace the original variables to populate the data table.
- Format a one-variable data table: After completing the data table, all values should be appropriately formatted.

3. Create a two-variable data table.

- A two-variable data table enables you to compare results for two variables at the same time but for only one result.
- Set up the substitution values for two variables: Use the top row for one variable's substitution values and the first column for the second variable's substitution values.
- Add a formula to the data table: Enter the required formula in the top-left corner of the data table.
- Calculate results for a two-variable data table: Select the data table boundaries, then choose Data Table from the What-If Analysis group.

4. Determine optimal input values using Goal Seek.

- Use Goal Seek to work backward with a problem when you know what you want for the result but you do not know the value of a variable to achieve that goal. If you accept the results, Excel enters the identified input value directly in the variable cell.

5. Use Scenario Manager.

- Use Scenario Manager to create a set of scenarios, each with multiple variables.
- The Scenario Manager dialog box enables you to add, delete, and change scenarios.
- For each scenario, you specify a name, the changing cells, and the values for those changing cells.
- Create scenarios: Use the Scenario Manager Dialog box to create scenarios to help analyze possible outcomes.
- Add and edit scenarios: Sometimes analysis environments evolve and additional scenarios are required. Scenarios can be added or edited from the Scenario Manager Dialog box.
- View scenarios: After scenarios are created they can be reviewed in the Scenario Manager Dialog box.
- Generate a scenario summary report: After you create the scenarios with specific values, you can generate a summary report.
- Excel creates the summary report in a structured format on a new worksheet and displays the values for the changing cells and their effects on the results cells so that you can compare the results easily.

6. Load the Solver add-in.

- Solver is an add-in program for Excel. When you enable Solver, Excel places Solver in the Analyze group on the Data tab.

7. Optimize results with Solver.

- Solver is an optimization tool that enables you to maximize or minimize the value of an objective function, such as profit or cost. Solver uses an iterative process to use different values for variable cells until it finds the optimum objective value within the constraints you set.
- Identify the objective cell and changing cells: The objective cell contains the information that is to be set to value of, minimum, or maximum by Solver.
- Define constraints: Set in the Solver dialog box, constraints are limitations that are imposed on Solver.
- Create a Solver report: In the Solver Results dialog box, choose an option under Reports to have Excel create a report on a new worksheet.
- Configure Solver: Solver's calculation settings can be configured by clicking Options in the Solver Parameters dialog box.
- Save and restore a Solver model: A Solver model can be imported or exported by clicking Load/Save in the Solver Parameters dialog box.

Key Terms Matching

Match the key terms with their definitions. Write the key term letter by the appropriate numbered definition.

a. Add-in

b. Binding constraint

c. Changing variable cells

d. Constraint

e. Goal Seek

f. Nonbinding constraint

g. Objective cell

h. One-variable data table

i. Optimization model

j. Range name

k. Scenario

l. Scenario Manager

m. Scenario summary report

n. Solver

o. Substitution value

p. Two-variable data table

q. Variable

r. What-if analysis

1. _____ A constraint that Solver must enforce to reach the target value. **p. 433**

2. _____ A cell containing a variable whose value changes until Solver optimizes the value in the objective cell. **p. 429**

3. _____ An add-in application that manipulates variables based on constraints to find the optimal solution to a problem. **p. 428**

4. _____ A data analysis tool that provides various results based on changing one variable. **p. 406**

5. _____ A set of values that represent a possible situation. **p. 419**

6. _____ The cell that contains the formula-based value that you want to maximize, minimize, or set to a value in Solver. **p. 429**

7. _____ Finds the highest, lowest, or exact value for one particular result by adjusting values for selected variables. **p. 428**

8. _____ A constraint that does not restrict the target value that Solver finds. **p. 433**

9. _____ The process of changing variables to observe how changes affect calculated results. **p. 406**

10. _____ A value that you can change to see how that change affects other values. **p. 406**

11. _____ Replaces the original value of a variable in a data table. **p. 406**

12. _____ A limitation that imposes restrictions on Solver. **p. 430**

13. _____ A program that can be added to Excel to provide enhanced functionality. **p. 428**

14. _____ A worksheet that contains scenario results. **p. 421**

15. _____ A data analysis tool that provides results based on changing two variables. **p. 410**

16. _____ A tool that identifies the necessary input value to obtain a desired goal. **p. 418**

17. _____ Enables you to define and manage scenarios to compare how they affect results. **p. 419**

18. _____ A word or string of characters that represents one or more cells. **p. 398**

Multiple Choice

1. Which what-if analysis tool is the best option for complex calculations requiring constrained optimization?

   (a) Goal Seek
   (b) Scenario Manager
   (c) Data Tables
   (d) Solver

2. What tool is used to edit pre-existing range names? (Check all that apply)

   (a) Name Box
   (b) Scenario Manager
   (c) Name Manager
   (d) Solver

3. Which tool is most effective when comparing the impact of various combinations of interest rates and down payments on a mortgage?

   (a) Goal Seek
   (b) Solver
   (c) Two-variable data table
   (d) Scenario Manager

4. This tool calculates the value required in a single cell to produce a desired result within a related cell.

   (a) Goal Seek
   (b) Solver
   (c) One- or two-variable data table
   (d) Scenario Manager

5. This analysis tool has the ability to handle multiple adjustable cells while minimizing, maximizing, or meeting goals.

   (a) Goal Seek
   (b) Solver
   (c) One- or two-variable data table
   (d) Scenario Manager

6. Which of the following is an Excel add-in?

   (a) Goal Seek
   (b) Solver
   (c) One- or two-variable data table
   (d) Scenario Manager

7. Which of the following is not an acceptable range name?

   (a) Apr
   (b) Rate_2018
   (c) 2018_Rate
   (d) Payment

8. What is the keyboard shortcut to paste range names?

   (a) F2
   (b) F3
   (c) F4
   (d) F5

9. Which of the following tools can incorporate constraints?

   (a) Goal Seek
   (b) Solver
   (c) Data Tables
   (d) Scenario Manager

10. How can you determine if the Solver add-in is active?

    (a) Solver is an option on the Home tab.
    (b) Solver is available via right-click.
    (c) Solver appears on the Data tab.
    (d) Solver appears in the Goal Seek dialog box to make it appear as a label.

Practice Exercises

1   Monthly Commission

You are a sales rep for Speedway International auto sales, an auto dealership that specializes in online sales. Each month you are paid 2% commission on all sales and you pay 4% income tax based on your current home office. You have decided to create an Excel worksheet and use one- and two-variable data tables to help predict your net income due to the variability in monthly sales and tax rate based on the sales location. You will also use Solver to help determine the exact amount of sales required to meet your monthly income goal and create range names to make your references easier to understand within your financial calculations. Refer to Figure 6.42 as you complete this exercise.

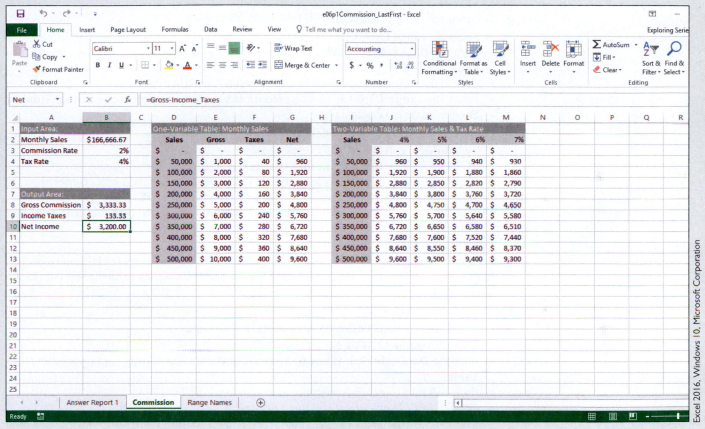

FIGURE 6.42

a. Open *e06p1Commission* and save it as **e06p1Commission_LastFirst**.

b. Select the **ranges A2:B4** and **A8:B10**. Click the **Formulas tab**, click **Create from Selection** in the Defined Names group, and click **OK**.

c. Click **Name Manager** and edit each of the newly created range names to the following then click close:

- **Commission_Rate = Commission**
- **Gross_Commission = Gross**
- **Net_Income = Net**
- **Monthly_Sales = Sales**

d. Use the named ranges created in the prior step to enter formulas in the following cells:

- **B8 = Sales*Commission**
- **B9 = Gross*Tax_Rate**
- **B10 = Gross-Income_Taxes**

e. Click **cell D3** and complete the following steps to enter a series of substitution values for the bonus percentage:

- Type **0.00** and press **Ctrl+Enter** to keep **cell D3** active.
- Click **Fill** in the Editing group on the Home tab and select **Series**.
- Click **Columns** in the *Series in* section, type **50000** in the *Step value* box, type **500000** in the *Stop value box*, and then click **OK**.
- Adjust the width of Column D to **11**

f. Enter the references to formulas in the following cells:

- **Cell E2: =Gross**
- **Cell F2: =Income_Taxes**
- **Cell G2: =Net**

g. Complete the one-variable data table by doing the following:

- Select the **range D2:G13**.
- Click the **Data tab**, click **What-If Analysis** in the Forecast group, and then select **Data Table**.
- Click in the **Column input cell box**, click **cell B2**, and then click **OK**.
- Select the **range E3:G13**, click the **Home tab**, and then select **Accounting Number Format** with zero decimal places.

h. Create column headings for the data table by doing the following:

- Type **Sales** in **cell D2**.
- Click **cell E2** and click the **Number Dialog Box Launcher** in the Number group.
- Click **Custom** in the Category list, scroll up in the Type list, and then select **General**.
- Select **General** in the Type box, type **"Gross"**, and then click **OK**.
- Adapt the above steps to create a custom number format to display **Taxes** in cell F2 and **Net** in cell G2.
- Center and bold the range D2:G2.

i. Set up the variables for the two-variable data table by copying the range D3:D13 and pasting it in the range I3:I13. Enter **4%** in cell J2 and use the Series dialog box to fill the row data to **7%** in steps of **1%**.

j. Type **=Net** in **cell I2**.

k. Complete the two-variable data table by doing the following:

- Select the **range I2:M13**.
- Click the **Data tab**, click **What-If Analysis** in the Forecast group, and then select **Data Table**.
- Click **cell B4** to enter that reference in the *Row input cell* box.
- Click in the **Column input cell box**, click **cell B2**, and then click **OK**.
- Select the **range J3:M13** and apply **Accounting Number Format** with zero decimal places.
- Apply a custom number format to display **"Sales"**, which was created in Step h, to cell I2. Bold and center data in this cell.

l. Select **cell B10**, click the **Data tab**, select **Solver** in the Analyze group and enter the following parameters.

- **Set Objective = Net**
- **To Value of: = 3200**
- **By Changing Variable Cells: Sales, Tax_Rate**

m. Click **Add** and enter the constraint **Tax_Rate <= 7%**.

n. Click **Add**, enter the constraint **Tax_Rate >=4%**, and click **OK**.

o. Click **Solve** and create an Answer Report.

p. Create a new worksheet named **Range Names**. Click **cell A1** and paste a list of the range names in the newly created worksheet.

q. Create a footer with your name on the left side, the sheet name code in the center, and the file name code on the right side.

r. Save and close the workbook. Based on your instructor's directions, submit e06p1Commission_LastFirst.

Sue has opened a bakery specializing in cupcakes. Her budget must account for fixed expenses, such as her facility lease, utilities, and credit card equipment fees. In addition, she accounts for variable costs including cost of goods sold and credit card processing fees. You will use Goal Seek to determine how many cupcakes she must sell to earn a net profit of $3,500. You then will use Scenario Manager to evaluate several possible situations. Refer to Figure 6.43 as you complete this exercise.

	A	B	C
1			
2	Sue's Bakery Budget		
3			
4	**Forecasts**		
5	Cupcakes sold (units sold)	1260	
6	Unit price	$ 0.75	
7	Sales price	$ 4.25	
8	Percentage of credit card sales per month	95%	
9	Credit Card Swipes per Month	375	
10	Credit Card Transaction Rate	1.25%	
11	Credit Card Cost per Swipe	$ 0.15	
12			
13	**Income**		
14	Income from cash	$ 267.75	
15	Income from credit	$5,087.25	
16	**Total income**	$5,355.00	
17			
18	**Fixed Costs**		
19	Lease	$ 525.00	
20	Utilities	$ 250.00	
21	Credit Card Equipment Fee	$ 15.00	
22	**Total**	$ 790.00	
23			
24	**Variable Costs**		
25	Costs of goods sold	$ 945.00	
26	Credit Card Processing Fees	$ 120.00	
27	**Total**	$1,065.00	
28			
29	**Net Profit**	$3,500.00	
30			
31			

Scenario Summary | **Budget**

Ready

Excel 2016, Windows 10, Microsoft Corporation

FIGURE 6.43

a. Open *e06p2Bakery* and save it as **e06p2Bakery_LastFirst**.

b. Enter the following formulas:
- **Cell B14**: **=B16-B16*B8** to calculate the projected cash sales amount of the total sales.
- **Cell B15**: **=B16-B14** to calculate the amount of income from credit card transactions.
- **Cell B25**: **=B5*B6** to calculate the cost of goods sold, which is the product of the units sold and unit cost.
- **Cell B26**: **=(B10*B15)+(B9*B11)** to calculate credit card processing fees, which are currently 1.25% of credit card amounts and $0.15 cents per transaction.
- **Cell B29**: **=B16-B22-B27** to calculate the net profit.

c. Click the **Data tab**, click **What-If Analysis** in the Forecast group, and then select **Goal Seek**.

d. Complete the Goal Seek by doing the following:
- Click **cell B29** to add the cell reference to the *Set cell* box.
- Click in the **To value box** and type **3500**.
- Click in the **By changing cell box** and click **cell B5**.
- Click **OK** in the Goal Seek dialog box and click **OK** in the Goal Seek Status dialog box. How many cupcakes must Sue sell to reach her net profit goal of $3,500? Answer: 1,260.

e. Click **What-If Analysis** in the Forecast group and select **Scenario Manager**.

f. Create the first scenario by doing the following:
- Click **Add** and type **Current Conditions** in the Scenario name box.
- Click in the **Changing cells box**, select the **range B5:B7**, and then press and hold **Ctrl** while you select the **range B9:B10**.
- Click in the **Comment box** edit it to reflect your name, such as "Created by Jason Davidson on 9/4/2018," and then click **OK**.
- Type **700** in the $B$5 box, leave the other current values intact, and then click **OK**.

g. Create the following three scenarios, clicking either **Add** or **OK** as indicated:

Scenario Name	Ideal Case	Increased Costs	Low Sales
$B$5	1,260	700	500
$B$6	.75	.75	.75
$B$7	4.25	4.50	4.00
$B$9	375	275	150
$B$10	1.25%	2.49%	1.25%

h. Click **Summary**, select and delete the suggested range in the Result cells box, press and hold **Ctrl** as you click **cells B16, B22, B27**, and **B29** to enter these cells, and then click **OK**.

i. Make these changes to the summary on the Scenario Summary worksheet:
- Delete the blank column A, the Current Values column, the blank row 1, and the notes in the **range A15:A17**.
- Click in **cell A5**, type **Units Sold**, and then press **Enter**.
- Type **Unit Cost**, **Sale Price**, **Credit Card Swipes**, and **Card Transaction Rate** in the range A6:A9.
- Type **Gross Sales**, **Fixed Costs**, **Variable Costs**, and **Profit** in the range A11:A14.
- Increase the width of column A to display the labels.
- Delete column B containing the cell references because these references would have no meaning if you distribute only the scenario summary worksheet to others.

j. Create a footer with your name on the left side, the sheet name code in the center, and the file name code on the right side.

k. Save and close the workbook. Based on your instructor's directions, submit e06p2Bakery_LastFirst.

Mid-Level Exercises

1 Housing Construction Cost Variables

Your friends, Elijah and Valerie Foglesong, want to build their dream house. They identified tentative costs, but they cannot afford the $414,717 estimated cost. You will use Goal Seek to determine an estimate of the total finished square footage they can afford. To help provide more flexibility in their decision making, you will create a data table listing various finished square footages and their effects on the base house cost and total cost. Finally, you will create another data table showing combinations of square footages and lot prices to identify total costs. Although a builder's overall house design specifies the square footage, the Foglesongs can use your data tables to help guide them in their decision.

a. Open *e06m1House* and save it as **e06m1House_LastFirst**.

b. Select the **cells B9, B15, B21, B23**, and assign appropriate range names.

c. Click **cell B25** and use the newly created range names to create a formula to calculate the total house cost.

d. Use Goal Seek to determine the total finished square footage to meet the total cost goal of $350,000.

e. Enter a series of total square footages ranging from 1,800 to 3,600 in increments of 200 in the range D6:D15. Apply **Blue font color** and **Comma Style** with zero decimal places to the series. Enter references to the base cost and total cost in the appropriate cells on row 5.

f. Complete the data table using the appropriate input cell. Apply custom number formats to give appropriate descriptions to the second and third columns. Apply these formats to the headings: bold, center, and **Blue font color**.

g. Identify the square footage, base price, and total cost that come closest to their goal. Apply **Blue, Accent 1, Lighter 40% fill color** to those cells in the data table.

h. Copy the square footage substitution values to the range H6:H15 and remove the fill color. Enter these lot price substitution values in the range I5:K5: **90000, 96000**, and **102675**. Format these values with **Accounting Number Format** with zero decimal places and **Blue font color**.

i. Enter the reference to the total cost formula in the appropriate location for the second data table. Complete the data table using the appropriate input cells. Apply a custom number format to the reference to the formula cell. Apply bold and **Blue font color** to that cell. Apply **Blue, Accent 1, Lighter 40% fill color** to the total price in each column that comes closest to their goal.

j. Format results in both tables with **Accounting Number Format** with zero decimal places.

k. Create a footer with your name on the left side, the sheet name code in the center, and the file name code on the right side. Adjust the orientation, margins, and scaling to fit on one page.

l. Save and close the workbook. Based on your instructor's directions, submit e06m1House_LastFirst.

2 Viking Heating and Air

ANALYSIS CASE

You are the chief financial officer for Viking Heating and Air. You were given the task of increasing gross income from $91,000 to $120,000 per year. Viking's income is earned through service calls. Customers are charged trip and hourly charges as pictured in the table below. Your goal is to create a spreadsheet to enable you to evaluate the most economically feasible option for increasing gross income while adhering to the following constraints. The maximum amount of hours billed without hiring additional technicians is 2,500. The trip charge may not exceed $50.00, and the service hourly rate/trip charge must all be whole numbers. The calls/hourly rate/trip charge must all be whole numbers.

a. Open *e06m2VikingAC* and save it as **e06m2VikingAC_LastFirst**.

b. Create range names based on the values in the **range A2:B5**.

c. Use the formula **Service_calls * Trip_charge + Hourly_rate* Hours_billed** to determine gross income.

d. Load the Solver add-in.

e. Set the objective cell to **$120,000**.

f. Set constraints to ensure service calls, hourly rate, and trip charge are integers.

g. Set a constraint to ensure hours billed cannot exceed 2,500.

h. Set a constraint to ensure the trip charge does not exceed $50.00.

i. Set a constraint to ensure hourly rate does not drop below $30.00.

j. Create an Answer Report to outline your findings.

DISCOVER

k. After solving, answer the questions in the Q&A section.

l. Create a footer with your name on the left side, the sheet name code in the center, and the file name code on the right side.

m. Save and close the file. Based on your instructor's directions, submit e06m2VikingAC_LastFirst.

---

3 College Budget

COLLABORATION CASE

FROM SCRATCH

You are beginning your freshman year of college. Prior to leaving for school, you worked a summer job and were able to save $1,500 for expenses such as books, supplies, and a university parking pass. After arriving on campus, you discover your computer is out of date, and you need to purchase a newer model. Your books cost $700, a mini-fridge for your room costs $250, and you are estimating your parking pass will cost $350. After researching pricing for newer computers, you determine a new computer will cost $750. Your parents have agreed to give you the additional money required to purchase the computer; however, they will only do so if you send them an Excel workbook outlining your expenses and the amount of money that they must contribute to the purchase. You have decided to create this document and then share the file with your parents through your family's OneDrive account. Before sharing the final document, you will first send the file to a classmate for additional assistance in researching prices.

Student 1:

a. Open Excel and create a blank workbook. Save this document as **e06m3CollegeBudget_LastFirst**.

b. Type headings for item Description and Expense in the **range A1:B1**.

c. Click in cell A2, type the name of your first expense—for example, **Parking Pass**—and then enter the corresponding cost in cell B2.

d. Continue entering your expenses in cells A3:B3 for books and in cell A4:B4 for the mini-fridge. Type **Total expenses** in cell A5, and enter a SUM function in cell B5 to total your expenses.

e. Highlight cells A5:B5 and apply the **Bad cell style** from the Styles group located in the Home tab.

f. Click **cell D1**, type **Summer Savings**, and then type **1500** in cell D2. Then complete the following tasks:
- Type **Savings after expenses** in cell A6.
- Type **Computer cost** in cell A7.
- Type **Parental contribution** in cell A8.
- Type **Deficit** in cell A9.
- Type **750** in cell B7.
- Type **0** in cell B8.

g. Click in **cell B6** and type the following formula: **=D2-B5**. This calculates the remaining savings after expenses.

h. Click in **cell B9** and type the following formula: **=B7-B6-B8**. This calculates the financial deficit after the computer has been purchased. The goal is for this cell to have a value of zero after your parents' contribution.

i. Use Goal Seek to set the deficit to **0** by changing your parents' contribution amount.

j. Format the worksheet with the font and color of your choice. Apply **Accounting Number Format** to all numbers.

k. Save the workbook to OneDrive and share the file with student 2.

Student 2:

l. Open the worksheet and review the proposed budget.

m. Based on the budget, search the Web for going rates on a college-size mini-fridge. If you are able to locate a better price, update the dollar amount and upload back to OneDrive.

n. Save the workbook to OneDrive and share a link to the file via email with your instructor.

Beyond the Classroom

Too Cold to Snow
GENERAL CASE

Have you ever wondered whether it could be too cold to snow? Actually, it is much more likely to snow if the temperature is close to freezing than if it is much below. The reason is that the air gets too dry to snow. As the air gets colder, it holds less water vapor for making snow. This explains why Nashville, Tennessee, typically gets more snowfall each year than frigid Barrow, Alaska! Because snow in northern Alaska does not melt as quickly as snow in Nashville, the area appears to get more snow.

You are a high school science teacher preparing a lesson on the effect of temperature and water vapor on snowfall. The dew point is the temperature at which water vapor condenses and forms into liquid or frozen precipitation, and the wet bulb temperature is the lowest temperature that can be reached by the evaporation of water only. Typically, the greater the difference between wet bulb and air temperatures, the drier the air. Because drier air is less likely to produce snow, you will use the wet bulb temperature to approximate the dryness of the air and the potential for snow. Use the Internet to find the temperature and dew point of Nashville on January 6 of the current year and develop an estimate of the wet bulb temperature.

Open *e06b1Snow* and save it as **e06b1Snow_LastFirst**. Use Scenario Manager to create a Most Likely and Least Likely projection of wet bulb temperature for Nashville. The Most Likely statistics are those that you identified for January 6. The Least Likely statistics are a temperature of 18° and a dew point of 5°. Wet bulb temperature is calculated by subtracting dew point from temperature and dividing the result by 3. Edit the summary as specified in the *Generating Scenario Summary Reports* section in the chapter. Insert a text box and write an analysis about your results. Create a footer with your name, the sheet name code, and the file name code. Save and close the file. Based on your instructor's directions, submit e06b1Snow_LastFirst.

IT Management
DISASTER RECOVERY

You work as an IT manager for Bower Industries, a Web hosting company that provides off-site Web hosting for online business. Your current service level agreement promises customers 24/7 server availability; however, in the unlikely event of a server outage, you need to gauge the economic impact. Based on your current user base, you estimate a cost of $1,500 an hour in customer refunds if an outage were to occur. You have decided to create a one-variable data table to further estimate the economic impact of outages between 1 and 5 hours in length. Open *e06b2NetworkOutage* and save it as **e06b2NetworkOutage_LastFirst**. Add appropriate range names to the inputs **Cost Per Hour** and **Outage Duration**. Next create a formula to calculate total cost for an outage the lasts 3 hours. Your last step is to create a one-variable data table to detail the sensitivity of expense based on an outage range of 1–5 hours based on half-hour increments. Add appropriate labels as needed, then create a footer with your name, the sheet name code, and the file name code. Save and close the file. Based on your instructor's directions, submit e06b2NetworkOutage_LastFirst.

Capstone Exercise

You are the production manager for Delta Paint, a regional manufacturing company that specializes in customized paints. Your company sells paint by the gallon, and you have the task of forecasting the best production blends to maximize profit and most effectively utilize resources.

Range Names

Before using Excel's Analysis tools to help complete your forecasts, you will create range names for key input cells to simplify the creation of formulas moving forward.

a. Open *e06c1Manufacturing* and save it as **e06c1Manufacturing_LastFirst**.

b. Create appropriate range names for Total Production Cost (**cell B18**) and Gross Profit (**cell B21**).

c. Edit the existing name range **Employee_Hourly_Wage** to reflect the current year. Example: Hourly_Wages2018.

d. Use the newly created range names to create a formula to calculate Net Profit (**cell B22**).

e. Create a new worksheet labeled **Range Names**, paste the newly created range name information in **cell A1**, and resize the columns as needed for proper display.

Goal Seek

Currently, the company has 15,000 gallons of raw materials available for production. One gallon of paint requires 3 units of raw materials. Your next task is to determine how many units to produce in order to completely exhaust the resources available.

a. Use Goal Seek to determine the units that must be sold to exhaust the total inventory of raw materials.

b. Enter the values in the Q&A worksheet.

One-Variable Data Table

Your maximum weekly production capability is 200 gallons. You would like to create a one-variable data table to measure the impact of Production Cost, Gross Profit, and Net Profit based on selling between 10 and 200 gallons of paint within a week.

a. Start in cell E3. Complete the series of substitution values ranging from 10 to 200 at increments of 10 gallons vertically down column E.

b. Enter references to the **Total Production Cost**, **Gross Profit**, and **Net Profit** in the correct location for a one-variable data table.

c. Complete the one-variable data table, and then format the results with **Accounting Number Format** with two decimal places.

d. Apply custom number formats to make the formula references appear as descriptive column headings. Bold and center the headings and substitution values.

e. Answer question 2 on the Q&A worksheet. Save the workbook.

Two-Variable Data Table

Your company is considering raising the manufacturing employees' hourly wages. Employees are currently earning $15 per hour; however, you would like to review the impact of profit if the salaries were between $15 and $40 per hour. You will create a two-variable data table to complete the task.

a. Copy the number of gallons produced substitution values from the one-variable data table, and then paste the values starting in cell E26.

b. Type **$15** in cell F25. Complete the series of substitution values from $15 to $40 at $5 increments.

c. Enter the reference to net profit formula in the correct location for a two-variable data table.

d. Complete the two-variable data table and format the results with **Accounting Number Format** with two decimal places.

e. Apply a custom number format to make the formula reference appear as a descriptive column heading. Bold and center the headings and substitution values.

f. Answer questions 3 and 4 on the Q&A worksheet. Save the workbook.

Scenario Manager

To this point you have created forecasts based on static production amounts; however, it is important to plan for both positive and negative outcomes. To help you analyze best, worst, and most likely outcomes, you will use Scenario Manager.

a. Create a scenario named **Best Case**, using Units Sold, Unit Selling Price, and Employee Hourly Wage. Enter these values for the scenario: **200**, **30**, and **15**.

b. Create a second scenario named **Worst Case**, using the same changing cells. Enter these values for the scenario: **100**, **25**, and **20**.

c. Create a third scenario named **Most Likely**, using the same changing cells. Enter these values for the scenario: **150**, **25**, and **15**.

d. Generate a scenario summary report using the Total Production Cost and Net Income.

e. Format the summary as discussed in the chapter.

f. Answer question 5 on the Q&A worksheet. Save the workbook.

Use Solver

You realize the best-case scenario may not be realistic. You have decided to continue your analysis by using Solver to determine the perfect production blend to maximize net income while most efficiently using raw materials and labor hours.

a. Load the Solver add-in if it is not already loaded.

b. Set the objective to calculate the highest Net Income possible.

c. Use the units sold as changing variable cells.

d. Use the Limitations section of the spreadsheet model to set a constraint for raw materials.

e. Set constraints for labor hours.

f. Set constraints for maximum production capability.

g. Solve the problem. Generate the Answer Report. If you get an internal memory error message, remove Solver as an add-in, close the workbook, open the workbook, add Solver in again, and finish using Solver.

h. Answer questions 6 through 8 on the Q&A worksheet. Apply **landscape orientation** to the Q&A worksheet. Save the workbook.

i. Create a footer on all five worksheets with your name on the left side, the sheet name code in the center, and the file name code on the right side.

j. Save and close the file. Based on your instructor's directions, submit e06c1Manufacturing_LastFirst.

Excel

Specialized Functions

LEARNING OUTCOME: You will manipulate data using date, logical, lookup, database, and financial functions.

OBJECTIVES & SKILLS: After you read this chapter, you will be able to:

CASE STUDY | Transpayne Filtration

You are an assistant accountant in the Human Resources (HR) Department for Transpayne Filtration, a company that sells water filtration systems to residential customers. Transpayne has locations in Atlanta, Boston, and Chicago, with a manager at each location who oversees several account representatives. You have an Excel workbook that contains names, locations, titles, hire dates, and salaries for the 20 managers and account representatives. To prepare for your upcoming salary analyses, you downloaded salary data from the corporate database into the workbook.

The HR manager wants you to perform several tasks based on locations and job titles. You will use logical functions to calculate annual bonus amounts and database functions to help analyze the data. Finally, you will review financial aspects of automobiles purchased for each manager.

CHAPTER 7

Using Date, Logical, Lookup, Database, and Financial Functions

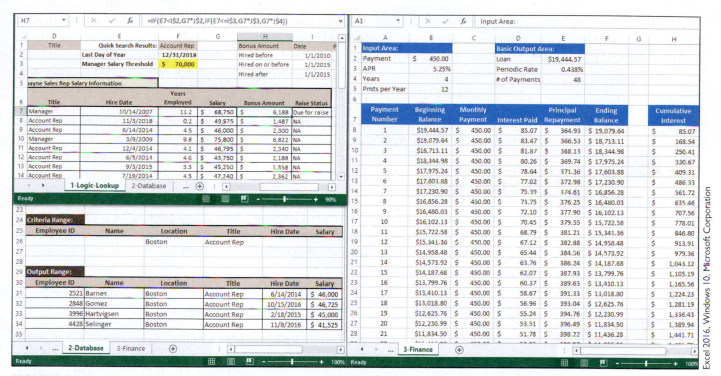

FIGURE 7.1 Transpayne Filtration Workbook

Case Study | Transpayne Filtration

Starting File	File to be Submitted
e07h1Salary	e07h3Salary_LastFirst

Date, Logical, and Lookup Functions

As you have learned, dates are stored as serial numbers. This method of storing dates enables you to perform calculations using cells that contain dates. The Date & Time category in the Function Library contains a variety of functions that work with dates. Previously, you used the TODAY function to return the current date and the NOW function to display the current date and time.

Logical functions enable you to test conditions to determine if a condition is true or false. You have used the IF function, which is the most commonly used logical function. Excel enables you to use two or more functions together to perform complex calculations. For example, people commonly use other functions within an IF function to evaluate complex logical conditions for multiple outcomes.

You have also used lookup and reference functions to look up a value contained elsewhere in a workbook. For example, you are familiar with the VLOOKUP and HLOOKUP functions, which take an identified value, such as the number of months for a certificate of deposit (CD) to mature, look up that value in a vertical or horizontal lookup table, and then obtain a related value, such as the annual percentage rate (APR). Excel contains additional logical functions to perform for more complicated referencing.

In this section, you will learn about some useful date functions and how to include a function as an argument inside another function. In addition, you will learn how to use the MATCH and INDEX lookup functions.

Using Date Functions

The Date & Time category in Excel's Function Library group includes a variety of date and time functions. You can use these functions to calculate when employees are eligible for certain benefits, what the date is six months from now, or what day of the week a particular date falls on.

Calculate Days and Years Between Dates

STEP 1 ❱❱ You might want to calculate the number of days or years between two dates. For example, if you work for a credit card company, you might want to calculate the number of days from a payment due date and the actual payment date. The **DAYS function** calculates the number of days between two dates where the most recent date is entered in the end_date argument and the older date is entered in the start_date argument. For example, if the end date is 9/30/2018 and the start date is 9/1/2018, the DAYS function calculates 29 days between those two dates (see the range A1:B3 in Figure 7.2). In cell E3, the DAYS function calculates 1,276 days between 1/1/2015 and 6/30/2018.

◢	A	B	C	D	E	F
1	Start Date	9/1/2018			1/1/2015	
2	End Date	9/30/2018			6/30/2018	
3	DAYS Function	29	=DAYS(B2,B1)		1276	=DAYS(E2,E1)
4	YEARFRAC Function	0.08	=YEARFRAC(B1,B2)		3.50	=YEARFRAC(E1,E2)
5						

FIGURE 7.2 DAYS and YEARFRAC Functions

Excel 2016, Windows 10, Microsoft Corporation

Instead of calculating the exact number of days between dates, you might want to calculate the fraction of a year or the number of years between two dates. The **YEARFRAC function** calculates the fraction of a year between two dates based on the number of whole days using the start_date and end_date arguments. In Figure 7.2, the YEARFRAC function in cell B4 calculates 8% of the year exists between 9/1/2018 and 9/30/2018. In cell E4, the YEARFRAC function calculates 3.5 years exist between 1/1/2015 and 6/30/2018. The DAYS and YEARFRAC functions use the same arguments (start_date and end_date) but in reverse order.

=DAYS(end_date,start_date)

=YEARFRAC(start_date,end_date)

Extract Day, Month, and Year

Often, a cell contains an exact date, such as 9/1/2018. However, you might want to extract part of the date, such as just the month, day, or year. For example, if you own a wedding catering business, you might review historical data to identify which month had the most weddings to cater. To do so, you would extract the months from dates when you catered weddings. The **DAY function** displays the day (1–31) within a given date. The **MONTH function** displays the month (1–12), where 1 is January and 12 is December, for a specific date. The **YEAR function** displays the year (such as 2018) for a specific date. Figure 7.3 illustrates two dates and the results of using the DAY, MONTH, and YEAR functions. The serial_number argument refers to the cell containing a date. If you want to enter a date directly in the argument, you must enclose the date in quotation marks, such as =DAY("6/30/2018").

=DAY(serial_number)

=MONTH(serial_number)

=YEAR(serial_number)

⊿	A	B	C	D	E	F
1	Dates	9/1/2018			30-Jun-18	
2						
3	DAY function	1	=DAY(B1)		30	=DAY(E1)
4	MONTH function	9	=MONTH(B1)		6	=MONTH(E1)
5	YEAR function	2018	=YEAR(B1)		2018	=YEAR(E1)

FIGURE 7.3 DAY, MONTH, and YEAR Functions

Excel 2016, Windows 10, Microsoft Corporation

TIP: EDATE AND EOMONTH FUNCTIONS

Two other date functions are useful. **EDATE** displays a date in the future or past, given a specific number of months. **EOMONTH** displays the last day of a month for a specified number of months from a particular date. For example, =EDATE("9/1/2018",3) displays 12/1/2018, three months from 9/1/2018, whereas =EOMONTH("9/1/2018",3) displays 12/31/2018, the end of the month three months from 9/1/2018.

The default result displays as a serial number, such as 43435 if the cell containing the function is formatted with General number format. To display the actual date, format the cell with Short Date number format.

Creating a Nested Logical Function

Recall from previous experience that the IF function contains three arguments: logical_test, value_if_true, and value_if_false. You can enter formulas within both the value_if_true and value_if_false arguments to perform calculations. For situations with multiple outcomes based on conditions, you can nest IF functions within the value_if_true and value_if_false arguments. A **nested function** is a function that is embedded within an argument of another function. You can nest up to 64 IF functions in the value_if_true and value_if_false arguments.

Nested IF Within an IF Function

STEP 2 ▶▶ When you have three outcomes for a situation, you can test one condition in the logical_test argument, display results if that condition is true in the value_if_true argument, and then test another condition by entering a nested IF function in the value_if_false argument. While the nested IF function can go in either the value_if_true or value_if_false argument, it helps for comprehending a nested IF function to keep the value_if_true argument simple.

For example, assume you want to calculate bonuses for employees based on hire date. You divided the hire dates into three timelines. If an employee was hired before 1/1/2010, the employee receives 9% of her or his salary as a bonus. If an employee was hired between 1/1/2010 and 1/1/2015, the employee earns a 5% bonus. Finally, employees hired after 1/1/2015 receive a 3% bonus (see Figure 7.4). Because this scenario has three possible outcomes for calculating bonuses, you use logical tests for two of the outcomes. If both logical tests are false, the third outcome is the result.

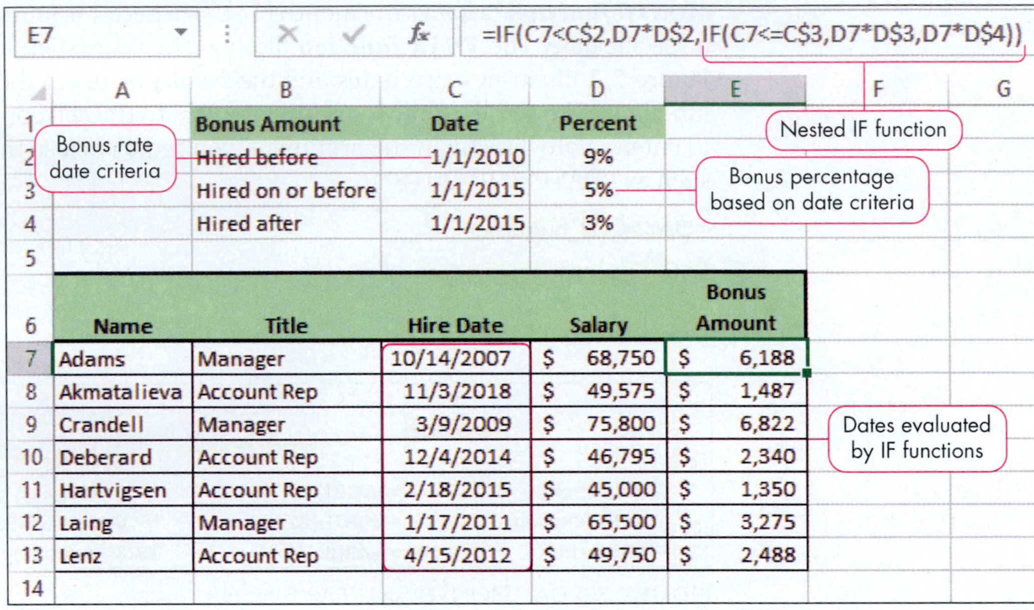

E7		×	✓	fx	=IF(C7<C$2,D7*D$2,IF(C7<=C$3,D7*D$3,D7*D$4))	

	A	B	C	D	E	F	G
1		Bonus Amount	Date	Percent			
2	Bonus rate date criteria	Hired before	1/1/2010	9%	Nested IF function		
3		Hired on or before	1/1/2015	5%	Bonus percentage based on date criteria		
4		Hired after	1/1/2015	3%			
5							
6	Name	Title	Hire Date	Salary	Bonus Amount		
7	Adams	Manager	10/14/2007	$ 68,750	$ 6,188		
8	Akmatalieva	Account Rep	11/3/2018	$ 49,575	$ 1,487		
9	Crandell	Manager	3/9/2009	$ 75,800	$ 6,822	Dates evaluated by IF functions	
10	Deberard	Account Rep	12/4/2014	$ 46,795	$ 2,340		
11	Hartvigsen	Account Rep	2/18/2015	$ 45,000	$ 1,350		
12	Laing	Manager	1/17/2011	$ 65,500	$ 3,275		
13	Lenz	Account Rep	4/15/2012	$ 49,750	$ 2,488		
14							

FIGURE 7.4 Nested IF Function Results

Figure 7.5 illustrates the bonus-calculation process as a flowchart. Diamonds are logical_test arguments, and rectangles are value_if_true and value_if_false arguments. The first logical_test evaluates if the employee was hired before 1/1/2010 (C7<C$2). If that test is TRUE, the salary is multiplied by 9% (D7*D$2). If that test is FALSE, the nested IF function in the value_if_false argument is executed. Figure 7.6 illustrates the bonus-calculation process with cell references.

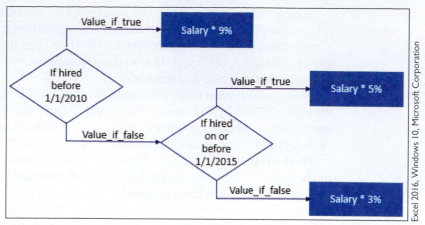

FIGURE 7.5 Nested IF Function Flowchart

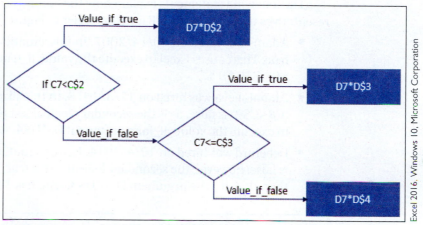

FIGURE 7.6 Nested IF Function Flowchart with Cell References

Figure 7.7 shows the nested IF function as the argument in the Value_if_false box in the Function Arguments dialog box. In the Formula Bar, the nested IF statement looks like this:

=IF(C7<C$2,D7*D$2,IF(C7<=C$3,D7*D$3,D7*D$4))

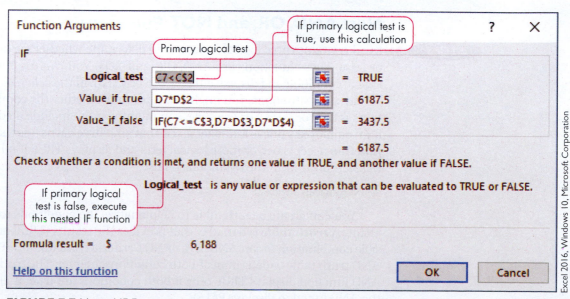

FIGURE 7.7 Nested IF Function

The function uses relative cell references for the hire date (cell C7) so that the cell reference will change to the next hire date when you copy the formula down the column. The formula uses mixed references for the date thresholds (C$2 and C$3) and for the bonus rates (D$2, D$3, and D$4) so that the references will point to the same rows when you copy the formulas down the column.

Because you have three outcomes, you need two logical tests: one for the primary IF function (C7<C$2) and one for the nested IF function (C7<=C$3). The primary logical test evaluates whether the hire date in cell C7 is older than the date in cell C2. If the logical test is true, Excel multiplies the salary in cell D7 by the rate in cell D2.

If the primary logical test (C7<C$2) is false, Excel executes the nested IF function in the value_if_false argument. The nested IF function then evaluates whether the hire date in cell C7 is older than or equal to the date in cell C3. If the logical test is true, Excel multiplies the salary by the rate in cell D3. If the logical test is false, Excel multiples the salary by the rate in cell D4. You do not need a third logical test to execute the remaining outcome.

The following statements explain how the bonus is calculated for the individual representatives using the nested IF function (refer to Figure 7.4):

- Adams was hired on 10/14/2007. In this situation, the logical test (C7<C$2) is true. This causes Excel to execute the value_if_true argument D7*D$2, which is $68,750 * 9%.

- Akmatalieva was hired on 11/3/2018. In this situation, the logical test (C8<C$2) is false, as is the secondary logical test (C8<=C$3). This causes Excel to execute the value_if_false argument D8*D$4, which is $49,575 * 3%.

- Deberard was hired on 12/4/2014. In this situation, the logical test (C10<C$2) is false; however, the secondary logical test is true. This causes Excel to execute the value_if_true argument D10*D$3, which is $46,795 * 5%.

> **TIP: HOW MANY LOGICAL TESTS?**
>
> To determine how many logical tests you need, count the number of outcomes and subtract one. For example, if you have three outcomes (such as Exceeds Expectations, Meets Expectations, and Below Expectations), you need only two logical tests. The first logical test produces one outcome (Exceeds Expectations). The nested logical test produces a second outcome (Meets Expectations) if true or produces the third outcome (Below Expectations) if false. Therefore, you do not need a third logical test to produce the third outcome.

Nest AND, OR, and NOT Functions

STEP 3 ▶▶ Excel contains three logical functions to determine whether certain conditions are true or false. These functions are AND, OR, and NOT. You can use these functions to test a logical condition and display either TRUE or FALSE in the cell.

In some situations, you might want to know whether the combination of two conditions is true or false. For example, you might want to include a column to display TRUE if an employee's title is Manager *and* if that employee earns less than $70,000. The ***AND function*** accepts two or more logical tests and displays TRUE if all conditions are true or FALSE if any one of the conditions is false.

=AND(logical1,logical2)

You can create a truth table to help analyze the conditions to determine the overall result. A ***truth table*** is a matrix that provides the results (TRUE or FALSE) for every possible combination for an AND, OR, or NOT criteria combination. Table 7.1 illustrates the AND truth table to determine if both conditions are met. The truth table reveals that the AND function displays TRUE only if both conditions are true. If either condition is false, the AND function displays FALSE.

TABLE 7.1 AND Truth Table

	Current Salary	
Type of Employee	**Less than $70,000**	**$70,000 or more**
Manager	TRUE	FALSE
Other Employees	FALSE	FALSE

Figure 7.8 shows the AND function is used in column E. Adams and Laing are the only managers who earn less than $70,000. Although Crandell is a manager, she earns more than $70,000. Although Lenz earns only $49,750, he is not a manager.

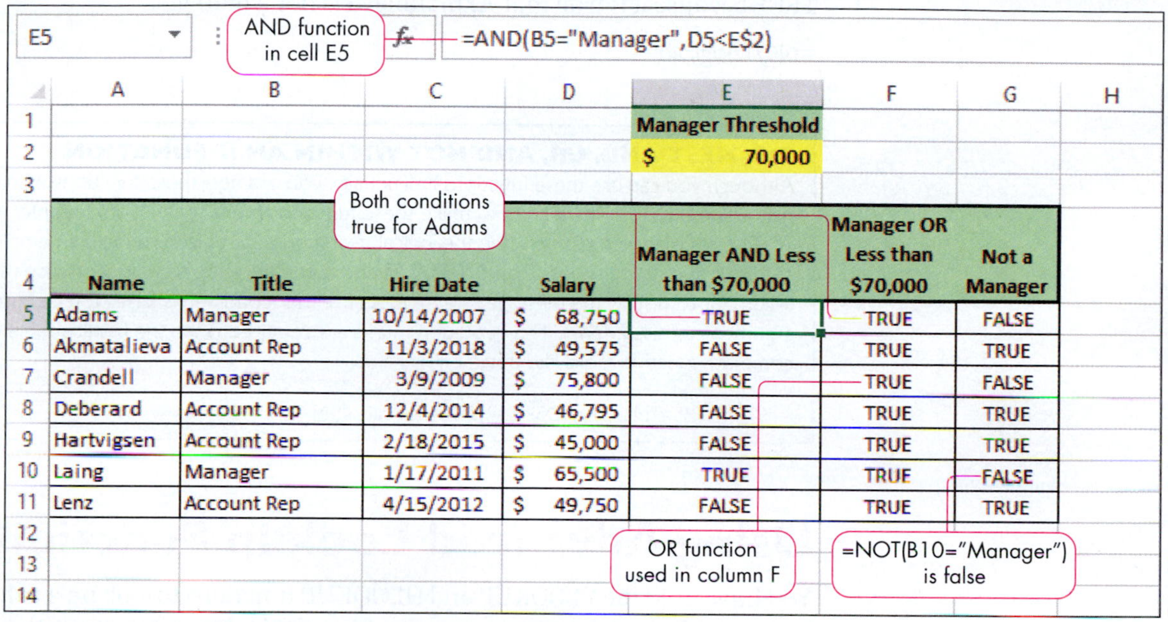

	A	B	C	D	E	F	G	H
1					Manager Threshold			
2					$ 70,000			
3								
4	Name	Title	Hire Date	Salary	Manager AND Less than $70,000	Manager OR Less than $70,000	Not a Manager	
5	Adams	Manager	10/14/2007	$ 68,750	TRUE	TRUE	FALSE	
6	Akmatalieva	Account Rep	11/3/2018	$ 49,575	FALSE	TRUE	TRUE	
7	Crandell	Manager	3/9/2009	$ 75,800	FALSE	TRUE	FALSE	
8	Deberard	Account Rep	12/4/2014	$ 46,795	FALSE	TRUE	TRUE	
9	Hartvigsen	Account Rep	2/18/2015	$ 45,000	FALSE	TRUE	TRUE	
10	Laing	Manager	1/17/2011	$ 65,500	TRUE	TRUE	FALSE	
11	Lenz	Account Rep	4/15/2012	$ 49,750	FALSE	TRUE	TRUE	
12								
13								
14								

FIGURE 7.8 AND Function

Unlike the AND function where *all* conditions must be true, the ***OR function*** evaluates to TRUE if *any* of the conditions are true. It returns FALSE only if all conditions are false. For example, you might want to identify employees who are either managers or who earn less than $70,000.

=OR(logical1,logical2)

Table 7.2 illustrates the OR truth table to determine if either condition is met. The truth table reveals that the OR function displays TRUE if at least one condition is true. The only time the OR function displays FALSE is if both conditions are false.

TABLE 7.2 OR Truth Table

	Current Salary	
Type of Employee	**Less than $70,000**	**$70,000 or more**
Manager	TRUE	TRUE
Other Employees	TRUE	FALSE

In Figure 7.8, column F uses the OR function to determine if employees are either managers or earn less than $70,000. The results indicate that either condition is met for all employees. That is, all employees are either managers or earn less than $70,000. Table 7.3 displays the differences between AND and OR functions.

Pearson Education, Inc.

TABLE 7.3   AND vs. OR

	All conditions are true	At least one condition is true	At least one condition is false	All conditions are false
AND	TRUE	FALSE	FALSE	FALSE
OR	TRUE	TRUE	TRUE	FALSE

The **NOT function** evaluates only one logical test and reverses the truth of the logical test. If the logical argument is true, the NOT function returns FALSE, and if the logical argument is false, the NOT function returns TRUE. For example, cell G5 contains =NOT(B5="Manager"). The result is false because Adams is a manager. Cell G6 displays TRUE because it is true that Akmatalieva is not a manager.

=NOT(logical)

TIP: NEST AND, OR, AND NOT WITHIN AN IF FUNCTION

Although you can use these functions individually, you can nest these functions within the logical_test argument of an IF function to make these functions more useful. For example, you can nest AND(B5="Manager",D5<E$2) in the logical_test argument to determine if an employee is (1) a manager and (2) earns less than $70,000. If both conditions are true, you can use the value_if_true argument to display the message *Due for raise*. If either condition is false, you can use the value_if_false argument to display *N/A*. The quotation marks are required when the result should display text. The complete function looks like this:

=IF(AND(B5="Manager",D5<E$2),"Due for raise","N/A")

Using Advanced Lookup Functions

You have used the VLOOKUP and HLOOKUP functions to look up a value, compare it to a lookup table, and then return a result from the lookup table. Two other lookup functions that are helpful are INDEX and MATCH.

Use the Index Function

When you work with a dataset, you might want to display content of a cell in a particular column on a particular row. For example, if a list contains agent names in the first column and their sales in the second column, you might want to know sales amount for the person on the third row. You can use the **INDEX function** to return a value at the intersection of a specified row and column. The following list explains the arguments of the INDEX function.

=INDEX(array,row_num,[column_num])

- **Array.** This argument is one or more ranges. In Figure 7.9, the array argument in the INDEX function in cell B7 is the range containing the agents and their respective sales: A2:B5.

- **Row_num.** This argument identifies the row number within the array range. In the INDEX function in cell B7 in Figure 7.9, the row_num is 3 to specify the third row in the array.

- **Column_num.** This argument identifies the column within the reference that contains the value you want. In Figure 7.9, the column_num is 2 to specify the second column within the range A2:B5.

	A	B	C
1	**Agent**	**Sales**	
2	Judi	$ 10,521	
3	Peyton	$ 14,147	
4	Kenneth	$ 8,454	
5	Cheri	$ 9,254	
6			
7	Value at specific row & column	$ 8,454	=INDEX(A2:B5,3,2)

FIGURE 7.9 INDEX Function

The INDEX function in cell B7 finds the intersection of the third row and second column in the array. In this case, cell B4 is at that intersection within the range. The INDEX function then returns the data contained in that cell, which is $8,454.

Use the MATCH Function

You might want to look up a particular value, but you do not know where it is located in a dataset. You can use the MATCH function to help look up the position of the data you want. The **MATCH function** searches through a range for a specific value and returns the relative position of that value within the range. Think of the MATCH function like a reverse phone number lookup. Instead of using directory assistance to look up a person's phone number, it would be like using the phone number to look up the person. For example, you can use the MATCH function to identify what row contains the value $8,454. The MATCH function contains three arguments: lookup_value, lookup_array, and match_type. The following list explains the arguments of the MATCH function.

=MATCH(lookup_value,lookup_array,[match_type])

- **Lookup_value.** This argument is the value that you want to find in the array or list. It can be a value, label, logical value, or cell reference that contains one of these items. In Figure 7.10, cell B8 contains the MATCH function. The lookup_value argument refers to the cell reference (B7) that contains the value to look up. In this case, you want to look up the value $8,454.

- **Lookup_array.** This argument is a range that contains a dataset. In the MATCH function in cell B8 in Figure 7.10, the lookup_array argument is the range containing the sales values, B2:B5.

- **Match_type.** This argument is 1, 0, or −1 to indicate which value to return. Use 1 to find the largest value that is less than or equal to the lookup_value when the values in the lookup_array are arranged in ascending order. Use −1 to find the smallest value that is greater than or equal to the lookup_value when the values in the lookup_array are in descending order. Use 0 to find the first value that is identical to the lookup_value when the values in the lookup_array have no particular order. In the MATCH function in cell B8 in Figure 7.10, the match_type is 0 to find an exact match of the highest sales.

	A	B	C
1	**Agent**	**Sales**	
2	Judi	$ 10,521	
3	Peyton	$ 14,147	
4	Kenneth	$ 8,454	
5	Cheri	$ 9,254	
6			
7	Value to look up	$ 8,454	
8	Position of particular value	3	=MATCH(B7,B2:B5,0)

FIGURE 7.10 MATCH Function

The MATCH function in cell B8 looks up the value stored in cell B7 ($8,454), compares it to the range B2:B5, and then finds an exact match on the third row of that range. Therefore, the MATCH function displays 3.

Create a Nested Function

STEP 4 ❯❯ In isolation, the INDEX and MATCH functions seem limited in usage. However, you can use the results (position of a value) from the MATCH function as an argument within the INDEX function to identify data related to that matching value. You can use three separate functions to identify a label related to a value. In Figure 7.11, cell B8 contains the MAX function to identify the highest sales ($14,147) in the range B2:B5. The MATCH function in cell B9 uses the results from the MAX function to find the position (2) of the highest sales within the range B2:B5. Then the INDEX function in cell B10 uses the position returned from the MATCH function to identify the agent (Peyton) responsible for the highest sales.

▲	A	B	C
1	Agent	Sales	
2	Judi	$ 10,521	
3	Peyton	$ 14,147	
4	Kenneth	$ 8,454	
5	Cheri	$ 9,254	
6			
7	Condition	Results	Formula
8	High Sales Amount	$ 14,147	=MAX(B2:B5)
9	Position of High Sales	2	=MATCH(B8,B2:B5,0)
10	Rep w/ Highest Sales	Peyton	=INDEX(A2:B5,B9,1)
11	Rep w/ Highest Sales	Peyton	=INDEX(A2:B5,MATCH(MAX(B2:B5),B2:B5,0),1)

Excel 2016, Windows 10, Microsoft Corporation

FIGURE 7.11 MATCH, INDEX, and Nested Functions

To reduce the number of cells containing functions, you can nest the MAX function within the MATCH function, and nest the MATCH function as the second argument in the INDEX function. This nested function will identify the highest sales, identify the position of the highest sales, and then return the name of the agent responsible for those sales. In Figure 7.11, cell B11 contains the nested function: =INDEX(A2:B5,MATCH(MAX(B2:B5),B2:B5,0),1).

The MAX function is nested within the MATCH function as the lookup_value argument. The MAX function returns $14,147 from the lookup_array range B2:B5. The match_type argument 0 indicates the function is looking for an exact match to the lookup_value. The MATCH function returns 2, the position of $14,147.

The INDEX function uses the entire dataset A2:B5 as the Array. The row_num argument is the position (2) returned from the MATCH function. Once the match is found, the INDEX function returns the contents in the first column, specified by the column_num argument 1. In this dataset, the INDEX function displays Peyton.

You can use the Insert Function and Function Arguments dialog boxes to insert functions as arguments for another function instead of typing the entire nested function directly in the Formula Bar.

To create a nested function using dialog boxes, complete the following steps:

1. Click Insert Function, select the outer function, such as INDEX, in the Insert Function dialog box and then click OK. When you select INDEX, the Select Arguments message box displays to select the argument type. Leave the default option selected and click OK to open the Function Arguments dialog box.

2. Click in the argument box where the nested function is needed, click the Name Box arrow on the Formula Bar, and then select the desired function from the list of recently used functions, or select More Functions from the Name Box list and select the function, such as MATCH, to open the Function Arguments dialog box for the nested function.

3. Enter the arguments for the nested function. Click in the outer function's name, INDEX, in the Formula Bar to display the Function Arguments dialog box for the outer function again.

4. Continue entering or nesting other arguments.

5. Click OK in the outer function's Function Arguments dialog box when the entire function is complete.

Quick Concepts

1. What is the difference between a single IF statement and a nested IF statement? *p. 457*

2. In what situation would you use an AND function instead of a nested IF statement? *p. 460*

3. What is the benefit of nesting the MATCH function inside the INDEX function? *p. 464*

Hands-On Exercises

 Watch the Video for this Hands-On Exercise!

 MyITLab® HOE1 Training

Skills covered: Use the YEARFRAC Function • Create a Nested IF Function • Nest an AND Function • Create a Lookup Field • Use the INDEX Function • Use the MATCH Function

1 Date, Logical, and Lookup Functions

As the Transpayne accounting assistant, you have been asked to identify underpaid account representatives to bring their salaries up to a new minimum standard within the corporation. In addition, you want to calculate annual bonus amounts based on hire date as well as create a quick search lookup field to allow for instant access to individual information.

STEP 1 >> USE THE YEARFRAC FUNCTION

Your first task is to calculate how long each manager and representative has worked for the company. You will use the YEARFRAC function to calculate the difference between an employee's hire date and December 31, 2018. Refer to Figure 7.12 as you complete Step 1.

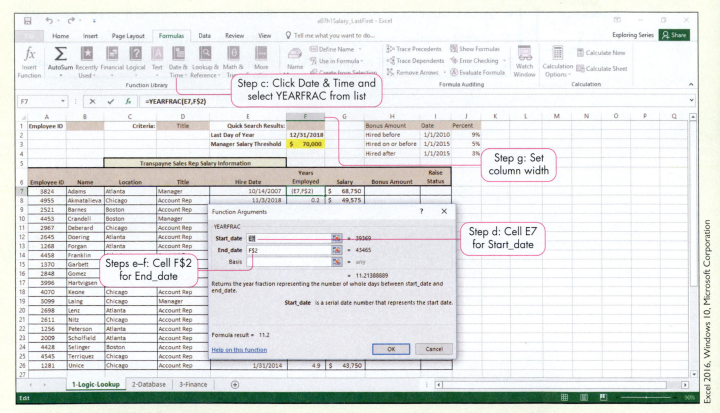

FIGURE 7.12 YEARFRAC Function

a. Open *e07h1Salary* and save it as **e07h1Salary_LastFirst**.

> **TROUBLESHOOTING:** If you make any major mistakes in this exercise, you can close the file, open *e07h1Salary* again, and then start this exercise over.

b. Click **cell F7** in the 1-Logic-Lookup worksheet.

c. Click the **Formulas tab**, click **Date & Time** in the Function Library group, scroll through the list of functions, and then select **YEARFRAC**.

The Function Arguments dialog box opens for the YEARFRAC function. The two required arguments are start_date and end_date.

d. Click **cell E7** to enter it in the Start_date box.

Cell E7 contains the hire (start) date for Adams. Adams started working for the company on 10/14/2007.

e. Click in the **End_date box** and click **cell F2**.

Cell F2 contains the comparison date of 12/31/2018.

f. Press **F4** twice to change the reference from F2 to F$2.

The mixed reference F$2 keeps the reference to row 2 absolute so that it does not change when you copy the formula down the column.

g. Click **OK**.

The formula indicates that Adams has worked at the company 11.2 years.

h. Click the **Home tab**, click the **Number Format arrow** in the Number group, and then select **Number**. Click **Decrease Decimal** in the Number group one time. Copy the function to the **range F8:F26**. Change the width of column F to **11.43**. Save the workbook.

Because Adams has the earliest hire date, he has worked at the company the longest (indicated by 11.2 years). Akmatalieva was recently hired and has the lowest number in the Years Employed column.

STEP 2 ›› CREATE A NESTED IF FUNCTION

Your next task is to calculate the annual bonus amount for each employee. The company uses a tiered bonus system that awards a specific percentage of salary based on hire date. Employees hired before 1/1/2010 receive 9%. Employees hired on or before 1/1/2015 receive 5%, and employees that were hired after 1/1/2015 receive 3%. You will use a nested IF function to calculate each employee's bonus. Refer to Figure 7.13 as you complete Step 2.

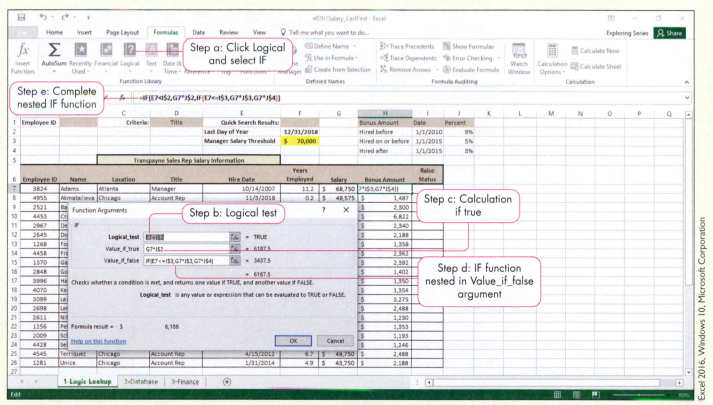

FIGURE 7.13 Nested IF Function

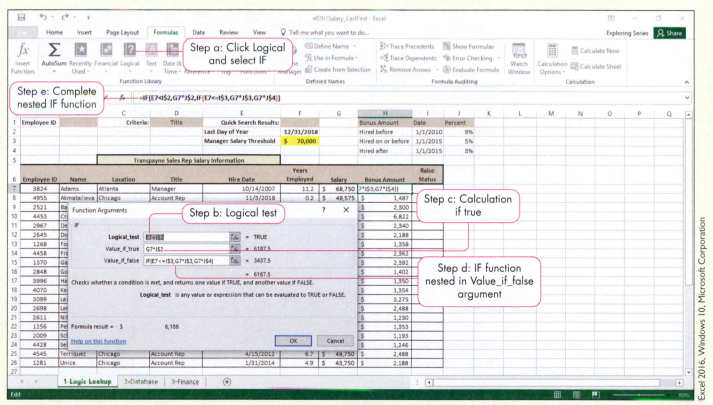

a. Click **cell H7**, click the **Formulas tab**, click **Logical** in the Function Library group, and then select **IF**.

b. Type **E7<I$2** in the Logical_test box.

The logical test compares the hire date to the first bonus threshold, 1/1/2010. Because you will copy the formula down the column and want to make sure the reference to the employee's hire date changes, use a relative cell reference to cell E7. To ensure that the reference to the date threshold remains constant, use a mixed cell reference to cell I$2. You could use an absolute reference, but because you are copying the formula down, the column letter I will remain the same. Using a mixed reference keeps the formula shorter and easier to read.

c. Type **G7*J$2** in the Value_if_true box.

This will multiply the salary by the bonus percentage if the logical test provided is true. If the logical test is not true, it will move on to the next argument created in Step d.

d. Click in the **Value_if_false box**, click the **Name Box arrow** above column A, and then select **IF**.

Excel opens another Function Arguments dialog box so that you can enter the arguments for the nested IF function.

e. Type **E7<=I$3** in the Logical_test box, type **G7*J$3** in the Value_if_true box, type **G7*J$4** in the Value_if_false box, and then click **OK**.

The Function Arguments dialog box closes, and Excel enters the nested IF function in cell H7. By entering an IF statement in the main IF function's Value_if_false box, you created a nested function that evaluates the second threshold, 1/1/2015 (cell I3). If the hire date does not fall within the first or second thresholds defined by the primary and secondary logical tests, it will then by default trigger the value_if_false, (G7*J$4). This formula will calculate the bonus based on the lowest bonus amount, 3% (cell J4).

Use relative cell references for the employee's hire date (cell E7), because it should change when you copy the formula down the column. Use a mixed (or an absolute) reference for the threshold date (cell I$3) to ensure it does not change as you copy the formula down the column. Again, using mixed references keeps the formula shorter and easier to read than absolute references, but both produce the same results.

The function returns the value $6,188. This is calculated by multiplying the current salary, $68,750 (cell G7), by the bonus percentage rate of 9% (cell J2).

f. Click the **Home tab**, click **Accounting Number Format** in the Number group, and then click **Decrease Decimal** two times in the Number group.

g. Double-click the **cell H7 fill handle** to copy the function to the **range H8:H26**. Save the workbook.

The Human Resources Director recommends that the company pay managers at least $70,000. You will nest an AND function inside an IF function to determine which managers should receive pay raises based on their current salary level. The salary threshold is located in cell F3 in the 1-Logic-Lookup worksheet. Refer to Figure 7.14 as you complete Step 3.

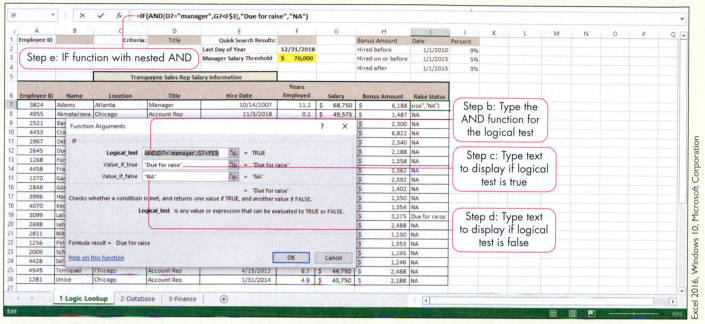

FIGURE 7.14 Nested AND Function Within IF Function

a. Click **cell I7**, click the **Formulas tab**, click **Logical** in the Function Library group, and then select **IF**.

b. Type **AND(D7="manager",G7<F$3)** in the Logical_test box.

Nesting the AND function in the logical test enables you to specify two conditions that must be true: the employee is a manager (D7="manager") and makes less than $70,000 (G7<F$3). You use a mixed reference in cell F3 to ensure that row number 3 does not change when you copy the formula down the column.

> **TROUBLESHOOTING:** Do not make cells D7 or G7 absolute or mixed. If you do, the function will use the incorrect cell references when you copy the function down the column.

c. Type **"Due for raise"** in the Value_if_true box.

If both conditions specified in the AND function are true, the employee is eligible for a raise.

d. Type **"NA"** in the Value_if_false box.

e. Click **OK**, double-click the **cell I7 fill handle** to copy the formula to the **range I8:I26**, change the width of column I to **11.86**, and then save the workbook.

The function now evaluates the employee's title and salary. If both arguments in the AND function are true, then *Due for raise* is displayed; if not, *NA* is displayed.

You want to provide a simple search feature so that users can enter an employee number in cell B1 and then display employee title information in cell F1. For example, if Employee ID 4070 is entered in cell B1, cell F1 displays Account Rep. Refer to Figure 7.15 as you complete Step 4.

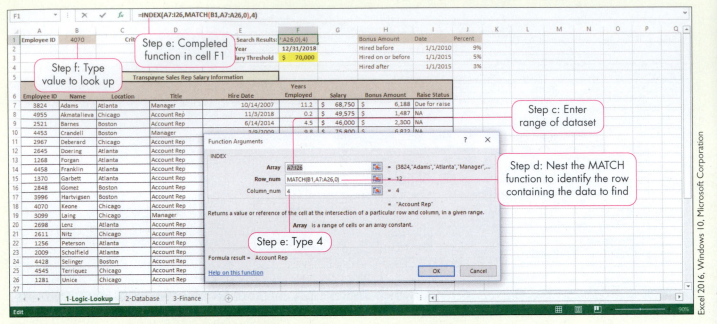

FIGURE 7.15 Nested MATCH and INDEX Functions

a. Click **cell F1**, click **Lookup & Reference** in the Function Library group, and then select **INDEX**.

The Select Arguments message box opens so that you can select the type of arguments to build the function.

b. Select **array,row_num,column_num** and click **OK**.

This argument specifies the array or range to evaluate first, followed by identifying the row number and column number to index. The Function Arguments dialog box opens so that you can enter the required arguments for the INDEX function.

c. Type **A7:I26** in the Array box.

This range defines the location from which Excel will extract information.

d. Type **MATCH(B1,A7:A26,0)** in the Row_num box.

If you nest the MATCH function in the Row_num box of the index function, Excel will look up the position of the employee number in cell B1 within the range A7:A26 and return the relative position, which for employee 4070 is 12.

e. Type **4** in the Column_num box. Click **OK**.

You entered the number 4 in the Column_num box so that the function will return information from the fourth column in the dataset. Currently, the function returns #N/A because cell B1 is blank.

f. Click **cell B1**, type **4070**, and then press **Enter.**

Cell F1 now displays the current position of employee 4070. It does this by matching the Employee ID in column A to the Title in column D.

g. Save the workbook. Keep the workbook open if you plan to continue with the next Hands-On Exercise. If not, close the workbook and exit Excel.

Database Filtering and Functions

Databases store and manipulate data, such as inventory details about automobiles at a particular dealership or financial transaction details for your credit card. While Microsoft Access is more appropriate for relational database modeling, people often use Excel for basic database storage and manipulation. You have some experience in using Excel tables to perform basic database tasks, such as sorting and filtering data. However, you may need to perform more advanced filtering or calculations.

In this section, you will learn how to use advanced filtering techniques and insert database functions. Specifically, you will define a criteria range and extract data that meet certain criteria. Then you will insert the DSUM and DAVERAGE functions to calculate results based on filtered data.

Applying Advanced Filtering

Data become more useful in decision making when you reduce the records to a subset of data that meets specific conditions. For example, a manager might want to identify account reps who earn more than $30,000 in Chicago. The manager can use the filter arrows to filter the table data by job title, salary, and location, and Excel will filter the original dataset by hiding records that do not meet the conditions. Sometimes, however, it may be important to keep the original dataset visible and create a copy of only those records that meet these conditions in another location of the worksheet. To do so, the manager can use advanced filtering techniques.

Define a Criteria Range

STEP 1 ❯❯ Before you apply advanced filtering techniques, you must define a criteria range. A *criteria range* is a group of two or more adjacent cells that specifies the conditions used to control the results of a filter. The criteria row is often located below the dataset. A criteria range must contain at least two rows and one column. The first row contains the column labels as they appear in the dataset, and the second row contains the conditions (e.g., values) for filtering the dataset. Figure 7.16 shows the original dataset, criteria range, and copy of records that meet the conditions.

	A	B	C	D	E
6	Employee ID	Name	Location	Title	Salary
7	3824	Adams	Atlanta	Manager	$ 68,750
8	4955	Akmatalieva	Chicago	Account Rep	$ 49,575
9	2521	Barnes	Boston	Account Rep	$ 46,000
10	4453	Crandell	Boston	Manager	$ 75,800
11	2967	Deberard	Chicago	Account Rep	$ 46,795
12	2645	Doering	Atlanta	Account Rep	$ 43,750
13	1268	Forgan	Atlanta	Account Rep	$ 45,250
14	4458	Franklin	Atlanta	Account Rep	$ 47,240
15	1370	Garbett	Atlanta	Account Rep	$ 47,835
16	2848	Gomez	Boston	Account Rep	$ 46,725
17	3996	Hartvigsen	Boston	Account Rep	$ 45,000
18	4070	Keone	Chicago	Account Rep	$ 45,125
19	3099	Laing	Chicago	Manager	$ 65,500
20			Labels on first row of criteria range	Criteria set on second row of criteria range	
21					
22	Employee ID	Name	Location	Title	Salary
23			Chicago	Account Rep	>30000
24					
25	Employee ID	Name	Location	Title	Salary
26	4955	Akmatalieva	Chicago	Account Rep	$ 49,575
27	2967	Deberard	Chicago	Account Rep	$ 46,795
28	4070	Keone	Chicago	Account Rep	$ 45,125
29					
30				Output area: copy of records meeting criteria	
31		Original data			
32					
33					
34					

FIGURE 7.16 Data, Criteria Range, and Output

Because you want to display records that meet all three conditions (Location, Title, and Salary), you enter the conditions on the second row of the criteria range, immediately below their respective labels: Chicago below Location, Account Rep below Title, and >30000 below Salary. By default, Excel looks for an exact match. If you want to avoid an exact match for values, enter relational operators. For example, entering >30000 sets the condition for salaries that are greater than $30,000. You can use <, >, <=, >=, and <> relational operators, similar to using relational operators in the logical_test argument of an IF function.

Excel copies only the records that meet all three conditions. Therefore, Adams earning $68,750 from Atlanta is excluded because Adams is a manager, not an account rep, and is not from Chicago. You can set an OR condition in the criteria range. For example, you want to display (a) Chicago account reps who earn more than $30,000 or (b) Atlanta account reps regardless of salary. Figure 7.17 shows the conditions in the criteria range. Notice that the criteria range contains three rows: column labels on the first row, the first set of conditions on the second row, and the second set of conditions on the third row. Each row of conditions sets an AND condition; that is, each criterion must be met. Each additional row sets an OR condition.

	Employee ID	Name	Location	Title	Salary
6	**Employee ID**	**Name**	**Location**	**Title**	**Salary**
7	3824	Adams	Atlanta	Manager	$ 68,750
8	4955	Akmatalieva	Chicago	Account Rep	$ 49,575
9	2521	Barnes	Boston	Account Rep	$ 46,000
10	4453	Crandell	Boston	Manager	$ 75,800
11	2967	Deberard	Chicago	Account Rep	$ 46,795
12	2645	Doering	Atlanta	Account Rep	$ 43,750
13	1268	Forgan	Atlanta	Account Rep	$ 45,250
14	4458	Franklin	Atlanta	Account Rep	$ 47,240
15	1370	Garbett	Atlanta	Account Rep	$ 47,835
16	2848	Gomez	Boston	Account Rep	$ 46,725
17	3996	Hartvigsen	Boston	Account Rep	$ 45,000
18	4070	Keone	Chicago	Account Rep	$ 45,125
19	3099	Laing	Chicago	Manager	$ 65,500
20					
21					

First set of criteria creates AND condition for each item in the row

	Employee ID	Name	Location	Title	Salary
22	**Employee ID**	**Name**	**Location**	**Title**	**Salary**
23			Chicago	Account Rep	>30000
24			Atlanta	Account Rep	
25					

Copy of records meeting either condition

Second set of criteria creates OR condition

	Employee ID	Name	Location	Title	Salary
26	**Employee ID**	**Name**	**Location**	**Title**	**Salary**
27	4955	Akmatalieva	Chicago	Account Rep	$ 49,575
28	2967	Deberard	Chicago	Account Rep	$ 46,795
29	2645	Doering	Atlanta	Account Rep	$ 43,750
30	1268	Forgan	Atlanta	Account Rep	$ 45,250
31	4458	Franklin	Atlanta	Account Rep	$ 47,240
32	1370	Garbett	Atlanta	Account Rep	$ 47,835
33	4070	Keone	Chicago	Account Rep	$ 45,125
34					
35					

FIGURE 7.17 Criteria Range with AND and OR Conditions

Excel 2016, Windows 10, Microsoft Corporation

TIP: USING = AND <>

Using equal (=) and unequal (<>) symbols with the criteria values selects records with empty and nonempty fields, respectively. An equal with nothing after it will return all records with no entry in the designated column. An unequal with nothing after it will select all records with an entry in the column. An empty cell in the criteria range returns every record in the list.

Apply the Advanced Filter

STEP 2 ▸▸ After you create the criteria range, you are ready to apply the advanced filter using the Advanced Filter dialog box. This dialog box enables you to filter the table in place or copy the selected records to another area in the worksheet, specify the list range, specify the criteria range, or display unique records only.

To apply the advanced filter, complete the following steps:

1. Click a cell in the data table.
2. Click the Data tab and click Advanced in the Sort & Filter group.
3. Click the desired action: *Filter the list, in-place* to filter the range by hiding rows that do not match your criteria or *Copy to another location* if you want to copy the rows that match your criteria instead of filtering the original dataset.
4. Ensure the List range displays the range containing the original dataset, including the column headings.
5. Enter the criteria range, including the criteria labels, in the Criteria range box. To perform the advanced filter for the OR condition in Figure 7.17, you must select all three rows of the criteria range: the column labels, the row containing the criteria for Chicago account reps earning more than $30,000, and the row containing criteria for Atlanta account reps.
6. Specify the Copy to range if you selected *Copy to another location* in Step 3. Enter only the starting row. Excel will copy the column labels and fill in the rows below the heading with the records that meet the conditions you set. Make sure the Copy to range contains sufficient empty rows to accommodate the copied records. If you do not include enough rows, Excel will replace existing data with the copied records. Click OK.

Figure 7.18 shows the Advanced Filter dialog box with settings to produce the advanced filter shown in Figure 7.17. The List range box contains $A$6:$E$19 for the dataset. The Criteria range box contains $A$22:SE$24 for the criteria range labels and conditions. The Copy to box contains $A$26:$E$26 for the labels in the output range.

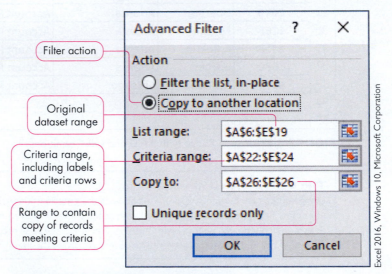

FIGURE 7.18 Advanced Filter Dialog Box

TIP: AUTO RANGE NAMES
When you use the Advanced Filter dialog box, Excel assigns the range name Criteria to the criteria range and Extract to the output range.

Manipulating Data with Database Functions

Database functions analyze data for selected records in a dataset. These functions are similar to statistical functions (SUM, AVERAGE, MAX, MIN, COUNT) except that database functions restrict the results to data that meets specific criteria. Data not meeting the specified criteria are filtered out. All database functions use a criteria range that defines the conditions for filtering the data to be used in the calculations. Database functions have three arguments: database, field, and criteria.

- **Database.** The database argument is the entire dataset, including column labels and all data, on which the function operates. The database reference may be represented by a range name. In Figure 7.19, the database argument is A6:E19.

- **Field.** The field argument is the column that contains the values operated on by the function. You can enter either the name of the column label in quotation marks, such as "Salary" or the number that represents the location of that column within the table. For example, if the Salary column is the fifth column in the table, you can enter a 5 for the field argument. You can also enter a cell reference containing the column label, for example, E6, as shown in Figure 7.19.

- **Criteria.** The criteria argument defines the conditions to be met by the function. This range must contain at least one column label and a cell below the label that specifies the condition. The criteria argument may include more than one column with conditions for each column label, indicated by a range, such as A22:E23 or a range name. In Figure 7.19, the criteria range specifies Atlanta as the location and Account Rep as the title.

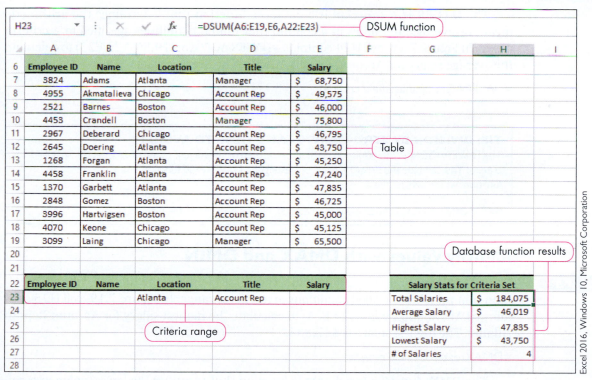

FIGURE 7.19 Database Functions

> **TIP: USING FORMULA AUTOCOMPLETE**
> Instead of using the Formulas tab to begin creating a function, you can type = and the first letter of a function. Excel displays the Formula AutoComplete list, showing a list of functions that start with the letter you typed. For example, if you type =D, Excel displays a list of functions that start with the letter D, including most database functions. Select the appropriate function from the list.

> **TIP: USING RANGE NAMES**
> You can assign range names to the dataset and criteria range to simplify the construction of the arguments in database functions.

Use DSUM and DAVERAGE Functions

STEP 3 The **DSUM function** is a database function that adds the values in a column that match conditions specified in a criteria range. In Figure 7.19, cell H23 contains =DSUM(A6:E19,E6,A22:E23) to calculate the total salaries for Account Reps in Atlanta. The total salaries paid is $184,075.

=DSUM(database,field,criteria)

The **DAVERAGE function** is a database function that determines the arithmetic mean, or average, of values in a column that match conditions specified in a criteria range. In Figure 7.19, cell H24 contains =DAVERAGE(A6:E19,E6,A22:E23) to calculate the average salary for Account Reps in Atlanta. The average salary is $46,019.

=DAVERAGE(database,field,criteria)

> **TIP: DIVISION BY ZERO—#DIV/0—AND HOW TO AVOID IT**
> The DAVERAGE function displays a division-by-zero error message if no records meet the specified criteria. You can hide the error message by nesting the DAVERAGE function inside the IFERROR function, which detects the error:
>
> =IFERROR(DAVERAGE(A6:E19,"Salary",A22:E23),"No Records Match the Criteria")

Identify Values with DMAX and DMIN

STEP 4 The **DMAX function** is a database function that identifies the highest value in a column that matches specified conditions in a criteria range. In Figure 7.19, cell H25 contains =DMAX(A6:E19,E6,A22:E23) to calculate the highest salary for Account Reps in Atlanta. The highest salary is $47,835.

=DMAX(database,field,criteria)

The **DMIN function** is a database function that identifies the lowest value in a column that matches specified conditions in a criteria range. In Figure 7.19, cell H26 contains =DMIN(A6:E19,E6,A22:E23) to calculate the lowest salary for Account Reps in Atlanta. The lowest salary is $43,750.

=DMIN(database,field,criteria)

Identify the Total Number with DCOUNT

The **DCOUNT function** is a database function that counts the cells that contain numbers in a column that matches specified conditions in a criteria range. In Figure 7.19, cell H27 contains =DCOUNT(A6:E19,E6,A22:E23) to count the number of Account Reps in Atlanta, which is 4. However, if one of the records is missing a value, DCOUNT excludes that record from being counted. If after completing the DCOUNT, you decide you would like to change the match conditions, you can do so by altering the information entered in the criteria area. To count records containing an empty cell, use DCOUNTA instead.

=DCOUNT(database,field,criteria)

=DCOUNTA(database,field,criteria)

TIP: ADDITIONAL DATABASE FUNCTIONS

Excel contains additional database functions, such as DSTDEV to calculate the sample population standard deviation for values in a column and DVAR to estimate the sample population variance for values in a column when specified conditions are met.

Quick Concepts

4. Why would you use advanced filtering instead of basic filtering? *p. 471*

5. What are the benefits of using database functions? *p. 475*

6. Why would you use a database function instead of advanced filtering? *p. 475*

Skills covered: Create Criteria and Output Ranges • Apply an Advanced Filter • Use the DAVERAGE Function • Use the DMIN Function • Use the DMAX Function • Use the DCOUNT Function

2 Database Filtering and Functions

Other assistant accountants want to be able to enter criteria to see a list of records that meet the conditions they specify. In addition, these assistants then want to calculate summary statistics based on the filtered results.

STEP 1 ›› **CREATE CRITERIA AND OUTPUT RANGES**

You want to set up the workbook with a criteria range and an output range. This will enable other assistant accountants to enter criteria of their choosing to filter the list of salary data. Refer to Figure 7.20 as you complete Step 1.

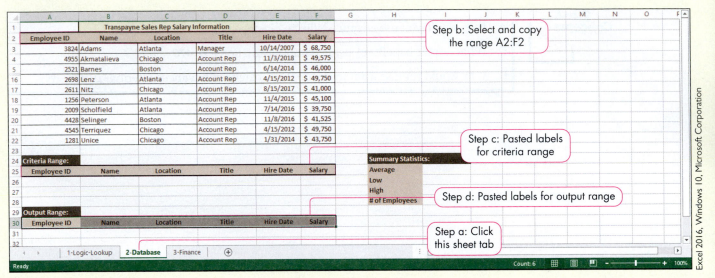

FIGURE 7.20 Criteria and Output Ranges

a. Open *e07h1Salary_LastFirst* if you closed it at the end of Hands-On Exercise 1, and save it as **e07h2Salary_LastFirst**, changing h1 to h h2. Click the **2-Database sheet tab**.

   Use this worksheet to preserve the work you did on the first worksheet.

b. Select the **range A2:F2** and click **Copy** in the Clipboard group on the Home tab.

   You copied the range containing the column labels.

c. Click **cell A25** and click **Paste** in the Clipboard group on the Home tab.

   You pasted the range containing the column labels for the criteria range.

d. Click **cell A30**, paste another copy of the data, and then press **Esc**. Save the workbook.

   You pasted another copy of the column labels for the output range in cells A30:F30.

You are ready to enter conditions to restrict the output list to Account Reps in Boston. Refer to Figure 7.21 as you complete Step 2.

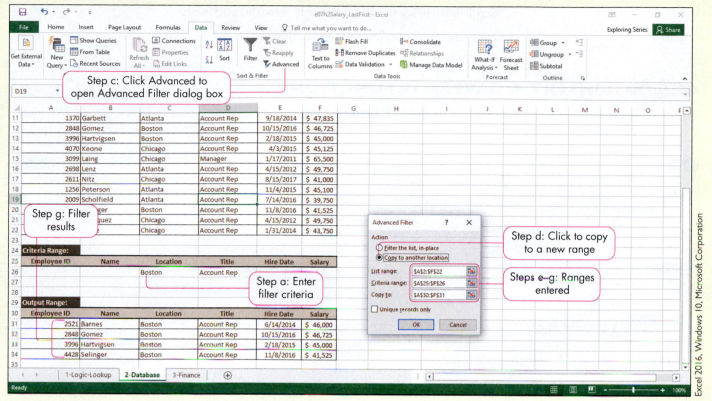

FIGURE 7.21 Conditions and Output

a. Type **Boston** in **cell C26** and type **Account Rep** in **cell D26**.

You entered the conditions on the first row below the labels in the criteria range. Because you entered both conditions on the same row, you created an AND condition. Both conditions must be met in order to display employee data in the output range.

b. Click **cell D19** (or any cell within the dataset).

c. Click the **Data tab** and click **Advanced** in the Sort & Filter group.

The Advanced Filter dialog box opens so that you can specify the desired filter action, the list, the criteria range, and other details.

d. Click **Copy to another location**.

This action will copy the records that meet the conditions to a new location instead of filtering the original dataset.

e. Click in the **List range box** and select the **range A2:F22**.

This range contains the original dataset. The List range box may display the sheet name along with the range, such as '2-Database'!$A$2:$F$22.

f. Click in the **Criteria range box** and select the **range A25:F26**.

You selected the labels and the row containing the conditions for the criteria range. The Criteria range box may display the sheet name along with the range, such as '2-Database'!$A$25:$F$26.

g. Click in the **Copy to box**, select the **range A30:F30**, and then click **OK**.

Make sure you select only the labels for the output range. The Copy to box may display the sheet name along with the range, such as '2-Database'!$A$30:$F$30. Excel copies the records that meet the condition below the output range labels.

h. Scroll down to see the output records. Save the workbook.

Four employees are Account Reps in Boston.

INSERT A DAVERAGE FUNCTION

Regardless of the criteria entered in the criteria range A25:F26, you want to calculate the average salary for the records that meet those conditions. You will insert a DAVERAGE function to perform the calculation. Refer to Figure 7.22 as you complete Step 3.

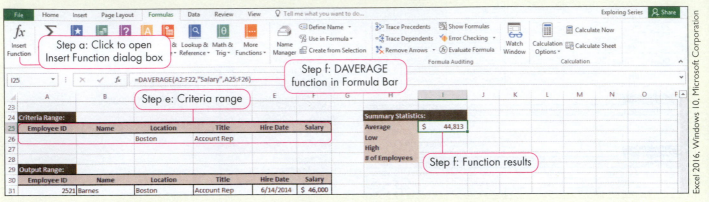

FIGURE 7.22 DAVERAGE Function

a. Click **cell I25**, click the **Formulas tab**, and then click **Insert Function** in the Function Library group.

The Insert Function dialog box opens so that you can select a function category and function.

b. Click the **Or select a category arrow**, select **Database**, select **DAVERAGE** in the *Select a function* list, and then click **OK**.

The Function Arguments dialog box opens so that you can specify the arguments for the DAVERAGE function.

c. Select the **range A2:F22** to enter that range in the Database box.

The Database argument must include the column labels and original dataset.

d. Click in the **Field box**, type **Salary**, and then press **Tab**.

Excel enters the quotation marks around the word Salary for you.

> **TROUBLESHOOTING:** If you type the function instead of using the dialog box, make sure you type the double quotation marks (") around text. Otherwise, Excel will display an error message.

e. Select the **range A25:F26** to enter in the Criteria box.

Excel displays Criteria instead of A25:F26 in the Criteria box because you had previously defied the criteria range in Step 2.

f. Click **OK**. Save the workbook.

The average salary of account reps in Boston is $44,813.

STEP 4 » USE DMIN, DMAX, AND DCOUNT FUNCTIONS

The other accounting assistants would like to see the lowest and highest salaries based on the database conditions. In addition, you want to insert the DCOUNT function to count the number of records that meet the specified conditions. Refer to Figure 7.23 as you complete Step 4.

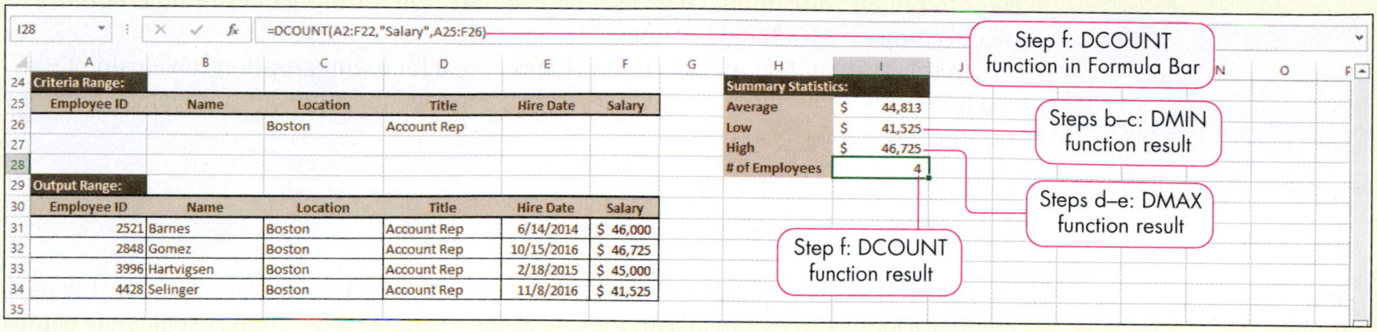

Excel 2016, Windows 10, Microsoft Corporation

FIGURE 7.23 DMIN, DMAX, DCOUNT Functions

a. Click **cell I26** and click **Insert Function** in the Function Library group.

The Database functions should be listed because that was the last function category you selected.

b. Select **DMIN** in the *Select a function* list and click **OK**.

The Function Arguments dialog box opens so that you can specify the arguments for the DMIN function.

c. Select the **range A2:F22** in the Database box, select the **cell F2** in the Field box, select the range **A25:F26** in the Criteria box, and then click **OK**.

The lowest salary for account reps in Boston is $41,525.

d. Click **cell I27** and click **Insert Function** in the Function Library group. Select **DMAX** in the *Select a function* list and click **OK**.

The Function Arguments dialog box opens so that you can specify the arguments for the DMAX function.

e. Select the **range A2:F22** in the Database box, select the **cell F2** in Field box, select the **range A25:F26** in the Criteria box, and then click **OK**.

The highest salary for account reps in Boston is $46,725.

f. Type **=DCOUNT(A2:F22,"Salary",A25:F26)** in **cell I28** and then press **Enter**.

The company has four account reps in the Boston location.

g. Save the workbook. Keep the workbook open if you plan to continue with the next Hands-On Exercise. If not, close the workbook and exit Excel.

Financial Functions

Excel's financial functions are helpful for business financial analysts and for you in your personal financial management. Knowing what different financial functions can calculate and how to use them will benefit you as you plan retirement savings, identify best rates to obtain your financial goals, and evaluate how future values of different investments compare with today's values.

In this section, you will learn how to prepare a loan amortization table using financial functions. In addition, you will use other financial functions to complete investment analyses.

Using Financial Functions

Previously, you worked with the PMT financial function to calculate the monthly payment of a loan. The Financial category includes a variety of functions to calculate details for investments. For example, you can calculate present or future values, rates, and number of payment periods. Figure 7.24 illustrates the results of several financial functions. Some of the arguments for the PMT function are similar to the arguments for other financial functions.

1	**Present Value**		
2	Lump Sum	$ 1,000,000.00	
3	Present Value	$ 1,246,221.03	=-PV(B6,B5,B4)
4	Per Year	$ 100,000.00	
5	No. of Years	20	
6	Rate	5%	
7			
8	**Future Value**		
9	Yearly Contribution	$ 3,000.00	
10	No. of Years	40	
11	APR	7%	
12	Future Value	$ 598,905.34	=-FV(B11,B10,B9)
13	Total Contributed	$ 120,000.00	=B9*B10
14	Interest	$ 478,905.34	=B12-B13
15			
16	**Net Present Value**		
17	Invest End of Year	$ 3,000.00	
18	Yearly Income	$ 1,200.00	
19	Rate	3%	
20	Net Present Value	$ 382.85	=NPV(B19,-B17,B18,B18,B18)
21			

FIGURE 7.24 Financial Functions

Excel 2016, Windows 10, Microsoft Corporation

Calculate Present and Future Values

STEP 1 ➤➤ The **PV function** calculates the total present (current) value of an investment with a fixed rate, specified number of payment periods, and a series of identical payments that will be made in the future. This function illustrates the time value of money in which the value of $1 today is worth more than the value of $1 received at some time in the future, given that you can invest today's $1 to earn interest in the future. For example, you might want to use the PV function to compare a lump-sum payment versus annual payments if you win the lottery to see which is better: receiving $100,000 per year for the next 20 years or $1 million now.

The PV function has three required arguments (rate, nper, and pmt) and two optional arguments (fv and type). The rate, nper, and type arguments have the same definitions as in other financial functions. The pmt argument is the fixed periodic payment. The fv argument represents the future value of the investment. If you do not know the payment, you must enter a value for the fv argument. In Figure 7.24 cell B3 contains the PV function. The yearly payments of $100,000 invested at 5% yield a higher present value ($1,246,221.03) than the $1 million lump-sum payment.

=PV(rate,nper,pmt,[fv],[type])

> **TIP: NEGATIVE SIGN IN FUNCTION**
>
> For many financial functions, the calculated results display as a negative value. The negative result occurs because Excel interprets these calculations as a negative cash flow (money leaving your account). To make the results easier to work with, a negative sign is placed after the = or before any of the arguments so that the results display as a positive result.

The **FV function** calculates the future value of an investment, given a fixed interest rate, term, and identical periodic payments. Use the FV function to determine how much an individual retirement account (IRA) would be worth at a future date. The FV function has three required arguments (rate, nper, and pmt) and two optional arguments (pv and type). If you omit the pmt argument, you must enter a value for the pv argument.

=FV(rate,nper,pmt,[pv],[type])

Assume that you plan to contribute $3,000 a year to an IRA for 40 years and that you expect the IRA to earn 7% interest annually. The future value of that investment—the amount you will have 40 years later—would be $598,905.34. In Figure 7.24, cell B12 contains the FV function. You would have contributed $120,000 ($3,000 a year for 40 years). The extra $478,905.34 results from compound interest you will earn over the life of your $120,000 investment.

The **NPV function** calculates the net present value of an investment, given a fixed rate (rate of return) and future payments that may be identical or different. It considers periodic future income and payments. The NPV and PV functions are very similar in concept. The difference is that the PV function requires equal payments at the end of a payment period, whereas the NPV function can have unequal but constant payments. The NPV function contains two required arguments (rate and value1) and additional optional arguments (such as value2). If an investment returns a positive net present value, the investment is profitable. If an investment returns a negative net present value, the investment will lose money.

=NPV(rate,value1,value2,)

- **Rate.** The rate argument is the interest rate for one period. It is also called the rate of return or the percentage return on your investment. If an investment pays 12% per year and each period is one month, the rate is 1%.

- **Value1.** The value arguments represent a sequence of payments and income during the investment period. To provide an accurate net present value, the cash flows must occur at equally spaced-out time periods and must occur at the end of each period.

Assume you invest $3,000 at the end of the first year and receive $1,200 during the second, third, and fourth years with a 3% rate. In Figure 7.24, cell B20 contains the NPV function. The net present value would be $382.85. However, if you pay the $3,000 at the beginning of the first year instead of the end of the first year, you cannot discount the $3,000 since it is already in today's value. You would then subtract it after the function: =NPV(B19,B18,B18,B18)–B17. By investing $3,000 immediately, the net present value is higher at $394.33.

Use NPER and RATE Functions

In some situations, you might have a payment goal and know the stated interest rate, but you need to calculate how many payments you will make. In other situations, you might know the payment and number of payments, but you need to calculate the rate. The NPER and RATE functions are useful in these situations.

The **NPER function** calculates the number of payment periods for an investment or loan given a fixed interest rate, periodic payment, and present value. You can use NPER to calculate the number of monthly payments given a car loan of $30,000, an APR of 5.25%, and a monthly payment of $694.28. In Figure 7.25, cell B6 contains the NPER function. The NPER would be 48.0001, or about 48 payments. The NPER function contains three required arguments (rate, pmt, and pv) and two optional arguments (fv and type).

=NPER(rate,pmt,pv,[fv],[type])

1	Number of Periods			
2	Loan	$	30,000.00	
3	APR		5.25%	
4	No. of Payment Periods in Year		12	
5	Monthly Payment	$	694.28	
6	Number of Periods		48	=NPER(B3/B4,-B5,B2)
7				
8	Rate			
9	Loan	$	30,000.00	
10	Monthly Payment	$	694.28	
11	No. of Periods in Year		12	
12	Years		4	
13	Periodic Rate		0.44%	=RATE(B11*B12,-B10,B9)
14	APR		5.25%	=B11*B13
15				
16				
17				

Excel 2016, Windows 10, Microsoft Corporation

FIGURE 7.25 NPER and RATE Functions

The **RATE function** calculates the periodic rate for an investment or loan given the number of payment periods, a fixed periodic payment, and present value. Use RATE to calculate the periodic rate of a four-year car loan of $30,000 and a monthly payment of $694.28. In Figure 7.25, cell B13 contains the RATE function. The periodic (monthly) rate would be 0.44%. The APR (5.25%) is found by multiplying the periodic rate by 12. The RATE function contains three required arguments (nper, pmt, and pv) and two optional arguments (fv and type).

=RATE(nper,pmt,pv,[fv],[type])

Creating a Loan Amortization Table

You used the PMT function to calculate the monthly payment for an automobile or house loan with a fixed interest rate (such as 5.75% APR) for a specified period of time (such as 30 years). Although knowing the monthly payment is helpful to analyze a potential loan, you might want to know how much of that payment contains interest and how much goes toward principal (or paying off the loan balance). Recall that a portion of the monthly payment covers the interest you owe and a portion of the monthly payment pays down your principal.

While the monthly payment is constant throughout the life of the loan, the interest and principal portions are not the same every month of the loan. With each payment, you decrease the balance of the loan. The interest is calculated on the balance of the loan, so as you continue making monthly payments, the loan balance continually decreases; therefore, the interest portion decreases and the principal portion increases each month.

To see the interest and principal portions of each monthly payment and the reduction in the loan amount, you can create a **loan amortization table**, which is a schedule that calculates the interest per payment period, principal repayment for each payment, and remaining balance after each payment is made. Figure 7.26 shows the top and bottom portions of an amortization schedule (rows 18:49 are hidden) for an automobile loan of $30,000 with an APR of 2.74% for a four-year loan with a monthly payment of $660.59, rounded to the nearest penny. The borrower pays a total of $31,708.23 (48 payments of $660.59). These payments equal the principal of $30,000 plus $1,708.23 in interest over the life of the loan.

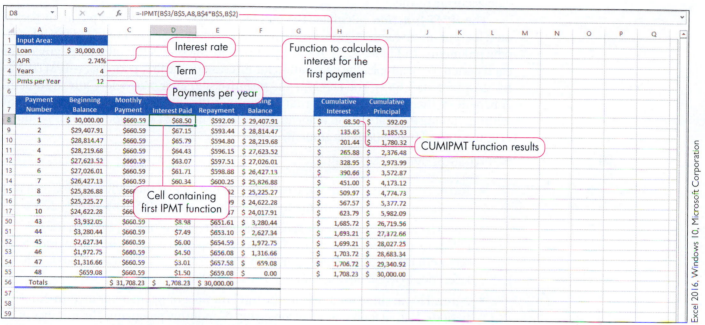

FIGURE 7.26 Loan Amortization Table

Perform Internal Calculations

STEP 2 ▸▸ The body of the worksheet reflected in Figure 7.26 shows how principal and interest comprise each payment. The balance of the loan at the beginning of the first period is $30,000. The monthly payment includes interest and principal repayment. The interest for the first month ($68.50) is calculated by multiplying the beginning loan balance for the period, which is the original loan amount ($30,000) by the monthly interest rate (2.74%/12).

The principal repayment is the amount of the monthly payment that is left over after deducting the monthly interest. For the first payment, the principal repayment is $592.09 ($660.59 − $68.50).

The remaining balance is the difference between the previous remaining balance and the principal repayment. For the first month, subtract the principal repayment from the original loan amount ($30,000 − $592.09).

The interest for the second month ($67.15) is less than interest for the previous period. This is because the balance to start the second period ($29,407.91) is less than the loan balance for the first period ($30,000) because $592.09 was paid in principal with the first payment.

Calculate Interest and Principal Payments with IPMT and PPMT Functions

The financial category contains additional functions to calculate results for loan payments: IPMT and PPMT. You can use these functions in isolation or within the body of a loan amortization table if the table does not allow additional principal payments. If the loan amortization enables you to pay additional principal, these functions will not provide accurate results.

The ***IPMT function*** calculates the periodic interest for a specified payment period on a loan or an investment given a fixed interest rate, specified term, and identical periodic payments. In Figure 7.26, the IPMT function calculates the interest payment for each period. For example, the calculation for interest for the first period is: =-IPMT(B$3/B$5,A8,B$4*B$5,B$2). You can type the negative sign after = or before any argument. A benefit of the IPMT function is that it identifies the interest for any given payment without having to create a loan amortization table. The IPMT function has four required arguments and two optional arguments.

=IPMT(rate,per,nper,pv,[fv],[type])

- **Rate.** The rate argument is the periodic interest rate. If the APR is 2.74% (cell B3) and monthly payments are made, the rate is 2.74%/12 (B$3/B$5), or 0.228%.

- **Per.** The per argument is the specific payment or investment period to use to calculate the interest where the first payment period is 1. It is best to include a payment number column as shown in Figure 7.26. You can use a relative cell reference to avoid having values in the argument.

- **Nper.** This argument represents the total number of payment or investment periods. With a four-year loan consisting of monthly payments, the number of payment periods is 48. You should perform the calculation using the input cells, such as B$4*B$5, in the nper argument instead of typing 48 in case the number of years or number of payments per year changes.

- **Pv.** This argument represents the present value of the loan or investment.

- **Fv.** The optional fv argument represents the future value of the loan or investment. If you omit this argument, Excel defaults to 0. For loan payments, the balance should be zero after you pay off your loan.

- **Type.** The optional type argument represents the timing of the payments. Enter 0 if the payments are made at the end of the period, or enter 1 if the payments are made at the beginning of the period. If you omit this argument, Excel assumes a default of 0.

The ***PPMT function*** calculates the principal payment for a specified payment period on a loan or an investment given a fixed interest rate, specified term, and identical periodic payments. As shown in Figure 7.26, you can use the PPMT function to calculate the principal repayment in column E. For example, cell E8 contains =-PPMT(B$3/B$5,A8,B$4*B$5,B$2). You can type the negative sign after = or before any argument. The first month's total payment of $660.59 includes $592.09 principal repayment. The PPMT function has the same four required arguments and two optional arguments as the IPMT function.

=PPMT(rate,per,nper,pv,[fv],[type])

Calculate Cumulative Interest with the CUMIPMT Function

STEP 3 ▶▶ Although the IPMT function calculates the amount of interest paid in one particular loan payment, it does not determine the amount of interest paid over a specific number of payments. You can use the **CUMIPMT function** to calculate the cumulative interest through a specified payment period. This function accumulates the interest paid between selected payments or throughout the entire loan. For the first payment, the cumulative interest is the same as the periodic interest. From that point on, you can calculate the cumulative interest, such as the sum of the interest paid for the first two periods, as shown in cell H9 in Figure 7.26. If you do not want to calculate a running total for the entire loan, you can specify the interest between two periods, such as between payment periods 13 and 24, to calculate the total interest paid for the second year of the loan. The CUMIPMT contains six arguments.

=CUMIPMT(rate,nper,pv,start_period,end_period,type)

The rate, nper, pv, and type arguments are the same arguments that you use in the IPMT and PPMT functions. The start_period argument specifies the first period you want to start accumulating the interest, and the end_period argument specifies the last payment period you want to include. In Figure 7.26, the first cumulative interest payment formula in cell H8 uses 1 for both the start_period and end_period arguments. From that point on, the start_period is still 1, but the end_period changes to reflect each payment period, using the payment numbers in column A.

Calculate Cumulative Principal Payments with the CUMPRINC Function

STEP 4 ▶▶ You can use the **CUMPRINC function** to calculate the cumulative principal through a specified payment period. This function accumulates the principal repayment between selected payments or throughout the entire loan. For the first payment, the cumulative principal paid is the same as the first principal repayment. From that point on, you can calculate the cumulative principal payment, such as the sum of the principal repayment paid for the first two periods, as shown in cell I9 in Figure 7.26. If you do not want to calculate a running total for the entire loan, you can specify the principal repayment between two periods, such as between payment periods 13 and 24, to calculate the total principal repaid for the second year of the loan.

The CUMPRINC contains six arguments. The rate, nper, pv, start_period, end_period, and type arguments are the same arguments that you use in the CUMIPMT function.

=CUMPRINC(rate,nper,pv,start_period,end_period,type)

Quick Concepts

7. What is the difference between PV and NPV calculations? *p. 483*

8. In what situation would you use IPMT and PPMT? *p. 486*

9. What is the difference between IPMT and CUMIPMT? *p. 487*

Hands-On Exercises

Skills covered: Use the PV Function • Enter Formulas in the Amortization Table • Use the IPMT Function • Use the PPMT Function • Use the CUMIPMT Function • Use the CUMPRINC Function

3 Financial Functions

The location managers want new company cars. Angela Khazen, the chief financial officer, has determined that the company can afford $450 monthly payments based on a 5.25% APR for four-year loans. She wants you to prepare a loan amortization table and running totals for interest and principal repayment.

STEP 1 ▶▶ CALCULATE THE PRESENT VALUE

Because Angela determined the monthly payment for an automobile, you must use the PV function to calculate the loan amount. Other variables, such as trade-in value of the current vehicle, need to be considered, but you will exclude those variables at the moment. Refer to Figure 7.27 as you complete Step 1.

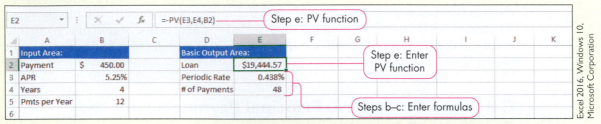

FIGURE 7.27 PV Function

a. Open *e07h2Salary_LastFirst* if you closed it at the end of Hands-On Exercise 2. and save it as **e07h3Salary_LastFirst**, changing h2 to h3. Click the **3-Finance sheet tab**.

You will calculate the periodic interest rate and number of payment periods before you can calculate the present value of the loan.

b. Click **cell E3**, type **=B3/B5**, and then press **Enter**.

The periodic rate, 0.438%, is the result of dividing the APR by the number of payments per year.

c. Type **=B4*B5** in **cell E4** and press **Enter**.

The total number of monthly payments, 48, is the product of the number of years the loan is outstanding and the number of payments per year.

d. Click **cell E2**, click **Financial** in the Function Library group on the Formulas tab, scroll through the list, and then select **PV**.

e. Click **cell E3** to enter that cell reference in the Rate box, click in the **Nper box**, and then click **cell E4**. Click in the **Pmt box**, type **B2**, and then click **OK**.

f. Edit the function by typing – between = and PV. Press **Enter**. Save the workbook.

The result is $19,444.57 based on four years of $450 monthly payments with an APR of 5.25%. You entered a negative sign after = to display the result as a positive value. If you do not enter a negative sign, Excel will display the loan as a negative value.

Angela wants you to create an amortization table. The column labels and payment numbers have already been entered into the worksheet. Now you will enter formulas to show the beginning loan balance for each payment, the monthly payment, interest paid, and principal repayment. Refer to Figure 7.28 as you complete Step 2.

| | D8 | | ▼ | ⋮ | × | ✓ | f_x | =-IPMT(E$3,A8,E$4,E$2) | Step c: IPMT function |

	A	B	C	D	E	F
1	**Input Area:**			**Basic Output Area:**		
2	Payment	$ 450.00		Loan	$19,444.57	
3	APR	5.25%		Periodic Rate	0.438%	
4	Years	4		# of Payments	48	
5	Pmts per Year	12				
6						
7	Payment Number	Beginning Balance	Monthly Payment	Interest Paid	Principal Repayment	Ending Balance
8	1	$19,444.57	$ 450.00	$ 85.07	$ 364.93	$ 19,079.64
9	2	$19,079.64	$ 450.00	$ 83.47	$ 366.53	$ 18,713.11
10	3	$18,713.11	$ 450.00	$ 81.87	$ 368.13	$ 18,344.98
48	41	$3,530.15	$ 450.00	$ 15.44	$ 434.56	$ 3,095.59
49	42	$3,095.59	$ 450.00	$ 13.54	$ 436.46	$ 2,659.13
50	43	$2,659.13	$ 450.00	$ 11.63	$ 438.37	$ 2,220.77
51	44	$2,220.77	$ 450.00	$ 9.72	$ 440.28	$ 1,780.48
52	45	$1,780.48	$ 450.00	$ 7.79	$ 442.21	$ 1,338.27
53	46	$1,338.27	$ 450.00	$ 5.85	$ 444.15	$ 894.13
54	47	$894.13	$ 450.00	$ 3.91	$ 446.09	$ 448.04
55	48	$448.04	$ 450.00	$ 1.96	$ 448.04	$ (0.00)
56	Totals		$ 21,600.00	$ 2,155.43	$ 19,444.57	
57						

Step a: Reference to original loan amount

Step e: =B8-E8 formula

Step d: PPMT function

Step f: =F8 formula

Step i: Total principal repaid

Step i: Total paid

Step i: Total interest

FIGURE 7.28 Loan Amortization Table

Excel 2016, Windows 10, Microsoft Corporation

a. Click **cell B8**, type **=E2**, and then press **Tab**.

You entered a reference to the original loan amount because that is the beginning balance to start the first payment period. Referencing the original cell is recommended instead of typing the value directly in the cell due to internal rounding. Furthermore, if you change the original input values, the calculated loan amount will change in both cells B8 and E2.

b. Type **=B$2** in **cell C8** and press **Ctrl+Enter**. Drag the **cell C8 fill handle** to copy the payment to the **range C9:C55**.

The monthly payment is $450.00. You entered a reference to the original monthly payment so that if you change it in cell B2, Excel will update the values in the Monthly Payment column automatically. The cell reference must be a mixed (B$2) or absolute ($B$2) reference to prevent the row number from changing when you copy the formula down the column later.

c. Click **cell D8**, click **Financial** in the Function Library, select **IPMT** to open the Function Arguments dialog box, type **E$3** in the Rate box, type **A8** in the Per box, type **E$4** in the Nper box, type **E$2** in the PV box, and then click **OK**. Edit the function by typing – between = and IPMT to convert the results to a positive value. Press **Ctrl+Enter**. Drag the **cell D8 fill handle** to copy the **IPMT** function to the **range D9:D55**.

The IPMT function calculates the interest of a specific payment based on the starting balance of $19,444.57 with a periodic interest of .438% over 48 payments. By not making cell A8 absolute, the function is able to adjust the period to match the specific period of evaluation.

d. Click **cell E8**, click **Financial** in the Function Library, select **PPMT** to open the Function Arguments dialog box, type **E$3** in the Rate box, type **A8** in the Per box, type **E$4** in the Nper box, type **E$2** in the PV box, and then click **OK**. Edit the function by typing – between = and PPMT to convert the results to a positive value. Press **Ctrl+Enter**. Drag the **cell E8 fill handle** to copy the PPMT function to the **range E9:E55**.

To calculate the principal repayment, subtract the interest of the first payment $85.07 from the monthly payment of $450. The remaining portion of the payment $364.93 goes toward paying down the principal owed. Using the PPMT function automatically completed these calculations.

e. Click in **cell F8** and type **=B8-E8**.

This calculates the ending balance after the first payment is made. The ending balance of $19,079.64 is calculated by subtracting the amount of principal in the payment $364.93 from the balance currently owed $19,444.57.

f. Click in **cell B9**, type **=F8**, and then press **Ctrl+Enter**.

The beginning balance of the second payment is also the ending balance of the first payment. The easiest method to populate the column is by referencing the ending balance from the prior month (cell F8). However, this can also be calculated by subtracting the previous principal repayment value (such as $364.93) from the previous month's beginning balance (such as $19,444.57).

g. Drag the **cell B9 fill handle** to copy the cell reference to the **range B10:B55**.

h. Drag the **cell F8 fill handle** to copy the formula to the **range F9:F55**.

The ending balance in cell F55 should be $0, indicating that the loan has been completely paid off.

i. Type SUM functions in **cells C56, D56**, and **E56**. Select the **range A56:F56** and apply the **Top and Double Bottom Border**. Save the workbook.

You calculated totals for the appropriate columns, noting that column B is a running balance and cannot be logically totaled. Figure 7.28 shows the top and bottom portions of the amortization table with rows 11 through 47 hidden.

The loan amortization table shows how much of each payment is interest and how much pays down the principal. However, Angela wants you to include a column to show the cumulative interest after each payment. Refer to Figure 7.29 as you complete Step 3.

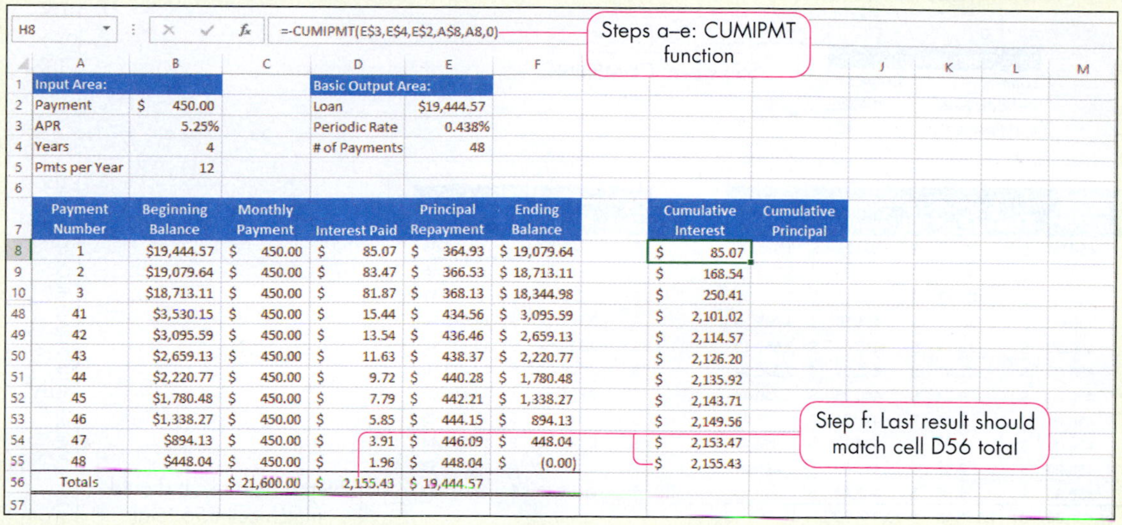

FIGURE 7.29 Cumulative Interest

a. Click **cell H8**, click **Financial** in the Function Library group on the Formulas tab, and then select **CUMIPMT**.

The Function Arguments dialog box displays so that you can enter the arguments for the CUMIPMT function.

b. Type the following arguments: **E$3** in the Rate box, **E$4** in the Nper box, **E$2** in the Pv box, and **A$8** in the Start_period box.

Make sure the cell references you enter in Rate, Nper, Pv, and Start_period boxes are mixed as shown to prevent the row number from changing as you copy the formula down the column.

> **TIP: MIXED OR ABSOLUTE REFERENCES**
> You can also use absolute references; however, the entire formula is easier to read (and is shorter) in the Formula Bar when you use mixed instead of absolute references.

c. Type **A8** in the End_period box.

This reference should be relative so that it reflects the current month's payment number as you copy the formula down the column.

d. Press **Tab**, type **0** in the Type box, and then click **OK**.

The cumulative interest for the first payment is the same as the first payment's interest. However, the formula displays a negative result, as indicated by the parentheses.

e. Edit the function by typing **-** between = and CUMIPMT to convert the results to a positive value. Press **Enter**.

The cumulative interest at the end of the first payment is identical to the interest on the first payment.

f. Copy the formula through **cell H55**. Save the workbook.

The cumulative interest in cell H55 should match the total interest paid calculated in cell D56: $2,155.43.

STEP 4 » CALCULATE CUMULATIVE PRINCIPAL PAID

Angela wants to see the cumulative principal paid after making each loan payment. You will use the CUMPRINC function to calculate the cumulative principal paid. Refer to Figure 7.30 as you complete Step 4.

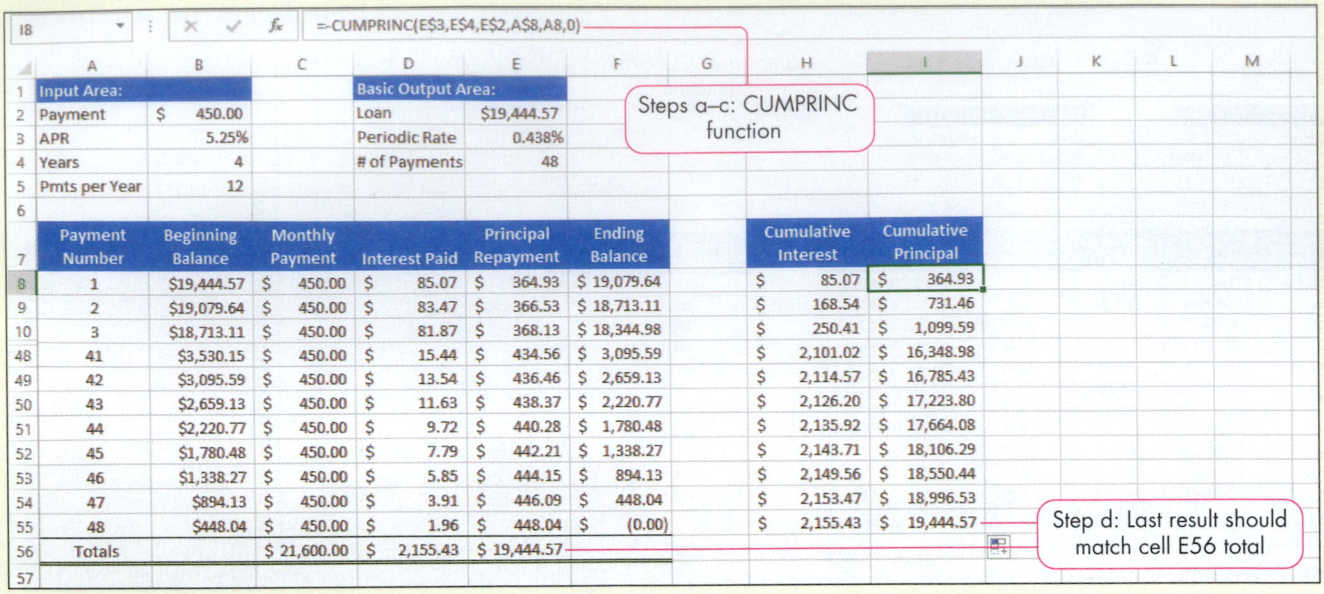

	A	B	C	D	E	F	G	H	I
1	Input Area:			Basic Output Area:					
2	Payment	$ 450.00		Loan	$19,444.57				
3	APR	5.25%		Periodic Rate	0.438%				
4	Years	4		# of Payments	48				
5	Pmts per Year	12							
6									
7	Payment Number	Beginning Balance	Monthly Payment	Interest Paid	Principal Repayment	Ending Balance		Cumulative Interest	Cumulative Principal
8	1	$19,444.57	$ 450.00	$ 85.07	$ 364.93	$ 19,079.64		$ 85.07	$ 364.93
9	2	$19,079.64	$ 450.00	$ 83.47	$ 366.53	$ 18,713.11		$ 168.54	$ 731.46
10	3	$18,713.11	$ 450.00	$ 81.87	$ 368.13	$ 18,344.98		$ 250.41	$ 1,099.59
48	41	$3,530.15	$ 450.00	$ 15.44	$ 434.56	$ 3,095.59		$ 2,101.02	$ 16,348.98
49	42	$3,095.59	$ 450.00	$ 13.54	$ 436.46	$ 2,659.13		$ 2,114.57	$ 16,785.43
50	43	$2,659.13	$ 450.00	$ 11.63	$ 438.37	$ 2,220.77		$ 2,126.20	$ 17,223.80
51	44	$2,220.77	$ 450.00	$ 9.72	$ 440.28	$ 1,780.48		$ 2,135.92	$ 17,664.08
52	45	$1,780.48	$ 450.00	$ 7.79	$ 442.21	$ 1,338.27		$ 2,143.71	$ 18,106.29
53	46	$1,338.27	$ 450.00	$ 5.85	$ 444.15	$ 894.13		$ 2,149.56	$ 18,550.44
54	47	$894.13	$ 450.00	$ 3.91	$ 446.09	$ 448.04		$ 2,153.47	$ 18,996.53
55	48	$448.04	$ 450.00	$ 1.96	$ 448.04	$ (0.00)		$ 2,155.43	$ 19,444.57
56	Totals		$ 21,600.00	$ 2,155.43	$ 19,444.57				
57									

FIGURE 7.30 Cumulative Principal

a. Click **cell I8**, click **Financial** in the Function Library group, and then select **CUMPRINC**.

The Function Arguments dialog box displays so that you can enter the arguments for the CUMPRINC function.

b. Type the following arguments: **E$3** in the Rate box, **E$4** in the Nper box, **E$2** in the Pv box, **A$8** in the Start_period box, **A8** in the End_period box, and **0** in the Type box.

c. Click **OK** and edit the function by typing - between = and CUMPRINC. Press **Ctrl+Enter**.

d. Copy the formula from **cell I8** to the **range I9:I55**.

The cumulative principal in cell I55 should match the total principal repayment calculated in cell E56: $19,444.57.

e. Save and close the file. Based on your instructor's directions, submit e07h3Salary_LastFirst.

Chapter Objectives Review

After reading this chapter, you have accomplished the following objectives:

1. Use date functions.

- Calculate days and years between dates: The DAYS function calculates the number of days between two dates, and the YEARFRAC function calculates the fraction of a year between two dates.
- Extract day, month, and year: The DAY function displays the day (1–31) within a month. The MONTH function displays the month (1–12) where 1 is January and 12 is December for a date. The YEAR function displays the year such as 2018 for a specific date.

2. Create a nested logical function.

- A nested IF function is one that contains one or more additional IF functions nested inside one or more arguments. This type of nested function helps derive calculations for complex situations with multiple outcomes.
- Nested IF within an IF function: When more than two outcomes are possible, you can nest an additional IF function within the value_if_true argument and/or value_if_false argument an IF function.
- Nest AND, OR, and NOT functions: Nested AND, OR, and NOT statements give you the ability to evaluate multiple conditions at the same time. The AND function returns TRUE if all conditions are true. The OR function returns TRUE if any condition is true. The NOT function returns TRUE if the statement is false and FALSE if the statement is true.

3. Use advanced lookup functions.

- Use the INDEX function: The INDEX function returns a value or the reference to a value within a range.
- Use the MATCH function: The MATCH function returns the position of a value in a list.
- Create a nested function: Nest the MATCH function inside the INDEX function to identify a location and then return related data.

4. Apply advanced filtering.

- Define a criteria range: Before you apply advanced filtering, you must define the criteria range that is separate from the table or list, contains column labels, and lists the conditions on the row(s) immediately below the column labels in the criteria range. Conditions listed on the same row form an AND condition. Conditions on multiple rows form an OR condition.
- Apply the Advanced Filter: Once applied, the Advanced Filter only displays information that meets predefined criteria. The output can filter the original table or copy records that meet the conditions in the output area.

5. Manipulate data with database functions.

- Use DSUM and DAVERAGE functions: The DSUM function adds the values in a database column based on specified conditions. The DAVERAGE function averages the values in a numeric database based on specified conditions.
- Identify values with DMAX and DMIN: The DMAX function returns the highest value in a database column that matches specified criteria. In contrast, the DMIN function returns the lowest value in a database column that matches specified criteria.
- Identify the total number with DCOUNT: The DCOUNT function counts the cells that contain numbers in a database column that match specified criteria.

6. Use financial functions.

- Calculate present and future values: The FV function calculates the future value of an investment. The PV function calculates the present value of an investment. These functions require a fixed rate, specified term, and identical periodic payments. The NPV function calculates net present value for an investment with a fixed rate where future payments may be identical or different.
- Use NPER and RATE functions: The NPER function calculates the number of payment periods for a loan or an investment with a fixed rate, present value, and identical periodic payments. The RATE function calculates the periodic interest rate for an investment or loan with a given number of payment periods, a fixed period payment, and present value.

7. Create a loan amortization table.

- A loan amortization table is a schedule of monthly payments, interest per period, principal repayment per period, and balances.
- Perform internal calculations: Use basic arithmetic operations to manually calculate interest and principal payments.
- Calculate interest and principal payments with IPMT and PPMT functions: The IPMT function calculates the periodic interest for a specified payment period on a loan or investment. The PPMT function calculates the principal payment for a specified payment period on a loan or investment.
- Calculate cumulative interest with CUMIPMT function: The CUMIPMT function calculates the cumulative interest for a specific period on a loan or investment.
- Calculate cumulative principal payments with the CUMPRIN function: The CUMPRINC function calculates the cumulative principal for a specific payment period.

Key Terms Matching

Match the key terms with their definitions. Write the key term letter by the appropriate numbered definition.

a. AND function
b. CUMIPMT function
c. CUMPRINC function
d. DAVERAGE function
e. DCOUNT function
f. DMAX function
g. DMIN function
h. DSUM function
i. FV function
j. INDEX function

k. IPMT function
l. Loan amortization table
m. MATCH function
n. NOT function
o. NPER function
p. NPV function
q. OR function
r. PPMT function
s. PV function
t. YEARFRAC function

1. _____ Calculates the number of periods for an investment or loan given a fixed rate, period payment, and present value. **p. 484**

2. _____ Calculates the future value of an investment given a fixed rate, a term, and identical periodic payments. **p. 483**

3. _____ Calculates the net present value of an investment with a fixed rate and periodic payments that may be identical or different. **p. 483**

4. _____ Calculates cumulative principal for a specified payment period. **p. 487**

5. _____ Calculates the present value of an investment with a fixed rate, specified number of periods, and identical periodic payments that will be made in the future. **p. 482**

6. _____ Calculates cumulative interest for a specified payment period. **p. 487**

7. _____ A schedule showing monthly payments, interest per payment, amount toward paying off the loan, and the remaining balance for each payment. **p. 485**

8. _____ Calculates the principal payment for a specified payment period on a loan or an investment given a fixed rate, a specified term, and identical periodic payments. **p. 486**

9. _____ Calculates periodic interest for a specific payment period on a loan or investment with a fixed rate, a specified term, and identical periodic payments. **p. 486**

10. _____ Counts the cells that contain a number in a database column that matches specified conditions. **p. 477**

11. _____ Identifies the highest value in a database column that matches specified conditions. **p. 476**

12. _____ Identifies the lowest value in a database column that matches specified conditions. **p. 476**

13. _____ Averages values in a database column that match specified conditions. **p. 476**

14. _____ Adds values in a database column that match specified conditions. **p. 476**

15. _____ Calculates the fraction of a year between two dates based on the number of whole days. **p. 456**

16. _____ Returns a value or reference to a value within a range based on the intersection of a specific row and column. **p. 462**

17. _____ Identifies the position of a value in a list based on a lookup value, a lookup array, and a match type. **p. 463**

18. _____ Returns TRUE if the argument is false and FALSE if the argument is true. **p. 462**

19. _____ Returns TRUE if any argument is true and returns FALSE if all arguments are false. **p. 461**

20. _____ Returns TRUE when all arguments are true and FALSE when at least one argument is false. **p. 460**

Multiple Choice

1. Today's date (February 12, 2018) is stored in cell B1. The last day of the semester (May 4, 2018) is stored in cell B2. You want to know how many days until the end of the semester? Which function should you use?

   (a) =DAYS(B1,B2)

   (b) =DAYS(B2,B1)

   (c) =YEARFRAC(B1,B2)

   (d) =DAY(B1)

2. The date 5/12/2018 is stored in cell C1. What function should you use to extract just 12?

   (a) =YEAR(C1)

   (b) =MONTH(C1)

   (c) =DAYS(B1,C1)

   (d) =DAY(C1)

3. Your workbook contains a list of artwork. Column B lists Sold Out if the piece is sold out, Available if it is still readily available, or Limited if only a few pieces are available. In the third column, you want to display TRUE if the art is not sold out. What function would produce the same results as =OR(B1="Available",B1="Limited")?

   (a) =AND(B1="Available",B1="Limited")

   (b) =IF(B1="Sold Out","TRUE", "FALSE")

   (c) =NOT(B1="Sold Out")

   (d) =TRUE(B1<>"Sold Out")

4. A workbook contains a list of members in the Computer Club. You want to identify the number of students who are freshmen who are Information Systems majors. Without filtering the dataset, what function should you use?

   (a) DCOUNT

   (b) COUNTA

   (c) DSUM

   (d) COUNT

5. A worksheet contains the times in which runners completed a race, with the times organized from fastest to slowest. You will use the MATCH function to identify what place a runner came in given a time of 4:05 (four minutes and five seconds). Which argument should contain the specific runner's time?

   (a) Lookup_array

   (b) Lookup_value

   (c) Match_type

   (d) Row_num

6. What function would you use to calculate the total interest paid for the first year of a mortgage?

   (a) CUMIPMT

   (b) IPMT

   (c) PPMT

   (d) CUMPRINC

7. When you are performing an advanced filter, where do you enter the range for the dataset?

   (a) Criteria range

   (b) Output range

   (c) List range

   (d) Copy to range

8. The original mortgage loan was for $300,000 with a 5% APR for 30 years. You want to calculate the interest on the last monthly payment at the end of the 15th year. What value should be referenced for the per argument in the IPMT function?

   (a) 15

   (b) 180

   (c) 30

   (d) 0.05/12

9. A local police office wants to create a rule that if an officer pulls over a person for exceeding the speed limit by at least five miles per hour or if that person has two or more speeding violations on record, the officer will fine the speeder the higher of $200 or $50 for each mile over the speed limit. Otherwise, the fine is $45. The speed limit is entered in cell B5, the person's speed is entered in cell B10, and the person's number of previous tickets is entered in cell B11. What function derives the correct answer?

   (a) =IF(AND(B10>B5,B11>=2),200,45)

   (b) =IF(AND(B10-B5>=5,B11<2),MAX(200, (B10-B5)*50),45)

   (c) =IF(OR(B10-B5>=5,B11>=2),MAX(200, (B10-B5)*50),45)

   (d) =IF(OR(B10>B5,B11>=2),MAX(200,50),45)

10. What function would you use to calculate the total number of periods in a loan or investment?

    (a) NPER

    (b) RATE

    (c) PV

    (d) FV

1 Furniture Sales

As the manager of Reid's Furniture Store, you track sales transactions by sales person, department, amount, and payment type. Customers either finance their purchase through your store or pay in full at the time of purchase. You will calculate down payments and balances for all transactions. If a transaction is paid in full, the balance is zero. Customers who finance their transactions must pay off the balance within four years from the transaction date. You want to review paid-in-full transactions above $4,000, identify the highest cash transaction, and identify which sales person was responsible for that sale. Refer to Figure 7.31 as you complete this exercise.

	A	B	C	D	E	F	G	H	I	J	K	L
I113					fx	=IF(H113>0,EDATE(C113,48),"-")						
1	Reid Furniture Store											
2												
3	Required Down Payment:		10%									
4	No. of Monthly Payments:		48									
5												
6	Number	Salesperson	Date	Department	Type	Amount	Down Paym	Balance	Last PMT Date			
106	2018-096	Gruenewald	3/29/2018	Bedroom	Finance	3,285	$ 328.50	2,956.50	3/29/2022			
107	2018-097	Gruenewald	3/29/2018	Bedroom	Finance	14,321	$ 1,432.10	12,888.90	3/29/2022			
108	2018-098	Gallagher	3/30/2018	Dining Room	Finance	2,480	$ 248.00	2,232.00	3/30/2022			
109	2018-099	Gallagher	3/30/2018	Bedroom	Finance	1,425	$ 142.50	1,282.50	3/30/2022			
110	2018-100	Desmarais	3/30/2018	Bedroom	Finance	11,234	$ 1,123.40	10,110.60	3/30/2022			
111	2018-101	Gruenewald	3/31/2018	Bedroom	Finance	5,773	$ 577.30	5,195.70	3/31/2022			
112	2018-102	Desmarais	3/31/2018	Bedroom	Paid in Full	2,000	$ 2,000.00	-	-			
113	2018-103	Gruenewald	3/31/2018	Living Room	Finance	2,505	$ 250.50	2,254.50	3/31/2022			
114												
115												
116	Number	Salesperson	Date	Department	Type	Amount	Down Paym	Balance	Last PMT Date			
117					Paid in Full	>4000						
118												
119												
120	Number	Salesperson	Date	Department	Type	Amount	Down Paym	Balance	Last PMT Date		Paid-in-Full Transactions	
121	2018-014	Gallagher	3/3/2018	Dining Room	Paid in Full	4,550	$ 4,550.00	-	-		No. of Paid-in-Full Transactions	7
122	2018-026	Gruenewald	3/7/2018	Living Room	Paid in Full	7,690	$ 7,690.00	-	-		Average Amount Above $4,000	$ 6,450.29
123	2018-075	Sardelis	3/24/2018	Living Room	Paid in Full	4,275	$ 4,275.00	-	-		Highest Paid-in-Full Transaction Amount	$11,972.00
124	2018-078	Desmarais	3/24/2018	Bedroom	Paid in Full	4,200	$ 4,200.00	-	-		Salesperson for Highest Cash Payment	Sardelis
125	2018-086	Sardelis	3/26/2018	Bedroom	Paid in Full	8,340	$ 8,340.00	-	-			
126	2018-088	Desmarais	3/26/2018	Bedroom	Paid in Full	4,125	$ 4,125.00	-	-			
127	2018-089	Sardelis	3/26/2018	Bedroom	Paid in Full	11,972	$11,972.00	-	-			
128												

March Data

Ready

Excel 2016, Windows 10, Microsoft Corporation

FIGURE 7.31 Furniture Store

a. Open *e07p1Furniture* and save it as **e07p1Furniture_LastFirst**.

b. Calculate the down payment for all sales. If a transaction is not financed, the down payment is identical to the amount. If the transaction is financed, the down payment is 10% of the amount purchased. Complete the following steps:

- Click **cell G7**.
- Click the **Formulas tab**, click **Logical** in the Function Library, and then select **IF**.
- Type **NOT(E7="Finance")** in the Logical_test box in the Function Arguments dialog box.
- Press **Tab** and type **F7** in the Value_if_true box.
- Press **Tab** and type **F7*C$3** to multiply the amount purchased by the down payment percentage rate in cell C3. Click **OK**.
- Double-click the **cell G7 fill handle** to copy the formula to the **range G8:G113**.

c. Click **cell H7**, type **=F7-G7**, and press **Ctrl+Enter**. Copy the formula to the **range H8:H113**. Notice that paid-in-full transactions show a negative sign (–) instead of a value.

d. Click **cell I7** and calculate the date the payment is due by completing the following steps:

- Click **Logical** in the Function Library and select **IF**.
- Type **H7>0** in the Logical_test box in the Function Arguments dialog box.
- Click in the **Value_if_true box**, click the **Name Box arrow**, select **More Functions**, type **EDATE**, click **Go**, and then click **OK**.
- Type **C7** in the Start_date box.
- Click in the **Months box**, type **C$4**, and then click **OK**.
- Edit the function to look like this: **=IF(H7>0,EDATE(C7,48),"-")**
- Double-click the **cell I7 fill handle** to copy the formula to the **range I8:I113**.

e. Create a criteria range that specifies Paid In Full transaction types and amounts greater than $4,000 by completing the following steps:

- Select the **range A6:I6** and click **Copy** in the Clipboard group on the Home tab.
- Click **cell A116** and click **Paste** in the Clipboard group on the Home tab to create the header for the criteria range.
- Click **cell A120** and click **Paste** in the Clipboard group on the Home tab to create the header for the output range. Press **Esc**.
- Click **cell E117** and type **Paid in Full**.
- Click **cell F117** and type **>4000**.

f. Apply an advanced filter by completing the following steps:

- Click **cell F113**, click the **Data tab**, and click **Advanced** in the Sort & Filter group.
- Click **Copy to another location**.
- Click in the **List range box** and select the **range A6:I113**.
- Click in the **Criteria range box** and select the **range A116:I117**.
- Click in the **Copy to box** and select the **range A120:I120**. Click **OK**.

g. Calculate the number of paid-in-full transactions by completing the following steps:

- Click **cell L121**, click **Insert Function**, click the **Or select a category arrow**, select **Database**, select **DCOUNT**, and then click **OK**.
- Type **A6:I113** in the Database box.
- Click in the **Field box** and type **"Amount"**.
- Click in the **Criteria box** and type **A116:I117**. Click **OK**.

h. Calculate the average amount for paid-in-full transactions over $4,000 by completing the following steps:

- Click **cell L122**, click **Insert Function**, select **DAVERAGE**, and then click **OK**.
- Type **A6:I113** in the Database box.
- Click in the **Field box** and type **"Amount"**.
- Click in the **Criteria box** and type **A116:I117**. Click **OK**.

i. Calculate the largest amount for paid-in-full transactions over $4,000 by completing the following steps:

- Click **cell L123**, click **Insert Function**, select **DMAX**, and then click **OK**.
- Type **A6:I113** in the Database box.
- Click in the **Field box** and type **"Amount"**.
- Click in the **Criteria box** and type **A116:I117**. Click **OK**.

j. Identify the sales person who completed the largest paid-in-full transaction by completing the following steps:

- Click **cell L124**, click the **Formulas tab**, click **Lookup & Reference** in the Function Library, select **INDEX**, and then click **OK**. Select **array,row_num,colum_num**. Click **OK**.
- Type **A6:I113** in the Array box.
- Click in the **Row_num box** and type **MATCH(L123,F6:F113,0)** to identify the row that contains the largest cash amount.
- Click in the **Col_num box**, type **2** to specify that the second column of the dataset contains the salespeople's names, and then click **OK**. The completed function looks like this: **=INDEX(A6:I113,MATCH(L123,F6:F113,0),2)**. Sardelis is the salesperson who completed the largest paid-in-full transaction.

k. Create a footer with your name on the left side, the sheet name code in the center, and the file name code on the right side.

l. Save and close the file. Based on your instructor's directions, submit e07p1Furniture_LastFirst.

2 Detailed Loan Amortization

You are planning to buy a house soon, so you want to set up a detailed loan amortization table. So far, you have designed a worksheet with a loan parameters area (i.e., input area), a summary area, and amortization table column labels. You want to build in mechanisms to prevent formula errors if input data are missing and to hide zeros from displaying if you take out a shorter-term loan or pay it off early. However, you must keep formulas in place for a traditional 30-year loan. In addition, you will notice overpayments on the last payment if you pay extra toward the principal each month. To make the amortization table as flexible as possible and to avoid errors, you will create several nested IF functions. Refer to Figure 7.32 as you complete this exercise.

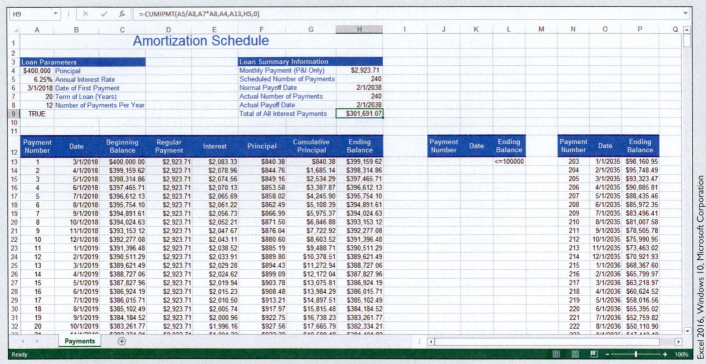

FIGURE 7.32 Detailed Amortization Table

a. Open *e07p2House* and save it as **e07p2House_LastFirst**.

b. Click in each cell in the **range B13:F13** to look at the formulas in the Formula Bar. Delete the contents of **cell A7** and look at the #NUM! errors.

c. Click **cell A9**, click the **Formulas tab**, click **Logical**, and then select **AND**. In the Function Arguments dialog box, complete the following steps:

- Type **A4>0** in the Logical1 box.
- Type **A5>0** in the Logical2 box.
- Type **A6>0** in the Logical3 box.
- Type **A7>0** in the Logical4 box.
- Type **A8>0** in the Logical5 box and click **OK**.

The arguments ensure that if any required input value is missing, the AND function returns FALSE. You will use cell A10's results to avoid error messages in calculated cells. Currently, the result is FALSE because you deleted the contents of cell A7.

d. Assign the range name **DataEntered** to **cell A9** so that you can use a range name in formulas that refer to this cell.

e. Enter the following replacement functions on row 13 to test if data have been entered or if cell A13 contains a value greater than zero. If data have been entered, calculations occur. If not, the functions return zeros:

- **Cell A13**: **=IF(DataEntered,1,0)**

  If DataEntered (cell A9) is TRUE, Excel will display 1 for first payment number. If DataEntered is FALSE, Excel will display 0 for first payment number.

- **Cell B13**: **=IF(A13>0,A6,"")**

  If cell A13 is greater than 0, Excel will display date of first payment entered in cell A6. If cell A13 contains a value of 0, Excel displays an empty cell.

- **Cell C13**: **=IF(A13>0,A4,0)**
- **Cell D13**: **=IF(A13>0,H$4,0)**
- **Cell E13**: **=IF(A13>0,IPMT(A$5/A$8,A13,H$5,-A$4),0)**
- **Cell F13**: **=IF(A13>0,PPMT(A$5/A$8,A13,H$5,-A$4,0),0)**
- **Cell G13**: **=IF(A13>0,-CUMPRINC(A$5/A$8,H$5,A$4,A$13,A13,0),0)**
- **Cell H13**: **=C13-F13**

f. Edit the formula in **cell H4** to be **=IF(DataEntered,PMT(A5/A8,H5,-A4),0)**. Edit the formula in **cell H5** to be **=IF(DataEntered,A7*A8,0)**.

All error messages should be gone now.

g. Type **30** in **cell A7** to see calculated results appear.

Because all required input values are entered, the AND function in cell A10 indicates TRUE, which is then used in several IF functions that display calculated results if all required inputs are entered.

h. Type the following formulas on row 14 to calculate values for the second payment:

- **Cell A14**: **=IF(H13>1,A13+1,0)**
  This function calculates the next payment number only if the previous ending balance is greater than one. (The ending balance in cell H13 may display $0, but due to rounding, the actual value may be one or two cents. This is why the logical argument is H13>1).

- **Cell B14**: **=IF(A14>0,DATE(YEAR(B13),MONTH(B13)+1,DAY(B13)),0)**
  The date functions identify the specific year, month, and day and add 1 to increase each due date to the next month. The result is 43191 because it is a serial date so far. You will format it soon.

- **Cell C14**: **=IF(A14>0,H13,0)**
  The beginning balance is equal to the ending balance from the previous period.

i. Format **cell B14** as **Short Date** and format **range C13:H14** as **Currency** (not Accounting Number Format).

j. Select the **range D13:H13** and drag the fill handle down to copy the formulas to row 14. Select the **range A14:H14** and drag the fill handle down to copy the formulas to row 373— one row after the end of the 360th payment in which the 30-year loan is paid off.

k. Click **cell A7** and change the value to **20** years. Scroll down the amortization table to row 252—the end of the 240th payment in which the 20-year loan is paid off. Notice that rows 253 through 372 contain zeros because the loan is paid off.

l. Click the **File tab**, click **Options**, and then click **Advanced** to see Advanced Options for working with Excel.

m. Scroll through the options to see *Display options for this worksheet: Payments*, click the **Show a zero in cells that have zero value check box** to deselect it, and then click **OK**. Deselecting this option hides the zeros in rows 253 through 372, but Excel keeps the formulas intact in case the results change. If you change the term to 30 years again, the results will display in the otherwise empty cells.

n. Click **cell D13** and type **=IF(A13>0,IF(C13>$H$4,$H$4,C13*A$5/A$8+C13),0)**. If cell A13 is 0, then the result shows zero. If the logical_test is true, the nested IF statement checks the current balance against the regular monthly payment. If the balance is greater, you pay the monthly payment. If the monthly payment is higher, you pay the balance plus the interest on the balance only to avoid overpayment. Double-click the **cell D13 fill handle** to copy the formula down the column through **cell D373**.

o. Click **cell H6**, type **=IF(DataEntered,DATE(YEAR(A6),MONTH(A6)+(A7-1)*A8+11,DAY(A6)),0)**, and then format it as **Short Date** to determine the normal payoff date if you do not make any extra payments.

p. Click **cell H7** and type **=IF(DataEntered,MATCH(0,BeginningBalance,0)-1,0)**. The MATCH function searches the existing range name BeginningBalance for the smallest value that is greater than or equal to zero. The balance never goes exactly to zero because of a rounding error. Thus, the row above the match corresponds to the number of actual payments.

q. Click **cell H8** and type **=IF(DataEntered,INDEX(AmortizationTable,H7,2),0)**. Apply the **Short Date format** to **cell H8**. The INDEX function returns the date from column 2 of the row within the table that was returned by the MATCH function in the above step.

r. Click **cell H9**, type **=-CUMIPMT(A5/A8,A7*A8,A4,A13,H5,0)**, and then format it as **Currency**.

s. Complete the criteria range by typing **<=100000** in **cell L13**. You want to locate the payments where the ending balance is less than $100,000.

t. Perform an advanced filter by completing the following steps:

- Click **cell H13**, click the **Data tab**, and then click **Advanced**.
- Click **Copy to another location**.
- Make sure the **List range** is $A$12:$H$373.
- Click in the **Criteria range box** and select the **range J12:L13**.
- Click in the **Copy to box** and select the **range N12:P12**. Click **OK**.

u. Create a footer with your name on the left side, the sheet name code in the center, and the file name code on the right side.

v. Save and close the file. Based on your instructor's directions, submit e07p2House_LastFirst.

3 Financial Investments

Some of your friends are in a business finance class. They are studying for their first test and will have to use financial calculators. As they practice for the test, they want to make sure they are calculating investment variables correctly. You volunteered to set up an investment model in which they enter the input variables to check their answers against formula calculations you will enter. Refer to Figure 7.33 as you complete this exercise.

E11 | =-FV(E7,E9,E10,E5)

	A	B	C	D	E	F
1	**Instructions:**	Enter input values in cells with light blue.				
2						
3	**Investment Variable**	**PMT/FV**	**PV**	**NPER/FV**	**RATE/FV**	
4	Payments Per Year	12	12	12	12	
5	Present Value	$ 100,000.00	**$ 100,000.00**	$ 100,000.00	$ 100,000.00	
6	APR	10.00%	10.00%	10.00%	**10.00%**	
7	Rate	**0.83%**	**0.83%**	**0.83%**	**0.83%**	
8	Term	20	20	**20**	20	
9	No. of Payments	**240**	**240**	**240**	**240**	
10	Periodic Payment	**$ 965.02**	$ 965.02	$ 965.02	$ 965.02	
11	Future Value	**$1,465,614.73**	$ 1,465,614.73	**$1,465,614.73**	**$1,465,614.73**	
12						

Excel 2016, Windows 10, Microsoft Corporation

FIGURE 7.33 Financial Functions

a. Open *e07p3Finance* and save it as **e07p3Finance_LastFirst**.

b. Calculate the periodic rate, number of periods, periodic payment, and future value in column B by completing the following steps:

- Click **cell B7** and type **=B6/B4** to calculate the periodic rate.
- Click **cell B9** and type **=B8*B4** to calculate the number of payment periods.
- Click **cell B10**, click the **Formulas tab**, click **Financial** in the Function Library group, scroll down, and then select **PMT**. Type **B7** in the Rate box, type **B9** in the Nper box, and then type **-B5** in the PV box. Click **OK** to calculate the monthly payment.
- Click **cell B11**, click **Financial** in the Function Library group, and then select **FV**. Type **B7** in the Rate box, type **B9** in the Nper box, type **B10** in the Pmt box, and then type **B5** in the Pv box. Click **OK** and edit the formula by typing - on the right side of **=**.

c. Calculate the number of payments, periodic rate, and present value in column C by completing the following steps:

- Click **cell C9** and type **=C8*C4** to calculate the number of payment periods.
- Click **cell C7** and type **=C6/C4** to calculate the periodic rate.
- Click **cell C5**, click **Financial** in the Function Library group, and then select **PV**. Type **C7** in the Rate box, type **C9** in the Nper box, and then type **C10** in the Pmt box. Click **OK** and edit the formula by typing - on the right side of **=**.

d. Calculate the rate, number of payment periods, term, and future value in column D by completing the following steps:

- Click **cell D7** and type **=D6/D4** to calculate the periodic rate.
- Click **cell D9**, click **Financial** in the Function Library group, and then select **NPER**. Type **D7** in the Rate box, type **D10** in the Pmt box, type **-D5** in the Pv box, and then click **OK**.
- Click **cell D8** and type **=D9/D4** to calculate the term (i.e., number of years).
- Click **cell D11** and type **=-FV(D7,D9,D10,D5)** to calculate the future value.

e. Calculate the number of payment periods, rate, APR, and future value in column E by completing the following steps:

- Click **cell E9** and type **=E8*E4** to calculate the number of payment periods.
- Click **cell E7**, click **Financial** in the Function Library group, and then select **RATE**. Type **E9** in the Nper box, type **-E10** in the Pmt box, type **E5** in the Pv box, and then click **OK**.
- Click **cell E6** and type **=E7*E4** to calculate the APR.
- Click **cell E11** and type **=-FV(E7,E9,E10,E5)** to calculate the future value.

f. Create a footer with your name on the left side, the sheet name code in the center, and the file name code on the right side.

g. Save and close the file. Based on your instructor's directions, submit e07p3Finance_LastFirst.

Mid-Level Exercises

1 West Coast University Admissions Office

You work in the Admissions Office for West Coast University, a mid-sized regional university in California. Your assistant entered a list of college applicants for the Fall 2018 semester. You determine if a student qualifies for early admission or early rejection based on SAT and GPA. After determining the immediate admissions and rejections, you calculate a total score based on SAT and GPA to determine regular admissions and rejections.

a. Open *e07m1Admissions* and save it as **e07m1Admissions_LastFirst**.

b. Enter a date function in **cell E14** that calculates the number of days between the Initial Deadline and the Date Received. Copy the function to the **range E15:E513**. A negative value indicates the application was received after the initial deadline.

c. Enter a nested logical function in **cell H14** to display either Yes or No in the Admit Early column. The university admits a student early if that student meets both the Early Admission criteria for the SAT (cell B6) and GPA (cell B7). That is, the student's SAT score must be 2000 or higher, and the GPA must be 3.80 or higher. Use relative and mixed references to the cells in the Admission Criteria range. Based on the requirements, the first student, Frank Aaron, will not be admitted early. Copy the function to the **range H15:H513**.

d. Enter a nested logical function in **cell I14** to display either Yes or No in the Reject Early column. The university rejects a student early if that student has either an SAT score less than 1000 (cell C6) or a GPA below 1.80 (C7). Use relative and mixed references to the cells in the Admission Criteria range. Copy the function to the **range I15:I513**.

e. Enter a formula in **cell J14** to calculate an applicant's Score. Apply the multiplier (found in the Miscellaneous Standards & Filter range) to the student's GPA and add that score to the SAT. Frank Aaron's score is 3496. Copy the function to the **range J15:J513**.

f. Enter a nested IF function inside a main IF function in **cell K14** (the Final Decision column). The decision text should be one of the following: Early Admission, Early Rejection, Admit, or Reject. Hint: Two logical tests are based on the Yes/No displayed in the Admit Early and Reject Early columns. For regular admission, a student must have a combined admission score that is 2900 or higher. A student is rejected if his or her score is lower than the threshold. Use a mixed reference to the cell in the Miscellaneous Standards & Filter range. Copy the function, select the **range K15:K513**, click **Paste** on the Home tab, and then click **Formulas** to copy just the formulas. If you use a regular Paste option, the double bottom borders will copy with the formulas.

g. Type the criteria in Criteria Range 1:
   - **>=2900** in **cell L6**
   - **Early Admission** in **cell M6**

h. Enter a database function in **cell H6** to count the total number of early admissions with >= the threshold score. Use the **range L5:M6** for the criteria range.

i. Enter a database function in **cell I6** to calculate the average SAT score for early admissions with >= threshold score. Use the **range L5:M6** for the criteria range.

j. Enter a database function in **cell J6** to calculate the average GPA for early admissions with >= threshold score. Use the **range L5:M6** for the criteria range.

k. Type the criteria in Criteria Range 2:
   - **In State** in **cell L10**
   - **Early Admission** in **cell M10**

l. Enter a database function in **cell H7** to count the total number of in-state early admissions. Use the **range L9:M10** for the criteria range.

m. Enter a database function in **cell I7** to calculate the average SAT for early in-state admissions. Use the **range L9:M10** for the criteria range.

n. Enter a database function in **cell J7** to calculate the average GPA for all in-state early admissions. Use the **range L9:M10** for the criteria range.

o. Enter a database function in **cell H9** to calculate the highest score for all in-state early admissions. Use the **range L9:L10** for the criteria range.

p. Enter an INDEX function with a nested MATCH function in **cell H10** to identify the last name of the person who had the highest overall score for in-state early admissions. The function should display Alevy.

q. Create a footer with your name on the left side, Page 1 of 28 codes in the middle, and the file name code on the right side.

r. Save and close the file. Based on your instructor's directions, submit e07m1Admissions_LastFirst.

2 Artwork Database

You are an analyst for an art gallery that is an authorized Greenwich Workshop fine art dealer (www.greenwichworkshop.com). Customers in your area are especially fond of James C. Christensen's art. You prepared a list of artwork: art, type, edition size, release date, issue price, and estimated market value. You want to identify highly sought-after pieces based on age, percentage of value increase, and sold-out status. In addition, you want to apply an advanced filter and identify specific details from the filtered data.

a. Open *e07m2Art* and save it as **e07m2Art_LastFirst**.

DISCOVER

b. Make sure the Valuable worksheet is active and enter the YEARFRAC function in **cell G2** to calculate the number of years from the release date and the date in **cell Q2**. Use relative and mixed references correctly. Format the value with **Comma Style** with one decimal place. Copy the function to the **range G3:G165**.

c. Enter a nested logical function in **cell L2** to display **Highly Valuable** if either condition is met:
  • The release date is on or before December 31, 1989, or
  • The sold-out status is Yes *and* the percentage increase in value is at least 500% *and* the Edition Size was less than 400.

Enter an empty text string if the conditions are not met. Hint: You will need to nest two logical functions within the logical test argument. Use cell references to the two conditions.

d. Copy the function from **cell L2** to the **range L3:165**.

e. Click **cell O10** and enter the database function to count the number of art pieces where the comment is Highly Valuable. The criteria range is located in the range N6:N7.

f. Click **cell O11** and enter the database function to calculate the average of art pieces where the comment is Highly Valuable. The criteria range is located in the range N6:N7.

g. Click **cell O12** and enter the database function to calculate the total estimated value of art pieces where the comment is Highly Valuable. The criteria range is located in the range N6:N7.

h. Display the Database worksheet. Assign a range name called **database** to the **range A14:J178**. Assign a range name called **Criteria** to the **range A7:J9**.

i. Create column labels for the criteria range and replace the Edition Size with a second Release Date column label. Set the following conditions in the criteria range:
  • Sold-out limited-edition canvases released after 1/1/2000 and before 12/31/2003
  • Sold-out limited-edition prints released after 1/1/2000 and before 12/31/2003

j. Create an advanced filter using the database list and criteria range. Filter the records in place.

k. Enter the appropriate database function in **cell C2** in the Summary Statistics area to calculate the highest estimated value of the filtered records. Apply **Currency** format and left-align the value.

DISCOVER

l. Enter a nested function using INDEX and MATCH to display the title (in cell C3) and the release date (in cell C4) for highest estimated valued filtered artwork. Left-align and format the date.

m. Create a footer with your name on the left side, the sheet name code in the center, and the file name code on the right side on each worksheet.

n. Save and close the file. Based on your instructor's directions, submit e07m2Art_LastFirst.

An out-of-state family member asked for your assistance with financial planning. First, he is considering purchasing a house and would like you to create a detailed amortization table and calculate cumulative principal paid, as well as cumulative interest throughout the loan, total amount of interest, and interest for selected years. In addition, he is considering a five-year investment in which you invest $75 per month. He would like you to calculate the interest earned per month and the ending values. Once you have completed the work, you will upload your file to OneDrive to allow for review.

Student 1:

a. Open *e07m3Personal* and save it as **e07m3Personal_LastFirst**.

b. Enter formulas on the Loan worksheet to complete the Calculations area, which is **range E2:E5**.

c. Enter values 1 through **360** in the Payment Number column, starting in **cell A10**.

d. Calculate values for the first payment on row 10 using appropriate relative, mixed, and absolute references:
   - Beginning Balance: Create a reference to the appropriate value above the amortization table.
   - Monthly Payment: Enter a reference to the calculated monthly payment.
   - Interest Paid: Use the appropriate financial function to calculate the interest payment for the given period.
   - Principal Repayment: Use the appropriate financial function to calculate the principal repayment for the given period.
   - Ending Balance: Enter the formula to calculate the ending balance after you make the first payment.

e. Type a reference to display the beginning balance for the second period. Copy formulas down their respective columns to row 369. Apply **Accounting Number Format** to the monetary values.

f. Calculate the following cumulative values:
   - Total Interest: Enter the appropriate financial function to calculate the total interest for the entire loan in **cell I6**.
   - Cumulative Interest: Use the appropriate financial function to calculate the cumulative interest for each period, starting in **cell H10**. The final value in cell H369 should be identical to the value calculated in cell I6.
   - Cumulative Principal: Use the appropriate financial function to calculate the cumulative principal for each period, starting in **cell I10**. The final value in cell I369 should match the loan amount in cell E3.
   - Interest Paid Summary: Enter individual financial functions to calculate total interest paid during specific years in the **range I2:I5**. The first function calculates total interest for the fifth year only, which is $13,441.15.

g. Format monetary values with **Accounting Number Format**.

h. Set appropriate margins and page scaling to fit one page so that if you decide to print the Loan worksheet, all columns fit across each page. Repeat the headings on row 9 on all pages. Create a footer with your name and the worksheet tab code on the right side of the Loan worksheet.

i. Save the file to OneDrive to share with student 2.

Student 2:

j. Open *e07m3Personal_LastFirst* and save it as **e07m3Personal_LastFirst_LastFirst,** using your name after the first student's name.

k. Display the Investment worksheet and in **cell A12**, enter a reference to the original start of the first investment period date. In **cell A13**, enter the DATE function with nested YEAR, MONTH, and DAY functions with appropriate arguments. Ensure that the month number represents the next month. Copy the formula down the column and apply different but complementary shading, such as starting with **Dark Blue, Text 2, Lighter 80%** for the first 12 months, applying

Dark Blue, Text 2, Lighter 60% to the next 12 months, and continuing to apply darker shades for to each 12-month period of dates. Apply right horizontal alignment and increase the indent three times for the dates in column A.

l. Enter formulas for the first period:

- Beginning Value: Type **0**.
- Interest Earned: Enter a formula to calculate the interest for the first period. Use relative and mixed references only.
- End-of-Period Invest: Enter a reference to the Deposit per Period found in the Input Area.
- Ending Value: Calculate the Ending Value, which includes the Beginning Value, Interest Earned, and End-of-Period Invest.

m. Calculate the second period's Beginning Value by referencing the previous period's Ending Value. Copy formulas down the columns.

n. Enter the appropriate financial function in **cell E75** to calculate the final value of the investment. This value should be identical to the value shown in cell E71.

o. Format monetary values with **Accounting Number Format**.

p. Adjust margins and insert a page break so that the first three years of investment display on page 1. Center the worksheet data between the left and right margins, and repeat the column headings at the top of page 2. Create a footer with your name on the left side, the sheet name code in the center, and the file name code on the right side of all worksheets.

 q. Answer the questions on the Q&A worksheet as you make these changes:

- Click the Loan worksheet and change the value in **cell B2** to **$350,000**.
- Click the Investment worksheet and change **cell B5** to **$125.00**.
- Click the Investment worksheet and change **cell B3** to **10**. After answering Question 3 on the Q&A worksheet, change the **cell B3** back to **5**.

r. Save and close the file. Based on your instructor's directions, submit e07m3Personal_LastFirst_LastFirst.

Beyond the Classroom

Studio Recording Equipment

GENERAL CASE

You own a recording studio and are considering purchasing some new recording equipment. Open *e07b1Studio* and save it as **e07b1Studio_LastFirst**. Use the Loan worksheet to complete the loan amortization table. Use a combination of mixed and absolute references. Use financial functions for the Interest Paid, Principal Reduction, and Cumulative Principal columns. Calculate cumulative interest for each 12-month period (not after each payment). Calculate totals for appropriate columns and ensure the Interest Paid and Cumulative Yearly Interest column totals match. Apply Accounting Number Format for monetary values and apply other formatting consistent with existing formatting.

Enter the EDATE function in cell F5 to calculate the last payment date. Subtract 1 from the EDATE result to display the correct final payment date. Enter the MATCH function in cell F7 to determine which payment number results in a cumulative principal of at least $5,000. Add one to the function result to get the correct payment number.

Create a criteria range in the **range A77:H78**. Enter **>0** for the Cumulative Yearly Interest criterion. Create an output range in the **range A81:H81**. Apply an advanced filter using the dataset, criteria range, and output range. The filter should display only five payment rows plus the total row.

Use the PV and NPV worksheet to complete a yearly analysis assuming you pay for the equipment upfront (instead of taking out a loan) and want to compare estimated income and expenses related to the equipment for a five-year period. Calculate the net yearly benefit, the present value of net income, the present value of upfront cost, and the present value of recurring costs. Total the Present Value column. In cell I15, use the NPV function to calculate the net present value of all income and costs. Use Help to find an example of upfront costs combined with yearly income and expenses. The NPV result should be identical to the total of the Present Value column. Adjust margins, column widths, and page setup options as needed. Create a footer with your name, the sheet name code, and the file name code on each worksheet. Save and close the file. Based on your instructor's directions, submit e07b1Studio_LastFirst.

Cruises

DISASTER RECOVERY

You just started working for a travel agency that specializes in working with cruise companies departing from Miami and traveling to the Caribbean and Mexico/Central America. Carter, your predecessor, created a database in Excel that lists details about each cruise, such as number of days of the cruise, departure date, destination, cruise line, ship name, and posted rates by cabin type. In addition, Carter calculated 10% discounts on Outside and Balcony cabins and discounts for Interior and Deluxe cabins based on these rules:

- 15% discount on Deluxe/Suite cabins for either 4- OR 5-day cruises
- 20% discount on Interior cabins with both (a) 7 or more day cruise AND (b) 4 rating
- 25% discount on Interior cabins with both (a) 7 or more day cruise AND (b) 3.5 rating

Open *e07b2Cruises* and save it as **e07b2Cruises_LastFirst**. Insert a date function in column A to replace the days that are currently entered as values. Correct the errors with the discount formula in the Adj-Suite column and in the Adj-Interior column. Insert comments in **cells L10 and O10** describing the errors and what you did to correct the errors. Carter also created a criteria range to be able to filter records for seven-day cruises to the Caribbean that depart before May 1, 2018, with a rating of either 4 or 5. Correct and document errors in this range and apply the advanced filter again, copying the results in the output range. Carter created an Adjusted Rate Statistics area using database functions to identify the lowest, highest, and average adjusted rates for the four cabin types that meet the conditions in the criteria range. In addition, he calculated the number of cruises meeting the criteria. Correct and document errors in this section. Create a footer with your name, the sheet name, and the file name. Adjust the scaling so that the worksheet data fit on seven pages. Save and close the file. Based on your instructor's directions, submit e07b2Cruises_LastFirst.

Capstone Exercise

You own five apartment complexes in Colorado. You created a dataset listing the apartment numbers, apartment complex names, number of bedrooms, rental price, whether the apartment is occupied or not, and the date the apartment was last remodeled. You want to insert some functions to perform calculations to help you decide which apartments need to be remodeled.

To focus on the apartments that need to be remodeled, you will use advanced filtering and database functions for your analysis. Finally, you are considering purchasing a sixth apartment complex. You will perform some financial calculations and analyses to help you decide if you will purchase the complex.

Perform Calculations

You want to calculate the number of years ago before 1/1/2018 that each apartment was last remodeled. In addition, you will update the pet deposit based on how long ago the apartment was remodeled. Recently remodeled apartments with two or more bedrooms will require a $275 deposit, whereas apartments remodeled over 10 years ago will require only a $200 deposit. Finally, you will display a comment *Need to Remodel* if an apartment is not occupied and was last remodeled over 10 years ago. The Constants for Formulas range contains values to use in formulas.

a. Open *e07c1Apartment* and save it as **e07c1Apartment_LastFirst**.

b. Make sure the Summary worksheet is active.

c. Insert a date function in **cell G8** to calculate the number of years between the current date (1/1/2018) and the last remodel date in the Last Remodel column. Use relative and mixed references correctly. Copy the function to the **range G9:G57**. Unit 101 was last remodeled 13.75 years ago.

d. Insert a nested logical function in **cell H8** to display the required pet deposit for each unit. If the unit has two or more bedrooms and was remodeled within the past 10 years from 1/1/2018, the deposit is $275; if not, it is $200. The pet deposit for Unit 101 is $200.

e. Enter a nested logical function in **cell I8** to display **Need to Remodel** if the apartment is unoccupied and was last remodeled more than 10 years ago from the 1/1/2018 date. For all other apartments, display **No Change**. Although Unit 101 was last remodeled over 10 years, the recommendation is No Change because the unit is occupied.

f. Copy the functions in the **range H8:I8** to the **range H9:I57**.

Create a Search Area

You want to be able to perform a simple search to enter an apartment unit number and display the rent for that apartment.

a. Type **101** in **cell B2**; this is the cell where you enter an apartment unit #.

b. Insert a nested MATCH function within an INDEX function in **cell B3** that will look up the rental price in column D using the apartment number referenced in cell B2. With 101 entered in cell B2, the lookup function displays $950.00.

Manage a Database List

The Database worksheet contains an identical list of apartments. You want to know how many two- and three-bedroom apartments should be remodeled, the value of lost rent, and the year of the oldest remodel on those units. You need to apply an advanced filter and enter some database functions to address the owner's concerns.

a. Click the **Database sheet tab**.

b. Enter conditions in the criteria range for unoccupied two- and three-bedroom apartments that need to be remodeled.

c. Apply an advanced filter based on the criteria range. Filter the existing database in place.

d. Enter a database function in **cell C8** to calculate the number of apartments that need to be remodeled based on the advanced filter you created.

e. Enter a database function in **cell C9** to calculate the total value of monthly rent lost for the apartments that need to be remodeled based on the advanced filter you created.

f. Enter a database function in **cell C10** to calculate the date of the apartment that had the oldest remodel date based on the filtered data.

Loan Amortization

You are considering purchasing a sixth apartment complex for $1,850,000 with a down payment of $750,000 for 30 years at 4.75%, with the first payment due on March 20, 2018. You will perform internal calculations and build a loan amortization table.

a. Click the **Loan sheet tab**.

b. Enter the loan parameters in the Input Area and insert formulas to perform calculations in the Summary Calculations. Format the monetary values with **Accounting Number Format**.

c. Complete the loan amortization table. In **cell C11**, enter a formula to reference the date stored in cell B7. Insert a nested date function in **cell C12** to calculate the date for the next payment. Copy the function to the **range C13:C370**.

d. Enter a formula in **cell D11** to reference the value stored in cell E2. Insert a formula in **cell D12** that references the ending balance for the previous payment row. Copy the formula to the **range D13:D370**.

e. Enter a financial function in **cell E11** to calculate the interest paid. Copy the formula to the **range E12:E370**.

f. Enter a financial function in **cell F11** to calculate the principal payment. Copy the function to the **range F12:F370**.

g. Enter a formula in **cell G11** to calculate the ending balance. Copy the formula to the **range G12:G370**. The last ending balance should be $0. Adjust the width of column G, if needed, to display the values.

h. Select the **range D11:G370** and apply **Accounting Number Format**.

Finance Function

You want to calculate the present value of potential monthly rent of $2,000 for 8 apartments for 30 years.

a. Enter the monthly rent per unit in **cell I2** and number of units in **cell I3**.

b. Click **cell I4** and insert a financial function to calculate the present value of the total monthly rent you will collect for the 8 units for 30 years. Use the number of periods and monthly rate from the Summary Calculations section.

c. Select **cells I2** and **I4** and apply **Accounting Number Format**.

Workbook Completion

You are ready to complete the workbook by adding a footer with identifying information.

a. Create a footer with your name on the left side, the sheet name code in the center, and the file name code on the right side of each worksheet.

b. Set **0.4"** left and right margins for the Database sheet.

c. Set **0.5"** left and right margins and repeat row 10 on all pages in the Loan sheet.

d. Save and close the file. Based on your instructor's directions, submit e07c1Apartment_LastFirst.

Statistical Functions

LEARNING OUTCOME You will employ statistical functions to analyze data for decision making.

OBJECTIVES & SKILLS: After you read this chapter, you will be able to:

CASE STUDY | Education Evaluation

You are the superintendent of schools for Banton School System, a K–12 school district in Erie, Pennsylvania. You and your team have the task of evaluating student and teacher performance across schools in your district. As part of your evaluation you would like to perform several statistical calculations based on location, age, and test scores.

First, you will evaluate teachers' performance rankings and salary quartiles. You then plan to assess middle school students' standardized testing performance. As part of this analysis, you will perform basic descriptive statistical calculations. You will also compare performance to attendance and test the correlation between test scores and daily turnout. Last, you will perform more advanced evaluation of high school students' performance using the Analysis ToolPak.

Analyzing Statistics

High School Educator Information				
Last Name	Hire Date	Salary	Township	Salary Rank
Kato	12/22/2007	$61,065.00	Veigo	4
Han	10/20/2015	$59,913.00	Jackson	7
Yoon	4/23/2014	$64,052.00	Jackson	3
Lopez	7/30/1999	$45,305.00	Veigo	30
Yamamoto	12/29/2002	$52,691.00	Veigo	23
Lee	4/16/2014	$38,827.00	Veigo	39
Garcia	4/23/2000	$57,307.00	Veigo	12
Thomas	10/2/2002	$48,384.00	Acorn	28
Gao	7/16/2006	$37,575.00	Jackson	41
Cruz	8/6/2011	$60,913.00	Veigo	6
Cruz	9/11/2006	$58,134.00	Acorn	9
Ortiz	8/16/2005	$57,394.00	Jackson	11
Rodriguez	8/4/2008	$43,815.00	Veigo	32
Ma	1/21/2010	$36,288.00	Jackson	42
Young	5/4/2010	$50,920.00	Veigo	26
Jhadav	8/3/2006	$55,953.00	Veigo	14
Jayaraman	10/14/2003	$64,261.00	Acorn	2
Sanchez	5/30/2009	$34,301.00	Acorn	47
Li	5/30/1999	$55,257.00	Veigo	18
He	1/17/2002	$44,450.00	Acorn	31
Mehta	1/13/2014	$35,259.00	Jackson	44
Hamade	8/17/2003	$58,478.00	Jackson	8
Bhatnagar	11/30/2011	$35,015.00	Jackson	45
Takahashi	12/17/2010	$53,994.00	Jackson	20
Young	4/17/2001	$40,878.00	Veigo	36
Park	5/25/2011	$31,386.00	Jackson	49
Matsumoto	5/11/2005	$41,571.00	Jackson	35

Summary Information	Hired before 1/1/2005	
Count		16
Total payroll	$	790,922.00
Average Salary	$	49,432.63
Acorn Township High School Teachers	Hired before 1/1/2005	
Count		6
Total Payroll	$	289,587.00
Average Salary	$	48,264.50
Quartile	Salary (QUARTILE.EXC)	
1	$	39,203.50
2	$	51,775.00
3	$	57,278.50

Test scores Analysis			Bins
Student ID	SAT Score	Absences	0
1397	2200	0	5
1840	2312	0	10
2047	2332	0	
2053	2390	0	
2987	2205	0	
3028	2119	0	
3546	2141	0	
3590	2260	0	
4334	2114	0	
4437	2280	0	
4543	2119	0	
4945	2061	0	
1704	1832	1	
1760	1880	1	
1795	1835	1	
1809	1855	1	
2030	1842	1	
2389	1984	1	
2812	1989	1	
3556	1944	1	
4193	1821	1	
4329	1861	1	

	SAT Score	Absences
SAT Score	217099.9604	
Absences	-1484.57	10.58333333

Bin	Frequency	Cumulative %
0	12	8.00%
5	57	46.00%
10	81	100.00%
More	0	100.00%

FIGURE 8.1 Education Evaluation Math and Statistical Functions

CASE STUDY | Education Evaluation

Starting File	File to be Submitted
e08h1Assessment	**e08h3Assessment_LastFirst**

Math and Statistical Functions

Do not let the term *statistics* scare you. Every day, you rely on statistics to make routine decisions. When you purchase a car, you compare the average miles per gallon (MPG) among several vehicles. The automobile manufacturer conducted multiple test drives, recorded the MPG under various driving conditions, and then calculated the MPG statistic based on average performance. Statistics involve analyzing a collection of data and making inferences to draw conclusions about a dataset.

You have already learned to use the SUM, AVERAGE, MIN, MAX, MEDIAN, and COUNT statistical functions. However, sometimes you might want to calculate a statistic based on a particular condition. Excel's math and statistical function categories contain functions that enable you to perform conditional calculations, such as calculating a total only when a particular circumstance or set of circumstances exists.

In this section, you will use math and statistical functions—SUMIF, AVERAGEIF, COUNTIF, SUMIFS, AVERAGEIFS, and COUNTIFS—to perform conditional statistical calculations. In addition, you will use relative-standing functions, such as RANK, PERCENTRANK, PERCENTILE, and QUARTILE.

Using Conditional Math and Statistical Functions

When you use SUM, AVERAGE, and COUNT functions, Excel calculates the respective total, the mathematical average, and the number of values for all values in the range specified in the function's arguments. The math and statistical function categories contain related functions—SUMIF, AVERAGEIF, COUNTIF, SUMIFS, AVERAGEIFS, and COUNTIFS—that perform similar calculations but based on a condition. These functions are similar to the logical function IF. As you recall, the IF function evaluates a logical test to determine if it is true or false. If the logical test is true, Excel returns one result; if the logical test is false, it returns a different result. These conditional math and statistical functions are a hybrid of math/statistical and logical functionality. Basically, instead of delivering a value of true or false, these functions perform a specific calculation when specified conditions are met. Figure 8.2 shows a salary table for educators in the district and the results of these math and statistical functions.

| | D15 | | ▾ | : | × | ✓ | f_x | =SUMIF(C2:C13,"high school",D2:D13) | | | Function in cell D15 | |

	A	B	C	D	E	F	G	H	I	J	K	L
1	Last Name	Township	Teaching Assignment	Salary								
2	Daniels	Jackson	elementary	$ 37,367.00								
3	Jackson	Jackson	intermediate	$ 55,452.00								
4	Williams	Jackson	intermediate	$ 47,036.00								
5	Davis	Jackson	high school	$ 48,456.00								
6	Attucks	Jackson	high school	$ 40,590.00								
7	Johnson	Viego	high school	$ 57,912.00								
8	Lewis	Viego	elementary	$ 47,393.00								
9	Vong	Viego	high school	$ 47,759.00								
10	Officer	Viego	intermediate	$ 45,490.00								
11	Stephenson	Acorn	intermediate	$ 39,213.00								
12	Crandell	Acorn	high school	$ 52,730.00								
13	Mitchell	Acorn	elementary	$ 44,966.00								
14							Functions with one condition					
15	Total salary of high school teachers			$247,447.00		=SUMIF(C2:C13,"high school",D2:D13)						
16	Average salary of high school teachers			$ 49,489.40		=AVERAGEIF(C2:C13,"high school",D2:D13)						
17	Total number of high school teachers			5		=COUNTIF(C2:C13,"high school")						
18							Functions with two conditions					
19	Total salary of high school teachers from Jackson Township			$ 89,046.00		=SUMIFS(D2:D13,C2:C13,"high school",B2:B13,"Jackson")						
20	Average salary of high school teachers from Jackson Township			$ 44,523.00		=AVERAGEIFS(D2:D13,C2:C13,"high school",B2:B13,"Jackson")						
21	Total number of high school teachers from Jackson Township			2		=COUNTIFS(C2:C13,"high school",B2:B13,"Jackson")						

FIGURE 8.2 Math and Statistical Functions

Use the SUMIF, AVERAGEIF, and COUNTIF Functions

STEP 1 ❱❱ The **SUMIF function** is a statistical function similar to the SUM function except that it calculates the total of a range of values when a specified condition is met. For example, in Figure 8.2, if you want to calculate the total salaries for all high school teachers in the district, you cannot use the SUM function because it would calculate the total salaries for teachers in the district's elementary and intermediate schools as well. However, you can complete the task using the SUMIF function. In Figure 8.2, cell D15 contains the results of the function =SUMIF(C2:C13,"high school",D2:D13) to sum the Salary column (D2:D13) if the Teaching Assignment column (C2:C13) contains the text *high school*. The total value of salaries for high school teachers is $247,447.00. The SUMIF function contains three required arguments:

=SUMIF(range,criteria,sum_range)

- **Range.** The range argument specifies the range of cells you want to evaluate to determine if the values meet a particular condition. In Figure 8.2, the SUMIF function's range is C2:C13, the range containing the teaching assignments.
- **Criteria.** The criteria argument specifies the condition that imposes limitations on what values Excel sums. The criteria can be a value, date, text, or another cell containing a value, date, or text. In Figure 8.2, the SUMIF function criterion is the text *high school*. Excel restricts the totaling to rows in which the range contains only *high school*. When you use text as a criterion, you must enclose it

within quotation marks. When you use values as criteria, do not use quotation marks. You can also create an input range to specify the condition and then simply use a cell reference as the criteria argument in the SUMIF function.

- **Sum_range.** The sum_range argument designates the cells containing values to add if the condition is met. In Figure 8.2, the SUMIF function's sum_range is D2:D13, the range containing the salaries.

> **TIP: QUOTATION MARKS**
>
> When entering criteria that contain text, a date, or an operator such as <, you must surround the criteria with quotation marks. If you enter the criteria using the Function Argument box, Excel will automatically add quotation marks. If you type the function from scratch instead of using the insert function button, you must type the quotation marks manually.

The **AVERAGEIF function** calculates the average, or arithmetic mean, of all cells in a range that meet a specific condition. In Figure 8.2, cell D16 contains =AVERAGEIF(C2:C13,"high school",D2:D13) to calculate the average value in the Salary column (D2:D13) when the Teaching Assignment column (C2:C13) contains the text *high school*. The average high school teacher's salary is $49,489.40.

=AVERAGEIF(range,criteria,average_range)

The AVERAGEIF function contains three required arguments: range, criteria, and average_range. The range and criteria arguments have the same meanings as the same arguments in the SUMIF function. The average_range argument specifies the range containing values that you want to average if the condition is met. In the AVERAGEIF function, the average_range is D2:D13.

> **TIP: REFERENCING THE INPUT RANGE**
>
> When using the SUMIF, AVERAGEIF, and COUNTIF functions, you can create an input range to specify the condition and then simply use a cell reference as the criteria argument in the function. This allows the user the flexibility to change the criteria and receive instant calculation updates.

The **COUNTIF function** is a statistical function, similar to the COUNT function except that it counts the number of cells in a range when a specified condition is met. In Figure 8.2, cell D17 contains =COUNTIF(C2:C13,"high school") to count the number of high school teachers, which is five.

=COUNTIF(range,criteria)

The COUNTIF function contains only two arguments: range and criteria. Similar to the SUMIF and AVERAGEIF functions, the range argument for the COUNTIF function specifies the range of cells you want to evaluate to see if the values meet a particular condition. The criteria argument specifies the condition to be met in order to count cells in the designated range.

Use the SUMIFS, AVERAGEIFS, and COUNTIFS Functions

STEP 2 ⟩⟩ Whereas the previously described functions enable you to perform conditional calculations, they can address only a single condition. Similar math and statistical functions enable you to specify more than one condition: SUMIFS, AVERAGEIFS, and COUNTIFS.

The **SUMIFS function** calculates the total value of cells in a range that meet multiple criteria. In Figure 8.2, cell D19 contains =SUMIFS(D2:D13,C2:C13,"high school",B2:B13,"Jackson"). This function sums the Salary range if the teaching assignment range contains *high school* and if the township range contains *Jackson*. The total salary of high school teachers in Jackson Township is $89,046.00. The SUMIFS function contains at least five arguments: sum_range, criteria_range1, criteria1, criteria_range2, and criteria2. Additional ranges and their criteria may be included. All conditions must be met in order to include values in the sum_range in the total.

=SUMIFS(sum_range,criteria_range1,criteria1,criteria_range2,criteria2…)

- **Sum_range.** The sum_range argument designates the cells containing values to add if the condition is met. In the SUMIFS function, the sum_range argument is the first argument instead of the last argument as in the SUMIF function. In Figure 8.2, the SUMIFS function's sum_range is D2:D13, the range containing the salaries.

- **Criteria_range1.** The range argument specifies the first range of cells you want to evaluate to see if the values meet a particular condition. The range must contain values, range names, arrays, or references that contain numbers, dates, or text. In Figure 8.2, the criteria_range1 is C2:C13, the range containing the teaching assignments.

- **Criteria1.** The criteria1 argument specifies the condition for the criteria_range1 argument that imposes limitations on what values are summed. In Figure 8.2, the SUMIFS function's criteria1 argument is *high school*.

- **Criteria_range2.** The range argument specifies the second range of cells you want to evaluate to see if the values meet a particular condition. The range must contain values, range names, arrays, or references that contain numbers, dates, or text. In Figure 8.2, the SUMIFS function's criteria_range2 is B2:B13, the range containing the township.

- **Criteria2.** The criteria2 argument specifies the condition that imposes limitations on what values are summed. In Figure 8.2, the SUMIFS function's criteria2 is *Jackson*.

The **AVERAGEIFS function** calculates the average value of cells in a range that meet multiple criteria. In Figure 8.2, cell D20 contains =AVERAGEIFS(D2:D13,C2:C13,"high school",B2:B13,"Jackson"). This function calculates the average value in the Salary range if the teaching assignment is *high school* and if the township is *Jackson*. The average salary of high school teachers in Jackson Township is $44,523. The AVERAGEIFS function contains at least five arguments. The average_range argument specifies the range of cells containing values that will be averaged when multiple conditions specified by the criteria ranges and criteria are met.

=AVERAGEIFS(average_range,criteria_range1,criteria1,criteria_range2,criteria2…)

The **COUNTIFS function** counts the number of cells in a range that meet multiple criteria. In Figure 8.2, cell D21 contains =COUNTIFS(C2:C13,"high school",B2:B13,"Jackson"). This function counts the number of high school teachers in Jackson Township, which is two. The COUNTIFS function contains at least four arguments: two ranges and their respective criteria.

=COUNTIFS(criteria_range1,criteria1,criteria_range2,criteria2…)

TIP: ADDITIONAL CRITERIA

Whereas the syntax shows only two criteria for SUMIFS, AVERAGEIFS, and COUNTIFS, you can continue adding criteria ranges and criteria. If you type the function in a cell, separate criteria ranges and criteria with commas. If you use the Function Arguments dialog box, it expands to display another Criteria box as you enter data in existing boxes, or you can press Tab within the dialog box to see additional criteria ranges and criteria boxes.

Enter Math and Statistical Functions

Excel organizes the conditional functions in the math and statistical function categories. The SUMIF and SUMIFS functions are math functions and are located in Math & Trig in the Function Library group. The AVERAGEIF, AVERAGEIFS, COUNTIF, and COUNTIFS functions are statistical functions. To locate these functions, click More Functions in the Function Library group, and then click Statistical.

Calculating Relative Standing with Statistical Functions

Often people analyze a single data point compared to the entire dataset. You do not have to be a statistician to need to use statistical calculations. For example, a professor might want to rank students in a chemistry class, or a medical doctor might want to identify diabetic patients' blood sugar levels based on what quartile they fall in. You can use the RANK.EQ, PERCENTRANK, QUARTILE, and PERCENTILE functions to analyze data.

Use the RANK and PERCENTRANK Functions

STEP 3 Excel contains two rank functions: RANK.EQ and RANK.AVG. As shown in Figure 8.3, the ***RANK.EQ function*** identifies a value's rank within a list of values, omitting the next rank when tie values exist. For example, the rank of 1 appears in E13. Figure 8.3 indicates that the $57,912.00 salary is the highest-ranking salary in the list, $55,452.00 is the second-highest-ranking salary, and so on. If the range of values contains duplicate numbers (such as $44,966.00 in cells D5 and D6), both values receive the same rank (8), the next ranking (9) is skipped, and the next value ($40,590) is assigned the ranking of 10.

The ***RANK.AVG function*** identifies the rank of a value but assigns an average rank when identical values exist. In Figure 8.3, column F shows the results of the RANK.AVG function in which both $44,966 values have a ranking of 8.5—the average of rankings 8 and 9—instead of a rank of 8. Some statisticians consider the RANK.AVG function results to be more accurate than the RANK.EQ function results.

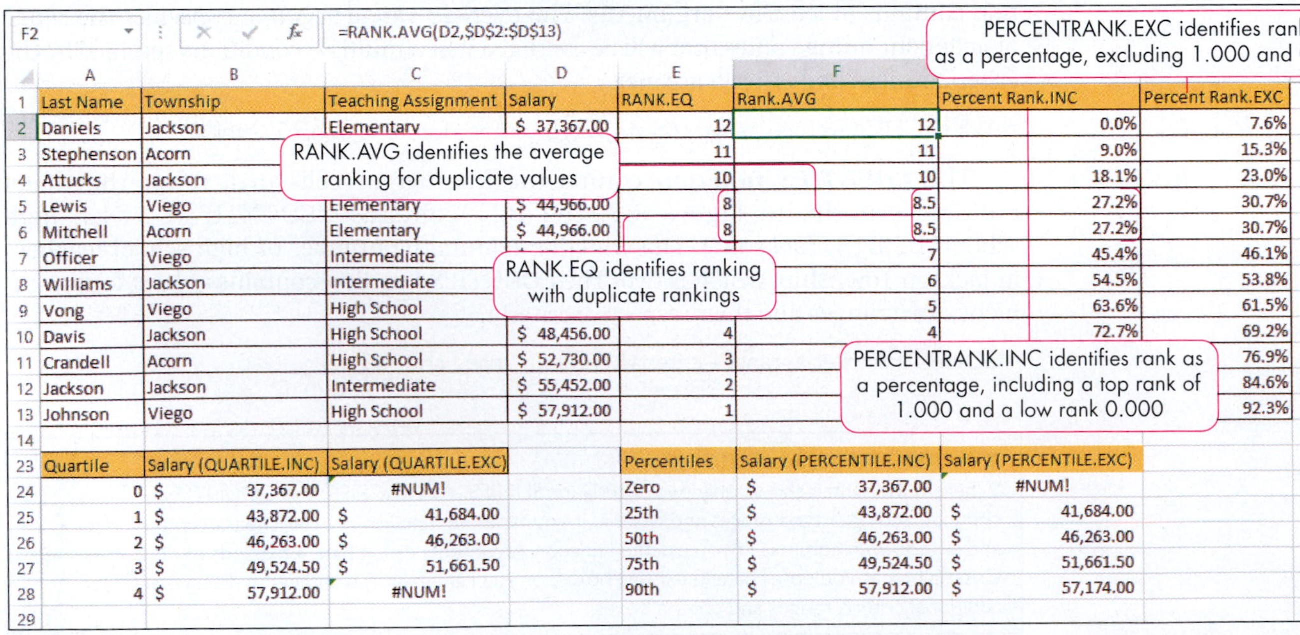
F2 | =RANK.AVG(D2,$D$2:$D$13)

	A	B	C	D	E	F	G	H
1	Last Name	Township	Teaching Assignment	Salary	RANK.EQ	Rank.AVG	Percent Rank.INC	Percent Rank.EXC
2	Daniels	Jackson	Elementary	$ 37,367.00	12	12	0.0%	7.6%
3	Stephenson	Acorn			11	11	9.0%	15.3%
4	Attucks	Jackson			10	10	18.1%	23.0%
5	Lewis	Viego	Elementary	$ 44,966.00	8	8.5	27.2%	30.7%
6	Mitchell	Acorn	Elementary	$ 44,966.00	8	8.5	27.2%	30.7%
7	Officer	Viego	Intermediate			7	45.4%	46.1%
8	Williams	Jackson	Intermediate			6	54.5%	53.8%
9	Vong	Viego	High School			5	63.6%	61.5%
10	Davis	Jackson	High School	$ 48,456.00	4	4	72.7%	69.2%
11	Crandell	Acorn	High School	$ 52,730.00	3			76.9%
12	Jackson	Jackson	Intermediate	$ 55,452.00	2			84.6%
13	Johnson	Viego	High School	$ 57,912.00	1			92.3%
14								
23	Quartile	Salary (QUARTILE.INC)	Salary (QUARTILE.EXC)		Percentiles	Salary (PERCENTILE.INC)	Salary (PERCENTILE.EXC)	
24	0	$ 37,367.00	#NUM!		Zero	$ 37,367.00	#NUM!	
25	1	$ 43,872.00	$ 41,684.00		25th	$ 43,872.00	$ 41,684.00	
26	2	$ 46,263.00	$ 46,263.00		50th	$ 46,263.00	$ 46,263.00	
27	3	$ 49,524.50	$ 51,661.50		75th	$ 49,524.50	$ 51,661.50	
28	4	$ 57,912.00	#NUM!		90th	$ 57,912.00	$ 57,174.00	
29								

FIGURE 8.3 RANK and PERCENTRANK Functions

Both the RANK.EQ and RANK.AVG functions contain two arguments (number and ref) and one optional argument (order).

=RANK.EQ(number,ref,[order])

=RANK.AVG(number,ref,[order])

- **Number.** The number argument specifies the cell containing the value you want to rank, such as cell D2.

- **Ref.** The ref argument specifies the range of values, such as $D$2:$D$13, that you want to use to identify their rankings. Absolute references are used so that the row numbers do not change as the formula is copied down the column.

- **Order.** The optional order argument enables you to specify how you want to rank the values. The implied default is 0, which ranks the values as if the values were listed in descending order. Because the order argument was omitted in Figure 8.3, the first-rank salary is the highest salary value of $57,912. If you enter any nonzero value for the order argument, Excel ranks the values as if the values were listed in ascending order (i.e., low to high). If the order argument were 2, the first-ranked salary would be the lowest value, which is $37,367.

Some functions have a descriptor added to the function name to further clarify the function's purpose and to distinguish functions that perform similar tasks but have subtle differences. The .INC descriptor indicates *inclusive* functions, that is, the functions *include* particular parameters. The .EXC descriptor indicates *exclusive* functions, that is, functions that *exclude* particular parameters.

The ***PERCENTRANK.INC function*** displays a value's rank as a percentile of the range of data in the dataset. In other words, you can use this function to identify a value's relative standing compared to other values in the dataset. Excel displays ranks as decimal values between 0 and 1, but you can format the results with Percent Number Style. The first rank is 1.000, and the lowest percent rank is 0.000, because the .INC descriptor *includes* 0 and 1. The percent rank correlates with the rank of a value. For example, in Figure 8.3, the $57,912 salary is the highest-ranking salary; its percent rank is 1.00 or 100% percentile. The $55,452 value is the second-highest-ranking salary; its percent rank is 0.909, indicating that this salary is the 90.9% percentile.

The ***PERCENTRANK.EXC function*** is similar to PERCENTRANK.INC in that it returns a value's rank as a percent. This function adheres to best practices in that a percent rank is between 0 and 1 because the EXC descriptor *excludes* the 0 and 1. For this function, the $57,912 salary has a percent rank of 0.923 or is in the 92.3% percentile.

Both PERCENTRANK.INC and PERCENTRANK.EXC functions contain two required arguments (array and x) and one optional argument (significance).

=PERCENTRANK.INC(array,x,[significance])

=PERCENTRANK.EXC(array,x,[significance])

- **Array.** The array argument specifies the range that contains the values to compare, such as D$2:D$13.

- **x.** The x argument specifies an individual's salary, such as cell D2.

- **Significance.** The optional significance argument designates the number of significant digits for precision. If you omit the significance argument, Excel displays three significant digits.

Use the QUARTILE and PERCENTILE Functions

STEP 4 ›› A *quartile* is a value used to divide a range of numbers into four equal groups. The **QUARTILE.INC function** identifies the value at a specific quartile for a dataset, *including* quartile 0 for the lowest value and quartile 4 for the highest value in the dataset. The **QUARTILE.EXC function** is similar in that it returns the value at a specific quartile, but it *excludes* quartiles 0 and 4. These functions contain two required arguments: array and quart. The array argument specifies the range of values. The quart argument is a number that represents a specific quartile (see Table 8.1).

=QUARTILE.INC(array,quart)

=QUARTILE.EXC(array,quart)

TABLE 8.1 Quart Argument

Argument Value	Description
0	Lowest value in the dataset. Identical to using the MIN function. Allowed in QUARTILE.INC only.
1	First quartile of the dataset. Identifies the value at the 25th percentile.
2	Second quartile or median value within the dataset. Identifies the value at the 50th percentile.
3	Third quartile of the dataset. Identifies the value at the 75th percentile.
4	Fourth quartile or highest value within the dataset. Identical to using the MAX function. Allowed in QUARTILE.INC only.

Pearson Education, Inc.

In Figure 8.4, cell B24 contains =QUARTILE.INC(D$2:D$13,A24), where cell A24 contains the quartile of Salary. The function returns $37,367, which is the lowest salary in the range. Cell B25 contains =QUARTILE.INC(D$2:D$13,A25) to identify the top salary in the first quartile, which is $43,872. Look at column G, which contains the PERCENTRANK.INC function, and column H, which contains the PERCENTRANK.EXC function. Any salaries with 25% or less fall in the first quartile, salaries above 25% and up to 50% fall in the second quartile, salaries above 50% and up to 75% fall in the third quartile, and salaries above 75% fall in the fourth (or top) quartile. The dataset is sorted in ascending order by salary, and the data in columns D and H are color coded to help you identify values within each quartile.

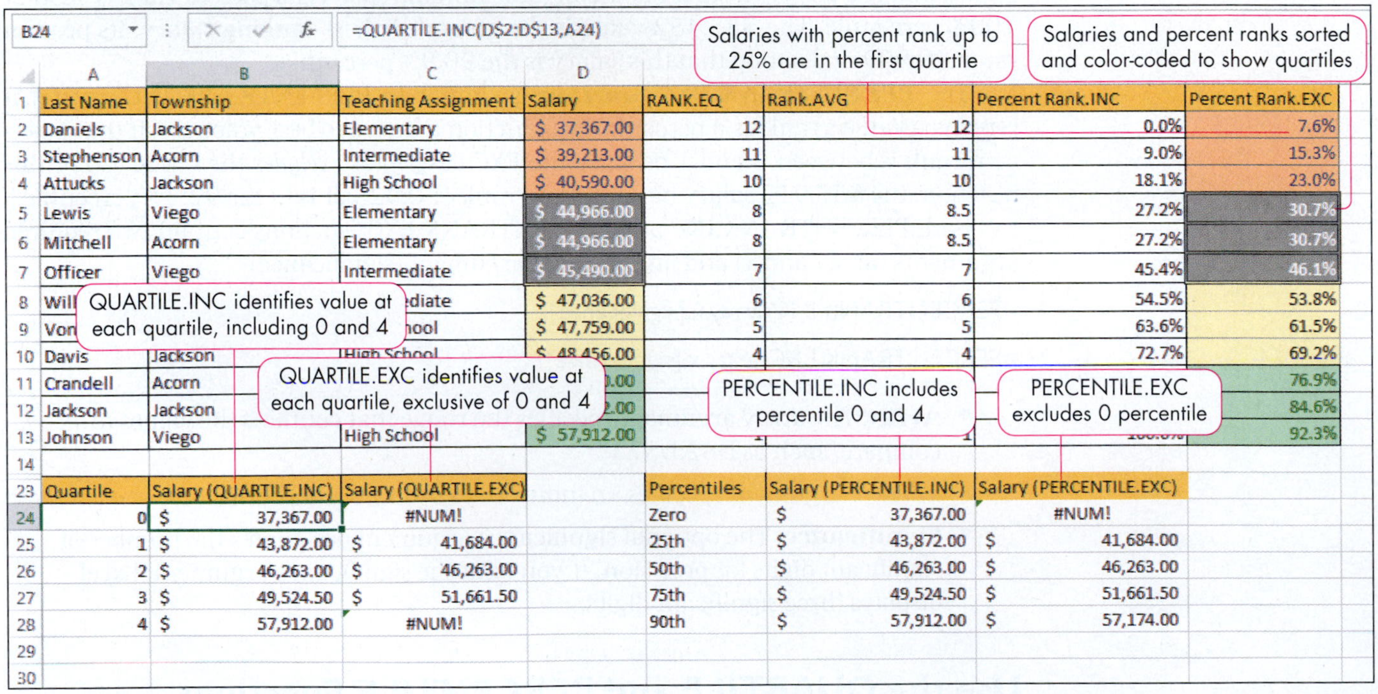

FIGURE 8.4 QUARTILE and PERCENTILE Functions

Range C24:C28 contains the QUARTILE.EXC function. For example, cell C24 contains =QUARTILE.EXC(D$2:D$13,A24). Because QUARTILE.EXC excludes 0 and 4, the function returns #NUM! error messages when 0 and 4 are used as the quart argument in cells C24 and C28. The salaries at the second quartiles are identical for either QUARTILE function; however, the salaries for the quartiles differ based on which function you use. Table 8.2 summarizes the findings from the QUARTILE.INC functions.

TABLE 8.2 Quartile Grouping

Quartile	Salary at Top of Quartile	Salaries
1 (0.25 or lower)	$43,872.00	$37,367
		$39,213
		$40,590
2 (between 0.251 and 0.5)	$46,263.50	$44,966
		$44,966
		$45,490
3 (between 0.501 and 0.75)	$49,524.50	$47,036
		$47,759
		$48,456
4 (above 0.75)	$57,912.00	$52,730
		$55,452
		$57,912

Pearson Education, Inc.

The **PERCENTILE.INC function** identifies the *k*th percentile of a specified value within a list of values, including the 0th and 100th percentiles. College admissions offices find this function helpful when identifying college applicants' percentiles to determine which candidates to admit to their college. For example, a college might have a policy to admit only candidates who fall within the 80th percentile. The **PERCENTILE.EXC function** also identifies a value at a specified percentile; however, the .EXC *excludes* 0th and 100th percentiles.

The PERCENTILE functions contain two required arguments: array and *k*. The array argument specifies the range containing values to determine individual standing. For the PERCENTILE.INC function, the *k* argument specifies the percentile value from 0 to 1. For the PERCENTILE.EXC function, the *k* argument *excludes* values 0 and 1. For example, 0.25 represents the 25th percentile. In Figure 8.4, cell F25 contains =PERCENTILE. INC(D$2:D$13,0.25) to identify the value at the 25th percentile. Note that this salary ($43,872) is the same as the value returned by =QUARTILE.INC(D$2:D$13,A25). However, unlike the QUARTILE.INC function that has distinct quartiles (0, 1, 2, 3, 4), you can specify any decimal value for the *k* argument in the PERCENTILE functions, such as =PERCENTILE.INC(D$2:D$13,0.9) to find the value at the 90th percentile. The PERCENTILE.EXC returns different values than PERCENTILE.INC at the higher percentiles. Also, =PERCENTILE.EXC(D$2:D$13,0) returns an error since the .EXC descriptor excludes 0 as a legitimate parameter.

=PERCENTILE.INC(array,k)

=PERCENTILE.EXC(array,k)

Quick Concepts

1. When would you use SUMIFS instead of SUMIF? **pp. 513–514**

2. When would you use RANK.AVG instead of RANK.EQ? **p. 516**

3. What is the difference between PERCENTRANK.INC versus PERCENTRANK.EXC? **p. 517**

Hands-On Exercises

Watch the Video for this Hands On Exercise!

MyITLab®
HOE1 Training

Skills covered: Use the SUMIF, AVERAGEIF, and COUNTIF Functions • Use the SUMIFS, AVERAGEIFS, and COUNTIFS Functions • Enter Math and Statistical Functions • Use the Rank and PERCENTRANK Functions • Use the QUARTILE and PERCENTILE Functions

1 Math and Statistical Functions

For the first step of your assessment, you calculate summary statistics of the teachers' salaries. First, you want to calculate statistics, such as average salary for teachers hired before 2005. You then will turn your attention to the Acorn Township, the township with the fewest teachers, as you perform statistical calculations. Finally, you want to rank each person's salary compared to the other salaries and identify the salary ranges for each quartile.

STEP 1 ›› USE SUMIF, AVERAGEIF, AND COUNTIF FUNCTIONS

You want to calculate the number of high school teachers that were hired before 1/1/2005. You also want to calculate the average salary and total payroll for all high school teachers hired before 1/1/2005. You will use SUMIF, COUNTIF, and AVERAGEIF to complete the calculations. Refer to Figures 8.5 and 8.6 as you complete Step 1.

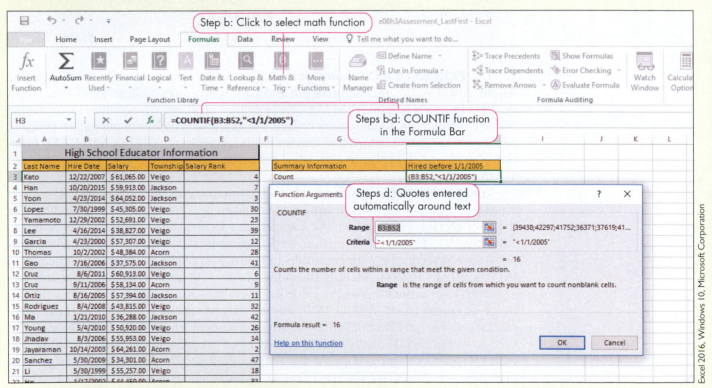

FIGURE 8.5 COUNTIF Function

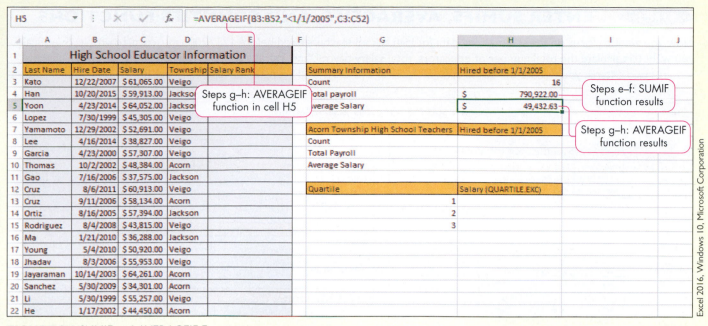

FIGURE 8.6 SUMIF and AVERAGEIF Functions

a. Open *e08h1Assessment* and save it as **e08h1Assessment_LastFirst**. Ensure the **Educator Assessment worksheet tab** is displayed.

> **TROUBLESHOOTING:** If you make any major mistakes in this exercise, you can close the file, open *e08h1Assessment* again, and then start this exercise over.

b. Click **cell H3**, click the **Formulas tab**, click **More Functions** in the Function Library group, point to **Statistical**, scroll through the list, and then select **COUNTIF**.

Cell H3 is the cell in which you want to calculate the total number of high school teachers hired before 1/1/2005. The Function Arguments dialog box opens so that you can enter the range and criteria arguments.

c. Select the **range B3:B52** to enter it in the Range box.

The range B3:B52 contains the data array that contains the values to be counted.

d. Click in the Criteria box, type **<1/1/2005**, and then click **OK**.

The newly created function indicates there are 16 teachers that meet the criteria requirements.

e. Click **cell H4**, click **Math & Trig** in the Function Library group, and then select **SUMIF**.

The Function Arguments dialog box displays so that you can enter the range, criteria, and sum_range arguments.

f. Type **B3:B52** in the Range box, type **<1/1/2005** in the Criteria box, and then type **C3:C52** in the Sum_range box: Click **OK** to exit the Function Arguments box.

The total salaries paid to high school teachers hired before 1/1/2005 is $790,922.00.

g. Ensure **cell H5** is selected. Click **More Functions** in the Function Library group, point to **Statistical**, and then select **AVERAGEIF**.

h. Type **B3:B52** in the Range box, type **<1/1/2005** in the Criteria box, and then type **C3:C52** in the Average_range box. Click **OK** to exit the Function Arguments box.

The average salary for high school teachers hired before 1/1/2005 is $49,432.63.

STEP 2 » ENTER SUMIFS, AVERAGEIFS, AND COUNTIFS FUNCTIONS

Now you want to focus on the summarizing data for high school teachers hired before 1/1/2005 in Acorn Township. Specifically, you want to calculate the total number of educators, total salary payroll, and average salary. Because each of these calculations requires two criteria, you will use the SUMIFS, AVERAGEIFS, and COUNTIFS functions. Refer to Figure 8.7 as you complete Step 2.

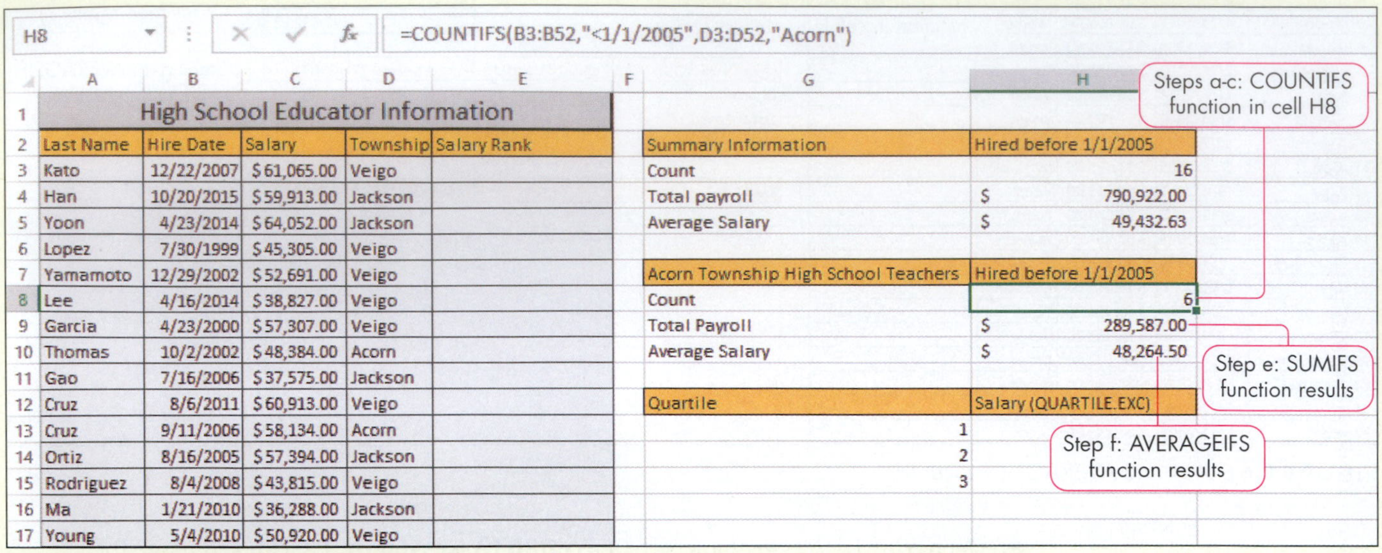

H8 =COUNTIFS(B3:B52,"<1/1/2005",D3:D52,"Acorn")

	A	B	C	D	E	F	G	H
1	High School Educator Information							
2	Last Name	Hire Date	Salary	Township	Salary Rank		Summary Information	Hired before 1/1/2005
3	Kato	12/22/2007	$ 61,065.00	Veigo			Count	16
4	Han	10/20/2015	$ 59,913.00	Jackson			Total payroll	$ 790,922.00
5	Yoon	4/23/2014	$ 64,052.00	Jackson			Average Salary	$ 49,432.63
6	Lopez	7/30/1999	$ 45,305.00	Veigo				
7	Yamamoto	12/29/2002	$ 52,691.00	Veigo			Acorn Township High School Teachers	Hired before 1/1/2005
8	Lee	4/16/2014	$ 38,827.00	Veigo			Count	6
9	Garcia	4/23/2000	$ 57,307.00	Veigo			Total Payroll	$ 289,587.00
10	Thomas	10/2/2002	$ 48,384.00	Acorn			Average Salary	$ 48,264.50
11	Gao	7/16/2006	$ 37,575.00	Jackson				
12	Cruz	8/6/2011	$ 60,913.00	Veigo			Quartile	Salary (QUARTILE.EXC)
13	Cruz	9/11/2006	$ 58,134.00	Acorn			1	
14	Ortiz	8/16/2005	$ 57,394.00	Jackson			2	
15	Rodriguez	8/4/2008	$ 43,815.00	Veigo			3	
16	Ma	1/21/2010	$ 36,288.00	Jackson				
17	Young	5/4/2010	$ 50,920.00	Veigo				

FIGURE 8.7 SUMIFS, AVERAGEIFS, and COUNTIFS Functions

a. Click **cell H8**, click **More Functions** and point to **Statistical** in the Function Library group, scroll through the list, and then select **COUNTIFS**.

b. Type **B3:B52** in the Criteria_range1 box, click in the Criteria1 box, and then type **<1/1/2005**.

Similar to the COUNTIF function, COUNTIFS has the ability to count data points in a range that match specified criteria. In this step the first criterion is <1/1/2005.

c. Click in the Criteria_range2 box and type **D3:D52**. Type **Acorn** in the Criteria 2 box and click **OK**.

The function returns 6, the total number of high school teachers in Acorn Township hired before 1/1/2005, by using the criteria <1/1/2005 and Acorn to filter the data ranges B3:B52 and D3:D52.

d. Click **cell H9**, click **Math & Trig** in the Function Library group, and then select **SUMIFS**.

e. Type **C3:C52** in the Sum_range box, type **B3:B52** in the Criteria_range1 box, type **<1/1/2005** in the Criteria1 box, type **D3:D52** in the Criteria_range2 box, type **Acorn** in the Criteria2 box, and then click **OK**.

The total payroll for high school teachers in Acorn Township hired before 1/1/2005 is $289,587.00.

TROUBLESHOOTING: If you misspell criterion text, such as the township name, the results will display 0. Always check the criterion text to make sure it matches text in the respective column.

f. Click **cell H10**,type **=AVERAGEIFS(C3:C52,B3:B52,"<1/1/2005",D3:D52, "Acorn")**, and press **Ctrl+Enter** manually.

The average salary of high school teachers in Acorn Township hired before 1/1/2005 is $48,264.50.

g. Save the workbook.

You want to identify the rank of each teacher's salary. Doing so will enable you to later compare salaries with classroom performance. Refer to Figure 8.8 as you complete Step 3.

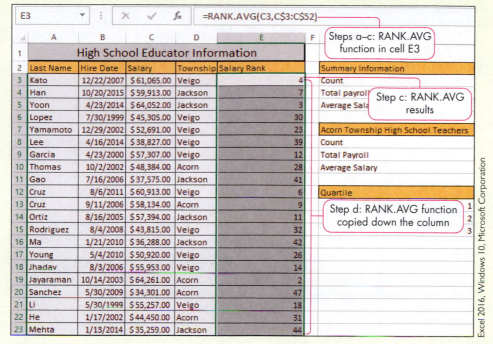

FIGURE 8.8 Salary Ranks

a. Ensure **cell E3** is selected. Click **More Functions** in the Function Library group, point to **Statistical**, and then select **RANK.AVG**.

b. Click **cell C3** to enter it in the Number box.

Excel uses the individual salary to compare it to a list of salaries to identify its rank.

c. Click in the Ref box, type **C$3:C$52**, and then click **OK**.

You use the mixed reference C$3:C$52 to prevent the row numbers from changing when you copy the function down the column. You do not have to use absolute references since the column letters will be the same as you copy the function down the same column.

Kato's salary of $61,065 is ranked fourth out of the entire list of salaries.

d. Double-click the fill handle in cell E3 to copy the function down the rank column.

e. Save the workbook.

You want to see what salary ranges fall within each quartile. You will use the QUARTILE function to identify the ranges and to identify the lowest and highest salaries. Refer to Figure 8.9 as you complete Step 4.

| H13 | ▼ | : | × | ✓ | *fx* | =QUARTILE.EXC(C$3:C$52,G13) | | | | |

Steps c-e: QUARTILE.EXC function

Step f: QUARTILE.EXC results

	A	B	C	D	E	F		H
1	High School Educator Information							
2	Last Name	Hire Date	Salary	Township	Salary Rank		Summary Information	Hired before 1/1/2005
3	Kato	12/22/2007	$61,065.00	Veigo		4	Count	16
4	Han	10/20/2015	$59,913.00	Jackson		7	Total payroll	$ 790,922.00
5	Yoon	4/23/2014	$64,052.00	Jackson		3	Average Salary	$ 49,432.63
6	Lopez	7/30/1999	$45,305.00	Veigo		30		
7	Yamamoto	12/29/2002	$52,691.00	Veigo		23	Acorn Township High School Teachers	Hired before 1/1/2005
8	Lee	4/16/2014	$38,827.00	Veigo		39	Count	6
9	Garcia	4/23/2000	$57,307.00	Veigo		12	Total Payroll	$ 289,587.00
10	Thomas	10/2/2002	$48,384.00	Acorn		28	Average Salary	$ 48,264.50
11	Gao	7/16/2006	$37,575.00	Jackson		41		
12	Cruz	8/6/2011	$60,913.00	Veigo		6	Quartile	Salary (QUARTILE.EXC)
13	Cruz	9/11/2006	$58,134.00	Acorn		9	Step e: Quart box criteria 1	$ 39,203.50
14	Ortiz	8/16/2005	$57,394.00	Jackson		11	2	$ 51,775.00
15	Rodriguez	8/4/2008	$43,815.00	Veigo		32	3	$ 57,278.50
16	Ma	1/21/2010	$36,288.00	Jackson		42		
17	Young	5/4/2010	$50,920.00	Veigo		26		

FIGURE 8.9 Top Salaries at Each Quartile

Excel 2016, Windows 10, Microsoft Corporation

a. Click **cell H13**, the cell to contain the top salary for the first quartile.

b. Click **Insert Function** on the Formulas tab. In the Insert Function dialog box, click the **Or select a category arrow** and select **Statistical**.

c. Scroll through the *Select a function* list, select **QUARTILE.EXC**, and then click **OK**.

   The Function Arguments dialog box opens so that you can enter the array and quart arguments.

d. Type the range **C$3:C$52** to enter it in the Array box.

e. Click in the Quart box, type **G13**, and then click **OK**.

   Cell G13 contains 1, which reflects Quartile 1. The highest salary in the first quartile is $39,203.50. This would be the salary at the 25th percentile. Note that because QUARTILE.EXC was used, quartiles 0 and 4 were omitted.

f. Double-click the **cell H13 fill handle** to copy the function for the rest of the quartiles.

   The array argument remains the same in the copied functions, but the quart argument changes to reflect the correct quartile values in column G.

g. Save the workbook. Keep the workbook open if you plan to continue with the next Hands-On Exercise. If not, close the workbook, and exit Excel.

Descriptive Statistical Functions

Attempting to make decisions based on datasets with hundreds if not thousands of entries can be a daunting task. Analyzing, summarizing, and describing a large dataset would be close to impossible without the right set of tools. Descriptive statistics provide the tools that help analyze and describe large datasets in pockets of manageable and usable information. While descriptive statistics like average and quartile are useful in defining the characteristics of a specific dataset, they are only calculations that describe the data and do not provide insight that is applicable into data outside the dataset. For example, a survey of high school teachers' opinions on dress code in Ohio would not provide any insight into high school teachers' opinions in Arkansas.

In this section, you will use statistical functions—VARIANCE, STANDARD DEVIATION, CORREL, and FREQUENCY —to measure central tendencies of datasets. In addition, you will also learn how calculation methods differ when working population and sample data.

Measuring Central Tendency

Functions used earlier in the chapter such as AVERAGEIF, QUARTILE, and RANK. AVG are all tools to measure central tendency. To add to these functions, Excel offers FREQUENCY, VARIANCE, standard deviation (STDEV), and CORREL to help define the shape and variation of a population or a sample of data. A **population** is a dataset that contains all the data you would like to evaluate. A **sample** is a smaller, more manageable portion of the population. For example, all educators in the state of Pennsylvania constitute an example of a population. A survey of 10% of the educators of each city in Pennsylvania is a sample.

Use the Standard Deviation and Variance Functions

STEP 1 ▶▶ **Variance** is a measure of a dataset's dispersion, such as the difference between the highest and lowest test scores in a class. **Standard deviation** is the measure of how far the data sample is spread around the mean, which is also referred to as μ, when using statistics. If calculated manually, the standard deviation is the square root of the variance.

> **TIP: μ (MU)**
> When working in formal statistical applications the Greek letter μ often appears. The symbol μ, pronounced "MU," is another method of describing the average or mean of a range of numbers.

Standard deviation and variance are two of the most popular tools to measure variations within a dataset. Recall that when working in descriptive statistics, the statistician can utilize data from the entire population or from a portion of the population, called a sample. Excel offers a variety of functions for these calculations based on the use of a sample or a population. Table 8.3 details the options available in Excel.

TABLE 8.3	Standard Deviation and Variance	
	Function	**Description**
Standard Deviation	STDEVA	Standard deviation of a sample including logical values and text
	STDEVPA	Standard deviation of a population including logical values and text
	STDEV.P	Standard deviation of a population
	STDEV.S	Standard deviation of a sample
Variance	VARA	Variance of a sample including logical values and text
	VARPA	Variance of a population including logical values and text
	VAR.P	Variance of a population
	VAR.S	Variance of a sample

Pearson Education, Inc.

The variance of a sample is the summation of the squared deviations divided by the size of the sample ($n - 1$) in which n is the number of data points. The variance describes how the data points compare to the mean. For example, a large variance indicates the data points are spread farther from the average, while a small variance indicates the data points are very close to the average. The standard deviation also describes the same data spread as the variance; however, the advantage is the calculated value uses the same units of measure as the original data points and is easier to understand. This value is calculated mathematically by determining the square root of the variance. While calculating standard deviation and variance mathematically may seem daunting, in Excel the functions are no more complicated than using a SUM function.

=STDEV.P(number1,number2)

=VAR.P(number1,number2)

The STDEV.P and VAR.P functions return values for an entire population. Recall that a population is the entire dataset that is possible. While it would be ideal to have access to 100% of all data that involves your study, it is often not realistic and in many cases sample data must be used. Excel does contain functions to calculate sample variations as well, as described in Table 8.3 and as displayed in syntax below.

=STDEV.S(number1,number2)

=VAR.S(number1,number2)

Use the CORREL Function

STEP 2 ▶▶ The **CORREL function**, short for "correlation coefficient," helps determine the strength of a relationship between two variables. When used to compare datasets, the function will return a value between −1 and 1. The closer the value is to 1, the stronger the relationship. For example, Figure 8.10 depicts the strength of the relationship between salary and credit score. Cell D3 contains a calculated correlation of .91313591. This would indicate a strong correlation between salary and a high credit score. In other words, this indicates that people with high salaries are more likely to have better credit scores.

The input variables for the CORREL function are entered in arrays. For example, the ranges B2:B15, C7:C10, and D16:D27 are all arrays.

=CORREL(array1,array2)

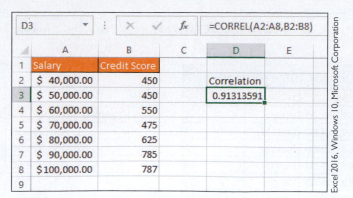

FIGURE 8.10 CORREL Function

Use the FREQUENCY Function

STEP 3 ❯❯ The **FREQUENCY function** is a descriptive statistical function in Excel that determines the frequency distribution of a dataset. The frequency distribution is a meaningful descriptive tool because it determines how often a set of numbers appears within a dataset. For example, you may want to determine how many student GPAs fall within a specific range. FREQUENCY is used to determine how many students earned As, Bs, and Cs. Using the FREQUENCY function is somewhat unique because it returns the frequency of numerical occurrence in bins. **Bins** are data ranges in which values can be categorized and counted. For example, when evaluating GPAs, bin 100%-90% would contain the number of students that received an A.

In Figure 8.11, the FREQUENCY function returns the number of occurrences of each salary in the dataset as determined by quartiles. In this scenario, there are 12 occurrences of salaries that are less than or equal to $39,203.50 which fall within the first quartile.

	A	B	C	D	E	F	G	H	I
	I4		fx {=FREQUENCY(C3:C52,H4:H6)}					FREQUENCY function	
1	**High School Educator Information**								
2	Last Name	Hire Date	Salary	Township	Salary rank		Quartile	Salary	Frequency
3	Kato	12/22/2007	$61,065.00	Veigo	4		1	$39,203.50	12
4	Han	10/20/2015	$59,913.00	Jackson	7		2	$51,775.00	13
5	Yoon	4/23/2014	$64,052.00	Jackson	3		3	$57,278.50	13
6	Lopez	7/30/1999	$45,305.00	Veigo	30				
7	Yamamoto	12/29/2002	$52,691.00	Veigo	23				
8	Lee	4/16/2014	$38,827.00	Veigo	39				
9	Garcia	4/23/2000	$57,307.00	Veigo	12				
10	Thomas	10/2/2002	$48,384.00	Acorn	28				

Bins array — Data array — Frequency distribution results

FIGURE 8.11 FREQUENCY Function

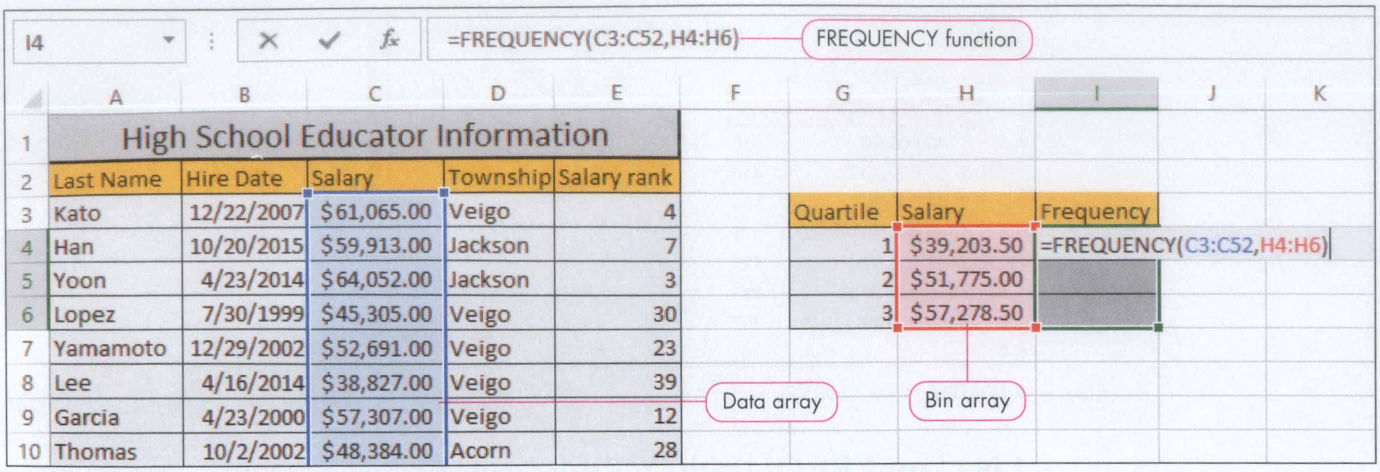

FIGURE 8.12 Frequency Function Input Variables

As shown in Figure 8.12 the FREQUENCY function requires two input variables, the data_array and the bins_array.

=FREQUENCY(data_array,bins_array)

- **Data_array.** The data_array is the range of cells that contain the values that are being evaluated for frequency of occurrence. In Figure 8.12, the data_array C3:C52 is being evaluated to determine how many salaries fall within the first, second, or third quartile.

- **Bins_array.** The bins_array argument is the range of numbers that specify the bins in which the data should be counted. Similar to a VLOOKUP table, data bins must be defined in the worksheet prior to using the FREQUENCY function. Furthermore, the data must be expressed in breakpoints and cannot be summarized in ranges. For example, see Table 8.4. In Figure 8.12, the range H4:H6 displays the quartile values that will be used as bins to determine frequency of occurrence within the data array.

TABLE 8.4 Bins_array Examples

Correct	Incorrect
0%	0%–60%
60%	61%–70%
70%	71%–80%
80%	81%–90%
90%	91%–100%
100%	

The benefit of FREQUENCY over COUNTIF, which could perform a similar calculation, is its ability to evaluate an entire dataset in one calculation. Unlike other Excel functions, you do not simply type the FREQUENCY function in a cell and press Enter. Instead, you must first select the cells in which you want to put the FREQUENCY function, type the formula, and then press Ctrl+Shift+Enter. This will return calculation results for all bins defined in the function. If you simply press Enter, then FREQUENCY will only calculate the frequency of the data that fall in the first cell bins_array.

To use the FREQUENCY function, complete the following steps:

1. Select a blank range of cells to output results.
2. Type =FREQUENCY in the first cell of the output range and press Tab.
3. Select the data_array and press comma.
4. Select the bins_array and type).
5. Press Ctrl+Shift+Enter.

TIP: NUMERICAL OUTLIERS

The FREQUENCY function will not return values that are higher than the highest number in the bins_array. If you are interested in documenting the numbers that fall outside the predefined bins_array, select one additional cell in the return range. This cell will populate with a count of the numbers that fall outside the highest number in the bins_array. For example, in Figure 8.13, there are 12 salaries that are outside the third quartile.

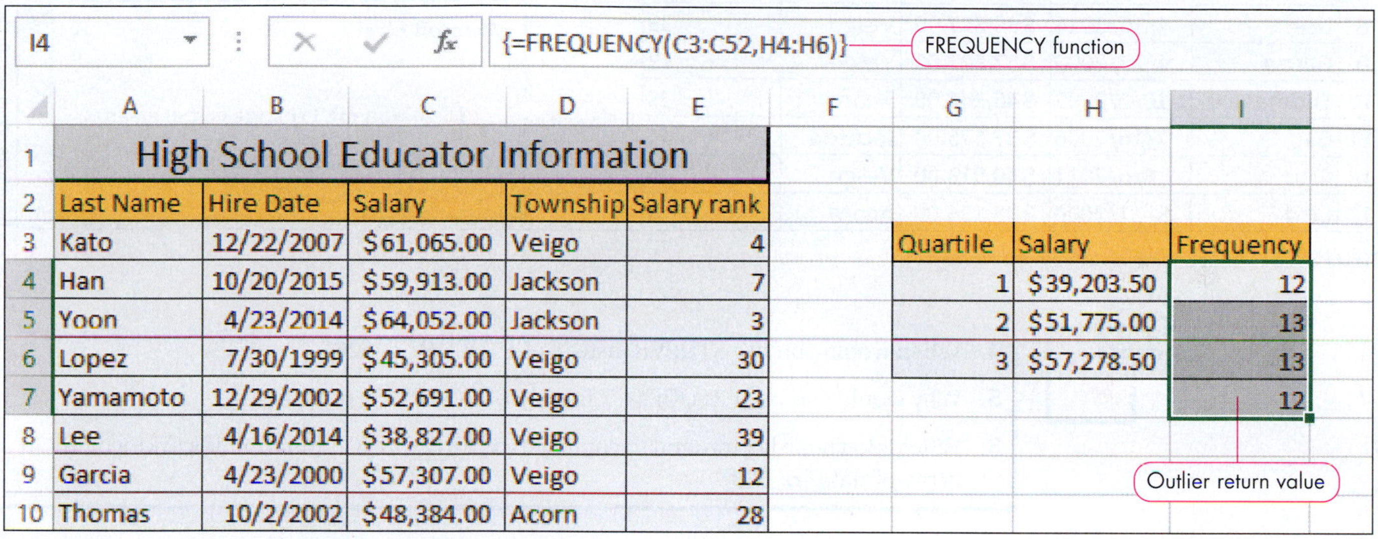

I4   fx   {=FREQUENCY(C3:C52,H4:H6)}   FREQUENCY function

	A	B	C	D	E	F	G	H	I
1	High School Educator Information								
2	Last Name	Hire Date	Salary	Township	Salary rank				
3	Kato	12/22/2007	$61,065.00	Veigo	4		Quartile	Salary	Frequency
4	Han	10/20/2015	$59,913.00	Jackson	7		1	$39,203.50	12
5	Yoon	4/23/2014	$64,052.00	Jackson	3		2	$51,775.00	13
6	Lopez	7/30/1999	$45,305.00	Veigo	30		3	$57,278.50	13
7	Yamamoto	12/29/2002	$52,691.00	Veigo	23				12
8	Lee	4/16/2014	$38,827.00	Veigo	39				
9	Garcia	4/23/2000	$57,307.00	Veigo	12			Outlier return value	
10	Thomas	10/2/2002	$48,384.00	Acorn	28				

FIGURE 8.13 Numerical Outliers

TIP: CHANGING AN ARRAY

As shown in Figure 8.14, Excel does not allow partial edits of an array, such as the one created when using the FREQUENCY function. In order to change or delete array calculations made with the FREQUENCY function, all data results must be simultaneously deleted.

	A	B	C	D	E	F	G	H	I	J
1	High School Educator Information									
2	Last Name	Hire Date	Salary	Township	Salary rank					
3	Kato	12/22/2007	$61,065.00	Veigo	4		Quartile	Salary	Frequency	
4	Han	10/20/2015	$59,913.00	Jackson	7		1	$39,203.50	12	
5	Yoon	4/23/2014	$64,052.00	Jackson	3		2	$51,775.00	13	
6	Lopez	7/30/1999	$45,305.00	Veigo	30		3	$57,278.50	13	
7	Yamamoto	12/29/2002	$52,691.00	Veigo	23					
8	Lee	4/16/2014	$38,827.00	Veigo	39					
9	Garcia	4/23/2000	$57,307.00	Veigo	12					
10	Thomas	10/2/2002	$48,384.00	Acorn	28					
11	Gao	7/16/2006	$37,575.00	Jackson	41					
12	Cruz	8/6/2011	$60,913.00	Veigo	6					
13	Cruz	9/11/2006	$58,134.00	Acorn	9					

Microsoft Excel — Edit warning — You can't change part of an array. — OK

Excel 2016, Windows 10, Microsoft Corporation

FIGURE 8.14 Changing an Array

Quick Concepts

4. When would you use STDEV.S instead of STDEV.P? *p. 526*

5. Why would you use FREQUENCY instead of COUNTIF? *p. 528*

6. What is keyboard command to complete the FREQUENCY function if working with an array of data? *p. 528*

Hands-On Exercises

Watch the Video
for this Hands On
Exercise!

MyITLab®
HOE2 Training

Skills covered: Use the
Standard Deviation Function
• Use the Variance Function • Use
the CORREL Function • Use the
FREQUENCY Function

2 Descriptive Statistical Functions

As the superintendent, you have been tasked with evaluating student performance. You have decided to base your assessment on standardized test scores and total attendance. You will also test the correlation between test scores and attendance. You plan to base your calculations on a sample of 50 students from the district.

STEP 1 » **CALCULATE STANDARD DEVIATION AND VARIANCE**

The sample you have collected contains test scores as well as attendance information of sixth- through eighth-grade students across the district. You will calculate the standard deviation of the test scores within the sample. Refer to Figure 8.15 as you complete Step 1.

	A	B	C	D	E	F	G	H	I	J
1										
2				6-8 Test Scores						
3		Student ID	Test Score	Township	School #	Days Absent				
4		1075	725	Acorn	24	2		Max Test Score	Sample Size	Average
5		1912	325	Acorn	24	10		800	50	517
6		4196	648	Acorn	24	6		Steps b-c: Standard deviation		
7		4483	750	Acorn	24	0		of test scores		
8		6237	585	Acorn	24	2		Standard Deviation	Variance	Correlation
9		6284	325	Acorn	24	9		181	32803	
10		6285	707	Acorn	24	1				
11		6312	684	Acorn	24	2		Days Absent	Frequency	
12		6353	407	Acorn	24	10		0		Steps d-e: Variance
13		6747	501	Acorn	26	6		5		of test scores
14		6778	282	Acorn	26	5		10		
15		7025	596	Acorn	26	2				
16		7284	789	Acorn	26	9				
17		7486	621	Acorn	26	0				

Excel 2016, Windows 10, Microsoft Corporation

FIGURE 8.15 Calculate Standard Deviation and Variance

a. Open *e08h1Assessment_LastFirst* if you closed it at the end of Hands-On Exercise 1, and save it as **e08h2Assessment_LastFirst**, changing h1 to h2.

b. Click the **Test Scores worksheet**. Click **cell H9**, click the **Formulas tab**, click **More Functions** in the Function Library group, point to **Statistical**, and then click **STDEV.S**.

STDEV.S is being used because the data is a random sample of 50 test scores. If every test score were included in the dataset, STDEV.P would be used.

c. Select the **range C4:C53** and click **OK**. With **cell H9** still selected, click **Decrease Decimal** in the Number group on the Home tab until no decimal points are displayed.

The standard deviation for the sample is 181. Therefore, assuming the distribution is normal, about 66% of students will receive a test score between 336 and 698. This is calculated by adding the standard deviation, 181, to the average test score of 517 to determine the high end of the range and subtracting 181 from 517 to determine the low end of the range.

d. Tab to **cell I9**, click the **Formulas tab**, click **More Functions** in the Function Library group, point to **Statistical**, and then select **VAR.S**.

e. Type **C4:C53** in the Number box 1 and click **OK**. With **cell I9** still selected, click **Decrease Decimal** located in the Number group on the Home tab until no decimal points are displayed.

The larger the variance, the greater the dispersion of data around the mean test score. The results of the VAR.S function (32803) would indicate a large dispersion.

f. Save the workbook.

STEP 2 ›› CALCULATE CORRELATION COEFFICIENT

After calculating the standard deviation and variance to help determine the data points' distance from the mean, you would like to test for a correlation between test scores and attendance. Refer to Figure 8.16 as you complete Step 2.

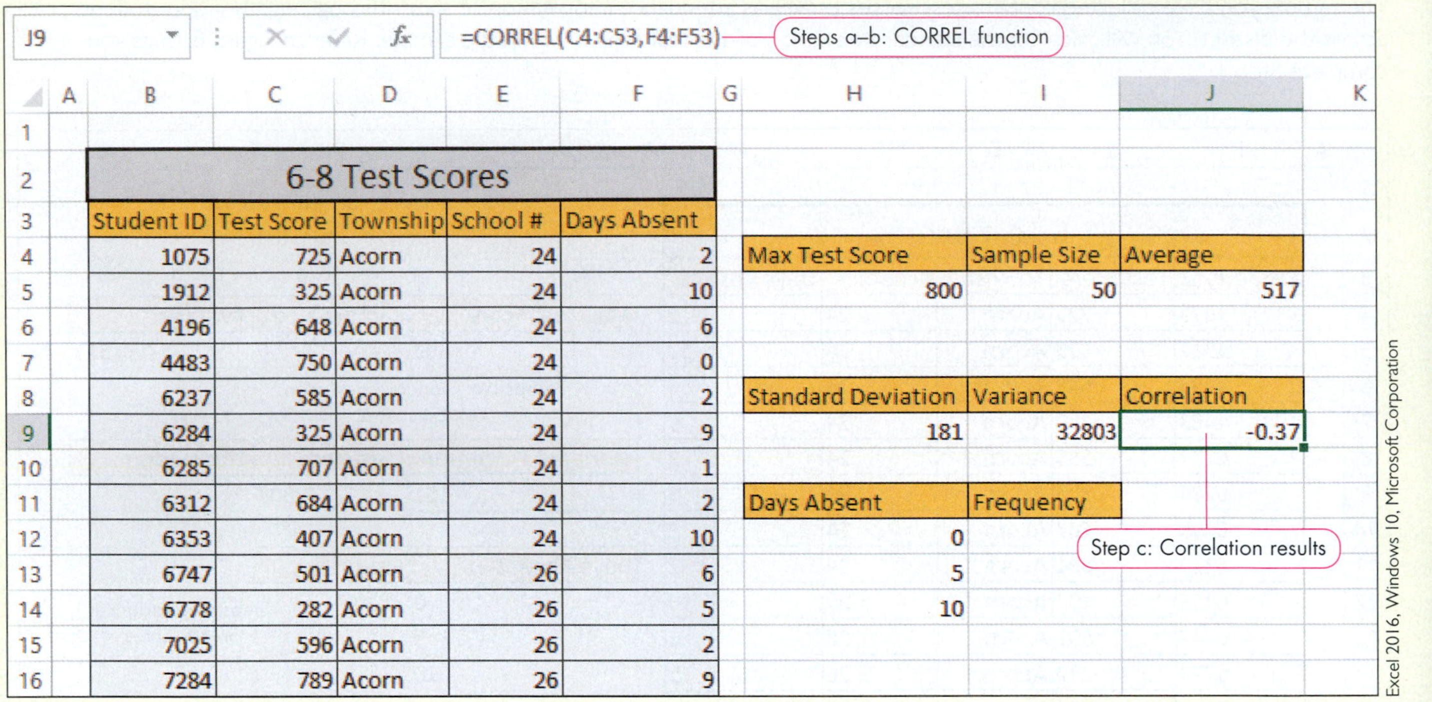

FIGURE 8.16 Use the CORREL Function

a. Click **cell J9**, ensure the Formulas tab is active, click **More Functions** in the Function Library group, point to **Statistical**, and then select **CORREL**.

b. Select **C4:C53** in the Array1 box, select **F4:F53** in the Array2 box, and then click **OK**.

c. Keep **cell J9** selected and click **Decrease Decimal** in the Number group on the Home tab until two decimal positions are displayed.

The result is −0.37. This means that there is a slightly negative correlation between attendance and test scores. Thus, the more days a student is absent, the lower the test scores received.

d. Save the workbook.

You want to determine the frequency of student absences based on the criteria of perfect attendance which will be used as bins, 0, 1 to 5 days absent, and 6 to 10 days absent. To do this, you will use the FREQUENCY function. Refer to Figure 8.17 as you complete Step 3.

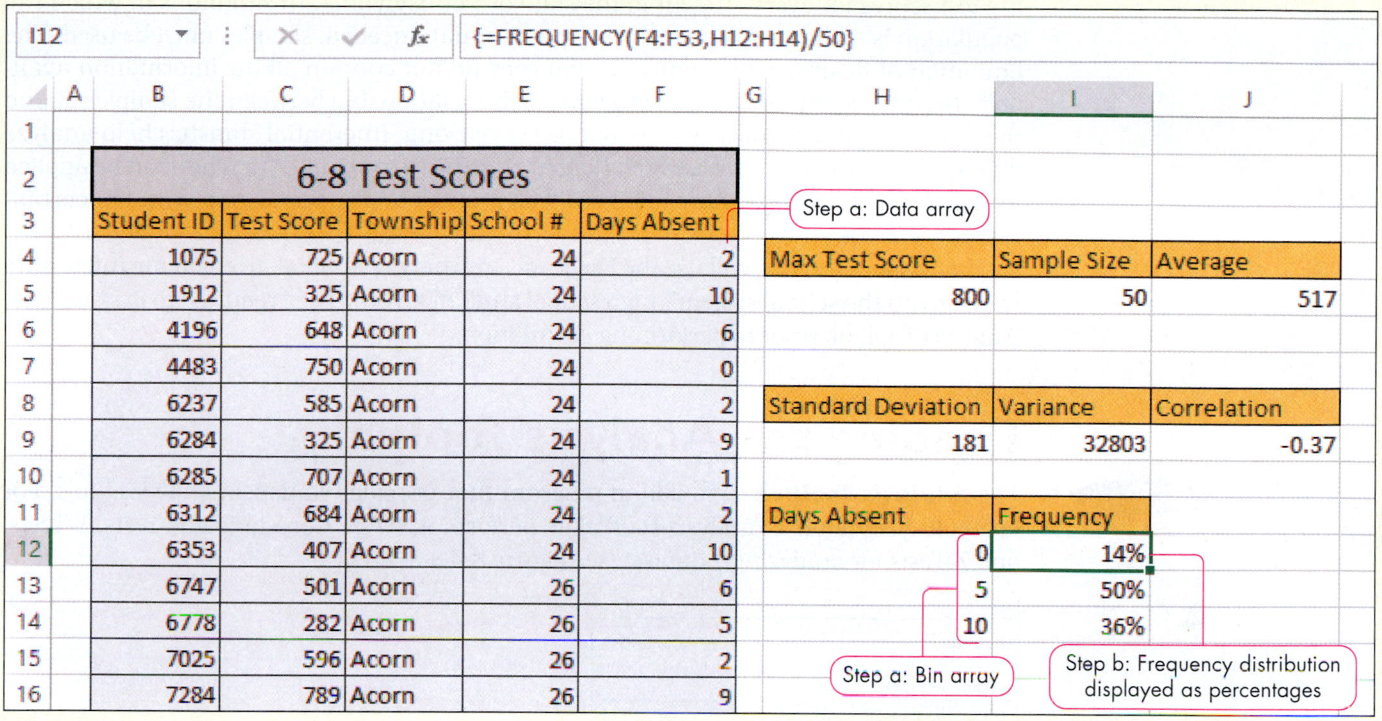

	A	B	C	D	E	F	G	H	I	J
I12						fx	{=FREQUENCY(F4:F53,H12:H14)/50}			

6-8 Test Scores

Student ID	Test Score	Township	School #	Days Absent					
1075	725	Acorn	24	2		Max Test Score		Sample Size	Average
1912	325	Acorn	24	10			800	50	517
4196	648	Acorn	24	6					
4483	750	Acorn	24	0					
6237	585	Acorn	24	2		Standard Deviation		Variance	Correlation
6284	325	Acorn	24	9			181	32803	-0.37
6285	707	Acorn	24	1					
6312	684	Acorn	24	2		Days Absent		Frequency	
6353	407	Acorn	24	10		0		14%	
6747	501	Acorn	26	6		5		50%	
6778	282	Acorn	26	5		10		36%	
7025	596	Acorn	26	2					
7284	789	Acorn	26	9					

Step a: Data array
Step a: Bin array
Step b: Frequency distribution displayed as percentages

FIGURE 8.17 Frequency Distribution

a. Select the **range I12:I14** and type **=FREQUENCY(F4:F53,H12:H14)/50**. Type a comma (), Type , and then press **Ctrl+Shift+Enter**. Refer to Figure 8.17 to check your function.

The range I12:I14 was selected in order to return all results. If only I12 were selected, the function would return data just for students with 1 to 5 absences. You divided the FREQUENCY function by the number of data points in the sample (50) so that the results are calculated as percentages.

> **TROUBLESHOOTING:** Make sure you add the right parenthesis after the bins_array but before adding /50. This will complete the FREQUENCY function before dividing the results by 50 to calculate the percentage.

b. Ensure the **range I12:I14** is still selected and apply the **Percentage Number Format** in the Number group on the Home tab.

From the results, you can determine that 14% of the students had perfect attendance, 50% missed between 1 to 5 days, and 36% missed between 5 and 10 days.

c. Save the workbook. Keep the workbook open if you plan to continue with the next Hands-On Exercise. If not, close the workbook, and exit Excel.

Excel 2016, Windows 10, Microsoft Corporation

Inferential Statistics

Descriptive statistics help define characteristics of a population such as mean, standard deviation, and variance. However, in many situations, you may want to research a population that you may not have the time or resources to evaluate—for example, evaluating test scores for every student in the state of Pennsylvania. In situations in which the population is too large to acquire every point of data needed, samples must be used. The limitation of dealing with samples is that they do not contain all the information available. Depending on the sample set selected, the relationship between the sample set and the entire population may or may not be very strong. Inferential statistics help analyze differences between groups and relationships within groups of data. They can be applied to samples to help make more informed statements about a population within a certain margin of error.

In this section, you will use the Excel add-in Analysis ToolPak to calculate inferential statistics on the school system's high school students. You will be required to first load the Analysis ToolPak prior to performing calculations.

Loading the Analysis ToolPak

STEP 1 ›› The **Analysis ToolPak** is an add-in program that provides statistical analysis tools. For example, you can use Analysis ToolPak to perform ANOVA, Correlation, F-Tests, T-Tests, and Z-Tests for analyzing a dataset (see Figure 8.18).

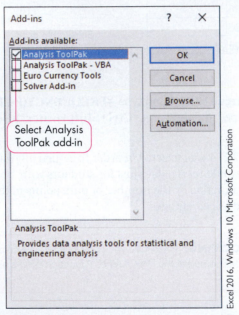

Excel 2016, Windows 10, Microsoft Corporation

FIGURE 8.18 Analysis ToolPak

> **To enable the Analysis ToolPak add-in, complete the following steps:**
>
> 1. Click the File tab and click Options.
> 2. Select Add-ins on the left side.
> 3. Ensure that Excel Add-ins is selected in the Manage box and click Go.
> 4. Click the Analysis ToolPak check box to select it and click OK.

Performing Analysis Using the Analysis ToolPak

The Analysis ToolPak offers 19 tools that fit a variety of needs across all professions. In Excel, there are alternate options to many of these tools, such as the FREQUENCY function versus the Histogram summary in the ToolPak. The benefit of using the Analysis ToolPak versus the corresponding function is that the ToolPak will generate reports while the function equivalents only return values.

Perform Analysis of Variance (ANOVA)

STEP 2 ›› In statistics, it is common to compare the means between two or more sample groups of data—for example, comparing test scores from a cross-sectional sample of multiple high schools in the same district or comparing test scores in a time-series sample over a period of years from the same high school. A common tool to compare these samples is analysis of variance, also abbreviated as ANOVA.

ANOVA is a statistical hypothesis test that helps determine if samples of data were taken from the same population. In practical use, it can be used to accept or reject a hypothesis. There is no one function to calculate ANOVA in Excel; however, you can create an ANOVA report using the Analysis ToolPak.

Three types of ANOVA calculations can be performed:

- Single factor
- Two factor with replication
- Two factor without replication

Single-factor ANOVA is a popular option because it provides information to compare the differences in a dataset based on a single variable.

> **To use the Analysis ToolPak to create a single-factor ANOVA report, complete the following steps:**
>
> 1. Click the Data tab and select Data Analysis in the Analysis group.
> 2. Select Anova: Single Factor in the Data Analysis dialog box and click OK.
> 3. Click the Input Range selection box and select the range of data you want to analyze.
> 4. Select either Grouped By Columns or Grouped By Rows based on your data layout.
> 5. Choose the default Alpha 0.05 (meaning there is a 5% chance of rejecting the null hypothesis).
> 6. Select an output option.
> 7. Click OK.

Excel will place the results on a new worksheet in the same workbook if the *New Worksheet Ply* option is selected. The results of the sample test scores can be viewed in Figure 8.19. The summary portion of the report provides basic descriptive statistics of each group analyzed. The ANOVA portion of the report breaks the data into two sets, between groups and within groups. ANOVA analysis within groups measures random variation. ANOVA analysis between groups measures variation due to differences within the group. Table 8.4 provides further detail on the ANOVA summary information.

TABLE 8.4 ANOVA Summary Report

Abbreviation	Full name	Explanation
SS	Sum of squares	Sum of the squares of the data points in the sample
df	Degrees of freedom	The number of data points in the sample − 1 (N − 1)
MS	Mean square	The means of the sample squared
F	F ratio	Equal to the mean square between/mean square within
P-value	Probability	Probability of population being similar to the sample
F crit	Critical value of F	Used to determine if the F_Test is significant

	A	B	C	D	E	F	G
1	Anova: Single Factor						
2							
3	SUMMARY						
4	*Groups*	*Count*	*Sum*	*Average*	*Variance*		
5	High School 1	50	64632	1292.64	250915.7		
6	High School 2	50	61331	1226.62	220865.5		
7	High School 3	50	66208	1324.16	187754.1		
8							
9							
10	ANOVA						
11	*Source of Variation*	*SS*	*df*	*MS*	*F*	*P-value*	*F crit*
12	Between Groups	247770	2	123885	0.563511	0.570432	3.057621
13	Within Groups	32317224	147	219845.1			
14							
15	Total	32564994	149				

FIGURE 8.19 ANOVA Results

Calculate COVARIANCE

STEP 3 ▶▶ *Covariance* is similar to correlation. It is a measure of how two sets of data vary simultaneously. It is calculated by taking the average of each product of the deviation of a data point. In Excel, there are COVARIANCE.P and COVARIANCE.S functions that can calculate covariance, and there is also a covariance reporting feature included in the Analysis ToolPak. While both the Analysis ToolPak and COVARIANCE functions will return the covariance, the Analysis ToolPak will also calculate the variance in the output in a preformatted report.

For example, you may hypothesize that the more days of school missed by a student, the lower the student's SAT scores. The CORREL function would return a numerical value that analyzes the strength of the relation. The covariance analysis will produce a matrix that shows how the datasets change together (see Figure 8.20). A positive covariance indicates a positive relationship, a negative value indicates an inverse relationship, and a 0 value indicates no relationship. For example, the relationship −1484.57 indicates a negative relationship between test scores and attendance.

Test scores Analysis

Student ID	SAT Score	Absences
1003	485	10
1016	1749	2
1017	1586	3
1030	1016	8
1114	1761	2
1129	868	9
1169	1328	5
1234	1226	6
1236	761	10
1246	1038	7

Negative covariance indicates negative relationship

Variance within data

	SAT Score	Absences
SAT Score	217099.9604	
Absences	-1484.57	10.58333333

Excel 2016, Windows 10, Microsoft Corporation

FIGURE 8.20 COVARIANCE Results

Create a Histogram

STEP 4 ▶▶ A *histogram* is a visual display of tabulated frequencies (see Figure 8.21). There are several ways to create a histogram in Excel; however, one of the simplest methods is by using the Analysis ToolPak. Creating a histogram is somewhat similar to using the FREQUENCY function in that it requires bins to tabulate the data and will return a frequency distribution table. Figure 8.21 depicts a completed histogram.

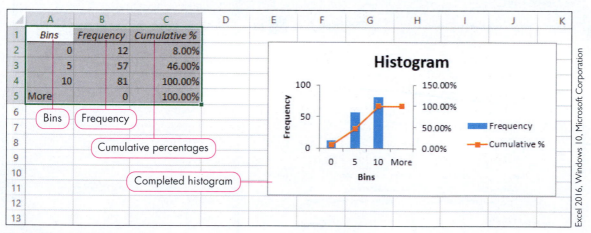

FIGURE 8.21 Histogram Results

To create a histogram, complete the following steps:

1. Click the Data tab, click Data Analysis, and then choose Histogram.
2. Enter the Input Range in the Input Range box.
3. Enter the Bin Range in the Bin Range box.
4. Click the Labels box.
5. Select the output options of your choice.
6. Choose Chart Output to display the visual histogram in the output.
7. Click OK.

Creating a Forecast Sheet

STEP 5 ➤➤ Excel 2016 offers a new business intelligence feature that has the ability to create a forecast worksheet to detail trends based on historical data. The new feature extrapolates information based on given data and can generate a worksheet that details the predictions. For example, say you track average SAT test scores over the years as they compare to average teacher salaries. As shown in Figure 8.22, the Forecast Sheet feature will generate a chart and corresponding table to provide a future forecast based on given data. The worksheet will provide information with a default confidence level of 95% and gives the user the option of setting start values, end values, and chart type within the forecast.

To create a Forecast worksheet, complete the following steps:

1. Sort the data in chronological order.
2. Select the data range for the desired forecast.
3. Click the Data tab and select Forecast Sheet.
4. Set the desired Forecast End.
5. Click Create.

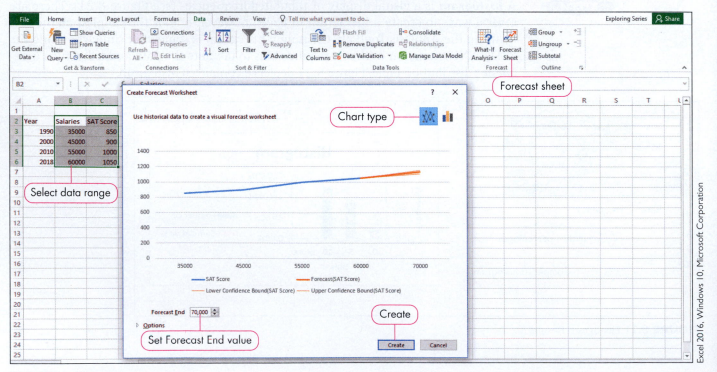

FIGURE 8.22 Forecast Worksheet

TABLE 8.5	New Forecasting Functions in Excel 2016
Name	**Description**
FORECAST.ETS	Returns the forecasted values for a specific future target date using exponential smoothing method.
FORECAST.ETS.CONFINT	Returns a confidence interval for the forecast value at the specified target date.
FORECAST.ETS. SEASONALITY	Returns the length of the repetitive pattern Microsoft Excel detects for the specified time series.
FORECAST.ETS. STAT	Returns the requested statistic for the forecast.
FORECAST.LINEAR	Calculates, or predicts, a future value along a linear trend by using existing values.

Pearson Education, Inc.

Quick Concepts

7. What is the difference between inferential statistics and descriptive statistics? **p. 534**

8. What is the benefit of using the Analysis ToolPak over Excel functions? **p. 535**

9. What is the difference between COVARIANCE and CORREL? **p. 536**

Hands-On Exercises

Skills covered: Perform Analysis of Variance (ANOVA) • Calculate COVARIANCE • Create a Histogram • Create a Forecast Sheet

3 Inferential Statistics

For the last portion of your educational assessment, you would like to analyze SAT data across multiple high schools in the district. As part of the analysis, you are going to use the Analysis ToolPak to calculate an ANOVA report as well as test the variation of test scores and SAT results using covariance. You will create a histogram of all SAT scores in the sample, and last you will use the new Forecast sheet feature to forecast the outcomes of absences on test scores.

STEP 1 ›› LOAD THE ANALYSIS TOOLPAK ADD-IN

Before you begin your calculations, you need to enable the Analysis ToolPak add-in. If the ToolPak is already loaded, skip to Step 2. Refer to Figure 8.23 as you complete Step 1.

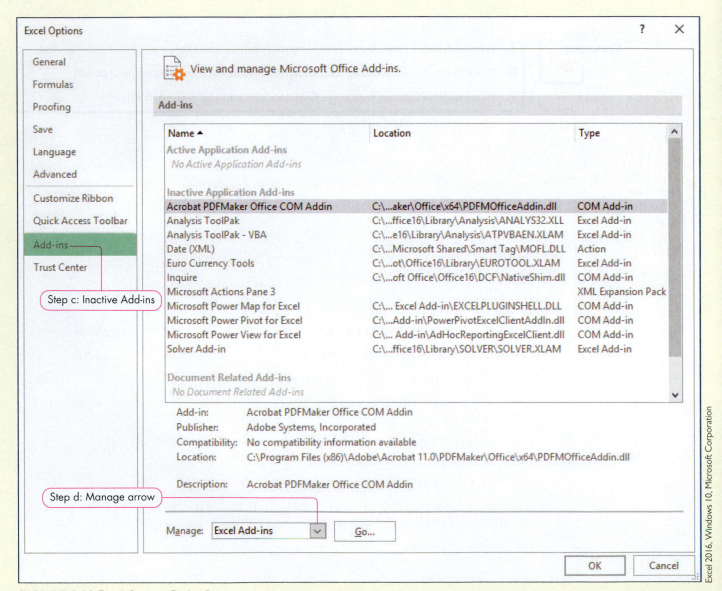

FIGURE 8.23 Excel Options Dialog Box

a. Open *e08h2Assessment_LastFirst* if you closed it at the end of Hands-On Exercise 2, and save it as **e08h3Assessment_LastFirst,** changing h2 to h3.

b. Make the **High School Samples** worksheet active, click the **File tab,** and then select **Options**.

c. Click **Add-ins** on the left side.

The Excel Options dialog box displays a list of active and inactive application add-ins.

d. Click the **Manage arrow**, select **Excel Add-ins**, and then click **Go**.

The Add-ins dialog box opens, containing a list of available add-in applications.

e. Click the **Analysis ToolPak check box** in the *Add-ins available* list to select it and click **OK**.

f. Save the workbook.

STEP 2 ▶▶ **PERFORMING ANALYSIS OF VARIANCE**

You are ready to create an analysis of variance using the Analysis ToolPak. You will analyze a cross-section data sample of SAT scores from three high schools in the school district. Refer to Figure 8.24 as you complete Step 2.

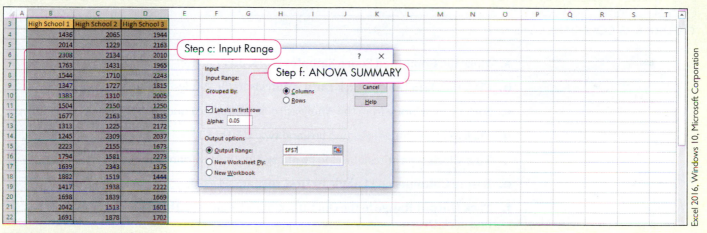

FIGURE 8.24 ANOVA Summary

a. Click the **Data tab** and click **Data Analysis** in the Analysis group.

b. Select **Anova: Single Factor** from the Analysis Tools options box and click **OK**.

c. Type **B3:D53** in the Input Range box.

This selects the entire dataset to be utilized for the ANOVA.

d. Click the **Labels in First Row** check box to select it and leave the *Alpha* setting at the default 0.05.

e. Click **Output Range** in the *Output options* section and type **F7** in the Output Range box. Click **OK**.

This embeds the ANOVA output on the current worksheet.

f. Ensure the **range F7:L21** is still selected, click the **Home tab**, and then select **Auto-Fit Column Width** from the Format menu in the Cells group.

g. Save the workbook.

Your next assessment is an analysis of trends between SAT scores and attendance. To complete this task, you will create a covariance summary. Refer to Figure 8.25 as you complete Step 3.

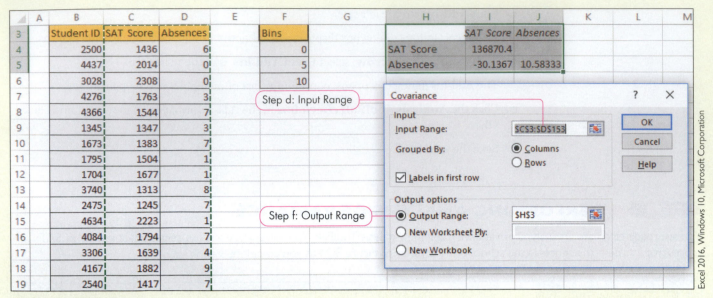

FIGURE 8.25 COVARIANCE Summary

a. Make the **Combined Score Samples worksheet** active.

b. Click the **Data tab** and click **Data Analysis** in the Analysis group.

c. Select **Covariance** from the Analysis Tools options box and click **OK**.

d. Click in Input Range selection box and type **C3:D153**.

This selects the entire dataset to be utilized for the covariance summary.

e. Ensure **Columns** and **Labels in first row** are selected.

f. Click **Output Range** in the Output options section, type **H3** in the Output Range box, and click **OK**.

By selecting cell H3 for the output range, you place the summary starting in cell H3 on the worksheet. The covariance of −1484.57 indicates a negative relationship between attendance and test scores.

g. Resize **columns I:J** width to 13.

h. Save the workbook.

Your next task is to create a histogram to document the frequency of absences in the high school. To complete the task, you will organize the data into bins for perfect attendance, 1 to 5 absences, and 5 to 10 absences. Refer to Figure 8.26 as you complete Step 4.

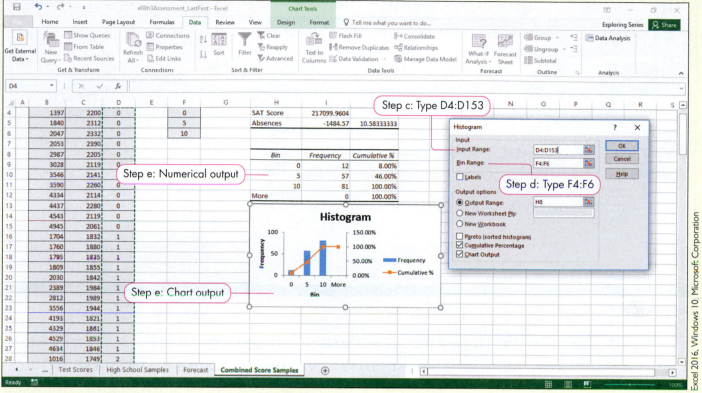

FIGURE 8.26 Complete Histogram

a. Ensure the **Combined Score Samples** worksheet is still active and click **Data Analysis** in the Analysis group.

b. Select **Histogram** from the Analysis Tools options box and click **OK**.

c. Type **D4:D153** in the Input Range box.

d. Type **F4:F6** in the Bin Range box.

e. Click **Output Range** in the Output options section, type **H8**, click **Cumulative Percentage**, click **Chart Output option**, and then click **OK**.

f. Move the newly created histogram chart so that the top-left corner is in cell H13.

g. Save the workbook.

Your last task is creating a forecast sheet to predict the impact of attendance on SAT scores. To complete the task, you will sort the data and create a forecast sheet ending with a forecast of 15 absences. Refer to Figure 8.27 as you complete Step 5.

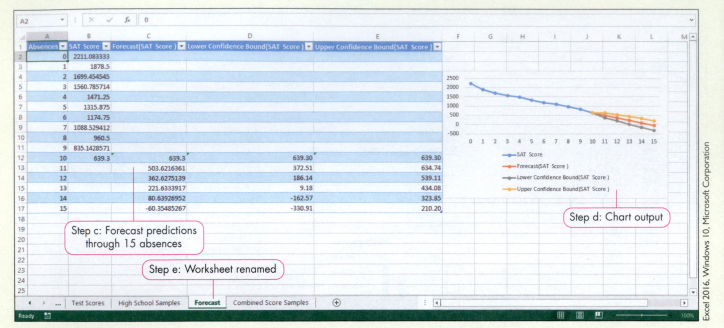

FIGURE 8.27 Create Forecast Sheet

a. Click **cell D4**. Click **Sort Smallest to Largest** in the Editing group on the Home tab.

b. Select the **range C3:D153,** click the **Data tab,** and then click **Forecast Sheet** in the Forecast group.

c. Type **15** in the Forecast End box and click **Create**.

d. Click the newly created chart, click the **Design tab** and select **Chart Style 12** in the Chart Styles group. Position the chart so the top-left corner is starting in **cell F4** and resize so it fills the **range F4:L16**.

e. Rename the worksheet **Forecast**.

f. Save and close the file. Based on your instructor's directions, submit e08h3Assessment_LastFirst.

Chapter Objectives Review

After reading this chapter, you have accomplished the following objectives:

I. Use conditional math and statistical functions.

- Use the SUMIF, AVERAGEIF, and COUNTIF functions: These functions require a range argument to specify the range of values to evaluate and a criteria argument that specifies the condition for the range.
- Use the SUMIFS, AVERAGEIFS, and COUNTIFS functions: These functions contain arguments to specify the range of values to sum, average, or count. When more than one condition must be met, use SUMIFS, AVERAGEIFS, and COUNTIFS.
- AVERAGEIF, AVERAGEIFS, COUNTIF, and COUNTIFS are considered statistical functions. These functions are located in the Statistical category under More Functions in the Function Library group.

2. Calculate relative standing with statistical functions.

- Use the RANK and PERCENTRANK functions: The RANK.EQ and RANK.AVG functions calculate ranking for individual values within a list. PERCENTRANK.INC and PERCENTRANK.EXC calculate rank as a percentage for each value in a list.
- Use the QUARTILE and PERCENTILE functions: The QUARTILE.INC and QUARTILE.EXC functions identify the value at a specific quartile. PERCENTILE.INC and PERCENTILE.EXC identify the kth percentile of a value.

3. Measure central tendency.

- Measures of central tendency define basic characteristics of a population or sample of data.
- Use the standard deviation and variance functions: The STDEV.S and STDEV.P functions help determine variations in a data series, specifically how far the sample is spread around the mean. The VAR.S and VAR.P functions determine the summation of the squared deviations divided by the amount of the sample – 1 or the total population.
- Use the CORREL function: The CORREL function determines the correlation coefficient. The value returned will be between –1 and 1. The closer the value is to 1, the stronger the positive relationship between datasets.

- Use the FREQUENCY function: The FREQUENCY function is an array function that calculates the number of occurrences of specific values of data that appear in a data series.

4. Load the Analysis ToolPak.

- The Analysis ToolPak is an Excel add-in that must be loaded before use. To activate the add-in, go to Options in Backstage view, click Add-ins, click Excel Add-ins from the Manage list, click Go, and then select Analysis ToolPak.

5. Perform analysis using the Analysis ToolPak.

- There are 19 tools available for use within the Analysis ToolPak. Many of the tools have function counterparts that can be used. The benefit of using the ToolPak over the functions is the final summary report options in the ToolPak.
- Perform analysis of variance (ANOVA): ANOVA is an abbreviation of analysis of variance. This statistical tool compares the means between two data samples to determine if they were derived from the same population.
- Calculate COVARIANCE: COVARIANCE is a measure of how two sample sets of data vary simultaneously. COVARIANCE.P can be used to calculate the COVARIANCE of a dataset that encompass the entire population. COVARIANCE.S calculates the COVARIANCE of a sample datasets.
- Create a histogram: A histogram is a tabular display of data frequencies organized into bins. The histogram feature of the Analysis ToolPak is comparable to the FREQUENCY function. It will return the number of occurrences of data points based on predefined bins. It also has charting capabilities.

6. Create a Forecast Sheet.

- Excel 2016 offers a new business intelligence feature that creates a numerical and visual forecast based on the seasonality of historical data. This feature can be used as a stand-alone tool or in conjunction with new time-series forecasting functions.

Key Terms Matching

Match the key terms with their definitions. Write the key term letter by the appropriate numbered definition.

a. Analysis ToolPak
b. ANOVA
c. AVERAGEIF function
d. CORREL function
e. COUNTIF function
f. Covariance
g. FREQUENCY function
h. Histogram
i. PERCENTILE.EXC function
j. PERCENTILE.INC function

k. PERCENTRANK.EXC function
l. PERCENTRANK.INC function
m. QUARTILE.EXC function
n. QUARTILE.INC function
o. RANK.AVG function
p. RANK.EQ function
q. Standard Deviation
r. SUMIF function
s. SUMIFS function
t. Variance

1. _____ A visual display of tabulated frequencies. **p. 537**

2. _____ Measure of how two sample sets of data vary simultaneously. **p. 536**

3. _____ A statistical tool that compares the means between two data samples to determine if they were derived from the same population. **p. 535**

4. _____ An add-in program that contains tools for performing complex statistical analysis. **p. 534**

5. _____ A measure of a dataset's dispersion, such as the difference between the highest and lowest points in the data. **p. 525**

6. _____ Measures how far the data sample is spread around the mean. **p. 525**

7. _____ Determines the number of occurrences of numerical values in a dataset based on predetermined bins. **p. 527**

8. _____ Calculates the correlation coefficient of two data series. **p. 526**

9. _____ Calculates the total of a range of values when a specified condition is met. **p. 514**

10. _____ A statistical function that identifies the rank of a value, omitting the next rank when tie values exist. **p. 516**

11. _____ Identifies the rank of a value, providing an average ranking for identical values. **p. 516**

12. _____ Identifies the value at a specific quartile. **p. 517**

13. _____ A statistical function that identifies the value at a specific quartile, exclusive of 0 and 4. **p. 517**

14. _____ A statistical function that returns the percentile of a range including the 0 or 100% percentile. **p. 517**

15. _____ A statistical function that returns the percentile of a range excluding the 0 or 100% percentile. **p. 517**

16. _____ Counts the number of cells in a range when a specified condition is met. **p. 514**

17. _____ Calculates the average of values in a range when a specified condition is met. **p. 513**

18. _____ Identifies the *k*th percentile of a specified value within a list of values, including the 0th and 100th percentiles. **p. 519**

19. _____ A statistical function that returns the percentile of a range excluding the 0 or 100% percentile. **p. 519**

20. _____ Calculates the total value of cells in a range that meet multiple criteria. **p. 514**

Multiple Choice

1. A workbook contains sales information for the first quarter and you are interested in finding the total sales generated in January by the sales rep Jim Anderson. What function is best suited to handle the task?

   (a) SUMIFS

   (b) AVERAGEIFS

   (c) DCOUNT

   (d) COUNTIFS

2. What function would you use to identify a value's rank as a percent, excluding 0 and 1?

   (a) QUARTILE.INC

   (b) PERCENTRANK.EXC

   (c) PERCENTRANK.INC

   (d) RANK.EQ

3. What does a negative COVARIANCE indicate?

   (a) No relationship between the datasets

   (b) A positive relationship between datasets

   (c) An inverse relationship between the datasets

   (d) A statistically insignificant dataset

4. A worksheet contains sales dollars for agents with your company. The values are $1,250, $1,090, $985, $985, $880, $756, $675, $650, and $600. Using the RANK. AVG function that is considered a best practice, what is the rank of the third values which are both 985?

   (a) 2

   (b) 3

   (c) 2.5

   (d) None of the above

5. What function would you use to calculate the strength of a relationship between two or more variables?

   (a) STDEV.S

   (b) CORREL

   (c) STDEV.P

   (d) FREQUENCY

6. You hypothesize that there is a relationship between lack of regular exercise and illness. To research this theory, you have compiled a sample set of data that contains numbers of days in which an hour or more of exercise is completed as well as numbers of days sick within a calendar year. What tools in Excel could you use to investigate the relationships between the data?

   (a) CORREL

   (b) PERCENTRANK.INC

   (c) VAR.S

   (d) SUMIFS

7. Which of the following functions has the ability to calculate the μ (MU) of a dataset based on a user defined set of criteria?

   (a) AVERAGE

   (b) SUMIFS

   (c) COUNTIFS

   (d) AVERAGEIFS

8. What is the difference between STDEV.S and STDEV.P?

   (a) STDEV.S calculates standard deviation of a sample; STDEV.P calculates the standard deviation of a population.

   (b) STDEV.P calculates the standard deviation of a population; STDEV.S calculates average variation.

   (c) STDEV.P calculates the standard deviation of a population; STDEV.S calculates variance.

   (d) There is no difference.

9. What is the difference between a sample and a population?

   (a) A sample contains all data you want to evaluate, while a population contains a portion of data available.

   (b) A population contains all data you want to evaluate, while a sample contains a portion of the data.

   (c) A sample contains all data from the population except statistical outliers.

   (d) There is no difference.

10. What keystroke combination is required to calculate a Frequency data array?

    (a) Ctrl+Enter

    (b) Alt+Enter

    (c) Ctrl+Shift+Enter

    (d) Ctrl+Shift+Delete

Practice Exercises

1 Sociology Textbooks

As vice president of the Sociology Division at Ivory Halls Publishing Company, you monitor sales of textbooks published by your division. The division categorizes textbooks by discipline (such as criminal justice and family) and then further classifies books by an area within the discipline. Your assistant downloaded and formatted the latest sales figures. Now you want to calculate some summary statistics for the introductory discipline and then, more specifically, the general area. Refer to Figure 8.28 as you complete this exercise.

	A	B	C	D	E	F	G	H
1	**Quartiles**					**Summary Statistics**		
2	Quartiles	Total Sales					Intro	Intro-General
3	1	$ 564,103				Total Sales	$17,876,251	$ 11,198,548
4	2	$ 1,154,422				Average Sales	$ 1,489,688	$ 2,239,710
5	3	$ 2,064,113				# of Books	12	5
6								
7	Discipline	Area	Book Title	Edition	Sales: Wholesale	Sales: Retail	Total Book Sales	Rank
8	Introductory	General	Contemporary Sociology	1	$ 3,740,000	$ 130,000	$ 3,870,000	1
9	Aging/Death	Death and Dying	Interpretations in Grief and Loss	7	$ 3,564,000	$ 187,187	$ 3,751,187	2
10	Race/Class/Gender	Race/Ethnicity	Bridging the Gap in Racial Groups	10	$ 3,218,750	$ 201,142	$ 3,419,892	3
11	Introductory	General	Sociology: An Introduction	8	$ 3,051,685	$ 294,500	$ 3,346,185	4
12	Research/Stats	Research Methods	Researching in Social Sciences	10	$ 3,016,575	$ 226,688	$ 3,243,263	5
13	Research/Stats	Social Statistics	Introductory Statistics in Social Research	8	$ 2,946,875	$ 202,935	$ 3,149,810	6
14	Race/Class/Gender	Gender Issues	Gender Roles in Society	5	$ 2,973,750	$ 169,000	$ 3,142,750	7
15	Social Psychology	General	Modern Perspectives on Social Psychology	1	$ 2,988,045	$ 127,950	$ 3,115,995	8
16	Introductory	General	Sociology 101	8	$ 2,724,777	$ 79,335	$ 2,804,112	9
17	Criminal Justice	Deviance	Deviant Behavior	9	$ 2,512,500	$ 280,849	$ 2,793,349	10
18	Social Psychology	General	An Introduction to Symbolic Interactionism	5	$ 2,531,250	$ 180,048	$ 2,711,298	11
19	Research/Stats	Social Statistics	Behavioral and Social Sciences Statistics	6	$ 2,569,675	$ 109,800	$ 2,679,475	12
20	Aging/Death	Death and Dying	Death in Society	2	$ 2,625,000	$ 16,851	$ 2,641,851	13
21	Social Psychology	Symbolic Interactionism	Symbolic Interactionism: An Introduction	7	$ 2,368,750	$ 269,602	$ 2,638,352	14
22	Family	Family Interaction	Trends in Family Interactions	10	$ 2,187,500	$ 201,142	$ 2,388,642	15

Books Summary

Excel 2016, Windows 10, Microsoft Corporation

FIGURE 8.28 Sociology Statistics

a. Open *e08p1Books* and save it as **e08p1Books_LastFirst**. If prompted, enable editing.

b. Click **cell F3** and click the **Formulas tab**.

c. Click **Math & Trig** in the Function Library group, scroll through the list, and then select **SUMIF**. Do the following:
   - Select the **range A8:A93** to enter the range in the Range box.
   - Type **Introductory** in the Criteria box.
   - Press **Tab**, select the **range G8:G93** to enter the range in the Sum_range box, and then click **OK**.

d. Click **cell F4**, click **More Functions** in the Function Library group, point to **Statistical**, and then select **AVERAGEIF**. Do the following:
   - Select the **range A8:A93** to enter the range in the Range box.
   - Press **Tab** and type **Introductory** in the Criteria box.
   - Press **Tab**, select the **range G8:G93** to enter the range in the Average_range box, and then click **OK**.

e. Click **cell F5**, click **More Functions** in the Function Library group, point to **Statistical**, and then select **COUNTIF**. Do the following:
   - Select the **range A8:A93** to enter the range in the Range box.
   - Press **Tab**, type **Introductory** in the Criteria box, and then click **OK**.

f. Click **cell G3**, click **Math & Trig** in the Function Library group, scroll through the list, and then select **SUMIFS**. Do the following:

- Select the **range G8:G93** to enter the range in the Sum_range box.
- Press **Tab** and select the **range A8:A93** to enter the range in the Criteria_range1 box.
- Press **Tab** and type **Introductory** in the Criteria1 box.
- Press **Tab** and select the **range B8:B93** to enter the range in the Criteria_range2 box.
- Press **Tab**, type **General** in the Criteria2 box, and then click **OK**.

g. Click **cell G4**, click **More Functions** in the Function Library group, point to **Statistical**, and then select **AVERAGEIFS**. Do the following:

- Select the **range G8:G93** to enter the range in the Average_range box.
- Press **Tab** and select the **range A8:A93** to enter the range in the Criteria_range1 box.
- Press **Tab** and type **Introductory** in the Criteria1 box.
- Press **Tab** and select the **range B8:B93** to enter the range in the Criteria_range2 box.
- Press **Tab**, type **General** in the Criteria2 box, and then click **OK**.

h. Click **cell G5**, click **More Functions** in the Function Library group, point to **Statistical**, scroll through the list, and then select **COUNTIFS**. Do the following:

- Select the **range A8:A93** to enter the range in the Criteria_range1 box.
- Press **Tab** and type **Introductory** in the Criteria1 box.
- Press **Tab** and select the **range B8:B93** to enter the range in the Criteria_range box.
- Press **Tab**, type **General** in the Criteria2 box, and then click **OK**.

i. Select the **range F3:G4**, apply **Accounting Number Format** with zero decimal places, and then adjust column widths as needed.

j. Click **cell H8**, type **=rank**, and then double-click **RANK.AVG** from the Formula AutoComplete list. Click **G8**, press comma, select the **range G8:G93**, press **F4** to make the range absolute, and then press **Ctrl+Enter** to enter =RANK.AVG(G8,$G$8:$G$93).

k. Double-click the **cell H8 fill handle** to copy the formula down the Rank column. Sort the list in ascending order by the Rank column.

l. Click **cell B3**. Click the **Formulas tab**, click **More Functions** in the Function Library group, point to **Statistical**, and then scroll through the list.

m. Select **QUARTILE.EXC** and type **G$8:G$93** in the Array box to create a mixed reference in which row numbers will not change when you copy the formula down. Press **Tab**, type **A3** in the Quart box to refer to the first quartile, and then click **OK**. Fill the formula to complete the **range B4:B5**. The array argument does not change, but the quart argument changes to reflect the correct quartile.

n. Format the **range B3:B5** with **Accounting Number Format** and zero decimal places. Apply the **Bottom Border style** to **cell B5**.

o. Create a footer with your name on the left side, the sheet name code in the center, and the file name code on the right side.

p. Save and close the workbook. Based on your instructor's directions, submit e08p1Books_LastFirst.

You have been hired to analyze the effectiveness of carbon hardening additives to Indy car tires. The added carbon increases the puncture strength and you will analyze its impact on burn temperature and weight. You will use Excel's statistical functions and the Analysis ToolPak to complete the next steps. Refer to Figure 8.29 as you complete this exercise.

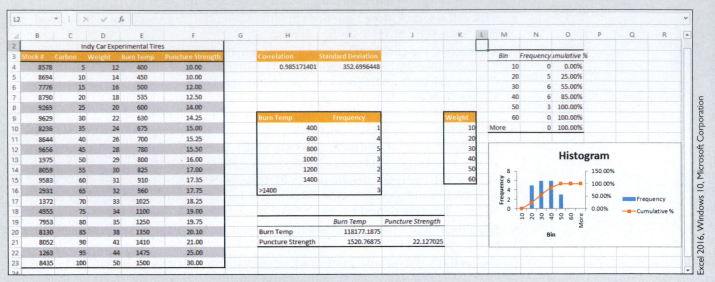

FIGURE 8.29 Indy Car Tire Analysis

a. Open *e08p2IndyCar* and save it as **e08p2IndyCar_LastFirst**.

b. Click **cell H4** in the Tires worksheet. Type **=CORREL** and press **Tab**. Select the **range C4:C23** for the first argument, press **comma,** and then select the **range E4:E23** for the second argument. Press **CTRL+Enter**.

c. Click **cell I4**. Type **=STDEV.S** and press **Tab**. Select the **range E4:E23** and press **Ctrl+Enter**.

d. Select the **range I10:I16**. Type **=FREQUENCY** and press **Tab**. Select the **range E4:E23** and press **comma**. Select the **range H10:H15** and press **Ctrl+Shift+Enter**.

e. Load the Analysis ToolPak by completing the following steps, or if it is already available, skip to Step f.

 • Click the **File tab**.
 • Click **Options** and select **Add-ins** on the left side of the Excel Options dialog box.
 • Select **Excel Add-ins** in the Manage box and click **Go**.
 • Click **Analysis ToolPak** in the Add-ins window and click **OK**.

f. Click the **Data tab** and click **Data Analysis** in the Analysis group. Select **Histogram**, click **OK**, and then complete the following steps:

 • Type **D4:D23** in the Input Range box.
 • Type **K10:K15** in the Bin Range box.
 • Type **M3** in the Output Range box.
 • Click the **Cumulative Percentage** option.
 • Click **chart**.
 • Click **OK**.
 • Position the chart so the upper-left corner starts in **cell M12** and resize it so the chart fills the **range M12:R20**.

g. Click the **Data tab** and click **Data Analysis** in the Analysis group. Select **Covariance**, click **OK**, and then complete the following steps:

- Type **E3:F23** in the Input Range box.
- Click **Columns.**
- Click **Labels in first row**.
- Type **H19** in the Output Range box.
- Click **OK**.
- Resize **columns H:J** and **M:O** as needed.

h. Click the **Test Drive worksheet**. Click the **Data tab** and click **Data Analysis** in the Analysis group. Select **ANOVA: Single Factor**, click **OK**, and then complete the following steps:

- Type **C2:E21** in the Input Range box.
- Click **Columns**.
- Click **Labels in first row**.
- Type **G2** in the Output Range box.
- Click **OK**.
- Resize **Columns G:M** as needed.

i. Select the **range B2:C21**, click **Data tab,** click **Forecast Sheet**, and click **Create.**

j. Rename the newly created worksheet **Forecast** and resize the chart as needed.

k. Create a footer on all worksheets with your name on the left side, the sheet name code in the center, and the file name code on the right side.

l. Save and close the workbook. Based on your instructor's directions, submit e08p2IndyCar_LastFirst.

Mid-Level Exercises

1 Investment Banking

You are an investment banker and you would like to put together a brief statistical report of the most viewed stock quotes for the day. To complete this task, you will research stock prices at www.nasdaq.com/quotes and create a report using the Analysis ToolPak.

a. Open Excel and create a new workbook. Save the workbook as **e08m1Stocks_LastFirst**.

b. Use your browser to open www.nasdaq.com/quotes/real-time.aspx and locate the four most-viewed stock prices for the day.

c. Type **Symbol** in **cell B2**, type **Last Sale Price** in **cell C2**, and type **Rank** in **cell D2**.

d. Type the corresponding stock symbols and prices from the website in **columns B** and **C**.

e. Use the RANK.AVG function to calculate the rank of the first stock in **cell D3** and copy the formula down to complete the column.

f. Click **cell B8**, type **Average value,** and in **cell C8** type **> 100** . In **cell B9**, use the **AVERAGEIF** function to calculate the average value of stocks that sell for less than $100.00 using the criteria in **cell C8**. Appropriately format the results.

g. Load the Analysis ToolPak add-in, if it is not available, as described in the chapter.

DISCOVER

h. Click **Data Analysis** in the Analysis Group in the Data tab. Select **Descriptive Statistics** from the Analysis Tools box, and use the following specifications:

* Select the range **C2:C6** as the Input Range.
* Select or deselect the **Labels in first row check box**, based on the input data you selected.
* Select the **Output Range F2**.
* Select **Summary statistics**.

i. Rename the worksheet **Stock Quotes** and apply the following formatting:

* Apply **Accent 2 Themed Cell Style** format to the **ranges B2:D2** and **B8:C8**.
* Apply **Top and Bottom Borders** to the **ranges B8:C8** and **B2:D2**.
* Apply **Thick Bottom Border** to the **range B6:D6**.

Create a footer with your name on the left side, the name of the worksheet in the middle, and the file name code on the right side.

j. Save and close the workbook. Based on your instructor's directions, submit e08m1Stocks_LastFirst.

2 Reading Comprehension Scores

ANALYSIS CASE

As an elementary school principal, you are concerned about students' reading comprehension. You brought in a reading consultant to help design an experimental study to compare the current teaching method (the control group), a stand-alone computer-based training (CBT) program, and a combination of the traditional teaching method and CBT (hybrid). The consultant randomly assigned 72 third-grade students into three groups of 24 each. During the two-week study, students were taught reading comprehension skills based on the respective methodology. At the end of the two-week period, students completed a standardized reading comprehension test. The consultant prepared a worksheet listing the test scores for each group. No student names or IDs were reported to you.

Now you want to calculate some general statistics and then conduct a one-way analysis of variance (ANOVA). Doing so will enable you to compare the three sample group means and evaluate the variances within each group compared to the variances among the three groups.

a. Open *e08m2Stats* and save it as **e08m2Stats_LastFirst**.

b. Calculate the descriptive statistics in the range F2:H8. For the variance and standard deviation, use the functions that include the *.S* descriptor. Format the values with **Comma Style** with three decimal places.

c. Check the Data tab to see if it contains the Data Analysis command. If not, load the Analysis ToolPak add-in program as directed in the chapter.

d. Use the Data Analysis ToolPak and select the **ANOVA: Single Factor**. Use the following specifications:
- Select the range **A1:C25** as the Input Range.
- Select the **Labels in first row check box**.
- Confirm the alpha value is **0.05**.
- Place the **Output Range** starting in **cell E11**.

e. Apply **Comma Style** with three decimal places to the averages and variances in the ANOVA table. Verify that the averages and variances in the ANOVA table match those you calculated in the *General Stats* section. If they do not match, correct the functions in the *General Stats* section. If needed, format the P-value (cell J22) with **Comma format** with six decimal places.

 f. Answer the questions on the Q&A worksheet.

g. Apply **Landscape orientation** to the Math Performance Scores worksheet.

h. Create a footer on all worksheets with your name on the left side, the sheet name code in the center, and the file name code on the right side.

i. Save and close the workbook. Based on your instructor's directions, submit e08m2Stats_LastFirst.

 Portfolio Analysis

COLLABORATION CASE

You are a financial advisor, and a client would like you to complete an analysis of his portfolio. As part of the analysis, you will perform basic analysis of value by type of commodity, calculate basic descriptive statistics with the Analysis ToolPak, create a stock forecast sheet, and answer client questions. Your client is located in DC and you are in New York, so you have decided to send him the completed file via OneDrive after completion for review.

Student 1:

a. Open *e08m3Portfolio* and save it as **e08m3Portfolio_LastFirst**.

b. Use the **RANK.AVG** function in **cell F6** to calculate the rank of the current values of each investment. Use the fill handle to complete the column.

c. Use the **COUNTIFS** function to determine the total number of bonds in the portfolio with a value greater than 50 in **cell I6**.

d. Use the fill handle to copy the function down the **range I7:I8**. Be sure to use the appropriate absolute or mixed cell references.

e. Use the **QUARTILE.INC** function in **cell I11** to determine the 0 quartile value of all commodities in the portfolio.

f. Use the fill handle to copy the function down the **range I12:I15**. Be sure to use the appropriate absolute or mixed cell references.

g. Use the **STDEV.S** function to calculate the standard deviation between the current values of all commodities.

h. Ensure the Analysis ToolPak is loaded.

i. Create a descriptive statistics summary based on the current value of investments in column E. Display the output in **cell H20**.

j. Format the mean, median, mode, standard deviation, minimum, maximum, and sum in the report as **Accounting Number Format**.

k. Use the **FREQUENCY** function to calculate the frequency distribution of commodity values based on the values located in the **range K6:K10**.

l. Click the **Trend** worksheet and use the **CORREL** function to calculate the correlation of purchase price and current value listed in the range C3:D10.

m. Create a **Forecast Sheet** displaying a forecast of purchase price through 1/1/2020.

 n. Answer the questions in the Q&A worksheet.

o. Save the document to your OneDrive account and share the file with Student 2.

Student 2:

p. Open the workbook located on OneDrive and save it as **e08m3PortfolioReview_LastFirst**.

q. Make the Portfolio worksheet active and sort column F from smallest to largest.

r. Locate the three lowest-valued commodities and apply the **Bad Cell Style** to the entire range.

s. Type **Sell assets highlighted in red** in cell D25.

t. Save and close the workbook. Based on your instructor's directions, submit the following:
e08m3PortfolioReview_LastFirst
e08m3Portfolio_LastFirst

Beyond the Classroom

Stock Market Research

GENERAL CASE

You want to conduct research on the stocks that make up the Dow Jones Industrial Average. As part of your research, you will group the prices into quartiles and use the Analysis ToolPak to calculate a descriptive statistics summary. Open *e08b1Market-Research*, click Enable Content, and save it as **e08b1MarketResearch_LastFirst**. The stock prices in the current data file may not be up to date. To check and import current prices, navigate to http://money.cnn.com/data/dow30/. Once you have ensured the prices are up to date, create a function in cell K4 to calculate the value in the lowest quartile based on stock prices in column B. Next, use the fill handle to copy the quartile function into the range K5:K8. Be sure to use the appropriate absolute or mixed cell references. For your last step, you will use the Analysis ToolPak to create a descriptive statistics summary. Place the summary in cell J10. Use the input range B4:B33. Format the mean, median, mode, minimum, maximum, and sum in Accounting Number Format. Create a footer with your name, the sheet name, and the file name on each worksheet. Save and close the workbook. Based on your instructor's directions, submit e08b1MarketResearch_LastFirst.

Taste Test

DISASTER RECOVERY

After receiving negative feedback on their older menu items, Lecxe Bakery decided to create a new menu of desserts. Before taking their desserts to production, they decided to conduct a taste-test survey based on a random cross-section sample of their client base. Your task as production manager is to analyze the results. You will calculate the frequency of responses as percentages as well as complete an ANOVA summary of the data using the Analysis ToolPak. Open *e08b2Survey* and save it as **e08b2Survey_LastFirst**. Using the response options in the range F6:F10, create a frequency that calculates the percentage of respondents that answered 1 through 5. Be sure to format the results with **Percentage Number Format**. Next, set columns F and G to **AutoFit Column Width**. Create a pie chart with the appropriate labels to visually document the information.

Your last step is to complete an ANOVA summary using the Analysis ToolPak. Create an ANOVA report starting in cell F23 using the range B5:D35. Create a footer with your name, the sheet name, and the file name on each worksheet. Save and close the workbook. Based on your instructor's directions, submit e08b2Survey_LastFirst.

Capstone Exercise

You have been hired to analyze the effectiveness of a local restaurant's drive-through service. As part of your analysis, you will evaluate customer satisfaction. You hypothesize that customer satisfaction decreases as wait time increases. You also believe there is a correlation between the quality of the food and overall satisfaction. You have collected a cross-section sample of 30 customers' wait time and satisfaction level surveys based on the range of 1 to 5, with 1 being least satisfied and 5 being most satisfied. You have also pulled a random sample of 10 surveys to evaluate wait time satisfaction.

Use Conditional Math and Statistical Functions

You would like to calculate basic demographic information about the sample you have collected.

a. Open *e08c1CustomerService* and save it as **e08c1CustomerService_LastFirst**.

b. Enter a conditional function in **cell M3** to calculate average satisfaction of service for store 251. Format the results with the **Number Format** with two decimal points.

c. Use the fill handle in **cell M3** to copy the function down to complete the calculations. Be sure to use the appropriate mixed or absolute referencing.

d. Enter a function in **cell M11** to calculate the number of survey responses in which restaurant 251 received a 2 or less in wait time and service.

e. Use the fill handle in **cell M11** to copy the function down to complete the calculations. Be sure to use the appropriate mixed or absolute referencing.

Calculate Relative Standing with Statistical Functions

To continue your analysis, you will calculate rankings based on average service satisfaction.

a. Enter a function in **cell N3** that calculates the rank of store 251 based on the averages in the **range M3:M5**.

b. Use the fill handle to copy the function down **column N**. Be sure to include the appropriate absolute or mixed cell references.

c. Click the **Wait Time** worksheet and enter a function in **cell F6** that calculates the wait time value of the first quartile.

d. Copy the function down to complete the column and return to the **Survey** worksheet.

Measure of Central Tendency

You would like to determine the frequency distribution of the satisfaction scores received by all restaurants combined. You would also like to test the strength of the relationship between wait time and satisfaction. You will use the CORREL and FREQUENCY functions to complete your calculation.

a. Enter a function in the **range J4:J8** to calculate the frequency of service ratings from 1 to 5 received by all restaurants.

b. Enter a function in **cell G11** to calculate the correlation between **columns C** and **E**.

c. Format the results as **Number Format** with two decimal positions.

d. Click the **Wait Time** worksheet and enter a function in **cell E3** to calculate the standard deviation between satisfaction scores of the wait time sample.

e. Enter a function in **cell F3** to calculate the variance between satisfaction scores of the wait time sample.

Using the Analysis ToolPak and Forecast Sheet

You will use the Analysis ToolPak to calculate covariance between wait time and customer satisfaction. You will also use the new Forecast Sheet feature to add satisfaction predictions based on wait time. Be sure to activate the Analysis ToolPak add-in before beginning the next steps.

a. Make the **Wait Time** worksheet active.

b. Click the **Data tab** and select **Data Analysis**. Select **Covariance** and click **OK**.

c. Complete the input criteria using the wait time and customer satisfaction data in **columns B** and **C**.

d. Set the output functions to display in **cell E10**. Resize the columns as needed to display the results.

e. Create a **Forecast** sheet that predicts customer satisfaction ending at a duration of 2:30 based on the time-series data provided in **columns B** and **C**.

f. Name the newly created worksheet **Forecast** and resize the chart to fill the **range A17:C30**.

g. Save the workbook and return to the **Survey** worksheet.

Create a Histogram

Your last step is to create a histogram with the Analysis ToolPak, to document the frequency of all survey responses by each category.

a. Click the **Data tab** and select **Data Analysis**. Select **Histogram** and click **OK**.

b. Use the survey data in the **range C4:E33** as the input range.

c. Use the ratings in the **range G4: G8** as the bin range.

d. Output the data in **cell G14**. Be sure to include a cumulative percentage and chart in the output.

e. Format the chart and output table accordingly.

f. Save and close the workbook. Based on your instructor's directions, submit e08c1CustomerService_LastFirst.

Multiple-Sheet Workbook Management

CASE STUDY | Circle City Sporting Goods

You are the regional manager of Circle City Sporting Goods (CSG), which has locations in Indianapolis, Bloomington, and South Bend. CSG is a comprehensive retailer that sells athletic apparel, exercise equipment, footwear, camping gear, sports gear, and sports nutrition items. Each store manager gathers monthly data for every department and prepares a quarterly worksheet. Because each store contains the same departments, the worksheets are identical to help you consolidate sales data for all three locations.

You want to review sales data for the past fiscal year. Before consolidating data, you will format the worksheets, copy data to the summary sheet, and then insert hyperlinks from the summary sheet back to the individual quarterly sheets in the Indianapolis workbook. Later, you will consolidate data from the Indianapolis, Bloomington, and South Bend workbooks into a regional workbook. Finally, you will use auditing tools to identify errors in the Bloomington workbook and add validation to ensure users enter correct data.

Everything possible/
Shutterstock

Ensuring Quality Control

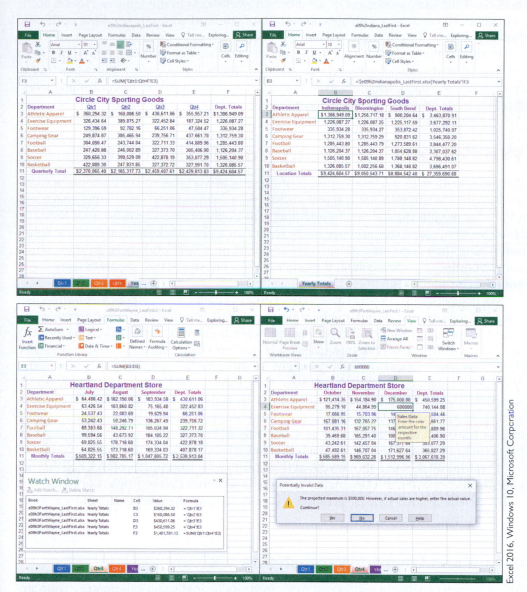

FIGURE 9.1 Circle City Sporting Goods Workbook

Excel 2016, Windows 10, Microsoft Corporation

CASE STUDY | Circle City Sporting Goods

Starting Files	Files to be Submitted
e09h1Indianapolis e09h2Bloomington e09h2SouthBend e09h2Indiana e09h3FortWayne	e09h2IndianaFiles_LastFirst.zip e09h3FortWayne_LastFirst

Multiple Worksheets

A workbook can contain one or more worksheets of related data. Deciding how to structure data into multiple worksheets and how to manage these worksheets is important. You should determine how much data to enter on each worksheet, when to divide data among several worksheets, and how to format worksheets efficiently. You might also want to create links among the worksheets to enable efficient navigation. For example, you can create a documentation worksheet and then insert links to each worksheet.

When you are working with a large dataset in a worksheet, you need to see multiple sections of the same worksheet or see different worksheets in the same workbook at the same time. You can open multiple copies of the same workbook and use View options to display portions of worksheets at the same time.

In this section, you will work with multiple worksheets and insert hyperlinks from one worksheet to other worksheets. In addition, you will group worksheets together to enter data and apply formatting. Finally, you will manage windows by controlling worksheet visibility, opening and arranging windows, and splitting a window.

Working with Grouped Worksheets

You often work with workbooks that contain several worksheets. For example, a workbook might contain sales data on one worksheet, a column chart on another sheet, and a PivotTable on a third sheet. In addition, you might create scenarios with Scenario Manager, generate a scenario summary report on a new worksheet or create a Solver model, and then generate a Solver answer report on a new worksheet. In these situations, in order to organize data, the original data are stored into separate worksheets from the consolidated analysis.

Worksheets within a workbook often contain similar content and formatting. For example, a budget workbook might contain detailed monthly data on separate worksheets. By placing monthly data on separate worksheets, you can focus on one month's data at a time instead of presenting the entire year's worth of data on only one worksheet. When worksheets contain similar data but for different time periods (such as months) or different locations (such as department store locations in several states), you should structure and format the data the same on all worksheets. For example, each monthly worksheet in the yearly budget workbook should contain an identical structure and format for the list of income and expenses. The only differences among the worksheets are the actual values and the column labels that identify the respective months.

Creating worksheets with identical structure and formatting provides consistency and continuity when working with the same type of data on multiple worksheets. In addition, it helps you locate particular items quickly on all worksheets because you know the structure is identical.

Group and Ungroup Worksheets

 Although you can design and format worksheets individually, you can improve your productivity by designing and formatting the worksheets as a group. *Grouping* is the process of selecting two or more worksheets so that you can perform the same action at the same time on all selected worksheets. Table 9.1 describes how to group worksheets. When you group worksheets, all worksheet tabs display as the active worksheet. That is, the bottom of all (active) grouped sheet tabs contain a green horizontal bar. The word [Group] displays between the filename and Excel in the title bar, such as Circle City Budget [Group] – Excel.

Pearson Education, Inc.

TABLE 9.1	Grouping Worksheets
To Group:	**Do This:**
All worksheets	Right-click a sheet tab and select Select All Sheets.
Adjacent worksheets	Click the first sheet tab, press and hold Shift, and then click the last sheet tab.
Nonadjacent worksheet tabs	Click the first sheet tab, press and hold Ctrl, and then click each additional sheet tab.

When you are done working on grouped worksheets, you should ungroup them. *Ungrouping* is the process of deselecting grouped worksheets so that actions performed on one sheet do not affect other worksheets.

To ungroup worksheets, complete one of the following steps:

- Click a sheet tab for a sheet that is not grouped.
- Right-click a sheet tab and select Ungroup Sheets.

> **TIP: CAUTION WITH GROUPING!**
> Make sure that you ungroup worksheets when you want to perform a task on only one worksheet. If you forget to ungroup sheets, you could potentially ruin several worksheets by overwriting data on all worksheets instead of just one worksheet.

Enter Data and Format Grouped Worksheets

STEP 2 ❱❱ Grouping worksheets enables you to improve your productivity by performing the same tasks on the grouped worksheets at the same time instead of performing the tasks individually on each worksheet. Whatever you do to the displayed worksheet also affects the other grouped worksheets.

You can enter labels, values, dates, and formulas efficiently on grouped worksheets, saving you from entering the same data on each worksheet individually. For example, if you enter row labels in the range A5:A10 to describe the different types of monthly income and expenses, Excel enters the same row labels in the same location (the range A5:A10) on the other grouped worksheets. When you enter a formula on grouped worksheets, Excel enters the formula in the same cell address on all grouped worksheets. For example, if you enter =A4-B4 in cell C4 on the active worksheet, Excel enters =A4-B4 in cell C4 on all grouped worksheets. The formulas use the values on the respective worksheets.

When you group similar worksheets, you can make structural changes for all worksheets at the same time. For example, if you insert a row between rows 4 and 5, and widen column B on the displayed worksheet, Excel inserts a row between rows 4 and 5, and widens column B on all grouped worksheets. You can cut, copy, and paste data to the same locations, and delete cell contents, rows, and columns on grouped worksheets.

You can apply text formatting, alignment settings, and number formats in the same cells on grouped worksheets. Figure 9.2 shows worksheets that were grouped to enter and format data.

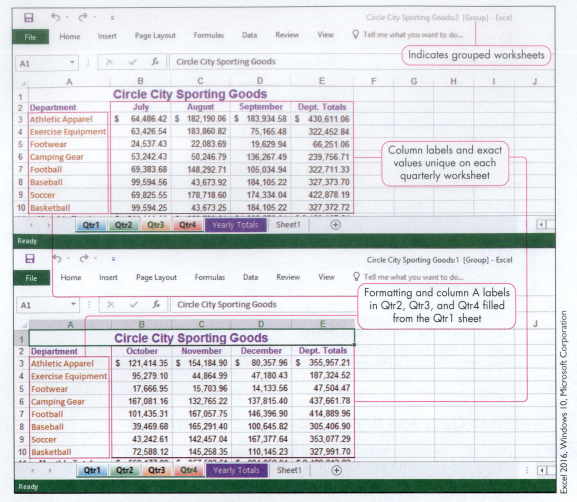

FIGURE 9.2 Multiple Worksheets Grouped

You can select Page Setup options for grouped worksheets. You can insert identical headers, set the page orientation, set the print areas, and adjust the scaling all at one time instead of applying these page layouts individually to each worksheet. After grouping worksheets, you can display them in Print Preview, select print settings, and then finally print the grouped worksheets.

> **TIP: UNAVAILABLE TASKS**
> Some tasks are not available on grouped worksheets. These tasks are grayed out on the Ribbon or in menus. For example, you cannot apply conditional formatting or format data as a table on grouped worksheets. Most commands such as PivotTable on the Insert tab are unavailable for grouped worksheets.

Fill Across Worksheets

The previous discussion assumes you are entering new data or formatting existing data across several worksheets at the same time. However, you might have created and formatted only one worksheet, and now you want to copy the data and formats to other worksheets. Instead of using the Copy and Paste commands or copying the entire worksheet, you can fill the data to other worksheets to save time and reduce potential errors, such as formatting the wrong area or neglecting to format a worksheet.

To fill data and/or formats from one sheet to other sheets, complete the following steps:

1. Click the sheet tab that contains the data and/or formats you want to copy. Select the range that you want to fill across the worksheets.

2. Press Ctrl while you click the destination sheet tabs—the worksheets to which you want to copy the data and/or formats.

3. Click the Home tab, click Fill ⬇ in the Editing group, and then select Across Worksheets to open the Fill Across Worksheets dialog box (see Figure 9.3).

4. Select one option in the dialog box:

   • Click All to copy data and formatting from the current worksheet to the grouped worksheets.

   • Click Contents to copy the data only from the current worksheet to the grouped worksheets without copying the formatting to the other worksheets.

   • Click Formats to copy only the formatting from the current worksheet to the grouped worksheets. The data is not copied to the grouped worksheets.

5. Click OK.

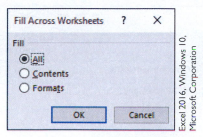

FIGURE 9.3 Fill Across Worksheets Dialog Box

Excel copies the data and/or formatting to the same cells in the other worksheets. For example, cell A1 contains the text Circle City Sporting Goods bold, centered, and in 14-pt font. When you select All in the Fill Across Worksheets dialog box, Excel copies text and formatting from cell A1 in the current worksheet to cell A1 in the grouped worksheets.

TIP: CONDITIONAL FORMATTING

Excel disables the Conditional Formatting feature when you group worksheets. You cannot group worksheets and then create and manage conditional formats. However, you can create a conditional formatting rule on one worksheet, group the worksheets, click Fill, select Fill Across Worksheets, and then select Formats to replicate the conditional formatting rule to a range on other worksheets.

Inserting Hyperlinks

STEP 3 ❯❯ When you create a workbook that has multiple worksheets, you might want to include a documentation worksheet that is similar to a table of contents. On the documentation worksheet, enter labels to describe each worksheet, and then create hyperlinks to the respective worksheets. A *hyperlink* is an electronic link that, when clicked, goes to another location in the same or a different worksheet, opens another file, opens a webpage in a Web browser, or opens an email client and inserts an email address into the To box.

To create a hyperlink, complete the following steps:

1. Click the cell that will contain the hyperlink or select an object, such as an image, that you want to use as the hyperlink, and then do one of the following to open the Insert Hyperlink dialog box (see Figures 9.4 and 9.5):
   - Click the Insert tab and click Hyperlink in the Links group.
   - Right-click the cell or object and select Hyperlink.
   - Press Ctrl+K.

2. Click the type of link on the left side of the dialog box: Existing File or Web Page, Place in This Document, Create New Document, or E-mail Address.

3. Click the specific location. For example, if you clicked Existing File or Web Page in Step 2, you can select Current Folder, Browsed Pages, or Recent Files. Select other options or specify the URL in the Address box. If you selected Place in This Document type, specify a target location, such as a cell reference, worksheet, or range name.

4. Click ScreenTip to open the Set Hyperlink ScreenTip dialog box, type the text you want to display in the ScreenTip text box, and then click OK.

5. Click OK in the Insert Hyperlink dialog box.

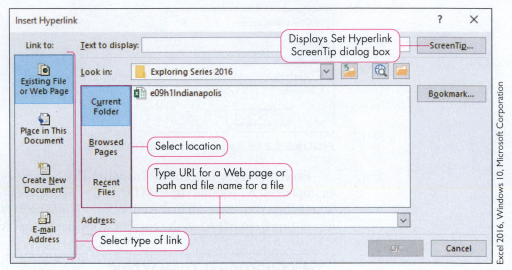

FIGURE 9.4 Insert Hyperlink Dialog Box (Existing File or Web Page)

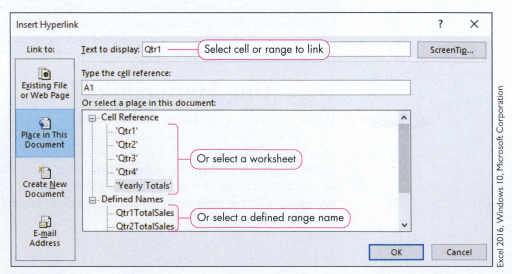

FIGURE 9.5 Insert Hyperlink Dialog Box (Place in This Document)

Workbook hyperlinks are similar to hyperlinks on a webpage. Text hyperlinks are blue with a blue underline until you click the hyperlink. When you point to a hyperlink, the pointer looks like a hand, and Excel displays either a default ScreenTip indicating the link's destination or a custom ScreenTip if you created one in the Set Hyperlink ScreenTip dialog box (see Figure 9.6). Click the hyperlink to visit the link's destination. After you click a text hyperlink, the color changes to purple to distinguish between links you have clicked and links you have not clicked. The hyperlink color changes back to blue if you edit the hyperlink or close the workbook and open it again.

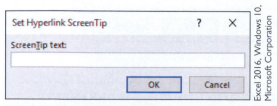

FIGURE 9.6 Set Hyperlink ScreenTip Dialog Box

Managing Windows

Because a workbook may contain several worksheets, you need to be able to manage the worksheets onscreen to help you focus on particular worksheets and reduce information overload. To help you manage worksheet windows, you can control worksheet visibility, open and arrange windows for ease of use, split a window to see different parts of a worksheet, and save the layout of the worksheet windows.

Control Visibility of Worksheets

STEP 4 ⟫ If a workbook contains so many worksheets that each corresponding tab is not visible, use the worksheet scroll buttons on the left side of the worksheet tabs to find the worksheet you need. If you do not need to view a worksheet, you can hide it. Hiding worksheets minimizes scrolling through worksheet tabs or when you want to display worksheets on a projector in a meeting but you do not want to accidently click a worksheet containing confidential data.

To hide a worksheet, complete the following steps:

1. Select the worksheet or worksheets you want to hide.
2. Click the Home tab and click Format in the Cells group.
3. Point to Hide & Unhide and select Hide Sheet.

To display a hidden worksheet again, complete the following steps:

1. Click Format in the Cells group.
2. Point to Hide & Unhide and select Unhide Sheet to open the Unhide dialog box (see Figure 9.7).
3. Select the worksheet that you want to display and click OK.

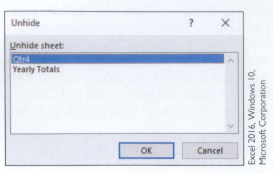

FIGURE 9.7 Unhide Dialog Box

> **TIP: HIDING AND UNHIDING WORKSHEETS**
> You can right-click a sheet tab and select Hide. To unhide a worksheet, you can right-click any visible tab, select Unhide, and then select the worksheet to unhide.

Open and Arrange Windows

You might want to see the contents of two worksheets in the same workbook at the same time. For example, you might want to compare the Qtr1 and Qtr2 worksheets simultaneously. Instead of clicking back and forth between worksheet tabs, you can open another window of the same workbook and display different worksheets within each window. To open another window of the current workbook, click New Window in the Window group on the View tab. Excel opens another window of the current workbook. The title bar adds *:1* to the original workbook view and *:2* to the second window. Although only one window appears maximized, both windows are open.

To see all windows of the same workbook, complete the following steps:

1. Click Arrange All in the Window group.
2. Select one of the options from the Arrange Windows dialog box (see Figure 9.8). You can display windows in a tiled arrangement, horizontally, vertically, or in a cascaded view. If you have other workbooks open when you click Arrange All, Excel includes those workbook windows.
3. Click the *Windows of active workbook* check box to select it to display windows for the current workbook only.

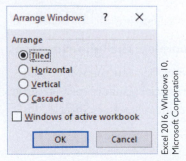

FIGURE 9.8 Arrange Windows Dialog Box

Split a Window

When you work with very large, complex worksheets, you may want to view different sections at the same time. For example, you may need to look at input data on rows 5 and 6 and see how changing the data affects overall results on row 361. To see these different worksheet sections at the same time, split the worksheet window. *Splitting* is the process of dividing a worksheet window into two or four resizable panes so you can view separate parts of a worksheet at the same time. Figure 9.9 shows the worksheet split between rows 13 and 361 to display the input area, first four payments, last nine payments, and the totals. To split a worksheet into panes, use the Split command in the Window group on the View tab. All panes are part of the same worksheet. Any changes you make to one pane affect the entire worksheet.

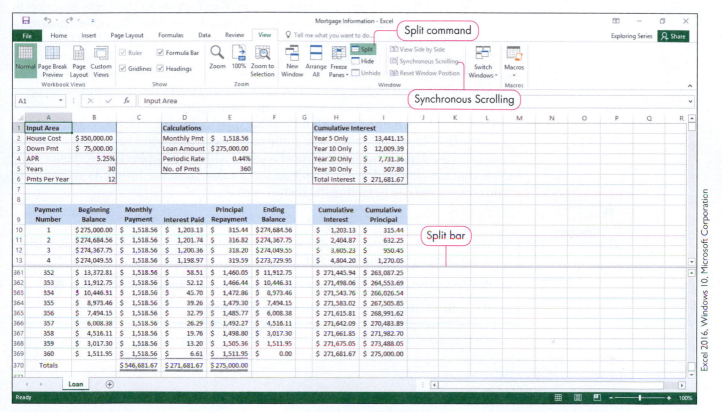

FIGURE 9.9 Split Panes

Depending on which cell is the active cell, Excel splits the worksheet into two or four panes with *split bars*—vertical and horizontal lines that frame the panes—above and to the left of the active cell. If the active cell is in row 1 (except cell A1), the worksheet displays in two vertical panes. For example, if the active cell is D1, the split bar displays between columns C and D. If the active cell is in column A (except cell A1), the worksheet displays in two horizontal panes. For example, if the active cell is A10, the split bar displays between rows 9 and 10. If the active cell is cell A1 or any cell other than the first row or first column, the worksheet displays in four panes.

Once the window is split, you can further customize the display by dragging a split bar between the panes. Drag the vertical split bar to divide the worksheet into left and right (vertical) panes. Drag the horizontal split bar to divide the worksheet into upper and lower (horizontal) panes. While the active cell will be mirrored across all split panes, you can scroll each pane to the desired range you want to see.

To remove panes, click Split in the Window group on the View tab or double-click the split bar. You can also remove panes by dragging the vertical split bar to the left or right edge of the window or a horizontal split bar to the top or bottom of the window.

Apply Other Window Settings

The Window group on the View tab contains additional commands. If you have two or more workbooks open, you can click View Side by Side to display the Compare Side by Side dialog box to select which workbook you want to display side by side with the active workbook. This view is helpful when comparing related data, such as budgets from two different years.

When you use the View Side by Side command, Synchronous Scrolling is activated. When you scroll through one workbook window, Excel scrolls in the same direction in the other workbook window at the same time. If you do not want the other window to remain stationary, click Synchronous Scrolling in the Window group to disable it.

After you open multiple windows, you might rearrange or resize the windows. For example, you might reduce the window size for a monthly workbook and enlarge the size of a quarterly workbook. You can click Reset Window Position in the Window group to make the side-by-side workbooks windows equal size again.

When you have multiple workbooks open, you can change which window is active. Click Switch Windows in the Window group and select which window you want to be the active Excel window. Using this command is useful when you display two workbooks side by side that are almost identical. Selecting the window from the Switch Windows command ensures you will be editing the correct workbook.

Quick Concepts

1. What are the benefits of grouping worksheets? What precautions should be taken when using grouped worksheets? *p. 560*

2. Besides linking inside a worksheet, where else can hyperlinks lead the user? *p. 563*

3. What are the benefits of using split windows? *p. 567*

Hands-On Exercises

Watch the Video for this Hands-On Exercise!

MyITLab®
HOE1 Training

Skills covered: Group Worksheets • Fill Across Worksheets • Enter and Format Data Across Worksheets • Insert Hyperlinks • Open and Arrange Worksheets

1 Multiple Worksheets

After reviewing last year's fiscal data, you want to improve the appearance of the worksheets for Circle City Sporting Goods. You want to enter a missing heading on the summary worksheet and enter formulas across the quarterly worksheets. To save time, you will group the worksheets to perform tasks on all grouped worksheets at the same time. After you complete the quarterly worksheets, you will insert hyperlinks from the yearly worksheet to the quarterly worksheets.

STEP 1 ›› GROUP AND FILL ACROSS WORKSHEETS

You noticed that the main title and the row headings are displayed only in the Qtr1 worksheet in the Indianapolis workbook. You will fill in the title and row headings for the other three quarterly and the yearly worksheets. Refer to Figure 9.10 as you complete Step 1.

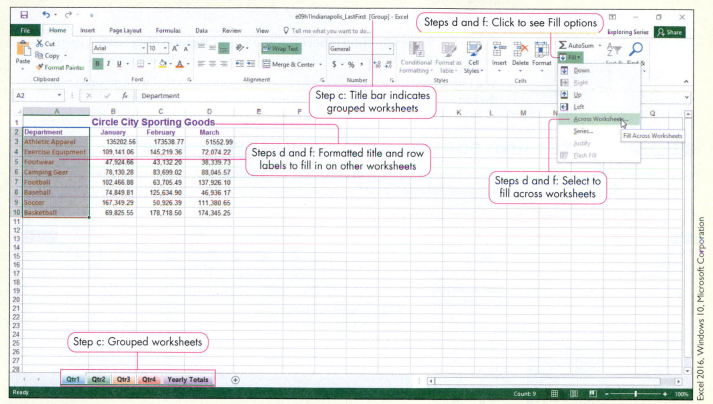

FIGURE 9.10 Formatted Title and Row Headings

a. Open *e09h1Indianapolis* and save it as **e09h1Indianapolis_LastFirst**.

> **TROUBLESHOOTING:** If you make any major mistakes in this exercise, you can close the file, open *e09h1Indianapolis* again, and then start this exercise over.

b. Click the **Qtr1 sheet tab** and click each worksheet tab to see the differences.

The Qtr1 worksheet contains a title and row labels, whereas the Qtr2, Qtr3, and Qtr4 worksheets are missing the title, row labels, and number formatting. The Yearly Totals worksheet is empty.

c. Click the **Qtr1 sheet tab**, press and hold **Shift**, and then click the **Yearly Totals sheet tab**.

You grouped all worksheets together. Anything you do now affects all grouped worksheets. The title bar displays [Group] after the file name.

d. Click **cell A1** in the Qtr1 worksheet to select it, click **Fill** [image] in the Editing group on the Home tab, and then select **Across Worksheets**.

The Fill Across Worksheets dialog box opens so that you can select what to fill from the active worksheet to the other grouped worksheets. The default option is All, which will fill in both the content and the formatting.

e. Click **OK**. Keep the worksheets grouped for the next step.

Excel fills in the formatted title from the Qtr1 worksheet to the other worksheets.

f. Select the **range A2:A10** on the Qtr1 worksheet, click **Fill** in the Editing group on the Home tab, select **Across Worksheets**, and then click **OK**.

> **TROUBLESHOOTING:** Do not select the range A1:D10 to fill across worksheets. If you do, you will overwrite the other worksheet data with the January, February, and March labels and data. If this happens, click Undo to restore data in the other worksheets.

g. Right-click the **Yearly Totals sheet tab** and select **Ungroup Sheets**. Click each worksheet to review the results. Save the workbook once review is complete.

You ungrouped the worksheets. Now all of the worksheets that were grouped contain the formatted title and row labels that were copied across worksheets.

STEP 2 ▶▶ **ENTER AND FORMAT DATA ACROSS WORKSHEETS**

You will regroup the worksheets so that you can increase the width of column A. In addition, you want to insert monthly and department totals for the quarterly worksheets. Refer to Figure 9.11 as you complete Step 2.

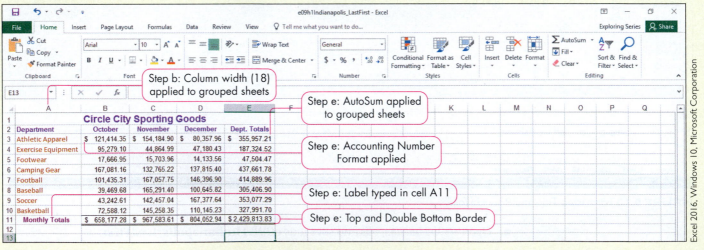

FIGURE 9.11 Data and Formatting Filled in Qtr4 Worksheet

a. Right-click the **Yearly Totals sheet tab** and select **Select All Sheets**.

b. Click **cell A2**, click **Format** in the Cells group on the Home tab, select **Column Width**, type **18** in the Column width box, and then click **OK**.

Although width of column A is 18 in the Qtr1 worksheet, the column width of A in the other worksheets was not 18. You set the column width to 18 for the first column in the grouped worksheets, ensuring that width of column A is identical among the worksheets.

c. Right-click the **Qtr1 sheet tab** and select **Ungroup Sheets**.

d. Press and hold **Shift** and click the **Qtr4 sheet tab**.

You have to ungroup sheets and group only the four quarterly worksheets to perform the tasks in Step e.

e. Do the following to the grouped quarterly worksheets:

- Select the **range B3:E11** and click **AutoSum** in the Editing group on the Home tab to insert department totals in column E and monthly totals in row 11.
- Apply **Accounting Number Format** to the **ranges B3:E3** and **B11:E11** to display a dollar sign and commas for the first and total rows.
- Type **Monthly Totals** in **cell A11**. Apply **bold** and click **Increase Indent** in the Alignment group on the Home tab.
- Type **Dept. Totals** in **cell E2**.
- Select the **range B11:E11**, click the **Border arrow** in the Font group, and then select **Top and Double Bottom Border**.
  You applied the Top and Double Bottom Border style to the monthly totals to conform to standard accounting formatting practices.

f. Right-click the **Qtr4 sheet tab**, select **Ungroup Sheets**, click each quarterly worksheet tab to ensure the formats were applied to each worksheet, and then save the workbook.

STEP 3 ›› **INSERT HYPERLINKS**

You want to insert hyperlinks on the Yearly Totals worksheet so that you can click a hyperlink to jump back to the respective quarterly worksheet quickly. Refer to Figure 9.12 as you complete Step 3.

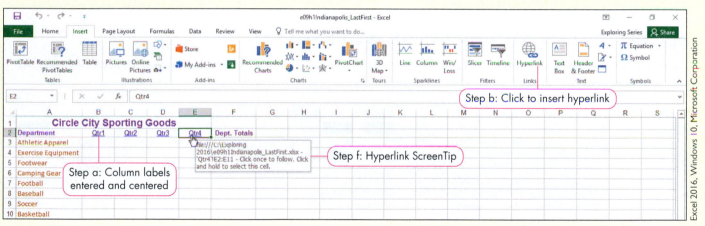

FIGURE 9.12 Hyperlinks

a. Click the **Yearly Totals sheet tab** and complete the following steps:

- Type **Qtr1** in **cell B2**, and then drag the **cell B2 fill handle** to fill in the remaining quarter labels in the **range C2:E2**.
- Type **Dept. Totals** in **cell F2**. Apply **bold** and **Purple font color** to **cell F2**.
- Select the **range B2:F2** and click **Center** in the Alignment group on the Home tab.
- Increase the width of column F to **12**.

b. Click **cell B2**, click the **Insert tab**, and then click **Hyperlink** in the Links group.

The Insert Hyperlink dialog box opens so that you can specify the destination when the user clicks the hyperlink.

c. Click **Place in This Document** in the *Link to* section on the left side of the dialog box.

d. Click in the **Type the cell reference box**, delete **A1**, type **E2:E11**, click **'Qtr1'** in the *Or select a place in this document* list, and then click **OK**.

You created a hyperlink to the range E2:E11 in the Qtr1 worksheet. Note that if you do not specify a reference cell for the link, it will default to cell A1.

e. Create the following hyperlinks by adapting steps b through d:

- **Cell C2**: Create a hyperlink to the **range E2:E11** in the Qtr2 worksheet.
- **Cell D2**: Create a hyperlink to the **range E2:E11** in the Qtr3 worksheet.
- **Cell E2**: Create a hyperlink to the **range E2:E11** in the Qtr4 worksheet.

f. Point to **cell E2** to display the ScreenTip.

The ScreenTip displays the hyperlink's destination (see Figure 9.12). The path and file name shown on your screen will differ from those shown in the figure. If you created a ScreenTip in the Insert Hyperlink dialog box, that text would display instead of the destination.

g. Click **cell E2**.

The hyperlink jumps to the destination: the range E2:E11 in the Qtr4 worksheet.

h. Click the **Yearly Totals sheet tab** and click the other hyperlinks to ensure they work. When you are done, click the **Yearly Totals sheet tab** and save the workbook.

> **TROUBLESHOOTING:** If a hyperlink does not display the correct range and worksheet, right-click the cell containing the incorrect hyperlink, select Edit Hyperlink, and then edit the hyperlink in the Edit Hyperlink dialog box.

STEP 4 ›› OPEN AND ARRANGE WORKSHEETS

You want to see the four quarterly sales data worksheets at the same time. To do this, you will need to open additional windows of the workbook and then arrange them. Refer to Figure 9.13 as you complete Step 4.

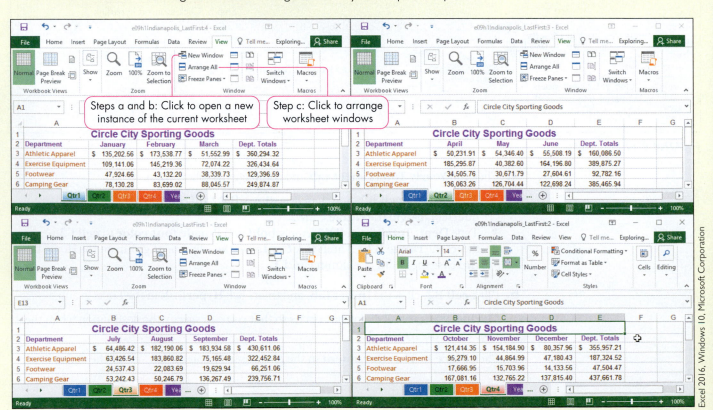

FIGURE 9.13 Worksheet Windows

a. Click the **View tab** and click **New Window** in the Window group.

You opened another window of the same workbook. The title bar displays the same file name with :2 at the end of the name. The Home tab displays in the new window.

b. Repeat Step a two times.

Two new windows open with :3 and :4 at the end of each file name. You now have four windows open of the same workbook.

c. Click the **View tab** and click **Arrange All** in the Window group.

The Arrange Windows dialog box opens so you can specify how you want to arrange the open worksheet windows.

d. Ensure **Tiled** is selected, click the **Windows of active workbook check box** to select it, and then click **OK**.

Clicking the *Windows of active workbook* check box ensures that the windows display for the active workbook. If other workbooks are open, those windows do not display. Excel arranges the four windows of the same workbook. Currently, all the Excel windows display the Yearly Totals worksheet.

e. Click the **Qtr1 sheet tab** twice in the top-left window, click the **Qtr2 sheet tab** twice in the top-right window, click the **Qtr3 sheet tab** twice in the bottom-left window, and click the **Qtr4 sheet tab** twice in the bottom-right window.

Each window displays a different quarterly worksheet.

f. Close three of the open windows so that you have one window of the workbook. Maximize the window.

g. Save the workbook. Keep the workbook open if you plan to continue with the next Hands-On Exercise. If not, close the workbook and exit Excel.

3-D Formulas and Linked Workbooks

Excel workbooks often contain data for different time periods, geographic regions, or products. For example, a workbook might contain a worksheet to store data for each week in a month, data for each location of a chain of department stores, or data for sales of each type of automobile produced by one manufacturer. While you have experience creating formulas and functions to perform calculations within one worksheet, you need to be able to consolidate, or combine, data from multiple worksheets into one. For example, you might want to consolidate sales data from all of your department store locations into one worksheet for the year.

Additional data analysis occurs over time. To avoid overloading a workbook with detailed sales data for several years, you might have detailed annual sales data in individual worksheets in one workbook. You then might want to insert a new worksheet and consolidate the data and compute the average yearly sales for the past 10 years on that new sheet.

In this section, you will create a formula with a 3-D reference to consolidate data from several worksheets. In addition, you will learn how to link data from several workbooks to one workbook.

Inserting Formulas and Functions with 3-D References

So far, you have created formulas that reference cells in the same worksheet to make it easier to update or apply changes automatically when performing what-if analyses. For example, when you created a one-variable data table, you entered a reference, such as =B12, to display the contents of a formula in cell B12 instead of performing the calculation again in the one-variable data table. The reference to cell B12 is a two-dimensional reference where the column is one dimension and the row number is the second dimension. At times, you may need to reference data from another worksheet as you create a formula on the current worksheet.

Insert a Formula with a 3-D Reference

STEP 1 ›› When a workbook contains multiple worksheets, you can create a ***3-D reference***, which is a reference within a formula or function on one worksheet that includes the name of another worksheet, column letter, and row number located within the workbook. The term 3-D reference comes from having a reference with three dimensions: worksheet name, column letter, and row number. For example, cell B4 in the October worksheet might contain a value that you need in the November worksheet. Instead of retyping the value in the November worksheet, you can create a 3-D reference, such as =October!B4. Doing so is efficient because if the value in cell B4 in the October worksheet changes, you do not have to edit the value in the November worksheet; the reference does that for you automatically.

If worksheet names include spaces, the 3-D reference includes single quotation marks before and after the worksheet name, such as 'October Sales'. The 3-D reference includes an exclamation point to separate the worksheet name and the cell reference.

='Worksheet Name'!RangeOfCells

TIP: PASCAL CASE AND CAMELCASE NOTATION

Pascal Case notation is a naming convention used when the name is comprised of multiple words. Pascal Case eliminates spaces and capitalizes the first letter of each word, such as OctoberSales versus October sales. By using a naming convention such as Pascal Case, you can reduce some of the complexity of a reference formula by eliminating the need for single quotation marks. Sometimes Camel Case is used, which is similar to Pascal Case, where the first letter of the combined word is lowercase, such as octoberSales.

What you have learned in previous chapters about using cell references in formulas applies to 3-D references. You can use a 3-D reference to build formulas using data from multiple worksheets, such as adding values from two different worksheets. For example, the formula =October!B4+November!B4 adds the values stored in cells B4 on both worksheets.

You can also create a formula that references a value on another worksheet and then performs a calculation using a value on the current worksheet. For example, you might set a goal to increase sales by 3% over last month's sales. Figure 9.14 shows the formula with the 3-D reference. The sales goal of 103% is entered in cell B2 in the November sheet. The formula to calculate the sales goal for the Athletic Department in cell B4 is =October!B4*November!B$2. The value stored in cell B4 in the October worksheet is multiplied by the value stored in cell B2 in the November sheet.

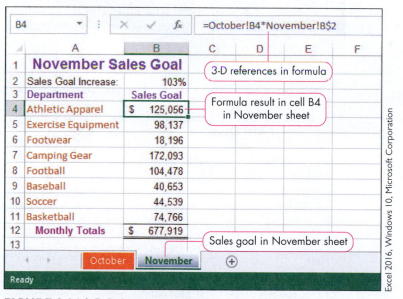

FIGURE 9.14 3-D Reference in a Formula

Insert a Function with 3-D References

STEP 2 ▶▶ An advantage of including several related worksheets in one workbook is that you can consolidate data from the worksheets into a summary worksheet. For example, with the Circle City Sporting Goods workbook, you might want to generate the fourth quarter totals from three monthly totals.

When individual worksheets have an identical structure (i.e., totals for the Athletic Apparel department are in cell B4 in each quarterly worksheet), you can use a 3-D reference in the SUM function that refers to the same cell or range in the October, November, and December worksheets. As you know, using functions improves efficiency in performing calculations. Instead of entering =October!B4+November!B4+December!B4, you can use the SUM function with 3-D references to the same cells in the other worksheets. The SUM function with 3-D references would be =SUM(October:December!B4).

The function =SUM(October:December!B4) includes 3-D references that add the values in cell B4 in each worksheet, starting in the October worksheet and ending in the December worksheet, including any worksheets between those two worksheets. You can type a function with 3-D references directly into a cell, but using the semi-selection method is more efficient.

=SUM('First Worksheet:Last Worksheet'!RangeOfCells)

To build a function using 3-D references, complete the following steps:

1. Click the cell in which you will enter the 3-D formula.
2. Type =, type the name of the function, such as SUM, and then type an opening parenthesis.
3. Click the first sheet tab, such as October.
4. Press and hold Shift as you click the last sheet tab for adjacent worksheets, or press and hold Ctrl as you click nonadjacent sheet tabs.
5. Click the cell or select the range that contains the value(s) you want to use in the function argument and press Enter. Figure 9.15 shows the fourth quarter worksheet that includes the SUM function with 3-D references.

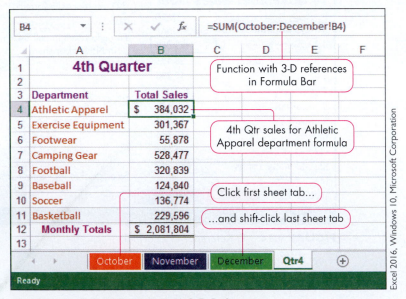

FIGURE 9.15 SUM Function with 3-D References

You can use a variety of functions with 3-D references. Some of these functions include SUM, AVERAGE, COUNT, MIN, MAX, and some standard deviation and variance functions. Other functions, such as PMT, VLOOKUP, and COUNTIF, do not work with 3-D references.

> **TIP: 3-D FORMULA ADVANTAGES**
>
> When you have a function such as =SUM(B1:B5) and insert a new fourth row, Excel modifies the SUM function to include the new row: =SUM(B1:B6). Similarly, if you insert or copy a worksheet between the beginning and ending worksheet references, the function containing the 3-D references automatically includes those worksheet data points in the calculation. If you move a worksheet out of the range, Excel excludes that worksheet's values from the formula containing the 3-D references. Finally, if you move or delete an endpoint worksheet, Excel adjusts the 3-D references for you. Go to www.support.office.com and search for the topic *Create a 3-D reference to the same cell range on multiple worksheets* for more information on 3-D references, how they work, and what functions can work with 3-D references.

Linking Workbooks

Workbook linking is another way of consolidating data. When you link workbooks, you consolidate the data from several workbooks into another workbook. *Linking* is the process of creating external cell references from worksheets in one workbook to cells on a worksheet in another workbook. For example, you might have three workbooks—Indianapolis, Bloomington, and South Bend—one for each store location. Each store manager maintains a workbook to record sales by department—such as exercise equipment, footwear, and camping gear—for a particular time period. As district manager, you want to consolidate the data from each workbook into one workbook. Instead of reentering the data, you can create links from specific cells of data in the individual workbooks to your active workbook.

Before creating links, identify the source and destination files. A *source file* is one that contains original data that you need in another file. For example, the individual department store workbooks—Indianapolis, Bloomington, and South Bend—are source files. The *destination file* is a file containing a link to receive data from the source files—that is, the target file that needs the data. When you link workbooks, you create a connection between the source and destination files. If data change in the source file, the data in the destination file is updated also. Linking ensures that the destination file always contains the most up-to-date data.

Create an External Reference

STEP 3 ▶▶ When you create a link between source and destination files, you establish an external reference or pointer to one or more cells in another workbook. The external reference is similar to the worksheet reference that you created for 3-D formulas. However, an external reference must include the workbook name to identify which workbook contains the linked worksheet and cell reference. For example, to create a link to cell E3 in the Qtr3 worksheet in the Indianapolis file, type =[Indianapolis.xlsx]Qtr3!E3. You must type the workbook name, including the file name extension, between brackets, such as [Indianapolis.xlsx]. After the closing bracket, type the worksheet name, such as Qtr3, followed by an exclamation mark and the cell reference, such as E3. Table 9.2 lists additional rules to follow when entering external references.

=[WorkbookName]WorksheetName!RangeOfCells

TABLE 9.2 External References

Situation	Rule	Example
Workbook and worksheet names do not contain spaces; source and destination files are in the same folder.	Type brackets around the workbook name and an exclamation mark between the worksheet name and range.	[Indianapolis.xlsx]Qtr3!A1
Workbook or worksheet name contains spaces; source and destination files are in the same folder.	Type single quotation marks on the left side of the opening bracket and the right side of the worksheet name.	'[South Bend.xlsx]Qtr3'!A1
Worksheet name contains spaces; source and destination files are in the same folder.	Type single quotation marks on the left side of the opening bracket and the right side of the worksheet name.	'[Bloomington.xlsx]Qtr 3 Sales'!A1
Source workbook is in a different folder from the destination workbook.	Type a single quotation mark, and then the full path—drive letter and folder name—before the opening bracket and a single quotation mark after the worksheet name.	'C:\Data[Indianapolis.xlsx]Sheet1'!A1

Pearson Education, Inc.

Excel displays formulas with external references in two ways, depending on whether the source workbook is open or closed. When the source is open, the external reference shows the file name, worksheet, and cell reference. When the source workbook is closed, the external reference shows the full path name in the Formula Bar. By default, Excel creates absolute cell references in the external reference. However, you can edit the external reference to create a relative or mixed cell reference.

To create an external reference between cells in different workbooks, complete the following steps:

1. Open the destination workbook and all source workbooks.
2. Select the cell to hold the external reference.
3. Type =. If you want to perform calculations or functions on the external references, type the expression or function.
4. Switch to the source workbook and click the sheet tab for the worksheet that contains the cells to which you want to link.
5. Select the cells to which you want to link and press Enter.

TIP: DRIVE AND FOLDER REFERENCE
Excel updates an external reference regardless of whether the source workbook is open. The source workbooks must be in the same folder location as when you created the link to update the destination workbook. If the location of the workbooks changes, as may happen if you copy the workbooks to a different folder, click Edit Links in the Connections group on the Data tab.

Manage and Update Linked Workbooks

STEP 4 ❯❯ If you create an external reference when both the source and destination files are open, changes you make to the source file occur in the destination file as well. However, if the destination file is closed when you change data in the source file, the destination file is not automatically updated to match the source file. Excel does not update linked data in a destination workbook automatically to protect the workbook against malicious activity, such as viruses.

When you open the destination file the first time, Excel displays the Security Warning Message Bar between the Ribbon and Formula Bar with the message *Automatic updates of links has been disabled*. If you are confident that the source files contain safe data, enable the links in the destination file. Click Enable Content to update the links and save the workbook (see Figure 9.16). The next time you open the destination file, Excel displays a message box that prompts the user to update, do not update, or select help. Click Update to update the links.

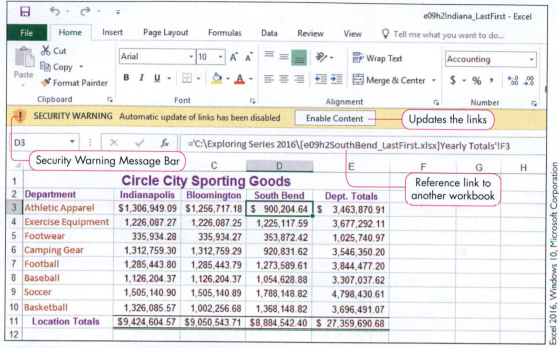

FIGURE 9.16 Security Warning to Update Links

If you rename the source workbook, you must edit the reference in the destination file to match the name of the source workbook. Otherwise, when you open the destination file, Excel displays an error message, *This workbook contains one or more links that cannot be updated*.

To edit a link to a source file, complete the following steps:

1. Click Edit Links to display the Edit Links dialog box (see Figure 9.17).
2. Select the source where the Status column indicates an error.
3. Click Change Source to open the Change Source dialog box.
4. Navigate through your folders to find the source file, select the source file, and then click OK.
5. Click Close in the Edit Links dialog box.

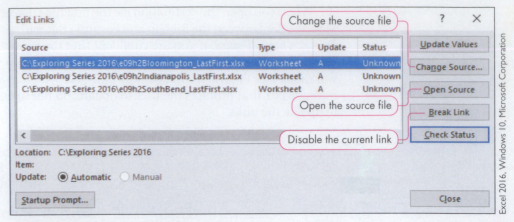

FIGURE 9.17 Edit Links Dialog Box

In the Edit Links dialog box, the Status column displays OK if the external reference link to the source file still works. If a problem exists, the Status column indicates the type of error, such as *Error: Source not found*.

Quick Concepts

4. Why should you create a 3-D reference (=JuneSales!F15) in one worksheet (Year) that refers to a cell in another worksheet (JuneSales) instead of just typing a value in the second worksheet (Year)? **p. 574**

5. How should worksheets within a workbook be structured to build a function (such as AVERAGE) using 3-D references? **p. 576**

6. Describe what happens when you open a workbook with links to other workbooks where the other workbooks have been moved to a different folder on your computer. **p. 577**

Watch the Video for this Hands-On Exercise!

MyITLab®
HOE2 Training

Skills covered: Insert a 3-D Reference in a Formula • Insert 3-D References in a Function • Link Workbooks • Complete the Linked Workbook

2 3-D Formulas and Linked Workbooks

Previously, you set up the four quarterly worksheets and the yearly total worksheet for Circle City Sporting Goods. Next, you want to calculate total yearly sales for each department as well as the overall total sales. In addition, you want to link sales data from all three locations into one workbook.

STEP 1 ›› INSERT A 3-D REFERENCE IN A FORMULA

Each quarterly worksheet calculates the quarterly sales totals for a three-month period for each department. You want to insert 3-D references from each quarterly worksheet to consolidate the quarterly sales on the Yearly Totals worksheet. Refer to Figure 9.18 as you complete Step 1.

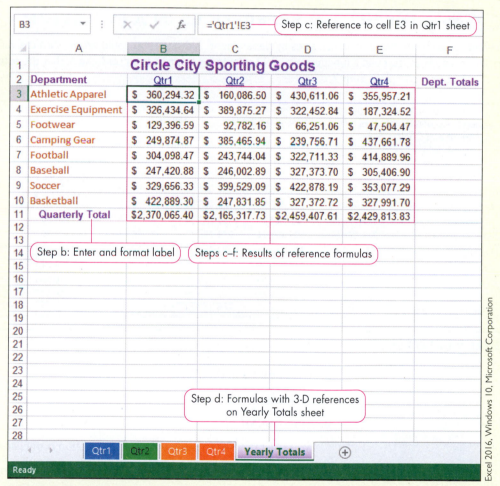

FIGURE 9.18 Worksheet References

a. Open *e09h1Indianapolis_LastFirst* if you closed it at the end of Hands-On Exercise 1, and save it as **e09h2Indianapolis_LastFirst**, changing h1 to h2.

b. Click the **Yearly Totals sheet tab**. Type **Quarterly Total** in cell **A11**. Apply **bold**, **indent**, and **Purple font color** to the label.

c. Click cell **B3**, type =, click the **Qtr1 sheet tab**, click **cell E3** in that worksheet, and then press **Ctrl+Enter**.

Look at the Formula Bar. The formula is ='Qtr1'!E3, where Qtr1 refers to the worksheet, and E3 refers to the cell within that worksheet.

d. Double-click the **cell B3 fill handle** to copy the formula down the column. Ignore ##### in cell B11 for now.

The formula's cell reference is relative, so it changes as you copy the formula down the column. The formula in cell B4 is ='Qtr1'!E4.

e. Click **cell C3** in the Yearly Totals worksheet, type **=**, click the **Qtr2 sheet tab**, click **cell E3** in that worksheet, and then press **Ctrl+Enter**. Double-click the **cell C3 fill handle** to copy the formula down the column.

Look at the Formula Bar. The formula is ='Qtr2'!E3, where Qtr2 refers to the worksheet and E3 refers to the cell within that worksheet.

f. Adapt Step e to enter references to the appropriate totals in the Qtr3 and Qtr4 worksheets.

g. Increase widths of the four quarterly columns to **13**. Save the workbook.

STEP 2 ›› **INSERT 3-D REFERENCES IN A FUNCTION**

You want to calculate the total annual sales by department. Although you could simply sum the values in the Yearly Totals worksheet, you want to build a function with 3-D references to provide a cross-check that the totals are correct. Refer to Figure 9.19 as you complete Step 2.

F3	Step f: Accounting Number Format and Comma Style	fx	=SUM('Qtr1:Qtr4'!E3)	Step d: Formula with 3-D reference		
	A		C	D	Step e: 3-D formulas copied with the fill handle	G
1		**Circle City Sporting Goods**				
2	Department	Qtr1	Qtr2	Qtr3	Qtr4	Dept. Totals
3	Athletic Apparel	$ 360,294.32	$ 160,086.50	$ 430,611.06	$ 355,957.21	$1,306,949.09
4	Exercise Equipment	326,434.64	389,875.27	322,452.84	187,324.52	1,226,087.27
5	Footwear	129,396.59	92,782.16	66,251.06	47,504.47	335,934.28
6	Camping Gear	249,874.87	385,465.94	239,756.71	437,661.78	1,312,759.30
7	Football	304,098.47	243,744.04	322,711.33	414,889.96	1,285,443.80
8	Baseball	247,420.88	246,002.89	327,373.70	305,406.90	1,126,204.37
9	Soccer	329,656.33	399,529.09	422,878.19	353,077.29	1,505,140.90
10	Basketball	422,889.30	247,831.85	327,372.72	327,991.70	1,326,085.57
11	Quarterly Total	$2,370,065.40	$2,165,317.73	$2,459,407.61	$2,429,813.83	$9,424,604.57
12						

FIGURE 9.19 3-D Formulas

Excel 2016, Windows 10, Microsoft Corporation

a. Click **cell F3** in the Yearly Totals worksheet.

You want to calculate the yearly sales for the Athletic Apparel department.

b. Type **=SUM(**.

You start the 3-D formula with =, the function name, and the opening parenthesis.

c. Click the **Qtr1 sheet tab**, press and hold **Shift**, and then click the **Qtr4 sheet tab**.

You grouped the worksheets together so that you can use a common cell reference for the range of cells to sum.

d. Click **cell E3**, the cell containing the quarterly sales, and press **Ctrl+Enter**.

Look at the Formula Bar. The function is =SUM('Qtr1:Qtr4'!E3). If you select the range B3:E3 in the Yearly Totals worksheet, the status bar shows that the sum is $1,306,949.09, the same value that displays when you inserted the 3-D formula.

e. Double-click the **cell F3 fill handle** to copy the formula down the column.

The cell reference is relative, so it changes as you copy the function.

f. Apply **Accounting Number Format** to the **ranges B3:F3** and **B11:F11**. Apply **Comma Style** to the **range B4:F10**. Increase the width of column F to **13**. Apply the **Top and Double Bottom Border** to the **range B11:F11**. Save the workbook.

STEP 3 »» **LINK WORKBOOKS**

You want to link the Indianapolis, Bloomington, and South Bend workbooks to display their totals in the Indiana workbook. The South Bend and Bloomington workbooks have the same structure as the Indianapolis workbook on which you have been working. Refer to Figure 9.20 as you complete Step 3.

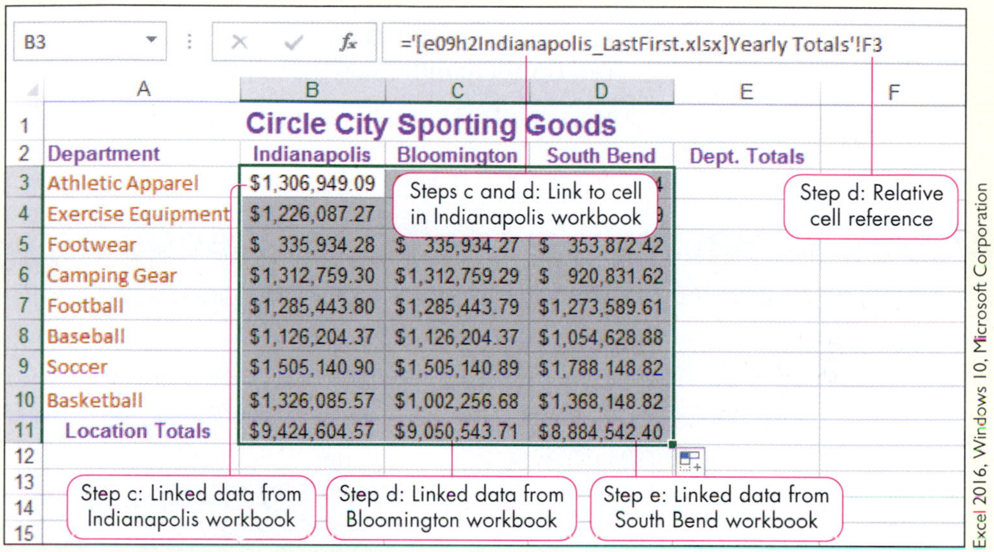

FIGURE 9.20 Linked Workbooks

a. Open *e09h2Bloomington* and save it as **e09h2Bloomington_LastFirst**; open *e09h2SouthBend* and save it as **e09h2SouthBend_LastFirst**; and then open *e09h2Indiana* and save it as **e09h2Indiana_LastFirst**, making sure you save the workbooks in the same folder as your e09h2Indianapolis_LastFirst workbook.

b. Click **e09h2Indiana_LastFirst** on the taskbar to make it the active workbook.

This workbook will contain the links to the three location workbooks.

c. Click **cell B3**, type **=**, point to the Excel icon on the Windows taskbar, select the **e09h2Indianapolis_LastFirst workbook**, click the **Yearly Totals sheet tab**, click **cell F3** containing the yearly department totals, and then press **Ctrl+Enter**.

The formula ='[e09h2Indianapolis_LastFirst.xlsx]Yearly Totals'!$F$3 creates a link to the Indianapolis workbook.

d. Edit the cell reference in the formula to make the cell F3 reference relative and press **Ctrl+Enter**.

You must make this cell reference relative before copying it down the column in Step f. Otherwise, the results will show the value for cell F3 for the other Indianapolis departments.

e. Click **cell C3**, type **=**, click the **View tab**, click **Switch Windows**, select the **e09h2Bloomington_LastFirst workbook**, click the **Yearly Totals sheet tab**, click **cell F3**, and then press **Ctrl+Enter**.

You created a link to the Bloomington workbook. The formula looks like ='[e09h2Bloomington_LastFirst.xlsx]Yearly Totals'!$F$3.

f. Edit the cell reference in the formula to make the cell F3 reference relative.

g. Click **cell D3**, type **=**, point to the Excel icon on the Windows taskbar, select the **e09h2SouthBend_LastFirst workbook**, click the **Yearly Totals sheet tab**, click **cell F3**, and then press **Ctrl+Enter**. Edit the cell reference in the formula to make cell F3 reference relative.

You created a link to the South Bend workbook. The formula looks like ='[e09h2SouthBend_LastFirst.xlsx]Yearly Totals'!F3.

h. Select the **range B3:D3** in the e09h2Indiana_LastFirst workbook and double-click the **cell D3 fill handle**. Save the workbook.

You copied the formulas down the columns in the e09h2Indiana_LastFirst workbook.

STEP 4 ›› **COMPLETE THE LINKED WORKBOOK**

You want to insert department totals for all three locations and format the linked workbook. Refer to Figure 9.21 as you complete Step 4.

E3		fx	=SUM(B3:D3)	Step b: SUM function	

⊿	A	B	C	D	E	F
1			Circle City Sporting Goods			
2	Department	Indianapolis	Bloomington	South Bend	Dept. Totals	
3	Athletic Apparel	$1,306,949.09	$1,256,717.18	$ 900,204.64	$ 3,463,870.91	
4	Exercise Equipment	1,226,087.27	1,226,087.25	1,225,117.59	3,677,292.11	
5	Footwear	335,934.28	335,934.27	353,872.42	1,025,740.97	
6	Camping Gear	1,312,759.30	1,312,759.29	920,831.62	3,546,350.20	
7	Football	1,285,443.80	1,285,443.79	1,273,589.61	3,844,477.20	
8	Baseball	1,126,204.37	1,126,204.37	1,054,628.88	3,307,037.62	
9	Soccer	1,505,140.90	1,505,140.89	1,788,148.82	4,798,430.61	
10	Basketball	1,326,085.57	1,002,256.68	1,368,148.82	3,696,491.07	
11	Location Totals	$9,424,604.57	$9,050,543.71	$8,884,542.40	$ 27,359,690.68	
12						
13		Step c: Comma Style		Step d: Top and Double Bottom		
14				Border for column totals		

Excel 2016, Windows 10, Microsoft Corporation

FIGURE 9.21 Completed Linked Workbooks

a. Click **cell E3** in the e09h2Indiana_LastFirst workbook.

b. Type **=SUM(B3:D3)** and press **Enter**. Copy the formula down column E. Adjust the width of column E to **15**.

You calculated the total yearly sales across all three locations by department.

c. Format the **range B4:E10** with **Comma Style**.

d. Apply the **Top and Double Bottom Border** to the **range B11:E11**.

e. Save and close the files. Open File Explorer. Select **e09Bloomington_LastFirst**, **e09h2Indiana_LastFirst**, **e09h2Indianapolis_LastFirst**, and **e09h2SouthBend_LastFirst**. Right-click one of the selected files, select **Send to**, select **Compressed (zipped) folder**, type **e09h2IndianaFiles_LastFirst**, and press **Enter**.

f. Keep Excel open if you plan to continue with the next Hands-On Exercise. If not, exit Excel.

Formula Audits and Data Validation

Errors can occur in a worksheet in several ways. Sometimes, an error may occur with a function name, such as =AVG(B1:E1) when the formula should be =AVERAGE(B1:E1). A ***syntax error*** is an error that occurs because a formula or function violates correct construction rules; for example, by containing a misspelled function name. Another common type of error is a ***run-time error***, which occurs while Excel tries to execute a syntactically correct formula or function, but the formula or function contains a cell reference with invalid or missing data. For example, if you create a formula that divides a value stored in a cell by a cell that does not contain a value, a divide-by-zero error occurs.

Excel helps you detect and correct syntax and run-time errors. For example, Excel displays #DIV/0! if the formula divides a value by zero to inform you that a result cannot be calculated. Table 9.3 lists some common syntax and run-time errors and the reasons for those errors.

TABLE 9.3 Syntax and Run-Time Errors Explained

Error	Reasons
#DIV/0!	Formula attempts to divide a value by zero or an empty cell
#NAME?	Misspelled or invalid range name Misspelled or invalid or function name, such as VLOKUP instead of VLOOKUP Parentheses missing for function, such as =TODAY instead of =TODAY( ) Omitted quotation marks around text, such as using *text* instead of *"text"* in the function =IF(A4="text",A5,A6) Missing colon in a range reference, such as =SUM(A1A8)
#N/A	Function is missing one or more required arguments VLOOKUP, HLOOKUP, or MATCH functions do not return a match when trying to find an exact match in an unsorted list
#NULL!	Incorrect range separator, such as using a semicolon instead of a colon within a reference to a range Formula requires cell ranges to intersect and they do not
#NUM!	Invalid numeric value contained in a formula or a function Invalid arguments used in a function
#REF!	Formula contains a reference to a cell that was deleted or replaced with other data
#VALUE!	Incorrect type of data used in an argument, such as referring to a cell that contains text instead of a value

Pearson Education, Inc.

Results that appear to be correct but are not create an error that is more difficult to detect. For example, entering an incorrect range, such as =AVERAGE(B1:D1) when the range should be =AVERAGE(B1:E1) is more challenging to detect. ***Logic errors*** are the result of a syntactically correct formula but logically incorrect construction, which produces inaccurate results. Logic errors occur when a formula contains a wrong cell reference or wrong operator (such as dividing instead of multiplying). Another type of error is a ***circular reference***, which occurs when a formula contains a direct or an indirect reference to the cell containing the formula. For example, in Figure 9.22, the formula in cell A4 contains a circular reference because A4 is in the formula =SUM(A1:A4).

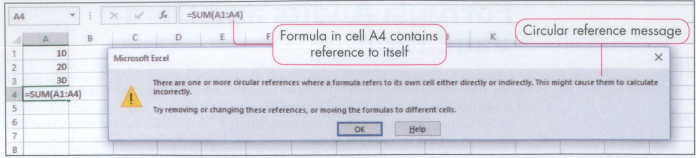

FIGURE 9.22 Circular Reference

Circular references usually cause inaccurate results. Excel displays a warning message when you enter a formula containing a circular reference or when you open an Excel workbook that contains an existing circular reference. Click Help to display the *Find and fix a circular reference* topic or click OK to accept the circular reference. Until you resolve a circular reference, the status bar indicates the location of a circular reference, such as *Circular References: A4*.

You can design worksheets to help facilitate correct data entry, such as ensuring that a user enters a value, not text. Doing so helps prevent formula errors because the user must enter valid data. Although you can design workbooks to require valid data, you might work with workbooks that other people created that contain errors in the formulas.

In this section, you will learn how to use formula auditing tools to detect errors. You will also apply data validation rules to make sure users enter correct data into input cells.

Auditing Formulas

Recall that you can press Ctrl+` (grave accent key) or click Show Formulas in the Formula Auditing group on the Formulas tab to display cell formulas. Displaying the formulas may help you identify some errors, but you might not be able to detect all errors immediately. To help you detect and correct errors in formulas, you can use ***formula auditing***, a set of tools that enable you to display or trace relationships for formula cells, show formulas, check for errors, and evaluate formulas. The Formula Auditing group on the Formulas tab contains commands to help you audit a workbook (see Figure 9.23).

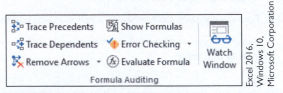

FIGURE 9.23 Formula Auditing Group

> **TIP: GREEN TRIANGLE**
> Excel detects potential logic errors even if the formula does not contain a syntax error. For example, Excel might detect that =SUM(B2:B5) contains a potential error if cell B1 contains a value, assuming the possibility that the function might need to include B1 in the range of values to add. When this occurs, Excel displays a green triangle in the top-left corner of the cell. Click the cell containing the green triangle and click the error icon, the yellow diamond with the exclamation mark, to see a list of options to correct the error.

Trace Precedents and Dependents

Although Excel displays error messages, you might not know which cell is causing the error. Even if your worksheet does not contain errors, you might want to use formula auditing tools to identify which cells are used in formulas. Formulas involve both

precedent and dependent cells. **Precedent cells** are cells that are referenced by a formula in another cell. For example, assume an hourly pay rate ($10.25) is stored in cell A1, hours worked (40) is stored in cell A2, and the formula =*A2 is stored in cell A3 to calculate the gross pay. Cells A1 and A2 are precedent cells to the formula in cell A3. **Dependent cells** contain formulas that *depend* on other cells to generate their values. For example, if cell A3 contains the formula =A1*A2, cell A3 is a dependent of cells A1 and A2.

You use Trace Precedents and Trace Dependents to display **tracer arrows**, colored lines that show the relationship between precedent and dependent cells (see Figure 9.24). The tracer starts in a precedent cell with the arrowhead ending in the dependent cell. The tracer arrows help you identify cells that cause errors. Blue arrows show cells with no errors. Red arrows show cells that cause errors.

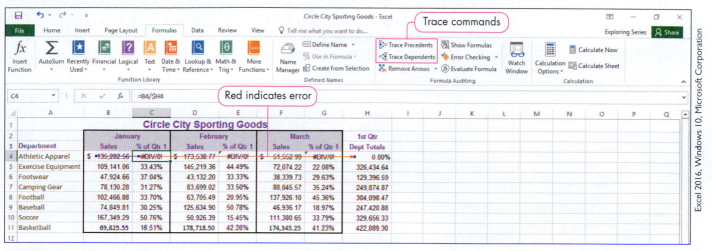

FIGURE 9.24 Trace Precedents

To trace precedents, complete the following steps:

1. Select the cell that contains the formula for which you want to find precedent cells.
2. Click the Formulas tab.
3. Click Trace Precedents in the Formula Auditing group.

To trace dependent cells, complete the following steps:

1. Click the cell for which you want to find dependents.
2. Click the Formulas tab.
3. Click Trace Dependents in the Formula Auditing group.

> **TIP: REMOVE TRACER ARROWS**
> Click Remove Arrows in the Formula Auditing group on the Formulas tab to remove all tracer arrows, or click the Remove Arrows arrow and select Remove Arrows, Remove Precedent Arrows, or Remove Dependent Arrows.

Check for and Repair Errors

STEP 2 When the tracing of precedents or dependents shows errors in formulas, or if you want to check for errors that have occurred in formulas anywhere in a worksheet, you can click Error Checking in the Formula Auditing group on the Formulas tab. The Error Checking dialog box opens (see Figure 9.25), identifies the first cell containing an error, and describes the error.

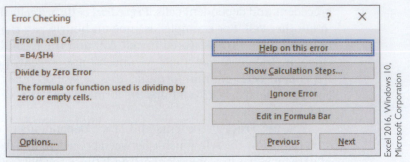

FIGURE 9.25 Error Checking Dialog Box

Excel 2016, Windows 10, Microsoft Corporation

Click *Help on this error* to see a description of the error. Click Show Calculation Steps to open the Evaluate Formula dialog box (see Figure 9.26), which provides an evaluation of the formula and shows which part of the evaluation will result in an error. Clicking Ignore Error either moves to the next error or indicates that Error Checking is complete. When you click Edit on the Formula Bar, you can correct the formula in the Formula Bar.

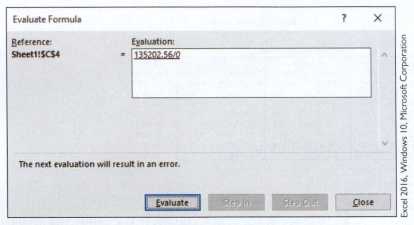

FIGURE 9.26 Evaluate Formula Dialog Box

Excel 2016, Windows 10, Microsoft Corporation

Evaluate a Formula

Understanding how a nested formula is calculated is difficult because intermediate calculations and logic tests exist. You can use the Evaluate Formula dialog box to view different parts of a nested formula and evaluate each part.

To use the Evaluate Formula dialog box, complete the following steps:

1. Select the cell you want to evaluate.
2. Click Evaluate Formula in the Formula Auditing group on the Formulas tab to display the Evaluate Formula dialog box (refer to Figure 9.26).
3. Click Evaluate to examine the value of the reference that is underlined.
4. Click Step In to display the other formula in the Evaluation box if the underlined part of the formula is a reference to another formula.
5. Click Step Out to return to the previous cell and formula.
6. Continue clicking Step In and Step Out until you have evaluated the entire formula and click Close.

Use the IFERROR Function to Detect Errors

If you create a workbook for others to use, you should anticipate errors the users will introduce so that you can provide a way to identify and correct those errors. The *IFERROR function* is a logic function that checks a cell to determine if that cell contains an error or if a formula will result in an error. If no error exists, the IFERROR function returns the value of the formula. The Value argument contains the value being checked for an error, and the Value_if_error argument is the value to return if the formula evaluates to an error. IFERROR detects the following types of errors: #N/A, #VALUE!, #REF!, #DIV/0!, #NUM!, #NAME?, and #NULL, although the output does not indicate the type of error.

Typically, you use a text string enclosed in quotation marks to return an error message. For example, if you divide the contents of cells in row 2 by cell B1 and anticipate that a #DIV/0! error might occur, you can use =IFERROR(A2/B1,"You cannot divide by zero. Change the value of cell B1 to a value higher than 0.").

`=IFERROR(value,value_if_error)`

> **TIP: INFORMATION FUNCTIONS**
> The Information functions contain additional functions you can use for error checking. Of particular interest are the ERROR.TYPE and ISERROR functions. Use Help to learn how to incorporate these functions in error-checking tasks.

Setting Up a Watch Window

STEP 3 ▶▶ When you work with a worksheet containing a large dataset, you can view formulas in cells that are not visible onscreen using the Watch Window instead of constantly scrolling back and forth through the worksheet or multiple worksheets to check how changes affect formula results. A *Watch Window* is a separate window from the worksheet window that displays the workbook name, worksheet name, cell addresses, values, and formulas so you can monitor and examine formula calculations involving cells not immediately visible on the screen. The Watch Window adds a watch for every cell in the selected range. Any time you make a change to the watched cell(s), the Watch Window shows you the current value of the watched cell(s). You can double-click a cell in the Watch Window to jump to that cell quickly.

To add cells to the Watch Window, complete the following steps:

1. Click Watch Window in the Formula Auditing group on the Formulas tab.
2. Click Add Watch in the Watch Window.
3. Select the cells to watch in the Add Watch dialog box and click Add. The Watch Window shows the cells and formulas you selected to watch (see Figure 9.27).

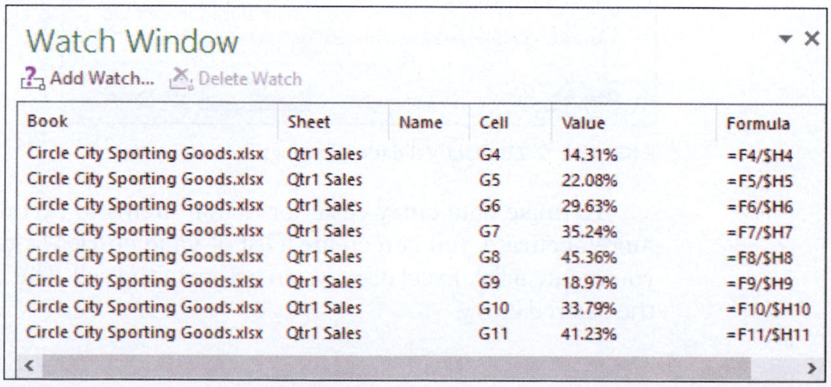

Book	Sheet	Name	Cell	Value	Formula
Circle City Sporting Goods.xlsx	Qtr1 Sales		G4	14.31%	=F4/$H4
Circle City Sporting Goods.xlsx	Qtr1 Sales		G5	22.08%	=F5/$H5
Circle City Sporting Goods.xlsx	Qtr1 Sales		G6	29.63%	=F6/$H6
Circle City Sporting Goods.xlsx	Qtr1 Sales		G7	35.24%	=F7/$H7
Circle City Sporting Goods.xlsx	Qtr1 Sales		G8	45.36%	=F8/$H8
Circle City Sporting Goods.xlsx	Qtr1 Sales		G9	18.97%	=F9/$H9
Circle City Sporting Goods.xlsx	Qtr1 Sales		G10	33.79%	=F10/$H10
Circle City Sporting Goods.xlsx	Qtr1 Sales		G11	41.23%	=F11/$H11

FIGURE 9.27 Watch Window

Validating Data

STEP 4 ▷▷ **_Data validation_** is a feature that requires specified rules be followed in order to allow data to be entered in a cell. It warns and prevents people from entering "wrong" data in a cell, or it can provide a list of valid data from which to choose. Data validation enables you to specify and correct the kind of data that can be entered, specify an input message alerting users when they click a cell that only specific types of data can be entered in that cell, and specify error messages that display when others persist and attempt to enter incorrect data.

> **To set up a data validation rule, complete the following steps:**
>
> 1. Click the cell for which the rule will be applied.
> 2. Click the Data tab.
> 3. Click Data Validation in the Data Tools group.
> 4. Select validation criteria.
> 5. Click the Input Message tab and enter the input message specifications.
> 6. Click the Error Alert tab and enter the error alert specifications.
> 7. Click OK.

Specify Data Validation Criteria

In the Data Validation dialog box, use the Settings tab to specify the **_validation criteria_**—the rules that dictate the type of data that can be entered in a cell. Click the Allow arrow to specify what type of data you will allow the user to enter, such as a whole number, a value that is part of a specific list, or a date that is within a particular date range. For example, if you specify whole number and the user attempts to enter a decimal, Excel displays an error message. You can also specify that the data must be between two values and specify the minimum and maximum values permitted. Figure 9.28 shows a validation rule in which the cell contents must be (a) a whole number and (b) within a minimum and maximum value, which are stored respectively in cells G5 and G6.

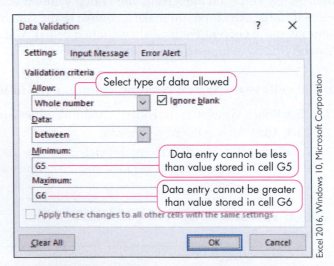

FIGURE 9.28 Data Validation Settings Tab: Criteria

To make data entry easier or to limit items to certain defined items and thereby be more accurate, you can create a list of valid entries from data contained in cells. When you create a list, Excel displays an arrow in the cell. The user clicks the arrow and selects the desired entry.

To create a list of valid entries and set up a validation rule for a list of valid entries, complete the following steps:

1. Create a list of valid entries in a single column or row without blank cells.
2. Click the cell for which you want to create a validation rule.
3. Click the Data tab and click Data Validation in the Data Tools group to display the Data Validation dialog box.
4. Click the Settings tab, click the Allow arrow, and then select List.
5. Click in the Source box and select the range that you created in Step 1 (see Figure 9.29).
6. Ensure that the *In-cell dropdown* check box is selected and that the *Ignore blank* check box is not selected. Click OK.

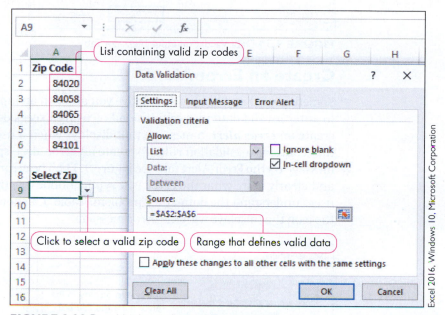

FIGURE 9.29 Data Validation Settings Tab: In-Cell Dropdown

Create an Input Message

STEP 5 ▶▶ **Input messages** are descriptive text or instructions that inform a user about the restrictions for entering data in a cell. You add input messages to cells, and Excel displays these messages when a user moves to a cell that has a data-entry restriction. Input messages consist of two parts: a title and an input message (see Figure 9.30). These messages should describe the data validation and explain or show how to enter data correctly. For example, an input message might be *Enter hire date in the format: mm/dd/yyyy* or *Enter Employee name: last name, first name.*

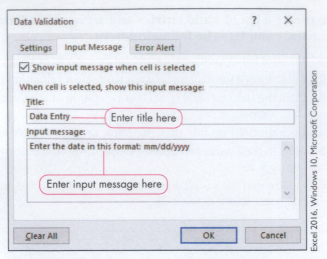

FIGURE 9.30 Data Validation Input Message Tab

Create an Error Alert

Sometimes, no matter how descriptive you are with an input message, users will attempt to enter invalid data in a cell. Instead of using Excel's default error message, you can create an **error alert**, a message that displays when a user enters invalid data in a cell that contains a validation rule. To create an error alert, specify the style, title, and error message on the Error Alert tab (see Figure 9.31). The error alert message should be polite and clearly state what the error is. Cryptic, nondescriptive alert messages do not help users understand the data-entry problem. Table 9.4 shows the error styles that control the icon that displays with the error message.

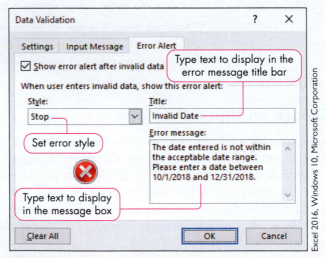

FIGURE 9.31 Data Validation Error Tab

TABLE 9.4	Error Style	
Icon	**Style**	**Description**
⊗	Stop	Prevents the user from entering invalid data
⚠	Warning	Accepts invalid data but warns user that data are invalid
ⓘ	Information	Accepts invalid data but provides information to the user

Quick Concepts

7. What is the difference between precedent and dependent cells? *p. 587*

8. What is the benefit of setting up a Watch Window? *p. 589*

9. What is the benefit of using data validation? *p. 590*

Hands-On Exercises

Watch the Video for this Hands-On Exercise!

MyITLab® HOE3 Training

Skills covered: Trace Precedents and Dependents • Check for Errors • Set Up a Watch Window • Create a Validation Rule • Specify Inputs and Alerts

3 Formula Audits and Data Validation

A colleague prepared a worksheet based on projected data if the company opened a store in Fort Wayne. Unfortunately, your colleague introduced several errors in the worksheet. You will use auditing tools to identify and correct the errors. In addition, you will insert validation rules to ensure only valid data are entered in the future.

STEP 1 ›› TRACE PRECEDENTS AND DEPENDENTS

You want to display precedent and dependent arrows to identify sources and destinations for cells being used in formulas in the Fort Wayne workbook. Refer to Figure 9.32 as you complete Step 1.

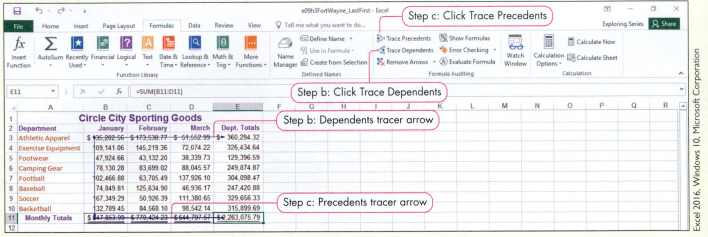

FIGURE 9.32 Dependent and Precedent Arrows

a. Open *e09h3FortWayne*, click **OK** when prompted to fix a circular error, and then save it as **e09h3FortWayne_LastFirst**.

b. Ensure that the Qtr1 worksheet is active, click **cell B3**, click the **Formulas tab**, and then click **Trace Dependents** in the Formula Auditing group.

Excel displays tracer arrows from cell B3 to cells E3 and B11, indicating that value in cell B3 is used in formulas in cells E3 and B11.

c. Click **cell E11** and click **Trace Precedents** in the Formula Auditing group.

Excel displays a tracer arrow, showing that the values in the range B11:D11 are used within the current cell's formula.

d. Click **Remove Arrows** in the Formula Auditing group. Save the workbook.

The Qtr2 worksheet contains errors. You will use the Error Checking dialog box and trace precedents to identify the errors. Refer to Figure 9.33 as you complete Step 2.

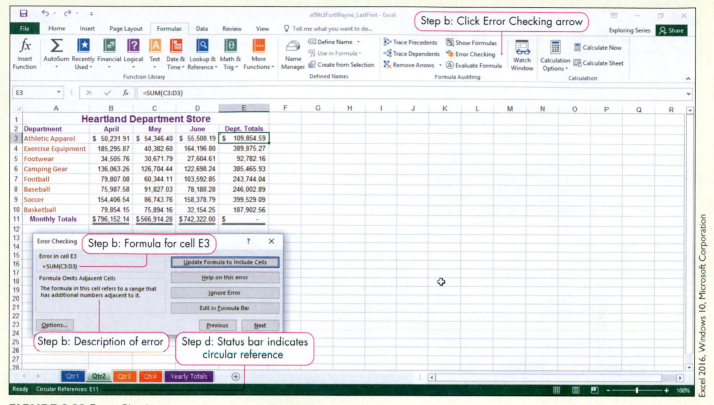

FIGURE 9.33 Error Checking

a. Click the **Qtr2 sheet tab**, look for the green error checking indicator in cell E3, and then click **cell A1**.

b. Click the **Error Checking arrow** in the Formula Auditing group and select **Error Checking**.

The Error Checking dialog box opens, indicating an error exists in cell E3. Excel detects that the formula omits an adjacent cell.

c. Click **Update Formula to Include Cells**.

Excel modifies the formula from =SUM(C3:D3) to =SUM(B3:D3) to include the April sales.

d. Click **OK** in the message box that informs you that error checking is complete.

When you opened the workbook, an error message stated that the workbook contains a circular reference. However, the Error Checking dialog box did not locate that circular reference. The status bar still indicates that a circular reference exists.

e. Click the **Error Checking arrow** in the Formula Auditing group, point to **Circular References**, and then select **$E$11**.

A circular reference occurs when a formula refers to itself. In this case, the formula in cell E11 includes a reference to E11 in the function argument.

f. Change the formula to **=SUM(B11:D11)**. Save the workbook.

The circular reference notation on the status bar disappears.

You want to set up a Watch Window to watch the results of formulas in the Yearly Totals worksheet when you change values in another worksheet. Refer to Figure 9.34 as you complete Step 3.

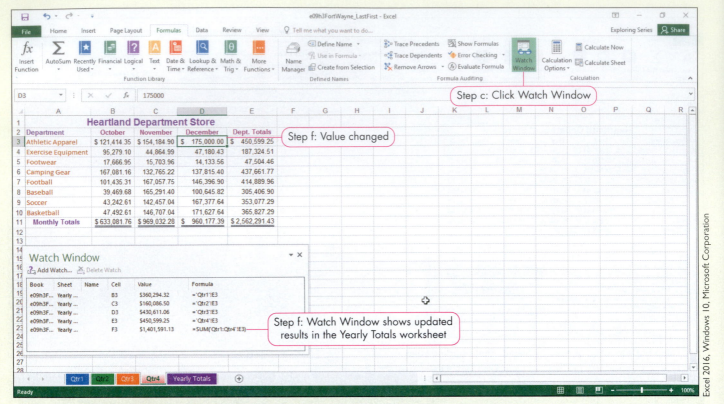

FIGURE 9.34 Watch Window

a. Click the **Yearly Totals sheet tab**.

b. Select the **range B3:F3**.

> You selected the range you want to watch to ensure formulas work correctly.

c. Click the **Formulas tab**, click the **Watch Window** in the Formula Auditing group, and click **Add Watch** in the Watch Window.

> The Add Watch dialog box opens, indicating the worksheet and cells you selected.

d. Click **Add**.

> The Watch Window adds a watch for every cell in the selected range. It shows the workbook name, worksheet name, cell address, current value, and formula.

e. Click the **Qtr4 sheet tab**.

> The Watch Window remains onscreen. The current Athletic apparel total is $355,957.21, shown in cell E3 and in the Watch Window. The Watch Window also shows the Athletic Apparel Yearly Total to be $1,306,949.08.

f. Click **cell D3**, type **175000**, and then press **Ctrl+Enter**.

> The Qtr4 Athletic Apparel total changed to $450,599.25 in cell E3 and in the Watch Window. The Watch Window also shows that the total Athletic Apparel sales are now $1,401,591.13.

g. Click **Watch Window** in the Formula Auditing group to hide the Watch Window. Save the workbook.

You want to insert a validation rule for the Exercise Equipment, Footwear, and Camping Gear values on the Qtr4 worksheet. Based on projections, you believe the maximum revenue would be no more than $500,000. Refer to Figure 9.35 as you complete Step 4.

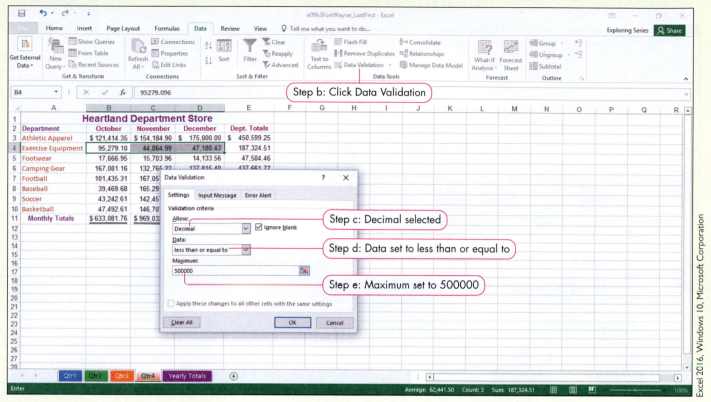

FIGURE 9.35 Data Validation

a. Select the **range B4:D4** on the Qtr4 worksheet.

b. Click the **Data tab** and click **Data Validation** in the Data Tools group.

The Data Validation dialog box opens.

c. Click the **Allow arrow** and select **Decimal** to allow for dollar-and-cents entries.

The dialog box displays Data, Minimum, and Maximum options.

d. Click the **Data arrow** and select **less than or equal to**.

e. Click in the **Maximum box** and type **500000**. Keep the Data Validation dialog box open for the next step.

You will specify the input message and an alert if a user enters more than 500,000, however, you will let the incorrect value be entered. Refer to Figure 9.36 as you complete Step 5.

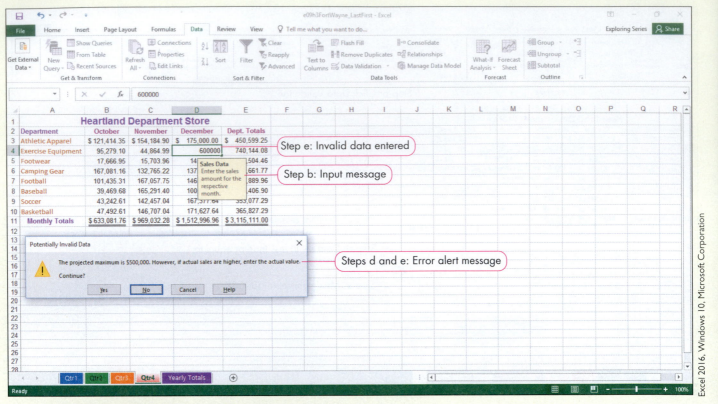

FIGURE 9.36 Error Alert Message

a. Click the **Input Message tab** in the Data Validation dialog box.

If you want to edit the validation message that was set up after completing the prior step, you can edit the validation rule by opening the Data Validation dialog box again.

b. Click in the **Title box** and type **Sales Data**. Click in the **Input message box** and type **Enter the sales amount for the respective month.**

c. Click the **Error Alert tab** in the Data Validation dialog box, click the **Style arrow**, and then select **Warning**.

The stop style would prevent values outside the acceptable maximum from being entered. However, your sales projections might be wrong, so you want to allow values over the maximum.

d. Click in the **Title box** and type **Potentially Invalid Data**. Click in the **Error Message box** and type **The projected maximum is $500,000. However, if actual sales are higher, enter the actual value.** Click **OK**.

e. Click **cell D4**, notice the input message you created from Step b, type **600000**, and then press **Enter**.

The error message you created displays (refer to Figure 9.36).

f. Click **Yes**.

Note that even though 600000 is beyond the validation limit, the user is still able to enter the number by clicking Yes.

g. Click the **Data Validation arrow** in the Data Tools group and select **Circle Invalid Data**.

Excel circles the value in cell D4, indicating that the value violates the validation rule.

h. Save and close the file. Based on your instructor's directions, submit the following:
e09h2IndianaFiles_LastFirst.zip
e09h3FortWayne_LastFirst.

Chapter Objectives Review

After reading this chapter, you have accomplished the following objectives:

1. Work with grouped worksheets.

- Group and ungroup worksheets: Grouping worksheets enables you to perform the same action simultaneously to grouped worksheets. When you group worksheets, [Group] displays after the file name on the title bar. After performing actions on grouped worksheets, remember to ungroup the worksheets before performing an action on an individual worksheet.

- Enter data and format grouped worksheets: Any changes you make while worksheets are grouped will affect all grouped worksheets. Grouping worksheets enables you to quickly enter data, make structural changes such as changing column width, adjust formatting such as applying borders, and change page layouts.

- Fill across worksheets: If you have already entered or formatted data on one sheet, you can copy that data or formatting to other sheets. Group the worksheets, select the range that contains the data or format you want to copy, and select Fill Across Worksheets to copy data and formatting across the grouped worksheets.

2. Insert hyperlinks.

- Hyperlinks are electronic links that, when clicked, connect one cell to another cell in the same worksheet, different worksheet, or different worksheet in another workbook. You can also create hyperlinks to link to webpages or email addresses.

3. Manage windows.

- Control visibility of worksheets: You hide worksheets so that the sheet tabs are not visible. It is beneficial to hide worksheets containing confidential information if you need to display other worksheets to an audience.

- Open and arrange windows: The Arrange Window dialog box enables you to display multiple windows as tiled, horizontal, vertical, or cascade. You can select an option to display multiple windows of the same workbook.

- Split a window: When you work with large worksheets, you can split the worksheet window into resizable panes. Horizontal and vertical split bars display so that you can move them to show more of one part of the window. You can double-click a split bar to remove it.

4. Insert formulas and functions with 3-D references.

- Insert a formula with a 3-D reference: A 3-D reference includes the worksheet name, the column letter, and the row number. A formula with a 3-D reference is useful to obtain the value from a cell or range in another worksheet. The formula contains the worksheet name, an exclamation point, and the cell reference, such as ='October Sales'!E15.

- Insert a function with 3-D references: A function may contain 3-D references to consolidate data from two or more worksheets. If the data are structured in identical cells on all worksheets, you can use a function such as SUM to total the values in the same cell on all worksheets. A function with a 3-D reference looks something like this: =SUM('Qtr1:Qtr4'!E3) where cell E3 in all sheets from Qtr1 to Qtr4 are included the range.

5. Link workbooks.

- Create an external reference: You can establish an external reference or pointer to one or more cells in an external worksheet. If the source data are changed, the destination data are also changed.

- Manage and update linked workbooks: When a destination file is first opened, you will be prompted to enable automatic link updates. You can edit links if you have moved source files and the destination file does not recognize the change in location.

6. Audit formulas.

- Trace precedent and dependents: You can display arrows that depict the relationships between precedent and dependent cells so that you can identify cells used in formulas. Precedent cells are cells referenced in a formula; dependent cells contain formulas that refer to other cells.

- Check for and repair errors: Check and repair errors by selecting *Error checking* in the Formula Auditing group on the Formulas tab. The dialog box enables you to obtain help on the error, show calculation steps, ignore the error, or edit the error in the Formula Bar.

- Evaluate a formula: Use the Evaluate Formula command to provide an evaluation of a formula that shows the portion that returns an error.

- Use IFERROR function to detect errors: The IFERROR function checks a value and returns the results, if possible, or an error message.

7. Set up a Watch Window.

- When you work with large datasets, you can watch formulas in cells that are not visible by using the Watch Window feature. The Watch Window displays the worksheet and cells containing formulas that you set to watch. When changes are made to precedent cells, the Watch Window indicates how that affects the results of formulas.

8. Validate data.

- Specify data validation criteria: To specify criteria, use the Settings tab in the Data Validation dialog box. For example, you can restrict data entry to a whole number between values stored in two cells.

- Create an input message: An input message is descriptive text or instructions for data entry. The Data Validation dialog box enables you to enter a title and an input message to display when a user clicks the cells that contains the input message.

- Create an error alert: An error alert is a message that displays when a user enters invalid data. An error alert displays a style (Stop, Warning, or Information), a title, and the error message.

Key Terms Matching

Match the key terms with their definitions. Write the key term letter by the appropriate numbered definition.

a. 3-D reference

b. Data validation

c. Dependent cell

d. Destination file

e. Error alert

f. Formula auditing

g. Grouping

h. Hyperlink

i. IFERROR function

j. Input message

k. Linking

l. Logic error

m. Precedent cell

n. Source file

o. Split bar

p. Splitting

q. Syntax error

r. Tracer arrow

s. Ungrouping

t. Validation criteria

1. _____ Occurs when a formula or function violates construction rules. **p. 585**

2. _____ An electronic link that, when clicked, goes to another location in the same or a different worksheet, opens another file, opens a webpage in a Web browser, or opens an email client and inserts an email address into the To box. **p. 563**

3. _____ Rules that dictate the type of data that can be entered in a cell. **p. 590**

4. _____ Checks a cell and returns the result, if possible, or returns an error message. **p. 589**

5. _____ A file that contains a link to retrieve data from a source file. **p. 577**

6. _____ A feature that requires specified rules be followed in order to allow data to be entered in a cell. **p. 590**

7. _____ Tools to enable you to detect and correct errors in formulas by identifying relationships among cells. **p. 586**

8. _____ A colored line that shows relationships between precedent and dependent cells. **p. 587**

9. _____ The process of creating external cell references from worksheets in one workbook to cells on a worksheet in another workbook. **p. 577**

10. _____ The process of selecting two or more worksheets so that you can perform the same action at the same time on all selected worksheets. **p. 560**

11. _____ The process of dividing a worksheet window into two or four resizable panes so you can view separate parts of a worksheet at the same time. **p. 567**

12. _____ The process of deselecting grouped worksheets so that actions performed on one sheet do not affect other worksheets. **p. 561**

13. _____ A vertical or horizontal line that frames panes in a worksheet and enables the user to resize the panes. **p. 567**

14. _____ A cell containing a formula that relies on other cells to obtain its value. **p. 587**

15. _____ Occurs when a formula uses incorrect cell references and produces inaccurate results. **p. 585**

16. _____ A reference within a formula or function on one worksheet that includes the name of another worksheet, column letter, and row number located within a workbook. **p. 574**

17. _____ A file that contains original data that you need in another file. **p. 577**

18. _____ A cell that is referenced by a formula in another cell. **p. 587**

19. _____ A message that displays when the user enters invalid data in a cell containing a validation rule. **p. 592**

20. _____ Descriptive text or instructions that inform a user about the restrictions for entering data in a cell. **p. 591**

Multiple Choice

1. You have a workbook that contains sales data for different regional sales reps of a company. Which task is the *least likely* to be done while the worksheets are grouped?

   (a) Fill the sales categories across the worksheets.

   (b) Format the column and row labels at the same time.

   (c) Enter specific values for the first sales rep.

   (d) Format the values with an appropriate number style.

2. Your manager sent you a workbook that contains data validation rules. One rule specifies a maximum value of 15% with a warning alert. You try to enter 22% in that cell. What happens?

   (a) Excel enters the 22% with no message boxes.

   (b) Excel informs you that your entry violates the validation rule.

   (c) Excel displays a message box and prevents you from entering 22%.

   (d) Excel displays a message box informing you the value is above the maximum value and lets you choose to go ahead and enter that value or a different value.

3. The function =FV(D10,D8,-D5) is entered in cell D12. Which cell is a dependent of cell D8?

   (a) D10

   (b) D12

   (c) D5

   (d) D1

4. If you want to display a portion of all three worksheets in a workbook, what should you do?

   (a) Open two new workbook windows, arrange windows, and then click a different worksheet tab in each window.

   (b) Use the Freeze Panes option and cascade the title bars of all open workbooks.

   (c) Double-click the split boxes to display four window panes, click within each pane, and then click the worksheet tab to display its content.

   (d) Use the Split, Freeze Panes, and Arrange All commands at the same time.

5. Cell B15 contains the formula =B14+B15. You created a:

   (a) 3-D formula

   (b) Circular reference

   (c) Syntax error

   (d) Reference formula

6. A personal trainer stores how much weight each person can lift in several categories. Each week's data are stored in a separate worksheet within the same workbook, and each worksheet has an identical structure. Assume cell F5 contains the weight the first person can bench press. What function can identify that person's highest amount bench-pressed in all worksheets?

   (a) =COUNT(Week 1,Week4:F5)

   (b) =SUM(Week 1:Week4:F5)

   (c) =MAX('Week 1:Week 4'!F5)

   (d) =MAX(Week1:Week4:'F5')

7. You want to create a hyperlink on the Summary worksheet to a cell in the Data worksheet within the same workbook. Which type of link do you create?

   (a) Existing File or Web Page

   (b) Place in This Document

   (c) Create New Document

   (d) E-mail Address

8. You want to create a situation so that you can monitor the results of cell formulas on a different worksheet as you change data on another worksheet. You should create a:

   (a) Data validation window

   (b) Hyperlink between worksheets

   (c) Watch Window

   (d) Circular Reference Window

9. You created several workbooks (Accounting, Finance, Management, and Marketing) in the same folder as the main workbook SchoolOfBusiness. What formula correctly links to cell D20 in the Fall 2018 worksheet within the Finance workbook?

   (a) =[Finance]Fall 2018$D$20

   (b) ="Finance[Fall 2018]"!D20

   (c) =[Finance.xlsx:Fall 2018]!$D$20

   (d) ='[Finance.xlsx]Fall 2018'!$D$20

10. You want to restrict data entry to whole numbers greater than 100. What do you create to enforce this data-entry restriction?

    (a) Validation criteria

    (b) An input message

    (c) An error alert

    (d) Watch Window

Practice Exercises

1 Organic Foods Corporation

The Organic Foods Corporation operates three stores in different areas of Portland. The manager of each store prepared a workbook that summarizes the first-quarter results. As the assistant to the general manager, you need to complete the Downtown workbook and link data from the three workbooks to a consolidated workbook. Refer to Figure 9.37 as you complete this exercise.

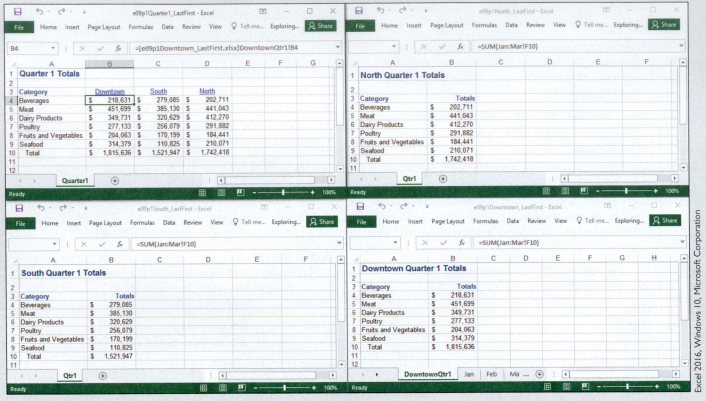

FIGURE 9.37 Organic Foods Corporation

a. Open *e09p1Downtown* and save it as **e09p1Downtown_LastFirst**. Click each sheet tab to see what work has been done and what work you will do.

b. Click the **Jan sheet tab**, press and hold **Shift**, click the **Mar sheet tab**, and then complete the following steps:
  - Click **cell A1**, click **Fill** in the Editing group on the Home tab, and then select **Across Worksheets**. Click **Formats** in the Fill Across Worksheets dialog box and click **OK**.
  - Select the **range B10:F10**, click **Fill** in the Editing group, and then select **Across Worksheets**. Click **Formats** in the Fill Across Worksheets dialog box and click **OK**.
  - Select the **range F1:F9**, click **Fill** in the Editing group, and then select **Across Worksheets**. Click **Formats** in the Fill Across Worksheets dialog box and click **OK**.
  - Select the **range B4:F10** and click **Sum** in the Editing group.

c. Click the **DowntownQtr1 sheet tab**, click **cell B4**, and then insert a function with a 3-D reference by completing the following steps:
  - Type **=SUM(**
  - Click the **Jan sheet tab**, press and hold **Shift**, and then click the **Mar sheet tab**.
  - Click **cell F4** and press **Ctrl+Enter**.
  - Double-click the **cell B4 fill handle** to copy the formula to the **range B5:B10**.

d. Open *e09p1South* and save it as **e09p1South_LastFirst**, open *e09p1North* and save it as **e09p1North_LastFirst**, and then open *e09p1Quarter1* and save it as **e09p1Quarter1_LastFirst**.

e. Click the **View tab**, click **Switch Windows** in the Window group, and then select **e09p1North_LastFirst**.

f. Click the **Jan sheet tab**, press and hold **Shift**, and then click the **Mar sheet tab** to group the worksheets. Right-click the **Jan sheet tab** and select **Hide** to hide the grouped worksheets.

g. Adapt Steps e and f to switch to the e09p1South_LastFirst workbook and hide the Jan, Feb, and Mar worksheets in that workbook.

h. Click the **View tab**, click **Switch Windows** in the Window group, and select **e09p1Quarter1_LastFirst**.

i. Click **Arrange All** in the Window group, ensure that the **Windows of active workbook check box** is not selected, and then click **OK** in the dialog box.

j. Add links by completing the following steps in the e09p1Quarter1_LastFirst workbook:

- Click **cell B4** in the Quarter1 worksheet. Type =, display e09p1Downtown_LastFirst, click **cell B4** in the DowntownQtr1 worksheet, and then press **Ctrl+Enter**. Edit the formula to change $B$4 to **B4**. Copy the formula down the Downtown column to the **range B5:B10**.
- Click **cell C4** in the Quarter1 worksheet. Type =, display e09p1South_LastFirst, click **cell B4** in the Qtr1 worksheet, and then press **Ctrl+Enter**. Edit the formula to change $B$4 to **B4**. Copy the formula down the South column to the **range B5:B10**.
- Click **cell D4** in the Quarter1 worksheet. Type =, display e09p1North_LastFirst, click **cell B4** in the Qtr1 worksheet, and then press **Ctrl+Enter**. Edit the formula to change $B$4 to **B4**. Copy the formula down the North column to the **range B5:B10**.
- Format the monetary values in the **range B4:D10** with **Accounting Number Format** with zero decimal places in the Quarter1 worksheet.

k. Click **cell B3** in the Quarter1 worksheet, click the **Insert tab**, click **Links**, click **Hyperlink** in the Links group, scroll through the list of files, locate and select **e09p1Downtown_LastFirst**, and then click **OK**.

l. Adapt Step k to create hyperlinks in **cells C3** and **C4** to their respective files.

m. Create a footer with your name on the left side, the sheet name code in the center, and the file name code on the right side of the Quarter1 worksheet.

n. Save and close the files. Open File Explorer and complete the following steps:

- Select **e09p1Downtown_LastFirst**, **e09p1North_LastFirst**, **e09p1Quarter1_LastFirst**, and **e09p1South_LastFirst**.
- Right-click a selected file.
- Select **Send to**, select **Compressed (zipped) Folder**, type **e09p1OrganicFiles_LastFirst**, and press **Enter**.

o. Based on your instructor's directions, submit e09p1OrganicFiles_LastFirst.zip.

2 Retirement Planning

An associate created a workbook to help people plan retirement based on a set of annual contributions to a retirement account. A user indicates the age to start contributions, projected retirement age, the number of years in retirement, and the rate of return expected to earn on the money when the user retires. The worksheet determines the total amount the user will have contributed, the amount the user will have accumulated, and the value of the monthly retirement amount. You will fill a title across worksheets and enter formulas with 3-D references. However, other formulas in the worksheet contain errors. You will use the auditing tools to identify and correct the errors. You then will specify validation rules to ensure users enter valid data. Refer to Figure 9.38 as you complete this exercise.

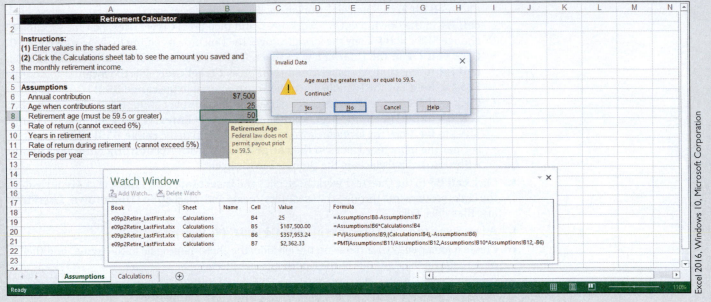

FIGURE 9.38 Retirement Planning

a. Open *e09p2Retire* and save it as **e09p2Retire_LastFirst**.

b. Ensure cell A1 is the active cell in the Assumptions worksheet. Complete the following steps to fill the title and formats to the Calculations worksheet:

- Press **Ctrl** and click the **Calculations sheet tab**.
- Click **Fill** in the Editing group on the Home tab and select **Across Worksheets**.
- Click **OK** in the Fill Across Worksheets dialog box.
- Right-click the **Calculations sheet tab** and select **Ungroup Sheets**. Notice the formatted title in cell A1.

c. Click **cell B4** in the Calculations sheet and insert a formula with 3-D references by completing the following steps:

- Type **=**
- Click the **Assumptions sheet tab** and click **cell B8**.
- Type **–**, click **cell B7**, and press **Enter** in the Assumptions worksheet to calculate the number of years until retirement.

d. Click **cell B5** in the Calculations sheet and insert a formula with 3-D references by completing the following steps:

- Type **=**
- Click the **Assumptions sheet tab** and click **cell B6**.
- Type *****, click the **Calculations sheet tab**, click **cell B4**, and then press **Enter** to calculate the total amount contributed into your retirement account.

e. Click **cell B7** in the Calculations sheet, click the **Formulas tab**, and then click **Trace Precedents** in the Formula Auditing group. Excel displays a worksheet icon with the tracer line to indicate the precedents are on another worksheet.

f. Click the **Error Checking arrow** in the Formula Auditing group and select **Error Checking**.

g. Click **Show Calculation Steps** in the Error Checking dialog box. The Evaluate Formula dialog box opens, showing the formula and stating that the next evaluation will result in an error. Complete the following steps:

- Click **Evaluate** to see the error replace the argument in the function: #DIV/0!.
- Click **Step In** to see the value and click **Step Out** to return to the evaluation.
- Repeat the Step In and Step Out process and click **Close**.
- Click **Next** in the Error Checking dialog box and click **OK** in the message box.
- Click the **Assumptions sheet tab**, click **cell B12**, type **12**, and then press **Enter**.

h. Click the **Calculations Sheet tab** to notice that the function now calculates the monthly retirement income in **cell B7**.

i. Click **Remove Arrows** in the Formula Auditing group to remove the precedents arrow.

j. Click **Watch Window** in the Formula Auditing group and complete the following steps:

- Click **Add Watch**.
- Move the dialog boxes so that you can see the data.
- Select the **range B4:B7** in the Calculations worksheet and click **Add**.
- Resize the dialog box so that you can see most of the details.
- Click the **Assumptions sheet tab** and move the Watch Window below the input area.

k. Create a data validation rule to ensure the retirement age is greater than or equal to 59.5 by completing the following steps:

- Click **cell B8**, click the **Data tab**, and then click **Data Validation** in the Data Tools group.
- Click the **Settings tab**, click the **Allow arrow**, and then select **Decimal**.
- Click the **Data arrow** and select **greater than or equal to**.
- Click in the **Minimum box** and type **59.5**.
- Click the **Input Message tab**, click in the **Title box**, and then type **Retirement Age**.
- Click in the **Input message box** and type **Federal law does not permit payout prior to 59.5.**
- Click the **Error Alert tab**, click the **Style arrow**, and then select **Warning**.
- Click in the **Title box** and type **Invalid Data**.
- Click in the **Error message box** and type **Age must be greater than or equal to 59.5.** and then click **OK**.

l. Create a data validation rule to ensure the rate of return cannot exceed 6% by completing the following steps:

- Click **cell B9**, click the **Data tab**, and then click **Data Validation** in the Data Tools group.
- Click the **Settings tab**, click the **Allow arrow**, and then select **Decimal**.
- Click the **Data arrow** and select **less than or equal to**.
- Click in the **Maximum box** and type **0.06**.
- Click the **Input Message tab**, click in the **Title box**, and then type **Rate of Return**.
- Click in the **Input message box** and type **The rate of return cannot exceed 6%.**
- Click the **Error Alert tab**, click the **Style arrow**, and then select **Warning**.
- Click in the **Title box** and type **Invalid Data**. Click in the **Error message box**, type **Rate must be less than or equal to 6%**, and then click **OK**.

m. Adapt Step l to create a validation rule for **cell B11** to ensure the rate of return during retirement will not exceed 5%. Include appropriate titles and messages.

n. Type **50** in **cell B8** and press **Enter**. Click **No** when the error message displays, change the value to **60**, and then press **Enter**.

o. Type **8.5%** in **cell B9**. Click **No** when the error message displays, change the value to **6%**, and then press **Enter**.

p. Type **5.1%** in **cell B11**. Click **No** when the error message displays, change the value to **5%**, and then press **Enter**. Close the Watch Window.

q. Create a footer with your name on the left side, the sheet name code in the center, and the file name code on the right side of both worksheets.

r. Save and close the file. Based on your instructor's directions, submit e09p2Retire_LastFirst.

Mid-Level Exercises

1 Sales Data

ANALYSIS CASE

You are an accountant for a pharmaceutical sales company. As one of your tasks, you compile an annual report that documents regional sales information into one standardized worksheet. As part of this process, you group the worksheets and insert descriptive rows and columns, apply formatting, and insert functions. Your last step is to create a sales summary worksheet and provide basic information for management to evaluate.

a. Open *e09m1Sales* and save it as **e09m1Sales_LastFirst**.

b. Group the five regional worksheets and complete the following steps:

- Insert a new row above row 1 of the existing data. Type **Agent** in **cell A1**. Apply the **Heading 2 style** in the Styles group on the Home tab.
- Type **Qtr1** in **cell B1**. Use the fill handle to add Qtr2-Qtr4 in **cells C1:E1**. Apply the **Heading 3 style** and apply center horizontal alignment to **cells B1:E1**.
- Type **Total** in **cell F1**. Apply the **Heading 2 style** and horizontal center alignment.
- Click **cell F2**, type **=SUM(B2:E2)**, and press **Enter**. Use the fill handle to complete the summary information to the **range B3:B19**.

c. Keep the five worksheets grouped (not including the Summary sheet) and complete the following steps:

- Type **Total** in **cell A20**. In **cell B20**, insert a function to total Qtr1 sales. Copy the function to the **range C20:F20**.
- Format the **ranges B2:F2** and **B20:F20** with **Accounting Number Format** and zero decimal places.
- Format the **range B3:F19** with **Comma Style** and zero decimal places.
- Add Top and Double Bottom Border to **cells B20:F20**.

d. Ungroup the worksheets and click the **Summary sheet tab**.

e. Build formulas with 3-D references by completing the following steps:

- Click **cell B2** and enter a formula that refers to cell B20 in the North Region worksheet.
- Click **cell B3** and enter a formula that refers to cell B20 in the East Region worksheet.
- Click **cell B4** and enter a formula that refers to cell B20 in the South Region worksheet.
- Click **cell B5** and enter a formula that refers to cell B20 in the Midwest Region worksheet.
- Click **cell B6** and enter a formula that refers to cell B20 in the West Region worksheet.
- Select the **range B2:B6** and copy the formulas to the **range C2:F20**.

f. Apply **Accounting Number Format** with zero decimal places to the **range B2:F2** and **Comma Style** with zero decimal places to the **range B3:F6**. Adjust the column widths if they are too narrow to display the formula results.

DISCOVER

g. Create a hyperlink in each cell in the range A2:A6 to cell A1 in the respective worksheet.

h. Edit each hyperlink to create a ScreenTip such as **Click to see North Region sales**.

i. Set a Watch Window to watch the formulas in the **range B2:F6** on the Summary sheet.

 j. Use the data in the Summary sheet to answer the summary questions 1, 3, and 4 in the **Q&A sheet**.

k. Click the **North Region sheet tab**, change the value in **cell B2** to **3,000,000**, and observe the changes in the Watch Window. Go to the **Q&A sheet** and answer question 2.

l. Create a footer with your name on the left side, the sheet name code in the center, and the file name code on the right side of the Summary and Q&A sheets.

m. Save and close the file. Based on your instructor's directions, submit e09m1Sales_LastFirst.

As a weather analyst, you have been tracking daily high and low temperatures for Oklahoma City, Tulsa, and Lawton during June, July, and August. Each month's data is stored in its own workbook, with each city's data stored in its own worksheet. You want to apply consistent formatting and enter formulas for all worksheets. On each workbook, you need to create the summary worksheet to identify the record high and low temperatures by day and identify the respective cities. Finally, you will link the data to a master workbook.

a. Open *e09m2June* and save it as **e09m2June_LastFirst**.

b. Group the city worksheets and complete the following steps:

- Fill the formatting of **cells A1**, **A2**, and **A5:C5** from the OKC worksheet to the other city worksheets.
- Enter dates **6/1** to **6/30** in this date format (no year) in the Date column. Apply **Orange, Accent 6, Lighter 60% fill** to the dates.
- Split the window after the date 6/10. Scroll down in the second window to see the Monthly Records section. Note that only the active window in the grouped worksheets is split.
- Enter a function in **cell B39** to calculate the highest temperature of the month. Enter a function in **cell C39** to calculate the lowest temperature of the month.
- Use a nested MATCH function within the INDEX function in **cell B40** to identify the date for the highest temperature. The dataset may contain several identical highest temperatures, but the nested function will identify the first date containing the match.
- Use a nested MATCH function within the INDEX function in **cell C40** to identify the date for the lowest temperature.
- Right-click the **OKC sheet tab** and select **Ungroup**.

DISCOVER

DISCOVER

c. Use a Web browser to go to www.wunderground.com, a weather website. Locate and click the **History Data link** below the Local Weather menu and search for **OKC**. Copy the URL and create a hyperlink to this webpage in **cell A3** on the OKC worksheet. Add a ScreenTip stating **Click to see weather history for Oklahoma City.**

d. Adapt Step c to create hyperlinks for the Tulsa and Lawton worksheets as well. Continue to use **www.wunderground.com** for the weather link. Check each hyperlink to ensure it works correctly.

e. Enter the functions with 3-D references in the Summary worksheet by completing the following steps:

- **Cell B6**: Calculate the highest temperature from the three cities for 6/1. Copy the formula down the High column.
- **Cell D6**: Calculate the lowest temperature from the three cities for 6/1. Copy the formula down the Low column.

DISCOVER

- **Cell C6**: Enter a nested IF function to determine which city had the highest temperature. Remember to enclose city names in double quotation marks. Use Help if needed to help you understand a nested IF function. Copy the function down the High-City column.
- **Cell E6**: Enter a nested IF function to determine which city had the lowest temperature. Copy the formula down the Low-City column.

f. Enter formulas in the shaded *Monthly Records* section (below the daily data) on the summary worksheet to identify the highest and lowest temperatures. Enter nested INDEX and MATCH functions to identify the dates and cities for the respective highest and lowest temperatures.

g. Create a footer with your name on the left side, the sheet name code in the center, and the file name code on the right side of each worksheet. Select the option to center the worksheet data horizontally on each sheet. Save the workbook.

h. Open *e09m2July* and save it as **e09m2July_LastFirst**. Open *e09m2August* and save it as **e09m2August_LastFirst**. Study the workbooks and adapt Steps b and e above as necessary to enter formulas on grouped city worksheets and to enter 3-D formulas on the Summary worksheets for these two workbooks. The formatting and hyperlinks are done for you. Add your name on the left side of the footer for each worksheet.

i. Open *e09m2Summer* and save it as **e09m2Summer_LastFirst**. Insert external reference links to the respective cells on the monthly Summary worksheets. Format dates and labels appropriately. Enter your name on the left side of the footer. Save the workbook.

j. Save and close the files. Open File Explorer, select the four e09m2 files, and create a compressed (zipped) folder named **e09m2SummerFiles_LastFirst**.

k. Based on your instructor's directions, submit e09m2SummerFiles_LastFirst.zip.

3 Book Club

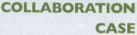
COLLABORATION CASE

FROM SCRATCH

You have decided to join a book club. As part of the book club, each member has the option to choose a book from any popular genre. To help make the decision process easier, you have decided to create an Excel spreadsheet that has links to popular media websites to allow members of the club to browse the available titles. You will save this file on OneDrive to allow each member to access the links as needed.

Student 1

a. Log in to your OneDrive account using your Windows ID. Do the following to create a shared folder for the rest of the participants:

- Click **New**, click **Folder**, and then type **Book Club shared folder**.
- Click the newly created folder, click **New**, and click **Excel workbook** from the Create menu.
- Save the newly created file as **e09m3BookClub_LastFirst**.

b. Type **Popular book websites** in cell A1.

c. Expand the width of column A to display the full text.

d. Name the worksheet **Book Links**.

e. Close the workbook to return to the OneDrive home screen. On the home screen, complete the following steps:

- Right-click the **e09m3BookClub_LastFirst** file and click **Share**.
- Type the email address of a student you will be collaborating with in the pop-up window and click **Share**.

Student 2

a. Open the email that contains the shared Excel workbook and save the file as **e09m3Book-Club_LastFirst_LastFirst**, where you add your name after the name of the first student.

b. Click **Edit in Excel Online** on the Edit Workbook menu.

c. Click **cell A2**. Click the **Insert tab** and create a hyperlink to **www.amazon.com**.

d. Click **cell A3** and create a hyperlink to **www.barnesandnoble.com**.

e. Click **cell A4** and create a hyperlink to **www.ebookstore.sony.com**.

f. Click **cell A5** and create a hyperlink to **www.apple.com/apps/ibooks**.

g. Save and close the file. Based on your instructor's directions, submit e09m3BookClub_LastFirst_LastFirst.

Beyond the Classroom

Pizza Sales

GENERAL CASE

You manage a chain of pizza restaurants in Augusta, Lewiston, and Portland, Maine. Each store manager created a workbook containing the quarterly sales for each type of sale (dine-in, carry-out, and delivery). You want to create links to a summary workbook for the yearly totals. Open *e09b1Augusta* and save it as **e09b1Augusta_LastFirst**, open *e09b1Lewiston* and save it as **Lewiston_LastFirst**, and open *e09b1Portland* and save it as **e09b1Portland_LastFirst**. In each file, calculate totals in the ranges F4:F6 and B7:F7. Type your name on the left side of the header for each worksheet.

Open *e09b1Pizza* and save it as **e09b1Pizza_LastFirst**. In the Augusta worksheet, insert a link to the Dine-In total in cell F4 in the *e09b1Augusta_LastFirst* workbook. Edit the formula to make the cell reference absolute, copy the formula, and use the paste option to paste the Formula to the range B5:B7 to preserve the existing formatting. Repeat this process to create links in the Lewiston and Portland worksheets. Group the Lewiston and Summary worksheets and fill the formats of the range A1:B7 from Lewiston to the Summary worksheet. Ungroup the worksheets, wrap text in cell A1 in the Summary worksheet, and increase the height of row 1 to 35. In cell B4 of the Summary worksheet, insert a 3-D reference to sum the Dine-In totals for all three city worksheets. Copy the formula in cell B4 and use the paste option to paste Formulas in the range B5:B7 to preserve the formatting. On the Contents worksheet, insert hyperlinks in the range A3:A6 to the grand total within each respective worksheet.

Create a footer with your name on the left side, the sheet name code in the center, and the file name code on the right side of each worksheet in the e09b1Pizza_LastFirst workbook. Save and close the file. In File Explorer, select the four e09b1 files, send them to a compressed folder named **e09b1PizzaFiles_LastFirst**. Based on your instructor's directions, submit e09b1PizzaFiles_LastFirst.zip.

Gradebook Errors

DISASTER RECOVERY

You are taking a teaching methods course at your college to prepare you to be a secondary education teacher. One course module teaches students about gradebook preparation, in which you learn how to create formulas to assign grades based on course assessment instruments. Your methods professor assigned a flawed gradebook to see how well you and the other future teachers will do in identifying and correcting the errors. Open *e09b2Grades* and save it as **e09b2Grades_LastFirst**. Set validation rules for the range of quiz and final exam scores to accept whole number scores between 0 and 100 only. Create appropriate input and error messages. Use the feature to circle invalid data. Use the Windows Snipping Tool to capture a screenshot of the Excel window, copy it, and paste it in cell N2. Adjust the height of the screenshot to 3.5" and crop off the image to the right of column M. Insert a comment in each cell containing invalid data describing what is wrong with the data and how to fix it. Then fix the data-entry errors.

Use the auditing tools to find errors and display precedents and dependents to identify errors. Use the Windows Snipping Tool to capture a screenshot of the Excel window, copy it, and paste it in cell N21. Adjust the height of the screenshot to 3.5" and crop off the image to the right of column M. Correct the errors in the formulas. Insert comments indicating the errors found and how you corrected the formulas. Create a footer with your name on the left side, the sheet name code in the center, and the file name code on the right side of the worksheet. Save and close the file. Based on your instructor's directions, submit e09b2Grades_LastFirst.

Capstone Exercise

You are the financial manager for the School of Information Sciences. Your school has three divisions: Information Management, Information Systems, and Information Technology. You need to complete a workbook to track faculty professional development expenses for each division. You will then link the individual division workbooks to a master workbook for the School of Information Sciences.

Data Validation

You are concerned that faculty are requesting professional memberships that cost more than the allocated budget. You want to create a validation rule to prompt the user with information if invalid data is entered. Because you might provide an exception to the rule, you want to warn, not stop, the user from entering data.

a. Open *e09c1IM* and save it as **e09c1IM_LastFirst**.

b. Display the **Bonnet sheet** and create a validation rule in **cell B3** with these specifications:
   - Whole number less than or equal to **$350**.
   - Input message title **Professional Membership** and input message **Enter the amount of the annual professional membership dues.**
   - Error alert style **Warning**, alert title **Too Expensive**, and error message **The amount you tried to enter exceeds $350. Please select a less expensive membership.**

c. Group the four faculty worksheets, fill the contents of **cell B3** from the Bonnet worksheet to the other three faculty worksheets. Use the option that fills all. Ungroup the worksheets and change the values in **cell B3** in these sheets:
   - Hoffman: **$200**
   - Myeong: **$350**
   - Stathopoulos: **$400**

   When the error message displays, click **No**, type **350**, and press **Enter**.

d. Activate the feature that circles invalid data on the Bonnet worksheet. Save the workbook.

Group Worksheets, Fill Data, and Enter Formulas

The Bonnet worksheet contains formatted labels in column A and the range B1:C1. You want to copy the formatted data to the other faculty worksheets. In addition, you will insert a function to calculate the total expenses for the faculty while the worksheets are grouped. Finally, you will format the values.

a. Group the four faculty worksheets.

b. Select the **range A1:A6** in the Bonnet worksheet and fill across the other grouped worksheets.

c. Change the width of column A to **26**.

d. Enter the SUM function in **cell B6** of the Bonnet worksheet to total her expenses.

e. Format **cells B3** and **B6** with **Accounting Number Format** with zero decimal places. Format the **range B4:B5** with **Comma Style** with zero decimal places.

f. Apply **Underline** to **cell B5** and **Double Accounting Underline** to **cell B6**.

g. Ungroup the worksheets and save the workbook.

Create 3-D References

You want to enter formulas that reference cells on other worksheets. That way, if the values for the individual faculty change, those changes will be reflected in the IM Division worksheet.

a. Click the **IM Division sheet tab**.

b. Enter each formula with a 3-D reference:
   - Cell B4: reference Bonnet's professional membership dues
   - Cell C4: reference Hoffman's professional membership dues
   - Cell D4: reference Myeong's professional membership dues
   - Cell E4: reference Stathopoulos's professional membership dues

c. Select the **range B4:E4** and copy the formulas to the **range B5:E7**.

d. Create a function in **cell F4** with 3-D references to the other worksheets. Use the SUM function to calculate the total professional membership dues for all four faculty. Copy the function to the **range F5:F7**. The copied functions should calculate the total reference books, total travel expenses, and the grand total for all faculty.

e. Format the **ranges B4:F4** and **B7:F7** with **Accounting Number Format** with zero decimal places.

f. Format the **range B6:F6** with **Comma Style** with zero decimal places.

g. Apply **Underline** to the **range B6:F6** and **Double Accounting Underline** to the **range B7:F7**. Save the workbook.

Create Hyperlinks

The Documentation sheet is the first sheet. You want to create hyperlinks from this sheet to the total cells for the respective faculty and for the IM Division.

a. Select the **Documentation sheet tab**, enter your name and the current date in the respective cells.

b. Create the following hyperlinks in the Documentation worksheet to the other worksheets:
- **Cell B7**: to **cell B6** in the Bonnet sheet
- **Cell B8**: to **cell B6** in the Hoffman sheet
- **Cell B9**: to **cell B6** in the Myeong sheet
- **Cell B10**: to **cell B6** in the Stathopoulos sheet
- **Cell B11**: to **cell F7** in the IM Division sheet

c. Edit the hyperlink in **cell B11** to display a ScreenTip **Click to see division totals.**

d. Test all hyperlinks and make any necessary corrections. Save the workbook.

Audit a Workbook

You want to audit formulas in the Information Systems workbook. You will correct errors while using the Error Checking feature.

a. Open *e09c1IS* and save the workbook as **e09c1IS_LastFirst**.

b. Show dependents for **cell B4** to see that the formulas in cells B7 and F7 rely on the value in cell B4.

c. Activate the Error Checking dialog box to find the first potential error. Click **Help on this Error** to display a Help window. Correct the function to total the range B4:E4.

d. Use Error Checking to identify a circular reference. Display the precedents arrow and fix the error. Save the workbook.

Link Workbooks

You want to consolidate division totals into the professional development workbook using links. To make it easier to create the links, you will tile windows.

a. Open *e09c1IT* and save it as **e09c1IT_LastFirst**.

b. Open *e09c1ProDevelop* and save it as **e09c1ProDevelop_LastFirst**.

c. Tile the four windows, making sure the division totals worksheets are active.

d. Create a link in **cell B4** in the e09c1ProDevelop_LastFirst workbook to the cell containing the total Professional Membership dues for the IM Division. Edit the formula to change the cell reference from absolute to relative. Then copy the formula to the **range B5:B7**.

e. Create a link in **cell C4** in the e09c1ProDevelop_LastFirst workbook to the cell containing the total professional dues for the IS Division. Remove the arrows and edit the formula to change the cell reference from absolute to mixed. Then copy the formula to the **range C5:C7**.

f. Create a link in **cell D4** in the e09c1ProDevelop_LastFirst workbook to the cell containing the total professional dues for the IT Division. Edit the formula to change the cell reference from absolute to mixed. Then copy the formula to the **range D5:D7**.

g. Create a function in **cell E4** for the total professional dues. Copy the function to the **range E5:E7**.

h. Set up a Watch Window to watch the formulas in the e09c1ProDevelop_LastFirst workbook.

Finalize the Workbooks

You are ready to finalize the workbooks by adding a footer to the worksheets. In addition, you will compress the files into one zip folder.

a. Create a footer on all worksheets with your name on the left side, the sheet name code in the center, and the file name code on the right side. Save and close the workbooks.

b. Open File Explorer, select the four e09c1 files with your name and compress them into a folder named **e09c1BudgetFiles_LastFirst**.

c. Based on your instructor's directions, submit e09c1BudgetFiles_LastFirst.zip.

Imports, XML, and Power Add-Ins

OBJECTIVES & SKILLS: After you read this chapter, you will be able to:

CASE STUDY | Stock Analysis

You are a financial analyst for a brokerage firm. Your manager wants you to analyze commodities sales patterns of his top five brokers for the first quarter. Unfortunately, the data required to complete the analysis are distributed between several key data sources. You received basic broker information through an email and transaction information from an Access database, and you will be required to retrieve real-time NASDAQ trading information from the Web. You do not want to simply copy and paste the data into the worksheet; you want to import current data into Excel so that the constantly changing values are always up to date. Your assistant compiled some historical data and saved it in an XML format. You will import that data into your workbook for additional analysis.

In addition to creating links to external data, you need to format the worksheet data. One challenge you will face is separating column data on the broker information worksheet. After separating the data, you will use text functions for additional formatting. Finally, you will use the new Power BI Add-ins Power Pivot, Power View, and Power Query to shape your data and complete the analysis.

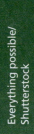

Managing Data

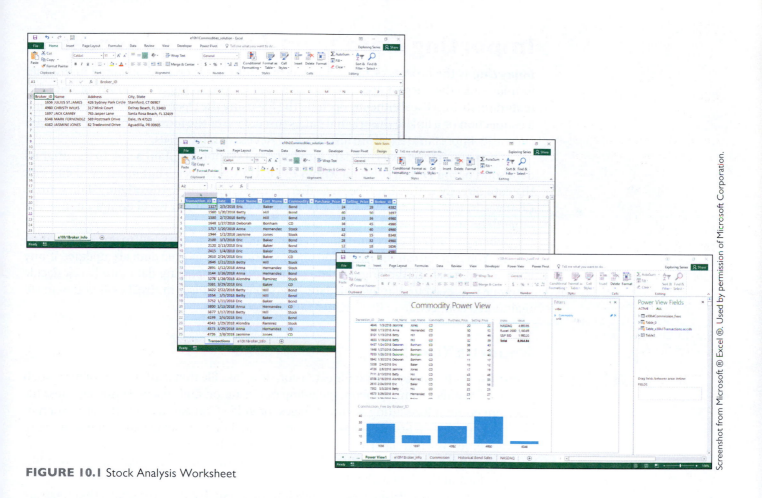

FIGURE 10.1 Stock Analysis Worksheet

CASE STUDY | Stock Analysis

Starting Files	File to be Submitted
e10h1Broker_Info.txt e10h1Transactions.accdb e10h3FourthQuarter.xml e10h4Commission_Fees.csv	e10h4Commodities_LastFirst

External Data

Data originate from, and are stored in, a variety of locations and formats. When you use Excel to manipulate data and perform quantitative analyses, you might obtain data that originate in an external source—somewhere besides an Excel workbook. For example, you might download customer data from a large database stored on your organization's server, or you might receive a text file containing data you need to manipulate in Excel.

External data may not be properly formatted for your Excel worksheet, but importing external data and formatting them in Excel maintains greater accuracy than if you manually enter the data. Furthermore, importing external data into a worksheet enables you to update the worksheet data based on changes from the external source.

In this section, you will learn how to import external data into an Excel workbook. Specifically, you will learn how to import text files and Access database tables.

Importing Data from External Sources

Importing is the process of inserting external data—data created or stored in another format—into the current application. Excel enables you to import a variety of data formats directly into Excel either by opening the file using the Open dialog box or by creating a connection or a link to the original data source. Two of the most common file types you can easily import into Excel are text files and Access database files.

When you import external data into Excel but do not maintain a link to the original data source, you *embed* the data within the Excel worksheet. That means you can edit the data directly within Excel because there is no connection to the original data source. Changes in the original data source or the embedded data in Excel do not change the other data; they are two separate datasets.

When you import external data as a connection, you create a link to the original data source. You can refresh the Excel worksheet so that the imported data are updated if any changes are made to the original data source. Before importing data into Excel, decide whether you need to manage the data as a separate dataset in Excel or if you want to maintain a connection to the original data source.

Import a Text File

STEP 1 ›› A *text file* (indicated by the .txt file extension) is a data file that contains characters, such as letters, numbers, and symbols, including punctuation and spaces. However, a text file does not contain formatting, sound, images, or video. You can use a text editor, such as Notepad, to create a text file, or you can download data from an organization's database or Web server as a text file. The benefit of a text file is that you can import a text file easily into a variety of programs, such as Excel or Access. After importing data from a text file, you can format the data within Excel.

Text files contain *delimiters*, special characters (such as a tab or space) that separate data. A *tab-delimited file* uses tabs to separate data into columns. Figure 10.2 shows a tab-delimited file in Notepad and the imported data in Excel. In the tab-delimited file, the columns do not align; only one tab separates columns. If the user had pressed Tab multiple times to align the data, the data would not have been imported correctly into Excel because Excel counts the number of tabs to determine the column into which the data is imported. An extra tab in a text file imports as a blank cell in Excel.

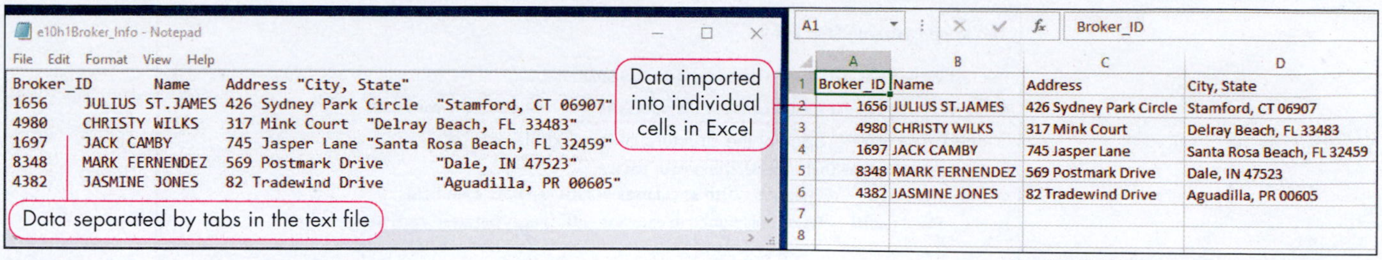

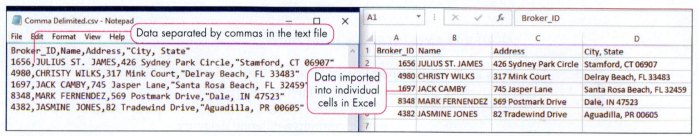

FIGURE 10.2 Tab-Delimited Text File and Data Imported into Excel

Excel 2016, Windows 10, Microsoft Corporation

The ***comma-separated values (CSV) file*** uses commas to separate data into columns and a newline character to separate data into rows. A ***newline character*** is a special character that designates the end of a line and separates data for the next line or row. Many websites, such as census.gov, contain links to download a text file directly into Excel. Figure 10.3 shows a CSV file in Notepad and the imported data in Excel. In the CSV file, commas are used only to separate data; commas are *not* used as the thousands separators in values or as punctuation marks. Otherwise, Excel would separate data at the commas used for punctuation or in values.

FIGURE 10.3 Comma Delimited Text File and Data Imported into Excel

Excel 2016, Windows 10, Microsoft Corporation

To import data from a text file into a new Excel workbook, complete the following steps:

1. Click the File tab and click Open.
2. Click the File Type arrow that currently displays *All Excel Files* and select Text Files.
3. Navigate to the folder that contains the text file, select it, and then click Open.

If you open a file with the .CSV file extension, Excel opens the data immediately in Excel. Because commas delimit the data, data between commas in the CSV file are imported into individual cells in Excel. Each line within the CSV file becomes a row within Excel.

If you open a file with the .txt file extension, the Text Import Wizard opens, prompting you to specify the data type and other instructions for importing the data during these three major steps:

Step 1: Select Delimited or Fixed width based on how the data are structured in the text file. Most text files use delimiters to separate data; therefore, you usually select Delimited to import text data. If data in each column contain the same number of characters and spaces are used only to separate columns, you can choose Fixed width. A ***fixed-width text file*** is a file in which each column contains a specific number of characters, such as 5 characters for the first column, 20 for the second column, and so on, to separate the fields.

Set the *Start import at row* value to where you want the data to begin (see Figure 10.4). Look at the *Preview of file* section to see the data in the text file and how they will be imported based on the *Start import at row* setting. If the text file contains a title or extraneous data extending across multiple columns, do not import from row 1; start importing from the row that contains the actual data. Click the *My data has headers* check box, if the text file contains column headings that describe the contents of each column.

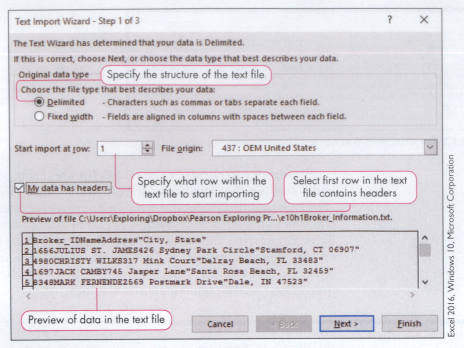

FIGURE 10.4 Step 1 of the Text Import Wizard

Step 2: The Text Import Wizard offers two options for importing (see Figure 10.5).

- Click the appropriate delimiter check box, such as Tab, if the text file is delimited. Click the *Other* check box and type the specific character in the box, if the text file contains a different delimiter.
- Move the column break lines to where the columns begin and end, if the text file contains fixed-width columns.

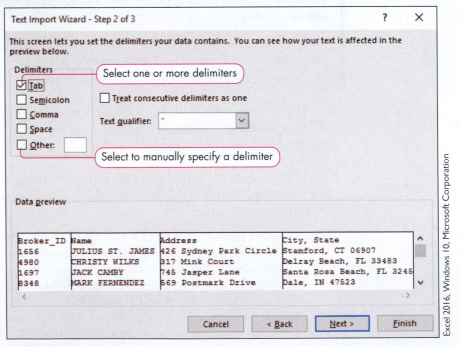

FIGURE 10.5 Step 2 of the Text Import Wizard

Step 3: Select an option in the *Column data format* section for each column you want to import in the Text Import Wizard (see Figure 10.6).

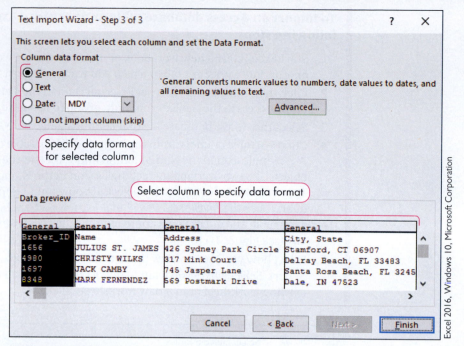

Excel 2016, Windows 10, Microsoft Corporation

FIGURE 10.6 Step 3 of the Text Import Wizard

Click the column heading in the Data preview window and select an option in the *Column data format* section. If you do not want to import a column, select the column and click *Do not import column (skip)*. The default column data format is General, but you can apply a different format. For example, you might want a column of dates to have the Date format.

After you import data from a text file, review the data in Excel. Typically, you will need to adjust column widths and format the data, such as by centering column labels and applying the Accounting Number Format to monetary data. Check for and correct any data errors if the data was not imported correctly.

Import an Access Database Table or Query

STEP 2 ❯❯ Large amounts of data are often stored in databases, such as an Access database table. However, database programs are not intuitive about manipulating data for quantitative analyses or do not contain the capabilities to do so. For example, a car dealership might use a database to maintain an inventory of new cars on the lot, but to analyze monthly sales by car model, the manager uses Excel and creates a PivotTable.

When importing an Access database table or query into Excel, you can maintain a connection to the Access data so that the Excel worksheet data are always current.

To import an Access database table or query into Excel, complete the following steps:

1. Start Excel, start a new workbook or open an existing workbook, and then click the appropriate worksheet tab to which you want to import the data.

2. Click the Data tab and click Get External Data in the Get & Transform group. Click From Access in the Get External Data group to open the Select Data Source dialog box.

3. Select the Access database file that contains data you want to import and click Open.

4. Choose a table or query from the list in the Select Table dialog box (see Figure 10.7). A rectangle icon in the Name column and TABLE in the Type column indicate a table object. The two overlapping rectangles icon in the Name column and VIEW in the Type column indicate a query object. If you want to import more than one table or query, click the *Enable selection of multiple tables* check box and click the check box for each table and query you want to import. Click OK to display the Import Data dialog box (see Figure 10.8).

5. Select how you want to view the data in your workbook, such as Table or PivotTable Report. Select where you want to import the data, such as starting in cell A1 in an existing worksheet or in a new worksheet. Click OK.

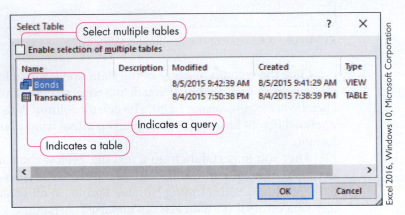

FIGURE 10.7 Select Table Dialog Box

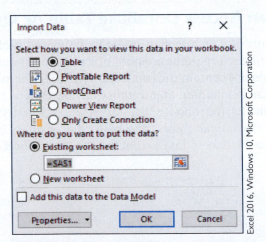

FIGURE 10.8 Import Data Dialog Box

If you import the data as a table, Excel formats the data using a default Excel table style. In addition, Excel displays the Table Tools Design tab as well as the filter arrows so that you can sort and filter data. The Table Name box indicates the data type, such as Table, an underscore, and the name of the Access object (see Figure 10.9).

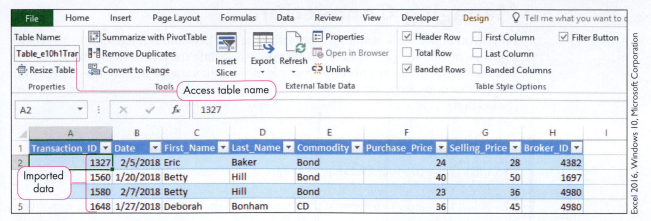

FIGURE 10.9 Imported Access Table

TIP: COPYING DATA FROM AN ACCESS TABLE

If you do not want to create a link to the Access database table, you can open the table in Access, select the table including field names, copy it, and then paste the data in Excel.

Import Data from Other Sources

You can import data from sources other than text files and Access databases (see Figure 10.10). Click Get External Data in the Get & Transform group and click From Other Sources in the Get External Data group to display a list of additional sources, as shown in Figure 10.10.

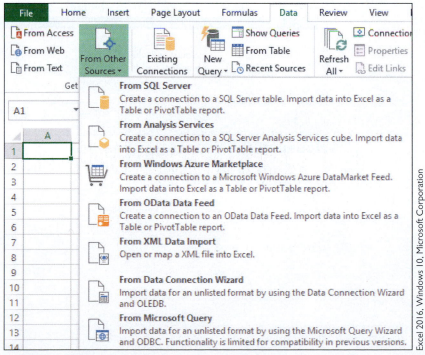

FIGURE 10.10 Import Data from Other Sources

Use Help to learn about each source and the type of data you can import. Some services require a username and password. Some marketplace datasets require a fee to obtain.

Managing Connections

When you import data using the options in the Get External Data group, Excel creates a link to the original data source so that you can update the data quickly in Excel. After you create the initial connection, you might want to view or modify the connection. The Connections group on the Data tab contains options to manage your external data connections.

To display a list of all connections in a workbook, complete the following steps:

1. Click Connections in the Connections group on the Data tab to display the Workbook Connections dialog box (see Figure 10.11).
2. Select the connection name in the top portion of the dialog box to see where a specific connection is located.
3. Click *Click here to see where the selected connections are used.* The dialog box shows the sheet name, connection name, and range in the worksheet.

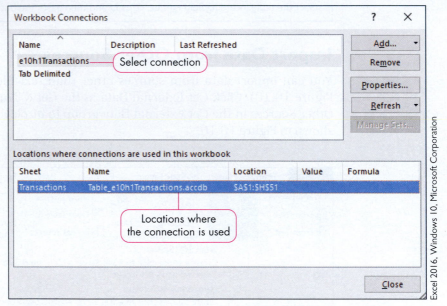

FIGURE 10.11 Workbook Connection Dialog Box

You can remove a connection if you no longer want to link the data to the external data source. After you disconnect the data in Excel from the external data source, you will not be able to refresh the data. To remove a connection, select it in the Workbook Connections dialog box, click Remove, click OK in the warning message box, and then click Close in the Workbook Connections dialog box.

Set Connection Properties

STEP 3 ⟩⟩ *Data range properties* are settings that control how imported data in cells connect to their source data. These properties also specify how the data display in Excel, how often the data are refreshed, and what happens if the number of rows in the data range changes based upon the current data in the external data source.

> **To display the data range properties, complete one of the following steps:**
>
> - Click Connections in the Connections group and click Properties.
> - Click Properties in the Connections group. When you click Properties in the Connections group, the External Data Properties dialog box displays (see Figure 10.12). This dialog box looks slightly different based on the type of external data you imported and based on which option you use to display the dialog box. For example, the dialog box has fewer options for a connection to an Access database table than it does for a text file.
> - Click the Refresh All arrow and select Connection Properties.

Data in a database or data in an external text file may be updated periodically. Although you created a connection to the external data within Excel, it will not be automatically updated. For example, if you created a connection to a database containing sales information, if a new sale is recorded it will not automatically appear in the Excel workbook. To ensure that the Excel data is current, you need to refresh the connections to the original external data source periodically. Refreshing the connection updates the linked data in an Excel workbook with the most up-to-date information.

> **To refresh data in a worksheet, complete one of the following steps:**
>
> - Click Refresh All in the Connections group to refresh all connections in the active workbook.
> - Click the Refresh All arrow in the Connections group and select Refresh to update data for the range containing the active cell.
> - Right-click in a range of data and select Refresh to update that data only.

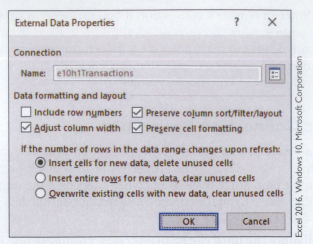

FIGURE 10.12 External Data Range Properties Dialog Box

Quick Concepts

1. What is the purpose of delimiters in a text file? Name two common text file delimiters. *p. 618*

2. What is the difference between opening a text file directly in Excel and using the Get External Data option to import text file data? *p. 624*

3. In what situation would you want to refresh a connection to external data? *p. 625*

Hands-On Exercises

Watch the Video for this Hands-On Exercise!

MyITLab®
HOE1 Training

Skills covered: Import a Text File • Import an Access Database Table or Query• Set Connection Properties

1 External Data

To begin your analysis report, you will import the text file of broker information you received via email. You will then add first quarter transaction information that is stored in an Access database table. Your last step is to configure the data connection as you will need to refresh the connection to import the most up-to-date data into your worksheet when the file is opened.

STEP 1 ►► IMPORT A TEXT FILE

A coworker created a list of broker contact information in Notepad, so your first task is to import the data into Excel. You do not need to create a connection to the text file because there is no plan to update the text file. You will simply open the file directly from the Open dialog box in Excel. Refer to Figure 10.13 as you complete Step 1.

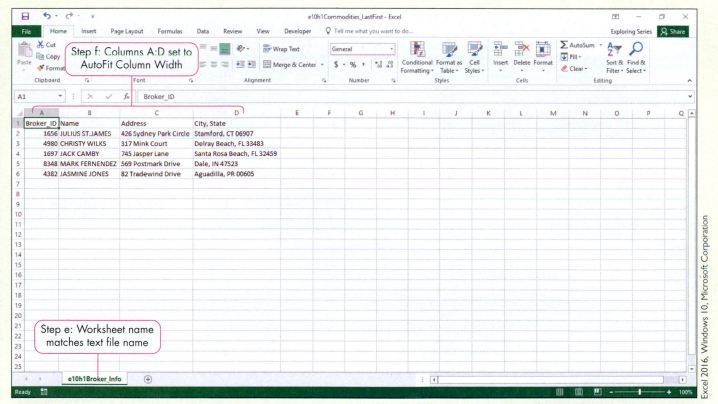

FIGURE 10.13 Imported Data from a Text File

a. Start Excel, click **Open Other Workbooks** in the bottom-left corner of the start window, and then double-click **This PC** to display the Open dialog box.

b. Click the **File Type arrow** that currently displays *All Excel Files*. Select **Text Files**, select *e10h1Broker_Info.txt*, and then click **Open**. The Text Import Wizard dialog box opens. Accept the defaults: Delimited as the file type and 1 as *Start import at row*.

c. Click the **My data has headers check box** to select it and click **Next**.

There are headers in the original file you received via email. When you click *My data has headers* Excel will use the first row provided as column headings.

d. Ensure that **Tab** is selected in the Delimiters section and click **Next**.

The Text Import Wizard – Step 2 of 3 dialog box contains options to specify the type of delimiter(s) contained in the text file. This text file contains tab delimiters.

e. Ensure **General** is selected in the *Column data format* section and click **Finish**.

The Text Import Wizard – Step 3 of 3 dialog box enables you to select each column and specify its data type. Excel imports the data from the text file into the first column of the worksheet. The worksheet name matches the name of the text file: e10h1Broker_Information.

f. Select columns **A:D**. Click the **Home tab**, click **Format** in the Cells group, and then select **AutoFit Column Width**.

g. Click the **File tab**. Click **Save As**, and then click **Browse**. Type **e10h1Commodities_LastFirst** in the File name box, click the **Save as type arrow**, select **Excel Workbook**, and then click **Save**.

STEP 2 >> IMPORT AN ACCESS DATABASE TABLE

Commodity transaction information is stored in an Access database table. You want to import that into the Excel workbook so that you will be able to better analyze the data. Refer to Figure 10.14 as you complete Step 2.

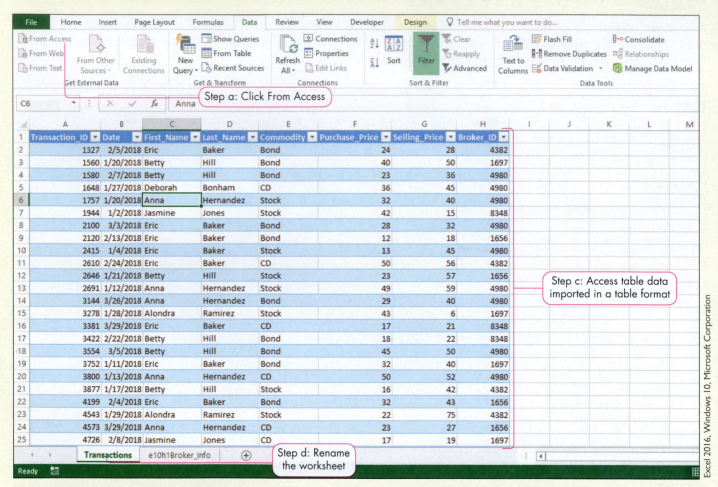

FIGURE 10.14 Access Table Imported

a. Click the **Data tab** in the Get External Data group and click **From Access**.

> **TROUBLESHOOTING:** If using a lower resolution monitor, the Get External Data group will be compressed into an icon. This icon must be clicked to display External Data options.

b. Navigate to your student data files. Select *e10h1Transactions.accdb* in the Select Data Source dialog box and click **Open**.

The Import Data dialog box opens so that you can specify how to view the data and where to place it.

c. Ensure **Table** is selected, click **New worksheet**, and then click **OK**.

You imported the Access data in a new worksheet. Notice that when you import data from a text file, the data import into a range of cells, whereas the Access import formats data as a table.

> **TROUBLESHOOTING:** If you accepted the default set to *Existing worksheet* and =$A$1, Excel will import the data starting in cell A1 and move the existing data to the right. If this happens, select columns A:H, delete them, and then start Step a over again.

d. Double-click the **Sheet1 tab**, type **Transactions**, and then press **Enter** to rename the worksheet.

e. Save the workbook.

STEP 3 ›› SET CONNECTION PROPERTIES

You want to change the refresh property so that it will refresh the data from the Access database when the workbook is opened. This change will enable you to monitor stock price changes throughout the day. Refer to Figure 10.15 as you complete Step 3.

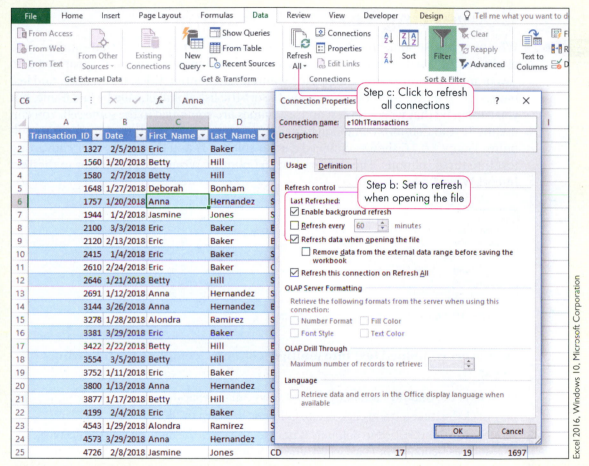

FIGURE 10.15 Maintaining Connections

a. Click **cell A2** on the Transactions sheet tab. Click the **Data tab**, click **Properties** in the Connections group, and then click the **Connection Properties** icon to the right of the Name box.

The Connection Properties dialog box opens so that you can modify the properties.

b. Click to select **Refresh data when opening the file**, click **OK** to exit the Connections Properties, and then click **OK** again to exit the External Data Properties dialog box.

The table imported from the database will update every time the workbook is opened.

c. Click **Refresh All** in the Connections group.

The status bar displays *Running background query* and the connected data is updated.

d. Save the workbook. Keep the workbook open if you plan to continue with the next Hands-On Exercise. If not, close the workbook, and exit Excel.

Text Manipulation

When you import data from external sources or need to modify a workbook created by someone else, the data may not be structured in a way that meets your needs. For example, data might import into one column instead of multiple columns, which would facilitate sorting and filtering at deeper levels. Furthermore, external data might be in all capital letters, and you want to display the data in title case—text in which the first letter of each major word is capitalized but prepositions such as *in* and *on* are lowercase—so that the data are easier to read. Excel contains features to help you manipulate text to fit your needs.

In this section, you will learn how to separate text stored in one column into multiple columns. In addition, you will use some text functions to manipulate text in a worksheet.

Converting Text to Columns

STEP 1 ›› Whether you use someone else's workbook or import data from external sources, data might be displayed in one column when they would be more useful if separated into two or more columns. For example, a column might contain titles, first names, and last names, such as Mr. John Doe. You want to sort the list alphabetically by last name, but you cannot do that when the first and last names are combined in the same cell. You can use the Text to Columns command to split the contents in one column into separate columns. Figure 10.16 shows combined data in column A and the results after converting text into three columns. The Convert Text to Columns Wizard is very similar to the Text Import Wizard.

	A	B
1	Original Data	Empty Columns
2	Mr. John Doe	
3	Dr. Jackie Doe	
4	Ms. Jill Doe	
5	Dr. Jay Doe	
6		

	A	B	C
1	Original Data	Originally Empty	
2	Mr.	John	Doe
3	Dr.	Jackie	Doe
4	Ms.	Jill	Doe
5	Dr.	Jay	Doe
6			

Excel 2016, Windows 10, Microsoft Corporation

FIGURE 10.16 Combined and Separated Data

To convert combined text into multiple columns, complete the following steps:

1. Select the column containing the text you want to separate.
2. Click the Data tab and click Text to Columns in the Data Tools group.
3. Use the Convert Text to Columns Wizard to distribute the data. Specify the file type, such as Delimited or Fixed width, and click Next.
4. Specify the delimiters, such as a Tab or Space, in the Convert Text to Columns Wizard—Step 2 of 3. The data shown in Figure 10.16 are delimited by spaces. The wizard can use the space to separate the title and first and last names in this example. Click Next.
5. Select the column data format, such as Text, in the Convert Text to Columns Wizard—Step 3 of 3, and click Finish.

TIP: ALLOW ROOM FOR SEPARATION

Allow enough columns to the right of the column containing text to separate to avoid overwriting data. Excel does *not* insert new columns. It separates data by placing them into adjoining columns. If you have a first name, middle name, and last name all in one column and you separate to get a first name column, middle name column, and last name column, you must have two empty columns. If the columns on the right side of the original column to split are not empty, Excel will overwrite existing data.

Manipulating Text with Functions

Excel has 27 functions that are specifically designed to change or manipulate text strings. The Function Library group on the Formulas tab contains a Text command that, when clicked, displays a list of text functions. You can also access the text functions from the Insert Function dialog box. Some of the most commonly used text functions are CONCATENATE, PROPER, UPPER, LOWER, and SUBSTITUTE.

Combine Text with the CONCATENATE Function

Text labels are often called text strings. A text string is not used for calculation. You can combine text strings stored in two or more cells into one cell. For example, you might want to combine a last name (e.g., Doe) and first name (e.g., John) stored in two cells into one text string to look like this: *Doe, John*. In this example, a comma and a space are placed after the last name. The **CONCATENATE function** joins between 2 and 255 individual text strings into one text string. In Figure 10.17, the first name is in cell B2, the last name is in cell C2, and cell E2 contains the =CONCATENATE(C2,", ",B2) function. The comma and space included inside quotes produce *Doe, John*. When constructing a CONCATENATE function, place any text (such as commas and spaces) correctly within quotation marks so that you get the desired result. The text items can be strings of text, numbers, or single-cell references.

=CONCATENATE(text1,text2)

	A	B	C	D	E
1	Title	First	Last	Concatenated	
2	Mr.	John	Doe	Doe, John	
3	Dr.	Jackie	Doe	Doe, Jackie	
4	Ms.	Jill	Doe	Doe, Jill	
5	Dr.	Jay	Doe	Doe, Jay	

D2 | fx =CONCATENATE(C2,", ",B2)

Excel 2016, Windows 10, Microsoft Corporation

FIGURE 10.17 Concatenation: Join Text Strings

> **TIP: ANOTHER WAY TO CONCATENATE**
> Use the ampersand (&) operator instead of the CONCATENATE function to join text items. For example, =A4&B4 returns the same value as =CONCATENATE(A4,B4).

Change Text Case with Text Functions

STEP 2 ▶▶ Data come in a variety of case or capitalization styles, such as ALL CAPS, Title Case, and lowercase. Depending on your usage of data, you may need to change the case in a worksheet. Excel contains three functions to change the case or capitalization of text: PROPER, UPPER, and LOWER. Figure 10.18 illustrates the results of these three functions.

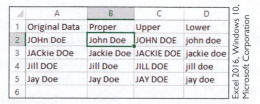

	A	B	C	D
1	Original Data	Proper	Upper	Lower
2	JOHn DoE	John Doe	JOHN DOE	john doe
3	JACkie DOe	Jackie Doe	JACKIE DOE	jackie doe
4	Jill DOE	Jill Doe	JILL DOE	jill doe
5	Jay Doe	Jay Doe	JAY DOE	jay doe
6				

Excel 2016, Windows 10, Microsoft Corporation

FIGURE 10.18 Results of Text Functions

Large amounts of capitalized text are difficult to read. Use the **PROPER function** to capitalize the first letter of each word in a text string, including the first letter of prepositions (such as *of*) and articles (such as *a*). The PROPER function converts all other letters to lowercase. The text argument is a text string that must be enclosed in quotation marks, a formula that returns text, or a reference to a cell that contains text that you want to partially capitalize. In Figure 10.18, cell B2 contains =PROPER(A2) to change the case of the content in cell A2 to proper case, such as *John Doe*.

`=PROPER(text)`

The **UPPER function** converts text strings to uppercase letters. The text argument is the text to be converted to all capitals and can be a reference or text string. Use this function to convert text in a cell or a range to all uppercase letters. In Figure 10.18, cell C2 contains =UPPER(A2) to change the case of the contents in cell A2 to uppercase letters, such as *JOHN DOE*.

`=UPPER(text)`

The **LOWER function** converts text in a cell or range to all lowercase. In Figure 10.18, cell D2 contains =LOWER(A2) to change the case of the text in cell A2 to lowercase letters, such as *john doe*.

`=LOWER(text)`

Use the Substitute Function

STEP 3 ▶▶ The **SUBSTITUTE function** substitutes, or replaces, new text for old text in a text string. For example, if a company changes its name, you can use the SUBSTITUTE function to replace the old company name with the new company name.

`=SUBSTITUTE(text,old_text,new_text,instance_num)`

Text is the original text or reference to a cell that contains the characters to be substituted, *old_text* is the text to be replaced, and *new_text* is the text you want to replace old_text with. *Instance_num* specifies which occurrence of old_text you want to replace with new_text. When instance_num is specified, only that instance is changed. If you do not include instance_num, all occurrences are changed.

Use Other Text Functions

STEP 4 ▶▶ Other text functions help you achieve a variety of text manipulations. Table 10.1 lists a few other common text functions and their descriptions.

TABLE 10.1 Additional Text Functions	
Function	**Description**
TRIM(Text)	Removes leading and trailing spaces in a text string but maintains spaces between words in a text string
LEFT(Text,Num_chars)	Returns the specified number of characters from the start of a text string
RIGHT(Text, Num_chars)	Returns the specified number of characters from the end of a text string
MID(Text,Start_num,Num_chars)	Returns the specified number of characters from the middle of a text string, based on a starting position and number of characters

Pearson Education, Inc.

Using Flash Fill

STEP 5 ▶▶ *Flash Fill* is a productivity feature that enables you to enter data in one or two cells to provide a pattern which is used by Excel to complete the data entry. Often, you use Flash Fill in conjunction with data in existing columns. Flash Fill has the ability to separate text into multiple columns, combine text into one column, automatically complete text or dates, automatically format phone numbers, and match any additional user defined patterns as long as the data is structured in a similar way for Flash Fill to recognize data patterns. For example, in Figure 10.19, column A contains cities and state abbreviations. Instead of using Text to Columns, you can type the first city name in a column adjacent to the dataset and use Flash Fill to create a column of city names only.

To use Flash Fill, complete the following steps:

1. Enter data that use part of existing data in a column in the dataset.
2. Press Enter and start typing the second sample data.
3. Click Fill on the home tab and select Flash Fill.

If you type only one sample entry and leave that as the active cell, you can click Fill in the Editing group on the Home tab and select Flash Fill to complete the rest of the column. If Excel can detect a pattern, it will fill in the data in the rest of the column.

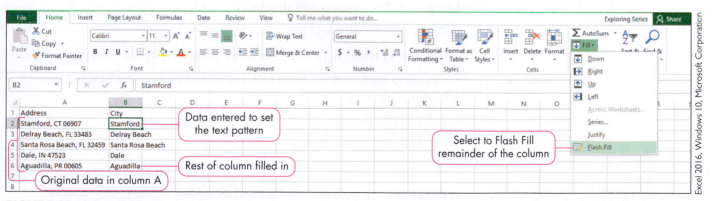

FIGURE 10.19 Flash Fill Results

Quick Concepts

4. What is the purpose of the Text to Columns feature? Provide one example of when it would be useful. *p. 630*

5. What is the difference among the PROPER, UPPER, and LOWER functions? *p. 632*

6. How can Flash Fill be used to replace text functions such as PROPER? *p. 633*

Hands-On Exercises

Skills covered: Convert Text to Columns • Change Text Case with Text Functions • Use the SUBSTITUTE Function • Use Other Text Functions • Use Flash Fill

2 Text Manipulation

After importing the broker information, you want to use text functions to manipulate the text within the worksheet. You want to make the data easier to access and display in multiple formats for future usage.

STEP 1 ›› CONVERT TEXT TO COLUMNS

Currently, the Broker Information worksheet contains the broker's first and last name in the same column. You want to separate the names so you can sort or filter by last name in the future. You also want to separate City and State information for the same purpose. Refer to Figure 10.20 as you complete Step 1.

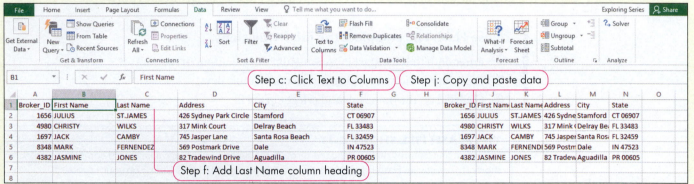

FIGURE 10.20 Separated into Columns

Excel 2016, Windows 10, Microsoft Corporation

a. Open *e10h1Commodities_LastFirst* if you closed it at the end of Hands-On Exercise 1 and save it as **e10h2Commodities_LastFirst**, changing h1 to h2. Click the **e10h1Broker_Information worksheet tab**.

b. Select **column C**, right-click, and then select **Insert**.

   You inserted a new column to place the results of separating the first and last names.

c. Select the **range B1:B6**, click the **Data tab,** and then click **Text to Columns** in the Data Tools group.

   The Convert Text to Columns Wizard dialog box opens.

d. Ensure Delimited is selected and click **Next**.

   The broker names are separated with a space that will be used as a delimiter.

e. Deselect the **Tab check box**, click the **Space check box** to select it, and then click **Finish**.

   Once completed, first names appear in column B and last names appear in column C.

f. Click **cell B1** and type **First Name**. Click **cell C1** and type **Last Name**.

g. Select the **range E1:E6** and click **Text to Columns** in the Data Tools group.

   The Convert Text to Columns Wizard dialog box opens.

h. Ensure Delimited is selected and click **Next**.

i. Deselect the Space check box, click the **Comma check box** to select it, and then click **Finish**.

Unlike broker information, the City and State information is separated by commas.

j. Select the **range A1:F6**, which contains the broker information. Copy the data and paste them starting in **cell I1**.

Before continuing to the next step, you copied the data for future reference in this exercise.

k. Press **Esc** and save the workbook.

STEP 2 ›› USE THE PROPER FUNCTION

You want to improve the readability of the broker first and last names by displaying the data in title case using the PROPER function. Refer to Figure 10.21 as you complete Step 2.

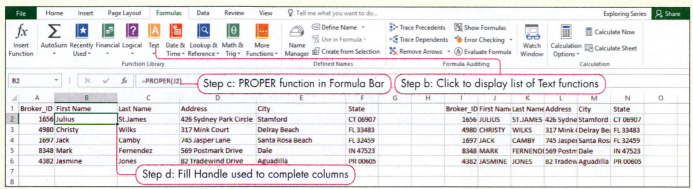

FIGURE 10.21 PROPER Function Results

Excel 2016, Windows 10, Microsoft Corporation

a. Select the **range B2:C6** and press **Delete**.

b. Click **cell B2**. Click the **Formulas tab**, click **Text** in the Function Library group, and then select **PROPER**.

The Function Arguments dialog box opens.

c. Click **cell J2** to enter it in the Text box and click **OK**.

The results of the PROPER function return the proper case of JULIUS as Julius.

d. Use the fill handle to copy the formula down and then over to complete the fill in **range B2:C6**.

Using the fill handle copies the formula to complete the first and last name columns.

e. Save the workbook.

STEP 3 ›› USE THE SUBSTITUTE FUNCTION

You received a recent email that broker Christy Wilks has recently married and her last name is now Davis. You could manually change the name; however, you have decided to practice by using the SUBSTITUTE function, as it can be used to replace large amounts of data as well. Refer to Figure 10.22 as you complete Step 3.

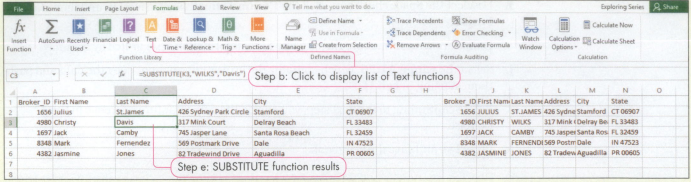

FIGURE 10.22 SUBSTITUTE Function Results

Excel 2016, Windows 10, Microsoft Corporation

a. Click **cell C3** and press **Delete**.

b. Click **Text** in the Function Library group and select **SUBSTITUTE**.

The Function Arguments dialog box opens so that you can specify the arguments for the SUBSTITUTE function.

c. Click **cell K3** to enter it in the Text box.

d. Press **Tab** and type **WILKS** in the Old_text box.

e. Press **Tab** and type **Davis** in the New_text box and click **OK**

You are replacing her prior last name with her married name Davis.

> **TROUBLESHOOTING:** Note that the SUBSTITUTE function is case sensitive. Because you are referencing WILKS in cell K3, it must be entered exactly the same in the function.

f. Click the warning box that appears next to **cell C3** and click **Ignore Error**.

The warning box appears because cell C3 no longer contains the PROPER function that is used in the rest of the column. This was done on purpose; therefore it is OK to ignore the warning message.

g. Save the workbook.

STEP 4 ▶▶ **USE OTHER TEXT FUNCTIONS**

In step 1 you separated city and state into two columns. You have decided to further separate the data by removing the zip code from the state column. There are several methods that could be used to complete this task and you have chosen to use the LEFT function. Refer to Figure 10.23 as you complete Step 4.

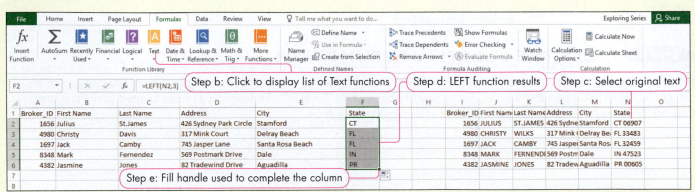

FIGURE 10.23 Use Other Text Functions

Excel 2016, Windows 10, Microsoft Corporation

a. Select the **range F2:F6** and press **Delete**.

b. Click **cell F2**, click **Text** in the Function Library group, and then select **LEFT**.

  The Function Arguments dialog box opens so that you can specify the arguments for the LEFT function.

c. Click **cell N2** to enter it in the Text box.

d. Press **Tab**, type **3** in the Num_chars box, and then click **OK**.

  The LEFT function displays the leading space and first two characters of the data in cell N2.

e. Double-click the **fill handle** in **cell F2** to copy the function down completing column F.

f. Save the workbook.

STEP 5 ▶▶ USE FLASH FILL

While you have been using text functions, you want to experiment with using Flash Fill to add the zip code information. Refer to Figure 10.24 as you complete Step 4.

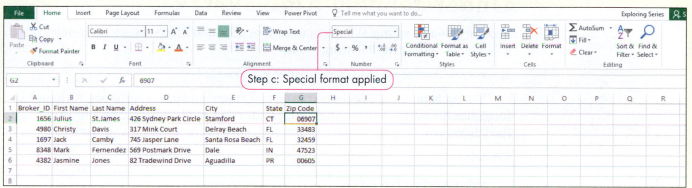

FIGURE 10.24 Final Results

Excel 2016, Windows 10, Microsoft Corporation

a. Click **cell O1**, type **Zip Code**, and press **Enter**.

b. Type **06907** and press **Ctrl+Enter**.

c. Click the **Home tab**. Click the **Number Format Dialog Box Launcher**, click **Special**, select **Zip Code**, and then click **OK**.

  You apply the zip code special format to ensure the zip codes display properly.

d. Click **Fill** in the Editing group and select **Flash Fill**.

  Flash fill completes the column by adding the remaining zip codes.

e. Select the **range O1:O6** and click **Copy** in the Clipboard group.

f. Click **cell G1** and click **Paste** in the Clipboard group.

  This copies the edited data to the correct location in the workbook.

g. Select the **range A1:G6**. Click **Copy**, click the **Paste arrow** in the Clipboard group, and then select **Values**.

  This copies the data and pastes it in the same location without the underlying functions.

h. Press **Esc**, select the **range I1:O6**, and then press **Delete**.

i. Save the workbook. Keep the workbook open if you plan to continue with the next Hands-On Exercise. If not, close the workbook and exit Excel.

XML

Organizations run a variety of applications on different hardware and operating systems. Individuals access the same data from different cities or countries, using laptops, desktops, smartphones, and other mobile devices. The hardware and software vary greatly, but they share a common element: They access and manipulate data. Faced with the challenge of creating data that people can use on these various systems, the World Wide Web Consortium (W3C) developed a solution to standardize file formats using Extensible Markup Language.

Extensible Markup Language (XML) is an industry standard for structuring data across applications, operating systems, and hardware. It enables data to be sent and retrieved between otherwise incompatible systems. XML describes the structure of data but not the appearance or formatting. Individual users, rather than a central authority, create the XML elements.

In this section, you will learn how to interpret XML tags and how to import XML data into an Excel worksheet.

Understanding XML Syntax

You are probably asking: What is markup language and what makes it extensible? Why is it flexible? Consider the following example:

3bedrooms/2bathrooms–$1,000permonth–(305)555-1234

You probably recognize the text as an advertisement for an apartment. Although you recognize the advertisement, the computer needs a method to interpret it. Using XML, the advertisement would appear as this, with no space between the tags and the data:

```
<Apartment>
    <Bedrooms>3</Bedrooms>
    <Bathrooms>2</Bathrooms>
    <Rent>$1,000</Rent>
    <Telephone>(305) 555-1234</Telephone>
</Apartment>
```

The data have been marked up with various tags (enclosed in angled brackets) to give it structure. A ***tag*** is a user-defined marker that identifies the beginning or ending of a piece of data in an XML document. Various tags are nested within one another; for example, the Bedrooms, Bathrooms, Rent, and Telephone tags are nested within the Apartment tag. The tags are relatively obvious and can be read by any XML-compliant application for further processing. The XML document does not contain any information about *how* to display the data; XML *describes* the data itself rather than the formatting of the data.

HTML uses a finite set of predefined tags, such as <b></b> and <i></i> for bold and italic, respectively. XML, however, is much more general because it has an infinite number of tags that are defined as necessary by the user in different applications. In other words, XML is ***extensible***, meaning it can be expanded as necessary to include additional data, such as adding elements for the apartment number.

Figure 10.25 displays an XML document that was created in Notepad. The question mark and angled brackets are part of the optional ***XML declaration***, which specifies the XML version and character encoding used. The document also contains a comment in the second line to identify the author. The indentation throughout the document makes it easier to read but is not required.

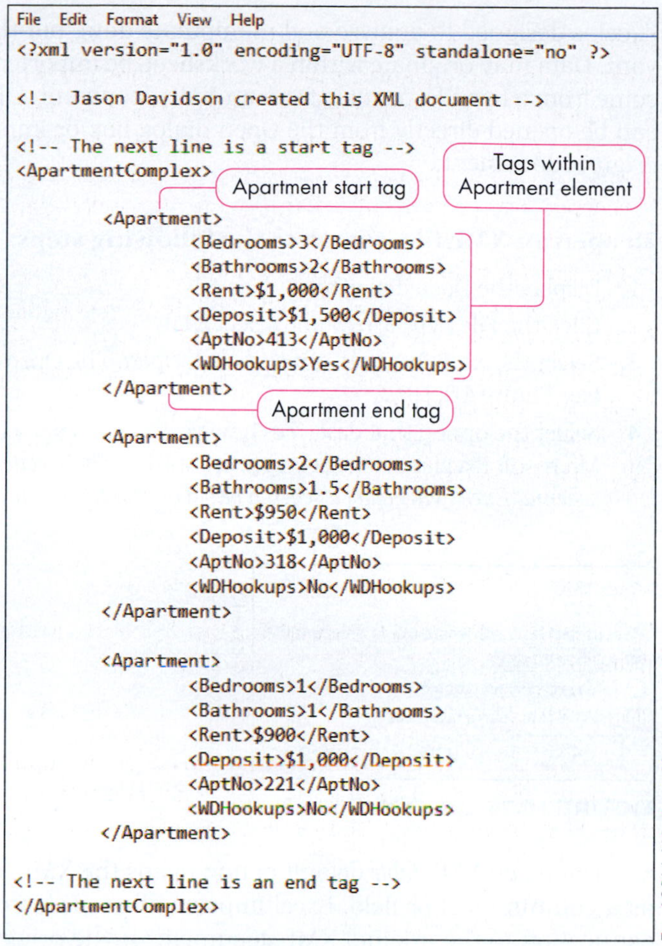

```
 File  Edit  Format  View  Help
<?xml version="1.0" encoding="UTF-8" standalone="no" ?>

<!-- Jason Davidson created this XML document -->

<!-- The next line is a start tag -->
<ApartmentComplex>

        <Apartment>
                <Bedrooms>3</Bedrooms>
                <Bathrooms>2</Bathrooms>
                <Rent>$1,000</Rent>
                <Deposit>$1,500</Deposit>
                <AptNo>413</AptNo>
                <WDHookups>Yes</WDHookups>
        </Apartment>

        <Apartment>
                <Bedrooms>2</Bedrooms>
                <Bathrooms>1.5</Bathrooms>
                <Rent>$950</Rent>
                <Deposit>$1,000</Deposit>
                <AptNo>318</AptNo>
                <WDHookups>No</WDHookups>
        </Apartment>

        <Apartment>
                <Bedrooms>1</Bedrooms>
                <Bathrooms>1</Bathrooms>
                <Rent>$900</Rent>
                <Deposit>$1,000</Deposit>
                <AptNo>221</AptNo>
                <WDHookups>No</WDHookups>
        </Apartment>

<!-- The next line is an end tag -->
</ApartmentComplex>
```

Callouts: Apartment start tag · Tags within Apartment element · Apartment end tag

Excel 2016, Windows 10, Microsoft Corporation

FIGURE 10.25 XML Coding

- An XML document is divided into elements. Each ***element*** contains a start tag, an end tag, and the associated data. The ***start tag*** contains the name of the element, such as Rent. The ***end tag*** contains the name of the element preceded by a slash, such as /Rent.

- XML tags are case sensitive. In Figure 10.25, <Rent> and </Rent> use the same case. However, <Rent> $1,000 </rent> would be incorrect because the start and end tags are not the same case.

- XML elements can be nested to any depth, but each inner element (or child) must be entirely contained within the outer element (or parent). For example, the Bedrooms and Rent elements are nested within the Apartment element.

- Indenting indicates the hierarchy structure. For example, elements for a particular month are indented one or two levels so that the start <Month> and end </Month> tags stand out. The outer element tags are aligned for readability.

- An XML comment is optional data that provide explanatory information about the coding. An XML comment starts with <!-- and ends with -->.

TIP: CREATING AN XML DOCUMENT

Typically, people use Notepad, or any text editor, to create an XML document, switch to a Web browser, such as Microsoft Edge, to view the XML document, and then switch back to Notepad to make any changes.

Importing XML Data into Excel

STEP 1 ▶▶ Excel is designed to analyze and manipulate data, but the source of that data is irrelevant. Data may originate within a worksheet, be imported from an Access table or query, come from a text file, or come from an XML document. Like a text file, an XML document can be opened directly from the Open dialog box or imported with a connection to the original document.

> **To open an XML file, complete the following steps:**
>
> 1. Display the Open dialog box.
> 2. Click the File Type arrow and select XML Files.
> 3. Select the XML file you want and click Open. The Open XML dialog box opens (see Figure 10.26).
> 4. Select the option that describes how you want to open the file and click OK. If the Microsoft Excel message box appears stating *The specified XML source does not refer to a schema. Excel will create a schema based on the XML source data*, click OK.

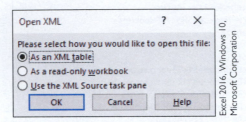

FIGURE 10.26 Open XML Dialog Box

The *As an XML table* default option opens the XML file as a table with each element as a column label or field. Excel imports all records from the source file without any connection to the original XML document. If the original XML document is changed, those changes will not be updated in the Excel workbook. You may have to format some imported XML data. For example, if you import the XML data shown in Figure 10.25, the monetary values import as text. You will then have to apply a number format to use the data as values.

If you select the *Use the XML Source task pane* option, Excel opens a new workbook and displays the XML Source task pane on the right side (see Figure 10.27). The data do not import by default.

> **To map XML elements to worksheet cells and import data, complete the following steps:**
>
> 1. Drag an element to the desired cell in the worksheet. You do not have to use all XML elements, and you can drag them in any sequence.
> 2. Right-click on a cell that contains XML data and point to XML.
> 3. Select Import, find the XML file containing the data you want to import, and then click OK. Excel imports the data that match the elements and sequence you specified.

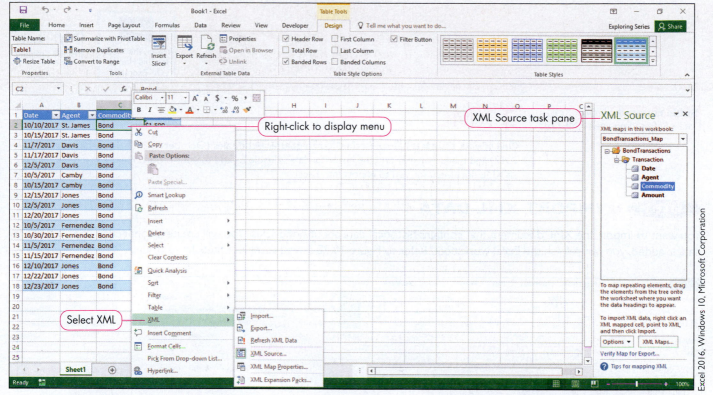

FIGURE 10.27 XML Elements Mapped

> **To import XML data while maintaining the connection, complete the following steps:**
>
> 1. Click the Data tab, and click Get External Data in the Get & Transform group. Click From Other Sources in the Get External Data group, and then select From XML Data Import.
> 2. Select the XML document you want to import in the Select Data Source dialog box and click Open.
> 3. Select the desired options from the Import Data dialog box and click OK. Excel imports the XML data in the sequence of the original XML file and displays the XML Source task pane on the right side.

Refresh Imported XML Data

STEP 2 ❯❯ If XML data is imported into Excel instead of opened, the connection is maintained and will be updated when the data is refreshed. There are several methods to refresh the connection.

> **To refresh data that is imported from XML, complete one of the following steps:**
>
> - Click the Data tab and click Refresh All in the Connections group.
> - Click the Data tab, click Connections, select the XML document, and click Refresh.
> - Right-click the data table that was created from the XML document and select Refresh.

Quick Concepts

7. What is the benefit of using XML? *p. 638*

8. What is the standard formatting for elements within an element? *p. 639*

9. If you want to maintain a connection to the original XML file, how should you import it? *p. 641*

Hands-On Exercises

Skills covered: Import XML Data • Refresh Imported XML Data

3 XML

One of your assistants has researched fourth-quarter bond sales (October 1, 2017 through December 31, 2017) and thinks you may find the historical data valuable to add to your report. He has saved the data in an XML document for you to import into Excel.

STEP 1 ▶▶ IMPORT XML DATA

You want to import the XML document that contains historical data about bond sales. You will create a connection so that if more data is added, you can refresh the Excel worksheet. Refer to Figure 10.28 as you complete Step 1.

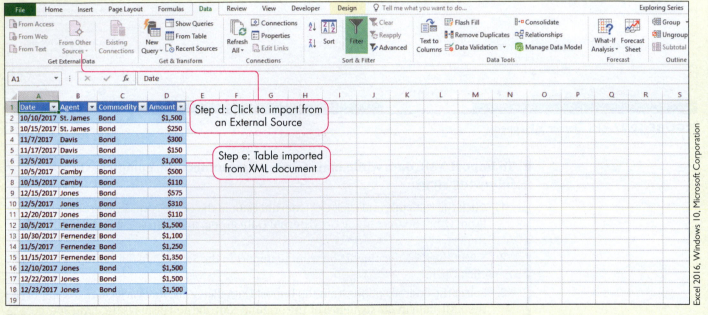

FIGURE 10.28 XML Imported

a. Open *e10h2Commodities_LastFirst* if you closed it at the end of Hands-On Exercise 2, and save it as **e10h3Commodities_LastFirst**, changing h2 to h3.

b. Locate the file *e10h3FourthQuarter* in your student data files, copy the file, and rename the copy **e10h3FourthQuarter_LastFirst**.

c. Click **New sheet**, rename the worksheet **Historical Bond Sales,** and then select **cell A1**.

d. Click the **Data tab**. Click **From Other Sources** and select **From XML Data Import**.

The Select Data Source dialog box opens.

e. Select *e10h3FourthQuarter_LastFirst.xml* from your data files, click **Open**, click **OK** in the message box informing you that the XML source does not refer to a schema, and then click **OK** in the Import Data dialog box.

The data is imported into the Historical Bond Sales worksheet.

f. Select the **range D2:D18**, click the **yellow warning icon**, and then select **Convert to Number**.

The number values in column D were originally imported as text. Clicking Convert to Number removes the error and converts the data to numerical values.

g. Save the workbook.

You notice that the data that was imported was created before broker Christy Davis was married and still uses her maiden name Wilks. You realize this should be corrected. You will modify the original XML document, save the changes, and refresh the data. Refer to Figure 10.29 as you complete Step 2.

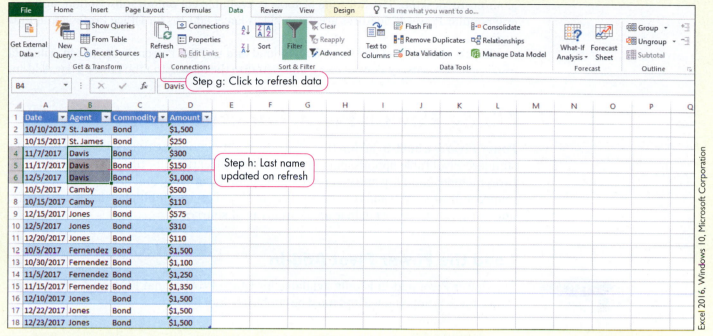

FIGURE 10.29 XML File Changes Updated in Excel Workbook

a. Right-click the **Windows Start menu**, click **Search**, and in the search box type **Notepad**, and open Notepad.

You will use Notepad to edit the original XML file.

b. Click **File**, click **Open**, and then click the **File Type arrow**.

c. Select **All Files**, locate your student data files, and then select *e10h3FourthQuarter_LastFirst*.

d. Click **Edit** and select **Replace** to open the Replace dialog box.

> **TROUBLESHOOTING:** Be careful when editing the XML document that you do not delete any of the tags. If so, you will need to retype the tags to avoid error messages.

e. Type **Wilks** in the Find what box, type **Davis** in the Replace with box, click the **Match case check box** to select it, and then click **Replace All**.

You replace Christy's prior name with her new last name Davis.

f. Click **Cancel**, save the XML document in Notepad, and then close Notepad.

> **TROUBLESHOOTING:** If you are unable to save the XML file in Notepad, close the Excel workbook, save the XML file in Notepad, and then open the Excel workbook again.

g. Return to Excel. Click **cell A2**, click the **Data tab**, and then click the **Refresh All arrow** in the Connections group.

h. Select **Refresh**.

Excel refreshes only the XML data in the workbook.

i. Select the **range D2:D18**, click the **error icon**, and then select **Convert to Number**.

j. Save the workbook. Keep the workbook open if you plan to continue with Hands-On Exercise 4. If not, close the workbook and exit Excel.

Power Add-Ins

Microsoft's **Power BI** (Business Intelligence) is an online application suite designed to help users manage, supplement, visualize, and analyze data. A free visualization application, Microsoft's Power BI desktop is available for download at https://powerbi.microsoft.com/en-us/desktop. The full suite of tools is available via online subscription, and several popular Power BI features are available as Excel add-ins for Office Professional Plus users.

In this section, you will learn how to load and use the Power Pivot Add-in. You will also import data using Power Query, and visualize the data using the Power View Add-in.

Using Power Pivot Functionality

Power Pivot is a built-in add-in that offers the key functionality that is included in Excel's standard PivotTable options, plus a variety of useful features for the power user. Key features include: handling and compressing big data, identifying and displaying key performance indicators, the ability to create relationships between multiple related data tables, and the ability to import data from a vast array of sources.

Load the Power Pivot Add-In

 The Power Pivot add-in is only available for Office Professional Plus users. By default, Power Pivot is not enabled and must be enabled before use.

To enable the Power Pivot add-in, complete the following steps:

1. Click the File tab and click Open Other Workbooks.
2. Select Options.
3. Select Add-Ins.
4. Select COM Add-Ins in the Manage box and click Go.
5. Click to select Microsoft Office Power Pivot and click OK.

Import Data with Power Pivot

 Excel's default functionality enables you to import data from a variety of sources such as text files, Access databases, and XML. Power Pivot expands this functionality to add a variety of different import source options.

To import data using Power Pivot, complete the following steps.

1. Click the Power Pivot tab.
2. Click Manage in the Data Model group.
3. Click Get External Data and select the desired data source.
4. Select the file path from the Table Import Wizard and click Finish.

See Table 10.2 for a full list of Power Pivots import capabilities.

TABLE 10.2	Power Pivot Import Options
From Database	From SQL Server
	From Access
	From Analysis Services or Power Pivot
From Data Services	From Microsoft Azure Marketplace
	Suggest Related Data
	From OData Data Feed
From Other Sources	Microsoft SQL Server
	Microsoft SQL Azure
	Microsoft SQL Server Parallel Data Warehouse
	Microsoft Access
	Oracle
	Teradata
	Sybase
	Informix
	IBM DB2
	Others (OLEDB/ODBC)
Multidimensional Sources	Microsoft Analysis Services
Data Feeds	Report
	From Microsoft Azure Marketplace
	Suggest Related Data
	Other Feeds
Text Files	Excel File
	Text File

Pearson Education, Inc.

Create Relationships with Power Pivot

A key feature of Power Pivot is the ability to create relationships among multiple data sources that share common fields. For example, suppose that one table contains commodity broker names and IDs. A related table contains the sales dates and sales amounts but only the brokers' IDs to avoid the mistyping of a person's name. If you want to create a separate dataset that includes just the broker names and related sales data, you need to pull the data from two tables. So the data aligns properly, you must create a relationship based on a common field (such as ID) between the tables. A **relationship** is an association between two related tables where both tables contain a related field of data, such as IDs.

After you create a relationship between tables, you can use Power Pivot to create a PivotTable that uses the common fields to display the sales reps' names instead of their IDs in the final data table.

Create a PivotTable with Power Pivot

After you create a relationship between the tables, you can use Power Pivot to create a PivotTable based on the related tables The PivotTable created with Power Pivot will have the same functionality as if it were created from one set of data or a single data table without relationships.

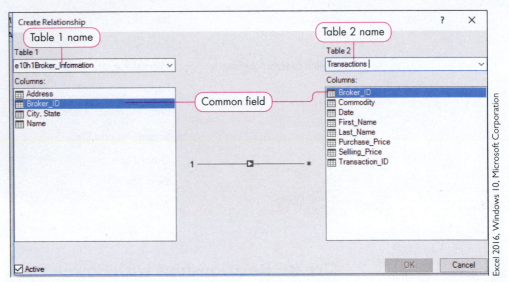

FIGURE 10.30 Create Relationships with Power Pivot

Importing Data with Power Query

Power Query is a new feature added to Excel 2016. *Power Query* is a business intelligence tool that provides the user with the ability to import, shape, cleanse, and query data. While some of the import capabilities overlap with Excel's basic external import options, the true benefit of Power Query is in its ability to manipulate the data before import. For example, suppose you want to import all transactions for the year that involved savings bonds. If all commodity sales are stored in an Access table you would have no choice but to import all transactions and filter after the import, or create a query in Access before importing. In contrast, Power Query enables you to select exactly the information you want to import before it is placed in an Excel worksheet. Furthermore, you can add additional data from multiple sources, edit formatting, and add calculated fields before completing the import.

> **To import data using Power Query (as shown in Figure 10.31), complete the following steps:**
>
> 1. Click the Data tab.
> 2. Click New Query in the Get & Transform group.
> 3. Select the desired data source.
> 4. Format the import data in the Query Editor to desired criteria (see Figure 10.32).
> 5. Click Close & Load.

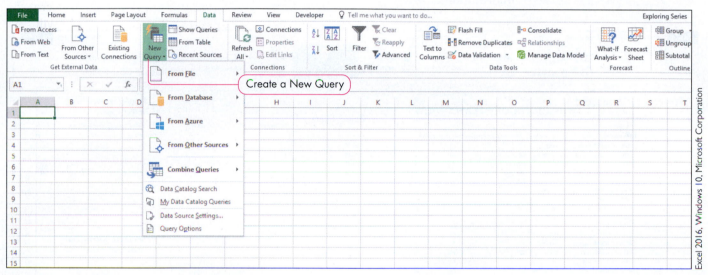

FIGURE 10.31 Create a Query with Power Query

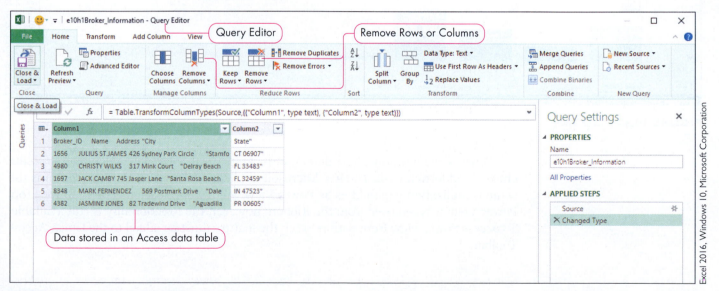

FIGURE 10.32 Shape Data with Power Query

Visualizing Data with Power View

Power View is an Excel add-in that enables the user to create a visual dashboard with the functionality of a PivotTable. Similar to Power Pivot and Power Query, Power View utilizes data from multiple data sources using relationships. Power Views are displayed on the Canvas. The **Canvas** is the area that contains the dashboard data visualizations. **Visualizations** are data fields and tables added to the Power View canvas. As shown in Figure 10.33, once a Power View is created, it can be filtered to only display desired information.

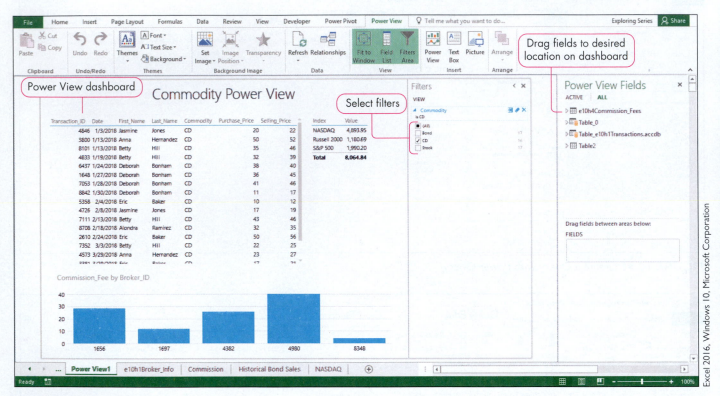

FIGURE 10.33 Power View

Power View not only filters data, it also can perform aggregate calculations, create charts, and format data. The free Microsoft application Power BI Desktop contains the same visualization capabilities as Power View. With the release of Power BI Desktop, Power View was removed from the Ribbon; however, the functionality is still available. To access Power View from within Excel, the feature must be added to the Quick Access Toolbar.

To create a Power View, complete the following steps:

1. Load the Power View add-in.
2. Add Power View to the Quick Access Toolbar.
3. Select the data you want to summarize.
4. Click Power View on the Quick Access Toolbar.
5. Drag the required fields from the Power View Fields box to the desired location on the Power View dashboard.
6. Click each field that contains data in the Power View Fields window and set the desired aggregate calculations.
7. Add additional formatting as needed.

Quick Concepts

10. What is the benefit of using Power Pivot? *p. 644*

11. Why would you use Power Query over Excel's external import features? *p. 646*

12. When would you use Power View instead of a PivotTable? *p. 648*

Watch the Video for this Hands-On Exercise!

MyITLab®
HOE4 Training

Skills covered: Load the Power Pivot Add-In • Import Data with Power Pivot • Create Relationships with Power Pivot • Create a PivotTable with Power Pivot • Import Data with Power Query • Visualize Data with Power View

4 Power Add-Ins

As your last step, you have decided to enhance your report with Excel Power Add-Ins. You will import commission fee information and create a relationship to existing data in a PivotTable using Power Pivot, import stock prices using Power Query, and create a dashboard using Power View.

STEP 1 ›› LOAD POWER ADD-INS

Your business computer does not currently have any of Microsoft's Power Add-Ins enabled. Your first step is to enable the Power Pivot and Power View Add-Ins. Refer to Figure 10.34 as you complete Step 1.

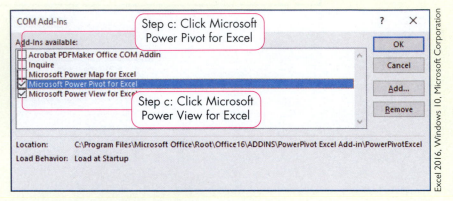

FIGURE 10.34 Enable Power Add-Ins

a. Open *e10h3Commodities_LastFirst* if you closed it at the end of Hands-On Exercise 3, and save it as **e10h4Commodities_LastFirst**, changing h3 to h4.

b. Click the **Insert tab**, click the **My Add-Ins arrow** in the Add-ins group, select **Manage Other Add-Ins**. Select **COM Add-Ins** from the Manage box, and click **Go**.

c. Select **Microsoft Power Pivot for Excel** and **Microsoft Power View for Excel**, and click **OK.** Click Continue if you receive the Enable Power View Reports prompt.

The Power Pivot tab will display on the ribbon and Power View must be added to the Quick Access Toolbar.

d. Click the **File tab**, click **Options**, and then select **Quick Access Toolbar**.

e. Select **Power View Tab** from the *Choose commands from:* box, select **Insert a Power View Report**, and then click **Add**. Click **OK**.

With the development of the Power BI Desktop download, Power View was removed from the Ribbon. To Access Power View directly from within Excel without an additional download, the Power View button is added to the Quick Access Toolbar.

f. Save the workbook.

STEP 2 ›› CREATE A PIVOTTABLE USING POWER PIVOT

You are interested in the amount of commission earned during the first week of the new year. You want to add the commission information to a PivotTable for more detailed analysis. You will use Power Pivot to create the PivotTable because the data is stored as a text file and will be displayed with information from an Access database. Refer to Figure 10.35 as you complete Step 2.

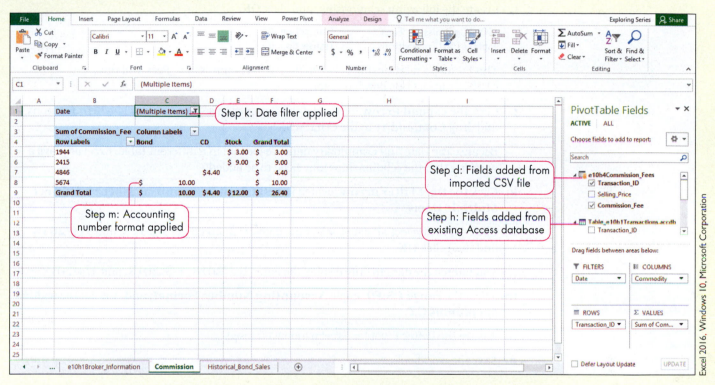

FIGURE 10.35 Create a PivotTable Using Power Pivot

a. Click the **Power Pivot tab**, click **Manage** in the Data Model group, and click the **Home tab** in the Power Pivot for Excel window.

The Power Pivot for Excel window opens.

b. Click **Get External Data**, click **From Other Sources**, scroll down, and then click **Text File**. Click **Next** to advance to the next step.

The Table Import Wizard opens to import the CSV text file.

c. Click **Browse** in the Table Import Wizard, select **Comma Separated Files** from the File Type box, and then select *e10h4Commission_Fees.csv*. Click **Open** to advance to the next step.

d. Ensure that Comma is selected from the Column Separator box, and Use first row as column headers is selected, click **Finish**, and then click **Close**.

You will return to the Power Pivot for Excel window and the external data will be displayed for additional manipulation.

e. Click **Home**, click **PivotTable** in the PivotTable group, and then select **New Worksheet**.

f. Click **OK** and rename the worksheet **Commission**.

A new worksheet is created with a blank PivotTable.

g. Click the **expand arrow** for the e10h4Commission_Fees table in the PivotTable Fields task pane, drag the **Transaction_ID** field to the ROWS box, and **Commission_Fee** to the VALUES box.

The Transaction_ID numbers appear as row headings in the table and the corresponding commission fee appears in the second column of the PivotTable. Next you will add the related fields from a different data source.

h. Click the **expand arrow** for the database imported earlier, Table_e10h1Transactions, drag the **Date field** to the FILTERS box, and then click **CREATE** in the PivotTable Fields Relationship warning message.

i. Create the following relationship, and click **OK**.

| e10h4Commission_Fees | Transaction_ID |
| Table_e10h1Transactions | Transaction_ID |

This creates a relationship between the e10h4Commission_Fees and the e10h1Transactions database table.

j. Click the **expand arrow** for the database imported earlier, Table_e10h1Transactions, and drag **Commodity** to the COLUMNS box.

Because the Date and Commodity data are located in a different table, Excel displays a warning that the relationships may need to be added.

k. Click the **Date Filter arrow** located in **cell C1**, click **Expand**, and then click **Select Multiple Items**.

l. Click **All** to deselect all dates, select the dates **1/2/2018**, **1/3/2018**, and **1/4/2018**, and then click **OK**.

You filtered the data to only display the dates 1/2/2018, 1/3/2018, and 1/4/2018.

m. Select the **range C5:F9**, apply **Accounting Number Format**, and AutoFit the widths of **columns C:F**.

n. Ensure the Power Pivot for Excel window is closed.

o. Save the workbook.

You want to import data into your report to show the current value and change information of the NASDAQ, S&P 500, and Russell 2000. To complete this task, you will use Power Query to create the connection and edit the data before import. Refer to Figure 10.36 as you complete Step 3.

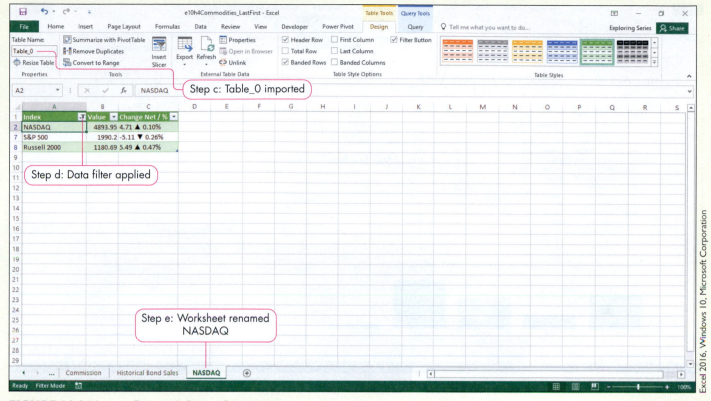

FIGURE 10.36 Import Data with Power Query

a. Click the **Data tab**. Click **New Query** in the Get & Transform group, point to **From Other Sources**, and then select **From Web**.

   The From Web dialog box opens, enabling you to enter a URL.

b. Type **http://www.nasdaq.com** and click **OK**.

   The Power Query Navigator screen opens displaying the tables that have information available to import.

c. Click **Table 0** and click **Load**.

   Table_0 is imported into Excel and is now available to be edited via Query Tools.

d. Click the **filter arrow** in **cell A1**. Filter the data to only display **NASDAQ**, **Russell 2000**, and **S&P 500**. Click **OK**.

e. Rename the worksheet **NASDAQ**.

f. Save the workbook.

As your last step, you have decided to build a dashboard to better visualize your data. To complete the task, you will use the existing connections and the new Excel add-in, Power View. Refer to Figure 10.37 as you complete Step 4.

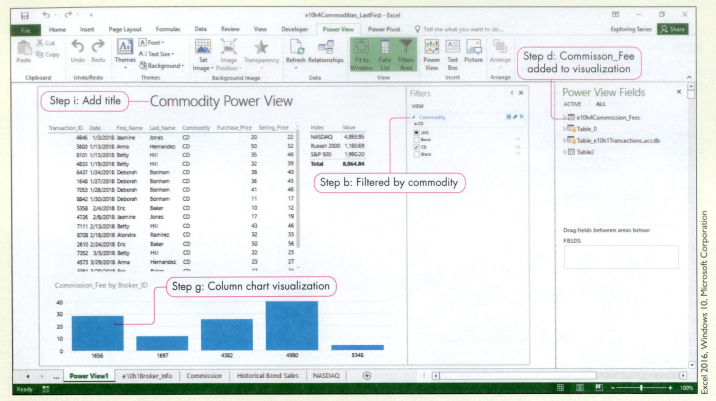

FIGURE 10.37 Create Power View

a. Click the **Transactions worksheet**, click **Power View** on the Quick Access Toolbar.

A Power View will be created with the original table displayed.

b. Click the **expand arrow** for Table_e10h1Transactions.accdb, add the **Selling Price** field to the existing visualization, add the **Commodity** field to the FILTERS area, and click **CD**.

The selling price appears in the existing data table and the entire dataset is now filtered to only display CD information.

c. Click **All** in the Power View Fields task pane, click the **expand arrow** for Table_0. Drag the Index and Value fields to the upper-right corner of the Power View.

d. Click the **filter arrow** for the newly added data, and select **NASDAQ**, **Russell 2000**, and **SP 500**. Resize as needed.

Value information for the NASDAQ, Russell 2000, and S&P 500 are now displayed.

e. Add the **Broker_ID** from the Table_e10h1Transactions.accdb to the lower-left corner of the Power View, then add **Commission Fee** from the e10h4Commission_Fees table next to Broker_ID.

A new table is displayed in the Power View showing Broker ID and Commission fee.

f. Click **Broker_ID** arrow in the FIELDS area of the Power View Fields window and select **Do Not Summarize Field**.

You stopped the newly created table from aggregating by Broker_ID number.

g. Ensure the new visualization is still selected, click **Column Chart,** and then select **Stacked Column**.

The Commission_Fee by Broker_ID table is now displayed as a column chart.

h. Resize the column chart to fill the lower half of the Power View.

i. Click the **Power View title** and type **Commodity Power View**.

j. Close the Workbook Query task pane and the Power View Fields task pane.

k. Create a footer with your name on the left side, the sheet name code in the center, and the file name code on the right side of all worksheets excluding the Power View.

l. Save and close the file. Based on your instructor's directions, submit e10h4Commodities_LastFirst.

Chapter Objectives Review

After reading this chapter, you have accomplished the following objectives:

1. Import data from external sources.

- Import a text file: Text files contain delimiters to separate data. A tab-delimited file is a text file that uses tabs to separate data, and a comma-separated value file is a text file that uses commas to separate data. The Text Import Wizard guides you through importing data and selecting the delimiter.

- Import an Access database table or query: You can copy data from an Access table into Excel. If you want to maintain a connection to the Access table, import it using the Get External Data command. You can then select the table or query, how to view the data, and where to place it.

- Import data from other sources: You can import data from other sources, such as an SQL server or from Windows Azure Marketplace.

2. Manage connections.

- The Workbook Connections dialog box lists the connections within the workbook. You can click a connection to see where it is located in the workbook.

- Set connection properties: Display the external Data Range Properties dialog box to specify the query definition, refresh control, and other attributes for a specific data import.

- Click Refresh All to refresh all connections or click the Refresh All arrow to select a specific refresh option.

3. Convert text to columns.

- When you import data or receive a workbook, data might be stored in one column that would be easier to use if in multiple columns. Use the Text to Columns command to separate data into multiple columns. Specify a delimiter and format the columns in the Convert Text to Columns Wizard.

4. Manipulate text with functions.

- Combine text with the CONCATENATE function: This function joins two or more text strings into one text string.

- Change text case with text functions: Use the PROPER, LOWER, and UPPER functions to control the case of text.

- Use the SUBSTITUTE function: The SUBSTITUTE function substitutes new text for old text in a text string.

- Use other text functions: Other useful text functions include TRIM, LEFT, RIGHT, and MID.

5. Use Flash Fill.

- The Flash Fill feature enables you to enter data into two or more cells that use part of data in a previous column. The data in the previous column must be similarly structured. The Flash Fill command can then be used to quickly fill the new column with the same type of data typed in the first cell.

6. Understand XML syntax.

- Extensible Markup Language (XML) is a standard file format that enables data sharing across hardware, operating systems, and applications.

- An XML document contains user-defined tags to mark the beginning and ending of data elements, such as a person's name.

- The start tag contains the name of the element, such as <Rent>, and the end tag contains a slash and the element name, such as </Rent>. Tags are case sensitive; that is, <Rent> is different from <rent>.

7. Import XML data into Excel.

- Use the Open dialog box to import XML data into a new blank workbook.

- Refresh XML data: Once a connection has been created to an external XML document, the data can be refreshed if the original document is edited.

8. Use Power Pivot functionality.

- Load the Power Pivot add-in: Power Pivot is not loaded as part of the default installation of Excel. In order to access the add-in, it must first be loaded.

- Import data with Power Pivot: One of the benefits of Power Pivot is its ability to import data from a variety of sources. This allows you to easily build a PivotTable based on multiple data sources.

- Create relationships with Power Pivot: Power Pivot has the ability to create relationships between multiple data sources that share common fields. This allows you to build PivotTables based on linked data without needing to combine the data sources.

- Create a PivotTable with Power Pivot: Power Pivot has the ability to create PivotTables that utilize multiple data sources linked through relationships with common fields.

9. Import data with Power Query.

- Power Query is a new add-in with Excel 2016. It enables you to import, query, and edit data.

10. Visualize data with Power View

- Power View is a new add-in with Excel 2016. It has the ability to create visualizations based on data tables in the worksheet. It also has the ability to utilize multiple external data sources as well as create relationships between data.

Key Terms Matching

Match the key terms with their definitions. Write the key term letter by the appropriate numbered definition.

a. Comma separated values (CSV) file

b. CONCATENATE function

c. Delimiter

d. Element

e. End tag

f. Extensible Markup Language (XML)

g. Fixed-width text file

h. Flash Fill

i. Importing

j. LOWER function

k. Power Pivot

l. PROPER function

m. Refresh

n. Start tag

o. SUBSTITUTE function

p. Tab-delimited file

q. Tag

r. Text file

s. UPPER function

1. _____ A function that converts all uppercase letters to lowercase. **p. 632**

2. _____ An XML component, including the start tag, an end tag, and associated data. **p. 639**

3. _____ An XML code indicating an element's starting point and element's name. **p. 639**

4. _____ A file that uses commas to separate text into columns. **p. 619**

5. _____ A file that contains letters, numbers, and symbols only; it does not contain formatting, sound, or video. **p. 618**

6. _____ A character used to separate data in a text file. **p. 618**

7. _____ A function that capitalizes the first letter of each word in a test string. **p. 632**

8. _____ A file that uses tabs to separate text into columns. **p. 618**

9. _____ An XML code indicating an element's ending point and name. **p. 639**

10. _____ A function that joins two or more text strings into one text string. **p. 631**

11. _____ An Excel add-in that has the ability to import data from various sources into PivotTables. **p. 644**

12. _____ A data-structuring standard for sharing data across applications, operating systems, and hardware. **p. 638**

13. _____ A user-defined marker that identifies the beginning or ending of a piece of XML data. **p. 638**

14. _____ A file that stores data in columns that have a specific number of characters designated for each column. **p. 619**

15. _____ The process of updating data in Excel to match current data in an external data source. **p. 625**

16. _____ The process of inserting data from one application or file into another. **p. 618**

17. _____ A function that inserts new text for old text in a text string. **p. 632**

18. _____ A feature that fills in data or values automatically based on one or two examples you enter. **p. 633**

19. _____ A function that converts text to uppercase letters. **p. 632**

Multiple Choice

1. A text file separates data by a special character called a:

   (a) Position holder.

   (b) Delimiter.

   (c) Column spacer.

   (d) Start tag.

2. Which of the following file formats can be imported using Power Query?

   (a) XML

   (b) HTML

   (c) CSV

   (d) All of the above

3. Which of the following Power Add-ins is best suited for editing data before import?

   (a) Power Pivot

   (b) Power View

   (c) Power Query

   (d) PivotTables

4. Your coworker created a workbook with a list of names and addresses. The state abbreviation and zip code are stored in one cell per customer, such as NC 27215. You need to be able to sort these data by postal code to use bulk-rate mailing. The appropriate Excel action is to:

   (a) Type 27215 in the cell to the right of NC 27215 and use Flash Fill.

   (b) Copy the data to another column and edit each cell to delete the state abbreviations.

   (c) Use the BREAK APART function to separate the state abbreviation and zip code.

   (d) Insert a new column and retype the postal codes.

5. A workbook contains addresses in column C. The addresses use commas after the street, city, and state, such as 129 Elm Street, Burlington, NC, 27215. Column D contains the phone number. You instruct Excel to divide the data into multiple columns using comma delimiters. You successfully divide the column into four columns. What happens to the phone numbers in column D?

   (a) Excel inserts new columns for each comma so the phone numbers will move to column G.

   (b) The phone numbers are overwritten by the cities.

   (c) Nothing will happen to the phone numbers.

   (d) The phone numbers will be converted to commas.

6. You have client last names stored in column A and the date of their first purchase in column B. You would like to create a custom account number by combining the client's last

name and date. What function would you use to complete the task?

   (a) CONCATENATE

   (b) LEFT

   (c) SUBSTITUTE

   (d) PROPER

7. You have a dataset that contains sales information including transactions and corresponding buyer names. One buyer, Sandy Yang, has recently married and would like to have her last name changed to Benson. Which function would you use to complete the task?

   (a) LEFT

   (b) SUBSTITUTE

   (c) PROPER

   (d) UPPER

8. One advantage of using XML data is that:

   (a) Data are not dependent on a specific operating system.

   (b) XML contains instructions on how the data should be formatted.

   (c) People must use identical tag names.

   (d) Once coded, XML data cannot be expanded.

9. Which of the following tools is best suited for visualizing data?

   (a) Power Pivot

   (b) Power View

   (c) Power Query

   (d) PivotTables

10. Examine the following XML code and select the *true* statement.

    ```
    <internship>
        <position>Help Desk Trainee</position>
        <pay>10.50</pay>
        <payperiod>hour</payperiod>
        <hours>mornings</hours>
    </internship>
    ```

    (a) Position, pay, payperiod, and hours will appear as fields if imported into Excel.

    (b) The nested tags (position, pay, payperiod, and hours) have no connection to the internship.

    (c) Only applicants available in the mornings will be considered.

    (d) Adding <b> before and after <hours> will create boldfaced type.

Practice Exercises

1 Earline's Bakery

You are the head baker for Earline's bakery, a local bakery that specializes in gluten-free desserts. You have decided to perform analysis on your sales information and product inventory using Power Add-Ins in Excel. You will import data from various sources into an Excel workbook, and then use Power Pivot to create a PivotTable that focuses on sales for your bakery bonanza sale (6/12/2018), Power Query to edit import data, and Power View to create a dashboard. Refer to Figure 10.38 as you complete this exercise.

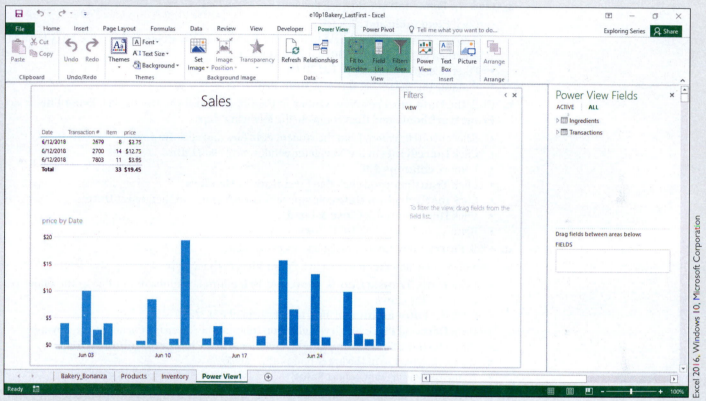

FIGURE 10.38 Earline's Bakery

a. Start a new blank workbook and save it as **e10p1Bakery_LastFirst**.

b. Click the **File tab**, click **Options**, and click **Add-ins**.

c. Select **Com Add-ins** from the Manage box and click **Go**.

d. Select **Microsoft Power Pivot for Excel** and **Microsoft Power View for Excel** and click **OK**.

e. Click the **File tab**, click **Options**, and click the **Quick Access Toolbar**.

f. Select **Power View Tab** from the *Choose commands from:* box, select **Insert a Power View Report**, and click **Add**.

g. Click **OK** and rename Sheet1 as **Products** and save the workbook.

h. Click the **Data tab** and click **From Text** in the Get External Data group.

i. Locate *e10p1Bakery.csv* in your student data files and click **Import**.

j. Click the **My data has headers checkbox** to select it, click **Next**.

k. Ensure Comma on step 2 of the Text Import Wizard is selected, and click **Finish**.

l. Place the data in **cell A1** of the Products worksheet and click **OK**.

m. Copy the **range B2:B16** and paste it in the **range E2:E16**.

n. Click **cell B2**, type **=TRIM(E2)**, and then use the **Fill handle** to copy the function down to **cell B16**.

o. Select the **range B2:B16**, press **Ctrl+C**.

p. Click the **Home tab**, click the **Paste arrow** in the Clipboard group, and select **Values**.

q. Delete the **range E2:E16**.

r. Click the **Power Pivot tab**, click **Manage** in the data model group, and do the following:

- Click **Home**, click **Get External Data**, click **From Database**, and then select **From Access**.
- Click **Browse**, select *e10p1Bakery.accdb* from the student data files, and click **Open**.
- Click **Next**, click **Next** again, click **Finish**, and then click **Close**.

s. Click the **Home tab** and do the following:

- Click **PivotTable** and click **OK**.
- Add the **Transaction #** field to the ROWS area, add the **Price field** to the VALUES area, and then add the **Date field** to the FILTERS area.
- Filter to display the date **6/12/2018**.
- Rename the worksheet **Bakery_Bonanza**.

t. Click the **Data tab**, click **New Query** in the Get & Transform group, click **From File**, select **From Workbook**, and then complete the following steps:

- Select *e10p1Inventory* from the student data files and click **Import**.
- Click **Ingredients** in the Navigator window and click **Edit**.
- Remove **columns 4:9**.
- Click **Transform** and click **Use First Row As Headers**.
- Click the **Expiration Date** column, click **Data Type**, and then select **Date**.
- Click **Home** and click **Close & Load**.
- Rename the worksheet **Inventory**.

u. Click **Power View tab** on the Quick Access Toolbar.

v. Complete the following steps to add a Power View to the workbook:

- Drag **Date**, **Transaction #**, **Item**, and **Price** into a visualization table in the upper-left corner of the canvas.
- Click the **Filter arrow** and filter to only display 6/12/2018.
- Drag **Date** and **Price** into a visualization table on the lower-left corner of the canvas.
- Click **Design**, click **Column Chart**, and then select **Clustered Column Chart**.
- Resize the chart to fit the lower half of the canvas.
- Name the Power View report **Sales**.

w. Save and close the workbook. Based on your instructors directions, submit e10p1Bakery_LastFirst.

2 New Employees

One of your jobs in the IT Department is to create email addresses for new employees. You received a text file containing a list of new employees. You will use text functions to convert the data to columns, create a list with surnames first in proper case, create a list of email addresses, and then create a list of alternate email addresses since your company provides two email addresses per person: one with an underscore between the first and last names and one with a period between the first and last names. Refer to Figure 10.39 as you complete this exercise.

	A	B	C	D	E
1	FIRST	LAST	NAMES	E-MAIL ADDRESS	ALTERNATE E-EMAIL ADDRESS
2	FRANK	BAILEY	Bailey, Frank	frank_bailey@ourcompany.com	frank.bailey@ourcompany.com
3	RENA	BERKOWICZ	Berkowicz, Rena	rena_berkowicz@ourcompany.com	rena.berkowicz@ourcompany.com
4	HEATHER	BOND	Bond, Heather	heather_bond@ourcompany.com	heather.bond@ourcompany.com
5	JEFF	BOROW	Borow, Jeff	jeff_borow@ourcompany.com	jeff.borow@ourcompany.com
6	ZEV	BOROW	Borow, Zev	zev_borow@ourcompany.com	zev.borow@ourcompany.com
7	ARIEL	BOROW	Borow, Ariel	ariel_borow@ourcompany.com	ariel.borow@ourcompany.com
8	LARRY	BRAGG	Bragg, Larry	larry_bragg@ourcompany.com	larry.bragg@ourcompany.com
9	HARRY	BUNTING	Bunting, Harry	harry_bunting@ourcompany.com	harry.bunting@ourcompany.com
10	JEFF	COTTRELL	Cottrell, Jeff	jeff_cottrell@ourcompany.com	jeff.cottrell@ourcompany.com
11	SARAH	COULTER	Coulter, Sarah	sarah_coulter@ourcompany.com	sarah.coulter@ourcompany.com
12	MARY	COULTER	Coulter, Mary	mary_coulter@ourcompany.com	mary.coulter@ourcompany.com

Excel 2016, Windows 10, Microsoft Corporation

FIGURE 10.39 Names and Email Addresses

a. Open Excel, click **Open Other Workbooks**, and navigate to your student data files.

b. Click the **File Type arrow**, select **Text Files**, and select *e10p2Names.txt*.

c. Click **Open**, click to select the **My data has headers check box**, and then click **Next**.

d. Deselect all check boxes in the Delimiters section and click **Next**.

e. Click **Text** in the Column data format section and click **Finish**.

f. Click the **File tab**, select **Save As**, and then click **Browse**.

g. Navigate to the location where you save your files, type **e10p2Names_LastFirst** in the File Name box, and click the **Save as type arrow**. Select **Excel Workbook** and click **Save**.

h. Click the **column A header**, click the **Data tab**, and then click **Text to Columns** in the Data Tools group to open the *Convert Text to Columns Wizard* dialog box.

i. Ensure Delimited is selected and click **Next**.

j. Select the **Space check box**, deselect the other check boxes, and then click **Next**.

k. Click **Text** to select the data format for the first column, click the **General column** in the Data preview section, and then click **Text** to select the data format for the second column.

l. Click **Finish** and select **columns A and B**.

m. Click the **Home tab**, click **Format** in the Cells group, and then select **AutoFit Column Width**.

n. Click **cell C1**, type **Last, First**, and then press **Ctrl+Enter**.

o. Click the **Home tab**, click **Fill** in the Editing group, and then select **Flash Fill** to fill the names down the column.

p. Select **column C**. Click the **Home tab**, click **Format** in the cells group, and then select **AutoFit Column Width**.

q. Click **cell D2**, type **=LOWER(CONCATENATE(A2,"_",B2,"@ourcompany.com"))**, and then press **Ctrl+Enter**. Copy the formula down the column, and Autofit column D.

r. Click **cell E2**, type **=SUBSTITUTE(D2,"_",".")**, and then press **Ctrl+Enter**. Copy the formula down the column and Autofit column E.

s. Type **NAMES** in **cell C1**, **EMAIL ADDRESS** in **cell D1**, and **ALTERNATE EMAIL ADDRESS** in **cell E1**. Bold and center the labels on the first row.

t. Click the **Page Layout tab**, click **Orientation,** and then select **Landscape orientation**.

u. Create a footer with your name on the left side, the sheet name code in the center, and the file name code on the right side for each worksheet.

v. Save and close the file. Based on your instructor's directions, submit e10p2Names_LastFirst.

3 Years on the Job

You manage a local bank in Kansas City. Employee retention is a concern. You are considering providing incentives to employees who have worked for the bank for more than five years. The HR director provided a list of employees and dates they were hired in an XML document. You will import the data into Excel and create a formula to calculate the number of years each employee has worked. In addition, you will count the number of employees by years on the job and apply a conditional format for employees who have worked more than five years. Refer to Figure 10.40 as you complete this exercise.

⊿	A	B	C	D
1	Input:			
2	Today's Date	8/1/2018		
3				
4	Counts:			
5	Less than 1 Year	0		
6	1-4.9 Years	7		
7	5 or More Years	5		
8				
9	Lastname ▼	Firstname ▼	DateHired ▼	Years ▼
10	Smith	Joe	4/1/2003	15.33
11	Dobsen	Doreen	4/1/2004	14.33
12	Martin	Cammie	12/10/2011	6.64
13	Lenz	Cherie	10/9/2015	2.81
14	Butterfield	Troy	6/18/2009	9.12
15	Anderson	Carl	5/1/2014	4.25
16	Jennings	Alesha	8/24/2013	4.94
17	Wilson	Kevin	7/11/2014	4.06
18	Forgan	Drew	9/27/2010	7.84
19	Rehm	Brad	3/11/2014	4.39
20	Barksdale	Claudia	12/15/2013	4.63
21	Galan	Nicole	1/15/2014	4.54
22				

Excel 2016, Windows 10, Microsoft Corporation

FIGURE 10.40 Names and Email Addresses

a. Copy *e10p3People* and rename the copied file as **e10p3People_LastFirst**.

b. Open *e10p3Employees* in Excel and save it as **e10p3Employees_LastFirst**.

c. Import the XML data by doing the following:
- Click the **Data tab**, click **Get External Data**, and then click **From Other Sources**.
- Select **From XML Data Import**, select *e10p3People_LastFirst*, and then click **Open**.
- Click **OK** in the Microsoft Excel message box.
- Type **A9** in the XML table in existing worksheet box and click **OK**.

d. Type **Years** in **cell D9** and press **Enter**.

e. Calculate and conditionally format the number of years by doing the following:
- Type **=YEARFRAC(C10,B$2)** in **cell D10** and press **Ctrl+Enter**.
- Select the **range D10:D21** and apply the **Comma Style**.
- Click **Conditional Formatting** in the Styles group on the Home tab, point to **Highlight Cells Rules**, select **Greater Than**, type **4.99** in the Format cells that are Greater Than dialog box, and then click **OK**.

f. Enter functions to count the number of employees by year by doing the following:
- Type **=COUNTIF(D10:D21,"<1")** in **cell B5**.
- Type **=COUNTIFS(D10:D21,">=1",D10:D21,"<5")** in **cell B6**.
- Type **=COUNTIF(D10:D21,">=5")** in **cell B7**.

g. Double-click between the column A and B column headings to increase the width of column A.

h. Save the workbook. Open *e10p3People_LastFirst* in Notepad. Change Cheri Lenz's hire date to **10/9/2015**. Change Drew Forgan's hire date to **9/27/2010**. Be careful not to delete any XML tags. Press **Ctrl+S** to save the XML document and then close it.

i. Click the **Data tab** and click **Refresh All** in the Connections group. If warning messages appear, click **OK** in each message box and save the workbook. Autofit the width of column A.

j. Create a footer with your name on the left side, the sheet name code in the center, and the file name code on the right side of the worksheet.

k. Save and close the workbook. Based on your instructor's directions, submit the following:
e10p3People_LastFirst
e10p3Employees_LastFirst

Mid-Level Exercises

1 DOW Jones Industrial Average

FROM SCRATCH

You are an intern for Hicks Financial, a small trading company located in Toledo, Ohio. Your intern supervisor wants you to create a report that details all trades made in February using current pricing information from the Dow Jones Index. To complete the task, you will import and shape data using Power Query. Then you will create data connections and visualizations of the data.

a. Open Excel and create a new blank workbook.

b. Save the workbook as **e10m1Dow_LastFirst**.

c. Use Power Query to import the Dow Index information located in Table 2 from the URL http://money.cnn.com/data/markets/dow.

d. Use the Query Editor to remove the columns **P/E, Volume, and YTD change**. Name the query **Dow** and load the data.

e. Name the newly created table **Dow** and name the worksheet **Current_Price**.

f. Use Power Query to import trade data located in the workbook *e10m1TradeInformation*.

g. Use the Query Editor to remove the **NULL value columns**, Use the **First Row As Headers**, and **split column 3** by the left most **space delimiter**.

h. Use the Query Editor to set the Date column Data Type to **Date**.

i. Use the Query Editor to rename the fourth column, **Company Name**. Load the data and rename the worksheet **Trades**.

j. Create a Power View with a Staked Bar Visualization that compares the trading price of Apple and Coca-Cola stocks.

k. Add the title **Trading Report**.

l. Create a footer for all worksheets with your name on the left side, the sheet name code in the center, and the file name code on the right side.

m. Save and close the workbook. Based on your instructor's directions, submit e10m1Dow_LastFirst.

2 Animal Shelter

ANALYSIS CASE

FROM SCRATCH

You manage a small animal shelter in Dayton, Ohio. Your assistant created an XML document that lists some of the recent small animals that your shelter took in. In particular, the XML document lists the animal type (such as cat); the age, sex, name, color, and date the animal was brought in; and the date the animal was adopted. You want to manage the data in an Excel worksheet, so you will create a link to the original data source in case the data changes.

a. Use Windows File Explorer to copy the *e10m2Animals* file and rename the copied file **e10m2Animals_LastFirst**.

b. Open the XML document *e10m2Animals_LastFirst* into Sheet1 of a new workbook. Rename Sheet1 **Animals**.

c. Save the workbook as **e10m2Shelter_LastFirst**.

DISCOVER

d. Create a PivotTable on a new worksheet from the imported data, placing the animal type and sex as row labels and counting names as values. Use the adoption date as a report filter and set a filter to show those animals that have *not* been adopted. Rename the PivotTable worksheet **PivotTable**.

e. Open *e10m2Animals_LastFirst* in Notepad. Edit the XML document by adding **3/25/2018** for the adoption date for Paws the cat. Edit Fido's data by entering his age: **6 months**. Edit Twerpy's color as **Orange**. Edit Misty's adoption date of **3/31/2018**. Save the XML file and close Notepad.

f. Display the Animals worksheet in Excel and refresh the connection. Display the PivotTable worksheet and refresh the PivotTable.

g. Display the PivotTable worksheet, type labels **Most Available Animals** and **Most Adopted Animals**, in the **range A15:B15**. Type answers to these questions in the **range B15:B16**.

h. Display the Animals worksheet and type **Name, Type** as a column label in **cell H1**. In **cell H2**, type **Paws, Cat**. Use Flash Fill to complete the rest of the data entry in this column. Adjust the column width to adequately display the data.

i. Create a footer with your name on the left side, the sheet name code in the center, and the file name code on the right side of each worksheet.

j. Save and close the workbook. Based on your instructor's directions, submit the following:

e10m2Animals_LastFirst

e10m2Shelter_LastFirst

---

3 Favorite Movies

COLLABORATION CASE

FROM SCRATCH

It is interesting to find out what people's favorite movies are. Work with a classmate to create an Access database table of favorite movies that you can import into an Excel workbook.

a. Create a blank Access database named **e10m3Movies_LastFirst**.

b. Create a table with these fields: Movie Title, Genre, Rating, Year Released, Lead Actor, and Lead Actress. Save the table as **Favorite Movies_Last First**.

c. Enter 10 records in the table, one for each of your favorite 10 movies.

d. Close the Access database and upload it to a OneDrive where you give your team member privileges to read and write files.

e. Download your team member's Access file and rename it by adding your last name after his or her name in the file name.

f. Start a new Excel workbook and save it as **e10m3Movies_LastFirst**.

g. Import your team member's Access database table into your Excel workbook.

h. Create a footer with your name on the left side, the sheet name code in the center, and the file name code on the right side of the worksheet. Save the workbook.

i. Open the Access database file *e10m3Movies_LastFirst*.

j. Add five of your favorite movies to the list. Make sure they do not duplicate any existing data. Sort the table in alphabetical order by movie title. Close the database.

k. Refresh the connection in Excel so that the data are updated to match the changes you made to the database.

l. Upload your completed files to the OneDrive account so that your team member can access your files to see what movies you added.

m. Based on your instructor's directions, submit the following:

e10m3Movies_LastFirst.accdb

e10m3Movies_LastFirst.xlsx

Beyond the Classroom

Text Functions vs. Flash Fill

After learning about text functions and Flash Fill in Excel, you would like to experiment with its capabilities compared to text functions. Open *e10b1TextFlash* and save it as **e10b1TextFlash_LastFirst**. The first column contains invoice numbers, such as 20181201, which represent the year (2018), the month (12 for December), and the invoice within that month (01).

Research the text functions that were not covered in Hands-On Exercise 2 and use text functions to separate the invoices to display the year, month, and invoice number in the range B4:D16. Answer the question by typing your responses in the range A19:E21. Use Flash Fill to complete data in the range H4:J16. Answer the questions by typing your responses in the range H19:J21.

Create a footer with your name on the left side, the sheet name code in the center, and the file name code on the right side of the worksheet. Save and close the workbook. Based on your instructor's directions, submit e10b1TextFlash_LastFirst.

Personal Book Library

Your friend Jeromy wants to create a list of books in his personal home library. His brother created an XML document containing data for a few of Jeromy's books. Unfortunately, the document contains errors. Use Windows File Explorer to copy the XML file *e10b2Books* and rename the copied file **e10b2Books_LastFirst**. Open the XML document in Notepad. Identify the errors. Insert XML-style comments that describe the errors. XML-style comments begin with <!-- and end with -->. Also, insert comments on style issues, although these issues are not programming errors. Fix the errors and style issues and save the XML document. Import the XML document into a new Excel workbook and name the workbook **e10b2Books_LastFirst** in the Excel Workbook format. Rename Sheet1 **Book List**. Create a footer with your name on the left side, the sheet name code in the center, and the file name code on the right side of the worksheet. Save and close the workbook. Based on your instructor's directions, submit the following:

e10b2Books_LastFirst.xml
e10b2Books_LastFirst

Capstone Exercise

You are a volunteer for Health Right, a nonprofit company that provides free physical fitness classes to schools that do not have a physical education facility. As part of your duties you generate weekly reports that detail donation pledge calls placed, as well as pledge dollars received. You also maintain pledge drive agent personal information and manage the thank-you gifts agents receive for volunteering their time. This week you have decided to overhaul your report by updating agent contact information, importing data previously stored outside your old report, implementing a PivotTable using Power Pivot, and utilize Power Add-ins to edit and visualize the week's data.

Import Data from an External Source

You plan to start creating your new report by importing volunteer information. The current contact information for volunteers that place pledge calls is stored in a CSV file. In addition, you want to separate the city, state, and zip code information into separate columns.

a. Open Excel and create a new workbook and save the workbook as **e10c1PledgeDrive_LastFirst**.

b. Import the file *e10c1VolunteerInfo.CSV*. Be sure to use a method that creates a connection to the external file.

c. Rename the worksheet **Volunteer Information**.

d. Use Text to Columns to separate the values in column D into three separate columns for city, state, and zip.

e. Set the External Data Range Properties to **Refresh data when opening the file.**

f. Resize the columns as needed.

Manipulate Text with Functions

After importing the data, you notice the volunteer's last names are uppercase in your document. To make the data more aesthetically pleasing, you will use a text function to display the last name in a more formal format.

a. Copy the **range B2:B7** and paste it in the **range I2:I7**.

b. Delete the original **range B2:B7**.

c. Enter a function in **cell B2** that formats the data in **cell I2** in a traditionally formal format.

d. Copy the function down to complete the column.

e. Copy the **range B2:B7** and paste the values back into the **range B2:B7** to remove the underlying functions.

f. Delete the values in column I.

Import XML Data

Volunteer reward information is saved in an XML document. You would like to import the data into Excel in order to keep the data in one document. You also notice there is a spelling error in the XML document. After creating the connection, you will open the original XML document, make the spelling correction, and refresh the data.

a. Create a new worksheet and name it **Rewards**.

b. Create a connection to the *e10c1Rewards.xml* file in the Rewards worksheet.

c. Apply Accounting Number Format to the dollar amounts imported into column A.

d. Open the document *e10c1Rewards* using Notepad. Locate the spelling error in line 18 (Sweet Shirt) and edit the data to Sweat Shirt.

e. Save the XML file and close it.

f. Refresh the XML connection only.

Create a PivotTable Using Power Pivot

All information regarding pledge dollars and transaction information is stored in an Access database. You will use Power Pivot to import the data into a PivotTable.

a. Ensure the Power Pivot Add-In is loaded.

b. Use Power Pivot to import the Access database *e10c1PledgeDollars.accdb* into a PivotTable.

c. Place the PivotTable on a new worksheet named **Pledge Dollars**.

d. Add the **Date** field to the FILTERS area, add **Operator_ID** to the ROWS area, and add **Pledge_Amount** to the VALUES area.

e. Add appropriate row and column headings and save the workbook.

Import Data with Power Query

You want to add contact information for new potential donation leads to your report. The data is currently stored in an Access database along with income information. You only want to add contact information, so you plan to use Power Query to shape the data before adding it to the report.

a. Ensure that the Power Query Add-In is enabled.

b. Use Power Query to open the database *e10c1Contacts .accdb*.

c. Use the Query editor to remove the Income and Dependents fields.

d. Close & Load the data.

e. Rename the worksheet **Pledge Leads**.

Visualize Data with Power View

As your last step you would like to create a dashboard to visualize pledge information using the new Power View. You will use the data from the Transactions table to complete the task.

a. Create a new Power View.

b. Create a visualization table in the upper left corner that displays **Operator_ID** and corresponding **Pledge_Amount** dollars. Do not summarize the Operator_ID column. Format the Operator_ID column with General Number Format.

c. Create a visualization pie chart that displays **Pledge_Amount** by operator in the upper right corner.

d. Create a visualization column chart that spans the lower half of the canvas. The chart should display **Pledge_Amount** and **Transaction_ID**.

e. Add an appropriate title to the dashboard.

Finalize the Workbook

You are ready to finalize the workbook.

a. Create a footer with your name on the left side, the sheet name code in the center, and the file name code on the right side of each worksheet.

b. Save and close the file. Based on your instructor's directions, submit e10c1PledgeDrive_LastFirst.

Excel

Collaboration and Workbook Distribution

LEARNING OUTCOME You will share, compare, merge, protect, and distribute workbooks for collaboration with others.

OBJECTIVES & SKILLS: After you read this chapter, you will be able to:

CASE STUDY | Marching Band Senior Dinner

As a senior member of the marching band, you are organizing a dinner fundraiser to purchase new uniforms. Each dinner ticket is $100, but you will provide a few complimentary tickets to current benefactors of the program. The dinner will be held in the university ballroom. The university waives the standard room rental fee, but the Facilities Department charges for table and chair rentals, linen cleaning, and cleanup. A grocery store donates the ingredients for the food, and a decorator prepares and donates a variety of decorations. Additional expenses include beverages, flowers, table decorations, and various publicity costs.

As the event coordinator, you have developed a workbook that contains an input section for the number of tables, chairs, complimentary tickets, and ticket price. In addition, you have itemized revenue, donations, expenses, and net income. To ensure the budget is accurate and complete, you will share the workbook with other students to get their feedback using collaborative tools. After updating the workbook, you will check for issues, protect the workbook from unauthorized modification, save the workbook in several formats, and distribute the final workbook to other people who have a vested interest in the success of the event.

Sharing Data with Others

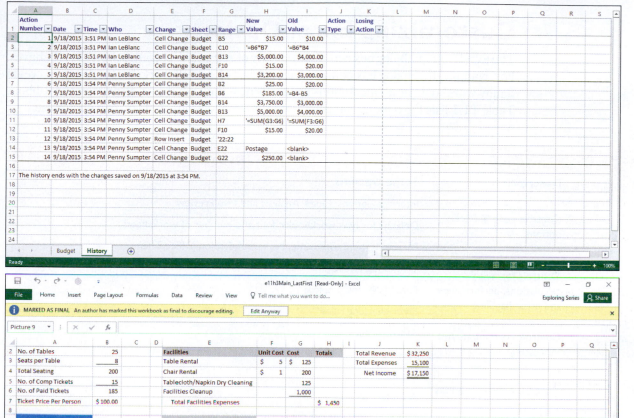

	Action Number	Date	Time	Who	Change	Sheet	Range	New Value	Old Value	Action Type	Losing Action
2	1	9/18/2015	3:51 PM	Ian LeBlanc	Cell Change	Budget	B5	$15.00	$10.00		
3	2	9/18/2015	3:51 PM	Ian LeBlanc	Cell Change	Budget	C10	'=B6*B7	'=B6*B4		
4	3	9/18/2015	3:51 PM	Ian LeBlanc	Cell Change	Budget	B13	$5,000.00	$4,000.00		
5	4	9/18/2015	3:51 PM	Ian LeBlanc	Cell Change	Budget	F10	$15.00	$20.00		
6	5	9/18/2015	3:51 PM	Ian LeBlanc	Cell Change	Budget	B14	$3,200.00	$3,000.00		
7	6	9/18/2015	3:54 PM	Penny Sumpter	Cell Change	Budget	B2	$25.00	$20.00		
8	7	9/18/2015	3:54 PM	Penny Sumpter	Cell Change	Budget	B6	$185.00	'=B4-B5		
9	8	9/18/2015	3:54 PM	Penny Sumpter	Cell Change	Budget	B14	$3,750.00	$3,000.00		
10	9	9/18/2015	3:54 PM	Penny Sumpter	Cell Change	Budget	B13	$5,000.00	$4,000.00		
11	10	9/18/2015	3:54 PM	Penny Sumpter	Cell Change	Budget	H7	'=SUM(G3:G6)	'=SUM(F3:G6)		
12	11	9/18/2015	3:54 PM	Penny Sumpter	Cell Change	Budget	F10	$15.00	$20.00		
13	12	9/18/2015	3:54 PM	Penny Sumpter	Row Insert	Budget	'22:22				
14	13	9/18/2015	3:54 PM	Penny Sumpter	Cell Change	Budget	E22	Postage	<blank>		
15	14	9/18/2015	3:54 PM	Penny Sumpter	Cell Change	Budget	G22	$250.00	<blank>		

17 The history ends with the changes saved on 9/18/2015 at 3:54 PM.

Budget   **History**

---

e11h3Main_LastFirst [Read-Only] - Excel

File   Home   Insert   Page Layout   Formulas   Data   Review   View   ♀ Tell me what you want to do...   Exploring Series   ☇ Share

ⓘ MARKED AS FINAL   An author has marked this workbook as final to discourage editing.   Edit Anyway   ✕

Picture 9

	A	B	C	D	E	F	G	H	I	J	K
2	No. of Tables	25			Facilities	Unit Cost	Cost	Totals		Total Revenue	$ 32,250
3	Seats per Table	8			Table Rental	$ 5	$ 125			Total Expenses	15,100
4	Total Seating	200			Chair Rental	$ 1	200			Net Income	$17,150
5	No. of Comp Tickets	15			Tablecloth/Napkin Dry Cleaning		125				
6	No. of Paid Tickets	185			Facilities Cleanup		1,000				
7	Ticket Price Per Person	$ 100.00			Total Facilities Expenses			$ 1,450			
8											
9	Revenue				Meal						
10	Ticket Revenue		$ 18,500		Food Ingredients	$ 15	3,000				
11					Beverages	$ 2	400				
12	Donations Income				Total Meal Expenses			3,400			
13	Decorations Donation	$ 5,000									
14	Food Donation	3,750			Decorations						
15	Corporate Sponsor	5,000			Flowers		3,500				
16	Total Contributions		13,750		Other Special Decorations		5,000				
17					Table Decorations	$ 10	250				
18	Total Revenue Generated		$ 32,250		Total Decorations Expenses			8,750			
19											
20					Publicity						
21					Photocopying/Printing		500				
22					Postage		250				
23					Newspaper Advertisement		750				
24					Total Publicity Expenses		1,500				
25	X										
26	Exploring Series				Total Expenses			$ 15,100			
27											

Budget

Ready

FIGURE 11.1 Marching Band Senior Dinner Workbook

Case Study | Marching Band Senior Dinner

Starting Files	File to be Submitted
e11h1Dinner e11h2Main e11h2Main_Ian e11h2Main_Penny	e11h4DinnerFiles_LastFirst.zip

Workbook Customization

You can customize Excel through the Excel Options dialog box. Think of the Excel Options dialog box as the control center that manages the behavior and settings of Excel—the color scheme, formula rules, automatic corrections, AutoComplete rules, and items that display onscreen. In addition to customizing the Excel program, you might want to personalize workbooks that you create.

In this section, you will customize Microsoft Office by entering your name as the user name. In addition, you will view and add properties to describe a workbook.

Customizing Excel Options

The Excel Options dialog box contains a variety of settings that control how Excel behaves. For example, the dialog box controls the number of default worksheets when you create a new workbook, how calculations are performed, and what tabs display on the Ribbon. Table 11.1 lists the options categories and some key options that you can customize.

TABLE 11.1	Excel Options Categories	
Category	**Description**	**Some Options**
General	Controls general Excel options	Interface options: Quick Analysis and Live Preview
		Defaults for new workbooks: font and number of worksheets
		Personalization: user name, background color, Office Theme
Formulas	Controls formula calculations, performance, and error handling	Workbook calculation
		Formula AutoComplete
		Error checking rules
Proofing	Controls corrections and formatting	AutoCorrect
		Spelling
Save	Controls how workbooks are saved	File format
		AutoRecover rules
		Offline editing options for server files
Language	Specifies language preferences	Editing languages
		ScreenTip language
Advanced	Controls advanced settings	Editing options
		Cut, copy, and paste
		Chart options
		Display settings
		Formula settings
Customize Ribbon	Enables users to customize the Ribbon	Commands, tabs, and groups
		Reset customizations
		Import and export a customization file
Quick Access Toolbar	Enables users to customize the Quick Access Toolbar	Commands
		Reset
		Import/Export
Add-ins	Manages add-in programs	Active and inactive add-ins
Trust Center	Keeps documents safe	Security settings
		Microsoft Excel Trust Center

Personalize Your Copy of Microsoft Office

STEP 1 ▶▶ When you create an Excel workbook or any Office document, the file is coded with identification information, such as the default user. When a person creates a new Excel workbook, the user name is associated as the author of the workbook, or if a person modifies an existing workbook, the user name is used to identify the last person to modify the workbook. Within an Office document, the user name shows up in comments, tracked changes, and document properties. In File Explorer, the user name is listed when you display file properties. You should personalize your copy of Microsoft Office so that the files you create or edit will include your name. Because people share files with each other within an organization, it is important to know who created or edited a particular file. For example, you want to add your name as the author of the Marching Band Senior Dinner workbook so that others will know that you created the budget.

The General section of the Excel Options dialog box enables you to change the user name. In Microsoft Word, PowerPoint, and Access, you can also enter your first and last initials in the Initials box. When you select *Always use these values regardless of sign in to Office*, files created or edited will reflect the user name rather than the Windows sign-in name.

To change the user name, complete the following steps:

1. Click the File tab to display Backstage view.
2. Click Options to open the Excel Options dialog box, which shows the General options for working with Excel (see Figure 11.2).
3. Type your name in the User name box in the *Personalize your copy of Microsoft Office* section.
4. Click OK.

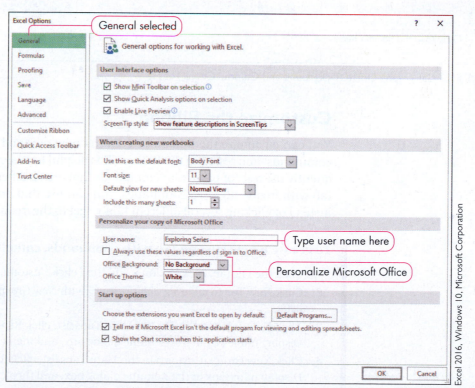

FIGURE 11.2 Excel Options Dialog Box

Note that the user name you enter in the Options dialog box is not the account name that displays below the sizing buttons in the top-right corner of Excel. The name in that location reflects the person who signed into Microsoft Office.

You can further personalize Microsoft Office by changing the Office Background and the Office Theme in the Options dialog box, or by clicking the File tab and clicking Account. The **Office Background** controls the faint background image, if any, in the top-right corner of the title bar. The default is No Background, but you can select settings such as Calligraphy to add a design to the title bar for personal interest. The **Office Theme** controls the overall appearance and color of the title bar and interface for Office programs. This book displays figures with the White theme where the title bar, Ribbon background, row and column headings, and scroll bars are white, and the status bar is green. You can change the Office Theme to Colorful to show program-specific color for the title bar. In Excel, the Colorful theme creates a green background for the title bar and tabs on the Ribbon (see Figure 11.3), whereas in Word the title bar and tabs on the Ribbon are blue. In Excel, the Ribbon, active tab, row and column headings, and the status bar display in gray when the Colorful theme is applied.

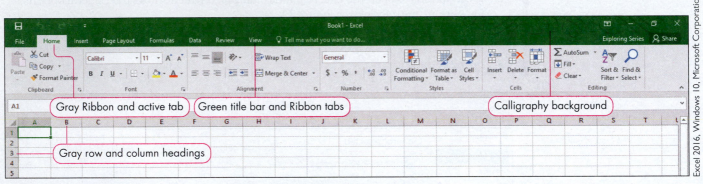

FIGURE 11.3 Calligraphy Office Background and Colorful Office Theme

Customize the Ribbon

You can customize the Ribbon by creating new tabs and groups, adding and removing commands, and resetting the Ribbon. It is helpful to customize the Ribbon when you frequently use a set of particular commands that are on different tabs. By creating a custom tab with frequently used commands, you can use that one tab to do most of your work instead of clicking several different tabs to get to the frequently used commands.

To create a new custom tab with commands, complete the following steps:

1. Click the File tab, click Options, and then click Customize Ribbon (see Figure 11.4).
2. Click New Tab to add *New Tab (Custom)* with *New Group (Custom)* to the Main Tabs list.
3. Click New Tab (Custom) in the Main Tabs list, click Rename, type a name in the Display name box in the Rename dialog box, and then click OK.
4. Click New Group (Custom) in the Main Tabs list, click Rename, type a name in the Display name box in the Rename dialog box, and then click OK.
5. Click a group name, select a category from the *Choose commands from* list, select a command in the commands list on the left side, and then click Add.
6. Click OK after adding commands to each new group.

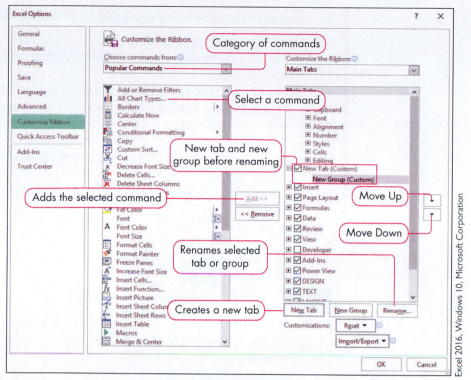

FIGURE 11.4 Customize the Ribbon Options

Click Move Up to move the selected tab up or click Move Down to move the selected tab down the Main Tabs list. Figure 11.5 shows the Exploring custom tab on the Ribbon.

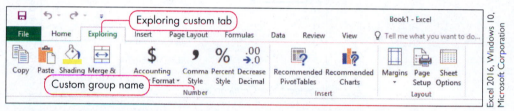

FIGURE 11.5 Customized Exploring Tab

> **TIP: RESET THE RIBBON AND HIDE A CUSTOM TAB**
> You can reset customizations if you no longer need them. To reset changes made to an original tab, select the tab in the Main Tabs list, click Reset, and then select *Reset only selected Ribbon tab*. To remove all customizations and return to the original settings, including new tabs created and Quick Access Toolbar customizations, click Reset, select *Reset all customizations*, and then click Yes. To remove a custom tab, right-click the tab in the dialog box and select Remove.
>
> If you want to remove a custom tab, display the Options dialog box, click Customize Ribbon, and then click to deselect the check box for the particular tab you want to hide, and then click OK.

Customize the Quick Access Toolbar

By default, the Quick Access Toolbar contains three commands: Save, Undo, and Redo. You can customize the Quick Access Toolbar to add any frequently used commands. For example, you could add the Spelling command for easy access to check the spelling in your worksheets to correct any spelling errors.

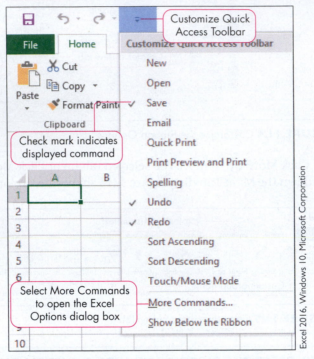

FIGURE 11.6 Customizing the Quick Access Toolbar

Alternatively, you can right-click a command on the Quick Access Toolbar and select Customize Quick Access Toolbar, or you can click the File tab, click Options, and then click Quick Access Toolbar. The Excel Options dialog box opens so that you can add or remove options from the Quick Access Toolbar. Use Help to learn how to change the order of commands or group commands by adding a separator.

TIP: IMPORT AND EXPORT SETTINGS

After customizing the Quick Access Toolbar or Ribbon, you can share the custom settings with other people. Click Import/Export within the Excel Options dialog box, select *Export all customizations*, enter a file name in the File Save dialog box, and then click Save. The file is saved as an Exported Office UI File format. To import the customizations file on another computer, click Import/Export within the Excel Options dialog box, select *Import customization file*, select the file in the File Open dialog box, and then click Open. The custom settings are then applied for Excel on that computer.

Customize Other Options

You might want to customize other options. In the Proofing category, deselect the *Ignore words in UPPERCASE* option so that the Spelling command will detect misspelled words that are typed in all uppercase letters. In the Save category, consider changing the *Default local file location* if you frequently save files in a particular folder. The Advanced category contains a lot of options. For example, you can change the number of recently used files in the *Show this number of Recent Workbooks* setting (see Figure 11.7) to control the number of recently used files listed when you start Excel.

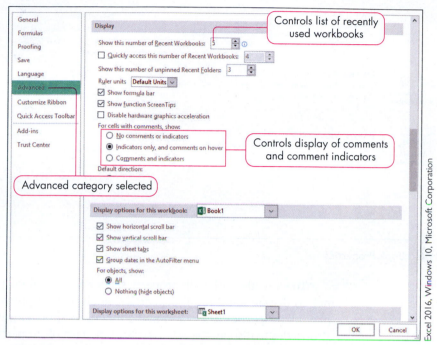

FIGURE 11.7 Advanced Settings

Changing Properties

STEP 2 ▶▶ When you create or edit a file, **metadata** (data that describe other data) or **document properties** are attached to that file. Document properties that describe or identify a file include details such as the author's name, title, subject, company, creation date, revision date, and keywords. Including document properties for your workbooks helps you classify your files. In addition, you can perform a search to find files that contain particular properties. For example, you can use Windows to perform a search for all files authored by a coworker or all files that contain *marching band* as keywords.

Display Properties in Backstage View

When you click the File tab, document information for the current workbook is displayed on the right side of Backstage view (see Figure 11.8). You can enter or edit standard properties, such as Title, Categories, and Author, by pointing to the respective property, clicking, and typing the information. You are not able to directly change certain properties, such as Size, Last Modified, and Last Printed. These properties change based on when you last perform an action, such as saving the workbook. When you save the workbook, the document properties are saved as part of the workbook too.

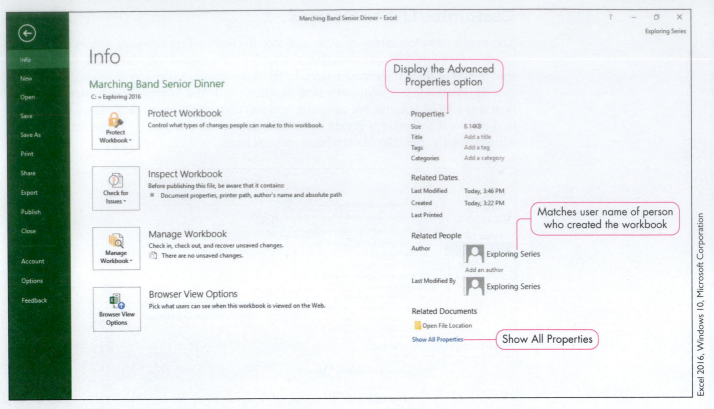

FIGURE 11.8 Workbook Properties

To view all workbook properties, click Show All Properties in the bottom-right corner to display additional properties, such as Company and Manager. When you display all properties, the command changes to Show Fewer Properties. Click Show Fewer Properties to display the original shortened list of properties again.

Use the Properties Dialog Box

STEP 3 ❯❯ You may want to see more property details than what is shown in Backstage view. The Properties dialog box provides more details than the property list.

> **To open the Properties dialog box, complete the following steps:**
> 1. Click the File tab.
> 2. Click Properties on the right side of Backstage view and select Advanced Properties.

The Properties dialog box contains five tabs to organize various properties: General, Summary, Statistics, Contents, and Custom (see Figure 11.9), and the dialog box title bar reflects the workbook name, such as Marching Band Senior Dinner Properties. Table 11.2 lists the tab names and describes the options on each tab.

FIGURE 11.9 Properties Dialog Box

TABLE 11.2	Properties Dialog Box Options
Category	**Description**
General	Displays the file name, file type, location, size, creation date, modification date, and last accessed date.
	Indicates the attributes, such as Read only or Hidden.
	General properties are created automatically and cannot be changed directly by the user.
Summary	Displays properties the user can enter and change, such as title, subject, author, manager, company, category, keywords, and comments.
	Keywords describe the document and help you find files that contain particular keywords.
Statistics	Displays creation, modified, accessed, and printed dates.
	Displays the author who last saved the file, revision number, and total editing time, if tracked.
Contents	Displays the worksheet names contained in the workbook.
Custom	Enables the user to create and maintain custom properties for the current workbook, such as Department, Project, and Purpose.

> **TIP: FILE EXPLORER**
> Some of the properties you set in the Properties dialog box in Excel display in a properties list when you select a file in File Explorer. The keywords you entered in the Excel Properties dialog box display in the Tags section in File Explorer. You can also change file properties for the Title, Authors, Tags, Categories, Content status, Subject, and Comments in File Explorer.

Quick Concepts ✓

1. What is the purpose of changing the user name settings in the Excel Options dialog box? **p. 673**

2. Why would a user customize the Ribbon by creating a custom tab? **p. 674**

3. What is the purpose of metadata? **p. 677**

Hands-On Exercises

Watch the Video for this Hands-On Exercise!

MyITLab®
HOE1 Training

Skills covered: Enter a User Name • Display and Add Properties • Add Advanced Properties

1 Workbook Customization

You want to personalize Microsoft Office on your computer so that your name will appear in the Author property on new files you create in any Microsoft Office application. In addition, you want to add some properties to the Marching Band Senior Dinner workbook.

STEP 1 ›› ENTER A USER NAME

Before working on the Marching Band Senior Dinner workbook, you want to enter your name as the user name for Microsoft Office on your computer. Refer to Figure 11.10 as you complete Step 1.

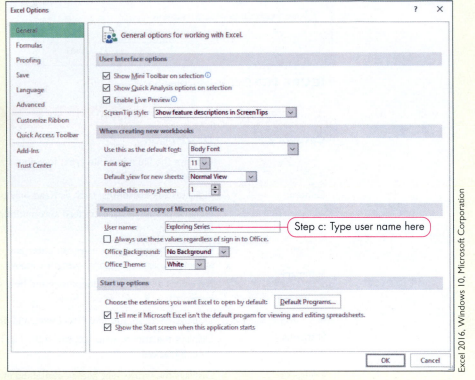

FIGURE 11.10 Excel Options

a. Open *e11h1Dinner* and save it as **e11h1Dinner_LastFirst**.

> **TROUBLESHOOTING:** If you make any major mistakes in this exercise, you can close the file, open *e11h1Dinner* again, and then start this exercise over.

b. Click the **File tab** and click **Options**.

The Excel Options dialog box opens. General is the default category on the left side.

c. Select any existing text in the **User name box**, type your name, and then click **OK**. Save the workbook.

You want to display the document properties for the Marching Band Senior Dinner workbook. Because the workbook was created before you entered your name as the user name, you want to edit the Author property. In addition, you want to enter information about the Senior Dinner in the Title property. Refer to Figure 11.11 as you complete Step 2.

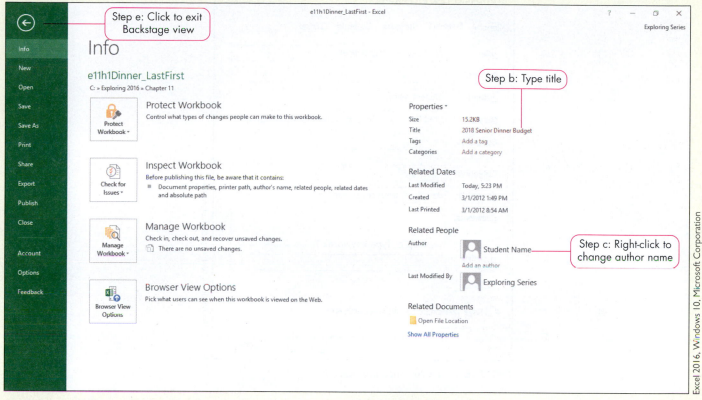

FIGURE 11.11 Document Properties

a. Click the **File tab**.

b. Click **Add a title** that displays next to the Title property, type **2018 Senior Dinner Budget**, and then press **Enter**.

The Title property displays the text you entered.

c. Right-click **Exploring Series**, the currently listed Author property, and select **Edit Property**.

The Edit person dialog box opens.

d. Select the text in the **Enter names or e-mail addresses box**, type your name, and then click **OK**.

e. Click **Back** to exit Backstage view. Save the workbook.

You want to add some additional properties to the workbook. Specifically, you want to enter Chef Dan as the manager. In addition, you want to enter keywords, such as donations, ticket prices, and expenses. Refer to Figure 11.12 as you complete Step 3.

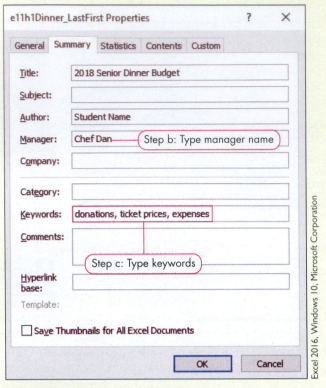

FIGURE 11.12 Advanced Properties

a. Click the **File tab**, click **Properties**, and then select **Advanced Properties**.

   The Properties dialog box for the current workbook opens. The options in the Summary tab are displayed.

b. Click in the **Manager box** and type **Chef Dan**.

c. Click in the **Keywords box** and type **donations, ticket prices, expenses**.

d. Click **OK** in the e11h1Dinner_LastFirst Properties dialog box.

   The keywords you entered in the Properties dialog box now display in the Tags section of the list of properties.

e. Click **Back** to close Backstage view.

f. Save the workbook. Keep the workbook open if you plan to continue with the next Hands-On Exercise. If not, close the workbook and exit Excel.

Collaboration

Collaboration is the process by which two or more individuals work together to achieve an outcome or goal by using software technology and features to share and edit the contents of a file. Often, the contents of a complex workbook result from the collaborative efforts of a team of people. Team members work together to plan, develop spreadsheets, conduct quantitative research, enter data, and analyze the results. For example, you are working with a team of students to prepare and finalize the Senior Dinner workbook. Together, your team obtains cost estimates, facilities expenses, meal expenses, decorations, publicity, projected donations, and revenue from ticket sales to prepare the budget worksheet.

You can share workbooks with other people and merge their workbooks into one workbook. In addition, Excel includes two key features that facilitate the collaborative process: comments and track changes. These features enable you and your team members to provide feedback and identify each other's suggested changes in a workbook.

In this section, you will learn how to share workbooks with others, compare and merge workbooks, and insert and edit comments. In addition, you will learn how to track changes made by team members and how to accept or reject their suggestions.

Inserting Comments

STEP 1 >> You can insert notes to yourself or make suggestions to another team member by inserting comments into a cell. A *comment* is a note or annotation to ask a question or provide a suggestion to another person about content in a worksheet cell. Comments help document a worksheet by providing additional information or clarification of the data, formula results, or labels. For example, in the Senior Dinner workbook, you want to insert the comment in cell C18 regarding income.

To insert a comment, complete the following steps:

1. Click the cell in which you want to insert the comment.
2. Click the Review tab and click New Comment in the Comments group or right-click the cell and select Insert Comment.
3. Type the text that you want to appear in the comment box and click outside the comment box (see Figure 11.13).

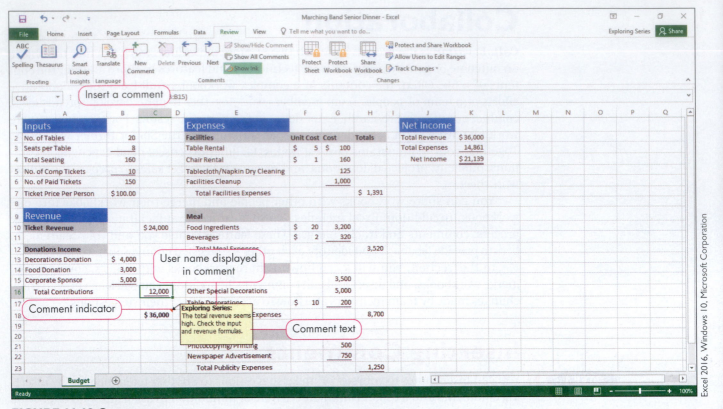

FIGURE 11.13 Comment

Format the comment text, if desired. Select the comment text, right-click the selected text, select Format Comment, select formats in the Format Comment dialog box, and then click OK. Alternatively, select comment text and apply font attributes, such as bold and font size, from the Font group on the Home tab.

Show and Hide Comments

A red triangle, known as a ***comment indicator***, appears in the top-right corner of a cell containing a comment. A comment box displays the user name in bold followed by the comments the user made. When you click outside the comment box, it closes, but the comment indicator remains in the cell. Point to that cell to display the comment again. Other comments remain hidden unless you show them. Table 11.3 lists steps to show and hide comments onscreen.

TABLE 11.3	Show and Hide Comments	
Action	**Ribbon Method**	**Shortcut Method**
Show a comment	Click the cell containing the comment.	Right-click the cell containing the comment.
	Click Show/Hide Comment in the Comments group on the Review tab.	Select Show/Hide Comments.
Hide a comment	Click the cell containing the comment.	Right-click the cell containing the comment.
	Click Show/Hide Comment in the Comments group.	Select Hide Comment.
Display or hide all comments in the entire workbook	Click Show All Comments in the Comments group.	Not applicable

To advance through a series of comments without clicking each one individually, click Next in the Comments group on the Review tab to go to the cell containing the next comment or click Previous to go to the cell containing the previous comment. When you click these commands, Excel selects the respective cell and displays the comment box.

> **TIP: COMMENT BOX**
> If the comment box obstructs the view of a cell you would like to see, you can reposition it by clicking the outer edge of the comment box and dragging to a new location. You can also drag a selection handle on the outer edge of a comment box to increase or decrease the size of the comment box.

Edit and Delete Comments

You may need to edit the comment text if information changes. You might have originally inserted a general comment such as *Some decorations will be donated*. A few days later, another team member identifies a supply store called Party America that is willing to donate some decorations. Therefore, you can edit the comment to display *Party America will provide $500 worth of decorations*.

To edit a comment, complete the following steps:

1. Click the cell that contains the comment you want to edit.
2. Click the Review tab and click Edit Comment in the Comments group, or right-click the cell and select Edit Comment.
3. Edit the comment text.
4. Click outside the comment box after you edit the comment.

After you read a comment, take the appropriate action. When you no longer need a comment, you can delete it.

To delete a comment, complete the following steps:

1. Click the cell that contains the comment you want to delete.
2. Click the Review tab and click Delete in the Comments group, or right-click the cell and select Delete Comment.

Excel immediately deletes the comment without providing a warning. If you need to restore the comment, immediately click Undo on the Quick Access Toolbar.

> **TIP: REMOVING ALL COMMENTS**
> To remove all comments at the same time, press Ctrl+G to display the Go To dialog box, click Special, ensure that Comments is selected, and then click OK. This selects all cells containing comments in the current worksheet. Click the Home tab, click Clear in the Editing group, and then select Clear Comments.

Print Comments

When you print a worksheet, comments do not print by default. The Sheet tab in the Page Setup dialog box contains two options for printing comments. The default Comments setting is (None). If you choose *As displayed on sheet*, the visible comment boxes appear where they are located onscreen. Hidden comments do not print. Choose *At end of sheet* to print the comments on a separate page (see Figure 11.14). This printout includes the cell reference and the comment text for each comment on the active worksheet, even if the comments are hidden.

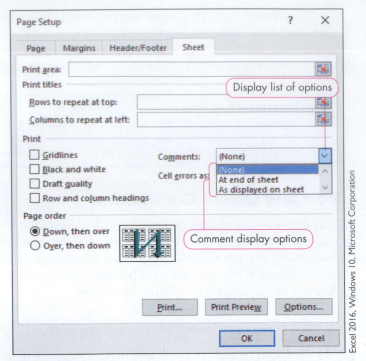

FIGURE 11.14 Page Setup Dialog Box with Comments Options

Sharing and Merging Workbooks

STEP 2 ❯❯ One way to collaborate on a workbook is to create a shared workbook. In Excel, a ***shared workbook*** is designated as sharable and is stored on an organization's network that is accessible to multiple people who can edit the workbook at the same time. All users must have access to the same network to share the workbook. Often people within the same department are on the same network; however, people in different departments may be on different networks, which would prevent workbook sharing.

> **TIP: HOME NETWORK**
> You might want to create a network drive to share files with family members or roommates at home. Use Help to learn how to create a network drive through Windows 10 and provide access to a shared folder. You can then store files in that network drive to share with other members of your household.

When you create a shared workbook, users can see changes made by other users. The person who creates the workbook and designates it as a shared workbook is the owner. The owner controls user access and resolves any conflicting changes made.

To share a workbook, complete the following steps:

1. Click the Review tab and click Share Workbook in the Changes group to open the Share Workbook dialog box.
2. Click the *Allow changes by more than one user at the same time* check box to select it and click the Advanced tab (see Figure 11.15) to specify the settings that control the shared workbook.
3. Specify how long, if at all, you want to keep a history of the changes made in the *Track changes* section. By default, Excel keeps track of changes in shared workbooks for only 30 days.
4. Specify how often to update changes in the *Update changes* section.
5. Select one of the settings in the *Conflicting changes between users* section and click OK. Click OK if a message box opens informing you that the workbook will be saved.

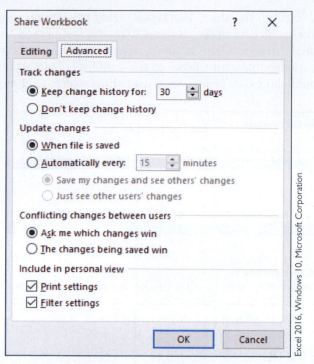

FIGURE 11.15 Share Workbook Dialog Box

After sharing a workbook on a network, you might want to know who is currently working on it. Click Share Workbook in the Changes group on the Review tab and then click the Editing tab. The *Who has this workbook open now* list displays names of people who have the workbook open (see Figure 11.16).

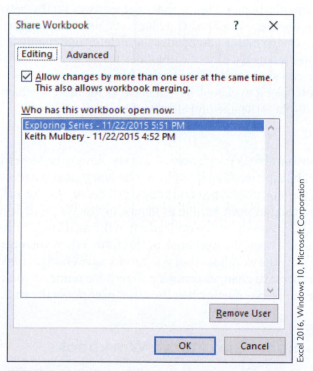

FIGURE 11.16 Share Workbook Dialog Box: Editing Tab

Understand Conflicts and Network Issues

Conflicts can arise when several users are working with shared workbooks. If multiple users attempt to change the same cell at the same time, a Resolve Conflicts dialog box opens for the second user (see Figure 11.17). The change is resolved based on the settings you select in the Share Workbook dialog box. When several people on a network share a workbook and make changes to it, the last person to make changes decides which changes to accept. This becomes a problematic situation when the last person is the least knowledgeable about Excel or the contents of a particular workbook. Therefore, you should allow only people you trust to have access to change your workbooks.

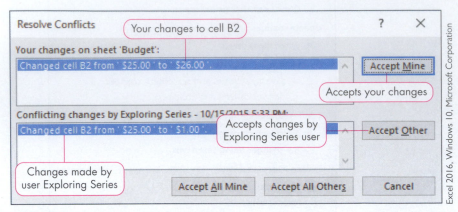

FIGURE 11.17 Resolve Conflicts Dialog Box

Issues with network permissions also may arise when storing and using files on a network. The network administrator usually sets permissions attributes that control who has rights to open and modify files versus who has read-only rights. Furthermore, workbooks that have not been designated as sharable may still be able to be modified by various users.

Network Permissions A network drive is a storage location on a local area network in an organization or a home that enables users on the network to share files. The network drive may be set to Read-Only for some users and as Owner for other users. People who have Owner rights can open, save, delete, and modify files. People who have Read-Only rights can open a file but cannot delete it or save changes back to that location; however, they can save changes to another location such as their own hard drive or a flash drive. If you open a workbook from a network location of which you are not an owner, the title bar displays [Read-Only] after the file name.

Nonsharable Workbook A workbook may be stored on a network that you can access, but the workbook might not be designated as a shared workbook. If another user has the workbook open and you try to open it, the File in Use dialog box will display. Click Read Only to open the file in Read-Only mode, or click Notify to open the workbook in Read-Only mode and be notified when the workbook is no longer being used, or click Cancel to not open the workbook at this time. When you open a file in Read-Only mode, you can view the workbook, but you cannot save changes under the same file name. However, you can save changes using a different file name. If you click Notify, the File Now Available dialog box opens when the other user closes the workbook.

Compare and Merge Workbooks

When you share a workbook with others, you might want to see what each person changed in the workbook instead of allowing immediate changes to the original workbook. You can use Compare and Merge Workbooks to combine the shared workbooks into one workbook so that you can compare the changes to decide which ones to keep. The Compare and Merge command works only with copies of a shared workbook; it does not work on workbooks that have not been designated as shared.

Each user must save a copy of the shared workbook with a unique name, such as Senior Dinner Jaime and Senior Dinner Mary, so that these names differ from the original file name. These files must be stored in the same folder that contains the shared workbook. The Compare and Merge command is not on the Ribbon by default. However, you can add the command to either the Ribbon or the Quick Access Toolbar.

To add the Compare and Merge command to the Quick Access Toolbar, complete the following steps:

1. Click Customize Quick Access Toolbar on the right side of the Quick Access Toolbar and select More Commands.
2. Click the *Choose commands from* arrow and select *Commands Not in the Ribbon*.
3. Scroll through the list and select *Compare and Merge Workbooks*.
4. Click Add and click OK.

The Compare and Merge Workbooks command looks like a green circle on the Quick Access Toolbar when you open a shared workbook (see Figure 11.18). It appears dimmed when you work with regular workbooks.

FIGURE 11.18 Shared Workbook

After adding the Compare and Merge Workbooks command to the Quick Access Toolbar, you can use it to merge copies of a shared workbook.

To merge the workbooks, complete the following steps:

1. Open the original shared workbook.
2. Click Compare and Merge Workbooks on the Quick Access Toolbar.
3. Click OK if the message box *This action will now save the workbook. Do you want to continue?* displays. The Select Files to Merge Into Current Workbook dialog box opens.
4. Click the file you want to merge. To select multiple files, press and hold Ctrl as you click the files. Click OK.

Changes are indicated by different color borders and top-left triangles, representing the different users who made changes to the shared workbook (see Figure 11.19).

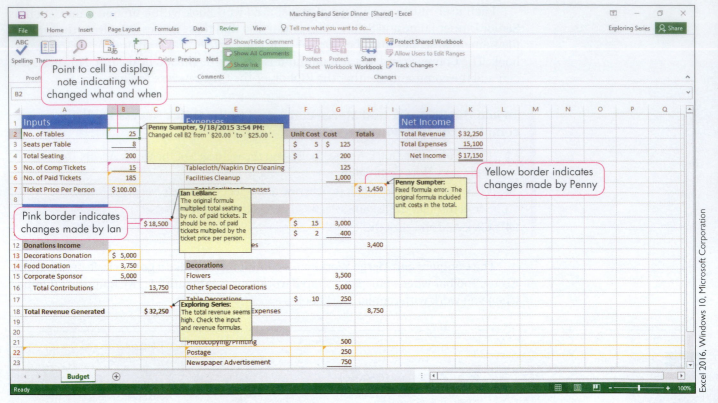

FIGURE 11.19 Merged Workbook

Tracking Changes

Although comments are helpful for posing questions or suggestions, you may want to create a log that identifies changes you and other people make in a workbook. *Track Changes* is a feature that records particular changes made in a workbook. It tracks changes to cell contents, row and column insertions and deletions, and copied and moved data. With several team members contributing to the Senior Dinner workbook, you can activate Track Changes to see who makes what change, such as changing the value of the price per person from $75 to $100.

Excel does not track all changes. For example, it does not track formatting changes such as applying bold or Accounting Number Format, or adjusting column width or row height. Because Excel does not track these types of changes, keep a copy of the original workbook. You can compare the original workbook to the workbook of your team members to see if they made any formatting changes.

To activate the Track Changes feature, complete the following steps:

1. Click the Review tab.
2. Click Track Changes in the Changes group and select Highlight Changes. The Highlight Changes dialog box opens.
3. Click to select the *Track changes while editing. This also shares your workbook* check box. The remaining options are now available (see Figure 11.20).
4. Click OK. If prompted, enter the name of the workbook and click Save.

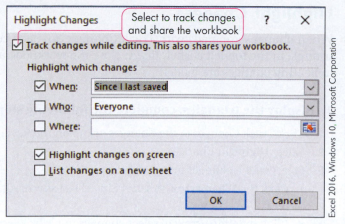

FIGURE 11.20 Highlight Changes Dialog Box

You can track changes only in a shared workbook. When you activate Track Changes, [Shared] appears on the right side of the file name on the title bar. Shared workbooks are often stored on a network server so that several people can simultaneously edit the workbook. However, you can track changes in a workbook stored on a local hard drive or external storage device.

A small triangle appears in the top-left corner of a cell when an edit is made and Track Changes is enabled. When you point to that cell, a yellow message box similar to a comment box displays the name of the person who made the change, the date and time the change was made, and the type of change made.

When you share a workbook or activate Track Changes, some Excel features are disabled, indicated by dimmed commands on the Ribbon. You cannot do the following tasks when you turn on Track Changes:

- Merge cells together or split merged cells into several cells.
- Add or change conditional formats.
- Format a range as an Excel table.
- Delete, protect, or unprotect worksheets.
- Change the tab color for worksheets.
- Create or change charts, PivotTables, PivotCharts, shapes, pictures, objects, and hyperlinks.
- Apply, change, or remove passwords.
- Import or link external data, display connections, or edit links.
- Add, modify, or remove data validation rules.
- Create, edit, delete, or view scenarios.
- Group, ungroup, or subtotal tables.
- Edit a macro, insert controls, and assign a macro to a control.

> **TIP: TURNING OFF CHANGE TRACKING**
> After reviewing the changes, you can turn off Track Changes by clicking Track Changes in the Changes group, selecting Highlight Changes, clicking the *Track changes while editing* check box to deselect it in the Highlight Changes dialog box, and then clicking OK. If you turn off Track Changes, the workbook is no longer shared, the history of changes made is lost, and other users who are sharing the workbook will not be able to save the changes they have made.

Highlight Changes

STEP 5 ▶▶ When changes are made with Track Changes on, each cell changed contains a colored triangle in the top-left corner. If you close the workbook and open it again, the triangles indicating changes are hidden.

> **To display the triangles, complete the following steps:**
>
> 1. Click Track Changes in the Changes group on the Review tab.
> 2. Select Highlight Changes.
> 3. Select which changes to highlight:
>   - Click the When arrow to select Since I last saved, All, Not yet reviewed, or Since date.
>   - Click the Who arrow to select changes made by Everyone or Everyone but Me.
>   - Click Where and select a range of cells to indicate whether changes are made to those respective cells.
> 4. Click OK.

By default, the *Highlight changes on screen* check box is selected in the Highlight Changes dialog box to ensure that changes display onscreen. You can then review the changes in any sequence by pointing to the cells containing blue triangles. Click *List changes on a new sheet* to create a list of changes made on a new worksheet.

Accept and Reject Changes

STEP 6 ▶▶ You can view changes in sequence through a dialog box that enables you to accept or reject changes. When you accept a change, the change is no longer indicated by the colored triangle; the change is accepted as part of the worksheet. When you reject a change, the suggested change is removed from the worksheet. For example, if someone made a change by deleting a row and you reject that change, the row is restored.

> **To accept and reject changes, complete the following steps:**
>
> 1. Click Track Changes in the Changes group on the Review tab. If you have not saved the workbook, you will be prompted to do so.
> 2. Select Accept/Reject Changes. The Select Changes to Accept or Reject dialog box opens (see Figure 11.21).
> 3. Click the check boxes for the type of changes to accept and reject and specify their settings. Click OK. The Accept or Reject Changes dialog box opens (see Figure 11.22), displaying the change number, who made the change, and what the person changed.
> 4. Click Accept to accept the change, click Reject to reject that change and move to the next change, click Accept All to accept all changes made, or click Reject All to reject all changes made. The dialog box closes automatically after all changes have been either accepted or rejected.

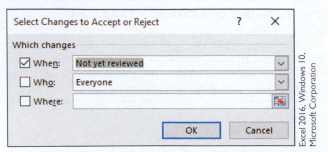

FIGURE 11.21 Select Changes to Accept or Reject Dialog Box

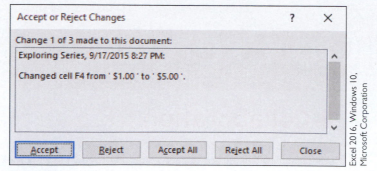

FIGURE 11.22 Accept or Reject Changes Dialog Box

Before accepting or rejecting changes, you might want to create a list of changes in a **history worksheet**. Within the Highlight Changes dialog box, click *List changes on a new sheet*. When you click OK, Excel creates a History worksheet that lists the changes made to the workbook, such as value changes, inserted and deleted columns and rows, and some formula changes. Note that changes made to formulas that are dependent on other cells, also known as dependent values, are not listed. The log does not track font changes or hiding/unhiding columns or rows. Figure 11.23 shows a change log in a new worksheet named History. The change log shows the dates, times, new and original values, and other details about all the changes. The History worksheet is temporary; Excel removes it when you close the workbook. However, you can copy and paste the values into a new worksheet that will remain when the workbook is saved.

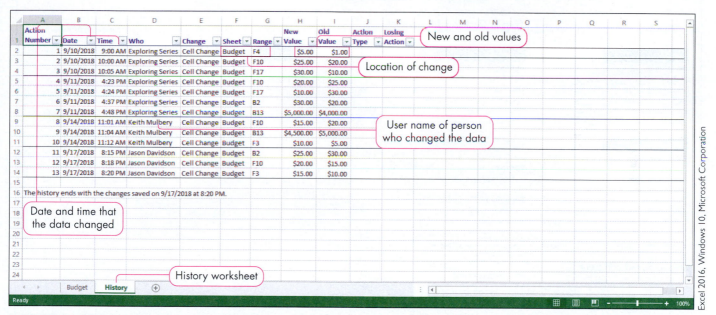

FIGURE 11.23 Change Log

Quick Concepts ✓

4. What is the purpose of inserting comments in a worksheet? *p. 683*

5. What are challenges of using a shared workbook on a network? *p. 688*

6. What are the benefits of using the Track Changes feature? *p. 690*

Hands-On Exercises

Watch the Video for this Hands-On Exercise!

MyITLab®
HOE2 Training

Skills covered: Insert a Comment • Edit a Comment • Share the Workbook • Add the Compare and Merge Workbooks Command to the Quick Access Toolbar • Compare and Merge Workbooks • Highlight Changes • Create a History Worksheet • Accept and Reject Changes

2 Collaboration

You want to insert some comments and then share the Senior Dinner workbook with Penny and Ian, two other marching band senior students. After they review the workbook, you will merge and combine the workbooks to see what comments they have. Finally, you will accept and reject changes as necessary.

STEP 1 ▸▸ INSERT AND EDIT A COMMENT

You notice that the total revenue generated seems high. Because you do not have time to check the worksheet formulas now, you will insert a comment to remind you to review the formulas later. Refer to Figure 11.24 as you complete Step 1.

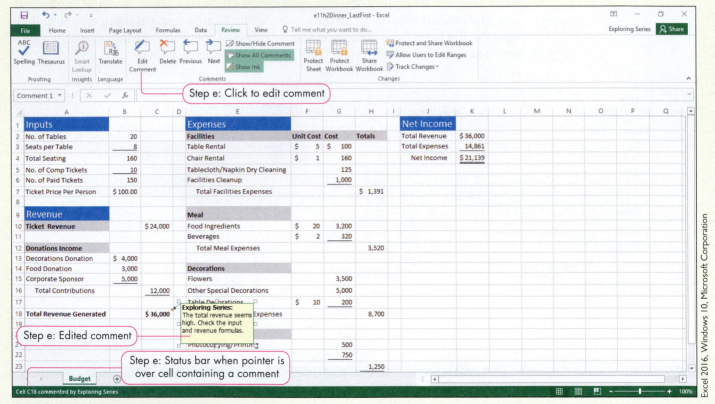

FIGURE 11.24 Edited Comment

a. Open *e11h1Dinner_LastFirst* and save it as **e11h2Dinner_LastFirst**.

b. Click **cell C18**.

c. Click the **Review tab** and click **New Comment** in the Comments group.

Excel displays a comment indicator in the top-right corner of cell C18 and a comment box containing your name.

d. Type **This seems high.** and click **cell C18** again.

The New Comment command in the Comments group changes to Edit Comment.

e. Click **Edit Comment** in the Comments group and change the comment text to **The total revenue seems high. Check the input and revenue formulas.** Save the workbook.

When you point to a cell containing a comment, the status bar displays the cell reference and the user who inserted the comment, such as *Cell C18 commented by Exploring Series.*

STEP 2 ➤➤ **SHARE THE WORKBOOK**

You want to designate the Senior Dinner workbook as sharable so that other team members can review it and offer suggestions. Refer to Figure 11.25 as you complete Step 2.

FIGURE 11.25 Shared Workbook

a. Click **Share Workbook** in the Changes group on the Review tab.

The Share Workbook dialog box opens.

b. Click the **Editing tab** within the dialog box and click to select the **Allow changes by more than one user at the same time check box**.

c. Click **OK** in the Share Workbook dialog box and click **OK** when prompted to save the workbook.

Excel displays [Shared] after the file name on the title bar.

d. Save the workbook.

You received an updated workbook from two team members. Before you can combine the separate workbooks into one workbook, you need to add the Compare and Merge Workbooks command to the Quick Access Toolbar. Refer to Figure 11.26 as you complete Step 3.

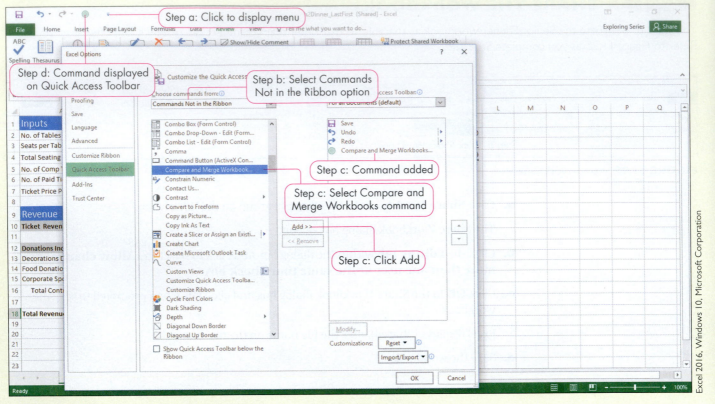

FIGURE 11.26 Compare and Merge Command

a. Click **Customize Quick Access Toolbar** on the right side of the Quick Access Toolbar and select **More Commands**.

The Excel Options dialog box opens, displaying the Quick Access Toolbar options.

b. Click the **Choose commands from arrow** and select **Commands Not in the Ribbon**.

c. Scroll through the commands list, select **Compare and Merge Workbooks**, and then click **Add**.

Excel adds an icon for the Compare and Merge Workbooks command to the Customize Quick Access Toolbar list.

d. Click **OK**.

The Compare and Merge Workbooks command displays as a circular icon on the Quick Access Toolbar.

e. Click **Save** on the Quick Access Toolbar. Click the **File tab** and click **Close**. You will submit the file at the end of the last Hands-On Exercise. Keep Excel open.

You closed the workbook and will use different workbooks for the next step.

You need to merge Ian's and Penny's workbooks into your workbook so that you can see the changes they made to the Senior Dinner budget. Refer to Figure 11.27 as you complete Step 4.

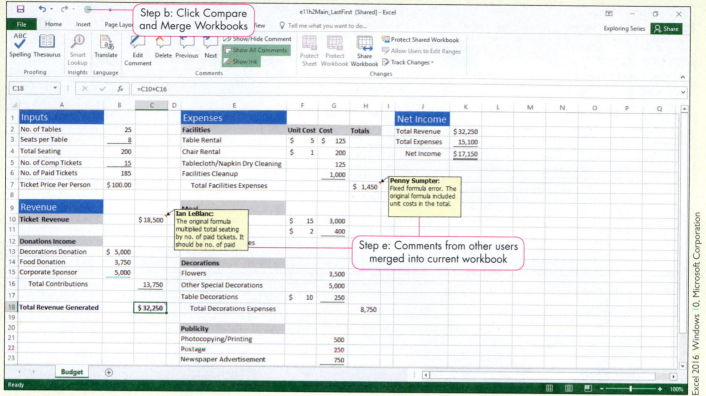

FIGURE 11.27 Workbooks Merged

a. Open *e11h2Main* and save it as **e11h2Main_LastFirst**.

    This shared workbook is almost identical to the one you saved and closed. Because you are not sending your workbook to Ian and Penny in real time, the publisher is providing an equivalent workbook that was used to share with Ian and Penny so that you can merge three workbooks into one.

b. Click **Compare and Merge Workbooks** on the Quick Access Toolbar.

    The Select Files to Merge Into Current Workbook dialog box opens.

> **TROUBLESHOOTING:** If Compare and Merge Workbooks is grayed out on the Quick Access Toolbar, click Share Workbook in the Changes group on the Review tab.

c. Navigate to the folder containing your data files.

    You need to select the files that Ian and Penny edited and returned to you.

d. Select *e11h2Main_Ian*, press and hold **Ctrl**, and then click *e11h2Main_Penny* in the Select Files to Merge Into Current Workbook dialog box.

e. Click **OK** and save the e11h2Main_LastFirst workbook.

    The results of each individual worksheet have now been merged into one combined worksheet. The merged workbook shows comment indicators that were added from merging workbooks. Other changes are not noticeable yet.

STEP 5 ▶▶ HIGHLIGHT CHANGES

You want to highlight the changes that Ian and Penny made to the shared workbook. In addition, you want to generate a change log in a History worksheet. Refer to Figures 11.28 and 11.29 as you complete Step 5.

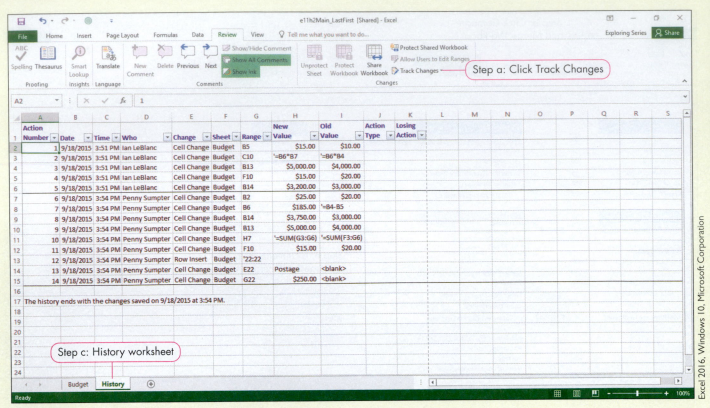

FIGURE 11.28 History Worksheet

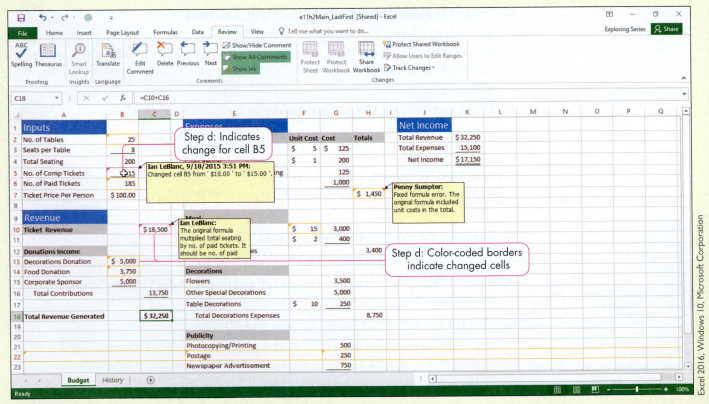

FIGURE 11.29 Changes Highlighted in Budget Worksheet

a. Click **Track Changes** in the Changes group on the Review tab and select **Highlight Changes**.

The Highlight Changes dialog box opens.

b. Click the **When check box** to deselect it.

By deselecting the When check box, all changes will be shown in the History worksheet.

c. Click to select the **List changes on a new sheet check box** and click **OK**. *Do not save the workbook.*

Excel creates a History worksheet that lists the changes (refer to Figure 11.28).

TROUBLESHOOTING: If you accidently clicked Save, repeat Steps a–c but do not save the workbook so that the History worksheet stays onscreen.

---

d. Click the **Budget sheet tab**, point to **cell B5**, and then compare your screen to Figure 11.29.

Excel highlights changes in the Budget worksheet with color-coded outlines and triangles. The colors may differ on your screen.

e. Click the **History sheet tab**. Open Word and create a new document. Click the **Insert tab**, click **Screenshot** in the Illustrations group, and then click **e11h2Main_LastFirst [Shared] – Excel** on the gallery.

You inserted a screenshot of the Excel window into the Word document. This document is evidence that you created a History worksheet.

f. Save the Word document as **e11h2History_LastFirst** and exit Word. You will submit the file at the end of the last Hands-On Exercise. Save the Excel workbook.

Excel removes the History worksheet when you save the shared workbook, but the changes remain in the Budget worksheet.

As you review Ian's and Penny's changes, you will accept and reject them, based on your decisions. Refer to Figure 11.30 as you complete Step 6.

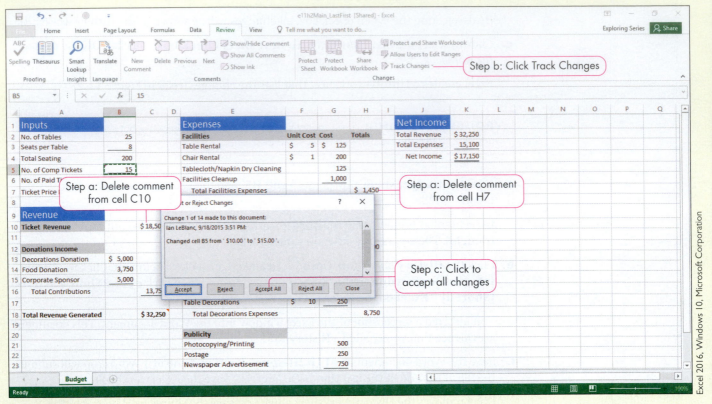

FIGURE 11.30 Accepting Changes

a. Point to **cell C10** to see Ian's comment about the formula. After reading his comment about the inaccurate formula, right-click **cell C10** and select **Delete Comment**. Click **cell H7**, read Penny's comment, right-click **cell H7**, and then select **Delete Comment**.

b. Click **Track Changes** in the Changes group on the Review tab and select **Accept/ Reject Changes**. Click **OK** in the Select Changes to Accept or Reject dialog box.

This opens the Accept or Reject Changes dialog box that you will use to review changes (refer to Figure 11.30). The dialog box displays the first change made. Ian changed cell B5 from $10 to $15.

c. Click **Accept All** to accept all changes that have been made to the worksheet.

Normally you should review each change separately and accept or reject each as needed. The color-coded borders display again to indicate cells that contain changes for the shared workbook. The color-coding will be removed when you close the workbook and open it again.

d. Save the workbook. Keep the workbook open if you plan to continue with the next Hands-On Exercise. If not, close the workbook and exit Excel.

Workbook Information

When you prepare to share an electronic copy of a workbook with others, you should run some checking tools to review your workbook for particular issues that might reveal personal information or create problems with other users. For example, if you are conducting a confidential analysis for a client or if you have a confidentiality agreement with a client, that client probably does not want to reveal that you did some analysis. You should remove your "fingerprints" from the file by removing any properties or identifying attributes that indicate your work on the workbook. After reviewing and updating a workbook, you can protect the integrity of the workbook. For example, you can save the workbook with a password or restrict who is able to edit or print the workbook.

In this section, you will prepare a workbook for sharing and then protect a workbook. In particular, you will use tools to check for issues and then mark a workbook as final.

Checking for Issues

Often, people prepare and distribute workbooks to others inside and outside their organizations. For example, you might distribute the Senior Dinner budget to some of the donors. Excel contains three tools—Document Inspector, Accessibility Checker, and Compatibility Checker—that check the workbook for issues and then alert you so that you can make any necessary changes before distributing the workbook.

Use Document Inspector

STEP 1 ⟫ Recall that document properties contain details about a workbook, such as the author and organization, which you may not want publicized. The *Document Inspector* is a tool that reviews a workbook for hidden or personal data stored in the workbook or personal document properties, such as author, and then informs you of these details so that you can select what data to remove. Document Inspector finds and removes comments and annotations, document properties, user names, document server properties, header and footer information, and hidden rows and columns. However, you cannot remove these elements if the workbook is a shared workbook.

> **TIP: MAKE A DUPLICATE!**
> Before using Document Inspector, you should save a copy of the workbook and then run Document Inspector on the duplicate workbook, because you cannot always restore all data that Document Inspector removes.

To use Document Inspector, complete the following steps:

1. Click the File tab.
2. Click Check for Issues and select Inspect Document to open the Document Inspector dialog box (see Figure 11.31). Excel will prompt you to save the workbook if you have made any changes that have not been saved yet.
3. Select the check boxes for the types of document content you want to inspect.
4. Click Inspect to display the inspection results.
5. Click Remove All for the types of content that you want to remove. Keep in mind that you might not be able to undo the changes. Use Help to learn more about hidden data and personal information that can be contained in a workbook.

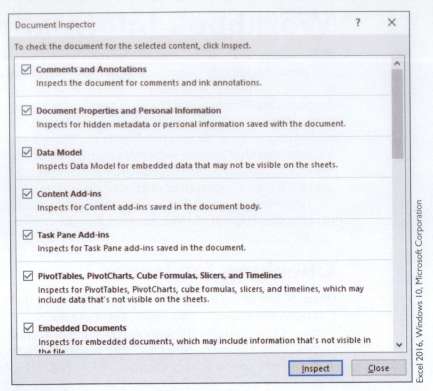

FIGURE 11.31 Document Inspector

Check Accessibility

STEP 2 ❱❱ Many organizations provide electronic documents for the public to download from websites or as email attachments. With a diverse audience of people using technology today, you should ensure your documents are accessible by everyone. The *Accessibility Checker* is a tool that reviews a workbook to detect potential issues that could hinder the ability of users who access your public files and then alerts you to these issues so that you can address them. The Accessibility Checker identifies the following types of issues, among others:

- Objects (such as charts and tables) that do not contain alternative (alt) text that make files more accessible to users who have disabilities
- Tables containing header rows
- Tables containing merged cells
- Hyperlinks that do not have ScreenTips

Accessibility Checker provides three types of feedback for each issue:

- **Error.** Content that creates extreme difficulty or impossibility for persons with disabilities to view correctly.
- **Warning.** Content that is difficult for users to comprehend.
- **Tip.** Content that is understandable but could be presented or organized differently to maximize comprehension.

> **To use the Accessibility Checker, complete the following steps:**
>
> 1. Click the File tab.
> 2. Click Check for Issues and select Check Accessibility. The Accessibility Checker task pane opens on the right side of the worksheet window, showing the results (see Figure 11.32).
> 3. Click a listed issue to see feedback in the Additional Information window. This window tells you why you should fix the problem and how to fix it.

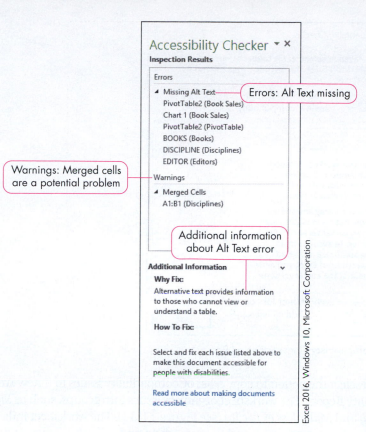

Accessibility Checker ▾ ✕
Inspection Results

Errors

◢ Missing Alt Text ——— Errors: Alt Text missing
PivotTable2 (Book Sales)
Chart 1 (Book Sales)
PivotTable2 (PivotTable)
BOOKS (Books)
DISCIPLINE (Disciplines)
EDITOR (Editors)

Warnings

Warnings: Merged cells are a potential problem

◢ Merged Cells
A1:B1 (Disciplines)

Additional information about Alt Text error

Additional Information ⌄

Why Fix:

Alternative text provides information to those who cannot view or understand a table.

How To Fix:

Select and fix each issue listed above to make this document accessible for people with disabilities.

Read more about making documents accessible

Excel 2016, Windows 10, Microsoft Corporation

FIGURE 11.32 Accessibility Checker

Check Compatibility

When you provide an Excel workbook for others to use, be aware that the recipients may have an older version of Excel installed on their computers. Because each new version of Excel contains new features, you may be using features that are not compatible with previous versions. For example, you may be using a chart style or PivotTable feature that was not available in previous versions of Excel. The ***Compatibility Checker*** is a tool that evaluates the workbook's contents to identify what data and features are not compatible with previous versions. By default, Compatibility Checker selects all Excel versions 97 through 2013. However, you can select a particular version to review for your workbook. The Compatibility Checker summarizes the issues that it finds within the dialog box and can create a worksheet that contains a list of issues.

To use Compatibility Checker, complete the following steps:

1. Click the File tab.
2. Click Check for Issues and select Check Compatibility. The Microsoft Excel - Compatibility Checker dialog box opens, showing a list of issues (see Figure 11.33).
3. Click the *Check compatibility when saving this workbook* check box if you want to check compatibility every time you save the workbook. Leave the check box blank if you do not want to check the workbook automatically upon saving.
4. Click Copy to New Sheet to create a report on a separate worksheet that lists the issues.
5. Click OK after reviewing the issues so that you can address them in the workbook.

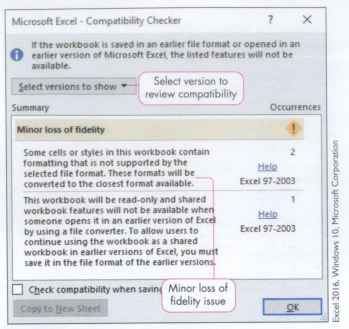

FIGURE 11.33 Compatibility Checker Dialog Box

It is helpful to select the option to copy a list of compatibility issues to a new worksheet named Compatibility Report. The worksheet organizes issues into groups, such as *Significant loss of functionality* and *Minor loss of fidelity* (see Figure 11.34). The worksheet indicates the number of occurrences per issue type and the worksheet and cell reference containing the issue. The last column indicates which version(s) of Excel are not compatible with that issue.

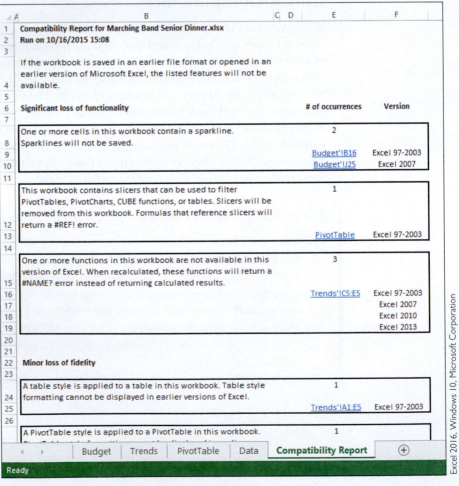

FIGURE 11.34 Compatibility Report Worksheet

Protecting a Workbook

You can protect a workbook to ensure the integrity of its contents. Workbook protection includes marking the workbook as final with an easy-to-remove Read-Only mode and inserting a digital signature that ensures the workbook's integrity and verifies that it has not been changed since it was signed electronically. The type of protection you add depends on the level of security you need to place on the workbook's contents.

Encrypt a Workbook with a Password

You can protect a workbook by restricting its access to authorized people only. To do this, you can encrypt the workbook with a password the user is required to enter in order to open the workbook. However, you cannot encrypt a file with a password if you have already marked it as final.

To encrypt a workbook with a password, complete the following steps:

1. Click the File tab.
2. Click Protect Workbook and select Encrypt with Password. The Encrypt Document dialog box opens (see Figure 11.35) so that you can enter a password in the Password box.
3. Type a password and click OK to display the Confirm Password dialog box. Type the same password in the *Reenter password* box and click OK. The Permissions area of Backstage view displays *A password is required to open this workbook.*

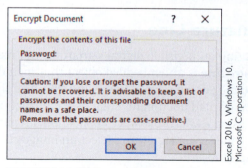

FIGURE 11.35 Encrypt Document Dialog Box

When you attempt to open a password-protected workbook, the Password dialog box opens. Enter the password and click OK. If you forget the password, you cannot recover the workbook.

Add a Digital Signature

A *digital signature* is an electronic, encrypted notation that stamps a document to authenticate the contents, confirms that a particular person authorized it, and marks the workbook as final. Use a digital signature to ensure that a workbook is authentic and that the content has not been changed since the signature was added. Your digital signature is valid until you make changes and resave the file. For example, an auditor might add a digital signature to a company's year-end financial statements to confirm that no changes have been made after the audit.

To digitally sign a workbook, you must obtain a certificate from a certified authority who can verify your signature. Adding a digital signature is similar to having your signature notarized. Digital signatures may be either visible or invisible. An invisible digital signature means that a signature is not added as a graphic object in the workbook. The digital signature is an electronic tag or attribute added to the workbook.

To add a digital signature through a third-party certificate authority, complete the following steps:

1. Click the File tab.
2. Click Protect Workbook and select Add a Digital Signature. If you have not saved the file, you will be prompted to do so. The Microsoft Excel message box displays, stating *To sign a Microsoft Office document you need a digital ID, would you like to get one from a Microsoft Partner now?*
3. Click Yes to open a Web browser with a list of digital ID services listed on support.office.com to select a service to issue a digital ID for you, or click OK to continue.

When the person electronically signs the document, Microsoft Office adds a digital signature indicating the time signed as a means to authenticate the person's identity. In addition, Microsoft Office designates the file as read-only and displays the Marked as Final Message Bar.

Add a Signature Line

STEP 3 ›› Instead of creating an invisible digital signature, you may want to include a signature line. A *signature line* is an embedded object that includes X, a line for a signature on a printout, and the person's typed name and title. The signature line is similar to a signature line in a printed document, such as a contract or legal document. In all documents created using a Microsoft Office application, an author can create a signature line to request someone type a signature, select an image containing a signature, or write a signature using a tablet PC.

To create a signature line, complete the following steps:

1. Click the Insert tab.
2. Click Add a Signature Line ⊠▾ in the Text group. The Signature Setup dialog box opens (see Figure 11.36).
3. Enter information in the appropriate boxes and click OK. The signature line displays as an object in the worksheet. You can move it within the worksheet.

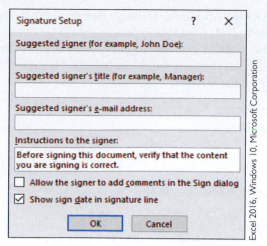

FIGURE 11.36 Signature Setup Dialog Box

When you save the workbook and open it again, the Signatures message bar appears, stating *This document needs to be signed.* Note, you only receive this message after closing and reopening the workbook. Click View Signatures to complete the process.

If you obtain a digital ID from a service provider, you can right-click the signature line and select Sign. You can then type your name next to the X for a printed version of your signature, select an image of your signature, or add a handwritten signature if you are using a tablet or touch device. Use Help to learn more about digital signatures.

Mark a Workbook as Final

STEP 4 After completing a workbook, you may want to communicate that it is a final version of the workbook. The Mark as Final command communicates that it is a final version and makes the file read-only. Excel prevents users from typing in and editing the workbook, displays a Marked as Final icon to the right of Ready on the status bar, and sets the Status document property as Final. If a workbook is shared, you cannot mark it as final; you must first remove the sharing attribute.

To mark a workbook as final, complete the following steps:

1. Click the File tab.
2. Click Protect Workbook and select Mark as Final. A warning message box appears, stating *This workbook will be marked as final and then saved.*
3. Click OK. If you have not saved the file, you will be prompted to do so. Excel then displays an information message box (see Figure 11.37).
4. Click OK. The Permissions area of Backstage view displays *This workbook has been marked as final to discourage editing.*

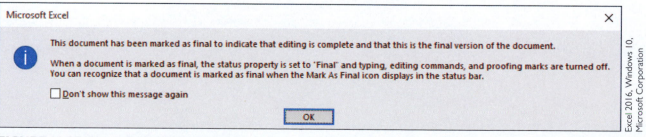

FIGURE 11.37 Mark as Final Verification Box

The MARKED AS FINAL Message Bar displays below the Ribbon, stating that *An author has marked this workbook as final to discourage editing*. A user can click Edit Anyway to remove the marked-as-final indication and begin editing the workbook. The Ribbon tabs are visible, but the commands are hidden. The title bar displays [Read-Only] after the filename (see Figure 11.38).

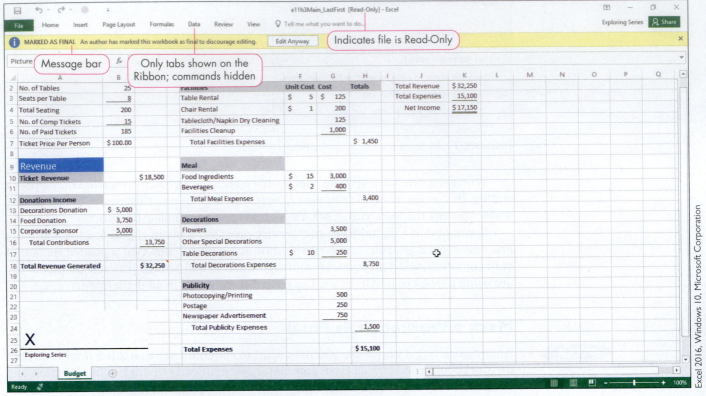

FIGURE 11.38 Workbook Marked as Final

Quick Concepts

7. What is the purpose of the Document Inspector? *p. 701*

8. Why is it important to check compatibility? *p. 703*

9. What indicators are present that a document has been marked as final? *p. 708*

Skills covered: Use the Document Inspector • Check Accessibility • Check Compatibility • Add a Signature Line • Mark as Final

3 Workbook Information

To prepare your Senior Dinner budget workbook to share the updates with other students, chefs, and donors, you need to check for and resolve issues. Then you will mark the budget as being final and add a digital signature.

STEP I ›› USE THE DOCUMENT INSPECTOR

Your budget may contain some items that you do not want to appear in the workbook you distribute to others. In particular, you want to make sure all comments are removed. Refer to Figure 11.39 as you complete Step 1.

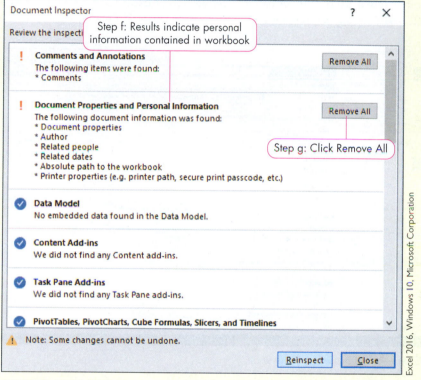

FIGURE 11.39 Document Inspector Results

a. Open *e11h2Main_LastFirst* and save it as **e11h3Main_LastFirst**.

> **TROUBLESHOOTING:** If you closed and reopened *e11h2Main_LastFirst*, make sure the file is still sharable, as indicated by [Shared] on the title bar. If not, complete the process to share the workbook again that was detailed in Hands-On Exercise 2, Step 2.

b. Click the **File tab**, click **Check for Issues**, and then select **Inspect Document**.

The Document Inspector dialog box opens.

c. Ensure all the check boxes are selected and click **Inspect**.

The Document Inspector results indicate that some hidden information cannot be removed because the workbook is shared.

d. Click **Close** to close the Document Inspector and click **Back** to return to the worksheet.

e. Click the **Review tab**, click **Share Workbook** in the Changes group, click the **Allow changes by more than one user at the same time check box** to deselect it, and then click **OK**. Click **Yes** when a message box opens.

f. Click the **File tab**, click **Check for Issues**, select **Inspect Document**, and then click **Inspect**.

The Document Inspector results with a red exclamation point indicate that it found Comments and Annotations and Document Properties and Personal Information, such as Author.

g. Click **Remove All** in the Document Properties and Personal Information section.

h. Click **Close**, click **Back**, and then save the workbook.

You want to make sure the Senior Dinner budget does not contain any content that might cause difficulties for users. In addition, you know that another senior band member has an older version of Excel, so you want to make sure the workbook does not have critical features that might not appear in the workbook when she opens it. Refer to Figure 11.40 as you complete Step 2.

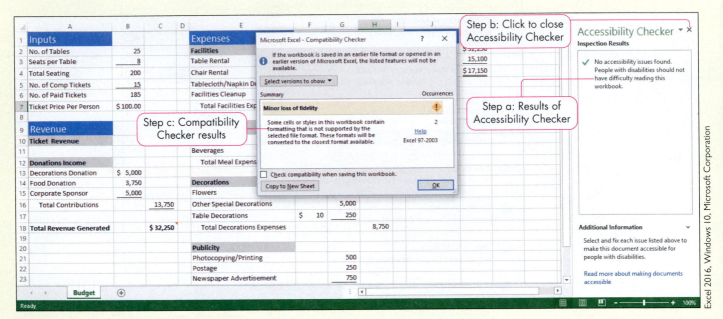

FIGURE 11.40 Check Accessibility and Compatibility

a. Click the **File tab**, click **Check for Issues**, and then select **Check Accessibility**.

The Accessibility Checker task pane displays on the right side. The inspection results indicate that no issues were found.

b. Close the Accessibility Checker task pane.

c. Click the **File tab**, click **Check for Issues**, and then select **Check Compatibility**.

The Microsoft Excel - Compatibility Checker dialog box opens. It did not find any critical losses of fidelity. It did find minor compatibility issues with Excel 97-2003 compatibility. This is not an issue, as all members of your project are using at least Excel 2010.

d. Click **OK** and save the workbook.

You want to add a signature line to indicate that you approve the dinner budget. Refer to Figure 11.41 as you complete Step 3.

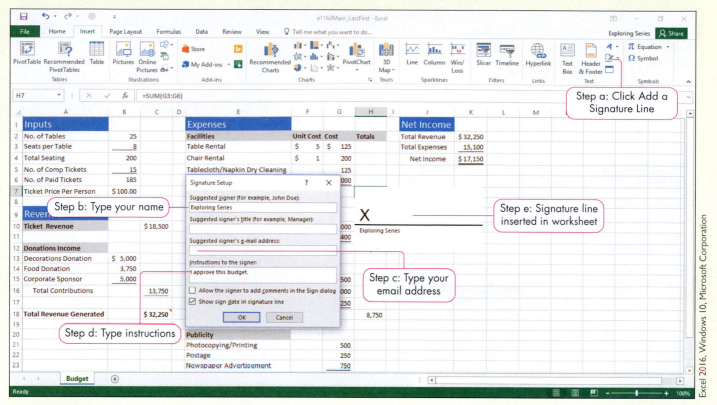

FIGURE 11.41 Signed Workbook

a. Click the **Insert tab** and click **Add a Signature Line** in the Text group.

The Signature Setup dialog box opens so that you can specify settings for the signature line.

b. Click in the **Suggested signer box** and type your name.

Your name will display on the signature line in the worksheet when you close the Signature Set dialog box.

c. Click in the **Suggested signer's e-mail address box** and type your address.

d. Delete the text in the **Instructions to the signer box** and type **I approve this budget.**

e. Click **OK.**

You will now see the signature box appear in the spreadsheet. Your name displays in the signature box; however, your email address and instructions to the signer do not display in the signature box.

f. Press **Alt** while dragging the signature box to snap it to the top corner of **cell A23** and save the workbook.

In this step, you created a signature line only. If you want to add an official digital signature, you need to obtain a signature ID from a Microsoft partner that supports digital signatures in Excel.

STEP 4 ›› MARK AS FINAL

You want the recipients of your workbook to know that it is a final budget. Refer to Figure 11.42 as you complete Step 4.

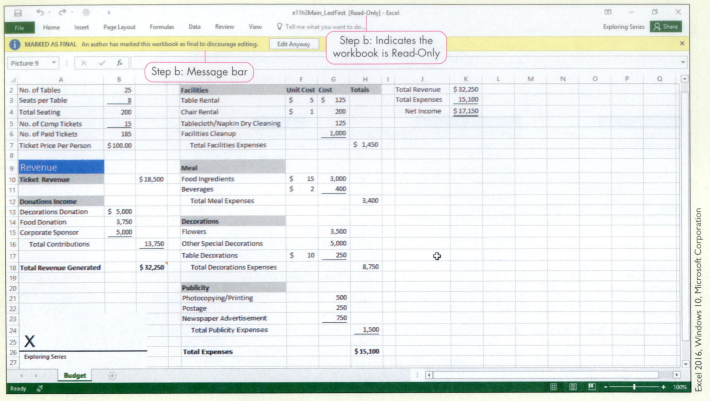

FIGURE 11.42 Marked as Final

a. Click the **File tab**, click **Protect Workbook**, and then select **Mark as Final**.

A message box appears, indicating that *This workbook will be marked as final and then saved.*

b. Click **OK**.

Excel saves the workbook. Another message box displays *This document has been marked as final to indicate that editing is complete and that this is the final version of the document.*

c. Click **OK**.

The Ribbon collapses, and a message bar displays below the Ribbon tab names. The title bar displays Read-Only.

d. Keep the workbook open if you plan to continue with the next Hands-On Exercise. If not, close the workbook and exit Excel.

Workbook Distribution

Some people prefer different formats for files they receive. While you are primarily working in Excel, you might need to save a file in other formats for the convenience of other users. Excel provides the means for you to change the file type and create different types of files from your Excel workbooks. If you do not provide data in a file format your recipients can manipulate, the data are useless to them. After saving a workbook, you are ready to distribute it. Excel provides a variety of distribution methods so that you can provide others with easy access to your workbooks, whether that is as an email attachment or uploaded to a server.

In this section, you will learn how to save a workbook in different file formats and how to send the workbook to others electronically.

Saving a Workbook in Different Formats

When you save a workbook in Excel 2016, you save the workbook in the default 2016 file format, which ends with the .xlsx extension. Excel 2013, 2010, and 2007 also save files in the .xlsx format. However, previous versions of Excel saved workbooks with the .xls extension. The primary reasons that the .xlsx file format is better than the .xls format are that the .xlsx files are smaller in size because the .xlsx format uses a built-in compression feature, and content images and macros are stored separately to enable increased probability of data recovery if a file becomes corrupted. In addition, any Office version beginning with 2007 uses XML (Extensible Markup Language), a standardized way of tagging data so that programs can automatically extract data from workbooks.

Although you use the default .xlsx file format when you save most Excel 2016 workbooks, you might need to save a workbook in another format. Excel enables you to save workbooks in many different formats. Table 11.4 lists and describes some of the most commonly used file formats.

TABLE 11.4	File Formats	
Format	**Extension**	**Description**
Excel Workbook	.xlsx	Default Office Excel 2007–2016 XML-based file format.
Excel 97-2003 Workbook	.xls	Binary file format used for Excel 97-2003 workbooks.
OpenDocument Spreadsheet	.ods	Format for spreadsheet applications such as Google Docs and OpenOffice.
Excel Template	.xltx	The default Office Excel 2007–2016 file format for an Excel template.
Excel Macro-Enabled Workbook	.xlsm	XML-based and macro-enabled format to save embedded macros for Excel 2007–2016.
Excel Binary Workbook	.xlsb	Binary file format for Excel 2007–2016.
Text (Tab delimited)	.txt	Tab-delimited format so that the file contents can be used with other Microsoft Windows programs. Uses the tab character as a delimiter to separate data into columns. Saves only the active worksheet.
CSV (Comma delimited)	.csv	Comma-delimited text file for use with other Windows programs. Uses the comma as a delimiter to separate data into columns. Saves only the active worksheet.
Formatted Text (Space delimited)	.prn	Lotus space-delimited format. Saves only the active worksheet.
Portable Document Format	.pdf	File format that preserves layout and formatting, ensure content is not easily changed, enables viewing on the Web.

Save a Workbook for Previous Excel Versions

More people are upgrading to Excel 2013 or 2016. However, some people will continue to use previous versions of Excel. You can open a workbook saved in Excel 2003 format within Excel 2016 and save it in the .xlsx format. However, Excel 2016 workbooks are not by default backward compatible with Excel 2003 and previous versions. If you need to send a workbook to someone who is using a previous version of Excel, you can save the workbook in the Excel 97-2003 Workbook format (.xls).

To save a workbook in an older version of Excel, complete the following steps:

1. Click the File tab and click Export.
2. Click Change File Type. Backstage view displays a column of File Types (see Figure 11.43).
3. Select Excel 97-2003 Workbook in the *Change File type* list.
4. Click Save As below the Change File type list, navigate to the folder in which you want to store the file, and type an appropriate name in the File name box.
5. Click Save in the Save As dialog box to save the workbook.

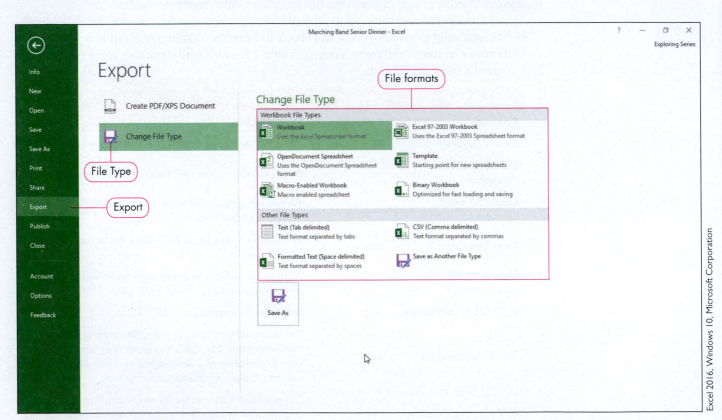

FIGURE 11.43 File Types

Save a Workbook as a PDF File

STEP 1 >> Sometimes you may want to save an Excel workbook so those who do not have Excel can display and print the file. The most common and best way to enable non–Excel users to display and print Excel workbooks is to save the Excel file in **Portable Document Format (PDF)**, a standard file format that preserves the document's data and formatting as originally intended in the source program and ensures that other people cannot edit the original data or see proprietary formulas. People can view PDF files correctly on various computer systems and platforms, even if the user does not have the source program. Saving a workbook as a PDF file saves the formatting that you used in an Excel workbook and enables non-Windows users to display and print the file because Adobe Systems Incorporated designed PDF as a universal file format.

You can also print to **XML Paper Specification (XPS)**, an electronic format created by Microsoft that preserves document formatting and is viewable and printable in any platform. XPS is an alternative to PDF. Like PDF, an XPS document is designed to be viewed and shared regardless the platform a recipient of your file is using. An XPS document can be viewed with the XPS Viewer, a Windows 10 accessory program that should have been installed with Windows 10; otherwise, it is available as a free download at www.microsoft.com/whdc/xps/viewxps.mspx.

> **To save a file in the PDF format, complete the following steps:**
>
> 1. Click the File tab and click Export.
> 2. Click Create PDF/XPS Document in the Export section. Backstage view displays the Create a PDF/XPS Document button.
> 3. Click Create PDF/XPS to open the Publish as PDF or XPS dialog box.
> 4. Click the *Save as type* arrow and select PDF if it is not already selected.
> 5. Navigate to the folder in which you want to store the file and type an appropriate name in the File name box. If you want to see how the file looks in PDF format after publishing it, click the *Open file after publishing* check box to select it.
> 6. Click Options to open the Options dialog box. Select appropriate settings, such as the page range, and click OK.
> 7. Click Publish in the Publish as PDF or XPS dialog box to save the workbook in PDF format.

> **TIP: PRINT TO PDF**
> If you have Adobe Acrobat (not just Adobe Reader) or other third-party applications that create PDF files installed, you can create a file through the Print options. Click the File tab, click Print, click the Printer arrow, select Adobe PDF, and then click Print. You will be prompted to enter a file name for the PDF file.

Sending a Workbook to Others

Excel provides multiple methods for sharing your workbook with other people. You can share your workbook as an email attachment or as an Internet fax. In addition, you can save a file on a OneDrive location so that you can share that file with others. Furthermore, you can email a workbook as an email attachment, send a link to a shared drive where the file is saved, send as a PDF email attachment, send as an XPS attachment, or send as an Internet fax.

Send a Workbook by Email

You can email the workbook to others so that they can collaborate on the contents of the workbook. While it is possible to send an Excel workbook as an attachment to an email message, it is often more convenient to send the email directly from Excel, as long as you have configured Outlook as your email client. When you start Outlook for the first time, you will be prompted to complete the Microsoft Outlook Startup Wizard to configure the program. Follow the prompts, enter the required information to connect your existing email account to Outlook, download the Outlook Connector (if prompted), restart your computer, and then start Outlook.

When you send a workbook as an attachment, keep in mind you are sending separate copies of the workbook to others. The recipients can save the workbook on their computer systems and modify it as they wish. If you want to incorporate their changes, the recipients will need to email their modified copy back to you so that you can compare and merge the workbook with yours.

To send an Excel workbook as an attachment by email, complete the following steps (make sure your Outlook client is connected to an email account):

1. Click the File tab and click Share.
2. Click Email in the Share section.
3. Click Send as Attachment, Send a Link, Send as PDF, Send as XPS, or Send as Internet Fax. If a dialog box opens to prompt you to enter your Microsoft account credentials, enter your credentials. The workbook file name appears in the Attached box (see Figure 11.44).
4. Type the recipient's email address in the To box.
5. Change the default subject line to an appropriate title.
6. Compose a message that informs the recipient of the workbook attachment and what you want the recipient to do with the workbook.
7. Click Send to send the email message with the attached Excel workbook.

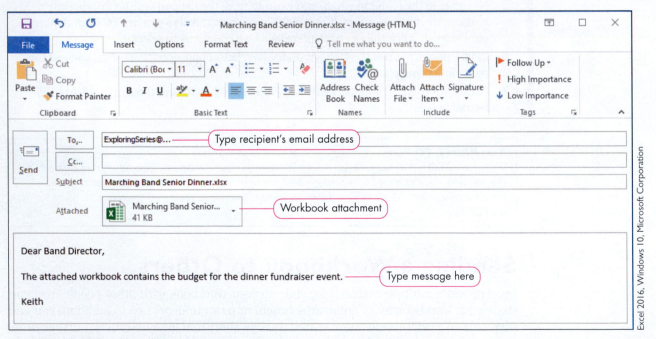

FIGURE 11.44 Email Interface

TIP: SENDING AN ATTACHED WORKBOOK WITHOUT OUTLOOK

If Outlook is not installed as your default email client, you may not be able to use the Share Email option to start the email program and attach the workbook. Instead, you should close the workbook, open your email client, and then click the Attach button or command in that window to send the workbook as an email attachment.

Share Workbooks Through OneDrive

 You might need files when you are away from your home or office computer. For example, you might save your homework for your Excel class on your home computer, but then you need to work on it between classes on campus. However, you might not want to carry a flash drive or external drive with you. You can save a workbook to **OneDrive**, an online storage location in which you can save and access files. Saving to OneDrive is an effective way to access your files from any device, including your smartphone or tablet, when you synchronize the devices.

To save a workbook to OneDrive, complete the following steps:

1. Click the File tab and click Save As.
2. Double-click OneDrive from the top of the Save As list (see Figure 11.45) in Backstage view.
3. Click the folder, such as Exploring, to which you want to save the workbook, or click New folder if you want to create a new folder on your OneDrive.
4. Enter a file name in the File name box in the Save As dialog box and click Save.

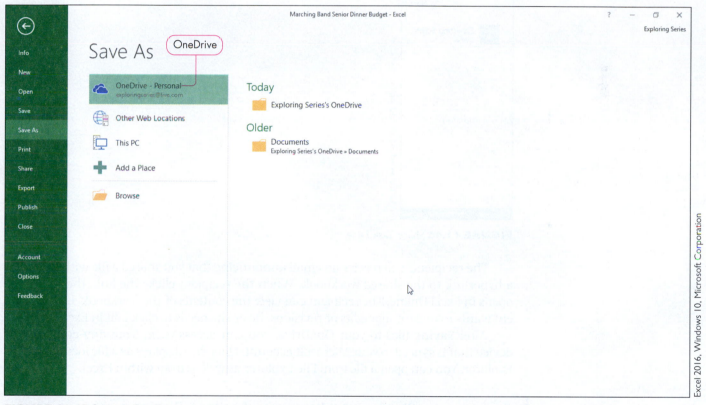

FIGURE 11.45 Save to OneDrive

> **TIP: ACCESSING WINDOWS LIVE ACCOUNT**
> When Microsoft Office 2016 is installed, you are required to create or sign in with an existing Microsoft account. This enables you to access OneDrive without additional logins. If you attempt to access your OneDrive account remotely, you will need to enter your user name and password.

Once a file is saved to OneDrive, it can be easily shared with others by clicking the Share button in the top-right corner of the Ribbon. You can then invite others to collaborate on, or just view, the workbook. Giving others editing privileges enables multiple people to work on the same workbook. This approach may be preferable to sending an email attachment and then consolidating changes from multiple workbooks later.

When you open an Excel workbook from OneDrive and click the Share button, the Share task pane lets you invite other people to share the file (see Figure 11.46). You can either type in an email address or search through your address book to select an address. After selecting a person to invite, select either *Can edit* or *Can view* to specify the level of rights the person has for that workbook. You can also include a message with the invitation. You can also click the File tab, click Share, and then click Share with People to display the Share task pane on the right side of the worksheet

FIGURE 11.46 Share Task Pane

The recipients will receive an email announcing that you shared a file with them and a hyperlink to the shared workbook. When the recipient clicks the link, the workbook opens in Excel Online. The recipient can view the contents of the workbook. If the recipient wants to make major edits or revisions, he or she needs to click Edit in Excel.

After saving files to your OneDrive, you can access them from any computer or device that is synced to your Microsoft account. OneDrive displays as a file location in File Explorer. You can open a file from File Explorer as well as from within Excel.

To access your files from OneDrive, complete the following steps:

1. Open File Explorer.
2. Double-click OneDrive in the navigation pane on the left side of File Explorer.
3. Double-click the file you want to open.

Quick Concepts

10. What is the benefit of exporting a file as a PDF? *p. 715*

11. Why would you choose to send a workbook as an email attachment? *p. 715*

12. What is the benefit of saving an Excel workbook to OneDrive? *p. 717*

Hands-On Exercises

Skills covered: Create a PDF File • Save a Workbook to OneDrive • Share a Workbook Through OneDrive

4 Workbook Distribution

You want to send the workbook to several people for reference. To ensure the recipients can see the data in the same format and to prevent them from changing the data, you will save the workbook as a PDF file. You will then save the workbook to OneDrive.

STEP 1 ›› CREATE A PDF FILE

You want to save the workbook as a PDF file so that the Senior Dinner donors can view but not change the budget. Refer to Figure 11.47 as you complete Step 1.

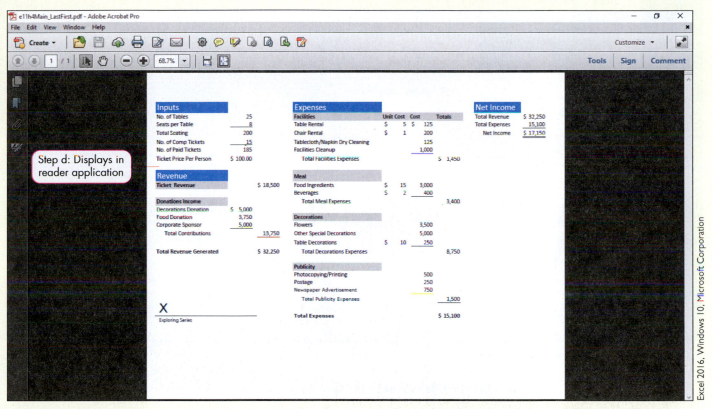

FIGURE 11.47 Workbook Saved as PDF

Excel 2016, Windows 10, Microsoft Corporation

a. Open *e11h3Main_LastFirst*. Do not save the file with a different name at this time.

> **TROUBLESHOOTING:** If you open the *e11h3Main_LastFirst* workbook and try to save it as another file name, Excel will remove the marked-as-final indication and the digital signature. You need to preserve those settings so that your instructor can verify that you completed those steps in Hands-On Exercise 3.

b. Click the **File tab** and click **Export**.

c. Click **Create PDF/XPS Document** and click **Create PDF/XPS** on the right side of Backstage view.

d. Change the name in the File name box to **e11h4Main_LastFirst**. Navigate to the folder containing your files, click the **Open file after publishing check box** to select it, and then click **Publish**.

The PDF opens in Adobe Reader, Adobe Acrobat, or Microsoft Reader, depending on what is installed on your computer.

e. Close the newly created PDF. You will submit the file at the end of the last Hands-On Exercise. Keep e11h3Main_LastFirst open in Excel to continue with the next step.

STEP 2 ▶▶ **SAVE A WORKBOOK TO ONEDRIVE**

You want to save the workbook to OneDrive so that the head chef can review the final dinner budget. Refer to Figure 11.48 as you complete Step 2.

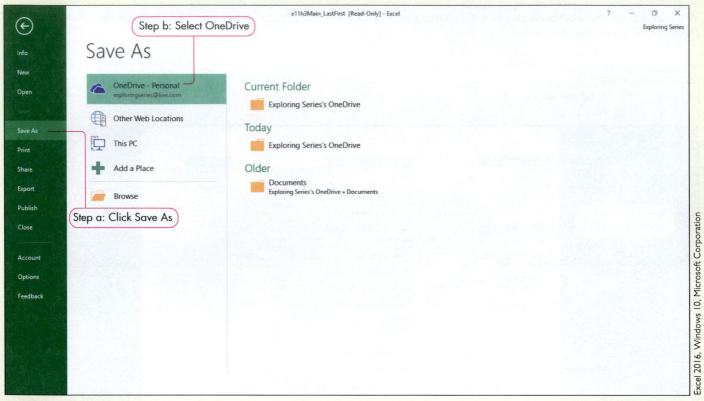

FIGURE 11.48 Save to OneDrive

a. Click the **File tab** and click **Save As**.

b. Double-click **OneDrive** at the top of Backstage view.

c. Select a folder in which to save your document and click **Save**.

d. Keep the workbook open.

Because you invite others to share the workbook you saved on OneDrive, you want to create an invitation to yourself to make sure the sharing capabilities work. You will then compress several files so that you can submit the compressed file to your instructor. Refer to Figure 11.49 as you complete Step 2.

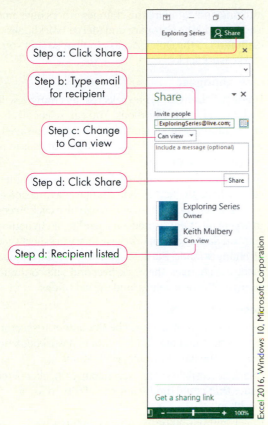

Step a: Click Share

Step b: Type email for recipient

Step c: Change to Can view

Step d: Click Share

Step d: Recipient listed

Excel 2016, Windows 10, Microsoft Corporation

FIGURE 11.49 Share Through OneDrive

a. Click **Share** on the top-right corner of the Ribbon.

The Share task pane opens and displays options to invite people to share the workbook.

b. Click in the **Invite people box** and type your email address.

You are entering your email so that you can test that you receive an email with a link to share the file.

c. Click the **Can edit arrow** and select **Can view.**

d. Click **Share** in the Share task pane.

Your name displays in the Share task pane, indicating that the file has been shared with you and that you can view the file.

e. Close the workbook and exit Excel.

f. Open File Explorer and navigate to where you saved your files. Press and hold down **Ctrl** as you click to select **e11h2Dinner_LastFirst**, **e11h2History_LastFirst.docx**, **e11h2Main_LastFirst**, **e11h3Main_LastFirst**, and **e11h4Main_LastFirst.pdf**.

g. Right-click one of the selected files, select **Send to**, select **Compressed (zipped) folder**, type **e11h4DinnerFiles_LastFirst**, and press **Enter**. Based on your instructor's directions, submit e11h4DinnerFiles_LastFirst.zip.

Chapter Objectives Review

After reading this chapter, you have accomplished the following objectives:

1. Customize Excel Options.
- Personalize your copy of Microsoft Office: You can personalize your copy of Microsoft Office by entering your name as the user name. You can further personalize Office by selecting an Office Background to display a faint design in the top-right corner of the title bar and select an Office Theme to change the main color scheme of Microsoft Office.
- Customize the Ribbon: You can create a new tab on the Ribbon through the Excel Options dialog box. After you create the new tab, you can name it, add new groups, and then add commands within the groups.
- Customize the Quick Access Toolbar: You can add frequently used commands to the Quick Access Toolbar. For example, you might add the Print command or Spelling command to the Quick Access Toolbar.
- Customize other options: You can customize other options, such as ensuring the Spelling command checks words in uppercase. In addition, you can specify the number or recently used files to display when opening Excel.

2. Change properties.
- Display properties in Backstage view: When you create or edit a file, document properties are attached to the file. For example, document properties include the author's name, title, subject, company, creation date, revision date, and keywords.
- Use the Properties dialog box: The Properties dialog box enables you to display properties such as the file type, location, size, and creation date. You can also enter and change summary properties, such as a title or subject, view statistics, and display worksheet names.

3. Insert comments.
- Show and hide comments: A comment indicator displays in the top-right corner of a cell that contains a comment. You can use the Ribbon or the shortcut menu to display or hide a comment.
- Edit and delete comments: If you need to change the text in a comment, you can edit it. If you no longer need a comment, you can delete it from the cell.
- Print comments: By default, comments do not print with a worksheet. However, you can select an option in the Page Setup dialog box to print comments in a worksheet.

4. Share and merge workbooks.
- Understand conflicts and network issues: Conflicts may arise when several users are working with shared workbooks. Depending on the network permissions, some users may not be able to edit a workbook. However, they can open a workbook in Read-Only mode to view the workbook content.
- Compare and merge workbooks: Use the Compare and Merge Workbooks command to merge the workbooks into one and compare the changes others have made. You can add the Compare and Merge Workbooks command to the Quick Access Toolbar so that you can merge workbooks.

5. Track changes.
- Highlight changes: When selected, all changes will be highlighted in the workbook. You can select all changes or just changes made since the last time you saved a workbook. Color-coded borders display in cells to indicate which cells were changed
- Accept and reject changes: When you track changes, you can go through changes one change at a time and either accept or reject the change. You can also click Accept All to accept all changes made in a workbook. In addition, you can display a temporary History worksheet that lists all changes made, the dates and times of the changes, who made the changes, the worksheet and cells containing the changes, the new values, and the old values.

6. Check for issues.
- Use Document Inspector: The Document Inspector detects personal and hidden data in a workbook and removes the data to your specifications.
- Check accessibility: The Accessibility Checker detects issues that could hinder a user's ability to use a workbook.
- Check compatibility: The Compatibility Checker detects data and features that are not compatible with previous versions of Excel.

7. Protect a workbook.
- Encrypt a workbook with a password: For enhanced protection, you can password-protect a file. If a person does not enter the correct password, he or she cannot open the workbook.
- Add a digital signature: A digital signature indicates that the workbook is authentic and has not been changed since you added the signature.
- Add a signature line: A signature line is an object embedded within the worksheet that displays an X, a signature line, a name, and a title, similar to a typed signature line on a contract.
- Mark a workbook as final: You can mark a workbook as final to indicate that you approve that particular version of the workbook. Marking a workbook as final makes it a read-only file.

8. Save a workbook in different formats.
- Save a workbook for previous Excel versions: Save the workbook in a legacy format for compatibility with older versions of Excel.
- Save a workbook as a PDF file: Save a workbook as a Portable Document Format (PDF) file that can be viewed in Adobe Reader or Adobe Acrobat.

9. Send a workbook to others.

- Send a workbook by email: Use Outlook to send the file as an email attachment.
- Share a workbook Through OneDrive: You can save the file to a folder on OneDrive so that you can access the file with other devices that are synchronized with a Microsoft account. You can also share a workbook with others by displaying the Share task pane to specify an email address for a recipient, specify whether that person can edit or view the workbook, and include a message. When you click Share, the recipient will receive an email with a link to the shared workbook on your OneDrive.

Key Terms Matching

Match the key terms with their definitions. Write the key term number by the appropriate numbered definition.

a. Accessibility Checker
b. Collaboration
c. Comment
d. Comment indicator
e. Compatibility Checker
f. Digital signature
g. Document Inspector
h. Document property
i. History worksheet
j. Metadata

k. Office Background
l. Office Theme
m. OneDrive
n. Portable Document Format (PDF)
o. Shared workbook
p. Signature line
q. Track Changes

1. _____ A central online storage location in which you can store, access, and share files via an Internet connection. **p. 717**

2. _____ A tool that evaluates the workbook contents to identify what data and features are not compatible with previous versions. **p. 703**

3. _____ A tool that reviews a workbook for hidden properties or personal information and then displays a list of these details so that you can select what data to remove. **p. 701**

4. _____ A tool that reviews a workbook to detect potential issues that could hinder a user's ability to use a workbook. **p. 702**

5. _____ A setting that controls the overall appearance and color of the title bar and interface for Office programs. **p. 674**

6. _____ A worksheet created through the Track Changes feature that lists particular types of changes made to a workbook. The worksheet is temporary; it is deleted when you save the workbook. **p. 693**

7. _____ A collaboration feature that records certain types of changes made in a workbook. **p. 690**

8. _____ A notation attached to a cell to pose a question or annotation to ask a question or provide a suggestion. **p. 683**

9. _____ An electronic, encrypted notation that stamps a document to authenticate the contents, confirms that a particular person authorized it, and marks the workbook as final. **p. 706**

10. _____ Data, such as a keyword, that describes other data, such as the contents of a file. **p. 677**

11. _____ An embedded object that includes X, a line for a signature on a printout, the person's typed name and title. **p. 706**

12. _____ A process that occurs when multiple people work together to achieve a common goal by using technology to edit the contents of a file. **p. 683**

13. _____ A setting that controls the faint background image, if any, in the top-right corner of the title bar. **p. 674**

14. _____ An attribute, such as an author's name or keyword, that describes a file. **p. 677**

15. _____ A file that is designated as sharable and is stored on a network that is accessible to multiple people who can edit the workbook at the same time. **p. 686**

16. _____ A colored triangle in the top-right corner of a cell to indicate that the cell contains a comment. **p. 684**

17. _____ A standard file format that preserves a document's original data and formatting for multi-platform use. **p. 715**

Multiple Choice

1. Which category in the Excel Options dialog box contains the option to change the user name?

    (a) General

    (b) Account Settings

    (c) Advanced

    (d) Trust Center

2. You want to organize frequently used commands in groups on a new tab on the Ribbon. What is the first step?

    (a) Add commands to a blank Ribbon.

    (b) Create a group on an existing tab.

    (c) Add a new tab to the Ribbon.

    (d) Rename the default group name.

3. When you display the Backstage Info section, you *cannot* manually change which property?

    (a) Author

    (b) Created date

    (c) Title

    (d) Tag

4. What is the default setting for the amount of time to keep tracked changes in history for a shared workbook?

    (a) 7 days

    (b) 30 days

    (c) 1 year

    (d) No restriction

5. If comments are hidden in a worksheet, how do you know which cells contain comments?

    (a) There is no way to know if the comments are hidden.

    (b) A comment task pane displays a list of cells that contain comments.

    (c) A red border displays for cells that contain comments.

    (d) A comment indicator displays in the top-right corner of the cells.

6. The Track Changes feature does *not* detect what type of change?

    (a) Changing a value of a number from 10 to 25

    (b) Inserting a new row above row 18

    (c) Deleting text within a label

    (d) Applying Percent Style for the range B4:B10

7. Which tool detects issues that could hinder a user's ability to use a workbook?

    (a) Accessibility Checker

    (b) Compatibility Checker

    (c) Change tracker

    (d) Document Inspector

8. A workbook that has been marked as final:

    (a) Displays a nonstop, flashing Message Bar that the workbook is final.

    (b) Is password protected to make any changes.

    (c) Opens in Read-Only mode.

    (d) Must contain a digital signature.

9. The _____ tool detects particular properties, such as Author, and removes those properties from a file that you plan to distribute.

    (a) Compatibility Checker

    (b) Document Inspector

    (c) Advanced Properties

    (d) Accessibility Checker

10. If you want to save a file in a format that preserves worksheet formatting, prevents changes, and ensures that the document looks the same on most computers, save the workbook in the _____ file format.

    (a) .csv

    (b) Excel template

    (c) Excel 97-2003 workbook

    (d) .pdf

Practice Exercises

1 | Harper County Houses Sold

A real estate agent sent you a workbook containing sales in the county for the last year. You want to add document properties and then review it for accessibility and compatibility. You then will create a PDF file to save to OneDrive. Refer to Figure 11.50 as you complete this exercise.

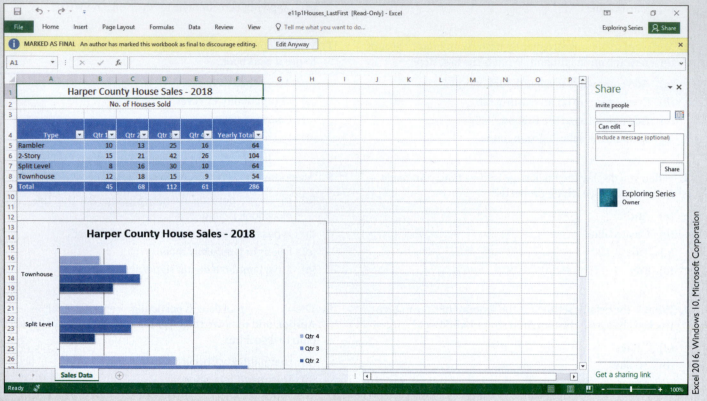

FIGURE 11.50 Harper County Houses Sold Workbook

a. Open *e11p1Houses* and save it as **e11p1Houses_LastFirst**. Type your name on the left side of the footer.

b. Click **File**, click **Properties**, and select **Advanced Properties**. Enter these properties:
- Type **2018 Harper County House Sales** in the Title box.
- Type your name in the Author box.

c. Click **OK**, click **Back**, and click **Save**.

d. Click **File**, click **Check for Errors**, and select **Inspect Document**. Click **Inspect** in the Document Inspector dialog box. The Document Inspector finds comments and annotations, document properties and personal information, headers and footers, and hidden rows and columns.

e. Scroll down to see the different items found by Document Inspector. Click **Remove All** to the right of Comments and Annotations. Click **Close** and click the **Back arrow**.

f. Click **Select All**, click **Format** in the Cells group on the Home tab, point to **Hide & Unhide**, and select **Unhide Rows**. Click **cell A1**.

g. Click **File**, click **Check for Issues**, and select **Check Accessibility**.

h. Complete the following set of steps to enter alternative text for the table:
- Double-click **Table1** in the Accessibility Checker task pane to select the table.
- Right-click the table, point to **Table**, and select **Alternative Text**.
- Type **2018 House Sales** in the Title box in the Alternative Text dialog box.

- Type **Number of houses sold in each category during each quarter.** in the Description box.
- Click **OK**.

i. Complete the following set of steps to enter alternative text for the chart:
- Double-click **Chart 1** in the Accessibility Checker task pane to select the chart.
- Double-click the **chart** to display the Format Chart Area task pane.
- Click **Size & Properties** and click **Alt Text**.
- Type **2018 House Sales** in the Title box.
- Type **Bar chart showing number of houses sold in each category during each quarter.** in the Description box.
- Close the Format Chart Area task pane.

j. Close the Accessibility Checker task pane and click any cell within the worksheet

k. Click the **File tab**, click **Protect Workbook**, and select **Mark as Final**. Click **OK** and then click **OK**.

l. Click the **File tab**, click **Export**, and then click **Create PDF/XPS**. Accept the default name, **e11p1Houses_LastFirst**, and click **Publish**. Close the PDF Reader program and keep the Excel workbook open.

m. Click **Share** in the top-right corner of the window and click **Save to Cloud**. Click **OneDrive Personal**, select a folder, and click **Save**. The Share task pane displays. Click in the **Invite people box** and enter your instructor's email address. Click **Share**.

n. Close the file. Based on your instructor's directions, submit the following:
e11p1Houses_LastFirst
e11p1Houses_LastFirst.pdf

2 Valentine's Day Dance

You are on the budget committee for the formal Valentine's Day Ball at your university. The ball includes dinner and dancing. Your committee prepared a tentative budget outlining income and expenses. The primary sources of income are contributions from student organizations and ticket sales. Expenses include the actual cost of the dinner, facilities, parking, and other costs at a luxurious hotel in the city. Your goal is to balance the income and expenses, decide on the most appropriate ticket price per student, and ensure your budget falls within the limitations. Refer to Figure 11.51 as you complete this exercise.

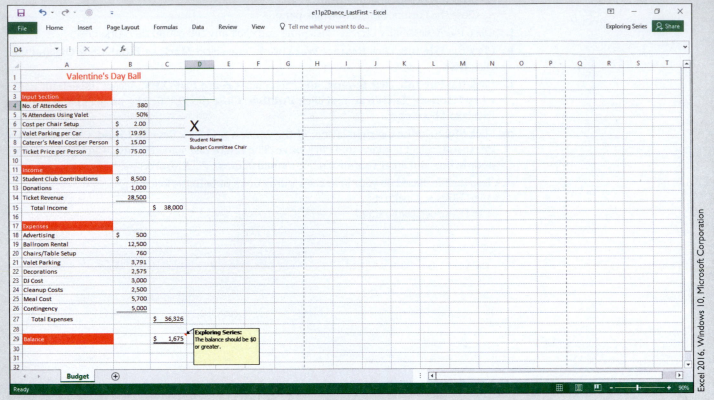

FIGURE 11.51 Valentine's Day Dance Budget

a. Open *e11p2Dance* and save it as **e11p2Dance_LastFirst**.

b. Click the **File tab**, click **Options**, select the text in the **User name box**, type your full name, and then click **OK**.

c. Look at the Quick Access Toolbar to see if it contains the Compare and Merge Workbooks command. If so, continue with Step d. If not, click **Customize Quick Access Toolbar** on the right side of the Quick Access Toolbar and select **More Commands**. Do the following in the Excel Options dialog box:
   - Click the **Choose commands from arrow** and select **Commands Not in the Ribbon**.
   - Scroll through the list, select **Compare and Merge Workbooks**, and then click **Add**.
   - Click **OK**.

d. Make the following changes:
   - Select and delete **rows 11 through 16**.
   - Click **cell A13** and right-click **row 13** and select **Insert**. Type **Donations** in **cell A13** and **1000** in **cell B13**.
   - Type **=SUM(B12:B14)** in **cell C15**.
   - Type **1500** in **cell B18** and **10000** in **cell B19**.
   - Type **=B4*B8** in **cell B25**.
   - Type **15** in **cell B8**. Save the workbook.

e. Click **Compare and Merge Workbooks** on the Quick Access Toolbar, select *e11p2Dance_Anita*, and then click **OK**.

f. Click the **Review tab**, select **Track Changes** in the Changes group, select **Highlight Changes**, deselect the **When check box**, click the **List changes on a new sheet check box** to select it, and then click **OK**.

g. Open the Snipping Tool in Windows. Click **New** and select **Window Snip**. Click the **Excel title bar**. Click **File** and select **Save As**. Click the **Save as type arrow** and select **Portable Network Graphic file (PNG)**. Save the image as **e11p2Dance_LastFirst**. Close the Snipping Tool.

h. Click the **Budget worksheet tab**, click **Track Changes** in the Changes group, select **Accept/Reject Changes**, and then click **OK**. Complete the following steps

- Click **Accept** to accept *Renamed sheet from 'Sheet1' to 'Budget'*. Click **Accept** for all of your changes. When prompted to select a value for cell B18, click **$500.00** by Anita and click **Accept**.
- Click **Accept** for Anita's change of cell B4 to 380.
- Click **Reject** for Anita's change to change cell B19 and delete row 19, click **Accept** on her change of cell B22 to $2,575, and then click **Reject** on her change for cell A23 to Live Band.

i. Click **Share Workbook** in the Changes group, click the **Editing tab**, deselect the **Allow changes by more than one user at a time check box**, and then click **OK**. Click **Yes**.

j. Click **cell C29**, click **New Comment** in the Comments group, and then type **The balance should be $0 or greater.**

k. Click **cell D4**, click the **Insert tab**, and then click **Add a Signature Line** in the Text group. Complete the following steps:

- Type your name in the Suggested signer box.
- Click in the **Suggested signer's title box** and type **Budget Committee Chair**.
- Click **OK**.

l. Create a footer with your name on the left side, the sheet name code in the center, and the file name code on the right side.

m. Save and close the file. Based on your instructor's directions, submit the following:
e11p2Dance_LastFirst
e11p2Dance_LastFirst.png

Mid-Level Exercises

1 House Sale Proceeds

You are an assistant at a local real estate firm. You and your colleague Jaime Acosta have been editing a shared workbook. You noticed some errors that need to be corrected. You will then combine and merge your workbook with the one Jaime sent to you.

a. Open *e11m1Proceeds* and save it as **e11m1Proceeds_LastFirst**. Open the Options dialog box and make sure your name is displayed in the User name box.

b. Use the Spelling command to detect and correct a spelling error.

c. Make the following changes:
   - Change the formula in **cell E3** to **=B2*B3**.
   - Change the formula in **cell E4** to **=B2*B4**.
   - Change the width of column D to **30**.

d. Insert a comment in **cell B6: Verify the number of months.**

e. Add the Compare and Merge Workbooks command to the Quick Access Toolbar. Compare and merge *e11m1Proceeds_Jaime* with your workbook.

f. Use Track Changes to display all changes and create a History worksheet. Use the Snipping Tool to create a screenshot of the History worksheet and save it as **e11m1Proceeds_LastFirst.png**. Close the Snipping Tool.

g. Activate Track Changes and accept the spelling error you corrected in cell A3 and the two formulas you corrected. Reject Jaime's change in cell B3 and accept his change to cell B5.

h. Remove the workbook from shared use.

i. Add the keywords in the properties: **commission rate**, **property tax**, **mortgage payoff**.

j. Use Accessibility Checker and correct the two warnings it detects. Close Accessibility Checker.

k. Click in **cell D12** and insert a signature line with your name and **Assistant** as your title.

l. Edit the footer to replace *Student Name* with your name. Save and mark the workbook as final.

m. Save and close the file. Based on your instructor's directions, submit the following:
   e11m1Proceeds_LastFirst
   e11m1Proceeds_LastFirst.png

2 Lecture Series Expenses

ANALYSIS CASE

The College of Science at Prestige University hosts a lecture series of guest presenters in the industry. As the fiscal manager, you are responsible for maintaining the budget, which includes the following expenses: lunches for the speakers and select faculty, printing costs for bulletin board fliers, travel accommodations for one out-of-state presenter per semester, and a gift pen set for each speaker. Your predecessor created a workbook containing expenses for the academic year; however, it contains errors. You and the associate dean, Sallie Hart, will review and correct the workbook. Then you will merge the two workbooks and accept and reject changes as needed. In addition, you need to prepare the workbook for distribution to the university's budget office and answer four questions on the data.

a. Open *e11m2Lecture* and save it as **e11m2Lecture_LastFirst**.

b. Ensure your name is the user name in the Excel Options dialog box.

c. Add the Compare and Merge Workbooks command to the Quick Access Toolbar. Compare and merge *e11m1Lecture_Sallie* with your workbook.

d. Insert the following comment in **cell C4** in the Spring worksheet: **We need to cut the budget another $200 next year.**

e. Activate the **Track Changes feature** so that you can accept and reject changes. Accept all changes except these four changes:

Description of Change	Action
Changed cell B2 to $120.00	Reject
Changed cell B29 from <blank> to $104.35	Reject
Changed cell B2 from $145.75 to $50.00	Reject
Changed cell B3 from $142.12 to $50.00	Reject

f. Change **cell B7** in the Gifts worksheet to **$122** and change **cell B8** in the Gifts worksheet to **$100**. Insert a comment in **cell C13** in the Spring worksheet: **Cut gift amounts for Spring semester to avoid going over budget.**

g. Display the Properties, type **Lecture Series Budget** in the Title box and **Budget** in the Categories box.

h. Select all worksheets and insert a footer with your name on the left side, the sheet name code in the center, and the file name code on the right side. Ungroup the worksheets.

i. Turn off workbook sharing. Run the Document Inspector but do not make any changes.

j. Click in **cell A18** in the Spring worksheet and insert a signature line with your name and **Fiscal Manager** as the title.

k. Answer the questions on the Q&A sheet. Then save the workbook.

l. Save the workbook on your OneDrive. Share this file with your instructor.

m. Save the workbook as an XPS document.

DISCOVER

n. Save and close the workbook. Based on your instructor's directions, submit the following:

e11m2Lecture_LastFirst

e11m2Lecture_LastFirst.xps

3 Ribbon Customization

COLLABORATION CASE

FROM SCRATCH

You and a coworker have been assigned to a team that manages financial sheets that must be merged and then emailed to management. To synchronize your efforts, you have decided to customize your Office Ribbon and then share the settings with your fellow team members. In addition, you will insert before and after screenshots into a Word document and change document properties.

Student 1

a. Start a new workbook.

b. Click the **File tab**, click **Options**, and then click **Customize Ribbon**.

c. Create a new tab and rename it as **Group Project**.

d. Rename the group on the Group Project tab as **Collaboration** and complete the following steps:

- Click **Choose commands from** and select **Main Tabs**.
- Add these Review Comments commands to the new group: **New Comment**, **Show/Hide Comment**, **Show All Comments**.
- Add these Review Changes commands to the new group: **Share Workbook** and **Track Changes**.
- Click **Choose commands from** and select **Commands Not in the Ribbon**. Add the **Compare and Merge Workbook command** to the new group you created.

e. Click **Import/Export** and select **Export all customizations**. Save the file as **e11m3Custom-Set_LastFirst** on your OneDrive. Obtain the email address of another student in your class and invite that person to share the file containing the custom Ribbon settings.

Student 2

f. Open Excel, create a new workbook, click the **File tab**, and then click **Options**. Click **Customize Ribbon**.

g. Click **Import/Export** and select **Import customization file**.

h. Import the file *e11m3CustomSet_LastFirst.exportedUI*. Click **Yes** when prompted to replace all existing Ribbon and Quick Access Toolbar customizations. Then display the newly customized tab.

i. Use the Snipping Tool to create a screenshot of the Excel window displaying the customized Ribbon. Save the screenshot as **e11m3CustomSet_LastFirst.png**.

j. Save and close the file. Based on your instructor's direction, submit the following:

e11m3CustomSet_LastFirst.exportedUI

e11m3CustomSet_LastFirst.png

Beyond the Classroom

Consulting Revenue

GENERAL CASE

You are a financial manager at a law firm in Denver. You have tracked the revenue from attorney consultations with clients for the past year. One of the partners of the firm wants to visit with you about the revenue this afternoon. You will add properties and comments before meeting with her. Open *e11b1Revenue* and save it as **e11b1Revenue_LastFirst**. Ensure that your name is stored as the user name. Type these keyword properties: **consultation, trends, revenue**. Type **Confidential revenue data** in the Comments property box. Type the comment **Check the transaction records. This amount seems low.** in **cell C7** in the Year Trends worksheet. Save the workbook.

The law firm has a strict procedure for managing and distributing files. Inspect the document; remove all comments, document properties, and custom XML data. Save the updated workbook as **e11b1RevenueDist_LastFirst**. Check accessibility and add alternative text for the chart with the title **Revenue Chart** and the description **Weekly consulting revenue by month**. Add alternative text for the table with the title **Revenue Table** and the description **Consulting revenue by week for each month**. Check compatibility with previous versions. Increase the height of the Compatibility Checker window to display all issues. Use the Snipping Tool to capture a screenshot of the Compatibility Checker window and paste it in the Compatibility worksheet. Adjust the size of the screenshot so that it will fit on one page. Add a Microsoft signature line with your name and type **Financial Manager** as the title below the sparklines in the Year Trends worksheet. Mark the workbook as final. Create a PDF file with the same file name. Ensure all worksheets are included in the PDF. Save and close the workbook and PDF. Based on your instructor's directions, submit the following:

> e11b1Revenue_FirstLast
> e11b1RevenueDist_LastFirst
> e11b1RevenueDist_LastFirst.pdf

Passenger Car Ratings

DISASTER RECOVERY

You work as an analyst for an independent automobile rating company that provides statistics to consumers. You prepared a worksheet containing the test results of five 2018 mid-sized passenger car models. Open *e11b2Autos* and save it as **e11b2Autos_LastFirst**. Make sure your name is the user name in Excel Options. Your assistant made some changes, but you think most of the changes are incorrect. Display a History worksheet. Use the Snipping Tool to capture a screenshot of the worksheet. Save the screenshot as **e11b2Autos_LastFirst.png** and close the Snipping Tool.

Use Track Changes to reject Jeff's changes to formulas and to the values in row 4. Accept his changes to correct spelling errors on row 3. Remove the workbook sharing. Insert a footer with your name on the left side, the sheet code in the center, and the file name code on the right side. Save and close the file. Based on your instructor's directions, submit the following:

> e11b2Autos_LastFirst
> e11b2Autos_LastFirst.png

Capstone Exercise

As the department head of the biology department at a university, you prepare and finalize the faculty teaching schedules. Recently, you prepared the first draft of the Spring class schedule. You will integrate changes from your assistant, add properties, check the workbook, finalize the schedule, and then share it with your faculty on OneDrive.

Customize Excel

Your first task is to ensure your name is entered as the user name in Excel. In addition, you will customize the Quick Access Toolbar to add the Compare and Merge Workbooks command.

a. Open *e11c1Classes* and save it as **e11c1Classes_LastFirst**.

b. Type your first name, middle initial, and last name as the user name in the Excel Options dialog box.

c. Ensure that the Compare and Merge Workbooks command is on the Quick Access Toolbar.

Compare and Merge Workbooks

You saved a sharable version of the schedule. Your assistant, Barbra Hoge, made some changes to her file and emailed the file back to you. You will compare and merge workbooks.

a. Compare and merge your open workbook with *e11c1Classes_Hoge*.

b. Activate the **Track Changes feature**, highlight all changes, click the **When check box** to deselect it, and then create a History worksheet.

c. Use the Snipping Tool to capture a screenshot of the History worksheet. Save the image as **e11c1History_LastFirst.png** and close the Snipping Tool.

Accept and Reject Changes

After studying the History worksheet that lists the changes Barbra Hoge made in the class schedule, you are ready to accept and reject changes.

a. Open the Select Changes to Accept or Reject dialog box and deselect all check boxes.

b. Accept the change in **cell J2** to STAFF.

c. Accept the change in **cell F22** to F.

d. Reject the change to delete row 40.

e. Accept the change in **cell J39** to Peterson, Rob.

f. Accept the change to delete row 37.

g. Reject the change to **cell J57**.

h. Turn off workbook sharing and save the workbook.

Comments and Properties

You want to insert a comment to remind you to assign faculty to classes indicated by STAFF. In addition, you will add document properties.

a. Insert the comment **Assign faculty to classes** in **cell J2**.

b. Type **Spring Biology Schedule** in the Title property box.

c. Edit the comment in **cell J2** by typing **listed as STAFF.** at the end of the existing comment text.

Check for Issues

Although the workbook is intended primarily for you, you want to check the workbook for potential problems. You will use Document Inspector, Accessibility Checker, and Compatibility Checker.

a. Run the Document Inspector. Insert a new sheet named **Checks** and move it to the right side of the other sheet tabs. Type **Document Inspector** in **cell A1** in the Checks worksheet and type the item noted as a concern by Document Inspector in **cell B1**. Widen the columns as needed.

b. Run Accessibility Checker. Type **Accessibility Checker** in **cell A2** in the Checks worksheet, and type the first sentence displayed in the Accessibility Checker task pane in **cell B2**. Close the Accessibility Checker task pane.

c. Run the Compatibility Checker. Type **Compatibility Checker** in **cell A3** in the Checks worksheet, and type the sentence displayed in the Compatibility Checker dialog box in **cell B3**.

d. Insert a footer with your name on the left side, the sheet name code in the center, and the file name code on the right side of all three worksheets.

e. Display the Faculty worksheet and use the Page Setup dialog box to repeat row 1 on each page.

f. Mark the workbook as final.

Distribute the Workbook

In case the clients do not have Excel 2016, you want to save the workbook as a PDF file. In addition, you will save the Excel workbook on your OneDrive and share that workbook with others.

a. Save the workbook as PDF with the name **e11c1Classes_LastFirst**. Only include the Faculty worksheet. Close the reader application.

b. Save the Excel workbook to your OneDrive. Share the workbook with your instructor by typing your instructor's email address in the invitation.

c. Close all open workbooks and files.

d. Save and close the file. Based on your instructor's directions, submit the following:

e11c1Classes_LastFirst
e11c1Classes_LastFirst.png
e11c1Classes_LastFirst.pdf

Templates, Styles, and Macros

CASE STUDY | Staff Accounting Services

Recently, you took a position as the manager of staff accounting at EBL, Ltd., a regional information technology company based in Denver, Colorado, with additional offices in Salt Lake City, Utah, and Reno, Nevada. The company provides computer and data network consultation services to individuals, small businesses, and nonprofits. The previous manager used a paper-based system to prepare expense reports, invoices, and payroll statements. However, this was a time-consuming process and required manual recalculation when any values changed.

Because of your extensive experience using Excel, you want to start automating these tasks. You decide to start with the monthly travel expense report form. Because each office utilizes the same procedures, you want to adapt an Excel template to use as a model for travel expense documentation. The template needs to be generic enough to accommodate a range of options, but it also needs to maintain a standard design to facilitate easy data entry.

You will customize the template by applying cell styles to give the form a more polished look and then create macros to perform a series of tasks, such as clearing the values to reset the form if needed and printing the expense report worksheet for management approval.

Standardizing Workbooks

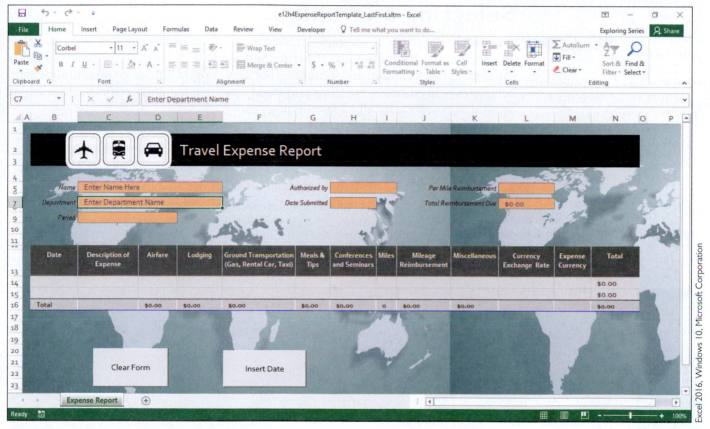

FIGURE 12.1 Staff Accounting Services Workbook

CASE STUDY | Staff Accounting Services

Starting Files	Files to be Submitted
e12h1ExpenseReport	e12h2ExpenseReportSample_LastFirst
e12h1Map	e12h4ExpenseReportTemplate_LastFirst
e12h4Calendar	

Templates, Themes, and Styles

Designing the perfect workbook can be time consuming. By now, you know you have to plan the layout before you enter data to minimize data-entry changes later. You decide what column and row labels are needed to describe the data, where to place the labels, and how to format the labels. In addition, you enter and format quantitative data, such as applying Accounting Number Format and decreasing the number of decimal places. The longer you work for the same department or organization, the more you will notice that you create the same types of workbooks. Excel has the right tools to improve your productivity in developing consistently formatted workbooks. Some of these tools include templates, themes, backgrounds, and styles.

In this section, you will select an Excel template. After opening the template, you will apply a theme, display a background, and apply cell styles.

Selecting a Template

STEP 1 A *template* is a partially completed document that you use as a model to create other documents that have the same structure and purpose. A template typically contains standard labels, formulas, and formatting but may contain little or no quantitative data. Templates help ensure consistency and standardization for similar workbooks, such as detailed sales reports for all 12 months of a year.

To create a new file based on a template, complete the following steps:

1. Start Excel, or if you are already working within a workbook, click the File tab and click New. Backstage view displays a gallery of featured templates (see Figure 12.2).
2. Select a template from templates you have recently used, sample templates that were installed with the software, or download new templates to meet the business need from Office.com. A window will display a sample of the selected template (see Figure 12.3).
3. Click Create to load the template data as a new workbook.

FIGURE 12.2 Template Thumbnails

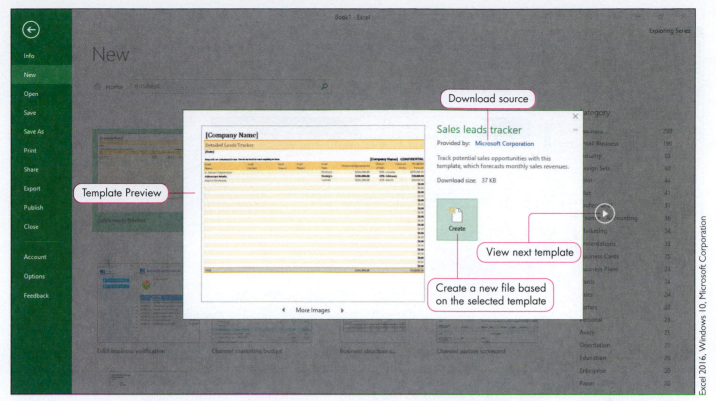

FIGURE 12.3 Preview of Template

The *Search for online templates* box enables you to search Office.com for a particular template by entering your search conditions and pressing Enter. Start searching, or you can select a template from a category, such as Business. These templates are created by Microsoft, a Microsoft partner, or a member of the Microsoft community.

Applying Themes and Backgrounds

STEP 2 ▶▶ In addition to selecting a template, you might want to apply a theme or insert a background to create a consistent look with the workbooks you create. A ***theme*** is a collection of formats that include coordinated colors, fonts, and special effects to provide a consistent appearance. You can apply a theme to a workbook to give it a consistent look with other workbooks used in your department or organization. Most organizations have a style that encompasses particular fonts, colors, and a logo or trademark on corporate stationery, advertisements, and webpages. You can use themes in Excel workbooks to match the corporate "look and feel." The Excel themes match the themes in other Office applications so that you can provide continuity and consistency with Word and PowerPoint files.

To apply a theme to all worksheets in a workbook, complete the following steps:

1. Click the Page Layout tab.
2. Click Themes in the Themes group. The Office theme is presented first; the other built-in themes are listed alphabetically in the Themes gallery (see Figure 12.4).
3. Point to each theme to display a Live Preview of how the theme would format existing data on the current worksheet.
4. Click a theme to make it active.

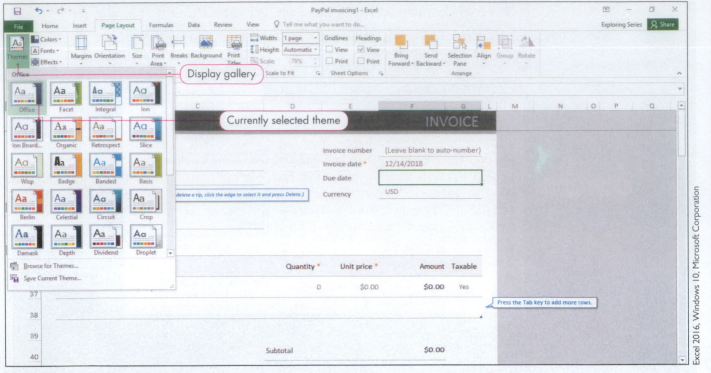

FIGURE 12.4 Themes Gallery

Customize a Theme

After applying a theme, you can customize the three elements that comprise the theme: colors, fonts, and effects. The Themes group on the Page Layout tab contains commands to customize the theme. When you click Colors, you can select from a gallery of color themes, or you can select Customize Colors to define the text, background, accent, hyperlink, and followed hyperlink colors. If you create and name your own color theme, that theme name will appear in the Custom section of the Colors menu.

Theme Fonts contain a coordinating heading and body text font for each theme. For example, the Office theme uses Calibri Light for headings and Calibri for cell entries. To select a theme font, click Fonts in the Themes group and select a theme font, or select Customize Fonts to define your own theme fonts.

Theme Effects are special effects that control the design differences in objects, such as shapes, SmartArt, and object borders. To select a theme effect, click Effects in the Themes group, point to an effect to see a Live Preview of how that effect will affect objects, and click the desired effect to apply it to your workbook.

Apply a Background

STEP 3 >> Excel enables you to use graphics as the background of a worksheet. The effect is similar to placing a background on a webpage. A *background* is an image placed behind the worksheet data. For example, you might want to use the corporate logo as your background, or you might want a "Confidential" graphic image to remind onscreen viewers that the worksheet contains corporate trade secrets. Be careful in selecting and using backgrounds, because the images can distract users and interfere with their comprehension of the quantitative data. A subtle, pale image is less likely to distract a workbook user than a bright, vividly colored image.

The image, like a background image on a webpage, is tiled across your worksheet (see Figure 12.5). The background image displays only in the worksheet onscreen; it does not print. If you want an image to appear behind data on a printed worksheet, insert the image as a watermark in a header. Notice that Delete Background replaces Background in the Page Setup group after you insert a background for a specific worksheet. If you want to remove a background picture, click Delete Background in the Page Setup group on the Page Layout tab.

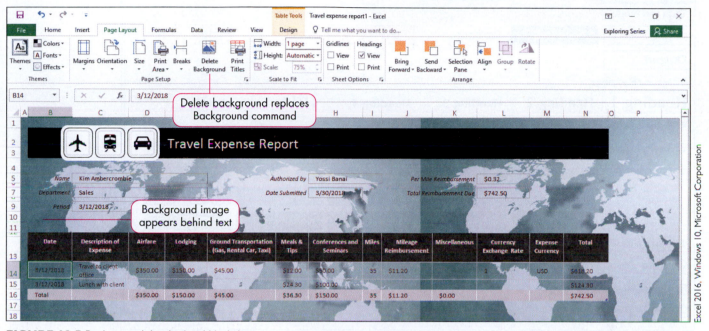

FIGURE 12.5 Background Applied to Worksheet

> **TIP: BACKGROUND VISIBILITY**
> You can turn off the gridlines to increase the visibility of the background image and the worksheet data. Click the Page Layout tab and deselect the Gridlines View check box in the Sheet Options group.

Applying Cell Styles

STEP 4 Different cell content often benefits from additional formatting. For example, titles may need to be centered and in a large font size; column labels may be bold and centered and in a darker hue; input cells may be formatted differently from output cells. To assist in applying these different formats consistently across worksheets and workbooks you can use a cell style. A ***cell style*** is a collection of format settings based on the currently selected theme to provide a consistent appearance within a worksheet and among similar workbooks. Cell styles control the following formats:

- Font attributes, such as font and font size
- Borders and fill styles and colors
- Vertical and horizontal cell alignment
- Number formatting, such as currency and number of decimal places
- Cell-protection settings

The currently selected theme controls the appearance of cell styles. If you change the theme, Excel updates cells formatted by cell styles to reflect the new theme. For example, if you change from Facet theme to Integral, particular fill colors change from shades of green to blue.

To apply a style to a cell or range of cells, complete the followings steps:

1. Click the Home tab and click Cell Styles in the Styles group to display the Cell Styles gallery (see Figure 12.6).
2. Point to a style name to see a Live Preview of how that style will affect the active cell.
3. Click a style to apply it to the active cell or range.

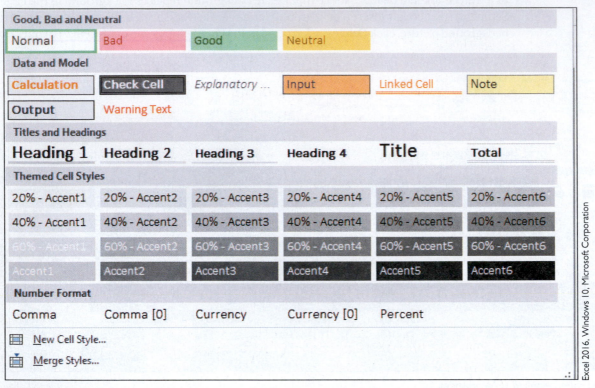

FIGURE 12.6 Cell Styles

The gallery contains the following five predefined cell categories:

- **Good, Bad, and Neutral:** Use to emphasize bad, good, or neutral results, or click Normal to reset a cell to its original default setting.
- **Data and Model:** Use to indicate special cell contents, such as a calculated result, input cell, output cell, or warning.
- **Titles and Headings:** Use to format titles and headings, such as column and row labels, for emphasis.
- **Themed Cell Styles:** Use Accent styles for visual emphasis. These cell styles are dependent on the currently selected theme.
- **Number Format:** Provide the same formatting as commands in the Number group on the Home tab.

Create Custom Cell Styles

You can create your own custom cell styles if the predefined cell styles do not meet your needs. For example, you might want to create custom cell styles that match the color, font, and design of your corporate logo or stationery to help brand your workbooks with the company image. After you create custom cell styles, you can apply them in multiple workbooks instead of formatting each workbook individually.

After you create a custom style, Excel displays another section, Custom, at the top of the Cell Styles gallery. This section lists the custom styles you create. A custom cell style can be created by duplicating and modifying an existing style. To duplicate a cell style, right-click a preset cell style and select duplicate.

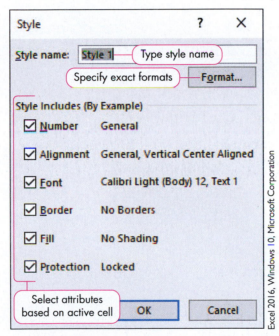

FIGURE 12.7 Style Dialog Box

Modify and Remove Cell Styles

After you create and apply cell styles to a worksheet, you might decide to change the format of a style. For example, you might want to change the font size or fill color. The primary advantage to creating and applying styles is that you can modify the style, and Excel updates all cells to which you applied the style automatically.

If you no longer need a cell style, you can delete it. However, if you delete a cell style that has been applied to worksheet cells, Excel will remove all formatting from those cells. To delete a cell style, right-click the style name in the Cell Styles gallery and select Delete. Excel does not ask for confirmation before deleting the style.

TIP: USE STYLES IN OTHER WORKBOOKS

When you create your own cell styles, the styles are saved with the workbook in which you created the styles. However, you may want to apply those styles in other workbooks as well. To do this, open the workbook that contains the custom cell styles (the source) and open the workbook in which you want to apply those custom styles (the destination). In the destination workbook, click Cell Styles in the Styles group on the Home tab. Select Merge Styles at the bottom of the Cell Styles gallery to open the Merge Styles dialog box. In the *Merge styles from* list, select the name of the workbook that contains the styles you want and click OK. When you click Cell Styles again, the custom styles appear in the gallery.

Quick Concepts

1. What are the benefits of using templates? *p. 738*

2. What are the benefits of using cell styles? *p. 741*

3. Why would you create a custom cell style? *p. 742*

MyITLab®
HOE1 Training

1 Templates, Themes, and Styles

You need to get up and running quickly since you took over at EBL, Ltd. You decide to use the Travel Expense Report template that is part of the Office template downloads. After opening the template, you will modify it by applying a theme, theme color, background, and cell styles.

STEP 1 ›› SELECT A TEMPLATE

To save time, you will create a new report using a template. After reviewing the templates available in the template gallery, you decide the Travel Expense Report template shown in Figure 12.8 is sufficient to build your company's report. Your first step is to open the Travel Expense Report template. Refer to Figure 12.8 as you complete Step 1.

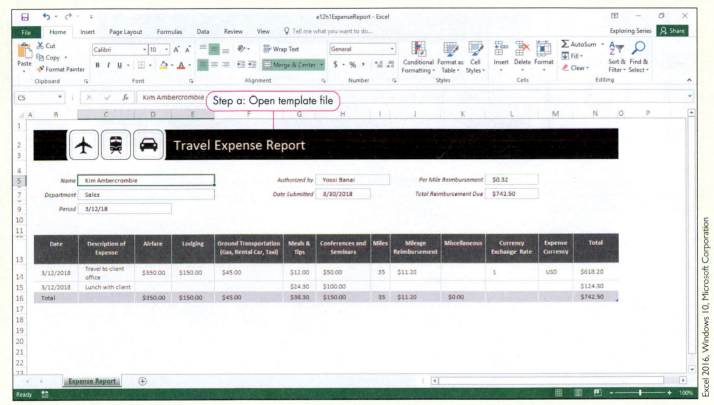

FIGURE 12.8 Travel Expense Template

a. Open Excel, click **Open Other Workbooks**, and then browse to the file *e12h1ExpenseReport*.

Microsoft Office templates are frequently added, removed, or edited. When searching online templates it is a good practice to make a back up copy of the original template as it may not always be available. The Travel Expense template is available for download, however, because Office templates are frequently edited a template file has been provided for consistency.

b. Click **Open** and review the original template provided.

Excel opens the Travel Expense Report template. The template can now be customized or saved as a standard Excel workbook.

c. Save the workbook as **e12h1ExpenseReport_LastFirst**.

The Travel Expense Report template provides the basic design you need, but you want to apply a different theme to the workbook. Refer to Figure 12.9 as you complete Step 2.

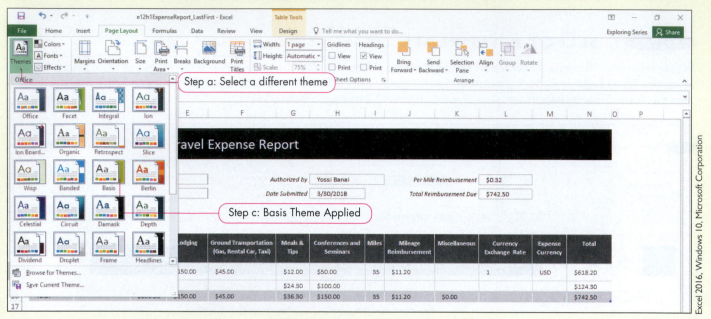

FIGURE 12.9 Theme Applied

a. Click the **Page Layout tab** and click **Themes** in the Themes group.

b. Point to the Office and Ion themes to see the Live Preview of how those themes will affect the workbook.

c. Click **Basis** to apply that theme to the workbook. Save the workbook.

To enhance the professional look and feel of the Travel Expense Report, you will add a background image. Refer to Figure 12.10 as you complete Step 3.

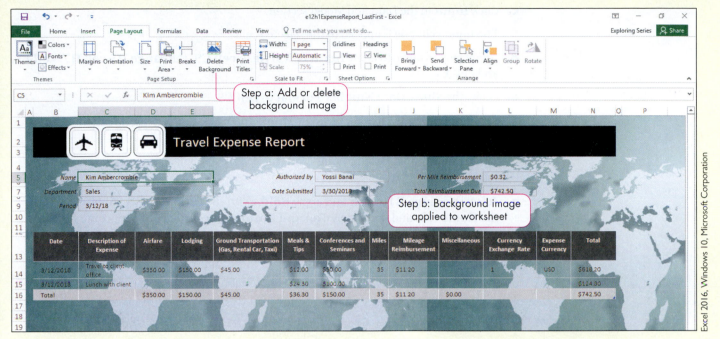

FIGURE 12.10 Background Applied

a. Click **Background** in the Page Setup group and then click **From a file**.

b. Navigate to the student data files, select *e12h1Map.jpg*, and then click **Insert**.

The image is tiled across and down the worksheet and appears behind the worksheet data. Because the original template did not include fill colors, the background image can be seen underneath the cells in the worksheet.

c. Save the workbook.

You want to further customize the Travel Expense Report workbook by applying different cell styles. Refer to Figure 12.11 as you complete Step 4.

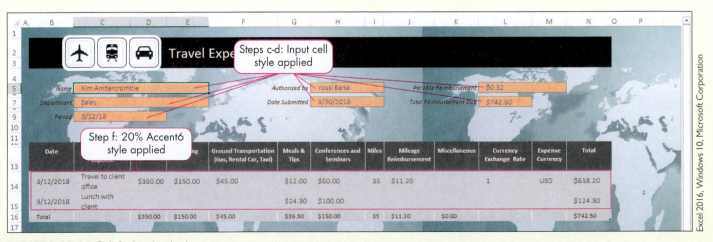

FIGURE 12.11 Cell Styles Applied

a. Select **cell C5**, press and hold **Ctrl**, and then select **cell C7**.

b. Click the **Home tab** and click **Cell Styles** in the Styles group.

The Cell Styles gallery opens so that you can apply a cell style to the selected cells.

c. Click **Input** in the Data and Model section.

The Input cell style is applied to the selected cells.

d. Adapt steps b and c to apply **Input cell style** to **cell C9**, the **range H5 cell H7**, **cell L5**, and **cell L7**.

e. Apply the **Short Date Number Format** to **cell C9**.

f. Select the **range B14:N15**. Click the **Home tab**, click **Cell Styles,** and then select **20% – Accent6 Cell Style**.

These ranges had no background. With the cell styles applied, they are now easier to read.

g. Select the **range B16:N16** and apply **Bold**. With the **range B16:N16** selected, click the **Home tab**, and then apply **Top and Bottom Border** in the Font group.

h. Save the workbook. Keep the workbook open if you plan to continue with the next Hands-On Exercise. If not, close the workbook and exit Excel.

Custom Templates and Workbook Protection

Using Excel templates helps save time when designing workbooks, but these templates will not always meet your needs. When this is the case, you can create a workbook with the specifications you need and save it as a template so that you can use it as a model to create identically structured workbooks for unique data. For example, after downloading the Travel Expense Report template, you applied a theme, a background, and several cell styles. You want the company's employees to be able to use this modified workbook to create individual reports. However, creating a new workbook from scratch for each employee is time consuming. When you find yourself needing the same workbook design for several unique workbooks, you should develop and use a template that can be accessed by each employee and modified as needed.

You can protect cells or worksheets from unauthorized or accidental changes. Doing so ensures that people do not change areas of a worksheet, such as formulas, when you distribute the worksheet on an organization's server.

In this section, you will learn how to save a workbook as a template. In the process, you will learn how to protect cells and worksheets from being changed.

Creating and Using a Template

The Travel Expense Report template you used contains labels, sample values, and formulas. The formulas calculate category totals, such as the total airfare and total of the lodging category expenses. You can remove the sample expenses from the workbook and save it as a template so that you have an empty report for each employee to fill out.

When you create a template from scratch instead of starting with an existing template, adhere to the following guidelines:

- Use formatted, descriptive labels, empty cells, and formulas.
- Avoid values when possible in formulas; use cell references instead.
- Use an appropriate function to trap errors.
- Include data-validation settings (valid data rules, warning messages, input messages).
- Include instructions for the template.
- Turn off worksheet gridlines, if desired, for clarity.
- Apply appropriate formatting to the template.
- Give worksheets meaningful names and delete worksheets that are not used.

After you finalize your workbook, you need to export it.

To save a workbook as a template, complete the following steps:

1. Click the File tab and click Export.
2. Click Change File Type.
3. Click Template in the Change File Type list and click Save As at the bottom of Backstage view to open the Save As dialog box. Notice that the *Save as type* is set to Excel Template.
4. Select the desired location, type a name in the File name box, and then click Save.

Templates use a different file extension (.xltx) than Excel workbooks (.xlsx). In order for your template to appear in the Template gallery in Backstage view, be sure to save it in the correct folder, C:\Users\username\Documents\Custom Office Templates in Windows 10. If you use File Explorer to find the Templates folder, you will need to display hidden folders to do so. If you save your custom templates in the correct location, you can use them to create new workbooks by clicking the File tab, clicking New, and then clicking Personal in the Templates gallery of Backstage view. The New dialog box displays thumbnails and names for the templates you created.

To save the template so that it automatically is included in the Templates gallery, complete the following steps:

1. Click Save As in Backstage view, click Save As, and then click This PC to open the Save As dialog box.
2. Click the *Save as type* arrow and select Excel Template. Excel then selects the C:\Users\username\Documents\Custom Office Templates folder automatically.
3. Type a name in the File name box and click Save.

Protecting a Cell, a Worksheet, and a Workbook

Most templates protect worksheets by enabling users to change only particular cells in a worksheet. For example, users are permitted to enter data in input cells, but they cannot change formulas or alter formatting or worksheet structure. It is considered a best practice to protect the formula cells in a template that you are distributing in the workplace. This will prevent users from changing the formulas. Protecting worksheets prevents modification of formulas and text but enables you to change values in unprotected cells.

Lock and Unlock Cells

STEP 1 ⟫ A *locked cell* is one that prevents users from editing the contents or formatting of that cell in a protected worksheet. By default, all cells in a workbook are locked. This is indicated by the blue border around the padlock icon for the Lock Cell option on the Format menu in the Cells group on the Home tab. Locked cells are not enforced until you protect the worksheet. Locking or unlocking cells has no effect if the worksheet has not been protected. Before protecting the worksheet, you should unlock the cells that you want users to be able to edit. For example, you will unlock the Per Mile Reimbursement and Date Submitted cells in the Travel Expense Report template so that users can enter unique values. However, you will keep the cells containing formulas locked.

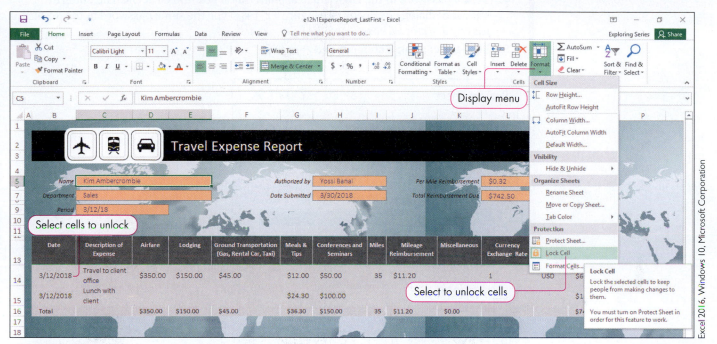

FIGURE 12.12 Process to Unlock Cells

To relock cells, repeat the above process.

> **TIP: USING THE FORMAT CELLS DIALOG BOX**
> Alternatively, after selecting a cell or range of cells to unlock, you can open the Format Cells dialog box, click the Protection tab, deselect the Locked check box, and then click OK.

Protect a Worksheet

STEP 2 After unlocking cells that you want the users to be able to modify, you are ready to protect the worksheet. When you protect a worksheet, you prevent users from altering the locked cells. During the process of protecting a worksheet, you can enter a password to ensure that only those who know the password can unprotect the worksheet. Protecting the template is typically the final step in the creation of a custom template because you need to enter standard labels, create formulas, and unprotect input cells first. If you protect the worksheet before finalizing the content, you will have to unprotect the worksheet, make content changes, and then protect the worksheet again.

To protect a worksheet, complete the following steps:

1. Click the Home tab and click Format in the Cells group.
2. Select Protect Sheet in the Protection section (or click Protect Sheet in the Changes group on the Review tab) to open the Protect Sheet dialog box (see Figure 12.13).
3. Select the check boxes for actions you want users to be able to do in the *Allow all users of this worksheet to* list.
4. Type a password in the *Password to unprotect sheet* box and click OK. The Confirm Password dialog box opens (see Figure 12.14). Type the same password in the *Reenter password to proceed* box.
5. Read the caution statement and click OK.

FIGURE 12.13 Protect Sheet Dialog Box

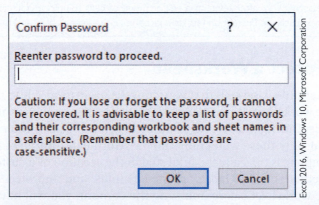

FIGURE 12.14 Confirm Passwords Dialog Box

TIP: PASSWORDS

Passwords can be up to 255 characters, including letters, numbers, and symbols. Passwords are case sensitive, so *passWORD* is not the same as *Password*. Make sure you record your password in a secure location or select a password that you will always remember. If you forget the password, you will not be able to unprotect the worksheet.

After you protect a worksheet, most commands on the Ribbon are dimmed, indicating that they are not available. If someone tries to enter or change data in a locked cell on a protected worksheet, Excel displays the warning message and instructs the user how to remove the protection (see Figure 12.15).

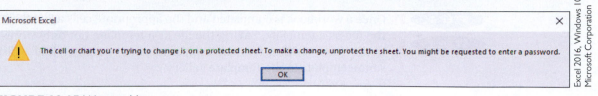

FIGURE 12.15 Warning Message

To unprotect a worksheet, complete the following steps:

1. Click Unprotect Sheet in the Changes group on the Review tab, or click Format in the Cells group on the Home tab and select Unprotect Sheet. The Unprotect Sheet dialog box opens.
2. Type the password in the Password box and click OK. The worksheet is then unprotected so that you can make changes.

Protect a Workbook

Although locking cells and protecting a worksheet prevents unauthorized modifications, users might make unwanted changes to other parts of the workbook. You can prevent users from inserting, deleting, renaming, moving, copying, and hiding worksheets within the workbook by protecting the workbook with a password. Protecting an entire workbook does not disable the unlocked cells within a workbook; it merely prevents worksheet manipulation from occurring. That is, individual cells must still be unlocked even if a workbook is unprotected.

To protect a workbook, complete the following steps:

1. Click the Review tab and click Protect Workbook in the Changes group. The Protect Structure and Windows dialog box opens (see Figure 12.16).
2. Click the check boxes for the desired action in the *Protect workbook for* section.
3. Type a password in the *Password (optional)* box and click OK. The Confirm Password dialog box opens.
4. Type the same password in the *Reenter password to proceed* box and click OK.

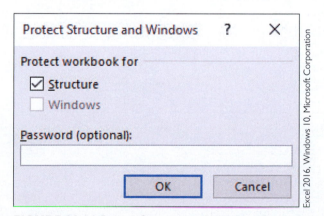

FIGURE 12.16 Protect Structure and Windows Dialog Box

Once a workbook is completed and the appropriate cells are locked, the last step is to save the file as a template. Saving the file as a template not only stores the file as a template in the Custom Office Templates folder on your computer, it also displays the file as a personal template in the Template gallery.

To save a workbook as a template, complete the following steps:

1. Click the File tab.
2. Click Save As, click This PC, and then click Browse.
3. Select Excel Template from the *Save as type* menu.
4. Click Save.

Quick Concepts

4. What is the default file extension for a template? *p. 750*

5. Where are templates saved in Windows 10? *p. 750*

6. Why would you protect a workbook? *p. 753*

Hands-On Exercises

Watch the Video for this Hands-On Exercise!

MyITLab®
HOE2 Training

Skills covered: Create and Use a Template • Lock and Unlock Cells • Protect a Worksheet • Protect a Workbook

2 Custom Templates and Workbook Protection

After customizing the Travel Expense Report, you want to ensure consistency of use within the company by saving the workbook as a template. As the manager, you do not want your staff deleting formulas or other required sections of the expense form you have created. Your next set of steps will include protecting the workbook and then saving it as a template.

STEP 1 ▶▶ UNLOCK INPUT CELLS

Before protecting the worksheet, you will unlock the input cells. You need to ensure the input cells are unlocked so that each employee can enter specific lodging, mileage, and miscellaneous costs. Refer to Figure 12.17 as you complete Step 1.

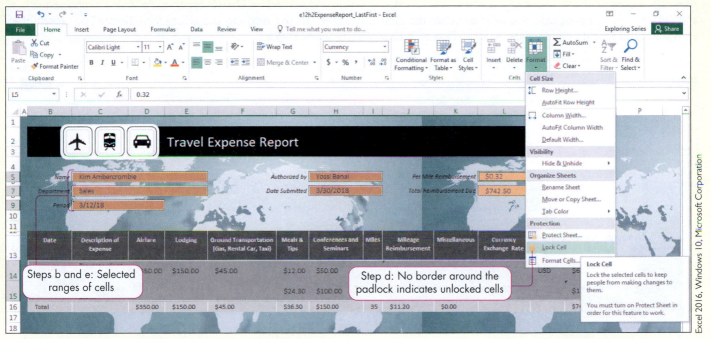

FIGURE 12.17 Unlock Input Cells

a. Open *e12h1ExpenseReport_LastFirst* if you closed it at the end of Hands-On Exercise 1, and save it as **e12h2ExpenseReport_LastFirst**, changing h1 to h2.

b. Click **cell C5**.

This cell will be the input area for the name of the creator of the report.

c. Ensure the Home tab is displayed, and click **Format** in the Cells group.

The Format menu opens.

d. Select **Lock Cell** in the Protection section.

The Lock Cell option does not change to Unlock Cell. However, when you unlock a cell, the Lock Cell command does not have a blue border around the padlock icon on the menu. The selected range of cells is unlocked and will remain unlocked when you protect the worksheet later.

e. Press **Ctrl** while selecting the following cells and range, and repeat Steps c and d to unlock the cells and range:

- **Cell C7**
- **Cell C9**
- **Cell H5**
- **Cell H7**
- **Cell L5**
- **Range B14:M15**

> **TROUBLESHOOTING:** If you unlock too many cells, select the cells that should be locked, click Format, and then select Lock Cell to lock them again.

f. Save the workbook.

STEP 2 ›› DELETE SAMPLE VALUES

Although you unlocked the input cells for Name, Department, Period, Authorized by, Date Submitted, Per Mile Reimbursement, and Total Reimbursement Due, you need to delete the sample values to create a ready-to-use empty form before you protect the worksheet and save it as a template. Refer to Figure 12.18 as you complete Step 2.

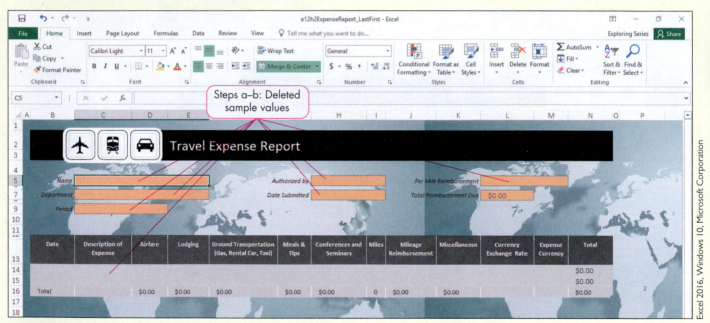

FIGURE 12.18 Sample Values Removed

a. Select **cell C5** and press **Delete**.

b. Delete the sample values in the following cells and range:

- **Cell C7**
- **Cell C9**
- **Cell H5**
- **Cell H7**
- **Cell L5**
- **Range B14:M15**

c. Save the workbook.

Now that you have unlocked the input cells and deleted sample expense values, you are ready to protect the Expense Report worksheet. The other cells in the worksheet still have the Lock Cell property enabled. So, after you protect the worksheet, users will not be able to modify those cells. Refer to Figure 12.19 as you complete Step 3.

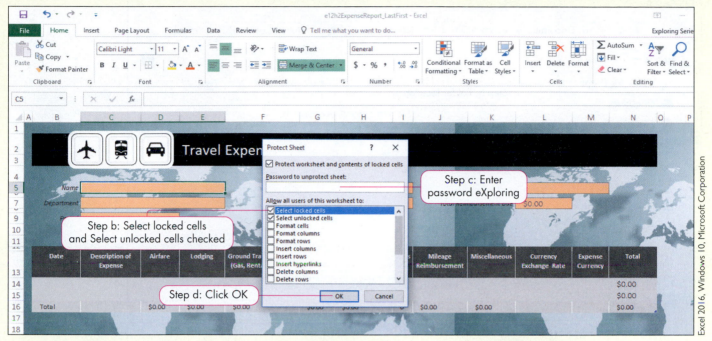

FIGURE 12.19 Protect the worksheet

a. Press **Ctrl+Home**.

b. Click **Format** in the Cells group and select **Protect Sheet**. Ensure the *Select locked cells* and *Select unlocked cells* check boxes are selected.

The Protect Sheet dialog box opens. The *Protect worksheet and contents of locked cells* check box is selected by default. In addition, the users are allowed to *Select locked cells* and *Select unlocked cells*. Although they can select locked cells, they will not be able to change those cells. Notice that users are not allowed to format data, insert columns or rows, or delete columns or rows.

c. Type **eXploring** in the *Password to unprotect sheet* box.

Remember that passwords are case sensitive and that you must remember the password. If you forget it, you will not be able to unprotect the sheet.

d. Click **OK**.

The Confirm Password dialog box opens with a caution.

e. Read the caution, type **eXploring** in the *Reenter password to proceed* box, and then click **OK**.

f. Click **cell N14** and try to type **1000**.

Excel displays the warning box that the cell is protected with instructions on how to unprotect the worksheet.

> **TROUBLESHOOTING:** If you are allowed to enter the new value without the warning box, the cell is not locked. Click Undo to restore the formula, review Step 1, and then lock this cell.

g. Click **OK** to close the warning box, and save the workbook.

You are ready to save the Travel Expense Report workbook as a template. Refer to Figure 12.20 as you complete Step 4.

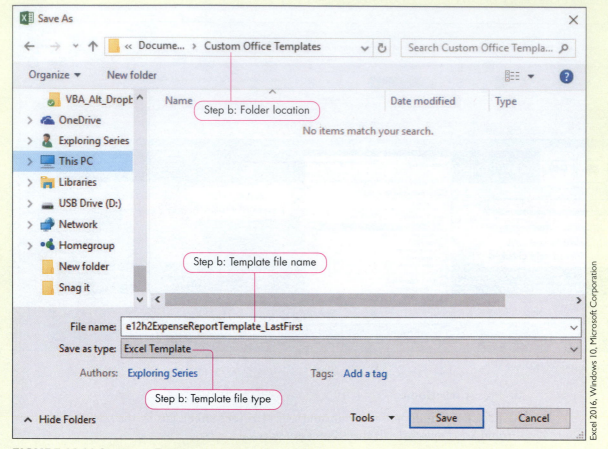

FIGURE 12.20 Saving as a Template

a. Click the **File tab**, click **Save As**, and then click **This PC**.

The Save As dialog box opens, displaying the current workbook name and Excel Workbook as the default file type.

b. Click the **Save as type arrow**, select **Excel Template**, and then save the file to the default folder, Custom Office Templates, as **e12h2ExpenseReportTemplate_ LastFirst**.

> **TROUBLESHOOTING:** When saving a template, Excel changes the file location to C:\Users\ Username\Documents\Custom Office Templates. You may not have the ability to save a template to the hard drive of your school's computer lab, or your instructor may request you submit the file. To ensure you do not lose the template, be sure to change the save location to your homework folder. Note that if you do change the default location, the template will not display in the Personal template gallery and you will need to manually open the file from your homework folder to continue.

c. Click **Save**.

This will save the workbook as a template and exit Backstage view.

d. Click the **File tab** and click **Close**.

STEP 5 ›› USE THE TEMPLATE TO CREATE A SAMPLE EXPENSE REPORT

Now that you have created a Travel Expense Report template, you are ready to enter data for one of your coworkers. Refer to Figure 12.21 as you complete Step 5.

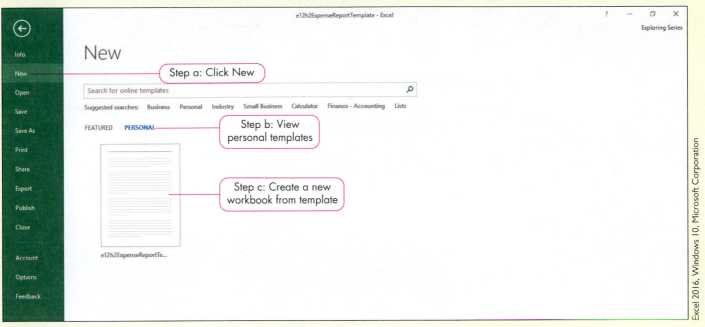

FIGURE 12.21 Create a New Workbook from a Personal Template

a. Click the **File tab** and click **New**.

Backstage view displays a gallery of available templates.

b. Click **PERSONAL** in the gallery section.

This displays personal templates saved on your computer.

> **TROUBLESHOOTING:** If you were not able to save the template to the Custom Office Templates folder in Step 4, you will not see the template in the Personal template gallery. If this is the case, the file can be located by searching Recent Workbooks from the Open menu in Backstage view.

c. Double-click *e12h2ExpenseReportTemplate_LastFirst*.

The template creates a new workbook based on the same file name but with a number appended to the end, such as *e12h2ExpenseReportTemplate_LastFirst1*.

d. Click the **File tab**, click **Save as**, double-click **This PC**, and then navigate to where you store your files.

e. Click the **Save as type arrow**, select **Excel Workbook**, and then save the file as **e12h2ExpenseReportSample_LastFirst**.

f. Click **Format** in the Cells group on the Home tab. Select **Unprotect Sheet** under Protection. Enter **eXploring** for the password and click **OK**.

g. Type **Your Name** in **cell C5**.

h. Type the following values in the appropriate cells:

Cell	Value
C7	Finance
H7	1/28/2018
L5	.35
B14	1/3/2018
C14	Sales Conference
D14	250.00
E14	125.00
F14	35.00

i. Press **Ctrl+Home**.

j. Save and close the file e12h2ExpenseReportSample. You will submit this file to your instructor at the end of the last Hands-On Exercise.

Macros

By now, you have used most of the tabs on the Ribbon to perform a variety of tasks. Often, you repeat the execution of the same commands as you develop and modify workbooks. Although the sequence to execute commands is easy, you lose productivity when you repeat the same procedures repeatedly. Previously, you learned how to apply styles and themes, and how to create and use templates as models to develop similar workbooks. In addition, you can automate other routine tasks to increase your productivity. For example, think about how often you set a print range, adjust scaling, set margins, insert a standard header or footer, and specify other page setup options prior to printing.

You can automate a series of routine or complex tasks by creating a macro. A *macro* is a set of instructions that executes a sequence of commands to automate repetitive or routine tasks. While the term *macro* often intimidates people, you should view macros as your personal assistants that do routine tasks for you! After you create a macro, you can execute the macro to perform all the tasks with minimal work on your part. As an additional benefit, macros can be saved in templates to automate tasks that may be time consuming or difficult for average users. When you run a macro, the macro executes all of the tasks the same way each time, and faster than you could execute the commands yourself, thus reducing errors while increasing efficiency.

The default Excel Workbook file format (.xlsx) cannot store macros. When you save a workbook containing macros, click the *Save as type* arrow in the Save As dialog box, and select one of the following file formats that support macros:

- Excel Macro-Enabled Workbook (.xlsm)
- Excel Binary Workbook (.xlsb)
- Excel Macro-Enabled Template (.xltm)

In this section, you will learn how to use the Macro Recorder to record a macro. You will also learn how to run a macro, edit a macro, create macro buttons, and review macro security issues.

Creating a Macro

Excel provides two methods for creating macros. You can either use the Macro Recorder or type instructions using *Visual Basic for Applications (VBA)*. VBA is a robust programming language that can be used within various software packages to enhance and automate functionality. While programmers use VBA to write macros, you do not need to be a programmer to create macros. It is relatively easy to use the *Macro Recorder* within Excel to record your commands, keystrokes, and mouse clicks to store Excel commands as VBA code within a workbook. Before you record a macro, keep the following points in mind:

- Once you begin recording a macro, most actions you take are recorded in the macro. If you click something in error, you have to edit the code or undo the action to correct it.
- Practice the steps before you start recording the macro so that you will know the sequence in which to perform the steps when you record the macro.
- Ensure your macros are broad enough to apply to a variety of situations or an action you perform often for the workbook.
- Determine whether cell references should be relative, absolute, or mixed if you include cell references in the macro.

Use the Macro Recorder

STEP 1 ▶▶ You can access the Macro Recorder in a variety of ways: from the View tab, from the Developer tab, or from the status bar. The following list briefly describes what each method includes:

- The View tab contains the Macros group with the Macros command. You can click the Macros arrow to view macros, record a macro, or use relative references.
- The Developer tab, when displayed, provides more in-depth tools that workbook developers use. The Code group contains the same commands as the Macros arrow on the View tab, but it also includes commands to open the Visual Basic Editor and set macro security.
- The status bar displays the Macro Recording button so that you can quickly click it to start and stop recording macros.

> **To display the Developer tab on the Ribbon, complete the following steps:**
>
> 1. Click the File tab and click Options to open the Excel Options dialog box.
> 2. Click Customize Ribbon on the left side to display the Customize the Ribbon options.
> 3. Click the Developer check box in the Main Tabs list to select it and click OK. Figure 12.22 shows the Developer tab.

FIGURE 12.22 Developer Tab

Excel 2016, Windows 10, Microsoft Corporation

Record a Macro

STEP 2 ▶▶ Recording a macro is relatively straightforward: You initiate the macro recording, perform a series of commands as you normally do, then stop the macro recording. Be careful and thorough when recording a macro to ensure that it performs the tasks it is designed to do and to avoid the need to edit the macro in the VBA Editor. Before recording a macro, you should practice it first and make sure you know the sequence of tasks you want to perform. After planning a macro, you are ready to record it.

> **To record a macro, complete the following steps:**
>
> 1. Click Record Macro using one of the methods described above. The Record Macro dialog box opens (see Figure 12.23 and Figure 12.24).
> 2. Type a name for the macro in the Macro name box. Macro names cannot include spaces or special characters and must start with a letter. Use Pascal Casing (capitalize the first letter of each word but without a space), a programming naming convention, to increase readability of the macro name.
> 3. Assign a keyboard shortcut, if desired, for your macro in the Shortcut key box. Use caution, because many Ctrl+ shortcuts are already assigned in Excel. To be safe, it is best to use Ctrl+Shift+, such as Ctrl+Shift+C instead of Ctrl+C, because Ctrl+C is the existing keyboard shortcut for the Copy command.
> 4. Click the *Store macro in* arrow and select a storage location, such as This Workbook.
> 5. Type a description of the macro and its purpose in the Description box and click OK to start recording the macro.
> 6. Perform the commands that you want to record.
> 7. Click the View tab, click Macros in the Macros group, and then select Stop Recording; or click the Developer tab and click Stop Recording in the Code group; or click Stop Recording on the status bar.

FIGURE 12.23 Status Bar

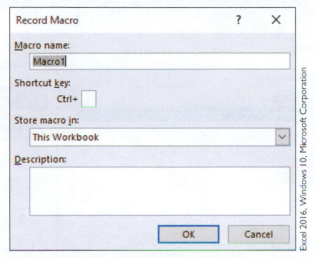

FIGURE 12.24 Record Macro Dialog Box

Use Relative References

It is important to determine if your macro should use relative, absolute, or mixed references as you record the macro. By default, when you select cells when recording a macro, the macro records the cells as absolute references. When you run the macro, the macro executes commands on the absolute cells, regardless of which cell is the active cell when you run the macro. For example, say you want to apply a macro that formats cells that are selected. If you want flexibility in that commands are performed relative to the active cell when you run the macro, click the Macros arrow in the Macros group on the View tab and select Use Relative References *before* you perform the commands. Be sure to turn relative references off when the feature is no longer needed.

Run a Macro

After you record a macro, you should run a test to see if it performs the commands as you had anticipated. When you run a macro, Excel performs the tasks in the sequence in which you recorded the steps.

To run a macro, complete the following steps:

1. Select the location where you will test the macro. It is recommended to test a macro in a new, blank workbook if you recorded it so that it is available for multiple workbooks. If you saved it to the current workbook only, insert a new worksheet to test the macro. Be sure to back up the workbook as macros cannot be undone.

2. Click the View tab, click the Macros arrow in the Macros group, and then select View Macros; or click the Developer tab and click Macros in the Code group. The Macro dialog box opens (see Figure 12.25).

3. Select the macro from the Macro name list and click Run.

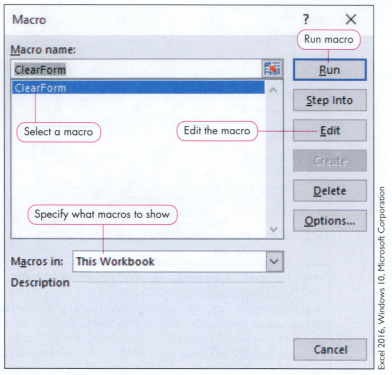

FIGURE 12.25 Macro Dialog Box

TIP: DELETE A MACRO

If you no longer need a macro, use the Macro dialog box to select the macro and click Delete. Excel will prompt you with a message box asking if you want to delete the selected macro. Click Yes to confirm the deletion.

Creating Macro Buttons

For the most part, it will be a rare macro that is so all-encompassing that it would rate a place on the Quick Access Toolbar. On the other hand, you may create a macro that is frequently used in a particular workbook such as a template. The easiest way to access frequently used macros within a workbook is to assign a macro to a button on a worksheet. That way, when you or other people use the workbook, it is easy to click the button to run the macro. Macros can also be assigned to objects within Excel such as text boxes or images.

To add a macro button to a worksheet, complete the following steps:

1. Click the Developer tab, click Insert in the Controls group, and then click Button (Form Control) in the Form Controls section of the Insert gallery (see Figure 12.26).
2. Drag the crosshair pointer to draw the button on the worksheet. When you release the mouse button, the Assign Macro dialog box opens (see Figure 12.27).
3. Select the macro to assign to the button and click OK.
4. Right-click the button, select Edit Text, delete the default text, and then type a more descriptive name for the button.
5. Click the worksheet to complete the button.
6. Click the cell that should be the active cell when the macro runs and click the button to execute the macro assigned to the button.

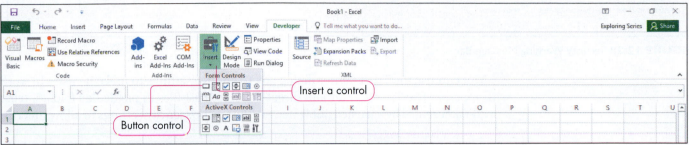

FIGURE 12.26 Form Controls

Excel 2016, Windows 10, Microsoft Corporation

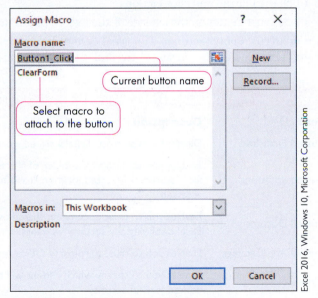

FIGURE 12.27 Assign Macro Dialog Box

Excel 2016, Windows 10, Microsoft Corporation

> **TIP: OTHER CONTROLS**
> You can insert other controls in a worksheet such as images and artwork and then assign macros to them. For example, you can insert combo boxes, check boxes, and option buttons by clicking Insert in the Controls group on the Developer tab and selecting the desired control. Drag an area on the worksheet to draw the control, right-click the object, and then select Assign Macro to assign a macro action for that particular control.

Setting Macro Security

Macro security is a concern for anyone who uses files containing macros. A macro virus is nothing more than actions written in VBA set to perform malicious actions when run. The proliferation of macro viruses has made people more cautious about opening workbooks that contain macros. By default, Excel automatically disables the macros and displays a security warning that macros have been disabled (see Figure 12.28). Click Enable Content to use the workbook and run macros.

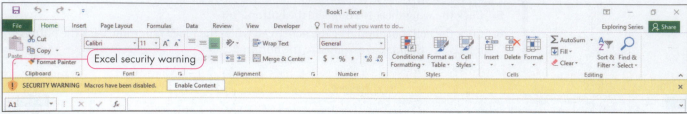

FIGURE 12.28 Security Warning Message Bar

Excel 2016, Windows 10, Microsoft Corporation

You can use the Trust Center dialog box to change settings to make it easier to work with macros. The Trust Center can direct Excel to trust files in particular folders, trust workbooks created by a trusted publisher, and lower the security settings to allow macros.

To open the Trust Center, complete the following steps:

1. Click the File tab and click Options.
2. Click Trust Center on the left side of the Excel Options dialog box.
3. Click Trust Center Settings. The Trust Center dialog box displays the sections described in Table 12.1 on the left side of the dialog box (see Figure 12.29).

TABLE 12.1 Trust Center Options

Item	Description
Trusted Publishers	Directs Excel to trust digitally signed workbooks by certain creators.
Trusted Locations	Enables you to designate a folder of files from trusted sources. Once a file is stored in a trusted location, it will not open in protected view when accessed.
Trusted Documents	Enables you to trust documents shared over a network to open without Excel displaying any security warnings.
Trusted App Catalogs	Enables you to trust third-party Office Apps that run inside Excel.
Add-Ins	Enables you to specify which add-ins will be allowed to run given the desired level of security.
ActiveX Settings	Enables you to adjust how Excel deals with ActiveX controls.
Macro Settings	Enables you to specify how Excel deals with macros.
Protected View	Opens potentially dangerous files in a restricted mode but without any security warnings.
Message Bar	Enables you to specify when Excel shows the message bar when it blocks macros.
External Content	Enables you to specify how Excel deals with links to other workbooks and data from other sources.
File Block Settings	Enables you to select which types of files, such as macros, to open in Protected View or which file type to prevent saving a file in.
Privacy Options	Enables you to deal with privacy issues that are not macro related.

Pearson Education, Inc.

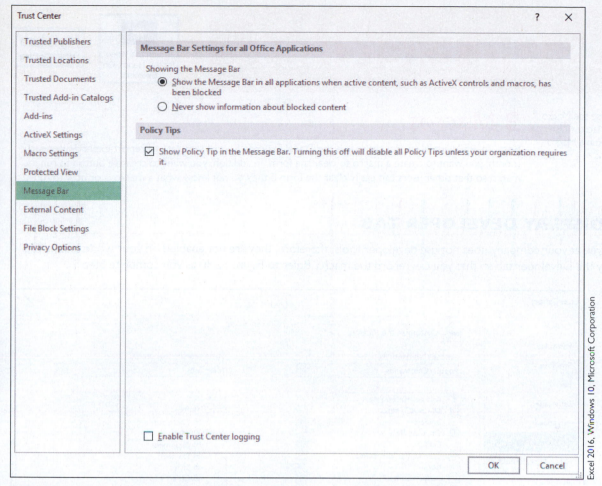

FIGURE 12.29 Trust Center Dialog Box

Quick Concepts

7. What is the purpose of a macro? *p. 761*

8. How are macros accessed after they have been recorded? *p. 764*

9. What potential risks are associated with macros? *p. 766*

Hands-On Exercises

 Watch the Video for this Hands-On Exercise!

 MyITLab® HOE3 Training

Skills covered: Use the Macro Recorder • Record a Macro • Use Relative References • Run a Macro • Create Macro Buttons

3 Macros

Because you want all employees to use the Travel Expense Report template to report expenditures each month, you want to create a macro to clear the form. In addition, you want to create a button to run the macro so that other users can easily clear the form if they do not know what a macro is or how to run it.

STEP 1 ▶▶ DISPLAY DEVELOPER TAB

The average employee at your company does not use developer tools; therefore, they are not enabled on your workstation. You would like to display the Developer tab so that you can record the macro. Refer to Figure 12.30 as you complete Step 1.

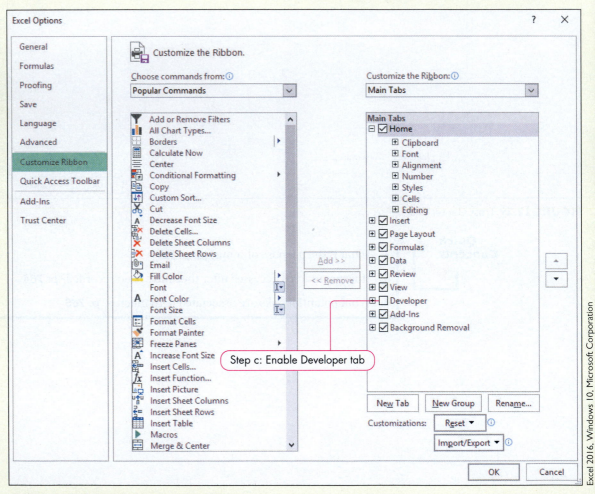

Excel 2016, Windows 10, Microsoft Corporation

FIGURE 12.30 Enable the Developer Tab

a. Open *e12h2ExpenseReportTemplate_LastFirst* and save it as **e12h3ExpenseReportTemplate_LastFirst**, changing h2 to h3.

When you use Open or Recent to open a template, you open it as a template to edit. When you use New, you make a copy of the template as a workbook.

> **TROUBLESHOOTING:** If you do not see Templates in Recent Places, click Open and navigate to the local directory that contains your student files.

b. Click the **File tab** and click **Options** to open the Excel Options dialog box.

c. Click **Customize Ribbon**, click the **Developer check box** in the Main Tabs list to select it, and then click **OK**.

The Developer tab is added to the Ribbon.

STEP 2 ›› **RECORD A MACRO**

You do not want to assume the level of Excel expertise throughout your company; therefore, you want to craft a macro that will automate as much as possible. The macro you would like to create needs to automatically clear existing values and then display an instruction for users to enter specific data. Although the template is empty to start, users might open the template, save a workbook, and then want to use that workbook to prepare future months' reports. Therefore, you need the macro to clear cells even though the original template has no values. Refer to Figure 12.31 as you complete Step 2.

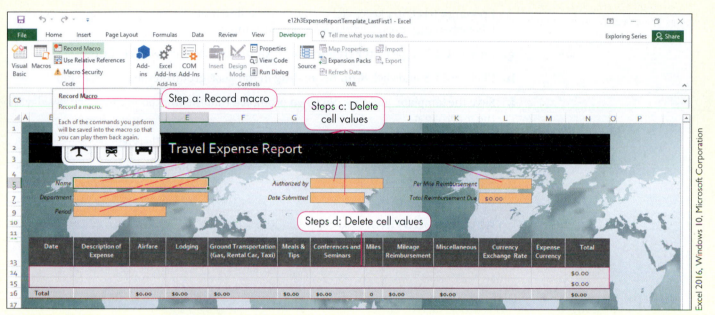

FIGURE 12.31 Record Macro

a. Click the **Developer tab**, and click **Record Macro** in the Code group.

The Record Macro dialog box opens so that you can name and describe the macro.

b. Type **ClearForm** in the Macro name box, click in the **Description box**, type **This macro clears existing values in the current Travel Expense Report**, and then click **OK**.

> **TROUBLESHOOTING:** Read through Steps c–g in advance before you proceed. Remember most actions taken in Excel are recorded by the Macro Recorder. Practice the steps below before activating the recorder. If you make a major mistake, delete the macro and repeat Steps b through j.

c. Select **cell C5** and press **Delete**.

Even though the cells are empty now, they may contain values at some point. You want the macro to delete any values that might exist in this range.

d. Adapt Step c for the following cells and ranges:

- **Cell C7**
- **Cell C9**
- **Cell H5**
- **Cell H7**
- **Cell L5**
- **Range B14:I15**
- **Range K14:M15**

You deleted ranges that might contain values after the user enters data into any workbooks created from the template. It is always good to plan for various possibilities in which data might be entered even if those ranges do not contain values now.

e. Press **Ctrl+G**, type **C5** in the Reference box of the Go To dialog box, and then click **OK**.

f. Type **Enter Name Here** in **cell C5** and press **Ctrl+Enter**.

Pressing Ctrl+Enter keeps cell C5 the active cell so that users can immediately enter the label when they open a workbook from the template.

g. Click **cell C7**, type **Enter Department Name**, and then press **Ctrl+Enter**.

h. Click **cell C5** and click **Stop Recording** in the Code group on the Developer tab.

i. Save the template, and click **No** when prompted that the workbook cannot be saved with the macro in it.

Excel opens the Save As dialog box so that you can select the file type.

j. Click the **Save as type arrow**, select **Excel Macro-Enabled Template**, and then click **Save**.

> **TROUBLESHOOTING:** Make sure you select Excel Macro-Enabled Template, not Excel Macro-Enabled Workbook, because you want the file saved as a template, not a workbook. Because the template contains macros, you must save it as an Excel Macro-Enabled Template, not just a template.

STEP 3 ⟩⟩ **RUN A MACRO**

You want to make sure the ClearForm macro does what you want it to do. First, you will add some sample data and run the macro. Refer to Figure 12.32 as you complete Step 3.

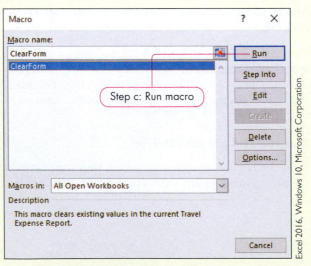

FIGURE 12.32 Run a Macro

a. Type your name in **cell C5**, type **Finance** in **cell C7**, type **1/25/2018** in **cell H7**, type **1/5/2018** in **cell B14**, type **Sales Meeting** in **cell C14**, and then type **$75.00** in **cell G14**.

You entered some sample values in various cells to test the ClearForm macro to verify if it will delete those values.

b. Ensure the Developer tab is displayed and click **Macros** in the Code group.

The Macro dialog box opens and displays the ClearForm macro, which should be selected in the Macro name box.

c. Select **ClearForm** and click **Run**.

The ClearForm macro quickly goes through the worksheet, erasing the values in the specified ranges, goes to cells C5 and C7, enters descriptive labels, and then stops.

> **TROUBLESHOOTING:** If the macro does not delete sample values, delete the macro and rerecord it.

d. Save the workbook.

STEP 4 ❱❱ **ADD A MACRO BUTTON**

Your colleagues may not be Excel experts and do not know how to run a macro. To make it easier to clear values from the form, you want to assign the ClearForm macro to a button. The users can then click the button to clear the form to use it for another month. You will also add an additional button to be utilized later in the project. Refer to Figure 12.33 as you complete Step 4.

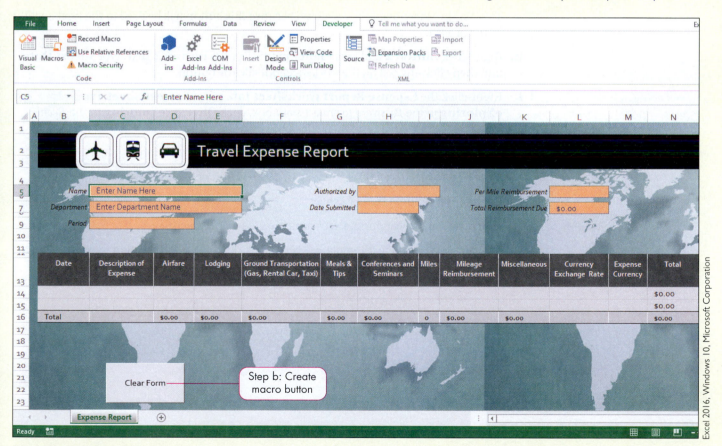

FIGURE 12.33 Macro Button

a. Click the **Home tab**, click **Format** in the Cells group, select **Unprotect Sheet**, type **eXploring** in the Password box in the Unprotect Sheet dialog box, and then click **OK**.

You have to unprotect the worksheet before you can insert a macro button.

b. Click the **Developer tab**, click **Insert** in the Controls group, and then click **Button (Form Control)** in the Form Controls section of the gallery.

c. Click the top of **cell C20** and drag down and to the right to the bottom of **cell D23** to create the area where the button will be placed.

The Assign Macro dialog box opens.

d. Select **ClearForm** in the Macro name list and click **OK**.

This action assigns the ClearForm macro to the button. The button appears in the range C20:D23, is selected, and displays *Button 1*. You will provide descriptive text to appear on the button.

e. Right-click **Button 1** and select **Edit Text**. Select the **Button 1 text**, type **Clear Form**, and then click any cell on the worksheet outside the button.

The button now shows *Clear Form*, which is more descriptive of the button's purpose than *Button 1*.

f. Click the **Developer tab**, click **Insert** in the Controls group, and then click **Button (Form Control)** in the Form Controls section of the gallery.

g. Click the top of **cell F20** and drag down and to the right to the bottom of **cell G23** to create the area where the button will be placed. Click **Cancel** in the Assign Macro dialog box.

The Assign Macro dialog box is closed because this button will be used in the next portion of the project.

h. Right-click **Button 2** and select **Edit Text**. Select the **Button 2 text**, type **Insert Date**, and then click any cell on the worksheet outside the button.

i. Right-click the **Expense Report worksheet tab**, select **Protect Sheet**, type **eXploring** in the *Password to protect sheet* box, click **OK**, type **eXploring** in the *Reenter password to proceed* box, and then click **OK**.

You need to protect the worksheet after creating the macro button.

j. Type **6/1/2018** in cell **B14** and type **6/29/2018** in **cell B15** to enter sample data.

k. Click **Clear Form** in the worksheet.

When you click Clear Form, Excel runs the ClearForm macro.

l. Save the Macro-Enabled Template. Keep the workbook open if you plan to continue with the next Hands-On Exercise. If not, close the workbook and exit Excel.

Visual Basic for Applications

As you perform commands while recording a macro, those commands are translated into Visual Basic for Applications (VBA). While many casual users will be able to complete required tasks using just the Macro Recorder, more advanced VBA macros can be created by authoring code directly into modules within the Visual Basic Editor. A *module* is a container in which VBA code is stored. The *Visual Basic Editor* is an application used to create, edit, execute, and debug Office application macros using programming code. These macros can then be used within a Macro-Enabled Workbook or Template.

The two types of VBA macros are sub procedures and custom functions. *Sub procedures*, which are also created when using the Macro Recorder, perform actions on a workbook but do not return specific values, such as the ClearForm example earlier in the chapter. For example, you can create a sub procedure to insert the current date in a worksheet. Similar to the hundreds of built-in functions in Excel, custom functions have the ability to manipulate input variables and return a value.

In this section, you will learn to use VBA to create and edit a sub procedure. You will also learn to create a custom function.

Creating a Sub Procedure

STEP 1 »» The first step to creating a sub procedure is inserting a new module or editing data in an existing module within the VBA Editor. To access the VBA Editor, press Alt+F11 on your keyboard. The left side of the VBA window contains the Project Explorer, which is similar in concept and appearance to the File Explorer except that it displays only open workbooks and/or other Visual Basic projects (see Figure 12.34).

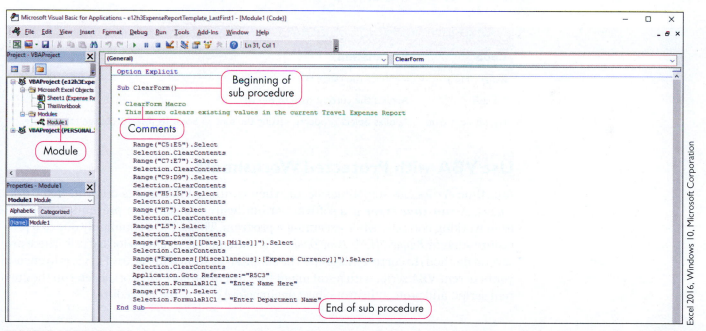

FIGURE 12.34 VBA Editor

The Visual Basic statements appear in the Text Editor window on the right side. In Excel, a Visual Basic module consists of at least one *procedure*, which is a named sequence of statements stored in a macro. In this example, Module1 contains the ClearForm procedure, which is also the name of the macro created in Excel. Module1 is stored in the Travel Expense Report workbook.

A procedure or macro always begins and ends with the Sub and End Sub statements. The Sub statement contains the name of the macro, such as Sub ClearForm() in Figure 12.32. The End Sub statement is the last statement and indicates the end of the macro. Sub and End Sub are Visual Basic keywords and appear in blue. **Keywords** are words or symbols reserved within a programming language for specific purposes.

Comments, which are indicated by an apostrophe and appear in green, provide information about the macro but do not affect its execution and are considered documentation. Comments can be entered manually or are inserted automatically by the macro recorder to document the macro name, its author, and shortcut key (if any). You can add, delete, or modify comments.

To create a basic sub procedure that would enter a date into a cell, complete the following steps:

1. Open the VBA Editor and select Module from the Insert menu.
2. Type *Sub CurrentDate()* and press Enter.
3. Type ' and add a descriptive comment.
4. Type *range("H7") = date* (replace *H7* with the cell address of the place where the date will appear) and press Enter.
5. Save and exit the Visual Basic Editor.

Table 12.2 explains some of the lines of code used to create the previous sub procedure. The first word, *range*, refers to an object. An **object** contains both data and code and represents an element of Excel such as Range or Selection. A period follows the object name, and the next word is often a method, such as Select or ClearContents, that describes a behavior or action performed on the object.

TABLE 12.2	VBA Editor Code
Code	**Explanation**
Range("H7")	Identifies the range H7
= Date	Applies the current date to the cell
Font.Bold = true	Applies object property, setting the font to bold. To disable, change *true* to *false*.

Pearson Education, Inc.

Use VBA with Protected Worksheets

Run-time errors can sometimes occur when running VBA scripts on protected worksheets. A **run-time error** is a software or hardware problem that prevents a program from working correctly while executing a program. This is most commonly due to a procedure such as *Range("H7").Font.Bold = true*, attempting to alter a locked cell. There are several methods to correct this issue. The simplest, as shown in Figure 12.35, is to encase your current VBA script with a statement that will unprotect the worksheet, run the current script, and protect the worksheet again before ending the procedure.

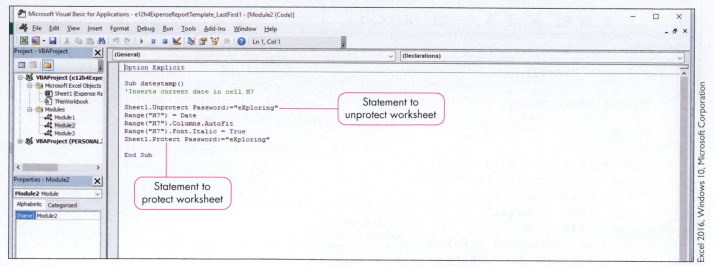

FIGURE 12.35 Unprotecting a Worksheet Using VBA

In the example, cell H7 is formatted. However, this will create a run-time error because the worksheet is protected. The statement *Sheet1.Unprotect Password:= "eXploring"* unprotects the worksheet to allow the format changes to occur. The statement *Sheet1.Protect Password:= "eXploring"* then protects the worksheet again.

Edit a Macro in the Visual Basic Editor

STEP 2 ⟫⟫ If you work with a workbook that has macros that were created by a coworker or you used the Macro Recorder, you can edit the existing macro using the Visual Basic Editor. For example, if you record a macro to apply bold, Arial font, 12-pt size, and Red font color, each command appears in a separate statement (see Figure 12.36). The two statements to apply bold and italic start with Selection.Font, indicating that a font attribute will be applied to the current selection. The statement continues with a period and behavior, such as *Bold = True*, indicating that bold is activated. If the sub procedure is turning off bold, the statement looks like this:

Selection.Font.Bold = False

The With statement enables you to perform multiple actions on the same object. All commands between the With and the corresponding End With statement are executed consecutively. Although the font and font size were changed in the macro, the macro also indicates that other attributes, such as superscript and subscript, are turned off. You can delete those lines of code if you want.

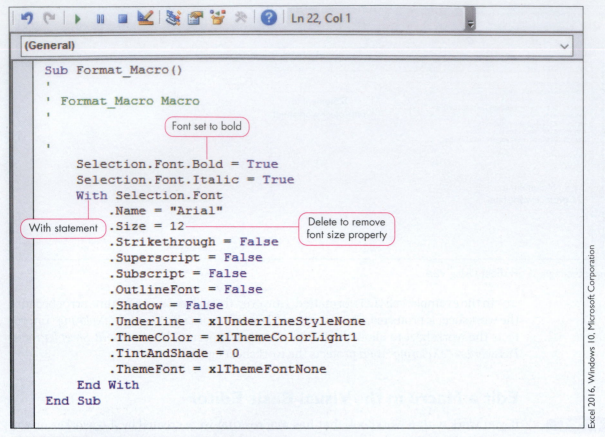

FIGURE 12.36 Edit Macro in VBA Editor

Creating a Custom Function

STEP 3 ▶▶ There are several hundred built-in functions in Excel that can perform tasks as simple as capitalizing the first letter of a word, such as the Proper function, or as complex as a multi-conditional sum, as created with SumIFs. In the event that one of the numerous built-in functions does not meet your needs, you can create your own custom function using VBA. Custom functions are virtually limitless. However, like sub procedures, they are still saved in modules. This means that if they are not saved to a Personal Macro Workbook, they will only be available within the Macro-Enabled Workbook in which they were created.

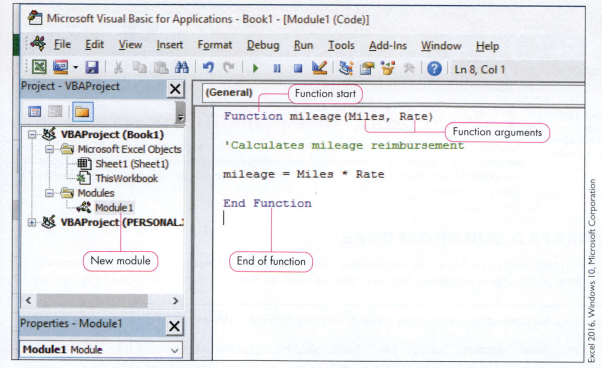

FIGURE 12.37 Create a VBA function

When creating a custom function in VBA, you must start by creating a new module and typing FUNCTION followed by the name of the function you are creating and the arguments that the function will use inside parentheses (refer to Figure 12.37).

After entering arguments on the next line, you add comments in the same manner they were added to sub procedures. Your next step is to enter the statement that defines your function such as:

*Mileage = Miles * Rate*

After completing the statement, you end the function by typing End Function. However, this step should automatically be completed by the VBA Editor.

Once a custom function is completed, it can be viewed within Excel under User Defined functions within the Insert Function command in the Function Library. Furthermore, you can access the function by simply typing = in the cell of your choice and the name of the function. This will allow you to use the custom function in the same manner as any of the built-in Excel functions.

Quick Concepts

10. When using Excel, why would you want to access the VBA Editor? *p. 775*

11. What is the difference between keywords and comments? *p. 774*

12. Why would it be necessary to create a custom function? *p. 776*

Watch the Video for this Hands-On Exercise!

 MyITLab® HOE4 Training

4 Visual Basic for Applications

You would like to automate as much of the Travel Expense Report as possible. Therefore, you will create a sub procedure assigned to a macro button to automatically insert the current date into the worksheet. You would also like to add an additional function that will allow the user to estimate mileage reimbursement prior to submission.

STEP 1 ›› CREATE A SUB PROCEDURE

Before you create the sub procedure, you will open the template you created in Hands-On Exercise 3 and save it as a template with another name to preserve the original template in case you make any mistakes. Refer to Figure 12.38 as you complete Step 1.

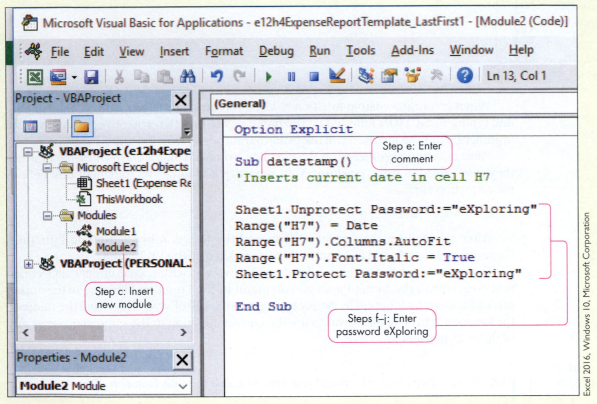

FIGURE 12.38 Create a Sub Procedure

a. Open the Macro-Enabled Template *e12h3ExpenseReportTemplate_LastFirst*, click **Enable Content** to activate the prior macro, and save it as **e12h4ExpenseReportTemplate_ LastFirst**, changing h3 to h4.

When you use Open or Recent to open a template, you open it as a template to edit. When you use New, you make a copy of the template as a workbook.

b. Press **Alt+F11** to open the Visual Basic Editor.

c. Click the **Insert menu** and select **Module**.

d. Type **Sub datestamp()** on the first line of the newly created module and press **Enter**.

e. Type **'Inserts current date in cell H7** and press **Enter**.

This adds a comment to the procedure you are creating that will make it easier for future users to understand your work.

f. Type **Sheet1.Unprotect Password:= "eXploring"** and press **Enter**.

This unprotects the workbook to allow the remaining changes to take place.

g. Type **range("H7") = Date** and press **Enter**.

This enters the current date.

h. Type **range("H7").Columns.Autofit** and press **Enter**.

This sets the selected column to AutoFit, which will ensure proper display of the date.

i. Type **range("H7").Font.Bold = True** and press **Enter**.

This sets the entered date to bold.

j. Type **Sheet1.Protect Password:="eXploring"** and press **Enter**.

k. Save the macro and press **F5** to test the macro.

When run, the sub procedure unprotects the worksheet, adds and formats the current date, sets the column width to auto, and protects the document.

l. Save the workbook.

STEP 2 ›› **EDIT A MACRO**

After running the sub procedure, you have decided that the inserted date should be italic instead of bold. You will make this change in the VBA Editor by changing the Bold property. Refer to Figure 12.39 as you complete Step 2.

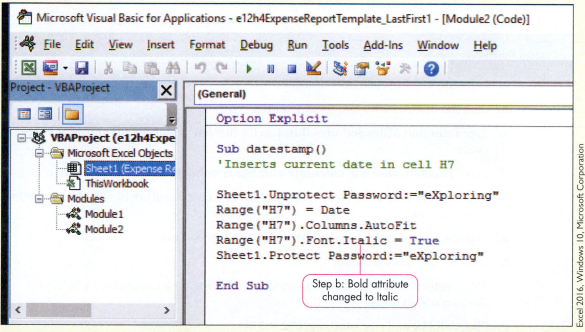

FIGURE 12.39 Edit a Macro

a. Ensure the VBA Editor is displayed by pressing **Alt+F11** to open the VBA Editor.

Excel opens the VBA Editor so that you can edit the macro programming language.

b. Click **Module2**, if it is not already selected, to display the sub procedure created in Step 1. Select the line **Range("H7").Font.Bold = True** and replace the word *Bold* with **Italic**.

This edits the command to set the inserted date to italic instead of bold.

c. Save and exit the VBA Editor.

d. Right-click **Button 2**. Select **Assign Macro**, select **DateStamp**, and then click **OK**.

This assigns the DateStamp macro to the Insert Date button created earlier in the exercise.

e. Click **Button 2** to verify the current date. Once the date is verified, click **Clear Form** and save the template.

f. Save the workbook.

STEP 3 ›› **CREATE A CUSTOM FUNCTION**

You have decided to create a custom function to enable users to manually calculate their mileage reimbursement if they choose. Refer to Figure 12.40 as you complete Step 4.

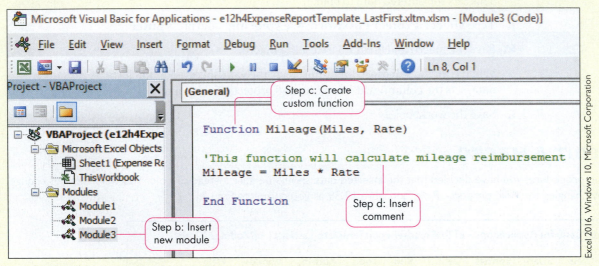

FIGURE 12.40 Create a Custom Function

a. Press **Alt +F11** to open the VBA Editor.

b. Click the **Insert menu** and select **Module**.

c. Type **Function Mileage(Miles,Rate)** on the first line of the module and press **Enter** twice.

d. Type **'This function will calculate mileage reimbursement**. Press **Enter**.

This will appear as a comment in the module. However, it will not impact the calculation of the function.

e. Type the statement **Mileage = Miles * Rate** and press **Enter**.

f. Save and exit the VBA Editor.

This creates a custom function that can be used in a similar fashion to any built-in function within Excel.

g. Click **cell J14** and type **=mileage(32,0.75)**.

This returns the value 24 and copies the function into cell J15. You entered 32 miles at the rate of $.75 per mile to test the newly created function.

h. Delete the contents of **cell J14** and **J15**.

i. Save and close all files. Based on your instructor's directions, submit the following:

e12h2ExpenseReportSample_LastFirst

e12h4ExpenseReportTemplate_LastFirst

Chapter Objectives Review

After reading this chapter, you have accomplished the following objectives:

1. Select a template.
- A template is a partially created workbook that you can use as a model to create a workbook. You can create a workbook based on sample templates stored on your computer, or you can download a template from Office.com to create a new workbook.

2. Apply themes and backgrounds.
- A theme is a collection of colors, fonts, and special effects. You can apply themes to various workbooks to develop a consistent look for your organization's workbooks.
- Customize a theme: After applying a theme, you can customize the colors, fonts, and effects.
- Apply a background: Excel can use graphics as a background of a worksheet.

3. Apply cell styles.
- A cell style is a collection of format settings to provide a consistent look for fonts, borders, fill colors, alignment, and number formatting.
- The Cell Styles gallery provides a variety of existing cell styles. If you change the cell style formatting, all cells affected by that style assume the new formatting, thus saving you valuable time so that you do not have to reformat cells individually.
- Create custom cell styles: You can create a new custom style from the Styles group in the Home tab.
- Modify and remove custom cell styles: Create custom styles that can be modified or removed by right-clicking the style and selecting the desired change in the Styles group.

4. Create and use a template.
- You can save a workbook as a template when existing templates do not provide the structure you need.
- When you save a template, Excel saves it in the C:\Users\username\Documents\Custom Office Templates folder so that the templates are available when you click the File tab and click New.
- Templates have an .xltx file name extension.

5. Protect a cell, a worksheet, and a workbook.
- Lock and unlock cells: By default, the Locked property is selected for all cells in all new workbooks you create; however, this property has no effect until you protect the worksheet.
- Before protecting the worksheet, you should unlock cells that you want a user to be able to change, such as input cells.

- Protect a worksheet: For greater security, you can assign a password that is required to unprotect the worksheet.
- Protect a workbook: For additional protection, you can protect an entire workbook to prevent users from inserting, deleting, renaming, or moving worksheets.

6. Create a macro.
- A macro is a stored procedure that performs multiple, routine, or complex tasks.
- Use the Macro Recorder: The Macro Recorder translates user actions into VBA.
- The Developer tab contains commands to record, run, and edit macros.
- Record a macro: When recording a macro, all user actions will be recorded by the Macro Recorder and stored in VBA.
- Use relative references: By default, when you select cells when recording a macro, the macro records the cells as absolute references. By recording the macro using relative references, you apply the macro to the cells you choose on execution.
- Run a macro: After macros are created, they can be run from the assigned keyboard shortcut, a macro button, or from the Macro dialog box.

7. Create macro buttons.
- To facilitate the running of a macro, you can assign a macro to a button. The Developer tab contains controls, such as buttons, you can insert in a worksheet.

8. Set macro security.
- The proliferation of Excel macro viruses has made it dangerous to open workbooks that contain macros. To counter this threat, Excel automatically disables the macros and displays a security warning message that macros have been disabled.

9. Creating a sub procedure.
- Sub procedures can be created using the Macro Recorder or entered manually in the VBA Editor. Sub procedures only perform actions and cannot return values.
- Edit a macro in the VBA Editor: After a sub procedure has been created, it can be edited in the VBA Editor.
- Use VBA with a protected worksheet: VBA can be used to protect and unprotect worksheets.

10. Creating a custom function.
- If the built-in Excel functions do not meet your needs, you can create a custom function using VBA.

Key Terms Matching

Match the key terms with their definitions. Write the key term letter by the appropriate numbered definition.

a. Background
b. Cell Style
c. Comment
d. Keyword
e. Locked Cell
f. Macro
g. Macro Recorder
h. Module
i. Object

j. Personal Macro Workbook
k. Procedure
l. Run-Time Error
m. Sub Procedure
n. Template
o. Theme
p. Visual Basic for Applications (VBA)
q. Visual Basic Editor

1. _____ A special workbook file used as a model to create similarly structured workbooks. **p. 738**

2. _____ A collection of formats that include coordinating colors, fonts, and special effects to provide a stylish appearance. **p. 739**

3. _____ An image that appears in the worksheet window behind the worksheet data onscreen. **p. 740**

4. _____ A collection of format settings based on the currently selected theme to provide a consistent appearance within a worksheet and among similar workbooks. **p. 741**

5. _____ Prevents users from making changes to a specific cell in a protected worksheet. **p. 750**

6. _____ A set of instructions that executes a sequence of commands to automate repetitive or routine tasks. **p. 761**

7. _____ A tool that records a series of commands in the sequence performed by a user and converts the commands into programming syntax. **p. 762**

8. _____ A hidden workbook stored in the XLSTART folder that contains macros and opens automatically when you start Excel. **p. 763**

9. _____ An application used to create, edit, execute, and debug Office applications macros using programming code. **p. 773**

10. _____ A named sequence of statements stored in a macro. **p. 773**

11. _____ A word or symbol reserved within a programming language for specific purposes. **p. 774**

12. _____ Documents programming code, starts with an apostrophe, and appears in green in the VBA Editor. **p. 774**

13. _____ A group of commands in the VBA Editor that have the ability to perform actions in Excel when the Sub is executed. **p. 773**

14. _____ An object that stores sub procedures and functions. **p. 773**

15. _____ A container that holds both data and code and represents an element of Excel. **p. 774**

16. _____ A software or hardware problem that prevents a program from working correctly. **p. 774**

17. _____ A robust programming language that can be used within various software packages to enhance and automate functionality. **p. 761**

Multiple Choice

1. How do you enable the Developer tab?

  (a) Open Backstage view, click Excel Options, click Customize Ribbon, and click Developer in the Customize the Ribbon window.

  (b) Open Backstage view, click Add-ins, and then click Developer.

  (c) Click the Data tab, Click Developer in the Get & Transform group.

  (d) Open Backstage view, click Options, and then choose the Office.com templates in the Template Manager.

2. You created an invoice template to prepare invoices for your consulting business. In Windows 10, where would you save the template so it is available in the available templates list in Backstage view?

  (a) C:\Users\user_name\Libraries\Documents

  (b) Submit it to Office.com.

  (c) C:\Users\username\Documents\Custom Office Templates

  (d) None of the above

3. How do you create a new workbook based on a template you personally created?

  (a) Click File and select new template from the template gallery.

  (b) Click New, search Office.com for the template, and click download.

  (c) Click File, click New, click PERSONAL, and select the template.

  (d) All of the above

4. How do you set a picture as the background of a worksheet?

  (a) In Print Options, select Background.

  (b) Click Page Layout, click Background.

  (c) Click the File tab, click Options, click Set Background.

  (d) Click Insert, click Background.

5. What is the keyboard shortcut to access the VBA Editor?

  (a) Alt+F8

  (b) F3

  (c) F4

  (d) Alt+F11

6. If you forget the password you used to protect an Excel worksheet, how do you reset it?

  (a) You cannot reset it.

  (b) You can reset it in Excel Options in Backstage view.

  (c) You can email it to Office.com for reset.

  (d) There is a password reset in the Properties pane for each Excel workbook.

7. In which programming language are Excel macros written?

  (a) Java

  (b) C++

  (c) VBA

  (d) SQL

8. Which of the following is *not* true about macros?

  (a) Macros are created using VBA.

  (b) Macros can be saved in XLSM workbooks.

  (c) Macros can use absolute or relative cell referencing.

  (d) Templates cannot contain macros.

9. Which of the following statements is *true* about macro security?

  (a) When you add a Macro-Enabled Workbook to the Trust Center, you must enable the content of that file each time you open it.

  (b) Setting your Trust Center options to include files in a specific folder and then saving macro-enabled files in that folder allows you to open those files with the content enabled.

  (c) Set macro security options on the Developer tab to Secured.

  (d) Macro-enabled files cannot contain viruses.

10. Which of the following workbook file extensions support macros?

  (a) .xlsm

  (b) .xlsb

  (c) .xltm

  (d) All of the above

Practice Exercises

1 Blood Pressure Tracker

FROM SCRATCH

Inner City Health Clinic is located in downtown San Francisco. As a physician's assistant, you help monitor each patient's blood pressure. It is important for some patients to track their blood pressure throughout the week between office visits, so you want to create a template that you can email to them. You will create a template from scratch, select a theme, add a background image, apply custom styles, and create a macro to format blood pressure readings that require further attention in red. After you are satisfied with the appearance, you will then save the workbook as a new template that you can email to your computer-savvy patients so that they can track their blood pressure at home. Refer to Figure 12.41 as you complete this exercise.

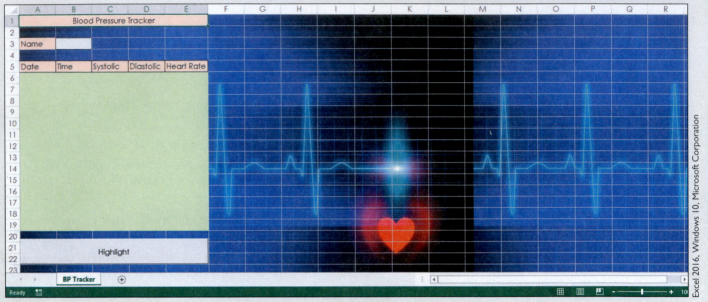

FIGURE 12.41 Blood Pressure Tracker Template

a. Start Excel and click **Blank workbook** in Backstage view.

b. Save the workbook as an Excel Macro-Enabled Template with the file name **e12p1BpTracker_LastFirst**.

c. Name the worksheet **BP Tracker**.

d. Click the **Page Layout tab**, click **Themes** in the Themes group, and then select **Slice**.

e. Click **Background** in the Page Setup group, click **Browse**, and then navigate to your student data files. Select *e12p1Bpressure.jpg* in the Sheet Background dialog box and click **Insert**.

f. Merge and center the **range A1:E1** and complete the following tasks:
   - Type **Blood Pressure Tracker** in **cell A1** and apply **20% – Accent5 cell style**.
   - Type **Name** in **cell A3** and apply **20% – Accent5 cell style**.
   - Apply the **Output cell style** to **cell B3**.

g. Select the **range A5:E5**, click the **Borders arrow** in the Font group on the Home tab, select **All Borders**, and then apply **20% – Accent5 cell style**.

h. Enter the following text as column headings in row 5:
   - **Cell A5: Date**
   - **Cell B5: Time**
   - **Cell C5: Systolic**
   - **Cell D5: Diastolic**
   - **Cell E5: Heart Rate**

i. Click **cell E5**, click the **Home tab**, and then click **Format** in the Cells group. Select **AutoFit Column Width**.

j. Select **range A6:E19**, click **Cell Styles**, select **New Cell Style**, name the new style **Data**, and do the following to complete the formatting tasks:

- Set the Font style to **Bold**
- Set the Fill color to **Dark Green, Accent 4, Lighter 80%** (Second row, third from the right).
- Click **OK** to exit the Format Cells window and click **OK** again to complete creating the new cell style.

k. Select **cell B3**, press and hold **Ctrl**, and then select the **range A6:E19**. Click **Format** in the Cells group on the Home tab and select **Lock Cell**.

l. Ensure the Developer tab is enabled. Click **Use Relative References**, click **Record Macro**, name the macro **Warning**, accept the default settings, and then click **OK** to activate the Macro Recorder.

m. Click the **Home tab**, click **Font Color** in the Font group, select **Red**, and then stop the Macro Recorder.

n. Ensure the **cell B3** and **range A6:E19** are still selected, click **Font Color**, and then select **Automatic**.

o. Click the **Developer tab**, click **Insert** in the Controls group, and then select **Button**.

p. Create a Form Control button that fills the **range A21:E22** and assign the Warning macro.

q. Right-click the **Form Control button**, select **Edit Text**, and then rename the button **Highlight**.

r. Protect the worksheet by completing the following tasks:

- Right-click the **BP Tracker sheet tab**, select **Protect Sheet**, type **eXploring** in the *Password (optional)* box, and then click **OK**.
- Type **eXploring** in the *Reenter password to proceed* box and click **OK**.

s. Click the **File tab** and click **Save As**. Click the **Save as type arrow**, navigate to your homework data files, and then select **Excel Macro-Enabled Template**. Keep the default name and then click **Save**.

t. Save and close the workbook. Based on your instructor's directions, submit e12p1BpTracker_LastFirst.

FROM
SCRATCH

You are the sales manager for Home Sites Inc., a regional construction company that specializes in building homes for first-time home owners. You have decided to create a sales worksheet to more efficiently manage your daily transactions. To accomplish this task, you will modify an existing Excel template. You will also use the Macro Recorder and VBA to automate clearing and protecting the workbook. You will then assign the macros to buttons. Refer to Figure 12.42 as you complete this exercise.

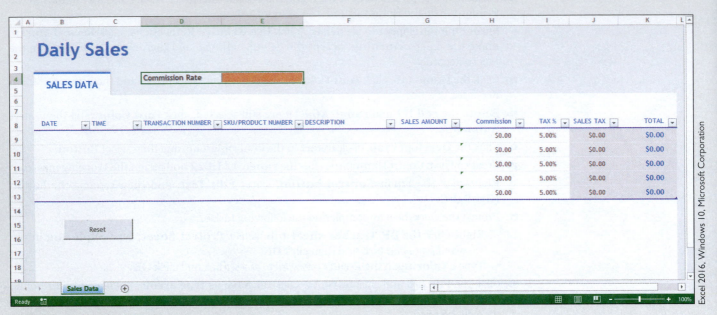

FIGURE 12.42 Daily Sales Template

a. Open Excel, type **Daily sales report** in the gallery search box, click **Daily sales report**, and click **Create**.

b. Save the workbook as a Macro-Enabled Template named **e12p2SalesTemplate_LastFirst**. Click **Yes** when prompted to clear external data.

c. Click **Page Layout**, click **Colors** in the Themes group, and then select **Blue Warm**.

d. Right-click the **Inventory worksheet**, select **Delete**, and then click **Delete** to remove the worksheet from the workbook.

e. Adapt the steps from above to delete the Sales Report worksheet.

f. Right-click the **Inventory button** on the Sales Data worksheet and click **Cut** to remove the button from the worksheet.

g. Right-click the **Sales Report button** and click **Cut** to remove the link from the worksheet.

h. Click **cell B2** and type **Daily Sales**.

i. Select the **range B9:G13**, press **Delete**, and then complete the following steps:
   - Insert a column before column H.
   - Click **cell H8** and type **COMMISSION**.
   - Apply **Currency Number Format** to the **range H9:H13**.

j. Select the **range B9:G13**, click the **Home tab**, click **Format** in the Cells group, and then select **Lock Cell**.

k. Press **Alt+F11**, click **Insert** in the Visual Basic Editor, and then select **Module**. Enter the following text to create a custom function:
   - Type **Function Commission (Sales, Rate)** and press **Enter** twice.
   - Type **Commission = Sales * Rate** and press **Enter**.

l. Click **Insert**, select **Module**, and then enter the following text to create a sub procedure to reset the worksheet:

- Type **Sub Reset()** and press **Enter** twice.
- Type **'Unprotect worksheet** and press **Enter**.
- Type **Sheet1.Unprotect Password:="eXploring"** and press **Enter** twice.
- Type **'Clear contents** and press **Enter**.
- Type **Range("B9:G13").ClearContents** and press **Enter** twice.
- Type **'Protect worksheet** and press **Enter**.
- Type **Sheet1.Protect Password:="eXploring"**.

m. Click **Save** and exit the Visual Basic Editor.

n. Click the **Developer tab**, click **Insert** and select **Button**.

o. Create a button that spans the **range B15:C16**, apply the Reset macro, and then edit the button title to **Reset**.

p. Click **cell D4**. Type **Commission Rate**, press **Ctrl+Enter**, and then apply the **Output cell style**.

q. Click **cell E4**, apply the **Input cell style**, and **Percent Style Number Format**.

r. Click **cell H9**, type **=commission(G9,$E$4)**, and then press **Ctrl+Enter**.

s. Click the **File tab**, click **Options**, and then click **Trust Center**. Click **Trust Center Settings**, click **Trusted Locations**, and click **Add new location**. Select the path where the workbook is saved and click **OK** on both windows to return to the workbook.

t. Create a footer with your name on the left side, the sheet name code in the center, and the file name code on the right side of the worksheets.

u. Save and close the workbook. Based on your instructor's directions, submit e12p2SalesTemplate_LastFirst.

Mid-Level Exercises

1 Little League Statistics

You have volunteered to coach for your community Little League program. You are working with the Pirates, a team of 10- to 12-year-olds who respond well to seeing their batting statistics. You created a workbook to record the Pirates' batting data and calculate their statistics. The recreation department manager is a friend of yours from high school and is impressed with your workbook. He wondered if you could make something similar for the other coaches when he saw how you were recording statistics.

a. Open *e12m1Pirates* and save it as **e12m1Pirates_LastFirst**.

b. Apply the **Title cell style** to **cell A1**, the **Heading 2 cell style** to the **range A2:R2**, the **Heading 4 cell style** to the **range A3:A20**, and **Output style** to the **range B3:R20**.

c. Apply the **Wood Type theme** and apply the **Red theme colors**.

d. Add *e12m1Pirate.jpg* as a background image for the worksheet.

e. Save the Excel workbook, and then also save it as a template named **e12m1Baseball_LastFirst**.

f. Delete the background from the Statistics worksheet and insert *e12m1Baseball.jpg* as the background image for the template before distributing the template to the other teams.

g. Select the **Game 1 worksheet**, delete all players' names and batting information from the **range A3:M16**. Right-align the labels in the **range C2:M2**.

h. Unlock **cell A1**, the **range A3:M16** of the Game 1 worksheet, and **cell A1** in the Statistics worksheet. Right-align the labels in the **range B2:R2** in the Statistics worksheet.

i. Set **0.2"** left and right margins on both worksheets. Set a width of **6.00** for columns B:H and J:O on the Statistics worksheet.

j. Create a footer with your name on the left side, the sheet name code in the center, and the file name code on the right side of both worksheets.

k. Protect all worksheets with the password **eXploring**. Enable all users to format cells, columns, and rows.

l. Save and close the template.

m. Create a new workbook from the *e12m1Baseball_LastFirst* template and save the workbook as **e12m1Broncos_LastFirst**.

n. Edit the league name from *Pirates* to **Broncos** in **cell A1** of each worksheet and enter player names and data for 14 players in the Game1 worksheet.

o. Save the workbook. Based on your instructor's directions, submit the following:

   e12m1Pirates_LastFirst

   e12m1Broncos_LastFirst

2 Shield Lawn Care

ANALYSIS CASE

You own a small landscaping business and have recently experienced an increase in new customers. To help manage the added workload, you will create an invoice template. The template will contain macros to both finalize the document and reset to default settings. To minimize the amount of development time required, you will download and edit an existing template from Office.com.

a. Open Excel, search and download the template **Invoice with finance charge (blue)**, and then click **Create**.

b. Save the file as a Macro-Enabled Template named **e12m2LawnCare_LastFirst**.

c. Change the template theme colors to **Green Yellow**.

d. Delete the logo placeholder located in the upper left corner and slogan place holder located in **cell C2**.

e. Edit the placeholder text in **cell B4** to reflect the company name **Shield Lawn Care** and apply the **Title cell style**.

f. Unlock **cell B19**, the **range B22:D30**, and **cell E7**.

g. Clear the contents of cells **B19**, **B22:D30**, **E12:E16**, and **cell E7**.

h. Create a macro named **Finalize**. The macro should insert the current date in **cell E7** and protect the workbook using the password **eXploring**.

i. Create a form control button that spans the **range B35:C36**, assign the Finalize macro, and edit the button text to **Finalize**.

j. Use the Visual Basic Editor to create a new module.

k. Create a new sub procedure within the module named **Reset**. The sub procedure should clear the contents of **cell E7**, the **ranges B19:C19**, and **B22:D30**.

l. Create a form control button that spans the **range D35:E36**, assign the Reset macro, and edit the button text to **Reset**.

m. Create a footer with your name on the left side, the sheet name code in the center, and the file name code on the right side on each worksheet.

n. Save and close the workbook. Based on your instructor's directions, submit e12m2LawnCare_LastFirst.

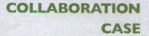

3 Fundraiser

COLLABORATION CASE

You work for a regional philanthropic organization that helps raise money for underprivileged youth. To help meet an end-of-the-year fundraising goal, you have decided to deploy regional donation agents to help collect contributions. You would like to make a worksheet to help track donations. Once the worksheet is completed, you will share the file via email with a collaborator in the region who will update the numbers.

Student 1:

a. Open *e12m3FundRaiser* and save it as **e12m3FundRaiser_LastFirst**.

b. Select **cell B2** and apply the **Heading 2 cell style**.

c. Select the **range B3:E10**, click the **Home tab**, click **Format** and then unlock the cells.

d. Click **Format** and protect the worksheet using the password **eXploring**.

e. Click the **File tab** and select **Share** in Backstage view.

f. Select **EMAIL** and choose **Send as Attachment**.

g. Email the worksheet to your collaborator.

Student 2:

h. Open the email and the attachment and enter the following data:

Date	Name	Donation	Collector
12/20/2018	Smith	$350.00	
12/22/2018	Williams	$125.00	
12/23/2018	Wilky	$110.00	
12/23/2018	Barns	$500.00	

i. Type your name as the **Collector** in column E.

j. Create a footer with your name on the left side, the sheet name code in the center, and the file name code on the right side on each worksheet.

k. Save and close the workbook. Based on your instructor's directions, submit e12m3FundRaiser_LastFirst.

Beyond the Classroom

Trust Center

So far, you have worked with the default Trust Center settings. You want to learn more about the Trust Center. Open the Trust Center dialog box in Excel and display the Macro Settings options. Start Word and insert a screenshot of the default Macro Settings. Set a **3"** shape height for the screenshot. Save the Word document as **e12b1Trust_LastFirst**. Compose a short explanation of the default Macro Settings option. In Excel, display the File Block Settings options and click to select the Excel 2007 and later Macro-Enabled Workbooks and Templates Open and Save check boxes. Insert a screenshot in your Word document and set a **3"** shape height. Click **OK** in each open dialog box.

In Excel, open *e12h3ExpenseReportTemplate_LastFirst*, the Macro-Enabled Template. In Word, explain what happens when you open this template and what happens when you try to run the macro by clicking **Clear Form**. Close the Macro-Enabled Template and deselect the check boxes you just selected in the File Block Settings. In the Word document, insert a footer with your name on the left side and a file name field on the right side. Save the document. Based on your instructor's directions, submit e12b1Trust_LastFirst.

Real Estate Listings

You are a real estate analyst who works for Mountain View Realty in the North Utah County area. Your assistant, Joey, compiled a list of houses sold during the past few months in a macro-enabled workbook. Joey created three macros: (1) a Clear macro to clear the existing Criteria Range and run the filter to empty the Output Range, (2) a CedarHills macro to set a criterion in the Criteria Range to filter the list for Cedar Hills only, and (3) a CityAgentCombo interactive macro with input boxes to prompt the user for the city and agent, enter those in respective cells, and run the advanced filter. In addition, Joey created three macro buttons, one to run each macro. However, the macros and buttons have errors. Open *e12b2RealEstate* and save it as a Macro-Enabled Workbook named **e12b2RealEstate_LastFirst**. Find the errors in the macros, document the problems in the macro code using programming comments, and then fix the errors. Find and correct the macro button errors. Create a footer with your name on the left side, the sheet name code in the center, and the file name code on the right side of the Input-Output worksheet. Save and close the workbook. Based on your instructor's directions, submit e12b2RealEstate_LastFirst.

Capstone Exercise

You are graduating from college, and moving into your first apartment. After moving into your apartment, your insurance agent has advised you to create an inventory of the contents of your home and their value. To complete this task, you will create a worksheet based on an Office.com template; you will also use the Macro Recorder and Visual Basic for Application to automate organization and calculations within the workbook.

Create a Template

You want to download an inventory template. In addition, you will apply cell styles to format the template.

a. Open Excel and search the template gallery for **Inventory of home contents**.

b. Create a new document based on the template and save it as a Macro-Enabled Template named **e12c1Inventory_LastFirst**.

c. Apply the **Droplet theme**.

d. Apply the **Title cell style** to the **cell B2**.

e. Apply the **Yellow Orange theme colors**.

f. Unlock the **range B15:K17** and **range D4:D12**.

g. Save the template.

Create the Sort Macro

You will sort the information in the template chronologically based on date purchased. To automate this task, you use the Macro Recorder and Developer Tools.

a. Record a macro named **Sort**.

b. Ensure the macro sorts the Inventory list in ascending order based on the dates listed in column F.

c. Create a form control button that spans the **range F5:G6**.

d. Assign the Sort macro and edit the button text to **Sort**.

Create a Custom Function

Along with calculating the total estimated value of your items, you also would like to calculate the depreciated value based on 5% depreciations. To complete this task, you will create a custom function using VBA and then use the function in the template.

a. Use the VBA Editor to create a new module.

b. Type the following VBA code to create a custom depreciation function:
   - **Function Depreciation (Value, Rate)**
   - **Depreciation = Value * Rate**

c. Save and exit the VBA Editor.

d. Insert two rows above row 12.

e. Enter the Row heading **DEPRECIATION RATE** in **cell B12** and **DEPRECIATION** in **cell B13**.

f. Use the Depreciation function in **cell D13** to calculate depreciation based on the Total Estimated Value on All Items (cell D14) and the Depreciation Rate (D12).

Finalize the Template

To finalize your inventory template, you will clear sample data and lock the workbook.

a. Clear the contents in the **range B17:K19**.

b. Protect the workbook using the password **eXploring**.

c. Save the file as **e12c1Inventory_LastFirst** in the Excel Macro-Enabled Template file format. Close the template. Based on your instructor's directions, submit e12c1Inventory_LastFirst.

Excel Introductory Capstone Exercise (Chs. 1–4)

You are a vice president for a publisher of software training books. Your division publishes three series that focus on Microsoft Office and Windows. You want to analyze the sales data and calculate author royalties. You will format the worksheet, insert formulas and functions to perform calculations, sort and filter data to review specific book sales, and prepare a chart that compares sales by series.

Format the Worksheet

Your assistant compiled the initial data and saved it in an Excel workbook. However, the column labels are hard to read because the full text does not display. You will use alignment and format options to make it easier to read the labels.

a. Open *eApp_Cap1_Publisher* and save it as **eApp_Cap1_Publisher_LastFirst**.

b. Select the **range A6:K6** on the Data worksheet.

c. Wrap the text and apply Center alignment to the selected range.

d. Change the row height to **30**.

Insert Formulas and Basic Functions

The Data worksheet contains the quantity of books sold, the number of books returned, and the unit price per book. You want to calculate the percentage of books that were returned from bookstores to your warehouse. Then you will also calculate the net sales, the amount of royalties to pay the authors, and the total author earnings. You want to insert functions to calculate the average, highest, and lowest net sales amounts. Use appropriate relative, absolute, and mixed references correctly in your formulas.

a. Click **cell F7** on the Data worksheet and insert a formula that calculates the percentage of books returned based on the number of books returned and the quantity sold. Copy the formula from cell F7 to the **range F8:F22**.

b. Click **cell H7** and insert a formula that calculates the net sales. This monetary amount reflects the number of books *not* returned and the unit price. Copy the formula from cell H7 to the **range H8:H22**.

c. Click **cell I7** and insert a formula that calculates the amount of the first author's royalties. An author's royalties are based on the Royalty Rate located in the Input Area and the respective Net Sales. Copy the formula from cell I7 to the **range I8:I22**.

d. Click **cell K7** and insert a formula that adds the first author's royalty amount to the bonus. Copy the formula from cell K7 to the **range K8:K22**.

e. Click **cell J2** and insert a function to calculate the average net sales.

f. Click **cell J3** and insert a function to calculate the highest net sales.

g. Click **cell J4** and insert a function to calculate the lowest net sales.

Move Data and Insert Functions

The legend that explains the abbreviations for each series would look better in a different location. You will insert a new column in the worksheet and insert a lookup function to display the full series names. Finally, you will replace the bonus with a function that calculates a bonus only if the return rate is less than 10%. Use relative, absolute, and mixed references correctly in your functions.

a. Select the **range L1:N2**, copy the selected data, and transpose the data when pasting it to **cell A2**. Delete the data in the **range L1:N2**.

b. Click **cell C6** and insert a column. Type **Series Name** in **cell C6**.

c. Click **cell C7** and insert a lookup function that identifies the series code, compares it to the series legend, and then returns the name of the series. Copy the function you entered from cell C7 to the **range C8:C22**.

d. Change the width of column C to **18**.

e. Click **cell K7** and insert an IF function that compares the percent returned for the first book to the return rate in the Input Area. If the percent returned is less than the return rate, the result is $500. Otherwise, the author receives no bonus. The only value you may type directly in the function is 0 where needed. Copy the function you entered from cell K7 to the **range K8:K22**.

Format Data

Most of the values were already formatted with Accounting Number Format, and when you inserted functions in the Net Sales area, Excel formatted the values for you because the source values were already formatted. However, you want to format the values in the Percent Returned and Bonus columns. In addition, you want to format the Series legend to match the other ranges at the top of the worksheet. You will merge and center the label and apply a border around the range.

a. Select the **range G7:G22** and apply the **Percent Style** format with one decimal place.

b. Select the **range K7:K22** and apply the **Accounting Number Format**.

c. Merge and center the label Series Legend in the **range A1:C1**.

d. Apply **Thick Outside Borders** to the **range A1:C4**.

Select Page Setup Options

Currently, the worksheet data would not fit on one printed page. You will change the orientation, scaling, and margins so that the data would fit on one page if you decide to print the worksheet.

a. Select **Landscape orientation**.

b. Adjust the scaling so that the data fits on one page.

c. Set **0.1"** left and right margins.

Insert a Table, Sort and Filter Data, and Apply Conditional Formatting

To preserve the integrity of the original data, you will work with a portion of the dataset in the Sales worksheet. First, you will convert the data to a table and apply a specific table style. Next, you will sort the data in a specific order and display the total net sales by series and within each series with the highest to lowest net sales. Then you will add a total row to display the total net sales. Finally, you want to apply a conditional format to focus on the book titles where 10% or more of the books were returned and then apply a filter to focus on the books with the lowest net sales.

a. Click the **Sales sheet tab** and convert the data to a table.

b. Apply **Table Style Light 9**.

c. Sort the data by Series Name in alphabetical order and then within Series Name, sort by Net Sales from largest to smallest.

d. Add a total row to display the sum of the Net Sales column. Change the column width to **14** for the Net Sales column.

e. Select the values in the Percent Returned column and apply conditional formatting to apply **Light Red Fill with Dark Red Text** for values that are greater than 9.9%.

f. Select the values in the Net Sales column and apply a filter to display only net sales that are less than $100,000.

Create a Column Chart

The Net Sales worksheet contains net sales organized by software and series. You will create a clustered column chart to compare the software sales across the series.

a. Click the **Net Sales sheet tab**.

b. Select the **range A3:D7** and create a clustered column chart.

c. Move the chart so that the top-left corner covers **cell A9**. Change the chart width to **4.66"** and the chart height to **2.9"**.

d. Link the chart title to **cell A1**.

e. Format the value axis to display whole numbers only.

f. Format the chart title, value axis, category axis, and legend with **Black, Text 1 font color**.

Create a Pie Chart

The Series Sales worksheet contains net sales organized by software and series. You will create a pie chart to determine the percentage of sales for each book within the Office Reference series.

a. Click the **Series Sales sheet tab**.

b. Select the **ranges A4:A7** and **C4:C7** and create a pie chart. Move the pie chart to a chart sheet named **Office Reference**. Move the Office Reference chart sheet to the right of the Series Sales sheet.

c. Change the chart title to **Office Reference Series**. Apply **bold** and change the font size to **18** for the chart title.

d. Apply the **Style 12** chart style and change the colors to **Color 4**.

e. Display data labels in the **Inside End** position. Display **Percentage** data labels; remove the Value data labels. Apply **bold**, change the font size to **18**, and then apply **White, Background 1** font color to the data labels.

f. Apply these fill colors: Excel data point **Green**, Access data point **Purple**, PowerPoint data point **Orange, Accent 2**.

Finish the Project

You want to insert a footer on each sheet.

a. Group the Data, Sales, Net Sales, and Series Sales sheet tabs.

b. Create a footer with your name on the left side, the sheet tab code in the center, and the file name code on the right side of each sheet.

c. Click the Office Reference chart sheet and create a footer with your name on the left side, the sheet tab code in the center, and the file name code on the right side.

d. Save and close the file. Based on your instructor's directions, submit eApp_Cap1_Publisher_LastFirst.

You have recently become the CFO for Beta Manufacturing, a small cap company that produces auto parts. As you step into your new position, you have decided to compile a report that details all aspects of the business, including: employee tax withholding, facility management, sales data, and product inventory. To complete the task, you will duplicate existing formatting, utilize various conditional logic functions, complete an amortization table with financial functions, visualize data with PivotTables and Power View, and lastly, import data from an Access database.

Format the Workbook

You will format the worksheets in the workbook by duplicating existing formatting.

a. Open the file name *eApp_Cap2_Manufacturing* and save it as **eApp_Cap2_Manufacturing_LastFirst**.

b. Group all the worksheets in the workbook and fill the **range A1:F1** from the Insurance worksheet across all worksheets, maintaining the formatting.

c. Save the workbook.

Perform Lookup Functions and Conditional Math

You will first calculate employee deductions. You will also determine additional statistical information about full-time employees. To complete the task, you will use a variety of lookup and conditional math functions.

a. Ungroup the worksheets and ensure the Insurance worksheet is active.

b. Click **cell I5** and enter a function that determines the number of full-time employees, (FT).

c. Enter a function in **cell I6** that determines the average salary of all full-time employees. Format the results in **Accounting Number Format**.

d. Enter a lookup function in **cell E5** that returns the tax deduction amount for the number of dependents listed in **cell C5**. Use the table in **range H13:I17** to complete the function. The maximum deduction is $500.00; therefore, employees with more than four dependents will receive no additional deductions.

e. Use **Flash Fill** to copy down the function, completing column E. Be sure to use the appropriate cell referencing.

f. Format the data in column E with the **Accounting Number Format**.

g. Save the workbook.

Use Conditional Logic and Conditional Formatting

You will determine the employee withholding. You also want to highlight employees with more than three dependents. To complete the task, you will use conditional logic and conditional formatting.

a. Enter a logical function in **cell F5** that calculates employee FICA withholding. If the employee is full-time and has at least one dependent, then he or she pays 7% of the annual salary minus any deductions. All other employees pay 5% of the annual salary minus any deductions.

b. Format the data in column F with the **Accounting Number Format**.

c. Apply conditional formatting to the **range C4:C34** that highlights any dependents that are greater than 3 in **Red**.

d. Save the workbook.

Perform Advanced Filtering and Database Functions

You want to determine additional statistical information about full-time employees. Since you are interested in full-time employees with at least one dependent, you will use database functions and advanced filtering.

a. Click **cell H10** and enter a database function to determine the average salary of full-time employees with at least one dependent. Use the criteria in the **range H25:M25** to complete the function.

b. Format the results in **Accounting Number Format**.

c. Use Advanced Filtering to restrict the data to only display full-time employees with at least one dependent. Place the results in **cell A37**. Use the criteria in the **range H25:M25** to complete the function.

d. Save the workbook.

Use What-If Analysis

As part of your analysis, you are evaluating facility costs. You will use What-If Analysis to aid in your assessments.

a. Ensure that the Facilities worksheet is active.

b. Use Goal Seek to reduce the monthly payment in **cell B6** to the optimal value of $6,000. Complete this task by changing the Loan amount in **cell E6**.

c. Create the following three scenarios using Scenario Manager. The scenarios should change the **cells B7**, **B8**, and **E6**.

Good	Most Likely	Bad
B7 = .0325	B7 = .0575	B7 = .0700
B8 = 5	B8 = 5	B8 = 3
E6 = 275000	E6 = 312227.32	E6 = 350000

d. Create a Scenario Summary Report based on the value in **cell B6**.

e. Format the new report appropriately and save the workbook.

Complete an Amortization Schedule

To continue your analysis of facility expenditures you will complete an amortization table detailing payment, principal, interest, cumulative principle, and cumulative interest.

a. Ensure that the Facilities worksheet is active.

b. Enter a reference to the beginning loan balance in **cell B12**.

c. Enter a reference to the payment amount in **cell C12**.

d. Enter a function in **cell D12**, based on the payment and loan details, that calculates the amount of interest paid on the first payment. Be sure to use the appropriate absolute, relative, or mixed cell references.

e. Enter a function in **cell E12**, based on the payment and loan details, that calculates the amount of principal paid on the first payment. Be sure to use the appropriate absolute, relative, or mixed cell references.

f. Enter a formula in **cell F12** to calculate the remaining balance after the current payment. The remaining balance is calculated by subtracting the principal payment from the balance in column B.

g. Enter a function in **cell G12**, based on the payment and loan details, that calculates the amount of cumulative interest paid on the first payment. Be sure to use the appropriate absolute, relative, or mixed cell references.

h. Enter a function in **cell H12**, based on the payment and loan details, that calculates the amount of cumulative principal paid on the first payment. Be sure to use the appropriate absolute, relative, or mixed cell references.

i. Enter a reference to the remaining balance of payment 1 in **cell B13**.

j. Use the fill handle to copy down the functions created in the prior steps to complete the amortization table. Expand the width of **columns D:H** as needed.

k. Save the workbook.

Enter Specialized Functions and Data Validation

As part of your sales reporting you want to create custom transaction numbers. You also want to create a custom lookup that enables the user to look up transaction information based on user defined criteria.

a. Ensure the Sales worksheet is active.

b. Enter a nested function in **cell B8** to create a custom transaction number. The transaction number should be comprised of the item number listed in **cell C8** combined with the quantity in **cell D8** and the first initial of the payment type in **cell E1**.

c. Use Flash Fill to copy down the function, completing the data in column B.

d. Enter a nested function in **cell G8** that displays the word "Flag" if the Payment Type is Credit and the Amount is greater than or equal to $4,000.

e. Use Flash Fill to copy down the function, completing the data in column G.

f. Create a data validation list in **cell D5** that displays **Quantity**, **Payment Type**, and **Amount**.

g. Type the Trans# **30038C** in **cell B5** and select **Quantity** from the validation list in **cell D5**.

h. Enter a nested lookup function in **cell F5** that evaluates the Trans # in **cell B5** as well as the Category in **cell D5** and returns the results based on the data in the **range C8:F32**.

i. Save the workbook.

Create a PivotTable, PivotChart, and Slicer

You want to complete a detailed sales analysis. To complete the task, you will create a PivotTable, PivotChart, and corresponding Slicer.

a. Create a PivotTable based on the **range A7:G32**. Place the PivotTable in **cell I17** on the current worksheet.

b. Place Payment Type in the ROWS box and Amount in the VALUES box. Format the Amount with **Accounting Number Format**.

c. Insert a PivotChart using the Pie chart type based on the data. Place in the upper-left corner of the chart in **cell I23**.

d. Format the Legend of the PivotChart to appear at the bottom of the chart area.

e. Format the Data Labels to appear on the outside end of the chart.

f. Insert a Slicer based on Date. Place in the upper-left corner of the Slicer in **cell L9**.

g. Save the workbook.

Import an Access Database

All inventory data is stored in an external database. For your last task you will import the data into your workbook.

a. Ensure the Inventory worksheet is active.

b. Import the Access database *eApp_Cap2_Inventory* into the worksheet starting in **cell A3**.

c. Save the workbook.

Finalize the Workbook

a. Create a footer with your name on the left, the sheet code in the center, and the file name on the right for each worksheet.

b. Save and close the file. Based on your instructor's directions, submit eApp_Cap2_Manufacturing_LastFirst.

Microsoft Office 2016 Specialist Excel Core

Online Appendix materials can be found in the Student Resources located at www.pearsonhighered.com/exploring.

MOS Obj Number	Objective Text	Exploring Chapter	Exploring Section
1.0 Create and Manage Worksheets and Workbooks			
1.1 Create Worksheets and Workbooks			
1.1.1	create a workbook	**Chapter 1**, Introduction to Excel	Entering and Editing Cell Data
1.1.2	import data from a delimited text file	**Chapter 10**, Managing Data	Importing Data from External Sources
1.1.3	add a worksheet to an existing workbook	**Chapter 1**, Introduction to Excel	Managing Worksheets
1.1.4	copy and move a worksheet	**Chapter 1**, Introduction to Excel	Managing Worksheets
1.2 Navigate in Worksheets and Workbooks			
1.2.1	search for data within a workbook	**Chapter 1**, Office 2016 Common Features	Working with Files
1.2.2	navigate to a named cell, range, or workbook element	**Chapter 1**, Introduction to Excel	Exploring the Excel Window
1.2.3	insert and remove hyperlinks	**Chapter 9**, Multiple-Sheet Workbook Management	Inserting Hyperlinks
1.3 Format Worksheets and Workbooks			
1.3.1	change worksheet tab color	**Chapter 1**, Introduction to Excel	Managing Worksheets
1.3.2	rename a worksheet	**Chapter 1**, Introduction to Excel	Managing Worksheets
1.3.3	change worksheet order	**Chapter 1**, Introduction to Excel	Managing Worksheets
1.3.4	modify page setup	**Chapter 1**, Introduction to Excel	Selecting Page Setup Options
1.3.5	insert and delete columns or rows	**Chapter 1**, Introduction to Excel	Managing Columns and Rows
1.3.6	change workbook themes	**Chapter 1**, Introduction to Excel	Applying Cell Styles, Alignment, and Font Options
1.3.7	adjust row height and column width	**Chapter 1**, Introduction to Excel	Managing Columns and Rows
1.3.8	insert headers and footers	**Chapter 1**, Introduction to Excel	Selecting Page Setup Options
1.4 Customize Options and Views for Worksheets and Workbooks			
1.4.1	hide or unhide worksheets	**Chapter 9**, Multiple-Sheet Workbook Management	Managing Windows
1.4.2	hide or unhide columns and rows	**Chapter 1**, Introduction to Excel	Managing Columns and Rows
1.4.3	customize the Quick Access toolbar	**Chapter 1**, Office 2016 Common Features	Getting Started with Office Applications
1.4.4	change workbook views	**Chapter 1**, Introduction to Excel	Selecting Page Setup Options
1.4.5	change window views	**Chapter 1**, Office 2016 Common Features	Modifying Document Layout and Properties

MOS Obj Number	Objective Text	Exploring Chapter	Exploring Section
1.4.6	modify document properties	**Chapter 1**, Office 2016 Common Features	Modifying Document Layout and Properties
1.4.7	change magnification by using zoom tools	**Chapter 1**, Office 2016 Common Features	Modifying Document Layout and Properties
1.4.8	display formulas	**Chapter 1**, Introduction to Excel	Displaying Cell Formulas
1.5	**Configure Worksheets and Workbooks for Distribution**		
1.5.1	set a print area	**Chapter 1**, Introduction to Excel	Selecting Page Setup Options
1.5.2	save workbooks in alternative file formats	**Chapter 11**, Collaboration and Workbook Distribution	Saving a Workbook in Different Formats
1.5.3	print all or part of a workbook	**Chapter 1**, Introduction to Excel	Selecting Page Setup Options, Previewing and Printing a Worksheet
1.5.4	set print scaling	**Chapter 1**, Introduction to Excel	Selecting Page Setup Options
1.5.5	display repeating row and column titles on multipage worksheets	**Chapter 1**, Introduction to Excel	Selecting Page Setup Options
1.5.6	inspect a workbook for hidden properties or personal information	**Chapter 11**, Collaboration and Workbook Distribution	Using the Document Inspector
1.5.7	inspect a workbook for accessibility issues	Online Appendix	Online Appendix
1.5.8	inspect a workbook for compatibility issues	**Chapter 11**, Collaboration and Workbook Distribution	Checking Compatibility

2.0 Manage Data Cells and Ranges

MOS Obj Number	Objective Text	Exploring Chapter	Exploring Section
2.1	**Insert Data in Cells and Ranges**		
2.1.1	replace data	**Chapter 3**, Charts	Adding, Editing, and Formatting Chart Elements
2.1.2	cut, copy, or paste data	**Chapter 1**, Introduction to Excel	Selecting, Moving, Copying, and Pasting Data
2.1.3	paste data by using special paste options	**Chapter 1**, Introduction to Excel	Selecting, Moving, Copying, and Pasting Data
2.1.4	fill cells by using Auto Fill	**Chapter 1**, Introduction to Excel	Entering and Editing Cell Data
2.1.5	insert and delete cells	**Chapter 1**, Introduction to Excel	Managing Columns and Rows
2.2	**Format Cells and Ranges**		
2.2.1	merge cells	**Chapter 1**, Introduction to Excel	Applying Cell Styles, Alignment, and Font Options
2.2.2	modify cell alignment and indentation	**Chapter 1**, Introduction to Excel	Applying Cell Styles, Alignment, and Font Options
2.2.3	format cells by using Format Painter	**Chapter 1**, Office 2016 Common Features	Modifying Text
2.2.4	wrap text within cells	**Chapter 1**, Introduction to Excel	Applying Cell Styles, Alignment, and Font Options
2.2.5	apply number formats	**Chapter 1**, Introduction to Excel	Applying a Number Format
2.2.6	apply cell formats	**Chapter 1**, Introduction to Excel **Chapter 12**, Templates, Styles, and Macros	Applying Cell Styles, Alignment, and Font Options Applying Cell Styles
2.2.7	apply cell styles	**Chapter 1**, Introduction to Excel	Applying Cell Styles, Alignment, and Font Options

MOS Obj Number	Objective Text	Exploring Chapter	Exploring Section
2.3	**Summarize and Organize Data**		
2.3.1	insert sparklines	**Chapter 3**, Charts	Creating and Customizing Sparklines
2.3.2	outline data	**Chapter 5**, Summarizing And Analyzing Data	Subtiotaling Data, Grouping and Ungrouping Data
2.3.3	insert subtotals	Online Appendix	Online Appendix
2.3.4	apply conditional formatting	**Chapter 4**, Datasets and Tables	Applying Conditional Formatting

3.0   Create Tables

3.1	**Create and Manage Tables**		
3.1.1	create an Excel table from a cell range	**Chapter 4**, Datasets and Tables	Designing and Creating Tables
3.1.2	convert a table to a cell range	**Chapter 4**, Datasets and Tables	Designing and Creating Tables
3.1.3	add or remove table rows and columns	**Chapter 4**, Datasets and Tables	Designing and Creating Tables
3.2	**Manage Table Styles and Options**		
3.2.1	apply styles to tables	**Chapter 4**, Datasets and Tables	Applying a Table Style
3.2.2	configure table style options	**Chapter 4**, Datasets and Tables	Applying a Table Style
3.2.3	insert total rows	**Chapter 4**, Datasets and Tables	Adding a Total Row
3.3	**Filter and Sort a Table**		
3.3.1	filter records	**Chapter 4**, Datasets and Tables	Filtering Data
3.3.2	sort data by multiple columns	**Chapter 4**, Datasets and Tables	Sorting Data
3.3.3	change sort order	**Chapter 4**, Datasets and Tables	Sorting Data
3.3.4	remove duplicate records	**Chapter 4**, Datasets and Tables	Designing and Creating Tables

4.0   Perform Operations with Formulas and Functions

4.1	**Summarize Data by using Functions**		
4.1.1	insert references	**Chapter 2**, Formulas and Functions	Using Relative, Absolute, and Mixed Cell References in Formulas
4.1.2	perform calculations by using the SUM function	**Chapter 2**, Formulas and Functions	Inserting Basic Math and Statistics Functions
4.1.3	perform calculations by using MIN and MAX functions	**Chapter 2**, Formulas and Functions	Inserting Basic Math and Statistics Functions
4.1.4	perform calculations by using the COUNT function	**Chapter 2**, Formulas and Functions	Inserting Basic Math and Statistics Functions
4.1.5	perform calculations by using the AVERAGE function	**Chapter 2**, Formulas and Functions	Inserting Basic Math and Statistics Functions
4.2	**Perform Conditional Operations by using Functions**		
4.2.1	perform logical operations by using the IF function	**Chapter 2**, Formulas and Functions	Determining Results with the IF Function
4.2.2	perform logical operations by using the SUMIF function	**Chapter 8**, Statistical Functions	Using Conditional Math and Statistical Functions

MOS Obj Number	Objective Text	Exploring Chapter	Exploring Section
4.2.3	perform logical operations by using the AVERAGEIF function	**Chapter 8**, Statistical Functions	Using Conditional Math and Statistical Functions
4.2.4	perform statistical operations by using the COUNTIF function	**Chapter 8**, Statistical Functions	Using Conditional Math and Statistical Functions
4.3	**Format and Modify Text by using Functions**		
4.3.1	format text by using RIGHT, LEFT, and MID functions	**Chapter 10**, Managing Data	Manipulating Text with Functions
4.3.2	format text by using UPPER, LOWER, and PROPER functions	**Chapter 10**, Managing Data	Manipulating Text with Functions
4.3.3	format text by using the CONCATENATE function	**Chapter 10**, Managing Data	Manipulating Text with Functions

5.0   Create Charts and Objects

5.1   Create Charts

5.1.1	create a new chart	**Chapter 3**, Charts	Choosing a Chart Type
5.1.2	add additional data series	**Chapter 3**, Charts	Modifying the Data Source
5.1.3	switch between rows and columns in source data	**Chapter 1**, Introduction to Excel	Selecting, Moving, Copying, and Pasting Data
5.1.4	analyze data by using Quick Analysis	**Chapter 3**, Charts	Choosing a Chart Type

5.2   Format Charts

5.2.1	resize charts	**Chapter 3**, Charts	Moving, Sizing, and Printing a Chart
5.2.2	add and modify chart elements	**Chapter 3**, Charts	Adding, Editing, and Formatting Chart Elements
5.2.3	apply chart layouts and styles	**Chapter 3**, Charts	Adding, Editing, and Formatting Chart Elements
5.2.4	move charts to a chart sheet	**Chapter 3**, Charts	Moving, Sizing, and Printing a Chart

5.3   Insert and Format Objects

5.3.1	insert text boxes and shapes	**Chapter 3**, Charts	Beyond the Classroom
5.3.2	insert images	**Chapter 1**, Office 2016 Common Features	Working with Pictures and Graphics
5.3.3	modify object properties	**Chapter 3**, Charts **Chapter 1**, Office 2016 Common Features	Adding, Editing, and Formatting Chart Elements Working with Pictures and Graphics
5.3.4	add alternative text to objects for accessibility	**Chapter 3**, Charts	Adding, Editing, and Formatting Chart Elements

Microsoft Office 2016 Specialist
Excel Expert

MOS Obj Number	Objective Text	Exploring Chapter	Exploring Section
1.0 Manage Workbook Options and Settings			
1.1 Manage Workbooks			
1.1.1	save a workbook as a template	**Chapter 12**, Standardizing Workbooks	Creating and Using a Template
1.1.2	copy macros between workbooks	Online Appendix	Online Appendix
1.1.3	reference data in another workbook	**Chapter 9**, Multiple-Sheet Workbook Management	Inserting Hyperlinks, Linking Workbooks
1.1.4	reference data by using structured references	**Chapter 4**, Datasets and Tables	Creating Structured References in Formulas
1.1.5	enable macros in a workbook	**Chapter 12**, Standardizing Workbooks	Setting Macro Security
1.1.6	display hidden ribbon tabs	Online Appendix	Online Appendix
1.2 Manage Workbook Review			
1.2.1	restrict editing	**Chapter 12**, Standardizing Workbooks	Protecting a Cell, a Worksheet, and a Workbook
1.2.2	protect a worksheet	**Chapter 12**, Standardizing Workbooks	Protecting a Cell, a Worksheet, and a Workbook
1.2.3	configure formula calculation options	Online Appendix	Online Appendix
1.2.4	protect workbook structure	**Chapter 12**, Standardizing Workbooks	Protecting a Cell, a Worksheet, and a Workbook
1.2.5	manage workbook versions	Online Appendix	Online Appendix
1.2.6	encrypt a workbook with a password	**Chapter 12**, Standardizing Workbooks	Protecting a Cell, a Worksheet, and a Workbook
2.0 Apply Custom Data Formats and Layouts			
2.1 Apply Custom Data Formats and Validation			
2.1.1	create custom number formats	Online Appendix	Online Appendix
2.1.2	populate cells by using advanced Fill Series options	**Chapter 6**, What-If Analysis Online Appendix	Creating a One-Variable Data Table Online Appendix
2.1.3	configure data validation	**Chapter 9**, Multiple-Sheet Workbook Management	Validating Data
2.2 Apply Advanced Conditional Formatting and Filtering			
2.2.1	create custom conditional formatting rules	**Chapter 4**, Datasets and Tables	Applying Conditional Formatting, Creating a New Rule
2.2.2	create conditional formatting rules that use formulas	**Chapter 4**, Datasets and Tables	Creating a New Rule
2.2.3	manage conditional formatting rules	**Chapter 4**, Datasets and Tables	Applying Conditional Formatting, Creating a New Rule

MOS Obj Number	Objective Text	Exploring Chapter	Exploring Section
2.3	**Create and Modify Custom Workbook Elements**		
2.3.1	create custom color formats	Online Appendix	Online Appendix
2.3.2	create and modify cell styles	**Chapter 12**, Standardizing Workbooks	Applying Cell Styles
2.3.3	create and modify custom themes	**Chapter 12**, Standardizing Workbooks	Applying Themes and Backgrounds
2.3.4	create and modify simple macros	**Chapter 12**, Standardizing Workbooks	Creating a Macro
2.3.5	insert and configure form controls	**Chapter 12**, Standardizing Workbooks Online Appendix	Creating Macro Buttons Online Appendix
2.4	**Prepare a Workbook for Internationalization**		
2.4.1	display data in multiple international formats	Online Appendix	Online Appendix
2.4.2	apply international currency formats	Online Appendix	Online Appendix
2.4.3	manage multiple options for +Body and +Heading fonts	Online Appendix	Online Appendix
3.0	**Create Advanced Formulas**		
3.1	**Apply Functions in Formulas**		
3.1.1	perform logical operations by using AND, OR, and NOT functions	**Chapter 7**, Using Date, Logical, Lookup, Database, and Financial Functions	Creating a Nested Logical Function
3.1.2	perform logical operations by using nested functions	**Chapter 7**, Using Date, Logical, Lookup, Database, and Financial Functions Online Appendix	Creating a Nested Logical Function Online Appendix
3.1.3	perform statistical operations by using SUMIFS, AVERAGEIFS, and COUNTIFS functions	**Chapter 8**, Statistical Functions	Using Conditional Math and Statistical Functions
3.2	**Look Up Data by using Functions**		
3.2.1	look up data by using the VLOOKUP function	**Chapter 2**, Formulas and Functions	Using Lookup Functions
3.2.2	look up data by using the HLOOKUP function	**Chapter 2**, Formulas and Functions	Using Lookup Functions
3.2.3	look up data by using the MATCH function	**Chapter 7**, Using Date, Logical, Lookup, Database, and Financial Functions	Using Advanced Lookup Functions
3.2.4	look up data by using the INDEX function	**Chapter 7**, Using Date, Logical, Lookup, Database, and Financial Functions	Using Advanced Lookup Functions
3.3	**Apply Advanced Date and Time Functions**		
3.3.1	reference the date and time by using the NOW and TODAY functions	**Chapter 2**, Formulas and Functions	Using Date Functions

MOS Obj Number	Objective Text	Exploring Chapter	Exploring Section
3.3.2	serialize numbers by using date and time functions	**Chapter 7**, Using Date, Logical, Lookup, Database, and Financial Functions	Using Date Functions
3.4	**Perform Data Analysis and Business Intelligence**		
3.4.1	import, transform, combine, display, and connect to data	**Chapter 10**, Managing Data	Importing Data from External Sources
3.4.2	consolidate data	Online Appendix	Online Appendix
3.4.3	perform what-if analysis by using Goal Seek and Scenario Manager	**Chapter 6**, What-If Analysis	Determining Optimal Input Values Using Goal Seek, Using Scenario Manager
3.4.4	use cube functions to get data out of the Excel data model	Online Appendix	Online Appendix
3.4.5	calculate data by using financial functions	**Chapter 2**, Formulas and Functions **Chapter 7**, Using Date, Logical, Lookup, Database, and Financial Functions	Calculating Payments with the PMT Function, Using Financial Functions
3.5	**Troubleshoot Formulas**		
3.5.1	trace precedence and dependence	**Chapter 9**, Multiple-Sheet Workbook Management	Auditing Formulas
3.5.2	monitor cells and formulas by using the Watch Window	**Chapter 9**, Multiple-Sheet Workbook Management	Setting Up a Watch Window
3.5.3	validate formulas by using error checking rules	**Chapter 9**, Multiple-Sheet Workbook Management	Auditing Formulas, Validating Data
3.5.4	evaluate formulas	**Chapter 9**, Multiple-Sheet Workbook Management	Auditing Formulas
3.6	**Define Named Ranges and Objects**		
3.6.1	name cells	**Chapter 6**, What-If Analysis	Creating and Maintaining Range Names
3.6.2	name data ranges	**Chapter 6**, What-If Analysis	Creating and Maintaining Range Names
3.6.3	name tables	**Chapter 4**, Datasets and Tables	Rename a Table
3.6.4	manage named ranges and objects	**Chapter 6**, What-If Analysis	Creating and Maintaining Range Names

4.0 Create Advanced Charts and Tables

4.1 Create Advanced Charts

MOS Obj Number	Objective Text	Exploring Chapter	Exploring Section
4.1.1	add trendlines to charts	Online Appendix	Online Appendix
4.1.2	create dual-axis charts	**Chapter 3**, Charts	Choosing a Chart Type
4.1.3	save a chart as a template	Online Appendix	Online Appendix
4.2	**Create and Manage PivotTables**		
4.2.1	create PivotTables	**Chapter 5**, Summarizing and Analyzing Data	Creating a PivotTable
4.2.2	modify field selections and options	**Chapter 5**, Summarizing and Analyzing Data	Modifying a PivotTable

MOS Obj Number	Objective Text	Exploring Chapter	Exploring Section
4.2.3	create slicers	**Chapter 5**, Summarizing and Analyzing Data	Filtering and Slicing a PivotTable
4.2.4	group PivotTable data	**Chapter 5**, Summarizing and Analyzing Data	Creating a PivotTable, Modifying a PivotTable
4.2.5	reference data in a PivotTable by using the GETPIVOTDATA function	Online Appendix	Online Appendix
4.2.6	add calculated fields	**Chapter 5**, Summarizing and Analyzing Data	Creating a Calculated Field
4.2.7	format data	**Chapter 5**, Summarizing and Analyzing Data	Modifying a PivotTable, Changing the PivotTable Design
4.3 Create and Manage Pivot Charts			
4.3.1	create PivotCharts	**Chapter 5**, Summarizing and Analyzing Data	Creating a PivotChart
4.3.2	manipulate options in existing PivotCharts	**Chapter 5**, Summarizing and Analyzing Data	Creating a PivotChart
4.3.3	apply styles to PivotCharts	**Chapter 5**, Summarizing and Analyzing Data	Creating a PivotChart
4.3.4	drill down into PivotChart details	**Chapter 5**, Summarizing and Analyzing Data	Creating a PivotChart

Glossary

100% stacked column chart A chart type that places (stacks) data in one column per category, with each column the same height of 100%.

3-D reference A reference within a formula or function on one worksheet that includes the name of another worksheet, column letter, and row number located within the same workbook. The three dimensions include the worksheet name, the column, and the row.

Absolute cell reference A designation that indicates a constant reference to a specific cell location; the cell reference does not change when you copy the formula.

Access A relational database management system in which you can record and link data, query databases, and create forms and reports.

Accessibility Checker A tool that reviews a workbook to detect potential issues that could hinder a user's ability to use it.

Accounting Number Format A number format that displays $ on the left side of a cell, formats a value with a comma for every three digits on the left side of the decimal point, and displays two digits to the right of the decimal point.

Active cell The current cell in a worksheet. It is indicated by a dark green border, and the Name Box shows the location of the active cell.

Add-in A program that can be added to Excel to provide enhanced functionality.

Alignment The placement of data within the boundaries of a cell. By default, text aligns on the left side, and values align on the right side of a cell.

Alt text An accessibility compliance feature where you enter text and a description for an objective, such as a table or a chart. A special reader can read the alt text to a user.

Analysis ToolPak An add-in program that contains tools for performing complex statistical analysis, such as ANOVA, correlation, and histograms.

AND function A logical function that returns TRUE when all arguments are true and FALSE when at least one argument is false.

ANOVA An acronym for Analysis of Variance, which is a statistical tool that compares the means between two data samples to determine if they were derived from the same population.

Area chart A chart type that emphasizes magnitude of changes over time by filling in the space between lines with a color.

Argument A positional reference contained within parentheses in a function such as a cell reference or value, required to complete a function and produce output.

Auto Fill A feature that helps you complete a sequence of months, abbreviated months, quarters, weekdays, weekday abbreviations, or values. Auto Fill also can be used to fill or copy a formula down a column or across a row.

AutoComplete A feature that searches for and automatically displays any other label in that column that matches the letters you type.

AVERAGE function A statistical function that calculates the arithmetic mean, or average, of values in a range of cells.

AVERAGEIF function A statistical function that calculates the average, or arithmetic mean, of all cells in a range that meet a specific condition.

AVERAGEIFS function A statistical function that returns the average (arithmetic mean) of all cells that meet multiple criteria.

Axis title A label that describes either the category axis or the value axis. Provides clarity, particularly in describing the value axis.

Background An image placed behind the worksheet data.

Backstage view A component of Office that provides a concise collection of commands related to an open file.

Bar chart A chart type that compares values across categories using horizontal bars where the length represents the value; the longer the bar, the larger the value. In a bar chart, the horizontal axis displays values and the vertical axis displays categories.

Binding constraint A rule that Solver enforces to reach the objective value.

Bins Data ranges in which values can be categorized and counted.

Border A line that surrounds a cell or a range of cells to offset particular data from the rest of the data in a worksheet.

Breakpoint The lowest value for a category or in a series.

Calculated field A user-defined field that performs a calculation based on other fields in a PivotTable.

Cancel An icon between the Name Box and Formula Bar. When you enter or edit data, click Cancel to cancel the data entry or edit, and revert back to the previous data in the cell, if any. Cancel changes from gray to red when you position the pointer over it.

Canvas The area within a Power View that contains the dashboard data visualizations.

Category axis The chart axis that displays descriptive labels for the data points plotted in a chart. The category axis labels are typically text contained in the first column of worksheet data (such as job titles) used to create the chart.

Cell The intersection of a column and row in a table, such as the intersection of column B and row 5.

Cell address The unique identifier of a cell, starting with the column letter and then the row number, such as C6.

Cell style A collection of format settings based on the currently selected theme to provide a consistent appearance within a worksheet and among similar workbooks.

Changing variable cell A cell containing a variable whose value changes within the constraints until the objective cell reaches its optimum value.

Chart A visual representation of numerical data.

Chart area A container for the entire chart and all of its elements, including the plot area, titles, legends, and labels.

Chart element A component of a chart that helps complete or clarify the chart.

Chart filter A setting that controls what data series and categories are displayed or hidden in a chart.

Chart sheet A sheet within a workbook that contains a single chart and no spreadsheet data.

Chart style A collection of formatting that controls the color of the chart area, plot area, and data series.

Chart title The label that describes the entire chart. The title is usually placed at the top of the chart area.

Circular reference A situation that occurs when a formula contains a direct or an indirect reference to the cell containing the formula.

Clipboard An area of memory reserved to temporarily hold selections that have been cut or copied and allows you to paste the selections.

Cloud storage A technology used to store files and to work with programs that are stored in a central location on the Internet.

Clustered column chart A type of chart that groups, or clusters, columns set side by side to compare several data points among categories.

Collaboration A process that occurs when multiple people work together to achieve a goal by using technology to edit the contents of a file.

Collapse The process of hiding detailed rows or columns within subtotaled or an outlined dataset or within a PivotTable.

Color scale A conditional format that displays a particular color based on the relative value of the cell contents to the other selected cells.

Column chart A type of chart that compares values vertically in columns where the height represents the value; the taller the column, the larger the value. In a column chart, the vertical axis displays values and the horizontal axis displays categories.

Column heading The alphabetical letter above a column in a worksheet. For example, B is the column heading for the second column.

Column index number The column number in the lookup table that contains the return values.

Column width The horizontal measurement of a column in a table or a worksheet. In Excel, it is measured by the number of characters or pixels.

COLUMNS area A section within the PivotTable Fields List used to display columns of summarized data for the selected field(s) that will display labels to organize summarized data vertically in a PivotTable.

Combo chart A chart that combines two chart types, such as column and line, to plot different types of data, such as quantities and percentages.

Comma Style A number format that formats a value with a comma for every three digits on the left side of the decimal point and displays two digits to the right of the decimal point.

Comma-separated values (CSV) file A file type that uses commas to separate data into columns and a newline character to separate data into rows.

Command A button or area within a group that you click to perform tasks.

Comment (1) A notation attached to a cell to pose a question or provide a suggestion. (2) A line that documents programming code; it starts with an apostrophe and appears in green in the VBA Editor. It provides information about the macro but does not affect its execution.

Comment indicator A red triangle in the top-right corner of a cell that indicates the cell contains a comment.

Compatibility Checker A tool that evaluates the workbook's contents to identify what data and features are not compatible with previous versions.

CONCATENATE function A text function that joins between 2 and 255 individual text strings into one text string.

Conditional formatting A set of rules that applies specific formatting to highlight or emphasize cells that meet specific conditions.

Constraint Specifies the restrictions of limitations imposed on a spreadsheet model as Solver determines the optimum value for the objective cell.

Contextual tab A tab that contains a group of commands related to the selected object.

Copy A command used to duplicate a selection from the original location and place a copy in the Office Clipboard.

CORREL function A statistical function that determines the strength of a relationship between two variables.

COUNT function A statistical function that tallies the number of cells in a range that contain values you can use in calculations, such as numerical and date data, but excludes blank cells or text entries from the tally.

COUNTA function A statistical function that tallies the number of cells in a range that are not blank, that is, cells that contain data, whether a value, text, or a formula.

COUNTBLANK function A statistical function that tallies the number of cells in a range that are blank.

COUNTIF function A statistical function that counts the number of cells in a range when a specified condition is met.

COUNTIFS function A statistical function that applies criteria to cells across multiple ranges and counts the number of times all criteria are met.

Covariance A measure of how two sample sets of data vary simultaneously.

Criteria range A group of two or more adjacent cells that specifies the conditions used to control the results of a filter.

CUMIPMT function A financial function that calculates the cumulative interest through a specified payment period.

CUMPRINC function A financial function that calculates the cumulative principal through a specified payment period.

Cut A command used to remove a selection from the original location and place it in the Office Clipboard.

Data bar Data bar formatting applies a gradient or solid fill bar in which the width of the bar represents the current cell's value compared relatively to other cells' values.

Data label An identifier that shows the exact value of a data point in a chart. Appears above or on a data point in a chart. May indicate percentage of a value to the whole on a pie chart.

Data mining The process of analyzing large volumes of data using advanced statistical techniques to identify trends and patterns in the data.

Data model A collection of related tables that contain structured data used to create a database.

Data point A numeric value that describes a single value in a chart or worksheet.

Data range properties Excel settings that control how imported data in cells connect to their source data.

Data series A group of related data points that display in row(s) or column(s) in a worksheet.

Data structure The organization method used to manage multiple data points within a dataset.

Data table A grid that contains the data source values and labels to plot data in a chart. A data table may be placed below a chart or hidden from view.

Data validation A feature that requires specified rules be followed in order to allow data to be entered in a cell.

Database function A function that analyzes data for selected records in a dataset.

DAVERAGE function A database function that calculates the arithmetic mean, or average, of values in a column that match specified conditions in a criteria range.

DAY function A date function that displays the day (1-31) within a given date.

DAYS function A date function that calculates the number of days between two dates where the most recent date is entered in the end_date argument and the older date is entered in the start_date argument.

DCOUNT function A database function that counts the cells that contain numbers in a column that matches specified conditions in a criteria range.

Delimiter A special character (such as a tab or space) that separates data.

Dependent cell A cell containing a formula that relies on other cells to obtain its value.

Destination file A file that contains a link to receive data from a source file.

Dialog box A box that provides access to more precise, but less frequently used, commands.

Dialog Box Launcher A button that when clicked opens a corresponding dialog box.

Digital signature An electronic, encrypted notation that stamps a document to authenticate the contents, confirms that a particular person authorized it, and marks the workbook as final.

DMAX function A database function that identifies the highest value in a column that matches specified conditions in a criteria range.

DMIN function A database function that identifies the lowest value in a column that matches specified conditions in a criteria range.

Document Inspector A tool that reviews a workbook for hidden properties or personal information and then displays a list of these details so that you can select what data to remove.

Document property An attribute, such as an author's name or keyword, that describes a file.

DSUM function A database function that adds the values in a column that match specified conditions in a criteria range.

EDATE A date function that displays a date in the future or past, given a specific number of months.

EOMONTH A date function that displays the last day of a month for a specified number of months from a particular date.

Element An object that contains a start tag, an end tag, and the associated data in XML.

Embed The act of importing external data into Excel but not maintaining a link to the original data source.

End tag A portion of programming code that contains the name of an XML element preceded by a slash to indicate the end of the element data.

Enhanced ScreenTip A small message box that displays when you place the pointer over a command button. The purpose of the command, short descriptive text, or a keyboard shortcut if applicable will display in the box.

Enter An icon between the Name Box and Formula Bar. When you enter or edit data, click Enter to accept data typed in the active cell and keep the current cell active. Enter changes from gray to blue when you position the pointer over it.

Error alert A message that displays when a user enters invalid data in a cell that contains a validation rule.

Error bars Visual that indicates the standard error amount, a percentage, or a standard deviation for a data point or marker in a chart.

Excel An application that makes it easy to organize records, financial transactions, and business information in the form of worksheets.

Expand The process of displaying detailed rows or columns within subtotaled or an outlined dataset or within a PivotTable.

Exploded pie chart A chart type in which one or more pie slices are separated from the rest of the pie chart for emphasis.

Extensible The ability to be expanded as necessary to include additional data.

Extensible Markup Language (XML) An industry standard for structuring data across applications, operating systems, and hardware.

Field The smallest data element contained in a table, such as first name, last name, address, and phone number.

Fill color The background color that displays behind the data in a cell so that the data stands out.

Fill handle A small green square at the bottom-right corner of the active cell. You can position the pointer on the fill handle and drag it to repeat the contents of the cell to other cells or to copy a formula in the active cell to adjacent cells down the column or across the row.

Filtering The process of specifying conditions to display only those records that meet those conditions.

FILTERS area A section within the PivotTable Fields List used to place a field so that the user can then filter the data by that field. Displays top-level filters above the PivotTable so that you can set filters to display results based on particular conditions you set.

Fixed-width text file A file in which each column contains a specific number of characters.

Flash Fill A productivity feature that enables you to enter data in one or two cells to provide a pattern which is used by Excel to complete the data entry.

Footer Information that displays at the bottom of a document page.

Format Painter A feature that enables you to quickly and easily copy all formatting from one area to another in Word, PowerPoint, and Excel.

Formula A combination of cell references, operators, values, and/or functions used to perform a calculation.

Formula auditing Tools that enable you to display or trace relationships for formulas, show formulas, check for errors, and evaluate formulas.

Formula AutoComplete A feature that displays a list of functions and defined names that match letters as you type a formula.

Formula Bar An element located below the Ribbon and to the right of the Insert Function command. It shows the contents of the active cell. You enter or edit cell contents in the Formula Bar for the active cell.

Freezing The process of keeping rows and/or columns visible onscreen at all times even when you scroll through a large dataset.

FREQUENCY function A statistical function that determines the number of occurrences of numerical values in a dataset based on predetermined bins.

Fully qualified structured reference A structured formula that contains the table name.

Function A predefined computation that simplifies creating a complex calculation and produces a result based on inputs known as arguments.

Function ScreenTip A small pop-up description that displays the function's arguments.

FV function A financial function that calculates the future value of an investment, given a fixed interest rate, term, and identical periodic payments.

Gallery An area in Word which provides additional text styles. In Excel, the gallery provides a choice of chart styles, and in Power Point, the gallery provides transitions.

Goal Seek A tool that enables you to specify a desired amount from a formula without knowing what input value achieves that goal.

Gridline A horizontal or vertical line that extends from the horizontal or vertical axis through the plot area to guide the reader's eyes across the chart to identify values.

Group A subset of a tab that organizes similar tasks together.

Grouping (data) The process of joining rows or columns of related data into a single entity so that groups can be collapsed or expanded for data analysis.

Grouping (worksheets) The process of selecting two or more worksheets so that you can perform the same action at the same time on all selected worksheets.

Header An area with one or more lines of information at the top of each page.

Histogram A visual display of tabulated frequencies that is similar to a column chart. The category axis shows bin ranges (intervals) where data is aggregated into bins, and the vertical axis shows frequencies.

History worksheet A worksheet created through the Track Changes feature that lists particular types of changes made to a workbook. The worksheet is temporary; it is deleted when you save the workbook.

HLOOKUP function A lookup and reference function that accepts a value, looks the value up in a horizontal lookup table with data organized in rows, and returns a result.

Horizontal alignment The placement of cell data between the left and right cell margins. By default, text is left-aligned, and values are right-aligned.

Hyperlink An electronic link that, when clicked, goes to another location in the same or a different worksheet, opens another file, opens a webpage in a Web browser, or opens an email client and inserts an email address into the To box.

Icon set A set of symbols or signs that classify data into three, four, or five categories, based on values in a range.

IF function A logical function that evaluates a condition and returns one value if the condition is true and a different value if the condition is false.

IFERROR function A logic function that checks a cell to determine if that cell contains an error or if a formula will result in an error. If no error exists, the function returns the value of the formula. If an error exists, the function returns the type of error.

Importing The process of inserting external data—data created or stored in another format—into the current application.

Indent A format that offsets data from its default alignment. For example, if text is left-aligned, the text may be indented or offset from the left side to stand out. If a value is right-aligned, it can be indented or offset from the right side of the cell.

INDEX function A lookup and reference function that returns a value at the intersection of a specified row and column.

Input area A range of cells in a worksheet used to store and change the variables used in calculations.

Input message Descriptive text or instructions that inform a user about the restrictions for entering data in a cell.

Insert Function An icon between the Name Box and Formula Bar. Click Insert Function to open the Insert Function dialog box to search for and insert a particular function.

IPMT function A financial function that calculates the periodic interest for a specified payment period on a loan or an investment given a fixed interest rate, specified term, and identical periodic payments.

Keyword A word or symbol reserved within a programming language for specific purposes.

Landscape orientation A document layout when a page is wider than it is tall.

Legend A key that identifies the color, gradient, picture, texture, or pattern assigned to each data series in a chart.

Line chart A chart type that displays lines connecting data points to show trends over equal time periods, such as months, quarters, years, or decades.

Linking The process of creating external cell references from worksheets in one workbook to cells on a worksheet in another workbook.

Live Preview An Office feature that provides a preview of the results of a selection when you point to an option in a list or gallery. Using Live Preview, you can experiment with settings before making a final choice.

Loan amortization table A schedule showing monthly payments, interest per payment, amount toward paying off the loan, and the remaining balance after each payment for a loan.

Locked cell A cell that prevents users from editing the contents or formatting of that cell in a protected worksheet.

Logic error An error that occurs when a formula is syntactically correct but logically incorrect, which produces inaccurate results.

Logical test An expression that evaluates to true or false.

Lookup table A range that contains data for the basis of the lookup and data to be retrieved.

Lookup value The cell reference of the cell that contains the value to look up.

LOWER function An Excel function that converts all uppercase letters in a text string to lowercase.

Macro A set of instructions that executes a sequence of commands to automate repetitive or routine tasks.

Macro Recorder The Macro Recorder records your commands, keystrokes, and mouse clicks to store Excel commands as VBA code within a workbook.

Margin The area of blank space that displays to the left, right, top, and bottom of a document or worksheet.

MATCH function A lookup and reference function that searches through a range for a specific value and returns the relative position of a value within the range.

MAX function A statistical function that identifies the highest value in a range.

MEDIAN function A predefined formula that identifies the midpoint value in a set of values.

Metadata Data, such as a keyword, that describes other data, such as the contents of a file.

Microsoft Office A productivity software suite including a set of software applications, each one specializing in a particular type of output.

MIN function A predefined formula that displays the lowest value in a range.

Mini toolbar A toolbar that provides access to the most common formatting selections, such as adding bold or italic, or changing font type or color. Unlike the Quick Access Toolbar, the Mini toolbar is not customizable.

Mixed cell reference A designation that combines an absolute cell reference with a relative cell reference. The absolute part does not change but the relative part does when you copy the formula.

Module A container in which VBA code is stored.

MONTH function A date function that displays the month (1–12) where 1 is January and 12 is December for a specific date.

Name Box An element located below the Ribbon, which displays the address of the active cell.

Nested function A function that contains another function embedded inside one or more of it's arguments.

Newline character A special character that designates the end of a line and separates data for the next line or row.

New sheet An icon that, when clicked, inserts a new worksheet in the workbook.

Nonadjacent range A collection of multiple ranges (such as D5:D10 and F5:F10) that are not positioned in a contiguous cluster in an Excel worksheet.

Nonbinding constraint A constraint that does not restrict the target value that Solver finds.

Normal view (Excel) The default view of a worksheet that shows worksheet data but not margins, headers, footers, or page breaks.

NOT function A logical function that returns TRUE if the argument is false and FALSE if the argument is true.

NOW function A date and time function that calculates the current date and military time that you last opened the workbook using the computer's clock.

Nper Total number of payment periods.

NPER function A financial function that calculates the number of payment periods for an investment or loan given a fixed interest rate, periodic payment, and present value.

NPV function A financial function that calculates the net present value of an investment, given a fixed discount rate (rate of return) and future payments that may be identical or different.

Number format A setting that controls how a value appears in a cell.

Object An object contains both data and code and represents an element of Excel such as a Range or Selection.

Objective cell The cell that contains the formula-based value that you want to maximize, minimize, or set to a value by manipulating values of one or more variables.

Office Background A setting that controls the faint background image, if any, in the top-right corner of the title bar.

Office Theme A setting that controls the overall appearance and color of the title bar and interface for Office programs.

One-variable data table A structured range that contains different values for one variable to compare how the different values affect one or more calculated results.

OneDrive Microsoft's cloud storage system. Saving files to OneDrive enables them to sync across all Windows devices and to be accessible from any Internet-connected device.

Optimization model A model that finds the highest, lowest, or exact value for one particular result by adjusting values for selected variables.

OR function A logical function that returns TRUE if any argument is true and returns FALSE if all arguments are false.

Order of operations A rule that controls the sequence in which arithmetic operations are performed. Also called the *order of precedence*.

Outline A hierarchical structure of data that you can group related data to summarize. When a dataset has been grouped into an outline, you can collapse the outlined data to show only main rows such as subtotals or expand the outlined data to show all the details.

Output area The range of cells in an Excel worksheet that contain formulas dependent on the values in the input area.

Page break An indication of where data will start on another printed page.

Page Break Preview A view setting that displays the worksheet data and page breaks within the worksheet.

Page Layout view A view setting that displays the worksheet data, margins, headers, and footers.

Paste A command used to place a cut or copied selection into another location.

Paste Options button An icon that displays in the bottom-right corner immediately after using the Paste command. It enables the user to apply different paste options.

Percent Style A number format that displays a value as if it was multiplied by 100 and with the % symbol. The default number of decimal places is zero if you click Percent Style in the Number group or two decimal places if you use the Format Cells dialog box.

PERCENTILE.EXC function A statistical function that returns the percentile of a range excluding the 0 or 100% percentile.

PERCENTILE.INC function A statistical function that returns the percentile of a range including the 0 or 100% percentile.

PERCENTRANK.EXC function A statistical function that identifies a value's rank as a percentile, excluding 0 and 1, of a list of values.

PERCENTRANK.INC function A statistical function that displays a value's rank as a percentile of the range of data in the dataset.

Personal Macro Workbook A hidden workbook that allows user-created macros to be available at all times.

Picture A graphic file that is retrieved from storage media or the Internet and placed in an Office project.

Pie chart A chart type that shows each data point in proportion to the whole data series as a slice in a circle. A pie chart depicts only one data series.

PivotChart An interactive graphical representation of data in a PivotTable.

PivotTable Fields List A task pane that displays the fields in a dataset and enables a user to specify what fields are used to create a layout to organize the data in columns, rows, values, and filters in a PivotTable.

PivotTable report An interactive table that uses calculations to consolidate and summarize data from a data source into a separate table to enable a person to analyze the data in a dataset without altering the dataset itself. You can rotate or pivot the data in a PivotTable to look at the data from different perspectives. Also referred to simply as a *PivotTable*.

PivotTable style A set of formatting that controls bold, font colors, shading colors, and border lines.

PivotTable timeline A small window that starts with the first date and ends with the last date in the data source. It contains horizontal tiles that you can click to filter data by day, month, quarter, or year.

Plot area The region of a chart containing the graphical representation of the values in one or more data series. Two axes form a border around the plot area.

PMT function A financial function that calculates the periodic loan payment given a fixed rate, number of periods (also known as term), and the present value of the loan (the principal).

Pointing The process of using the pointer to select cells while building a formula. Also known as *semi-selection*.

Population A dataset that contains all the information you would like to evaluate.

Portable Document Format (PDF) A standard file format that preserves the document's data and formatting as originally intended in the source program and ensures that other people cannot edit the original data or see proprietary formulas.

Portrait orientation A document layout when a page is taller than it is wide.

Power BI (Business Intelligence) An online application suite designed to help users manage, supplement, visualize, and analyze data.

Power Pivot A built-in Add-in that offers the key functionality that is included in Excel's stock PivotTable options, plus a variety of useful features for the power user.

Power Query A business intelligence tool that provides the user with the ability to shape, cleanse, and query data.

Power View An Excel add-in that gives the user the ability to create a visual dashboard with the functionality of a PivotTable.

PowerPoint An application that enables you to create dynamic presentations to inform groups and persuade audiences.

PPMT function A financial function that calculates the principal payment for a specified payment period on a loan or an investment given a fixed interest rate, specified term, and identical periodic payments.

Precedent cell A cell that is referenced by a formula in another cell.

Print area The range of cells within a worksheet that will print.

Print order The sequence in which the pages are printed.

Procedure A named sequence of statements stored in a macro.

PROPER function An Excel function that capitalizes the first letter of each word in a text string, including the first letter of prepositions.

Pv An argument in the PMT function representing the present value of the loan.

PV function A financial function that calculates the total present (current) value of an investment with a fixed rate, specified number of payment periods, and a series of identical payments that will be made in the future.

Quartile A value used to divide a range of numbers into four equal groups.

QUARTILE.EXC function A statistical function that identifies the value at a specific quartile, exclusive of 0 and 4.

QUARTILE.INC function A statistical function that identifies the value at a specific quartile, *including* quartile 0 for the lowest value and quartile 4 for the highest value in the dataset.

Quick Access Toolbar A toolbar located at the top-left corner of any Office application window, this provides fast access to commonly executed tasks such as saving a file and undoing recent actions.

Quick Analysis A set of analytical tools you can use to apply formatting, create charts or tables, and insert basic functions.

Radar chart A chart type that compares aggregate values of three or more variables represented on axes starting from the same point.

Range A group of adjacent or contiguous cells in a worksheet. A range can be adjacent cells in a column (such as C5:C10), in a row (such as A6:H6), or a rectangular group of cells (such as G5:H10).

Range name A word or string of characters assigned to one or more cells.

Range_lookup An argument that determines how the VLOOKUP and HLOOKUP functions handle lookup values that are not an exact match for the data in the lookup table.

RANK.AVG function A statistical function that identifies the rank of a value, providing an average ranking for identical values.

RANK.EQ function A statistical function that identifies the rank of a value, omitting the next rank when tie values exist.

Rate The periodic interest rate; the percentage of interest paid for each payment period; the first argument in the PMT function.

RATE function A financial function that calculates the periodic rate for an investment or loan given the number of payment periods, a fixed periodic payment, and present value.

Record A group of related fields representing one entity, such as data for one person, place, event, or concept.

Refresh A tool that updates the linked data in an Excel workbook with the most up-to-date information.

Relationship An association or connection between two related tables where both tables contain a related field of data, such as IDs.

Relative cell reference A designation that indicates a cell's relative location from the original cell containing the formula; the cell reference changes when the formula is copied.

Ribbon The command center of Office applications. It is the long bar located just beneath the title bar, containing tabs, groups, and commands.

Row heading A number to the left side of a row in a worksheet. For example, 3 is the row heading for the third row.

Row height The vertical measurement of the row in a worksheet.

ROWS area A section within the PivotTable Fields List used to place a field that will display labels to organize data horizontally in a PivotTable. It groups the data into categories in the first column, listing each unique label only once regardless how many times the label is contained in the original dataset.

Run-time error An error that occurs when a syntactically correct formula or function contains a cell reference with invalid or missing data; an error that occurs when there is a problem with software or hardware while executing a program.

Sample A smaller portion of the population that is easier to evaluate.

Scenario Detailed sets of values that represent different possible situations.

Scenario Manager A what-if analysis tool that enables you to define and manage up to 32 scenarios to compare their side effects on calculated results.

Scenario summary report An organized structured table of the scenarios, their input values, and their respective results.

Select All The triangle at the intersection of the row and column headings in the top-left corner of the worksheet. Click it to select everything contained in the active worksheet.

Semi-selection The process of using the pointer to select cells while building a formula. Also known as *pointing*.

Shared workbook A file that is designated as sharable and is stored on a network that is accessible to multiple people who can edit the workbook at the same time.

Sheet tab A visual label that looks like a file folder tab. In Excel, a sheet tab shows the name of a worksheet contained in the workbook.

Sheet tab navigation Visual elements that help you navigate to the first, previous, next, or last sheet within a workbook.

Shortcut menu A menu that provides choices related to the selection or area at which you right-click.

Signature line An embedded object that includes X, a line for a signature on a printout, the person's typed name and title.

Sizing handles Eight circles that display on the outside border of a chart—one on each corner and one on each middle side—when the chart is selected; enables the user to adjust the height and width of the chart.

Slicer A small window containing one button for each unique item in a field so that you can filter the PivotTable quickly.

Slicer caption The text or field name that appears as a header or title at the top of a slicer to identify the data in that field.

Solver An add-in application that searches for the best or optimum solution to a problem by manipulating the values for several variables within restrictions that you impose.

Sorting The process of arranging records by the value of one or more fields within a table or data range.

Source file A file that contains original data that you need in another file.

Sparkline A small line, column, or win/loss chart contained in a single cell to provide a simple visual illustrating one data series.

Split bar The vertical or horizontal line that frames a split window. A vertical split bar splits the window into left and right panes. A horizontal split bar splits the window into top and bottom panes.

Splitting The process of dividing a worksheet window into two or four resizable panes so you can view separate parts of a worksheet at the same time. Any changes made in one pane affect the entire worksheet.

Spreadsheet An electronic file that contains a grid of columns and rows used to organize related data and to display results of calculations, enabling interpretation of quantitative data for decision making.

Stacked column chart A chart type that places stacks of data in segments on top of each other in one column, with each category in the data series represented by a different color.

Standard deviation A statistic that measures how far the data sample is spread around the mean.

Start tag A portion of programming code that contains the name of an XML element.

Status bar A bar located at the bottom of the program window that contains information relative to the open file. It also includes tools for changing the view of the file and for changing the zoom size of onscreen file contents.

Stock chart A chart type that shows fluctuation in stock prices.

Structured reference A tag or use of a table element, such as a field label, as a reference in a formula. Field labels are enclosed in square brackets, such as [Amount] within the formula.

Sub procedure Visual Basic code that performs actions on a workbook but does not return a specific value.

SUBSTITUTE function A text function that substitutes, or replaces, new text for old text in a text string.

Substitution value A value that replaces the original value of a variable in a data table.

SUBTOTAL function A predefined formula that calculates an aggregate value, such as totals, for displayed values in a range, a table, or a database. The first argument is a number that indicates the function. For example, the argument 9 represents the Sum function. The second argument represents a range of values to subtotal.

Subtotal row A row that contains at least one aggregate calculation, such as SUM or AVERAGE, that applies for a group of sorted data within a dataset.

SUM function A statistical function that calculates the total of values contained in one or more cells.

SUMIF function A statistical function that calculates the total of a range of values when a specified condition is met.

SUMIFS function A statistical function that calculates the cells in a range that meet multiple criteria.

Surface chart A chart type that displays trends using two dimensions on a continuous curve.

Syntax A set of rules that governs the structure and components for properly entering a function.

Syntax error An error that occurs when a formula or function violates construction rules; for example, by containing a misspelled a function name.

Tab Located on the Ribbon, each tab is designed to appear much like a tab on a file folder, with the active tab highlighted.

Tab-delimited file A technique that uses tabs to separate data into columns.

Table A structured range that contains related data organized in a method that increases the capability to manage and analyze information.

Table array The range that contains the lookup table.

Table style A named collection of color, font, and border designs that can be applied to a table.

Tag A user-defined marker that identifies the beginning or ending of a piece of data in an XML document.

***Tell me what you want to do* box** Located to the right of the last tab, this box enables you to search for help and information about a command or task you want to perform and also presents you with a shortcut directly to that command.

Template A predesigned file that incorporates formatting elements, such as a theme and layouts, that you can use as a model to create other documents that have the same structure and purpose; may include content that can be modified.

Text Any combination of letters, numbers, symbols, and spaces not used in Excel calculations.

Text file A data file (indicated by the .txt file extension) that contains characters, such as letters, numbers, and symbols, including punctuation and spaces.

Theme A collection of design formats that include colors, fonts, and special effects used to give a consistent appearance to a document, workbook, presentation, or database form or report.

Title bar The long bar at the top of each window that displays the name of the folder, file, or program displayed in the open window and the application in which you are working.

TODAY function A date and time function that displays the current date.

Toggle commands A button that acts somewhat like light switches that you can turn on and off. You select the command to turn it on, then select it again to turn it off.

Total row (Excel) A table row that appears below the last row of records in an Excel table and displays summary or aggregate statistics, such as a sum or an average.

Tracer arrow A colored line that shows relationships between precedent and dependent cells.

Track Changes A collaboration feature that records particular changes made in a workbook.

Trendline A line that depicts trends or helps forecast future data in a chart. For example, if the plotted data includes 2005, 2010, and 2015, a trendline can help forecast values for 2020 and beyond.

Truth table A matrix that provides the results (TRUE or FALSE) for every possible combination for an AND, OR, or NOT criteria combination.

Two-variable data table a structured range that contains different values for two variables to compare how these differing values affect the results for one calculated value.

Ungrouping The process of deselecting grouped worksheets so that actions performed on one sheet do not affect other worksheets.

Unqualified reference The use of field headings without row references in a structured formula.

UPPER function An Excel function that converts text strings to uppercase letters.

Validation criteria The rules that dictate the type of data that can be entered in a cell.

Value A number that represents a quantity or a measurable amount.

Value axis The chart axis that displays incremental numbers to identify approximate values, such as dollars or units, of data points in a chart.

VALUES area A section within the PivotTable Fields List used to place a field to display summary statistics, such as totals or averages, in a PivotTable.

Variable An input value that can change to other values to affect the results of a situation.

Variance A measure of a dataset's dispersion, such as the difference between the highest and lowest points in the dataset.

Vertical alignment The placement of cell data between the top and bottom cell margins.

View The various ways a file can appear on the screen.

View controls Icons on the right side of the status bar that enable you to change to Normal, Page Layout, or Page Break view to display the worksheet.

Visual Basic Editor An application used to create, edit, execute, and debug Office application macros using programming code.

Visual Basic for Applications (VBA) A robust programming language that can be used within various software packages to enhance and automate functionality.

Visualizations A view created from data fields and tables added to the Power View canvas.

VLOOKUP function A lookup and reference function that accepts a value, looks the value up in a vertical lookup table with data organized in columns, and returns a result.

Watch Window A separate window from the worksheet window that displays cell addresses, values, and formulas so you can monitor and examine formula calculations involving cells not immediately visible on the screen.

What-if analysis The process of changing variables to observe how changes affect calculated results.

Word An application that can produce all sorts of documents, including memos, newsletters, forms, tables, and brochures.

Workbook A collection of one or more related worksheets contained within a single file.

Worksheet A single spreadsheet that typically contains descriptive labels, numeric values, formulas, functions, and graphical representations of data.

Wrap text An Excel feature that makes data appear on multiple lines by adjusting the row height to fit the cell contents within the column width.

X Y (scatter) chart A chart type that shows a relationship between two variables using their X and Y coordinates. Excel plots one coordinate on the horizontal X-axis and the other variable on the vertical Y-axis. Scatter charts are often used to represent data in education, scientific, and medical experiments.

X-axis The horizontal border that provides a frame of reference for measuring data left to right on a chart.

XML declaration An opening statement of programming code that specifies the XML version and character encoding used.

XML Paper Specification (XPS) An electronic format created by Microsoft that preserves document formatting and is viewable and printable in any platform.

Y-axis The vertical border that provides a frame of reference for measuring data up and down on a chart.

YEAR function A date function that displays the year (such as 2018) for a specific date

YEARFRAC function A date function that calculates the fraction of a year between two dates based on the number of whole days using the start_date and end_date arguments.

Zoom control A control that enables you to increase or decrease the size of the worksheet data onscreen.

Zoom slider A feature that displays at the far right side of the status bar. It is used to increase or decrease the magnification of the file.

Index

= (equal sign), 84
logical operator, 175
(pound signs), 97

A

absolute cell references, 155–156
  input area and, 155
Access 2016, 4
access database table
  importing, 621–623
accessibility, checking, 702–703
Accessibility Checker, 702
accessibility compliance, 233
Accounting Number Format, 114, 115
active cell, 72
adding
  axis title, 226–228
  background, 741
  chart elements, 225–234
  data labels, 229–231
  fields, 278
  gridlines, 232
  records, 279
  scenarios, 420–421
add-ins
  defined, 428
  installing, 17–18
  loading the Solver, 428–429
alignment
  defined, 111
  horizontal cell alignment, 112
  options, 111
  vertical cell alignment, 112
  worksheets and, 110–111
analysis of variance (ANOVA). *see* ANOVA
Analysis ToolPak, 534
  loading, 534
  performing analysis using, 535–539
AND function, 460
ANOVA, 535–536
  calculations, 535
  results, 536
  single-factor, 535
  summary report, 536
  two factor without replication, 535
  two factor with replication, 535
area chart, 214
arguments
  database, 475
  field, 475
  logical test, 175
  nest functions as, 165, 176
  rate, 483
  value, 483
  value_if_false, 175–176

value_if_true, 175–176
arrows
  move down one cell, 73
  move left one cell, 73
  move right one cell, 73
  move up one cell, 73
auditing
  formulas, 586–589
AutoComplete, 75
  Formula AutoComplete, 161
Auto Fill, 75
AVERAGE function, 165
AVERAGEIF function, 513–514
AVERAGEIFS function, 514–515
axes
  formatting, 228–229
  X-, 201
  Y-axis, 201
axis title, 224
  adding, 226–228
  formatting, 226–228
  linking to cell, 226
  positioning, 226–228

B

background
  adding, 741
  applying, 740–741
  defined, 740
  visibility, 741
  in worksheets, 124
Backstage view, 42–44
  customizing application options, 43
bar chart, 208–209
binding constraint, 433
bins, 527
bold argument names, 162
borders
  cells, 113
[ ] brackets, 164
brackets [ ], 164
breakpoint, 179

C

calculated field
  creating, 359–362
Cancel icon, 71
Canvas, 648
category axis, 201
cell references
  absolute, 155–156
  in formulas, 83–84, 154–157
  mixed, 156–157
  relative, 154

toggle between relative, absolute, mixed
  cell references (F4), 157
cells, 72
  active, 72
  address, 72
  borders, 113
  chart title linking to, 226
  clearing contents, 78
  dependent, 587
  displaying formulas in, 86–87
  editing contents, 78
  Format Cells dialog box, 111, 115
  horizontal alignment, 112
  indenting contents, 112–113
  inserting, 93–94
  line break in, 112
  linking to axis title, 226
  locking, 750–751
  merge options, 111–112
  number formats, 113–115
  precedent, 587
  protecting, 750–751
  rotate data, 112
  unlocking, 750–751
  unmerge, 111–112
  vertical alignment, 112
  wrap text feature, 112
cell styles, 110
  applying, 741–744
  creating custom, 742–743
  defined, 741
  modifying, 743–744
  removing, 743–744
central tendency, measuring, 525–530
  CORREL function, 526–527
  FREQUENCY function, 527–530
  standard deviation and variance
    functions, 525–526
changing variable cells, 429–430
chart area, 201
  formatting, 232–233
chart elements, 224–234
  adding, 225–234
  axis title, 224
  chart title, 224
  data label, 224
  data table, 224
  defined, 224
  editing, 225–234
  error bars, 224
  formatting, 225–234
  gridlines, 224
  images/textures, 233
  legend, 224
  removing, 228
  trendline, 224